An Introduction to Shakespeare

revised edition

edited by
Hardin Craig
David Bevington
The University of Chicago

Scott, Foresman and Company   Glenview, Illinois

Dallas, Tex.   Oakland, N.J.   Palo Alto, Cal.   Tucker, Ga.   Brighton, England

For Philip, Joan, Ann, and Mark.

ISBN: 0-673-07972-4
Library of Congress Catalog Card Number 74-82772

Printed in the United States of America.

Acknowledgments

Cover: Drawing of the Globe Theatre, after Visscher's view of London. Courtesy of the Trustees, the British Museum.

Page 1: Sheldon tapestry owned by Mrs. Anthony Sheldon. Photograph courtesy Victoria and Albert Museum. Crown Copyright.

Pages 40–41: William Blake's "Oberon, Titania, and Puck with Fairies Dancing." Courtesy the Tate Gallery, London.

Preface

As in my recent revision of Hardin Craig's *The Complete Works of Shakespeare*, this revision of *An Introduction to Shakespeare* seeks to preserve the essence of Craig's work while at the same time bringing up to date his scholarship and criticism. This edition offers the reader eight plays and the sonnets, as in Craig's edition, and retains his choice of plays except that *A Midsummer Night's Dream* now takes the place of *Much Ado about Nothing*. The general introduction follows Craig's outline for the most part, although all the sections have been rewritten. The individual play introductions, which are substantially those of the *Complete Works*, offer critical essays in place of Craig's more historical and factual observations; but the valuable information he offered on text, dating, and sources has been preserved in a new set of appendices. Craig's text and his notes have been thoroughly revised and updated, but remain essentially his. Here is a detailed analysis of the revisions incorporated in this edition, so that the reader may know as precisely as possible what is Craig's and what is mine.

The General Introduction. The section entitled "Life in Shakespeare's England" retains Craig's ordering of topics, and much of the information he collected, but is substantially rewritten. The same is true of "London Theatres and Dramatic Companies," and the biographical surveys of the four periods of Shakespeare's life from "The Early Period, 1564–1594" through "The Period of Romances, 1609–1616." The essays on "Shakespeare's Texts" and on "Shakespeare's Dramatic Development," on the other hand, are essentially new. All of these essays closely resemble their counterparts in the revised *Complete Works*, though somewhat shortened and rearranged for inclusion in this present volume.

The Play Introductions. These are only slightly altered from the introductions to be found in the revised *Complete Works*. They are, however, substantially unlike those provided by Craig in his earlier edition. His emphasis was on historical information about dating, sources, and stage history. This present volume has transferred such materials to the new appendices (see below), and has instead focused the play introductions on matters of critical interpretation.

The Notes. Assisted by a panel of consultants whose names appear below, I have revised all of Craig's notes, retaining those that remain sound and pertinent while adding new information as required. The glossing of sexual double entendres, for example, is virtually all new; Craig silently overlooked such terms, as did most editors of his generation.

Text. The play texts in this volume are all taken without change from the revised *Complete Works*. As in that edition, I have based my text on Craig's edition of the famous Globe text of 1864, but have continued the process of modernization followed by Craig. In other words, like him I have reviewed the decisions of the Globe editors in the light of recent bibliographical research, and have introduced modifications throughout the volume (as recorded in the textual notes), but have tried to avoid changes that would interfere with the reference value of the Globe text. That edition has remained a standard for so many years, especially in its act, scene, and line numbering, that its preservation through a conservative updating seems a desirable goal. Accordingly I have approached the task of revising the text in such a way as to leave intact the essential features of the original (including line numbering).

In particular, I have corrected the Globe's tendency to be "eclectic" when dealing with two early texts—for example, to choose unsystematically between the readings of the 1608 quarto and the Folio texts of *King Lear*, first from one and then from the other. Modern bibliographical theory has shown the unlikelihood that such a method can recover what Shakespeare actually wrote; the more systematic method is to determine which early text is closest to Shakespeare's composition, and then to stay conservatively close to that copy text. Accordingly, I have moved the text of *King Lear* somewhat closer to its Folio original. Two plays in this edition are now more conservatively based on the quarto editions that have been shown to be the best copy texts: *Romeo and Juliet* (Q2, 1599) and *Hamlet* (Q2, 1604–1605). The changes are not extensive, however, and do not interfere with the lineation of the Globe text.

Other individual changes are to be found scattered throughout the volume, as in Craig's revision of the Globe text. Virtually all of my changes are restorations of the original textual reading; that is, I have rejected a number of emendations adopted by the Globe editors and retained by Craig. Some of these restorations deal with simple matters of consistency; for example, I have resisted the Globe editors' tendency to regularize or "improve" Shakespeare's use of *further* and *farther*, *show'd* and *shown*, *does* and *doth*, *seemeth* and *seems*, and the like. In such cases I have simply followed the original Folio or quarto text. In general I have held to the view that glossing of unfamiliar words should occur in the notes rather than by revising the text, and so I have restored *mushrump* for the Globe's *mushroom*, *Bristow* for *Bristol*, *whe'r* for *whether*, *strond* for *strand*, *wrack* for *wreck*, *moe* for *more*, and the like. These changes have been enumerated in the textual notes, so that the book can continue to be used as a Globe text for purposes of reference.

In addition I have introduced a number of nonsubstantive changes. Most important among these concerns elision. The Globe editors were not consistent in their use of elision. Although they adopted the system of eliding the *e* in a word like *enjoy'd*, as in the First Folio and quartos, to indicate that the word has two syllables rather than three, they often left words such as *loved* unelided even though the scansion and the original copy texts both demanded an elision. I have reviewed all such elisions, and have followed the original copy texts in elision as conservatively as possible. I have also followed the original copy in such words as *fall'n, t' account, scatt'red, suff'ring, y' are, th' art, th' abhorr'd, spak'st, 'a* (for *he*), and so on. I have not entered most such changes in the prose, however, since the Globe text adopted the common system of differentiating between prose (in which the elisions in the original text are in any case quite inconsistent) and verse (in which elision is crucial to proper scansion of the lines).

I have also followed the original texts faithfully on stage directions, and have employed square brackets to indicate editorial additions to the original stage directions (including indications of act and scene). In adopting this system, which preserves Shakespeare's own language in many cases, I have altered the language of the Globe stage directions as little as possible. The indications of place for each scene, though enclosed in square brackets, are with very few exceptions as they appear in the Globe text. The Globe-supplied lists of *dramatis personae* have similarly been placed in square brackets.

Appendices. The appendices are new to this edition and to the *Complete Works*, and are intended to provide further reference for students wishing to learn more about textual problems, dating, and sources. Appendix I provides a literal transcript of all the title pages of the relevant early texts, a feature contained in the play introductions of Craig's previous editions. Appendix II contains summaries of Shakespeare's sources, a new feature and one not found in most texts of Shakespeare today. Appendix III contains the Textual Notes.

Bibliographies. These lists of suggestions for further reading and research are new to this edition and to the *Complete Works*. Those for the individual plays are based on suggestions submitted by the consultants. The various lists also contain the names of many books to which I am personally indebted for information and ideas used in writing the introductions and other critical materials for this volume.

I take pleasure in acknowledging the generous assistance I have received in preparing this volume. A group of scholarly consultants read and criticized early drafts of the general introduction and the individual play introductions. These consultants also made up lists of recommended reading for the individual plays, carefully reviewed the notes, offered ideas on the editing of the texts, and assisted in many needful ways. Their names are as follows: for the general introduction, John Wasson of Washington State University (Pullman) and Michael Houlahan of North Park College; for *A Midsummer Night's Dream* and *Twelfth Night*, Neil Rudenstine of Princeton University; for *Richard II* and *1 Henry IV*, John Elliott of Syracuse University and Charles Forker of Indiana University; for *Romeo and Juliet*, George Williams of Duke University; for *Hamlet* and *King Lear*, Howard Felperin of Yale University; for *The Tempest*, Arthur Kirsch of the University of Virginia; and for the sonnets, Cyrus Hoy of the University of Rochester. I have also received valuable advice on the project as a whole from Madeleine Doran of the University of Wisconsin (Madison) and from C. L. Barber of the University of California (Santa Cruz). For other debts of gratitude, I refer the reader to the Preface of the *Complete Works*.

David Bevington

Contents

MIDDEL
SEXIAE
HARMSWORTH
HARLINGTON
SOVTHOLD
NORWOOD
HANWELL
HESTON
CRANFORD
HOWNSLEY
ASHFORD
FELTHAM
COLBROKE
HORTON
BEDSVNT

General Introduction

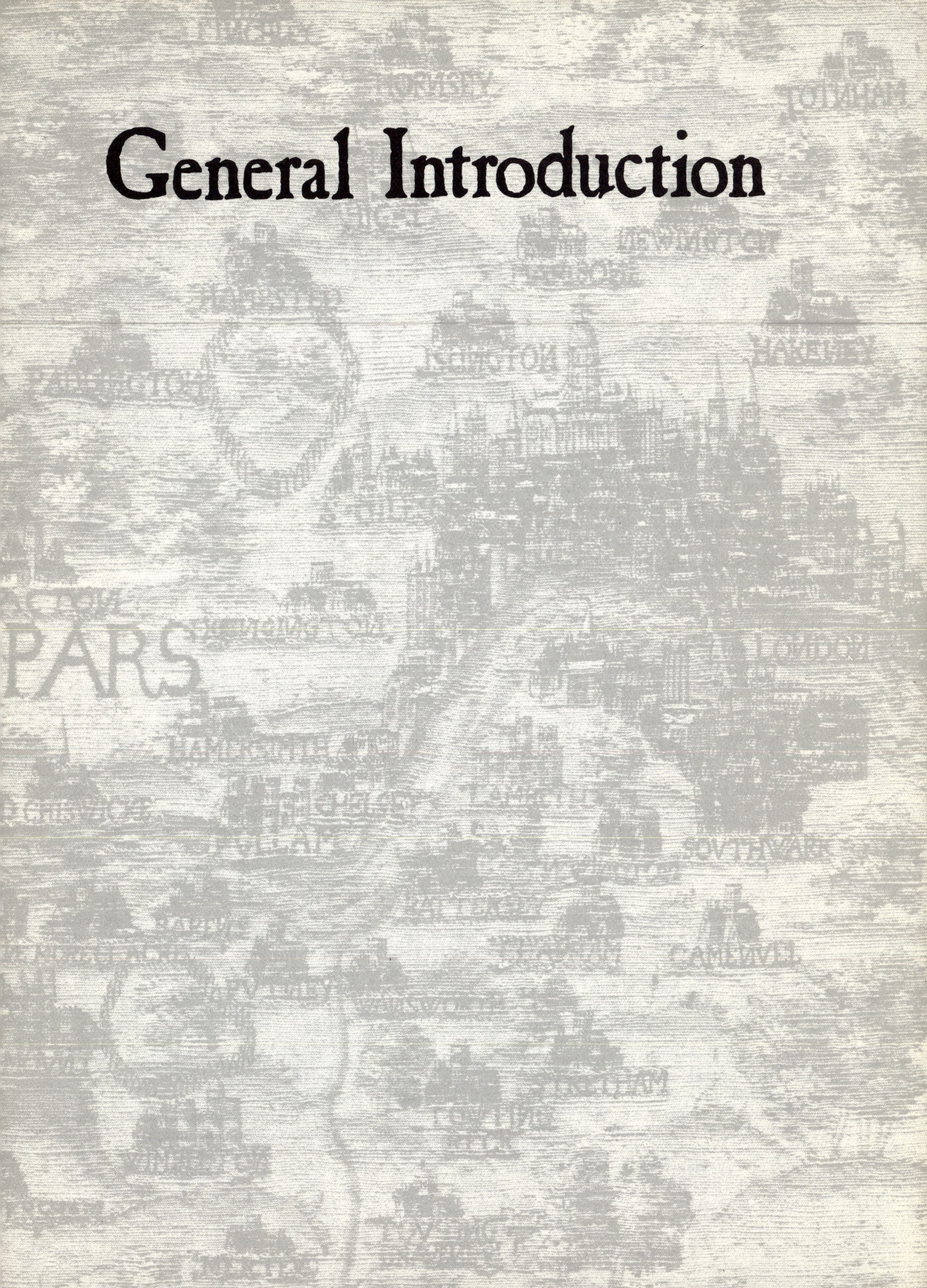

Shakespeare as an English Dramatist

LIFE IN SHAKESPEARE'S ENGLAND

England during Shakespeare's lifetime (1564–1616) was a proud nation with a strong sense of national identity, but she was also a small nation by modern standards. Probably not more than five million people lived in the whole of England, considerably fewer than now live in London. England's territories in France were no longer extensive, as they had been during the fourteenth century and earlier; in fact, by the end of Queen Elizabeth's reign (1558–1603), England had virtually retired from her once-great empire on the Continent. Her overseas empire in America had scarcely begun. Scotland was not yet a part of Great Britain; union with Scotland would not take place until 1707, despite the fact that King James VI of Scotland assumed the English throne in 1603 as James I of England. Ireland, although declared a kingdom under English rule in 1541, was more a source of trouble than of economic strength. The last years of Elizabeth's reign, especially from 1597 to 1601, were plagued by the rebellion of the Irish under Hugh O'Neill, Earl of Tyrone. Thus, England of the sixteenth and early seventeenth centuries was both small and isolated.

THE SOCIAL AND ECONOMIC BACKGROUND

By and large, England was a rural land. Much of the kingdom was still wooded, though timber was being used increasingly in manufacturing and shipbuilding. The area of the midlands, today heavily industrialized, was still at that time a region of great trees, green fields, and clear streams. England's chief means of livelihood was agriculture. This part of the economy was generally in a bad way, however, and Englishmen who lived off the land did not share in the prosperity of many Londoners. A problem throughout the sixteenth century was that of "enclosure": the conversion by rich landowners of crop lands into pasturage. Farmers and peasants complained bitterly that they were being dispossessed and starved for the benefit of livestock. Rural uprisings and food riots were common, to the dismay of the authorities. The agrarian poor of Oxfordshire arose in 1596, threatening to massacre the gentry and march on London; other riots had occurred in 1586 and 1591, provoking memories of the infamous May Day riots of 1517. Although the government did what it could to inhibit enclosure, the economic forces at work were too massive and too inadequately understood to be curbed by governmental fiat. Pasture was more profitable than crop land; it used large areas with greater efficiency than in crop farming, and required far less labor. The wool produced by the pasturing of sheep was needed in ever-increasing amounts for the manufacture of cloth.

The wool industry also experienced occasional economic difficulties, to be sure; overexpansion in the early years of the sixteenth century created a glutted market that had collapsed disastrously in 1551, creating widespread unemployment. Despite such fluctuations and reversals, however, the wool industry continued on the whole to expand and to provide handsome profits for landowners and middlemen. Mining and manufacture in coal, iron, tin, copper, and lead, although insignificant by modern standards, were also expanding at an enormous rate. Trading companies exploited the rich new resources of the Americas, as well as of Eastern Europe and the Orient. Queen Elizabeth aided economic development by keeping England out of war with her continental enemies as long as possible, despite provocations from those powers and despite the eagerness of some of her advisers to retaliate.

The new economic prosperity was not evenly distributed. Especially during Shakespeare's first years in London, in the late 1580's and the 1590's, the gap between rich and poor grew more and more extreme. Elizabeth's efforts at peacemaking were no longer able to prevent years of war with the Catholic powers of the Continent. Taxation grew heavier, and inflation proceeded at an unusually rapid rate during this period. A succession of bad harvests compounded the miseries of those who dwelled on the land. When the hostilities on the Continent ceased for a time in about 1597, a wave of returning veterans added to unemployment and crime. The rising prosperity experienced by Shakespeare and other fortunate Londoners was undeniably real, but it was not universal. Nowhere was the contrast between rich and poor more visible than in London.

London

Sixteenth-century London was at once more attractive and less attractive than twentieth-century London. It was full of trees and gardens; meadows and cultivated lands reached in some places to its very walls. Today we can perhaps imagine the way in which it bordered clear streams and green fields, when we approach from a distance some uncommercial provincial city such as Lincoln, York, or Hereford. Surrounded by its ancient wall, London was by no means a large metropolis. Although its population had expanded into the surrounding area in all directions, the city proper stretched along the north bank of the Thames River from the old Tower of London on the east to St. Paul's Cathedral and the Fleet Ditch on the west—a distance of little more than a mile. A visitor approaching London from the south bank of the Thames (the bankside), and crossing London Bridge, could see virtually all of this exciting city lying before him. London Bridge itself was one of the major attractions of the city, lined with shops and richly decorated on occasion for the triumphal entry of a king or queen.

Yet London had its grim and ugly side as well. On London Bridge could sometimes be seen the heads of executed traitors. The city's houses were generally small and crowded; its streets were often narrow and filthy. In the absence of sewers, open ditches in the streets served to collect and carry off refuse. Frequent epidemics of the bubonic plague were the inevitable result of unsanitary conditions and medical ignorance. Lighting of the streets at night was generally nonexistent, and the constabulary was notoriously unreliable. Shakespeare gives us unforgettable satires of night watchmen and bumbling police officials in *Much Ado about Nothing* (Dogberry and the night watch) and *Measure for Measure* (Constable Elbow). Prostitution thrived in the suburbs, conveniently located although beyond the reach of the London authorities. Houses of prostitution were often to be found in the vicinity of the public theatres, since the theatres also took advantage of suburban locations to escape the stringent regulations imposed by London's Lord Mayor and Council of Aldermen. The famous Globe Theatre, for example, was on the south bank of the Thames, a short distance to the west of London Bridge. Another theatrical building (called simply "The Theatre") used earlier by Shakespeare and the Lord Chamberlain's players was located in Finsbury Fields, a short distance across Moorfields from London's northeast corner. The suburbs also housed various con games and illegal operations.

London's population stood at perhaps one hundred thousand people within the walls and as many more in the suburbs. The royal palace of Whitehall, Westminster Abbey (then known as the Abbey Church of St. Peter), the Parliament House, and Westminster Hall were well outside London, two miles or so to the west on the Thames River. They remain today in the same location, in Westminster, although the metropolis of London has long since surrounded these official buildings.

Travel

Travel was still extremely painful and slow because of the unimproved condition of the roads. It was also dangerous on account of highway robbers, as we can see from Shakespeare's celebrated portrayal of the robbery at Gads Hill, in *1 Henry IV*. (This robbery occurs on the main road between London and Canterbury.) English inns seem to have been good, however, certainly much better than the inns of the Continent. Travel on horseback was the most common method, and probably the most comfortable, since coach building was a new and imperfect art. Coaches of state, some of which we see in prints and pictures of the era, were lumbering affairs, no doubt handsome enough in processions, but springless, unwieldy, and hard to transport. Carts and wagons were used for carrying merchandise, but packsaddles were safer and quicker. Under such difficulties, no metropolitan area such as London could possibly have thrived in the interior. London depended for its commercial greatness upon the Thames River and its access to the North Sea.

Commerce

When Elizabeth came to the English throne in 1558, England's chief foreign trade was with Antwerp, Bruges, and other Belgian cities. Antwerp was an especially important market for England's export of wool cloth. This market was a seriously threatened one, however, since the Low Countries were under the domination of the Catholic King of Spain, Philip II. When Philip shortsightedly undertook to punish his Protestant subjects in the Low Countries for their religious heresy, many of Elizabeth's counselors and subjects urged her to come to the defense of England's Protestant neighbors and trading allies. Elizabeth prudently held back. Philip's armies attacked Antwerp in 1576 and again in 1585, putting to an end the commercial ascendancy of that great northern European metropolis. Perhaps as many as one third of Antwerp's merchants and artisans settled in London, bringing with them their expert knowledge of commerce and manufacture. The influx of so many skilled workmen and merchants into London produced problems of unemployment and overcrowding, but contributed nevertheless to London's emergence as a leading port of trade.

English ships assumed a dominant position in Mediterranean trade, formerly carried on mainly by the Venetians. In the Baltic Sea, England captured trade that had previously been controlled by the Hanseatic League. Bristol thrived on commerce with Ireland

The illustration by Claes Janszoon de Visscher in the year of Shakespeare's death shows the London of 1616 as a thriving metropolis. The various boats on the Thames are evidence of the vital role the river played in the city's emergence as a center of international as well as national trade. The Globe Theatre appears on the near side of the river.

and subsequently on trade with the Western Hemisphere. Boston and Hull increased their business with Scandinavian ports. The Russia Company was founded in 1555; the Levant Company became the famous East India Company in 1600; and the Virginia Company opened up trade with the New World in the Western Hemisphere. Fisheries were developed in the North Sea, in the waters north of Ireland, and off the banks of Newfoundland. Elizabeth and her ministers wisely encouraged this commercial expansion.

The Poor Laws and Apprenticeship

Despite the new prosperity experienced by many Elizabethans, especially in London, unemployment remained a serious problem. The suppression of the monasteries in 1536–1539, as part of Henry VIII's reformation of the Catholic Church, had dispossessed a large class of persons who were not easily reemployed. Other causes of unemployment, such as the periodic collapses of the wool trade, dispossession of farm workers by enclosure of land, the sudden influx of skilled artisans from Antwerp, and the return of army veterans, have already been mentioned. Elizabethan Parliaments attempted to cope with the problem of unemployment, but did so in ways that seem unduly harsh today. In 1572 an act of Parliament made the mayors, magistrates, and county officials responsible for the care of their local poor and for the enforcement of stern measures against vagabonds. Under this act, vagabonds were arrested and sent back to their own parishes and there compelled to work. This localization of responsibility laid the basis for what has been known historically as the "poor rate" (a local tax levied for the support of the poor) and for that sinister institution, the workhouse. The provisions of the act of 1572 remained in force for centuries.

Regulations for apprentices were no less strict. An act of Parliament of 1563, known as the Statute of Artificers, gave the craft trades of England—still organized as medieval guilds—virtually complete authority over the young persons apprenticed to a trade. Apprenticeship usually began at the age of fourteen to seventeen, and lasted for a period of not less than seven years. During this time the young worker lived with the family of his master. Without

THE FOLGER SHAKESPEARE LIBRARY

such an extensive apprenticeship, entry into the skilled crafts was virtually impossible. Acting companies, such as the company Shakespeare joined, were similarly organized as guilds and took on boy actors in an apprenticeship role. We do not know, however, whether Shakespeare actually served such an indenture before becoming a full member of his acting company.

Social Change

The opportunities for rapid economic advance in Elizabethan England, though by no means available to all, did produce social change and a quality of restlessness in English society. "New men" at court were an increasing phenomenon under the Tudor monarchs, who tended to rely on loyal counselors of humble origin rather than on the once-too-powerful nobility. Cardinal Wolsey, for example, rose from obscurity to become the most mighty subject of Henry VIII's realm, with a newly built residence (Hampton Court) rivaling the splendor of the king's own palaces. He was detested as an upstart by old aristocrats such as the Duke of Norfolk, and his sudden fall was as spectacular as had been his rise to power. The Earl of Leicester, Queen Elizabeth's first favorite, was a descendant of the Edmund Dudley who had risen from unpretentious beginnings to great eminence under Henry VII, Queen Elizabeth's grandfather. Such new and influential families were numerous. Conversely, the ancient families discovered that they were no longer entrusted with positions of highest authority. To be sure, the aristocracy remained vitally important as the apex of England's social structure. New aspirants to power emulated the aristocracy by purchasing land and building splendid residences, rather than defining themselves as a rich new "middle class." Bourgeois status was something the new men put behind them as quickly as they could. Moreover, social mobility could work in both directions, both upward and downward. Many men were quickly ruined by the costly and competitive business of seeking favor at the Tudor court. Nonetheless, the Elizabethan era was one of greater opportunity for rapid social and economic advancement than England had heretofore known.

Increased economic contacts with the outside world inevitably led to the importation of new styles of living. Such new fashions, together with the rapid changes now possible in social position, produced a reaction of dismay from those who feared the destruction of traditional English values. Italy was particularly reviled, both as the home of the Catholic Church and as the originator of many supposedly decadent fashions. The word "Italianate" connoted a whole range of villainous practices, including diabolical

THE BRITISH LIBRARY BOARD

The wealthy felt little obligation to relieve the widespread poverty and unemployment of the times.

methods of torture and revenge: poisoned books of devotion which would kill the unsuspecting victims who kissed them, ingeniously contrived chairs that would close upon the person who sat in them, and the like. The revenge plays of Shakespeare's contemporaries, such as *Antonio's Revenge* by John Marston, *The Revenger's Tragedy* perhaps by Cyril Tourneur or Thomas Middleton, and *The White Devil* by John Webster, offer spectacular caricatures of the so-called Italianate style in murder. The name of Italy was also associated with licentiousness, immorality, and outlandish fashions in clothes. France, too, was accused of encouraging such extravagances in dress as ornamented headdresses, stiffly pleated ruffs, padded doublets, puffed or double sleeves, and richly decorated hose. Rapid changes in fashion added to the costliness of being up to date, and thereby increased the outcry against vanity in dress. Fencing, dicing, the use of cosmetics, the smoking of tobacco, the drinking of imported wines, and almost every vice known to man were attributed by angry moralists to the corrupting influence from abroad.

Not all Englishmen deplored continental fashion, of course. Persons of advanced taste saw the importation of European styles as a culturally liberating process. Fashion thus became a subject of debate between moral traditionalists and those who welcomed the new styles. The controversy was a bitter one, with religious overtones, in which the reformers' angry accusations became increasingly extreme. This attack on changing fashion was in fact an integral part of the Puritan movement. It therefore stressed the sinfulness not only of extravagance in clothing but of the costliness in building great houses and other such worldly pursuits. Those whose sympathies were Puritan became more and more disaffected with the cultural values represented by the court, and thus English society drifted further and further toward irreconcilable conflict.

Shakespeare's personal views on this controversy are hard to determine and do not bear importantly on his achievement as an artist. Generally, however, we can observe that his many references to changes in fashion cater neither to the avant-garde nor to reactionary traditionalists. Shakespeare's audience was after all a broadly national one. It included many ordinary Londoners who viewed "Italianate" fashion neither with enthusiasm nor with alarm, but with satiric laughter. Such spectators would certainly have seen the point, for example, in Mercutio's witty diatribe at the expense of the new French style in fencing. The object of his scorn is Tybalt, who, according to Mercutio, "fights as you sing prick-song" and fancies himself to be "the very butcher of a silk button." "Is not this a lamentable thing," asks Mercutio rhetorically, "that we should be thus afflicted with these strange flies, these fashion-mongers, these perdona-mi's, who stand so much on the new form, that they cannot sit at ease on the old bench?" (*Romeo and Juliet*, II,iv). In a similar vein, Shakespeare's audience would have appreciated the joking in *The Merchant of Venice* about England's servile imitation of continental styles in clothes. "What say you, then, to Falconbridge, the young baron of England?" asks Nerissa of her mistress Portia concerning one of Portia's many suitors. Portia replies, "How oddly he is suited! I think he bought his doublet in Italy, his round hose in France, his bonnet in Germany and his behaviour everywhere" (I,ii). Court butterflies in Shakespeare's plays who bow and scrape and fondle their plumed headgear, like Le Beau in *As You Like It* and Osric in *Hamlet*, are the objects of ridicule. Hotspur in *1 Henry IV*, though flawed by aristocratic pride, contrasts

THE BRITISH LIBRARY BOARD

The English usurer was seen by many as a social and religious outcast, defying biblical injunctions against the charging of interest or "use."

favorably with the effeminate courtier, "perfumed like a milliner," who has come from King Henry to discuss the question of prisoners (I,iii). Throughout Shakespeare's plays, the use of cosmetics generally has the negative connotation of artificial beauty used to conceal inward corruption, as in Claudius' reference to "the harlot's cheek, beautied with plast'ring art" (*Hamlet*, III,i). Yet Shakespeare's treatment of newness in fashion is never shrill in tone. Nor does he fail in his dramas to give an honorable place to the ceremonial use of wealth and splendid costuming. His plays thus avoid both extremes in the controversy over changing fashions, though they give plentiful evidence as to the liveliness and currency of the topic.

Shakespeare also reflects a contemporary interest in the problem of usury, especially in *The Merchant of Venice*. Although usury was becoming more and more of a necessity, emotional attitudes toward it changed only slowly. The traditional moral view condemned usury as forbidden by Christian teaching; on the other hand, European governments of the sixteenth century found themselves increasingly obliged to borrow large sums of money. The laws against usury were alternatively relaxed and enforced, according to the economic exigencies of the moment. Shakespeare's plays capture the Elizabethan ambivalence of attitude toward this feared but necessary practice. Similarly, most Englishmen had contradictory attitudes toward what we today would call the law of supply and demand in the marketplace. Conservative moralists complained bitterly when merchants exploited the scarcity of some commodity by forcing up prices; the practice was denounced as excessive profit-taking and declared to be sinful, like usury. In economic policy, then, as in matters of changing fashion or increased social mobility, the old-fashioned and disappearing world of late medieval England exerted a strong emotional appeal.

Elizabethan Houses

Those fortunate Englishmen who grew wealthy in the reign of Elizabeth took special pleasure in building themselves fine new houses. Chimneys were increasingly common, so that smoke no longer had to escape through a hole in the roof. Pewter, or even silver dishes, took the place of the wooden spoon and trencher. Beds and even pillows became common. Carpets were replacing rushes as covering for the floors; wainscoting, tapestries or hangings, and pictures appeared on the walls; and glass began to be used extensively for windows.

Despite the warnings of those moralists who preached against the vanity of worldly acquisition, domestic comfort made considerable progress in Elizabethan England. Many splendid Tudor mansions stand today, testifying to the important social changes that had taken place between the strife-torn fifteenth century and the era of relative peace under Elizabeth. The battlement, the moat, the fortified gate, and the narrow window used for archery or firearms generally disappeared in favor of handsome gardens and terraces. On a lower social scale, the peasant enjoyed greater physical security, and no longer needed to bring his cows, pigs, and poultry into his house at night in order to protect them from thieves. City houses, of which many exist today, were often large and imposing structures, three or four stories in height, and framed usually of strong oak with the walls filled in with brick and plaster. Although the frontage on the streets of London was usually narrow, many houses had trees and handsome gardens at the rear.

With these finer houses, too, came features of privacy that had been virtually unknown to previous generations. Life in the household of a medieval lord had generally focused on the great hall, which could serve variously as the kitchen, dining hall, and sitting room for the entire family and its retainers. The men drank in the hall in the evenings and slept there at night. The new dwellings of prosperous Elizabethans, on the other hand, featured private chambers into which the family and the chief guests could retire.

The Elizabethans built well. Not only do we still admire their houses, but we can see from their oriel windows and stained glass, their broad staircases, their jewels, and their costumes, that they treasured the new beauty of their lives made possible by the culture of the Renaissance. Although the graphic and plastic arts did not thrive in England to the same extent as in Italy, France, and the Low Countries, England made lasting achievements in architecture as well as in music, drama, and all forms of literature.

THE POLITICAL AND RELIGIOUS BACKGROUND

England under the Tudor kings suffered from almost unceasing religious conflict. The battle over religion affected every aspect of life, none more so than politics. At the very beginning of the Tudor reign, to be sure, England's problem was not religious but dynastic. Henry VII, the first of the Tudor kings, brought an end to the devastating civil wars of the fifteenth century by his overthrow of Richard III at the battle of Bosworth Field in 1485. The civil wars thus ended were the so-called Wars of the Roses, between the Lancastrian House of Henry VI (symbolized by the red rose) and the Yorkist House of Edward IV (symbolized by the white rose). Shakespeare chose these eventful struggles as the subject for his first series of English history plays, from *Henry VI* in three parts to *Richard III*. The House of Lancaster drew its title from John of Gaunt, Duke of Lancaster, father of Henry IV and great-grandfather of Henry VI; the House of York drew its title from Edmund Langley, Duke of York, great-grandfather of Edward IV and Richard III. Because John of Gaunt and Edmund Langley had been brothers, virtually all the noble contestants in this War of the Roses were cousins of

ENGLAND'S MONARCHS, 1377–1649

The House of Plantagenet	
Richard II	1377–1399
The House of Lancaster	
Henry IV	1399–1413
Henry V	1413–1422
Henry VI	1422–1461
The House of York	
Edward IV	1461–1483
Edward V	1483
Richard III	1483–1485
The House of Tudor	
Henry VII	1485–1509
Henry VIII	1509–1547
Edward VI	1547–1553
Mary	1553–1558
Elizabeth I	1558–1603
The House of Stuart	
James I	1603–1625
Charles I	1625–1649

For further details, see Genealogical Tables on pp. 38–39.

one another, caught in a senseless dynastic struggle for control of the English crown. Many of them lost their lives in the fighting. By 1485, England was exhausted from civil conflict. Although Henry VII's own dynastic claim to the throne was weak, he managed to suppress factional opposition and to give England the respite from war she so desperately needed. His son, Henry VIII, inherited a throne in 1509 that was more secure than it had been in nearly a century.

Henry VIII's notorious marital difficulties, however, soon brought an end to dynastic security and civil accord. Because he divorced his first wife, Katharine of Aragon, in 1530 without the consent of Rome, he was excommunicated from the Catholic Church; his response in 1534 was to have himself proclaimed "Protector and only Supreme Head of the Church and Clergy of England." This decisive act signaled the beginning of the Reformation in England, not many years after Martin Luther's momentous break with the Papacy in 1517 and the consequent beginning of Lutheran Protestantism on the Continent. In England, Henry's act of defiance split the church and the nation. Many men chose Sir Thomas More's path of martyrdom rather than submit to Henry's new title as supreme head of the English church. Henry's later years did witness a period of retrenchment in religion, after the downfall of Thomas Cromwell in 1540, and indeed Henry's break with Rome had had its origin in political and marital rivalries rather than in matters of dogma and liturgy. Nevertheless, the establishment of an Anglican church was now an accomplished fact. The accession of Henry's ten-year-old son Edward VI, in 1547, gave reformers an opportunity to bring about rapid changes in English Protestantism. Archbishop Cranmer's forty-two articles of religion (1551), and his prayer book, laid the basis for the Anglican church of the sixteenth century.

The death of the sickly Edward VI in 1553 brought with it an intense crisis in religious politics, and a temporary reversal of England's religious direction. For five years England returned to Catholicism under the rule of Edward's elder sister Mary, daughter of the Catholic Queen Katharine of Aragon. The crisis accompanying such changes of government during this midcentury period was greatly exacerbated by the fact that all three of Henry VIII's living children were considered illegitimate by one faction or another of the English people. In Protestant eyes, Mary was the daughter of the divorced Queen Katharine, whose marriage to Henry had never been valid because she had previously been the spouse of Henry VIII's older brother Arthur. This Arthur had died at a young age, in 1502, shortly after his state marriage to the Spanish princess. If, as the Protestants insisted, Arthur had consummated the marriage, then Katharine's subsequent union with her deceased husband's brother was invalid, and Henry was free instead to marry Anne Boleyn—the mother-to-be of Elizabeth. In Catholic eyes, however, both Elizabeth and her brother Edward VI (son of Jane Seymour, Henry VIII's third wife) were the bastard issue of Henry's bigamous marriages; Henry's one and only true marriage in the Catholic faith was that to Katharine of Aragon. Edward and Elizabeth were regarded by many Catholics, at home and abroad, not only as illegitimate children but as illegitimate rulers, to be disobeyed and even overthrown by force. Thus, dynastic and marital conflicts became matters of grave political consequence.

Because of these struggles, Elizabeth's accession to the throne in 1558 remained an uncertainty until the last moment. Once she actually became ruler, however, England returned once more to the Protestant faith. Even then, tact and moderation were required to prevent open religious war. Elizabeth's genius at compromise prompted her to seek a middle position for her church, one that combined an episcopal form of church government (owing no allegiance to the Pope) with an essentially traditional form of liturgy and dogma. As much as was practicable, she left matters up to individual conscience; she drew the line, however, where matters of conscience tended to "exceed their bounds and grow to be matter of faction." In practice this meant that she did not tolerate avowed Catholics on the religious right, or Brownists and Unitarians (who denied the doctrine of the Trinity) on the religious left. The foundation for this so-called Elizabethan compromise was the thirty-nine articles, adopted in 1563 and based in many respects upon the forty-two articles of 1551. The compromise did not please everyone, of course, but it did achieve a remarkable degree of consensus during Elizabeth's long reign.

Queen Elizabeth and Tudor Absolutism

Elizabeth had to cope with a religiously divided nation and with extremists of both right and left who wished her downfall. She was a woman, in an age openly skeptical of women's ability or right to rule. Her success in dealing with such formidable odds was in large measure the result of her personal style as a monarch. Her combination of imperious will and femininity and her brilliant handling of her many contending male admirers have become legendary. She remained unmarried throughout her life, in part at least because marriage would have upset the delicate balance she maintained among rival groups, both foreign and domestic. Marriage would have committed her irretrievably to either one foreign nation or to one constituency at home. She chose instead to bestow her favor on certain courtiers, notably Robert Dudley (whom she elevated to be the Earl of Leicester) and, after Leicester's death in 1588, Robert Devereux, second Earl of Essex. Her relationship with these men, despite her partiality to them, was marked by her outbursts of tempestuous jealousy. In addition, she relied on the staid counsel of her hardworking ministers: Lord Burghley, Sir Francis Walsingham, Burghley's son Robert Cecil, and a few others.

In theory, at least, Tudor England was an absolutist monarchy in an age when many of England's greatest rivals—France, Spain, the Holy Roman Empire—were also under absolutist rule. The rise of absolutism throughout Renaissance Europe was the result of an increase of centralized national power and a corresponding decrease in autonomous baronial influence. Henry VII's strong assertion of his royal authority at the expense of the feudal lords corresponded roughly in time with the ascendancy of Francis I of France (1515) and Charles V of the Holy Roman Empire (1519). Yet England had long enjoyed a tradition of rule by consensus. When Elizabeth came to the throne, England was already in some ways a "limited" monarchy. Parliament, and especially the members of the House of Commons, claimed prerogatives of their own and were steadily gaining in both experience and power. In the mid-1560's, for example, the Commons made repeated attempts to use their tax-levying authority as a means of obliging Elizabeth to name a Protestant successor to the throne. The attempt, despite its failure to achieve its immediate goal, was significant; the Commons had shown that they were a force to be reckoned with. Even though Elizabeth made skillful rhetorical use of the theory of absolutism, portraying herself as God's appointed deputy on earth, her idea of absolutism should not be confused with despotism. She needed all her considerable diplomatic skills in dealing with her Parliaments and with the English people, self-reliant and proud of their reputation for independence. Elizabeth had more direct authority over her Privy Council, since she could appoint its members herself; still, she consulted faithfully with them on virtually everything she did. Nor were her closest advisers reluctant to offer her advice. Many vocal leaders in her government, including Walsingham and Leicester, urged the queen during the 1570's and 1580's to undertake a more active military role on the Continent against the Catholic powers. So did her later favorite, the Earl of Essex. With remarkable tact, she managed to retain the loyalty of her militant and sometimes exasperated counselors, and yet to keep England out of war with Spain until that country actually launched an invasion attempt in 1588 (the Great Armada).

Catholic Opposition

During her early years, Elizabeth sought through her religious compromise to ease the divisions of her kingdom, and attempted to placate her enemies abroad (notably Philip of Spain) rather than involve England in a costly war. For about twelve years, while England's economy gained much-needed strength, this policy of temporizing succeeded. Yet Elizabeth's more extreme Catholic opponents at home and abroad could never be reconciled to the daughter of that Protestant "whore," Anne Boleyn. England's period of relative accommodation came to an end in 1569 and 1570, with Catholic uprisings in the north and with Papal excommunication of the English queen. As a declared heretic, Elizabeth's very life was in danger; her Catholic subjects were enjoined by Rome to disobey her and to seek means for her violent overthrow.

Conspirators did in fact make attempts on the queen's life, notably in the so-called Babington conspiracy of 1586. This plot, brought to light by Secretary of State Walsingham, sought to place Mary Queen of Scots on the English throne in Elizabeth's stead. Mary was Elizabeth's kinswoman; Mary's grandmother, sister to Henry VIII, had been married to James IV of Scotland. So long as Elizabeth remained childless, Mary was a prominent heir to the English throne. Catholics pinned their hopes on her succession, by force if necessary; Protestant leaders urged Elizabeth to marry and give birth to a Protestant heir, or at least name a Protestant successor. Mary had abdicated the Scottish throne in 1567, after the sensational murder of her Catholic counselor David Rizzio, the murder of Mary's husband the Earl of Darnley (in which Mary was widely suspected to have taken part), and her subsequent marriage to Darnley's slayer, the Earl of Bothwell. Taking refuge in England, Mary remained a political prisoner and the inevitable focus of Catholic plotting against Elizabeth for approximately two decades. All that long while Elizabeth resisted demands from her Protestant advisers that she execute her kinswoman and thereby end a constant threat to the throne. Finally, Mary's clear involvement in the Babington conspiracy led to her execution in 1587. By that time, Spain was mounting an invasion against England, and Elizabeth's temporizing tactics were no longer feasible. The long years of peace had done their work, however, and England was considerably stronger and more resolute than she had been thirty years before. With Elizabeth's tacit approval, Sir Francis Drake and other naval commanders carried the fighting to Spain's very shore and to her American colonies. In 1585, Elizabeth had permitted troops under the command of the Earl of Leicester to aid the Dutch against Spain. The war with Spain continued from 1588 until about 1597.

Protestant Opposition

The threat from the religious left was no less worrisome than that from the right. Protestant reformers had experienced their first taste of power at the time of Henry VIII's break with Rome in 1534. Under Thomas Cromwell, Cardinal Wolsey's successor as the king's chief minister, the monasteries were suppressed and William Tyndale's English Bible was authorized. The execution of Cromwell introduced a period of conservative retrenchment, but the accession of Edward VI in 1547 brought reform once more into prominence. Thereafter Mary's Catholic reign drove most of the reformers into continental exile. When they returned after 1558, many had been made more radical by their continental experience.

To be sure, reform covered a wide spectrum from moderation to radicalism. Some preferred to work within the existing hierarchical structure of church and state, whereas others were religious separatists. Only the more radical groups, such as the Brownists and Anabaptists, endorsed ideas of equality and communal living. The abusive epithet "Puritan," applied indiscriminately to all shades of reforming activity, tended to obscure the wide range of differences in the reform movement. The reformers were to some extent united by a dislike for formal ritual and ecclesiastical garments, by a preference for a simple and pious manner of living, and by a belief in the literal word of the Bible rather than the patristic teachings of the church. They stressed personal responsibility in religion and were Calvinist in their emphasis on human depravity and the need for grace through election. Yet at first only the more radical were involved in a movement to establish an entirely separate church.

The radicals on the religious left, even if they represented at first only a minority of the religious reformers, posed a serious threat to Elizabeth's government. Their program bore an ironic resemblance to that of the Catholic opposition on the religious right. In their theoretical writings, the extreme reformers justified overthrow of what they considered to be tyrannical rule, just as Catholic spokesmen had absolved Elizabeth's subjects of obedience to her on the grounds that she was illegitimate. Both extremes appealed to disobedience in the name of a higher religious law. Among the reforming theoreticians was John Ponet, whose *Shorte Treatise of Politike Power* (1556) argued that a monarch is subject to a social contract and must rule according to laws that are equally subscribed to by Parliament, the clergy, and the people.

The Doctrine of Passive Obedience

Elizabeth's government countered such assaults on its authority, from both the right and the left, with many arguments, of which perhaps the most central was that of passive obedience. This doctrine condemned rebellion under virtually all circumstances. Its basic assumption was that the king is God's appointed deputy on earth. To depose such a monarch must therefore be an act of disobedience against God's will. Since God is all-wise and all-powerful, his placing of an evil ruler in power must proceed from some divine intention such as the punishment of a wayward people. Rebellion against God's "scourge" merely displays further disobedience to God's will. A people suffering under a tyrant must wait patiently for God to remove the burden, which he will surely do when the proper time arrives.

This doctrine was included in the official book of homilies of the Church of England, and was read from the pulpit at regular intervals. The best-known such homily was entitled *Against Disobedience and Wilful Rebellion.* Shakespeare heard it often, and he expresses its ideas through several of his characters such as John of Gaunt in *Richard II* (I,ii). This is not to say that he endorses such ideas, however, for he sets them in dramatic opposition to other and more heterodox concepts. We can say, nevertheless, that Shakespeare's audience would have recognized in Gaunt's speeches a clear expression of a familiar and officially correct position.

The Political Ideas of Machiavelli

The orthodoxies of the Elizabethan establishment were under attack not only from the Catholic right and the Protestant left, but also from a new and revolutionary point of view that set aside all criteria of religious morality. Tudor defense of order was based, as we have seen, on the assumption that the monarch rules in accord with a divine plan, a higher Law of Nature to which every just ruler is attuned. Political morality must be at one with religious morality. Catholic and Protestant critiques of the Tudor establishment made similar assumptions, even though they appealed to revolution in the name of that religious morality. To Niccolò Machiavelli, however, politics was a manipulative science best governed by the dictates of social expediency. His philosophy did not, as many accusingly charged, lead necessarily to the cynical promotion of mere self-interest. Nevertheless, he did argue, in his *Discourses* and *The Prince*, that survival and political stability are the first obligations of any ruler. Machiavelli regarded religion as a tool of the enlightened ruler rather than as a morally absolute guide. He extolled in his ideal leader the quality of *virtù*—a mixture of cunning and forcefulness. He saw history as a subject offering practical lessons in the kind of pragmatic statecraft he proposed.

Machiavelli was a hated name in England, and his works were never available in an English printed edition during Shakespeare's lifetime. Nevertheless, his writings were available in Italian, French, and Latin editions, and in manuscript English translations. His ideas certainly had a profound impact on the England of the 1590's. Marlowe caricatures the Italian writer in his *The Jew of Malta*, but he clearly was fascinated by what Machiavelli had to say. Shakespeare too reveals a complex awareness. However much he may lampoon the type of conscienceless villain in *Richard III*, he shows us more plausible pragmatists in *Richard II* and *1 Henry IV*. Conservative theories of the divine right of kings are set in debate with the more heterodox ambitions of Henry Bolingbroke and his associates. Bolingbroke is not a very attractive figure, but he does succeed politically where Richard has failed.

Shakespeare thus reveals himself as less a defender of the established order than as a great dramatist able to give sympathetic expression to the aspirations of all sides in a tense political struggle. His history plays have been variously interpreted as defenses of monarchy and as subtle pleas for rebellion, but the consensus today is that they are plays about human conflict. Perhaps the plays do stress the painful consequences of disorder, and perhaps they present an admiring view of monarchy (especially in *Henry V*) despite the manifest limitations of that institution. Certainly we can sense that Shakespeare's history plays were written for a generation of Englishmen who had experienced political crisis, and who could perceive issues of statecraft in Shakespeare's plays that were relevant to England's struggles in the 1580's and the 1590's. For example, Elizabeth bitterly acknowledged the cogency of a popular analogy comparing her reign with that of King Richard II; and when Shakespeare's play about Henry IV's overthrow of Richard was apparently revived for political purposes shortly before the Earl of Essex' abortive rebellion against Elizabeth, Shakespeare's acting company had some explaining to do to the authorities (see Introduction to *Richard II*). Nevertheless, Shakespeare's attitudes toward the issues of his own day are ultimately unknowable and unimportant, since his main concern seems to have been with the dramatization of conflict rather than with the urging of a controversial position.

Shakespeare on Religion

Our impressions of Shakespeare's personal sympathies in religion are similarly obscured by his refusal to use his art for polemical purposes. Although various attempts have been made to prove him a Catholic sympathizer or a loyal moderate Anglican, we see in his plays a spectrum of religious attitudes portrayed with an extraordinary range of insight. Some Catholic prelates are schemers, like Pandulph in *King John*. Ordinarily, however, Shakespeare's satirical digs at ecclesiastical pomposity and hypocrisy have little to do with the Catholic question. Many of Shakespeare's nominally Catholic clerics, such as Friar Laurence in *Romeo and Juliet* or Friar Francis in *Much Ado about Nothing*, are gentle and well-intentioned people even if occasionally bumbling. We can certainly say that Shakespeare consistently avoids the chauvinistic anti-Catholic baiting so often found in the plays of his contemporaries.

The same avoidance of extremes can be seen in his portrayal of Protestant reformers, though the instances in this case are very few in number. Malvolio in *Twelfth Night* is fleetingly compared with a "Puritan," although Shakespeare insists that no extensive analogy can be made. Angelo in *Measure for Measure* is sometimes thought to be a critical portrait of the Puritan temperament. Even if so, Shakespeare's satire is extremely indirect compared with the lampoons written by his contemporaries Ben Jonson and Thomas Dekker.

Stuart Absolutism

Queen Elizabeth's successor, James I of the Scottish house of Stuarts, reigned from 1603 to 1625. Like Elizabeth, he was a strong believer in the divine right of kings. He did not possess Elizabeth's tact, however, in dealing with the heterogeneous and antagonistic forces that she had kept in precarious balance through the sheer force of her personality. At the Hampton Court Conference of 1604, James totally alienated the Puritan wing of the church and drove even its more moderate members into the arms of the separatists. He similarly antagonized an increasingly radical group in the House of Commons. In the widening rift between the absolutists and those who defended the supremacy of Parliament, James' court moved toward the right. Catholic sympathies at court became common. Open civil war and the beheading of King Charles I (James' son) would not occur until the 1640's, but throughout James' reign the sense of estrangement between the right and the left was becoming more and more extreme. The infamous Gunpowder Plot of 1605, in which Guy Fawkes and other Catholic conspirators were accused of having plotted to blow up the houses of Parliament, raised hysteria to a new level of intensity. Penal laws against papists were harshly enforced. The Parliament of 1614 included in its membership John Pym, Thomas Wentworth, and John Eliot, men who were to become turbulent spokesmen against taxes imposed without parliamentary grant, imprisonment without the stating of specific criminal charges, and other abuses of royal prerogative. The polarization of English society naturally affected the London theatres. Popular London audiences (often Puritan in sympathy) grew disaffected with the stage, while even the popular acting companies came under the increasing domination of the court. Shakespeare's late plays reflect the increasing influence of a courtly audience.

THE INTELLECTUAL BACKGROUND

Renaissance Cosmology

In learning, as in politics and religion, Shakespeare's England was a time of conflict and excitement. Medieval ideas of a hierarchical and ordered creation were under attack but were still widely prevalent, and were used to justify a hierarchical order in society itself. According to the so-called Ptolemaic system of the universe, formulated by Ptolemy of Alexandria in the second century A.D., the earth stood at the center of creation. Around it moved in nine concentric spheres the heavenly bodies of the visible universe, in order as follows (from the earth outward): the moon, Mercury, Venus, the sun, Mars, Jupiter, Saturn, the fixed stars on a single plane, and lastly the *primum mobile*, imparting motion to the whole system.

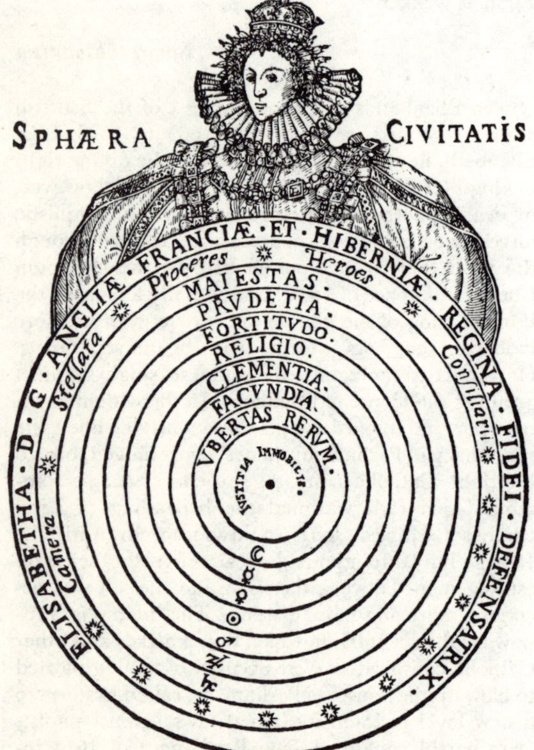

THE HUNTINGTON LIBRARY, SAN MARINO, CALIFORNIA

In this graphic analogy to a Ptolemaic universe, Elizabeth is shown as the primum mobile, *responsible for uniting and imparting motion to the spheres of state.*

Some medieval commentators proposed alternate arrangements or speculated as to the existence of one or two additional spheres, in particular a "crystalline sphere" between the fixed stars and the *primum mobile*, but they did not challenge the concept of an earth-centered cosmos.

The *primum mobile* was thought to turn the entire universe around the earth once every twenty-four hours. Simultaneously, the individual heavenly bodies moved more slowly around the earth on their individual spheres, constantly changing position with respect to the fixed stars. The moon, being the only heavenly body that seemed subject to change in its monthly waxing and waning, was thought to represent the boundary between the unchanging universe and the incessantly changing world. Beneath the moon, in the "sublunary" sphere, all creation was subject to death as a result of Adam's fall from grace; beyond the moon lay perfection. Hell was imagined to exist deep within the earth, as in Dante's *Inferno*, or else outside the *primum mobile* and far below the created universe in the realm of chaos, as in Milton's *Paradise Lost*.

Heaven or the Empyrean stood, according to most Ptolemaic systems, at the top of the universe. Between heaven and earth dwelled the nine angelic orders, each associated with one of the nine concentric spheres. Closest to God were the contemplative orders of Seraphim, Cherubim, and Thrones; next, the intermediate orders of Dominations, Powers, and Virtues; and finally the active orders of Principalities, Archangels, and Angels. These last served as God's messengers and intervened from time to time in the affairs of mortals. Ordered life among men, although manifestly imperfect when compared with the eternal bliss of the angelic orders, still modeled itself on that Platonic idea of perfect harmony. Thus the state, the church, and the family all resembled one another because they resembled (however distantly) the kingdom of God.

The devils of hell were fallen angels, with Satan as their leader. Such evil spirits might assume any number of shapes as demons, goblins, wizards, or witches. Believers in evil spirits generally made no distinction between orthodox Christian explanations of evil and the more primitive folklore of witchcraft. Belief in witchcraft was widespread indeed; King James I took the matter very seriously. On the other hand, a book like Reginald Scot's *Discoverie of Witchcraft* (1584) attempted to confute what the author regarded as ignorant superstition. Throughout Shakespeare's lifetime, belief and skepticism about such matters existed side by side.

A similar ambiguity pertained to belief in the Ptolemaic universe itself. All major poets of the Renaissance, including Shakespeare, Spenser, and Milton (who completed *Paradise Lost* after 1660), represented the universe in cosmic terms essentially as described by Ptolemy. Yet Nicolaus Copernicus' *De revolutionibus orbium coelestium* had been published in 1543, and

Galileo Galilei (who adopted the Copernican theory of a sun-centered system, though he was reluctant to speak out), published the results of his telescopic examinations of the moon in 1610. John Donne lamented in 1611–1612 that the "new philosophy" (i.e., the new science) "calls all in doubt." Skeptical uncertainty about the cosmos was on the rise. The poetic affirmations in Renaissance art of traditional ideas of the cosmos can best be understood as a response to uncertainty, a statement of faith in an age of increasing doubt.

Alchemy and Medicine

In all areas of Renaissance learning, the new and the old science were confusedly juxtaposed. Alchemy, for example, made important contributions to learning despite its superstitious character. Its chief goal was the transformation of base metals into gold, on the assumption that all metals were ranked on a hierarchical scale and could be raised from lower to higher positions on that scale by means of certain alchemical techniques. Other aims of alchemy included the discovery of a universal cure for diseases, and of a means for preserving life indefinitely. Such aims encouraged quackery and prompted various exposés, such as Chaucer's "The Canon's Yeoman's Tale" (late fourteenth century) and Jonson's *The Alchemist* (1610). Yet many of the procedures used in alchemy were essentially chemical procedures, and the science of chemistry received an invaluable impetus from constant experimentation.

In physics, medicine, and psychology, as well, older concepts vied with new. Traditional learning apportioned all physical matter into four elements, earth, air, fire, and water. Each of these was thought to be a different combination of the four "qualities" of the universe, hot, cold, moist, and dry. Earth combined cold and dry, air hot and moist, fire hot and dry, water cold and moist. Earth and water were the baser or lower elements, confined to the physical world; fire and air were aspiring elements, tending upward. Man, as a microcosm of the larger universe, contained in himself the four elements. The individual man's temperament, or "humour" or "complexion," depended on which "humour" predominated in him. The four humours in man corresponded to the four elements of physical matter. The blood was hot and moist, like air; yellow bile or choler was hot and dry, like fire; phlegm was cold and moist, like water; and black bile was cold and dry, like earth. A predominance of blood in an individual created a sanguine or cheerful temperament (or humour), yellow bile produced a choleric or irascible temperament, phlegm a phlegmatic or stolid temperament, and black bile a melancholic temperament. Diet could affect the balance among these humours, since an excess of a particular food would stimulate overproduction of one humour. The stomach and the liver, which converted food into humours, were regarded as the seat of

THE BODLEIAN LIBRARY

Alchemists employed relatively sophisticated equipment in their futile search for the "philosopher's stone."

human passions. A common remedy in medicine for illness was to let blood and thereby purge the body of unwanted humours.

The traditional name associated with such theories was that of Galen, the most celebrated of ancient writers on medicine (c. 130 A.D.). A more revolutionary name was that of Paracelsus, a famous German physician (c. 1493–1541), who attacked the Aristotelianism of his time and urged a more unfettered pragmatic research into pharmacy and medicine. Such experimentalism bore fruit in the anatomical research of Vesalius and in William Harvey's investigations of the circulation of the blood (c. 1616). Nevertheless, the practice of medicine in Renaissance times remained under the influence of the "humours" theory until quite late, and its ideas are to be found throughout Shakespeare's plays.

Learning

In learning generally, and in theories of education, new ideas conflicted with old. The curriculum of schools and colleges in the Renaissance was inherited largely from the Middle Ages and displayed many traditional characteristics. The curriculum consisted of the seven Liberal Arts: a lower division called the trivium, comprised of grammar, rhetoric, and logic, and an upper division called the quadrivium, comprised of arithmetic, geometry, astronomy, and music. In addition there were the philosophical studies, associated chiefly with Aristotle: natural philosophy, ethics, and metaphysics.

Aristotle's name had a towering influence in medieval times, and remained important to the Renaissance as well. Even among his Renaissance admirers, however, Aristotle proved more compelling in practical matters than in the abstract scholastic reasoning associated with his name in the Middle Ages. The Italian Aristotelians whose work made its way into England were interested primarily in the science of human behavior. Aristotelian ethics was for them a practical subject, telling men how to live usefully and well and how to govern themselves politically. Rhetoric was the science of persuasion, enabling men to use eloquence for socially useful goals. Poetry was a kind of rhetoric, a language of persuasion which dramatists too might use for morally pragmatic ends.

At the same time, new thinkers were daring to attack Aristotle by name as a symbol of traditional medieval thought. The attack was not always fair to Aristotle himself, whose work had been bent to the *a priori* purposes of much medieval scholasticism. Nevertheless, his name had assumed such symbolic importance that he had to be confronted directly. The Huguenot logician Petrus Ramus (1515–1572), defiantly proclaiming that "everything that Aristotle taught is false," argued for rules of logic as derived from observation. He urged, for example, that his students learn about rhetoric from observing in detail Cicero's effect on his listeners, rather than by the rote practice of syllogism. Actually, Ramus' thought was less revolutionary in its concepts of logic than in the tremendous ferment of opinion caused by his iconoclastic teaching.

THE FOLGER SHAKESPEARE LIBRARY

One Renaissance belief was that the useful exercise of knowledge gained through study was the only permanent thing in this life—all else was subject to Death's grip.

A basic issue at stake in the anti-Aristotelian movement was that of traditional authority versus independent observation. How does man best acquire true knowledge, through the teachings of his predecessors or through his own discovery? The issue had profound implications for religious truth as well: should the individual heed the collective wisdom of the earthly church, or read the Bible with his individual perceptions as his guide? Is "reason" an accretive wisdom handed down by authority or a quality of the individual soul? Obviously a middle ground exists between the two extremes, and no new thinker of the Renaissance professed to abandon entirely the use of ancient authority. For men like Henricus Agrippa (1486–1535) and Sir Francis Bacon (1561–1626), however, the weight of scholastic tradition had exerted its oppressive influence far too long. Authority needed to be examined critically and scientifically. Bacon, in his *The Advancement of Learning* (1605), fought against the blind acceptance of ancient wisdom, and argued that "knowledge derived from Aristotle, and exempted from liberty of examination, will not rise again higher than the knowledge of Aristotle." Sir Walter Ralegh and others joined in the excited new search for what human "reason" could discover when set free from scholastic restraint. The new learning did not seem to trouble these men in their religious faith, although a tension between scientific observation and faith in miracles was to become plentifully evident in the seventeenth century.

The Nature of Man

Another challenge to established concepts of thought came from Michel de Montaigne, Shakespeare's great French contemporary. In his "Apology for Raymond Sebond" and other of his essays, Montaigne questioned the assumption of man's superiority to the rest of the animal kingdom. That assumption rested on biblical and patristic teachings about the hierarchy of creation, in which man stood at the apex of physical creation nearest God and the angels. Man was thus supreme on earth in the so-called chain of being. His human reason, though subject to error because of his sinfulness, enabled man to aspire toward divinity. Man was, in the view of medieval philosophers, the great amphibian as well as the microcosm of the universe, part bestial and part immortal, doomed by Adam's fall to misery and death in this life but promised eternal salvation through Christ's atonement. Right reason, properly employed, could lead man to the truths of revealed Christianity and thus give him a glimpse of the heavenly perfection one day to be his. Renaissance neo-Platonism, as expounded, for example, in Castiglione's *The Courtier* (translated by Sir Thomas Hoby, 1561), offered man a vision of a Platonic ladder extending from the perception of a woman's beauty to the experiencing of God's transcendent love.

Montaigne, on the other hand, gave Shakespeare a fundamentally different way to consider the nature of man—a way that reflects itself, for example, in Hamlet's observations on man as a "quintessence of dust." Montaigne stressed man's arrogance, vanity, and frailty. He was unconvinced of man's purported moral superiority to the animals, and argued that animals are no less endowed with a soul. Montaigne destroyed, in other words, the hierarchy in which man was the unquestioned master of the physical world, just as Copernican science overturned the earth-centered cosmos and Machiavelli's political system dismissed as an improbable fiction the divinely constituted hierarchy of the state. Montaigne was followed in the seventeenth century by that overpowering iconoclast, Thomas Hobbes, who extended the concept of mechanical laws governing human society and human psychology. Hobbes postdates Shakespeare, to be sure, but one has only to consider Iago's philosophy of the assertive individual will (in *Othello*), or Edmund's contempt for his father Gloucester's astrological pieties (in *King Lear*), to see the enormous impact on Shakespeare of the new heterodoxies of his age. Shakespeare customarily puts such insidious philosophies in the mouths of his villains, and affirms more traditional values through contrastingly virtuous characters; nevertheless, the challenge to the older cosmos in a play like *King Lear* is profound.

LONDON THEATRES AND DRAMATIC COMPANIES

Throughout Shakespeare's life the propriety of acting any plays at all was a matter of bitter controversy. Indeed, when one considers the power and earnestness of the opposition, one is surprised that there could come into being such a wealth of dramatic excellence, and that Shakespeare's plays should reflect so little the bitterness of the controversy waged in his time.

RELIGIOUS AND MORAL OPPOSITION TO THE THEATRE

From the 1570's onward, and even earlier, the city fathers of London revealed an ever-increasing distrust of the public performance of plays. They fretted about the dangers of plague and of riotous assembly. They objected to apprentices idly wasting their time instead of working in their shops. And always the municipal authorities suspected immorality. Thus, by an order of the Common Council of London, dated December 6, 1574, the players were put under severe restrictions.

The order cites the reasons. The players, it was charged, had been acting in the innyards of the city, which in consequence were haunted by great multitudes of people, especially youths. These gatherings had been the occasions of frays and quarrels, "evil practices of incontinency in great inns"; the players published "uncomely and unshamefast speeches and doings," withdrew the queen's subjects from divine service on Sundays and holidays, wasted the money of "poor and fond persons," gave opportunity to pickpockets, uttered "busy and seditious matters," and injured and maimed people by engines, by the falling of their scaffolds, and by weapons and powder used in plays. The order goes on to state the Common Council's fear that if the plays, which had been forbidden on account of the plague, should be resumed, God's wrath would manifest itself by an increase of the infection. Therefore, no innkeeper, tavernkeeper, or other person might cause or suffer to be openly played "any play, interlude, comedy, tragedy, matter, or show" which had not been first licensed by the mayor and the court of aldermen.

The mayor and aldermen did not always state their case plainly, because Queen Elizabeth was a patron of the players, and because the players had friends and patrons in the Privy Council and among the nobility; sometimes, however, they did so quite boldly. One sees the case against plays stated syllogistically in the following words of Thomas White, a preacher at Paul's Cross in 1577.

> Looke but vppon the common playes of London, and see the multitude that flocketh to them and followeth them: beholde the sumptuous Theater houses, a continuall monument of London prodigalitie and folly. But I vnderstande they are now forbidden bycause of the plague. I like the pollicye well if it hold still, for a disease is but bodged or patched vp that is not cured in the cause, and the cause of plagues is sinne, if you looke to it well: and the cause of sinne are playes: therefore the cause of plagues are playes. (From *A Sermon preached at Paules Cross . . . in the time of the Plague*, 1578.)

Moved, no doubt, by the prohibition of the Common Council, James Burbage, with a company of actors under the patronage of the Earl of Leicester, leased a site in Shoreditch, a London suburb in Middlesex, beyond the immediate jurisdiction of the official enemies in the Common Council, whose authority extended only to the city limits. By 1576 he had completed the Theatre. He could call it "the Theatre" because there was no other; Burbage erected England's first permanent commercial theatrical building. In general, the building combined features of the innyard and the animal-baiting house, having a central and probably paved courtyard open to the sky (like an innyard) and surrounding galleries on all sides (like an animal-baiting house). Burbage erected a stage at one side of the circular arena, and put dressing rooms in back of it. His Theatre became the model for public playhouses such as the Curtain, the Swan, and the Globe, all constructed later.

THE FOLGER SHAKESPEARE LIBRARY

Because of restrictions placed on London street players such as these, England's first permanent theatre was erected for the Earl of Leicester's men in 1576.

Burbage had in this manner availed himself of that immunity from the enforcement of law which arises from indirect jurisdiction. The city fathers could not suppress plays or control them with perfect success if they were performed in Middlesex or on the famous Bankside across the Thames in Surrey. In order to get at them in these suburban regions it was necessary to petition the Queen's Privy Council to give orders to the magistrates and officers of the law in these counties. The queen's Privy Council, although always on the most polite terms with the Lord Mayor and his brethren of the city and always open to the argument that the assemblage of crowds caused the spread of the plague, were to a much less degree in sympathy with the moral scruples of the city. There were, moreover, current arguments for the plays, derived from the works of scholars, poets, and playwrights; namely, that there was precedent in antiquity for dramatic spectacles; that by drawing a true picture of both the bad and the good in life, plays enabled men to choose the good; that the people should have wholesome amusement; and that plays provided livelihood for loyal subjects of the queen.

Of these arguments the Privy Council made little use, resting the case for plays on what was no doubt an unanswerable argument—that, since the players were to appear before Her Majesty, the players needed practice in order to prepare themselves to please the royal taste. There was a good deal of politic fencing over the whole matter, and, so far as orders, complaints, and denunciations were concerned, the reforming opposition had much the better of it. The preachers thundered against plays. Pamphleteers denounced all matters pertaining to the stage: Stephen Gosson in *The Schoole of Abuse, Containing a pleasaunt invective against Poets, Pipers, Plaiers, Iesters and such like Caterpillers of a Commonwelth* (1579) and other works; Philip Stubbes in *The Anatomie of Abuses* (1583); and finally and most furiously of all, William Prynne in *Histrio-Mastix: the Players Scourge or Actors Tragedy* (1633). Gosson spoke of plays as "the inventions of the devil, the offerings of idolatry, the pomp of worldlings, the blossoms of vanity, the root of apostacy, food of iniquity, riot and adultery." "Detest them," he warns. "Players are masters of vice, teachers of wantonness, spurs to impurity, the sons of idleness."

Still, such diatribes represented an extreme reforming opinion that was not shared at first by a majority of London viewers. They kept coming to plays, and the public theatres continued to flourish, until the early reign of James I (1603–1625) when the rift between the Puritans and the court erupted into irreconcilable antagonism. After about 1604, when James openly alienated the Puritans at the Hampton Court Conference, popular London audiences fell away increasingly from the theatre. The acting companies, whether through choice or necessity, moved toward the precinct of the court. Opposition to the stage, which had become increasingly Puritan in character, forced the total closing of the theatres in 1642.

THE PUBLIC THEATRES

A year or more after Burbage built the Theatre in 1576, the Curtain was put up near it by Philip Henslowe, or possibly by Henry Laneman, or Lanman. About ten years later Henslowe built the Rose, the first playhouse on the Bankside (the southern bank of the Thames River). The Swan was built there in 1594. In 1599 Richard and Cuthbert Burbage, sons of James Burbage, the former being the great actor of Shakespeare's heroes, tore down the Theatre because of trouble about the lease of the land and rebuilt it as the Globe on the Bankside. This Globe was the theatre that burned June 29, 1613, from cannon wadding which set fire to the roof after the discharge of ordnance during the acting of a play called *All is True*, thought to be identical with Shakespeare's *Henry VIII.* The Globe was rebuilt, probably in its original polygonal form—that is, essentially round with a

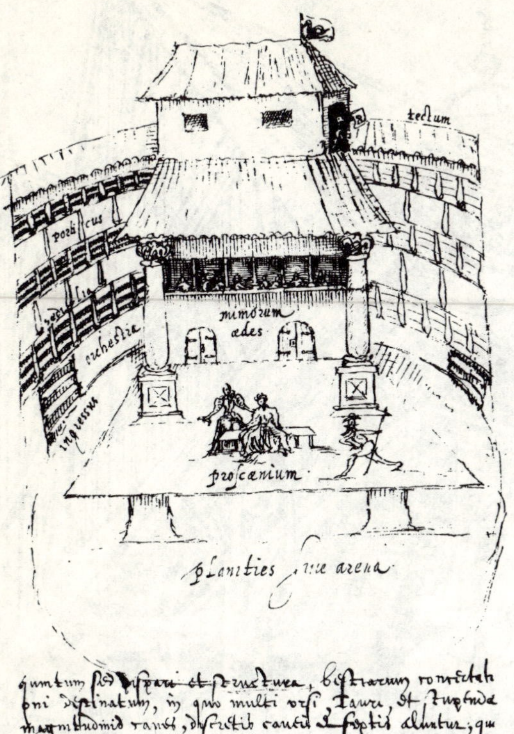

UTRECHT UNIVERSITY LIBRARY

The only extant illustration of the Swan; by Van Buchell (c. 1596), it may be based on several by De Witt.

large number of sides. In 1600 Henslowe built the Fortune, specifications for which have been preserved at Dulwich College with the other invaluable papers of the old theatre manager. This college, it may be said in passing, was founded by the munificence of the great actor Edward Alleyn, who had married Henslowe's stepdaughter.

Henslowe's Fortune Theatre was apparently a countermove to the activities of the Burbage group, who constituted a joint stock company for the support of the king's company, whereas Henslowe operated as theatre proprietor. He managed the Lord Admiral's men and secured, we may be sure, a large part of the profits of their activities. The contract for building the Fortune was let to the same contractor who had built the new Globe, and, since it was specified that it should be like the Globe in all its main features, except that it was to be square instead of polygonal, we may gain from these specifications an idea of the Globe. There is also preserved a drawing of the Swan which accompanies a description of the playhouse by Johannes De Witt, who visited London in 1596. The drawing, which was discovered in the University Library at Utrecht, is the work of one Van Buchell and may be based on drawings by De Witt himself. Besides these there are two or three little pictures of the Elizabethan public stage on the title pages of published plays, the most important being that on the title page of William Alabaster's *Roxana* (1632).

THE PUBLIC STAGE

From these documents and pictures, from scattered references to the theatres, and from extended studies of stage directions and scenic conditions in plays themselves, we have a fairly clear idea of the public stage. Its features are these: a pit about 70 feet in diameter, usually circular and open to the sky; surrounding this, galleries in three tiers, where were the most expensive seats; and a rectangular stage, about 43 by 27 feet, wider than it was deep, raised about 5½ feet above the surface of the yard, sometimes built on trestles so that it could be removed if the house was also customarily used for bearbaiting and bullbaiting.

THE FOLGER SHAKESPEARE LIBRARY

A drawing of the gallery seats or "Lord's room" (bottom row, middle panel) from the title page of Roxana *(1632).*

O
K
L
M
Q
O
J
E
E
N
H
G
F
C. WALTER
HODGES
A

The (Second) Globe Playhouse, 1614-1644.

Key.

AA. *Main entrances to auditorium.*
B. *Yard for standing spectators.*
CC. *Entrances to lowest gallery.*
DD. *Entrances to staircase leading to upper galleries.*
EE. *"Gentlemen's Rooms."*
F. *The stage.*
G. *The stage trap (leading from the "Hell" beneath the stage).*
H. *Curtained space for "discovery" scenes.*
J. *Upper stage.*
K. *The "Heavens." (This area probably often covered across with a stretched canopy painted to represent the sky.)*
L. *Backing painted with clouds. A shutter is here shown open to allow a god's throne to travel forward. (c.f. "Cymbeline," Act V sc. IV)*
M. *The throne about to descend to the stage.*
N. *Backstage area (or "Tiring-house").*
O. *Wardrobe and dressing-rooms.*
P. *Spectator galleries.*
Q. *"Fly" gallery in the Heavens.*
R. *Playhouse flag (reached from top landing of staircase, and raised to denote performance days).*

The second Globe Theatre, built in 1613 after a fire had destroyed the first Globe during a performance of Shakespeare's Henry VIII. *This building generally resembled its predecessor in the size of the stage and the "yard" for spectators, the location of stage doors and of a curtained area backstage for discovery scenes, etc. The upper acting station in this second Globe Theatre may, however, have been somewhat more elaborate than in the first Globe where spectators often sat above the stage (see pp. 17,20). In neither theatre was the upper acting station used extensively for dramatic presentation.*

ORIGINAL ILLUSTRATION COURTESY C. WALTER HODGES

The flat open stage usually contained one trap door. Part of the stage was roofed over by a wooden cover supported by posts, which might constitute "the heavens." Above this roof was a "hut" perhaps containing suspension gear for ascents and descents.

At the back of the stage was a partition wall, the "tiring-house façade," with at least two doors opening out of the actors' dressing rooms or "tiring house." Some theatres appear to have had no more than two doors, left and right, as shown in the Swan drawing; other theatres may have had a third door in the center. The arrangement of the Globe Theatre in this important matter cannot be finally determined, although some particular scenes from Shakespeare's plays seem to demand a third door. In any case, the so-called inner stage, long supposed to have stood at the rear of the Elizabethan stage, almost certainly did not exist. A more modest "discovery space" could be provided at one of the curtained doors when needed, as for example when Ferdinand and Miranda are suddenly "discovered" at their game of chess by Prospero in *The Tempest*. Such scenes never called for extensive action within the discovery space, however, and indeed the number of such discoveries in Elizabethan plays is very few. Well-to-do spectators who may have been seated in the gallery above the rear of the stage could not see into the discovery space. Accordingly it was used sparingly for brief visual effects. Otherwise, the actors performed virtually all their scenes on the open stage. Sometimes curtains were hung over the tiring-house façade between the doors to facilitate scenes of concealment, as when Polonius and Claudius eavesdrop on Hamlet and Ophelia.

An upper station was sometimes used as an acting space, but not nearly so often as was once supposed. The gallery seats above the stage, sometimes known as the "Lord's room," were normally sold to well-to-do spectators. (We can see such spectators in the Swan drawing and in Alabaster's *Roxana*.) Occasionally these box seats could be used by the actors, as when Juliet appears at her window (it is never called a balcony). In military sequences, as in the *Henry VI* plays, the tiring-house façade could represent the walls of a besieged city, with the city's defenders appearing "on the walls" (i.e., in the gallery above the stage) in order to parley with the besieging enemy standing below on the main stage. Such scenes were relatively infrequent, however, and usually required only a small number of persons to be aloft. A music room, when needed, could be located in one of the gallery boxes over the stage; but public theatres did not emulate the private stages with music rooms and entr' act music until some time around 1609.

The use of scenery was almost wholly unknown on the Elizabethan public stage, although we do find occasional hints of the use of labels to designate a certain door or area as a fixed location. For the most part, the scene was unlimited and the concept of space extremely fluid. No proscenium arch or curtain stood between the actors and audience, so the action could not be easily interrupted. Only belatedly did the public companies adopt the private-theatre practice of entr' act music, as we have seen. Most popular Elizabethan plays were written to be performed non-stop. Five-act structure had little currency, especially at first, and the divisions in Shakespeare's text of this kind are nonauthorial. Acting tempo was brisk. The Prologue of *Romeo and Juliet* speaks of "the two hours' traffic of our stage." Plays were performed in the afternoons, and had to be completed by dark in order to allow the audience to return safely to London. During the winter season playing time was severely restricted.

A capacity audience for the popular theatres came to about 3000 persons. The spectators represented a broad national cross-section, from the small shopkeepers and artisans who stood in the pit or yard for a penny, to the more substantial citizens who paid two pence or three pence for gallery seats, to the lords who occupied the elegant twelve-penny rooms. These spectators were lively, demanding, and intelligent. Although Shakespeare does allow Hamlet to refer disparagingly on one occasion to the "groundlings" who "for the most part are capable of nothing but inexplicable dumbshows and noise" (*Hamlet*, III,ii), Shakespeare wrote to please every level of his audience simultaneously, and thereby achieved a breadth of vision seldom found in continental courtly drama of the same period. The vitality and financial success of the Elizabethan public theatre is without parallel in English history. The city of London had only about 100,000 inhabitants, yet throughout Shakespeare's career several companies were competing simultaneously for this audience and constantly producing new plays. Most new plays ran for only a few performances, so that the acting companies were always in rehearsal with new shows. The actors needed phenomenal memories and a gift of improvisation as well. Their acting seems to have been of a high caliber despite the speed with which they worked. Among other things, many of them were expert fencers and singers.

LONDON PRIVATE THEATRES

Londoners could also enjoy the talents of boy actors in the so-called private theatres, especially at St. Paul's and at Blackfriars. The private theatre flourished during the 1580's and again after 1598–1599, having been closed down during most of the 1590's because of its satirical activities. Although a commercial theatre, it was "private" in its clientele because its high price of admission (sixpence) excluded those who could stand in the yards of the "public" theatres for a penny (roughly the equivalent of an hour's wage for a skilled worker). Plays written for the more select audiences of the "private" theatres tended to be more satirical and oriented to courtly values than those written for the "public" theatres, although the distinction is not absolute.

From 1576 to 1584 the Children of the Queen's Chapel, one of the two most important companies of boy actors, had used a hall in the precinct of Blackfriars in which to act their plays. In 1596 James Burbage purchased property in this precinct and seems to have spent a good deal of money in its adaptation for use as an indoor theatre (the so-called Second Blackfriars). He probably appreciated its advantages over Cripplegate or the Bankside, particularly for use in winter. But the aristocratic residents of the Blackfriars by petition to the Privy Council prevented him from making use of his theatre. Plays within the city proper had only recently been finally and successfully prohibited, and the petitioners no doubt objected to their intrusion into Blackfriars on the grounds that they and their crowds were a nuisance.

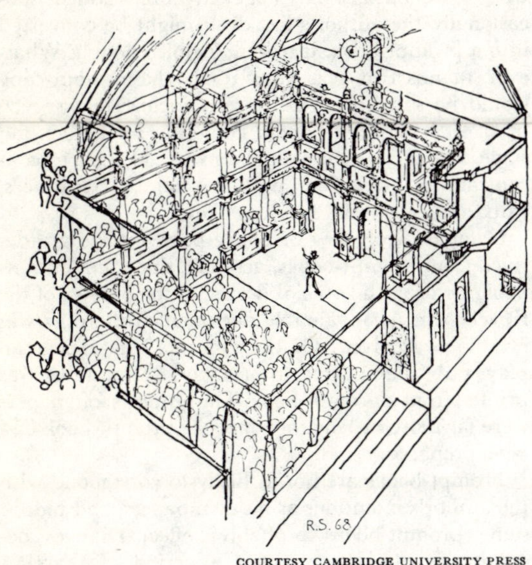

COURTESY CAMBRIDGE UNIVERSITY PRESS

A reconstruction of the Second Blackfriars, featuring a rectangular stage, a tiring house with three doors, and a gallery.

Burbage's new indoor theatre may have lain idle from the time of its preparation until 1600; but, in any case, in that year it became the scene of many plays. It was let by lease to a group of men for the use of the Children of the Chapel, who in 1604 became the Children of the Queen's Revels. These theatre managers brought into their service a number of new dramatists, Jonson, Marston, Chapman, and later Webster; the vogue of the plays acted by the Children of the Chapel was so great as to damage the patronage of the established companies and to compel them to go on the road. Out of this rivalry between the children and the adult actors arose that "War of the Theatres" alluded to in *Hamlet* (II,ii). In 1608 the Burbage interests secured the evacuation of the lease, so that the theatre in Blackfriars then became the winter playhouse of Shakespeare's company.

SHAKESPEARE'S TEXTS

The earliest complete edition of Shakespeare's plays was the so-called First Folio of 1623, sponsored by Shakespeare's theatrical colleagues John Heminges and Henry Condell. (A "folio" book was one in which the printing sheets were folded only once, each producing two "leaves" or four rather large printed pages of about 13½ x 8¼ inches. In a "quarto" book the sheets were folded twice, producing eight pages half the folio size.) The First Folio brought together eighteen plays that had previously been published in single quarto volumes, and eighteen plays that had never before been published. It did not include Shakespeare's nondramatic poetry, of which *Venus and Adonis* and *The Rape of Lucrece* had been published in 1593–1594 and the sonnets in 1609. Nor did it include *Pericles*.

The plays in the First Folio were printed from various sorts of copy: from authorial manuscripts, from manuscripts prepared for theatrical performance, and from quarto editions that had already been published before the appearance of the First Folio. Each of these sorts of copy left its own characteristic imprint on Shakespeare's text, altering it in ways that were often unfortunate. Today, the editor must face the difficulty of trying to recover what Shakespeare actually wrote, insofar as that is possible. Let us examine the kinds of problems one by one, following the Shakespearean manuscript through successive phases of staging, licensing, and printing.

MANUSCRIPTS: "FOUL PAPERS"

When Shakespeare had finished writing a play, he presumably submitted a readable manuscript to his acting company. This draft in his handwriting, or any earlier draft, went by the name of "foul papers," as distinguished from "fair papers" or a clean copy that might be prepared by the author or a playhouse scribe. Actually, the foul papers need not have been especially messy, although a certain amount of deletion, interlineation, inconsistency, and illegibility was inevitable. These foul papers were usually preserved by the acting company and were often turned over to the printer when the company decided to sell its rights in a play. The company usually preferred to hold on to its prompt-book copy of the play (see below), and to dispose of the foul papers as of little further value. A manuscript of this sort naturally posed some difficulties for the compositor.

At their best, foul papers are close to what Shakespeare wrote, but they are also potentially laden with error. Some foul-paper texts preserve Shakespeare's work in an early state of composition, such as *Timon of Athens*, whereas others, such as *1 Henry IV*, are very good texts. Foul papers therefore represent a whole spectrum of states from unrevised manuscript to a text that has been thoroughly worked over.

Unfortunately, no manuscript of a regular Shakespearean play has survived today. Other early dramatic manuscripts have survived, however, enabling textual scholars to determine when a printed text has been based upon foul papers. Among the telltale characteristics are vagueness in specifying the number of supernumeraries needed for a scene, lack of precision in the marking of entrances and especially exits, authorial stage-directions that tend to describe stage business or the emotional states of the characters more than a businesslike prompt-book would require, speech prefixes that inconsistently refer to a character both by his personal name and his generic title.

LICENSING FOR PERFORMANCE

Before a Shakespearean play could go into production, it had to be licensed by the Master of the Revels, an officer of the royal household responsible for supervising court entertainments. Since the beginning of Elizabeth's reign, and even earlier, dramatic performances throughout England had been made subject to governmental control. Elizabeth had authorized municipal and other local governments to scrutinize plays performed within their jurisdictions. In the vicinity of London, however, where municipal hostility toward the theatre was particularly strong, she took the unusual step in 1581 of transferring licensing power to her own Master of the Revels. Since many public plays came to court, as we have seen, Elizabeth was inclined to protect the players against the city authorities in this way, and to adopt the useful fiction that public performances were rehearsals of plays intended for her ultimate benefit.

The Master of the Revels did occasionally censor Shakespeare's plays. For example, the scene of Richard II's deposition, omitted from the three earliest quarto editions of the play, seems to have been disallowed for acting during Elizabeth's lifetime. (She was sensitive to a widespread and libelous analogy comparing her with Richard.) More often, one suspects, the mere threat of censorship was sufficient to keep the London dramatic companies in line. The Tudor establishment had no intention of tolerating openly seditious criticism. Generally, the Master of the Revels was more concerned with questions of religion and politics than with morals.

THE PROMPT-BOOK

The document on which the Master of the Revels affixed his seal of approval was the prompt-book or prompt-copy or playbook—that is, the version prepared by the acting company for use in actual production. Usually this version was a fair copy of the manuscript, readied for stage performance—that is, with the technical inconsistencies weeded out and with more businesslike stage directions added. Occasionally the author's last draft might be converted into a prompt-book, if it were legible enough. Whatever manuscript was thus used, the prompt-copy would be sure to normalize any inconsistent speech prefixes, in order to avoid confusion for actors and stage managers. Stage directions would tend to concentrate on technical matters such as entrances, exits, and occasional specific effects.

Comparatively few of Shakespeare's texts are derived from prompt-books, actually, since the prompt-book, bearing the official license of the Master of the Revels, was an invaluable document if the play was ever to be revived. Of the nineteen Shakespearean plays published in quarto prior to 1623, not one was printed from a prompt-book. The author's foul papers were far more expendable once the prompt-book had been prepared.

Prompt-books are not as likely to correspond with the author's intentions as his own papers, and indeed some prompt-books probably reflect changes occurring in the theatre over a period of years. A prompt-book might be altered for the revival of an old favorite, or might even represent a cut performance intended to be taken on tour.

THE BAD QUARTOS

An acting company did not normally like to see its plays in print. On occasion, to be sure, a company might disband and sell its plays, or experience financial difficulties and sell some older plays for ready money, but ordinarily the company regarded its plays as the very key to its economic prosperity. Popular plays that enjoyed long runs, and could later be revived, were especially valuable. Hence the company guarded carefully its authorial manuscripts and prompt-books, and did not usually permit other copies to be made or circulated.

By the same token, however, the temptation for some unscrupulous bookseller to pirate an edition of a popular play was obviously great. And, unfortunately, no copyright law protected the acting companies from such piracy. If a bookseller could obtain a dramatic text in any way, all he had to do was to present his book at Stationers' Hall and enter it in the Stationers' Register, or official record book of the London Company of Stationers (i.e., booksellers). By paying a fee, usually sixpence, he reserved the right to publish the work he had thus entered. This right had considerable legal force. Although authors and acting companies could not copyright their plays, the stationers or booksellers enjoyed a tight monopoly. Their London Company of Stationers had a patent from the crown to restrict the number of presses operating in London, the number of books that could be printed, and so on. Legal safeguards were all on the side of the booksellers.

To protect themselves, the acting companies sometimes formed friendly relationships with cooperative booksellers and entered agreements with them designed to forestall the piratical activities of less scrupulous publishers. The acting company might allow a friendly bookseller or printer to register a play for later publication. Despite such precautions, however, unauthorized or "bad" quartos were fairly common.

How were such pirated texts obtained? Textual scholarship now generally supports the findings of W. W. Greg that most pirated texts were put together by "memorial reconstruction." The usual culprits seem to have been one or more actors, in league with an unscrupulous printer. Most pirates were temporary actors hired to perform minor roles, rather than actor-sharers having a vested interest in the acting company and its stock of plays. Possibly one or more such minor actors got together and slowly recited what they could remember of a play, while a scribe took down what they recited. The reporter or reporters of a pirated text can sometimes tentatively be identified by the relative accuracy of certain roles. For example, the actor who perhaps doubled the minor parts of Marcellus and Lucianus in *Hamlet* may have helped in the memorial reconstruction of the bad quarto of that play.

A bad quarto put together by memorial reconstruction can be identified with some accuracy by modern textual methods. Such a text tends to give a fairly accurate rendition of the overall plot, but garbles some speeches, transfers or misplaces lines of dialogue or even whole scenes, borrows scraps of phrases from other plays in which the actor-reporters may have acted, mislineates blank verse or crudely versifies passages of prose, ad-libs freely in half-remembered parts of the play, and so on. A bad quarto is always shorter than the regular version. Visual impressions are often vivid, since the actor-reporters are remembering things they have seen on stage. The stage directions tend to be more frequent and more detailed than in either an author's manuscript or a prompt-book.

THE GOOD QUARTOS

Despite their general unwillingness to see their plays in print, acting companies did sometimes sell texts to the printers for ready cash or to correct bad quartos that had already appeared (as in the case of the good quartos of *Romeo and Juliet*, 1599 and *Hamlet*, 1604–1605). The good quartos were based generally on Shakespeare's own drafts, or transcripts of them. The list of good quartos is a short one, and sporadic in its time schedule; Shakespeare's company did not regularly dispose of its plays to the printers. Once a play had appeared in print, however, it was apt to be reprinted. Some quarto texts continued to appear after the Folio of 1623.

Before a play could be printed, it had to be licensed for publication. The licensing agency responsible for printed matter was a panel of London clergymen known as the "correctors of the press," operating under the authority of the Privy Council, the Bishop of London, the Archbishop of Canterbury, and the Lord Chamberlain. In 1606, Parliament passed a law forbidding references to the Deity in the texts of plays.

THE TEXTS USED FOR THE 1623 FOLIO

The idea of publishing a collected edition of Shakespeare's plays evidently did not originate with Heminges and Condell, the supervisors of the First Folio of 1623. A few years earlier, in 1619, a bookseller named Thomas Pavier and a printer named William Jaggard attempted to bring out ten plays (eight of them Shakespeare's) in a single volume. The scheme was frustrated, however, seemingly by the Lord Chamberlain at the instigation of Shakespeare's company. Pavier chose the expedient of publishing his plays separately, some with fraudulently early dates and names of publishers in an apparent attempt to obscure the fact of new publication. None of Pavier's texts provides any independent textual authority, for all were copied from earlier quartos.

Pavier's dubious and abortive undertaking may possibly have given impetus to a more legitimate edition of Shakespeare's collected plays, although Shakespeare's company may already have been contemplating such an honor to its famous playwright. Ben Jonson's folio collection of plays in 1616 had established a major precedent for such a volume, despite the scorn of those who regarded all plays as subliterary. The large folio format, normally reserved for edifying religious works and the like, might now be used also for a collection of plays.

The first task facing the supervisors of the Folio collection, Heminges and Condell, was the assembling of publishing rights to those eighteen Shakespearean plays that had already appeared in print. The most efficient means of doing so was to form a syndicate of publishers who already owned the rights to a large number of the plays. Some of the men who participated were William Jaggard, Edward Blount, John Smethwick, and William Aspley. The eighteen plays that had never before been printed were registered for publication in the Stationers' Register in November of 1623.

In addition to securing publishing rights, Heminges and Condell and their associates had the further task of selecting copy from which the printers were to set up their work. In the case of the eighteen as yet unpublished plays, the editors selected the best manuscripts they could find. The complicated choices involved plays that had already been published. Printers, then as now, preferred to work from printed copy because of its legibility. Yet some published

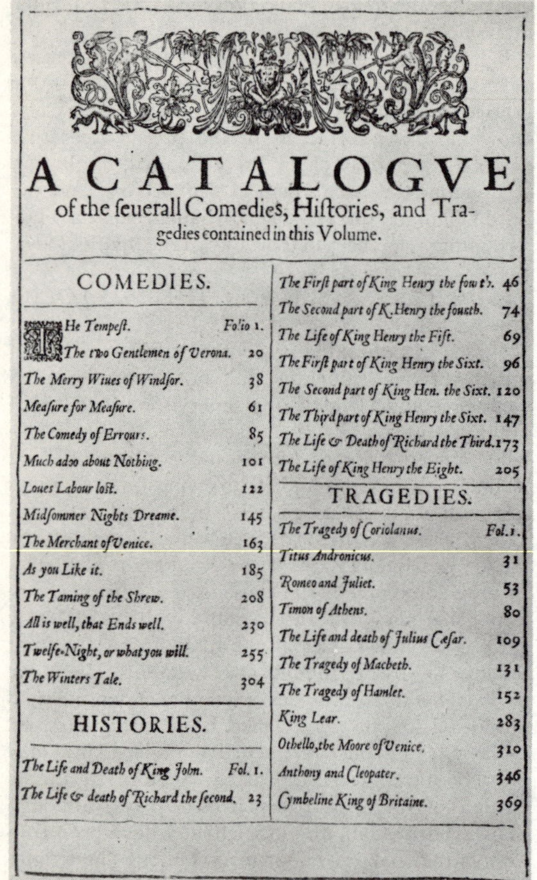

A CATALOGVE
of the ſeuerall Comedies, Hiſtories, and Tragedies contained in this Volume.

COMEDIES.

THe Tempeſt.	*Folio* 1.
The two Gentlemen of Verona.	20
The Merry Wiues of Windſor.	38
Meaſure for Meaſure.	61
The Comedy of Errours.	85
Much adoo about Nothing.	101
Loues Labour loſt.	122
Midſommer Nights Dreame.	145
The Merchant of Venice.	163
As you Like it.	185
The Taming of the Shrew.	208
All is well, that Ends well.	230
Twelfe-Night, or what you will.	255
The Winters Tale.	304

HISTORIES.

The Life and Death of King John.	*Fol.* 1.
The Life & death of Richard the ſecond.	23
The Firſt part of King Henry the fowrth.	46
The Second part of K. Henry the fourth.	74
The Life of King Henry the Fift.	69
The Firſt part of King Henry the Sixt.	96
The Second part of King Hen. the Sixt.	120
The Third part of King Henry the Sixt.	147
The Life & Death of Richard the Third.	173
The Life of King Henry the Eight.	205

TRAGEDIES.

The Tragedy of Coriolanus.	*Fol.* 1.
Titus Andronicus.	31
Romeo and Juliet.	53
Timon of Athens.	80
The Life and death of Julius Cæſar.	109
The Tragedy of Macbeth.	131
The Tragedy of Hamlet.	152
King Lear.	283
Othello, the Moore of Venice.	310
Anthony and Cleopater.	346
Cymbeline King of Britaine.	369

The printers of the First Folio arranged the plays into Comedies, Histories, and Tragedies. Troilus and Cressida, *inserted between the histories and tragedies, was omitted from the original table of contents.*

Shakespearean plays were bad quartos, the "stolne and surreptitious copies" that Heminges and Condell had vowed to replace with more perfect copies. Although one might suppose that Heminges and Condell would have set aside bad quartos entirely, they did not always do so, perhaps because the manuscript alternatives were illegible or defective. In other cases, the editors had to make a more subtle choice between a "good" quarto and a still better manuscript. What the editors sometimes did in such cases was to use the inferior printed text but to annotate it by reference to a superior manuscript. This process of annotation might vary widely in its degree of thoroughness.

THE PRINTING OF THE 1623 FOLIO

The printing of the 1623 Folio continued from April of 1621 to December of 1623 in the printing shop of William and Isaac Jaggard. The compositors who actually set the type were, according to Charlton Hinman (*The Printing and Proof-Reading of the First Folio of Shakespeare*, 2 vols., 1963), five in number. For convenient reference they are designated as compositors A through E. A and B were the principal workmen. E was evidently an inept apprentice, unfortunately brought into the project just in time to work on several of the tragedies.

Compositors had to rely on their ability to memorize whole lines of verse at a time, since they needed to look at the type they were setting manually. Hence, they were apt to make mistakes based on imperfect remembering. Less skillful compositors not infrequently introduced errors by transposing words in a line, substituting a new word for what was in the copy, or maiming the scansion of a line of verse by adding or subtracting syllables.

Compositors were largely responsible for the "pointing" or punctuation of the text. They also usually imposed their own normalized spelling practices on their copy. Since no copy editor went over the materials first to normalize spelling, the compositors did what they could. Elizabethan spelling was in any case chaotic by our standards. The modern textual business of identifying compositors relies mainly on discovering the characteristic spelling habits of each.

Rather than setting their pages in numbered sequence right through an entire play, as we would assume, the compositors of the Folio used a system known as "casting off": that is, they estimated the amount of copy needed to fill a page of type, and divided the whole text up into portions of the estimated correct length. They could then set page twelve right after they had set page one, and immediately start printing these two pages side by side on the same "forme" or side of a sheet. (When three large sheets are folded once and gathered together, the result is a "quire" of twelve pages with pages one and twelve printed on the outer side or "forme" of the outermost sheet, pages two and eleven on the inner forme of that same sheet, pages three and ten on the outer forme of the middle sheet, and so on.) Since type was expensive and in limited supply in a printing shop, the type had to be redistributed into the fonts as soon as the requisite number of copies of any forme had been run off. Casting off enabled the printers to print and redistribute the type of pages one and twelve without having to wait for all the intervening pages to be set up also. (The reappearance of distributed type is in fact the clue by which Hinman was able to discover that the Folio had been set up throughout by casting off rather than by printing in sequence.)

Despite the advantages of flexibility, casting off had its disadvantages. If a compositor discovered he had been given too little copy for a page of text, he had to stretch his material by heavy "leading." If, on the other hand, he discovered he had been given too much copy for a page, he had to crowd his lines, print verse as prose, or even eliminate words and lines.

THE FOLGER SHAKESPEARE LIBRARY

Although printing in Shakespeare's time was a cumbersome and time-consuming process usually conducted by press-operators more interested in profit than in accuracy and consistency, the printers of the First Folio seem to have been more conscientious and skilled than most.

Knowledge of this sort of printing information is useful to a modern editor, since it enables him to determine when the compositors may have interfered with the text that Shakespeare wrote.

When a compositor had completed one entire forme, consisting of two pages of text to be printed on one side of a large printing sheet, the forme went into the press and the requisite number of copies was run off by hand. One side of the sheet, either the inner or outer forme, was printed at a time. Proofreading, or "press correction," took place while the printing continued. At first, a number of sides of the sheet would be printed in their uncorrected state, that is, entirely unproofread. When the press corrector found errors, the presses would be stopped in order that the errors might be corrected, after which printing would continue. Such interruptions might occur several times. Uncorrected or partially corrected sheets were not destroyed, however; paper was too costly for that. Later, when the stack of sheets printed on one side were printed on the other side, errors would again be corrected as printing continued. Ultimately, when the sheets were gathered by three's into a quire of twelve pages and then sewn into a complete volume, no single copy of the Folio was apt to be exactly like another. In fact, the many copies of the First Folio extant today differ from one another in their press variants. Even though we might regard this as evidence of carelessness, Jaggard's work on the First Folio seems to have been scrupulous when judged by the standards of the day.

About 1200 copies of the First Folio were printed and sold for twenty shillings. Approximately 230 copies survive today, of which 80 are found in the collection of the Folger Library, Washington, D.C.

THE LATER FOLIOS

When after nine years the first edition of the Folio had been sold out, a second edition was printed in 1632 by Thomas Cotes. He had succeeded to the Jaggards' business after the death of Isaac in 1627. The Second Folio merely reprinted the text of the First Folio together with a considerable number of editorial emendations. These have no independent textual authority, although some of the more commonsense suggestions have since been adopted by modern editors. A third edition appeared in 1663, based on the second. A second issue of this same third edition in 1664 included seven new plays: *Pericles*, *The London Prodigal*, *Thomas Lord Cromwell*, *Sir John Oldcastle*, *The Puritan*, *A Yorkshire Tragedy*, and *Locrine*. Of these, only *Pericles* has gained general acceptance in the Shakespeare canon. A fourth edition of the Folio in 1685, based on the third, also included the seven new plays. Like the second and third editions, this fourth edition offered many emendations or new errors not based on any textual authority.

SHAKESPEARE'S DRAMATIC DEVELOPMENT

Critics once spoke of the periods of Shakespeare's creative life in biographical terms, as in Edward Dowden's fanciful evocation of the experimental years "In the Workshop" (1590–1594), the years of happy success at writing comedy and history "In the World" (1595–1601), the tragic period "De Profundis" or "Out of the Depths" (1602–1608), and the final years of serene resignation "On the Heights" (1608–1612). Such implicitly biographical explanations are now regarded with great skepticism. Still, most critics would agree that Shakespeare developed from phase to phase with extraordinary artistic consistency. Although we talk now in terms of genres rather than of Shakespeare's changing spiritual mood, we nevertheless generally recognize four discernible phases in his career.

1. The Early Period. Shakespeare's experimentalism is plainly evident in *The Comedy of Errors*, based chiefly on Plautus' *Menaechmi*, and in *Titus Andronicus*, a revenge play inspired partly by Thomas Kyd's *The Spanish Tragedy*. When he wrote *Love's Labour's Lost*, Shakespeare seems to have been especially impressed by John Lyly. The *Henry VI* plays and *Richard III* owe a lot to Marlowe and Peele. Shakespeare's genius is evident everywhere in these plays, but he has not yet developed fully his most distinctive genres. *The Two Gentlemen of Verona*, for example, is a romantic comedy containing many of the features Shakespeare later used to such marvelous effect—maidens disguised as young men, banishment to a forest, outlaws—and yet the lovers of this play do not achieve the poetic insights into the nature of love that we come to expect from Shakespeare's mature comedies.

2. The Period of Comedies and Histories. The greatest comedies and history plays were virtually all written between 1595 and 1601, beginning perhaps with *A Midsummer Night's Dream* and *Richard II* and continuing through *The Merchant of Venice*, *Much Ado about Nothing*, *As You Like It*, *Twelfth Night*, *Henry IV*, and *Henry V*. Shakespeare wrote virtually no tragedies during the entire first half of his career; we have only the early and experimental *Titus Andronicus*, and the exquisitely comic and touching *Romeo and Juliet*. Shakespeare may have had several reasons for concentrating so on the perfection of two genres only, romantic comedy and patriotic English history. For one thing, these genres were very much in vogue on the stage for which he wrote. The Spanish Armada victory of 1588 had helped launch the history play as an expression of England's jubilantly patriotic mood during much of the 1590's. By the time of Queen Elizabeth's death in 1603, however, the mood had shifted to doubt and uncertainty. Perhaps also the popular appetite for patriotic drama had simply been satiated. The children's companies, reopening in 1598–1599 after having been closed for most of the 1590's, were wholly uninterested in patriotic history drama; they preferred satires and revenge tragedies, following the new vogue. Shakespeare's *Henry V* in 1599 was not only his last history play except for the late and uncharacteristic *Henry VIII* (1613), but was one of the last popular history plays written by any Elizabethan dramatist. The genre came to an end, almost as abruptly as it had started. Similar changes in fashion affected romantic comedy. Shakespeare's masterpieces in the genre, composed from 1595 to 1601, coincided with the great age of romantic comedy in the Elizabethan theatre. Greene and Peele had preceded Shakespeare in this genre; Thomas Heywood, Thomas Dekker, and others were his contemporaries. In about 1600–1601 this genre too began to decline, partly because the great Puritan-leaning popular audiences of London were on the verge of renouncing the theatre.

3. The Period of Tragedies. The 1600's thus saw the theatres gravitate more and more to the tastes of courtly and intellectual audiences. Shakespeare's tragic period is characterized not only by the great tragedies of *Hamlet*, *Othello*, *King Lear*, and *Macbeth*, but also by the more ironic and iconoclastic Roman or classical plays: *Julius Caesar*, *Troilus and Cressida*, *Timon of Athens*, *Antony and Cleopatra*, *Coriolanus*. *Troilus and Cressida* seems to have been Shakespeare's experiment with avant-garde satire. He wrote perhaps two comedies during the tragic period, *All's Well That Ends Well* and *Measure for Measure*, but they are so affected by the dark preoccupations of Shakespeare's tragic period that they are often referred to as "problem comedies" or "problem plays."

4. The Period of Romances. Shakespeare's final phase was a return to comedy of a sort, but comedy with such leanings toward tragicomedy and miraculous circumstance that the final plays are often called romances to distinguish them from the earlier "festive" comedies. Here again Shakespeare both reflects and contributes to a shift in the artistic movements of his era; other dramatists such as Beaumont and Fletcher were showing a new interest in tragicomedy. Most of the late romances were evidently written with sophisticated Blackfriars audiences in mind, although these plays continued to be performed at the Globe Theatre as well.

Shakespeare's Life and Work

THE EARLY PERIOD, 1564–1594

William Shakespeare was baptized on April 26, 1564, in Stratford-upon-Avon, Warwickshire. Tradition assigns his actual birthdate to April 23, the feast day of St. George, England's patron saint. Shakespeare's father was John Shakespeare, a maker and seller of gloves and other leather goods, who rose to become one of Stratford's most prominent and successful citizens. At various times John Shakespeare was ale taster (inspector of bread and malt), burgess (petty constable), affeeror (assessor of fines), city chamberlain (treasurer), alderman, and high bailiff of the town—the highest municipal office in Stratford. Although his fortune began a sudden and mysterious decline some time around 1577 or 1578, he was a man of substance who was later granted the right to bear arms and style himself a gentleman. (His famous son carried through to completion the petition for this honor in 1596.) William's mother was Mary Arden, daughter of a wealthy landowner in the vicinity of Stratford.

SHAKESPEARE IN SCHOOL

Nicholas Rowe, who published in 1709 the first extensive biographical account of Shakespeare, reports the tradition that Shakespeare studied "for some time at a Free-School." Although the list of students who actually attended the King's New School at Stratford-upon-Avon in the late sixteenth century has not survived, we cannot doubt that Rowe is reporting accurately. Shakespeare's father, as a leading citizen of Stratford, would scarcely have spurned the benefits of one of Stratford's most prized institutions. The town had had a free school since the thirteenth century, at first under the auspices of the church. During the reign of King Edward VI (1547–1553), the church lands were expropriated by the crown and the town of Stratford was granted a corporate charter. At this time the school was reorganized as the King's New School, named in honor of the reigning monarch. It prospered. Its teachers or "masters" regularly held degrees from Oxford during Shakespeare's childhood and received salaries that were superior to those of most comparable schools.

Much has been learned about the curriculum of such a school. A child would first learn the rudiments of reading and writing English by spending two or three years in a "petty" or elementary school. The child learned to read from his "hornbook," a single sheet of paper mounted on a board and protected by a thin transparent layer of horn, on which was usually printed the alphabet in small and capital letters and the Lord's Prayer. The child would also practice his ABC book with catechism. When he had demonstrated the ability to read satisfactorily, he was admitted, at about the age of seven, to the grammar school proper. Here the day was a rigorous one, usually extending from 6 A.M. in the summer or 7 A.M. in the winter until 5 P.M. Intervals for food or brief recreation came at midmorning, noon, and midafternoon. Holidays occurred at Christmas, Easter, and Whitsuntide (usually late May and June), comprising perhaps forty days in all through the year. Discipline was strict and physical punishment was common.

Latin formed the basis of the grammar school curriculum. The scholars studied grammar, read ancient writers, recited, and learned to write in Latin. A standard text was the *Grammatica Latina* by William Lilly or Lyly, father of the later Elizabethan dramatist John Lyly. The scholars also became familiar with the *Disticha de Moribus* (moral proverbs) attributed to Cato, *Aesop's Fables*, the *Eclogues* of Baptista Spagnuoli Mantuanus or Mantuan (alluded to in *Love's Labour's Lost*), the *Eclogues* and *Aeneid* of Virgil, the comedies of Plautus or Terence (sometimes performed in Latin by the children), Ovid's *Metamorphoses* and other of his works, and possibly some Horace and Seneca.

Shakespeare plentifully reveals in his dramatic writings an awareness of many of these authors, especially Plautus (in *The Comedy of Errors*), Ovid (in *A Midsummer Night's Dream* and elsewhere), and Seneca (in *Titus Andronicus*). Although he often consulted translations of these authors, he seems to have known the originals as well. He had, in Ben Jonson's learned estimation, "small Latine and lesse Greeke"; the tone is condescending, but the statement does concede that Shakespeare had some of both. He would have acquired some Greek in the last years of his grammar schooling. By twentieth-century standards, Shakespeare had a fairly comprehensive amount of training in the ancient classics, certainly enough to account for the general if unscholarly references we find in the plays themselves.

SHAKESPEARE'S MARRIAGE

When Shakespeare was eighteen years old, he married Anne Hathaway, a woman eight years his senior. (The inscription on her grave states that she was sixty-seven when she died in August of 1623.) The bishop's register of Worcester, the central city of the diocese, shows for November 27, 1582, the issue of a bishop's license for the marriage of William Shakespeare and Anne Hathaway. She has been identified with all reasonable probability as Agnes (or Anne) Hathaway, daughter of the then recently deceased Richard Hathaway of the hamlet of Shottery, a short distance from Stratford.

The obtaining of a license was not normally required for a marriage. William Shakespeare and Anne Hathaway seem to have applied for a license on this occasion because they wished to be married after only one reading of the banns rather than the usual three. (The reading of the banns, or announcement in church of a forthcoming marriage, usually on three successive Sundays, enabled any party to object to the marriage if he knew of any legal impediment.) Since the reading of all banns was suspended for long periods during Advent (before Christmas) and Lent (before Easter), a couple intending to marry shortly before Christmas might have had to wait until April before the banns could be read thrice. Accordingly, the bishop not uncommonly granted a license permitting couples to marry during the winter season with only one reading of the banns. To obtain such a license, two friends of the bride's family had to sign a bond obligating themselves to pay the bishop up to forty pounds, should any impediment to the marriage result in a legal action against the bishop for having issued the license.

The actual record of the marriage in a parish register has not survived, but presumably the couple were joined in matrimony shortly after obtaining the license. They may have been married in Temple Grafton, where Anne had relatives. The couple took up residence in Stratford. Anne was already pregnant at the time of the marriage, for she gave birth to a daughter, Susanna, on May 26, 1583. The birth of a child six months after the wedding may explain the need for haste the previous November. These circumstances, and Anne's considerable seniority in age to William, have given rise to much speculation about matters that can never be satisfactorily resolved. We do know that a formal betrothal in the presence of witnesses could legally validate a binding relationship, enabling a couple to consummate their love without social stigma. We know also that Shakespeare dramatized the issue of premarital contract and pregnancy in *Measure for Measure*. Whether Shakespeare entered into such a formal relationship with Anne is, however, undiscoverable.

On February 2, 1585, Shakespeare's only other children, the twins Hamnet and Judith, were baptized in Stratford Church. The twins seem to have been named after Shakespeare's friends and neighbors, Hamnet Sadler, a baker, and his wife, Judith.

THE SEVEN "DARK" YEARS

From 1585, the year in which his twins were baptized, until 1592, when he is first referred to as an actor and dramatist of growing importance in London, Shakespeare's activities are wholly unknown. Presumably at some time during this period he made his way to London and entered its theatrical world, but otherwise we can only record traditions and guesses as to what he did between the ages of 21 and 28.

One of the oldest and most intriguing suggestions comes from John Aubrey, who, in collecting information about actors and dramatists for his "Minutes of Lives," sought the help of one William Beeston. John Dryden believed Beeston to be "the chronicle of the stage," and Aubrey seems also to have had a high opinion of Beeston's theatrical knowledge. In his manuscript, Aubrey made a note to himself: "W. Shakespeare—quære [i.e., inquire of] Mr. Beeston, who knows most of him." Aubrey then cites Beeston as his authority for this tradition about Shakespeare:

> Though, as Ben: Johnson sayes of him, that he had but little Latine and lesse Greek, He understood Latine pretty well: for he had been in his younger yeares a Schoolmaster in the Countrey.

Beeston had been a theatrical manager all his life. He was the son of the actor Christopher Beeston, who had been a member of Shakespeare's company probably from 1596 until 1602 and who therefore had occasion to know Shakespeare well.

Shakespeare's own grammar school education would not have qualified him to be the master of a school, but he could have served as "usher" or assistant to the master. The idea that Shakespeare may have taught in this way is not unattractive. Although, as we have seen, he had some acquaintance with Plautus, Ovid, and other classical writers through his own grammar school reading, a stint as schoolmaster would have made these authors more familiar and readily accessible to him when he began writing his plays and nondramatic poems. His earliest works—*The Comedy of Errors*, *Love's Labour's Lost*, *Titus Andronicus*, *Venus and Adonis*, *The Rape of Lucrece*—show most steadily and directly the effect of his classical reading. Schoolteaching experience might have encouraged his ambitions to be a writer, like Marlowe or Greene, who went to London not to be actors but to try their hands at poetry and playwriting. All in all, however, it seems more probable that Shakespeare became a young actor rather than a schoolteacher.

Another tradition about the years from 1585 to 1592 asserts that Shakespeare served part of an apprenticeship in Stratford. This suggestion comes to us from one John Dowdall who, traveling through Warwickshire in 1693, heard the story from an old parish clerk who was showing him around the town of Stratford. According to this parish clerk, Shakespeare had been bound as apprentice to a butcher, but ran away from his master to London where he was received into a playhouse as "serviture." John Aubrey records a similar tradition: "when he [Shakespeare] was a boy he exercised his father's Trade." Aubrey believed this trade to have been that of a butcher. Moreover, says Aubrey, "when he kill'd a Calfe, he would doe it in a *high style*, & make a Speech." No other evidence confirms, however, that Shakespeare was a runaway apprentice. Nor can we give much credence to the account set down by the Reverend Richard Davies, some time between 1688 and 1709, that Shakespeare was "much given to all unluckinesse in stealing venison & Rabbits, particularly from Sir ——— Lucy, who had him oft whipt & sometimes Imprisoned & at last made Him fly his Native Country, to his great Advancement."

SHAKESPEARE'S ARRIVAL IN LONDON

Because of the total absence of reliable information concerning the seven years from 1585 to 1592, we do not know how Shakespeare got his start in the theatrical world. He may have joined one of the touring companies that came to Stratford, and then accompanied the players to London. Edmund Malone offered the unsupported statement (in 1780) that Shakespeare's "first office in the theatre was that of prompter's attendant." Presumably a young man from the country would have had to begin at the bottom. Shakespeare's later work certainly reveals an intimate and practical acquaintance with technical matters of stagecraft. In any case, his rise to eminence as an actor and writer seems to have been rapid. He was fortunate also in having at least one prosperous acquaintance in London, Richard Field, formerly of Stratford and the son of an associate of Shakespeare's father. Field was a printer, and in 1593 and 1594 he published two handsome editions of Shakespeare's first serious poems, *Venus and Adonis* and *The Rape of Lucrece.*

"THE ONELY SHAKE-SCENE IN A COUNTREY"

The first allusion to Shakespeare after his Stratford days is a vitriolic attack on him. It occurs in *Greene's Groats-worth of Wit Bought with a Million of Repentance*, written by Robert Greene during the last months of his wretched existence (he died in poverty in September of 1592). A famous passage in this work lashes out at the actors of the public theatres for having deserted Greene and for bestowing their favor instead on a certain upstart dramatist. The passage warns three fellow dramatists and University Wits, Christopher Marlowe, Thomas Nashe, and George Peele, to abandon the writing of plays before they fall prey to a similar ingratitude. The diatribe runs as follows:

> . . . Base minded men all three of you, if by my miserie you be not warnd: for vnto none of you (like mee) sought those burres to cleaue: those Puppets (I meane) that spake from our mouths, those Anticks garnisht in our colours. Is it not strange, that I, to whom they all haue beene beholding: is it not like that you, to whome they all haue beene beholding, shall (were yee in that case as I am now) bee both at once of them forsaken? Yes trust them not: for there is an vpstart Crow, beautified with our feathers, that with his *Tygers hart wrapt in a Players hyde*, supposes he is as well able to bombast out a blanke verse as the best of you: and beeing an absolute *Iohannes fac totum*, is in his owne conceit the onely Shake-scene in a countrey.

The "burres" here referred to are the actors who have forsaken Greene in his poverty for the rival playwright "Shake-scene"—an obvious hit at Shakespeare. The sneer at a "Johannes fac totum" suggests another dig at Shakespeare for being a Jack-of-all-trades—actor, playwright, poet, and theatrical handyman in the directing and producing of plays. The most unmistakable reference to Shakespeare, however, is to be found in the burlesque line, "Tygers hart wrapt in a Players hyde," modeled after "O tiger's heart wrapt in a woman's hide!" from *3 Henry VI* (I,iv,137). Shakespeare's success as a dramatist has led to an envious outburst from an older, disappointed rival.

CHETTLE'S APOLOGY

Shakespeare may understandably have resented this attack on his professional reputation. Marlowe, too, had cause for grievance, since Greene had accused him in the same pamphlet of atheism. Greene died soon after he wrote *Groats-worth of Wit*, but some of his fellow dramatists were suspected of having had a hand in the libel. Thomas Nashe vigorously denied any responsibility. So did Henry Chettle, the man who saw Greene's manuscript through the press, although Chettle is even today under suspicion for having written the attack on Shakespeare and Marlowe himself. Whether or not Chettle was guilty, he quickly protected himself by denying in his *Kind-Harts Dreame* that he had done anything more than act as Greene's literary executor:

> . . . I had onely in the copy this share: it was il written, as sometime *Greenes* hand was none of the best; licensd it must be, ere it could bee printed, which could neuer be if it might not be read. To be breife, *I* writ it ouer; and as neare as *I* could, followed the copy; onely in that letter *I* put something out, but in the whole booke not a worde in: for I protest it was all *Greenes*, not mine nor Maister Nashes, as some vniustly haue affirmed.

Chettle professes not to have known Marlowe personally, and insists he has no desire to make the acquaintance of so notorious a person; but toward Shakespeare he expresses genuine concern and regret that the publishing incident took place:

The other, whome at that time I did not so much spare, as since I wish I had, for that as I haue moderated the heate of liuing writers, and might have vsde my owne discretion (especially in such a case) the Author beeing dead, that I did not, I am as sory as if the originall fault had beene my fault, because my selfe haue seene his demeanor no lesse ciuill than he exelent in the qualitie he professes: Besides, diuers of worship haue reported his uprightnes of dealing, which argues his honesty, and his facetious grace in writting, that approoues his Art.

This handsome apology reveals the young Shakespeare in a most attractive light. It suggests that Chettle, though not having known Shakespeare previously, has been impressed by Shakespeare's civility. Chettle also praises the young dramatist as "exelent in the qualitie he professes," that is, excellent as an actor. Chettle notes with approval that Shakespeare enjoys the favor of certain persons of importance, some of whom have borne witness to his uprightness in dealing. By "diuers of worship" Chettle does not mean actors or theatrical people, but persons of gentle blood. *Groats-worth of Wit*, then, with its rancorous attack on Shakespeare, has served paradoxically to reveal the fact that in 1592 Shakespeare was regarded as a man of pleasant demeanor, honest reputation, and acknowledged skill as an actor and writer.

THE PERIOD OF COMEDIES AND HISTORIES, 1595–1601

During the years from 1595 to 1601, Shakespeare seems to have prospered as an actor and writer for the Lord Chamberlain's men. Whether he had previously belonged to Lord Strange's company or to the Earl of Pembroke's company, or possibly to some other group, is uncertain; but we know that he took part in 1594 in the general reorganization of the companies out of which emerged the Lord Chamberlain's company. In 1595 his name appeared for the first time in the accounts of the Treasurer of the Royal Chamber, as a member of the Chamberlain's company of players who had presented two comedies before Queen Elizabeth at Greenwich in the Christmas season of 1594. This company usually performed at the Theatre, northeast of London, from 1594 until 1599, when they moved to the Globe theatre south of the Thames. They seem to have been the victors in the intense economic rivalry between themselves and the Lord Admiral's company at the Rose theatre under Philip Henslowe's management. Fortunately for all the adult companies, the boys' private theatrical companies were shut down during most of the 1590's. Shakespeare's company enjoyed a phenomenal success, and in short time became the most successful theatrical organization in England.

The nucleus of the Chamberlain's company in 1594 was the family of Burbage. James Burbage, the father, was owner of the Theatre, Cuthbert Burbage was a manager, and Richard Burbage became the principal actor of the troupe. Together the Burbages owned five "shares" in the company, entitling them to half the profits. Shakespeare and four other principal actors—John Heminges, Thomas Pope, Augustine Phillips, and Will Kempe—owned one share each. Not only was Shakespeare a full sharing actor, but he was also the principal playwright of the company. He was named as a chief actor in the 1616 edition of Ben Jonson's *Every Man in His Humour*, performed by the Chamberlain's company in 1598. Later tradition reports, with questionable reliability, that Shakespeare specialized in "kingly parts" or in the roles of older men, such as Adam in *As You Like It* and the Ghost in *Hamlet*. Shakespeare was more celebrated as a playwright than as an actor, and his acting responsibilities may well have diminished as his writing reputation grew. The last occasion on which he is known to have acted was in Jonson's *Sejanus* in 1603.

His prosperity appears in the first record of his residence in London. The tax returns, or Subsidy Rolls, of a parliamentary subsidy granted to Queen Elizabeth for the year 1596, show Shakespeare resident in the parish of St. Helen's, Bishopsgate, near the Theatre, and assessed at the respectable sum of £5. By the next year Shakespeare had evidently moved to Southwark near the Bear Garden, for the returns from

THE FOLGER SHAKESPEARE LIBRARY

The most famous comic of the time was Will Kempe of the Lord Chamberlain's men, for whom Shakespeare created several roles, probably including that of Bottom in A Midsummer Night's Dream.

Bishopsgate show his taxes delinquent. He was later located and the taxes paid.

In 1596 Shakespeare suffered a serious personal loss: the death of his only son Hamnet, at the age of eleven. Hamnet was buried at Stratford in August. Except for this misfortune, however, Shakespeare continued to prosper. In the following year he purchased New Place in Stratford, a house of importance and one of the two largest in the town. Shakespeare's family entered the house as residents shortly after the purchase and continued there until long after Shakespeare's death. The last of his family, his granddaughter, Lady Bernard, died in 1670, and New Place was sold.

Shakespeare was also interested in the purchase of land at Shottery in 1598. He was listed among the chief holders of corn and malt in Stratford that same year, and sold a load of stone to the Stratford corporation in 1599.

During this period Shakespeare's plays began to appear occasionally in print, attesting to his popularity as a dramatist. His name was becoming such a drawing card that it appeared on the title pages of the second and third quartos of *Richard II* (1598), the second quarto of *Richard III* (1598), *Love's Labour's Lost* (1598), and the second quarto of *1 Henry IV* (1599).

In 1599 the printer William Jaggard sought to capitalize unscrupulously on Shakespeare's growing reputation by bringing out a slender volume of twenty or twenty-one poems called *The Passionate Pilgrim*, attributed to Shakespeare. In fact, only five of the poems were assuredly his, and none of them was newly composed for the occasion. Three came from *Love's Labour's Lost* (published 1598) and two from Shakespeare's as yet unpublished sonnet sequence.

THE

Tragedie of King Richard the ſecond.

As it hath beene publikely acted by the Right Honourable the Lord Chamberlaine his ſeruants.

By William Shake-ſpeare.

LONDON

Printed by Valentine Simmes for Andrew Wiſe, and are to be ſold at his ſhop in Paules churchyard at the ſigne of the Angel.

1598.

THE FOLGER SHAKESPEARE LIBRARY

As Shakespeare grew in popularity, his name began to appear on the title pages of his published plays, as in this 1598 quarto of Richard II.

THE PERIOD OF TRAGEDIES, 1602–1608

When the Globe, the most famous of the London public playhouses, was built in 1599, one-half interest in the property was assigned to the brothers Cuthbert and Richard Burbage. The other half was divided among five actor-sharers: Shakespeare, Will Kempe, Thomas Pope, Augustine Phillips, and John Heminges. Kempe left the company, however, in 1599, and subsequently became a member of the Earl of Worcester's men. His place as leading comic actor was taken by Robert Armin, an experienced man of the theatre and occasional author whose comic specialty was the role of the wise fool. We can observe in Shakespeare's plays the effects of Kempe's departure and of Armin's arrival. Kempe had apparently specialized in clownish and rustic parts, such as those of Dogberry in *Much Ado*, Launcelot Gobbo in *The Merchant of Venice*, and Bottom in *A Midsummer Night's Dream*. (We know that he played Dogberry because his name appears in the play manuscript; similar evidence links his name to the role of Peter in *Romeo and Juliet*.) For Armin, on the other hand, Shakespeare evidently created such roles as Touchstone in *As You Like It*, Feste in *Twelfth Night*, Lavatch in *All's Well that Ends Well*, and the Fool in *King Lear*.

Other shifts in personnel can sometimes be traced in Shakespeare's plays, especially changes in the number and ability of the boy actors (whose voices would suddenly start to crack at puberty). Shakespeare makes an amusing point about the relative size of two boy actors, for example, in *A Midsummer Night's Dream* and in *As You Like It;* this option may have been available to him only at certain times. On the other hand, not all changes in the company roster can be related meaningfully to Shakespeare's dramatic development. Augustine Phillips, who died in 1605, was a full actor-sharer of long standing in the company, but his "type" of role was probably not sharply differ-

THE HUNTINGTON LIBRARY, SAN MARINO, CALIFORNIA

Unlike his predecessor Will Kempe, who left Shakespeare's company in 1599, Robert Armin specialized in comic roles emphasizing subtle wit and sharp repartee, such as the roles of Feste in Twelfth Night *and the Fool in* King Lear.

entiated from that of several of his associates. Shakespeare's plays, after all, involve many important supporting roles, and versatility in the undertaking of such parts must have been more common than specialization. (Phillips is remembered, however, for his last will and testament: he left a bequest of "a thirty shillings peece in gould" to "my Fellowe, William Shakespeare," and similar bequests to other members of the troupe.)

With the reopening of the boys' acting companies in 1598–1599, a serious economic rivalry sprang up between them and the adult companies. The Children of the Chapel Royal occupied the theatre in Blackfriars, and the Children of Paul's probably acted in their own singing school in St. Paul's churchyard. Their plays exploited a new vogue for satire. The satiric laughter was often directed at the city of London and its bourgeois inhabitants: socially ambitious tradesmen's wives, Puritan zealots, and the like. Other favorite targets included parvenu knights at court, would-be poets, and hysterical governmental officials. The price of admission at the private theatres was considerably higher than at the Globe or Rose, so that the clientele tended to be more fashionable. Sophisticated authors like Ben Jonson, George Chapman, and John Marston tended to find writing for the boy actors more literarily rewarding than writing for the adult players.

One manifestation of the rivalry between public and private theatres was the so-called War of the Theatres, or Psychomachia. In part this was a personal quarrel between Jonson on one side and Marston and Thomas Dekker on the other. Underlying this quarrel, however, was a serious hostility between a broadly based popular theatre and one that catered to the elite. Dekker, with Marston's encouragement, attacked Jonson as a literary dictator and snob, one who subverted public decency. Jonson replied with a fervent defense of the artist's right to criticize everything he sees wrong. The major plays in the exchange (1600–1601) were Jonson's *Cynthia's Revels*, Dekker's and Marston's *Satiromastix*, and Jonson's *The Poetaster*.

Shakespeare allows Hamlet to comment on the theatrical rivalry (II,ii), with seeming regret for the fact that the boys have been overly successful and that many adult troupes have been obliged to tour the provinces. Most of all, though, Hamlet's remarks deplore the needless bitterness on both sides. The tone of kindly remonstrance makes it seem unlikely that Shakespeare took an active part in the fracas. To be sure, in the Cambridge play *2 Return from Parnassus* (1601–1603) the character called Will Kempe does assert that his fellow actor Shakespeare had put down the famous Ben Jonson:

> Why, heres our fellow *Shakespeare* puts them all downe, I, and *Ben Ionson* too. O that *Ben Ionson* is a pestilent fellow, and he brought vp *Horace* giuing the Poets a pill, but our fellow *Shakespeare* hath giuen him a purge that made him bewray his credit.
>
> (ll. 1809–1813)

Nevertheless, no play exists in which Shakespeare did put down Jonson, and Kempe is probably thinking instead of *Satiromastix* which was performed by Shakespeare's company. In fact, Shakespeare and Jonson remained on cordial terms despite their profound differences in artistic outlook.

Upon the death of Queen Elizabeth in 1603 and the accession to the throne of King James I, Shakespeare's company added an important new success to their already great prosperity. According to a document of instruction from King James to his Keeper of the Privy Seal, dated May 19, 1603, and endorsed as "The Players' Privilege," the acting company that had formerly been the Lord Chamberlain's men now became the King's servants. The document names Shakespeare, Richard Burbage, Augustine Phillips, John Heminges, Henry Condell, Will Sly, Robert Armin, Richard Cowley, and Lawrence Fletcher—the last an actor who had played before the king and the Scottish court in 1599 and 1601. These players are accorded the usual privileges of exercising their art anywhere within the kingdom and are henceforth to be known as the King's company. As the King's servants, the principal members of the troupe were also appointed to the honorary rank of Grooms of the Royal Chamber. We therefore find them duly recorded in the Accounts of the Master of the Wardrobe on March 15, 1604, as recipients of the customary grants of red cloth, so that they, dressed in the royal livery, might take part in the approaching coronation procession of King James. The same men are mentioned in these grants as in the Players' Privilege. Shakespeare's name stands second in the former document and first in the latter. In a somewhat similar manner the king's players, as Grooms of the Royal Chamber, were called in attendance on the Spanish ambassador at Somerset House in August 1604.

The Revels Accounts of performances at court during the winter season of 1604–1605 contain an unusually full entry listing several of Shakespeare's plays. The list includes *Othello*, *The Merry Wives of Windsor*, *Measure for Measure*, "*The plaie of Errors*," *Love's Labour's Lost*, *Henry V*, and *The Merchant of Venice*. The last play was "Againe Commanded By the Kings Maiestie," and so was performed a second time. This list also sporadically notes the names of "the poets which mayd the plaies," ascribing three of these works to "Shaxberd." (Probably the final "d" is an error for "e," since the two characters are easily confused in Elizabethan handwriting; the word represents "Shaxbere" or "Shaxpere.") The entire entry was once called into question as a possible forgery, but is now generally regarded as authentic.

A number of records during this period show us glimpses of Shakespeare as a man of property. On May 1, 1602, John and William Combe conveyed to Shakespeare one hundred and seven acres of arable land plus twenty acres of pasture in the parish of Old Stratford, for the sizable payment of three hundred and twenty pounds. The deed was delivered to Shakespeare's brother Gilbert and not to the poet, who was probably at that time occupied in London. On September 28th of the same year Shakespeare acquired the title to "one cottage and one garden by estimation a quarter of an acre," located opposite his home (New Place) in Stratford.

Shakespeare made still other real-estate investments in his home town. In 1605 he purchased an interest in the tithes of Stratford and adjacent villages from one Ralph Huband for the considerable sum of four hundred and forty pounds. The purchasing of tithes was a common financial transaction in Shakespeare's time, though unknown today. Tithes were originally intended for the support of the church, but had in many cases become privately owned and hence negotiable. The owners of tithes paid a fixed rental sum for the right to collect as many of these taxes as they could, up to the total amount due under the law. Shakespeare seems, on this occasion in 1605, to have bought from Ralph Huband a one-half interest, or "moiety," in certain tithes of Stratford and vicinity. Later, probably in 1609, Shakespeare was one of those who brought a bill of complaint before the Lord Chancellor, requesting that certain other titheholders be required to come into the High Court of Chancery and make answer to the complaints alleged, namely, that they had not paid their proportional part of an annual rental of £27 13s. 4d. on the whole property in the tithes to one Henry Barker. This Barker had the

THE TATE GALLERY, LONDON

John Everett Millais' "Ophelia" (1851), a Pre-Raphaelite conception of her drowning in Hamlet, *Shakespeare's best-known tragedy.*

theoretical right to foreclose on the entire property if any one of the forty-two titheholders failed to contribute his share of the annual fee. The suit was in effect a friendly one, designed to ensure that all those who were supposed to contribute did so on an equitable and businesslike basis.

We learn from the Stratford Registers of baptism, marriage, and burial, of the changes in Shakespeare's family during this period. His father died in 1601, his brother Edmund in 1607, and his mother in 1608. On June 5, 1607, his daughter Susanna was married to Dr. John Hall in Holy Trinity Church, Stratford. Their first child and Shakespeare's first grandchild, Elizabeth, was christened in the same church on February 21, 1608.

THE PERIOD OF ROMANCES, 1609–1616

In the summer of 1608, Shakespeare's acting company signed a twenty-one-year lease for the use of the Blackfriars playhouse, an indoor and rather intimate, artificially lighted theatre inside the city of London, close to St. Paul's cathedral. A private theatre had existed on this spot since 1576, when the Children of the Chapel and then Paul's boys began acting their courtly plays for paying spectators in a building that had once belonged to the Dominicans, or Black Friars. James Burbage had begun construction in 1596 of the so-called Second Blackfriars theatre in the same building. Although James encountered opposition from the residents of the area and died before he could complete the work, James' son Richard did succeed in opening the new theatre in 1600. At first he leased it (for twenty-one years) to a children's company; but when that company was suppressed in 1608 for offending the French ambassador in a play by George Chapman, Burbage seized the opportunity to take back the unexpired lease and set up Blackfriars as the winter playhouse for his adult company, the King's men. By this time the adult troupes could plainly see that they needed to cater more directly to courtly audiences than they once had done. Their popular audiences were becoming increasingly disenchanted with the drama. Puritan fulminations against the stage gained in effect, especially when many playwrights refused to disguise their satirical hostility toward Puritans and the London bourgeoisie.

Several of Shakespeare's late plays may have been acted both at the Globe and at Blackfriars. The plays he wrote after 1608–1609, *Cymbeline*, *The Winter's Tale*, and *The Tempest*, all show the distinct influence of the dramaturgy of the private theatres. Also, we know that an increasing number of Shakespeare's plays were acted at the court of King James. *Othello*, *King Lear*, and *The Tempest* are named in court revels accounts, and *Macbeth* attentively flatters the Scottish royal ancestry of King James as though for a court performance. On the other hand, Shakespeare's plays certainly continued to be acted at the Globe to the very end of his career. The 1609 quarto of *Pericles* advertises that it was acted "by his Maiesties Seruants, at the Globe on the Banck-side." The 1608 quarto of *King Lear* mentions a performance at court and assigns the play to "his Maiesties seruants playing vsually at the Gloabe on the Bancke-side." Simon Forman saw *Macbeth*, *Cymbeline*, and *The Winter's Tale* at the Globe. Finally, a performance of *Henry VIII* on June 29, 1613, resulted in the burning of the Globe to the ground, though it was rebuilt soon after.

Shakespeare's last plays, written with a view to Blackfriars and the court as well as to the Globe, are usually called romances or tragicomedies or sometimes both. The term romance suggests a return to the kind of story Robert Greene had derived from Greek romance: tales of adventure, long separation, and tearful reunion, involving shipwreck, capture by pirates, riddling prophecies, children set adrift in boats or abandoned on foreign shores, the illusion of death and subsequent restoration to life, the revelation of the identity of long-lost children by birthmarks, and the like. The term tragicomedy suggests a play in which the protagonist commits a seemingly fatal error or crime, or (as in *Pericles*) suffers an extraordinarily adverse fortune to test his patience; in either event he must experience agonies of contrition and bereavement until he is miraculously delivered from his tribulations. The tone is deeply melancholy and resigned, although suffused also with a sense of gratitude for the harmonies that are mysteriously restored.

The appropriateness of such plays to the elegant atmosphere of Blackfriars and the court is subtle but real. Although one might suppose at first that old-fashioned naiveté would seem out of place in a sophisticated milieu, the naiveté is only superficial. Tragicomedy and pastoral romance were, in the period from 1606 to 1610, beginning to enjoy a fashionable courtly revival. The leading practitioners of the new genre were Beaumont and Fletcher, though Shakespeare made a highly significant contribution. Perhaps sophisticated audiences responded to pastoral and romantic drama as the nostalgic evocation of an idealized past, a chivalric "golden world" fleetingly recovered through an artistic journey back to naiveté and innocence. The evocation of such a world demands the kind of studied but informal artifice we find in many tragicomic plays of the period: the elaborate masques and allegorical shows, the descents of enthroned gods from the heavens (as in *Cymbeline*), the use of quaint Chorus figures like Old Gower or Time (in *Pericles* and *The Winter's Tale*), the quasi-operatic blend of music and spectacle. At their best, such plays powerfully compel belief in the artistic world thus artificially created. The very improbability of the story becomes, paradoxically, part of the means by which an audience must "awake its faith" in a mysterious truth.

Shakespeare did not merely ape the new fashion in tragicomedy and romance. In fact, he may have done much to establish it. His *Pericles*, written seemingly in about 1606–1608 for the public stage before Shakespeare's company acquired Blackfriars, anticipated many important features not only of Shakespeare's own later romances but of Beaumont and Fletcher's *The Maid's Tragedy* and *Philaster* (c. 1608–1611). Still, Shakespeare was on the verge of retirement, and the future belonged to Beaumont and Fletcher. Gradually Shakespeare disengaged himself, spending more and more time in Stratford. His last-known stint as an actor was in *Sejanus* in 1603. Some time in 1611 or 1612 he probably gave up his lodgings in London, though he still may have returned for such occasions as the opening performance of *Henry VIII* in 1613. He continued to be one of the proprietors of the newly rebuilt Globe, but his involvement in its day-to-day operations dwindled.

Shakespeare's last recorded investment in real estate was the purchase of a house in Blackfriars, London, in 1613. There is no indication he lived there, for he had retired to Stratford. He did not pay the full purchase price of £140, and the mortgage deed executed for the unpaid balance furnishes one of the six absolutely unquestioned examples of his signature.

John Combe, a wealthy bachelor of Stratford and Shakespeare's friend, left him a legacy of five pounds in his will at the time of Combe's death in 1613. At about the same time, John's kinsman William Combe began a controversial attempt to enclose Welcombe Common—that is, to convert narrow strips of arable land to pasture. Presumably Combe was interested in a more efficient use of the land. Enclosure was, however, an explosive issue, since many people feared they would lose the right to farm the land and be evicted to make room for cattle and sheep. Combe attempted to guarantee Shakespeare and other titheholders that they would lose no money. He offered similar assurances to the Stratford Council, but the townspeople were adamantly opposed. Shakespeare was consulted by letter as a leading titheholder. The letter is lost, but presumably it set forth the Council's reasons for objecting to enclosure. Shakespeare's views on the controversy remain unknown. Eventually the case went to the Privy Council, where Combe was ordered to restore the land to its original use.

One of the most interesting documents from the later period consists of the records of a lawsuit entered into in 1612 by Stephen Belott against his father-in-law Christopher Mountjoy, a Huguenot maker of woman's ornamental headdresses who resided on Silver Street, St. Olave's parish, London. Belott sought payment of a dower promised him at the time of his marriage to Mountjoy's daughter. In this suit Shakespeare was summoned as a witness and made deposition on five interrogatories. From this document we learn that Shakespeare was a lodger in Mountjoy's house at the time of the marriage in 1604 and probably for some time before that, since he states in his testimony that he had known Mountjoy for more than ten years. Shakespeare admitted that, at the solicitation of Mountjoy's wife, he had acted as an intermediary in the arrangement of the marriage between Belott and Mountjoy's daughter. Shakespeare declared himself unable, however, to recall the exact amount of the portion or the date on which it was to have been paid. Shakespeare's signature to his deposition is undoubtedly authentic, and one of the best samples of his handwriting that we have.

In January of 1615 or 1616, Shakespeare drew up his last will and testament with the assistance of his lawyer Francis Collins, who had aided him earlier in some of his transactions in real estate. On March 25, 1616, Shakespeare revised his will in order to provide for the marriage of his daughter Judith and Thomas Quiney in that same year. Shakespeare's three quavering signatures, one on each page of this document, suggest that he was in failing health. The cause of his death on April 23 is not known. An intriguing bit of Stratford gossip is reported by John Ward, vicar of Holy Trinity in Stratford from 1662 to 1689, in his diary: "Shakespear, Drayton, and Ben Jhonson, had a merry meeting, and itt seems drank too hard, for Shakespear died of a feavour there contracted." The report comes fifty years after Shakespeare's death, however, and is hardly an expert medical opinion.

The will disposes of all the property of which Shakespeare is known to have died possessed, the greater share of it going to his daughter Susanna. His recently married daughter Judith received a dowry, a provision for any children that might be born of her marriage, and other gifts. Ten pounds went to the poor of Stratford, Shakespeare's sword to Mr. Thomas Combe, 28s. 8d. apiece to Shakespeare's fellow actors Heminges, Burbage, and Condell to buy them mourning rings, and other small bequests to various other friends and relatives.

An interlineation contains the bequest of Shakespeare's "second best bed with the furniture," that is, the hangings, to his wife. Anne's name appears nowhere else in the will. Some scholars, beginning with Edmond Malone, have taken this reference as proof of an unhappy marriage, confirming earlier indications such as the hasty wedding to a woman who was William's senior by eight years, and his prolonged residence in London for twenty years or more seemingly without his family. The evidence is inconclusive, however. Shakespeare certainly supported his family handsomely, acquired much property in Stratford, and retired there when he might have remained still in London. Although he showed no great solicitude for Anne's well-being in the will, her rights were protected by law; a third of her husband's estate went to her without having to be mentioned in the will. New

Place was to be the home of Shakespeare's favorite daughter Susanna, wife of the distinguished Dr. John Hall. Anne Shakespeare would make her home with her daughter, and with her dower rights secured by law would be quite as wealthy as she needed to be.

The date of Shakespeare's death, April 23, 1616, is inscribed on his monument. This elaborate structure, still standing in the chancel of Trinity Church, Stratford, was erected some time before 1623 by the London stonecutting firm of Gheerart Janssen and his sons. Janssen's shop was in Southwark, near the Globe, and may have been familiar to the actors. The bust of Shakespeare is a conventional sort of statuary for its time. Still, it is one of the only two contemporary likenesses we have. The other is the Droeshout engraving of Shakespeare in the Folio of 1623.

The epitaph on the monument reads as follows:

Ivdicio Pylivm, genio Socratem, arte Maronem:
Terra tegit, popvlvs maeret, Olympvs habet.
Stay Passenger, why goest thov by so fast?
Read if thov canst, whom enviovs Death hath plast,
With in this monvment Shakspeare: with whome,
Quick natvre dide: whose name doth deck ys Tombe,
Far more then cost: sieh all, yt He hath writt,
Leaves living art, bvt page, to serve his witt.
Obiit anno domini 1616
Aetatis—53 die 23 April.

These lines, which seem to indicate, as well as anything could, the high reputation in which Shakespeare was held as a poet at the time of his death, are not so well known as those inscribed over Shakespeare's grave near the north wall of the chancel. A local tradition assigns them to Shakespeare himself and implies that he wrote them "to suit the capacity of clerks and sextons," whom he wished apparently to frighten out of the idea of opening the grave to make room for a new occupant:

Good frend for Iesvs sake forbeare,
To digg the dvst encloased heare.
Bleste be ye man yt spares thes stones,
And cvrst be he yt moves my bones.

Whether Shakespeare actually wrote these lines cannot, however, be determined.

SHAKESPEARE ALLUSIONS

Shakespeare enjoyed considerable fame during his lifetime, a fame that is all the more remarkable when we remember that dramatists were generally less highly regarded than nondramatic poets in Elizabethan times. The extent of Shakespeare's contemporary reputation can be measured by the number of notices and tributes he received. One of the earliest is to be found in an anonymous commendatory verse prefixed to Henry Willobie's *Willobie His Avisa* in 1594. Richard Barnfield, in his *Poems in Divers Humors* (1598), praised the "hony-flowing Vaine" of Shakespeare's *Venus and Adonis* and *The Rape of Lucrece*. Francis Meres insisted, in *Palladis Tamia*, 1598, that Shakespeare deserved to be compared not only with Ovid for his verse, but with Plautus and Seneca for his comedies and tragedies. Other tributes were written by John Weever, Gabriel Harvey, Anthony Scoloker, William Camden, John Davies of Hereford, Thomas Freeman, John Webster, and many others. Shakespeare's great contemporary Ben Jonson criticized Shakespeare for his lack of classical decorum and for carelessness in writing, but acknowledged that Shakespeare was worthy of comparison with the very greatest of classical writers. Indeed, said Jonson, as a comic writer Shakespeare had no rival even in "insolent *Greece* or haughtie *Rome*."

THE ANTI-STRATFORDIAN MOVEMENT

What we know of Shakespeare's life is really quite considerable. The information we have is just the kind one would expect. It hangs together and refers to one man and one career. Though lacking in the personal details we should like to have, it is both adequate and plausible. Yet the past hundred years or so have seen the growth of a tendency to doubt Shakespeare's authorship of the plays and poems ascribed to him. The phenomenon is sometimes called the "anti-Stratfordian" movement, since its attack is leveled at the literary credentials of the man who was born in Stratford and later became an actor in London. Although based on no reliable evidence, the movement has persisted long enough to become a kind of myth. It also has the appeal of a mystery thriller: who really wrote Shakespeare's plays? A brief account must be made here of the origins of the anti-Stratfordian movement.

Beginning in the late eighteenth century, and especially in the mid nineteenth century, a few admirers of Shakespeare began to be troubled by the scantiness of information about England's greatest author. Good reasons exist for that scarcity: the great London fire of 1666 that destroyed many records, the relatively low social esteem accorded to popular dramatists during the Elizabethan period, and the like. Also, we do actually know more about Shakespeare than about most of his contemporaries in the theatre, despite the difficulties imposed by the passage of time. Still, some nineteenth-century readers saw only that they knew far less about Shakespeare than about many authors of more recent date.

Moreover, the impressions of the man did not seem to square with his unparalleled literary greatness. William Shakespeare had been brought up in a small country town; were his parents cultured folk, or even literate? No record of his schooling has been preserved; was Shakespeare himself able to read and write, much less write immortal plays and poems? The anti-Stratfordians did not deny the existence of a man called Shakespeare from Stratford-upon-Avon, but they found it incredible that such a person should be connected with the works ascribed to him. Mark Twain, himself an anti-Stratfordian, was fond of joking that the plays were not by Shakespeare but by another person of the same name. Beneath the humor in this remark lies a deep-seated mistrust: how could a simple country boy have written so knowledgeably and eloquently about the lives of kings and queens? Where could such a person have learned so much about the law, about medicine, about the art of war, about heraldry? The puzzle seemed a genuine one, even though no one until the late eighteenth century had thought to question Shakespeare's authorship of the plays—least of all his colleagues and friends, such as Ben Jonson, who admitted that Shakespeare's classical learning was "small," but insisted that Shakespeare was an incomparable genius.

The first candidate put forward as the "real" author of the plays was Sir Francis Bacon, a reputable Elizabethan writer with connections at court and considerable cultural attainments. Yet the ascription of the plays to Bacon was based on no documentary evidence. It relied instead on the essentially snobbish argument that Bacon was better born and purportedly better educated than Shakespeare—an argument that appealed strongly to the nineteenth century in which a university education was becoming more and more a distinctive mark of the cultivated person. The assertion of Bacon's authorship was also based on a conspiratorial theory of history. That is, its believers had to assume the existence of a mammoth conspiracy in Elizabethan times in which Shakespeare would allow his name to be used by Bacon as a *nom de plume*, and in which Shakespeare's friends such as Ben Jonson would take part. (Jonson knew Shakespeare too well, after all, to have been duped for a period of almost twenty years.) The motive for such an arrangement, presumably, was that Bacon did not deign to lend his dignified name to the writing of popular plays (since they were considered subliterary) and so chose a common actor named Shakespeare to serve as his alter ego. This theory of an elaborate hoax involving England's greatest literary giant has proved powerfully attractive to modern writers like Mark Twain, who sometimes refer to themselves as rebels against the cultural "Establishment" of their own times.

Bacon's claim to have written Shakespeare was soon challenged by that of other prominent Elizabethans: the Earl of Oxford, the Earl of Southampton, Anthony Bacon, the Earl of Rutland, the Earl of Devonshire, Christopher Marlowe, and others. Since Bacon's documentary claims to Shakespearean greatness were nonexistent, other Elizabethans could be proposed to fill his role just as satisfactorily as Bacon himself. The anti-Stratfordian movement gained momentum and came to include several prominent persons including Delia Bacon and Sigmund Freud as well as Mark Twain. One of the appeals of the anti-Stratfordian movement in recent years has proved to be a kind of amateur sleuthing or scholarship carried on by professional lawyers, doctors, and the like, who have explored Shakespeare's interest in law and medicine as a hobby and have convinced themselves that Shakespeare's wisdom in these subjects entitles him to claim a better birth than that of a glover's son from Stratford. Absurdly ingenious efforts at "deciphering" hidden meanings in the works have been adduced to prove some authorship claim or other. The academic "Establishments" of modern universities have been accused of perpetuating Shakespeare's name out of mere vested self-interest: Shakespeare scholarship is an industry, and its busy workers need to preserve their source of income.

We must ask in all seriousness, however, whether such assertions are not offering answers to nonexistent questions. Responsible recent scholarship has admirably dispelled the seeming mystery of Shakespeare's humble beginnings. T. W. Baldwin, for example, in *William Shakspere's Petty School* (1943) and *William Shakspere's Small Latine and Lesse Greeke* (1944) has shown just what sort of classical training Shakespeare almost surely received in the free grammar school of Stratford. It is precisely the sort of training that would have enabled him to use classical authors as he does, with the familiarity of one who likes to read. His Latin and Greek were passable but not strong; he often consulted modern translations as well as classical originals. Just as importantly, Shakespeare's social background was in fact typical of many of the greatest writers of the English Renaissance. He earned his living by his writing, and thus had one of the strongest of motives for success. So did his contemporaries Marlowe (who came from a shoemakers' family) and Jonson (whose stepfather was a brickmason). Greene, Peele, Nashe, and many others sold plays and other writings for a livelihood. Although a few well-born persons such as Bacon and Sir Philip Sidney also made exceptional contributions to literature, and although a number of courtiers emulated Henry VIII and Elizabeth as gifted amateurs in the arts, the court was not the direct or major source of England's literary greatness. Most courtiers were not, like Shakespeare, professional writers. A man like Bacon lacked Shakespeare's connection with a commercial acting company. Surely the theatre was a more relevant "university" for Shakespeare than Oxford or Cambridge, where most of his studies would have been in ancient languages and in divinity.

THE ROYAL GENEALOGY OF ENGLAND, 1154–1625

THE PLANTAGENET KINGS

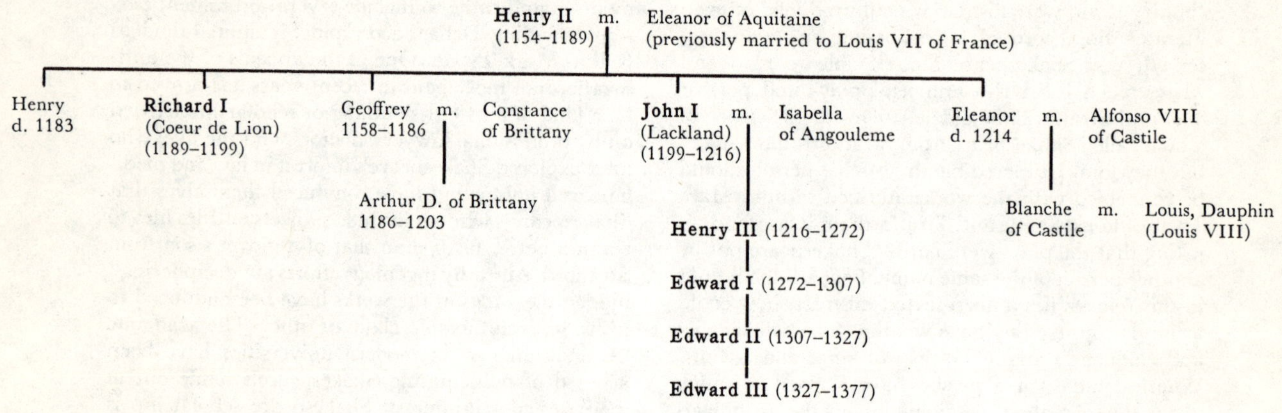

THE LANCASTRIAN KINGS

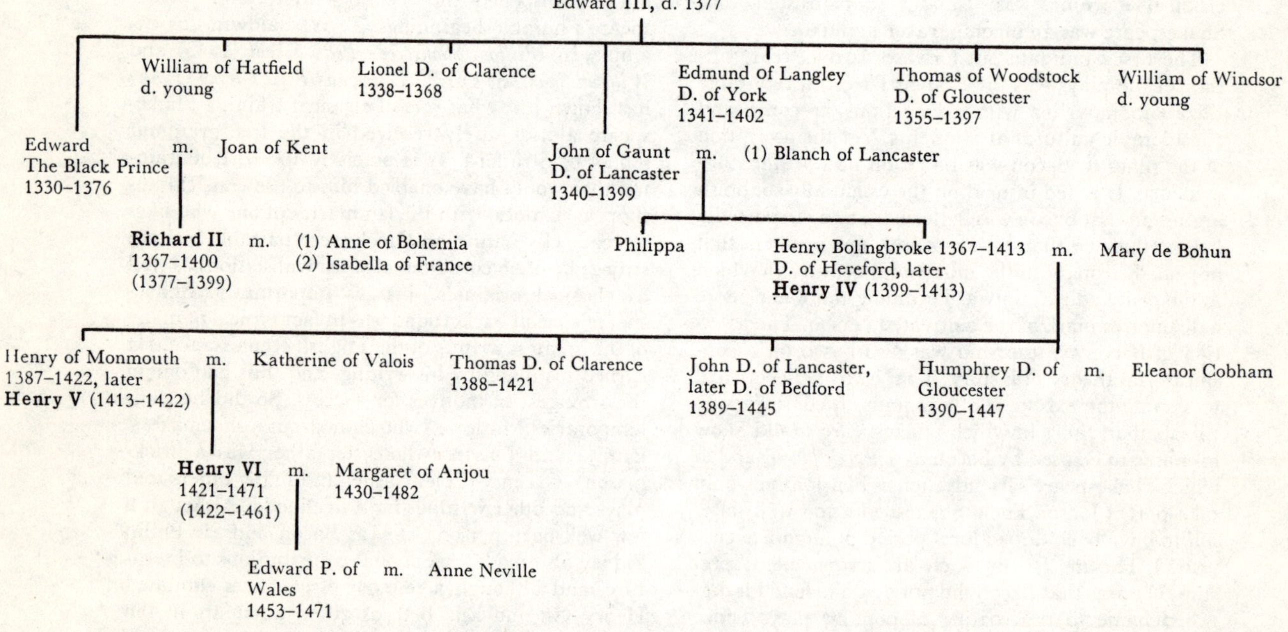

In these diagrams, reigning dates are given in parentheses; other dates indicate life span. Abbreviations: P. Prince, D. Duke, E. Earl, b. born, d. died, m. married. English monarchs are printed in boldface type. The spatial arrangement of names in a family usually but not always indicates order of birth.

In *1 Henry IV*, Shakespeare confuses the Edmund Mortimer who married Glendower's daughter, and died in 1409, with his nephew Edmund, fifth Earl of March, who asserted a claim to the English throne (see "The Yorkist Kings"). Shakespeare also refers to Henry Percy's (Hotspur's) wife as "Kate," though historically she was named Elizabeth.

Catherine Swynford, third wife of John of Gaunt (see "The Tudor Kings"), bore him children before their eventual marriage. These Beauforts, although later legitimized, were specifically barred from any claim to the English throne.

THE YORKIST KINGS

Edward III m. Philippa of Hainault
Edward
William
Lionel D. of Clarence m. Elizabeth de Burgh
John of Gaunt
Edmund Langley 1st D. of York m. Isabel of Castile
Thomas
Philippa m. Edmund Mortimer 3rd E. of March 1351–1381
Edward D. of Aumerle, later D. of York 1373–1415
Roger Mortimer 4th E. of March 1374–1398 m. Eleanor Holland
Edmund d. 1409 m. Daughter of Owen Glendower
Elizabeth m. Henry Percy (Hotspur)
Edmund Mortimer 5th E. of March 1391–1425
Anne Mortimer m. Richard E. of Cambridge 1375–1415
Richard Plantagenet E. of Cambridge, later D. of York 1411–1460 m. Cecily Neville
Edward, E. of March 1422–1483 Edward IV (1461–1483) m. Elizabeth Woodville Lady Grey
Edmund, E. of Rutland 1443–1460
George D. of Clarence 1449–1478 m. Isabell Neville, daughter of Richard E. of Warwick
Richard D. of Gloucester 1452–1485 Richard III (1483–1485)
Elizabeth b. 1465 m. Henry Tudor (Henry VII)
Edward V 1470–1483 (1483)
Richard k. 1483
Edward
Margaret

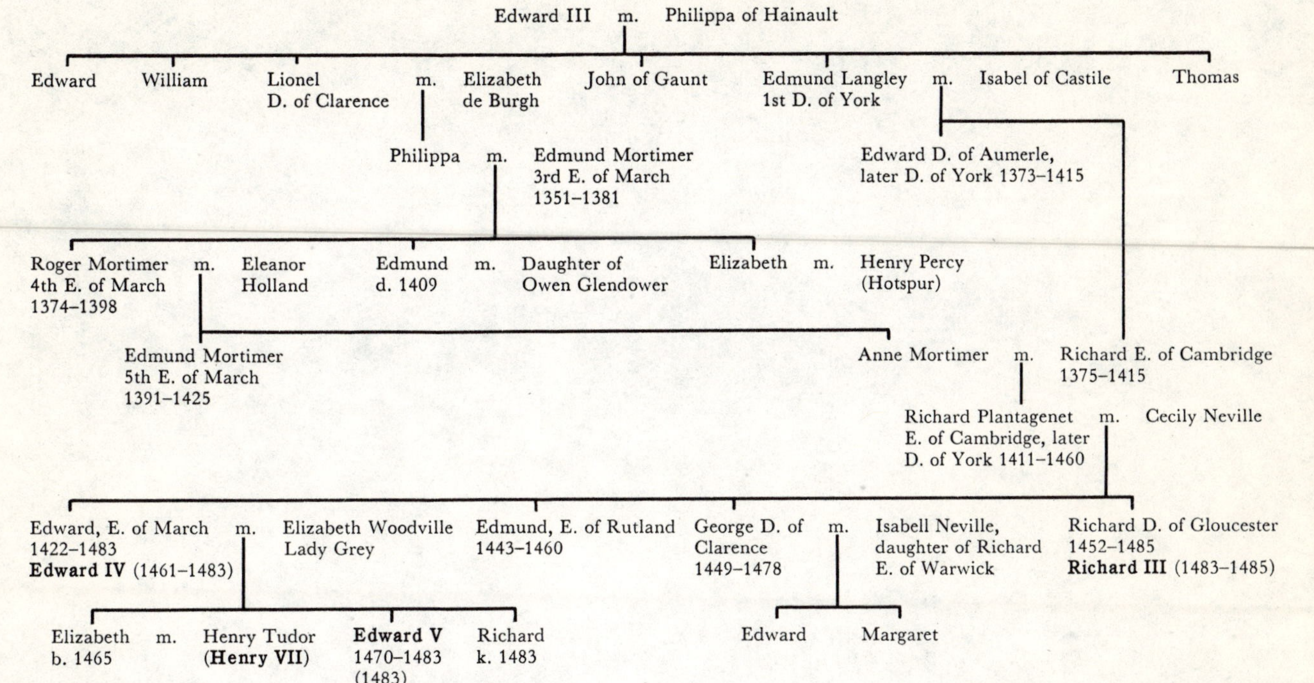

THE TUDOR KINGS

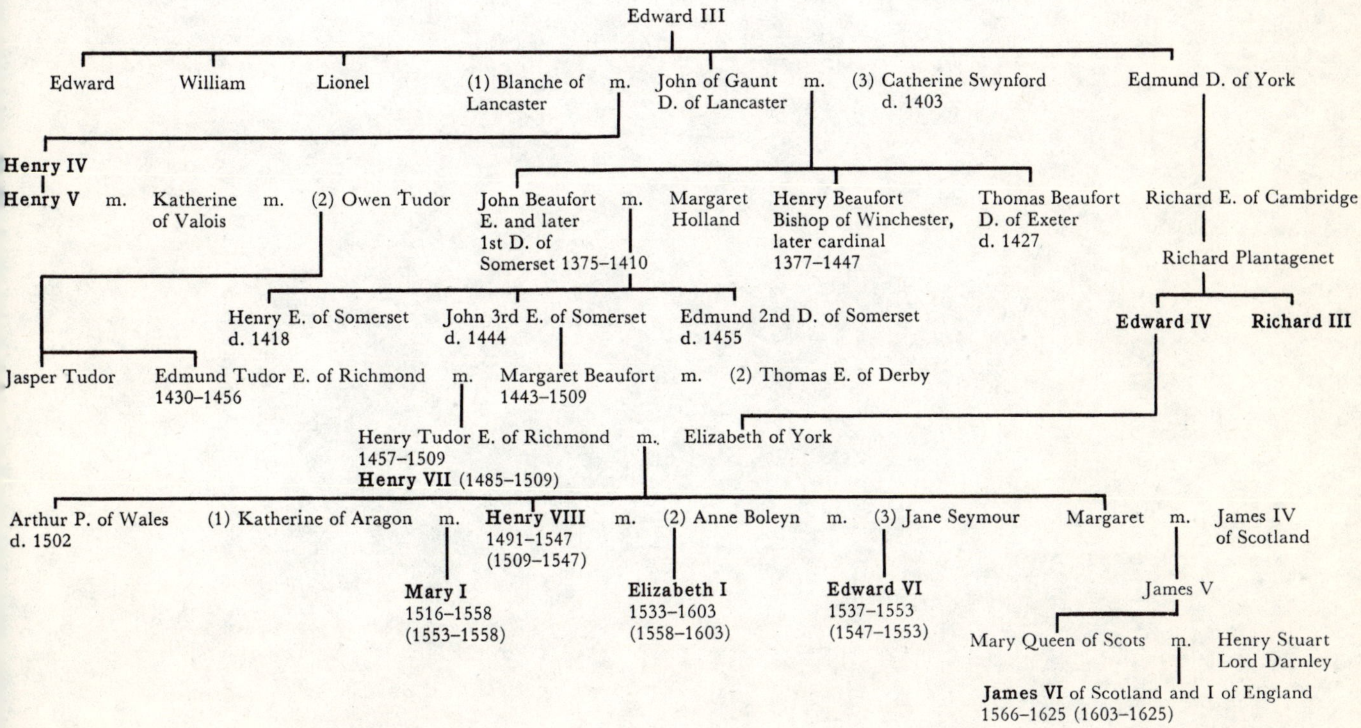

Edward III
Edward
William
Lionel
(1) Blanche of Lancaster m. John of Gaunt D. of Lancaster m. (3) Catherine Swynford d. 1403
Edmund D. of York
Henry IV
Henry V m. Katherine of Valois m. (2) Owen Tudor
John Beaufort E. and later 1st D. of Somerset 1375–1410 m. Margaret Holland
Henry Beaufort Bishop of Winchester, later cardinal 1377–1447
Thomas Beaufort D. of Exeter d. 1427
Richard E. of Cambridge
Richard Plantagenet
Henry E. of Somerset d. 1418
John 3rd E. of Somerset d. 1444
Edmund 2nd D. of Somerset d. 1455
Edward IV
Richard III
Jasper Tudor
Edmund Tudor E. of Richmond 1430–1456 m. Margaret Beaufort 1443–1509 m. (2) Thomas E. of Derby
Henry Tudor E. of Richmond 1457–1509 Henry VII (1485–1509) m. Elizabeth of York
Arthur P. of Wales d. 1502
(1) Katherine of Aragon m. Henry VIII 1491–1547 (1509–1547) m. (2) Anne Boleyn m. (3) Jane Seymour
Margaret m. James IV of Scotland
Mary I 1516–1558 (1553–1558)
Elizabeth I 1533–1603 (1558–1603)
Edward VI 1537–1553 (1547–1553)
James V
Mary Queen of Scots m. Henry Stuart Lord Darnley
James VI of Scotland and I of England 1566–1625 (1603–1625)

The Plays and Sonnets

Romeo and Juliet
A Midsummer Night's Dream
The Tragedy of King Richard the Second
The First Part of King Henry the Fourth
Twelfth Night; or, What You Will
Hamlet, Prince of Denmark
King Lear
The Tempest

The Sonnets

ROMEO AND JULIET

Though a tragedy, *Romeo and Juliet* is more closely comparable to Shakespeare's romantic comedies than to his other tragedies. Stylistically belonging to the years 1594–1596, it is in the lyric vein of the sonnets, *A Midsummer Night's Dream*, and *The Merchant of Venice*, all from the mid-1590's. Like them, it uses a variety of rhyme schemes (couplets, quatrains, octets, even sonnets) and revels in punning, flowery Petrarchan metaphor, and wit combat. It is separated in tone and in time from the earliest of the great tragedies, *Julius Caesar* and *Hamlet*, by almost half a decade, and, except for the experimental *Titus Andronicus*, it is Shakespeare's only tragedy (that is not also a "History") in the first decade of his productivity—a period devoted otherwise to exuberant comedy and patriotic English history.

Like many comedies, *Romeo and Juliet* is a love story, celebrating the exquisite brief joy of youthful passion. Even its tragic ending stresses the poignancy of that brief beauty, not the bitter futility of love as in *Troilus and Cressida* or *Othello*. The tragic ending of *Romeo and Juliet* underscores the observation made by a vexed lover in *A Midsummer Night's Dream* that "The course of true love never did run smooth" (I,i). True love in *Romeo and Juliet*, as in *A Midsummer*, is destined to be crossed by differences in "blood" or family background, differences in age, the arbitrary choice of family or friends, or other uncontrollable catastrophes such as war, death, and sickness. Love is thus, as in *A Midsummer*, "momentary as a sound, Swift as a shadow, short as any dream," swallowed up by darkness; "So quick bright things come to confusion." A dominant image pattern in *Romeo and Juliet* evokes a corresponding sense of suddenness and violence: fire, gunpowder, hot blood, lightning, the inconstant wind, the storm-tossed or shipwrecked vessel. Love so threatened and fragile is beautiful because it is brief. Tragic outcome therefore affirms the uniqueness and pristine youthful ecstasy of the experience. The flowering and fading of a joy "too rich for use, for earth too dear" (I,v), does not condemn the unfeeling world so much as it welcomes the martyrdom of literally dying for love.

As protagonists, Romeo and Juliet lack tragic stature by any classical definition or by the medieval convention of the Fall of Princes. The lovers are not extraordinary except in their passionate attachment to one another. By birth they are respectable citizens rather than nobility. Their dilemma of parental opposition is of the domestic sort often found in comedy. Accordingly, several characters in the play partly resemble the conventional character types of Plautus or Italian neoclassical comedy: the domineering father who insists that his daughter marry according to his choice, the unwelcome rival wooer, the garrulous and

RADIO TIMES HULTON PICTURE LIBRARY

Ford Madox Brown's painting of Romeo and Juliet shows their parting in Act III, scene v, after their wedding night.

bawdy nurse, and of course the lovers. The Italian *novella*, from which Shakespeare ultimately derived his plot, made use of these same types and paid little attention to classical precepts whereby the protagonists in a tragic story ought to be persons of lofty station who are humbled through some inner flaw or *hamartia*. Luigi da Porto told (c. 1530) of a feud between the two Veronese families of Montecchi and Cappelletti and of two young lovers, Romeo and Giulietta, who with a friar's help resorted to the dire expedient of a soporific drug. Luigi based his account on an older *novella* of Masuccio of Salerno (1476) and on the still older tradition of a sleeping potion as found in the Greek romance of *Ephesiaca* (by the fifth century A.D.). Luigi's version was followed in turn by Bandello in his famous *Novelle* of 1554, whence the story was translated into the French of Pierre Boaistuau (1559) and thus into English in the long narrative poem of Arthur Brooke called *The Tragicall Historye of Romeus and Juliet* (1562). Brooke mentions having seen a play on the subject, but we must doubt that Shakespeare made much use of this old play even if he knew it. Brooke's poem was his chief and probably only source. Shakespeare has condensed Brooke's action from nine months to less than a week, greatly expanded the role of Mercutio, and given to the Nurse a warmth and humorous richness not found in the usual Italian duenna or *balia*. He has also tidied up the friar's immorality and deleted the antipapal tone. Still, Shakespeare retains the basically romantic (rather than classically tragic) conception of love overwhelmed by external obstacles.

Like the romantic comedies, *Romeo and Juliet* is often funny and erotic. Samson and Gregory in the first scene are slapstick cowards, hiding behind the law and daring to quarrel only when reinforcements arrive. The Nurse delights us with her earthy recollection of the day she weaned Juliet: the child tasting "the wormwood on the nipple Of my dug," the hot Italian sun, an earthquake, the Nurse's husband telling his lame but often-repeated bawdy joke. Mercutio employs his inventive and sardonic humor to twit Romeo for lovesickness and the Nurse for her pomposity. She in turn scolds Peter, and plagues Juliet (who is breathlessly awaiting news from Romeo) with a history of her back ailments. Mercutio and the Nurse are among Shakespeare's bawdiest characters. Their wry and salacious view of love contrasts with the nobly innocent and yet physically passionate love of Romeo and Juliet. Mercutio and the Nurse cannot take part in the play's denouement; one dies, misinterpreting Romeo's appeasement of Tybalt, while the other proves insensitive to Juliet's spiritual needs. Yet the play loses much of its funniness and vitality with the disappearance of these engaging companions.

The lovers too are at first well suited to Shakespearean romantic comedy. When we meet Romeo he is not in love with Juliet at all, despite the play's title, but is mooning over a "hard-hearted wench" named Rosaline. This "goddess" appropriately never appears in the play; she is almost a disembodied idea in Romeo's mind, a typically Petrarchan scornful beauty like Phebe in *As You Like It*. Romeo's love for her is tedious and self-pitying, like that of the conventional Petrarchan wooer in a sonnet sequence. Juliet, although not yet fourteen years of age, must change all this by teaching him the nature of true love. She will have none of his shopworn clichés learned in the service of Rosaline, his flowery protestations and swearing by the moon, lest they prove to be love's perjuries. With her innocent candor she instead insists (like many heroines of the romantic comedies) on dispelling the mask of pretense that lovers too often show one another. "Capulet" and "Montague" are mere labels, not the inner self. Although Juliet would have been more coy, she confesses, had she known that Romeo was overhearing her, she will now "prove more true Than those that have more cunning to be strange." She is more practical than he in assessing danger and making plans. Later she also proves herself remarkably able to bear misfortune.

This comic mood of the play's first half is, of course, overshadowed by the certainty of disaster. The opening chorus plainly warns us that the lovers will die. They are "star-cross'd," and speak of themselves as such. Romeo fears "Some consequence yet hanging in the stars" when he reluctantly goes to the Capulets' feast (I,iv); after he has slain Tybalt, he cries "O, I am fortune's fool!" (III,i); and at the news of Juliet's supposed death he proclaims "Then I defy you, stars!" (V,i). Yet in what sense are Romeo and Juliet "star-cross'd"? The concept is deliberately broad in this play, encompassing many factors such as hatred, bumbling, bad luck, and simple lack of awareness.

The first scene presents feuding as a major cause in the tragedy. The quarrel between the two families is so ancient that the original motives are no longer even discussed. Inspired by the "fiery" Tybalt, factionalism pursues its mindless course despite the efforts of the Prince to end the slaughter. Although the elders of both families talk of peace, they draw their swords quickly enough when a fray begins. Still, this senseless hatred does not in itself lead to tragedy until its effects are fatally complicated through misunderstanding. With poignant irony, good intentions are repeatedly undermined by lack of knowledge. We can see why Juliet does not tell her family of her elopement with a presumably hated Montague, but in fact Capulet has accepted Romeo as a guest in his house, praising him as a "virtuous and well govern'd youth." For all his dictatorial ways, Capulet would never force his daughter into bigamy if he knew the truth. Not knowing, he and his wife can only interpret her refusal to marry Paris as exasperating caprice. Count Paris himself is perhaps the greatest victim of this tragedy of unawareness. He is an eminently suitable wooer for Juliet, rich and nobly born yet considerate, peace-loving, and deeply fond of Juliet (as he demonstrates by his private and sincere grief at her tomb). Certainly he would never force his attentions on a married young woman if he knew the truth. Not knowing, he must play the unattractive role of the rival wooer and must even die for it. Similarly, Mercutio cannot understand Romeo's seemingly craven behavior toward Tybalt, and so begins the duel that leads to Romeo's banishment. The final scene, with Friar Laurence's retelling of the tragic story, allows us to see the survivors confronted with what they have all unknowingly done.

Chance or "accident" plays a role of equal importance to that of hatred and unawareness. An outbreak of the plague prevents Friar John from conveying Friar Laurence's letter to Romeo at Mantua. Friar Laurence, dashing off at this news to the Capulets' tomb, arrives only minutes after Romeo has taken poison. Juliet awakens only moments later. As Friar Laurence laments, "what an unkind hour Is guilty of this lamentable chance!" (V,iii). Earlier, Capulet's decision to move the wedding date up one day has crucially affected the timing. Human miscalculation makes its contribution also to the catastrophe: Mercutio is killed under Romeo's arm, and Friar Laurence wonders unhappily if any of his complicated plans "Miscarried by my fault." Even character and human decision play a part in this tragedy, for Romeo should not have dueled with Tybalt no matter what the provocation. To blame the tragedy in Aristotelean fashion on his and Juliet's impulsiveness is, however, a desperate argument.

Instead, the ending of the play brings together a pattern out of the seeming welter of mistakes and animosities. "A greater power than we can contradict Hath thwarted our intents," says Friar Laurence, thus implying piously that the seeming bad luck of the delayed letter was in fact the intent of a mysterious higher intelligence. Prince Escalus identifies this "greater power" as divine providence. "See, what a scourge is laid upon your hate," he admonishes the Montagues and Capulets, "That heaven finds means to kill your joys with love." Romeo and Juliet are "Poor sacrifices of our enmity." As the Prologue had foretold, their deaths will "bury their parents' strife." The families' feud is a stubborn evil force "which, but their children's end, nought could remove." Order is preciously restored; the price is great, but the sacrifice nonetheless confirms a sense of meaning in a divinely ordained universe. Throughout the play, love and hate are interrelated opposites, yoked through the rhetorical device of oxymoron or inherent contradiction. Romeo apostrophizes "O brawling love, O loving hate," and Juliet later echoes his words: "My only love sprung from my only hate." This paradox expresses a conflict in man as in the universe itself. "Two such opposed kings encamp them still In man as well as herbs," says Friar Laurence, "grace and rude will." Through hatred and misunderstanding, man kills the things most dear to him, but he can at least learn from his wanton destructiveness to strive to be worthy of the sacrifice.

ROMEO AND JULIET

[*Dramatis Personae*

ESCALUS, *Prince of Verona.*
PARIS, *a young nobleman, kinsman to the prince.*
MONTAGUE, } *heads of two houses at variance*
CAPULET, } *with each other.*
An old man, *cousin to Capulet.*
ROMEO, *son to Montague.*
MERCUTIO, *kinsman to the prince, and friend to Romeo.*
BENVOLIO, *nephew to Montague, and friend to Romeo.*
TYBALT, *nephew to Lady Capulet.*
FRIAR LAURENCE, } *Franciscans.*
FRIAR JOHN, }
BALTHASAR, *servant to Romeo.*
SAMPSON, } *servants to Capulet.*
GREGORY, }
PETER, *servant to Juliet's nurse.*
ABRAHAM, *servant to Montague.*
An Apothecary.
Three Musicians.
Page to Paris; another Page; an Officer.

LADY MONTAGUE, *wife to Montague.*
LADY CAPULET, *wife to Capulet.*
JULIET, *daughter to Capulet.*
Nurse to Juliet.

Citizens of Verona; several Men *and* Women, relations to both houses; Maskers, Guards, Watchmen, *and* Attendants.

Chorus.

SCENE: *Verona: Mantua.*]

THE PROLOGUE.

[*Enter* CHORUS.]

Chorus. Two households, both alike in dignity,
In fair Verona, where we lay our scene,
From ancient grudge break to new mutiny,
Where civil blood makes civil hands unclean.
From forth the fatal loins of these two foes
A pair of star-cross'd lovers take their life;
Whose misadventur'd piteous overthrows
Doth with their death bury their parents' strife.
The fearful passage of their death-mark'd love,
And the continuance of their parents' rage
Which, but their children's end, nought could remove,
Is now the two hours' traffic of our stage;
The which if you with patient ears attend,
What here shall miss, our toil shall strive to mend. [*Exit.*]

[ACT I.

SCENE I. *Verona. A public place.*]

Enter SAMPSON *and* GREGORY, *with swords and bucklers, of the house of Capulet.*

Sam. Gregory, on my word, we'll not carry coals.
Gre. No, for then we should be colliers.
Sam. I mean, an we be in choler, we'll draw.
Gre. Ay, while you live, draw your neck out of collar.
Sam. I strike quickly, being moved.
Gre. But thou art not quickly moved to strike.
Sam. A dog of the house of Montague moves me.
Gre. To move is to stir; and to be valiant is to stand: therefore, if thou art moved, thou runn'st away.
Sam. A dog of that house shall move me to stand: I will take the wall of any man or maid of Montague's.
Gre. That shows thee a weak slave; for the weakest goes to the wall.
Sam. 'Tis true; and therefore women, being the weaker vessels, are ever thrust to the wall: therefore I will push Montague's men from the wall, and thrust his maids to the wall.
Gre. The quarrel is between our masters and us their men.
Sam. 'Tis all one, I will show myself a tyrant: when I have fought with the men, I will be civil with the maids—I will cut off their heads.
Gre. The heads of the maids?
Sam. Ay, the heads of the maids, or their maidenheads; take it in what sense thou wilt.
Gre. They must take it in sense that feel it.
Sam. Me they shall feel while I am able to stand: and 'tis known I am a pretty piece of flesh.
Gre. 'Tis well thou art not fish; if thou hadst, thou hadst been poor John. Draw thy tool; here comes two of the house of the Montagues.

Enter two other Servingmen [ABRAHAM *and* BALTHASAR].

Sam. My naked weapon is out: quarrel, I will back thee.
Gre. How! turn thy back and run?
Sam. Fear me not.
Gre. No, marry; I fear thee!
Sam. Let us take the law of our sides; let them begin.
Gre. I will frown as I pass by, and let them take it as they list.
Sam. Nay, as they dare. I will bite my thumb at them; which is disgrace to them, if they bear it.
Abr. Do you bite your thumb at us, sir?
Sam. I do bite my thumb, sir.
Abr. Do you bite your thumb at us, sir?
Sam. [*Aside to Gre.*] Is the law of our side, if I say ay?
Gre. No.
Sam. No, sir, I do not bite my thumb at you, sir, but I bite my thumb, sir.
Gre. Do you quarrel, sir?
Abr. Quarrel, sir! no, sir.
Sam. But if you do, sir, I am for you: I serve as good a man as you.
Abr. No better.
Sam. Well, sir.

Enter BENVOLIO.

Gre. Say 'better:' here comes one of my master's kinsmen.
Sam. Yes, better, sir.
Abr. You lie.
Sam. Draw, if you be men. Gregory, remember thy swashing blow. *They fight.*
Ben. Part, fools!
Put up your swords; you know not what you do.
[*Beats down their swords.*]

Enter TYBALT.

Tyb. What, art thou drawn among these heartless hinds?
Turn thee, Benvolio, look upon thy death.
Ben. I do but keep the peace: put up thy sword,
Or manage it to part these men with me.
Tyb. What, drawn, and talk of peace! I hate the word,
As I hate hell, all Montagues, and thee:
Have at thee, coward! [*They fight.*]

Enter [*an* Officer, *and*] *three or four* Citizens *with clubs or partisans.*

Officer. Clubs, bills, and partisans! strike! beat them down!
Down with the Capulets! down with the Montagues!

Enter old CAPULET *in his gown, and his* Wife.

Cap. What noise is this? Give me my long sword, ho!
La. Cap. A crutch, a crutch! why call you for a sword?
Cap. My sword, I say! Old Montague is come,
And flourishes his blade in spite of me.

Enter old MONTAGUE *and his* Wife.

Mon. Thou villain Capulet,—Hold me not, let me go.
La. Mon. Thou shalt not stir one foot to seek a foe.

Enter PRINCE ESCALUS, *with his train.*

Prin. Rebellious subjects, enemies to peace,
Profaners of this neighbour-stained steel,—
Will they not hear? What, ho! you men, you beasts,
That quench the fire of your pernicious rage
With purple fountains issuing from your veins,
On pain of torture, from those bloody hands
Throw your mistempered weapons to the ground,
And hear the sentence of your moved prince.
Three civil brawls, bred of an airy word,
By thee, old Capulet, and Montague,
Have thrice disturb'd the quiet of our streets,
And made Verona's ancient citizens
Cast by their grave beseeming ornaments,
To wield old partisans, in hands as old,

PROLOGUE. 3. **mutiny,** state of discord. 6. **star-cross'd,** thwarted by destiny. Shakespeare shows in this play particularly, and throughout his plays generally, the current belief in the influence of the stars. The idea blends with that of divine providence. 9. **fearful,** full of fear; see glossary. **passage,** progress. 12. **two hours' traffic of our stage.** This line is one of a small number of references which enable us to tell the length of time occupied by a Shakespearean play. If the time was nearer two hours than three, the play must have been rapidly recited, with little loss of time between scenes. The bareness of the stage and the lack of a curtain would have contributed to the speed of presentation.

ACT I. SCENE I. This scene serves to give us the atmosphere of the whole play, an atmosphere of feud. Sampson is a stupid bully, Gregory a merry one. 1. **carry coals,** endure insults. 4. **choler,** one of the four humors, productive of anger. 10. **moves,** incites; see glossary. 15. **take the wall,** take the side of the walk nearest the wall, an act of discourtesy. 37. **poor John,** hake salted and dried—a poor kind of food. 42. **Fear,** mistrust; see glossary. 43. **marry,** mild oath; see glossary. 47. **list,** please; see glossary. 48. **bite my thumb,** an insulting gesture. 70. **swashing,** crushing. 73. **drawn,** with drawn sword. **heartless hinds,** cowardly menials; see *hind* in glossary. 79. **Have at thee,** I shall attack thee, defend thyself; see glossary. 80.

Cank'red with peace, to part your cank'red hate:
If ever you disturb our streets again,
Your lives shall pay the forfeit of the peace.
For this time, all the rest depart away:
You, Capulet, shall go along with me:
And, Montague, come you this afternoon,
To know our further pleasure in this case,
To old Free-town, our common judgement-place.
Once more, on pain of death, all men depart.
Exeunt [all but Montague, Lady Montague, and Benvolio].
Mon. Who set this ancient quarrel new abroach?
Speak, nephew, were you by when it began?
Ben. Here were the servants of your adversary,
And yours, close fighting ere I did approach:
I drew to part them: in the instant came
The fiery Tybalt, with his sword prepar'd,
Which, as he breath'd defiance to my ears,
He swung about his head and cut the winds,
Who nothing hurt withal hiss'd him in scorn:
While we were interchanging thrusts and blows,
Came more and more and fought on part and part,
Till the prince came, who parted either part.
La. Mon. O, where is Romeo? saw you him to-day?
Right glad I am he was not at this fray.
Ben. Madam, an hour before the worshipp'd sun
Peer'd forth the golden window of the east,
A troubled mind drave me to walk abroad;
Where, underneath the grove of sycamore
That westward rooteth from the city's side,
So early walking did I see your son:
Towards him I made, but he was ware of me
And stole into the covert of the wood:
I, measuring his affections by my own,
Which then most sought where most might not be found,
[Being one too many by my weary self,]
Pursu'd my humour not pursuing his,
And gladly shunn'd who gladly fled from me.
Mon. Many a morning hath he there been seen,
With tears augmenting the fresh morning's dew,
Adding to clouds more clouds with his deep sighs;
But all so soon as the all-cheering sun
Should in the farthest east begin to draw
The shady curtains from Aurora's bed,
Away from light steals home my heavy son,
And private in his chamber pens himself,
Shuts up his windows, locks fair daylight out
And makes himself an artificial night:
Black and portentous must this humour prove,
Unless good counsel may the cause remove.
Ben. My noble uncle, do you know the cause?
Mon. I neither know it nor can learn of him.
Ben. Have you importun'd him by any means?
Mon. Both by myself and many other friends:
But he, his own affections' counsellor,
Is to himself—I will not say how true—
But to himself so secret and so close,
So far from sounding and discovery,
As is the bud bit with an envious worm,
Ere he can spread his sweet leaves to the air,
Or dedicate his beauty to the sun.
Could we but learn from whence his sorrows grow,
We would as willingly give cure as know.

Enter Romeo.

Ben. See, where he comes: so please you, step aside;
I'll know his grievance, or be much denied.
Mon. I would thou wert so happy by thy stay,
To hear true shrift. Come, madam, let 's away.
Exeunt [Montague and Lady].
Ben. Good morrow, cousin.
Rom. Is the day so young?
Ben. But new struck nine.
Rom. Ay me! sad hours seem long.
Was that my father that went hence so fast?
Ben. It was. What sadness lengthens Romeo's hours?
Rom. Not having that, which, having, makes them short.
Ben. In love?
Rom. Out—
Ben. Of love?
Rom. Out of her favour, where I am in love.
Ben. Alas, that love, so gentle in his view,
Should be so tyrannous and rough in proof!
Rom. Alas, that love, whose view is muffled still,
Should, without eyes, see pathways to his will!
Where shall we dine? O me! What fray was here?
Yet tell me not, for I have heard it all.
Here 's much to do with hate, but more with love.
Why, then, O brawling love! O loving hate!
O any thing, of nothing first create!
O heavy lightness! serious vanity!
Mis-shapen chaos of well-seeming forms!
Feather of lead, bright smoke, cold fire, sick health!
Still-waking sleep, that is not what it is!
This love feel I, that feel no love in this.
Dost thou not laugh?
Ben. No, coz, I rather weep.
Rom. Good heart, at what?
Ben. At thy good heart's oppression.
Rom. Why, such is love's transgression.
Griefs of mine own lie heavy in my breast,
Which thou wilt propagate, to have it prest
With more of thine: this love that thou hast shown
Doth add more grief to too much of mine own.
Love is a smoke rais'd with the fume of sighs;
Being purg'd, a fire sparkling in lovers' eyes;
Being vex'd, a sea nourish'd with lovers' tears:
What is it else? a madness most discreet,
A choking gall and a preserving sweet.
Farewell, my coz.
Ben. Soft! I will go along;
An if you leave me so, you do me wrong.
Rom. Tut, I have lost myself; I am not here;
This is not Romeo, he 's some other where.
Ben. Tell me in sadness, who is that you love.
Rom. What, shall I groan and tell thee?

Clubs, bills, and partisans, a rallying cry of London apprentices. *Bills* and *partisans* were long-handled spears with cutting blades. 83. **crutch,** i.e., a crutch would befit him better than a sword. 102. **Cank'red . . . cank'red,** corroded . . . malignant. 109. **Free-town,** Villa Franca in Brooke's poem *Romeus and Juliet*. 111. **set . . . abroach,** reopened. 119. **nothing,** not at all; see glossary. **withal,** with this; see glossary. 121. **on part and part,** on one side and the other. 133. **affections,** wishes, inclination; see glossary. 134. **Which then . . . self],** so Q_2; Globe follows F, which has only one line in place of two lines here. 135. **humour,** mood, whim; see glossary. 143. **heavy,** sad. 151. **means,** agency; see *mean* in glossary. 155. **close,** secret, private; see glossary. 157. **envious,** malicious; see glossary. 159. **sun,** so Theobald; Qq: *same*. 163. **denied,** refused; see *deny* in glossary. 165. **shrift,** confession. 166. **morrow,** morning. **cousin,** any relative not belonging to one's immediate family; see glossary. 174. **favour,** good will, liking; see glossary. 176. **proof,** experience; see glossary. 181-188. **Here 's . . . this.** These lines, abounding in paradoxical phrases called oxymoron, such as *loving hate*, *cold fire*, are characteristic of artificial love poetry. 183. **create,** created. 193. **propagate,** increase. 206. **sadness,** seriousness.

Ben. Groan! why, no:
But sadly tell me who.
Rom. Bid a sick man in sadness make his will:
Ah, word ill urg'd to one that is so ill!
In sadness, cousin, I do love a woman.
Ben. I aim'd so near, when I suppos'd you lov'd.
Rom. A right good mark-man! And she 's fair I love.
Ben. A right fair mark, fair coz, is soonest hit.
Rom. Well, in that hit you miss: she'll not be hit
With Cupid's arrow; she hath Dian's wit;
And, in strong proof of chastity well arm'd,
From love's weak childish bow she lives unharm'd.
She will not stay the siege of loving terms,
Nor bide th' encounter of assailing eyes,
Nor ope her lap to saint-seducing gold:
O, she is rich in beauty, only poor,
That when she dies with beauty dies her store.
Ben. Then she hath sworn that she will still live chaste?
Rom. She hath, and in that sparing makes huge waste,
For beauty starv'd with her severity
Cuts beauty off from all posterity.
She is too fair, too wise, wisely too fair,
To merit bliss by making me despair:
She hath forsworn to love, and in that vow
Do I live dead that live to tell it now.
Ben. Be rul'd by me, forget to think of her.
Rom. O, teach me how I should forget to think!
Ben. By giving liberty unto thine eyes;
Examine other beauties.
Rom. 'Tis the way
To call hers exquisite, in question more:
These happy masks that kiss fair ladies' brows
Being black put us in mind they hide the fair;
He that is strucken blind cannot forget
The precious treasure of his eyesight lost:
Show me a mistress that is passing fair,
What doth her beauty serve, but as a note
Where I may read who pass'd that passing fair?
Farewell: thou canst not teach me to forget.
Ben. I'll pay that doctrine, or else die in debt.
Exeunt.

[SCENE II. *A street.*]

Enter CAPULET, COUNTY PARIS, *and the Clown* [*a* Servant].

Cap. But Montague is bound as well as I,
In penalty alike; and 'tis not hard, I think,
For men so old as we to keep the peace.
Par. Of honourable reckoning are you both;
And pity 'tis you liv'd at odds so long.
But now, my lord, what say you to my suit?
Cap. But saying o'er what I have said before:
My child is yet a stranger in the world;
She hath not seen the change of fourteen years;
Let two more summers wither in their pride,
Ere we may think her ripe to be a bride.
Par. Younger than she are happy mothers made.
Cap. And too soon marr'd are those so early made.
The earth hath swallowed all my hopes but she,
She is the hopeful lady of my earth:
But woo her, gentle Paris, get her heart,
My will to her consent is but a part;
An she agree, within her scope of choice
Lies my consent and fair according voice.
This night I hold an old accustom'd feast,
Whereto I have invited many a guest,
Such as I love; and you, among the store,
One more, most welcome, makes my number more
At my poor house look to behold this night
Earth-treading stars that make dark heaven light:
Such comfort as do lusty young men feel
When well-apparell'd April on the heel
Of limping winter treads, even such delight
Among fresh fennel buds shall you this night
Inherit at my house; hear all, all see,
And like her most whose merit most shall be:
†Which on more view, of many mine being one
May stand in number, though in reck'ning none.
Come, go with me. [*To Serv., giving a paper.*] Go, sirrah, trudge about
Through fair Verona; find those persons out
Whose names are written there, and to them say,
My house and welcome on their pleasure stay.
Exit [*with Paris*].

Serv. Find them out whose names are written here! It is written, that the shoemaker should meddle with his yard, and the tailor with his last, the fisher with his pencil, and the painter with his nets; but I am sent to find those persons whose names are here writ, and can never find what names the writing person hath here writ. I must to the learned.—In good time.

Enter BENVOLIO *and* ROMEO.

Ben. Tut, man, one fire burns out another's burning,
One pain is less'ned by another's anguish;
Turn giddy, and be holp by backward turning;
One desperate grief cures with another's languish:
Take thou some new infection to thy eye,
And the rank poison of the old will die.
Rom. Your plaintain-leaf is excellent for that.
Ben. For what, I pray thee?
Rom. For your broken shin.
Ben. Why, Romeo, art thou mad?
Rom. Not mad, but bound more than a madman is;
Shut up in prison, kept without my food,
Whipp'd and tormented and—God-den, good fellow.
Serv. God gi' god-den. I pray, sir, can you read?
Rom. Ay, mine own fortune in my misery.
Serv. Perhaps you have learned it without book: but, I pray, can you read any thing you see?
Rom. Ay, if I know the letters and the language.
Serv. Ye say honestly: rest you merry!
Rom. Stay, fellow; I can read. *He reads the letter.*
'Signior Martino and his wife and daughters; County Anselme and his beauteous sisters; the lady

212. **fair,** beautiful; see glossary. 213. **fair,** clear, distinct; see glossary. 218. **stay,** submit to. 222. **store.** She will die without children and therefore her beauty will die with her. 223. **still,** always. 225. **starv'd,** allowed to die; see glossary. 235. **in question more,** even more strongly to my mind. 240. **passing,** surpassingly; see glossary. 244. **pay that doctrine,** give that instruction.

SCENE II. 4. **reckoning,** estimation, repute. 9. **fourteen years.** Juliet is younger than in Shakespeare's source, Brooke's *Romeus and Juliet*, where she is sixteen. 15. **hopeful . . . earth,** my heir and hope for posterity. 18. **An,** if; see glossary. **scope,** limit; see glossary. 29. **fennel,** flowering herb thought to have the power of awakening passion. Often emended to *female* (as in Q_1, Globe). 32-33. **Which. . . none.** Capulet may mean that his daughter will lose her identity by being swallowed up in a number of others. He is punning on the saying, "one is no number." Dowden places a comma after *of* and dashes after *many* and *one*. He explains *reckoning* to mean "estimation" (as in line 4, above), with word play, i.e., "counting heads." 34. **sirrah,** customary form of address to servants; see glossary. 48. **holp,** helped; see glossary. 51.

widow of Vitruvio; Signior Placentio and his lovely nieces; Mercutio and his brother Valentine; mine uncle Capulet, his wife, and daughters; my fair niece Rosaline; Livia; Signior Valentio and his cousin Tybalt; Lucio and the lively Helena.'
A fair assembly: whither should they come?
Serv. Up.
Rom. Whither? to supper?
Serv. To our house.
Rom. Whose house?
Serv. My master's.
Rom. Indeed, I should have ask'd you that before.
Serv. Now I'll tell you without asking: my master is the great rich Capulet; and if you be not of the house of Montagues, I pray, come and crush a cup of wine. Rest you merry! [*Exit.*]
Ben. At this same ancient feast of Capulet's
Sups the fair Rosaline whom thou so loves,
With all the admired beauties of Verona:
Go thither; and, with unattainted eye,
Compare her face with some that I shall show,
And I will make thee think thy swan a crow.
Rom. When the devout religion of mine eye
Maintains such falsehood, then turn tears to fires;
And these, who often drown'd could never die,
Transparent heretics, be burnt for liars!
One fairer than my love! the all-seeing sun
Ne'er saw her match since first the world begun.
Ben. Tut, you saw her fair, none else being by,
Herself pois'd with herself in either eye:
But in that crystal scales let there be weigh'd
Your lady's love against some other maid
That I will show you shining at this feast,
And she shall scant show well that now seems best.
Rom. I'll go along, no such sight to be shown,
But to rejoice in splendour of mine own. [*Exeunt.*]

[Scene iii. *A room in Capulet's house.*]

Enter Capulet's Wife *and* Nurse.

La. Cap. Nurse, where 's my daughter? call her forth to me.
Nurse. Now, by my maidenhead, at twelve year old,
I bade her come. What, lamb! what, ladybird!
God forbid! Where 's this girl? What, Juliet!

Enter Juliet.

Jul. How now! who calls?
Nurse. Your mother.
Jul. Madam, I am here.
What is your will?
La. Cap. This is the matter:—Nurse, give leave awhile,
We must talk in secret:—nurse, come back again;
I have remember'd me, thou 's hear our counsel.
Thou knowest my daughter 's of a pretty age.
Nurse. Faith, I can tell her age unto an hour.
La. Cap. She 's not fourteen.
Nurse. I'll lay fourteen of my teeth,—
And yet, to my teen be it spoken, I have but four,—
She is not fourteen. How long is it now
To Lammas-tide?
La. Cap. A fortnight and odd days.
Nurse. Even or odd, of all days in the year,
Come Lammas-eve at night shall she be fourteen.
Susan and she—God rest all Christian souls!—
Were of an age: well, Susan is with God;
She was too good for me: but, as I said,
On Lammas-eve at night shall she be fourteen;
That shall she, marry; I remember it well.
'Tis since the earthquake now eleven years;
And she was wean'd,—I never shall forget it,—
Of all the days of the year, upon that day:
For I had then laid wormwood to my dug,
Sitting in the sun under the dove-house wall;
My lord and you were then at Mantua:—
Nay, I do bear a brain:—but, as I said,
When it did taste the wormwood on the nipple
Of my dug and felt it bitter, pretty fool,
To see it tetchy and fall out with the dug!
'Shake' quoth the dove-house: 'twas no need, I trow,
To bid me trudge:
And since that time it is eleven years;
For then she could stand high lone; nay, by th' rood,
She could have run and waddled all about;
For even the day before, she broke her brow:
And then my husband—God be with his soul!
'A was a merry man—took up the child:
'Yea,' quoth he, 'dost thou fall upon thy face?
Thou wilt fall backward when thou hast more wit;
Wilt thou not, Jule?' and, by my holidame,
The pretty wretch left crying and said 'Ay.'
To see, now, how a jest shall come about!
I warrant, an I should live a thousand years,
I never should forget it: 'Wilt thou not, Jule?' quoth he;
And, pretty fool, it stinted and said 'Ay.'
La. Cap. Enough of this; I pray thee, hold thy peace.
Nurse. Yes, madam: yet I cannot choose but laugh,
To think it should leave crying and say 'Ay.'
And yet, I warrant, it had upon it brow
A bump as big as a young cock'rel's stone;
A perilous knock; and it cried bitterly:
'Yea,' quoth my husband, 'fall'st upon thy face?
Thou wilt fall backward when thou comest to age;
Wilt thou not, Jule?' it stinted and said 'Ay.'
Jul. And stint thou too, I pray thee, nurse, say I.
Nurse. Peace, I have done. God mark thee to his grace!
Thou wast the prettiest babe that e'er I nurs'd:
An I might live to see thee married once,
I have my wish.
La. Cap. Marry, that 'marry' is the very theme
I came to talk of. Tell me, daughter Juliet,
How stands your disposition to be married?
Jul. It is an honour that I dream not of.

rank, corrupt; see glossary. 57. **God-den,** good evening. **fellow,** usual term for a servant; see glossary. 66-74. **Signior . . . Helena,** actually, a verse passage. 86. **crush a cup of wine,** drink a cup of wine. Cf. "crack a bottle." 87. **ancient,** customary. 89. **admired,** wondered at; see glossary. 90. **unattainted,** impartial. 95. **these,** i.e., these eyes.

Scene iii. 3. **ladybird,** sweetheart; also, loose woman (used endearingly). 7. **give leave,** leave us. 9. **thou 's,** thou shalt. 13. **teen,** sorrow. 15. **Lammas-tide,** the time around Lammas, August 1. 18. **Susan,** the Nurse's own child who has evidently died. 29. **bear a brain.** The nurse prides herself on her memory. 31. **fool,** term of endearment; see glossary. 32. **tetchy,** fretful. 33. **trow,** believe; see glossary. 36. **high lone,** on her feet, without help. **rood,** cross. 38. **broke her brow,** banged her head (by falling). 40. **'A,** he. 43. **holidame,** same as "halidom," a relic or holy thing. 48. **stinted,** ceased. 52. **it,** so QqF; Globe: *its.* 53. **cock'rel's stone,** young rooster's testicle.

Nurse. An honour! were not I thine only nurse,
I would say thou hadst suck'd wisdom from thy teat.
La. Cap. Well, think of marriage now; younger than you,
Here in Verona, ladies of esteem,
Are made already mothers: by my count,
I was your mother much upon these years
That you are now a maid. Thus then in brief:
The valiant Paris seeks you for his love.
Nurse. A man, young lady! lady, such a man
As all the world—why, he 's a man of wax.
La. Cap. Verona's summer hath not such a flower.
Nurse. Nay, he 's a flower; in faith, a very flower.
La. Cap. What say you? can you love the gentleman?
This night you shall behold him at our feast;
Read o'er the volume of young Paris' face
And find delight writ there with beauty's pen;
Examine every married lineament
And see how one another lends content,
And what obscur'd in this fair volume lies
Find written in the margent of his eyes.
This precious book of love, this unbound lover,
To beautify him, only lacks a cover:
The fish lives in the sea, and 'tis much pride
For fair without the fair within to hide:
That book in many's eyes doth share the glory,
That in gold clasps locks in the golden story;
So shall you share all that he doth possess,
By having him, making yourself no less.
Nurse. No less! nay, bigger; women grow by men.
La. Cap. Speak briefly, can you like of Paris' love?
Jul. I'll look to like, if looking liking move:
But no more deep will I endart mine eye
Than your consent gives strength to make it fly.

Enter Servingman.

Serv. Madam, the guests are come, supper served up, you called, my young lady asked for, the nurse cursed in the pantry, and every thing in extremity. I must hence to wait; I beseech you, follow straight.

La. Cap. We follow thee. [*Exit Servingman.*] Juliet, the county stays.
Nurse. Go, girl, seek happy nights to happy days.
Exeunt.

[SCENE IV. *A street.*]

Enter ROMEO, MERCUTIO, BENVOLIO, *with five or six other* Maskers; Torch-bearers.

Rom. What, shall this speech be spoke for our excuse?
Or shall we on without apology?
Ben. The date is out of such prolixity:
We'll have no Cupid hoodwink'd with a scarf,
Bearing a Tartar's painted bow of lath,
Scaring the ladies like a crow-keeper;
Nor no without-book prologue, faintly spoke
After the prompter, for our entrance:
But let them measure us by what they will;
We'll measure them a measure, and be gone.
Rom. Give me a torch: I am not for this ambling;
Being but heavy, I will bear the light.
Mer. Nay, gentle Romeo, we must have you dance.
Rom. Not I, believe me: you have dancing shoes
With nimble soles: I have a soul of lead
So stakes me to the ground I cannot move.
Mer. You are a lover; borrow Cupid's wings,
And soar with them above a common bound.
Rom. I am too sore enpierced with his shaft
To soar with his light feathers, and so bound,
I cannot bound a pitch above dull woe:
Under love's heavy burden do I sink.
Mer. And, to sink in it, should you burden love;
Too great oppression for a tender thing.
Rom. Is love a tender thing? it is too rough,
Too rude, too boist'rous, and it pricks like thorn.
Mer. If love be rough with you, be rough with love;
Prick love for pricking, and you beat love down.
Give me a case to put my visage in:
A visor for a visor! what care I
What curious eye doth quote deformities?
Here are the beetle brows shall blush for me.
Ben. Come, knock and enter; and no sooner in,
But every man betake him to his legs.
Rom. A torch for me: let wantons light of heart
Tickle the senseless rushes with their heels,
For I am proverb'd with a grandsire phrase;
I'll be a candle-holder, and look on.
The game was ne'er so fair, and I am done.
Mer. Tut, dun 's the mouse, the constable's own word:
If thou art dun, we'll draw thee from the mire
Of this sir-reverence love, wherein thou stickest
Up to the ears. Come, we burn daylight, ho!
Rom. Nay, that 's not so.
Mer. I mean, sir, in delay
We waste our lights in vain, like lamps by day.
Take our good meaning, for our judgement sits
Five times in that ere once in our five wits.
Rom. And we mean well in going to this mask;
But 'tis no wit to go.
Mer. Why, may one ask?
Rom. I dream'd a dream to-night.
Mer. And so did I.
Rom. Well, what was yours?
Mer. That dreamers often lie.
Rom. In bed asleep, while they do dream things true.
Mer. O, then, I see Queen Mab hath been with you.
She is the fairies' midwife, and she comes
In shape no bigger than an agate-stone
On the fore-finger of an alderman,

76. **a man of wax,** such as one would picture in wax, i.e., handsome. 83. **married,** harmonized into mutual helpfulness (Hudson). 86. **margent,** commentary or marginal gloss. 89. **fish lives in the sea.** Shakespeare may mean that, just as the sea enfolds the fish, being thereby both handsome in appearance and rich in inner value, so Juliet is to enclose Paris in her arms and add beauty to his worth. 105. **county,** count.

SCENE IV. 1. **speech.** The older fashion was for maskers to be preceded by a messenger with a set speech, but *the date is out* for *such prolixity;* see *date* and *out* in glossary. 4. **hoodwink'd,** blindfolded. 5. **Tartar's painted bow.** Tartar's bows are said to have resembled the old Roman bow with which Cupid was pictured. 6. **crow-keeper,** scarecrow. 10. **measure . . . measure,** perform a dance; see glossary. 11. **ambling,** walking affectedly; used contemptuously of dancing. 21. **pitch,** height; see glossary. 30. **visor,** a mask, for an ugly masklike face. 31. **quote,** take notice of. 36. **rushes.** Rushes were used for floor coverings. 38. **candle-holder,** an allusion to the proverb "A good candle-holder (i.e., a mere onlooker) is a good gamester." 40. **dun 's the mouse,** a common phrase usually taken to mean "keep still." *Dun* (l. 41) alludes to a Christmas game, "Dun is in the mire," in which a heavy log was lifted by the players. 42. **sir-reverence,** corruption of "save-reverence" (*salve-reverentia*), an apology for something improper.

Drawn with a team of little atomies
Over men's noses as they lie asleep;
Her waggon-spokes made of long spinners' legs,
The cover of the wings of grasshoppers,
Her traces of the smallest spider web,
Her collars of the moonshine's wat'ry beams,
Her whip of cricket's bone, the lash of film,
Her waggoner a small grey-coated gnat,
Not half so big as a round little worm
Prick'd from the lazy finger of a maid;
Her chariot is an empty hazel-nut
Made by the joiner squirrel or old grub,
Time out o' mind the fairies' coachmakers.
And in this state she gallops night by night
Through lovers' brains, and then they dream of love;
O'er courtiers' knees, that dream on court'sies
straight,
O'er lawyers' fingers, who straight dream on fees,
O'er ladies' lips, who straight on kisses dream,
Which oft the angry Mab with blisters plagues,
Because their breaths with sweetmeats tainted are:
Sometime she gallops o'er a courtier's nose,
And then dreams he of smelling out a suit;
And sometime comes she with a tithe-pig's tail
Tickling a parson's nose as 'a lies asleep,
Then dreams he of another benefice:
Sometime she driveth o'er a soldier's neck,
And then dreams he of cutting foreign throats,
Of breaches, ambuscadoes, Spanish blades,
Of healths five-fathom deep; and then anon
Drums in his ear, at which he starts and wakes,
And being thus frighted swears a prayer or two
And sleeps again. This is that very Mab
That plats the manes of horses in the night,
And bakes the elf-locks in foul sluttish hairs,
Which once untangled much misfortune bodes:
This is the hag, when maids lie on their backs,
That presses them and learns them first to bear,
Making them women of good carriage:
This is she—

Rom. Peace, peace, Mercutio, peace!
Thou talk'st of nothing.

Mer. True, I talk of dreams,
Which are the children of an idle brain,
Begot of nothing but vain fantasy,
Which is as thin of substance as the air
And more inconstant than the wind, who wooes
Even now the frozen bosom of the north,
And, being anger'd, puffs away from thence,
Turning his side to the dew-dropping south.

Ben. This wind, you talk of, blows us from
ourselves;
Supper is done, and we shall come too late.

Rom. I fear, too early: for my mind misgives
Some consequence yet hanging in the stars
Shall bitterly begin his fearful date
With this night's revels and expire the term
Of a despised life clos'd in my breast
By some vile forfeit of untimely death.
But He, that hath the steerage of my course,
Direct my sail! On, lusty gentlemen.

Ben. Strike, drum.

They march about the stage, and [retire to one side].

[SCENE V. *A hall in Capulet's house.*]

Servingmen *come forth with napkins.*

First Serv. Where 's Potpan, that he helps not to take away? He shift a trencher? he scrape a trencher!

Sec. Serv. When good manners shall lie all in one or two men's hands and they unwashed too, 'tis a foul thing.

First Serv. Away with the joint-stools, remove the court-cupboard, look to the plate. Good thou, save me a piece of marchpane; and, as thou loves me, let the porter let in Susan Grindstone and Nell. Antony, and Potpan!

Sec. Serv. Ay, boy, ready.

First Serv. You are looked for and called for, asked for and sought for, in the great chamber.

Third Serv. We cannot be here and there too. Cheerly, boys; be brisk awhile, and the longer liver take all.

Exeunt.

Enter [CAPULET *and family and*] *all the* Guests *and* Gentlewomen *to the* Maskers.

Cap. Welcome, gentlemen! ladies that have their
toes
Unplagu'd with corns will walk about with you.
Ah ha, my mistresses! which of you all
Will now deny to dance? she that makes dainty,
She, I'll swear, hath corns; am I come near ye now?
Welcome, gentlemen! I have seen the day
That I have worn a visor and could tell
A whispering tale in a fair lady's ear,
Such as would please: 'tis gone, 'tis gone, 'tis gone:
You are welcome, gentlemen! Come, musicians,
play. *Music plays, and they dance.*
A hall, a hall! give room! and foot it, girls.
More light, you knaves; and turn the tables up,
And quench the fire, the room is grown too hot.
Ah, sirrah, this unlook'd-for sport comes well.
Nay, sit, nay, sit, good cousin Capulet;
For you and I are past our dancing days:
How long is 't now since last yourself and I
Were in a mask?

Sec. Cap. By 'r lady, thirty years.

Cap. What, man! 'tis not so much, 'tis not so much:
'Tis since the nuptial of Lucentio,
Come Pentecost as quickly as it will,
Some five and twenty years; and then we mask'd.

Sec. Cap. 'Tis more, 'tis more: his son is elder, sir;
His son is thirty.

Cap. Will you tell me that?

46-47. **Take . . . wits,** i.e., try to understand what I intend to say, relying on common sense rather than on one single mental faculty. (The five faculties were common sense, imagination, fantasy, judgment, and reason.) 53. **Queen Mab,** a name of Celtic origin for the fairy queen. 57. **atomies,** tiny creatures. 63. **film,** gossamer thread. 65. **worm.** This alludes to an ancient superstition that "worms breed in the fingers of the idle." 70. **state,** pomp, dignity; see glossary. 73. **straight,** immediately; see glossary. 77. **Sometime,** from time to time, sometimes; see glossary. 78. **suit,** a request or plea at court. 79. **tithe-pig's tail.** This alludes to the tenth pig given the parson as a church tax. 85. **anon,** by an by. 89. **plats the manes of horses,** an allusion to the familiar superstition of "witches stirrups," tangles in the manes of horses. 90. **elf-locks,** tangles. 93. **learns,** teaches; see glossary. 98. **vain,** empty, foolish. **fantasy,** imagination. 108. **date,** time. 109. **expire,** (transitive), bring to an end.

SCENE V. The action is continuous from the previous scene. 2. **trencher,** wooden dish or plate; see glossary. 7. **joint-stools,** stools, properly those made by a joiner. 8. **court-cupboard,** sideboard. 9. **marchpane,** cake made from sugar and almonds. 21. **makes dainty,** seems coyly reluctant (to dance). 29. **turn the tables up.** Tables were probably made of hinged leaves and placed on trestles. They were put aside for dancing.

His son was but a ward two years ago.
Rom. [*To a Servingman*] What lady 's that, which doth enrich the hand
Of yonder knight?
Serv. I know not, sir.
Rom. O, she doth teach the torches to burn bright!
It seems she hangs upon the cheek of night
As a rich jewel in an Ethiope's ear;
Beauty too rich for use, for earth too dear!
So shows a snowy dove trooping with crows,
As yonder lady o'er her fellows shows.
The measure done, I'll watch her place of stand,
And, touching hers, make blessed my rude hand.
Did my heart love till now? forswear it, sight!
For I ne'er saw true beauty till this night.
Tyb. This, by his voice, should be a Montague.
Fetch me my rapier, boy. What dares the slave
Come hither, cover'd with an antic face,
To fleer and scorn at our solemnity?
Now, by the stock and honour of my kin,
To strike him dead I hold it not a sin.
Cap. Why, how now, kinsman! wherefore storm you so?
Tyb. Uncle, this is a Montague, our foe,
A villain that is hither come in spite,
To scorn at our solemnity this night.
Cap. Young Romeo is it?
Tyb. 'Tis he, that villain Romeo.
Cap. Content thee, gentle coz, let him alone;
'A bears him like a portly gentleman;
And, to say truth, Verona brags of him
To be a virtuous and well govern'd youth:
I would not for the wealth of all this town
Here in my house do him disparagement:
Therefore be patient, take no note of him:
It is my will, the which if thou respect,
Show a fair presence and put off these frowns,
An ill-beseeming semblance for a feast.
Tyb. It fits, when such a villain is a guest:
I'll not endure him.
Cap. He shall be endur'd:
What, goodman boy! I say, he shall: go to;
Am I the master here, or you? go to.
You'll not endure him! God shall mend my soul!
You'll make a mutiny among my guests!
You will set cock-a-hoop! you'll be the man!
Tyb. Why, uncle, 'tis a shame.
Cap. Go to, go to;
You are a saucy boy: is 't so, indeed?
This trick may chance to scathe you, I know what:
You must contrary me! marry, 'tis time.
Well said, my hearts! You are a princox; go:
Be quiet, or—More light, more light! For shame!
I'll make you quiet. What, cheerly, my hearts!
Tyb. Patience perforce with wilful choler meeting
Makes my flesh tremble in their different greeting.
I will withdraw: but this intrusion shall
Now seeming sweet convert to bitt'rest gall. *Exit.*

Rom. [*To Juliet*] If I profane with my unworthiest hand
This holy shrine, the gentle sin is this:
My lips, two blushing pilgrims, ready stand
To smooth that rough touch with a tender kiss.
Jul. Good pilgrim, you do wrong your hand too much,
Which mannerly devotion shows in this;
For saints have hands that pilgrims' hands do touch,
And palm to palm is holy palmers' kiss.
Rom. Have not saints lips, and holy palmers too?
Jul. Ay, pilgrim, lips that they must use in pray'r.
Rom. O, then, dear saint, let lips do what hands do;
They pray, grant thou, lest faith turn to despair.
Jul. Saints do not move, though grant for prayers' sake.
Rom. Then move not, while my prayer's effect I take. [*Kiss.*]
Thus from my lips, by thine, my sin is purg'd.
Jul. Then have my lips the sin that they have took.
Rom. Sin from my lips? O trespass sweetly urg'd!
Give me my sin again. [*Kiss again.*]
Jul. You kiss by th' book.
Nurse. Madam, your mother craves a word with you.
Rom. What is her mother?
Nurse. Marry, bachelor,
Her mother is the lady of the house,
And a good lady, and a wise and virtuous:
I nurs'd her daughter, that you talk'd withal;
I tell you, he that can lay hold of her
Shall have the chinks.
Rom. Is she a Capulet?
O dear account! my life is my foe's debt.
Ben. Away, be gone; the sport is at the best.
Rom. Ay, so I fear; the more is my unrest.
Cap. Nay, gentlemen, prepare not to be gone;
We have a trifling foolish banquet towards.
Is it e'en so? why, then, I thank you all;
I thank you, honest gentlemen; good night.
More torches here! Come on then, let 's to bed.
Ah, sirrah, by my fay, it waxes late:
I'll to my rest. [*Exeunt all but Juliet and Nurse.*]
Jul. Come hither, nurse. What is yond gentleman?
Nurse. The son and heir of old Tiberio.
Jul. What 's he that now is going out of door?
Nurse. Marry, that, I think, be young Petrucio.
Jul. What 's he that follows there, that would not dance?
Nurse. I know not.
Jul. Go, ask his name: if he be married,
My grave is like to be my wedding bed.
Nurse. His name is Romeo, and a Montague;
The only son of your great enemy.
Jul. My only love sprung from my only hate!
Too early seen unknown, and known too late!
Prodigious birth of love it is to me,
That I must love a loathed enemy.

42. **ward,** a minor under guardianship. 49. **dear,** precious; see glossary. 50. **shows,** appears. 52. **The measure done,** when this dance is over. 58. **antic face,** fantastic mask. 59. **fleer,** to look mockingly. 68. **portly,** of good deportment. 79. **goodman boy.** "Goodman" applied to one below the rank of gentleman, but still of some substance, like a wealthy farmer. **go to,** an expression of impatience. 83. **You . . . cock-a-hoop,** i.e., you want to be cock of the walk. 86. **scathe,** harm. 91. **Patience perforce,** patience upon compulsion; see *perforce* in glossary; *patience* is a general word for self-control. 94. **convert,** change (to). 95-108. **If . . . take.** These lines are in the form of a sonnet. They afford an example of Shakespeare's early exuberance in poetic style. 96. **shrine,** i.e., Juliet's hand. 112. **book,** book of etiquette. 119. **chinks,** plenty of money. 120. **my foe's debt,** due to my foe, at his mercy. 124. **foolish,** insignificant. **banquet,** light refreshment. **towards,** in preparation; see glossary. 128. **fay,** faith.

Act II. prologue. This may be an addition to the original text. It provides no needed information, and interrupts a continuous scene. 10. **use to swear,** are in the habit of swearing; see *use* in glossary. 13. **passion,** feeling of love; see glossary.

Scene i. 2. **dull earth,** Romeo himself. **thy centre,** Juliet. The figure of speech is that of man as a microcosm or little world. 6. **conjure,** utter incantation. 12. **purblind,** completely blind. 13. **Abraham.**

Nurse. What 's this? what 's this?
Jul. A rhyme I learn'd even now
Of one I danc'd withal. *One calls within* 'Juliet.'
Nurse. Anon, anon!
Come, let 's away; the strangers all are gone. *Exeunt.*

[ACT II.

PROLOGUE.]

[*Enter*] Chorus.

Chor. Now old desire doth in his death-bed lie,
And young affection gapes to be his heir;
That fair for which love groan'd for and would die,
With tender Juliet match'd, is now not fair.
Now Romeo is belov'd and loves again,
Alike bewitched by the charm of looks,
But to his foe suppos'd he must complain,
And she steal love's sweet bait from fearful hooks:
Being held a foe, he may not have access
To breathe such vows as lovers use to swear;
And she as much in love, her means much less
To meet her new-beloved any where:
But passion lends them power, time means, to meet,
Temp'ring extremities with extreme sweet. [*Exit.*]

[SCENE I. *Near Capulet's orchard.*]

Enter ROMEO *alone.*

Rom. Can I go forward when my heart is here?
Turn back, dull earth, and find thy centre out.

Enter BENVOLIO *with* MERCUTIO. [ROMEO *retires.*]

Ben. Romeo! my cousin Romeo! Romeo!
Mer. He is wise;
And, on my life, hath stol'n him home to bed.
Ben. He ran this way, and leap'd this orchard wall:
Call, good Mercutio.
Mer. Nay, I'll conjure too.
Romeo! humours! madman! passion! lover!
Appear thou in the likeness of a sigh:
Speak but one rhyme, and I am satisfied;
Cry but 'Ay me!' pronounce but 'love' and 'dove;'
Speak to my gossip Venus one fair word,
One nick-name for her purblind son and heir,
Young Abraham Cupid, he that shot so true,
When King Cophetua lov'd the beggar-maid!
He heareth not, he stirreth not, he moveth not;
The ape is dead, and I must conjure him.
I conjure thee by Rosaline's bright eyes,
By her high forehead and her scarlet lip,
By her fine foot, straight leg and quivering thigh
And the demesnes that there adjacent lie,
That in thy likeness thou appear to us!
Ben. An if he hear thee, thou wilt anger him.
Mer. This cannot anger him: 'twould anger him
To raise a spirit in his mistress' circle
Of some strange nature, letting it there stand
Till she had laid it and conjur'd it down;
That were some spite: my invocation
Is fair and honest; in his mistress' name
I conjure only but to raise up him.
Ben. Come, he hath hid himself among these trees,
To be consorted with the humorous night:
Blind is his love and best befits the dark.
Mer. If love be blind, love cannot hit the mark.
Now will he sit under a medlar tree,
And wish his mistress were that kind of fruit
As maids call medlars, when they laugh alone.
O, Romeo, that she were, O, that she were
An open et cætera, thou a pop'rin pear!
Romeo, good night: I'll to my truckle-bed;
This field-bed is too cold for me to sleep:
Come, shall we go?
Ben. Go, then; for 'tis in vain
To seek him here that means not to be found.
Exit [*with Mercutio*].

[SCENE II. *Capulet's orchard.*]

[ROMEO *comes forward.*]

Rom. He jests at scars that never felt a wound.
[*Juliet appears above, as at a window.*]
But, soft! what light through yonder window breaks?
It is the east, and Juliet is the sun.
Arise, fair sun, and kill the envious moon,
Who is already sick and pale with grief,
That thou her maid art far more fair than she:
Be not her maid, since she is envious;
Her vestal livery is but sick and green
And none but fools do wear it; cast it off.
It is my lady, O, it is my love!
O, that she knew she were!
She speaks, yet she says nothing: what of that?
Her eye discourses; I will answer it.
I am too bold, 'tis not to me she speaks:
Two of the fairest stars in all the heaven,
Having some business, do entreat her eyes
To twinkle in their spheres till they return.
What if her eyes were there, they in her head?
The brightness of her cheek would shame those stars,
As daylight doth a lamp; her eyes in heaven
Would through the airy region stream so bright
That birds would sing and think it were not night.
See, how she leans her cheek upon her hand!
O, that I were a glove upon that hand,
That I might touch that cheek!
Jul. Ay me!
Rom. She speaks:
O, speak again, bright angel! for thou art
As glorious to this night, being o'er my head,
As is a winged messenger of heaven
Unto the white-upturned wond'ring eyes

Globe: *Adam*, supposing that Shakespeare was referring to Adam Bell, a famous archer in old ballads. "Abraham" may suggest that young Cupid is also very old. 14. **King Cophetua,** who in an old ballad falls in love with a beggar-maid and makes her his queen. 16. **ape,** used as a term of endearment. 20. **desmesnes,** regions, with bawdy suggestion that is continued in *raise, circle, stand, laid it, raise up.* 22. **An if,** if; see glossary. 25. **strange,** belonging to another person; see glossary. 27. **spite,** injury. 31. **consorted,** associated. **humorous,** moist; also, influenced by humor or mood. 34, 38. **medlar, pop'rin,** fruits used as slang terms for the sexual organs. The medlar was edible only when partly decayed; poperin, derived from *Poperinghe* in Flanders, has a bawdily suggestive sound. 39. **truckle-bed,** a bed on casters to be shoved under a standing bed.

SCENE II. There is no break in the action. A rhymed couplet links the two scenes. Romeo has been hiding from his friends as though concealed by the orchard wall. He speaks at once, then turns to observe Juliet. 13. **discourses,** speaks; see glossary. 17. **spheres,** transparent concentric shells supposed to carry the heavenly bodies with them in their revolution around the earth.

Of mortals that fall back to gaze on him
When he bestrides the lazy-pacing clouds
And sails upon the bosom of the air.
Jul. O Romeo, Romeo! wherefore art thou Romeo?
Deny thy father and refuse thy name;
Or, if thou wilt not, be but sworn my love,
And I'll no longer be a Capulet.
Rom. [*Aside*] Shall I hear more, or shall I speak at this?
Jul. 'Tis but thy name that is my enemy;
Thou art thyself, though not a Montague.
What 's Montague? it is nor hand, nor foot,
Nor arm, nor face, nor any other part
Belonging to a man. O, be some other name!
What 's in a name? that which we call a rose
By any other name would smell as sweet;
So Romeo would, were he not Romeo call'd,
Retain that dear perfection which he owes
Without that title. Romeo, doff thy name,
And for that name which is no part of thee
Take all myself.
Rom. I take thee at thy word:
Call me but love, and I'll be new baptiz'd;
Henceforth I never will be Romeo.
Jul. What man art thou that thus bescreen'd in night
So stumblest on my counsel?
Rom. By a name
I know not how to tell thee who I am:
My name, dear saint, is hateful to myself,
Because it is an enemy to thee;
Had I it written, I would tear the word.
Jul. My ears have not yet drunk a hundred words
Of thy tongue's uttering, yet I know the sound:
Art thou not Romeo and a Montague?
Rom. Neither, fair maid, if either thee dislike.
Jul. How camest thou hither, tell me, and wherefore?
The orchard walls are high and hard to climb,
And the place death, considering who thou art,
If any of my kinsmen find thee here.
Rom. With love's light wings did I o'erperch these walls;
For stony limits cannot hold love out,
And what love can do that dares love attempt;
Therefore thy kinsmen are no stop to me.
Jul. If they do see thee, they will murder thee.
Rom. Alack, there lies more peril in thine eye
Than twenty of their swords: look thou but sweet,
And I am proof against their enmity.
Jul. I would not for the world they saw thee here.
Rom. I have night's cloak to hide me from their eyes;
And but thou love me, let them find me here:
My life were better ended by their hate,
Than death prorogued, wanting of thy love.
Jul. By whose direction found'st thou out this place?
Rom. By love that first did prompt me to inquire;
He lent me counsel and I lent him eyes.
I am no pilot; yet, wert thou as far
As that vast shore wash'd with the farthest sea,
I should adventure for such merchandise.
Jul. Thou knowest the mask of night is on my face,
Else would a maiden blush bepaint my cheek
For that which thou hast heard me speak tonight.
Fain would I dwell on form, fain, fain deny
What I have spoke: but farewell compliment!
Dost thou love me? I know thou wilt say 'Ay,'
And I will take thy word: yet, if thou swear'st,
Thou mayst prove false; at lovers' perjuries,
They say, Jove laughs. O gentle Romeo,
If thou dost love, pronounce it faithfully:
Or if thou thinkest I am too quickly won,
I'll frown and be perverse and say thee nay,
So thou wilt woo; but else, not for the world.
In truth, fair Montague, I am too fond,
And therefore thou mayst think my 'haviour light:
But trust me, gentleman, I'll prove more true
Than those that have more cunning to be strange.
I should have been more strange, I must confess,
But that thou overheard'st, ere I was ware,
My true-love passion; therefore pardon me,
And not impute this yielding to light love,
Which the dark night hath so discovered.
Rom. Lady, by yonder blessed moon I vow
That tips with silver all these fruit-tree tops—
Jul. O, swear not by the moon, th' inconstant moon,
That monthly changes in her circled orb,
Lest that thy love prove likewise variable.
Rom. What shall I swear by?
Jul. Do not swear at all;
Or, if thou wilt, swear by thy gracious self,
Which is the god of my idolatry,
And I'll believe thee.
Rom. If my heart's dear love—
Jul. Well, do not swear: although I joy in thee,
I have no joy of this contract to-night:
It is too rash, too unadvis'd, too sudden;
Too like the lightning, which doth cease to be
Ere one can say 'It lightens.' Sweet, good night!
This bud of love, by summer's ripening breath,
May prove a beauteous flow'r when next we meet.
Good night, good night! as sweet repose and rest
Come to thy heart as that within my breast!
Rom. O, wilt thou leave me so unsatisfied?
Jul. What satisfaction canst thou have to-night?
Rom. Th' exchange of thy love's faithful vow for mine.
Jul. I gave thee mine before thou didst request it:
And yet I would it were to give again.
Rom. Wouldst thou withdraw it? for what purpose, love?
Jul. But to be frank, and give it thee again.
And yet I wish but for the thing I have:
My bounty is as boundless as the sea,
My love as deep; the more I give to thee,
The more I have, for both are infinite.
[*Nurse calls within.*]
I hear some noise within; dear love, adieu!
Anon, good nurse! Sweet Montague, be true.
Stay but a little, I will come again. [*Exit, above.*]
Rom. O blessed, blessed night! I am afeard,

30. **mortals,** human beings. 46. **owes,** owns; see glossary. 53. **counsel,** secret thought. 61. **dislike,** displease. 66. **o'er-perch,** fly over and perch beyond. 69. **stop,** hindrance. 73. **proof,** protected. 78. **prorogued,** postponed. **wanting,** lacking. 89. **compliment,** punctiliousness, ceremony. 98. **fond,** foolish; see glossary. 101. **strange,** reserved; see glossary. 106. **discovered,** revealed; see *discover* in glossary. 110. **orb,** equivalent to *sphere;* see above, line 17. 131. **frank,** liberal, bounteous. 143. **bent,** purpose; from the idea of the tension of a bow. 145. **procure,** provide for. 151. **By and by,** immediately. 160. **tassel-gentle,** tercel-gentle, the male of the goshawk. 173. **still,** always; see

Being in night, all this is but a dream,
Too flattering-sweet to be substantial.

[*Enter* JULIET, *above.*]

Jul. Three words, dear Romeo, and good night indeed.
If that thy bent of love be honourable,
Thy purpose marriage, send me word to-morrow,
By one that I'll procure to come to thee,
Where and what time thou wilt perform the rite;
And all my fortunes at thy foot I'll lay
And follow thee my lord throughout the world.

Nurse. [*Within*] Madam!

Jul. I come, anon.—But if thou meanest not well,
I do beseech thee—

Nurse. [*Within*] Madam!

Jul. By and by, I come:—
To cease thy suit, and leave me to my grief:
To-morrow will I send.

Rom. So thrive my soul—

Jul. A thousand times good night! [*Exit, above.*]

Rom. A thousand times the worse, to want thy light.
Love goes toward love, as schoolboys from their books,
But love from love, toward school with heavy looks.
[*Retiring.*]

Enter JULIET, [*above*] *again.*

Jul. Hist! Romeo, hist! O, for a falc'ner's voice,
To lure this tassel-gentle back again!
Bondage is hoarse, and may not speak aloud;
Else would I tear the cave where Echo lies,
And make her airy tongue more hoarse than mine,
With repetition of 'my Romeo!'

Rom. It is my soul that calls upon my name:
How silver-sweet sound lovers' tongues by night,
Like softest music to attending ears!

Jul. Romeo!

Rom. My dear?

Jul. What o'clock to-morrow
Shall I send to thee?

Rom. By the hour of nine.

Jul. I will not fail: 'tis twenty years till then.
I have forgot why I did call thee back.

Rom. Let me stand here till thou remember it.

Jul. I shall forget, to have thee still stand there,
Rememb'ring how I love thy company.

Rom. And I'll still stay, to have thee still forget,
Forgetting any other home but this.

Jul. 'Tis almost morning; I would have thee gone:
And yet no farther than a wanton's bird;
That lets it hop a little from her hand,
Like a poor prisoner in his twisted gyves,
And with a silken thread plucks it back again,
So loving-jealous of his liberty.

Rom. I would I were thy bird.

Jul. Sweet, so would I:
Yet I should kill thee with much cherishing.
Good night, good night! parting is such sweet sorrow,
That I shall say good night till it be morrow.
[*Exit, above.*]

Rom. Sleep dwell upon thine eyes, peace in thy breast!
Would I were sleep and peace, so sweet to rest!
Hence will I to my ghostly father's cell,
His help to crave, and my dear hap to tell. *Exit.*

[SCENE III. *Friar Laurence's cell.*]

Enter FRIAR [LAURENCE] *alone, with a basket.*

Fri. L. The grey-ey'd morn smiles on the frowning night,
Chequ'ring the eastern clouds with streaks of light,
And flecked darkness like a drunkard reels
From forth day's path and Titan's fiery wheels:
Now, ere the sun advance his burning eye,
The day to cheer and night's dank dew to dry,
I must up-fill this osier cage of ours
With baleful weeds and precious-juiced flowers.
The earth that 's nature's mother is her tomb;
What is her burying grave that is her womb,
And from her womb children of divers kind
We sucking on her natural bosom find,
Many for many virtues excellent,
None but for some and yet all different.
O, mickle is the powerful grace that lies
In plants, herbs, stones, and their true qualities:
For nought so vile that on the earth doth live
But to the earth some special good doth give,
Nor aught so good but strain'd from that fair use
Revolts from true birth, stumbling on abuse:
Virtue itself turns vice, being misapplied;
And vice sometime by action dignified.
Within the infant rind of this weak flower
Poison hath residence and medicine power:
For this, being smelt, with that part cheers each part;
Being tasted, slays all senses with the heart.
Two such opposed kings encamp them still
In man as well as herbs, grace and rude will;
And where the worser is predominant,
Full soon the canker death eats up that plant.

Enter ROMEO.

Rom. Good morrow, father.

Fri. L. Benedicite!
What early tongue so sweet saluteth me?
Young son, it argues a distempered head
So soon to bid good morrow to thy bed:
Care keeps his watch in every old man's eye,
And where care lodges, sleep will never lie;
But where unbruised youth with unstuff'd brain
Doth couch his limbs, there golden sleep doth reign:
Therefore thy earliness doth me assure
Thou art up-rous'd with some distemp'rature;
Or if not so, then here I hit it right,
Our Romeo hath not been in bed to-night.

Rom. That last is true; the sweeter rest was mine.

Fri. L. God pardon sin! wast thou with Rosaline?

Rom. With Rosaline, my ghostly father? no;
I have forgot that name, and that name's woe.

Fri. L. That 's my good son: but where hast thou been, then?

Rom. I'll tell thee, ere thou ask it me again.
I have been feasting with mine enemy,

glossary. 180. **gyves,** fetters. 189. **ghostly,** spiritual. 190. **dear hap,** good fortune.
SCENE III. 3. **flecked,** dappled. 4. **Titan's.** Helios, the sun god, was a descendant of the race of Titans. 7. **osier cage,** willow basket. 15. **mickle,** great. **grace,** beneficent virtue; see glossary. 16. **qualities,** properties; see glossary. 30. **canker,** cankerworm. 33. **distempered,** out of temper or balance, ill. 34. **good morrow,** good morning, i.e., farewell. 37. **unstuff'd,** not overcharged; another reference to the state of the humors.

Where on a sudden one hath wounded me,
That 's by me wounded: both our remedies
Within thy help and holy physic lies:
I bear no hatred, blessed man, for, lo,
My intercession likewise steads my foe.

Fri. L. Be plain, good son, and homely in thy drift;
Riddling confession finds but riddling shrift.

Rom. Then plainly know my heart's dear love is set
On the fair daughter of rich Capulet:
As mine on hers, so hers is set on mine;
And all combin'd, save what thou must combine
By holy marriage: when and where and how
We met, we woo'd and made exchange of vow,
I'll tell thee as we pass; but this I pray,
That thou consent to marry us to-day.

Fri. L. Holy Saint Francis, what a change is here!
Is Rosaline, that thou didst love so dear,
So soon forsaken? young men's love then lies
Not truly in their hearts, but in their eyes.
Jesu Maria, what a deal of brine
Hath wash'd thy sallow cheeks for Rosaline!
How much salt water thrown away in waste,
To season love, that of it doth not taste!
The sun not yet thy sighs from heaven clears,
Thy old groans ring yet in mine ancient ears;
Lo, here upon thy cheek the stain doth sit
Of an old tear that is not wash'd off yet:
If e'er thou wast thyself and these woes thine,
Thou and these woes were all for Rosaline:
And art thou chang'd? pronounce this sentence then,
Women may fall, when there 's no strength in men.

Rom. Thou chid'st me oft for loving Rosaline.

Fri. L. For doting, not for loving, pupil mine.

Rom. And bad'st me bury love.

Fri. L. Not in a grave,
To lay one in, another out to have.

Rom. I pray thee, chide not: she whom I love now
Doth grace for grace and love for love allow;
The other did not so.

Fri. L. O, she knew well
Thy love did read by rote, that could not spell.
But come, young waverer, come, go with me,
In one respect I'll thy assistant be;
For this alliance may so happy prove,
To turn your households' rancour to pure love.

Rom. O, let us hence; I stand on sudden haste.

Fri. L. Wisely and slow; they stumble that run fast.

Exeunt.

[SCENE IV. *A street.*]

Enter BENVOLIO *and* MERCUTIO.

Mer. Where the devil should this Romeo be?
Came he not home to-night?

Ben. Not to his father's; I spoke with his man.

Mer. Why, that same pale hard-hearted wench, that Rosaline,
Torments him so, that he will sure run mad.

Ben. Tybalt, the kinsman to old Capulet,
Hath sent a letter to his father's house.

Mer. A challenge, on my life.

Ben. Romeo will answer it.

Mer. Any man that can write may answer a letter.

Ben. Nay, he will answer the letter's master, how he dares, being dared.

Mer. Alas poor Romeo! he is already dead; stabbed with a white wench's black eye; run through the ear with a love-song; the very pin of his heart cleft with the blind bow-boy's butt-shaft: and is he a man to encounter Tybalt?

Ben. Why, what is Tybalt?

Mer. More than prince of cats, I can tell you. O, he's the courageous captain of complements. He fights as you sing prick-song, keeps time, distance, and proportion; he rests his minim rests, one, two, and the third in your bosom: the very butcher of a silk button, a duellist, a duellist; a gentleman of the very first house, of the first and second cause: ah, the immortal passado! the punto reverso! the hai!

Ben. The what?

Mer. The pox of such antic, lisping, affecting fantasticoes; these new tuners of accents! 'By Jesu, a very good blade! a very tall man! a very good whore!' Why, is not this a lamentable thing, grandsire, that we should be thus afflicted with these strange flies, these fashion-mongers, these perdona-mi's, who stand so much on the new form, that they cannot sit at ease on the old bench? O, their bones, their bones!

Enter ROMEO.

Ben. Here comes Romeo, here comes Romeo.

Mer. Without his roe, like a dried herring: O flesh, flesh, how art thou fishified! Now is he for the numbers that Petrarch flowed in: Laura to his lady was but a kitchen-wench; marry, she had a better love to be-rhyme her; Dido a dowdy; Cleopatra a gipsy; Helen and Hero hildings and harlots; Thisbe a grey eye or so, but not to the purpose. Signior Romeo, bon jour! there 's a French salutation to your French slop. You gave us the counterfeit fairly last night.

Rom. Good morrow to you both. What counterfeit did I give you?

Mer. The slip, sir, the slip; can you not conceive?

Rom. Pardon, good Mercutio, my business was great; and in such a case as mine a man may strain courtesy.

Mer. That 's as much as to say, such a case as yours constrains a man to bow in the hams.

Rom. Meaning, to court'sy.

Mer. Thou hast most kindly hit it.

Rom. A most courteous exposition.

Mer. Nay, I am the very pink of courtesy.

Rom. Pink for flower.

52. **physic,** medicine, healing property; see glossary. 54 **steads,** helps; see glossary. 88. **did read by rote,** was merely a matter of repeating conventional expressions of love. 93. **stand on,** am in need of.

SCENE IV. 15. **pin,** peg in the center of a target. 16. **butt-shaft,** an unbarbed arrow. 19. **prince of cats.** The name of the king of cats in *Reynard the Fox* was Tybalt or Tybert. 20. **captain of complements,** master of ceremony and outward show. 21. **prick-song,** music written out. 22. **proportion,** rhythm. 23. **minim,** short note in music. 24. **butcher of a silk button,** one able to strike a button on his adversary's person. 26. **first house,** possibly of the best school of fencing. **first and second cause,** ready to quarrel for a trifle; probably an allusion to the supposed code of quarreling. 27. **passado,** forward thrust. **punto reverso,** backhanded stroke. **hai,** home thrust. 30. **fantasticoes,** coxcombs. 31. **accents,** language. **tall,** valiant. 35. **flies,** parasites. **perdona-mi's,** Italian for "pardon me's"; a reference to the affectation of using foreign phrases. 36-37. **form . . . bench.** *Form* means both "fashion" and "bench." 37. **bones,** French *bon* with play on English "bone." 39. **Without his roe,** sometimes explained as a pun on first syllable of Romeo's name, in which case the last syllables might be taken as an expression of woe. 41. **Petrarch,** Italian poet of the Renaissance who addressed his sonnets to Laura. 45. **hildings,** good-for-nothings. 48. **slop,** loose trousers of French fashion. **fairly,** handsomely; see glossary. 51. **slip.** Counterfeit coins

Mer. Right.

Rom. Why, then is my pump well flowered.

Mer. Sure wit, follow me this jest now till thou hast worn out thy pump, that when the single sole of it is worn, the jest may remain after the wearing solely singular.

Rom. O single-soled jest, solely singular for the singleness!

Mer. Come between us, good Benvolio; my wits faint.

Rom. Swits and spurs, swits and spurs; or I'll cry a match.

Mer. Nay, if our wits run the wild-goose chase, I am done, for thou hast more of the wild-goose in one of thy wits than, I am sure, I have in my whole five: was I with you there for the goose?

Rom. Thou wast never with me for any thing when thou wast not there for the goose.

Mer. I will bite thee by the ear for that jest.

Rom. Nay, good goose, bite not.

Mer. Thy wit is a very bitter sweeting; it is a most sharp sauce.

Rom. And is it not, then, well served in to a sweet goose?

Mer. O, here 's a wit of cheveril, that stretches from an inch narrow to an ell broad!

Rom. I stretch it out for that word 'broad;' which added to the goose, proves thee far and wide a broad goose.

Mer. Why, is not this better now than groaning for love? now art thou sociable, now art thou Romeo; now art thou what thou art, by art as well as by nature: for this drivelling love is like a great natural, that runs lolling up and down to hide his bauble in a hole.

Ben. Stop there, stop there.

Mer. Thou desirest me to stop in my tale against the hair.

Ben. Thou wouldst else have made thy tale large.

Mer. O, thou art deceived; I would have made it short: for I was come to the whole depth of my tale; and meant, indeed, to occupy the argument no longer.

Rom. Here 's goodly gear!

Enter Nurse *and her Man* [Peter].

A sail, a sail!

Mer. Two, two; a shirt and a smock.

Nurse. Peter!

Peter. Anon!

Nurse. My fan, Peter.

Mer. Good Peter, to hide her face; for her fan 's the fairer face.

Nurse. God ye good morrow, gentlemen.

Mer. God ye good den, fair gentlewoman.

Nurse. Is it good den?

Mer. 'Tis no less, I tell ye, for the bawdy hand of the dial is now upon the prick of noon.

Nurse. Out upon you! what a man are you!

Rom. One, gentlewoman, that God hath made for himself to mar.

Nurse. By my troth, it is well said; 'for himself to mar,' quoth 'a? Gentlemen, can any of you tell me where I may find the young Romeo?

Rom. I can tell you; but young Romeo will be older when you have found him than he was when you sought him: I am the youngest of that name, for fault of a worse.

Nurse. You say well.

Mer. Yea, is the worst well? very well took, i' faith; wisely, wisely.

Nurse. If you be he, sir, I desire some confidence with you.

Ben. She will indite him to some supper.

Mer. A bawd, a bawd, a bawd! So ho!

Rom. What hast thou found?

Mer. No hare, sir; unless a hare, sir, in a lenten pie, that is something stale and hoar ere it be spent. [*Sings.*]

An old hare hoar,
And an old hare hoar,
Is very good meat in lent:
But a hare that is hoar
Is too much for a score,
When it hoars ere it be spent.

Romeo, will you come to your father's? we'll to dinner, thither.

Rom. I will follow you.

Mer. Farewell, ancient lady; farewell, [*singing*] 'lady, lady, lady.' *Exeunt* [*Mercutio and Benvolio*].

Nurse. Marry, farewell! I pray you, sir, what saucy merchant was this, that was so full of his ropery?

Rom. A gentleman, nurse, that loves to hear himself talk, and will speak more in a minute than he will stand to in a month.

Nurse. An 'a speak any thing against me, I'll take him down, an 'a were lustier than he is, and twenty such Jacks; and if I cannot, I'll find those that shall. Scurvy knave! I am none of his flirt-gills; I am none of his skains-mates. And thou must stand by too, and suffer every knave to use me at his pleasure?

Peter. I saw no man use you at his pleasure; if I had, my weapon should quickly have been out, I warrant you: I dare draw as soon as another man, if I see occasion in a good quarrel, and the law on my side.

Nurse. Now, afore God, I am so vexed, that every part about me quivers. Scurvy knave! Pray you, sir, a word: and as I told you, my young lady bid me inquire you out; what she bid me say, I will keep to myself: but first let me tell ye, if ye should lead her into a fool's paradise, as they say, it were a very gross kind of behaviour, as they say: for the gentlewoman is young; and, therefore, if you should deal double with her, truly it were an ill thing to be offered to any gentlewoman, and very weak dealing.

were called "slips." 56. **case,** situation; also, physical condition. 59. **kindly,** naturally; politely. 64. **is my pump well flowered.** The shoe is pinked or perforated in ornamental figures. 69. **single-soled,** thin; contemptible, with pun on "soul." 70. **singleness,** feebleness. 73. **Swits,** switches. 74. **cry a match,** claim a victory. 75. **wild-goose chase,** a horse race in which the leading rider might force his competitors to follow him wherever he went. 80. **goose,** prostitute. 83. **sweeting,** probably a pun on a tart-tasting apple called the "sweeting." 87. **cheveril,** kid leather. 96. **natural,** idiot. 97. **bauble,** a jester's wand; here with bawdy suggestion. 100. **against the hair,** against the grain (with a bawdy play on *tale, tail;* continued with *large, short, depth, occupy,* etc.). 107. **gear,** general word meaning "substance" or "stuff"; see glossary. 109. **a shirt . . . smock,** a man and a woman; see *smock* in glossary. 119. **prick,** point on the dial of a clock (with bawdy suggestion). 120. **Out upon you,** expression of indignation; see *out* in glossary. 134. **confidence,** the nurse's mistake for "conference." 135. **indite,** Benvolio's deliberate malapropism for "invite." 138. **hare,** used as a slang word for "courtesan." 144. **hoar,** moldy (with pun). 151. **'lady, lady, lady,'** refrain from the ballad *Chaste Susanna.* 153. **merchant,** fellow. 154. **ropery,** the nurse's mistake for "roguery." 160. **Jacks,** used as a term of disparagement. 162. **flirt-gills,** loose women. 163. **skains-mates,** perhaps dagger-mates, outlaws, or gangster molls.

Rom. Nurse, commend me to thy lady and mistress. I protest unto thee—

Nurse. Good heart, and, i' faith, I will tell her as much: Lord, Lord, she will be a joyful woman.

Rom. What wilt thou tell her, nurse? thou dost not mark me.

Nurse. I will tell her, sir, that you do protest; which, as I take it, is a gentlemanlike offer.

Rom. Bid her devise
Some means to come to shrift this afternoon;
And there she shall at Friar Laurence' cell
Be shriv'd and married. Here is for thy pains.

Nurse. No, truly, sir; not a penny.

Rom. Go to; I say you shall.

Nurse. This afternoon, sir? well, she shall be there.

Rom. And stay, good nurse, behind the abbey wall:
Within this hour my man shall be with thee,
And bring thee cords made like a tackled stair;
Which to the high top-gallant of my joy
Must be my convoy in the secret night.
Farewell; be trusty, and I'll quit thy pains:
Farewell; commend me to thy mistress.

Nurse. Now God in heaven bless thee! Hark you, sir.

Rom. What say'st thou, my dear nurse?

Nurse. Is your man secret? Did you ne'er hear say,
Two may keep counsel, putting one away?

Rom. I warrant thee, my man 's as true as steel.

Nurse. Well, sir; my mistress is the sweetest lady—Lord, Lord! when 'twas a little prating thing:—O, there is a nobleman in town, one Paris, that would fain lay knife aboard; but she, good soul, had as lief see a toad, a very toad, as see him. I anger her sometimes and tell her that Paris is the properer man; but, I'll warrant you, when I say so, she looks as pale as any clout in the versal world. Doth not rosemary and Romeo begin both with a letter?

Rom. Ay, nurse; what of that? both with an R.

Nurse. Ah, mocker! that 's the dog's name; R is for the—No; I know it begins with some other letter:—and she hath the prettiest sententious of it, of you and rosemary, that it would do you good to hear it.

Rom. Commend me to thy lady.

Nurse. Ay, a thousand times. [*Exit Romeo.*] Peter!

Pet. Anon!

Nurse. Peter, take my fan, and go before, and apace.
Exeunt.

[SCENE V. *Capulet's orchard.*]

Enter JULIET.

Jul. The clock struck nine when I did send the nurse;
In half an hour she promised to return.
Perchance she cannot meet him: that 's not so.
O, she is lame! love's heralds should be thoughts,
Which ten times faster glide than the sun's beams,
Driving back shadows over louring hills:
Therefore do nimble-pinion'd doves draw love,
And therefore hath the wind-swift Cupid wings.
Now is the sun upon the highmost hill
Of this day's journey, and from nine till twelve
Is three long hours, yet she is not come.
Had she affections and warm youthful blood,
She would be as swift in motion as a ball;
My words would bandy her to my sweet love,
And his to me:
†But old folks, many feign as they were dead;
Unwieldy, slow, heavy and pale as lead.
O God, she comes!

Enter Nurse [*and* PETER].

O honey nurse, what news?
Hast thou met with him? Send thy man away.

Nurse. Peter, stay at the gate. [*Exit Peter.*]

Jul. Now, good sweet nurse,—O Lord, why lookest thou sad?
Though news be sad, yet tell them merrily;
If good, thou shamest the music of sweet news
By playing it to me with so sour a face.

Nurse. I am a-weary, give me leave awhile:
Fie, how my bones ache! what a jaunce have I had!

Jul. I would thou hadst my bones, and I thy news.
Nay, come, I pray thee, speak; good, good nurse, speak.

Nurse. Jesu, what haste! can you not stay awhile?
Do you not see that I am out of breath?

Jul. How art thou out of breath, when thou hast breath
To say to me that thou art out of breath?
The excuse that thou dost make in this delay
Is longer than the tale thou dost excuse.
Is thy news good, or bad? answer to that;
Say either, and I'll stay the circumstance:
Let me be satisfied, is 't good or bad?

Nurse. Well, you have made a simple choice; you know not how to choose a man: Romeo! no, not he; though his face be better than any man's, yet his leg excels all men's; and for a hand, and a foot, and a body, though they be not to be talked on, yet they are past compare: he is not the flower of courtesy, but, I'll warrant him, as gentle as a lamb. Go thy ways, wench; serve God. What, have you dined at home?

Jul. No, no: but all this did I know before.
What says he of our marriage? what of that?

Nurse. Lord, how my head aches! what a head have I!
It beats as it would fall in twenty pieces.
My back a t' other side,—ah, my back, my back!
Beshrew your heart for sending me about,
To catch my death with jauncing up and down!

Jul. I' faith, I am sorry that thou art not well.
Sweet, sweet, sweet nurse, tell me, what says my love?

Nurse. Your love says, like an honest gentleman, and a courteous, and a kind, and a handsome, and, I warrant, a virtuous,—Where is your mother?

Jul. Where is my mother! why, she is within;
Where should she be? How oddly thou repliest!
'Your love says, like an honest gentleman,
Where is your mother?'

Nurse. O God's lady dear!
Are you so hot? marry, come up, I trow;

183. **protest,** vow. 188. **mark,** attend to. 201. **tackled stair,** rope ladder. 202. **top-gallant,** summit. 203. **convoy,** a thing that conducts. 204. **quit,** reward, requite; see glossary. 208. **secret,** trustworthy. 217. **properer,** handsomer; see glossary. 219. **clout,** rag; a proverbial expression. **versal,** universal. 220. **a,** the same. 223. **the dog's name.** The letter *R* was thought to resemble the dog's growl. 226. **sententious.** The nurse probably means "sentences," pithy sayings.

SCENE V. 7. **love,** Venus, whose chariot was drawn by doves. 14. **bandy,** toss to and fro. 16. **many,** Johnson: *marry.* 25. **give me leave,** let me alone. 26. **jaunce,** so Q_2; Globe: *jaunt.* 36. **stay the circumstance,** await details; see *circumstance* in glossary. 52. **Beshrew,** common objurgation meaning "ill-luck"; see glossary. 64. **come up,**

Is this the poultice for my aching bones?
Henceforward do your messages yourself.

Jul. Here 's such a coil! come, what says Romeo?

Nurse. Have you got leave to go to shrift to-day?

Jul. I have.

Nurse. Then hie you hence to Friar Laurence' cell;
There stays a husband to make you a wife:
Now comes the wanton blood up in your cheeks,
They'll be in scarlet straight at any news.
Hie you to church; I must another way,
To fetch a ladder, by the which your love
Must climb a bird's nest soon when it is dark:
I am the drudge and toil in your delight,
But you shall bear the burden soon at night.
Go; I'll to dinner; hie you to the cell.

Jul. Hie to high fortune! Honest nurse, farewell.

Exeunt.

[SCENE VI. *Friar Laurence's cell.*]

Enter FRIAR [LAURENCE] *and* ROMEO.

Fri. L. So smile the heavens upon this holy act,
That after hours with sorrow chide us not!

Rom. Amen, amen! but come what sorrow can,
It cannot countervail the exchange of joy
That one short minute gives me in her sight:
Do thou but close our hands with holy words,
Then love-devouring death do what he dare;
It is enough I may but call her mine.

Fri. L. These violent delights have violent ends
And in their triumph die, like fire and powder,
Which as they kiss consume: the sweetest honey
Is loathsome in his own deliciousness
And in the taste confounds the appetite:
Therefore love moderately; long love doth so;
Too swift arrives as tardy as too slow.

Enter JULIET.

Here comes the lady: O, so light a foot
Will ne'er wear out the everlasting flint:
A lover may bestride the gossamer
That idles in the wanton summer air,
And yet not fall; so light is vanity.

Jul. Good even to my ghostly confessor.

Fri. L. Romeo shall thank thee, daughter, for us both.

Jul. As much to him, else is his thanks too much.

Rom. Ah, Juliet, if the measure of thy joy
Be heap'd like mine and that thy skill be more
To blazon it, then sweeten with thy breath
This neighbour air, and let rich music's tongue
Unfold the imagin'd happiness that both
Receive in either by this dear encounter.

Jul. Conceit, more rich in matter than in words,
Brags of his substance, not of ornament:
They are but beggars that can count their worth;
But my true love is grown to such excess
I cannot sum up sum of half my wealth.

Fri. L. Come, come with me, and we will make short work;
For, by your leaves, you shall not stay alone
Till holy church incorporate two in one. [*Exeunt.*]

[ACT III.

SCENE I. *A public place.*]

Enter MERCUTIO, BENVOLIO, *and* Men.

Ben. I pray thee, good Mercutio, let 's retire:
The day is hot, the Capulets abroad,
And, if we meet, we shall not scape a brawl;
For now, these hot days, is the mad blood stirring.

Mer. Thou art like one of those fellows that when he enters the confines of a tavern claps me his sword upon the table and says 'God send me no need of thee!' and by the operation of the second cup draws him on the drawer, when indeed there is no need.

Ben. Am I like such a fellow?

Mer. Come, come, thou art as hot a Jack in thy mood as any in Italy, and as soon moved to be moody, and as soon moody to be moved.

Ben. And what to?

Mer. Nay, an there were two such, we should have none shortly, for one would kill the other. Thou! why, thou wilt quarrel with a man that hath a hair more, or a hair less, in his beard, than thou hast: thou wilt quarrel with a man for cracking nuts, having no other reason but because thou hast hazel eyes: what eye but such an eye would spy out such a quarrel? Thy head is as full of quarrels as an egg is full of meat, and yet thy head hath been beaten as addle as an egg for quarrelling: thou hast quarrelled with a man for coughing in the street, because he hath wakened thy dog that hath lain asleep in the sun: didst thou not fall out with a tailor for wearing his new doublet before Easter? with another, for tying his new shoes with old riband? and yet thou wilt tutor me from quarrelling!

Ben. An I were so apt to quarrel as thou art, any man should buy the fee-simple of my life for an hour and a quarter.

Mer. The fee simple! O simple!

Enter TYBALT *and others.*

Ben. By my head, here come the Capulets.

Mer. By my heel, I care not.

Tyb. Follow me close, for I will speak to them.
Gentlemen, good den: a word with one of you.

Mer. And but one word with one of us? couple it with something; make it a word and a blow.

Tyb. You shall find me apt enough to that, sir, an you will give me occasion.

Mer. Could you not take some occasion without giving?

Tyb. Mercutio, thou consortest with Romeo,—

Mer. Consort! what, dost thou make us minstrels? an thou make minstrels of us, look to hear nothing but discords: here 's my fiddlestick; here 's that shall make you dance. 'Zounds, consort!

Ben. We talk here in the public haunt of men:
Either withdraw unto some private place,

expressive of impatience like "go to." 67. **coil,** turmoil, bustle; see glossary.

SCENE VI. 4. **countervail,** equal. 9. **These violent delights,** etc., expresses a premonition of evil. 13. **confounds,** destroys; see glossary. 18. **gossamer,** spider's thread. 26. **blazon,** heraldic term meaning "to describe" or "to set forth." 28. **Unfold,** make known; see glossary.

30. **Conceit,** imagination, thought; see glossary.

ACT III. SCENE I. 9. **draws . . . drawer,** draws his sword against the waiter. 14. **moody,** angry. 47. **consortest.** *To consort* meant "to accompany" in a musical sense and also "to attend or wait upon." 52. **'Zounds,** a modified form of the oath, "by God's wounds."

Or reason coldly of your grievances,
Or else depart; here all eyes gaze on us.
Mer. Men's eyes were made to look, and let them gaze;
I will not budge for no man's pleasure, I.

Enter ROMEO.

Tyb. Well, peace be with you, sir: here comes my man.
Mer. But I'll be hang'd, sir, if he wear your livery:
Marry, go before to field, he'll be your follower;
Your worship in that sense may call him 'man.'
Tyb. Romeo, the love I bear thee can afford
No better term than this,—thou art a villain.
Rom. Tybalt, the reason that I have to love thee
Doth much excuse the appertaining rage
To such a greeting: villain am I none;
Therefore farewell; I see thou knowest me not.
Tyb. Boy, this shall not excuse the injuries
That thou hast done me; therefore turn and draw.
Rom. I do protest, I never injur'd thee,
But love thee better than thou canst devise,
Till thou shalt know the reason of my love:
And so, good Capulet,—which name I tender
As dearly as my own,—be satisfied.
Mer. O calm, dishonourable, vile submission!
Alla stoccata carries it away. [*Draws.*]
Tybalt, you rat-catcher, will you walk?
Tyb. What wouldst thou have with me?
Mer. Good king of cats, nothing but one of your nine lives; that I mean to make bold withal, and, as you shall use me hereafter, dry-beat the rest of the eight. Will you pluck your sword out of his pilcher by the ears? make haste, lest mine be about your ears ere it be out.
Tyb. I am for you. [*Drawing.*]
Rom. Gentle Mercutio, put thy rapier up.
Mer. Come, sir, your passado. [*They fight.*]
Rom. Draw, Benvolio; beat down their weapons.
Gentlemen, for shame, forbear this outrage!
Tybalt, Mercutio, the prince expressly hath
Forbid this bandying in Verona streets:
Hold, Tybalt! good Mercutio!
[*Tybalt under Romeo's arm stabs Mercutio, and flies with his followers.*]
Mer. I am hurt.
A plague o' both your houses! I am sped.
Is he gone, and hath nothing?
Ben. What, art thou hurt?
Mer. Ay, ay, a scratch, a scratch; marry, 'tis enough.
Where is my page? Go, villain, fetch a surgeon.
[*Exit Page.*]
Rom. Courage, man; the hurt cannot be much.
Mer. No, 'tis not so deep as a well, nor so wide as a church-door; but 'tis enough, 'twill serve: ask for me to-morrow, and you shall find me a grave man. I am peppered, I warrant, for this world. A plague o' both your houses! 'Zounds, a dog, a rat, a mouse, a cat, to scratch a man to death! a braggart, a rogue, a villain, that fights by the book of arithmetic! Why the devil came you between us? I was hurt under your arm.
Rom. I thought all for the best.
Mer. Help me into some house, Benvolio,
Or I shall faint. A plague o' both your houses!
They have made worms' meat of me: I have it,
And soundly too: your houses!
Exit [*supported by Benvolio*].
Rom. This gentleman, the prince's near ally,
My very friend, hath got this mortal hurt
In my behalf; my reputation stain'd
With Tybalt's slander,—Tybalt, that an hour
Hath been my cousin! O sweet Juliet,
Thy beauty hath made me effeminate
And in my temper soft'ned valour's steel!

Enter BENVOLIO.

Ben. O Romeo, Romeo, brave Mercutio is dead!
That gallant spirit hath aspir'd the clouds,
Which too untimely here did scorn the earth.
Rom. This day's black fate on moe days doth depend;
This but begins the woe others must end.

[*Enter* TYBALT.]

Ben. Here comes the furious Tybalt back again.
Rom. Alive, in triumph! and Mercutio slain!
Away to heaven, respective lenity,
And fire-ey'd fury be my conduct now!
Now, Tybalt, take the 'villain' back again,
That late thou gavest me; for Mercutio's soul
Is but a little way above our heads,
Staying for thine to keep him company:
Either thou, or I, or both, must go with him.
Tyb. Thou, wretched boy, that didst consort him here,
Shalt with him hence.
Rom. This shall determine that.
They fight; Tybalt falls.
Ben. Romeo, away, be gone!
The citizens are up, and Tybalt slain.
Stand not amaz'd: the prince will doom thee death,
If thou art taken: hence, be gone, away!
Rom. O, I am fortune's fool!
Ben. Why dost thou stay? *Exit Romeo.*

Enter Citizens.

First Cit. Which way ran he that kill'd Mercutio?
Tybalt, that murderer, which way ran he?
Ben. There lies that Tybalt.
First Cit. Up, sir, go with me;
I charge thee in the prince's name, obey.

Enter PRINCE [*attended*], *old* MONTAGUE, CAPULET, *their* Wives, *and all.*

Prin. Where are the vile beginners of this fray?
Ben. O noble prince, I can discover all
The unlucky manage of this fatal brawl:
There lies the man, slain by young Romeo,
That slew thy kinsman, brave Mercutio.
La. Cap. Tybalt, my cousin! O my brother's child!
O prince! O cousin! husband! O, the blood is spilt

61. **field,** field of encounter. 77. **Alla stoccata,** Italian, "with the thrust"; i.e., the fencing master wins the victory. 78. **rat-catcher,** an allusion to Tybalt as king of cats (see II, iv, 19). 81. **make bold,** make free with. 83. **dry-beat,** beat soundly. 84. **pilcher,** scabbard. 88. **passado,** forward thrust; used derisively. 94. **sped,** done for. 102. **grave man.** Mercutio thus makes puns with his last breath. 106. **by the book of arithmetic,** merely by theory. Back of the whole scene lies a current controversy between the old broadsword style of fencing and the new French style of rapier fencing. 114. **ally,** kinsman. 115. **very,** true. 124. **moe,** more; so Q_2F; Globe: *more.* 128. **respective lenity,** considerate gentleness. 129. **conduct,** guide. 139. **doom,** adjudge. 141. **fortune's fool.** At this crucial moment in the play Romeo again alludes to destiny. 148. **manage,** management; see glossary. 158. **fair,** civilly; see glossary. 159. **nice,** trivial; see glossary. 162. **take truce,** make peace. **unruly spleen,** ungovernable rage; see *spleen* in glossary. 163. **tilts,** strikes. 169. **Retorts,** throws back upon his

Of my dear kinsman! Prince, as thou art true,
For blood of ours, shed blood of Montague.
O cousin, cousin!
Prin. Benvolio, who began this bloody fray?
Ben. Tybalt, here slain, whom Romeo's hand did slay;
Romeo that spoke him fair, bade him bethink
How nice the quarrel was, and urg'd withal
Your high displeasure: all this uttered
With gentle breath, calm look, knees humbly bow'd,
Could not take truce with the unruly spleen
Of Tybalt deaf to peace, but that he tilts
With piercing steel at bold Mercutio's breast,
Who, all as hot, turns deadly point to point,
And, with a martial scorn, with one hand beats
Cold death aside, and with the other sends
It back to Tybalt, whose dexterity
Retorts it: Romeo he cries aloud,
'Hold, friends! friends, part!' and, swifter than his tongue,
His agile arm beats down their fatal points,
And 'twixt them rushes; underneath whose arm
An envious thrust from Tybalt hit the life
Of stout Mercutio, and then Tybalt fled;
But by and by comes back to Romeo,
Who had but newly entertain'd revenge,
And to 't they go like lightning, for, ere I
Could draw to part them, was stout Tybalt slain,
And, as he fell, did Romeo turn and fly.
This is the truth, or let Benvolio die.
La. Cap. He is a kinsman to the Montague;
Affection makes him false; he speaks not true:
Some twenty of them fought in this black strife,
And all those twenty could but kill one life.
I beg for justice, which thou, prince, must give;
Romeo slew Tybalt, Romeo must not live.
Prin. Romeo slew him, he slew Mercutio;
Who now the price of his dear blood doth owe?
Mon. Not Romeo, prince, he was Mercutio's friend;
His fault concludes but what the law should end,
The life of Tybalt.
Prin. And for that offence
Immediately we do exile him hence:
I have an interest in your hate's proceeding,
My blood for your rude brawls doth lie a-bleeding;
But I'll amerce you with so strong a fine
That you shall all repent the loss of mine:
I will be deaf to pleading and excuses;
Nor tears nor prayers shall purchase out abuses:
Therefore use none: let Romeo hence in haste,
Else, when he is found, that hour is his last.
Bear hence this body and attend our will:
Mercy but murders, pardoning those that kill. *Exeunt.*

[SCENE II. *Capulet's orchard.*]

Enter JULIET *alone.*

Jul. Gallop apace, you fiery-footed steeds,
Towards Phœbus' lodging: such a waggoner
As Phæthon would whip you to the west,
And bring in cloudy night immediately.
Spread thy close curtain, love-performing night,
That runaways' eyes may wink, and Romeo
Leap to these arms, untalk'd of and unseen.
Lovers can see to do their amorous rites
By their own beauties; or, if love be blind,
It best agrees with night. Come, civil night,
Thou sober-suited matron, all in black,
And learn me how to lose a winning match,
Play'd for a pair of stainless maidenhoods:
Hood my unmann'd blood, bating in my cheeks,
With thy black mantle; till strange love, grown bold,
Think true love acted simple modesty.
Come, night; come, Romeo; come, thou day in night;
For thou wilt lie upon the wings of night
Whiter than new snow upon a raven's back.
Come, gentle night, come, loving, black-brow'd night,
Give me my Romeo; and, when he shall die,
Take him and cut him out in little stars,
And he will make the face of heaven so fine
That all the world will be in love with night
And pay no worship to the garish sun.
O, I have bought the mansion of a love,
But not possess'd it, and, though I am sold,
Not yet enjoy'd: so tedious is this day
As is the night before some festival
To an impatient child that hath new robes
And may not wear them. O, here comes my nurse,

Enter Nurse, *with cords.*

And she brings news; and every tongue that speaks
But Romeo's name speaks heavenly eloquence.
Now, nurse, what news? What hast thou there? the cords
That Romeo bid thee fetch?
Nurse. Ay, ay, the cords.
[*Throws them down.*]
Jul. Ay me! what news? why dost thou wring thy hands?
Nurse. Ah, weraday! he's dead, he's dead, he's dead!
We are undone, lady, we are undone!
Alack the day! he 's gone, he 's kill'd, he 's dead!
Jul. Can heaven be so envious?
Nurse. Romeo can,
Though heaven cannot: O Romeo, Romeo!
Who ever would have thought it? Romeo!
Jul. What devil art thou, that dost torment me thus?
This torture should be roar'd in dismal hell.
Hath Romeo slain himself? say thou but 'I,'
And that bare vowel 'I' shall poison more
Than the death-darting eye of cockatrice:
I am not I, if there be such an I;
Or those eyes shut, that make thee answer 'I.'
If he be slain, say 'I'; or if not, no:
Brief sounds determine of my weal or woe.
Nurse. I saw the wound, I saw it with mine eyes,—
God save the mark!—here on his manly breast:
A piteous corse, a bloody piteous corse;

adversary. 176. **entertain'd,** harbored thoughts of; see glossary. 195. **amerce,** punish by fine. 198. **purchase out,** redeem, exempt from penalty. **abuses,** misdeeds; see glossary.

SCENE II. 2-3. **such . . . Phæthon,** i.e., a young man like Phæthon would understand our haste. Phæthon was son of the sun god, Helios, and was allowed to assume the reins of the sun for a day; not being able to restrain the steeds, he had to be slain by the thunderbolt of Jupiter. 6. **runaways.** Perhaps refers to the horses of the sun chariot which ran away with Phæthon. **wink,** shut; see glossary. 10. **civil,** well-ordered. 14. **Hood,** cover; term in falconry. The hawk's eyes were covered so that it would not bate or beat the wings. **unmann'd,** another term in falconry meaning "untamed." 37. **weraday,** Globe: *well-a-day.* 45. **'I,'** ay, yes. 47. **cockatrice,** basilisk, a fabulous serpent which could kill by its look. 53. **God save the mark,** God forbid; a familiar oath originally intended to avert ill omen.

Pale, pale as ashes, all bedaub'd in blood,
All in gore-blood; I swounded at the sight.

Jul. O, break, my heart! poor bankrout, break at once!
To prison, eyes, ne'er look on liberty!
Vile earth, to earth resign; end motion here;
And thou and Romeo press one heavy bier!

Nurse. O Tybalt, Tybalt, the best friend I had!
O courteous Tybalt! honest gentleman!
That ever I should live to see thee dead!

Jul. What storm is this that blows so contrary?
Is Romeo slaught'red, and is Tybalt dead?
My dearest cousin, and my dearer lord?
Then, dreadful trumpet, sound the general doom!
For who is living, if those two are gone?

Nurse. Tybalt is gone, and Romeo banished;
Romeo that kill'd him, he is banished.

Jul. O God! did Romeo's hand shed Tybalt's blood?

Nurse. It did, it did; alas the day, it did!

Jul. O serpent heart, hid with a flow'ring face!
Did ever dragon keep so fair a cave?
Beautiful tyrant! fiend angelical!
Dove-feather'd raven! wolvish-ravening lamb!
Despised substance of divinest show!
Just opposite to what thou justly seem'st,
A damned saint, an honourable villain!
O nature, what hadst thou to do in hell,
When thou didst bower the spirit of a fiend
In mortal paradise of such sweet flesh?
Was ever book containing such vile matter
So fairly bound? O, that deceit should dwell
In such a gorgeous palace!

Nurse. There 's no trust,
No faith, no honesty in men; all perjur'd,
All forsworn, all naught, all dissemblers.
Ah, where 's my man? give me some aqua vitæ:
These griefs, these woes, these sorrows make me old.
Shame come to Romeo!

Jul. Blister'd be thy tongue
For such a wish! he was not born to shame:
Upon his brow shame is asham'd to sit;
For 'tis a throne where honour may be crown'd
Sole monarch of the universal earth.
O, what a beast was I to chide at him!

Nurse. Will you speak well of him that kill'd your cousin?

Jul. Shall I speak ill of him that is my husband?
Ah, poor my lord, what tongue shall smooth thy name,
When I, thy three-hours wife, have mangled it?
But, wherefore, villain, didst thou kill my cousin?
That villain cousin would have kill'd my husband:
Back, foolish tears, back to your native spring;
Your tributary drops belong to woe,
Which you, mistaking, offer up to joy.
My husband lives, that Tybalt would have slain;
And Tybalt 's dead, that would have slain my husband:
All this is comfort; wherefore weep I then?
Some word there was, worser than Tybalt's death,
That murd'red me: I would forget it fain;
But, O, it presses to my memory,
Like damned guilty deeds to sinners' minds:
'Tybalt is dead, and Romeo—banished;'
That 'banished,' that one word 'banished,'
Hath slain ten thousand Tybalts. Tybalt's death
Was woe enough, if it had ended there:
Or, if sour woe delights in fellowship
And needly will be rank'd with other griefs,
Why followed not, when she said 'Tybalt 's dead,'
Thy father, or thy mother, nay, or both,
Which modern lamentation might have mov'd?
But with a rearward following Tybalt's death,
'Romeo is banished,' to speak that word,
Is father, mother, Tybalt, Romeo, Juliet,
All slain, all dead. 'Romeo is banished!'
There is no end, no limit, measure, bound,
In that word's death; no words can that woe sound.
Where is my father, and my mother, nurse?

Nurse. Weeping and wailing over Tybalt's corse:
Will you go to them? I will bring you thither.

Jul. Wash they his wounds with tears: mine shall be spent,
When theirs are dry, for Romeo's banishment.
Take up those cords: poor ropes, you are beguil'd,
Both you and I; for Romeo is exil'd:
He made you for a highway to my bed;
But I, a maid, die maiden-widowed.
Come, cords, come, nurse; I'll to my wedding-bed;
And death, not Romeo, take my maidenhead!

Nurse. Hie to your chamber: I'll find Romeo
To comfort you: I wot well where he is.
Hark ye, your Romeo will be here at night:
I'll to him; he is hid at Laurence' cell.

Jul. O, find him! give this ring to my true knight,
And bid him come to take his last farewell. *Exeunt.*

[SCENE III. *Friar Laurence's cell.*]

Enter FRIAR [LAURENCE.]

Fri. L. Romeo, come forth; come forth, thou fearful man:
Affliction is enamour'd of thy parts,
And thou art wedded to calamity.

[*Enter*] ROMEO.

Rom. Father, what news? what is the prince's doom?
What sorrow craves acquaintance at my hand,
That I yet know not?

Fri. L. Too familiar
Is my dear son with such sour company:
I bring thee tidings of the prince's doom.

Rom. What less than dooms-day is the prince's doom?

Fri. L. A gentler judgement vanish'd from his lips,
Not body's death, but body's banishment.

Rom. Ha, banishment! be merciful, say 'death;'
For exile hath more terror in his look,
Much more than death: do not say 'banishment.'

Fri. L. Hence from Verona art thou banished:
Be patient, for the world is broad and wide.

Rom. There is no world without Verona walls,
But purgatory, torture, hell itself.
Hence-banished is banish'd from the world,
And world's exile is death: then 'banished'
Is death mis-term'd; calling death 'banished,'

56. **gore-blood,** clotted blood. 59. **motion,** power of movement, life. 81. **bower,** give lodging to. 87. **naught,** worthless; see glossary. 117. **needly,** of necessity. 120. **modern,** ordinary; see glossary. 121. **rearward,** rear guard. 139. **wot,** know; see glossary.

SCENE III. 10. **vanish'd,** issued. 26. **rush'd,** thrust (aside). 33.

Thou cutt'st my head off with a golden axe,
And smilest upon the stroke that murders me.
Fri. L. O deadly sin! O rude unthankfulness!
Thy fault our law calls death; but the kind prince,
Taking thy part, hath rush'd aside the law,
And turn'd that black word death to banishment:
This is dear mercy, and thou seest it not.
Rom. 'Tis torture, and not mercy: heaven is here,
Where Juliet lives; and every cat and dog
And little mouse, every unworthy thing,
Live here in heaven and may look on her;
But Romeo may not: more validity,
More honourable state, more courtship lives
In carrion-flies than Romeo: they may seize
On the white wonder of dear Juliet's hand
And steal immortal blessing from her lips,
Who, even in pure and vestal modesty,
Still blush, as thinking their own kisses sin;
But Romeo may not; he is banished:
Flies may do this, but I from this must fly:
They are free men, but I am banished.
And sayest thou yet that exile is not death?
Hadst thou no poison mix'd, no sharp-ground knife,
No sudden mean of death, though ne'er so mean,
But 'banished' to kill me?—'banished'?
O friar, the damned use that word in hell;
Howlings attend it: how hast thou the heart,
Being a divine, a ghostly confessor,
A sin-absolver, and my friend profess'd,
To mangle me with that word 'banished'?
Fri. L. Thou fond mad man, hear me a little
speak.
Rom. O, thou wilt speak again of banishment.
Fri. L. I'll give thee armour to keep off that word;
Adversity's sweet milk, philosophy,
To comfort thee, though thou art banished.
Rom. Yet 'banished'? Hang up philosophy!
Unless philosophy can make a Juliet,
Displant a town, reverse a prince's doom,
It helps not, it prevails not: talk no more.
Fri. L. O, then I see that madmen have no ears.
Rom. How should they, when that wise men have no
eyes?
Fri. L. Let me dispute with thee of thy estate.
Rom. Thou canst not speak of that thou dost not feel:
Wert thou as young as I, Juliet thy love,
An hour but married, Tybalt murdered,
Doting like me and like me banished,
Then mightst thou speak, then mightst thou tear thy
hair,
And fall upon the ground, as I do now,
Taking the measure of an unmade grave.
Knock.
Fri. L. Arise; one knocks; good Romeo, hide thyself.
Rom. Not I; unless the breath of heart-sick groans,
Mist-like, infold me from the search of eyes. *Knock.*
Fri. L. Hark, how they knock! Who 's there?
Romeo, arise;
Thou wilt be taken. Stay awhile! Stand up; *Knock.*
Run to my study. By and by! God's will,
What simpleness is this! I come, I come! *Knock.*
Who knocks so hard? whence come you? what 's your
will?
Nurse. [*Within*] Let me come in, and you shall know
my errand;
I come from Lady Juliet.
Fri. L. Welcome, then.

Enter Nurse.

Nurse. O holy friar, O, tell me, holy friar,
Where is my lady's lord, where 's Romeo?
Fri. L. There on the ground, with his own tears
made drunk.
Nurse. O, he is even in my mistress' case,
Just in her case! O woful sympathy!
Piteous predicament! Even so lies she,
Blubb'ring and weeping, weeping and blubb'ring.
Stand up, stand up; stand, an you be a man:
For Juliet's sake, for her sake, rise and stand;
Why should you fall into so deep an O?
Rom. Nurse!
Nurse. Ah sir! ah sir! Well, death 's the end of all.
Rom. Spakest thou of Juliet? how is it with her?
Doth not she think me an old murderer,
Now I have stain'd the childhood of our joy
With blood remov'd but little from her own?
Where is she? and how doth she? and what says
My conceal'd lady to our cancell'd love?
Nurse. O, she says nothing, sir, but weeps and weeps;
And now falls on her bed; and then starts up,
And Tybalt calls; and then on Romeo cries,
And then down falls again.
Rom. As if that name,
Shot from the deadly level of a gun,
Did murder her; as that name's cursed hand
Murder'd her kinsman. O, tell me, friar, tell me,
In what vile part of this anatomy
Doth my name lodge? tell me that I may sack
The hateful mansion. [*Drawing his sword.*]
Fri. L. Hold thy desperate hand:
Art thou a man? thy form cries out thou art:
Thy tears are womanish; thy wild acts denote
The unreasonable fury of a beast:
Unseemly woman in a seeming man!
And ill-beseeming beast in seeming both!
Thou hast amaz'd me: by my holy order,
I thought thy disposition better temper'd.
Hast thou slain Tybalt? wilt thou slay thyself?
And slay thy lady that in thy life lives,
By doing damned hate upon thyself?
Why railest thou on thy birth, the heaven, and earth?
Since birth, and heaven, and earth, all three do meet
In thee at once; which thou at once wouldst lose.
Fie, fie, thou shamest thy shape, thy love, thy wit;
Which, like a usurer, abound'st in all,
And usest none in that true use indeed
Which should bedeck thy shape, thy love, thy wit:
Thy noble shape is but a form of wax,
Digressing from the valour of a man;
Thy dear love sworn but hollow perjury,
Killing that love which thou hast vow'd to cherish;
Thy wit, that ornament to shape and love,
Mis-shapen in the conduct of them both,
Like powder in a skilless soldier's flask,
Is set a-fire by thine own ignorance,
And thou dismemb'red with thine own defence.

validity, value. 34. **courtship,** both courtliness and wooing. 45. **mean . . . mean,** means . . . base; see glossary. 63. **dispute,** reason; see glossary. **estate,** situation. 94. **old,** (colloquial), real, actual. 103. **level,** aim. 107. **sack,** destroy. 123. **Which,** (you) who.

What, rouse thee, man! thy Juliet is alive,
For whose dear sake thou wast but lately dead;
There art thou happy: Tybalt would kill thee,
But thou slewest Tybalt; there art thou happy.
The law that threat'ned death becomes thy friend
And turns it to exile; there art thou happy:
A pack of blessings lights upon thy back;
Happiness courts thee in her best array;
But, like a misbehav'd and sullen wench,
Thou pout'st upon thy fortune and thy love:
Take heed, take heed, for such die miserable.
Go, get thee to thy love, as was decreed,
Ascend her chamber, hence and comfort her:
But look thou stay not till the watch be set,
For then thou canst not pass to Mantua;
Where thou shalt live, till we can find a time
To blaze your marriage, reconcile your friends,
Beg pardon of the prince, and call thee back
With twenty hundred thousand times more joy
Than thou went'st forth in lamentation.
Go before, nurse: commend me to thy lady;
And bid her hasten all the house to bed,
Which heavy sorrow makes them apt unto:
Romeo is coming.
Nurse. O Lord, I could have stay'd here all the night
To hear good counsel: O, what learning is!
My lord, I'll tell my lady you will come.
Rom. Do so, and bid my sweet prepare to chide.
Nurse. Here, sir, a ring she bid me give you, sir:
Hie you, make haste, for it grows very late. [*Exit.*]
Rom. How well my comfort is reviv'd by this!
Fri. L. Go hence; good night; and here stands all your state:
Either be gone before the watch be set,
Or by the break of day disguis'd from hence:
Sojourn in Mantua; I'll find out your man,
And he shall signify from time to time
Every good hap to you that chances here:
Give me thy hand; 'tis late: farewell; good night.
Rom. But that a joy past joy calls out on me,
It were a grief, so brief to part with thee:
Farewell. *Exeunt.*

[SCENE IV. *A room in Capulet's house.*]

Enter old CAPULET, *his* Wife, *and* PARIS.

Cap. Things have fall'n out, sir, so unluckily,
That we have had no time to move our daughter:
Look you, she lov'd her kinsman Tybalt dearly,
And so did I:—Well, we were born to die.
'Tis very late, she'll not come down to-night:
I promise you, but for your company,
I would have been a-bed an hour ago.
Par. These times of woe afford no times to woo.
Madam, good night: commend me to your daughter.
La. Cap. I will, and know her mind early to-morrow;
To-night she 's mew'd up to her heaviness.
Cap. Sir Paris, I will make a desperate tender
Of my child's love: I think she will be rul'd
In all respects by me; nay, more, I doubt it not.
Wife, go you to her ere you go to bed;
Acquaint her here of my son Paris' love;
And bid her, mark you me, on Wednesday next—
But, soft! what day is this?
Par. Monday, my lord.
Cap. Monday! ha, ha! Well, Wednesday is too soon,
A Thursday let it be: a Thursday, tell her,
She shall be married to this noble earl.
Will you be ready? do you like this haste?
We'll keep no great ado,—a friend or two;
For, hark you, Tybalt being slain so late,
It may be thought we held him carelessly,
Being our kinsman, if we revel much:
Therefore we'll have some half a dozen friends,
And there an end. But what say you to Thursday?
Par. My lord, I would that Thursday were to-morrow.
Cap. Well, get you gone: a Thursday be it, then.
Go you to Juliet ere you go to bed,
Prepare her, wife, against this wedding-day.
Farewell, my lord. Light to my chamber, ho!
Afore me! it is so very very late,
That we may call it early by and by.
Goodnight. *Exeunt.*

[SCENE V. *Capulet's orchard.*]

Enter ROMEO *and* JULIET *aloft* [*at the window*].

Jul. Wilt thou be gone? it is not yet near day:
It was the nightingale, and not the lark,
That pierc'd the fearful hollow of thine ear;
Nightly she sings on yond pomegranate-tree:
Believe me, love, it was the nightingale.
Rom. It was the lark, the herald of the morn,
No nightingale: look, love, what envious streaks
Do lace the severing clouds in yonder east:
Night's candles are burnt out, and jocund day
Stands tiptoe on the misty mountain tops.
I must be gone and live, or stay and die.
Jul. Yond light is not day-light, I know it, I:
It is some meteor that the sun exhales,
To be to thee this night a torch-bearer,
And light thee on thy way to Mantua:
Therefore stay yet; thou need'st not to be gone.
Rom. Let me be ta'en, let me be put to death;
I am content, so thou wilt have it so.
I'll say yon grey is not the morning's eye,
'Tis but the pale reflex of Cynthia's brow;
Nor that is not the lark, whose notes do beat
The vaulty heaven so high above our heads:
I have more care to stay than will to go:
Come, death, and welcome! Juliet wills it so.
How is 't, my soul? let 's talk; it is not day.
Jul. It is, it is: hie hence, be gone, away!
It is the lark that sings so out of tune,
Straining harsh discords and unpleasing sharps.
Some say the lark makes sweet division;
This doth not so, for she divideth us:
Some say the lark and loathed toad change eyes;
O, now I would they had chang'd voices too!
Since arm from arm that voice doth us affray,

151. **blaze,** publish, divulge. 157. **apt,** ready, inclined. 166. **here stands all your state,** your fortune depends on what follows.
SCENE IV. 11. **mew'd,** cooped; see glossary. 12. **desperate tender,** rash offer. 25. **held,** regarded. 34. **Afore me,** by my life.
SCENE V. 8. **lace,** stripe. 20. **Cynthia's,** the moon's. 28. **sharps,** high notes. 29. **division,** variations on a melody, made by dividing each note into notes of briefer duration. 31. **change eyes,** an allusion to a popular saying that the toad and the lark had changed eyes, since the lark has ugly eyes and the toad beautiful ones. 34. **hunt's-up,** a song or tune to awaken huntsmen. 57. **fails,** errs. 59. **Dry sorrow.**

Hunting thee hence with hunt's-up to the day.
O, now be gone; more light and light it grows.
Rom. More light and light; more dark and dark our woes!

Enter Nurse [*hastily*].

Nurse. Madam!
Jul. Nurse?
Nurse. Your lady mother is coming to your chamber:
The day is broke; be wary, look about. [*Exit.*]
Jul. Then, window, let day in, and let life out.
Rom. Farewell, farewell! one kiss, and I'll descend.
[*He goeth down.*]
Jul. Art thou gone so? love, lord, ay, husband, friend!
I must hear from thee every day in the hour,
For in a minute there are many days:
O, by this count I shall be much in years
Ere I again behold my Romeo!
Rom. Farewell!
I will omit no opportunity
That may convey my greetings, love, to thee.
Jul. O, think'st thou we shall ever meet again?
Rom. I doubt it not; and all these woes shall serve
For sweet discourses in our times to come.
Jul. O God, I have an ill-divining soul!
Methinks I see thee, now thou art so low,
As one dead in the bottom of a tomb:
Either my eyesight fails, or thou look'st pale.
Rom. And trust me, love, in my eye so do you:
Dry sorrow drinks our blood. Adieu, adieu! *Exit.*
Jul. O Fortune, Fortune! all men call thee fickle:
If thou art fickle, what dost thou with him
That is renown'd for faith? Be fickle, fortune;
For then, I hope, thou wilt not keep him long,
But send him back.

Enter Mother [LADY CAPULET].

La. Cap. Ho, daughter! are you up?
Jul. Who is 't that calls? It is my lady mother.
Is she not down so late, or up so early?
What unaccustom'd cause procures her hither?
La. Cap. Why, how now, Juliet!
Jul. Madam, I am not well.
La. Cap. Evermore weeping for your cousin's death?
What, wilt thou wash him from his grave with tears?
An if thou couldst, thou couldst not make him live;
Therefore, have done: some grief shows much of love;
But much of grief shows still some want of wit.
Jul. Yet let me weep for such a feeling loss.
La. Cap. So shall you feel the loss, but not the friend
Which you weep for.
Jul. Feeling so the loss,
I cannot choose but ever weep the friend.
La. Cap. Well, girl, thou weep'st not so much for his death,
As that the villain lives which slaughter'd him.
Jul. What villain, madam?
La. Cap. That same villain, Romeo.
Jul. [*Aside*] Villain and he be many miles asunder.—
God pardon him! I do, with all my heart;
And yet no man like he doth grieve my heart.
La. Cap. That is, because the traitor murderer lives.
Jul. Ay, madam, from the reach of these my hands:
Would none but I might venge my cousin's death!
La. Cap. We will have vengeance for it, fear thou not:
Then weep no more. I'll send to one in Mantua,
Where that same banish'd runagate doth live,
Shall give him such an unaccustom'd dram,
That he shall soon keep Tybalt company:
And then, I hope, thou wilt be satisfied.
Jul. Indeed, I never shall be satisfied
With Romeo, till I behold him—dead—
Is my poor heart so for a kinsman vex'd:
Madam, if you could find out but a man
To bear a poison, I would temper it;
That Romeo should, upon receipt thereof,
Soon sleep in quiet. O, how my heart abhors
To hear him nam'd, and cannot come to him,
To wreak the love I bore my cousin
Upon his body that hath slaughter'd him!
La. Cap. Find thou the means, and I'll find such a man.
But now I'll tell thee joyful tidings, girl.
Jul. And joy comes well in such a needy time:
What are they, beseech your ladyship?
La. Cap. Well, well, thou hast a careful father, child;
One who, to put thee from thy heaviness,
Hath sorted out a sudden day of joy,
That thou expects not nor I look'd not for.
Jul. Madam, in happy time, what day is that?
La. Cap. Marry, my child, early next Thursday morn,
The gallant, young and noble gentleman,
The County Paris, at Saint Peter's Church,
Shall happily make thee there a joyful bride.
Jul. Now, by Saint Peter's Church and Peter too,
He shall not make me there a joyful bride!
I wonder at this haste; that I must wed
Ere he, that should be husband, comes to woo.
I pray you, tell my lord and father, madam,
I will not marry yet; and, when I do, I swear,
It shall be Romeo, whom you know I hate,
Rather than Paris. These are news indeed!
La. Cap. Here comes your father; tell him so yourself,
And see how he will take it at your hands.

Enter CAPULET *and* Nurse.

Cap. When the sun sets, the earth doth drizzle dew;
But for the sunset of my brother's son
It rains downright.
How now! a conduit, girl? what, still in tears?
Evermore show'ring? In one little body
Thou counterfeits a bark, a sea, a wind;
For still thy eyes, which I may call the sea,
Do ebb and flow with tears; the bark thy body is,
Sailing in this salt flood; the winds, thy sighs;
Who, raging with thy tears, and they with them,
Without a sudden calm, will overset
Thy tempest-tossed body. How now, wife!
Have you delivered to her our decree?

The heat of the body in sorrow and despair was thought to descend into the bowels and dry up the blood. 67. **down,** in bed. 68. **procures,** induces to come. At this point Juliet, who has appeared until now at her "window" above the stage, probably descends to the main stage for the remainder of the scene. 84. **like,** so much as. 95. **dead.** This word is placed between the clauses so that it can be understood with either what precedes or what follows it. 98. **temper,** used equivocally, meaning "to mix" or "to alloy." 108. **careful,** provident. 112. **in happy time,** a vague expression like "by the way." 130. **conduit,** water pipe.

La. Cap. Ay, sir; but she will none, she gives you thanks.
I would the fool were married to her grave!
Cap. Soft! take me with you, take me with you, wife.
How! will she none? doth she not give us thanks?
Is she not proud? doth she not count her blest,
Unworthy as she is, that we have wrought
So worthy a gentleman to be her bridegroom?
Jul. Not proud, you have; but thankful, that you have:
Proud can I never be of what I hate;
But thankful even for hate, that is meant love.
Cap. How, how, how, how, chop-logic! What is this?
'Proud,' and 'I thank you,' and 'I thank you not;'
And yet 'not proud:' mistress minion, you,
Thank me no thankings, nor proud me no prouds,
But fettle your fine joints 'gainst Thursday next,
To go with Paris to Saint Peter's Church,
Or I will drag thee on a hurdle thither.
Out, you green-sickness carrion! out, you baggage!
You tallow-face!
La. Cap. Fie, fie! what, are you mad?
Jul. Good father, I beseech you on my knees,
Hear me with patience but to speak a word.
Cap. Hang thee, young baggage! disobedient wretch!
I tell thee what: get thee to church a Thursday,
Or never after look me in the face:
Speak not, reply not, do not answer me;
My fingers itch. Wife, we scarce thought us blest
That God had lent us but this only child;
But now I see this one is one too much,
And that we have a curse in having her:
Out on her, hilding!
Nurse. God in heaven bless her!
You are to blame, my lord, to rate her so.
Cap. And why, my lady wisdom? hold your tongue,
Good prudence; smatter with your gossips, go.
Nurse. I speak no treason.
Cap. O, God ye god-den!
Nurse. May not one speak?
Cap. Peace, you mumbling fool!
Utter your gravity o'er a gossip's bowl;
For here we need it not.
La. Cap. You are too hot.
Cap. † God's bread! it makes me mad:
†Day, night, hour, tide, time, work, play,
Alone, in company, still my care hath been
To have her match'd: and having now provided
A gentleman of noble parentage,
Of fair demesnes, youthful, and nobly train'd,
Stuff'd, as they say, with honourable parts,
Proportion'd as one's thought would wish a man;
And then to have a wretched puling fool,
A whining mammet, in her fortune's tender,
To answer 'I'll not wed; I cannot love,
I am too young; I pray you, pardon me.'
But, an you will not wed, I'll pardon you:
Graze where you will, you shall not house with me:
Look to 't, think on 't, I do not use to jest.
Thursday is near; lay hand on heart, advise:
An you be mine, I'll give you to my friend;
An you be not, hang, beg, starve, die in the streets,
For, by my soul, I'll ne'er acknowledge thee,
Nor what is mine shall never do thee good:
Trust to 't, bethink you; I'll not be forsworn. *Exit.*
Jul. Is there no pity sitting in the clouds,
That sees into the bottom of my grief?
O, sweet my mother, cast me not away!
Delay this marriage for a month, a week;
Or, if you do not, make the bridal bed
In that dim monument where Tybalt lies.
La. Cap. Talk not to me, for I'll not speak a word:
Do as thou wilt, for I have done with thee. *Exit.*
Jul. O God!—O nurse, how shall this be prevented?
My husband is on earth, my faith in heaven;
How shall that faith return again to earth,
Unless that husband send it me from heaven
By leaving earth? comfort me, counsel me.
Alack, alack, that heaven should practise stratagems
Upon so soft a subject as myself!
What say'st thou? hast thou not a word of joy?
Some comfort, nurse.
Nurse. Faith, here it is.
Romeo is banish'd; and all the world to nothing,
That he dares ne'er come back to challenge you;
Or, if he do, it needs must be by stealth.
Then, since the case so stands as now it doth,
I think it best you married with the county.
O, he 's a lovely gentleman!
Romeo 's a dishclout to him: an eagle, madam,
Hath not so green, so quick, so fair an eye
As Paris hath. Beshrew my very heart,
I think you are happy in this second match,
For it excels your first: or if it did not,
Your first is dead; or 'twere as good he were,
As living here and you no use of him.
Jul. Speak'st thou from thy heart?
Nurse. And from my soul too;
Else beshrew them both.
Jul. Amen!
Nurse. What?
Jul. Well, thou hast comforted me marvellous much.
Go in; and tell my lady I am gone,
Having displeas'd my father, to Laurence' cell,
To make confession and to be absolv'd.
Nurse. Marry, I will; and this is wisely done. [*Exit.*]
Jul. Ancient damnation! O most wicked fiend!
Is it more sin to wish me thus forsworn,
Or to dispraise my lord with that same tongue
Which she hath prais'd him with above compare
So many thousand times? Go, counsellor;
Thou and my bosom henceforth shall be twain.
I'll to the friar, to know his remedy:
If all else fail, myself have power to die. *Exit.*

[ACT IV.

SCENE I. *Friar Laurence's cell.*]

Enter FRIAR [LAURENCE] *and* COUNTY PARIS.

Fri. L. On Thursday, sir? the time is very short.

140. **will none,** refuses it. 142. **take me with you,** let me understand you. 145. **wrought,** procured. 150. **chop-logic,** a shallow and sophistical arguer. 152. **minion,** spoiled darling, minx. 154. **fettle,** make ready. 156. **hurdle,** a conveyance for criminals. 157. **green-sickness,** an anemic ailment of young women; it suggests Juliet's paleness. 170. **rate,** berate, scold; see glossary. 172. **smatter,** chatter. 175. **gravity,** wisdom; used contemptuously. 177. **God's bread,** an oath by the sacrament. 186. **mammet,** doll. **fortune's tender,** offer of good fortune. 207. **my faith in heaven.** Juliet refers to her marriage vows. 211. **practise,** scheme, contrive; see glossary. **stratagems,**

Par. My father Capulet will have it so;
And I am nothing slow to slack his haste.
Fri. L. You say you do not know the lady's mind:
Uneven is the course, I like it not.
Par. Immoderately she weeps for Tybalt's death,
And therefore have I little talk'd of love;
For Venus smiles not in a house of tears.
Now, sir, her father counts it dangerous
That she do give her sorrow so much sway,
And in his wisdom hastes our marriage,
To stop the inundation of her tears;
Which, too much minded by herself alone,
May be put from her by society:
Now do you know the reason of this haste.
Fri. L. [*Aside*] I would I knew not why it should be slow'd.—
Look, sir, here comes the lady toward my cell.

Enter JULIET.

Par. Happily met, my lady and my wife!
Jul. That may be, sir, when I may be a wife.
Par. That may be must be, love, on Thursday next.
Jul. What must be shall be.
Fri. L. That 's a certain text.
Par. Come you to make confession to this father?
Jul. To answer that, I should confess to you.
Par. Do not deny to him that you love me.
Jul. I will confess to you that I love him.
Par. So will ye, I am sure, that you love me.
Jul. If I do so, it will be of more price,
Being spoke behind your back, than to your face.
Par. Poor soul, thy face is much abus'd with tears.
Jul. The tears have got small victory by that;
For it was bad enough before their spite.
Par. Thou wrong'st it, more than tears, with that report.
Jul. That is no slander, sir, which is a truth;
And what I spake, I spake it to my face.
Par. Thy face is mine, and thou hast sland'red it.
Jul. It may be so, for it is not mine own.
Are you at leisure, holy father, now;
Or shall I come to you at evening mass?
Fri. L. My leisure serves me, pensive daughter, now.
My lord, we must entreat the time alone.
Par. God shield I should disturb devotion!
Juliet, on Thursday early will I rouse ye:
Till then, adieu; and keep this holy kiss. *Exit.*
Jul. O, shut the door! and when thou hast done so,
Come weep with me; past hope, past cure, past help!
Fri. L. Ah, Juliet, I already know thy grief;
It strains me past the compass of my wits:
I hear thou must, and nothing may prorogue it,
On Thursday next be married to this county.
Jul. Tell me not, friar, that thou hearest of this,
Unless thou tell me how I may prevent it:
If, in thy wisdom, thou canst give no help,
Do thou but call my resolution wise,
And with this knife I'll help it presently.
God join'd my heart and Romeo's, thou our hands;
And ere this hand, by thee to Romeo seal'd,
Shall be the label to another deed,
Or my true heart with treacherous revolt
Turn to another, this shall slay them both:
Therefore, out of thy long-experienc'd time,
Give me some present counsel, or, behold,
'Twixt my extremes and me this bloody knife
Shall play the umpire, arbitrating that
Which the commission of thy years and art
Could to no issue of true honour bring.
Be not so long to speak; I long to die,
If what thou speak'st speak not of remedy.
Fri. L. Hold, daughter: I do spy a kind of hope,
Which craves as desperate an execution
As that is desperate which we would prevent.
If, rather than to marry County Paris,
Thou hast the strength of will to slay thyself,
Then is it likely thou wilt undertake
A thing like death to chide away this shame,
That cop'st with death himself to scape from it;
And, if thou darest, I'll give thee remedy.
Jul. O, bid me leap, rather than marry Paris,
From off the battlements of any tower;
Or walk in thievish ways; or bid me lurk
Where serpents are; chain me with roaring bears;
Or hide me nightly in a charnel-house,
O'er-cover'd quite with dead men's rattling bones,
With reeky shanks and yellow chapless skulls;
Or bid me go into a new-made grave
And hide me with a dead man in his shroud;
Things that, to hear them told, have made me tremble;
And I will do it without fear or doubt,
To live an unstain'd wife to my sweet love.
Fri. L. Hold, then; go home, be merry, give consent
To marry Paris: Wednesday is to-morrow:
To-morrow night look that thou lie alone;
Let not thy nurse lie with thee in thy chamber:
Take thou this vial, being then in bed,
And this distilling liquor drink thou off;
When presently through all thy veins shall run
A cold and drowsy humour, for no pulse
Shall keep his native progress, but surcease:
No warmth, no breath, shall testify thou livest;
The roses in thy lips and cheeks shall fade
To paly ashes, thy eyes' windows fall,
Like death, when he shuts up the day of life;
Each part, depriv'd of supple government,
Shall, stiff and stark and cold, appear like death:
And in this borrowed likeness of shrunk death
Thou shalt continue two and forty hours,
And then awake as from a pleasant sleep.
Now, when the bridegroom in the morning comes
To rouse thee from thy bed, there art thou dead:
Then, as the manner of our country is,
In thy best robes uncovered on the bier
Thou shalt be borne to that same ancient vault
Where all the kindred of the Capulets lie.
In the mean time, against thou shalt awake,
Shall Romeo by my letters know our drift,
And hither shall he come: and he and I
Will watch thy waking, and that very night
Shall Romeo bear thee hence to Mantua.
And this shall free thee from this present shame;
If no inconstant toy, nor womanish fear,

dreadful deeds. 215. **all . . . nothing,** the odds are overwhelming.

ACT IV. SCENE I. 5. **Uneven,** not straightforward. 13. **minded,** thought about. 40. **entreat,** ask to have. 41. **shield,** prevent (that). 54. **presently,** at once; see glossary. 57. **label,** a strip attached to a deed to carry the seal. 61. **present,** instant; see glossary. 62. **extremes,** extreme difficulties. 64. **commission,** authority. 75. **cop'st,** encounters, negotiates. 81. **charnel house,** vault for old bones. 83. **reeky,** malodorous. **chapless,** without the lower jaw. 94. **distilling,** infusing. 97. **surcease,** cease. 119. **toy,** idle fancy; see glossary.

Abate thy valour in the acting it.

Jul. Give me, give me! O, tell not me of fear!

Fri. L. Hold; get you gone, be strong and prosperous
In this resolve: I'll send a friar with speed
To Mantua, with my letters to thy lord.

Jul. Love give me strength! and strength shall help afford.
Farewell, dear father! *Exeunt.*

[SCENE II. *Hall in Capulet's house.*]

Enter Father CAPULET, *Mother* [LADY CAPULET], Nurse, *and* Servingmen, *two or three.*

Cap. So many guests invite as here are writ. [*Exit First Servant.*]
Sirrah, go hire me twenty cunning cooks.

Sec. Serv. You shall have none ill, sir; for I'll try if they can lick their fingers.

Cap. How canst thou try them so?

Sec. Serv. Marry, sir, 'tis an ill cook that cannot lick his own fingers: therefore he that cannot lick his fingers goes not with me.

Cap. Go, be gone. [*Exit Sec. Servant.*]
We shall be much unfurnish'd for this time.
What, is my daughter gone to Friar Laurence?

Nurse. Ay, forsooth.

Cap. Well, he may chance to do some good on her:
A peevish self-will'd harlotry it is.

Enter JULIET.

Nurse. See where she comes from shrift with merry look.

Cap. How now, my headstrong! where have you been gadding?

Jul. Where I have learn'd me to repent the sin
Of disobedient opposition
To you and your behests, and am enjoin'd
By holy Laurence to fall prostrate here,
To beg your pardon: pardon, I beseech you!
Henceforward I am ever rul'd by you.

Cap. Send for the county; go tell him of this:
I'll have this knot knit up to-morrow morning.

Jul. I met the youthful lord at Laurence' cell;
And gave him what becomed love I might,
Not stepping o'er the bounds of modesty.

Cap. Why, I am glad on 't; this is well: stand up:
This is as 't should be. Let me see the county;
Ay, marry, go, I say, and fetch him hither.
Now, afore God! this reverend holy friar,
All our whole city is much bound to him.

Jul. Nurse, will you go with me into my closet,
To help me sort such needful ornaments
As you think fit to furnish me to-morrow?

La. Cap. No, not till Thursday; there is time enough.

Cap. Go, nurse, go with her: we'll to church to-morrow. *Exeunt* [*Juliet and Nurse*].

La. Cap. We shall be short in our provision:
'Tis now near night.

Cap. Tush, I will stir about,
And all things shall be well, I warrant thee, wife:
Go thou to Juliet, help to deck up her;
I'll not to bed to-night; let me alone;
I'll play the housewife for this once. What, ho!
They are all forth. Well, I will walk myself
To County Paris, to prepare him up
Against to-morrow: my heart is wondrous light,
Since this same wayward girl is so reclaim'd. *Exeunt.*

[SCENE III. *Juliet's chamber.*]

Enter JULIET *and* Nurse.

Jul. Ay, those attires are best: but, gentle nurse,
I pray thee, leave me to myself to-night;
For I have need of many orisons
To move the heavens to smile upon my state,
Which, well thou knowest, is cross and full of sin.

Enter Mother [LADY CAPULET].

La. Cap. What, are you busy, ho? need you my help?

Jul. No, madam; we have cull'd such necessaries
As are behoveful for our state to-morrow:
So please you, let me now be left alone,
And let the nurse this night sit up with you;
For, I am sure, you have your hands full all,
In this so sudden business.

La. Cap. Good night:
Get thee to bed, and rest; for thou hast need.
Exeunt [*Lady Capulet and Nurse*].

Jul. Farewell! God knows when we shall meet again.
I have a faint cold fear thrills through my veins,
That almost freezes up the heat of life:
I'll call them back again to comfort me:
Nurse!—What should she do here?
My dismal scene I needs must act alone.
Come, vial.
What if this mixture do not work at all?
Shall I be married then to-morrow morning?
No, no: this shall forbid it: lie thou there.
[*Laying down her dagger.*]
What if it be a poison, which the friar
Subtly hath minist'red to have me dead,
Lest in this marriage he should be dishonour'd,
Because he married me before to Romeo?
I fear it is: and yet, methinks, it should not,
For he hath still been tried a holy man.
How if, when I am laid into the tomb,
I wake before the time that Romeo
Come to redeem me? there 's a fearful point!
Shall I not, then, be stifled in the vault,
To whose foul mouth no healthsome air breathes in,
And there die strangled ere my Romeo comes?
Or, if I live, is it not very like,
The horrible conceit of death and night,
Together with the terror of the place,—
As in a vault, an ancient receptacle,
Where, for this many hundred years, the bones
Of all my buried ancestors are pack'd:
Where bloody Tybalt, yet but green in earth,

120. **Abate,** diminish; see glossary.

SCENE II. 14. **A . . . is,** i.e., she's a silly good-for-nothing. 26. **becomed,** befitting. 33. **closet,** private room. 35. **furnish,** fit out; see glossary.

SCENE III. 3. **orisons,** prayers. 5. **cross,** contrary. 8. **behoveful,** needful. 25. **minist'red,** administered (something healing or the reverse). 29. **tried,** proved. After this line, Q1: *I will not entertain so bad a thought.* 39. **As,** namely; see glossary. 47. **mandrakes'.** Mandragora or mandrake was a narcotic plant, the root of which resembled the human form; it was fabled to utter a shriek when torn from the ground. 50. **fears,** objects of fear; see glossary. 53. **rage,** madness; see glossary.

Lies fest'ring in his shroud; where, as they say,
At some hours in the night spirits resort;—
Alack, alack, is it not like that I,
So early waking, what with loathsome smells,
And shrieks like mandrakes' torn out of the earth,
That living mortals, hearing them, run mad:—
O, if I wake, shall I not be distraught,
Environed with all these hideous fears?
And madly play with my forefathers' joints?
And pluck the mangled Tybalt from his shroud?
And, in this rage, with some great kinsman's bone,
As with a club, dash out my desp'rate brains?
O, look! methinks I see my cousin's ghost
Seeking out Romeo, that did spit his body
Upon a rapier's point: stay, Tybalt, stay!
Romeo, I come! this do I drink to thee.
[*She falls upon her bed, within the curtains.*]

[SCENE IV. *Hall in Capulet's house.*]

Enter Lady of the House [LADY CAPULET] *and* Nurse.

La. Cap. Hold, take these keys, and fetch more spices, nurse.

Nurse. They call for dates and quinces in the pastry.

Enter old CAPULET.

Cap. Come, stir, stir, stir! the second cock hath crow'd,
The curfew-bell hath rung, 'tis three o'clock:
Look to the bak'd meats, good Angelica:
Spare not for cost.

Nurse. Go, you cot-quean, go,
Get you to bed; faith, you'll be sick to-morrow
For this night's watching.

Cap. No, not a whit: what! I have watch'd ere now
All night for lesser cause, and ne'er been sick.

La. Cap. Ay, you have been a mouse-hunt in your time;
But I will watch you from such watching now.
Exeunt Lady and Nurse.

Cap. A jealous-hood, a jealous-hood!

Enter three or four [Fellows] *with spits and logs, and baskets.*

Now, fellow,
What is there?

First Fellow. Things for the cook, sir; but I know not what.

Cap. Make haste, make haste. [*Exit First Fellow.*]
Sirrah, fetch drier logs:
Call Peter, he will show thee where they are.

Sec. Fellow. I have a head, sir, that will find out logs,
And never trouble Peter for the matter. [*Exit.*]

Cap. Mass, and well said; a merry whoreson, ha!
Thou shalt be logger-head. Good faith, 'tis day:
The county will be here with music straight,
For so he said he would: I hear him near.
Play music.
Nurse! Wife! What, ho! What, nurse, I say!

Enter Nurse.

Go waken Juliet, go and trim her up;
I'll go and chat with Paris: hie, make haste,
Make haste; the bridegroom he is come already:
Make haste, I say. [*Exit Capulet.*]

[SCENE V. *Juliet's chamber.*]

[*The* NURSE *goes to the curtains.*]

Nurse. Mistress! what, mistress! Juliet! fast, I warrant her, she:
Why, lamb! why, lady! fie, you slug-a-bed!
Why, love, I say! madam! sweet-heart! why, bride!
What, not a word? you take your pennyworths now;
Sleep for a week; for the next night, I warrant,
The County Paris hath set up his rest,
That you shall rest but little. God forgive me,
Marry, and amen, how sound is she asleep!
I must needs wake her. Madam, madam, madam!
Ay, let the county take you in your bed;
He'll fright you up, i' faith. Will it not be?
[*Undraws the curtains.*]
What, dress'd! and in your clothes! and down again!
I must needs wake you: Lady! lady! lady!
Alas, alas! Help, help! my lady 's dead!
O, weraday, that ever I was born!
Some aqua vitæ, ho! My lord! my lady!

[*Enter* LADY CAPULET.]

La. Cap. What noise is here?

Nurse. O lamentable day!

La. Cap. What is the matter?

Nurse. Look, look! O heavy day!

La. Cap. O me, O me! My child, my only life,
Revive, look up, or I will die with thee!
Help, help! Call help.

Enter Father [CAPULET].

Cap. For shame, bring Juliet forth; her lord is come.

Nurse. She 's dead, deceas'd, she 's dead; alack the day!

La. Cap. Alack the day, she 's dead, she 's dead, she 's dead!

Cap. Ha! let me see her: out, alas! she 's cold;
Her blood is settled, and her joints are stiff;
Life and these lips have long been separated:
Death lies on her like an untimely frost
Upon the sweetest flower of all the field.

Nurse. O lamentable day!

La. Cap. O woful time!

Cap. Death, that hath ta'en her hence to make me wail,
Ties up my tongue, and will not let me speak.

Enter FRIAR [LAURENCE] *and the* COUNTY [PARIS, *with* Musicians].

Fri. L. Come, is the bride ready to go to church?

Cap. Ready to go, but never to return.
O son! the night before thy wedding-day
Hath Death lain with thy wife. There she lies,
Flower as she was, deflowered by him.
Death is my son-in-law, Death is my heir;

SCENE IV. 2. **pastry,** room in which pastry was made. 4. **curfew-bell,** apparently rung at other times than at curfew. 5. **bak'd meats,** pies, pastry. 6. **cot-quean,** a man who acts the housewife. 8. **watching,** waking; see glossary. 11. **mouse-hunt,** hunter of women. 13. **jealous-hood,** (you wear) the cap of jealousy. 19. **Mass,** by the Mass. 20. **logger-head,** blockhead.

SCENE V. The action here is uninterrupted from the previous scene. The Nurse opens the curtains rear-stage where Juliet has lain since IV, iii. 1. **fast,** fast asleep. 4. **pennyworths,** small portions. 6. **set up his rest,** firmly resolved (with bawdy suggestion of readying a lance for the charge). 15. **weraday,** Globe: *well-a-day*. 26. **settled,** congealed.

My daughter he hath wedded: I will die,
And leave him all; life, living, all is Death's.
Par. Have I thought long to see this morning's face,
And doth it give me such a sight as this?
La. Cap. Accurs'd, unhappy, wretched, hateful day!
Most miserable hour that e'er time saw
In lasting labour of his pilgrimage!
But one, poor one, one poor and loving child,
But one thing to rejoice and solace in,
And cruel death hath catch'd it from my sight!
Nurse. O woe! O woful, woful, woful day!
Most lamentable day, most woful day,
That ever, ever, I did yet behold!
O day! O day! O day! O hateful day!
Never was seen so black a day as this:
O woful day, O woful day!
Par. Beguil'd, divorced, wronged, spited, slain!
Most detestable death, by thee beguil'd,
By cruel cruel thee quite overthrown!
O love! O life! not life, but love in death!
Cap. Despis'd, distressed, hated, martyr'd, kill'd!
Uncomfortable time, why cam'st thou now
To murder, murder our solemnity?
O child! O child! my soul, and not my child!
Dead art thou! Alack! my child is dead;
And with my child my joys are buried.
Fri. L. Peace, ho, for shame! confusion's cure lives not
In these confusions. Heaven and yourself
Had part in this fair maid; now heaven hath all,
And all the better is it for the maid:
Your part in her you could not keep from death,
But heaven keeps his part in eternal life.
The most you sought was her promotion;
For 'twas your heaven she should be advanc'd:
And weep ye now, seeing she is advanc'd
Above the clouds, as high as heaven itself?
O, in this love, you love your child so ill,
That you run mad, seeing that she is well:
She 's not well married that lives married long;
But she 's best married that dies married young.
Dry up your tears, and stick your rosemary
On this fair corse; and, as the custom is,
In all her best array bear her to church:
For though fond nature bids us all lament,
Yet nature's tears are reason's merriment.
Cap. All things that we ordained festival,
Turn from their office to black funeral;
Our instruments to melancholy bells,
Our wedding cheer to a sad burial feast,
Our solemn hymns to sullen dirges change,
Our bridal flowers serve for a buried corse,
And all things change them to the contrary.
Fri. L. Sir, go you in; and, madam, go with him;
And go, Sir Paris; every one prepare
To follow this fair corse unto her grave:
The heavens do lour upon you for some ill;
Move them no more by crossing their high will.
Exeunt. Mane[n]t [Musicians and Nurse].

First Mus. Faith, we may put up our pipes, and be gone.
Nurse. Honest good fellows, ah, put up, put up;
For, well you know, this is a pitiful case. *[Exit.]*
First Mus. Ay, by my troth, the case may be amended.

Enter PETER.

Pet. Musicians, O, musicians, 'Heart's ease, Heart's ease:' O, an you will have me live, play 'Heart's ease.'
First Mus. Why 'Heart's ease'?
Pet. O, musicians, because my heart itself plays 'My heart is full of woe:' O, play me some merry dump, to comfort me.
First Mus. Not a dump we; 'tis no time to play now.
Pet. You will not, then?
First Mus. No.
Pet. I will then give it you soundly.
First Mus. What will you give us?
Pet. No money, on my faith, but the gleek; I will give you the minstrel.
First Mus. Then will I give you the serving-creature.
Pet. Then will I lay the serving-creature's dagger on your pate. I will carry no crotchets: I'll re you, I'll fa you; do you note me?
First Mus. An you re us and fa us, you note us.
Sec. Mus. Pray you, put up your dagger, and put out your wit.
Pet. Then have at you with my wit! I will dry-beat you with an iron wit, and put up my iron dagger. Answer me like men:
'When griping grief the heart doth wound,
And doleful dumps the mind oppress,
Then music with her silver sound'—
why 'silver sound'? why 'music with her silver sound'? What say you, Simon Catling?
First Mus. Marry, sir, because silver hath a sweet sound.
Pet. Pretty! What say you, Hugh Rebeck?
Sec. Mus. I say 'silver sound,' because musicians sound for silver.
Pet. Pretty too! What say you, James Soundpost?
Third Mus. Faith, I know not what to say.
Pet. O, I cry you mercy; you are the singer: I will say for you. It is 'music with her silver sound,' because musicians have no gold for sounding:
'Then music with her silver sound
With speedy help doth lend redress.' *Exit.*
First Mus. What a pestilent knave is this same!
Sec. Mus. Hang him, Jack! Come, we'll in here; tarry for the mourners, and stay dinner. *Exeunt.*

[ACT V.

SCENE I. *Mantua. A street.*]

Enter ROMEO.

Rom. If I may trust the flattering truth of sleep,

41. **thought long,** looked forward to. 43. **unhappy,** fatal; see glossary. 61. **solemnity,** festivity. 65. **confusion's,** calamity's. 79. **rosemary,** symbol of immortality and enduring love; therefore used at both funerals and weddings. 83. **Yet . . . merriment.** Nature is here used as the opposite of reason. 101. **amended,** bettered. *Stage Direction: Enter* **Peter.** Q_2 has *Enter Will Kemp.* This well-known comic actor was a member of Shakespeare's company. Shakespeare evidently had Kemp (or Kempe) in mind when he wrote this part, and named him in the manuscript. 102. **'Heart's ease,'** popular tune, as also '*My heart is full of woe,*' line 107. 108. **dump,** mournful tune. 115. **gleek,** jest, gibe. 120. **carry,** endure; see glossary. **crotchets,** meaning both "quarter notes" and "whims." 122. **note,** set to music; used punningly. 124. **put out,** display. 128-130. **'When . . . sound.'** This is a part of a song by Richard Edwards preserved in the *Paradise of Daintie Devices* (1576). 132. **Catling.** A catling was a small lutestring made of catgut. 135. **Rebeck.** A rebeck was a fiddle with three strings. 139. **Soundpost.** A

My dreams presage some joyful news at hand:
My bosom's lord sits lightly in his throne;
And all this day an unaccustom'd spirit
Lifts me above the ground with cheerful thoughts.
I dreamt my lady came and found me dead—
Strange dream, that gives a dead man leave to
think!—
And breath'd such life with kisses in my lips,
That I reviv'd, and was an emperor.
Ah me! how sweet is love itself possess'd,
When but love's shadows are so rich in joy!

Enter ROMEO'*s Man* [BALTHASAR, *booted*].

News from Verona!—How now, Balthasar!
Dost thou not bring me letters from the friar?
How doth my lady? Is my father well?
How fares my Juliet? that I ask again;
For nothing can be ill, if she be well.
Bal. Then she is well, and nothing can be ill:
Her body sleeps in Capels' monument,
And her immortal part with angels lives.
I saw her laid low in her kindred's vault,
And presently took post to tell it you:
O, pardon me for bringing these ill news,
Since you did leave it for my office, sir.
Rom. Is it e'en so? then I defy you, stars!
Thou knowest my lodging: get me ink and paper,
And hire post-horses; I will hence to-night.
Bal. I do beseech you, sir, have patience:
Your looks are pale and wild, and do import
Some misadventure.
Rom. Tush, thou art deceiv'd:
Leave me, and do the thing I bid thee do.
Hast thou no letters to me from the friar?
Bal. No, my good lord.
Rom. No matter: get thee gone,
And hire those horses; I'll be with thee straight.
Exit [*Balthasar*].
Well, Juliet, I will lie with thee to-night.
Let 's see for means: O mischief, thou art swift
To enter in the thoughts of desperate men!
I do remember an apothecary,—
And hereabouts 'a dwells,—which late I noted
In tatt'red weeds, with overwhelming brows,
Culling of simples; meagre were his looks,
Sharp misery had worn him to the bones:
And in his needy shop a tortoise hung,
An alligator stuff'd, and other skins
Of ill-shap'd fishes; and about his shelves
A beggarly account of empty boxes,
Green earthen pots, bladders and musty seeds,
Remnants of packthread and old cakes of roses,
Were thinly scattered, to make up a show.
Noting this penury, to myself I said
'An if a man did need a poison now,
Whose sale is present death in Mantua,
Here lives a caitiff wretch would sell it him.'
O, this same thought did but forerun my need;
And this same needy man must sell it me.
As I remember, this should be the house.
Being holiday, the beggar's shop is shut.
What, ho! apothecary!

[*Enter* Apothecary.]

Ap. Who calls so loud?
Rom. Come hither, man. I see that thou art poor:
Hold, there is forty ducats: let me have
A dram of poison, such soon-speeding gear
As will disperse itself through all the veins
That the life-weary taker may fall dead
And that the trunk may be discharg'd of breath
As violently as hasty powder fir'd
Doth hurry from the fatal cannon's womb.
Ap. Such mortal drugs I have; but Mantua's law
Is death to any he that utters them.
Rom. Art thou so bare and full of wretchedness,
And fearest to die? famine is in thy cheeks,
Need and oppression starveth in thy eyes,
Contempt and beggary hangs upon thy back;
The world is not thy friend nor the world's law;
The world affords no law to make thee rich;
Then be not poor, but break it, and take this.
Ap. My poverty, but not my will, consents.
Rom. I pay thy poverty, and not thy will.
Ap. Put this in any liquid thing you will,
And drink it off; and, if you had the strength
Of twenty men, it would dispatch you straight.
Rom. There is thy gold, worse poison to men's souls,
Doing more murder in this loathsome world,
Than these poor compounds that thou mayst not sell.
I sell thee poison; thou hast sold me none.
Farewell: buy food, and get thyself in flesh.
Come, cordial and not poison, go with me
To Juliet's grave; for there must I use thee. *Exeunt.*

[SCENE II. *Friar Laurence's cell.*]

Enter FRIAR JOHN *to* FRIAR LAURENCE.

Fri. J. Holy Franciscan friar! brother, ho!

Enter [FRIAR] LAURENCE.

Fri. L. This same should be the voice of Friar John.
Welcome from Mantua: what says Romeo?
Or, if his mind be writ, give me his letter.
Fri. J. Going to find a bare-foot brother out,
One of our order, to associate me,
Here in this city visiting the sick,
And finding him, the searchers of the town,
Suspecting that we both were in a house
Where the infectious pestilence did reign,
Seal'd up the doors, and would not let us forth;
So that my speed to Mantua there was stay'd.
Fri. L. Who bare my letter, then, to Romeo?
Fri. J. I could not send it,—here it is again,—
Nor get a messenger to bring it thee,
So fearful were they of infection.
Fri. L. Unhappy fortune! by my brotherhood,

soundpost is the pillar or peg which supports the body of a stringed instrument. 141. **cry you mercy,** beg your pardon; see glossary. 143. **sounding,** playing music.

ACT V. SCENE I. 1. **flattering,** illusive. 2. **presage some joyful news.** The premonition here is ironical. 3. **bosom's lord,** heart. 11. **shadows,** phantoms; see glossary. 21. **took post,** started with post horses. 33. **straight,** immediately. 39. **weeds,** clothes. **overwhelming brows,** eyebrows jutting out over his eyes. 40. **simples,** medicinal herbs. 45. **beggarly account,** poor array. 47. **cakes of roses,** rose petals caked to be used as perfume. 51. **present,** immediate. 52. **caitiff,** miserable. 59. **ducats,** coins, usually gold, of varying value. 63. **trunk,** body. 67. **utters,** issues, gives out. 85. **cordial,** restorative.

SCENE II. 4. **mind,** thoughts, message; see glossary. 6. **associate,** accompany. 8. **searchers of the town,** town officials charged with public health (and especially concerned about the plague).

The letter was not nice but full of charge
Of dear import, and the neglecting it
May do much danger. Friar John, go hence;
Get me an iron crow, and bring it straight
Unto my cell.

Fri. J. Brother, I'll go and bring it thee. *Exit.*

Fri. L. Now must I to the monument alone;
Within this three hours will fair Juliet wake:
She will beshrew me much that Romeo
Hath had no notice of these accidents;
But I will write again to Mantua,
And keep her at my cell till Romeo come;
Poor living corse, clos'd in a dead man's tomb! *Exit.*

[SCENE III. *A Churchyard; in it a tomb belonging to the Capulets.*]

Enter PARIS, *and his* Page [*bearing flowers and a torch*].

Par. Give me thy torch, boy: hence, and stand aloof:
Yet put it out, for I would not be seen.
Under yond yew-trees lay thee all along,
Holding thine ear close to the hollow ground;
So shall no foot upon the churchyard tread,
Being loose, unfirm, with digging up of graves,
But thou shalt hear it: whistle then to me,
As signal that thou hearest something approach.
Give me those flowers. Do as I bid thee, go.

Page. [*Aside*] I am almost afraid to stand alone
Here in the churchyard; yet I will adventure. [*Retires.*]

Par. Sweet flower, with flowers thy bridal bed I strew,—
O woe! thy canopy is dust and stones;—
Which with sweet water nightly I will dew,
Or, wanting that, with tears distill'd by moans:
The obsequies that I for thee will keep
Nightly shall be to strew thy grave and weep.
Whistle Boy.
The boy gives warning something doth approach.
What cursed foot wanders this way to-night,
To cross my obsequies and true love's rite?
What, with a torch! muffle me, night, awhile. [*Retires.*]

Enter ROMEO *and* [BALTHASAR, *with a torch, mattock, &c.*].

Rom. Give me that mattock and the wrenching iron.
Hold, take this letter; early in the morning
See thou deliver it to my lord and father.
Give me the light: upon thy life, I charge thee,
Whate'er thou hearest or seest, stand all aloof,
And do not interrupt me in my course.
Why I descend into this bed of death,
Is partly to behold my lady's face;
But chiefly to take thence from her dead finger
A precious ring, a ring that I must use
In dear employment: therefore hence, be gone:
But if thou, jealous, dost return to pry
In what I further shall intend to do,
By heaven, I will tear thee joint by joint
And strew this hungry churchyard with thy limbs:
The time and my intents are savage-wild,
More fierce and more inexorable far
Than empty tigers or the roaring sea.

Bal. I will be gone, sir, and not trouble you.

Rom. So shalt thou show me friendship. Take thou that:
Live, and be prosperous: and farewell, good fellow.

Bal. [*Aside*] For all this same, I'll hide me hereabout:
His looks I fear, and his intents I doubt. [*Retires.*]

Rom. Thou detestable maw, thou womb of death,
Gorg'd with the dearest morsel of the earth,
Thus I enforce thy rotten jaws to open,
And, in despite, I'll cram thee with more food!
[*Opens the tomb.*]

Par. This is that banish'd haughty Montague,
That murd'red my love's cousin, with which grief,
It is supposed, the fair creature died;
And here is come to do some villanous shame
To the dead bodies: I will apprehend him.
[*Comes forward.*]
Stop thy unhallowed toil, vile Montague!
Can vengeance be pursued further than death?
Condemned villain, I do apprehend thee:
Obey, and go with me; for thou must die.

Rom. I must indeed; and therefore came I hither.
Good gentle youth, tempt not a desp'rate man;
Fly hence, and leave me: think upon these gone;
Let them affright thee. I beseech thee, youth,
Put not another sin upon my head,
By urging me to fury: O, be gone!
By heaven, I love thee better than myself;
For I come hither arm'd against myself:
Stay not, be gone; live, and hereafter say,
A madman's mercy bid thee run away.

Par. I do defy thy conjurations,
And apprehend thee for a felon here.

Rom. Wilt thou provoke me? then have at thee, boy!
[*They fight.*]

Page. O Lord, they fight! I will go call the watch.
[*Exit.*]

Par. O, I am slain! [*Falls.*] If thou be merciful,
Open the tomb, lay me with Juliet. [*Dies.*]

Rom. In faith, I will. Let me peruse this face.
Mercutio's kinsman, noble County Paris!
What said my man, when my betossed soul
Did not attend him as we rode? I think
He told me Paris should have married Juliet:
Said he not so? or did I dream it so?
Or am I mad, hearing him talk of Juliet,
To think it was so? O, give me thy hand,
One writ with me in sour misfortune's book!
I'll bury thee in a triumphant grave;
A grave? O, no! a lantern, slaught'red youth,
For here lies Juliet, and her beauty makes
This vault a feasting presence full of light.
Death, lie thou there, by a dead man interr'd.
[*Laying Paris in the tomb.*]
How oft when men are at the point of death
Have they been merry! which their keepers call
A lightning before death: O, how may I
Call this a lightning? O my love! my wife!
Death, that hath suck'd the honey of thy breath,
Hath had no power yet upon thy beauty:
Thou art not conquer'd; beauty's ensign yet
Is crimson in thy lips and in thy cheeks,

18. **nice,** trivial. **charge,** importance. 21. **iron crow,** crowbar.
SCENE III. 3. **all along,** at full length. 16. **obsequies,** dutiful acts performed in memory of the dead. 21. **muffle,** hide. 33. **jealous,** suspicious. 44. **doubt,** suspect; see glossary. 45. **womb,** belly. 68. **conjurations,** solemn appeals, which seem perhaps like incantations. 74. **peruse,** scrutinize. 84. **lantern,** a turret full of windows. 86. **presence,** presence chamber. 90. **lightning,** a shedding of light; also, a revival of the spirits. 110. **set up my everlasting rest.** See IV, v, 6.

And death's pale flag is not advanced there.
Tybalt, liest thou there in thy bloody sheet?
O, what more favour can I do to thee,
Than with that hand that cut thy youth in twain
To sunder his that was thine enemy?
Forgive me, cousin! Ah, dear Juliet,
Why art thou yet so fair? shall I believe
That unsubstantial Death is amorous,
And that the lean abhorred monster keeps
Thee here in dark to be his paramour?
For fear of that, I still will stay with thee;
And never from this pallet of dim night
Depart again: here, here will I remain
With worms that are thy chamber-maids; O, here
Will I set up my everlasting rest,
And shake the yoke of inauspicious stars
From this world-wearied flesh. Eyes, look your last!
Arms, take your last embrace! and, lips, O you
The doors of breath, seal with a righteous kiss
A dateless bargain to engrossing death!
Come, bitter conduct, come, unsavoury guide!
Thou desperate pilot, now at once run on
The dashing rocks thy sea-sick weary bark!
Here 's to my love! [*Drinks.*] O true apothecary!
Thy drugs are quick. Thus with a kiss I die. [*Dies.*]

Enter [*at the other end of the churchyard*] FRIAR [LAURENCE] *with lantern, crow, and spade.*

Fri. L. Saint Francis be my speed! how oft to-night
Have my old feet stumbled at graves! Who 's there?
Bal. Here 's one, a friend, and one that knows you well.
Fri. L. Bliss be upon you! Tell me, good my friend,
What torch is yond, that vainly lends his light
To grubs and eyeless skulls? as I discern,
It burneth in the Capels' monument.
Bal. It doth so, holy sir; and there 's my master,
One that you love.
Fri. L. Who is it?
Bal. Romeo.
Fri. L. How long hath he been there?
Bal. Full half an hour.
Fri. L. Go with me to the vault.
Bal. I dare not, sir:
My master knows not but I am gone hence;
And fearfully did menace me with death,
If I did stay to look on his intents.
Fri. L. Stay, then; I'll go alone. Fear comes upon me:
O, much I fear some ill unthrifty thing.
Bal. As I did sleep under this yew-tree here,
I dreamt my master and another fought,
And that my master slew him.
Fri. L. Romeo! [*Advances.*]
Alack, alack, what blood is this, which stains
The stony entrance of this sepulchre?
What mean these masterless and gory swords
To lie discolour'd by this place of peace? [*Enters the tomb.*]
Romeo! O, pale! Who else? what, Paris too?
And steep'd in blood? Ah, what an unkind hour
Is guilty of this lamentable chance!
The lady stirs. [*Juliet wakes.*]
Jul. O comfortable friar! where is my lord?
I do remember well where I should be,
And there I am. Where is my Romeo? [*Noise within.*]
Fri. L. I hear some noise. Lady, come from that nest
Of death, contagion, and unnatural sleep:
A greater power than we can contradict
Hath thwarted our intents. Come, come away.
Thy husband in thy bosom there lies dead;
And Paris too. Come, I'll dispose of thee
Among a sisterhood of holy nuns:
Stay not to question, for the watch is coming;
Come, go, good Juliet [*Noise again*], I dare no longer stay.
Jul. Go, get thee hence, for I will not away.
Exit [*Fri. L.*].
What 's here? a cup, clos'd in my true love's hand?
Poison, I see, hath been his timeless end:
O churl! drunk all, and left no friendly drop
To help me after? I will kiss thy lips;
Haply some poison yet doth hang on them,
To make me die with a restorative. [*Kisses him.*]
Thy lips are warm.
First Watch. [*Within*] Lead, boy: which way?
Jul. Yea, noise? then I'll be brief. O happy dagger!
[*Snatching Romeo's dagger.*]
This is thy sheath [*Stabs herself*]; there rust, and let me die. [*Falls on Romeo's body, and dies.*]

Enter [PARIS'] Boy *and* Watch.

Page. This is the place; there, where the torch doth burn.
First Watch. The ground is bloody; search about the churchyard:
Go, some of you, whoe'er you find attach.
Pitiful sight! here lies the county slain;
And Juliet bleeding, warm, and newly dead,
Who here hath lain these two days buried.
Go, tell the prince: run to the Capulets:
Raise up the Montagues: some others search:
We see the ground whereon these woes do lie;
But the true ground of all these piteous woes
We cannot without circumstance descry.

Enter [*some of the* Watch, *with*]ROMEO'S *Man* [BALTHASAR].

Sec. Watch. Here 's Romeo's man; we found him in the churchyard.
First Watch. Hold him in safety, till the prince come hither.

Enter FRIAR [LAURENCE], *and another* Watchman.

Third Watch. Here is a friar, that trembles, sighs, and weeps:
We took this mattock and this spade from him,
As he was coming from this churchyard side.
First Watch. A great suspicion: stay the friar too.

Enter the PRINCE [*and* Attendants].

Prince. What misadventure is so early up,
That calls our person from our morning's rest?

Enter CAPULET *and his* Wife [*with others*].

Cap. What should it be, that is so shriek'd abroad?
La. Cap. O, the people in the street cry Romeo,

The meaning is, "make my final determination," with allusion also to the idea of repose. 115. **dateless,** everlasting. **engrossing,** monopolizing. 121. **speed,** protector and assistant; see glossary. 122. **stumbled at graves,** a bad omen. 137. **yew-,** so Pope; Q_2F: *yong*.

162. **timeless,** everlasting, or untimely. 165. **Haply,** perhaps. 173. **attach,** arrest; see glossary.

Some Juliet, and some Paris; and all run,
With open outcry, toward our monument.
Prince. What fear is this which startles in our ears?
First Watch. Sovereign, here lies the County Paris slain;
And Romeo dead; and Juliet, dead before,
Warm and new kill'd.
Prince. Search, seek, and know how this foul murder comes.
First Watch. Here is a friar, and slaughter'd Romeo's man;
With instruments upon them, fit to open
These dead men's tombs.
Cap. O heavens! O wife, look how our daughter bleeds!
This dagger hath mista'en,—for, lo, his house
Is empty on the back of Montague,—
And it mis-sheathed in my daughter's bosom!
La. Cap. O me! this sight of death is as a bell,
That warns my old age to a sepulchre.

Enter MONTAGUE [*and others*].

Prince. Come, Montague; for thou art early up,
To see thy son and heir more early down.
Mon. Alas, my liege, my wife is dead tonight;
Grief of my son's exile hath stopp'd her breath:
What further woe conspires against mine age?
Prince. Look, and thou shalt see.
Mon. O thou untaught! what manners is in this,
To press before thy father to a grave?
Prince. Seal up the mouth of outrage for a while,
Till we can clear these ambiguities,
And know their spring, their head, their true descent;
And then will I be general of your woes,
And lead you even to death: meantime forbear,
And let mischance be slave to patience.
Bring forth the parties of suspicion.
Fri. L. I am the greatest, able to do least,
Yet most suspected, as the time and place
Doth make against me, of this direful murder:
And here I stand, both to impeach and purge
Myself condemned and myself excus'd.
Prince. Then say at once what thou dost know in this.
Fri. L. I will be brief, for my short date of breath
Is not so long as is a tedious tale.
Romeo, there dead, was husband to that Juliet;
And she, there dead, that Romeo's faithful wife:
I married them; and their stol'n marriage-day
Was Tybalt's dooms-day, whose untimely death
Banish'd the new-made bridegroom from this city,
For whom, and not for Tybalt, Juliet pin'd.
You, to remove that siege of grief from her,
Betroth'd and would have married her perforce
To County Paris: then comes she to me,
And, with wild looks, bid me devise some mean
To rid her from this second marriage,
Or in my cell there would she kill herself.
Then gave I her, so tutor'd by my art,
A sleeping potion; which so took effect
As I intended, for it wrought on her
The form of death: meantime I writ to Romeo,
That he should hither come as this dire night,
To help to take her from her borrowed grave,
Being the time the potion's force should cease.
But he which bore my letter, Friar John,
Was stay'd by accident, and yesternight
Return'd my letter back. Then all alone
At the prefixed hour of her waking,
Came I to take her from her kindred's vault;
Meaning to keep her closely at my cell,
Till I conveniently could send to Romeo:
But when I came, some minute ere the time
Of her awakening, here untimely lay
The noble Paris and true Romeo dead.
She wakes; and I entreated her come forth,
And bear this work of heaven with patience:
But then a noise did scare me from the tomb;
And she, too desperate, would not go with me,
But, as it seems, did violence on herself.
All this I know; and to the marriage
Her nurse is privy: and, if aught in this
Miscarried by my fault, let my old life
Be sacrific'd, some hour before his time,
Unto the rigour of severest law.
Prince. We still have known thee for a holy man.
Where 's Romeo's man? what can he say in this?
Bal. I brought my master news of Juliet's death;
And then in post he came from Mantua
To this same place, to this same monument.
This letter he early bid me give his father,
And threat'ned me with death, going in the vault,
If I departed not and left him there.
Prince. Give me the letter; I will look on it.
Where is the county's page, that rais'd the watch?
Sirrah, what made your master in this place?
Page. He came with flowers to strew his lady's grave;
And bid me stand aloof, and so I did:
Anon comes one with light to ope the tomb;
And by and by my master drew on him;
And then I ran away to call the watch.
Prince. This letter doth make good the friar's words,
Their course of love, the tidings of her death:
And here he writes that he did buy a poison
Of a poor 'pothecary, and therewithal
Came to this vault to die, and lie with Juliet.
Where be these enemies? Capulet! Montague!
See, what a scourge is laid upon your hate,
That heaven finds means to kill your joys with love.
And I for winking at your discords too
Have lost a brace of kinsmen: all are punish'd.
Cap. O brother Montague, give me thy hand:
This is my daughter's jointure, for no more
Can I demand.
Mon. But I can give thee more:
For I will raise her statue in pure gold;
That whiles Verona by that name is known,
There shall no figure at such rate be set
As that of true and faithful Juliet.
Cap. As rich shall Romeo's by his lady's lie;
Poor sacrifices of our enmity!
Prince. A glooming peace this morning with it brings;
The sun, for sorrow, will not show his head:
Go hence, to have more talk of these sad things;
Some shall be pardon'd, and some punished:
For never was a story of more woe
Than this of Juliet and her Romeo. [*Exeunt.*]

203. **house,** scabbard. 216. **outrage,** outcry. 226. **purge,** purify, cleanse. 247. **as this,** this very. 253. **prefixed,** agreed upon previously. 255. **closely,** secretly. 273. **post,** haste; see glossary. 297. **jointure,** marriage portion. 301. **rate,** value; see glossary.

A MIDSUMMER NIGHT'S DREAM

A Midsummer Night's Dream (c. 1594–1595) belongs to the period of transition from Shakespeare's experimental, imitative comedy to his mature, romantic, philosophical, "festive" vein. The play resembles Shakespeare's earlier attempts in its lighthearted presentation of love's tribulations. The two sets of lovers, scarcely distinguishable one from the other, are conventional figures. In them we find no hint of the profound self-discovery experienced by Beatrice and Benedick (*Much Ado about Nothing*) or Rosalind and Orlando (*As You Like It*). At the same time, this play develops the motif of love as an imaginative journey from reality into a fantasy world created by the artist, ending in return to a reality that has itself been partly transformed by the experience of the journey. (Shakespeare gives us an earlier hint of such an imaginary silvan landscape in *The Two Gentleman of Verona*.) This motif, with its contrasting worlds of social order and imaginative escape, remained an enduring vision for Shakespeare to the very last.

In construction, *A Midsummer Night's Dream* is a skillful interweaving of four plots involving four groups of characters: the court party of Duke Theseus, the four young lovers, the fairies, and the "rude mechanicals" or would-be actors. Mendelssohn's nineteenth-century incidental music evokes the contrasting textures of the various groups: Theseus' hunting horns and ceremonial wedding marches, the lovers' soaring and throbbing melodies, the fairies' pianissimo staccato, the tradesmen's clownish bassoon. Moreover, each plot is derived from its own set of source materials. The action involving Theseus and Hippolyta, for example, owes several details to Thomas North's translation (1579) of Plutarch's *Lives of the Noble Grecians and Romanes*, to Chaucer's *Knight's Tale* and perhaps his *Legend of Good Women*, and to Ovid's *Metamorphoses* (in the Latin text or in Golding's popular Elizabethan translation). The lovers' story, meanwhile, is Italianate and Ovidian in tone, and also in the broadest sense follows the conventions of plot in Plautus' and Terence's Roman comedies, although no particular source is known. Shakespeare's rich fairy lore, by contrast, is part folk tradition and part "learned." Although he certainly needed no books to tell him about mischievous spirits that could prevent churned milk from turning to butter, for instance, Shakespeare might have borrowed Oberon's name either from the French romance *Huon of Bordeaux* (translated into English by 1540), or from Greene's play *James IV* (c. 1591), or from Spenser's *The Fairie Queene*, II,i,8 (1590). Similarly, he may have taken Titania's name from the *Metamorphoses*, where it is used as an epithet for both Diana and Circe. Finally, for Bottom the Weaver and company, Shakespeare's primary inspiration was doubtless his own theatrical experience, although even here he is indebted to Ovid for the story of Pyramus and Thisbe, and probably to Apuleius' *Golden Ass* (translated by William Adlington, 1566) for Bottom's transformation.

Each of the four main plots in *A Midsummer Night's Dream* contains one or more pairs of lovers whose happiness has been frustrated by misunderstanding or parental opposition. Theseus and Hippolyta, once enemies in battle, become husband and wife; and their court marriage, constituting the "overplot" of the play, provides a framework for other dramatic actions that similarly oscillate between conflict and harmony. Theseus' actions are in fact instrumental in setting in motion and finally resolving the tribulations of the other characters. In the beginning of the play, for example, the lovers flee from Theseus' Athenian law; at the end, they are awakened by him from their dream. The king and queen of fairies come to Athens to celebrate Theseus' wedding, but quarrel with one another because Oberon has long been partial to Hippolyta, and Titania partial to Theseus. The Athenian tradesmen go off into the forest to rehearse their performance of "Pyramus and Thisbe" in anticipation of the wedding festivities.

The tragic love story of Pyramus and Thisbe, although it seems absurdly ill-suited for a wedding, simply reinforces by contrast the universal accord reuniting the other couples. Theseus, who originally won the Amazonian Hippolyta with his sword, doing her injuries, finally becomes the devoted husband. Hippolyta, legendary figure of woman's self-assertive longing to dominate the male, emerges as the happily submissive wife. The reconciliation of Oberon and Titania, meanwhile, reinforces this hierarchy of male over female. Having taught Titania a lesson concerning the changeling boy she tried to keep from him, Oberon relents and eventually frees Titania from her enchantment. Thus, the occasion of Theseus' wedding both initiates and brings to an end the difficulties that have beset the drama's various couples.

Despite Theseus' cheerful preoccupation with marriage, his court embodies at first a stern attitude toward young love. As administrator of the law, Theseus must accede to the remorseless demands of Hermia's father, Egeus. The inflexible Athenian law sides with parentage, age, wealth, and position against youth and romantic choice in love. The penalties are harsh: death, or perpetual virginity—and virginity is presented in this comedy (despite the nobly chaste examples of Christ, St. Paul, and Queen Elizabeth) as a fate worse than death. Egeus is a "blocking" or "heavy" character, the enemy of festival, the *alazon* of Plautus' or Terence's Latin versions of Grecian New Comedy. Indeed, the lovers' story is distantly derived from that New Comedy, which conventionally celebrated the triumph of young love over the machinations of age and wealth. Lysander reminds us that

A Midsommer nights dreame.

As it hath beene sundry times pub-
lickely acted, by the Right honoura-
ble, the Lord Chamberlaine his
seruants.

Written by William Shakespeare.

¶ Imprinted at London, for *Thomas Fisher*, and are to
be soulde at his shoppe, at the Signe of the White Hart,
in *Fleetestreete.* 1600.

The title page of the first quarto of A Midsummer Night's Dream, *published in 1600.*

"the course of true love never did run smooth," and he sees its enemies as being chiefly external: the conflicting interests of parents or friends, or mismating in respect of years and blood, or war, or death, or sickness (I,i). This description clearly applies to "Pyramus and Thisbe," and it is tested by the action of *A Midsummer Night's Dream* as a whole (as well as by other early Shakespearean plays, such as *Romeo and Juliet*). The archetypal story, whether ending happily or sadly, is an evocation of love's difficulties in the face of social hostility and indifference.

While Shakespeare uses several "New Comedy" elements in setting up the basic conflicts of his drama, however, he also introduces important modifications from the very beginning. For example, he discards one conventional confrontation of classical and neoclassical comedy in which the heroine must choose between an old, wealthy suitor supported by her family, and the young but impecunious darling of her heart. Lysander is equal to his rival in social position, income, and attractiveness. Egeus' demand, therefore —that Hermia marry Demetrius rather than Lysander—seems simply arbitrary and unjust. Shakespeare emphasizes in this way the irrationality of Egeus' harsh insistence on being obeyed, and Theseus' rather complacent acceptance of the law's inequity. Spurned by an unfeeling social order, Lysander and Hermia are compelled to elope. To be sure, Egeus proves at the last to be no formidable threat; even he must admit the logic of permitting the lovers to couple as they ultimately desire. Thus, the obstacles to love are from the start seen as fundamentally superficial and indeed almost whimsical. Egeus is as "heavy" a villain as we are likely to find in this *jeu d'esprit*. Moreover, the very irrationality of his position paves the way for an ultimate resolution of the conflict. Nevertheless, by the end of Act I the supposedly rational world of conformity and duty has, by its customary insensitivity to youthful happiness, set in motion a temporary escape to a fantasy world where the law cannot reach.

In the forest, all the lovers—including Titania and Bottom—undergo a transforming experience engineered by the mischievous Puck. This experience demonstrates the universal power of love, which can overcome the queen of fairies as readily as the lowliest of men. It also suggests the irrational nature of love and its affinity to enchantment, witchcraft, and even madness. Love is seen as an affliction taken in through the frail senses, particularly the eyes. When it strikes, the victim cannot choose but to embrace the object of his dotage. By his amusing miscalculations, Puck shuffles the four interchangeable lovers through various permutations with mathematical predictability. First, two gentlemen compete for one lady, leaving the second lady sadly unrequited in love; then everything is at cross-purposes, with each gentleman pursuing the lady who is in love with the other man; then the two gentlemen compete for the lady they both previously ignored. Finally, of course, Jack shall have his Jill—whom else should he have? The couples are properly united, as they evidently were at some time prior to the commencement of the play when Demetrius had made love to Helena, and Lysander and Hermia had preferred one another.

We sense that Puck is by no means unhappy about his knavish errors. "Lord, what fools these mortals be!" Along with the other fairies in this play, Puck takes his being and his complex motivation from many denizens of the invisible world. As the agent of all-powerful love, Puck compares himself to Cupid. The love-juice he administers comes from Cupid's flower, "love-in-idleness." Like Cupid, Puck acts at the behest of the gods, and yet he wields a power that the chiefest gods themselves cannot resist. Essentially, however, Puck is less a classical love deity than a prankish folk spirit, such as we find in every folklore: gremlin, leprechaun, hobgoblin, and the like. Titania's fairies recognize Puck as one who, for example, can deprive a beer barrel of its yeast so that it spoils rather than ferments. Puck characterizes himself as a practical joker, pulling stools out from behind old ladies.

Folk wisdom imagines the inexplicable and unaccountable events in life to be caused by invisible forces who laugh at man's discomfiture and mock him for mere sport. Puck is related to such mysterious forces dwelling in nature, who must be placated with gifts and ceremonies. Although Shakespeare restricts Puck to a benign sportive role in dealing with the lovers or with Titania, the actual folk legends about Puck mentioned in this play are frequently disquieting. Puck is known to "mislead night-wanderers, laughing at their harm"; indeed, he demonstrates as much with Demetrius and Lysander, engineering a confrontation that greatly oppresses the lovers even though we perceive the sportful intent. At the play's end, Puck links himself and his fellows with the ghoulish apparitions of death and night: wolves howling at the moon, screech-owls, shrouds, gaping graves. Associations of this sort go beyond mere sportiveness to the witchcraft and demonology practiced by spirits rising from the dead. Even Oberon's assurance that the fairies will bless all the marriages of this play, shielding their progeny against mole, harelip, or other birth defects, carries the implication that such misfortunes can be caused by offended spirits. The magic of this play is thus explicitly related to deep irrational powers and forces capable of doing great harm, although of course the spirit of comedy keeps such veiled threats safely at a distance in *A Midsummer Night's Dream*.

Oberon and Titania, in their view of the relationship between gods and men, reflect yet another aspect of the fairies' spiritual ancestry—one more nearly related to the gods and goddesses of the world of Greek mythology. The king and queen of fairies assert that, because they are immortal, their regal quarrels in love must inevitably have dire consequences on earth, either in the love relationship of Theseus and Hippolyta or in the management of the weather. Floods, storms, diseases, and sterility abound, "And this same progeny of evils comes From our debate, from our dissension; We are their parents and original" (II,i). Even though this motif of the gods' quarreling over human affairs is Homeric or Virgilian in conception, however, the motif in this lighthearted play is more nearly mock-epic than truly epic. The consequences of the gods' anger are simply mirth-provoking, most of all in Titania's love affair with Bottom the Weaver.

The "Bottom" incident is recognizably a "metamorphosis" in a playfully classical mode, a love affair between a god and an earthly creature, underscoring man's dual nature. Bottom is himself half man and half beast, although he is ludicrously unlike the centaurs, mermaids, and other half-human beings of classical mythology. Whereas the head should be the aspiring part of him and his body the bestial part, Bottom wears an ass's knoll on his shoulders. His very name suggests the solid nature of his fleshly being ("bottom" is also appropriately a weaving term). He and Titania represent the opposites of flesh and spirit.

A play bringing together fairies and mortals inevitably raises questions of illusion and reality. These questions reach their greatest intensity in the presentation of "Pyramus and Thisbe." This play within a play focuses our attention on the familiarly Shakespearean metaphor of art as illusion, and of the world itself as a stage on which men and women are merely players. As Theseus observes, apologizing for the ineptness of the tradesmen's performance, "the best in this kind are but shadows." That is, Shakespeare's own play is of the same order of reality as Bottom's play. Puck too, in his epilogue, enjoins any spectator offended by Shakespeare's play to dismiss it as a mere dream—as, indeed, the play's very title suggests. Theseus goes even further, linking dream to the essence of imaginative art, although he does so in a clearly critical and rather patronizing way. The artist, he says, is like the madman or the lover in his frenzy of inspiration, giving "to airy nothing A local habitation and a name" (V,i). Artistic achievements are too unsubstantial for Theseus; from his point of view they are the products of mere fantasy and irrationality, mere myths or fairy stories or old wives' tales. Behind this critical persona defending the "real" world of his court, however, we can hear Shakespeare's characteristically self-effacing. defense of "dreaming."

COURTESY OF THE NEWBERRY LIBRARY, CHICAGO

In an engraving from about 1800 of Act III, scene i, the buffoonish craftsmen surround Bottom the Weaver, who wears the ass's head magically placed there by the mischievous Puck, during their rehearsal of "Pyramus and Thisbe."

"Pyramus and Thisbe," like the larger play surrounding it, attempts to body forth "the forms of things unknown." The play within the play gives us personified moonshine, a speaking wall, and an apologetic lion. Of course it is an absurdly bad play, full of lame epithets, bombastic alliteration, and bathos. In part Shakespeare is here satirizing the abuses of a theatre he had helped reform. The players' chosen method of portraying imaginative matters is ridiculous, and calls forth deliciously wry comments from the courtly spectators on stage: "Would you desire lime and hair to speak better?" At the same time, those spectators on stage are actors in our play. Their sarcasms render them less sympathetic in our eyes; we see that their kind of sophistication is as restrictive as it is illuminating. Bottom and his friends have conceived moonshine and lion as they did because these simple men are so responsive to the terrifying power of art. A lion might frighten the ladies and get them all hanged. Theirs is a primitive faith, naive but strong, and in this sense it contrasts favorably with the jaded rationality of the court party. Theseus' valuable reminder, that all art is only "illusion," is thus juxtaposed with Bottom's insistence that imaginative art has a reality of its own.

Theseus above all embodies the sophistication of the court in his description of art as a frenzy of seething brains. Genially scoffing at "These antic fables" and "these fairy toys," he is unmoved by the lovers' account of their dreamlike experience. Limited by his own skepticism, Theseus has never experienced the enchantment of the forest. Even Bottom can claim more than that, for he has been lover of the queen of fairies; and, although his language cannot adequately describe the experience, Bottom will see it made into a ballad called "Bottom's Dream." Shakespeare leaves the status of his fantasy world deliberately complex; Theseus' lofty denial of dreaming is too abrupt. Even if the Athenian forest world can be made only momentarily substantial in the artifact of Shakespeare's play, we as audience respond to its tantalizing vision. We emerge back into our lives wondering if the fairies were "real," that is, puzzled by the relationship of these artistic symbols to the tangible concreteness of our daily existence. Unless our perceptions have been thus enlarged by sharing in the author's "dream," we have not surrendered to the imaginative experience.

A MIDSUMMER NIGHT'S DREAM

[*Dramatis Personae*

THESEUS, Duke of Athens.
EGEUS, *father to Hermia.*
LYSANDER, } *in love with Hermia.*
DEMETRIUS, }
PHILOSTRATE, *master of the revels to Theseus.*

QUINCE, *a carpenter.*
SNUG, *a joiner.*
BOTTOM, *a weaver.*
FLUTE, *a bellows-mender.*
SNOUT, *a tinker.*
STARVELING, *a tailor.*

HIPPOLYTA, *queen of the Amazons, betrothed to Theseus.*
HERMIA, *daughter to Egeus, in love with Lysander.*
HELENA, *in love with Demetrius.*

OBERON, *king of the fairies.*
TITANIA, *queen of the fairies.*
PUCK, *or Robin Goodfellow.*
PEASEBLOSSOM, }
COBWEB, } *fairies.*
MOTH, }
MUSTARDSEED, }
Other fairies attending their king and queen.

Attendants on Theseus and Hippolyta.

SCENE: *Athens, and a wood near it.*]

[ACT I.

SCENE I. *Athens. The palace of* THESEUS.]

Enter THESEUS, HIPPOLYTA, [PHILOSTRATE,] *with others.*

The. Now, fair Hippolyta, our nuptial hour
Draws on apace; four happy days bring in
Another moon: but, O, methinks, how slow
This old moon wanes! she lingers my desires,
Like to a step-dame or a dowager
Long withering out a young man's revenue.
Hip. Four days will quickly steep themselves in night;
Four nights will quickly dream away the time;
And then the moon, like to a silver bow
New-bent in heaven, shall behold the night
Of our solemnities.
The. Go, Philostrate,
Stir up the Athenian youth to merriments;
Awake the pert and nimble spirit of mirth:
Turn melancholy forth to funerals;
The pale companion is not for our pomp.
[*Exit Philostrate.*]
Hippolyta, I woo'd thee with my sword,
And won thy love, doing thee injuries;
But I will wed thee in another key,
With pomp, with triumph and with revelling.

Enter EGEUS *and his Daughter* HERMIA, *and* LYSANDER, *and* DEMETRIUS.

Ege. Happy be Theseus, our renowned duke!
The. Thanks, good Egeus: what 's the news with thee?
Ege. Full of vexation come I, with complaint
Against my child, my daughter Hermia.
Stand forth, Demetrius. My noble lord,
This man hath my consent to marry her.
Stand forth, Lysander: and, my gracious duke,
This man hath bewitch'd the bosom of my child:
Thou, thou, Lysander, thou hast given her rhymes
And interchang'd love-tokens with my child:
Thou hast by moonlight at her window sung
With feigning voice verses of feigning love,
And stol'n the impression of her fantasy
With bracelets of thy hair, rings, gawds, conceits,
Knacks, trifles, nosegays, sweetmeats, messengers
Of strong prevailment in unhardened youth:
With cunning hast thou filch'd my daughter's heart,
Turn'd her obedience, which is due to me,
To stubborn harshness: and, my gracious duke,
Be it so she will not here before your grace
Consent to marry with Demetrius,
I beg the ancient privilege of Athens,
As she is mine, I may dispose of her:
Which shall be either to this gentleman
Or to her death, according to our law
Immediately provided in that case.
The. What say you, Hermia? be advis'd, fair maid:
To you your father should be as a god;
One that compos'd your beauties, yea, and one
To whom you are but as a form in wax
By him imprinted and within his power
To leave the figure or disfigure it.
Demetrius is a worthy gentleman.
Her. So is Lysander.
The. In himself he is;
But in this kind, wanting your father's voice,
The other must be held the worthier.
Her. I would my father look'd but with my eyes.
The. Rather your eyes must with his judgement look.
Her. I do entreat your grace to pardon me.
I know not by what power I am made bold,
Nor how it may concern my modesty,
In such a presence here to plead my thoughts;
But I beseech your grace that I may know
The worst that may befall me in this case,

ACT I. SCENE I. 5. **step-dame,** stepmother. **dowager,** widow with a jointure or dower. 13. **pert,** lively, brisk. 19. **triumph,** public festivity. 27. **bosom,** here thought of as the seat of the passions. 32. **And . . . fantasy,** made her fall in love with you (imprinting your image on her fancy) by dishonest means; see *fantasy* in glossary. 33. **gawds,** playthings. 34. **Knacks,** knickknacks. 35. **prevailment,** power to persuade. 45. **Immediately,** expressly. 51. **disfigure,** obliterate. 54. **kind,** respect; see glossary. **voice,** authority, approval. 60. **concern,** befit.

If I refuse to wed Demetrius.
The. Either to die the death or to abjure
For ever the society of men.
Therefore, fair Hermia, question your desires;
Know of your youth, examine well your blood,
Whether, if you yield not to your father's choice,
You can endure the livery of a nun,
For aye to be in shady cloister mew'd,
To live a barren sister all your life,
Chanting faint hymns to the cold fruitless moon.
Thrice-blessed they that master so their blood,
To undergo such maiden pilgrimage;
But earthlier happy is the rose distill'd,
Than that which withering on the virgin thorn
Grows, lives and dies in single blessedness.
Her. So will I grow, so live, so die, my lord,
Ere I will yield my virgin patent up
Unto his lordship, whose unwished yoke
My soul consents not to give sovereignty.
The. Take time to pause; and, by the next new moon—
The sealing-day betwixt my love and me,
For everlasting bond of fellowship—
Upon that day either prepare to die
For disobedience to your father's will,
Or else to wed Demetrius, as he would;
Or on Diana's altar to protest
For aye austerity and single life.
Dem. Relent, sweet Hermia: and, Lysander, yield
Thy crazed title to my certain right.
Lys. You have her father's love, Demetrius;
Let me have Hermia's: do you marry him.
Ege. Scornful Lysander! true, he hath my love,
And what is mine my love shall render him.
And she is mine, and all my right of her
I do estate unto Demetrius.
Lys. I am, my lord, as well deriv'd as he,
As well possess'd; my love is more than his;
My fortunes every way as fairly rank'd,
If not with vantage, as Demetrius';
And, which is more than all these boasts can be,
I am belov'd of beauteous Hermia:
Why should not I then prosecute my right?
Demetrius, I'll avouch it to his head,
Made love to Nedar's daughter, Helena,
And won her soul; and she, sweet lady, dotes,
Devoutly dotes, dotes in idolatry,
Upon this spotted and inconstant man.
The. I must confess that I have heard so much,
And with Demetrius thought to have spoke thereof;
But, being over-full of self-affairs,
My mind did lose it. But, Demetrius, come;
And come, Egeus; you shall go with me,
I have some private schooling for you both.
For you, fair Hermia, look you arm yourself
To fit your fancies to your father's will;
Or else the law of Athens yields you up—
Which by no means we may extenuate—
To death, or to a vow of single life.
Come, my Hippolyta: what cheer, my love?
Demetrius and Egeus, go along:
I must employ you in some business
Against our nuptial and confer with you
Of something nearly that concerns yourselves.
Ege. With duty and desire we follow you.
Exeunt [*all but Lysander and Hermia*].
Lys. How now, my love! why is your cheek so pale?
How chance the roses there do fade so fast?
Her. Belike for want of rain, which I could well
Beteem them from the tempest of my eyes.
Lys. Ay me! for aught that I could ever read,
Could ever hear by tale or history,
The course of true love never did run smooth;
But, either it was different in blood,—
Her. O cross! too high to be enthrall'd to low.
Lys. Or else misgraffed in respect of years,—
Her. O spite! too old to be engag'd to young.
Lys. Or else it stood upon the choice of friends,—
Her. O hell! to choose love by another's eyes.
Lys. Or, if there were a sympathy in choice,
War, death, or sickness did lay siege to it,
Making it momentany as a sound,
Swift as a shadow, short as any dream;
Brief as the lightning in the collied night,
That, in a spleen, unfolds both heaven and earth,
And ere a man hath power to say 'Behold!'
The jaws of darkness do devour it up:
So quick bright things come to confusion.
Her. If then true lovers have been ever cross'd,
It stands as an edict in destiny:
Then let us teach our trial patience,
Because it is a customary cross,
As due to love as thoughts and dreams and sighs,
Wishes and tears, poor fancy's followers.
Lys. A good persuasion: therefore, hear me, Hermia.
I have a widow aunt, a dowager
Of great revenue, and she hath no child:
From Athens is her house remote seven leagues;
And she respects me as her only son.
There, gentle Hermia, may I marry thee;
And to that place the sharp Athenian law
Cannot pursue us. If thou lovest me then,
Steal forth thy father's house to-morrow night;
And in the wood, a league without the town,
Where I did meet thee once with Helena,
To do observance to a morn of May,
There will I stay for thee.
Her. My good Lysander!
I swear to thee, by Cupid's strongest bow,
By his best arrow with the golden head,
By the simplicity of Venus' doves,
By that which knitteth souls and prospers loves,
And by that fire which burn'd the Carthage queen,
When the false Troyan under sail was seen,
By all the vows that ever men have broke,

69. **Whether,** one syllable, like "where." 71. **mew'd,** shut in (as used of a hawk); see glossary. 74. **blood,** supposed source of passions; see glossary. 76. **earthlier happy,** happier as respects this world. 80. **patent,** privilege. 89. **protest,** vow. 92. **crazed,** unsound. 98. **estate unto,** settle or bestow upon. 99. **deriv'd,** descended, i.e., as well born; see glossary. 100. **As well possess'd,** possessed of as much wealth; see *possess* in glossary. 101. **fairly,** handsomely; see glossary. 102. **vantage,** superiority; see glossary. 106. **avouch . . . head,** declare it to his face. 117. **look,** take care; see glossary. 118. **fancies,** likings, thoughts of love. 120. **extenuate,** mitigate. 125. **Against,** in preparation for.

126. **nearly that,** that closely. 127. **duty,** reverence; see glossary. 130. **Belike,** very likely. 131. **Beteem,** grant. 137. **misgraffed,** badly matched. 143. **momentany,** lasting but a moment. 145. **collied,** blackened, darkened. 146. **spleen,** swift impulse. **unfolds,** discloses; see glossary. 149. **confusion,** ruin, destruction; see glossary. 150. **ever cross'd,** always tormented. 155. **fancy's,** amorous passion's; see glossary. 160. **respects,** regards, considers; see glossary. 167. **do . . . May,** perform the ceremonies of May Day. 171-251. **By the simplicity,** etc. The style here shifts to the rhymed couplet. While Theseus was on the scene and the business was serious, the play was

In number more than ever women spoke,
In that same place thou hast appointed me,
To-morrow truly will I meet with thee.

Lys. Keep promise, love. Look, here comes Helena.

Enter HELENA.

Her. God speed fair Helena! whither away?

Hel. Call you me fair? that fair again unsay.
Demetrius loves your fair: O happy fair!
Your eyes are lode-stars; and your tongue 's sweet air
More tuneable than lark to shepherd's ear,
When wheat is green, when hawthorn buds appear.
Sickness is catching: O, were favour so,
Yours would I catch, fair Hermia, ere I go;
My ear should catch your voice, my eye your eye,
My tongue should catch your tongue's sweet melody.
Were the world mine, Demetrius being bated,
The rest I 'ld give to be to you translated.
O, teach me how you look, and with what art
You sway the motion of Demetrius' heart.

Her. I frown upon him, yet he loves me still.

Hel. O that your frowns would teach my smiles such skill!

Her. I give him curses, yet he gives me love.

Hel. O that my prayers could such affection move!

Her. The more I hate, the more he follows me.

Hel. The more I love, the more he hateth me.

Her. His folly, Helena, is no fault of mine.

Hel. None, but your beauty: would that fault were mine!

Her. Take comfort: he no more shall see my face;
Lysander and myself will fly this place.
Before the time I did Lysander see,
Seem'd Athens as a paradise to me:
O, then, what graces in my love do dwell,
That he hath turn'd a heaven unto a hell!

Lys. Helen, to you our minds we will unfold:
To-morrow night, when Phœbe doth behold
Her silver visage in the wat'ry glass,
Decking with liquid pearl the bladed grass,
A time that lovers' flights doth still conceal,
Through Athens' gates have we devis'd to steal.

Her. And in the wood, where often you and I
Upon faint primrose-beds were wont to lie,
Emptying our bosoms of their counsel sweet,
There my Lysander and myself shall meet;
And thence from Athens turn away our eyes,
To seek new friends and stranger companies.
Farewell, sweet playfellow: pray thou for us;
And good luck grant thee thy Demetrius!
Keep word, Lysander: we must starve our sight
From lovers' food till morrow deep midnight.

Lys. I will, my Hermia. *Exit Herm.*
Helena, adieu:
As you on him, Demetrius dote on you! *Exit Lys.*

Hel. How happy some o'er other some can be!
Through Athens I am thought as fair as she.
But what of that? Demetrius thinks not so;
He will not know what all but he do know:
And as he errs, doting on Hermia's eyes,
So I, admiring of his qualities:
Things base and vile, holding no quantity,
Love can transpose to form and dignity:
Love looks not with the eyes, but with the mind;
And therefore is wing'd Cupid painted blind:
Nor hath Love's mind of any judgement taste;
Wings and no eyes figure unheedy haste:
And therefore is Love said to be a child,
Because in choice he is so oft beguil'd.
As waggish boys in game themselves forswear,
So the boy Love is perjur'd every where:
For ere Demetrius look'd on Hermia's eyne,
He hail'd down oaths that he was only mine;
And when this hail some heat from Hermia felt,
So he dissolv'd, and show'rs of oaths did melt.
I will go tell him of fair Hermia's flight:
Then to the wood will he to-morrow night
Pursue her; and for this intelligence
If I have thanks, it is a dear expense:
But herein mean I to enrich my pain,
To have his sight thither and back again. *Exit.*

[SCENE II. *Athens.* QUINCE'S *house.*]

Enter QUINCE *the Carpenter, and* SNUG *the Joiner, and* BOTTOM *the Weaver, and* FLUTE *the Bellows Mender, and* SNOUT *the Tinker, and* STARVELING *the Tailor.*

Quin. Is all our company here?

Bot. You were best to call them generally, man by man, according to the scrip.

Quin. Here is the scroll of every man's name, which is thought fit, through all Athens, to play in our interlude before the duke and the duchess, on his wedding-day at night.

Bot. First, good Peter Quince, say what the play treats on, then read the names of the actors, and so grow to a point.

Quin. Marry, our play is, The most lamentable comedy, and most cruel death of Pyramus and Thisby.

Bot. A very good piece of work, I assure you, and a merry. Now, good Peter Quince, call forth your actors by the scroll. Masters, spread yourselves.

Quin. Answer as I call you. Nick Bottom, the weaver.

Bot. Ready. Name what part I am for, and proceed.

Quin. You, Nick Bottom, are set down for Pyramus.

Bot. What is Pyramus? a lover, or a tyrant?

Quin. A lover, that kills himself most gallant for love.

Bot. That will ask some tears in the true performing of it: if I do it, let the audience look to their eyes; I will move storms, I will condole in some measure. To the rest: yet my chief humour is for a tyrant: I

in blank verse. The transition indicates the lighter import of the conversation of the lovers. 173, 174. **Carthage queen, false Troyan.** According to Virgil (*Aeneid* iv.) Dido, queen of Carthage, slew herself after desertion by the Trojan hero Aeneas. 182. **fair,** beauty; see glossary. 183. **lode-stars,** stars of guidance. 184. **tuneable,** tuneful. 186. **favour,** appearance; or, affection. 190. **bated,** excepted; see glossary. 193. **motion,** impulse; see glossary. 194-201. **I . . . mine.** Each character speaks one line of the dialogue. This artificiality of style is called stichomythia; it is characteristic of classical drama. 197. **affection,** passion; see glossary. **move,** arouse; see glossary. 209. **Phœbe,** Diana, the moon. 215. **faint,** pale. 231. **admiring of,** wondering at; see glossary. 237. **figure,** are a symbol of. 242. **eyne,** eyes; old form of plural. 249. **a dear expense,** a thing which will be costly to me; see *dear* in glossary.

SCENE II. 2. **generally,** Bottom's blunder for "severally." 3. **scrip,** writing, written list. 10. **grow to,** come to. 11. **Marry,** a mild oath; see glossary. 29. **condole,** grieve; here in some blundering sense. 30. **humour,** inclination, whim; see glossary.

could play Ercles rarely, or a part to tear a cat in, to make all split.

The raging rocks
And shivering shocks
Shall break the locks
Of prison gates;
And Phibbus' car
Shall shine from far
And make and mar
The foolish Fates.

This was lofty! Now name the rest of the players. This is Ercles' vein, a tyrant's vein; a lover is more condoling.

Quin. Francis Flute, the bellows-mender.

Flu. Here, Peter Quince.

Quin. Flute, you must take Thisby on you.

Flu. What is Thisby? a wandering knight?

Quin. It is the lady that Pyramus must love.

Flu. Nay, faith, let not me play a woman; I have a beard coming.

Quin. That 's all one: you shall play it in a mask, and you may speak as small as you will.

Bot. An I may hide my face, let me play Thisby too, I'll speak in a monstrous little voice, 'Thisne, Thisne;' 'Ah Pyramus, my lover dear! thy Thisby dear, and lady dear!'

Quin. No, no; you must play Pyramus: and, Flute, you Thisby.

Bot. Well, proceed.

Quin. Robin Starveling, the tailor.

Star. Here, Peter Quince.

Quin. Robin Starveling, you must play Thisby's mother. Tom Snout, the tinker.

Snout. Here, Peter Quince.

Quin. You, Pyramus' father: myself, Thisby's father. Snug, the joiner; you, the lion's part: and, I hope, here is a play fitted.

Snug. Have you the lion's part written? pray you, if it be, give it me, for I am slow of study.

Quin. You may do it extempore, for it is nothing but roaring.

Bot. Let me play the lion too: I will roar, that I will do any man's heart good to hear me; I will roar, that I will make the duke say 'Let him roar again, let him roar again.'

Quin. An you should do it too terribly, you would fright the duchess and the ladies, that they would shriek; and that were enough to hang us all.

All. That would hang us, every mother's son.

Bot. I grant you, friends, if that you should fright the ladies out of their wits, they would have no more discretion but to hang us: but I will aggravate my voice so that I will roar you as gently as any sucking dove; I will roar you an 'twere any nightingale.

Quin. You can play no part but Pyramus; for Pyramus is a sweet-faced man; a proper man, as one shall see in a summer's day; a most lovely gentleman-like man: therefore you must needs play Pyramus.

Bot. Well, I will undertake it. What beard were I best to play it in?

Quin. Why, what you will.

Bot. I will discharge it in either your straw-colour beard, your orange-tawny beard, your purple-in-grain beard, or your French-crown-colour beard, your perfect yellow.

Quin. Some of your French crowns have no hair at all, and then you will play barefaced. But, masters, here are your parts: and I am to entreat you, request you and desire you, to con them by to-morrow night; and meet me in the palace wood, a mile without the town, by moonlight; there will we rehearse, for if we meet in the city, we shall be dogged with company, and our devices known. In the meantime I will draw a bill of properties, such as our play wants. I pray you, fail me not.

Bot. We will meet; and there we may rehearse most obscenely and courageously. Take pains; be perfect: adieu.

Quin. At the duke's oak we meet.

Bot. Enough; hold or cut bow-strings. *Exeunt.*

[ACT II.

SCENE I. *A wood near Athens.*]

Enter a Fairy *at one door, and* ROBIN GOODFELLOW [PUCK] *at another.*

Puck. How now, spirit! whither wander you?

Fai. Over hill, over dale,
Thorough bush, thorough brier,
Over park, over pale,
Thorough flood, thorough fire,
I do wander every where,
Swifter than the moon's sphere;
And I serve the fairy queen,
To dew her orbs upon the green.
The cowslips tall her pensioners be:
In their gold coats spots you see;
Those be rubies, fairy favours,
In those freckles live their savours:
I must go seek some dewdrops here
And hang a pearl in every cowslip's ear.
Farewell, thou lob of spirits; I'll be gone:
Our queen and all her elves come here anon.

Puck. The king doth keep his revels here to-night:
Take heed the queen come not within his sight;
For Oberon is passing fell and wrath,
Because that she as her attendant hath
A lovely boy, stolen from an Indian king;
She never had so sweet a changeling;
And jealous Oberon would have the child
Knight of his train, to trace the forests wild;

31. **Ercles,** Hercules, a popular character in Tudor drama. From Seneca's *Hercules Furens* had come the tradition of ranting in this part, as in the case of Herod in the mystery plays. **tear a cat,** proverbial for "rant." 32. **make all split,** proverbial for "cause a commotion." 37. **Phibbus',** Phoebus'. 47. **wandering knight,** knight-errant. 54. **An,** if; see glossary. 84. **aggravate,** Bottom's blunder for "diminish." 88. **proper,** handsome; see glossary. 95. **discharge,** perform. 97. **purple-in-grain,** very deep red. **French-crown-colour,** color of a French crown; a gold coin. 99. **crowns,** heads bald from syphilis, the "French disease." 103. **con,** learn by heart. 107. **devices,** plans. 111. **obscenely,** Bottom's blunder for "obscurely" (?) 114. **hold . . . bow-strings,** an archer's expression not definitely explained, but easy to understand; Chambers suggests, "keep your promises, or give up the play."

ACT II. SCENE I. 3. **Thorough,** through; see glossary. 9. **orbs,** fairy rings. 10. **pensioners,** bodyguards of the sovereign; possible allusion to Queen Elizabeth's fifty gentlemen pensioners. 13. **savours,** sweet smells. 16. **lob,** country bumpkin. 17. **anon,** at once; see glossary. 20. **passing fell,** exceedingly angry; see *passing* in glossary. **wrath,** wrathful. 23. **changeling,** child left by fairies in exchange for one stolen; here, the stolen child. 26. **perforce,** forcibly; see glossary. 30. **square,** quarrel. 33. **shrewd,** mischievous; see glossary. 34. **Robin Goodfellow,** a mischievous household spirit of very ancient folklore; Shakespeare associates him with fairies. 35. **villagery,** villages or villagers collectively. 36. **quern,** handmill. 38. **sometime,** at times; see glossary. **barm,** yeast, froth. 47. **gossip's bowl,** drink of gossiping women. 48. **crab,** crab apple. 50. **dewlap,** loose skin on neck.

But she perforce withholds the loved boy,
Crowns him with flowers and makes him all her joy:
And now they never meet in grove or green,
By fountain clear, or spangled starlight sheen,
But they do square, that all their elves for fear
Creep into acorn-cups and hide them there.

Fai. Either I mistake your shape and making quite,
Or else you are that shrewd and knavish sprite
Call'd Robin Goodfellow: are not you he
That frights the maidens of the villagery;
Skim milk, and sometimes labour in the quern
And bootless make the breathless housewife churn;
And sometime make the drink to bear no barm;
Mislead night-wanderers, laughing at their harm?
Those that Hobgoblin call you and sweet Puck,
You do their work, and they shall have good luck:
Are you not he?

Puck. Thou speakest aright;
I am that merry wanderer of the night.
I jest to Oberon and make him smile
When I a fat and bean-fed horse beguile,
Neighing in likeness of a filly foal:
And sometime lurk I in a gossip's bowl,
In very likeness of a roasted crab,
And when she drinks, against her lips I bob
And on her withered dewlap pour the ale.
The wisest aunt, telling the saddest tale,
Sometime for three-foot stool mistaketh me;
Then slip I from her bum, down topples she,
And 'tailor' cries, and falls into a cough;
And then the whole quire hold their hips and laugh,
And waxen in their mirth and neeze and swear
A merrier hour was never wasted there.
But, room, fairy! here comes Oberon.

Fai. And here my mistress. Would that he were gone!

Enter [OBERON] *the King of Fairies at one door, with his train; and* [TITANIA] *the Queen at another, with hers.*

Obe. Ill met by moonlight, proud Titania.

Tita. What, jealous Oberon! Fairy, skip hence:
I have forsworn his bed and company.

Obe. Tarry, rash wanton: am not I thy lord?

Tita. Then I must be thy lady: but I know
When thou hast stolen away from fairy land,
And in the shape of Corin sat all day,
Playing on pipes of corn and versing love
To amorous Phillida. Why art thou here,
Come from the farthest steep of India?
But that, forsooth, the bouncing Amazon,
Your buskin'd mistress and your warrior love,
To Theseus must be wedded, and you come
To give their bed joy and prosperity.

Obe. How canst thou thus for shame, Titania,
Glance at my credit with Hippolyta,
Knowing I know thy love to Theseus?
Didst thou not lead him through the glimmering night
From Perigenia, whom he ravished?
And make him with fair Ægles break his faith,
With Ariadne and Antiopa?

Tita. These are the forgeries of jealousy:
And never, since the middle summer's spring,
Met we on hill, in dale, forest or mead,
By paved fountain or by rushy brook,
Or in the beached margent of the sea,
To dance our ringlets to the whistling wind,
But with thy brawls thou hast disturb'd our sport.
Therefore the winds, piping to us in vain,
As in revenge, have suck'd up from the sea
Contagious fogs; which falling in the land
Have every pelting river made so proud
That they have overborne their continents:
The ox hath therefore stretch'd his yoke in vain,
The ploughman lost his sweat, and the green corn
Hath rotted ere his youth attain'd a beard;
The fold stands empty in the drowned field,
And crows are fatted with the murrion flock;
The nine men's morris is fill'd up with mud,
And the quaint mazes in the wanton green
For lack of tread are undistinguishable:
The human mortals want their winter here;
No night is now with hymn or carol blest:
Therefore the moon, the governess of floods,
Pale in her anger, washes all the air,
That rheumatic diseases do abound:
And thorough this distemperature we see
The seasons alter: hoary-headed frosts
Fall in the fresh lap of the crimson rose,
And on old Hiems' thin and icy crown
An odorous chaplet of sweet summer buds
Is, as in mockery, set: the spring, the summer,
The childing autumn, angry winter, change
Their wonted liveries, and the mazed world,
By their increase, now knows not which is which:
And this same progeny of evils comes
From our debate, from our dissension;
We are their parents and original.

Obe. Do you amend it then; it lies in you:
Why should Titania cross her Oberon?
I do but beg a little changeling boy,
To be my henchman.

Tita. Set your heart at rest:
The fairy land buys not the child of me.
His mother was a vot'ress of my order:
And, in the spiced Indian air, by night,
Full often hath she gossip'd by my side,
And sat with me on Neptune's yellow sands,
Marking th' embarked traders on the flood,
When we have laugh'd to see the sails conceive
And grow big-bellied with the wanton wind;

51. **aunt,** old woman. 54. **'tailor' cries,** allusion obscure; *NED* suggests that *tailor* (corruption of *tailard*), means "one with a tail." 56. **neeze,** sneeze. 66, 68. **Corin, Phillida,** names of pastoral lovers. 67. **pipes of corn,** tubular wind instruments made of straw. 69. **steep,** mountain range; so F; Globe, following Q_1: *steppe.* 71. **buskin'd,** shod with half boots. 75. **Glance at,** hit at, reflect upon. 78. **Perigenia,** Perigouna (Grant White), daughter of the robber Sinnis; a story from Plutarch. 79. **Ægles,** a nymph beloved by Theseus, for whom he deserted Ariadne; QF: *Eagles*, corrected by Rowe; form should be *Aegles* as in Plutarch's *Life of Theseus*, from which Shakespeare took the names in this passage. 80. **Ariadne,** daughter of Minos, king of Crete; by her aid Theseus slew the Minotaur and escaped from the labyrinth. **Antiopa,** queen of the Amazons and wife of Theseus, elsewhere called Hippolyta. 82. **middle summer's spring,** beginning of midsummer. 85. **in,** on. **margent,** edge, border. 86. **ringlets.** See *orbs* above, line 9. 91. **pelting,** paltry. 92. **continents,** i.e., banks that contain them; see glossary. 97. **murrion,** murrain (plague); here, diseased. 98. **nine men's morris,** rustic game played on a board or on squares laid out on the village green with nine pebbles or pegs. 99. **quaint,** ingeniously wrought; see glossary. **mazes,** figures marked out on the village green for sports. **wanton,** luxuriant or sportive. 101. **want,** lack; see glossary. 106. **distemperature,** disturbance in nature. 109. **Hiems'.** Hiems is the god of winter. 112. **childing,** fruitful. 113. **mazed,** bewildered. 117. **original,** origin. 121. **henchman,** attendant, page.

Which she, with pretty and with swimming gait
Following,- -her womb then rich with my young squire,—
Would imitate, and sail upon the land,
To fetch me trifles, and return again,
As from a voyage, rich with merchandise.
But she, being mortal, of that boy did die;
And for her sake do I rear up her boy,
And for her sake I will not part with him.

Obe. How long within this wood intend you stay?

Tita. Perchance till after Theseus' wedding-day.
If you will patiently dance in our round
And see our moonlight revels, go with us;
If not, shun me, and I will spare your haunts.

Obe. Give me that boy, and I will go with thee.

Tita. Not for thy fairy kingdom. Fairies, away!
We shall chide downright, if I longer stay.

Exeunt [Titania with her train].

Obe. Well, go thy way: thou shalt not from this grove
Till I torment thee for this injury.
My gentle Puck, come hither. Thou remembʼrest
Since once I sat upon a promontory,
And heard a mermaid on a dolphin's back
Uttering such dulcet and harmonious breath
That the rude sea grew civil at her song
And certain stars shot madly from their spheres,
To hear the sea-maid's music.

Puck I remember.

Obe. That very time I saw, but thou couldst not,
Flying between the cold moon and the earth,
Cupid all arm'd: a certain aim he took
At a fair vestal throned by the west,
And loos'd his love-shaft smartly from his bow,
As it should pierce a hundred thousand hearts;
But I might see young Cupid's fiery shaft
Quench'd in the chaste beams of the wat'ry moon,
And the imperial vot'ress passed on,
In maiden meditation, fancy-free.
Yet mark'd I where the bolt of Cupid fell:
It fell upon a little western flower,
Before milk-white, now purple with love's wound,
And maidens call it love-in-idleness.
Fetch me that flow'r; the herb I shew'd thee once:
The juice of it on sleeping eye-lids laid
Will make or man or woman madly dote
Upon the next live creature that it sees.
Fetch me this herb; and be thou here again
Ere the leviathan can swim a league.

Puck. I'll put a girdle round about the earth
In forty minutes. [*Exit.*]

Obe. Having once this juice,
I'll watch Titania when she is asleep,
And drop the liquor of it in her eyes.
The next thing then she waking looks upon,
Be it on lion, bear, or wolf, or bull,
On meddling monkey, or on busy ape,
She shall pursue it with the soul of love:
And ere I take this charm from off her sight,
As I can take it with another herb,
I'll make her render up her page to me.
But who comes here? I am invisible;
And I will overhear their conference.

Enter Demetrius, Helena *following him.*

Dem. I love thee not, therefore pursue me not.
Where is Lysander and fair Hermia?
The one I'll slay, the other slayeth me.
Thou told'st me they were stol'n unto this wood;
And here am I, and wode within this wood,
Because I cannot meet my Hermia.
Hence, get thee gone, and follow me no more.

Hel. You draw me, you hard-hearted adamant;
But yet you draw not iron, for my heart
Is true as steel: leave you your power to draw,
And I shall have no power to follow you.

Dem. Do I entice you? do I speak you fair?
Or, rather, do I not in plainest truth
Tell you, I do not, nor I cannot love you?

Hel. And even for that do I love you the more.
I am your spaniel; and, Demetrius,
The more you beat me, I will fawn on you:
Use me but as your spaniel, spurn me, strike me,
Neglect me, lose me; only give me leave,
Unworthy as I am, to follow you.
What worser place can I beg in your love,—
And yet a place of high respect with me,—
Than to be used as you use your dog?

Dem. Tempt not too much the hatred of my spirit,
For I am sick when I do look on thee.

Hel. And I am sick when I look not on you.

Dem. You do impeach your modesty too much,
To leave the city and commit yourself
Into the hands of one that loves you not;
To trust the opportunity of night
And the ill counsel of a desert place
With the rich worth of your virginity.

Hel. Your virtue is my privilege: for that
It is not night when I do see your face,
Therefore I think I am not in the night;
Nor doth this wood lack worlds of company,
For you in my respect are all the world:
Then how can it be said I am alone,
When all the world is here to look on me?

Dem. I'll run from thee and hide me in the brakes,
And leave thee to the mercy of wild beasts.

Hel. The wildest hath not such a heart as you.
Run when you will, the story shall be chang'd:
Apollo flies, and Daphne holds the chase;
The dove pursues the griffin; the mild hind
Makes speed to catch the tiger; bootless speed,
When cowardice pursues and valour flies.

Dem. I will not stay thy questions; let me go:
Or, if thou follow me, do not believe
But I shall do thee mischief in the wood.

Hel. Ay, in the temple, in the town, the field,
You do me mischief. Fie, Demetrius!
Your wrongs do set a scandal on my sex:
We cannot fight for love, as men may do;
We should be woo'd and were not made to woo.

[*Exit Dem.*]

I'll follow thee and make a heaven of hell,

148-168. **Thou . . . love-in-idleness.** This famous passage contains an allusion to Queen Elizabeth and probably to some entertainment in her honor at Kenilworth in 1575, or more probably at Elvetham in 1591. 151. **breath,** voice, notes. 157. **all,** fully. 161. **might,** could; see glossary. 168. **love-in-idleness,** pansy, heartsease. 174. **leviathan,** sea monster. 176. **forty,** used indefinitely. 192. **wode,** mad; usual form, wood. 195. **adamant,** very hard stone; here lodestone. 197. **leave,** give up. 199. **fair,** courteously; see glossary. 220. **virtue,** goodness or power to attract. **privilege,** safeguard, warrant. **for that,** because. 224. **in my respect,** as far as I am concerned; or, in my opinion. 231. **Apollo . . . chase,** allusion to the story of Apollo's pursuit of Daphne; here Daphne *holds the chase*, or pursues, instead of Apollo. 232. **griffin,** a fabulous monster with the head of an eagle and the body of a lion. **hind,** female deer. 235. **stay,** wait for; see glossary. **questions,** talk or argu-

To die upon the hand I love so well. [*Exit.*]
Obe. Fare thee well, nymph: ere he do leave this grove,
Thou shalt fly him and he shall seek thy love.

Enter PUCK.

Hast thou the flower there? Welcome, wanderer.
Puck. Ay, there it is.
Obe. I pray thee, give it me.
I know a bank where the wild thyme blows,
Where oxlips and the nodding violet grows,
†Quite over-canopied with luscious woodbine,
With sweet musk-roses and with eglantine:
There sleeps Titania sometime of the night,
Lull'd in these flowers with dances and delight;
And there the snake throws her enamell'd skin,
Weed wide enough to wrap a fairy in:
And with the juice of this I'll streak her eyes,
And make her full of hateful fantasies.
Take thou some of it, and seek through this grove:
A sweet Athenian lady is in love
With a disdainful youth: anoint his eyes;
But do it when the next thing he espies
May be the lady: thou shalt know the man
By the Athenian garments he hath on.
Effect it with some care that he may prove
More fond on her than she upon her love:
And look thou meet me ere the first cock crow.
Puck. Fear not, my lord, your servant shall do so.
Exeunt.

[SCENE II. *Another part of the wood.*]

Enter TITANIA, *Queen of Fairies, with her train.*

Tita. Come, now a roundel and a fairy song;
Then, for the third part of a minute, hence;
Some to kill cankers in the musk-rose buds,
Some war with rere-mice for their leathern wings,
To make my small elves coats, and some keep back
The clamorous owl that nightly hoots and wonders
At our quaint spirits. Sing me now asleep;
Then to your offices and let me rest.

Fairies sing.

You spotted snakes with double tongue,
Thorny hedgehogs, be not seen;
Newts and blind-worms, do no wrong,
Come not near our fairy queen.
Philomel, with melody
Sing in our sweet lullaby;
Lulla, lulla, lullaby, lulla, lulla, lullaby:
Never harm,
Nor spell nor charm,
Come our lovely lady nigh;
So, good night, with lullaby.

First F. Weaving spiders, come not here;
Hence, you long-legg'd spinners, hence!
Beetles black, approach not near;
Worm nor snail, do no offence.
Philomel, with melody, &c.

Sec. F. Hence, away! now all is well:
One aloof stand sentinel.
[*Exeunt Fairies. Titania sleeps.*]

Enter OBERON [*and squeezes the flower on Titania's eyelids*].

Obe. What thou seest when thou dost wake,
Do it for thy true-love take,
Love and languish for his sake:
Be it ounce, or cat, or bear,
Pard, or boar with bristled hair,
In thy eye that shall appear
When thou wak'st, it is thy dear:
Wake when some vile thing is near. [*Exit.*]

Enter LYSANDER *and* HERMIA.

Lys. Fair love, you faint with wand'ring in the wood;
And to speak troth, I have forgot our way:
We'll rest us, Hermia, if you think it good,
And tarry for the comfort of the day.
Her. Be it so, Lysander: find you out a bed;
For I upon this bank will rest my head.
Lys. One turf shall serve as pillow for us both;
One heart, one bed, two bosoms and one troth.
Her. Nay, good Lysander; for my sake, my dear,
Lie further off yet, do not lie so near.
Lys. O, take the sense, sweet, of my innocence!
Love takes the meaning in love's conference.
I mean, that my heart unto yours is knit
So that but one heart we can make of it;
Two bosoms interchained with an oath;
So then two bosoms and a single troth.
Then by your side no bed-room me deny;
For lying so, Hermia, I do not lie.
Her. Lysander riddles very prettily:
Now much beshrew my manners and my pride,
If Hermia meant to say Lysander lied.
But, gentle friend, for love and courtesy
Lie further off; in human modesty,
Such separation as may well be said
Becomes a virtuous bachelor and a maid,
So far be distant; and, good night, sweet friend:
Thy love ne'er alter till thy sweet life end!
Lys. Amen, amen, to that fair prayer, say I;
And then end life when I end loyalty!
Here is my bed: sleep give thee all his rest!
Her. With half that wish the wisher's eyes be press'd!
[*They sleep.*]

Enter PUCK.

Puck. Through the forest have I gone,
But Athenian found I none,
On whose eyes I might approve
This flower's force in stirring love.
Night and silence.—Who is here?
Weeds of Athens he doth wear:
This is he, my master said,
Despised the Athenian maid;
And here the maiden, sleeping sound,
On the dank and dirty ground.
Pretty soul! she durst not lie

ment. 244. **upon,** by. 250. **oxlips,** flowers resembling cowslip and primrose. 251. **woodbine,** honeysuckle. 252. **eglantine,** sweetbriar. 254. **dances and delight,** delightful dances. 255. **throws . . . skin,** sloughs off her enamel-like skin. 256. **Weed,** garment; see glossary. 257. **streak,** stroke, touch softly. 266. **fond on,** doting on; see *fond* in glossary.

SCENE II. 1. **roundel,** dance in a ring. 3. **cankers,** cankerworms. 4. **rere-mice,** bats. 11. **Newts,** lizards. 13. **Philomel,** nightingale; Philomela, daughter of Pandion, was transformed into a nightingale in a familiar story in Ovid, *Metamorphoses*, vi. 30. **ounce,** lynx. 31. **Pard,** panther or leopard. 36. **troth,** truth. 42. **troth,** faith, troth-plight. 45. **sense,** import; see glossary. 51. **deny,** refuse; see glossary. 54. **beshrew,** curse (but mildly meant). 57. **human,** humane, courteous. 68. **approve,** test, prove.

Near this lack-love, this kill-courtesy.
Churl, upon thy eyes I throw
All the power this charm doth owe.
When thou wak'st, let love forbid
Sleep his seat on thy eyelid:
So awake when I am gone;
For I must now to Oberon. *Exit.*

Enter DEMETRIUS *and* HELENA, *running.*

Hel. Stay, though thou kill me, sweet Demetrius.
Dem. I charge thee, hence, and do not haunt me thus.
Hel. O, wilt thou darkling leave me? do not so.
Dem. Stay, on thy peril: I alone will go. [*Exit.*]
Hel. O, I am out of breath in this fond chase!
The more my prayer, the lesser is my grace.
Happy is Hermia, wheresoe'er she lies;
For she hath blessed and attractive eyes.
How came her eyes so bright? Not with salt tears:
If so, my eyes are oft'ner wash'd than hers.
No, no, I am as ugly as a bear;
For beasts that meet me run away for fear:
Therefore no marvel though Demetrius
Do, as a monster, fly my presence thus.
What wicked and dissembling glass of mine
Made me compare with Hermia's sphery eyne?
But who is here? Lysander! on the ground!
Dead? or asleep? I see no blood, no wound.
Lysander, if you live, good sir, awake.
Lys. [*Awaking*] And run through fire I will for thy sweet sake.
Transparent Helena! Nature shows art,
That through thy bosom makes me see thy heart.
Where is Demetrius? O, how fit a word
Is that vile name to perish on my sword!
Hel. Do not say so, Lysander; say not so.
What though he love your Hermia? Lord, what though?
Yet Hermia still loves you: then be content.
Lys. Content with Hermia! No; I do repent
The tedious minutes I with her have spent.
Not Hermia but Helena I love:
Who will not change a raven for a dove?
The will of man is by his reason sway'd;
And reason says you are the worthier maid.
Things growing are not ripe until their season:
So I, being young, till now ripe not to reason;
And touching now the point of human skill,
Reason becomes the marshal to my will
And leads me to your eyes, where I o'erlook
Love's stories written in love's richest book.
Hel. Wherefore was I to this keen mockery born?
When at your hands did I deserve this scorn?
Is 't not enough, is 't not enough, young man,
That I did never, no, nor never can,
Deserve a sweet look from Demetrius' eye,
But you must flout my insufficiency?
Good troth, you do me wrong, good sooth, you do,
In such disdainful manner me to woo.
But fare you well: perforce I must confess
I thought you lord of more true gentleness.
O, that a lady, of one man refus'd,
Should of another therefore be abus'd! *Exit.*
Lys. She sees not Hermia. Hermia, sleep thou there:
And never mayst thou come Lysander near!
For as a surfeit of the sweetest things
The deepest loathing to the stomach brings,
Or as the heresies that men do leave
Are hated most of those they did deceive,
So thou, my surfeit and my heresy,
Of all be hated, but the most of me!
And, all my powers, address your love and might
To honour Helen and to be her knight! *Exit.*
Her. [*Awaking*] Help me, Lysander, help me! do thy best
To pluck this crawling serpent from my breast!
Ay me, for pity! what a dream was here!
Lysander, look how I do quake with fear:
Methought a serpent eat my heart away,
And you sat smiling at his cruel prey.
Lysander! what, remov'd? Lysander! lord!
What, out of hearing? gone? no sound, no word?
Alack, where are you? speak, an if you hear;
Speak, of all loves! I swoon almost with fear.
No? then I well perceive you are not nigh:
Either death or you I'll find immediately. *Exit.*

[ACT III.

SCENE I. *The wood. Titania lying asleep.*]

Enter the Clowns [QUINCE, SNUG, BOTTOM, FLUTE, SNOUT, *and* STARVELING].

Bot. Are we all met?

Quin. Pat, pat; and here 's a marvellous convenient place for our rehearsal. This green plot shall be our stage, this hawthorn-brake our tiring-house; and we will do it in action as we will do it before the duke.

Bot. Peter Quince,—

Quin. What sayest thou, bully Bottom?

Bot. There are things in this comedy of Pyramus and Thisby that will never please. First, Pyramus must draw a sword to kill himself; which the ladies cannot abide. How answer you that?

Snout. By 'r lakin, a parlous fear.

Star. I believe we must leave the killing out, when all is done.

Bot. Not a whit: I have a device to make all well. Write me a prologue; and let the prologue seem to say, we will do no harm with our swords and that Pyramus is not killed indeed; and, for the more better assurance, tell them that I Pyramus am not Pyramus, but Bottom the weaver: this will put them out of fear.

Quin. Well, we will have such a prologue; and it shall be written in eight and six.

Bot. No, make it two more; let it be written in eight and eight.

Snout. Will not the ladies be afeard of the lion?

Star. I fear it, I promise you.

79. **owe,** own; see glossary. 86. **darkling,** in the dark. 89. **grace,** favor I obtain; see glossary. 90. **lies,** dwells; see glossary. 99. **sphery eyne,** starlike eyes. 103. **run through fire,** proverbial for any hard task. 118. **ripe,** usually understood as a verb in this passage meaning "grow ripe." 133. **of,** by; see glossary. 134. **abus'd,** maltreated; see glossary. 150. **prey,** act of preying upon. 154. **of all loves,** for all love's sake.

ACT III. SCENE I. 5. **tiring-house,** dressing room. 8. **bully,** term of companionship. 14. **By 'r lakin,** by our ladykin, i.e., the Virgin Mary. **parlous,** perilous. 25. **eight and six,** alternate lines of eight and six syllables, ballad measure. 32. **lion among ladies.** Malone called attention to a pamphlet (*Somers' Tracts*, ii, 179) which tells how at the christening of Prince Henry, eldest son of King James I, then James VI of Scotland, a "blackmoor" instead of a lion drew the triumphal chariot, since the lion's presence might have "brought some fear to the nearest." 33. **fearful,** fear-inspiring; see glossary. 40. **de-**

Bot. Masters, you ought to consider with yourselves: to bring in—God shield us!—a lion among ladies, is a most dreadful thing; for there is not a more fearful wild-fowl than your lion living; and we ought to look to 't.

Snout. Therefore another prologue must tell he is not a lion.

Bot. Nay, you must name his name, and half his face must be seen through the lion's neck: and he himself must speak through, saying thus, or to the same defect, —'Ladies,'—or 'Fair ladies,—I would wish you,'—or 'I would request you,'—or 'I would entreat you,—not to fear, not to tremble: my life for yours. If you think I come hither as a lion, it were pity of my life: no, I am no such thing; I am a man as other men are;' and there indeed let him name his name, and tell them plainly he is Snug the joiner.

Quin. Well, it shall be so. But there is two hard things; that is, to bring the moonlight into a chamber; for, you know, Pyramus and Thisby meet by moonlight.

Snout. Doth the moon shine that night we play our play?

Bot. A calendar, a calendar! look in the almanac; find out moonshine, find out moonshine.

Quin. Yes, it doth shine that night.

Bot. Why, then may you leave a casement of the great chamber window, where we play, open, and the moon may shine in at the casement.

Quin. Ay; or else one must come in with a bush of thorns and a lanthorn, and say he comes to disfigure, or to present, the person of Moonshine. Then, there is another thing: we must have a wall in the great chamber; for Pyramus and Thisby, says the story, did talk through the chink of a wall.

Snout. You can never bring in a wall. What say you, Bottom?

Bot. Some man or other must present Wall: and let him have some plaster, or some loam, or some rough-cast about him, to signify wall; and let him hold his fingers thus, and through that cranny shall Pyramus and Thisby whisper.

Quin. If that may be, then all is well. Come, sit down, every mother's son, and rehearse your parts. Pyramus, you begin: when you have spoken your speech, enter into that brake: and so every one according to his cue.

Enter ROBIN [PUCK].

Puck. What hempen home-spuns have we
swagg'ring here,
So near the cradle of the fairy queen?
What, a play toward! I'll be an auditor;
An actor too perhaps, if I see cause.

Quin. Speak, Pyramus. Thisby, stand forth.

Bot. Thisby, the flowers of odious savours sweet,—

Quin. Odours, odours.

Bot. —— odours savours sweet:
So hath thy breath, my dearest Thisby dear.
But hark, a voice! stay thou but here awhile,
And by and by I will to thee appear. *Exit.*

Puck. A stranger Pyramus than e'er played here.
[*Exit.*]

Flu. Must I speak now?

Quin. Ay, marry, must you; for you must understand he goes but to see a noise that he heard, and is to come again.

Flu. Most radiant Pyramus, most lily-white of hue,
Of colour like the red rose on triumphant brier,
Most brisky juvenal and eke most lovely Jew,
As true as truest horse that yet would never tire.
I'll meet thee, Pyramus, at Ninny's tomb.

Quin. 'Ninus' tomb,' man: why, you must not speak that yet; that you answer to Pyramus: you speak all your part at once, cues and all. Pyramus enter: your cue is past; it is, 'never tire.'

Flu. O,—As true as truest horse, that yet would
never tire.

[*Enter* PUCK, *and* PYRAMUS *with the ass head.*]

Bot. If I were fair, Thisby, I were only thine.

Quin. O monstrous! O strange! we are haunted. Pray, masters! fly, masters! Help!

[*Exeunt Quince, Snug, Flute, Snout, and Starveling.*]

Puck. I'll follow you, I'll lead you about a round,
Through bog, through bush, through brake,
through brier:
Sometime a horse I'll be, sometime a hound,
A hog, a headless bear, sometime a fire;
And neigh, and bark, and grunt, and roar, and burn,
Like horse, hound, hog, bear, fire, at every turn. *Exit.*

Bot. Why do they run away? this is a knavery of them to make me afeard.

Enter SNOUT.

Snout. O Bottom, thou art changed! what do I see on thee?

Bot. What do you see? you see an ass-head of your own, do you? [*Exit Snout.*]

Enter QUINCE.

Quin. Bless thee, Bottom! bless thee! thou art translated. *Exit.*

Bot. I see their knavery: this is to make an ass of me; to fright me, if they could. But I will not stir from this place, do what they can: I will walk up and down here, and I will sing, that they shall hear I am not afraid. [*Sings.*]

The ousel cock so black of hue,
With orange-tawny bill,
The throstle with his note so true,
The wren with little quill,—

Tita. [*Awaking*] What angel wakes me from my
flow'ry bed?

Bot. [*Sings*]
The finch, the sparrow and the lark,
The plain-song cuckoo gray,
Whose note full many a man doth mark,
And dares not answer nay;—
for, indeed, who would set his wit to so foolish a bird?

fect, Bottom's blunder for "effect." 44. **pity of my life,** i.e., my life would be in jeopardy. 61. **bush of thorns.** According to legend, the man in the moon was a person who had been banished there for gathering firewood on Sundays. 62. **disfigure,** blunder for "prefigure." **present,** represent; see glossary. 71. **rough-cast,** a mixture of lime and gravel used to plaster the outside of buildings. 81. **toward,** about to take place; see glossary. 97. **brisky juvenal,** brisk juvenile or youth. **Jew,** probably an absurd repetition of the first syllable of *juvenal*. 100. **'Ninus,'** mythical founder of Babylon, at which place the scene of the story of Pyramus and Thisbe is laid. 106. *Stage Direction:* **Pyramus... ass head.** As in F; indicates a particular stage property. 122. **translated,** transformed. 128. **ousel,** blackbird. 134. **plain-song,** melody without variations; here used as an adjective.

who would give a bird the lie, though he cry 'cuckoo' never so?

Tita. I pray thee, gentle mortal, sing again:
Mine ear is much enamoured of thy note;
So is mine eye enthralled to thy shape;
And thy fair virtue's force perforce doth move me
On the first view to say, to swear, I love thee.

Bot. Methinks, mistress, you should have little reason for that: and yet, to say the truth, reason and love keep little company together now-a-days; the more the pity that some honest neighbours will not make them friends. Nay, I can gleek upon occasion.

Tita. Thou art as wise as thou art beautiful.

Bot. Not so, neither: but if I had wit enough to get out of this wood, I have enough to serve mine own turn.

Tita. Out of this wood do not desire to go:
Thou shalt remain here, whether thou wilt or no.
I am a spirit of no common rate:
The summer still doth tend upon my state;
And I do love thee: therefore, go with me;
I'll give thee fairies to attend on thee,
And they shall fetch thee jewels from the deep,
And sing while thou on pressed flowers dost sleep:
And I will purge thy mortal grossness so
That thou shalt like an airy spirit go.
Peaseblossom! Cobweb! Moth! and Mustardseed!

Enter four Fairies [Peaseblossom, Cobweb, Moth, *and* Mustardseed].

Peas. Ready.
Cob. And I.
Moth. And I.
Mus. And I.
All. Where shall we go?

Tita. Be kind and courteous to this gentleman;
Hop in his walks and gambol in his eyes;
Feed him with apricocks and dewberries,
With purple grapes, green figs, and mulberries;
The honey-bags steal from the humble-bees,
And for night-tapers crop their waxen thighs
And light them at the fiery glow-worm's eyes,
To have my love to bed and to arise;
And pluck the wings from painted butterflies
To fan the moonbeams from his sleeping eyes:
Nod to him, elves, and do him courtesies.

Peas. Hail, mortal!
Cob. Hail!
Moth. Hail!
Mus. Hail!

Bot. I cry your worships mercy, heartily: I beseech your worship's name.

Cob. Cobweb.

Bot. I shall desire you of more acquaintance, good Master Cobweb: if I cut my finger, I shall make bold with you. Your name, honest gentleman?

Peas. Peaseblossom.

Bot. I pray you, commend me to Mistress Squash, your mother, and to Master Peascod, your father. Good Master Peaseblossom, I shall desire you of more acquaintance too. Your name, I beseech you, sir?

Mus. Mustardseed.

Bot. Good Master Mustardseed, I know your patience well: that same cowardly, giant-like ox-beef hath devoured many a gentleman of your house: I promise you your kindred hath made my eyes water ere now. I desire you of more acquaintance, good Master Mustardseed.

Tita. Come wait upon him; lead him to my bower.
The moon methinks looks with a wat'ry eye;
And when she weeps, weeps every little flower,
Lamenting some enforced chastity.
Tie up my lover's tongue, bring him silently. *Exeunt.*

[Scene II. *Another part of the wood.*]

Enter [Oberon,] *King of Fairies.*

Obe. I wonder if Titania be awak'd;
Then, what it was that next came in her eye,
Which she must dote on in extremity.

[*Enter*] Robin Goodfellow [Puck].

Here comes my messenger.
How now, mad spirit!
What night-rule now about this haunted grove?

Puck. My mistress with a monster is in love.
Near to her close and consecrated bower,
While she was in her dull and sleeping hour,
A crew of patches, rude mechanicals,
That work for bread upon Athenian stalls,
Were met together to rehearse a play
Intended for great Theseus' nuptial-day.
The shallowest thick-skin of that barren sort,
Who Pyramus presented, in their sport
Forsook his scene and ent'red in a brake:
When I did him at this advantage take,
An ass's nole I fixed on his head:
Anon his Thisby must be answered,
And forth my mimic comes. When they him spy,
As wild geese that the creeping fowler eye,
Or russet-pated choughs, many in sort,
Rising and cawing at the gun's report,
Sever themselves and madly sweep the sky,
So, at his sight, away his fellows fly;
And, at our stamp, here o'er and o'er one falls;
He murder cries and help from Athens calls.
Their sense thus weak, lost with their fears thus strong,
Made senseless things begin to do them wrong;
For briers and thorns at their apparel snatch;
Some sleeves, some hats, from yielders all things catch.
I led them on in this distracted fear,
And left sweet Pyramus translated there:
When in that moment, so it came to pass,
Titania wak'd and straightway lov'd an ass.

Obe. This falls out better than I could devise.
But hast thou yet latch'd the Athenian's eyes
With the love-juice, as I did bid thee do?

Puck. I took him sleeping,—that is finish'd too,—
And the Athenian woman by his side;
That, when he wak'd, of force she must be ey'd.

143. **thy fair virtue's force,** the power of thy beauty. 150. **gleek,** scoff, jest. 154. **serve . . . turn,** answer my purpose; see glossary. 157. **rate,** rank. 158. **still,** ever, always; see glossary. 191. **Squash,** unripe pea pod. 197. **patience,** what you have endured. 205. **enforced,** forced, violated.

Scene ii. 2. **next,** nearest, first. 3. **in extremity,** to the utmost degree. 5. **night-rule,** regular diversion for the night. 9. **patches,** clowns, fools. **mechanicals,** artisans, workingmen. 13. **barren sort,** stupid company or crew. 17. **nole,** head. 19. **mimic,** burlesque actor. 21. **choughs,** probably, jackdaws; Clarendon Press reads *russet-patted,* meaning "red-legged," to refer to the Cornish chough. 36. **latch'd,** caught and held fast as by a charm. 40. **of force,** perforce. 45. **use,** treat; see glossary. 57. **dead,** deadly. 65. **Out,** expression of impatience; see glossary. 70. **brave touch,** noble exploit. 71. **worm,**

Enter DEMETRIUS *and* HERMIA.

Obe. Stand close: this is the same Athenian.
Puck. This is the woman, but not this the man.
Dem. O, why rebuke you him that loves you so?
Lay breath so bitter on your bitter foe.
Her. Now I but chide; but I should use thee worse,
For thou, I fear, hast given me cause to curse.
If thou hast slain Lysander in his sleep,
Being o'er shoes in blood, plunge in the deep,
And kill me too.
The sun was not so true unto the day
As he to me: would he have stolen away
From sleeping Hermia? I'll believe as soon
This whole earth may be bor'd and that the moon
May through the centre creep and so displease
Her brother's noontide with th' Antipodes.
It cannot be but thou hast murd'red him;
So should a murderer look, so dead, so grim.
Dem. So should the murdered look, and so should I,
Pierc'd through the heart with your stern cruelty:
Yet you, the murderer, look as bright, as clear,
As yonder Venus in her glimmering sphere.
Her. What 's this to my Lysander? where is he?
Ah, good Demetrius, wilt thou give him me?
Dem. I had rather give his carcass to my hounds.
Her. Out, dog! out, cur! thou driv'st me past the bounds
Of maiden's patience. Hast thou slain him, then?
Henceforth be never numb'red among men!
O, once tell true, tell true, even for my sake!
Durst thou have look'd upon him being awake,
And hast thou kill'd him sleeping? O brave touch!
Could not a worm, an adder, do so much?
An adder did it; for with doubler tongue
Than thine, thou serpent, never adder stung.
Dem. You spend your passion on a mispris'd mood:
I am not guilty of Lysander's blood;
Nor is he dead, for aught that I can tell.
Her. I pray thee, tell me then that he is well.
Dem. An if I could, what should I get therefore?
Her. A privilege never to see me more.
And from thy hated presence part I so:
See me no more, whether he be dead or no. *Exit*.
Dem. There is no following her in this fierce vein:
Here therefore for a while I will remain.
So sorrow's heaviness doth heavier grow
For debt that bankrout sleep doth sorrow owe;
Which now in some slight measure it will pay,
If for his tender here I make some stay.
Lie down [*and sleep*].
Obe. What hast thou done? thou hast mistaken quite
And laid the love-juice on some true-love's sight:
Of thy misprision must perforce ensue
Some true love turn'd and not a false turn'd true.
Puck. Then fate o'er-rules, that, one man holding troth,
A million fail, confounding oath on oath.
Obe. About the wood go swifter than the wind,
And Helena of Athens look thou find:
All fancy-sick she is and pale of cheer,
With sighs of love, that costs the fresh blood dear:
By some illusion see thou bring her here:
I'll charm his eyes against she do appear.
Puck. I go, I go; look how I go,
Swifter than arrow from the Tartar's bow. [*Exit*.]
Obe. Flower of this purple dye,
Hit with Cupid's archery,
Sink in apple of his eye.
When his love he doth espy,
Let her shine as gloriously
As the Venus of the sky.
When thou wak'st, if she be by,
Beg of her for remedy.

Enter PUCK.

Puck. Captain of our fairy band,
Helena is here at hand;
And the youth, mistook by me,
Pleading for a lover's fee.
Shall we their fond pageant see?
Lord, what fools these mortals be!
Obe. Stand aside: the noise they make
Will cause Demetrius to awake.
Puck. Then will two at once woo one;
That must needs be sport alone;
And those things do best please me
That befal prepost'rously.

Enter LYSANDER *and* HELENA.

Lys. Why should you think that I should woo in scorn?
Scorn and derision never come in tears:
Look, when I vow, I weep; and vows so born,
In their nativity all truth appears.
How can these things in me seem scorn to you,
Bearing the badge of faith, to prove them true?
Hel. You do advance your cunning more and more.
When truth kills truth, O devilish-holy fray!
These vows are Hermia's: will you give her o'er?
Weigh oath with oath, and you will nothing weigh:
Your vows to her and me, put in two scales,
Will even weigh, and both as light as tales.
Lys. I had no judgement when to her I swore.
Hel. Nor none, in my mind, now you give her o'er.
Lys. Demetrius loves her, and he loves not you.
Dem. [*Awaking*] O Helen, goddess, nymph, perfect, divine!
To what, my love, shall I compare thine eyne?
Crystal is muddy. O, how ripe in show
Thy lips, those kissing cherries, tempting grow!
That pure congealed white, high Taurus' snow,
Fann'd with the eastern wind, turns to a crow
When thou hold'st up thy hand: O, let me kiss
This princess of pure white, this seal of bliss!
Hel. O spite! O hell! I see you all are bent
To set against me for your merriment:
If you were civil and knew courtesy,
You would not do me thus much injury.
Can you not hate me, as I know you do,
But you must join in souls to mock me too?
If you were men, as men you are in show,

serpent. 74. **passion,** violent feelings; see glossary. **misprised,** mistaken. 86-87. **Which . . . stay,** i.e., if he waits until sleep "tenders" itself, he will derive some relief for his sorrow. 90. **misprision,** mistake. 93. **confounding . . . oath,** i.e., invalidating one oath with another; see *confound* in glossary. 96. **fancy-sick,** lovesick. **cheer,** face. 97. **sighs . . . blood,** allusion to the physiological theory that each sigh cost the heart a drop of blood. 101. **Tartar's bow.** Tartars were famed for their skill with the bow. 114. **fond pageant,** foolish exhibition; see *fond* and *pageant* in glossary. 121. **prepost'rously,** in inverted order. 124-125. **vows . . . appears,** i.e., vows made by one who is weeping give evidence thereby of their sincerity. 135. **mind,** opinion; see glossary. 141. **Taurus',** a lofty mountain range in Asia Minor. 144. **seal,** pledge, covenant.

You would not use a gentle lady so;
To vow, and swear, and superpraise my parts,
When I am sure you hate me with your hearts.
You both are rivals, and love Hermia;
And now both rivals, to mock Helena:
A trim exploit, a manly enterprise,
To conjure tears up in a poor maid's eyes
With your derision! none of noble sort
Would so offend a virgin and extort
A poor soul's patience, all to make you sport.
Lys. You are unkind, Demetrius; be not so;
For you love Hermia; this you know I know:
And here, with all good will, with all my heart,
In Hermia's love I yield you up my part;
And yours of Helena to me bequeath,
Whom I do love and will do till my death.
Hel. Never did mockers waste more idle breath.
Dem. Lysander, keep thy Hermia; I will none:
If e'er I lov'd her, all that love is gone.
My heart to her but as guest-wise sojourn'd,
And now to Helen is it home return'd,
There to remain.
Lys. Helen, it is not so.
Dem. Disparage not the faith thou dost not know,
Lest, to thy peril, thou aby it dear.
Look, where thy love comes; yonder is thy dear.

Enter HERMIA.

Her. Dark night, that from the eye his function takes,
The ear more quick of apprehension makes;
Wherein it doth impair the seeing sense,
It pays the hearing double recompense.
Thou art not by mine eye, Lysander, found;
Mine ear, I thank it, brought me to thy sound.
But why unkindly didst thou leave me so?
Lys. Why should he stay, whom love doth press to go?
Her. What love could press Lysander from my side?
Lys. Lysander's love, that would not let him bide,
Fair Helena, who more engilds the night
Than all yon fiery oes and eyes of light.
Why seek'st thou me? could not this make thee know,
The hate I bear thee made me leave thee so?
Her. You speak not as you think: it cannot be.
Hel. Lo, she is one of this confederacy!
Now I perceive they have conjoin'd all three
To fashion this false sport, in spite of me.
Injurious Hermia! most ungrateful maid!
Have you conspir'd, have you with these contriv'd
To bait me with this foul derision?
Is all the counsel that we two have shar'd,
The sisters' vows, the hours that we have spent,
When we have chid the hasty-footed time
For parting us,—O, is it all forgot?
All school-days' friendship, childhood innocence?
We, Hermia, like two artificial gods,
Have with our needles created both one flower,
Both on one sampler, sitting on one cushion,
Both warbling of one song, both in one key,
As if our hands, our sides, voices and minds,
Had been incorporate. So we grew together,
Like to a double cherry, seeming parted,
But yet an union in partition;
Two lovely berries moulded on one stem;
So, with two seeming bodies, but one heart;
Two of the first, like coats in heraldry,
Due but to one and crowned with one crest.
And will you rent our ancient love asunder,
To join with men in scorning your poor friend?
It is not friendly, 'tis not maidenly:
Our sex, as well as I, may chide you for it,
Though I alone do feel the injury.
Her. I am amazed at your passionate words.
I scorn you not: it seems that you scorn me.
Hel. Have you not set Lysander, as in scorn,
To follow me and praise my eyes and face?
And made your other love, Demetrius,
Who even but now did spurn me with his foot,
To call me goddess, nymph, divine and rare,
Precious, celestial? Wherefore speaks he this
To her he hates? and wherefore doth Lysander
Deny your love, so rich within his soul,
And tender me, forsooth, affection,
But by your setting on, by your consent?
What though I be not so in grace as you,
So hung upon with love, so fortunate,
But miserable most, to love unlov'd?
This you should pity rather than despise.
Her. I understand not what you mean by this.
Hel. Ay, do, persever, counterfeit sad looks,
Make mouths upon me when I turn my back;
Wink each at other; hold the sweet jest up:
This sport, well carried, shall be chronicled.
If you have any pity, grace, or manners,
You would not make me such an argument.
But fare ye well: 'tis partly my own fault;
Which death or absence soon shall remedy.
Lys. Stay, gentle Helena; hear my excuse:
My love, my life, my soul, fair Helena!
Hel. O excellent!
Her. Sweet, do not scorn her so.
Dem. If she cannot entreat, I can compel.
Lys. Thou canst compel no more than she entreat:
Thy threats have no more strength than her weak prayers.
Helen, I love thee; by my life, I do:
I swear by that which I will lose for thee,
To prove him false that says I love thee not.
Dem. I say I love thee more than he can do.
Lys. If thou say so, withdraw, and prove it too.
Dem. Quick, come!
Her. Lysander, whereto tends all this?
Lys. Away, you Ethiope!
Dem. †No, no; he'll . . .
Seem to break loose; take on as you would follow,
But yet come not: you are a tame man, go!
Lys. Hang off, thou cat, thou burr! vile thing, let loose,
Or I will shake thee from me like a serpent!
Her. Why are you grown so rude? what change is this?

153. **superpraise,** overpraise. **parts,** qualities. 157. **trim,** pretty; used ironically. 169. **will none,** i.e., of her. 175. **aby,** pay for. 177. **his,** its; see glossary. 188. **oes,** general word for "circles" and "orbs." 195. **Injurious,** insulting. 196. **contriv'd,** plotted; see glossary. 203. **artificial,** skilled in art. 208. **incorporate,** united in one body. 213. **Two of the first,** i.e., two bodies, referred to like colors in the description of a coat-of-arms. "The first" is the color first mentioned.

237. **persever,** persevere; accented on the second syllable. **sad,** grave, serious; see glossary. 238. **Make mouths upon,** make faces at. 240. **carried,** managed; see glossary. 242. **argument,** subject for a story; see glossary. 257. **No, no; he'll.** Q: *No, no: heele.* F: *No, no, Sir;* text apparently corrupt. We may understand that Demetrius first addresses Helena and breaks off, then turns to chide Lysander. 260. **Hang off,** let go. 272. **what news?** What is the matter? 274.

Sweet love,—
Lys. Thy love! out, tawny Tartar, out!
Out, loathed med'cine! O hated potion, hence!
Her. Do you not jest?
Hel. Yes, sooth; and so do you.
Lys. Demetrius, I will keep my word with thee.
Dem. I would I had your bond, for I perceive
A weak bond holds you: I'll not trust your word.
Lys. What, should I hurt her, strike her, kill her dead?
Although I hate her, I'll not harm her so.
Her. What, can you do me greater harm than hate?
Hate me! wherefore? O me! what news, my love!
Am not I Hermia? are not you Lysander?
I am as fair now as I was erewhile.
Since night you lov'd me; yet since night you left me:
Why, then you left me—O, the gods forbid!—
In earnest, shall I say?
Lys. Ay, by my life;
And never did desire to see thee more.
Therefore be out of hope, of question, of doubt;
Be certain, nothing truer; 'tis no jest
That I do hate thee and love Helena.
Her. O me! you juggler! you cankerblossom!
You thief of love! what, have you come by night
And stol'n my love's heart from him?
Hel. Fine, i' faith!
Have you no modesty, no maiden shame,
No touch of bashfulness? What, will you tear
Impatient answers from my gentle tongue?
Fie, fie! you counterfeit, you puppet, you!
Her. Puppet? why so? ay, that way goes the game.
Now I perceive that she hath made compare
Between our statures; she hath urg'd her height;
And with her personage, her tall personage,
Her height, forsooth, she hath prevail'd with him.
And are you grown so high in his esteem,
Because I am so dwarfish and so low?
How low am I, thou painted maypole? speak;
How low am I? I am not yet so low
But that my nails can reach unto thine eyes.
Hel. I pray you, though you mock me, gentlemen,
Let her not hurt me: I was never curst;
I have no gift at all in shrewishness;
I am a right maid for my cowardice:
Let her not strike me. You perhaps may think,
Because she is something lower than myself,
That I can match her.
Her. Lower! hark, again.
Hel. Good Hermia, do not be so bitter with me.
I evermore did love you, Hermia,
Did ever keep your counsels, never wrong'd you;
Save that, in love unto Demetrius,
I told him of your stealth unto this wood.
He followed you; for love I followed him;
But he hath chid me hence and threat'ned me
To strike me, spurn me, nay, to kill me too:
And now, so you will let me quiet go,
To Athens will I bear my folly back
And follow you no further: let me go:
You see how simple and how fond I am.
Her. Why, get you gone: who is 't that hinders you?
Hel. A foolish heart, that I leave here behind.
Her. What, with Lysander?
Hel. With Demetrius.
Lys. Be not afraid; she shall not harm thee, Helena.
Dem. No, sir, she shall not, though you take her part.
Hel. O, when she 's angry, she is keen and shrewd!
She was a vixen when she went to school;
And though she be but little, she is fierce.
Her. 'Little' again! nothing but 'low' and 'little'!
Why will you suffer her to flout me thus?
Let me come to her.
Lys. Get you gone, you dwarf;
You minimus, of hind'ring knot-grass made;
You bead, you acorn.
Dem. You are too officious
In her behalf that scorns your services.
Let her alone: speak not of Helena;
Take not her part; for, if thou dost intend
Never so little show of love to her,
Thou shalt aby it.
Lys. Now she holds me not;
Now follow, if thou dar'st, to try whose right,
Of thine or mine, is most in Helena. [*Exit.*]
Dem. Follow! nay, I'll go with thee, cheek by jowl.
[*Exit, following Lysander.*]
Her. You, mistress, all this coil is 'long of you:
Nay, go not back.
Hel. I will not trust you, I,
Nor longer stay in your curst company.
Your hands than mine are quicker for a fray,
My legs are longer though, to run away. [*Exit.*]
Her. I am amaz'd, and know not what to say. *Exit.*
Obe. This is thy negligence: still thou mistak'st,
Or else committ'st thy knaveries wilfully.
Puck. Believe me, king of shadows, I mistook.
Did not you tell me I should know the man
By the Athenian garments he had on?
And so far blameless proves my enterprise,
That I have 'nointed an Athenian's eyes;
And so far am I glad it so did sort
As this their jangling I esteem a sport.
Obe. Thou see'st these lovers seek a place to fight:
Hie therefore, Robin, overcast the night;
The starry welkin cover thou anon
With drooping fog as black as Acheron,
And lead these testy rivals so astray
As one come not within another's way.
Like to Lysander sometime frame thy tongue,
Then stir Demetrius up with bitter wrong;
And sometime rail thou like Demetrius;
And from each other look thou lead them thus,
Till o'er their brows death-counterfeiting sleep
With leaden legs and batty wings doth creep:
Then crush this herb into Lysander's eye;
Whose liquor hath this virtuous property,
To take from thence all error with his might,
And make his eyeballs roll with wonted sight.
When they next wake, all this derision
Shall seem a dream and fruitless vision,
And back to Athens shall the lovers wend,

erewhile, just now. 288. **puppet.** This word, *Ethiope* (l. 257), and *dwarfish* (l. 295) indicate that Hermia is short and dark. 300. **curst,** shrewish; see glossary. 302. **right,** true. 304. **something,** somewhat; see glossary. 310. **stealth,** stealing away. 329. **minimus,** diminutive creature. **knot-grass,** a weed (*polygonum aviculare*), an infusion of which was thought to stunt the growth. 333. **intend,** give sign of. 338. **cheek by jowl,** side by side. 339. **coil,** turmoil, dissension; see glossary. **'long of you,** on account of you; see glossary. 347. **king of shadows.** Note the suggestion in this and other passages of a larger aspect of Oberon's power. 352. **sort,** turn out. 356. **welkin,** sky; see glossary. 357. **Acheron,** river of hell, which Shakespeare seems to have thought of as a pit or lake. 359. **As,** so that; see glossary. 370. **derision,** four syllables.

With league whose date till death shall never end.
Whiles I in this affair do thee employ,
I'll to my queen and beg her Indian boy;
And then I will her charmed eye release
From monster's view, and all things shall be peace.
Puck. My fairy lord, this must be done with haste,
For night's swift dragons cut the clouds full fast,
And yonder shines Aurora's harbinger;
At whose approach, ghosts, wand'ring here and there,
Troop home to churchyards: damned spirits all,
That in crossways and floods have burial,
Already to their wormy beds are gone;
For fear lest day should look their shames upon,
They wilfully themselves exile from light
And must for aye consort with black-brow'd night.
Obe. But we are spirits of another sort:
I with the morning's love have oft made sport,
And, like a forester, the groves may tread,
Even till the eastern gate, all fiery-red,
Opening on Neptune with fair blessed beams,
Turns into yellow gold his salt green streams.
But, notwithstanding, haste; make no delay:
We may effect this business yet ere day. [*Exit.*]
Puck. Up and down, up and down,
I will lead them up and down:
I am fear'd in field and town:
Goblin, lead them up and down.
Here comes one.

Enter LYSANDER.

Lys. Where art thou, proud Demetrius? speak thou now.
Puck. Here, villain; drawn and ready. Where art thou?
Lys. I will be with thee straight.
Puck. Follow me, then,
To plainer ground. [*Exit Lysander, as following the voice.*]

Enter DEMETRIUS.

Dem. Lysander! speak again:
Thou runaway, thou coward, art thou fled?
Speak! In some bush? Where dost thou hide thy head?
Puck. Thou coward, art thou bragging to the stars,
Telling the bushes that thou look'st for wars,
And wilt not come? Come, recreant; come, thou child,
I'll whip thee with a rod: he is defil'd
That draws a sword on thee.
Dem. Yea, art thou there?
Puck. Follow my voice: we'll try no manhood here.
Exeunt.

[*Enter* LYSANDER.]

Lys. He goes before me and still dares me on:
When I come where he calls, then he is gone.
The villain is much lighter-heel'd than I:
I followed fast, but faster he did fly;
That fallen am I in dark uneven way,
And here will rest me. [*Lies down.*] Come, thou gentle day!
For if but once thou show me thy grey light,
I'll find Demetrius and revenge this spite. [*Sleeps.*]

[*Enter*] ROBIN [PUCK] *and* DEMETRIUS.

Puck. Ho, ho, ho! Coward, why com'st thou not?
Dem. Abide me, if thou dar'st; for well I wot
Thou runn'st before me, shifting every place,
And dar'st not stand, nor look me in the face.
Where art thou now?
Puck. Come hither: I am here.
Dem. Nay, then, thou mock'st me. Thou shalt buy this dear,
If ever I thy face by daylight see:
Now, go thy way. Faintness constraineth me
To measure out my length on this cold bed.
By day's approach look to be visited.
[*Lies down and sleeps.*]

Enter HELENA.

Hel. O weary night, O long and tedious night,
Abate thy hours! Shine comforts from the east,
That I may back to Athens by daylight,
From these that my poor company detest:
And sleep, that sometimes shuts up sorrow's eye,
Steal me awhile from mine own company.
[*Lies down and*] *sleep*[*s*].
Puck. Yet but three? Come one more;
Two of both kinds makes up four.
Here she comes, curst and sad:
Cupid is a knavish lad,
Thus to make poor females mad.

[*Enter* HERMIA.]

Her. Never so weary, never so in woe,
Bedabbled with the dew and torn with briers,
I can no further crawl, no further go;
My legs can keep no pace with my desires.
Here will I rest me till the break of day.
Heavens shield Lysander, if they mean a fray!
[*Lies down and sleeps.*]
Puck. On the ground
Sleep sound:
I'll apply
To your eye,
Gentle lover, remedy.
[*Squeezing the juice on Lysander's eyes.*]
When thou wak'st,
Thou tak'st
True delight
In the sight
Of thy former lady's eye:
And the country proverb known,
That every man should take his own,
In your waking shall be shown:
Jack shall have Jill;
Nought shall go ill;
The man shall have his mare again, and all shall be well. [*Exit.*]

---

373. **date,** term of existence; see glossary. 379. **dragons,** supposed by Shakespeare to be yoked to the car of the goddess of night. 380. **Aurora's harbinger,** the morning star. 383. **crossways . . . burial.** Those who had committed suicide were buried at crossways, with a stake driven through them; those drowned, i.e., buried in floods or great waters, would be condemned to wander disconsolate for want of burial rites. 389. **morning's love,** Cephalus, a beautiful youth beloved by Aurora; sometimes taken to refer to the goddess herself. 402. **drawn,** with drawn sword. 403. **straight,** immediately; see glossary. 409. **recreant,** cowardly wretch; see glossary. 422. **wot,** know; see glossary. 432. **Abate,** lessen; see glossary.

ACT IV. SCENE I. 2. **coy,** caress. 20. **neaf,** fist. 21. **leave your courtesy,** put on your hat. 25. **Cavalery,** cavalero, gentleman; form of address. 31. **tongs . . . bones,** instruments for rustic music, the

[ACT IV.

SCENE I. *The same.* LYSANDER, DEMETRIUS, HELENA, *and* HERMIA *lying asleep.*]

Enter [TITANIA,] *Queen of Fairies, and* [BOTTOM *the*] *Clown, and* Fairies; *and* [OBERON,] *the King, behind them.*

Tita. Come, sit thee down upon this flow'ry bed,
While I thy amiable cheeks do coy,
And stick musk-roses in thy sleek smooth head,
And kiss thy fair large ears, my gentle joy.

Bot. Where 's Peaseblossom?

Peas. Ready.

Bot. Scratch my head, Peaseblossom.
Where 's Mounsieur Cobweb?

Cob. Ready.

Bot. Mounsieur Cobweb, good mounsieur, get you your weapons in your hand, and kill me a red-hipped humble-bee on the top of a thistle; and, good mounsieur, bring me the honey-bag. Do not fret yourself too much in the action, mounsieur; and, good mounsieur, have a care the honey-bag break not; I would be loath to have you overflown with a honey-bag, signior. Where 's Mounsieur Mustardseed?

Mus. Ready.

Bot. Give me your neaf, Mounsieur Mustardseed. Pray you, leave your courtesy, good mounsieur.

Mus. What 's your will?

Bot. Nothing, good mounsieur, but to help Cavalery Cobweb to scratch. I must to the barber's, mounsieur; for methinks I am marvellous hairy about the face; and I am such a tender ass, if my hair do but tickle me, I must scratch.

Tita. What, wilt thou hear some music, my sweet love?

Bot. I have a reasonable good ear in music. Let 's have the tongs and the bones.

Tita. Or say, sweet love, what thou desirest to eat.

Bot. Truly, a peck of provender: I could munch your good dry oats. Methinks I have a great desire to a bottle of hay: good hay, sweet hay, hath no fellow.

Tita. I have a venturous fairy that shall seek
The squirrel's hoard, and fetch thee new nuts.

Bot. I had rather have a handful or two of dried peas. But, I pray you, let none of your people stir me: I have an exposition of sleep come upon me.

Tita. Sleep thou, and I will wind thee in my arms.
Fairies, be gone, and be all ways away. [*Exeunt fairies.*]
So doth the woodbine the sweet honeysuckle
Gently entwist; the female ivy so
Enrings the barky fingers of the elm.
O, how I love thee! how I dote on thee! [*They sleep.*]

Enter ROBIN GOODFELLOW [PUCK].

Obe. [*Advancing*] Welcome, good Robin. See'st thou this sweet sight?
Her dotage now I do begin to pity:
For, meeting her of late behind the wood,
Seeking sweet favours for this hateful fool,
I did upbraid her and fall out with her;
For she his hairy temples then had rounded
With coronet of fresh and fragrant flowers;
And that same dew, which sometime on the buds
Was wont to swell like round and orient pearls,
Stood now within the pretty flouriets' eyes
Like tears that did their own disgrace bewail.
When I had at my pleasure taunted her
And she in mild terms begg'd my patience,
I then did ask of her her changeling child;
Which straight she gave me, and her fairy sent
To bear him to my bower in fairy land.
And now I have the boy, I will undo
This hateful imperfection of her eyes:
And, gentle Puck, take this transformed scalp
From off the head of this Athenian swain;
That, he awaking when the other do,
May all to Athens back again repair
And think no more of this night's accidents
But as the fierce vexation of a dream.
But first I will release the fairy queen.
Be as thou wast wont to be;
See as thou wast wont to see:
Dian's bud o'er Cupid's flower
Hath such force and blessed power.
Now, my Titania; wake you, my sweet queen.

Tita. My Oberon! what visions have I seen!
Methought I was enamour'd of an ass.

Obe. There lies your love.

Tita. How came these things to pass?
O, how mine eyes do loathe his visage now!

Obe. Silence awhile. Robin, take off this head.
Titania, music call; and strike more dead
Than common sleep of all these five the sense.

Tita. Music, ho! music, such as charmeth sleep! [*Music.*]

Puck. Now, when thou wak'st, with thine own fool's eyes peep.

Obe. Sound, music! Come, my queen, take hands with me,
And rock the ground whereon these sleepers be. [*Dance.*]
Now thou and I are new in amity
And will to-morrow midnight solemnly
Dance in Duke Theseus' house triumphantly
And bless it to all fair prosperity:
There shall the pairs of faithful lovers be
Wedded, with Theseus, all in jollity.

Puck. Fairy king, attend, and mark:
I do hear the morning lark.

Obe. Then, my queen, in silence sad,
Trip we after night's shade:
We the globe can compass soon,
Swifter than the wand'ring moon.

Tita. Come, my lord, and in our flight
Tell me how it came this night
That I sleeping here was found
With these mortals on the ground. *Exeunt.*
Wind horn [*within*].

Enter THESEUS *and all his train* [; HIPPOLYTA, EGEUS].

The. Go, one of you, find out the forester;
For now our observation is perform'd;

former described as an instrument played like the triangle; the latter are bones held between the fingers and used as clappers. 35. **bottle,** bundle (of hay). 36. **fellow,** equal; see glossary. 42. **exposition,** Bottom's word for "disposition." 44. **all ways,** in all directions. 52. **favours,** i.e., nosegays of flowers. 57. **orient pearls,** i.e., the most beautiful of all pearls, those coming from the Orient. 58. **flouriets',** flowerets'. 69. **other,** others. 76. **Dian's bud,** sometimes defined as *agnus castus* or chaste-tree, which could preserve chastity; perhaps simply invented by Shakespeare to correspond to Cupid's flower. 85. **these five,** i.e., the four lovers and Bottom. 100. **night's,** dissyllable. 108. **observation,** i.e., *observance to a morn of May* (I, i, 167).

And since we have the vaward of the day,
My love shall hear the music of my hounds.
Uncouple in the western valley; let them go:
Dispatch, I say, and find the forester. [*Exit an Attendant.*]
We will, fair queen, up to the mountain's top
And mark the musical confusion
Of hounds and echo in conjunction.

Hip. I was with Hercules and Cadmus once,
When in a wood of Crete they bay'd the bear
With hounds of Sparta: never did I hear
Such gallant chiding; for, besides the groves,
The skies, the fountains, every region near
Seem'd all one mutual cry: I never heard
So musical a discord, such sweet thunder.

The. My hounds are bred out of the Spartan kind,
So flew'd, so sanded, and their heads are hung
With ears that sweep away the morning dew;
Crook-knee'd, and dew-lapp'd like Thessalian bulls;
Slow in pursuit, but match'd in mouth like bells,
Each under each. A cry more tuneable
Was never holla'd to, nor cheer'd with horn,
In Crete, in Sparta, nor in Thessaly:
Judge when you hear. But, soft! what nymphs are these?

Ege. My lord, this is my daughter here asleep;
And this, Lysander; this Demetrius is;
This Helena, old Nedar's Helena:
I wonder of their being here together.

The. No doubt they rose up early to observe
The rite of May, and, hearing our intent,
Came here in grace of our solemnity.
But speak, Egeus; is not this the day
That Hermia should give answer of her choice?

Ege. It is, my lord.

The. Go, bid the huntsmen wake them with their horns.

Shout within. They all start up. Wind horns.

Good morrow, friends. Saint Valentine is past:
Begin these wood-birds but to couple now?

Lys. Pardon, my lord. [*They kneel.*]

The. I pray you all, stand up.
I know you two are rival enemies:
How comes this gentle concord in the world,
That hatred is so far from jealousy,
To sleep by hate, and fear no enmity?

Lys. My lord, I shall reply amazedly,
Half sleep, half waking: but as yet, I swear,
I cannot truly say how I came here;
But, as I think,—for truly would I speak,
And now I do bethink me, so it is,—
I came with Hermia hither: our intent
Was to be gone from Athens, where we might,
Without the peril of the Athenian law.

Ege. Enough, enough, my lord; you have enough:
I beg the law, the law, upon his head.
They would have stol'n away; they would, Demetrius,
Thereby to have defeated you and me,
You of your wife and me of my consent,
Of my consent that she should be your wife.

Dem. My lord, fair Helen told me of their stealth,
Of this their purpose hither to this wood;
And I in fury hither followed them,
Fair Helena in fancy following me.
But, my good lord, I wot not by what power,—
But by some power it is,—my love to Hermia,
Melted as the snow, seems to me now
As the remembrance of an idle gawd
Which in my childhood I did dote upon;
And all the faith, the virtue of my heart,
The object and the pleasure of mine eye,
Is only Helena. To her, my lord,
Was I betroth'd ere I saw Hermia:
But, like in sickness, did I loathe this food;
But, as in health, come to my natural taste,
Now I do wish it, love it, long for it,
And will for evermore be true to it.

The. Fair lovers, you are fortunately met:
Of this discourse we more will hear anon.
Egeus, I will overbear your will;
For in the temple, by and by, with us
These couples shall eternally be knit:
And for the morning now is something worn,
Our purpos'd hunting shall be set aside.
Away with us to Athens; three and three,
We'll hold a feast in great solemnity.
Come, Hippolyta.

[*Exeunt Theseus, Hippolyta, Egeus, and train.*]

Dem. These things seem small and undistinguishable,
Like far-off mountains turned into clouds.

Her. Methinks I see these things with parted eye,
When every thing seems double.

Hel. So methinks:
And I have found Demetrius like a jewel,
Mine own, and not mine own.

Dem. Are you sure
That we are awake? It seems to me
That yet we sleep, we dream. Do not you think
The duke was here, and bid us follow him?

Her. Yea; and my father.

Hel. And Hippolyta.

Lys. And he did bid us follow to the temple.

Dem. Why, then, we are awake: let 's follow him;
And by the way let us recount our dreams. [*Exeunt.*]

Bot. [*Awaking*] When my cue comes, call me, and I will answer: my next is, 'Most fair Pyramus.' Heigh-ho! Peter Quince! Flute, the bellows-mender! Snout, the tinker! Starveling! God 's my life, stolen hence, and left me asleep! I have had a most rare vision. I have had a dream, past the wit of man to say what dream it was: man is but an ass, if he go about to expound this dream. Methought I was—there is no man can tell what. Methought I was,—and methought I had,—but man is but a patched fool, if he will offer to say what methought I had. The eye of man hath not heard, the ear of man hath not seen, man's hand is not able to taste, his tongue to conceive, nor his heart to report, what my dream was. I

109. **vaward,** vanguard, i.e., earliest part. 116-122. **I was . . . thunder.** This reminiscence, which brings such unlikely huntsmen into the field together, is probably of Shakespeare's invention. Hounds of Crete and of Sparta were alike celebrated, the Spartan the more famous. 124. **flew'd,** with large overhanging jaws. **sanded,** of sandy color. 127. **mouth,** voice (of hounds). 128. **Each under each,** with differing notes. **cry,** pack of hounds. 138. **solemnity,** i.e., solemnization of their marriage. 143. **Saint Valentine.** Birds were supposed to choose their mates on St. Valentine's Day. 156. **where,** wherever. 157. **Without,** outside of, beyond. 158. **Enough,** i.e., evidence to convict him. 161. **defeated,** ruined, thwarted; see glossary. 212. **go about,** attempt. 216. **patched,** wearing motley, i.e., a dress of various colors. **offer,** venture. 226. **her,** Thisbe's (?).

Scene II. 4. **transported,** carried off, or possibly, transformed. 20. **sixpence a day,** i.e., as a royal pension. 26. **hearts,** good fellows. 27. **courageous,** used blunderingly. 29. **discourse,** relate; see glossary. 38. **presently,** immediately; see glossary. 40. **preferred,** selected for consideration.

will get Peter Quince to write a ballad of this dream: it shall be called Bottom's Dream, because it hath no bottom; and I will sing it in the latter end of a play, before the duke: peradventure, to make it the more gracious, †I shall sing it at her death. [*Exit.*]

[SCENE II. *Athens.* QUINCE'S *house.*]

Enter QUINCE, FLUTE [, SNOUT, *and* STARVELING].

Quin. Have you sent to Bottom's house? is he come home yet?

Star. He cannot be heard of. Out of doubt he is transported.

Flu. If he come not, then the play is marred: it goes not forward, doth it?

Quin. It is not possible: you have not a man in all Athens able to discharge Pyramus but he.

Flu. No, he hath simply the best wit of any handicraft man in Athens.

Quin. Yea, and the best person too; and he is a very paramour for a sweet voice.

Flu. You must say 'paragon:' a paramour is, God bless us, a thing of naught.

Enter SNUG *the Joiner.*

Snug. Masters, the duke is coming from the temple, and there is two or three lords and ladies more married: if our sport had gone forward, we had all been made men.

Flu. O sweet bully Bottom! Thus hath he lost sixpence a day during his life; he could not have 'scaped sixpence a day: an the duke had not given him sixpence a day for playing Pyramus, I'll be hanged; he would have deserved it: sixpence a day in Pyramus, or nothing.

Enter BOTTOM.

Bot. Where are these lads? where are these hearts?

Quin. Bottom! O most courageous day! O most happy hour!

Bot. Masters, I am to discourse wonders: but ask me not what; for if I tell you, I am not true Athenian. I will tell you every thing, right as it fell out.

Quin. Let us hear, sweet Bottom.

Bot. Not a word of me. All that I will tell you is, that the duke hath dined. Get your apparel together, good strings to your beards, new ribbons to your pumps; meet presently at the palace; every man look o'er his part; for the short and the long is, our play is preferred. In any case, let Thisby have clean linen; and let not him that plays the lion pare his nails, for they shall hang out for the lion's claws. And, most dear actors, eat no onions nor garlic, for we are to utter sweet breath; and I do not doubt but to hear them say, it is a sweet comedy. No more words: away! go, away! [*Exeunt.*]

[ACT V.

SCENE I. *Athens. The palace of* THESEUS.]

Enter THESEUS, HIPPOLYTA, *and* PHILOSTRATE [, Lords, *and* Attendants].

Hip. 'Tis strange, my Theseus, that these lovers
speak of.
The. More strange than true: I never may believe
These antique fables, nor these fairy toys.
Lovers and madmen have such seething brains,
Such shaping fantasies, that apprehend
More than cool reason ever comprehends.
The lunatic, the lover and the poet
Are of imagination all compact:
One sees more devils than vast hell can hold,
That is, the madman: the lover, all as frantic,
Sees Helen's beauty in a brow of Egypt:
The poet's eye, in a fine frenzy rolling,
Doth glance from heaven to earth, from earth to
heaven;
And as imagination bodies forth
The forms of things unknown, the poet's pen
Turns them to shapes and gives to airy nothing
A local habitation and a name.
Such tricks hath strong imagination,
That, if it would but apprehend some joy,
It comprehends some bringer of that joy;
Or in the night, imagining some fear,
How easy is a bush suppos'd a bear!
Hip. But all the story of the night told over,
And all their minds transfigur'd so together,
More witnesseth than fancy's images
And grows to something of great constancy;
But, howsoever, strange and admirable.

Enter lovers: LYSANDER, DEMETRIUS, HERMIA, *and* HELENA.

The. Here come the lovers, full of joy and mirth.
Joy, gentle friends! joy and fresh days of love
Accompany your hearts!
Lys. More than to us
Wait in your royal walks, your board, your bed!
The. Come now; what masques, what dances shall
we have,
To wear away this long age of three hours
Between our after-supper and bed-time?
Where is our usual manager of mirth?
What revels are in hand? Is there no play,
To ease the anguish of a torturing hour?
Call Philostrate.
Phil. Here, mighty Theseus.
The. Say, what abridgement have you for this
evening?
What masque? what music? How shall we beguile
The lazy time, if not with some delight?
Phil. There is a brief how many sports are ripe:
Make choice of which your highness will see first.
[*Giving a paper.*]

ACT V. SCENE I. 2. **may,** can; see glossary. 3. **antique,** strange, grotesque. **toys,** trifles; see glossary. 4-22. **Lovers . . . bear.** These lines furnish a probable illustration of the discoveries of the bibliographical students of Shakespeare. If lines 4-6, 9-11, and 18-22 are read consecutively without paying attention to the lines omitted, it will be found that they make complete sense, and that they refer only to the madman and the lover. The other lines, which refer to the poet, are found in the earliest printed texts of the play to be slightly deranged in verse form. It is inferred that Shakespeare's first draft introduced only the figures of the lover and the madman, and that he subsequently expanded them in his happiest vein with the lines referring to the poet, writing the new lines on the margin. The printers, working from the original playbook, were unable to get them exactly correct in the alignment of the verse. 8. **compact,** formed, composed. 11. **Helen's,** i.e., Helen of Troy, pattern of beauty. **brow of Egypt,** i.e., the face of a gypsy. 21. **fear,** object of fear; see glossary. 25. **images,** creations of the imagination; see glossary. 26. **constancy,** certainty. 39. **abridgement,** pastime. 42. **brief,** short written statement.

The. [*Reads*] 'The battle with the Centaurs, to be sung
By an Athenian eunuch to the harp.'
We'll none of that: that have I told my love,
In glory of my kinsman Hercules.
[*Reads*] 'The riot of the tipsy Bacchanals,
Tearing the Thracian singer in their rage.'
That is an old device; and it was play'd
When I from Thebes came last a conqueror.
[*Reads*] 'The thrice three Muses mourning for the death
Of Learning, late deceas'd in beggary.'
That is some satire, keen and critical,
Not sorting with a nuptial ceremony.
[*Reads*] 'A tedious brief scene of young Pyramus
And his love Thisby; very tragical mirth.'
Merry and tragical! tedious and brief!
That is, hot ice and wondrous strange snow.
How shall we find the concord of this discord?
Phil. A play there is, my lord, some ten words long,
Which is as brief as I have known a play;
But by ten words, my lord, it is too long,
Which makes it tedious; for in all the play
There is not one word apt, one player fitted:
And tragical, my noble lord, it is;
For Pyramus therein doth kill himself.
Which, when I saw rehears'd, I must confess,
Made mine eyes water; but more merry tears
The passion of loud laughter never shed.
The. What are they that do play it?
Phil. Hard-handed men that work in Athens here,
Which never labour'd in their minds till now,
And now have toil'd their unbreathed memories
With this same play, against your nuptial.
The. And we will hear it.
Phil. No, my noble lord;
It is not for you: I have heard it over,
And it is nothing, nothing in the world;
Unless you can find sport in their intents,
Extremely stretch'd and conn'd with cruel pain,
To do you service.
The. I will hear that play;
For never anything can be amiss,
When simpleness and duty tender it.
Go, bring them in: and take your places, ladies.
[*Exit Philostrate.*]
Hip. I love not to see wretchedness o'er-charg'd
And duty in his service perishing.
The. Why, gentle sweet, you shall see no such thing.
Hip. He says they can do nothing in this kind.
The. The kinder we, to give them thanks for nothing.
Our sport shall be to take what they mistake:
And what poor duty cannot do, noble respect
†Takes it in might, not merit.
Where I have come, great clerks have purposed
To greet me with premeditated welcomes;
Where I have seen them shiver and look pale,
Make periods in the midst of sentences,
Throttle their practis'd accent in their fears
And in conclusion dumbly have broke off,
Not paying me a welcome. Trust me, sweet,
Out of this silence yet I pick'd a welcome;
And in the modesty of fearful duty
I read as much as from the rattling tongue
Of saucy and audacious eloquence.
Love, therefore, and tongue-tied simplicity
In least speak most, to my capacity.

[*Enter* PHILOSTRATE.]

Phil. So please your grace, the Prologue is address'd.
The. Let him approach. [*Flourish of trumpets.*]

Enter the Prologue [QUINCE].

Pro. If we offend, it is with our good will.
That you should think, we come not to offend,
But with good will. To show our simple skill,
That is the true beginning of our end.
Consider then we come but in despite.
We do not come as minding to content you,
Our true intent is. All for your delight
We are not here. That you should here repent you,
The actors are at hand and by their show
You shall know all that you are like to know.

The. This fellow doth not stand upon points.

Lys. He hath rid his prologue like a rough colt; he knows not the stop. A good moral, my lord: it is not enough to speak, but to speak true.

Hip. Indeed he hath played on his prologue like a child on a recorder; a sound, but not in government.

The. His speech was like a tangled chain; nothing impaired, but all disordered. Who is next?

Enter PYRAMUS *and* THISBY, *and* WALL, *and* MOONSHINE, *and* LION.

Pro. Gentles, perchance you wonder at this show;
But wonder on, till truth make all things plain.
This man is Pyramus, if you would know;
This beauteous lady Thisby is certain.
This man, with lime and rough-cast, doth present
Wall, that vile Wall which did these lovers sunder;
And through Wall's chink, poor souls, they are content
To whisper. At the which let no man wonder.
This man, with lanthorn, dog, and bush of thorn,
Presenteth Moonshine; for, if you will know,
By moonshine did these lovers think no scorn
To meet at Ninus' tomb, there, there to woo.
This grisly beast, which Lion hight by name,
The trusty Thisby, coming first by night,
Did scare away, or rather did affright;
And, as she fled, her mantle she did fall,
Which Lion vile with bloody mouth did stain.
Anon comes Pyramus, sweet youth and tall,
And finds his trusty Thisby's mantle slain:
Whereat, with blade, with bloody blameful blade,
He bravely broach'd his boiling bloody breast;

44. **battle with the Centaurs,** probably refers to the battle of the Centaurs and the Lapithae, as narrated in Ovid, *Metamorphoses*, Bk. xii. 47. **kinsman.** Plutarch's *Life of Theseus* states that Hercules and Theseus were near kinsmen. 48-49. **tipsy . . . singer.** This was the story of the death of Orpheus, as told in *Metamorphoses*, Bk. xi. 52-53. **'The . . . beggary.'** These two lines were long thought to have some reference to Spenser's *Teares of the Muses* (1591) and were connected by Knight with the death in poverty of the learned poet, Robert Greene. The editors of the New Cambridge Shakespeare see in the lines following, which describe the piece as a satire, a mild retaliation on Shakespeare's part for Greene's attack on Shakespeare as "an upstart crow"; see Shakespeare's Life and Work, Early Period. 55. **Not sorting with,** not befitting. 74. **unbreathed,** unexercised. 80. **stretch'd,** strained. 92. **Takes . . . merit,** values it for the effort made rather than for the excellence achieved (?). 93. **clerks,** learned men. 96. **periods,** full stops. 100. **I pick'd a welcome.** In the kindly speech of Theseus we are probably to see a tribute to the graciousness of Queen Elizabeth. Attempts have been made to see in the passage a reference to a particular occasion. 105. **to my capacity,** as far as I am able to understand. 106. **Prologue,** speaker of the Prologue. **address'd,** ready. 108-117. **If . . . to know.** The humor of the passage is in the blunders of its punctuation. There is a similar piece in *Ralph Roister Doister*, which is

And Thisby, tarrying in mulberry shade,
His dagger drew, and died. For all the rest,
Let Lion, Moonshine, Wall, and lovers twain
At large discourse, while here they do remain.
Exeunt Lion, Thisby, and Moonshine.

The. I wonder if the lion be to speak.

Dem. No wonder, my lord: one lion may, when many asses do.

Wall. In this same interlude it doth befall
That I, one Snout by name, present a wall;
And such a wall, as I would have you think,
That had in it a crannied hole or chink,
Through which the lovers, Pyramus and Thisby,
Did whisper often very secretly.
This loam, this rough-cast and this stone doth show
That I am that same wall; the truth is so:
And this the cranny is, right and sinister,
Through which the fearful lovers are to whisper.

The. Would you desire lime and hair to speak better?

Dem. It is the wittiest partition that ever I heard discourse, my lord.

[PYRAMUS *comes forward.*]

The. Pyramus draws near the wall: silence!

Pyr. O grim-look'd night! O night with hue so black!
O night, which ever art when day is not!
O night, O night! alack, alack, alack,
I fear my Thisby's promise is forgot!
And thou, O wall, O sweet, O lovely wall,
That stand'st between her father's ground and mine!
Thou wall, O wall, O sweet and lovely wall,
Show me thy chink, to blink through with mine eyne! [*Wall holds up his fingers.*]
Thanks, courteous wall: Jove shield thee well for this!
But what see I? No Thisby do I see.
O wicked wall, through whom I see no bliss!
Curs'd be thy stones for thus deceiving me!

The. The wall, methinks, being sensible, should curse again.

Pyr. No, in truth, sir, he should not. 'Deceiving me' is Thisby's cue: she is to enter now, and I am to spy her through the wall. You shall see, it will fall pat as I told you. Yonder she comes.

Enter THISBY.

This. O wall, full often hast thou heard my moans,
For parting my fair Pyramus and me!
My cherry lips have often kiss'd thy stones,
Thy stones with lime and hair knit up in thee.

Pyr. I see a voice: now will I to the chink,
To spy an I can hear my Thisby's face.
Thisby!

This. My love thou art, my love I think.

Pyr. Think what thou wilt, I am thy lover's grace;
And, like Limander, am I trusty still.

This. And I like Helen, till the Fates me kill.

Pyr. Not Shafalus to Procrus was so true.

This. As Shafalus to Procrus, I to you.

Pyr. O, kiss me through the hole of this vile wall!

This. I kiss the wall's hole, not your lips at all.

Pyr. Wilt thou at Ninny's tomb meet me straightway?

This. 'Tide life, 'tide death, I come without delay.
[*Exeunt Pyramus and Thisby.*]

Wall. Thus have I, Wall, my part discharged so;
And, being done, thus Wall away doth go. [*Exit.*]

The. Now is the mural down between the two neighbours.

Dem. No remedy, my lord, when walls are so wilful to hear without warning.

Hip. This is the silliest stuff that ever I heard.

The. The best in this kind are but shadows; and the worst are no worse, if imagination amend them.

Hip. It must be your imagination then, and not theirs.

The. If we imagine no worse of them than they of themselves, they may pass for excellent men. Here come two noble beasts in, a man and a lion.

Enter LION *and* MOONSHINE.

Lion. You, ladies, you, whose gentle hearts do fear
The smallest monstrous mouse that creeps on floor,
May now perchance both quake and tremble here,
When lion rough in wildest rage doth roar.
Then know that I, as Snug the joiner, am
A lion fell, nor else no lion's dam;
For, if I should as lion come in strife
Into this place, 'twere pity on my life.

The. A very gentle beast, and of a good conscience.

Dem. The very best at a beast, my lord, that e'er I saw.

Lys. This lion is a very fox for his valour.

The. True; and a goose for his discretion.

Dem. Not so, my lord; for his valour cannot carry his discretion; and the fox carries the goose.

The. His discretion, I am sure, cannot carry his valour; for the goose carries not the fox. It is well: leave it to his discretion, and let us listen to the moon.

Moon. This lanthorn doth the horned moon present;—

Dem. He should have worn the horns on his head.

The. He is no crescent, and his horns are invisible within the circumference.

Moon. This lanthorn doth the horned moon present;
Myself the man i' th' moon do seem to be.

The. This is the greatest error of all the rest: the man should be put into the lanthorn. How is it else the man i' the moon?

Dem. He dares not come there for the candle; for, you see, it is already in snuff.

Hip. I am aweary of this moon: would he would change!

quoted in Wilson's *Arte of Rhetoric*, which Shakespeare probably knew. 113. **minding,** intending; see glossary. 118. **not stand upon points,** quibbling upon the two meanings (1) "to be overscrupulous" and (2) "to mind his stops in reading." 123. **recorder,** a wind instrument like a flute or flageolet. 124. **government,** control. 140. **hight,** is called. 143. **fall,** let fall; see glossary. 145. **tall,** courageous. 148. **broach'd,** stabbed; used rantingly. 152. **At large,** in full; see *large* in glossary. 164. **sinister,** left. 168. **partition,** wall, and section of a learned book. 171. **grim-look'd,** grim-looking. 183. **sensible,** capable of feeling; see glossary. 198-199. **Limander . . . Helen,** blunders for "Leander" and "Hero." 201. **Shafalus to Procrus,** blunder for "Cephalus" to "Procris," also famous lovers. 205. **'Tide life, 'tide death,** whether life or death betide. 213. **shadows,** likenesses, representations; see glossary. 214. **if imagination amend them.** The idea in this passage is fundamental in art and recurs so frequently in Shakespeare as to be a recognizable article of his faith. 227. **lion fell,** fierce lion (with pun on *fell,* skin). 244. **horns on his head,** the customary jest about the horns of the cuckold. 253. **for,** because of. 254. **in snuff,** pun on the meanings "to be offended" and "to be in need of snuffing."

The. It appears, by his small light of discretion, that he is in the wane; but yet, in courtesy, in all reason, we must stay the time.

Lys. Proceed, Moon.

Moon. All that I have to say, is, to tell you that the lanthorn is the moon; I, the man in the moon; this thorn-bush, my thorn-bush; and this dog, my dog.

Dem. Why, all these should be in the lanthorn; for all these are in the moon. But, silence! here comes Thisby.

Enter THISBY.

This. This is old Ninny's tomb. Where is my love?
Lion. [*Roaring*] Oh—— [*Thisby runs off.*]
Dem. Well roared, Lion.
The. Well run, Thisby.

Hip. Well shone, Moon. Truly, the moon shines with a good grace.

[*The Lion shakes Thisby's mantle, and exit.*]

The. Well moused, Lion.
Dem. And then came Pyramus.
Lys. And so the lion vanished.

Enter PYRAMUS.

Pyr. Sweet Moon, I thank thee for thy sunny beams;
I thank thee, Moon, for shining now so bright;
For, by thy gracious, golden, glittering gleams,
I trust to take of truest Thisby sight.
But stay, O spite!
But mark, poor knight,
What dreadful dole is here!
Eyes, do you see?
How can it be?
O dainty duck! O dear!
Thy mantle good,
What, stain'd with blood!
Approach, ye Furies fell!
O Fates, come, come,
Cut thread and thrum;
Quail, crush, conclude, and quell!

The. This passion, and the death of a dear friend, would go near to make a man look sad.

Hip. Beshrew my heart, but I pity the man.

Pyr. O wherefore, Nature, didst thou lions frame?
Since lion vile hath here deflower'd my dear:
Which is—no, no—which was the fairest dame
That liv'd, that lov'd, that lik'd, that look'd with cheer.
Come, tears, confound;
Out, sword, and wound
The pap of Pyramus;
Ay, that left pap,
Where heart doth hop: [*Stabs himself.*]
Thus die I, thus, thus, thus.
Now am I dead,
Now am I fled;
My soul is in the sky:
Tongue, lose thy light;
Moon, take thy flight: [*Exit Moonshine.*]
Now die, die, die, die, die. [*Dies.*]

Dem. No die, but an ace, for him; for he is but one.

Lys. Less than an ace, man; for he is dead; he is nothing.

The. With the help of a surgeon he might yet recover, and prove an ass.

Hip. How chance Moonshine is gone before Thisby comes back and finds her lover?

The. She will find him by starlight. Here she comes; and her passion ends the play.

[*Enter* THISBY.]

Hip. Methinks she should not use a long one for such a Pyramus: I hope she will be brief.

Dem. A mote will turn the balance, which Pyramus, which Thisby, is the better; he for a man, God warrant us; she for a woman, God bless us.

Lys. She hath spied him already with those sweet eyes.

Dem. And thus she means, videlicet:—

This. Asleep, my love?
What, dead, my dove?
O Pyramus, arise!
Speak, speak. Quite dumb?
Dead, dead? A tomb
Must cover thy sweet eyes.
These lily lips,
This cherry nose,
These yellow cowslip cheeks,
Are gone, are gone:
Lovers, make moan:
His eyes were green as leeks.
O Sisters Three,
Come, come to me,
With hands as pale as milk;
Lay them in gore,
Since you have shore
With shears his thread of silk.
Tongue, not a word:
Come, trusty sword;
Come, blade, my breast imbrue: [*Stabs herself.*]
And, farewell, friends;
Thus Thisby ends:
Adieu, adieu, adieu. [*Dies.*]

The. Moonshine and Lion are left to bury the dead.

Dem. Ay, and Wall too.

Bot. [*Starting up*] No, I assure you; the wall is down that parted their fathers. Will it please you to see the epilogue, or to hear a Bergomask dance between two of our company?

The. No epilogue, I pray you; for your play needs no excuse. Never excuse; for when the players are all dead, there need none to be blamed. Marry, if he that writ it had played Pyramus and hanged himself in Thisby's garter, it would have been a fine tragedy: and so it is, truly; and very notably discharged. But, come, your Bergomask; let your epilogue alone.

[*A dance.*]

283. **dole,** grief. 291. **thread and thrum,** the warp in weaving and the loose end of the warp; Bottom was a weaver. 292. **Quail,** overpower. **quell,** kill, destroy. 299. **cheer,** countenance. 312. **ace,** the side of the die containing the single pip, or spot. 330. **means,** moans, laments. 343. **Sisters Three,** the Fates. 347. **shore,** shorn. 351. **imbrue,** stain with blood. 360. **Bergomask dance,** dance named from Bergamo, a province in the state of Venice, noted for the rusticity of its manners. The New Cambridge edition points out that this rustic dance is the antimasque, or grotesque contrasting measure, to the dance of the fairies that is to follow. 363. **excuse,** seek to extenuate (a fault); see glossary. 370. **told,** counted; see *tell* in glossary. 374. **palpable-gross,** palpably gross, obviously crude. 381. **fordone,** exhausted. 391. **triple Hecate's.** Hecate ruled in three capacities: as Luna or Cynthia in heaven, as Diana on earth, and as Proserpina in hell. 394. **frolic,** merry. 397. **sweep the dust behind the door,** i.e., where it would not show. Robin Goodfellow was a household spirit and helped good housemaids and punished lazy ones. 398-407. **Through . . . place.** The editors of the New Cambridge Shakespeare find

The iron tongue of midnight hath told twelve:
Lovers, to bed; 'tis almost fairy time.
I fear we shall out-sleep the coming morn
As much as we this night have overwatch'd.
This palpable-gross play hath well beguil'd
The heavy gait of night. Sweet friends, to bed.
A fortnight hold we this solemnity,
In nightly revels and new jollity. *Exeunt.*

Enter PUCK.

Puck. Now the hungry lion roars,
And the wolf behowls the moon;
Whilst the heavy ploughman snores,
All with weary task fordone.
Now the wasted brands do glow,
Whilst the screech-owl, screeching loud,
Puts the wretch that lies in woe
In remembrance of a shroud.
Now it is the time of night
That the graves all gaping wide,
Every one lets forth his sprite,
In the church-way paths to glide:
And we fairies, that do run
By the triple Hecate's team,
From the presence of the sun,
Following darkness like a dream,
Now are frolic: not a mouse
Shall disturb this hallowed house:
I am sent with broom before,
To sweep the dust behind the door.

Enter [OBERON *and* TITANIA,] *King and Queen of Fairies, with all their train.*

Obe. Through the house give glimmering light,
By the dead and drowsy fire:
Every elf and fairy sprite
Hop as light as bird from brier;
And this ditty, after me,
Sing, and dance it trippingly.
Tita. First, rehearse your song by rote,
To each word a warbling note:
Hand in hand, with fairy grace,
Will we sing, and bless this place. [*Song and dance.*]
Obe. Now, until the break of day,
Through this house each fairy stray.
To the best bride-bed will we,
Which by us shall blessed be;
And the issue there create
Ever shall be fortunate.
So shall all the couples three
Ever true in loving be;
And the blots of Nature's hand
Shall not in their issue stand;
Never mole, hare lip, nor scar,
Nor mark prodigious, such as are
Despised in nativity,
Shall upon their children be.
With this field-dew consecrate,
Every fairy take his gait;
And each several chamber bless,
Through this palace, with sweet peace;
And the owner of it blest
Ever shall in safety rest.
Trip away; make no stay;
Meet me all by break of day.
Exeunt [*Oberon, Titania, and train*].
Puck. If we shadows have offended,
Think but this, and all is mended,
That you have but slumb'red here
While these visions did appear.
And this weak and idle theme,
No more yielding but a dream,
Gentles, do not reprehend:
If you pardon, we will mend:
And, as I am an honest Puck,
If we have unearned luck
Now to 'scape the serpent's tongue,
We will make amends ere long;
Else the Puck a liar call:
So, good night unto you all.
Give me your hands, if we be friends,
And Robin shall restore amends. [*Exit.*]

in this passage evidence that the play was written for performance in the great chamber of some private house on the occasion of the celebration of a marriage. Theseus and the court leave the stage; the lights are extinguished, all but one; the fairies enter, kindle their torches at the remaining flame, place them on their heads and exhibit their dance; then depart as if to bless the bridal chamber. 412. **create,** created. 419. **prodigious,** monstrous, unnatural. 422. **consecrate,** consecrated. 424. **several,** separate; see glossary. 432. **That . . . here,** i.e., that it is a "midsummer-night's dream." 440. **serpent's tongue,** hissing. 444. **Give . . . hands,** applaud by clapping.

THE TRAGEDY OF KING RICHARD THE SECOND

Richard II (c. 1595–1596) is the first in Shakespeare's great four-play historical saga, or tetralogy, that continues with the two parts of *Henry IV* (c. 1596–1598) and concludes with *Henry V* (1599). This second tetralogy completes the action of Shakespeare's great cycle on the Wars of the Roses, begun in the earlier tetralogy on Henry VI and Richard III (c. 1589–1594). Both sequences move from an outbreak of civil faction to the eventual triumph of political stability. Together, they comprise the story of England's long century of political turmoil from the 1390's until Henry Tudor's victory over Richard III in 1485. Yet Shakespeare chose to relate the two halves of this chronicle in reverse order. His crowning statement about kingship in *Henry V* focuses on the education and kingly success of Prince Hal.

With *Richard II*, then, Shakespeare returns to the events which had launched England's century of crisis. These events were still fresh and relevant to Elizabethan minds. Richard and Bolingbroke's contest for the English crown provided a "mirror for magistrates": a sobering example of political wrongdoing and, at least by implication, a rule for political right conduct. One prominent reason for studying history, to an Elizabethan, was to avoid errors of the past. What are the rights and wrongs of Richard's deposition, and to what extent can political lessons be drawn from Shakespeare's presentation?

To begin with, we should not underestimate Richard's attractive qualities, as a man and even as a king. Throughout the play, Richard is consistently more impressive and majestic in appearance than his rival Bolingbroke. Richard fascinates us with his verbal sensitivity, his poetic insight, and his dramatic self-consciousness. He eloquently expounds a sacramental view of kingship, according to which "Not all the water in the rough rude sea Can wash the balm off from an anointed king" (III,ii). Bolingbroke can depose Richard but can never capture the aura of majesty Richard possesses; Bolingbroke may succeed politically, but only at the expense of desecrating an idea. Richard is much more interesting to us as a man than Bolingbroke, more capable of grief, more tender in his personal relationships, more in need of being understood. Indeed, a major factor in Richard's tragedy is the conflict between his public role (wherein he sees himself as divinely appointed, almost superhuman) and his private role (wherein he is emotionally dependent and easily hurt). Although Richard sometimes indulges in childish sentimentality, at his best he is superbly refined, perceptive, and poetic.

These qualities notwithstanding, Richard is an incompetent ruler compared with the man who supplants him. Richard himself confesses to the prodigal expense of "too great a court." In order to raise funds, he has been obliged to "farm our royal realm": that is, sell for ready cash the right of collecting taxes to individual courtiers, who are then free to extort what the market will bear (I,iv). Similarly, Richard proposes to issue "blank charters" to his minions, who will then be authorized to fill in the amount of tax to be paid by any hapless subject. These abuses were infamous to Elizabethan audiences as symbols of autocratic misgovernment. No less heinous is Richard's seizure of the dukedom of Lancaster from his cousin Bolingbroke. Although Richard does receive the consent of his council to banish Bolingbroke, he violates the very idea of inheritance of property when he takes away Bolingbroke's title and lands. And, as his uncle the Duke of York remonstrates, Richard's own right to the throne depends on that idea of due inheritance. By offending against the most sacred concepts of order and degree, he teaches others to rebel.

Richard's behavior even prior to the commencement of the play arouses suspicion. The nature of his complicity in the death of his uncle Thomas of Woodstock, Duke of Gloucester, is perhaps never entirely clear, and Gloucester may have given provocation. Indeed, one can sympathize with the predicament of a very young ruler prematurely thrust into the center of power by the untimely death of his father, the crown prince, now having to cope with an array of worldly-wise, advice-giving uncles. Nevertheless, Richard is unambiguously guilty of murder in the eyes of Gloucester's widow and of her brother-in-law John of Gaunt, Duke of Lancaster. Apparently, too, Gaunt's son Bolingbroke believes Richard to be a murderer, and brings accusation against Thomas Mowbray, Duke of Norfolk, partly as a means of embarrassing the king whom he cannot accuse directly. Mowbray's lot is an unenviable one: he was in command at Calais when Gloucester was executed there, and he hints that Richard ordered the execution (even though Mowbray alleges that he himself did not carry out the order). For his part, Richard is only too glad to banish the man suspected of having been his agent in murder. Mowbray is a convenient scapegoat.

The polished, ceremonial tone of the play's opening is vitiated, then, by our growing awareness of some very dirty politics going on beneath the surface. Our first impression of Richard is of a king devoted to the public display of conciliatory evenhandedness. He listens to the claims and counterclaims of Bolingbroke and Mowbray, and, when he cannot manage to reconcile them peacefully, he allows a trial by combat. This trial (I,iii) is replete with ceremonial repetition and ritual. The combatants are duly sworn in the justice of their cause, and God is to decide the merits of the quarrel by awarding victory to the champion who speaks the truth. Richard, the presiding officer, is God's anointed deputy on earth. Yet it becomes evident in due course that Richard is a major perpetrator of injustice rather than an impartial judge, that Bolingbroke is after greater stakes than he acknowledges even to himself, and that the banishment of the two contenders is Richard's desperate way of sweeping his problems under the carpet. His uncles reluctantly consent to the banishment only because they too see that disaffection has reached alarming proportions.

Bolingbroke's motivation in these opening scenes is perhaps even more obscure than that of Richard. Our first impression of Bolingbroke is of forthrightness, moral indignation, and patriotic zeal. In fact we never really question the earnestness of his outrage at Richard's misgovernance, his longing to avenge a family murder (for Gloucester was his uncle, too), or his bitter disappointment at being banished from his fatherland. Yet we are prompted to ask further: what is the essential cause of the enmity between Bolingbroke and Richard? If Mowbray is only a stalking-horse, is not Gloucester's death also the excuse for pursuing a preexistent animosity? Richard, for one, appears to think so. His portrayal of Bolingbroke as a scheming politician, one who curries favor with the populace in order to build a power base against the king himself, is telling and prophetic. Bolingbroke, says Richard, acts "As were our England in reversion his, And he our subjects' next degree in hope" (I,iv). This unflattering appraisal might be ascribed to malicious envy on Richard's part, were it not proved by subsequent events to be wholly accurate.

Paradoxically, Richard is far the more prescient of the two contenders for the English throne. It is he, in fact, who perceives from the start that the conflict between them is irreconcilable. He banishes Bolingbroke as his chief rival, and does not doubt what motives will call Bolingbroke home again. Meanwhile, Bolingbroke disclaims any motive for his deed other than love of country and hatred of injustice. Although born with a political sixth sense that Richard lacks, Bolingbroke does not theorize about the consequences of his acts. As a man of action, he lives in the present. Richard, conversely, a person of exquisite contemplative powers and poetic imagination, does not deign to cope with the practical. He both envies and despises Bolingbroke's easy way with the commoners. Richard cherishes kingship for the majesty and the royal prerogative it confers, not for the power to govern wisely. Thus it is that, despite his perception of what will follow, Richard habitually indulges his worst instincts, buying a moment of giddy pleasure at the expense of long-term disaster.

We cannot doubt Richard's incompetence as a ruler. Does this incompetence condone Bolingbroke's armed rebellion? According to John of Gaunt, to York (despite his later shift of allegiance), and to the Bishop of Carlisle, it does not. The attitude of these men can be summed up by the phrase "passive obedience." As Gaunt expresses the concept, "God's is the quarrel." Because Richard is God's anointed deputy on earth, only God may punish the king's wrongdoing. Gaunt does not question Richard's guilt, but he does not question God's ability to avenge, either. Gaunt sees human intervention in God's affair as blasphemous: "for I may never lift An angry arm against His minister" (I,ii). To be sure, Gaunt does acknowledge a solemn duty to offer frank advice to extremists of both sides, and he does so unsparingly. He consents to the banishment of his son, and he rebukes Richard savagely with his dying breath.

This doctrine of passive obedience was familiar to Elizabethans, for they heard it in church periodically in official homilies against rebellion. It was the Tudor state's answer to those who asserted a right to overthrow reputedly evil kings. The argument was logically ingenious. Why are evil rulers permitted to govern from time to time? Presumably because God wishes to test a people or punish them for waywardness. Any king performing such chastisement is a divine "scourge." Accordingly, the worst thing a people can do is to rebel against God's scourge, thereby manifesting more waywardness. Instead, they must attempt to remedy the insolence in their hearts, advise the king to mend his ways, and patiently await God's pardon. If they do so they will not long be disappointed. The doctrine is essentially conservative, defending the Establishment. Nevertheless, in *Richard II* it is a moderate position between the extremes of tyranny and rebellion, and is expressed by thoughtful, selfless men. We might be tempted to label it the authorial viewpoint, if we did not also perceive that the doctrine is continually placed in ironic conflict with harsh political realities. The character who most reflects the ironies and even ludicrous incongruities of the situation is the Duke of York.

York is to an extent a choric character—that is, one who helps direct our viewpoint—because his transfer of loyalties from Richard to Bolingbroke structurally delineates the decline of Richard's fortunes and the concurrent rise of Bolingbroke's. At first York shares with his brother Gaunt a dismay at Richard's willfulness, together with a reluctance to act. It is only when Richard seizes the dukedom of Lancaster that York can no longer hold his tongue. His condemnation is as bitter as that of Gaunt, hinting even at loss of allegiance (II,i). Still, he accepts the responsibility, so cavalierly bestowed by Richard, of governing England in the king's absence. He musters what force he can to oppose Bolingbroke's advance, and lectures against this rebellion with the same vehemence he had used against Richard's despotism. Yet when faced with Bolingbroke's overwhelming military superiority, he accedes rather than fight in behalf of a lost cause. However much this may resemble cowardice or mere expediency, it also displays a pragmatic logic. Once Bolingbroke has become *de facto* king, in York's view he must be acknowledged and obeyed. By a kind of analogy to the doctrine of passive obedience (which more rigorous theorists would never allow), York accepts the status quo as inevitable. He is vigorously ready to defend the new regime, just as he earlier defended Richard's rule.

When, however, this conclusion brings York to the point of turning in his own son Aumerle for a traitor, and quarreling with his wife as to whether their son shall live, the ironic absurdity is apparent. King Henry himself is amused, in one of the play's rare lighthearted moments (V,iii). When a family and a kingdom are divided against one another, there can be no really satisfactory resolution.

We are never entirely convinced that all the fine old medieval theories surrounding kingship—divine right, passive obedience, trial by combat, and the like—can ever wholly explain or remedy the complex and nasty political situation afflicting England. The one man capable of decisive action, in fact, is he who never theorizes at all: Bolingbroke. As we have seen, his avowed motive for opposing Mowbray—simple patriotic indignation—is uttered with such earnestness that we wonder if indeed Bolingbroke has examined in himself those political ambitions so plainly visible to Richard and others. This same discrepancy between surface and depth applies to Bolingbroke's motives in returning to England. With seemingly passionate sincerity he protests to York that he comes only for his dukedom of Lancaster (II,iii). But does he seriously think he can reclaim that dukedom by force, and then yield to Richard without either maintaining Richard as a puppet king or placing himself in intolerable jeopardy? And can he suppose that his allies, Northumberland and the rest, who have now openly defied the king, will countenance the return to power of one who would never trust them again? It is in this context that York protests, "Well, well, I see the issue of these arms." Not only the deposition of Richard, but Richard's death, are foregone conclusions once Bolingbroke has succeeded in an armed rebellion. There can be no turning back. Yet Bolingbroke simply will not theorize in these terms. He repeatedly admonishes Northumberland for treating Richard harshly, even though Northumberland is only taking upon himself the unpleasant but unavoidable duty of arresting and impeaching a king. When the new King Henry discovers—to his surprise, evidently—that Richard's life is now a burden to the state, he ponders aloud, "Have I no friend will rid me of this living fear?" and then rebukes Exton for proceeding on cue.

The phrase for Bolingbroke's pragmatic spirit, and for his new government, is "*de facto*." Ultimately, the justification for his rule is the very fact of its existence, its functioning. Bolingbroke is the man of the hour. In Yeats' fine maxim, Bolingbroke is the vessel of clay, Richard the vessel of porcelain. One is durable and utilitarian, yet unattractive; the other is exquisite, fragile, impractical. The comparison does not force us to prefer one to the other, even though Yeats himself characteristically sided with beauty against politics. Rather, Shakespeare gives us our choice, allowing us to see in ourselves an inclination toward political and social stability or toward artistic temperament.

The paradox may suggest that the qualities of a good administrator are not those of a sensitive, thoughtful man. However hopeless as a king, Richard stands before us increasingly as an introspective and fascinating person. When his power crumbles, his spirit is enhanced, as though loss of power and royal identity were necessary for the discovery of true values.

In this there is a faint anticipation of King Lear's self-learning, fearfully and preciously bought. The trace is only slight here, because in good part *Richard II* is a political history play rather than a tragedy, and because Richard's self-realization is imperfect. Nevertheless, when Richard faces deposition and separation from his queen, and especially when he is alone in prison expecting to die, he strives to understand his life and through it the general condition of humanity. He perceives a contradiction in heaven's assurances about salvation: on the one hand Christ promises to receive all God's children, whereas He also warns that it is as hard for a rich man to enter heaven as for a camel to thread a needle's eye (V,v). The paradox echoes the Beatitudes: the last shall be first, the meek shall inherit the earth. Richard, now one of the downtrodden, gropes for an understanding of the vanity of human achievement whereby he can aspire to the victory Christ promised. At his death, that victory seems to him assured: his soul will mount to its seat on high "Whilst my gross flesh sinks downward, here to die."

In this triumph of spirit over flesh, the long downward motion of Richard's worldly fortune is crucially reversed. By the same token, the worldly success of Bolingbroke is shown to be no more than that:

THE FOLGER SHAKESPEARE LIBRARY

Holbein's "Dance of Death" (1538)—the king, despite power and wealth, is stalked by Death; see III,ii,155 ff.

worldly success. His archetype is Cain, the primal murderer of a brother. To the extent that the play is a history, Bolingbroke's *de facto* success is still a matter of political relevance; but in the belated movement toward Richard's personal tragedy, we experience a profound countermovement that partly achieves a purgative sense of atonement and reassurance. Whatever Richard may have lost, his gain is also great.

The image patterns of *Richard II* reinforce structure and meaning. The play is unusual for its extensive use of blank verse and rhyme, and for its interwoven sets of recurring images. England is a garden mismanaged by her royal gardener, so that weeds and caterpillars (e.g., Bushy, Bagot, and Green) flourish. She is also a sick body ill-tended by her royal physician, and a family divided against itself yielding abortive and sterile progeny. Her political ills are attested to by disorders in the cosmos: comets, shooting stars, withered bay trees, weeping rains. Night owls, associated with death, prevail over the larks of morning. The sun, royally associated at first with Richard, deserts him for Bolingbroke and leaves Richard as the Phaëthon who has mishandled the sun-god's chariot and so scorched the earth. Linked to the sun image is the prevalent *leit-motif* of ascent and descent. And, touching upon all these, a cluster of Biblical images sees England as a despoiled garden of Eden witnessing a second fall of man. Richard repeatedly brands his enemies and deserters as Judases and Pilates, not always fairly; nonetheless, in his last agony he finds genuine consolation in Christ's example. This poetic method is intensely suitable for a man so self-absorbed in the drama of his existence.

The poetry also confirms the date of *Richard II* as of the so-called lyric period, c. 1594–1596, that also produced *Romeo and Juliet* and *A Midsummer Night's Dream*. The play, registered and carefully published in quarto form in 1597, appears to have drawn on Samuel Daniel's *Civill Wars* (1595) as well as Holinshed's *Chronicles*. For its structure it surely owed something to Marlowe's *Edward II* (c. 1592), and it may have relied on the anonymous *Thomas of Woodstock* (c. 1591–1595) for an understanding of the occasionally obscure events surrounding the death of Richard's uncle. Shakespeare must have known he was dealing with a politically explosive topic often used as a libelous analogy against Queen Elizabeth. The deposition scene is missing from the earlier quartos, as though it had been excised by the censor. And in 1601 the Earl of Essex commissioned Shakespeare's company to perform a revived play about Richard II on the eve of an abortive rebellion, presumably as a means of inciting to riot. Whether the play was Shakespeare's is not certain, but seems likely. The acting company was ultimately exonerated, but not before Elizabeth believed that she was being compared to Richard. However little Shakespeare may have intended the analogy when he wrote, he chose a subject of intense political relevance to Elizabethans, for which the greatest tact was needed.

THE TRAGEDY OF KING RICHARD THE SECOND

[*Dramatis Personae*

KING RICHARD the Second.
JOHN OF GAUNT, Duke of Lancaster, } *uncles to the King.*
EDMUND OF LANGLEY, Duke of York, } *uncles to the King.*
HENRY, *surnamed* BOLINGBROKE, Duke of Hereford, *son to John of Gaunt; afterwards* KING HENRY IV.
DUKE OF AUMERLE, *son to the Duke of York.*
THOMAS MOWBRAY, Duke of Norfolk.
DUKE OF SURREY.
EARL OF SALISBURY.
LORD BERKELEY.
BUSHY, BAGOT, GREEN, } *servants to King Richard.*
EARL OF NORTHUMBERLAND.
HENRY PERCY, *surnamed* Hotspur, *his son.*
LORD ROSS.
LORD WILLOUGHBY.
LORD FITZWATER.
Bishop of Carlisle.
Abbot of Westminster.
Lord Marshal.
SIR STEPHEN SCROOP.
SIR PIERCE of Exton.
Captain of a band of Welshmen.

QUEEN to King Richard.
DUCHESS OF YORK.
DUCHESS OF GLOUCESTER.
Ladies attending on the Queen.

Lords, Heralds, Officers, Soldiers, Gardeners, Keeper, Messenger, Groom, *and other* Attendants.

SCENE: *England and Wales.*]

[ACT I.

SCENE I. *London.* KING RICHARD'S *palace.*]

Enter KING RICHARD, JOHN OF GAUNT, *with other* Nobles *and* Attendants.

K. Rich. Old John of Gaunt, time-honoured Lancaster,
Hast thou, according to thy oath and band,
Brought hither Henry Hereford thy bold son,
Here to make good the boist'rous late appeal,
Which then our leisure would not let us hear,
Against the Duke of Norfolk, Thomas Mowbray?
Gaunt. I have, my liege.
K. Rich. Tell me, moreover, hast thou sounded him,
If he appeal the duke on ancient malice;

Or worthily, as a good subject should,
On some known ground of treachery in him?
Gaunt. As near as I could sift him on that argument,
On some apparent danger seen in him
Aim'd at your highness, no inveterate malice.
K. Rich. Then call them to our presence; face to face,
And frowning brow to brow, ourselves will hear
The accuser and the accused freely speak:
High-stomach'd are they both, and full of ire,
In rage deaf as the sea, hasty as fire.

Enter BOLINGBROKE *and* MOWBRAY.

Boling. Many years of happy days befal
My gracious sovereign, my most loving liege!
Mow. Each day still better other's happiness;
Until the heavens, envying earth's good hap,
Add an immortal title to your crown!
K. Rich. We thank you both: yet one but flatters us,
As well appeareth by the cause you come;
Namely, to appeal each other of high treason.
Cousin of Hereford, what dost thou object
Against the Duke of Norfolk, Thomas Mowbray?
Boling. First, heaven be the record to my speech!
In the devotion of a subject's love,
Tend'ring the precious safety of my prince,
And free from other misbegotten hate,
Come I appellant to this princely presence.
Now, Thomas Mowbray, do I turn to thee,
And mark my greeting well; for what I speak
My body shall make good upon this earth,
Or my divine soul answer it in heaven.
Thou art a traitor and a miscreant,
Too good to be so and too bad to live,
Since the more fair and crystal is the sky,
The uglier seem the clouds that in it fly.
Once more, the more to aggravate the note,
With a foul traitor's name stuff I thy throat;
And wish, so please my sovereign, ere I move,
What my tongue speaks my right drawn sword may prove.
Mow. Let not my cold words here accuse my zeal:
'Tis not the trial of a woman's war,
The bitter clamour of two eager tongues,
Can arbitrate this cause betwixt us twain;
The blood is hot that must be cool'd for this:
Yet can I not of such tame patience boast
As to be hush'd and nought at all to say:
First, the fair reverence of your highness curbs me
From giving reins and spurs to my free speech;
Which else would post until it had return'd
These terms of treason doubled down his throat.
Setting aside his high blood's royalty,
And let him be no kinsman to my liege,
I do defy him, and I spit at him;
Call him a slanderous coward and a villain:
Which to maintain I would allow him odds,
And meet him, were I tied to run afoot
Even to the frozen ridges of the Alps,
Or any other ground inhabitable,
Where ever Englishman durst set his foot.
Mean time let this defend my loyalty,
By all my hopes, most falsely doth he lie.
Boling. Pale trembling coward, there I throw my gage,
Disclaiming here the kindred of the king,
And lay aside my high blood's royalty,
Which fear, not reverence, makes thee to except.
If guilty dread have left thee so much strength
As to take up mine honour's pawn, then stoop:
By that and all the rites of knighthood else,
Will I make good against thee, arm to arm,
What I have spoke, or thou canst worse devise.
Mow. I take it up; and by that sword I swear,
Which gently laid my knighthood on my shoulder,
I'll answer thee in any fair degree,
Or chivalrous design of knightly trial:
And when I mount, alive may I not light,
If I be traitor or unjustly fight!
K. Rich. What doth our cousin lay to Mowbray's charge?
It must be great that can inherit us
So much as of a thought of ill in him.
Boling. Look what I speak, my life shall prove it true;
That Mowbray hath receiv'd eight thousand nobles
In name of lendings for your highness' soldiers,
The which he hath detain'd for lewd employments,
Like a false traitor and injurious villain.
Besides I say and will in battle prove,
Or here or elsewhere to the furthest verge
That ever was survey'd by English eye,
That all the treasons for these eighteen years
Complotted and contrived in this land
Fetch from false Mowbray their first head and spring.
Further I say and further will maintain
Upon his bad life to make all this good,
That he did plot the Duke of Gloucester's death,
Suggest his soon-believing adversaries,
And consequently, like a traitor coward,
Sluic'd out his innocent soul through streams of blood:
Which blood, like sacrificing Abel's, cries,
Even from the tongueless caverns of the earth,
To me for justice and rough chastisement;
And, by the glorious worth of my descent,
This arm shall do it, or this life be spent.
K. Rich. How high a pitch his resolution soars!
Thomas of Norfolk, what say'st thou to this?
Mow. O, let my sovereign turn away his face

ACT I. SCENE I. *Stage Direction: London.* Holinshed places this scene at Windsor; he is followed by many editors. 1. **Old John of Gaunt,** born in 1340 at Ghent; hence the surname *Gaunt.* At this time, April 29, 1398, he was only fifty-eight, although Shakespeare represents him as being very old. 2. **band,** bond. 4. **appeal,** accusation, formal challenge or impeachment which the accuser was obliged to maintain in combat. 9. **appeal,** accuse. 12. **sift,** discover true motives by questioning. **argument,** subject. 13. **apparent,** obvious. 18. **High-stomach'd,** haughty, having an appetite for combat. 23. **hap,** fortune. 32. **Tend'ring,** holding dear. 34. **appellant,** in accusation, as the accuser. 43. **note,** reproach. 46. **right drawn,** justly or rightly drawn. 47. **accuse my zeal,** accuse me of wanting zeal. 49. **eager,** sharp, biting. 58. **Setting . . . royalty,** disregarding Bolingbroke's royal blood. 59. **let him be,** suppose him to be. 63. **tied,** obliged. 65. **inhabitable,** uninhabitable. 67. **this,** i.e., his sword, or his assertion of Bolingbroke's guilt. 69. **gage,** a gauntlet as a sign of the pledge to combat. 72. **except,** use as an excuse. 74. **pawn,** i.e., his gage. 82. **light,** dismount. 85. **inherit,** put in possession of. 88. **nobles,** gold coins worth twenty groats or 6s. 8d. 89. **lendings,** money advanced to soldiers when the regular pay cannot be given (Onions). 90. **lewd,** vile, base. 97. **head and spring,** synonymous words meaning "origin." 100. **Duke of Gloucester's death.** Thomas of Woodstock, Duke of Gloucester, sixth (or seventh) son of Edward III and brother of John of Gaunt, was murdered at Calais in September 1397. 101. **Suggest,** prompt, incite. 102. **consequently,** afterwards. 104. **Abel's.** See Genesis 4:3-12. 105. **tongueless,** resonant but without articulate speech.

And bid his ears a little while be deaf,
Till I have told this slander of his blood,
How God and good men hate so foul a liar.

K. Rich. Mowbray, impartial are our eyes and ears:
Were he my brother, nay, my kingdom's heir,
As he is but my father's brother's son,
Now, by my sceptre's awe, I make a vow,
Such neighbour nearness to our sacred blood
Should nothing privilege him, nor partialize
The unstooping firmness of my upright soul:
He is our subject, Mowbray; so art thou:
Free speech and fearless I to thee allow.

Mow. Then, Bolingbroke, as low as to thy heart,
Through the false passage of thy throat, thou liest!
Three parts of that receipt I had for Calais
Disburs'd I duly to his highness' soldiers;
The other part reserv'd I by consent,
For that my sovereign liege was in my debt
Upon remainder of a dear account,
Since last I went to France to fetch his queen:
Now swallow down that lie. For Gloucester's death,
I slew him not; but to my own disgrace
Neglected my sworn duty in that case.
For you, my noble Lord of Lancaster,
The honourable father to my foe,
Once did I lay an ambush for your life,
A trespass that doth vex my grieved soul;
But ere I last receiv'd the sacrament
I did confess it, and exactly begg'd
Your grace's pardon, and I hope I had it.
This is my fault: as for the rest appeal'd,
It issues from the rancour of a villain,
A recreant and most degenerate traitor:
Which in myself I boldly will defend;
And interchangeably hurl down my gage
Upon this overweening traitor's foot,
To prove myself a loyal gentleman
Even in the best blood chamber'd in his bosom.
In haste whereof, most heartily I pray
Your highness to assign our trial day.

K. Rich. Wrath-kindled gentlemen, be rul'd by me;
Let's purge this choler without letting blood:
This we prescribe, though no physician;
Deep malice makes too deep incision;
Forget, forgive; conclude and be agreed;
Our doctors say this is no month to bleed.
Good uncle, let this end where it begun;
We'll calm the Duke of Norfolk, you your son.

Gaunt. To be a make-peace shall become my age:
Throw down, my son, the Duke of Norfolk's gage.

K. Rich. And, Norfolk, throw down his.

Gaunt. When, Harry, when?
Obedience bids I should not bid again.

K. Rich. Norfolk, throw down, we bid; there is no boot.

Mow. Myself I throw, dread sovereign, at thy foot.
My life thou shalt command, but not my shame:
The one my duty owes; but my fair name,
Despite of death that lives upon my grave,
To dark dishonour's use thou shalt not have.
I am disgrac'd, impeach'd and baffled here,
Pierc'd to the soul with slander's venom'd spear,
The which no balm can cure but his heart-blood
Which breath'd this poison.

K. Rich. Rage must be withstood:
Give me his gage: lions make leopards tame.

Mow. Yea, but not change his spots: take but my shame,
And I resign my gage. My dear dear lord,
The purest treasure mortal times afford
Is spotless reputation: that away,
Men are but gilded loam or painted clay.
A jewel in a ten-times-barr'd-up chest
Is a bold spirit in a loyal breast.
Mine honour is my life; both grow in one;
Take honour from me, and my life is done:
Then, dear my liege, mine honour let me try;
In that I live and for that will I die.

K. Rich. Cousin, throw up your gage; do you begin.

Boling. O, God defend my soul from such deep sin!
Shall I seem crest-fallen in my father's sight?
Or with pale beggar-fear impeach my height
Before this out-dar'd dastard? Ere my tongue
Shall wound my honour with such feeble wrong,
Or sound so base a parle, my teeth shall tear
The slavish motive of recanting fear,
And spit it bleeding in his high disgrace,
Where shame doth harbour, even in Mowbray's face.
[*Exit Gaunt.*]

K. Rich. We were not born to sue, but to command;
Which since we cannot do to make you friends,
Be ready, as your lives shall answer it,
At Coventry, upon Saint Lambert's day:
There shall your swords and lances arbitrate
The swelling difference of your settled hate:
Since we can not atone you, we shall see
Justice design the victor's chivalry.
Lord marshal, command our officers at arms
Be ready to direct these home alarms. *Exit* [*with others*].

[SCENE II. *The* DUKE OF LANCASTER'S *palace.*]

Enter JOHN OF GAUNT *with the* DUCHESS OF GLOUCESTER.

Gaunt. Alas, the part I had in Woodstock's blood
Doth more solicit me than your exclaims,
To stir against the butchers of his life!
But since correction lieth in those hands
Which made the fault that we cannot correct,
Put we our quarrel to the will of heaven;
Who, when they see the hours ripe on earth,
Will rain hot vengeance on offenders' heads.

Duch. Finds brotherhood in thee no sharper spur?
Hath love in thy old blood no living fire?
Edward's seven sons, whereof thyself art one,
Were as seven vials of his sacred blood,

113. **slander of,** disgrace or reproach to. 126. **receipt,** thing received. 132-134. **For . . . case.** Mowbray's excuse is at the king's expense; he vaguely hints at the king's connivance. In Holinshed Mowbray ignores the charge. 140. **exactly,** explicitly, formally. 144. **recreant,** cowardly. 146. **interchangeably,** in exchange. 153. **choler,** excess of the humor choler, anger. **letting blood,** used with a quibble on the sense of "mortal combat." 156. **conclude,** come to a final agreement. 157. **no month to bleed.** Spring and autumn were regarded as the proper times to bleed patients. Ff: *time;* Q_1: *month.* 160. **make-peace,** peacemaker. 164. **boot,** alternative, remedy. 170. **impeach'd,** called into question, discredited. **baffled,** disgraced, as of a recreant knight. A part of the punishment of coward knights was hanging by the heels, which is the original meaning of the word. 174. **lions, leopards.** The royal arms showed a rampant lion; the Norfolk arms may have shown a leopard. 184. **try,** put to the test. 189. **beggar-fear,** a beggar's fear. **height,** high position. 190. **out-dar'd,** dared down, cowed. 192. **parle,** parley, overture to peace. 193. **motive,** instrument. 199. **Saint Lambert's day,** September 17. 203. **design,** point out.

Or seven fair branches springing from one root:
Some of those seven are dried by nature's course,
Some of those branches by the Destinies cut;
But Thomas, my dear lord, my life, my Gloucester,
One vial full of Edward's sacred blood,
One flourishing branch of his most royal root,
Is crack'd, and all the precious liquor spilt,
Is hack'd down, and his summer leaves all faded,
By envy's hand and murder's bloody axe.
Ah, Gaunt, his blood was thine! that bed, that womb,
That metal, that self mould, that fashioned thee
Made him a man; and though thou livest and
    breathest,
Yet art thou slain in him: thou dost consent
In some large measure to thy father's death,
In that thou seest thy wretched brother die,
Who was the model of thy father's life.
Call it not patience, Gaunt; it is despair:
In suff'ring thus thy brother to be slaught'red,
Thou showest the naked pathway to thy life,
Teaching stern murder how to butcher thee:
That which in mean men we intitle patience
Is pale cold cowardice in noble breasts.
What shall I say? to safeguard thine own life,
The best way is to venge my Gloucester's death.
Gaunt. God's is the quarrel; for God's substitute,
His deputy anointed in His sight,
Hath caus'd his death: the which if wrongfully,
Let heaven revenge; for I may never lift
An angry arm against His minister.
Duch. Where then, alas, may I complain myself?
Gaunt. To God, the widow's champion and defence.
Duch. Why, then, I will. Farewell, old Gaunt.
Thou goest to Còventry, there to behold
Our cousin Hereford and fell Mowbray fight:
O, sit my husband's wrongs on Hereford's spear,
That it may enter butcher Mowbray's breast!
Or, if misfortune miss the first career,
Be Mowbray's sins so heavy in his bosom,
That they may break his foaming courser's back,
And throw the rider headlong in the lists,
A caitiff recreant to my cousin Hereford!
Farewell, old Gaunt: thy sometimes brother's wife
With her companion Grief must end her life.
Gaunt. Sister, farewell; I must to Coventry:
As much good stay with thee as go with me!
Duch. Yet one word more: grief boundeth where it
    falls,
Not with the empty hollowness, but weight:
I take my leave before I have begun,
For sorrow ends not when it seemeth done.
Commend me to thy brother, Edmund York.
Lo, this is all:—nay, yet depart not so;
Though this be all, do not so quickly go;
I shall remember more. Bid him—ah, what?—
With all good speed at Plashy visit me.
Alack, and what shall good old York there see
But empty lodgings and unfurnish'd walls,
Unpeopled offices, untrodden stones?
And what hear there for welcome but my groans?
Therefore commend me; let him not come there,
To seek out sorrow that dwells every where.
Desolate, desolate, will I hence and die:
The last leave of thee takes my weeping eye. *Exeunt.*

[SCENE III. *The lists at Coventry.*]

Enter Lord Marshal *and the* DUKE [OF] AUMERLE.

Mar. My Lord Aumerle, is Harry Hereford arm'd?
Aum. Yea, at all points; and longs to enter in.
Mar. The Duke of Norfolk, sprightfully and bold,
Stays but the summons of the appellant's trumpet.
Aum. Why, then, the champions are prepar'd, and
    stay
For nothing but his majesty's approach.

The trumpets sound, and the KING *enters with his nobles* [GAUNT, BUSHY, BAGOT, GREEN, *and others*]. *When they are set, enter* [MOWBRAY] *the* DUKE OF NORFOLK *in arms, defendant* [*with a* Herald].

K. Rich. Marshal, demand of yonder champion
The cause of his arrival here in arms:
Ask him his name and orderly proceed
To swear him in the justice of his cause.
Mar. In God's name and the king's, say who thou
    art
And why thou comest thus knightly clad in arms,
Against what man thou com'st, and what thy quarrel:
Speak truly, on thy knighthood and thy oath;
As so defend thee heaven and thy valour!
Mow. My name is Thomas Mowbray, Duke of
    Norfolk;
Who hither come engaged by my oath—
Which God defend a knight should violate!—
Both to defend my loyalty and truth
To God, my king and my succeeding issue,
Against the Duke of Hereford that appeals me;
And, by the grace of God and this mine arm,
To prove him, in defending of myself,
A traitor to my God, my king, and me:
And as I truly fight, defend me heaven!

The trumpets sound. Enter [BOLINGBROKE,] DUKE OF HEREFORD, *appellant, in armour* [*with a* Herald].

K. Rich. Marshal, ask yonder knight in arms,
Both who he is and why he cometh hither
Thus plated in habiliments of war,
And formally, according to our law,
Depose him in the justice of his cause.
Mar. What is thy name? and wherefore com'st thou
    hither,
Before King Richard in his royal lists?
Against whom comest thou? and what 's thy quarrel?
Speak like a true knight, so defend thee heaven!
Boling. Harry of Hereford, Lancaster and Derby
Am I; who ready here do stand in arms,
To prove, by God's grace and my body's valour,

SCENE II. 1. **part . . . blood,** my kinship with Woodstock (the Duke of Gloucester; see I, i, 100, note). 2. **exclaims,** exclamations. 4. **those hands,** i.e., Richard's, whom he charges with responsibility for Gloucester's death. Gaunt is more explicit in lines 37-41. 23. **self mould,** selfsame mold. 28. **model,** likeness. 36. **venge,** avenge. 47. **O . . . spear.** The duchess regards Bolingbroke as the family champion, as he seems to regard himself (I, i, 104-108). 49. **career,** the charge of the horse in the tourney or combat. 53. **caitiff,** cowardly. 58. **boundeth,** bounces. 62. **Edmund York,** Edmund of Langley, fifth son of Edward III. 66. **Plashy,** Gloucester's seat in Essex. 68. **unfurnish'd,** bare. 69. **offices,** servants' quarters. 73. **will I hence.** The adverb of place is used here, as frequently in Shakespeare, without the verb of motion.

SCENE III. The events of this scene took place historically on September 16, 1398. 3. **sprightfully,** with high spirit. 7-10. **Marshal . . . cause.** One finds here, as elsewhere in Richard's public behavior, an illustration of what Coleridge calls his "attention to decorum and high feeling of kingly dignity." 28. **plated,** clothed in armor. 30. **Depose,** put under oath.

In lists, on Thomas Mowbray, Duke of Norfolk,
That he is a traitor, foul and dangerous,
To God of heaven, King Richard and to me;
And as I truly fight, defend me heaven!
Mar. On pain of death, no person be so bold
Or daring-hardy as to touch the lists,
Except the marshal and such officers
Appointed to direct these fair designs.
Boling. Lord marshal, let me kiss my sovereign's hand,
And bow my knee before his majesty:
For Mowbray and myself are like two men
That vow a long and weary pilgrimage;
Then let us take a ceremonious leave
And loving farewell of our several friends.
Mar. The appellant in all duty greets your highness,
And craves to kiss your hand and take his leave.
K. Rich. We will descend and fold him in our arms.
Cousin of Hereford, as thy cause is right,
So be thy fortune in this royal fight!
Farewell, my blood; which if to-day thou shed,
Lament we may, but not revenge thee dead.
Boling. O, let no noble eye profane a tear
For me, if I be gor'd with Mowbray's spear:
As confident as is the falcon's flight
Against a bird, do I with Mowbray fight.
My loving lord, I take my leave of you;
Of you, my noble cousin, Lord Aumerle;
Not sick, although I have to do with death,
But lusty, young, and cheerly drawing breath.
Lo, as at English feasts, so I regreet
The daintiest last, to make the end most sweet:
O thou, the earthly author of my blood,
Whose youthful spirit, in me regenerate,
Doth with a twofold vigour lift me up
To reach at victory above my head,
Add proof unto mine armour with thy prayers;
And with thy blessings steel my lance's point,
That it may enter Mowbray's waxen coat,
And furbish new the name of John a Gaunt,
Even in the lusty haviour of his son.
Gaunt. God in thy good cause make thee prosperous!
Be swift like lightning in the execution;
And let thy blows, doubly redoubled,
Fall like amazing thunder on the casque
Of thy adverse pernicious enemy:
Rouse up thy youthful blood, be valiant and live.
Boling. Mine innocency and Saint George to thrive!
Mow. However God or fortune cast my lot,
There lives or dies, true to King Richard's throne,
A loyal, just and upright gentleman:
Never did captive with a freer heart
Cast off his chains of bondage and embrace
His golden uncontroll'd enfranchisement,
More than my dancing soul doth celebrate
This feast of battle with mine adversary.
Most mighty liege, and my companion peers,
Take from my mouth the wish of happy years:
As gentle and as jocund as to jest
Go I to fight: truth hath a quiet breast.
K. Rich. Farewell, my lord: securely I espy
Virtue with valour couched in thine eye.
Order the trial, marshal, and begin.
Mar. Harry of Hereford, Lancaster and Derby,
Receive thy lance; and God defend the right!
Boling. Strong as a tower in hope, I cry amen.
Mar. Go bear this lance to Thomas, Duke of Norfolk.
First Her. Harry of Hereford, Lancaster and Derby,
Stands here for God, his sovereign and himself,
On pain to be found false and recreant,
To prove the Duke of Norfolk, Thomas Mowbray,
A traitor to his God, his king and him;
And dares him to set forward to the fight.
Sec. Her. Here standeth Thomas Mowbray, Duke of Norfolk,
On pain to be found false and recreant,
Both to defend himself and to approve
Henry of Hereford, Lancaster, and Derby,
To God, his sovereign and to him disloyal;
Courageously and with a free desire
Attending but the signal to begin.
Mar. Sound, trumpets; and set forward, combatants. [*A charge sounded.*]
Stay, the king hath thrown his warder down.
K. Rich. Let them lay by their helmets and their spears,
And both return back to their chairs again:
Withdraw with us: and let the trumpets sound
While we return these dukes what we decree.
[*A long flourish.*]
Draw near,
And list what with our council we have done.
For that our kingdom's earth should not be soil'd
With that dear blood which it hath fostered;
And for our eyes do hate the dire aspect
Of civil wounds plough'd up with neighbours' sword;
And for we think the eagle-winged pride
Of sky-aspiring and ambitious thoughts,
With rival-hating envy, set on you
To wake our peace, which in our country's cradle
Draws the sweet infant breath of gentle sleep;
Which so rous'd up with boist'rous untun'd drums,
With harsh-resounding trumpets' dreadful bray,
And grating shock of wrathful iron arms,
Might from our quiet confines fright fair peace
And make us wade even in our kindred's blood;
Therefore, we banish you our territories:
You, cousin Hereford, upon pain of life,
Till twice five summers have enrich'd our fields
Shall not regreet our fair dominions,
But tread the stranger paths of banishment.
Boling. Your will be done: this must my comfort be,
That sun that warms you here shall shine on me;
And those his golden beams to you here lent
Shall point on me and gild my banishment.

43. **daring-hardy,** daringly bold, reckless. 59. **profane,** be profaned by. 66. **cheerly,** cheerfully. 67. **regreet,** greet, salute. 70. **regenerate,** born anew. 73. **proof,** invulnerability. 75. **waxen,** penetrable, soft. 77. **haviour,** behavior, deportment. 81. **amazing,** confusing, bewildering. **casque,** helmet. 95. **jest,** take part in a play or pastime. 97. **securely,** confidently. 102. **Strong . . . hope,** an allusion to Psalms 61:3. 106. **On pain to be,** at the risk of being. 112. **approve,** prove. 118. **Stay . . . down.** Shakespeare fails to disclose Richard's motive here. According to Froissart, several noblemen of the king's party warned him not to let the combat proceed because the people were aroused on Bolingbroke's behalf. The victory of either knight would be perilous to the king's own safety. **warder,** staff or truncheon borne by the king when presiding over a trial by combat. 122. **While,** until. 124. **list,** hear. 134-137. **Which . . . peace.** Syntactically the antecedent of *which* is *peace*, line 132. Both the syntax and the metaphor have gone astray. Note the figurative representation of *peace*, lines 132-133. 139. **we . . . territories.** Richard shows what Gardiner calls the "unwise cunning of a madman" and takes the one course which would be sure

K. Rich. Norfolk, for thee remains a heavier doom,
Which I with some unwillingness pronounce:
The sly slow hours shall not determinate
The dateless limit of thy dear exile;
The hopeless word of 'never to return'
Breathe I against thee, upon pain of life.
Mow. A heavy sentence, my most sovereign liege,
And all unlook'd for from your highness' mouth:
A dearer merit, not so deep a maim
As to be cast forth in the common air,
Have I deserved at your highness' hands.
The language I have learn'd these forty years,
My native English, now I must forego:
And now my tongue's use is to me no more
Than an unstringed viol or a harp,
Or like a cunning instrument cas'd up,
Or, being open, put into his hands
That knows no touch to tune the harmony:
Within my mouth you have engaol'd my tongue,
Doubly portcullis'd with my teeth and lips;
And dull unfeeling barren ignorance
Is made my gaoler to attend on me.
I am too old to fawn upon a nurse,
Too far in years to be a pupil now:
What is thy sentence then but speechless death,
Which robs my tongue from breathing native breath?
K. Rich. It boots thee not to be compassionate:
After our sentence plaining comes too late.
Mow. Then thus I turn me from my country's light,
To dwell in solemn shades of endless night.
K. Rich. Return again, and take an oath with thee.
Lay on our royal sword your banish'd hands;
Swear by the duty that you owe to God—
Our part therein we banish with yourselves—
To keep the oath that we administer:
You never shall, so help you truth and God!
Embrace each other's love in banishment;
Nor never look upon each other's face;
Nor never write, regreet, nor reconcile
This louring tempest of your home-bred hate;
Nor never by advised purpose meet
To plot, contrive, or complot any ill
'Gainst us, our state, our subjects, or our land.
Boling. I swear.
Mow. And I, to keep all this.
Boling. Norfolk, so far as to mine enemy:—
By this time, had the king permitted us,
One of our souls had wand'red in the air,
Banish'd this frail sepulchre of our flesh,
As now our flesh is banish'd from this land:
Confess thy treasons ere thou fly the realm;
Since thou hast far to go, bear not along
The clogging burthen of a guilty soul.
Mow. No, Bolingbroke: if ever I were traitor,
My name be blotted from the book of life,
And I from heaven banish'd as from hence!
But what thou art, God, thou, and I do know;
And all too soon, I fear, the king shall rue.
Farewell, my liege. Now no way can I stray;
Save back to England, all the world 's my way. *Exit.*
K. Rich. Uncle, even in the glasses of thine eyes
I see thy grieved heart: thy sad aspect
Hath from the number of his banish'd years
Pluck'd four away. [*To Boling.*] Six frozen winters spent,
Return with welcome home from banishment.
Boling. How long a time lies in one little word!
Four lagging winters and four wanton springs
End in a word: such is the breath of kings.
Gaunt. I thank my liege, that in regard of me
He shortens four years of my son's exile:
But little vantage shall I reap thereby;
For, ere the six years that he hath to spend
Can change their moons and bring their times about,
My oil-dried lamp and time-bewasted light
Shall be extinct with age and endless night;
My inch of taper will be burnt and done,
And blindfold death not let me see my son.
K. Rich. Why, uncle, thou hast many years to live.
Gaunt. But not a minute, king, that thou canst give:
Shorten my days thou canst with sullen sorrow,
And pluck nights from me, but not lend a morrow;
Thou canst help time to furrow me with age,
But stop no wrinkle in his pilgrimage;
Thy word is current with him for my death,
But dead, thy kingdom cannot buy my breath.
K. Rich. Thy son is banish'd upon good advice,
Whereto thy tongue a party-verdict gave:
Why at our justice seem'st thou then to lour?
Gaunt. Things sweet to taste prove in digestion sour.
You urg'd me as a judge; but I had rather
You would have bid me argue like a father.
O, had it been a stranger, not my child,
To smooth his fault I should have been more mild:
A partial slander sought I to avoid,
And in the sentence my own life destroy'd.
Alas, I look'd when some of you should say,
I was too strict to make mine own away;
But you gave leave to my unwilling tongue
Against my will to do myself this wrong.
K. Rich. Cousin, farewell; and, uncle, bid him so:
Six years we banish him, and he shall go.
[*Flourish. Exit King Richard with his train.*]
Aum. Cousin, farewell: what presence must not know,
From where you do remain let paper show.
Mar. My lord, no leave take I; for I will ride,
As far as land will let me, by your side.
Gaunt. O, to what purpose dost thou hoard thy words,
That thou returnest no greeting to thy friends?
Boling. I have too few to take my leave of you,
When the tongue's office should be prodigal
To breathe the abundant dolour of the heart.
Gaunt. Thy grief is but thy absence for a time.
Boling. Joy absent, grief is present for that time.

to work injustice to both men. 150. **determinate,** put an end to. 151. **dear,** costly, severe. 174. **boots,** avails. 175. **plaining,** complaining. 202. **book of life.** See Revelation 3:5. 204-205. **But . . . rue.** The historical Richard probably meant to recall Mowbray and make Bolingbroke's exile permanent; but such an intention is not implied in this play. 208. **glasses,** mirrors. 210. **banish'd years,** years of banishment. *Banish'd* is not a past participle, but an adjective. 211. **Pluck'd four away.** According to Holinshed the amelioration of Bolingbroke's sentence took place later, at Eltham, when the king was taking leave of Bolingbroke. 214. **wanton,** luxuriant. 230. **But . . . pilgrimage,** efface no wrinkle that comes with time. 231. **current,** i.e., as good as current coin. 234. **a party-verdict,** one person's share in a joint verdict. 241. **partial slander,** accusation of partiality. Cf. line 210. 244. **too strict to make,** i.e., in making; a gerundive use of the infinitive, common in Shakespeare. 249. **what . . . know,** what I cannot learn from you in person.

Gaunt. What is six winters? they are quickly gone.
Boling. To men in joy; but grief makes one hour ten.
Gaunt. Call it a travel that thou tak'st for pleasure.
Boling. My heart will sigh when I miscall it so,
Which finds it an inforced pilgrimage.
Gaunt. The sullen passage of thy weary steps
Esteem as foil wherein thou art to set
The precious jewel of thy home return.
Boling. Nay, rather, every tedious stride I make
Will but remember me what a deal of world
I wander from the jewels that I love.
Must I not serve a long apprenticehood
To foreign passages, and in the end,
Having my freedom, boast of nothing else
But that I was a journeyman to grief?
Gaunt. All places that the eye of heaven visits
Are to a wise man ports and happy havens.
Teach thy necessity to reason thus;
There is no virtue like necessity.
Think not the king did banish thee,
But thou the king. Woe doth the heavier sit,
Where it perceives it is but faintly borne.
Go, say I sent thee forth to purchase honour
And not the king exil'd thee; or suppose
Devouring pestilence hangs in our air
And thou art flying to a fresher clime:
Look what thy soul holds dear, imagine it
To lie that way thou goest, not whence thou com'st:
Suppose the singing birds musicians,
The grass whereon thou tread'st the presence strew'd,
The flowers fair ladies, and thy steps no more
Than a delightful measure or a dance;
For gnarling sorrow hath less power to bite
The man that mocks at it and sets it light.
Boling. O, who can hold a fire in his hand
By thinking on the frosty Caucasus?
Or cloy the hungry edge of appetite
By bare imagination of a feast?
Or wallow naked in December snow
By thinking on fantastic summer's heat?
O, no! the apprehension of the good
Gives but the greater feeling to the worse:
Fell sorrow's tooth doth never rankle more
Than when he bites, but lanceth not the sore.
Gaunt. Come, come, my son, I'll bring thee on thy way:
Had I thy youth and cause, I would not stay.
Boling. Then, England's ground, farewell; sweet soil, adieu;
My mother, and my nurse, that bears me yet!
Where'er I wander, boast of this I can,
Though banish'd, yet a trueborn Englishman. *Exeunt.*

[SCENE IV. *The court.*]

Enter the KING, *with* BAGOT, [GREEN,] *&c. at one door; and the* LORD AUMERLE *at another.*

K. Rich. We did observe. Cousin Aumerle,
How far brought you high Hereford on his way?
Aum. I brought high Hereford, if you call him so,
But to the next highway, and there I left him.
K. Rich. And say, what store of parting tears were shed?
Aum. Faith, none for me; except the northeast wind,
Which then blew bitterly against our faces,
Awak'd the sleeping rheum, and so by chance
Did grace our hollow parting with a tear.
K. Rich. What said our cousin when you parted with him?
Aum. 'Farewell:'
And, for my heart disdained that my tongue
Should so profane the word, that taught me craft
To counterfeit oppression of such grief
That words seem'd buried in my sorrow's grave.
Marry, would the word 'farewell' have length'ned hours
And added years to his short banishment,
He should have had a volume of farewells;
But since it would not, he had none of me.
K. Rich. He is our cousin, cousin; but 'tis doubt,
When time shall call him home from banishment,
Whether our kinsman come to see his friends.
Ourself and Bushy, Bagot here and Green
Observ'd his courtship to the common people;
How he did seem to dive into their hearts
With humble and familiar courtesy,
What reverence he did throw away on slaves,
Wooing poor craftsmen with the craft of smiles
And patient underbearing of his fortune,
As 'twere to banish their affects with him.
Off goes his bonnet to an oyster-wench;
A brace of draymen bid God speed him well
And had the tribute of his supple knee,
With 'Thanks, my countrymen, my loving friends;'
As were our England in reversion his,
And he our subjects' next degree in hope.
Green. Well, he is gone; and with him go these thoughts.
Now for the rebels which stand out in Ireland,
Expedient manage must be made, my liege,
Ere further leisure yield them further means
For their advantage and your highness' loss.
K. Rich. We will ourself in person to this war:
And, for our coffers, with too great a court
And liberal largess, are grown somewhat light,
We are inforc'd to farm our royal realm;
The revenue whereof shall furnish us
For our affairs in hand: if that come short,
Our substitutes at home shall have blank charters;
Whereto, when they shall know what men are rich,
They shall subscribe them for large sums of gold
And send them after to supply our wants;
For we will make for Ireland presently.

266. **foil,** metal surface used in setting gems to show off their luster; hence, that which sets something off to advantage. 272. **passages,** wanderings, experiences. 274. **journeyman,** laborer hired by the day; at the end of such service would come the settlement in his trade. 289. **presence strew'd,** i.e., the royal presence chamber strewn with rushes. 292. **gnarling,** snarling, growling. 299. **fantastic,** imaginary. 300. **apprehension,** idea, product of mere imagination. 302-303. **Fell . . . sore,** i.e., never poisons more than when it irritates the sore instead of lancing to cure it. 302. **rankle,** cause to fester, i.e., produce irritation by poison.

SCENE IV. 8. **rheum,** tears. 12-13. **for . . . word.** This clause is the antecedent of *that*. Aumerle says he pretended to be overcome by grief in order to avoid saying "Farewell" to Bolingbroke. 23. **Ourself . . . Green:** so Q_5; QF: *Our selfe, and Bushy: heere. Bagot and Greene*, which may be construed by omitting punctuation except comma after *heere*. 24. **his courtship to the common people.** Compare Bolingbroke's own account, *1 Henry IV*, III, ii, 46 ff. 29. **underbearing,** bearing, enduring. 30. **affects,** affections. 35. **reversion,** right of future possession. 37. **go,** let go. 38. **rebels . . . Ireland.** Many of the colonies planted by Henry II in the "English Pale" had thrown off their allegiance and were in rebellion. 39. **Expedient manage,** expeditious management. 43. **too great a court.** Holinshed says that Richard "kept the greatest court, and mainteined the most plentiful house that euer any king in England did either before his time or since." 45. **farm,**

Enter BUSHY.

Bushy, what news?
Bushy. Old John of Gaunt is grievous sick, my lord,
Suddenly taken; and hath sent post haste
To entreat your majesty to visit him.
K. Rich. Where lies he?
Bushy. At Ely House.
K. Rich. Now put it, God, in the physician's mind
To help him to his grave immediately!
The lining of his coffers shall make coats
To deck our soldiers for these Irish wars.
Come, gentlemen, let 's all go visit him:
Pray God we may make haste, and come too late!
[*All.*] Amen. *Exeunt.*

[ACT II.

SCENE I. *Ely House.*]

Enter JOHN OF GAUNT *sick, with the* DUKE OF YORK, *&c.*

Gaunt. Will the king come, that I may breathe my last
In wholesome counsel to his unstaid youth?
York. Vex not yourself, nor strive not with your breath;
For all in vain comes counsel to his ear.
Gaunt. O, but they say the tongues of dying men
Enforce attention like deep harmony:
Where words are scarce, they are seldom spent in vain,
For they breathe truth that breathe their words in pain.
He that no more must say is listened more
Than they whom youth and ease have taught to glose;
More are men's ends mark'd than their lives before:
The setting sun, and music at the close,
As the last taste of sweets, is sweetest last,
Writ in remembrance more than things long past:
Though Richard my life's counsel would not hear,
My death's sad tale may yet undeaf his ear.
York. No; it is stopp'd with other flattering sounds,
As praises, of whose taste the wise are fond,
Lascivious metres, to whose venom sound
The open ear of youth doth always listen;
Report of fashions in proud Italy,
Whose manners still our tardy apish nation
Limps after in base imitation.
Where doth the world thrust forth a vanity—
So it be new, there 's no respect how vile—
That is not quickly buzz'd into his ears?
Then all too late comes counsel to be heard,
Where will doth mutiny with wit's regard.
Direct not him whose way himself will choose:
'Tis breath thou lack'st, and that breath wilt thou lose.
Gaunt. Methinks I am a prophet new inspir'd
And thus expiring do foretell of him:
His rash fierce blaze of riot cannot last,
For violent fires soon burn out themselves;
Small show'rs last long, but sudden storms are short;
He tires betimes that spurs too fast betimes;
With eager feeding food doth choke the feeder:
Light vanity, insatiate cormorant,
Consuming means, soon preys upon itself.
This royal throne of kings, this scept'red isle,
This earth of majesty, this seat of Mars,
This other Eden, demi-paradise,
This fortress built by Nature for herself
Against infection and the hand of war,
This happy breed of men, this little world,
This precious stone set in the silver sea,
Which serves it in the office of a wall
Or as a moat defensive to a house,
Against the envy of less happier lands,
This blessed plot, this earth, this realm, this England,
This nurse, this teeming womb of royal kings,
Fear'd by their breed and famous by their birth,
Renowned for their deeds as far from home,
For Christian service and true chivalry,
As is the sepulchre in stubborn Jewry
Of the world's ransom, blessed Mary's Son,
This land of such dear souls, this dear dear land,
Dear for her reputation through the world,
Is now leas'd out, I die pronouncing it,
Like to a tenement or pelting farm:
England, bound in with the triumphant sea,
Whose rocky shore beats back the envious siege
Of wat'ry Neptune, is now bound in with shame,
With inky blots and rotten parchment bonds:
That England, that was wont to conquer others,
Hath made a shameful conquest of itself.
Ah, would the scandal vanish with my life,
How happy then were my ensuing death!

Enter KING [RICHARD] *and* QUEEN, [AUMERLE, BUSHY, GREEN, BAGOT, ROSS, *and* WILLOUGHBY,] *&c.*

York. The king is come: deal mildly with his youth;
For young hot colts being †rag'd do rage the more.
Queen. How fares our noble uncle, Lancaster?
K. Rich. What comfort, man? how is 't with aged Gaunt?
Gaunt. O, how that name befits my composition!
Old Gaunt indeed, and gaunt in being old:
Within me grief hath kept a tedious fast;
And who abstains from meat that is not gaunt?
For sleeping England long time have I watch'd;
Watching breeds leanness, leanness is all gaunt:
The pleasure that some fathers feed upon,
Is my strict fast; I mean, my children's looks;
And therein fasting, hast thou made me gaunt:

to let the right of collecting taxes, for a present cash payment, to the highest bidder. 48. **blank charters,** ready-drawn obligations, blank spaces being left for the names of the parties and the sums they were to provide. 50. **subscribe them,** make them write their names under. 58. **Ely House,** palace of the bishop of Ely in Holborn. 61. **lining,** contents (with pun on lining for coats).

ACT II. SCENE I. 2. **unstaid,** thoughtless, rash. 9. **listened,** listened to. 10. **glose,** flatter, deceive in speech. 12. **close,** harmonious chords at the end of a piece of music. 16. **undeaf,** make capable of hearing. 19. **venom,** pernicious, poisonous. 21. **proud Italy.** Ascham, Lyly, and other sixteenth-century writers complain of the growing influence of Italian luxury. 22. **still,** always. **tardy apish,** imitative but behind the times. 26. **buzz'd,** whispered; used contemptuously. 28. **with wit's regard,** against the consideration due to reason. 33. **riot,** profligacy. 36. **betimes,** soon, early. 38. **cormorant,** glutton. 40-55. **This . . . Jewry.** These lines, except line 50, were published in *England's Parnassus* (1600) and attributed to M. Dr. (Michael Drayton). 44. **infection,** pollution; possibly, plague. 52. **breed,** ancestral reputation for warlike prowess. 55. **stubborn Jewry,** Judea, called stubborn because it resisted Christianity. 60. **tenement,** land held by a tenant. **pelting,** paltry. 70. **rag'd,** enraged. 73. **composition,** constitution. 77. **watch'd,** stayed awake at night.

Gaunt am I for the grave, gaunt as a grave,
Whose hollow womb inherits nought but bones.
K. Rich. Can sick men play so nicely with their names?
Gaunt. No, misery makes sport to mock itself:
Since thou dost seek to kill my name in me,
I mock my name, great king, to flatter thee.
K. Rich. Should dying men flatter with those that live?
Gaunt. No, no, men living flatter those that die.
K. Rich. Thou, now a-dying, sayest thou flatterest me.
Gaunt. O, no! thou diest, though I the sicker be.
K. Rich. I am in health, I breathe, and see thee ill.
Gaunt. Now He that made me knows I see thee ill;
Ill in myself to see, and in thee seeing ill.
Thy death-bed is no lesser than thy land
Wherein thou liest in reputation sick;
And thou, too careless patient as thou art,
Commit'st thy anointed body to the cure
Of those physicians that first wounded thee:
A thousand flatterers sit within thy crown,
Whose compass is no bigger than thy head;
And yet, incaged in so small a verge,
The waste is no whit lesser than thy land.
O, had thy grandsire with a prophet's eye
Seen how his son's son should destroy his sons,
From forth thy reach he would have laid thy shame,
Deposing thee before thou wert possess'd,
Which art possess'd now to depose thyself.
Why, cousin, wert thou regent of the world,
It were a shame to let this land by lease;
But for thy world enjoying but this land,
Is it not more than shame to shame it so?
Landlord of England art thou now, not king:
Thy state of law is bondslave to the law;
And thou—
K. Rich. A lunatic lean-witted fool,
Presuming on an ague's privilege,
Darest with thy frozen admonition
Make pale our cheek, chasing the royal blood
With fury from his native residence.
Now, by my seat's right royal majesty,
Wert thou not brother to great Edward's son,
This tongue that runs so roundly in thy head
Should run thy head from thy unreverent shoulders.
Gaunt. O, spare me not, my brother Edward's son,
For that I was his father Edward's son;
That blood already, like the pelican,
Hast thou tapp'd out and drunkenly carous'd:
My brother Gloucester, plain well-meaning soul,
Whom fair befal in heaven 'mongst happy souls!
May be a precedent and witness good
That thou respect'st not spilling Edward's blood:
Join with the present sickness that I have;
And thy unkindness be like crooked age,
To crop at once a too long withered flower.
Live in thy shame, but die not shame with thee!
These words hereafter thy tormentors be!
Convey me to my bed, then to my grave:
Love they to live that love and honour have.
Exit [borne off by his Attendants].
K. Rich. And let them die that age and sullens have;
For both hast thou, and both become the grave.
York. I do beseech your majesty, impute his words
To wayward sickliness and age in him:
He loves you, on my life, and holds you dear
As Harry Duke of Hereford, were he here.
K. Rich. Right, you say true: as Hereford's love, so his;
As theirs, so mine; and all be as it is.

[Enter NORTHUMBERLAND.]

North. My liege, old Gaunt commends him to your majesty.
K. Rich. What says he?
North. Nay, nothing; all is said:
His tongue is now a stringless instrument;
Words, life and all, old Lancaster hath spent.
York. Be York the next that must be bankrout so!
Though death be poor, it ends a mortal woe.
K. Rich. The ripest fruit first falls, and so doth he;
His time is spent, our pilgrimage must be.
So much for that. Now for our Irish wars:
We must supplant those rough rug-headed kerns,
Which live like venom where no venom else
But only they have privilege to live.
And for these great affairs do ask some charge,
Towards our assistance we do seize to us
The plate, coin, revenues and moveables,
Whereof our uncle Gaunt did stand possess'd.
York. How long shall I be patient? ah, how long
Shall tender duty make me suffer wrong?
Not Gloucester's death, nor Hereford's banishment,
Not Gaunt's rebukes, nor England's private wrongs,
Nor the prevention of poor Bolingbroke
About his marriage, nor my own disgrace,
Have ever made me sour my patient cheek,
Or bend one wrinkle on my sovereign's face.
I am the last of noble Edward's sons,
Of whom thy father, Prince of Wales, was first:
In war was never lion rag'd more fierce,
In peace was never gentle lamb more mild,
Than was that young and princely gentleman.
His face thou hast, for even so look'd he,
Accomplish'd with the number of thy hours;
But when he frown'd, it was against the French
And not against his friends; his noble hand
Did win what he did spend and spent not that
Which his triumphant father's hand had won;
His hands were guilty of no kindred blood,
But bloody with the enemies of his kin.
O Richard! York is too far gone with grief,
Or else he never would compare between.

83. **inherits,** possesses. 84. **nicely,** delicately, fantastically. 86. **kill my name in me,** i.e., by banishing my son. 102. **verge,** circle, ring; technically, "the compass about the king's court which extended for twelve miles." 103. **waste,** a legal use meaning "destruction of houses, woods, lands, etc., done by a tenant to the prejudice of the heir" (Onions). 109. **cousin,** any kinsman not of the immediate family. 114. **Thy state . . . law,** i.e., your legal status as king is now subservient to and at the mercy of the law governing contracts, such as blank charters. 118. **Make pale our cheek.** Richard's physical sensitiveness, which caused him to turn pale readily (see III, ii, 75; III, iii, 67), is recorded by Froissart and other chroniclers. 122. **roundly,** unceremoniously; see glossary. 126. **pelican,** allusion to the belief that the pelican fed its young on its own blood; accordingly, the bird was seen as an emblem of Christian sacrifice. 133. **unkindness,** unnaturalness. 139. **sullens,** moroseness, sullenness. 144. **As Harry Duke of Hereford,** i.e., as he holds Harry, etc. Richard purposely misinterprets the ambiguous speech of York. 156. **rug-headed,** rough-haired. **kerns,** Irish foot soldiers. 157. **no venom else,** allusion to the freedom of Ireland from reptiles, traditionally ascribed to St. Patrick. 159. **charge,** expense. 166. **Gaunt's rebukes,** i.e., the rebuke given to Gaunt. 173. **rag'd,** may equal *enraged*, as in line 70, or we may understand a relative pronoun *that* omitted after lion. 177. **Accomplish'd . . . hours,** i.e., when

K. Rich. Why, uncle, what 's the matter?
York. O my liege,
Pardon me, if you please; if not, I, pleas'd
Not to be pardoned, am content withal.
Seek you to seize and gripe into your hands
The royalties and rights of banish'd Hereford?
Is not Gaunt dead, and doth not Hereford live?
Was not Gaunt just, and is not Harry true?
Did not the one deserve to have an heir?
Is not his heir a well-deserving son?
Take Hereford's rights away, and take from Time
His charters and his customary rights;
Let not to-morrow then ensue to-day;
Be not thyself; for how art thou a king
But by fair sequence and succession?
Now, afore God—God forbid I say true!—
If you do wrongfully seize Hereford's rights,
Call in the letters patents that he hath
By his attorneys-general to sue
His livery, and deny his off'red homage,
You pluck a thousand dangers on your head,
You lose a thousand well-disposed hearts
And prick my tender patience to those thoughts
Which honour and allegiance cannot think.
K. Rich. Think what you will, we seize into our hands
His plate, his goods, his money and his lands.
York. I'll not be by the while: my liege, farewell:
What will ensue hereof, there 's none can tell;
But by bad courses may be understood
That their events can never fall out good. *Exit.*
K. Rich. Go, Bushy, to the Earl of Wiltshire straight:
Bid him repair to us to Ely House
To see this business. To-morrow next
We will for Ireland; and 'tis time, I trow:
And we create, in absence of ourself,
Our uncle York lord governor of England;
For he is just and always lov'd us well.
Come on, our queen: to-morrow must we part;
Be merry, for our time of stay is short.
[*Flourish.*] *Exeunt King and Queen. Manet Northumberland* [*with Willoughby and Ross*].
North. Well, lords, the Duke of Lancaster is dead.
Ross. And living too; for now his son is duke.
Willo. Barely in title, not in revenues.
North. Richly in both, if justice had her right.
Ross. My heart is great; but it must break with silence,
Ere 't be disburdened with a liberal tongue.
North. Nay, speak thy mind; and let him ne'er speak more
That speaks thy words again to do thee harm!
Willo. Tends that thou wouldst speak to the Duke of Hereford?
If it be so, out with it boldly, man;
Quick is mine ear to hear of good towards him.
Ross. No good at all that I can do for him;
Unless you call it good to pity him,
Bereft and gelded of his patrimony.
North. Now, afore God, 'tis shame such wrongs are borne
In him, a royal prince, and many moe
Of noble blood in this declining land.
The king is not himself, but basely led
By flatterers; and what they will inform,
Merely in hate, 'gainst any of us all,
That will the king severely prosecute
'Gainst us, our lives, our children, and our heirs.
Ross. The commons hath he pill'd with grievous taxes,
†And quite lost their hearts: the nobles hath he fin'd
For ancient quarrels, and quite lost their hearts.
Willo. And daily new exactions are devis'd,
As blanks, benevolences, and I wot not what:
But what, o' God's name, doth become of this?
North. Wars hath not wasted it, for warr'd he hath not,
But basely yielded upon compromise
That which his noble ancestors achiev'd with blows:
More hath he spent in peace than they in wars.
Ross. The Earl of Wiltshire hath the realm in farm.
Willo. The king 's grown bankrout, like a broken man.
North. Reproach and dissolution hangeth over him.
Ross. He hath not money for these Irish wars,
His burthenous taxations notwithstanding,
But by the robbing of the banish'd duke.
North. His noble kinsman: most degenerate king!
But, lords, we hear this fearful tempest sing,
Yet seek no shelter to avoid the storm;
We see the wind sit sore upon our sails,
And yet we strike not, but securely perish.
Ross. We see the very wrack that we must suffer;
And unavoided is the danger now,
For suffering so the causes of our wrack.
North. Not so; even through the hollow eyes of death
I spy life peering; but I dare not say
How near the tidings of our comfort is.
Willo. Nay, let us share thy thoughts, as thou dost ours.
Ross. Be confident to speak, Northumberland:
We three are but thyself; and, speaking so,
Thy words are but as thoughts; therefore, be bold.
North. Then thus: I have from Le Port Blanc, a bay
In Brittaine receiv'd intelligence
That Harry Duke of Hereford, Rainold Lord Cobham,
†. . . . . . .
That late broke from the Duke of Exeter,
His brother, Archbishop late of Canterbury,
Sir Thomas Erpingham, Sir John Ramston,
Sir John Norbery, Sir Robert Waterton and Francis Quoint,
All these well furnish'd by the Duke of Brittaine

he was your age. 185. **compare between,** draw comparisons. 190. **royalties,** privileges belonging to a member of the royal house. 197. **ensue,** follow upon. 202. **Call . . . patents.** This occurred some six weeks after Gaunt's death. **letters patents,** letters addressed by a sovereign to the patentee granting him some dignity, office, or privilege. 203. **attorneys-general,** deputies, legal substitutes. 227. **if . . . right.** This conversation marks the beginning of the counterplot. 242. **inform,** charge against (used technically); see glossary. 246. **pill'd,** plundered, robbed. 247. **And . . . fin'd.** This line is defective in meter, and is probably corrupt; Pope omitted *quite*. 250. **blanks,** *cartes blanches*, referred to in I, iv, 48. **wot,** know. 253. **basely yielded,** allusion to Richard's unpopular foreign policy of peace with France. 266. **strike,** furl (of sails) (with pun on striking blows). **securely,** heedlessly, overconfidently. 268. **unavoided,** unavoidable. 280. The break indicated here may be due to an omission of a line by the printer. Holinshed records that "the earle of Arundels sonne, named Thomas, which was kept in the duke of Exeters house, escaped out of the realme . . . and went to his vncle Thomas Arundell late archbishop of Canturburie." Malone supplying this detail from Holinshed inserts here the line, "The son of Richard Earle of Arundel." This puts the text into accord with Holinshed, since it is this Thomas and not Lord Cobham who escaped from the Duke of Exeter.

With eight tall ships, three thousand men of war,
Are making hither with all due expedience
And shortly mean to touch our northern shore:
Perhaps they had ere this, but that they stay
The first departing of the king for Ireland.
If then we shall shake off our slavish yoke,
Imp out our drooping country's broken wing,
Redeem from broking pawn the blemish'd crown,
Wipe off the dust that hides our sceptre's gilt
And make high majesty look like itself,
Away with me in post to Ravenspurgh;
But if you faint, as fearing to do so,
Stay and be secret, and myself will go.

Ross. To horse, to horse! urge doubts to them that fear.

Willo. Hold out my horse, and I will first be there.

Exeunt.

[SCENE II. *Windsor Castle.*]

Enter the QUEEN, BUSHY, [*and*] BAGOT.

Bushy. Madam, your majesty is too much sad:
You promis'd, when you parted with the king,
To lay aside life-harming heaviness
And entertain a cheerful disposition.

Queen. To please the king I did; to please myself
I cannot do it; yet I know no cause
Why I should welcome such a guest as grief,
Save bidding farewell to so sweet a guest
As my sweet Richard: yet again, methinks,
Some unborn sorrow, ripe in fortune's womb,
Is coming towards me, and my inward soul
With nothing trembles: at some thing it grieves,
More than with parting from my lord the king.

Bushy. Each substance of a grief hath twenty shadows,
Which shows like grief itself, but is not so;
For sorrow's eye, glazed with blinding tears,
Divides one thing entire to many objects;
Like perspectives, which rightly gaz'd upon
Show nothing but confusion, ey'd awry
Distinguish form: so your sweet majesty,
Looking awry upon your lord's departure,
Find shapes of grief, more than himself, to wail;
Which, look'd on as it is, is nought but shadows
Of what it is not. Then, thrice-gracious queen,
More than your lord's departure weep not: more 's not seen;
Or if it be, 'tis with false sorrow's eye,
Which for things true weeps things imaginary.

Queen. It may be so; but yet my inward soul
Persuades me it is otherwise: howe'er it be,
I cannot but be sad; so heavy sad
As, though on thinking on no thought I think,
Makes me with heavy nothing faint and shrink.

Bushy. 'Tis nothing but conceit, my gracious lady.

Queen. 'Tis nothing less: conceit is still deriv'd
From some forefather grief; mine is not so,
For nothing hath begot my something grief;
Or something hath the nothing that I grieve:
'Tis in reversion that I do possess;
But what it is, that is not yet known; what
I cannot name; 'tis nameless woe, I wot.

[*Enter* GREEN.]

Green. God save your majesty! and well met, gentlemen:
I hope the king is not yet shipp'd for Ireland.

Queen. Why hopest thou so? 'tis better hope he is;
For his designs crave haste, his haste good hope:
Then wherefore dost thou hope he is not shipp'd?

Green. That he, our hope, might have retir'd his power,
And driven into despair an enemy's hope,
Who strongly hath set footing in this land:
The banish'd Bolingbroke repeals himself,
And with uplifted arms is safe arriv'd
At Ravenspurgh.

Queen. Now God in heaven forbid!

Green. Ah, madam, 'tis too true: and that is worse,
The Lord Northumberland, his son young Henry Percy,
The Lords of Ross, Beaumond, and Willoughby,
With all their powerful friends, are fled to him.

Bushy. Why have you not proclaim'd Northumberland
And all the rest revolted faction traitors?

Green. We have: whereupon the Earl of Worcester
Hath broken his staff, resign'd his stewardship,
And all the household servants fled with him
To Bolingbroke.

Queen. So, Green, thou art the midwife to my woe,
And Bolingbroke my sorrow's dismal heir:
Now hath my soul brought forth her prodigy,
And I, a gasping new-deliver'd mother,
Have woe to woe, sorrow to sorrow join'd.

Bushy. Despair not, madam.

Queen. Who shall hinder me?
I will despair, and be at enmity
With cozening hope: he is a flatterer,
A parasite, a keeper back of death,
Who gently would dissolve the bands of life,
Which false hope lingers in extremity.

[*Enter* YORK.]

Green. Here comes the Duke of York.

Queen. With signs of war about his aged neck:
O, full of careful business are his looks!
Uncle, for God's sake, speak comfortable words.

York. Should I do so, I should belie my thoughts:
Comfort 's in heaven; and we are on the earth,
Where nothing lives but crosses, cares and grief.
Your husband, he is gone to save far off,
Whilst others come to make him lose at home:
Here am I left to underprop his land,
Who, weak with age, cannot support myself:
Now comes the sick hour that his surfeit made;

287. **expedience,** expedition, swiftness. 292. **Imp out,** piece out; a term from falconry meaning to attach new feathers to a disabled wing of a bird. 293. **broking pawn,** the security held by a broker; used scornfully. 294. **gilt,** gold (with pun on *guilt*). 296. **Away . . . Ravenspurgh.** The Earl of Northumberland, head of the powerful family of the Percys, is the leader among the nobles in the rebellion against Richard; see V, i, 55 ff. *Ravenspurgh* was a busy seaport in Yorkshire on the Humber, destroyed since by the sea. 300. **Hold out my horse,** if my horse holds out.

SCENE II. 18. **perspectives,** pictures of figures made to appear distorted or confused except when seen from a special point of view. **rightly,** directly, straight. 20. **Distinguish form,** make the form distinct. 31. **As . . . think,** as though in thinking, I fix my thoughts on nothing. 33. **conceit,** fancy. 34. **'Tis nothing less,** i.e., it is anything but that. 36-38. **For . . . possess.** As in line 12, the queen's play on the antithesis between *something* and *nothing* is confusing. She says: Either *nothing* caused her real grief, or else there is *something* in this unknown subject of her grief. The cause of the grief can only be revealed in the future

Now shall he try his friends that flatter'd him.

[*Enter a* Servingman.]

Serv. My lord, your son was gone before I came.
York. He was? Why, so! go all which way it will!
The nobles they are fled, the commons they are cold,
And will, I fear, revolt on Hereford's side.
Sirrah, get thee to Plashy, to my sister Gloucester;
Bid her send me presently a thousand pound:
Hold, take my ring.
Serv. My lord, I had forgot to tell your lordship,
To-day, as I came by, I called there;
But I shall grieve you to report the rest.
York. What is 't, knave?
Serv. An hour before I came, the duchess died.
York. God for his mercy! what a tide of woes
Comes rushing on this woeful land at once!
I know not what to do: I would to God,
So my untruth had not provok'd him to it,
The king had cut off my head with my brother's.
What, are there no posts dispatch'd for Ireland?
How shall we do for money for these wars?
Come, sister,—cousin, I would say,—pray, pardon me.
Go, fellow, get thee home, provide some carts
And bring away the armour that is there.
[*Exit Servingman.*]
Gentlemen, will you go muster men?
If I know how or which way to order these affairs
Thus disorderly thrust into my hands,
Never believe me. Both are my kinsmen:
Th' one is my sovereign, whom both my oath
And duty bids defend; t' other again
Is my kinsman, whom the king hath wrong'd,
Whom conscience and my kindred bids to right.
Well, somewhat we must do. Come, cousin, I'll
Dispose of you.
Gentlemen, go, muster up your men,
And meet me presently at Berkeley.
I should to Plashy too;
But time will not permit: all is uneven,
And every thing is left at six and seven.
Exeunt Duke [of York], Queen. Manent Bushy, [Bagot,] Green.
Bushy. The wind sits fair for news to go to Ireland,
But none returns. For us to levy power
Proportionable to the enemy
Is all unpossible.
Green. Besides, our nearness to the king in love
Is near the hate of those love not the king.
Bagot. And that 's the wavering commons: for their love
Lies in their purses, and whoso empties them
By so much fills their hearts with deadly hate.
Bushy. Wherein the king stands generally condemn'd.
Bagot. If judgement lie in them, then so do we,
Because we ever have been near the king.
Green. Well, I will for refuge straight to Bristol castle:
The Earl of Wiltshire is already there.
Bushy. Thither will I with you; for little office
The hateful commons will perform for us,
Except like curs to tear us all to pieces.
Will you go along with us?
Bagot. No; I will to Ireland to his majesty.
Farewell: if heart's presages be not vain,
We three here part that ne'er shall meet again.
Bushy. That 's as York thrives to beat back Bolingbroke.
Green. Alas, poor duke! the task he undertakes
Is numb'ring sands and drinking oceans dry:
Where one on his side fights, thousands will fly.
Farewell at once, for once, for all, and ever.
Bushy. Well, we may meet again.
Bagot. I fear me, never. [*Exeunt.*]

[SCENE III. *Wilds in Gloucestershire.*]

Enter [BOLINGBROKE, DUKE OF] HEREFORD, [*and*] NORTHUMBERLAND [*with Forces*].

Boling. How far is it, my lord, to Berkeley now?
North. Believe me, noble lord,
I am a stranger here in Gloucestershire:
These high wild hills and rough uneven ways
Draws out our miles, and makes them wearisome;
And yet your fair discourse hath been as sugar,
Making the hard way sweet and delectable.
But I bethink me what a weary way
From Ravenspurgh to Cotshall will be found
In Ross and Willoughby, wanting your company,
Which, I protest, hath very much beguil'd
The tediousness and process of my travel:
But theirs is sweet'ned with the hope to have
The present benefit which I possess;
And hope to joy is little less in joy
Than hope enjoy'd: by this the weary lords
Shall make their way seem short, as mine hath done
By sight of what I have, your noble company.
Boling. Of much less value is my company
Than your good words. But who comes here?

Enter HARRY PERCY.

North. It is my son, young Harry Percy,
Sent from my brother Worcester, whencesoever.
Harry, how fares your uncle?
Percy. I had thought, my lord, to have learn'd his health of you.
North. Why, is he not with the queen?
Percy. No, my good lord; he hath forsook the court,
Broken his staff of office and dispers'd
The household of the king.
North. What was his reason?
He was not so resolv'd when last we spake together.
Percy. Because your lordship was proclaimed traitor.
But he, my lord, is gone to Ravenspurgh,
To offer service to the Duke of Hereford,
And sent me over by Berkeley, to discover

(*in reversion*). 46. **retir'd,** drawn back. 59. **broken his staff,** i.e., in token of the resignation of his office of Lord High Steward. Thomas Percy, Earl of Worcester, brother of the Earl of Northumberland, provokes the rebellion of the Percys in *1* and *2 Henry IV*. 64. **prodigy,** monstrous birth. 69. **cozening,** cheating. 72. **lingers,** causes to linger. 74. **signs of war.** York is in armor. 76. **comfortable,** affording comfort. 86. **your son,** the Duke of Aumerle, who had accompanied Richard to Ireland. 90. **sister,** sister-in-law. 96. **knave,** familiar term in addressing servants (without evil significance). 97. **the duchess died.** The death of the Duchess of Gloucester is anticipated by several months (in order to add to York's consternation). 101. **untruth,** disloyalty. 122. **at six and seven,** at sixes and sevens, in confusion. 125. **Proportionable,** proportionate.

SCENE III. 9. **Cotshall,** Cotswold, hilly district in Gloucestershire. 12. **tediousness and process,** tedious process. 15. **joy,** enjoy. 22. **whencesoever,** from wherever he is.

What power the Duke of York had levied there;
Then with directions to repair to Ravenspurgh.
North. Have you forgot the Duke of Hereford, boy?
Percy. No, my good lord, for that is not forgot
Which ne'er I did remember: to my knowledge,
I never in my life did look on him.
North. Then learn to know him now; this is the duke.
Percy. My gracious lord, I tender you my service,
Such as it is, being tender, raw and young;
Which elder days shall ripen and confirm
To more approved service and desert.
Boling. I thank thee, gentle Percy; and be sure
I count myself in nothing else so happy
As in a soul rememb'ring my good friends;
And, as my fortune ripens with thy love,
It shall be still thy true love's recompense:
My heart this covenant makes, my hand thus seals it.
North. How far is it to Berkeley? and what stir
Keeps good old York there with his men of war?
Percy. There stands the castle, by yon tuft of trees,
Mann'd with three hundred men, as I have heard;
And in it are the Lords of York, Berkeley, and Seymour;
None else of name and noble estimate.

[*Enter* ROSS *and* WILLOUGHBY.]

North. Here come the Lords of Ross and Willoughby,
Bloody with spurring, fiery-red with haste.
Boling. Welcome, my lords. I wot your love pursues
A banish'd traitor: all my treasury
Is yet but unfelt thanks, which more enrich'd
Shall be your love and labour's recompense.
Ross. Your presence makes us rich, most noble lord.
Willo. And far surmounts our labour to attain it.
Boling. Evermore thanks, the exchequer of the poor;
Which, till my infant fortune comes to years,
Stands for my bounty. But who comes here?

[*Enter* BERKELEY.]

North. It is my Lord of Berkeley, as I guess.
Berk. My Lord of Hereford, my message is to you.
Boling. My lord, my answer is—to Lancaster;
And I am come to seek that name in England;
And I must find that title in your tongue,
Before I make reply to aught you say.
Berk. Mistake me not, my lord; 'tis not my meaning
To rase one title of your honour out:
To you, my lord, I come, what lord you will,
From the most gracious regent of this land,
The Duke of York, to know what pricks you on
To take advantage of the absent time
And fright our native peace with self-born arms.

[*Enter* YORK *attended.*]

Boling. I shall not need transport my words by you;
Here comes his grace in person.
My noble uncle! [*Kneels.*]
York. Show me thy humble heart, and not thy knee,
Whose duty is deceivable and false.
Boling. My gracious uncle—
York. Tut, tut!
Grace me no grace, nor uncle me no uncle:
I am no traitor's uncle; and that word 'grace'
In an ungracious mouth is but profane.
Why have those banish'd and forbidden legs
Dar'd once to touch a dust of England's ground?
But then more 'why?' why have they dar'd to march
So many miles upon her peaceful bosom,
Frighting her pale-fac'd villages with war
And ostentation of despised arms?
Com'st thou because the anointed king is hence?
Why, foolish boy, the king is left behind,
And in my loyal bosom lies his power.
Were I but now the lord of such hot youth
As when brave Gaunt, thy father, and myself
Rescued the Black Prince, that young Mars of men,
From forth the ranks of many thousand French,
O, then how quickly should this arm of mine,
Now prisoner to the palsy, chastise thee
And minister correction to thy fault!
Boling. My gracious uncle, let me know my fault:
On what condition stands it and wherein?
York. Even in condition of the worst degree,
In gross rebellion and detested treason:
Thou art a banish'd man, and here art come
Before the expiration of thy time,
In braving arms against thy sovereign.
Boling. As I was banish'd, I was banish'd Hereford;
But as I come, I come for Lancaster.
And, noble uncle, I beseech your grace
Look on my wrongs with an indifferent eye:
You are my father, for methinks in you
I see old Gaunt alive; O, then, my father,
Will you permit that I shall stand condemn'd
A wandering vagabond; my rights and royalties
Pluck'd from my arms perforce and given away
To upstart unthrifts? Wherefore was I born?
If that my cousin king be King of England,
It must be granted I am Duke of Lancaster.
You have a son, Aumerle, my noble cousin;
Had you first died, and he been thus trod down,
He should have found his uncle Gaunt a father,
To rouse his wrongs and chase them to the bay.
I am denied to sue my livery here,
And yet my letters-patents give me leave:
My father's goods are all distrain'd and sold,
And these and all are all amiss employ'd.
What would you have me do? I am a subject,
And I challenge law: attorneys are denied me;
And therefore personally I lay my claim
To my inheritance of free descent.
North. The noble duke hath been too much abus'd.
Ross. It stands your grace upon to do him right.
Willo. Base men by his endowments are made great.

42. **raw and young.** Henry Percy, called "Hotspur," was born in 1364; Prince Hal in 1387. Shakespeare represents them as of the same age. 45-49. **I thank . . . recompense.** Cf. *1 Henry IV*, I, iii, 251 ff., where Hotspur bitterly recalls this speech. 56. **name,** rank, title. 61. **unfelt,** impalpable, not perceived. 70. **Lancaster.** Bolingbroke will enter into no negotiations unless his proper title is given him. 75. **rase,** erase. 79. **the absent time,** the time of the king's absence. 80. **native,** entitled (i.e., to peace) by birth, rightful. **self-born,** indigenous, home-sprung (Clark and Wright); some editors read *self-borne*, i.e., borne for himself, not for the king. 84. **deceivable,** deceptive. 91. **dust,** a particle of dust. 92. **more 'why?'** more questions to ask. 114. **I come for Lancaster,** i.e., in the character of Lancaster. Compare *2 Henry IV*, IV, v, 184-186. 116. **indifferent,** impartial. 122. **unthrifts,** spendthrifts, prodigals. 128. **to the bay,** to the extremity where the hunted animal turns on its pursuers. 129. **sue my livery,** sue for legal delivery of my freehold as heir. 131. **distrain'd,** seized by legal process. 134. **challenge,** claim. 138. **stands . . . upon,** is incumbent upon. 139. **his endowments,** i.e., his properties which they have seized. 154. **ill left,** left with inadequate means. 159. **neuter,** neutral. 164. **Bristow,** Bristol. 165. **Bagot.** He had gone to Ireland, not to Bristol; see II, ii, 141.

York. My lords of England, let me tell you this:
I have had feeling of my cousin's wrongs
And labour'd all I could to do him right;
But in this kind to come, in braving arms,
Be his own carver and cut out his way,
To find out right with wrong, it may not be;
And you that do abet him in this kind
Cherish rebellion and are rebels all.

North. The noble duke hath sworn his coming is
But for his own; and for the right of that
We all have strongly sworn to give him aid;
And let him never see joy that breaks that oath!

York. Well, well, I see the issue of these arms:
I cannot mend it, I must needs confess,
Because my power is weak and all ill left:
But if I could, by Him that gave me life,
I would attach you all and make you stoop
Unto the sovereign mercy of the king;
But since I cannot, be it known to you
I do remain as neuter. So, fare you well;
Unless you please to enter in the castle
And there repose you for this night.

Boling. An offer, uncle, that we will accept:
But we must win your grace to go with us
To Bristow castle, which they say is held
By Bushy, Bagot and their complices,
The caterpillars of the commonwealth,
Which I have sworn to weed and pluck away.

York. It may be I will go with you: but yet I'll pause;
For I am loath to break our country's laws.
Nor friends nor foes, to me welcome you are:
Things past redress are now with me past care. *Exeunt.*

[SCENE IV. *A camp in Wales.*]

Enter EARL OF SALISBURY *and a* Welsh Captain.

Cap. My Lord of Salisbury, we have stay'd ten days,
And hardly kept our countrymen together,
And yet we hear no tidings from the king;
Therefore we will disperse ourselves: farewell.

Sal. Stay yet another day, thou trusty Welshman:
The king reposeth all his confidence in thee.

Cap. 'Tis thought the king is dead; we will not stay.
The bay-trees in our country are all wither'd
And meteors fright the fixed stars of heaven;
The pale-fac'd moon looks bloody on the earth
And lean-look'd prophets whisper fearful change;
Rich men look sad and ruffians dance and leap,
The one in fear to lose what they enjoy,
The other to enjoy by rage and war:
These signs forerun the death or fall of kings.
Farewell: our countrymen are gone and fled,
As well assur'd Richard their king is dead. [*Exit.*]

Sal. Ah, Richard, with the eyes of heavy mind
I see thy glory like a shooting star
Fall to the base earth from the firmament.
Thy sun sets weeping in the lowly west,
Witnessing storms to come, woe and unrest:
Thy friends are fled to wait upon thy foes,
And crossly to thy good all fortune goes. [*Exit.*]

[ACT III.

SCENE I. *Bristol. Before the castle.*]

Enter [BOLINGBROKE,] DUKE OF HEREFORD, YORK, NORTHUMBERLAND, [ROSS, PERCY, WILLOUGHBY, *with*] BUSHY *and* GREEN, *prisoners.*

Boling. Bring forth these men.
Bushy and Green, I will not vex your souls—
Since presently your souls must part your bodies—
With too much urging your pernicious lives,
For 'twere no charity; yet, to wash your blood
From off my hands, here in the view of men
I will unfold some causes of your deaths.
You have misled a prince, a royal king,
A happy gentleman in blood and lineaments,
By you unhappied and disfigured clean:
You have in manner with your sinful hours
Made a divorce betwixt his queen and him,
Broke the possession of a royal bed
And stain'd the beauty of a fair queen's cheeks
With tears drawn from her eyes by your foul wrongs.
Myself, a prince by fortune of my birth,
Near to the king in blood, and near in love
Till you did make him misinterpret me,
Have stoop'd my neck under your injuries,
And sigh'd my English breath in foreign clouds,
Eating the bitter bread of banishment;
Whilst you have fed upon my signories,
Dispark'd my parks and fell'd my forest woods,
From my own windows torn my household coat,
Ras'd out my imprese, leaving me no sign,
Save men's opinions and my living blood,
To show the world I am a gentleman.
This and much more, much more than twice all this,
Condemns you to the death. See them delivered over
To execution and the hand of death.

Bushy. More welcome is the stroke of death to me
Than Bolingbroke to England. Lords, farewell.

Green. My comfort is that heaven will take our souls
And plague injustice with the pains of hell.

Boling. My Lord Northumberland, see them dispatch'd.
[*Exeunt Northumberland and others, with the prisoners.*]
Uncle, you say the queen is at your house;
For God's sake, fairly let her be entreated:
Tell her I send to her my kind commends;
Take special care my greetings be delivered.

York. A gentleman of mine I have dispatch'd
With letters of your love to her at large.

Boling. Thanks, gentle uncle. Come, lords, away,
To fight with Glendower and his complices:

complices, accomplices.

SCENE IV. 8. **bay-trees.** In this yeare . . . old baie trees withered, and afterwards . . . grew greene againe; a strange sight, and supposed to import some vnknowne euent (Holinshed; in second edition, 1587, only). 11. **lean-look'd,** lean-looking. 24. **crossly,** adversely.

ACT III. SCENE I. 3. **presently,** immediately. 4. **urging,** emphasizing as reasons (for your executions). 9. **happy,** fortunate. 10. **unhappied,** made wretched, ruined. **clean,** completely. 12. **Made a divorce.** There is no basis for this charge; but see V, i, 71 ff. It may have been suggested by the situation in Marlowe's *Edward II.* 14. **fair queen's.** Queen Isabella, daughter of Charles VI of France and consort of Richard II, was historically only eleven years old at this time. 22. **signories,** lordships, estates. 23. **Dispark'd,** destroyed the enclosures and thrown the parks open. 24. **my household coat,** coat of arms, frequently emblazoned on stained or painted windows. 25. **Ras'd,** erased. **imprese,** device, emblematic design. 37. **entreated,** treated. 43. **Glendower.** Owen Glendower was not at this time in arms against Bolingbroke; perhaps Bolingbroke thinks he is the Welsh commander (see preceding scene).

Awhile to work, and after holiday. *Exeunt.*

[SCENE II. *The coast of Wales, near Barkloughly castle.*]

[*Drum: flourish and colours.*] *Enter the* KING, AUMERLE, [*the* BISHOP OF] CARLISLE, *&c.* [*with* Soldiers].

K. Rich. Barkloughly castle call they this at hand?
Aum. Yea, my lord. How brooks your grace the air,
After your late tossing on the breaking seas?
K. Rich. Needs must I like it well: I weep for joy
To stand upon my kingdom once again.
Dear earth, I do salute thee with my hand,
Though rebels wound thee with their horses' hoofs:
As a long-parted mother with her child
Plays fondly with her tears and smiles in meeting,
So, weeping, smiling, greet I thee, my earth,
And do thee favours with my royal hands.
Feed not thy sovereign's foe, my gentle earth,
Nor with thy sweets comfort his ravenous sense;
But let thy spiders, that suck up thy venom,
And heavy-gaited toads lie in their way,
Doing annoyance to the treacherous feet
Which with usurping steps do trample thee:
Yield stinging nettles to mine enemies;
And when they from thy bosom pluck a flower,
Guard it, I pray thee, with a lurking adder
Whose double tongue may with a mortal touch
Throw death upon thy sovereign's enemies.
Mock not my senseless conjuration, lords:
This earth shall have a feeling and these stones
Prove armed soldiers, ere her native king
Shall falter under foul rebellion's arms.
Car. Fear not, my lord: that Power that made you king
Hath power to keep you king in spite of all.
The means that heaven yields must be embrac'd,
And not neglected; else, if heaven would,
And we will not, heaven's offer we refuse,
The proffered means of succour and redress.
Aum. He means, my lord, that we are too remiss;
Whilst Bolingbroke, through our security,
Grows strong and great in substance and in power.
K. Rich. Discomfortable cousin! know'st thou not
That when the searching eye of heaven is hid,
Behind the globe, that lights the lower world,
Then thieves and robbers range abroad unseen
In murders and in outrage, boldly here;
But when from under this terrestrial ball
He fires the proud tops of the eastern pines
And darts his light through every guilty hole,
Then murders, treasons and detested sins,
The cloak of night being pluck'd from off their backs,
Stand bare and naked, trembling at themselves?
So when this thief, this traitor, Bolingbroke,
Who all this while hath revell'd in the night
Whilst we were wand'ring with the antipodes,
Shall see us rising in our throne, the east,
His treasons will sit blushing in his face,
Not able to endure the sight of day,
But self-affrighted tremble at his sin.
Not all the water in the rough rude sea
Can wash the balm off from an anointed king;
The breath of worldly men cannot depose
The deputy elected by the Lord:
For every man that Bolingbroke hath press'd
To lift shrewd steel against our golden crown,
God for his Richard hath in heavenly pay
A glorious angel: then, if angels fight,
Weak men must fall, for heaven still guards the right.

Enter SALISBURY.

Welcome, my lord: how far off lies your power?
Sal. Nor near nor farther off, my gracious lord,
Than this weak arm: discomfort guides my tongue
And bids me speak of nothing but despair.
One day too late, I fear me, noble lord,
Hath clouded all thy happy days on earth:
O, call back yesterday, bid time return,
And thou shalt have twelve thousand fighting men!
To-day, to-day, unhappy day, too late,
O'erthrows thy joys, friends, fortune and thy state:
For all the Welshmen, hearing thou wert dead,
Are gone to Bolingbroke, dispers'd and fled.
Aum. Comfort, my liege: why looks your grace so pale?
K. Rich. But now the blood of twenty thousand men
Did triumph in my face, and they are fled;
And, till so much blood thither come again,
Have I not reason to look pale and dead?
All souls that will be safe fly from my side,
For time hath set a blot upon my pride.
Aum. Comfort, my liege; remember who you are.
K. Rich. I had forgot myself: am I not king?
Awake, thou coward majesty! thou sleepest.
Is not the king's name twenty thousand names?
Arm, arm, my name! a puny subject strikes
At thy great glory. Look not to the ground,
Ye favourites of a king: are we not high?
High be our thoughts: I know my uncle York
Hath power enough to serve our turn. But who comes here?

Enter SCROOP.

Scroop. More health and happiness betide my liege
Than can my care-tun'd tongue deliver him!
K. Rich. Mine ear is open and my heart prepar'd:
The worst is worldly loss thou canst unfold.
Say, is my kingdom lost? why, 'twas my care;
And what loss is it to be rid of care?
Strives Bolingbroke to be as great as we?
Greater he shall not be; if he serve God,
We'll serve Him too and be his fellow so:
Revolt our subjects? that we cannot mend;
They break their faith to God as well as us:
Cry woe, destruction, ruin and decay;
The worst is death, and death will have his day.
Scroop. Glad am I that your highness is so arm'd

SCENE II. 1. **Barkloughly,** probably Harlech, a castle in Wales between Caernarvon and Aberystwyth. 2. **brooks,** enjoys. 3. **late,** recent. 21. **double,** forked. **mortal,** deadly. 23. **senseless conjuration.** adjuration of senseless things. 25. **native,** entitled (to the crown) by birth, rightful. 33. **He . . . remiss.** The stern, practical bishop has attempted to bring Richard back to reality; Richard hardly understands; Aumerle interprets in this line. 34. **security,** confidence, heedlessness. 36. **Discomfortable,** uncomforting. 38. **that lights the lower world.** This clause modifies *eye of heaven*. 55. **balm,** consecrated oil used in anointing a king. 58. **press'd,** impressed, forced into the ranks. 64. **near,** nearer. 65. **discomfort,** discouragement. 76. **twenty thousand men.** Holinshed puts Salisbury's force at forty thousand. 76-81. **But . . . pride.** Note that Richard's highly emotional speech is in the form of a sestet. 112. **thin,** thin-haired (Schmidt); possibly, shrunken to thinness. 114. **clap,** thrust. **female,** weak and delicate like a woman, implying their youth. 116. **beadsmen,** almsmen whose duty it was to pray for the king. 117. **double-fatal,** doubly fatal (since the wood of the yew was used for bows and the berry as poison). 118. **manage,** wield. **bills,** weapons used by infantry; a *bill* was a long-handled ax with hook-shaped blade and spearhead. 122. **Bagot.** Bagot's name seems in-

To bear the tidings of calamity.
Like an unseasonable stormy day,
Which makes the silver rivers drown their shores,
As if the world were all dissolv'd to tears,
So high above his limits swells the rage
Of Bolingbroke, covering your fearful land
With hard bright steel and hearts harder than steel.
White-beards have arm'd their thin and hairless scalps
Against thy majesty; boys, with women's voices,
Strive to speak big and clap their female joints
In stiff unwieldy arms against thy crown:
Thy very beadsmen learn to bend their bows
Of double-fatal yew against thy state;
Yea, distaff-women manage rusty bills
Against thy seat: both young and old rebel,
And all goes worse than I have power to tell.

K. Rich. Too well, too well thou tell'st a tale so ill.
Where is the Earl of Wiltshire? where is Bagot?
What is become of Bushy? where is Green?
That they have let the dangerous enemy
Measure our confines with such peaceful steps?
If we prevail, their heads shall pay for it:
I warrant they have made peace with Bolingbroke.

Scroop. Peace have they made with him indeed, my lord.

K. Rich. O villains, vipers, damn'd without redemption!
Dogs, easily won to fawn on any man!
Snakes, in my heart-blood warm'd, that sting my heart!
Three Judases, each one thrice worse than Judas!
Would they make peace? terrible hell make war
Upon their spotted souls for this offence!

Scroop. Sweet love, I see, changing his property,
Turns to the sourest and most deadly hate:
Again uncurse their souls; their peace is made
With heads, and not with hands: those whom you curse
Have felt the worst of death's destroying wound
And lie full low, grav'd in the hollow ground.

Aum. Is Bushy, Green, and the Earl of Wiltshire dead?

Scroop. Ay, all of them at Bristow lost their heads.

Aum. Where is the duke my father with his power?

K. Rich. No matter where; of comfort no man speak:
Let 's talk of graves, of worms and epitaphs;
Make dust our paper and with rainy eyes
Write sorrow on the bosom of the earth,
Let 's choose executors and talk of wills:
And yet not so, for what can we bequeath
Save our deposed bodies to the ground?
Our lands, our lives and all are Bolingbroke's,
And nothing can we call our own but death
And that small model of the barren earth
Which serves as paste and cover to our bones.
For God's sake, let us sit upon the ground
And tell sad stories of the death of kings:
How some have been depos'd; some slain in war;
Some haunted by the ghosts they have depos'd;
Some poisoned by their wives; some sleeping kill'd;
All murdered: for within the hollow crown
That rounds the mortal temples of a king
Keeps Death his court and there the antic sits,
Scoffing his state and grinning at his pomp,
Allowing him a breath, a little scene,
To monarchize, be fear'd and kill with looks,
Infusing him with self and vain conceit,
As if this flesh which walls about our life
Were brass impregnable, and humour'd thus
Comes at the last and with a little pin
Bores through his castle wall, and farewell king!
Cover your heads and mock not flesh and blood
With solemn reverence: throw away respect,
Tradition, form and ceremonious duty,
For you have but mistook me all this while:
†I live with bread like you, feel want,
Taste grief, need friends: subjected thus,
How can you say to me, I am a king?

Car. My lord, wise men ne'er sit and wail their woes,
But presently prevent the ways to wail.
To fear the foe, since fear oppresseth strength,
Gives in your weakness strength unto your foe,
And so your follies fight against yourself.
Fear, and be slain; no worse can come to fight:
And fight and die is death destroying death;
Where fearing dying pays death servile breath.

Aum. My father hath a power; inquire of him,
And learn to make a body of a limb.

K. Rich. Thou chid'st me well: proud Bolingbroke, I come
To change blows with thee for our day of doom.
This ague fit of fear is over-blown;
An easy task it is to win our own.
Say, Scroop, where lies our uncle with his power?
Speak sweetly, man, although thy looks be sour.

Scroop. Men judge by the complexion of the sky
The state and inclination of the day:
So may you by my dull and heavy eye,
My tongue hath but a heavier tale to say.
I play the torturer, by small and small
To lengthen out the worst that must be spoken:
Your uncle York is join'd with Bolingbroke,
And all your northern castles yielded up,
And all your southern gentlemen in arms
Upon his party.

K. Rich. Thou hast said enough.
Beshrew thee, cousin, which didst lead me forth [*To Aumerle.*]
Of that sweet way I was in to despair!
What say you now? what comfort have we now?
By heaven, I'll hate him everlastingly
That bids me be of comfort any more.
Go to Flint castle: there I'll pine away;
A king, woe's slave, shall kingly woe obey.
That power I have, discharge; and let them go
To ear the land that hath some hope to grow,

advertently mentioned here. The king speaks, line 132, of *three Judases;* Aumerle does not ask about Bagot in line 141. 125. **peaceful,** unopposed. 135. **property,** distinctive quality. 153. **model,** may refer to Richard's own mortal body, or to the grave mound. 162. **Death.** Douce called attention to a print in the *Imagines Mortis* of a king sitting on a throne, sword in hand, surrounded by courtiers, with a grinning skeleton arising from his crown. **antic,** grotesque figure. 163. **Scoffing,** scoffing at. 164. **breath,** breathing space, moment. 166. **self and vain conceit,** selfish and vain conceit. 168. **humour'd,** having satisfied his humor or whim (referring to Death); sometimes defined as "humored" or "indulged" (referring to the king). 176. **subjected,** made subject to grief, want, etc. (with pun on "being treated like a subject"). 183-185. **Fear . . . breath.** To die fighting is to triumph over death; to fear death is to become its slave. 189. **change,** exchange. 198. **by small and small,** little by little. 211. **That power . . . discharge,** discharge what army I have. 212. **ear,** plough. (Richard suggests bitterly that his followers pursue Bolingbroke's prospects for hope and growth.) **grow,** produce fruit.

For I have none: let no man speak again
To alter this, for counsel is but vain.
Aum. My liege, one word.
K. Rich. He does me double wrong
That wounds me with the flatteries of his tongue.
Discharge my followers: let them hence away,
From Richard's night to Bolingbroke's fair day.
[*Exeunt.*]

[SCENE III. *Wales. Before Flint castle.*]

Enter [*with drum and colours*] BOLINGBROKE, YORK, NORTHUMBERLAND[, Attendants, *and forces*].

Boling. So that by this intelligence we learn
The Welshmen are dispers'd, and Salisbury
Is gone to meet the king, who lately landed
With some few private friends upon this coast.
North. The news is very fair and good, my lord:
Richard not far from hence hath hid his head.
York. It would beseem the Lord Northumberland
To say 'King Richard:' alack the heavy day
When such a sacred king should hide his head.
North. Your grace mistakes; only to be brief,
Left I his title out.
York. The time hath been,
Would you have been so brief with him, he would
Have been so brief with you, to shorten you,
For taking so the head, your whole head's length.
Boling. Mistake not, uncle, further than you should.
York. Take not, good cousin, further than you should,
Lest you mistake the heavens are over our heads.
Boling. I know it, uncle, and oppose not myself
Against their will. But who comes here?

Enter PERCY.

Welcome, Harry: what, will not this castle yield?
Percy. The castle royally is mann'd, my lord,
Against thy entrance.
Boling. Royally!
Why, it contains no king?
Percy. Yes, my good lord,
It doth contain a king; King Richard lies
Within the limits of yon lime and stone:
And with him are the Lord Aumerle, Lord Salisbury,
Sir Stephen Scroop, besides a clergyman
Of holy reverence; who, I cannot learn.
North. O, belike it is the Bishop of Carlisle.
Boling. Noble lords,
Go to the rude ribs of that ancient castle;
Through brazen trumpet send the breath of parley
Into his ruin'd ears, and thus deliver:
Henry Bolingbroke
On both his knees doth kiss King Richard's hand
And sends allegiance and true faith of heart
To his most royal person, hither come
Even at his feet to lay my arms and power,
Provided that my banishment repeal'd
And lands restor'd again be freely granted:
If not, I'll use the advantage of my power
And lay the summer's dust with show'rs of blood
Rain'd from the wounds of slaughtered Englishmen:
The which, how far off from the mind of Bolingbroke
It is, such crimson tempest should bedrench
The fresh green lap of fair King Richard's land,
My stooping duty tenderly shall show.
Go, signify as much, while here we march
Upon the grassy carpet of this plain.
Let 's march without the noise of threat'ning drum,
That from this castle's tattered battlements
Our fair appointments may be well perus'd.
Methinks King Richard and myself should meet
With no less terror than the elements
Of fire and water, when their thund'ring shock
At meeting tears the cloudy cheeks of heaven.
Be he the fire, I'll be the yielding water:
The rage be his, whilst on the earth I rain
My waters; on the earth, and not on him.
March on, and mark King Richard how he looks.

The trumpets sound [*a parle without and within, then a flourish.* KING] RICHARD *appeareth on the walls* [*with the* BISHOP OF CARLISLE, AUMERLE, SCROOP, *and* SALISBURY].

See, see, King Richard doth himself appear,
As doth the blushing discontented sun
From out the fiery portal of the east,
When he perceives the envious clouds are bent
To dim his glory and to stain the track
Of his bright passage to the occident.
York. Yet looks he like a king: behold, his eye,
As bright as is the eagle's, lightens forth
Controlling majesty: alack, alack, for woe,
That any harm should stain so fair a show!
K. Rich. We are amaz'd; and thus long have we stood
To watch the fearful bending of thy knee, [*To North.*]
Because we thought ourself thy lawful king:
And if we be, how dare thy joints forget
To pay their awful duty to our presence?
If we be not, show us the hand of God
That hath dismiss'd us from our stewardship;
For well we know, no hand of blood and bone
Can gripe the sacred handle of our sceptre,
Unless he do profane, steal, or usurp.
And though you think that all, as you have done,
Have torn their souls by turning them from us,
And we are barren and bereft of friends;
Yet know, my master, God omnipotent,
Is mustering in his clouds on our behalf
Armies of pestilence; and they shall strike
Your children yet unborn and unbegot,
That lift your vassal hands against my head
And threat the glory of my precious crown.
Tell Bolingbroke—for yon methinks he stands—
That every stride he makes upon my land
Is dangerous treason: he is come to open
The purple testament of bleeding war;

SCENE III. 6. **Richard . . . head.** The plot here diverges from Holinshed. Richard fled to Conway Castle, where he found Salisbury. To this place, then, Bolingbroke dispatched Northumberland, who induced Richard to a conference, assuring him that Bolingbroke came merely to demand his rights and advising that a parliament should be called to restore order to the kingdom. On their riding forth from Conway, Northumberland led Richard into an ambush, by which means Richard was taken to Flint Castle as a prisoner. Later he was taken to Chester and to London. The divergence in plot may be accounted for by a marginal note in Holinshed which reads: "K. Richard stealeth awaie from his armie, and taketh the castell of Flint." 62-67. **See . . . occident,** assigned by Dyce to Percy, by Warburton and Hanmer to York; but Bolingbroke is everywhere sensitive to Richard's personal charm. See IV, i, 304; V, vi, 40. 69. **lightens forth,** flashes out, like lightning. 76. **awful,** reverential. 81. **profane,** commit sacrilege. 83. **torn their souls,** injured their souls by treason to the king. 93-94. **open The purple testament,** begin to carry out a bequest of blood to England. Blood was often said to be purple. 97. **flower of England's face,** the

But ere the crown he looks for live in peace,
Ten thousand bloody crowns of mothers' sons
Shall ill become the flower of England's face,
Change the complexion of her maid-pale peace
To scarlet indignation and bedew
Her pastures' grass with faithful English blood.
North. The king of heaven forbid our lord the king
Should so with civil and uncivil arms
Be rush'd upon! Thy thrice noble cousin
Harry Bolingbroke doth humbly kiss thy hand;
And by the honourable tomb he swears,
That stands upon your royal grandsire's bones,
And by the royalties of both your bloods,
Currents that spring from one most gracious head,
And by the buried hand of warlike Gaunt,
And by the worth and honour of himself,
Comprising all that may be sworn or said,
His coming hither hath no further scope
Than for his lineal royalties and to beg
Enfranchisement immediate on his knees:
Which on thy royal party granted once,
His glittering arms he will commend to rust,
His barbed steeds to stables, and his heart
To faithful service of your majesty.
This swears he, as he is a prince, is just;
And, as I am a gentleman, I credit him.
K. Rich. Northumberland, say thus the king returns:
His noble cousin is right welcome hither;
And all the number of his fair demands
Shall be accomplish'd without contradiction:
With all the gracious utterance thou hast
Speak to his gentle hearing kind commends.
We do debase ourselves, cousin, do we not,
[*To Aumerle.*]
To look so poorly and to speak so fair?
Shall we call back Northumberland, and send
Defiance to the traitor, and so die?
Aum. No, good my lord; let 's fight with gentle words
Till time lend friends and friends their helpful swords.
K. Rich. O God, O God! that e'er this tongue of mine,
That laid the sentence of dread banishment
On yon proud man, should take it off again
With words of sooth! O that I were as great
As is my grief, or lesser than my name!
Or that I could forget what I have been,
Or not remember what I must be now!
Swell'st thou, proud heart? I'll give thee scope to beat,
Since foes have scope to beat both thee and me.
Aum. Northumberland comes back from Bolingbroke.
K. Rich. What must the king do now? must he submit?
The king shall do it: must he be depos'd?
The king shall be contented: must he lose
The name of king? a God's name, let it go:
I'll give my jewels for a set of beads,
My gorgeous palace for a hermitage,
My gay apparel for an almsman's gown,
My figur'd goblets for a dish of wood,
My sceptre for a palmer's walking-staff,
My subjects for a pair of carved saints
And my large kingdom for a little grave,
A little little grave, an obscure grave;
Or I'll be buried in the king's highway,
Some way of common trade, where subjects' feet
May hourly trample on their sovereign's head;
For on my heart they tread now whilst I live;
And buried once, why not upon my head?
Aumerle, thou weep'st, my tender-hearted cousin!
We'll make foul weather with despised tears;
Our sighs and they shall lodge the summer corn,
And make a dearth in this revolting land.
Or shall we play the wantons with our woes,
And make some pretty match with shedding tears?
As thus, to drop them still upon one place,
Till they have fretted us a pair of graves
Within the earth; and, therein laid,—there lies
Two kinsmen digg'd their graves with weeping eyes.
Would not this ill do well? Well, well, I see
I talk but idly, and you laugh at me.
Most mighty prince, my Lord Northumberland,
What says King Bolingbroke? will his majesty
Give Richard leave to live till Richard die?
You make a leg, and Bolingbroke says ay.
North. My lord, in the base court he doth attend
To speak with you; may it please you to come down.
K. Rich. Down, down I come; like glist'ring Phaethon,
Wanting the manage of unruly jades.
In the base court? Base court, where kings grow base,
To come at traitors' calls and do them grace.
In the base court? Come down? Down, court! down, king!
For night-owls shriek where mounting larks should sing. [*Exeunt from above.*]
Boling. What says his majesty?
North. Sorrow and grief of heart
Makes him speak fondly, like a frantic man:
Yet he is come.

[*Enter* King Richard *and his attendants below.*]

Boling. Stand all apart,
And show fair duty to his majesty. *He kneels down.*
My gracious lord,—
K. Rich. Fair cousin, you debase your princely knee
To make the base earth proud with kissing it:
Me rather had my heart might feel your love
Than my unpleas'd eye see your courtesy.
Up, cousin, up; your heart is up, I know,
Thus high at least, although your knee be low.
Boling. My gracious lord, I come but for mine own.
K. Rich. Your own is yours, and I am yours, and all.
Boling. So far be mine, my most redoubted lord,
As my true service shall deserve your love.
K. Rich. Well you deserve: they well deserve to have,

blooming face of England. Cf. Daniel, *Civil Wars*, I, 118: "Th' vngodly bloodshed that . . . did marre the flowre of thy chiefe pride . . ." The abundance of Richard's metaphors is startling. Blood, which disfigures war and also the heads of ten thousand Englishmen, stains purple the will or testament, makes the face of England scarlet with indignation, and bedews the grass of the pastures. 102. **civil,** used in civil strife. **uncivil,** barbarous, violent. 114. **Enfranchisement,** recall from banishment and restoration to his rights. 116. **commend,** give over. 117. **barbed,** armed. 121. **returns,** answers. 136. **sooth,** cajolery, flattery.

162. **lodge,** beat down. 167. **fretted,** eaten away, worn. 175. **make a leg,** assent by making an obeisance or curtsy. 176. **base court,** outer or lower court of a castle. 178. **glist'ring,** glistening. **Phaethon,** son of the sun-god Helios, who, unable to control the horses of the sun, was hurled from the chariot by Jupiter. 179. **Wanting,** lacking. **jades,** worthless horses. 192. **Me rather had,** a construction resulting from a combination of "me were liefer" and "I had rather." 195. **Thus high.** Richard touches his crown here.

That know the strong'st and surest way to get.
Uncle, give me your hands: nay, dry your eyes;
Tears show their love, but want their remedies.
Cousin, I am too young to be your father,
Though you are old enough to be my heir.
What you will have, I'll give, and willing too;
For do we must what force will have us do.
Set on towards London, cousin, is it so?

Boling. Yea, my good lord.

K. Rich. Then I must not say no.

[*Flourish. Exeunt.*]

[SCENE IV. *Langley. The* DUKE OF YORK's *garden.*]

Enter the QUEEN *with* [*two* Ladies,] *her Attendants.*

Queen. What sport shall we devise here in this garden,
To drive away the heavy thought of care?

Lady. Madam, we'll play at bowls.

Queen. 'Twill make me think the world is full of rubs,
And that my fortune runs against the bias.

Lady. Madam, we'll dance.

Queen. My legs can keep no measure in delight,
When my poor heart no measure keeps in grief:
Therefore, no dancing, girl; some other sport.

Lady. Madam, we'll tell tales.

Queen. Of sorrow or of joy?

Lady. Of either, madam.

Queen. Of neither, girl:
For if of joy, being altogether wanting,
It doth remember me the more of sorrow;
Or if of grief, being altogether had,
It adds more sorrow to my want of joy:
For what I have I need not to repeat;
And what I want it boots not to complain.

Lady. Madam, I'll sing.

Queen. 'Tis well that thou hast cause;
But thou shouldst please me better, wouldst thou weep.

Lady. I could weep, madam, would it do you good.

Queen. And I could sing, would weeping do me good,
And never borrow any tear of thee.

Enter Gardeners [*a Master and two Men*].

But stay, here come the gardeners:
Let's step into the shadow of these trees.
My wretchedness unto a row of pins,
They will talk of state; for every one doth so
Against a change; woe is forerun with woe.

[*Queen and Ladies retire.*]

Gard. Go, bind thou up yon dangling apricocks,
Which, like unruly children, make their sire
Stoop with oppression of their prodigal weight:
Give some supportance to the bending twigs.
Go thou, and like an executioner,
Cut off the heads of too fast growing sprays
That look too lofty in our commonwealth:
All must be even in our government.
You thus employ'd, I will go root away
The noisome weeds, which without profit suck
The soil's fertility from wholesome flowers.

Man. Why should we in the compass of a pale
Keep law and form and due proportion,
Showing, as in a model, our firm estate,
When our sea-walled garden, the whole land,
Is full of weeds, her fairest flowers chok'd up,
Her fruit-trees all unprun'd, her hedges ruin'd,
Her knots disordered and her wholesome herbs
Swarming with caterpillars?

Gard. Hold thy peace:
He that hath suffered this disordered spring
Hath now himself met with the fall of leaf:
The weeds which his broad-spreading leaves did shelter,
That seem'd in eating him to hold him up,
Are pluck'd up root and all by Bolingbroke,
I mean the Earl of Wiltshire, Bushy, Green.

Man. What, are they dead?

Gard. They are; and Bolingbroke
Hath seiz'd the wasteful king. O, what pity is it
That he had not so trimm'd and dress'd his land
As we this garden! We at time of year
Do wound the bark, the skin of our fruit-trees,
Lest, being over-proud in sap and blood,
With too much riches it confound itself:
Had he done so to great and growing men,
They might have liv'd to bear and he to taste
Their fruits of duty: superfluous branches
We lop away, that bearing boughs may live:
Had he done so, himself had borne the crown,
Which waste of idle hours hath quite thrown down.

Man. What, think you the king shall be depos'd?

Gard. Depress'd he is already, and depos'd
'Tis doubt he will be: letters came last night
To a dear friend of the good Duke of York's,
That tell black tidings.

Queen. O, I am press'd to death through want of speaking! [*Coming forward.*]
Thou, old Adam's likeness, set to dress this garden,
How dares thy harsh rude tongue sound this unpleasing news?
What Eve, what serpent, hath suggested thee
To make a second fall of cursed man?
Why dost thou say King Richard is depos'd?
Dar'st thou, thou little better thing than earth,
Divine his downfall? Say, where, when, and how,
Cam'st thou by this ill tidings? speak, thou wretch.

Gard. Pardon me, madam: little joy have I
To breathe this news; yet what I say is true.
King Richard, he is in the mighty hold
Of Bolingbroke: their fortunes both are weigh'd:
In your lord's scale is nothing but himself,
And some few vanities that make him light;
But in the balance of great Bolingbroke,
Besides himself, are all the English peers,
And with that odds he weighs King Richard down.
Post you to London, and you will find it so;
I speak no more than every one doth know.

Queen. Nimble mischance, that art so light of foot,
Doth not thy embassage belong to me,

---

203. **Tears . . . remedies,** tears show love, but offer no remedies. 204. **too . . . father.** Bolingbroke was born in 1367, and Richard a few months later in 1368.

SCENE IV. 13. **wanting,** lacking. 14. **remember,** remind. 18. **boots,** avails. 28. **Against,** anticipating. 29. **apricocks,** apricots. 40. **pale,** enclosure. 46. **knots,** laid-out garden plots. 69. **doubt,** feared likely. 72. **press'd to death,** allusion to the *peine forte et dure,* inflicted by pressure of heavy weights upon the chests of indicted persons who refused to plead. 75. **suggested,** tempted. 79. **Divine,** foretell prophetically. 93. **embassage,** message. 105. **rue,** "herb of grace," a plant symbolical of repentance, ruth, or sorrow for another's misery.

ACT IV. SCENE I. *Stage Direction:* ***Westminster Hall.*** It had just been rebuilt by King Richard's orders. 5. **timeless,** untimely; also, eternal. 10. **dead time,** past time (?) night time (?). 14. **that very**

And am I last that knows it? O, thou thinkest
To serve me last, that I may longest keep
Thy sorrow in my breast. Come, ladies, go,
To meet at London London's king in woe.
What, was I born to this, that my sad look
Should grace the triumph of great Bolingbroke?
Gard'ner, for telling me these news of woe,
Pray God the plants thou graft'st may never grow.
Exit [*with Ladies*].

Gard. Poor queen! so that thy state might be no worse,
I would my skill were subject to thy curse.
Here did she fall a tear; here in this place
I'll set a bank of rue, sour herb of grace:
Rue, even for ruth, here shortly shall be seen,
In the remembrance of a weeping queen. *Exeunt.*

[ACT IV.

SCENE I. *Westminster Hall.*]

Enter BOLINGBROKE *with the Lords* [AUMERLE, NORTHUMBERLAND, PERCY, FITZWATER, SURREY, *the* BISHOP OF CARLISLE, *the* ABBOT OF WESTMINSTER, *and another* Lord, Herald, Officers] *to Parliament*.

Boling. Call forth Bagot.

Enter [Officers *with*] BAGOT.

Now, Bagot, freely speak thy mind;
What thou dost know of noble Gloucester's death,
Who wrought it with the king, and who perform'd
The bloody office of his timeless end.

Bagot. Then set before my face the Lord Aumerle.

Boling. Cousin, stand forth, and look upon that man.

Bagot. My Lord Aumerle, I know your daring tongue
Scorns to unsay what once it hath deliver'd.
In that dead time when Gloucester's death was plotted,
I heard you say, 'Is not my arm of length,
That reacheth from the restful English court
As far as Calais, to mine uncle's head?'
Amongst much other talk, that very time,
I heard you say that you had rather refuse
The offer of an hundred thousand crowns
Than Bolingbroke's return to England;
Adding withal, how blest this land would be
In this your cousin's death.

Aum. Princes and noble lords,
What answer shall I make to this base man?
Shall I so much dishonour my fair stars,
On equal terms to give him chastisement?
Either I must, or have mine honour soil'd
With the attainder of his slanderous lips.
There is my gage, the manual seal of death,
That marks thee out for hell: I say, thou liest,
And will maintain what thou hast said is false
In thy heart-blood, though being all too base
To stain the temper of my knightly sword.

Boling. Bagot, forbear; thou shalt not take it up.

Aum. Excepting one, I would he were the best
In all this presence that hath mov'd me so.

Fitz. If that thy valour stand on sympathy,
There is my gage, Aumerle, in gage to thine:
By that fair sun which shows me where thou stand'st,
I heard thee say, and vauntingly thou spak'st it,
That thou wert cause of noble Gloucester's death.
If thou deniest it twenty times, thou liest;
And I will turn thy falsehood to thy heart,
Where it was forged, with my rapier's point.

Aum. Thou dar'st not, coward, live to see that day.

Fitz. Now, by my soul, I would it were this hour.

Aum. Fitzwater, thou art damn'd to hell for this.

Percy. Aumerle, thou liest; his honour is as true
In this appeal as thou art all unjust;
And that thou art so, there I throw my gage,
To prove it on thee to the extremest point
Of mortal breathing: seize it, if thou dar'st.

Aum. An if I do not, may my hands rot off
And never brandish more revengeful steel
Over the glittering helmet of my foe!

Another Lord. I task the earth to the like, forsworn Aumerle;
And spur thee on with full as many lies
As may be holloa'd in thy treacherous ear
From sun to sun: there is my honour's pawn;
Engage it to the trial, if thou darest.

Aum. Who sets me else? by heaven, I'll throw at all:
I have a thousand spirits in one breast,
To answer twenty thousand such as you.

Surrey. My Lord Fitzwater, I do remember well
The very time Aumerle and you did talk.

Fitz. 'Tis very true: you were in presence then;
And you can witness with me this is true.

Surrey. As false, by heaven, as heaven itself is true.

Fitz. Surrey, thou liest.

Surrey. Dishonourable boy!
That lie shall lie so heavy on my sword,
That it shall render vengeance and revenge
Till thou the lie-giver and that lie do lie
In earth as quiet as thy father's skull:
In proof whereof, there is my honour's pawn;
Engage it to the trial, if thou dar'st.

Fitz. How fondly dost thou spur a forward horse!
If I dare eat, or drink, or breathe, or live,
I dare meet Surrey in a wilderness,
And spit upon him, whilst I say he lies,
And lies, and lies: there is my bond of faith,
To tie thee to my strong correction.
As I intend to thrive in this new world,
Aumerle is guilty of my true appeal:
Besides, I heard the banish'd Norfolk say
That thou, Aumerle, didst send two of thy men
To execute the noble duke at Calais.

Aum. Some honest Christian trust me with a gage,
That Norfolk lies: here do I throw down this,
If he may be repeal'd, to try his honour.

Boling. These differences shall all rest under gage
Till Norfolk be repeal'd: repeal'd he shall be,
And, though mine enemy, restor'd again
To all his lands and signories: when he is return'd,

time. An inconsistency; Gloucester's death occurred before Bolingbroke left England. 21. **stars,** i.e., his sphere or fortune. 24. **attainder,** dishonoring accusation. 25. **manual seal of death,** death warrant. 33. **sympathy,** correspondence, or equality, of blood or rank. 52. **task the earth,** charge the earth with the task of bearing my gage. 53. **full as many lies,** giving the lie as many times. 56. **Engage,** take up (a pledge). 57. **sets,** challenges to a game (properly, by laying down stakes). 60. ***Surrey,*** Richard's nephew, who with Aumerle represents the Yorkist faction. 67. **vengeance and revenge,** possibly tautological, meaning "furious revenge." 72. **fondly,** foolishly. 80. **Besides, I heard,** etc. John Hall, a groom of Mowbray's at Calais, confessed on October 18, 1399, that he and two servants murdered Gloucester. They were sent, Mowbray told him, by Aumerle. 85. **repeal'd,** recalled from exile.

Against Aumerle we will enforce his trial.
Car. That honourable day shall ne'er be seen.
Many a time hath banish'd Norfolk fought
For Jesu Christ in glorious Christian field,
Streaming the ensign of the Christian cross
Against black pagans, Turks, and Saracens;
And toil'd with works of war, retir'd himself
To Italy; and there at Venice gave
His body to that pleasant country's earth,
And his pure soul unto his captain Christ,
Under whose colours he had fought so long.
Boling. Why, bishop, is Norfolk dead?
Car. As surely as I live, my lord.
Boling. Sweet peace conduct his sweet soul to the bosom
Of good old Abraham! Lords appellants,
Your differences shall all rest under gage
Till we assign you to your days of trial.

Enter YORK [*attended*].

York. Great Duke of Lancaster, I come to thee
From plume-pluck'd Richard; who with willing soul
Adopts thee heir, and his high sceptre yields
To the possession of thy royal hand:
Ascend his throne, descending now from him;
And long live Henry, fourth of that name!
Boling. In God's name, I'll ascend the regal throne.
Car. Marry, God forbid!
Worst in this royal presence may I speak,
Yet best beseeming me to speak the truth.
Would God that any in this noble presence
Were enough noble to be upright judge
Of noble Richard! then true noblesse would
Learn him forbearance from so foul a wrong.
What subject can give sentence on his king?
And who sits here that is not Richard's subject?
Thieves are not judg'd but they are by to hear,
Although apparent guilt be seen in them;
And shall the figure of God's majesty,
His captain, steward, deputy-elect,
Anointed, crowned, planted many years,
Be judg'd by subject and inferior breath,
And he himself not present? O, forfend it, God,
That in a Christian climate souls refin'd
Should show so heinous, black, obscene a deed!
I speak to subjects, and a subject speaks,
Stirr'd up by God, thus boldly for his king.
My Lord of Hereford here, whom you call king,
Is a foul traitor to proud Hereford's king:
And if you crown him, let me prophesy:
The blood of English shall manure the ground,
And future ages groan for this foul act;
Peace shall go sleep with Turks and infidels,
And in this seat of peace tumultuous wars
Shall kin with kin and kind with kind confound;
Disorder, horror, fear and mutiny
Shall here inhabit, and this land be call'd
The field of Golgotha and dead men's skulls.
O, if you raise this house against this house,
It will the woefullest division prove
That ever fell upon this cursed earth.
Prevent it, resist it, let it not be so,
Lest child, child's children, cry against you 'woe!'
North. Well have you argued, sir; and, for your pains,
Of capital treason we arrest you here.
My Lord of Westminster, be it your charge
To keep him safely till his day of trial.
May it please you, lords, to grant the commons' suit.
Boling. Fetch hither Richard, that in common view
He may surrender; so we shall proceed
Without suspicion.
York. I will be his conduct. *Exit.*
Boling. Lords, you that here are under our arrest,
Procure your sureties for your days of answer.
Little are we beholding to your love,
And little look'd for at your helping hands.

Enter RICHARD *and* YORK [*with* Officers *bearing the regalia*].

K. Rich. Alack, why am I sent for to a king,
Before I have shook off the regal thoughts
Wherewith I reign'd? I hardly yet have learn'd
To insinuate, flatter, bow, and bend my limbs:
Give sorrow leave awhile to tutor me
To this submission. Yet I well remember
The favours of these men: were they not mine?
Did they not sometime cry, 'all hail!' to me?
So Judas did to Christ: but he, in twelve,
Found truth in all but one; I, in twelve thousand, none.
God save the king! Will no man say amen?
Am I both priest and clerk? well then, amen.
God save the king! although I be not he;
And yet, amen, if heaven do think him me.
To do what service am I sent for hither?
York. To do that office of thine own good will
Which tired majesty did make thee offer,
The resignation of thy state and crown
To Henry Bolingbroke.
K. Rich. Give me the crown. Here, cousin, seize the crown;
Here, cousin;
On this side my hand, and on that side yours.
Now is this golden crown like a deep well
That owes two buckets, filling one another,
The emptier ever dancing in the air,
The other down, unseen and full of water:
That bucket down and full of tears am I,
Drinking my griefs, whilst you mount up on high.
Boling. I thought you had been willing to resign.
K. Rich. My crown I am; but still my griefs are mine:

91-100. **That . . . long.** This year (1399) Thomas Mowbraie, Duke of Norffolke, died in exile at Venice (Holinshed). Norffolk . . . died at Venice in his return from Jerusalem (Stow, *Annals*). 94. **Streaming,** flying. 96. **toil'd,** wearied. 104. **good old Abraham.** See Luke 16:22. **Lords appellants,** lords who appear as formal accusers. 108. **plume-pluck'd,** humbled. 113. **In . . . throne.** Shakespeare gives no ground for Henry's claim; in Holinshed he claims the throne as descended from Henry III according to a false tradition that his ancestor, Edward Crouchback, was older than his brother Edward I, but was set aside on account of physical deformity. 114. **Marry, God forbid,** etc. Carlisle's speech, according to Holinshed, from whom it is largely taken, was made on October 22, three weeks before the deposition. 115. **Worst,** least in rank. 119. **noblesse,** noble birth, nobleness. 120. **Learn,** teach. 123. **but,** unless. 124. **apparent,** manifest. 125. **figure,** image. 129. **forfend,** forbid. 131. **obscene,** odious, repulsive. 141. **kin,** relationship (of family). **kind,** relationship (of race and nation). 144. **Golgotha,** "the place of a skull," Calvary. See Mark 15:22. 145. **house . . . house.** See Mark 3:25. 152. **My . . . charge.** Carlisle was committed to the Abbey of St. Albans and some months later transferred to the Abbey of Westminster. 154-318. Omitted from Q_{1-2}. That they belonged originally to the play is clear from line 321. 154. **commons' suit,** i.e., request that the charges against Richard be publicly aired. 156-

You may my glories and my state depose,
But not my griefs; still am I king of those.
Boling. Part of your cares you give me with your crown.
K. Rich. Your cares set up do not pluck my cares down.
My care is loss of care, by old care done;
Your care is gain of care, by new care won:
The cares I give I have, though given away;
They tend the crown, yet still with me they stay.
Boling. Are you contented to resign the crown?
K. Rich. Ay, no; no, ay; for I must nothing be;
Therefore no no, for I resign to thee.
Now mark me, how I will undo myself:
I give this heavy weight from off my head
And this unwieldy sceptre from my hand,
The pride of kingly sway from out my heart;
With mine own tears I wash away my balm,
With mine own hands I give away my crown,
With mine own tongue deny my sacred state,
With mine own breath release all duteous oaths:
All pomp and majesty I do forswear;
My manors, rents, revenues I forego;
My acts, decrees, and statutes I deny:
God pardon all oaths that are broke to me!
God keep all vows unbroke are made to thee!
Make me, that nothing have, with nothing griev'd,
And thou with all pleas'd, that hast all achiev'd!
Long mayst thou live in Richard's seat to sit,
And soon lie Richard in an earthy pit!
God save King Henry, unking'd Richard says,
And send him many years of sunshine days!
What more remains?
North. No more, but that you read
These accusations and these grievous crimes
Committed by your person and your followers
Against the state and profit of this land;
That, by confessing them, the souls of men
May deem that you are worthily depos'd.
K. Rich. Must I do so? and must I ravel out
My weav'd-up folly? Gentle Northumberland,
If thy offences were upon record,
Would it not shame thee in so fair a troop
To read a lecture of them? If thou wouldst,
There shouldst thou find one heinous article,
Containing the deposing of a king
And cracking the strong warrant of an oath,
Mark'd with a blot, damn'd in the book of heaven:
Nay, all of you that stand and look upon,
Whilst that my wretchedness doth bait myself,
Though some of you with Pilate wash your hands
Showing an outward pity; yet you Pilates
Have here deliver'd me to my sour cross,
And water cannot wash away your sin.
North. My lord, dispatch; read o'er these articles.
K. Rich. Mine eyes are full of tears, I cannot see:
And yet salt water blinds them not so much
But they can see a sort of traitors here.
Nay, if I turn mine eyes upon myself,
I find myself a traitor with the rest;
For I have given here my soul's consent
To undeck the pompous body of a king;
Made glory base and sovereignty a slave,
Proud majesty a subject, state a peasant.
North. My lord,—
K. Rich. No lord of thine, thou haught insulting man,
Nor no man's lord; I have no name, no title,
No, not that name was given me at the font,
But 'tis usurp'd: alack the heavy day,
That I have worn so many winters out,
And know not now what name to call myself!
O that I were a mockery king of snow,
Standing before the sun of Bolingbroke,
To melt myself away in water-drops!
Good king, great king, and yet not greatly good,
An if my word be sterling yet in England,
Let it command a mirror hither straight,
That it may show me what a face I have,
Since it is bankrout of his majesty.
Boling. Go some of you and fetch a looking-glass.
[*Exit an attendant*.]
North. Read o'er this paper while the glass doth come.
K. Rich. Fiend, thou torments me ere I come to hell!
Boling. Urge it no more, my Lord Northumberland.
North. The commons will not then be satisfied.
K. Rich. They shall be satisfied: I'll read enough,
When I do see the very book indeed
Where all my sins are writ, and that 's myself.

Enter one with a glass.

Give me the glass, and therein will I read.
No deeper wrinkles yet? hath sorrow struck
So many blows upon this face of mine,
And made no deeper wounds? O flattering glass,
Like to my followers in prosperity,
Thou dost beguile me! Was this face the face
That every day under his household roof
Did keep ten thousand men? was this the face
That, like the sun, did make beholders wink?
Was this the face that fac'd so many follies,
And was at last out-fac'd by Bolingbroke?
A brittle glory shineth in this face:
As brittle as the glory is the face;
[*Dashes the glass against the ground*.]
For there it is, crack'd in a hundred shivers.
Mark, silent king, the moral of this sport,
How soon my sorrow hath destroy'd my face.
Boling. The shadow of your sorrow hath destroy'd
The shadow of your face.

157. **we . . . suspicion.** The deposition scene is without historical basis. Richard signed, perhaps under compulsion, an act of abdication, but before witnesses in the Tower. Daniel (*Civil Wars*) gives an elaborate description of the scene. 160. **beholding,** obliged, indebted. 165. **insinuate,** wheedle, ingratiate oneself. 168. **favours,** faces; also, benefits. 185. **owes,** owns, has. 195. **cares.** Three meanings of "care" are involved in the word play which follows: "care" in the sense of responsibility; in the sense of duty or task; in the sense of grief. 201-202. **Ay,** i.e., I. But *I*=nothing; therefore *Ay*=I=no. 204-221. **I give . . . days.** The speech follows with some faithfulness the formula of abdication, as recorded in the Rolls of Parliament. 210. **duteous oaths;** so F; Q_{3-4} and Globe: *duty's rites*. 215. **are made;** so F; Q_{3-4} and Globe: *that swear*. 220. **Henry,** so F; Q_{3-4} and Globe: *Harry*. 232-233. **wouldst . . . shouldst.** In modern usage these words would be reversed. 239. **wash your hands.** See Matthew 27:24. Richard persistently compares himself with Christ; see also III, ii, 24, 61; IV, i, 170. 254. **haught,** haughty, proud. 255. **I have no name.** Richard laments that his whole being and identity are dependent on his now-lost title. 260. **mockery,** counterfeit. 265. **straight,** at once. 267. **bankrout,** bankrupt. 281. **Was this . . . face.** An echo of Marlowe's *Doctor Faustus*. 285. **fac'd,** countenanced. 292. **shadow,** outward show. 293. **shadow,** reflection (in the mirror).

K. Rich. Say that again.
The shadow of my sorrow! ha! let 's see:
'Tis very true, my grief lies all within;
And these external manners of laments
Are merely shadows to the unseen grief
That swells with silence in the tortur'd soul;
There lies the substance: and I thank thee, king,
For thy great bounty, that not only giv'st
Me cause to wail but teachest me the way
How to lament the cause. I'll beg one boon,
And then be gone and trouble you no more.
Shall I obtain it?
Boling. Name it, fair cousin.
K. Rich. 'Fair cousin'? I am greater than a king:
For when I was a king, my flatterers
Were then but subjects; being now a subject,
I have a king here to my flatterer.
Being so great, I have no need to beg.
Boling. Yet ask.
K. Rich. And shall I have?
Boling. You shall.
K. Rich. Then give me leave to go.
Boling. Whither?
K. Rich. Whither you will, so I were from your sights.
Boling. Go, some of you convey him to the Tower.
K. Rich. O, good! convey? conveyers are you all,
That rise thus nimbly by a true king's fall.
[*Exeunt King Richard, some Lords, and a Guard.*]
Boling. On Wednesday next we solemnly set down
Our coronation: lords, prepare yourselves.
Exeunt. Manent [*the Abbot of*] *Westminster,* [*the Bishop of*] *Carlisle, Aumerle.*
Abbot. A woeful pageant have we here beheld.
Car. The woe 's to come; the children yet unborn
Shall feel this day as sharp to them as thorn.
Aum. You holy clergymen, is there no plot
To rid the realm of this pernicious blot?
Abbot. My lord,
Before I freely speak my mind herein,
You shall not only take the sacrament
To bury mine intents, but also to effect
Whatever I shall happen to devise.
I see your brows are full of discontent,
Your hearts of sorrow and your eyes of tears:
Come home with me to supper; and I'll lay
A plot shall show us all a merry day. *Exeunt.*

[ACT V.

SCENE I. *London. A street leading to the Tower.*]

Enter the QUEEN *with* [Ladies,] *her Attendants.*

Queen. This way the king will come; this is the way
To Julius Cæsar's ill-erected tower,
To whose flint bosom my condemned lord
Is doom'd a prisoner by proud Bolingbroke:
Here let us rest, if this rebellious earth
Have any resting for her true king's queen.

Enter RICHARD [*and* Guard].

But soft, but see, or rather do not see,
My fair rose wither: yet look up, behold,
That you in pity may dissolve to dew,
And wash him fresh again with true-love tears.
Ah, thou, the model where old Troy did stand,
Thou map of honour, thou King Richard's tomb,
And not King Richard; thou most beauteous inn,
Why should hard-favour'd grief be lodg'd in thee,
When triumph is become an alehouse guest?
K. Rich. Join not with grief, fair woman, do not so,
To make my end too sudden: learn, good soul,
To think our former state a happy dream;
From which awak'd, the truth of what we are
Shows us but this: I am sworn brother, sweet,
To grim Necessity, and he and I
Will keep a league till death. Hie thee to France
And cloister thee in some religious house:
Our holy lives must win a new world's crown,
Which our profane hours here have stricken down.
Queen. What, is my Richard both in shape and mind
Transform'd and weak'ned? hath Bolingbroke depos'd
Thine intellect? hath he been in thy heart?
The lion dying thrusteth forth his paw,
And wounds the earth, if nothing else, with rage
To be o'erpow'r'd; and wilt thou, pupil-like,
Take thy correction mildly, kiss the rod,
And fawn on rage with base humility,
Which art a lion and the king of beasts?
K. Rich. A king of beasts, indeed; if aught but beasts,
I had been still a happy king of men.
Good sometime queen, prepare thee hence for France:
Think I am dead and that even here thou takest,
As from my death-bed, thy last living leave.
In winter's tedious nights sit by the fire
With good old folks and let them tell thee tales
Of woeful ages long ago betid;
And ere thou bid good night, to quite their griefs,
Tell thou the lamentable tale of me
And send the hearers weeping to their beds:
For why, the senseless brands will sympathize
The heavy accent of thy moving tongue
And in compassion weep the fire out;
And some will mourn in ashes, some coal-black,
For the deposing of a rightful king.

Enter NORTHUMBERLAND [*and* others].

North. My lord, the mind of Bolingbroke is chang'd;
You must to Pomfret, not unto the Tower.
And, madam, there is order ta'en for you;
With all swift speed you must away to France.
K. Rich. Northumberland, thou ladder wherewithal
The mounting Bolingbroke ascends my throne,
The time shall not be many hours of age

308. **to my flatterer,** as, or in the capacity of, my flatterer. 316. **convey,** escort. 317. **convey,** steal, with a play upon the normal sense of the word.

ACT V. SCENE I. 1. **This . . . come.** There is no historical authority for this interview between Richard and the queen; they did not meet again after Richard left for Ireland. In Daniel, *Civil Wars*, II, 89-94, the queen visits him in prison, and there is a striking parallel to Daniel in the passage (II, 66 ff.) where she watches the king ride into the city. 2. **Julius Cæsar's.** The Tower, ascribed by tradition to Julius Caesar, was built by William the Conqueror to hold the city in subordination. **ill-erected,** erected for evil ends, or under evil auspices. 8. **My fair rose.** Hotspur calls Richard *that sweet lovely rose, 1 Henry IV*, I, iii, 175. 11. **thou . . . stand,** thou ruined majesty that resemblest the desolate waste where Troy once stood (Malone). 12. **map of honour,** i.e., the mere outline. 13. **inn,** mansion, abode (with some sense, however, of its more common meaning). 20. **sworn brother,** allusion to the *fratres jurati* of chivalry. 24. **new world's,** heaven's. 42. **betid,** past; happened. 43. **quite their griefs,** make return for their tragic tales. 46. **For why,**

More than it is ere foul sin gathering head
Shall break into corruption: thou shalt think,
Though he divide the realm and give thee half,
It is too little, helping him to all;
And he shall think that thou, which knowest the way
To plant unrightful kings, wilt know again,
Being ne'er so little urg'd, another way
To pluck him headlong from the usurped throne.
The love of wicked men converts to fear;
That fear to hate, and hate turns one or both
To worthy danger and deserved death.
North. My guilt be on my head, and there an end.
Take leave and part; for you must part forthwith.
K. Rich. Doubly divorc'd! Bad men, you violate
A twofold marriage, 'twixt my crown and me,
And then betwixt me and my married wife.
Let me unkiss the oath 'twixt thee and me;
And yet not so, for with a kiss 'twas made.
Part us, Northumberland; I towards the north,
Where shivering cold and sickness pines the clime;
My wife to France: from whence, set forth in pomp,
She came adorned hither like sweet May,
Sent back like Hallowmas or short'st of day.
Queen. And must we be divided? must we part?
K. Rich. Ay, hand from hand, my love, and heart from heart.
Queen. Banish us both and send the king with me.
North. That were some love but little policy.
Queen. Then whither he goes, thither let me go.
K. Rich. So two, together weeping, make one woe.
Weep thou for me in France, I for thee here;
Better far off than near, be ne'er the near.
Go, count thy way with sighs; I mine with groans.
Queen. So longest way shall have the longest moans.
K. Rich. Twice for one step I'll groan, the way being short,
And piece the way out with a heavy heart.
Come, come, in wooing sorrow let 's be brief,
Since, wedding it, there is such length in grief:
One kiss shall stop our mouths, and dumbly part;
Thus give I mine, and thus take I thy heart.
Queen. Give me mine own again; 'twere no good part
To take on me to keep and kill thy heart.
So, now I have mine own again, be gone,
That I may strive to kill it with a groan.
K. Rich. We make woe wanton with this fond delay:
Once more, adieu; the rest let sorrow say. *Exeunt.*

[SCENE II. *The* DUKE OF YORK'S *palace.*]

Enter DUKE OF YORK *and the* DUCHESS.

Duch. My lord, you told me you would tell the rest,
When weeping made you break the story off,
Of our two cousins coming into London.
York. Where did I leave?
Duch. At that sad stop, my lord,
Where rude misgovern'd hands from windows' tops
Threw dust and rubbish on King Richard's head.
York. Then, as I said, the duke, great Bolingbroke,
Mounted upon a hot and fiery steed
Which his aspiring rider seem'd to know,
With slow but stately pace kept on his course,
Whilst all tongues cried 'God save thee, Bolingbroke!'
You would have thought the very windows spake,
So many greedy looks of young and old
Through casements darted their desiring eyes
Upon his visage, and that all the walls
With painted imagery had said at once
'Jesu preserve thee! welcome, Bolingbroke!'
Whilst he, from the one side to the other turning,
Bareheaded, lower than his proud steed's neck,
Bespake them thus: 'I thank you, countrymen:'
And thus still doing, thus he pass'd along.
Duch. Alack, poor Richard! where rode he the whilst?
York. As in a theatre, the eyes of men,
After a well-grac'd actor leaves the stage,
Are idly bent on him that enters next,
Thinking his prattle to be tedious;
Even so, or with much more contempt, men's eyes
Did scowl on gentle Richard; no man cried 'God save him!'
No joyful tongue gave him his welcome home:
But dust was thrown upon his sacred head;
Which with such gentle sorrow he shook off,
His face still combating with tears and smiles,
The badges of his grief and patience,
That had not God, for some strong purpose, steel'd
The hearts of men, they must perforce have melted
And barbarism itself have pitied him.
But heaven hath a hand in these events,
To whose high will we bound our calm contents.
To Bolingbroke are we sworn subjects now,
Whose state and honour I for aye allow.
Duch. Here comes my son Aumerle.
York. Aumerle that was;
But that is lost for being Richard's friend,
And, madam, you must call him Rutland now:
I am in parliament pledge for his truth
And lasting fealty to the new made king.

[*Enter* AUMERLE.]

Duch. Welcome, my son: who are the violets now
That strew the green lap of the new come spring?
Aum. Madam, I know not, nor I greatly care not:
God knows I had as lief be none as one.
York. Well, bear you well in this new spring of time,
Lest you be cropp'd before you come to prime.
What news from Oxford? Do those justs and triumphs hold?
Aum. For aught I know, my lord, they do.
York. You will be there, I know.
Aum. If God prevent not, I purpose so.
York. What seal is that, that hangs without thy bosom?

because. **brands,** firebrands. **sympathize,** respond to. 52. **Pomfret,** Pontefract in Yorkshire, twenty-two miles from York. 53. **order ta'en,** arrangements made. 55. **Northumberland, thou ladder,** etc. Henry recalls this speech, quoting lines 55 and 56 in altered form, in *2 Henry IV*, III, i, 70. 59. **corruption,** putrid matter, pus. 66. **converts,** changes to, turns to. 74. **unkiss,** annul with a kiss (regarded as the seal of a ceremonial bond). 77. **pines,** afflicts, distresses. 80. **Hallowmas,** All Saints' Day (November 1); regarded as the beginning of winter; ten days later in the old calendar than it is now. 88. **Better . . . near,** better be far off than near and yet be unable to meet. The second *near* is the old short comparative form for "nearer."

SCENE II. 4. **leave,** leave off. 20. **Bespake,** spoke to. 25. **idly,** indifferently. 40. **allow,** acknowledge. 41. **Aumerle that was.** Aumerle, with others of Richard's party, lost all titles and honors conferred upon him by King Richard. 44. **truth,** loyalty. 46-47. **who are . . . spring?** Who are the favorites of the new king?

Yea, look'st thou pale? let me see the writing.
Aum. My lord, 'tis nothing.
York. No matter, then, who see it:
I will be satisfied; let me see the writing.
Aum. I do beseech your grace to pardon me:
It is a matter of small consequence,
Which for some reasons I would not have seen.
York. Which for some reasons, sir, I mean to see.
I fear, I fear,—
Duch. What should you fear?
'Tis nothing but some bond, that he is ent'red into
For gay apparel 'gainst the triumph day.
York. Bound to himself! what doth he with a bond
That he is bound to? Wife, thou art a fool.
Boy, let me see the writing.
Aum. I do beseech you, pardon me; I may not show it.
York. I will be satisfied; let me see it, I say.
He plucks it out of his bosom and reads it.
Treason! foul treason! Villain! traitor! slave!
Duch. What is the matter, my lord?
York. Ho! who is within there?

[*Enter a* Servant.]

Saddle my horse.
God for his mercy, what treachery is here!
Duch. Why, what is it, my lord?
York. Give me my boots, I say; saddle my horse.
[*Exit Servant.*]
Now, by mine honour, by my life, by my troth,
I will appeach the villain.
Duch. What is the matter?
York. Peace, foolish woman.
Duch. I will not peace. What is the matter, Aumerle?
Aum. Good mother, be content; it is no more
Than my poor life must answer.
Duch. Thy life answer!
York. Bring me my boots: I will unto the king.

His Man *enters with his boots.*

Duch. Strike him, Aumerle. Poor boy, thou art amaz'd.— [*To York's Man.*]
Hence, villain! never more come in my sight.
York. Give me my boots, I say.
Duch. Why, York, what wilt thou do?
Wilt thou not hide the trespass of thine own?
Have we more sons? or are we like to have?
Is not my teeming date drunk up with time?
And wilt thou pluck my fair son from mine age,
And rob me of a happy mother's name?
Is he not like thee? is he not thine own?
York. Thou fond mad woman,
Wilt thou conceal this dark conspiracy?
A dozen of them here have ta'en the sacrament,
And interchangeably set down their hands,
To kill the king at Oxford.
Duch. He shall be none;
We'll keep him here: then what is that to him?
York. Away, fond woman! were he twenty times my son,
I would appeach him.
Duch. Hadst thou groan'd for him
As I have done, thou wouldst be more pitiful.
But now I know thy mind; thou dost suspect
That I have been disloyal to thy bed,
And that he is a bastard, not thy son:
Sweet York, sweet husband, be not of that mind:
He is as like thee as a man may be,
Not like to me, or any of my kin,
And yet I love him.
York. Make way, unruly woman! *Exit.*
Duch. After, Aumerle! mount thee upon his horse;
Spur post, and get before him to the king,
And beg thy pardon ere he do accuse thee.
I'll not be long behind; though I be old,
I doubt not but to ride as fast as York:
And never will I rise up from the ground
Till Bolingbroke have pardon'd thee. Away, be gone!
[*Exeunt.*]

[SCENE III. *A royal palace.*]

Enter [BOLINGBROKE, *now*] *the* KING, *with his* Nobles [PERCY *and others*].

Boling. Can no man tell me of my unthrifty son?
'Tis full three months since I did see him last:
If any plague hang over us, 'tis he.
I would to God, my lords, he might be found:
Inquire at London, 'mongst the taverns there,
For there, they say, he daily doth frequent,
With unrestrained loose companions,
Even such, they say, as stand in narrow lanes,
And beat our watch, and rob our passengers;
Which he, young wanton and effeminate boy,
Takes on the point of honour to support
So dissolute a crew.
Percy. My lord, some two days since I saw the prince,
And told him of those triumphs held at Oxford.
Boling. And what said the gallant?
Percy. His answer was, he would unto the stews,
And from the common'st creature pluck a glove,
And wear it as a favour; and with that
He would unhorse the lustiest challenger.
Boling. As dissolute as desperate; yet through both
I see some sparks of better hope, which elder years
May happily bring forth. But who comes here?

Enter AUMERLE, *amazed.*

Aum. Where is the king?
Boling. What means our cousin, that he stares and looks
So wildly?
Aum. God save your grace! I do beseech your majesty,
To have some conference with your grace alone.

78. **troth,** faith, allegiance. 79. **appeach,** inform against. 80. **Peace,** keep silent. 85. **Strike him,** i.e., strike the servant. **amaz'd,** confused, bewildered. 90. **Have we more sons.** Historically this Duchess of York was the duke's second wife and was not Aumerle's mother. 91. **teeming date,** period of childbearing. 97-99. **A . . . Oxford.** Hervpon was an indenture sextipartite made, sealed with their seales, and signed with their hands, in the which each stood bound to other, to do their whole indeuor for the accomplishing of their purposed exploit (Holinshed). 99. **none,** not one of them. 111. **his horse,** i.e., one of York's horses.

SCENE III. 1. **my unthrifty son.** Prince Henry was twelve years old at this time. Shakespeare has in mind the traditions of Prince Hal's wayward youth followed in the later plays of the series. 6. **frequent,** be there as a matter of habit. 9. **passengers,** passers-by, wayfarers. 10-12. **Which . . . crew.** This passage will not construe in strict syntax, *which* and *crew* both standing as objects of *support.* 10. **wanton,** spoiled or pampered person. **effeminate,** licentious (?) 13. **I saw the prince.** This is the first bringing together of Hotspur and Prince Hal.

Boling. Withdraw yourselves, and leave us here alone. [*Exeunt Percy and Lords.*]
What is the matter with our cousin now?
Aum. For ever may my knees grow to the earth,
My tongue cleave to my roof within my mouth,
Unless a pardon ere I rise or speak.
Boling. Intended or committed was this fault?
If on the first, how heinous e'er it be,
To win thy after-love I pardon thee.
Aum. Then give me leave that I may turn the key,
That no man enter till my tale be done.
Boling. Have thy desire.
[*Aumerle locks the door.*] *The Duke of York knocks at the door and crieth.*
York. [*Within*] My liege, beware; look to thyself;
Thou hast a traitor in thy presence there.
Boling. Villain, I'll make thee safe. [*Drawing.*]
Aum. Stay thy revengeful hand; thou hast no cause to fear.
York. [*Within*] Open the door, secure, foolhardy king:
Shall I for love speak treason to thy face?
Open the door, or I will break it open.

[*Enter* YORK.]

Boling. What is the matter, uncle? speak;
Recover breath; tell us how near is danger,
That we may arm us to encounter it.
York. Peruse this writing here, and thou shalt know
The treason that my haste forbids me show.
Aum. Remember, as thou read'st, thy promise pass'd:
I do repent me; read not my name there;
My heart is not confederate with my hand.
York. It was, villain, ere thy hand did set it down.
I tore it from the traitor's bosom, king;
Fear, and not love, begets his penitence:
Forget to pity him, lest thy pity prove
A serpent that will sting thee to the heart.
Boling. O heinous, strong and bold conspiracy!
O loyal father of a treacherous son!
Thou sheer, immaculate and silver fountain,
From whence this stream through muddy passages
Hath held his current and defil'd himself!
Thy overflow of good converts to bad,
And thy abundant goodness shall excuse
This deadly blot in thy digressing son.
York. So shall my virtue be his vice's bawd;
And he shall spend mine honour with his shame,
As thriftless sons their scraping fathers' gold.
Mine honour lives when his dishonour dies,
Or my sham'd life in his dishonour lies:
Thou kill'st me in his life; giving him breath,
The traitor lives, the true man 's put to death.
Duch. [*Within*] What ho, my liege! for God's sake, let me in.
Boling. What shrill-voic'd suppliant makes this eager cry?
Duch. A woman, and thy aunt, great king; 'tis I.
Speak with me, pity me, open the door:
A beggar begs that never begg'd before.
Boling. Our scene is alt'red from a serious thing,
And now chang'd to 'The Beggar and the King.'
My dangerous cousin, let your mother in:
I know she is come to pray for your foul sin.
York. If thou do pardon, whosoever pray,
More sins for this forgiveness prosper may.
This fest'red joint cut off, the rest rest sound;
This let alone will all the rest confound.

[*Enter* DUCHESS.]

Duch. O king, believe not this hard-hearted man!
Love loving not itself none other can.
York. Thou frantic woman, what dost thou make here?
Shall thy old dugs once more a traitor rear?
Duch. Sweet York, be patient. Hear me, gentle liege. [*Kneels.*]
Boling. Rise up, good aunt.
Duch. Not yet, I thee beseech:
For ever will I walk upon my knees,
And never see day that the happy sees,
Till thou give joy; until thou bid me joy,
By pardoning Rutland, my transgressing boy.
Aum. Unto my mother's prayers I bend my knee. [*Kneels.*]
York. Against them both my true joints bended be. [*Kneels.*]
Ill mayst thou thrive, if thou grant any grace!
Duch. Pleads he in earnest? look upon his face;
His eyes do drop no tears, his prayers are in jest;
His words come from his mouth, ours from our breast:
He prays but faintly and would be denied;
We pray with heart and soul and all beside:
His weary joints would gladly rise, I know;
Our knees shall kneel till to the ground they grow:
His prayers are full of false hypocrisy;
Ours of true zeal and deep integrity.
Our prayers do out-pray his; then let them have
That mercy which true prayer ought to have.
Boling. Good aunt, stand up.
Duch. Nay, do not say, 'stand up;'
Say 'pardon' first, and afterwards 'stand up.'
An if I were thy nurse, thy tongue to teach,
'Pardon' should be the first word of thy speech.
I never long'd to hear a word till now;
Say 'pardon,' king; let pity teach thee how:
The word is short, but not so short as sweet;
No word like 'pardon' for kings' mouths so meet.
York. Speak it in French, king; say 'pardonne moi.'
Duch. Dost thou teach pardon pardon to destroy?
Ah, my sour husband, my hard-hearted lord,
That sets the word itself against the word!
Speak 'pardon' as 'tis current in our land;
The chopping French we do not understand.
Thine eye begins to speak; set thy tongue there;

See Bolingbroke's reflection on Hal and Hotspur in *1 Henry IV*, I, i, 78-90; and the tavern view of the matter from the same play, II, iv, 114-121. 16. **stews,** houses of ill fame. 22. **happily,** haply; possibly, combining also the modern sense of the word. 31. **My . . . mouth.** See Psalms 137:6. 43. **secure,** unsuspecting, heedless. 44. **speak . . . face,** i.e., by calling him *secure* and *foolhardy*. 58. **serpent,** allusion to the fable of the *Countryman and the Viper*. See also III, ii, 131. 61-66. **Thou . . . son.** Chambers quotes a parallel passage from Lyly's *Euphues* (Arbor ed., page 191): "As the water that springeth from the fountain's head," etc. 61. **sheer,** clear, pure. 66. **digressing,** transgressing. 69. **scraping,** parsimonious. 80. **'The Beggar and the King,'** one of the many allusions in Shakespeare to the ballad of *King Cophetua and the Beggar Maid*; see *Love's Labour's Lost*, I, ii, 114 ff.; *Romeo and Juliet*, II, i, 14; *2 Henry IV*, V, iii, 106. 88. **Love . . . can.** He who does not love his own kin can love no one else, not even the king. 119. **'pardonne moi,'** excuse me (affectedly polite refusal). 124. **chopping,** jerky, shifting suddenly; also, changing (the sense of words).

Or in thy piteous heart plant thou thine ear;
That hearing how our plaints and prayers do pierce,
Pity may move thee 'pardon' to rehearse.
Boling. Good aunt, stand up.
Duch. I do not sue to stand;
Pardon is all the suit I have in hand.
Boling. I pardon him, as God shall pardon me.
Duch. O happy vantage of a kneeling knee!
Yet am I sick for fear: speak it again;
Twice saying 'pardon' doth not pardon twain,
But makes one pardon strong.
Boling. With all my heart
I pardon him.
Duch. A god on earth thou art. [*Rises.*]
Boling. But for our trusty brother-in-law and the abbot,
With all the rest of that consorted crew,
Destruction straight shall dog them at the heels.
Good uncle, help to order several powers
To Oxford, or where'er these traitors are:
They shall not live within this world, I swear,
But I will have them, if I once know where.
Uncle, farewell: and, cousin too, adieu:
Your mother well hath pray'd, and prove you true.
Duch. Come, my old son: I pray God make thee new. *Exeunt.*

[SCENE IV. *The same.*]

Enter SIR PIERCE EXTON *and* [Servant].

Exton. Didst thou not mark the king, what words he spake,
'Have I no friend will rid me of this living fear?'
Was it not so?
Ser. These were his very words.
Exton. 'Have I no friend?' quoth he: he spake it twice,
And urg'd it twice together, did he not?
Serv. He did.
Exton. And speaking it, he wishtly look'd on me,
As who should say, 'I would thou wert the man
That would divorce this terror from my heart;'
Meaning the king at Pomfret. Come, let 's go:
I am the king's friend, and will rid his foe. [*Exeunt.*]

[SCENE V. *Pomfret castle.*]

Enter RICHARD *alone.*

K. Rich. I have been studying how I may compare
This prison where I live unto the world:
And for because the world is populous
And here is not a creature but myself,
I cannot do it; yet I'll hammer it out.
My brain I'll prove the female to my soul,
My soul the father; and these two beget
A generation of still-breeding thoughts,
And these same thoughts people this little world,
In humours like the people of this world,
For no thought is contented. The better sort,
As thoughts of things divine, are intermix'd
With scruples and do set the word itself
Against the word:
As thus, 'Come, little ones,' and then again,
'It is as hard to come as for a camel
To thread the postern of a small needle's eye.'
Thoughts tending to ambition, they do plot
Unlikely wonders; how these vain weak nails
May tear a passage through the flinty ribs
Of this hard world, my ragged prison walls,
And, for they cannot, die in their own pride.
Thoughts tending to content flatter themselves
That they are not the first of fortune's slaves,
Nor shall not be the last; like seely beggars
Who sitting in the stocks refuge their shame,
That many have and others must sit there;
And in this thought they find a kind of ease,
Bearing their own misfortunes on the back
Of such as have before endur'd the like.
Thus play I in one person many people,
And none contented: sometimes am I king;
Then treasons make me wish myself a beggar,
And so I am: then crushing penury
Persuades me I was better when a king;
Then am I king'd again: and by and by
Think that I am unking'd by Bolingbroke,
And straight am nothing: but whate'er I be,
Nor I nor any man that but man is
With nothing shall be pleas'd, till he be eas'd
With being nothing. Music do I hear? *The music plays.*
Ha, ha! keep time: how sour sweet music is,
When time is broke and no proportion kept!
So is it in the music of men's lives.
And here have I the daintiness of ear
To check time broke in a disordered string;
But for the concord of my state and time
Had not an ear to hear my true time broke.
I wasted time, and now doth time waste me;
For now hath time made me his numb'ring clock:
My thoughts are minutes; and with sighs they jar
Their watches on unto mine eyes, the outward watch,
Whereto my finger, like a dial's point,
Is pointing still, in cleansing them from tears.
Now sir, the sound that tells what hour it is
Are clamorous groans, which strike upon my heart,
Which is the bell: so sighs and tears and groans
Show minutes, times, and hours: but my time
Runs posting on in Bolingbroke's proud joy,
While I stand fooling here, his Jack of the clock.
This music mads me; let it sound no more;
For though it have holp madmen to their wits,
In me it seems it will make wise men mad.
Yet blessing on his heart that gives it me!

130. **suit,** petition (with play upon the term as used at cards). 137. **our trusty brother-in-law,** the Duke of Fxeter, who had married Bolingbroke's sister. 138. **consorted,** confederate. 145. **prove you true.** Aumerle, as Duke of York, died leading the van at Agincourt.

SCENE IV. 7. **And speaking it,** etc. Cf. Daniel's *Civil Wars*, II, 57:

"And wisht that some would so his life esteeme,
As *ridde* him of these feares wherein he stood:
And there-with eyes a knight, that then was by,
Who soone could learne his lesson by his eye."

wishtly, intently; also, wistfully.

SCENE V. 1. **I have been studying,** etc. Daniel (III, 64-69) presents Richard soliloquizing, "Conferring captiue-Crownes with freedome poore," somewhat in the spirit of this passage. 15-17. **Come, little . . . eye.** See Matthew 19:14, 24. 21. **ragged,** rugged. 25. **seely,** simpleminded. 26. **refuge,** protect themselves from. 50. **numb'ring clock.** Henley explains thus: " . . . his sighs correspond to the jarring of the pendulum, which, at the same time that it watches or numbers the seconds, marks also their progress in minutes on the dial or outward watch, to which the king compares his eyes; and their want of figures is supplied by a succession of tears, or, to use the expression of Milton, minute-drops; his finger, by as regularly wiping these tears

For 'tis a sign of love; and love to Richard
Is a strange brooch in this all-hating world.

Enter a Groom of the Stable.

Groom. Hail, royal prince!
K. Rich. Thanks, noble peer;
The cheapest of us is ten groats too dear.
What art thou? and how comest thou hither,
Where no man never comes but that sad dog
That brings me food to make misfortune live?
Groom. I was a poor groom of thy stable, king,
When thou wert king; who, travelling towards York,
With much ado at length have gotten leave
To look upon my sometimes royal master's face.
O, how it ern'd my heart when I beheld
In London streets, that coronation-day,
When Bolingbroke rode on roan Barbary,
That horse that thou so often hast bestrid,
That horse that I so carefully have dress'd!
K. Rich. Rode he on Barbary? Tell me, gentle friend,
How went he under him?
Groom. So proudly as if he disdain'd the ground.
K. Rich. So proud that Bolingbroke was on his back!
That jade hath eat bread from my royal hand;
This hand hath made him proud with clapping him.
Would he not stumble? would he not fall down,
Since pride must have a fall, and break the neck
Of that proud man that did usurp his back?
Forgiveness, horse! why do I rail on thee,
Since thou, created to be aw'd by man,
Wast born to bear? I was not made a horse;
And yet I bear a burthen like an ass,
Spurr'd, gall'd, and tir'd by jauncing Bolingbroke.

Enter one [*a* Keeper] *to* Richard *with meat.*

Keep. Fellow, give place; here is no longer stay.
K. Rich. If thou love me, 'tis time thou wert away.
Groom. What my tongue dares not, that my heart shall say. *Exit Groom.*
Keep. My lord, will 't please you to fall to?
K. Rich. Taste of it first, as thou art wont to do.
Keep. My lord, I dare not: Sir Pierce of Exton, who lately came from the king, commands the contrary.
K. Rich. The devil take Henry of Lancaster and thee!
Patience is stale, and I am weary of it. [*Beats the keeper.*]
Keep. Help, help, help!

The Murderers [Exton *and* Servants] rush in.

K. Rich. How now! what means death in this rude assault?
Villain, thy own hand yields thy death's instrument.
[*Snatching an axe from a Servant and killing him.*]
Go thou, and fill another room in hell.
[*He kills another.*] *Here Exton strikes him down.*
That hand shall burn in never-quenching fire
That staggers thus my person. Exton, thy fierce hand
Hath with the king's blood stain'd the king's own land.
Mount, mount, my soul! thy seat is up on high;
Whilst my gross flesh sinks downward, here to die.
[*Dies.*]
Exton. As full of valour as of royal blood:
Both have I spill'd; O would the deed were good!
For now the devil, that told me I did well,
Says that this deed is chronicled in hell.
This dead king to the living king I'll bear:
Take hence the rest, and give them burial here.
[*Exeunt.*]

[Scene vi. *Windsor castle.*]

[*Flourish.*] *Enter* Bolingbroke [*as King*], *with the* Duke of York [*,other* Lords, *and* Attendants].

Boling. Kind uncle York, the latest news we hear
Is that the rebels have consum'd with fire
Our town of Cicester in Gloucestershire;
But whether they be ta'en or slain we hear not.

Enter Northumberland.

Welcome, my lord: what is the news?
North. First, to thy sacred state wish I all happiness.
The next news is, I have to London sent
The heads of Oxford, Salisbury, Blunt, and Kent:
The manner of their taking may appear
At large discoursed in this paper here.
Boling. We thank thee, gentle Percy, for thy pains;
And to thy worth will add right worthy gains.

Enter Lord Fitzwater.

Fitz. My lord, I have from Oxford sent to London
The heads of Brocas and Sir Bennet Seely,
Two of the dangerous consorted traitors
That sought at Oxford thy dire overthrow.
Boling. Thy pains, Fitzwater, shall not be forgot;
Right noble is thy merit, well I wot.

Enter Henry Percy [*and the* Bishop of Carlisle].

Percy. The grand conspirator, Abbot of Westminster,
With clog of conscience and sour melancholy
Hath yielded up his body to the grave;
But here is Carlisle living, to abide
Thy kingly doom and sentence of his pride.
Boling. Carlisle, this is your doom:
Choose out some secret place, some reverend room,
More than thou hast, and with it joy thy life;
So as thou liv'st in peace, die free from strife:
For though mine enemy thou hast ever been,
High sparks of honour in thee have I seen.

Enter Exton, *with* [*persons bearing*] *the coffin.*

Exton. Great king, within this coffin I present
Thy buried fear: herein all breathless lies
The mightiest of thy greatest enemies,

away performs the office of the dial point; his clamorous groans are the sounds that tell the hour." 51. **jar,** tick. 60. **Jack of the clock,** a figure which struck the bell on a clock. 62. **holp madmen to their wits,** probable allusion to the story of the cure of Saul by David. 66. **brooch,** ornament (worn in a man's hat). 68. **ten groats too dear.** There is a pun on *royal* and *noble* in the preceding lines. Though a royal (10s.) is worth 10 groats (ten times 4d.) more than a noble (6s. 8d.) is, a noble itself is 10 groats too high a price for either Richard or the Groom. 76. **ern'd,** grieved. 78. **roan Barbary.** Boswell-Stone suggests that the story of "roan Barbary" may come from an account repeated in Froissart of a greyhound, Mathe, which forsook his old master, Richard, and followed Bolingbroke. 94. **gall'd,** annoyed; literally, made sore by rubbing. **jauncing,** making prance up and down (of a horse); here, hard-riding. 108. **room,** a particular place assigned to a person. 115. **O . . . good!** It is said, that sir Piers of Exton, after he had thus slaine him, wept right bitterlie, as one stricken with the pricke of a giltie conscience, for murthering him, whom he had so long time obeied as king (Holinshed).

Scene vi. 8. **Oxford.** No such name occurs in Holinshed; F reads *Spencer*. Shakespeare antedates the death of Richard, since the conspiracy was put down before his death. 15. **consorted,** confederate.

Richard of Bordeaux, by me hither brought.
Boling. Exton, I thank thee not; for thou hast wrought
A deed of slander with thy fatal hand
Upon my head and all this famous land.
Exton. From your own mouth, my lord, did I this deed.
Boling. They love not poison that do poison need,
Nor do I thee: though I did wish him dead,
I hate the murderer, love him murdered.
The guilt of conscience take thou for thy labour,
But neither my good word nor princely favour:
With Cain go wander thorough shades of night,
And never show thy head by day nor light.
Lords, I protest, my soul is full of woe,
That blood should sprinkle me to make me grow:
Come, mourn with me for that I do lament,
And put on sullen black incontinent:
I'll make a voyage to the Holy Land,
To wash this blood off from my guilty hand:
March sadly after; grace my mournings here;
In weeping after this untimely bier. [*Exeunt*.]

48. **incontinent,** immediately. 49-50. **I'll . . . hand.** Henry never fulfilled his vow, though he had it always in mind; see *1 Henry IV*, I, i, 19 ff.; *2 Henry IV*, III, i, 108; IV, iv, 3; v, 210 ff. and 233 ff. 52. **In . . . bier.** Richard probably died in January 1400; he was buried at Pomfret. His body was then carried to London, displayed in Cheapside and St. Paul's on March 12, 1400, and buried in an obscure grave at Langley. Through the piety of Henry v, his body was placed in the tomb in Westminster Abbey that Richard himself had built for his first queen, Anne of Bohemia.

THE FIRST PART OF KING HENRY THE FOURTH

The opening of *1 Henry IV* is taut and grave in tone. England is "shaken" and "wan with care." The troubles of *Richard II*, to which this play (1596–1597) is a close sequel, have not been left behind. However much King Henry would prefer to unite his countrymen against a common foreign enemy, in a crusade to the holy lands, he is prevented from doing so by uninterrupted war. The impassioned rhetoric of his opening speech proclaiming a new era of peace can only end in anticlimax, for the actual purpose of this meeting in council is to receive and assess reports of military action against the throne.

Henry's current troubles are in the far reaches of his kingdom: Scots in the north, Welsh in the west. Fighting for Henry on these two fronts are the nobles of the Percy family who helped him to power: Henry Percy ("Hotspur"), his father the Earl of Northumberland, his uncle the Earl of Worcester, and his brother-in-law Edmund Mortimer the Earl of March. Apparently they have fought bravely. Yet we soon sense that all is not well between the new king and those who rebelled with him against Richard. A quarrel breaks out because Hotspur refuses to deliver to Henry some prisoners as required by feudal obedience. The matter of the ransom money is only a technicality; what is really at issue? In part, it is Henry's insistence on being obeyed on principle. Admiring Hotspur inordinately, the king feels he must discipline affectionately this fine young warrior as a father would discipline his son. Even more deeply, however, the issue of the prisoners galls Henry because of the proviso that he ransom Mortimer, captured by the Welsh. Henry does not forget that Mortimer is his chief rival for the English crown, being descended from the Duke of Clarence (elder brother to Henry's father, Gaunt), and proclaimed by Richard heir to the throne. Mortimer is the last person Henry would wish ransomed. Moreover, the king suspects Mortimer of having fought with something less than total zeal against the Welsh Glendower. Mortimer's marriage to Glendower's daughter starkly confirms the king's worst fears. Henry knows Northumberland and Worcester to be expert in treasonous plotting, since they conspired with him to overthrow Richard. Now, Henry believes, these Percys are extending their alliance by a series of calculated marriages in order to seize power once again. This time their claimant is Mortimer.

RADIO TIMES HULTON PICTURE LIBRARY

George Cruikshank's etching of Falstaff playing the role of Hal's father, the King.

Shakespeare's sympathies are many-sided. The Percy clan is in fact organizing against Henry, but not without cause. As they see it, the man they helped to the throne has done precious little for them since. His manner of disciplining them sounds too much like hostility and ingratitude. Other counselors attend the king constantly while Worcester is banished from court. In such an atmosphere of distrust, suspicion breeds still more suspicion. The situation has polarized, surely more than either party originally intended.

Hotspur is the most attractive of the rebels, to us as to King Henry. He is outspoken, courageous, witty, domineering in conversation. Above all, he is a disciple of manliness, loyalty, chivalry, bravery in battle—the attributes of an upstanding and somewhat old-fashioned sense of honor. Yet a fatal defect dwells even in these attractive qualities. Hotspur is impatient, proud, unwilling to tolerate a rival—be it Glendower or Prince Hal. In his very first speech, purporting to explain his refusal to deliver the prisoners, he brilliantly satirizes an effete courtier who had come to him from King Henry in the midst of a battle. The satire betrays many harsh qualities in Hotspur: the self-indulgent wrath which returns fully to him even in recollection of the encounter, the pride in his own stoical indifference to suffering, and especially the obsessive character (revealed in the repetitive pattern of the rhetoric) of his contempt for courtiers generally. Surely his scorn for stay-at-home politicians is directed in part at King Henry himself. All courtiers are to Hotspur effeminate, perfume-wearing, affected in mannerism and speech, scarcely masculine. This obsession of Hotspur makes him extraordinarily prone to one-sided judgments. Like most excessive devotees of chivalry, he divides mankind into sheep and goats: those who are gentlemen, like himself, and those who are beneath contempt. The "vile politician" Bolingbroke and his son the "sword-and-buckler Prince of Wales" fall into the latter category.

Prone as he is to such an overly simple view of political behavior, Hotspur can see no good in the king's cause and no evil in his own. He is a poor listener because of his obsession, and yet an easy prey to his uncle and father who desperately require his leadership for their cause. They need only implant the suggestion that King Henry is trying to pull a political maneuver in his refusal to ransom Mortimer, and Hotspur is ready to leap incautiously to the defense of their cause. The great irony is that Hotspur fails to read political motives in his own relatives' machinations. While he fights for bright honor, they jockey cautiously for position and prove uncertain allies when the hour of battle approaches. Most crucially, they betray Hotspur in the pre-battle negotiations, at which he is not present. As Worcester explains to Vernon during their return to rebel headquarters (V,ii), they cannot let Hotspur know of the king's offer to settle matters by a general pardon. Although, as they realize, the king could pardon Hotspur's youth, there can be no turning back for themselves. Thus the honor for which Hotspur fights is at bottom a lie, and the mutual esteem that might have grown between him and a much-reformed Prince of Wales is thwarted by the polarization of attitudes in the two camps. Hotspur's brand of honor is the victim of its own excess, and lends some credence to Falstaff's wry conclusion that honor "is a mere scutcheon."

The contrasting of Falstaff and Hotspur on the theme of honor suggests that they are dramatic "foils" to one another, representing extremes of life-styles between which Hal must choose. Shakespeare uses this "foil" device structurally and consciously; for example, he has considerably reduced the age of the Hotspur he found in Holinshed's *Chronicles* in order to accentuate the similarity of age between Hotspur and Hal. Conversely, to emphasize the contrast between Falstaff and Hotspur, Shakespeare envisages Falstaff as old (nearly sixty, by his own admission), fat, humorous, and without honor. Falstaff's vices are Hotspur's virtues, and vice versa. Whereas Hotspur offers to Hal a model of chivalric striving and attention to duty, Falstaff is a highwayman and liar. On the other hand, Hotspur is a fanatic, unbending and self-absorbed even in the company of his sprightly wife Kate, irritated by music and poetry; Falstaff is the epitome of merriment and *joi de vivre*. We excuse much in him because he lusts after life with such an appetite, and ingratiates himself to others by inviting them to laugh at his expense.

The two most pronounced motifs of the first scene between Hal and Falstaff (I,ii) are the hanging of thieves and temptation to sinfulness. Beneath the gay surface of their raillery, the two are already debating the need for the ultimate rejection of Falstaff. Can their relationship continue unchanged into the reign of Henry v? Will there be gallows standing, and justice for highwaymen? Will "Monsieur Remorse," as Poins calls Falstaff, ever sincerely repent? Will the prince, for that matter? It is to allay our fears in this regard that Hal comes before us in soliloquy at the scene's end, vowing his determination to use these scapegrace companions as mere "foils" to his triumphal reformation at the appropriate time. But this explanation raises an opposite danger in our sympathies: is he callously using his companions merely to create a public-relations myth of Prince Hal, the Politician with the Common Touch? Since the rejection of Falstaff is, by Hal's own words, a foregone conclusion, can we credit him with a serious friendship? Where do Shakespeare's sympathies lie, with the need for political order or with the hedonistic spirit of youth? Perhaps he recognizes the validity of both, and accordingly shows us a prince who is genuinely fond of Falstaff's exuberant company, but who also knows that he is a king's son and must sooner or later accept the consequences of that unsought role. Falstaff's gift to him is youthful irresponsibility, which must be cherished (by all of us) even though it cannot last.

In the Gadshill robbery episode, Falstaff reveals

that his "cowardice" differs from the natural craven fear of Bardolph and Peto. He fights no longer than he sees "reason," that is, not against unfair odds such as two athletic young men in the dark (or later, at Shrewsbury, against the burly Scots giant, the Douglas). A man could get killed that way. Falstaff's cowardice, then, is philosophic, seen by himself in a humorous perspective. The same is true of his lying about the robbery. However much Hal exults in exposing Falstaff as a fraud, we cannot dismiss the possibility that Falstaff may see through the prince's scheme, and may then feed Hal the expectedly outlandish lie (two men in buckram green become eleven men) as a means of begging for affection. Falstaff's only way of pleading his cause is to tickle the prince's fancy, in his role as a kind of court fool. What Fal-

PRINTS DIVISION, THE NEW YORK PUBLIC LIBRARY, ASTOR, LENOX AND TILDEN FOUNDATION

Irresponsible, fleshy, mendacious Jack Falstaff, despite his faults, or perhaps because of them, remains Shakespeare's most popular comic character.

staff most wants is to be loved and retained for what he is; and that, poignantly enough, is the one thing the mature Henry v cannot grant.

Falstaff is a foil not only to Hotspur, but to Henry iv, and (in *2 Henry IV*) to the Lord Chief Justice; perhaps also to Prince John of Lancaster. Three of these are father-figures. All offer Hal varying models of conduct which he alone must adapt and transform. Just as he must achieve Hotspur's bright honor without the fanaticism, he must discover his father's sense of responsibility without yielding to the political expediency and drabness of the older man (balefully bequeathed to Hal's brother Prince John). Hal must ultimately reject Falstaff and adopt instead the counsel of the Lord Chief Justice, but must attempt to do so without becoming priggish or complacent. Unquestionably the rejection of Falstaff does impose on Hal the loss of his attractively irresponsible qualities. The carefree pleasures Hal knew as a private person must dwindle when he accepts his new role as ruler and statesman. If Hal undertakes his awesome obligations with an awareness of the loss to himself, however, we can applaud the wisdom of his maturation even while we lament the passing of his youthful spontaneity.

THE FIRST PART OF KING HENRY THE FOURTH

[*Dramatis Personae*

KING HENRY the Fourth.
HENRY, Prince of Wales, } *sons to the King.*
JOHN of Lancaster, }
EARL OF WESTMORELAND.
SIR WALTER BLUNT.
THOMAS PERCY, Earl of Worcester.
HENRY PERCY, Earl of Northumberland.
HENRY PERCY, *surnamed* HOTSPUR, *his son.*
EDMUND MORTIMER, Earl of March.
RICHARD SCROOP, Archbishop of York.
ARCHIBALD, Earl of DOUGLAS.
OWEN GLENDOWER.
SIR RICHARD VERNON.
SIR JOHN FALSTAFF.
SIR MICHAEL, *a friend to the Archbishop of York.*
POINS.
GADSHILL.
PETO.
BARDOLPH.

LADY PERCY, *wife to Hotspur, and sister to Mortimer.*
LADY MORTIMER, *daughter to Glendower, and wife to Mortimer.*
MISTRESS QUICKLY, *hostess of a tavern in Eastcheap.*

Lords, Officers, Sheriff, Vintner, Chamberlain, Drawers, *two* Carriers, Travellers, *and* Attendants.

SCENE: *England and Wales.*]

[ACT I.

SCENE I. *London. The palace.*]

Enter the KING, LORD JOHN OF LANCASTER, [*the*] EARL OF WESTMORELAND, [SIR WALTER BLUNT,] *with others.*

King. So shaken as we are, so wan with care,
Find we a time for frighted peace to pant,
And breathe short-winded accents of new broils
To be commenc'd in stronds afar remote.
†No more the thirsty entrance of this soil
Shall daub her lips with her own children's blood;
No more shall trenching war channel her fields,
Nor bruise her flow'rets with the armed hoofs
Of hostile paces: those opposed eyes,
Which, like the meteors of a troubled heaven,
All of one nature, of one substance bred,
Did lately meet in the intestine shock

And furious close of civil butchery
Shall now, in mutual well-beseeming ranks,
March all one way and be no more oppos'd
Against acquaintance, kindred and allies:
The edge of war, like an ill-sheathed knife,
No more shall cut his master. Therefore, friends,
As far as to the sepulchre of Christ,
Whose soldier now, under whose blessed cross
We are impressed and engag'd to fight,
Forthwith a power of English shall we levy;
Whose arms were moulded in their mothers' womb
To chase these pagans in those holy fields
Over whose acres walk'd those blessed feet
Which fourteen hundred years ago were nail'd
For our advantage on the bitter cross.
But this our purpose now is twelve month old,
And bootless 'tis to tell you we will go:
Therefore we meet not now. Then let me hear
Of you, my gentle cousin Westmoreland,
What yesternight our council did decree
In forwarding this dear expedience.

West. My liege, this haste was hot in question,
And many limits of the charge set down
But yesternight: when all athwart there came
A post from Wales loaden with heavy news;
Whose worst was, that the noble Mortimer,
Leading the men of Herefordshire to fight
Against the irregular and wild Glendower,
Was by the rude hands of that Welshman taken,
A thousand of his people butchered;
Upon whose dead corpse there was such misuse,
Such beastly shameless transformation,
By those Welshwomen done as may not be
Without much shame retold or spoken of.

King. It seems then that the tidings of this broil
Brake off our business for the Holy Land.

West. This match'd with other did, my gracious lord;
For more uneven and unwelcome news
Came from the north and thus it did import:
On Holy-rood day, the gallant Hotspur there,
Young Harry Percy and brave Archibald,
That ever-valiant and approved Scot,
At Holmedon met,
Where they did spend a sad and bloody hour;
As by discharge of their artillery,
And shape of likelihood, the news was told;
For he that brought them, in the very heat
And pride of their contention did take horse,
Uncertain of the issue any way.

King. Here is a dear, a true industrious friend,
Sir Walter Blunt, new lighted from his horse,
Stain'd with the variation of each soil
Betwixt that Holmedon and this seat of ours;
And he hath brought us smooth and welcome news.
The Earl of Douglas is discomfited:
Ten thousand bold Scots, two and twenty knights,
Balk'd in their own blood did Sir Walter see
On Holmedon's plains. Of prisoners, Hotspur took
Mordake the Earl of Fife, and eldest son
To beaten Douglas; and the Earl of Athol,
Of Murray, Angus, and Menteith:
And is not this an honourable spoil?
A gallant prize? ha, cousin, is it not?

West. In faith,
It is a conquest for a prince to boast of.

King. Yea, there thou mak'st me sad and mak'st me sin
In envy that my Lord Northumberland
Should be the father to so blest a son,
A son who is the theme of honour's tongue;
Amongst a grove, the very straightest plant;
Who is sweet Fortune's minion and her pride:
Whilst I, by looking on the praise of him,
See riot and dishonour stain the brow
Of my young Harry. O that it could be prov'd
That some night-tripping fairy had exchang'd
In cradle-clothes our children where they lay,
And call'd mine Percy, his Plantagenet!
Then would I have his Harry, and he mine.
But let him from my thoughts. What think you, coz,
Of this young Percy's pride? the prisoners,
Which he in this adventure hath surpris'd,
To his own use he keeps; and sends me word,
I shall have none but Mordake Earl of Fife.

West. This is his uncle's teaching: this is Worcester,
Malevolent to you in all aspects;
Which makes him prune himself, and bristle up
The crest of youth against your dignity.

King. But I have sent for him to answer this;
And for this cause awhile we must neglect
Our holy purpose to Jerusalem.
Cousin, on Wednesday next our council we
Will hold at Windsor; so inform the lords:
But come yourself with speed to us again;
For more is to be said and to be done
Than out of anger can be uttered.

West. I will, my liege. *Exeunt.*

[SCENE II. *London. An apartment of the Prince's.*]

Enter PRINCE OF WALES *and* SIR JOHN FALSTAFF.

Fal. Now, Hal, what time of day is it, lad?

Prince. Thou art so fat-witted, with drinking of old sack and unbuttoning thee after supper and sleeping upon benches after noon, that thou hast forgotten to demand that truly which thou wouldst truly know. What a devil hast thou to do with the time of the day? Unless hours were cups of sack and minutes capons and clocks the tongues of bawds and dials the signs of leaping-houses and the blessed sun himself a fair hot wench in flame-coloured taffeta, I see no reason why thou shouldst be so superfluous to demand the time of the day.

ACT I. SCENE I. 4. **stronds,** shores. 9. **opposed,** hostile (of enemies). 12. **intestine,** internal. 13. **close,** encounter. 22. **power,** army. 28. **twelve month,** a year; used collectively. 29. **bootless,** useless. 33. **dear expedience,** urgent expedition. 34. **hot in question,** being hotly debated. 35. **limits of the charge,** military arrangements; possibly, estimates of expense. 36. **athwart,** frustrating, interrupting. 38. **worst,** i.e., worst news. 40. **irregular,** lawless. 43-46. **Upon . . . spoken of.** Holinshed also says that the outrages are unmentionable. 49. **This . . . other,** this piece of news matched with another. 50. **uneven,** embarrassing. 55. **Holmedon,** Humbleton, a town in Northumberland. 57. **by,** i.e., judging from. 64. **the variation of each,** every kind of. 66. **smooth,** flattering, pleasant. 69. **Balk'd,** heaped up in balks or ridges. 71. **Mordake,** i.e., Murdoch. 95. **none but Mordake.** Since the prisoner in question was of royal blood, being grandson to Robert II, Hotspur could not claim him as his prisoner. 97. **Malevolent, aspects,** astrological terms. 98. **prune,** preen (as a bird its feathers).

SCENE II. 8. **sack,** a Spanish white wine. 9. **dials,** sundials. 9-10. **leaping-houses,** houses of prostitution. 11. **taffeta,** commonly worn by prostitutes.

Fal. Indeed, you come near me now, Hal; for we that take purses go by the moon and the seven stars, and not by Phœbus, he, 'that wandering knight so fair.' And, I prithee, sweet wag, when thou art king, as, God save thy grace,—majesty I should say, for grace thou wilt have none,—

Prince. What, none?

Fal. No, by my troth, not so much as will serve to be prologue to an egg and butter.

Prince. Well, how then? come, roundly, roundly.

Fal. Marry, then, sweet wag, when thou art king, let not us that are squires of the night's body be called thieves of the day's beauty: let us be Diana's foresters, gentlemen of the shade, minions of the moon; and let men say we be men of good government, being governed, as the sea is, by our noble and chaste mistress the moon, under whose countenance we steal.

Prince. Thou sayest well, and it holds well too; for the fortune of us that are the moon's men doth ebb and flow like the sea, being governed, as the sea is, by the moon. As, for proof, now: a purse of gold most resolutely snatched on Monday night and most dissolutely spent on Tuesday morning; got with swearing 'Lay by' and spent with crying 'Bring in;' now in as low an ebb as the foot of the ladder and by and by in as high a flow as the ridge of the gallows.

Fal. By the Lord, thou sayest true, lad. And is not my hostess of the tavern a most sweet wench?

Prince. As the honey of Hybla, my old lad of the castle. And is not a buff jerkin a most sweet robe of durance?

Fal. How now, how now, mad wag! what, in thy quips and thy quiddities? what a plague have I to do with a buff jerkin?

Prince. Why, what a pox have I to do with my hostess of the tavern?

Fal. Well, thou hast called her to a reckoning many a time and oft.

Prince. Did I ever call for thee to pay thy part?

Fal. No; I'll give thee thy due, thou hast paid all there.

Prince. Yea, and elsewhere, so far as my coin would stretch; and where it would not, I have used my credit.

Fal. Yea, and so used it that, were it not here apparent that thou art heir apparent—But, I prithee, sweet wag, shall there be gallows standing in England when thou art king? and resolution thus fubbed as it is with the rusty curb of old father antic the law? Do not thou, when thou art king, hang a thief.

Prince. No; thou shalt.

Fal. Shall I? O rare! By the Lord, I'll be a brave judge.

Prince. Thou judgest false already: I mean, thou shalt have the hanging of the thieves and so become a rare hangman.

Fal. Well, Hal, well; and in some sort it jumps with my humour as well as waiting in the court, I can tell you.

Prince. For obtaining of suits?

Fal. Yea, for obtaining of suits, whereof the hangman hath no lean wardrobe. 'Sblood, I am as melancholy as a gib cat or a lugged bear.

Prince. Or an old lion, or a lover's lute.

Fal. Yea, or the drone of a Lincolnshire bagpipe.

Prince. What sayest thou to a hare, or the melancholy of Moor-ditch?

Fal. Thou hast the most unsavoury similes and art indeed the most comparative, rascalliest, sweet young prince. But, Hal, I prithee, trouble me no more with vanity. I would to God thou and I knew where a commodity of good names were to be bought. An old lord of the council rated me the other day in the street about you, sir, but I marked him not; and yet he talked very wisely, but I regarded him not; and yet he talked wisely, and in the street too.

Prince. Thou didst well; for wisdom cries out in the streets, and no man regards it.

Fal. O, thou hast damnable iteration and art indeed able to corrupt a saint. Thou hast done much harm upon me, Hal; God forgive thee for it! Before I knew thee, Hal, I knew nothing; and now am I, if a man should speak truly, little better than one of the wicked. I must give over this life, and I will give it over: by the Lord, an I do not, I am a villain: I'll be damned for never a king's son in Christendom.

Prince. Where shall we take a purse to-morrow, Jack?

Fal. 'Zounds, where thou wilt, lad; I'll make one; an I do not, call me villain and baffle me.

Prince. I see a good amendment of life in thee; from praying to purse-taking.

Fal. Why, Hal, 'tis my vocation, Hal; 'tis no sin for a man to labour in his vocation.

Enter Poins.

Poins! Now shall we know if Gadshill have set a match. O, if men were to be saved by merit, what hole in hell were hot enough for him? This is the most omnipotent villain that ever cried 'Stand' to a true man.

Prince. Good morrow, Ned.

Poins. Good morrow, sweet Hal. What says Monsieur Remorse? what says Sir John Sack and Sugar? Jack! how agrees the devil and thee about thy soul, that thou soldest him on Good-Friday last for a cup of Madeira and a cold capon's leg?

Prince. Sir John stands to his word, the devil shall have his bargain; for he was never yet a breaker of proverbs: he will give the devil his due.

Poins. Then art thou damned for keeping thy word with the devil.

Prince. Else he had been damned for cozening the devil.

Scene ii. 14. **you come near me now,** you've scored a point on me. Prince Hal's speech has been full of extravagant abuse; Falstaff parries by taking it in a sense of his own. 16. **the seven stars,** the Pleiades. **Phœbus,** the sun. 17-18. **'that . . . fair,'** a line from some ballad. 19. **grace,** royal highness, with pun on spiritual grace and also on "grace" or blessing before a meal. 23. **prologue,** punning allusion to grace before meat. 24. **roundly,** out with it. It is a wit combat. 29. **Diana's.** Diana was goddess of the moon, of chastity, and of the hunt. 30. **minions,** favorites. 33. **steal,** move quietly; also, take purses. 40. **'Lay by,'** a cry of highwaymen, like "Hands up!" 41. **'Bring in,'** i.e., the orders in the tavern. 47. **Hybla,** a mountain region in Sicily near Syracuse, famed for honey. 48. **old lad of the castle,** a pun on the name, Sir John Oldcastle, borne by Falstaff in the earlier versions of the Henry iv plays; also on The Castle, a famous brothel in Southwark. **buff jerkin,** a leather jacket worn by officers of the law; a *robe of durance* in two senses, since *durance* means "imprisonment" and "durability." 51. **quips,** jests. **quiddities,** subtleties of speech. 67-68. **resolution,** courage (of a highwayman). 68. **fubbed,** cheated. 69. **antic,** buffoon. 80. **suits,** suits at court and suits of clothes. 82. **'Sblood,** an oath. 83. **gib cat,** tomcat. **lugged bear,** bear tied to a stake and baited by

Poins. But, my lads, my lads, to-morrow morning, by four o'clock, early at Gadshill! there are pilgrims going to Canterbury with rich offerings, and traders riding to London with fat purses: I have vizards for you all; you have horses for yourselves: Gadshill lies to-night in Rochester: I have bespoke supper to-morrow night in Eastcheap: we may do it as secure as sleep. If you will go, I will stuff your purses full of crowns; if you will not, tarry at home and be hanged.

Fal. Hear ye, Yedward; if I tarry at home and go not, I'll hang you for going.

Poins. You will, chops?

Fal. Hal, wilt thou make one?

Prince. Who, I rob? I a thief? not I, by my faith.

Fal. There 's neither honesty, manhood, nor good fellowship in thee, nor thou camest not of the blood royal, if thou darest not stand for ten shillings.

Prince. Well then, once in my days I'll be a madcap.

Fal. Why, that 's well said.

Prince. Well, come what will, I'll tarry at home.

Fal. By the Lord, I'll be a traitor then, when thou art king.

Prince. I care not.

Poins. Sir John, I prithee, leave the prince and me alone: I will lay him down such reasons for this adventure that he shall go.

Fal. Well, God give thee the spirit of persuasion and him the ears of profiting, that what thou speakest may move and what he hears may be believed, that the true prince may, for recreation sake, prove a false thief; for the poor abuses of the time want countenance. Farewell: you shall find me in Eastcheap.

Prince. Farewell, thou latter spring! farewell, All-hallown summer! [*Exit Falstaff*.]

Poins. Now, my good sweet honey lord, ride with us to-morrow: I have a jest to execute that I cannot manage alone. Falstaff, Bardolph, Peto and Gadshill shall rob those men that we have already waylaid; yourself and I will not be there; and when they have the booty, if you and I do not rob them, cut this head off from my shoulders.

Prince. How shall we part with them in setting forth?

Poins. Why, we will set forth before or after them, and appoint them a place of meeting, wherein it is at our pleasure to fail, and then will they adventure upon the exploit themselves; which they shall have no sooner achieved, but we'll set upon them.

Prince. Yea, but 'tis like that they will know us by our horses, by our habits and by every other appointment, to be ourselves.

Poins. Tut! our horses they shall not see; I'll tie them in the wood; our vizards we will change after we leave them: and, sirrah, I have cases of buckram for the nonce, to immask our noted outward garments.

Prince. Yea, but I doubt they will be too hard for us.

Poins. Well, for two of them, I know them to be as true-bred cowards as ever turned back; and for the third, if he fight longer than he sees reason, I'll forswear arms. The virtue of this jest will be, the incomprehensible lies that this same fat rogue will tell us when we meet at supper: how thirty, at least, he fought with; what wards, what blows, what extremities he endured; and in the reproof of this lies the jest.

Prince. Well, I'll go with thee: provide us all things necessary and meet me to-morrow night in Eastcheap; there I'll sup. Farewell.

Poins. Farewell, my lord. *Exit Poins*.

Prince. I know you all, and will awhile uphold
The unyok'd humour of your idleness:
Yet herein will I imitate the sun,
Who doth permit the base contagious clouds
To smother up his beauty from the world,
That, when he please again to be himself,
Being wanted, he may be more wond'red at,
By breaking through the foul and ugly mists
Of vapours that did seem to strangle him.
If all the year were playing holidays,
To sport would be as tedious as to work;
But when they seldom come, they wish'd for come,
And nothing pleaseth but rare accidents.
So, when this loose behaviour I throw off
And pay the debt I never promised,
By how much better than my word I am,
By so much shall I falsify men's hopes;
And like bright metal on a sullen ground,
My reformation, glitt'ring o'er my fault,
Shall show more goodly and attract more eyes
Than that which hath no foil to set it off.
I'll so offend, to make offence a skill;
Redeeming time when men think least I will. *Exit*.

[SCENE III. *London. The palace.*]

Enter the KING, NORTHUMBERLAND, WORCESTER, HOTSPUR, SIR WALTER BLUNT, *with others*.

King. My blood hath been too cold and temperate,
Unapt to stir at these indignities,
And you have found me; for accordingly
You tread upon my patience: but be sure
I will from henceforth rather be myself,
Mighty and to be fear'd, than my condition;
Which hath been smooth as oil, soft as young down,
And therefore lost that title of respect
Which the proud soul ne'er pays but to the proud.

Wor. Our house, my sovereign liege, little deserves
The scourge of greatness to be us'd on it;
And that same greatness too which our own hands
Have holp to make so portly.

North. My lord,—

King. Worcester, get thee gone; for I do see

dogs. 88. **Moor-ditch,** a foul ditch draining Moorfields. 99. **wisdom cries out,** etc., an allusion to Proverbs 1:20-24. 103. **much harm upon me.** Oldcastle was traditionally a religious hypocrite and a Lollard, or follower of John Wycliffe; Falstaff retains his faculty for insincere repentance. 112. **'Zounds,** an oath, "God's wounds." 113. **baffle,** hang up by the heels as a recreant knight. 116. **vocation,** a cant term for religious conversion. 119. **set a match,** arranged a robbery. In the old play *The Famous Victories of Henry V* Gadshill is called a "setter." 136. **cozening,** cheating. 139. **Gadshill,** a town near Rochester on the road from London to Canterbury. (One of the highwaymen is also called Gadshill.) 142. **vizards,** masks. 149. **Yedward,** Edward; a colloquialism. 151. **chops,** apparently alluding to Falstaff's fat jaws. 170, 171. **spirit of persuasion, ears of profiting,** cant phrases of religious connotation. 175. **want countenance,** lack encouragement and protection from men of rank. 178. **All-hallown summer.** Falstaff's summer (his youth) has lasted to All Saints' Day, November 1st. 182. **Bardolph, Peto,** so Theobald; QF: *Harvey*, *Rossill*. 201. **cases,** suits. 202. **noted,** known. 208. **incomprehensible,** unlimited.

SCENE III. 3. **found me,** i.e., found me so. 13. **portly,** prosperous, with a suggestion of overprosperity.

Danger and disobedience in thine eye:
O, sir, your presence is too bold and peremptory,
And majesty might never yet endure
The moody frontier of a servant brow.
You have good leave to leave us: when we need
Your use and counsel, we shall send for you. *Exit Wor.*
You were about to speak. [*To North.*]
North. Yea, my good lord.
Those prisoners in your highness' name demanded,
Which Harry Percy here at Holmedon took,
Were, as he says, not with such strength denied
As is delivered to your majesty:
Either envy, therefore, or misprision
Is guilty of this fault and not my son.
Hot. My liege, I did deny no prisoners.
But I remember, when the fight was done,
When I was dry with rage and extreme toil,
Breathless and faint, leaning upon my sword,
Came there a certain lord, neat, and trimly dress'd,
Fresh as a bridegroom; and his chin new reap'd
Show'd like a stubble-land at harvest-home;
He was perfumed like a milliner;
And 'twixt his finger and his thumb he held
A pouncet-box, which ever and anon
He gave his nose and took 't away again;
Who therewith angry, when it next came there,
Took it in snuff; and still he smil'd and talk'd,
And as the soldiers bore dead bodies by,
He call'd them untaught knaves, unmannerly,
To bring a slovenly unhandsome corse
Betwixt the wind and his nobility.
With many holiday and lady terms
He questioned me; amongst the rest, demanded
My prisoners in your majesty's behalf.
I then, all smarting with my wounds being cold,
To be so pest'red with a popinjay,
Out of my grief and my impatience,
Answer'd neglectingly I know not what,
He should, or he should not; for he made me mad
To see him shine so brisk and smell so sweet
And talk so like a waiting-gentlewoman
Of guns and drums and wounds,—God save the mark!—
And telling me the sovereignest thing on earth
Was parmaceti for an inward bruise;
And that it was great pity, so it was,
This villanous salt-petre should be digg'd
Out of the bowels of the harmless earth,
Which many a good tall fellow had destroy'd
So cowardly; and but for these vile guns,
He would himself have been a soldier.
This bald unjointed chat of his, my lord,
I answer'd indirectly, as I said;
And I beseech you, let not his report
Come current for an accusation
Betwixt my love and your high majesty.
Blunt. The circumstance considered, good my lord,
Whate'er Lord Harry Percy then had said
To such a person and in such a place,
At such a time, with all the rest retold,
May reasonably die and never rise
To do him wrong or any way impeach
What then he said, so he unsay it now.
King. Why, yet he doth deny his prisoners,
But with proviso and exception,
That we at our own charge shall ransom straight
His brother-in-law, the foolish Mortimer;
Who, on my soul, hath wilfully betray'd
The lives of those that he did lead to fight
Against that great magician, damn'd Glendower,
Whose daughter, as we hear, that Earl of March
Hath lately married. Shall our coffers, then,
Be emptied to redeem a traitor home?
Shall we buy treason? and indent with fears,
When they have lost and forfeited themselves?
No, on the barren mountains let him starve;
For I shall never hold that man my friend
Whose tongue shall ask me for one penny cost
To ransom home revolted Mortimer.
Hot. Revolted Mortimer!
He never did fall off, my sovereign liege,
But by the chance of war: to prove that true
Needs no more but one tongue for all those wounds,
Those mouthed wounds, which valiantly he took,
When on the gentle Severn's sedgy bank,
In single opposition, hand to hand,
He did confound the best part of an hour
In changing hardiment with great Glendower:
Three times they breath'd and three times did they drink,
Upon agreement, of swift Severn's flood;
Who then, affrighted with their bloody looks,
Ran fearfully among the trembling reeds,
And hid his crisp head in the hollow bank
Bloodstained with these valiant combatants.
Never did base and rotten policy
Colour her working with such deadly wounds;
Nor never could the noble Mortimer
Receive so many, and all willingly:
Then let not him be slandered with revolt.
King. Thou dost belie him, Percy, thou dost belie him;
He never did encounter with Glendower:
I tell thee,
He durst as well have met the devil alone
As Owen Glendower for an enemy.
Art thou not asham'd? But, sirrah, henceforth
Let me not hear you speak of Mortimer:
Send me your prisoners with the speediest means
Or you shall hear in such a kind from me
As will displease you. My Lord Northumberland,
We license your departure with your son.
Send us your prisoners, or you will hear of it.
Exit King [*with Blunt, and train*].
Hot. An if the devil come and roar for them,
I will not send them: I will after straight
And tell him so; for I will ease my heart,
Albeit I make a hazard of my head.

19. **moody,** passionate, angry. **frontier,** outwork or fortification; here with play on the word *front* or *brow*. 27. **envy,** malice. **misprision,** misunderstanding. 34. **reap'd,** i.e., with beard newly trimmed according to the latest fashion, not like a soldier's beard. 35. **Show'd,** looked. **harvest-home,** end of harvest, fields being neat and bare. 36. **milliner,** man dealing in fancy articles. 38. **pouncet-box,** perfume box with perforated lid. 40. **Who,** i.e., his nose. 41. **Took it in snuff,** proverbially meaning to take offense, but here with literal meaning also; the nose sniffs in the perfume. (This snuff is not tobacco, but perfumed herbs.) 46. **lady,** ladylike. 50. **popinjay,** parrot. 51. **grief,** pain. 56. **God save the mark.** Probably originally a formula to avert evil omen; here, an expression of impatience. 57. **sovereignest,** most efficacious. 58. **parmaceti,** spermaceti, sperm from the whale. 80, 84. **Mortimer, Earl of March.** There were two Edmund Mortimers; Shakespeare confuses them and combines their stories. It was the uncle (1378-1409?) who was captured by Glendower and married Glen-

North. What, drunk with choler? stay and pause awhile:
Here comes your uncle.

Enter WORCESTER.

Hot. Speak of Mortimer!
'Zounds, I will speak of him; and let my soul
Want mercy, if I do not join with him:
Yea, on his part I'll empty all these veins,
And shed my dear blood drop by drop in the dust,
But I will lift the down-trod Mortimer
As high in the air as this unthankful king,
As this ingrate and cank'red Bolingbroke.
North. Brother, the king hath made your nephew mad.
Wor. Who struck this heat up after I was gone?
Hot. He will, forsooth, have all my prisoners;
And when I urg'd the ransom once again
Of my wife's brother, then his cheek look'd pale,
And on my face he turn'd an eye of death,
Trembling even at the name of Mortimer.
Wor. I cannot blame him: was not he proclaim'd
By Richard that dead is the next of blood?
North. He was; I heard the proclamation:
And then it was when the unhappy king,—
Whose wrongs in us God pardon!—did set forth
Upon his Irish expedition;
From whence he intercepted did return
To be depos'd and shortly murdered.
Wor. And for whose death we in the world's wide mouth
Live scandaliz'd and foully spoken of.
Hot. But, soft, I pray you; did King Richard then
Proclaim my brother Edmund Mortimer
Heir to the crown?
North. He did; myself did hear it.
Hot. Nay, then I cannot blame his cousin king,
That wish'd him on the barren mountains starve.
But shall it be, that you, that set the crown
Upon the head of this forgetful man
And for his sake wear the detested blot
Of murderous subornation, shall it be,
That you a world of curses undergo,
Being the agents, or base second means,
The cords, the ladder, or the hangman rather?
O, pardon me that I descend so low,
To show the line and the predicament
Wherein you range under this subtle king;
Shall it for shame be spoken in these days,
Or fill up chronicles in time to come,
That men of your nobility and power
Did gage them both in an unjust behalf,
As both of you—God pardon it!—have done,
To put down Richard, that sweet lovely rose,
And plant this thorn, this canker, Bolingbroke?
And shall it in more shame be further spoken,
That you are fool'd, discarded and shook off
By him for whom these shames ye underwent?
No; yet time serves wherein you may redeem
Your banish'd honours and restore yourselves
Into the good thoughts of the world again,
Revenge the jeering and disdain'd contempt
Of this proud king, who studies day and night
To answer all the debt he owes to you
Even with the bloody payment of your deaths:
Therefore, I say,—
Wor. Peace, cousin, say no more:
And now I will unclasp a secret book,
And to your quick-conceiving discontents
I'll read you matter deep and dangerous,
As full of peril and adventurous spirit
As to o'er-walk a current roaring loud
On the unsteadfast footing of a spear.
Hot. If he fall in, good night! or sink or swim:
Send danger from the east unto the west,
So honour cross it from the north to south,
And let them grapple: O, the blood more stirs
To rouse a lion than to start a hare!
North. Imagination of some great exploit
Drives him beyond the bounds of patience.
Hot. By heaven, methinks it were an easy leap,
To pluck bright honour from the pale-fac'd moon,
Or dive into the bottom of the deep,
Where fathom-line could never touch the ground,
And pluck up drowned honour by the locks;
So he that doth redeem her thence might wear
Without corrival all her dignities:
But out upon this half-fac'd fellowship!
Wor. He apprehends a world of figures here,
But not the form of what he should attend.
Good cousin, give me audience for a while.
Hot. I cry you mercy.
Wor. Those same noble Scots
That are your prisoners,—
Hot. I'll keep them all;
By God, he shall not have a Scot of them!
No, if a Scot would save his soul, he shall not:
I'll keep them, by this hand!
Wor. You start away
And lend no ear unto my purposes.
Those prisoners you shall keep.
Hot. Nay, I will; that 's flat:
He said he would not ransom Mortimer;
Forbad my tongue to speak of Mortimer;
But I will find him when he lies asleep,
And in his ear I'll holla 'Mortimer!'
Nay,
I'll have a starling shall be taught to speak
Nothing but 'Mortimer,' and give it him,
To keep his anger still in motion.
Wor. Hear you, cousin; a word.
Hot. All studies here I solemnly defy,
Save how to gall and pinch this Bolingbroke:
And that same sword-and-buckler Prince of Wales,
But that I think his father loves him not
And would be glad he met with some mischance,
I would have him poisoned with a pot of ale.
Wor. Farewell, kinsman: I'll talk to you

dower's daughter; it was the nephew (1391-1425), fifth Earl of March, who had been proclaimed heir to King Richard II. 87. **indent,** bargain, make an indenture. 101. **changing hardiment,** exchanging blows. 102. **breath'd,** paused for breath. 108. **policy,** cunning. 137. **cank'red,** spoiled, malignant. 149. **in us,** caused by our doings. 163. **murderous subornation,** the suborning of or inciting to murder. 168. **line,** rank; also, hangman's rope. **predicament,** dilemma, dangerous situation; also, category. 173. **gage,** pledge. 176. **canker,** canker rose, dog rose, wild and unfragrant; also, ulcer. 183. **disdain'd,** disdainful. 194. **or sink or swim,** i.e., such a man, walking over a roaring stream, is doomed if he fall in, whether he sink or swim. 207. **corrival,** rival, competitor. 208. **But . . . fellowship,** i.e., down with this business of sharing glory with others. 230. **sword-and-buckler,** arms improper for a prince, who should carry rapier and dagger.

When you are better temper'd to attend.
North. Why, what a wasp-stung and impatient fool
Art thou to break into this woman's mood,
Tying thine ear to no tongue but thine own!
Hot. Why, look you, I am whipp'd and scourg'd with rods,
Nettled and stung with pismires, when I hear
Of this vile politician, Bolingbroke.
In Richard's time,—what do you call the place?—
A plague upon it, it is in Gloucestershire;
'Twas where the madcap duke his uncle kept,
His uncle York; where I first bow'd my knee
Unto this king of smiles, this Bolingbroke,—
'Sblood!—
When you and he came back from Ravenspurgh.
North. At Berkeley castle.
Hot. You say true:
Why, what a candy deal of courtesy
This fawning greyhound then did proffer me!
'Look when his infant fortune came to age,'
And 'gentle Harry Percy,' and 'kind cousin;'
O, the devil take such cozeners! God forgive me!
Good uncle, tell your tale; I have done.
Wor. Nay, if you have not, to it again;
We will stay your leisure.
Hot. I have done, i' faith.
Wor. Then once more to your Scottish prisoners.
Deliver them up without their ransom straight,
And make the Douglas' son your only mean
For powers in Scotland; which, for divers reasons
Which I shall send you written, be assur'd,
Will easily be granted. You, my lord,
[*To Northumberland.*]
Your son in Scotland being thus employ'd,
Shall secretly into the bosom creep
Of that same noble prelate, well belov'd,
The archbishop.
Hot. Of York, is it not?
Wor. True; who bears hard
His brother's death at Bristow, the Lord Scroop.
I speak not this in estimation,
As what I think might be, but what I know
Is ruminated, plotted and set down,
And only stays but to behold the face
Of that occasion that shall bring it on.
Hot. I smell it: upon my life, it will do well.
North. Before the game is afoot, thou still let'st slip.
Hot. Why, it cannot choose but be a noble plot:
And then the power of Scotland and of York,
To join with Mortimer, ha?
Wor. And so they shall.
Hot. In faith, it is exceedingly well aim'd.
Wor. And 'tis no little reason bids us speed,
To save our heads by raising of a head;
For, bear ourselves as even as we can,
The king will always think him in our debt,
And think we think ourselves unsatisfied,
Till he hath found a time to pay us home:
And see already how he doth begin
To make us strangers to his looks of love.
Hot. He does, he does: we'll be reveng'd on him.
Wor. Cousin, farewell: no further go in this
Than I by letters shall direct your course.
When time is ripe, which will be suddenly,
I'll steal to Glendower and Lord Mortimer;
Where you and Douglas and our pow'rs at once,
As I will fashion it, shall happily meet,
To bear our fortunes in our own strong arms,
Which now we hold at much uncertainty.
North. Farewell, good brother: we shall thrive, I trust.
Hot. Uncle, adieu: O, let the hours be short
Till fields and blows and groans applaud our sport!
Exeunt.

[ACT II.

SCENE I. *Rochester. An inn yard.*]

Enter a Carrier *with a lantern in his hand.*

First Car. Heigh-ho! an it be not four by the day, I'll be hanged: Charles' wain is over the new chimney, and yet our horse not packed. What, ostler!

Ost. [*Within*] Anon, anon.

First Car. I prithee, Tom, beat Cut's saddle, put a few flocks in the point; poor jade, is wrung in the withers out of all cess.

Enter another Carrier.

Sec. Car. Peas and beans are as dank here as a dog, and that is the next way to give poor jades the bots: this house is turned upside down since Robin Ostler died.

First Car. Poor fellow, never joyed since the price of oats rose; it was the death of him.

Sec. Car. I think this be the most villanous house in all London road for fleas: I am stung like a tench.

First Car. Like a tench! by the mass, there is ne'er a king christen could be better bit than I have been since the first cock.

Sec. Car. Why, they will allow us ne'er a jordan, and then we leak in your chimney; and your chamber-lie breeds fleas like a loach.

First Car. What, ostler! come away and be hanged! come away.

Sec. Car. I have a gammon of bacon and two razes of ginger, to be delivered as far as Charing-cross.

First Car. God's body! the turkeys in my pannier are quite starved. What, ostler! A plague on thee! hast thou never an eye in thy head? canst not hear? An 'twere not as good deed as drink, to break the pate on thee, I am a very villain. Come, and be hanged! hast no faith in thee?

Enter GADSHILL.

240. **pismires,** ants. 241. **politician,** deceitful schemer. 244. **kept,** dwelled. 251. **candy,** sugared, flattering. 255. **cozeners,** cheats, with pun on "cousins." 261. **mean,** i.e., means of procuring. 272. **estimation,** guesswork. 278. **let'st slip,** i.e., let loose the dogs.

ACT II. SCENE I. *Stage Direction:* **Carrier,** one whose trade was conveying goods, usually by pack horses. 1-2. **by the day,** in the morning. 2. **Charles' wain,** the constellation of the Great Bear. 3. **horse,** horses. 6. **beat,** soften. **Cut's saddle,** packsaddle of the horse named *Cut*, meaning "bob-tailed." 7. **flocks,** locks of wool. **point,** pommel of the saddle. **wrung,** chafed. 8. **cess,** measure, estimate. 10. **next,** nearest, quickest. 11. **bots,** a disease of horses. 17. **tench,** a kind of fish; probably an allusion to an ancient belief that the spots on certain fishes were due to flea bites. 19. **christen,** in Christendom. 20. **first cock,** i.e., midnight. 22. **jordan,** chamberpot. 23. **chamber-lie,** urine. **loach,** a prolific fish. 26. **gammon,** side. 27. **razes,** roots. 30. **pannier,** basket. 43. **Ay, when? canst tell?** Don't you wish I would? 51, 64. **charge,** baggage. 53. **At hand, quoth pick-purse,** slang expression for "Coming immediately." Gadshill's reply shows the chamberlain's alliance with the robbers. 60. **holds current,** holds true. 61. **franklin,** a farmer owning his own land. **wild of Kent,**

Gads. Good morrow, carriers. What 's o'clock?

First Car. I think it be two o'clock.

Gads. I prithee, lend me thy lantern, to see my gelding in the stable.

First Car. Nay, by God, soft; I know a trick worth two of that, i' faith.

Gads. I pray thee, lend me thine.

Sec. Car. Ay, when? canst tell? Lend me thy lantern, quoth he? marry, I'll see thee hanged first.

Gads. Sirrah carrier, what time do you mean to come to London?

Sec. Car. Time enough to go to bed with a candle, I warrant thee. Come, neighbour Mugs, we'll call up the gentlemen: they will along with company, for they have great charge. *Exeunt* [*Carriers*].

Gads. What, ho! chamberlain!

Enter Chamberlain.

Cham. At hand, quoth pick-purse.

Gads. That 's even as fair as—at hand, quoth the chamberlain; for thou variest no more from picking of purses than giving direction doth from labouring; thou layest the plot how.

Cham. Good morrow, Master Gadshill. It holds current that I told you yesternight: there 's a franklin in the wild of Kent hath brought three hundred marks with him in gold: I heard him tell it to one of his company last night at supper; a kind of auditor; one that hath abundance of charge too, God knows what. They are up already, and call for eggs and butter: they will away presently.

Gads. Sirrah, if they meet not with Saint Nicholas' clerks, I'll give thee this neck.

Cham. No, I'll none of it: I pray thee, keep that for the hangman; for I know thou worshippest Saint Nicholas as truly as a man of falsehood may.

Gads. What talkest thou to me of the hangman? if I hang, I'll make a fat pair of gallows; for if I hang, old Sir John hangs with me, and thou knowest he is no starveling. Tut! there are other Troyans that thou dreamest not of, the which for sport sake are content to do the profession some grace; that would, if matters should be looked into, for their own credit sake, make all whole. I am joined with no foot land-rakers, no long-staff sixpenny strikers, none of these mad mustachio purple-hued malt-worms; but with nobility and tranquillity, burgomasters and great oneyers, such as can hold in, such as will strike sooner than speak, and speak sooner than drink, and drink sooner than pray: and yet, 'zounds, I lie; for they pray continually to their saint, the commonwealth; or rather, not pray to her, but prey on her, for they ride up and down on her and make her their boots.

Cham. What, the commonwealth their boots? will she hold out water in foul way?

Gads. She will, she will; justice hath liquored her. We steal as in a castle, cocksure; we have the receipt of fern-seed, we walk invisible.

Cham. Nay, by my faith, I think you are more beholding to the night than to fern-seed for your walking invisible.

Gads. Give me thy hand: thou shalt have a share in our purchase, as I am a true man.

Cham. Nay, rather let me have it, as you are a false thief.

Gads. Go to; 'homo' is a common name to all men. Bid the ostler bring my gelding out of the stable. Farewell, you muddy knave. [*Exeunt.*]

[Scene ii. *The highway, near Gadshill.*]

Enter Prince, Poins, *and* Peto, *&c.*

Poins. Come, shelter, shelter: I have removed Falstaff's horse, and he frets like a gummed velvet.

Prince. Stand close.

Enter Falstaff.

Fal. Poins! Poins, and be hanged! Poins!

Prince. Peace, ye fat-kidneyed rascal! what a brawling dost thou keep!

Fal. Where 's Poins, Hal?

Prince. He is walked up to the top of the hill: I'll go seek him. [*Steps aside.*]

Fal. I am accursed to rob in that thief's company: the rascal hath removed my horse, and tied him I know not where. If I travel but four foot by the squier further afoot, I shall break my wind. Well, I doubt not but to die a fair death for all this, if I 'scape hanging for killing that rogue. I have forsworn his company hourly any time this two and twenty years, and yet I am bewitched with the rogue's company. If the rascal have not given me medicines to make me love him, I'll be hanged; it could not be else; I have drunk medicines. Poins! Hal! a plague upon you both! Bardolph! Peto! I'll starve ere I'll rob a foot further. An 'twere not as good a deed as drink, to turn true man and to leave these rogues, I am the veriest varlet that ever chewed with a tooth. Eight yards of uneven ground is threescore and ten miles afoot with me; and the stony-hearted villains know it well enough: a plague upon it when thieves cannot be true one to another! (*They whistle.*) Whew! A plague upon you all! Give me my horse, you rogues; give me my horse, and be hanged!

Prince. [*Comes forward*] Peace, ye fat-guts! lie down; lay thine ear close to the ground and list if thou canst hear the tread of travellers.

Fal. Have you any levers to lift me up again, being down? 'Sblood, I'll not bear mine own flesh so far afoot again for all the coin in thy father's exchequer. What a plague mean ye to colt me thus?

Prince. Thou liest; thou art not colted, thou art uncolted.

Fal. I prithee, good Prince Hal, help me to my horse, good king's son.

weald (wooded region) of Kent. 62. **marks,** coins of the value in that day of 13s. 6d. 68. **Saint Nicholas' clerks,** highwaymen. St. Nicholas was vulgarly supposed the patron of thieves. 77. **Troyans,** slang for "thieves." 81. **foot land-rakers,** footpads. 82. **long-staff sixpenny strikers,** robbers with long staves who would knock down their victims for sixpence. 83. **mustachio purple-hued malt-worms,** common drunkards with mustaches stained with drink. 84. **tranquillity,** those who lead easy lives. 85. **oneyers,** many conjectures; possibly, a coinage from *ones* with pun on *owner* (White). **hold in,** keep confidence. 91. **boots,** booty, with pun on "boots." 95. **liquored,** made waterproof by oiling, and made drunk. 96. **of fern-seed,** i.e., of becoming invisible, since fern seed was popularly supposed to render its possessor invisible. 104. **'homo' . . . men,** i.e., the Latin name for man applies to all types.

Scene ii. 2. **frets,** chafes, with pun on another meaning of the word applying to velvet with the nap awry. 13. **squier,** square, measure. 20. **medicines,** love potions. 25. **turn true man,** turn honest man; also, turn informer. 40. **colt,** cheat.

Prince. Out, ye rogue! shall I be your ostler?

Fal. Go hang thyself in thine own heir-apparent garters! If I be ta'en, I'll peach for this. An I have not ballads made on you all and sung to filthy tunes, let a cup of sack be my poison: when a jest is so forward, and afoot too! I hate it.

Enter GADSHILL [*and* BARDOLPH].

Gads. Stand.

Fal. So I do, against my will.

Poins. O, 'tis our setter: I know his voice. Bardolph, what news?

Bard. Case ye, case ye; on with your vizards: there 's money of the king's coming down the hill; 'tis going to the king's exchequer.

Fal. You lie, ye rogue; 'tis going to the king's tavern.

Gads. There 's enough to make us all.

Fal. To be hanged.

Prince. Sirs, you four shall front them in the narrow lane; Ned Poins and I will walk lower: if they 'scape from your encounter, then they light on us.

Peto. How many be there of them?

Gads. Some eight or ten.

Fal. 'Zounds, will they not rob us?

Prince. What, a coward, Sir John Paunch?

Fal. Indeed, I am not John of Gaunt, your grandfather; but yet no coward, Hal.

Prince. Well, we leave that to the proof.

Poins. Sirrah Jack, thy horse stands behind the hedge: when thou needest him, there thou shalt find him. Farewell, and stand fast.

Fal. Now cannot I strike him, if I should be hanged.

Prince. [*To Poins*] Ned, where are our disguises?

Poins. [*To Prince*] Here, hard by: stand close.

[*Exeunt Prince and Poins*.]

Fal. Now, my masters, happy man be his dole, say I: every man to his business.

Enter the Travellers.

First Trav. Come, neighbour: the boy shall lead our horses down the hill; we'll walk afoot awhile, and ease our legs.

Thieves. Stand!

Travellers. Jesus bless us!

Fal. Strike; down with them; cut the villains' throats: ah! whoreson caterpillars! bacon-fed knaves! they hate us youth: down with them; fleece them.

Travellers. O, we are undone, both we and ours for ever!

Fal. Hang ye, gorbellied knaves, are ye undone? No, ye fat chuffs; I would your store were here! On, bacons, on! What, ye knaves! young men must live. You are grandjurors, are ye? we'll jure ye, 'faith.

Here they rob them and bind them. Exeunt.

Enter the PRINCE *and* POINS.

Prince. The thieves have bound the true men. Now could thou and I rob the thieves and go merrily to London, it would be argument for a week, laughter for a month and a good jest for ever.

Poins. Stand close; I hear them coming.

Enter the Thieves again.

Fal. Come, my masters, let us share, and then to horse before day. An the Prince and Poins be not two arrant cowards, there 's no equity stirring: there 's no more valour in that Poins than in a wild-duck.

Prince. Your money!

Poins. Villains!

As they are sharing, the Prince and Poins set upon them; they all run away; and Falstaff, after a blow or two, runs away too, leaving the booty behind them.

Prince. Got with much ease. Now merrily to horse:
The thieves are all scattered and possess'd with fear
So strongly that they dare not meet each other;
Each takes his fellow for an officer.
Away, good Ned. Falstaff sweats to death,
And lards the lean earth as he walks along:
Were 't not for laughing, I should pity him.

Poins. How the fat rogue roar'd! *Exeunt.*

[SCENE III. *Warkworth castle.*]

Enter HOTSPUR, *solus, reading a letter.*

Hot. 'But, for mine own part, my lord, I could be well contented to be there, in respect of the love I bear your house.' He could be contented: why is he not, then? In respect of the love he bears our house: he shows in this, he loves his own barn better than he loves our house. Let me see some more. 'The purpose you undertake is dangerous;'—why, that 's certain: 'tis dangerous to take a cold, to sleep, to drink; but I tell you, my lord fool, out of this nettle, danger, we pluck this flower, safety. 'The purpose you undertake is dangerous; the friends you have named uncertain; the time itself unsorted; and your whole plot too light for the counterpoise of so great an opposition.' Say you so, say you so? I say unto you again, you are a shallow cowardly hind, and you lie. What a lack-brain is this! By the Lord, our plot is a good plot as ever was laid; our friends true and constant: a good plot, good friends, and full of expectation; an excellent plot, very good friends. What a frosty-spirited rogue is this! Why, my lord of York commends the plot and the general course of the action. 'Zounds, an I were now by this rascal, I could brain him with his lady's fan. Is there not my father, my uncle and myself? lord Edmund Mortimer, my lord of York and Owen Glendower? is there not besides the Douglas? have I not all their letters to meet me in arms by the ninth of the next month? and are they not some of them set forward already? What a pagan rascal is this! an infidel! Ha! you shall see now in very sincerity of fear and cold heart, will he to the king and lay open all our proceedings. O, I could divide myself and go to buffets, for moving such a dish of skim milk with so honourable an action! Hang him! let him tell the king: we are prepared. I will set forward to-night.

47. **peach,** inform on you. 53. **setter,** arranger of the robbery. 55. **Case ye,** put on your disguises. 70. **Gaunt,** with pun on *gaunt*, thin. 80. **happy man be his dole,** may happiness be his portion. 88. **caterpillars,** those who thrive off the commonwealth. 93. **gorbellied,** big-bellied. 94. **chuffs,** churls, rich but miserly. **store,** total wealth. 95. **bacons,** swine. 96. **grandjurors,** i.e., men of wealth, able to serve on juries. 100. **argument,** a subject for conversation. 107. **equity,** justice; variously interpreted. 116. **lards the lean earth,** an allusion to the practice on the part of butchers of inserting fat into lean meat. 118. **fat,** introduced by Neilson from a fragmentary QO; not in Globe.

SCENE III. 13. **unsorted,** unsuitable. 16. **hind,** menial. 34-35. **divide . . . buffets,** i.e., fight with myself. 50. **watch'd,** lain awake. 55. **palisadoes,** stakes set in the ground for defense. 56. **basilisks,** large cannon. **culverin,** long cannon. 58. **currents,** occurrences.

Enter his LADY.

How now, Kate! I must leave you within these two hours.
Lady. O, my good lord, why are you thus alone?
For what offence have I this fortnight been
A banish'd woman from my Harry's bed?
Tell me, sweet lord, what is 't that takes from thee
Thy stomach, pleasure and thy golden sleep?
Why dost thou bend thine eyes upon the earth,
And start so often when thou sit'st alone?
Why hast thou lost the fresh blood in thy cheeks;
And given my treasures and my rights of thee
To thick-ey'd musing and curs'd melancholy?
In thy faint slumbers I by thee have watch'd,
And heard thee murmur tales of iron wars;
Speak terms of manage to thy bounding steed;
Cry 'Courage! to the field!' And thou hast talk'd
Of sallies and retires, of trenches, tents,
Of palisadoes, frontiers, parapets,
Of basilisks, of cannon, culverin,
Of prisoners' ransom and of soldiers slain,
And all the currents of a heady fight.
Thy spirit within thee hath been so at war
And thus hath so bestirr'd thee in thy sleep,
That beads of sweat have stood upon thy brow,
Like bubbles in a late-disturbed stream;
And in thy face strange motions have appear'd,
Such as we see when men restrain their breath
On some great sudden hest. O, what portents are these?
Some heavy business hath my lord in hand,
And I must know it, else he loves me not.
Hot. What, ho!

[*Enter* Servant.]

Is Gilliams with the packet gone?
Serv. He is, my lord, an hour ago.
Hot. Hath Butler brought those horses from the sheriff?
Serv. One horse, my lord, he brought even now.
Hot. What horse? a roan, a crop-ear, is it not?
Serv. It is, my lord.
Hot. That roan shall be my throne.
Well, I will back him straight: O esperance!
Bid Butler lead him forth into the park. [*Exit Servant.*]
Lady. But hear you, my lord.
Hot. What say'st thou, my lady?
Lady. What is it carries you away?
Hot. Why, my horse, my love, my horse.
Lady. Out, you mad-headed ape!
A weasel hath not such a deal of spleen
As you are toss'd with. In faith,
I'll know your business, Harry, that I will.
I fear my brother Mortimer doth stir
About his title, and hath sent for you
To line his enterprize: but if you go,—
Hot. So far afoot, I shall be weary, love.
Lady. Come, come, you paraquito, answer me
Directly unto this question that I ask:
In faith, I'll break thy little finger, Harry,
An if thou wilt not tell me all things true.
Hot. Away,
Away, you trifler! Love! I love thee not,
I care not for thee, Kate: this is no world
To play with mammets and to tilt with lips:
We must have bloody noses and crack'd crowns,
And pass them current too. God 's me, my horse!
What say'st thou, Kate? what would'st thou have with me?
Lady. Do you not love me? do you not, indeed?
Well, do not then; for since you love me not,
I will not love myself. Do you not love me?
Nay, tell me if you speak in jest or no.
Hot. Come, wilt thou see me ride?
And when I am a-horseback, I will swear
I love thee infinitely. But hark you, Kate:
I must not have you henceforth question me
Whither I go, nor reason whereabout:
Whither I must, I must; and, to conclude,
This evening must I leave you, gentle Kate.
I know you wise, but yet no farther wise
Than Harry Percy's wife: constant you are,
But yet a woman: and for secrecy,
No lady closer; for I well believe
Thou wilt not utter what thou dost not know;
And so far will I trust thee, gentle Kate.
Lady. How! so far?
Hot. Not an inch further. But hark you, Kate:
Whither I go, thither shall you go too;
To-day will I set forth, to-morrow you.
Will this content you, Kate?
Lady. It must of force. *Exeunt.*

[SCENE IV. *The Boar's-Head Tavern, Eastcheap.*]

Enter PRINCE *and* POINS.

Prince. Ned, prithee, come out of that fat room, and lend me thy hand to laugh a little.

Poins. Where hast been, Hal?

Prince. With three or four loggerheads amongst three or four score hogsheads. I have sounded the very base-string of humility. Sirrah, I am sworn brother to a leash of drawers; and can call them all by their christen names, as Tom, Dick, and Francis. They take it already upon their salvation, that though I be but Prince of Wales, yet I am the king of courtesy; and tell me flatly I am no proud Jack, like Falstaff, but a Corinthian, a lad of mettle, a good boy, by the Lord, so they call me, and when I am king of England, I shall command all the good lads in Eastcheap. They call drinking deep, dyeing scarlet; and when you breathe in your watering, they cry 'hem!' and bid you play it off. To conclude, I am so good a proficient in one quarter of an hour, that I can drink with any tinker in his own language during my life. I tell thee, Ned, thou hast lost much honour, that thou wert not with me in this action. But, sweet Ned,—to sweeten which name of Ned, I give thee this pennyworth of sugar, clapped even now into

65. **hest,** command. 74. **esperance,** hope; the motto of the Percy family. 86. **line,** strengthen. 88. **paraquito,** little parrot; term of endearment. 95. **mammets,** dolls; or else breasts. 96. **crowns,** obvious pun on the coin called a "crown." 120. **of force,** of necessity.

SCENE IV. *Stage Direction:* **The Boar's-Head.** Never named as such in this play, but see *2 Henry IV*, II, ii, 159. 1. **fat,** stuffy; or, a vat-room. 4. **loggerheads,** blockheads. 7. **sworn brother,** allusion to the practice of becoming *fratres jurati.* **leash of drawers,** i.e., three waiters (like three greyhounds). 13. **Corinthian,** gay fellow, with suggestion of profligacy. 17. **breathe,** pause. 18. **watering,** drinking. 20-21. **tinker . . . language.** Tinkers' language was cant or jargon, and tinkers were proverbial drinkers.

my hand by an under-skinker, one that never spake other English in his life than 'Eight shillings and sixpence,' and 'You are welcome,' with this shrill addition, 'Anon, anon, sir! Score a pint of bastard in the Half-moon,' or so. But, Ned, to drive away the time till Falstaff come, I prithee, do thou stand in some by-room, while I question my puny drawer to what end he gave me the sugar; and do thou never leave calling 'Francis,' that his tale to me may be nothing but 'Anon.' Step aside, and I'll show thee a precedent.

Poins. Francis!

Prince. Thou art perfect.

Poins. Francis! [*Exit Poins.*]

Enter [FRANCIS, *a*] *Drawer.*

Fran. Anon, anon, sir. Look down into the Pomgarnet, Ralph.

Prince. Come hither, Francis.

Fran. My lord?

Prince. How long hast thou to serve, Francis?

Fran. Forsooth, five years, and as much as to—

Poins. [*Within*] Francis!

Fran. Anon, anon, sir.

Prince. Five year! by 'r lady, a long lease for the clinking of pewter. But, Francis, darest thou be so valiant as to play the coward with thy indenture and show it a fair pair of heels and run from it?

Fran. O Lord, sir, I'll be sworn upon all the books in England, I could find in my heart—

Poins. [*Within*] Francis!

Fran. Anon, sir.

Prince. How old art thou, Francis?

Fran. Let me see—about Michaelmas next I shall be—

Poins. [*Within*] Francis!

Fran. Anon, sir. Pray stay a little, my lord.

Prince. Nay, but hark you, Francis: for the sugar thou gavest me, 'twas a pennyworth, was 't not?

Fran. O Lord, I would it had been two!

Prince. I will give thee for it a thousand pound: ask me when thou wilt, and thou shalt have it.

Poins. [*Within*] Francis!

Fran. Anon, anon.

Prince. Anon, Francis? No, Francis; but to-morrow, Francis; or Francis, a Thursday; or indeed, Francis, when thou wilt. But, Francis!

Fran. My lord?

Prince. Wilt thou rob this leathern jerkin, crystal-button, not-pated, agate-ring, puke-stocking, caddis-garter, smooth-tongue, Spanish-pouch,—

Fran. O Lord, sir, who do you mean?

Prince. Why, then, your brown bastard is your only drink; for look you, Francis, your white canvas doublet will sully: in Barbary, sir, it cannot come to so much.

Fran. What, sir?

Poins. [*Within*] Francis!

Prince. Away, you rogue! dost thou not hear them call?

Here they both call him; the drawer stands amazed, not knowing which way to go.

Enter Vintner.

Vint. What, standest thou still, and hearest such a calling? Look to the guests within. [*Exit Francis.*] My lord, old Sir John, with half-a-dozen more, are at the door: shall I let them in?

Prince. Let them alone awhile, and then open the door. [*Exit Vintner.*] Poins!

Enter POINS.

Poins. Anon, anon, sir.

Prince. Sirrah, Falstaff and the rest of the thieves are at the door: shall we be merry?

Poins. As merry as crickets, my lad. But hark ye; what cunning match have you made with this jest of the drawer? come, what 's the issue?

Prince. I am now of all humours that have showed themselves humours since the old days of goodman Adam to the pupil age of this present twelve o'clock at midnight.

[*Enter* FRANCIS.]

What 's o'clock, Francis?

Fran. Anon, anon, sir. [*Exit.*]

Prince. That ever this fellow should have fewer words than a parrot, and yet the son of a woman! His industry is up-stairs and down-stairs; his eloquence the parcel of a reckoning. I am not yet of Percy's mind, the Hotspur of the north; he that kills me some six or seven dozen of Scots at a breakfast, washes his hands, and says to his wife 'Fie upon this quiet life! I want work.' 'O my sweet Harry,' says she, 'how many hast thou killed to-day?' 'Give my roan horse a drench,' says he; and answers 'Some fourteen,' an hour after; 'a trifle, a trifle.' I prithee, call in Falstaff: I'll play Percy, and that damned brawn shall play Dame Mortimer his wife. 'Rivo!' says the drunkard. Call in ribs, call in tallow.

Enter FALSTAFF [, GADSHILL, BARDOLPH, *and* PETO; FRANCIS *following with wine*].

Poins. Welcome, Jack: where hast thou been?

Fal. A plague of all cowards, I say, and a vengeance too! marry, and amen! Give me a cup of sack, boy. Ere I lead this life long, I'll sew nether stocks and mend them and foot them too. A plague of all cowards! Give me a cup of sack, rogue. Is there no virtue extant? *He drinketh.*

Prince. Didst thou never see Titan kiss a dish of butter? pitiful-hearted Titan, that melted at the sweet tale of the sun's! if thou didst, then behold that compound.

Fal. You rogue, here 's lime in this sack too: there is nothing but roguery to be found in villanous man: yet a coward is worse than a cup of sack with lime in

26. **under-skinker,** under-tapster. 31. **Score,** charge. **bastard,** sweet Spanish wine. **Half-moon,** name of a room in the inn. 42. **Pomgarnet,** pomegranate (another room in the inn). 78. **not-pated,** crop-haired. **puke-stocking,** woolen stocking. 79. **caddis-garter,** worsted garter. Since garters were worn in sight, they needed to be of better stuff than common worsted. The prince's epithets seem to apply to the vintner, the boy's master. 82-85. **Why . . . much.** The prince talks nonsense in order to bewilder Francis; but he also implies that Francis should endure his life as a drawer, not run away. 106. **goodman,** a sort of familiar title. **pupil age,** i.e., the day is young. 113. **parcel,** item. 123. **brawn,** fat boar. 124. **'Rivo!'** An interjection of doubtful meaning; certainly bacchanalian. 130. **nether stocks,** stockings. 134. **pitiful-hearted Titan.** Theobald suggested *butter* for *Titan*, which still seems the best way to explain this apparently contradictory passage. 137. **lime in this sack,** i.e., added to make it sparkle. 143. **shotten herring,** a herring that has cast its roe and is thin. 147. **weaver,** allusion to psalm-singing Protestants from Flanders, mainly weavers. 151. **dagger of lath.** The Vice in the interludes was

it. A villanous coward! Go thy ways, old Jack; die when thou wilt, if manhood, good manhood, be not forgot upon the face of the earth, then am I a shotten herring. There lives not three good men unhanged in England; and one of them is fat and grows old: God help the while! a bad world, I say. I would I were a weaver; I could sing psalms or any thing. A plague of all cowards, I say still.

Prince. How now, wool-sack! what mutter you?

Fal. A king's son! If I do not beat thee out of thy kingdom with a dagger of lath, and drive all thy subjects afore thee like a flock of wild-geese, I'll never wear hair on my face more. You Prince of Wales!

Prince. Why, you whoreson round man, what 's the matter?

Fal. Are not you a coward? answer me to that: and Poins there?

Poins. 'Zounds, ye fat paunch, and ye call me coward, by the Lord, I'll stab thee.

Fal. I call thee coward! I'll see thee damned ere I call thee coward: but I would give a thousand pound I could run as fast as thou canst. You are straight enough in the shoulders, you care not who sees your back: call you that backing of your friends? A plague upon such backing! give me them that will face me. Give me a cup of sack: I am a rogue, if I drunk to-day.

Prince. O villain! thy lips are scarce wiped since thou drunkest last.

Fal. All 's one for that. (*He drinketh.*) A plague of all cowards, still say I.

Prince. What 's the matter?

Fal. What 's the matter! there be four of us here have ta'en a thousand pound this day morning.

Prince. Where is it, Jack? where is it?

Fal. Where is it! taken from us it is: a hundred upon poor four of us.

Prince. What, a hundred, man?

Fal. I am a rogue, if I were not at half-sword with a dozen of them two hours together. I have 'scaped by miracle. I am eight times thrust through the doublet, four through the hose; my buckler cut through and through; my sword hacked like a hand-saw—ecce signum! I never dealt better since I was a man: all would not do. A plague of all cowards! Let them speak: if they speak more or less than truth, they are villains and the sons of darkness.

Prince. Speak, sirs; how was it?

Gads. We four set upon some dozen—

Fal. Sixteen at least, my lord.

Gads. And bound them.

Peto. No, no, they were not bound.

Fal. You rogue, they were bound, every man of them; or I am a Jew else, an Ebrew Jew.

Gads. As we were sharing, some six or seven fresh men set upon us—

Fal. And unbound the rest, and then come in the other.

Prince. What, fought you with them all?

Fal. All! I know not what you call all; but if I fought not with fifty of them, I am a bunch of radish: if there were not two or three and fifty upon poor old Jack, then am I no two-legged creature.

Prince. Pray God you have not murdered some of them.

Fal. Nay, that 's past praying for: I have peppered two of them; two I am sure I have paid, two rogues in buckram suits. I tell thee what, Hal, if I tell thee a lie, spit in my face, call me horse. Thou knowest my old ward; here I lay, and thus I bore my point. Four rogues in buckram let drive at me—

Prince. What, four? thou saidst but two even now.

Fal. Four, Hal; I told thee four.

Poins. Ay, ay, he said four.

Fal. These four came all a-front, and mainly thrust at me. I made me no more ado but took all their seven points in my target, thus.

Prince. Seven? why, there were but four even now.

Fal. In buckram?

Poins. Ay, four, in buckram suits.

Fal. Seven, by these hilts, or I am a villain else.

Prince. [*Aside to Poins*] Prithee, let him alone; we shall have more anon.

Fal. Dost thou hear me, Hal?

Prince. Ay, and mark thee too, Jack.

Fal. Do so, for it is worth the listening to. These nine in buckram that I told thee of—

Prince. So, two more already.

Fal. Their points being broken,—

Poins. Down fell their hose.

Fal. Began to give me ground: but I followed me close, came in foot and hand; and with a thought seven of the eleven I paid.

Prince. O monstrous! eleven buckram men grown out of two!

Fal. But, as the devil would have it, three misbegotten knaves in Kendal green came at my back and let drive at me; for it was so dark, Hal, that thou couldst not see thy hand.

Prince. These lies are like their father that begets them; gross as a mountain, open, palpable. Why, thou clay-brained guts, thou knotty-pated fool, thou whoreson, obscene, greasy tallow-catch,—

Fal. What, art thou mad? art thou mad? is not the truth the truth?

Prince. Why, how couldst thou know these men in Kendal green, when it was so dark thou couldst not see thy hand? come, tell us your reason: what sayest thou to this?

Poins. Come, your reason, Jack, your reason.

Fal. What, upon compulsion? 'Zounds, an I were at the strappado, or all the racks in the world, I would not tell you on compulsion. Give you a reason on compulsion! if reasons were as plentiful as blackberries, I would give no man a reason upon compulsion, I.

Prince. I'll be no longer guilty of this sin; this san-

so armed, as no doubt other clowns were. 182. **half-sword,** fighting at close quarters. 185. **doublet,** Elizabethan upper garment like a jacket. **hose,** close-fitting breeches. 187. **ecce signum,** behold the proof; familiar words from the Mass. 213. **buckram,** coarse linen cloth stiffened. 215. **ward,** guard in fencing. 223. **mainly,** powerfully. 224. **target,** shield; see glossary. 238. **points.** Falstaff uses *points* to mean "swords"; Poins' reply introduces a pun on the same word meaning the "laces" by which the hose were attached to the doublet and so supported. 240. **followed me,** a sort of reflexive or middle voice. 241-242. **with a thought,** quick as a thought. 246. **Kendal green,** green cloth worn by foresters. 251-252. **knotty-pated,** thickheaded. 253. **tallow-catch,** explained as "tallow-tub," and as "tallow-keech," a roll of fat delivered by the butcher to the tallow chandler. It has been pointed out that such breathless strings of epithets of abuse are characteristic of Latin comedy. 262. **strappado,** a kind of torture. 264. **reasons . . . blackberries.** Falstaff not only avoids the issue, but also turns it into a jest by punning on the word "raisins," which was pronounced nearly like *reasons*.

guine coward, this bed-presser, this horseback-breaker, this huge hill of flesh,—

Fal. 'Sblood, you starveling, you elf-skin, you dried neat's tongue, you bull's pizzle, you stock-fish! O for breath to utter what is like thee! you tailor's-yard, you sheath, you bow-case, you vile standing-tuck,—

Prince. Well, breathe awhile, and then to it again: and when thou hast tired thyself in base comparisons, hear me speak but this.

Poins. Mark, Jack.

Prince. We two saw you four set on four and bound them, and were masters of their wealth. Mark now, how a plain tale shall put you down. Then did we two set on you four; and, with a word, out-faced you from your prize, and have it; yea, and can show it you here in the house: and, Falstaff, you carried your guts away as nimbly, with as quick dexterity, and roared for mercy and still run and roared, as ever I heard bull-calf. What a slave art thou, to hack thy sword as thou hast done, and then say it was in fight! What trick, what device, what starting-hole, canst thou now find out to hide thee from this open and apparent shame?

Poins. Come, let 's hear, Jack; what trick hast thou now?

Fal. By the Lord, I knew ye as well as he that made ye. Why, hear you, my masters: was it for me to kill the heir-apparent? should I turn upon the true prince? why, thou knowest I am as valiant as Hercules: but beware instinct; the lion will not touch the true prince. Instinct is a great matter; I was now a coward on instinct. I shall think the better of myself and thee during my life; I for a valiant lion, and thou for a true prince. But, by the Lord, lads, I am glad you have the money. Hostess, clap to the doors: watch to-night, pray to-morrow. Gallants, lads, boys, hearts of gold, all the titles of good fellowship come to you! What, shall we be merry? shall we have a play extempore?

Prince. Content; and the argument shall be thy running away.

Fal. Ah, no more of that, Hal, an thou lovest me!

Enter Hostess.

Host. O Jesu, my lord the prince!

Prince. How now, my lady the hostess! what sayest thou to me?

Host. Marry, my lord, there is a nobleman of the court at door would speak with you: he says he comes from your father.

Prince. Give him as much as will make him a royal man, and send him back again to my mother.

Fal. What manner of man is he?

Host. An old man.

Fal. What doth gravity out of his bed at midnight? Shall I give him his answer?

Prince. Prithee, do, Jack.

Fal. 'Faith, and I'll send him packing. *Exit.*

Prince. Now, sirs: by 'r lady, you fought fair; so did you, Peto; so did you, Bardolph: you are lions too, you ran away upon instinct, you will not touch the true prince; no, fie!

Bard. 'Faith, I ran when I saw others run.

Prince. 'Faith, tell me now in earnest, how came Falstaff's sword so hacked?

Peto. Why, he hacked it with his dagger, and said he would swear truth out of England but he would make you believe it was done in fight, and persuaded us to do the like.

Bard. Yea, and to tickle our noses with spear-grass to make them bleed, and then to beslubber our garments with it and swear it was the blood of true men. I did that I did not this seven year before, I blushed to hear his monstrous devices.

Prince. O villain, thou stolest a cup of sack eighteen years ago, and wert taken with the manner, and ever since thou hast blushed extempore. Thou hadst fire and sword on thy side, and yet thou rannest away: what instinct hadst thou for it?

Bard. My lord, do you see these meteors? do you behold these exhalations?

Prince. I do.

Bard. What think you they portend?

Prince. Hot livers and cold purses.

Bard. Choler, my lord, if rightly taken.

Prince. No, if rightly taken, halter.

Enter FALSTAFF.

Here comes lean Jack, here comes bare-bone. How now, my sweet creature of bombast! How long is 't ago, Jack, since thou sawest thine own knee?

Fal. My own knee! when I was about thy years, Hal, I was not an eagle's talent in the waist; I could have crept into any alderman's thumb-ring: a plague of sighing and grief! it blows a man up like a bladder. There 's villanous news abroad: here was Sir John Bracy from your father; you must to the court in the morning. That same mad fellow of the north, Percy, and he of Wales, that gave Amamon the bastinado and made Lucifer cuckold and swore the devil his true liegeman upon the cross of a Welsh hook—what a plague call you him?

Poins. Owen Glendower.

Fal. Owen, Owen, the same; and his son-in-law Mortimer, and old Northumberland, and that sprightly Scot of Scots, Douglas, that runs a-horseback up a hill perpendicular,—

Prince. He that rides at high speed and with his pistol kills a sparrow flying.

Fal. You have hit it.

Prince. So did he never the sparrow.

Fal. Well, that rascal hath good mettle in him; he will not run.

Prince. Why, what a rascal art thou then, to praise him so for running!

Fal. A-horseback, ye cuckoo; but afoot he will not budge a foot.

Prince. Yes, Jack, upon instinct.

Fal. I grant ye, upon instinct. Well, he is there too, and one Mordake, and a thousand blue-caps more:

271. **neat's tongue,** ox tongue. 272. **stock-fish,** dried cod. 274. **standing-tuck,** rapier standing on end. 283. **out-faced,** frightened. 290. **starting-hole,** point of shelter (like a rabbit's hole). 306. **watch,** stay awake (see Matthew 26:41). 310. **argument,** subject. 321. **royal.** The man is a noble (6s. 8d); give him 3s. 4d. and he will be a *royal* (10s.) *man*. 348. **fire . . . side.** Bardolph is a drunkard, and his flaming face is continually harped upon. 351. **meteors,** i.e., the red blotches on Bardolph's face. 355. **Hot . . . purses,** livers made hot by drink, and purses made empty by spending. 356. **taken,** understood. 357. **halter.** The pun is on "collar" pronounced like *choler*, i.e., the hangman's noose. 359. **bombast,** cotton padding. 363. **talent,** talon. 370. **Amamon,** name of a demon. **bastinado,** beating with a cudgel. 372-373. **Welsh hook,** a weapon having no cross, such as a sword-hilt. 380. **pistol.** There were, of course, no pistols in the time of King Henry's reign. 392. **blue-caps,** Scottish soldiers. 414. **particulars,** details of a private nature; see glossary. 418. **joined-stool,**

Worcester is stolen away to-night; thy father's beard is turned white with the news: you may buy land now as cheap as stinking mackerel.

Prince. Why, then, it is like, if there come a hot June and this civil buffeting hold, we shall buy maidenheads as they buy hob-nails, by the hundreds.

Fal. By the mass, lad, thou sayest true; it is like we shall have good trading that way. But tell me, Hal, art not thou horrible afeard? thou being heir-apparent, could the world pick thee out three such enemies again as that fiend Douglas, that spirit Percy, and that devil Glendower? Art thou not horribly afraid? doth not thy blood thrill at it?

Prince. Not a whit, i' faith; I lack some of thy instinct.

Fal. Well, thou wilt be horribly chid to-morrow when thou comest to thy father: if thou love me, practise an answer.

Prince. Do thou stand for my father, and examine me upon the particulars of my life.

Fal. Shall I? content: this chair shall be my state, this dagger my sceptre, and this cushion my crown.

Prince. Thy state is taken for a joined-stool, thy golden sceptre for a leaden dagger, and thy precious rich crown for a pitiful bald crown!

Fal. Well, an the fire of grace be not quite out of thee, now shalt thou be moved. Give me a cup of sack to make my eyes look red, that it may be thought I have wept; for I must speak in passion, and I will do it in King Cambyses' vein.

Prince. Well, here is my leg.

Fal. And here is my speech. Stand aside, nobility.

Host. O Jesu, this is excellent sport, i' faith!

Fal. Weep not, sweet queen; for trickling tears are vain.

Host. O, the father, how he holds his countenance!

Fal. For God's sake, lords, convey my tristful queen;
For tears do stop the flood-gates of her eyes.

Host. O Jesu, he doth it as like one of these harlotry players as ever I see!

Fal. Peace, good pint-pot; peace, good tickle-brain. Harry, I do not only marvel where thou spendest thy time, but also how thou art accompanied: for though the camomile, the more it is trodden on the faster it grows, yet youth, the more it is wasted the sooner it wears. That thou art my son, I have partly thy mother's word, partly my own opinion, but chiefly a villanous trick of thine eye and a foolish hanging of thy nether lip, that doth warrant me. If then thou be son to me, here lies the point; why, being son to me, art thou so pointed at? Shall the blessed sun of heaven prove a micher and eat blackberries? a question not to be asked. Shall the son of England prove a thief and take purses? a question to be asked. There is a thing, Harry, which thou hast often heard of and it is known to many in our land by the name of pitch: this pitch, as ancient writers do report, doth defile; so doth the company thou keepest: for, Harry, now I do not speak to thee in drink but in tears, not in pleasure but in passion, not in words only, but in woes also: and yet there is a virtuous man whom I have often noted in thy company, but I know not his name.

Prince. What manner of man, an it like your majesty?

Fal. A goodly portly man, i' faith, and a corpulent; of a cheerful look, a pleasing eye and a most noble carriage; and, as I think, his age some fifty, or, by 'r lady, inclining to three score; and now I remember me, his name is Falstaff: if that man should be lewdly given, he deceiveth me; for, Harry, I see virtue in his looks. If then the tree may be known by the fruit, as the fruit by the tree, then, peremptorily I speak it, there is virtue in that Falstaff: him keep with, the rest banish. And tell me now, thou naughty varlet, tell me, where hast thou been this month?

Prince. Dost thou speak like a king? Do thou stand for me, and I'll play my father.

Fal. Depose me? if thou dost it half so gravely, so majestically, both in word and matter, hang me up by the heels for a rabbit-sucker or a poulter's hare.

Prince. Well, here I am set.

Fal. And here I stand: judge, my masters.

Prince. Now, Harry, whence come you?

Fal. My noble lord, from Eastcheap.

Prince. The complaints I hear of thee are grievous.

Fal. 'Sblood, my lord, they are false: nay, I'll tickle ye for a young prince, i' faith.

Prince. Swearest thou, ungracious boy? henceforth ne'er look on me. Thou art violently carried away from grace: there is a devil haunts thee in the likeness of an old fat man; a tun of man is thy companion. Why dost thou converse with that trunk of humours, that bolting-hutch of beastliness, that swollen parcel of dropsies, that huge bombard of sack, that stuffed cloak-bag of guts, that roasted Manningtree ox with the pudding in his belly, that reverend vice, that grey iniquity, that father ruffian, that vanity in years? Wherein is he good, but to taste sack and drink it? wherein neat and cleanly, but to carve a capon and eat it? wherein cunning, but in craft? wherein crafty, but in villany? wherein villanous, but in all things? wherein worthy, but in nothing?

Fal. I would your grace would take me with you: whom means your grace?

Prince. That villanous abominable misleader of youth, Falstaff, that old white-bearded Satan.

Fal. My lord, the man I know.

Prince. I know thou dost.

Fal. But to say I know more harm in him than in myself, were to say more than I know. That he is old, the more the pity, his white hairs do witness it; but that he is, saving your reverence, a whoremaster, that I utterly deny. If sack and sugar be a fault, God help the wicked! if to be old and merry be a sin, then many an old host that I know is damned: if to be fat be to be hated, then Pharaoh's lean kine are to be loved. No, my good lord; banish Peto, banish Bardolph, banish Poins: but for sweet Jack Falstaff, kind Jack Falstaff, true Jack Falstaff, valiant Jack Falstaff,

a stool made by a joiner, hence, of rough workmanship. 426. **King Cambyses' vein,** allusion to Thomas Preston's bombastic tragedy *Cambises*, still preserved. 427. **leg,** bow. 434. **tristful,** sorrowing. 437. **harlotry,** vagabond. 439. **tickle-brain,** strong drink. 441. **camomile.** This parodies an actual passage in Lyly's *Euphues* and exaggerates the balance and alliteration of the style. 450. **micher,** truant. 456-457. **pitch . . . defile,** an allusion to the familiar proverb from Ecclesiasticus 13:1, about the defilement of touching pitch. This proverb appears also in Lyly's *Euphues*. 480. **rabbit-sucker,** sucking rabbit. 481. **poulter's,** poulterer's. 495. **bolting-hutch,** large flour bin. 497. **bombard,** leathern drinking vessel. 498. **Manningtree ox.** Manningtree, a town in Essex, had noted fairs where, no doubt, oxen were roasted whole. 499-500. **vice . . . iniquity.** These terms suggest another feature of Manningtree, which was the acting of morality plays; the word *vanity* also suggests a character in such plays. 521. **Pharaoh's lean kine.** See Genesis 41:3-4, 18-21.

and therefore more valiant, being, as he is, old Jack Falstaff, banish not him thy Harry's company, banish not him thy Harry's company: banish plump Jack, and banish all the world.

Prince. I do, I will. [*A knocking heard.*]
[*Exeunt Hostess, Francis, and Bardolph.*]

Enter BARDOLPH, *running.*

Bard. O, my lord, my lord! the sheriff with a most monstrous watch is at the door.

Fal. Out, ye rogue! Play out the play: I have much to say in the behalf of that Falstaff.

Enter the Hostess.

Host. O Jesu, my lord, my lord!

Prince. Heigh, heigh! the devil rides upon a fiddlestick: what 's the matter?

Host. The sheriff and all the watch are at the door: they are come to search the house. Shall I let them in?

Fal. Dost thou hear, Hal? never call a true piece of gold a counterfeit: thou art essentially mad, without seeming so.

Prince. And thou a natural coward, without instinct.

Fal. I deny your major: if you will deny the sheriff, so; if not, let him enter: if I become not a cart as well as another man, a plague on my bringing up! I hope I shall as soon be strangled with a halter as another.

Prince. Go, hide thee behind the arras: the rest walk up above. Now, my masters, for a true face and good conscience.

Fal. Both which I have had: but their date is out, and therefore I'll hide me.

Prince. Call in the sheriff.
[*Exeunt all except the Prince and Peto.*]

Enter Sheriff *and the* Carrier.

Now, master sheriff, what is your will with me?

Sher. First, pardon me, my lord. A hue and cry
Hath followed certain men unto this house.

Prince. What men?

Sher. One of them is well known, my gracious lord,
A gross fat man.

Car. As fat as butter.

Prince. The man, I do assure you, is not here;
For I myself at this time have employ'd him.
And, sheriff, I will engage my word to thee
That I will, by to-morrow dinner-time,
Send him to answer thee, or any man,
For any thing he shall be charg'd withal:
And so let me entreat you leave the house.

Sher. I will, my lord. There are two gentlemen
Have in this robbery lost three hundred marks.

Prince. It may be so: if he have robb'd these men,
He shall be answerable; and so farewell.

Sher. Good night, my noble lord.

Prince. I think it is good morrow, is it not?

Sher. Indeed, my lord, I think it be two o'clock.
Exit [*with Carrier*].

Prince. This oily rascal is known as well as Paul's. Go, call him forth.

Peto. Falstaff!—Fast asleep behind the arras, and snorting like a horse.

Prince. Hark, how hard he fetches breath. Search his pockets. (*He searcheth his pockets, and findeth certain papers.*) What hast thou found?

Peto. Nothing but papers, my lord.

Prince. Let 's see what they be: read them.

Peto. [*Reads*]

Item, A capon, ...	2s. 2d.
Item, Sauce, ...	4d.
Item, Sack, two gallons, ...	5s. 8d.
Item, Anchovies and sack after supper, ...	2s. 6d.
Item, Bread, ...	ob.

Prince. O monstrous! but one half-pennyworth of bread to this intolerable deal of sack! What there is else, keep close; we'll read it at more advantage: there let him sleep till day. I'll to the court in the morning. We must all to the wars, and thy place shall be honourable. I'll procure this fat rogue a charge of foot; and I know his death will be a march of twelve-score. The money shall be paid back again with advantage. Be with me betimes in the morning; and so, good morrow, Peto.

Peto. Good morrow, good my lord. *Exeunt.*

[ACT III.

SCENE I. *Bangor. The Archdeacon's house.*]

Enter HOTSPUR, WORCESTER, LORD MORTIMER, *and* OWEN GLENDOWER.

Mort. These promises are fair, the parties sure,
And our induction full of prosperous hope.

Hot. Lord Mortimer, and cousin Glendower,
Will you sit down?
And uncle Worcester: a plague upon it!
I have forgot the map.

Glend. No, here it is.
Sit, cousin Percy; sit, good cousin Hotspur,
For by that name as oft as Lancaster
Doth speak of you, his cheek looks pale and with
A rising sigh he wisheth you in heaven.

Hot. And you in hell, as oft as he hears Owen Glendower spoke of.

Glend. I cannot blame him: at my nativity
The front of heaven was full of fiery shapes,
Of burning cressets; and at my birth
The frame and huge foundation of the earth
Shak'd like a coward.

Hot. Why, so it would have done at the same season, if your mother's cat had but kittened, though yourself had never been born.

Glend. I say the earth did shake when I was born.

Hot. And I say the earth was not of my mind,
If you suppose as fearing you it shook.

Glend. The heavens were all on fire, the earth did tremble.

Hot. O, then the earth shook to see the heavens on fire,

530. **watch,** a posse of constables. 534. **the devil . . . fiddlestick,** proverbial; suggesting, here's much ado about nothing. 539-541. **Dost . . . seeming so.** In this difficult passage, Falstaff seems to suggest that he is true gold, not counterfeit, and so should not be betrayed to the watch by the Prince who (he hopes) is not merely playacting at the tavern but is truly one of its madcap members. 544. **major,** major proposition. Falstaff denies that he is a natural coward; he does not deny that he is affected by instinct. 546. **cart,** hangman's cart, tumbril. 556. **hue and cry,** pursuit of criminals by horn and halloo; technical term. 575. **Paul's,** St. Paul's Cathedral, a familiar landmark. 577. **arras,** wall-hanging. 590. **ob.,** abbreviation for *obolus* (Greek coin) meaning "halfpenny." 592. **deal,** lot. 597. **charge of foot,** company of infantry. 598. **twelve-score,** i.e., yards; a distance familiar from its use in archery. 599-600. **advantage,** interest. **betimes,** early.

ACT III. SCENE I. 2. **induction,** beginning. 8. **Lancaster,** King

And not in fear of your nativity.
Diseased nature oftentimes breaks forth
In strange eruptions; oft the teeming earth
Is with a kind of colic pinch'd and vex'd
By the imprisoning of unruly wind
Within her womb; which, for enlargement striving,
Shakes the old beldam earth and topples down
Steeples and moss-grown towers. At your birth
Our grandam earth, having this distemp'rature,
In passion shook.
Glend. Cousin, of many men
I do not bear these crossings. Give me leave
To tell you once again that at my birth
The front of heaven was full of fiery shapes,
The goats ran from the mountains, and the herds
Were strangely clamorous to the frighted fields.
These signs have mark'd me extraordinary;
And all the courses of my life do show
I am not in the roll of common men.
Where is he living, clipp'd in with the sea
That chides the banks of England, Scotland, Wales,
Which calls me pupil, or hath read to me?
And bring him out that is but woman's son
Can trace me in the tedious ways of art
And hold me pace in deep experiments.
Hot. I think there 's no man speaks better Welsh.
I'll to dinner.
Mort. Peace, cousin Percy; you will make him mad.
Glend. I can call spirits from the vasty deep.
Hot. Why, so can I, or so can any man;
But will they come when you do call for them?
Glend. Why, I can teach you, cousin, to command
The devil.
Hot. And I can teach thee, coz, to shame the devil
By telling truth: tell truth and shame the devil.
If thou have power to raise him, bring him hither,
And I'll be sworn I have power to shame him hence.
O, while you live, tell truth and shame the devil!
Mort. Come, come, no more of this unprofitable chat.
Glend. Three times hath Henry Bolingbroke made head
Against my power; thrice from the banks of Wye
And sandy-bottom'd Severn have I sent him
Bootless home and weather-beaten back.
Hot. Home without boots, and in foul weather too!
How 'scapes he agues, in the devil's name?
Glend. Come, here is the map: shall we divide our right
According to our threefold order ta'en?
Mort. The archdeacon hath divided it
Into three limits very equally:
England, from Trent and Severn hitherto,
By south and east is to my part assign'd:
All westward, Wales beyond the Severn shore,
And all the fertile land within that bound,
To Owen Glendower: and, dear coz, to you
The remnant northward, lying off from Trent.
And our indentures tripartite are drawn;
Which being sealed interchangeably,
A business that this night may execute,
To-morrow, cousin Percy, you and I
And my good Lord of Worcester will set forth
To meet your father and the Scottish power,
As is appointed us, at Shrewsbury.
My father Glendower is not ready yet,
Nor shall we need his help these fourteen days.
Within that space you may have drawn together
Your tenants, friends and neighbouring gentlemen.
Glend. A shorter time shall send me to you, lords:
And in my conduct shall your ladies come;
From whom you now must steal and take no leave,
For there will be a world of water shed
Upon the parting of your wives and you.
Hot. Methinks my moiety, north from Burton here,
In quantity equals not one of yours:
See how this river comes me cranking in,
And cuts me from the best of all my land
A huge half-moon, a monstrous cantle out.
I'll have the current in this place damm'd up;
And here the smug and silver Trent shall run
In a new channel, fair and evenly;
It shall not wind with such a deep indent,
To rob me of so rich a bottom here.
Glend. Not wind? it shall, it must; you see it doth.
Mort. Yea, but
Mark how he bears his course, and runs me up
With like advantage on the other side;
Gelding the opposed continent as much
As on the other side it takes from you.
Wor. Yea, but a little charge will trench him here
And on this north side win this cape of land;
And then he runs straight and even.
Hot. I'll have it so: a little charge will do it.
Glend. I'll not have it alt'red.
Hot. Will not you?
Glend. No, nor you shall not.
Hot. Who shall say me nay?
Glend. Why, that will I.
Hot. Let me not understand you, then; speak it in Welsh.
Glend. I can speak English, lord, as well as you;
For I was train'd up in the English court;
Where, being but young, I framed to the harp
Many an English ditty lovely well
And gave the tongue a helpful ornament,
A virtue that was never seen in you.
Hot. Marry,
And I am glad of it with all my heart:
I had rather be a kitten and cry mew
Than one of these same metre ballad-mongers;
I had rather hear a brazen canstick turn'd,
Or a dry wheel grate on the axle-tree;
And that would set my teeth nothing on edge,
Nothing so much as mincing poetry:
'Tis like the forc'd gait of a shuffling nag.
Glend. Come, you shall have Trent turn'd.
Hot. I do not care: I'll give thrice so much land
To any well-deserving friend;
But in the way of bargain, mark ye me,

Henry IV, formerly Duke of Lancaster. 13. **at my nativity.** Holinshed recounts the happening of portents at Glendower's birth; Shakespeare has developed his vanity and strange rapt quality. 14. **front,** forehead. 15. **cressets,** beacons. 27-35. **Diseased . . . shook.** These lines give the currently accepted scientific explanation of earthquakes. 31. **enlargement,** release. 32. **beldam,** grandmother. 46. **read to,** instructed. 48. **trace,** follow. **tedious,** laborious. **art,** i.e., magic. 67. **Bootless,** without advantage. 72. **archdeacon,** an official of an Episcopal diocese.

The divisions of the Kingdom are really very ancient; they appear in Geoffrey of Monmouth's *Chronicle*, and are those into which King Lear divided his kingdom. 87. **father,** father-in-law. 98. **comes me cranking in,** comes bending in on my share; *me* is an ethical dative. 100. **cantle,** piece. 115. **charge,** expenditure. 131. **canstick,** candlestick.

I'll cavil on the ninth part of a hair.
Are the indentures drawn? shall we be gone?

Glend. The moon shines fair; you may away by night:
I'll haste the writer and withal
Break with your wives of your departure hence:
I am afraid my daughter will run mad,
So much she doteth on her Mortimer. *Exit.*

Mort. Fie, cousin Percy! how you cross my father!

Hot. I cannot choose: sometime he angers me
With telling me of the moldwarp and the ant,
Of the dreamer Merlin and his prophecies,
And of a dragon and a finless fish,
A clip-wing'd griffin and a moulten raven,
A couching lion and a ramping cat,
And such a deal of skimble-skamble stuff
As puts me from my faith. I tell you what;
He held me last night at least nine hours
In reckoning up the several devils' names
That were his lackeys: I cried 'hum,' and 'well, go to,'
But mark'd him not a word. O, he is as tedious
As a tired horse, a railing wife;
Worse than a smoky house: I had rather live
With cheese and garlic in a windmill, far,
Than feed on cates and have him talk to me
In any summer-house in Christendom.

Mort. In faith, he is a worthy gentleman,
Exceedingly well read, and profited
In strange concealments, valiant as a lion
And wondrous affable and as bountiful
As mines of India. Shall I tell you, cousin?
He holds your temper in a high respect
And curbs himself even of his natural scope
When you come 'cross his humour; faith, he does:
I warrant you, that man is not alive
Might so have tempted him as you have done,
Without the taste of danger and reproof:
But do not use it oft, let me entreat you.

Wor. In faith, my lord, you are too wilful-blame;
And since your coming hither have done enough
To put him quite besides his patience.
You must needs learn, lord, to amend this fault:
Though sometimes it show greatness, courage, blood,—
And that 's the dearest grace it renders you,—
Yet oftentimes it doth present harsh rage,
Defect of manners, want of government,
Pride, haughtiness, opinion and disdain:
The least of which haunting a nobleman
Loseth men's hearts and leaves behind a stain
Upon the beauty of all parts besides,
Beguiling them of commendation.

Hot. Well, I am school'd: good manners be your speed!
Here come our wives, and let us take our leave.

Enter GLENDOWER *with the ladies.*

Mort. This is the deadly spite that angers me;
My wife can speak no English, I no Welsh.

Glend. My daughter weeps: she will not part with you;
She'll be a soldier too, she'll to the wars.

Mort. Good father, tell her that she and my aunt Percy
Shall follow in your conduct speedily.

Glendower speaks to her in Welsh, and she answers him in the same.

Glend. She is desperate here; a peevish self-will'd harlotry, one that no persuasion can do good upon.

The lady speaks in Welsh.

Mort. I understand thy looks: that pretty Welsh
Which thou pourest down from these swelling heavens
I am too perfect in; and, but for shame,
In such a parley should I answer thee.

The lady again in Welsh.

I understand thy kisses and thou mine,
And that 's a feeling disputation:
But I will never be a truant, love,
Till I have learn'd thy language; for thy tongue
Makes Welsh as sweet as ditties highly penn'd,
Sung by a fair queen in a summer's bower,
With ravishing division, to her lute.

Glend. Nay, if you melt, then will she run mad.

The lady speaks again in Welsh.

Mort. O, I am ignorance itself in this!

Glend. She bids you on the wanton rushes lay you down
And rest your gentle head upon her lap,
And she will sing the song that pleaseth you
And on your eyelids crown the god of sleep,
Charming your blood with pleasing heaviness,
Making such difference 'twixt wake and sleep
As is the difference betwixt day and night
The hour before the heavenly-harness'd team
Begins his golden progress in the east.

Mort. With all my heart I'll sit and hear her sing:
By that time will our book, I think, be drawn.

Glend. Do so;
And those musicians that shall play to you
Hang in the air a thousand leagues from hence,
And straight they shall be here: sit, and attend.

Hot. Come, Kate, thou art perfect in lying down: come, quick, quick, that I may lay my head in thy lap.

Lady P. Go, ye giddy goose. *The music plays.*

Hot. Now I perceive the devil understands Welsh;
And 'tis no marvel he is so humorous.
By 'r lady, he is a good musician.

Lady P. Then should you be nothing but musical, for you are altogether governed by humours. Lie still, ye thief, and hear the lady sing in Welsh.

Hot. I had rather hear Lady, my brach, howl in Irish.

Lady P. Wouldst thou have thy head broken?

Hot. No.

Lady P. Then be still.

Hot. Neither; 'tis a woman's fault.

Lady P. Now God help thee!

Hot. To the Welsh lady's bed.

Lady P. What 's that?

143. **writer,** the scrivener who would be drawing the indentures. 144. **Break with,** communicate with. 149. **moldwarp,** mole. Holinshed tells us that the division was arranged because of a prophecy which represented King Henry as the mole and the others as the dragon, the lion, and the wolf, who should divide the land among them. 150. **Merlin,** the traditional bard and prophet of the Welsh. 152. **griffin,** a fabulous beast. 153. **ramping,** rampant, advancing on its hind legs. (Hotspur is ridiculing the heraldic emblems which Glendower holds so dear.) 154. **skimble-skamble,** confused and foolish. 163. **cates,** delicacies. 177. **wilful-blame,** to blame for excessive willfulness. 179. **besides,** out of. 182. **dearest grace,** best credit. 183. **present,** represent. 190. **be your speed,** give you good fortune. 199. **harlotry,** silly wench. 202. **heavens,** i.e., eyes. 203. **perfect,** proficient. 204. **such a parley,** i.e., the same language. 206. **disputation,** conversation. 211. **division,** variation (in music). 214. **wanton,** soft, luxurious. 224. **book,** document, indentures. 234. **humorous,** capricious. 240.

Hot. Peace! she sings. *Here the lady sings a Welsh song.*

Hot. Come, Kate, I'll have your song too.

Lady P. Not mine, in good sooth.

Hot. Not yours, in good sooth! Heart! you swear like a comfit-maker's wife. 'Not you, in good sooth,' and 'as true as I live,' and 'as God shall mend me,' and 'as sure as day,'
And givest such sarcenet surety for thy oaths,
As if thou never walk'st further than Finsbury.
Swear me, Kate, like a lady as thou art,
A good mouth-filling oath, and leave 'in sooth,'
And such protest of pepper-gingerbread,
To velvet-guards and Sunday-citizens.
Come, sing.

Lady P. I will not sing.

Hot. 'Tis the next way to turn tailor, or be red-breast teacher. An the indentures be drawn, I'll away within these two hours; and so, come in when ye will. *Exit.*

Glend. Come, come, Lord Mortimer; you are as slow
As hot Lord Percy is on fire to go.
By this our book is drawn; we'll but seal,
And then to horse immediately.

Mort. With all my heart. *Exeunt.*

[SCENE II. *London. The palace.*]

Enter the KING, PRINCE OF WALES, *and others.*

King. Lords, give us leave; the Prince of Wales and I
Must have some private conference: but be near at hand,
For we shall presently have need of you. *Exeunt Lords.*
I know not whether God will have it so,
For some displeasing service I have done,
That, in his secret doom, out of my blood
He'll breed revengement and a scourge for me;
But thou dost in thy passages of life
Make me believe that thou art only mark'd
For the hot vengeance and the rod of heaven
To punish my mistreadings. Tell me else,
Could such inordinate and low desires,
Such poor, such bare, such lewd, such mean attempts,
Such barren pleasures, rude society,
As thou art match'd withal and grafted to,
Accompany the greatness of thy blood
And hold their level with thy princely heart?

Prince. So please your majesty, I would I could
Quit all offences with as clear excuse
As well as I am doubtless I can purge
Myself of many I am charg'd withal:
Yet such extenuation let me beg,
As, in reproof of many tales devis'd,
Which oft the ear of greatness needs must hear,
By smiling pick-thanks and base newsmongers,
I may, for some things true, wherein my youth
Hath faulty wand'red and irregular,
Find pardon on my true submission.

King. God pardon thee! yet let me wonder, Harry,
At thy affections, which do hold a wing
Quite from the flight of all thy ancestors.
Thy place in council thou hast rudely lost,
Which by thy younger brother is supplied,
And art almost an alien to the hearts
Of all the court and princes of my blood:
The hope and expectation of thy time
Is ruin'd, and the soul of every man
Prophetically do forethink thy fall.
Had I so lavish of my presence been,
So common-hackney'd in the eyes of men,
So stale and cheap to vulgar company,
Opinion, that did help me to the crown,
Had still kept loyal to possession
And left me in reputeless banishment,
A fellow of no mark nor likelihood.
By being seldom seen, I could not stir
But like a comet I was wond'red at;
That men would tell their children 'This is he;'
Others would say 'Where, which is Bolingbroke?'
And then I stole all courtesy from heaven,
And dress'd myself in such humility
That I did pluck allegiance from men's hearts,
Loud shouts and salutations from their mouths,
Even in the presence of the crowned king.
Thus did I keep my person fresh and new;
My presence, like a robe pontifical,
Ne'er seen but wond'red at: and so my state,
Seldom but sumptuous, show'd like a feast
And won by rareness such solemnity.
The skipping king, he ambled up and down
With shallow jesters and rash bavin wits,
Soon kindled and soon burnt; carded his state,
Mingled his royalty with cap'ring fools,
Had his great name profaned with their scorns
And gave his countenance, against his name,
To laugh at gibing boys and stand the push
Of every beardless vain comparative,
Grew a companion to the common streets,
Enfeoff'd himself to popularity;
That, being daily swallowed by men's eyes,
They surfeited with honey and began
To loathe the taste of sweetness, whereof a little
More than a little is by much too much.
So when he had occasion to be seen,
He was but as the cuckoo is in June,
Heard, not regarded; seen, but with such eyes
As, sick and blunted with community,
Afford no extraordinary gaze,
Such as is bent on sun-like majesty
When it shines seldom in admiring eyes;
But rather drows'd and hung their eyelids down,
Slept in his face and rend'red such aspect
As cloudy men use to their adversaries,
Being with his presence glutted, gorg'd and full.
And in that very line, Harry, standest thou;
For thou hast lost thy princely privilege
With vile participation: not an eye
But is a-weary of thy common sight,

brach, bitch hound. 253. **comfit-maker's,** confectioner's. 256. **sarcenet,** soft, from the silken material known as "sarcenet." 257. **Finsbury,** an archery ground outside Moorgate, resorted to by citizens. 261. **velvet-guards,** wearers of velvet trimmings. 264. **turn tailor.** Tailors were noted for singing.

SCENE II. 1. **give us leave,** leave us. 6. **doom,** judgment. 8. **passages,** course, conduct. 25. **pick-thanks,** flatterers. 43. **to possession,** i.e., to Richard II's sovereignty. 50. **stole . . . heaven.** He assumed a bearing of the utmost graciousness. 60. **skipping,** flighty. 61. **bavin,** brushwood, soon burnt out. 62. **carded,** debased; a term applied to the adulteration of wool. 65. **name,** i.e., dignity. 66. **stand the push,** put up with the impudence. 67. **comparative,** rival (in wit). 69. **Enfeoff'd,** gave himself up to. 77. **community,** commonness. 83. **cloudy,** sullen (also referring back to the image of the sun). 87. **vile participation,** base association or companionship.

Save mine, which hath desir'd to see thee more;
Which now doth that I would not have it do,
Make blind itself with foolish tenderness.

Prince. I shall hereafter, my thrice gracious lord,
Be more myself.

King. For all the world
As thou art to this hour was Richard then
When I from France set foot at Ravenspurgh,
And even as I was then is Percy now.
Now, by my sceptre and my soul to boot,
He hath more worthy interest to the state
Than thou the shadow of succession;
For of no right, nor colour like to right,
He doth fill fields with harness in the realm,
Turns head against the lion's armed jaws,
And, being no more in debt to years than thou,
Leads ancient lords and reverend bishops on
To bloody battles and to bruising arms.
What never-dying honour hath he got
Against renowned Douglas! whose high deeds,
Whose hot incursions and great name in arms
Holds from all soldiers chief majority
And military title capital
Through all the kingdoms that acknowledge Christ:
Thrice hath this Hotspur, Mars in swathling clothes,
This infant warrior, in his enterprizes
Discomfited great Douglas, ta'en him once,
Enlarged him and made a friend of him,
To fill the mouth of deep defiance up
And shake the peace and safety of our throne.
And what say you to this? Percy, Northumberland,
The Archbishop's grace of York, Douglas, Mortimer,
Capitulate against us and are up.
But wherefore do I tell these news to thee?
Why, Harry, do I tell thee of my foes,
Which art my nearest and dearest enemy?
Thou that art like enough, through vassal fear,
Base inclination and the start of spleen,
To fight against me under Percy's pay,
To dog his heels and curtsy at his frowns,
To show how much thou art degenerate.

Prince. Do not think so; you shall not find it so:
And God forgive them that so much have sway'd
Your majesty's good thoughts away from me!
I will redeem all this on Percy's head
And in the closing of some glorious day
Be bold to tell you that I am your son;
When I will wear a garment all of blood
And stain my favours in a bloody mask,
Which, wash'd away, shall scour my shame with it:
And that shall be the day, whene'er it lights,
That this same child of honour and renown,
This gallant Hotspur, this all-praised knight,
And your unthought-of Harry chance to meet.
For every honour sitting on his helm,
Would they were multitudes, and on my head
My shames redoubled! for the time will come,
That I shall make this northern youth exchange
His glorious deeds for my indignities.
Percy is but my factor, good my lord,
To engross up glorious deeds on my behalf;
And I will call him to so strict account,
That he shall render every glory up,
Yea, even the slightest worship of his time,
Or I will tear the reckoning from his heart.
This, in the name of God, I promise here:
The which if He be pleas'd I shall perform,
I do beseech your majesty may salve
The long-grown wounds of my intemperance:
If not, the end of life cancels all bands;
And I will die a hundred thousand deaths
Ere break the smallest parcel of this vow.

King. A hundred thousand rebels die in this!
Thou shalt have charge and sovereign thrust herein.

Enter BLUNT.

How now, good Blunt? thy looks are full of speed.

Blunt. So hath the business that I come to speak of.
Lord Mortimer of Scotland hath sent word
That Douglas and the English rebels met
The eleventh of this month at Shrewsbury:
A mighty and a fearful head they are,
If promises be kept on every hand,
As ever off'red foul play in a state.

King. The Earl of Westmoreland set forth to-day;
With him my son, Lord John of Lancaster;
For this advertisement is five days old:
On Wednesday next, Harry, you shall set forward;
On Thursday we ourselves will march: our meeting
Is Bridgenorth: and, Harry, you shall march
Through Gloucestershire; by which account,
Our business valued, some twelve days hence
Our general forces at Bridgenorth shall meet.
Our hands are full of business: let 's away;
Advantage feeds him fat, while men delay. *Exeunt.*

[SCENE III. *Eastcheap. The Boar's-Head Tavern.*]

Enter FALSTAFF *and* BARDOLPH.

Fal. Bardolph, am I not fallen away vilely since this last action? do I not bate? do I not dwindle? Why, my skin hangs about me like an old lady's loose gown; I am withered like an old apple-john. Well, I'll repent, and that suddenly, while I am in some liking; I shall be out of heart shortly, and then I shall have no strength to repent. An I have not forgotten what the inside of a church is made of, I am a pepper-corn, a brewer's horse: the inside of a church! Company, villanous company, hath been the spoil of me.

Bard. Sir John, you are so fretful, you cannot live long.

Fal. Why, there is it: come sing me a bawdy song; make me merry. I was as virtuously given as a gentleman need to be; virtuous enough; swore little; diced not above seven times a week; went to a bawdy-house not above once in a quarter—of an hour; paid money that I borrowed, three or four times; lived well and in good compass: and now I live out of all order, out of all compass.

Bard. Why, you are so fat, Sir John, that you must needs be out of all compass, out of all reasonable compass, Sir John.

91. **tenderness,** i.e., tears. 98. **interest,** claim. 99. **shadow of succession.** Hal's claim is a shadow compared to the real services toward gaining the crown which Hotspur has rendered. 100. **colour,** pretense. 101. **harness,** armor. 109. **majority,** preëminence. 110. **capital,** chief. 112. **swathling,** swaddling. 120. **Capitulate,** form a league. 124. **vassal,** slavish. 125. **Base inclination,** inclination for baseness. **start of spleen,** perversity. 147. **factor,** agent. 172. **advertisement,** tidings, news. 180. **Advantage feeds him,** opportunity feeds itself.

SCENE III. 2. **bate,** lose weight. 5. **apple-john,** a kind of apple still in perfect condition even when shriveled and withered. 6. **liking,** (good) bodily condition. 10. **peppercorn,** grain of pepper. **brewer's horse,** one that is old, withered, and decrepit. 22. **good compass,** reasonable limits. 25. **compass,** girth, circumference. 28. **admiral,** flagship. 35. **memento mori,** reminder of death, such as skull and

Fal. Do thou amend thy face, and I'll amend my life: thou art our admiral, thou bearest the lantern in the poop, but 'tis in the nose of thee; thou art the Knight of the Burning Lamp.

Bard. Why, Sir John, my face does you no harm.

Fal. No, I'll be sworn; I make as good use of it as many a man doth of a Death's-head or a memento mori: I never see thy face but I think upon hell-fire and Dives that lived in purple; for there he is in his robes, burning, burning. If thou wert any way given to virtue, I would swear by thy face; my oath should be 'By this fire, that 's God's angel:' but thou art altogether given over; and wert indeed, but for the light in thy face, the son of utter darkness. When thou rannest up Gadshill in the night to catch my horse, if I did not think thou hadst been an ignis fatuus or a ball of wildfire, there 's no purchase in money. O, thou art a perpetual triumph, an everlasting bonfire-light! Thou hast saved me a thousand marks in links and torches, walking with thee in the night betwixt tavern and tavern: but the sack that thou hast drunk me would have bought me lights as good cheap at the dearest chandler's in Europe. I have maintained that salamander of yours with fire any time this two and thirty years; God reward me for it!

Bard. 'Sblood, I would my face were in your belly!

Fal. God-a-mercy! so should I be sure to be heart-burned.

Enter HOSTESS.

How now, Dame Partlet the hen! have you inquired yet who picked my pocket?

Host. Why, Sir John, what do you think, Sir John? do you think I keep thieves in my house? I have searched, I have inquired, so has my husband, man by man, boy by boy, servant by servant: the tithe of a hair was never lost in my house before.

Fal. Ye lie, hostess: Bardolph was shaved and lost many a hair; and I'll be sworn my pocket was picked. Go to, you are a woman, go.

Host. Who, I? no; I defy thee: God's light, I was never called so in mine own house before.

Fal. Go to, I know you well enough.

Host. No, Sir John; you do not know me, Sir John. I know you, Sir John: you owe me money, Sir John; and now you pick a quarrel to beguile me of it: I bought you a dozen of shirts to your back.

Fal. Dowlas, filthy dowlas: I have given them away to bakers' wives; they have made bolters of them.

Host. Now, as I am a true woman, holland of eight shillings an ell. You owe money here besides, Sir John, for your diet and by-drinkings, and money lent you, four and twenty pound.

Fal. He had his part of it; let him pay.

Host. He? alas, he is poor; he hath nothing.

Fal. How! poor? look upon his face; what call you rich? let them coin his nose, let them coin his cheeks: I'll not pay a denier. What, will you make a younker of me? shall I not take mine ease in mine inn but I shall have my pocket picked? I have lost a seal-ring of my grandfather's worth forty mark.

Host. O Jesu, I have heard the prince tell him, I know not how oft, that that ring was copper!

Fal. How! the prince is a Jack, a sneak-cup: 'sblood, an he were here, I would cudgel him like a dog, if he would say so.

Enter the PRINCE [*with* PETO], *marching, and* FALSTAFF *meets them playing on his truncheon like a fife.*

How now, lad! is the wind in that door, i' faith? must we all march?

Bard. Yea, two and two, Newgate fashion.

Host. My lord, I pray you, hear me.

Prince. What sayest thou, Mistress Quickly? How doth thy husband? I love him well; he is an honest man.

Host. Good my lord, hear me.

Fal. Prithee, let her alone, and list to me.

Prince. What sayest thou, Jack?

Fal. The other night I fell asleep here behind the arras and had my pocket picked: this house is turned bawdy-house; they pick pockets.

Prince. What didst thou lose, Jack?

Fal. Wilt thou believe me, Hal? three or four bonds of forty pound a-piece, and a seal-ring of my grandfather's.

Prince. A trifle, some eight-penny matter.

Host. So I told him, my lord; and I said I heard your grace say so: and, my lord, he speaks most vilely of you, like a foul-mouthed man as he is; and said he would cudgel you.

Prince. What! he did not?

Host. There 's neither faith, truth, nor womanhood in me else.

Fal. There 's no more faith in thee than in a stewed prune; nor no more truth in thee than in a drawn fox; and for womanhood, Maid Marian may be the deputy's wife of the ward to thee. Go, you thing, go.

Host. Say, what thing! what thing?

Fal. What thing? why, a thing to thank God on.

Host. I am no thing to thank God on, I would thou shouldst know it; I am an honest man's wife: and, setting thy knighthood aside, thou art a knave to call me so.

Fal. Setting thy womanhood aside, thou art a beast to say otherwise.

Host. Say, what beast, thou knave, thou?

Fal. What beast! why, an otter.

Prince. An otter, Sir John! why an otter?

Fal. Why, she 's neither fish nor flesh; a man knows not where to have her.

Host. Thou art an unjust man in saying so: thou or any man knows where to have me, thou knave, thou!

Prince. Thou sayest true, hostess; and he slanders thee most grossly.

Host. So he doth you, my lord; and said this other day you ought him a thousand pound.

Prince. Sirrah, do I owe you a thousand pound?

Fal. A thousand pound, Hal! a million: thy love is worth a million: thou owest me thy love.

crossbones. 36. **Dives,** the rich man referred to in Luke 16:19-31. 39. **'By . . . angel,'** allusion to Psalms 104:4 and Hebrews 1:7. 44-45. **ignis fatuus,** will-o'-the-wisp. 48. **links,** torches. 51. **good cheap,** cheap. 53. **salamander,** a fabled monster able to live in fire. 60. **Partlet,** traditional name of a hen. 66. **tithe,** tenth part. 79. **Dowlas,** a coarse kind of linen. 81. **bolters,** cloths for sifting meal. 82. **holland,** fine linen. 83. **ell,** a measure of a yard and a quarter. 91. **denier,** one twelfth of a sou; type of very small coin. 92. **younker,** youth, greenhorn. 99. **sneak-cup.** Nares defines this as "one who shirks his liquor"; Johnson modifies to *sneak-up,* meaning "a sneak." 104. **Newgate,** famous city prison in London. (Prisoners marched two by two.) 128. **stewed prune,** customarily served in bawdy houses. 129. **drawn fox,** fox driven from cover and wily in getting back. 147. **have,** understand (with suggestion of enjoying sexually). 152. **ought,** owed.

Host. Nay, my lord, he called you Jack, and said he would cudgel you.

Fal. Did I, Bardolph?

Bard. Indeed, Sir John, you said so.

Fal. Yea, if he said my ring was copper.

Prince. I say 'tis copper: darest thou be as good as thy word now?

Fal. Why, Hal, thou knowest, as thou art but man, I dare: but as thou art prince, I fear thee as I fear the roaring of the lion's whelp.

Prince. And why not as the lion?

Fal. The king himself is to be feared as the lion: dost thou think I'll fear thee as I fear thy father? nay, an I do, I pray God my girdle break.

Prince. O, if it should, how would thy guts fall about thy knees! But, sirrah, there 's no room for faith, truth, nor honesty in this bosom of thine; it is all filled up with guts and midriff. Charge an honest woman with picking thy pocket! why, thou whoreson, impudent, embossed rascal, if there were anything in thy pocket but tavern-reckonings, memorandums of bawdy-houses, and one poor penny-worth of sugar-candy to make thee long-winded, if thy pocket were enriched with any other injuries but these, I am a villain: and yet you will stand to it; you will not pocket up wrong: art thou not ashamed?

Fal. Dost thou hear, Hal? thou knowest in the state of innocency Adam fell; and what should poor Jack Falstaff do in the days of villany? Thou seest I have more flesh than another man, and therefore more frailty. You confess then, you picked my pocket?

Prince. It appears so by the story.

Fal. Hostess, I forgive thee: go, make ready breakfast; love thy husband, look to thy servants, cherish thy guests: thou shalt find me tractable to any honest reason: thou seest I am pacified still. Nay, prithee, be gone. (*Exit Hostess.*) Now, Hal, to the news at court: for the robbery, lad, how is that answered?

Prince. O, my sweet beef, I must still be good angel to thee: the money is paid back again.

Fal. O, I do not like that paying back; 'tis a double labour.

Prince. I am good friends with my father and may do any thing.

Fal. Rob me the exchequer the first thing thou doest, and do it with unwashed hands too.

Bard. Do, my lord.

Prince. I have procured thee, Jack, a charge of foot.

Fal. I would it had been of horse. Where shall I find one that can steal well? O for a fine thief, of the age of two and twenty or thereabouts! I am heinously unprovided. Well, God be thanked for these rebels, they offend none but the virtuous: I laud them, I praise them.

Prince. Bardolph!

Bard. My lord?

Prince. Go bear this letter to Lord John of Lancaster, to my brother John; this to my Lord of Westmoreland. [*Exit Bardolph.*] Go, Peto, to horse, to horse; for thou and I have thirty miles to ride yet ere dinner time. [*Exit Peto.*] Jack, meet me to-morrow in the Temple hall at two o'clock in the afternoon.
There shalt thou know thy charge; and there receive
Money and order for their furniture.
The land is burning; Percy stands on high;
And either we or they must lower lie. [*Exit.*]

Fal. Rare words! brave world! Hostess, my
breakfast, come!
O, I could wish this tavern were my drum! [*Exit.*]

[ACT IV.

SCENE I. *The rebel camp near Shrewsbury.*]

[*Enter* HOTSPUR, WORCESTER, *and* DOUGLAS.]

Hot. Well said, my noble Scot: if speaking truth
In this fine age were not thought flattery,
Such attribution should the Douglas have,
As not a soldier of this season's stamp
Should go so general current through the world.
By God, I cannot flatter; I do defy
The tongues of soothers; but a braver place
In my heart's love hath no man than yourself:
Nay, task me to my word; approve me, lord.

Doug. Thou art the king of honour:
No man so potent breathes upon the ground
But I will beard him.

Enter one with letters.

Hot. Do so, and 'tis well.—
What letters hast thou there?—I can but thank you.

Mess. These letters come from your father.

Hot. Letters from him! why comes he not himself?

Mess. He cannot come, my lord; he is grievous sick.

Hot. 'Zounds! how has he the leisure to be sick
In such a justling time? Who leads his power?
Under whose government come they along?

Mess. His letters bear his mind, not I, my lord.

Wor. I prithee, tell me, doth he keep his bed?

Mess. He did, my lord, four days ere I set forth;
And at the time of my departure thence
He was much fear'd by his physicians.

Wor. I would the state of time had first been whole
Ere he by sickness had been visited:
His health was never better worth than now.

Hot. Sick now! droop now! this sickness doth infect
The very life-blood of our enterprise;
'Tis catching hither, even to our camp.
†He writes me here, that inward sickness—
And that his friends by deputation could not
So soon be drawn, nor did he think it meet
To lay so dangerous and dear a trust
On any soul remov'd but on his own.
Yet doth he give us bold advertisement,
That with our small conjunction we should on,
To see how fortune is dispos'd to us;
For, as he writes, there is no quailing now,
Because the king is certainly possess'd

177. **embossed,** swollen (with fat). 182. **injuries,** i.e., those things you claim to have lost, thereby suffering harm. 183. **stand to it,** make a stand, insist on your supposed rights. **pocket up,** endure silently. 206. **with unwashed hands,** at once. 212. **thief,** i.e., to steal a horse. 226. **furniture,** equipment, provision. 230. **drum.** Possibly Falstaff means to say that he could wish that he might recruit his soldiers by means of this tavern.

ACT IV. SCENE I. 3. **attribution,** praise. 4-5. **stamp . . . current,** a figure of speech derived from coining, meaning to be widely accepted. 7. **soothers,** flatterers. 9. **task . . . word,** challenge me to make good my word. **approve,** test. 18. **justling,** jostling, busy. 36. **advertisement,** counsel, advice. 37. **conjunction,** joint force, with allusion to the conjunction of planets. 44. **want,** i.e., the lack of him. 47. **cast,** throw of the dice. **main,** stake in gambling; also, an army. 48. **nice,** precarious. 51. **list,** limit; see glossary. 53. **reversion,** part of an estate yet to be inherited; hope of future profit. 58. **big,** threateningly.

Of all our purposes. What say you to it?
Wor. Your father's sickness is a maim to us.
Hot. A perilous gash, a very limb lopp'd off:
And yet, in faith, it is not; his present want
Seems more than we shall find it: were it good
To set the exact wealth of all our states
All at one cast? to set so rich a main
On the nice hazard of one doubtful hour?
It were not good; †for therein should we read
The very bottom and the soul of hope,
The very list, the very utmost bound
Of all our fortunes.
Doug. 'Faith, and so we should;
Where now remains a sweet reversion:
†We may boldly spend upon the hope of what
Is to come in:
A comfort of retirement lives in this.
Hot. A rendezvous, a home to fly unto,
If that the devil and mischance look big
Upon the maidenhead of our affairs.
Wor. But yet I would your father had been here.
The quality and hair of our attempt
Brooks no division: it will be thought
By some, that know not why he is away,
That wisdom, loyalty and mere dislike
Of our proceedings kept the earl from hence:
And think how such an apprehension
May turn the tide of fearful faction
And breed a kind of question in our cause;
For well you know we of the off'ring side
Must keep aloof from strict arbitrement,
And stop all sight-holes, every loop from whence
The eye of reason may pry in upon us:
This absence of your father's draws a curtain,
That shows the ignorant a kind of fear
Before not dreamt of.
Hot. You strain too far.
I rather of his absence make this use:
It lends a lustre and more great opinion,
A larger dare to our great enterprise,
Than if the earl were here; for men must think,
If we without his help can make a head
To push against a kingdom, with his help
We shall o'erturn it topsy-turvy down.
Yet all goes well, yet all our joints are whole.
Doug. As heart can think: there is not such a word
Spoke of in Scotland as this term of fear.

Enter SIR RICHARD VERNON.

Hot. My cousin Vernon! welcome, by my soul.
Ver. Pray God my news be worth a welcome, lord.
The Earl of Westmoreland, seven thousand strong,
Is marching hitherwards; with him Prince John.
Hot. No harm: what more?
Ver. And further, I have learn'd,
The king himself in person is set forth,
Or hitherwards intended speedily,
With strong and mighty preparation.
Hot. He shall be welcome too. Where is his son,
The nimble-footed madcap Prince of Wales,
And his comrades, that daff'd the world aside,
And bid it pass?
Ver. All furnish'd, all in arms;
†All plum'd like estridges that with the wind
Bated like eagles having lately bath'd;
Glittering in golden coats, like images;
As full of spirit as the month of May,
And gorgeous as the sun at midsummer;
Wanton as youthful goats, wild as young bulls.
I saw young Harry, with his beaver on,
His cuisses on his thighs, gallantly arm'd,
Rise from the ground like feathered Mercury,
And vaulted with such ease into his seat,
As if an angel dropp'd down from the clouds,
To turn and wind a fiery Pegasus
And witch the world with noble horsemanship.
Hot. No more, no more: worse than the sun in March,
This praise doth nourish agues. Let them come;
They come like sacrifices in their trim,
And to the fire-ey'd maid of smoky war
All hot and bleeding will we offer them:
The mailed Mars shall on his altar sit
Up to the ears in blood. I am on fire
To hear this rich reprisal is so nigh
And yet not ours. Come, let me taste my horse,
Who is to bear me like a thunderbolt
Against the bosom of the Prince of Wales:
Harry to Harry shall, hot horse to horse,
Meet and ne'er part till one drop down a corse.
O that Glendower were come!
Ver. There is more news:
I learn'd in Worcester, as I rode along,
He cannot draw his power this fourteen days.
Doug. That 's the worst tidings that I hear of yet.
Wor. Ay, by my faith, that bears a frosty sound.
Hot. What may the king's whole battle reach unto?
Ver. To thirty thousand.
Hot. Forty let it be:
My father and Glendower being both away,
The powers of us may serve so great a day.
Come, let us take a muster speedily:
Doomsday is near; die all, die merrily.
Doug. Talk not of dying: I am out of fear
Of death or death's hand for this one-half year.
Exeunt.

[SCENE II. *A public road near Coventry.*]

Enter FALSTAFF, [*and*] BARDOLPH.

Fal. Bardolph, get thee before to Coventry; fill me a bottle of sack: our soldiers shall march through; we'll to Sutton Co'fil' to-night.

Bard. Will you give me money, captain?

Fal. Lay out, lay out.

Bard. This bottle makes an angel.

Fal. An if it do, take it for thy labour; and if it make twenty, take them all; I'll answer the coinage. Bid my lieutenant Peto meet me at town's end.

61. **hair,** kind, nature. 69. **off'ring side,** side which attacks. 70. **arbitrement,** just inquiry or investigation. 96. **daff'd,** put aside with a gesture. 97. **furnish'd,** equipped. 98. **like estridges,** a reference to ostrich plumes on crests. 99. **Bated,** flapped their wings. 100. **images,** gilded statues. 104. **beaver,** visor (of helmet); also, the helmet itself. 105. **cuisses,** armor for the thighs. 109. **wind a fiery Pegasus,** turn or wheel like the winged horse of Greek mythology. 110. **witch,** bewitch. 111-112. **worse . . . agues.** The spring sun was believed to give impetus to chills and fevers, by drawing up vapors. 113. **trim,** fine apparel, trappings. 114. **maid,** Bellona, goddess of war. 118. **reprisal,** prize. 126. **power,** army.

SCENE II. 3. **Sutton Co'fil',** Sutton Coldfield in Warwickshire near Coventry. 5. **Lay out,** pay yourself. 6. **makes an angel,** i.e., that I have spent. **angel,** coin worth ten shillings.

Bard. I will, captain: farewell. *Exit.*

Fal. If I be not ashamed of my soldiers, I am a soused gurnet. I have misused the king's press damnably. I have got, in exchange of a hundred and fifty soldiers, three hundred and odd pounds. I press me none but good householders, yeomen's sons; inquire me out contracted bachelors, such as had been asked twice on the banns; such a commodity of warm slaves, as had as lieve hear the devil as a drum; such as fear the report of a caliver worse than a struck fowl or a hurt wild-duck. I pressed me none but such toasts-and-butter, with hearts in their bellies no bigger than pins' heads, and they have bought out their services; and now my whole charge consists of ancients, corporals, lieutenants, gentlemen of companies, slaves as ragged as Lazarus in the painted cloth, where the glutton's dogs licked his sores; and such as indeed were never soldiers, but discarded unjust serving-men, younger sons to younger brothers, revolted tapsters and ostlers trade-fallen, the cankers of a calm world and a long peace, ten times more dishonourable ragged than an old faced ancient: and such have I, to fill up the rooms of them that have bought out their services, that you would think that I had a hundred and fifty tattered prodigals lately come from swine-keeping, from eating draff and husks. A mad fellow met me on the way and told me I had unloaded all the gibbets and pressed the dead bodies. No eye hath seen such scarecrows. I'll not march through Coventry with them, that 's flat: nay, and the villains march wide betwixt the legs, as if they had gyves on; for indeed I had the most of them out of prison. There 's but a shirt and a half in all my company; and the half shirt is two napkins tacked together and thrown over the shoulders like a herald's coat without sleeves; and the shirt, to say the truth, stolen from my host at Saint Alban's, or the red-nose innkeeper of Daventry. But that 's all one; they'll find linen enough on every hedge.

Enter the PRINCE [*and the*] Lord *of* WESTMORELAND.

Prince. How now, blown Jack! how now, quilt!

Fal. What, Hal! how now, mad wag! what a devil dost thou in Warwickshire? My good Lord of Westmoreland, I cry you mercy: I thought your honour had already been at Shrewsbury.

West. Faith, Sir John, 'tis more than time that I were there, and you too; but my powers are there already. The king, I can tell you, looks for us all: we must away all night.

Fal. Tut, never fear me: I am as vigilant as a cat to steal cream.

Prince. I think, to steal cream indeed, for thy theft hath already made thee butter. But tell me, Jack, whose fellows are these that come after?

Fal. Mine, Hal, mine.

Prince. I did never see such pitiful rascals.

Fal. Tut, tut; good enough to toss; food for powder, food for powder; they'll fill a pit as well as better: tush, man, mortal men, mortal men.

West. Ay, but, Sir John, methinks they are exceeding poor and bare, too beggarly.

Fal. 'Faith, for their poverty, I know not where they had that; and for their bareness, I am sure they never learned that of me.

Prince. No, I'll be sworn; unless you call three fingers in the ribs bare. But, sirrah, make haste: Percy is already in the field. *Exit.*

Fal. What, is the king encamped?

West. He is, Sir John: I fear we shall stay too long. [*Exit.*]

Fal. Well,
To the latter end of a fray and the beginning of a feast
Fits a dull fighter and a keen guest. *Exit.*

[SCENE III. *The rebel camp near Shrewsbury.*]

Enter HOTSPUR, WORCESTER, DOUGLAS, [*and*] VERNON.

Hot. We'll fight with him to-night.
Wor. It may not be.
Doug. You give him then advantage.
Ver. Not a whit.
Hot. Why say you so? looks he not for supply?
Ver. So do we.
Hot. His is certain, ours is doubtful.
Wor. Good cousin, be advis'd; stir not to-night.
Ver. Do not, my lord.
Doug. You do not counsel well:
You speak it out of fear and cold heart.
Ver. Do me no slander, Douglas: by my life,
And I dare well maintain it with my life,
If well-respected honour bid me on,
I hold as little counsel with weak fear
As you, my lord, or any Scot that this day lives:
Let it be seen to-morrow in the battle
Which of us fears.
Doug. Yea, or to-night.
Ver. Content.
Hot. To-night, say I.
Ver. Come, come, it may not be. I wonder much,
Being men of such great leading as you are,
That you foresee not what impediments
Drag back our expedition: certain horse
Of my cousin Vernon's are not yet come up:
Your uncle Worcester's horse came but to-day;
And now their pride and mettle is asleep,
Their courage with hard labour tame and dull,
That not a horse is half the half of himself.
Hot. So are the horses of the enemy
In general, journey-bated and brought low:
The better part of ours are full of rest.
Wor. The number of the king exceedeth ours:
For God's sake, cousin, stay till all come in.
The trumpet sounds a parley.

Enter SIR WALTER BLUNT.

Blunt. I come with gracious offers from the king,
If you vouchsafe me hearing and respect.
Hot. Welcome, Sir Walter Blunt; and would to God
You were of our determination!
Some of us love you well; and even those some

13. **soused gurnet,** a kind of fish pickled; opprobrious. 14. **king's press,** royal warrant for the impressment of troops. 16. **yeomen's,** small freeholders'. 17. **contracted,** engaged to be married. 21. **caliver,** musket or harquebus. **struck,** wounded. 26. **ancients,** ensigns, standardbearers. 28. **painted cloth,** hangings for a room; in this case painted with the story of Lazarus, Luke 16:20. 32. **cankers,** worms which destroy leaves and buds; used figuratively. 34. **old faced ancient,** defined as an old standard mended with new cloth, or as a standard presenting an old aspect. Cambridge reads *old feaz'd,* meaning "frayed." 37. **prodigals.** See Luke 15:15-16. 39. **draff,** hogwash. 44. **gyves,** fetters. 50, 51. **Saint Alban's, Daventry,** towns on the road from London to Coventry. 53. **blown,** swollen, inflated; also, short

Envy your great deservings and good name,
Because you are not of our quality,
But stand against us like an enemy.
Blunt. And God defend but still I should stand so,
So long as out of limit and true rule
You stand against anointed majesty.
But to my charge. The king hath sent to know
The nature of your griefs, and whereupon
You conjure from the breast of civil peace
Such bold hostility, teaching his duteous land
Audacious cruelty. If that the king
Have any way your good deserts forgot,
Which he confesseth to be manifold,
He bids you name your griefs; and with all speed
You shall have your desires with interest
And pardon absolute for yourself and these
Herein misled by your suggestion.
Hot. The king is kind; and well we know the king
Knows at what time to promise, when to pay.
My father and my uncle and myself
Did give him that same royalty he wears;
And when he was not six and twenty strong,
Sick in the world's regard, wretched and low,
A poor unminded outlaw sneaking home,
My father gave him welcome to the shore;
And when he heard him swear and vow to God
He came but to be Duke of Lancaster,
To sue his livery and beg his peace,
With tears of innocency and terms of zeal,
My father, in kind heart and pity mov'd,
Swore him assistance and perform'd it too.
Now when the lords and barons of the realm
Perceiv'd Northumberland did lean to him,
The more and less came in with cap and knee;
Met him in boroughs, cities, villages,
Attended him on bridges, stood in lanes,
Laid gifts before him, proffer'd him their oaths,
Gave him their heirs, as pages followed him
Even at the heels in golden multitudes.
He presently, as greatness knows itself,
Steps me a little higher than his vow
Made to my father, while his blood was poor,
Upon the naked shore at Ravenspurgh;
And now, forsooth, takes on him to reform
Some certain edicts and some strait decrees
That lie too heavy on the commonwealth,
Cries out upon abuses, seems to weep
Over his country's wrongs; and by this face,
This seeming brow of justice, did he win
The hearts of all that he did angle for;
Proceeded further; cut me off the heads
Of all the favourites that the absent king
In deputation left behind him here,
When he was personal in the Irish war.
Blunt. Tut, I came not to hear this.
Hot. Then to the point.
In short time after, he depos'd the king;
Soon after that, depriv'd him of his life;
And in the neck of that, task'd the whole state;
To make that worse, suff'red his kinsman March,
Who is, if every owner were well plac'd,
Indeed his king, to be engag'd in Wales,
There without ransom to lie forfeited;
Disgrac'd me in my happy victories,
Sought to entrap me by intelligence;
Rated mine uncle from the council-board;
In rage dismiss'd my father from the court;
Broke oath on oath, committed wrong on wrong,
And in conclusion drove us to seek out
This head of safety; and withal to pry
Into his title, the which we find
Too indirect for long continuance.
Blunt. Shall I return this answer to the king?
Hot. Not so, Sir Walter: we'll withdraw awhile.
Go to the king; and let there be impawn'd
Some surety for a safe return again,
And in the morning early shall mine uncle
Bring him our purposes: and so farewell.
Blunt. I would you would accept of grace and love.
Hot. And may be so we shall.
Blunt. Pray God you do. [*Exeunt*.]

[SCENE IV. *York. The* ARCHBISHOP'S *palace*.]

Enter [*the*] ARCHBISHOP OF YORK, [*and*] SIR MICHAEL.

Arch. Hie, good Sir Michael; bear this sealed brief
With winged haste to the lord marshal;
This to my cousin Scroop, and all the rest
To whom they are directed. If you knew
How much they do import, you would make haste.
Sir M. My good lord,
I guess their tenour.
Arch. Like enough you do.
To-morrow, good Sir Michael, is a day
Wherein the fortune of ten thousand men
Must bide the touch; for, sir, at Shrewsbury,
As I am truly given to understand,
The king with mighty and quick-raised power
Meets with Lord Harry: and, I fear, Sir Michael,
What with the sickness of Northumberland,
Whose power was in the first proportion,
And what with Owen Glendower's absence thence,
Who with them was a rated sinew too
And comes not in, o'er-rul'd by prophecies,
I fear the power of Percy is too weak
To wage an instant trial with the king.
Sir M. Why, my good lord, you need not fear;
There is Douglas and Lord Mortimer.
Arch. No, Mortimer is not there.
Sir M. But there is Mordake, Vernon, Lord Harry Percy,
And there is my Lord of Worcester and a head
Of gallant warriors, noble gentlemen.
Arch. And so there is: but yet the king hath drawn
The special head of all the land together:
The Prince of Wales, Lord John of Lancaster,
The noble Westmoreland and warlike Blunt;
And many moe corrivals and dear men
Of estimation and command in arms.
Sir M. Doubt not, my lord, they shall be well oppos'd.

of wind. 71. **toss,** i.e., on a pike.
SCENE III. 10. **well-respected,** well weighed or considered. 26. **journey-bated,** tired from the journey. 51. **suggestion,** instigation. 62. **sue his livery,** sue as an heir come of age for the delivery of his lands held by the crown. 68. **more and less,** persons of all ranks. 88. **personal,** in person. 92. **in . . . that,** next. **task'd,** laid taxes upon. 98. **intelligence,** secret information, i.e., from spies. 103. **head of safety,** armed force for their protection.
SCENE IV. 1. **brief,** letter, dispatch. 10. **bide the touch,** be put to the test (like gold). 17. **rated sinew,** main strength or support reckoned upon. 31. **moe corrivals,** more partners in the enterprise. 32. **estimation,** reputation, importance.

Arch. I hope no less, yet needful 'tis to fear;
And, to prevent the worst, Sir Michael, speed:
For if Lord Percy thrive not, ere the king
Dismiss his power, he means to visit us,
For he hath heard of our confederacy,
And 'tis but wisdom to make strong against him:
Therefore make haste. I must go write again
To other friends; and so farewell, Sir Michael. *Exeunt.*

[ACT V.

SCENE I. *The* KING'S *camp near Shrewsbury.*]

Enter the KING, PRINCE OF WALES, LORD JOHN OF LANCASTER, EARL OF WESTMORELAND, SIR WALTER BLUNT, [*and*] FALSTAFF.

King. How bloodily the sun begins to peer
Above yon busky hill! the day looks pale
At his distemp'rature.
Prince. The southern wind
Doth play the trumpet to his purposes,
And by his hollow whistling in the leaves
Foretells a tempest and a blust'ring day.
King. Then with the losers let it sympathise,
For nothing can seem foul to those that win.
The trumpet sounds.

Enter WORCESTER [*and* VERNON].

How now, my Lord of Worcester! 'tis not well
That you and I should meet upon such terms
As now we meet. You have deceiv'd our trust,
And made us doff our easy robes of peace,
To crush our old limbs in ungentle steel:
This is not well, my lord, this is not well.
What say you to it? will you again unknit
This churlish knot of all-abhorred war?
And move in that obedient orb again
Where you did give a fair and natural light,
And be no more an exhal'd meteor,
A prodigy of fear and a portent
Of broached mischief to the unborn times?
Wor. Hear me, my liege:
For mine own part, I could be well content
To entertain the lag-end of my life
With quiet hours; for I do protest,
I have not sought the day of this dislike.
King. You have not sought it! how comes it, then?
Fal. Rebellion lay in his way, and he found it.
Prince. Peace, chewet, peace!
Wor. It pleas'd your majesty to turn your looks
Of favour from myself and all our house;
And yet I must remember you, my lord,
We were the first and dearest of your friends.
For you my staff of office did I break
In Richard's time; and posted day and night
To meet you on the way, and kiss your hand,
When yet you were in place and in account
Nothing so strong and fortunate as I.
It was myself, my brother and his son,
That brought you home and boldly did outdare
The dangers of the time. You swore to us,
And you did swear that oath at Doncaster,
That you did nothing purpose 'gainst the state;
Nor claim no further than your new-fall'n right,
The seat of Gaunt, dukedom of Lancaster:
To this we swore our aid. But in short space
It rain'd down fortune show'ring on your head;
And such a flood of greatness fell on you,
What with our help, what with the absent king,
What with the injuries of a wanton time,
The seeming sufferances that you had borne,
And the contrarious winds that held the king
So long in his unlucky Irish wars
That all in England did repute him dead:
And from this swarm of fair advantages
You took occasion to be quickly woo'd
To gripe the general sway into your hand;
Forgot your oath to us at Doncaster;
And being fed by us you us'd us so
As that ungentle gull, the cuckoo's bird,
Useth the sparrow; did oppress our nest;
Grew by our feeding to so great a bulk
That even our love durst not come near your sight
For fear of swallowing; but with nimble wing
We were enforc'd, for safety sake, to fly
Out of your sight and raise this present head;
Whereby we stand opposed by such means
As you yourself have forg'd against yourself
By unkind usage, dangerous countenance,
And violation of all faith and troth
Sworn to us in your younger enterprise.
King. These things indeed you have articulate,
Proclaim'd at market-crosses, read in churches,
To face the garment of rebellion
With some fine colour that may please the eye
Of fickle changelings and poor discontents,
Which gape and rub the elbow at the news
Of hurlyburly innovation:
And never yet did insurrection want
Such water-colours to impaint his cause;
Nor moody beggars, starving for a time
Of pellmell havoc and confusion.
Prince. In both your armies there is many a soul
Shall pay full dearly for this encounter,
If once they join in trial. Tell your nephew,
The Prince of Wales doth join with all the world
In praise of Henry Percy: by my hopes,
This present enterprise set off his head,
I do not think a braver gentleman,
More active-valiant or more valiant-young,
More daring or more bold, is now alive
To grace this latter age with noble deeds.
For my part, I may speak it to my shame,
I have a truant been to chivalry;
And so I hear he doth account me too;
Yet this before my father's majesty—
I am content that he shall take the odds
Of his great name and estimation,
And will, to save the blood on either side,
Try fortune with him in a single fight.
King. And, Prince of Wales, so dare we venture thee,

ACT V. SCENE I. 2. **busky,** bosky, bushy. 3. **distemp'rature,** ill-humor, or possibly, inclemency. 4. **his,** its, the sun's. 17. **orb,** orbit, sphere of action. 19. **exhal'd meteor,** a phenomenon created by vapor drawn up by the sun and visible as streaks of light; regarded as an ill omen. 21. **broached,** already begun. 29. **chewet,** chough, jackdaw; piece of fried pie; also, here, a chatterer. 32. **remember,** remind. 51. **sufferances,** suffering, distress. 60. **gull,** unfledged nestling. **cuckoo's bird,** allusion to the cuckoo's habit of laying its eggs in the sparrow's nest. 69. **dangerous,** menacing. 72. **articulate,** set forth, specified. 74. **face,** trim, adorn. 77. **rub the elbow,** i.e., hug themselves with delight. 78. **innovation,** revolution. 79. **want,** lack. 88. **set off his head,** taken from his account. 102. **Albeit,** on the other

Albeit considerations infinite
Do make against it. No, good Worcester, no,
We love our people well; even those we love
That are misled upon your cousin's part;
And, will they take the offer of our grace,
Both he and they and you, yea, every man
Shall be my friend again and I'll be his:
So tell your cousin, and bring me word
What he will do: but if he will not yield,
Rebuke and dread correction wait on us
And they shall do their office. So, be gone;
We will not now be troubled with reply:
We offer fair; take it advisedly.
Exeunt Worcester [and Vernon].

Prince. It will not be accepted, on my life:
The Douglas and the Hotspur both together
Are confident against the world in arms.

King. Hence, therefore, every leader to his charge;
For, on their answer, will we set on them:
And God befriend us, as our cause is just!
Exeunt. Manent Prince, Falstaff.

Fal. Hal, if thou see me down in the battle and bestride me, so; 'tis a point of friendship.

Prince. Nothing but a colossus can do thee that friendship. Say thy prayers, and farewell.

Fal. I would 'twere bed-time, Hal, and all well.

Prince. Why, thou owest God a death. *[Exit.]*

Fal. 'Tis not due yet; I would be loath to pay him before his day. What need I be so forward with him that calls not on me? Well, 'tis no matter; honour pricks me on. Yea, but how if honour prick me off when I come on? how then? Can honour set to a leg? no: or an arm? no: or take away the grief of a wound? no. Honour hath no skill in surgery, then? no. What is honour? a word. What is in that word honour? what is that honour? air. A trim reckoning! Who hath it? he that died a Wednesday. Doth he feel it? no. Doth he hear it? no. 'Tis insensible, then? Yea, to the dead. But will it not live with the living? no. Why? detraction will not suffer it. Therefore I'll none of it. Honour is a mere scutcheon: and so ends my catechism. *Exit.*

[SCENE II. *The rebel camp.*]

Enter WORCESTER , [*and*] SIR RICHARD VERNON.

Wor. O, no, my nephew must not know, Sir Richard,
The liberal and kind offer of the king.

Ver. 'Twere best he did.

Wor. Then are we all undone.
It is not possible, it cannot be,
The king should keep his word in loving us;
He will suspect us still and find a time
To punish this offence in other faults:
Supposition all our lives shall be stuck full of eyes;
For treason is but trusted like the fox,
Who, ne'er so tame, so cherish'd and lock'd up,
Will have a wild trick of his ancestors.
Look how we can, or sad or merrily,
Interpretation will misquote our looks,
And we shall feed like oxen at a stall,
The better cherish'd, still the nearer death.
My nephew's trespass may be well forgot;
It hath the excuse of youth and heat of blood,
And an adopted name of privilege,
A hare-brain'd Hotspur, govern'd by a spleen:
All his offences live upon my head
And on his father's; we did train him on,
And, his corruption being ta'en from us,
We, as the spring of all, shall pay for all.
Therefore, good cousin, let not Harry know,
In any case, the offer of the king.

Enter HOTSPUR [*and* DOUGLAS].

Ver. Deliver what you will; I'll say 'tis so.
Here comes your cousin.

Hot. My uncle is return'd:
Deliver up my Lord of Westmoreland.
Uncle, what news?

Wor. The king will bid you battle presently.

Doug. Defy him by the Lord of Westmoreland.

Hot. Lord Douglas, go you and tell him so.

Doug. Marry, and shall, and very willingly.
Exit Doug.

Wor. There is no seeming mercy in the king.

Hot. Did you beg any? God forbid!

Wor. I told him gently of our grievances,
Of his oath-breaking; which he mended thus,
By now forswearing that he is forsworn:
He calls us rebels, traitors; and will scourge
With haughty arms this hateful name in us.

Enter DOUGLAS.

Doug. Arm, gentlemen; to arms! for I have thrown
A brave defiance in King Henry's teeth,
And Westmoreland, that was engag'd, did bear it;
Which cannot choose but bring him quickly on.

Wor. The Prince of Wales stepp'd forth before the king,
And, nephew, challeng'd you to single fight.

Hot. O, would the quarrel lay upon our heads,
And that no man might draw short breath to-day
But I and Harry Monmouth! Tell me, tell me,
How show'd his tasking? seem'd it in contempt?

Ver. No, by my soul; I never in my life
Did hear a challenge urg'd more modestly,
Unless a brother should a brother dare
To gentle exercise and proof of arms.
He gave you all the duties of a man;
Trimm'd up your praises with a princely tongue,
Spoke your deservings like a chronicle,
Making you ever better than his praise
By still dispraising praise valued with you;
And, which became him like a prince indeed,
He made a blushing cital of himself;
And chid his truant youth with such a grace
As if he mast'red there a double spirit
Of teaching and of learning instantly.
There did he pause: but let me tell the world,
If he outlive the envy of this day,
England did never owe so sweet a hope,
So much misconstrued in his wantonness.

hand, were it not that. 111. **wait on us,** are in attendance upon us. 126. **thou . . . death,** proverbial, with a pun on "debt." 131. **prick me off,** mark me off as one dead. 142. **detraction,** slander. 143. **scutcheon,** emblem or hatchment carried in funerals. It was the lowest form of symbol, having no pennon or other insignia.

SCENE II. 8. **Supposition,** suspicious conjecture. 18. **adopted name of privilege.** Hotspur has taken a nickname, "hotspur," to justify his rashness. 21. **train,** incite, draw. 51. **tasking,** challenge. 62. **cital,** impeachment. 68. **owe,** own.

Hot. Cousin, I think thou art enamoured
On his follies: never did I hear
Of any prince so wild a libertine.
But be he as he will, yet once ere night
I will embrace him with a soldier's arm,
That he shall shrink under my courtesy.
Arm, arm with speed: and, fellows, soldiers, friends,
Better consider what you have to do
Than I, that have not well the gift of tongue,
Can lift your blood up with persuasion.

Enter a Messenger.

Mess. My lord, here are letters for you.
Hot. I cannot read them now.
O gentlemen, the time of life is short!
To spend that shortness basely were too long,
If life did ride upon a dial's point,
Still ending at the arrival of an hour.
An if we live, we live to tread on kings;
If die, brave death, when princes die with us!
Now, for our consciences, the arms are fair,
When the intent of bearing them is just.

Enter another [Messenger].

Mess. My lord, prepare; the king comes on apace.
Hot. I thank him, that he cuts me from my tale,
For I profess not talking; only this—
Let each man do his best: and here draw I
A sword, whose temper I intend to stain
With the best blood that I can meet withal
In the adventure of this perilous day.
Now, Esperance! Percy! and set on.
Sound all the lofty instruments of war,
And by that music let us all embrace;
For, heaven to earth, some of us never shall
A second time do such a courtesy.
Here they embrace. The trumpets sound. [*Exeunt.*]

[SCENE III. *Plain between the camps.*]

The KING *enters with his power. Alarum to the battle. Then enter* DOUGLAS *and* SIR WALTER BLUNT.

Blunt. What is thy name, that in the battle thus
Thou crossest me? what honour dost thou seek
Upon my head?
Doug. Know then, my name is Douglas;
And I do haunt thee in the battle thus
Because some tell me that thou art a king.
Blunt. They tell thee true.
Doug. The Lord of Stafford dear to-day hath bought
Thy likeness, for instead of thee, King Harry,
This sword hath ended him: so shall it thee,
Unless thou yield thee as my prisoner.
Blunt. I was not born a yielder, thou proud Scot;
And thou shalt find a king that will revenge
Lord Stafford's death. *They fight. Douglas kills Blunt.*

Then enter HOTSPUR.

Hot. O Douglas, hadst thou fought at Holmedon thus,
I never had triumph'd upon a Scot.
Doug. All 's done, all 's won; here breathless lies the king.
Hot. Where?
Doug. Here.
Hot. This, Douglas? no: I know this face full well:
A gallant knight he was, his name was Blunt;
Semblably furnish'd like the king himself.
Doug. A fool go with thy soul, whither it goes!
A borrowed title hast thou bought too dear:
Why didst thou tell me that thou wert a king?
Hot. The king hath many marching in his coats.
Doug. Now, by my sword, I will kill all his coats;
I'll murder all his wardrobe, piece by piece,
Until I meet the king.
Hot. Up, and away!
Our soldiers stand full fairly for the day. [*Exeunt.*]

Alarum. Enter FALSTAFF, *solus.*

Fal. Though I could 'scape shot-free at London, I fear the shot here; here 's no scoring but upon the pate. Soft! who are you? Sir Walter Blunt: there 's honour for you! here 's no vanity! I am as hot as molten lead, and as heavy too: God keep lead out of me! I need no more weight than mine own bowels. I have led my ragamuffins where they are peppered: there 's not three of my hundred and fifty left alive; and they are for the town's end, to beg during life. But who comes here?

Enter the PRINCE.

Prince. What, stand'st thou idle here? lend me thy sword:
Many a nobleman lies stark and stiff
Under the hoofs of vaunting enemies,
Whose deaths are yet unrevenged: I prithee, lend me thy sword.

Fal. O Hal, I prithee, give me leave to breathe awhile. Turk Gregory never did such deeds in arms as I have done this day. I have paid Percy, I have made him sure.

Prince. He is, indeed; and living to kill thee. I prithee, lend me thy sword.

Fal. Nay, before God, Hal, if Percy be alive, thou get'st not my sword; but take my pistol, if thou wilt.

Prince. Give it me: what, is it in the case?

Fal. Ay, Hal; 'tis hot, 'tis hot; there 's that will sack a city.

The Prince draws it out, and finds it to be a bottle of sack.

Prince. What, is it a time to jest and dally now?
He throws the bottle at him. Exit.

Fal. Well, if Percy be alive, I'll pierce him. If he do come in my way, so: if he do not, if I come in his willingly, let him make a carbonado of me. I like not such grinning honour as Sir Walter hath: give me life: which if I can save, so; if not, honour comes unlooked for, and there 's an end. [*Exit.*]

[SCENE IV. *Another part of the field.*]

Alarum. Excursions. Enter the KING, *the* PRINCE, LORD JOHN OF LANCASTER, [*and*] EARL OF WESTMORELAND.

King. I prithee,

84. **dial's point,** hand of watch or clock.
SCENE III. 21. **Semblably furnish'd,** similarly accoutered. 30. **shot-free,** without paying the bill. 31. **scoring,** marking up of charges (often on the inn door). 46. **Turk Gregory,** a sort of combined allusion to the famous pope Gregory the Great, and to the Grand Turk. 59. **Percy . . . pierce.** Current pronunciation probably rendered the pun more obvious than it is now. 62. **carbonado,** meat scored across for broiling.
SCENE IV. 5. **make up,** go forward. 6. **amaze,** alarm. 22. **mainte-**

Harry, withdraw thyself; thou bleedest too much.
Lord John of Lancaster, go you with him.
Lan. Not I, my lord, unless I did bleed too.
Prince. I beseech your majesty, make up,
Lest your retirement do amaze your friends.
King. I will do so.
My Lord of Westmoreland, lead him to his tent.
West. Come, my lord, I'll lead you to your tent.
Prince. Lead me, my lord? I do not need your help:
And God forbid a shallow scratch should drive
The Prince of Wales from such a field as this,
Where stain'd nobility lies trodden on,
And rebels' arms triumph in massacres!
Lan. We breathe too long: come, cousin Westmoreland,
Our duty this way lies; for God's sake, come.
[*Exeunt Prince John and Westmoreland.*]
Prince. By God, thou hast deceiv'd me, Lancaster;
I did not think thee lord of such a spirit:
Before, I lov'd thee as a brother, John;
But now, I do respect thee as my soul.
King. I saw him hold Lord Percy at the point
With lustier maintenance than I did look for
Of such an ungrown warrior.
Prince. O, this boy
Lends mettle to us all! *Exit.*

[*Enter* DOUGLAS.]

Doug. Another king! they grow like Hydra's heads:
I am the Douglas, fatal to all those
That wear those colours on them: what art thou,
That counterfeit'st the person of a king?
King. The king himself; who, Douglas, grieves at heart
So many of his shadows thou hast met
And not the very king. I have two boys
Seek Percy and thyself about the field:
But, seeing thou fall'st on me so luckily,
I will assay thee: so, defend thyself.
Doug. I fear thou art another counterfeit;
And yet, in faith, thou bearest thee like a king:
But mine I am sure thou art, whoe'er thou be,
And thus I win thee.
They fight; the King being in danger, enter Prince of Wales.
Prince. Hold up thy head, vile Scot, or thou art like
Never to hold it up again! the spirits
Of valiant Shirley, Stafford, Blunt, are in my arms:
It is the Prince of Wales that threatens thee;
Who never promiseth but he means to pay.
They fight: Douglas flieth.
Cheerly, my lord: how fares your grace?
Sir Nicholas Gawsey hath for succour sent,
And so hath Clifton: I'll to Clifton straight.
King. Stay, and breathe awhile:
Thou hast redeem'd thy lost opinion,
And show'd thou mak'st some tender of my life,
In this fair rescue thou hast brought to me.
Prince. O God! they did me too much injury
That ever said I heark'ned for your death.
If it were so, I might have let alone
The insulting hand of Douglas over you,
Which would have been as speedy in your end
As all the poisonous potions in the world
And sav'd the treacherous labour of your son.
King. Make up to Clifton: I'll to Sir Nicholas Gawsey. *Exit King.*

Enter HOTSPUR.

Hot. If I mistake not, thou art Harry Monmouth.
Prince. Thou speak'st as if I would deny my name.
Hot. My name is Harry Percy.
Prince. Why, then I see
A very valiant rebel of the name.
I am the Prince of Wales; and think not, Percy,
To share with me in glory any more:
Two stars keep not their motion in one sphere;
Nor can one England brook a double reign,
Of Harry Percy and the Prince of Wales.
Hot. Nor shall it, Harry; for the hour is come
To end the one of us; and would to God
Thy name in arms were now as great as mine!
Prince. I'll make it greater ere I part from thee;
And all the budding honours on thy crest
I'll crop, to make a garland for my head.
Hot. I can no longer brook thy vanities. *They fight.*

Enter FALSTAFF.

Fal. Well said, Hal! to it, Hal! Nay, you shall find no boy's play here, I can tell you.

Enter DOUGLAS. *He fighteth with* FALSTAFF, *who falls down as if he were dead.* [*Exit* DOUGLAS.] *The* PRINCE *killeth* PERCY.

Hot. O, Harry, thou hast robb'd me of my youth!
I better brook the loss of brittle life
Than those proud titles thou hast won of me;
They wound my thoughts worse than thy sword my flesh:
But thought 's the slave of life, and life time's fool;
And time, that takes survey of all the world,
Must have a stop. O, I could prophesy,
But that the earthy and cold hand of death
Lies on my tongue: no, Percy, thou art dust,
And food for— [*Dies.*]
Prince. For worms, brave Percy: fare thee well, great heart!
Ill-weav'd ambition, how much art thou shrunk!
When that this body did contain a spirit,
A kingdom for it was too small a bound;
But now two paces of the vilest earth
Is room enough: this earth that bears thee dead
Bears not alive so stout a gentleman.
If thou wert sensible of courtesy,
I should not make so dear a show of zeal:
But let my favours hide thy mangled face;
And, even in thy behalf, I'll thank myself
For doing these fair rites of tenderness.
Adieu, and take thy praise with thee to heaven!
Thy ignominy sleep with thee in the grave,
But not remember'd in thy epitaph!
He spieth Falstaff on the ground.
What, old acquaintance! could not all this flesh
Keep in a little life? Poor Jack, farewell!
I could have better spar'd a better man:
O, I should have a heavy miss of thee,
If I were much in love with vanity!

nance, bearing, demeanor. 25. **Hydra's heads,** allusion to the Lernean Hydra, whose heads grew again as fast as they were cut off. 49. **mak'st some tender,** hast some care for. 52. **heark'ned,** listened (as for welcome intelligence). 65. **Two . . . sphere,** proverbial allusion to the fact that each planet has its own orbit. 81-83. **But . . . stop.** Thought ends with life, and life is ended by time; and time, though it serve as the measure for the world, must itself come to an end. 93. **stout,** valiant. 96. **favours,** knots of ribbon, scarf, etc.

Death hath not struck so fat a deer to-day,
Though many dearer, in this bloody fray.
Embowell'd will I see thee by and by:
Till then in blood by noble Percy lie. *Exit.*

Falstaff riseth up.

Fal. Embowelled! if thou embowel me to-day, I'll give you leave to powder me and eat me too to-morrow. 'Sblood, 'twas time to counterfeit, or that hot termagant Scot had paid me scot and lot too. Counterfeit? I lie, I am no counterfeit: to die, is to be a counterfeit; for he is but the counterfeit of a man who hath not the life of a man: but to counterfeit dying, when a man thereby liveth, is to be no counterfeit, but the true and perfect image of life indeed. The better part of valour is discretion; in the which better part I have saved my life. 'Zounds, I am afraid of this gunpowder Percy, though he be dead: how, if he should counterfeit too and rise? by my faith, I am afraid he would prove the better counterfeit. Therefore I'll make him sure; yea, and I'll swear I killed him. Why may not he rise as well as I? Nothing confutes me but eyes, and nobody sees me. Therefore, sirrah [*stabbing him*], with a new wound in your thigh, come you along with me.

He takes up Hotspur on his back.

Enter PRINCE [*and*] JOHN OF LANCASTER.

Prince. Come, brother John; full bravely hast thou flesh'd
Thy maiden sword.

Lan. But, soft! whom have we here?
Did you not tell me this fat man was dead?

Prince. I did; I saw him dead,
Breathless and bleeding on the ground. Art thou alive?
Or is it fantasy that plays upon our eyesight?
I prithee, speak; we will not trust our eyes
Without our ears: thou art not what thou seem'st.

Fal. No, that 's certain; I am not a double man: but if I be not Jack Falstaff, then am I a Jack. There is Percy [*throwing the body down*]: if your father will do me any honour, so; if not, let him kill the next Percy himself. I look to be either earl or duke, I can assure you.

Prince. Why, Percy I killed myself and saw thee dead.

Fal. Didst thou? Lord, Lord, how this world is given to lying! I grant you I was down and out of breath; and so was he: but we rose both at an instant and fought a long hour by Shrewsbury clock. If I may be believed, so; if not, let them that should reward valour bear the sin upon their own heads. I'll take it upon my death, I gave him this wound in the thigh: if the man were alive and would deny it, 'zounds, I would make him eat a piece of my sword.

Lan. This is the strangest tale that ever I heard.

Prince. This is the strangest fellow, brother John.
Come, bring your luggage nobly on your back:
For my part, if a lie may do thee grace,
I'll gild it with the happiest terms I have.

A retreat is sounded.

The trumpet sounds retreat; the day is ours.
Come, brother, let us to the highest of the field,
To see what friends are living, who are dead.

Exeunt [*Prince of Wales and Lancaster*].

Fal. I'll follow, as they say, for reward. He that rewards me, God reward him! If I do grow great, I'll grow less; for I'll purge, and leave sack, and live cleanly as a nobleman should do. *Exit* [*with body*].

[SCENE V. *Another part of the field.*]

The trumpets sound. Enter the KING, PRINCE OF WALES, LORD JOHN OF LANCASTER, EARL OF WESTMORELAND, *with* WORCESTER *and* VERNON *prisoners.*

King. Thus ever did rebellion find rebuke.
Ill-spirited Worcester! did not we send grace,
Pardon and terms of love to all of you?
And wouldst thou turn our offers contrary?
Misuse the tenour of thy kinsman's trust?
Three knights upon our party slain to-day,
A noble earl and many a creature else
Had been alive this hour,
If like a Christian thou hadst truly borne
Betwixt our armies true intelligence.

Wor. What I have done my safety urg'd me to;
And I embrace this fortune patiently,
Since not to be avoided it falls on me.

King. Bear Worcester to the death and Vernon too:
Other offenders we will pause upon.

[*Exeunt Worcester and Vernon, guarded.*]

How goes the field?

Prince. The noble Scot, Lord Douglas, when he saw
The fortune of the day quite turn'd from him,
The noble Percy slain, and all his men
Upon the foot of fear, fled with the rest;
And falling from a hill, he was so bruis'd
That the pursuers took him. At my tent
The Douglas is; and I beseech your grace
I may dispose of him.

King. With all my heart.

Prince. Then, brother John of Lancaster, to you
This honourable bounty shall belong:
Go to the Douglas, and deliver him
Up to his pleasure, ransomless and free:
His valours shown upon our crests to-day
Have taught us how to cherish such high deeds
Even in the bosom of our adversaries.

Lan. I thank your grace for this high courtesy,
Which I shall give away immediately.

King. Then this remains, that we divide our power.
You, son John, and my cousin Westmoreland
Towards York shall bend you with your dearest speed,
To meet Northumberland and the prelate Scroop,
Who, as we hear, are busily in arms:
Myself and you, son Harry, will towards Wales,
To fight with Glendower and the Earl of March.
Rebellion in this land shall lose his sway,
Meeting the check of such another day:
And since this business so fair is done,
Let us not leave till all our own be won. *Exeunt.*

109. **Embowell'd,** disemboweled, i.e., for burial. 112. **powder,** salt. 114. **termagant,** violent; derived from the name of a heathen god of the Saracens in the miracle play of St. Nicholas. 115. **scot and lot,** used figuratively to denote complete payment. "Scot" and "lot" were parish taxes. 132. *Stage Direction:* ***He takes up,*** etc. Bodies of slain persons had to be removed from the stage in the Elizabethan theatre. This is a famous example of Shakespeare's skill in having the duty performed naturally. 138. **fantasy,** hallucination. 141. **double man,** spectre; also, two men. 143. **Jack,** knave.

SCENE V. 20. **Upon the foot of fear,** in flight.

TWELFTH NIGHT; OR, WHAT YOU WILL

Twelfth Night is possibly the latest in the festive group of comedies, including *Much Ado about Nothing* and *As You Like It*, with which Shakespeare climaxed his distinctively philosophical and joyous vein of comic writing. Performed on February 2, 1602, at the Middle Temple and written possibly as early as 1599, *Twelfth Night* is usually dated 1600 or 1601. This play is indeed the most festive of the lot. Its keynote is Saturnalian release and the innocently carnival pursuit of youth, love, and mirth. Along with such familiar motifs (found, for example, in *As You Like It* and *The Merchant of Venice*) as the plucky heroine disguised as a man, *Twelfth Night* also returns to the more hilariously farcical routines of mistaken identity found in Shakespeare's early comedy. As a witness of the 1602 performance, John Manningham,

THE TATE GALLERY, LONDON

This detail from a painting by Maclise shows Malvolio, Olivia's haughty steward, in yellow stockings "cross-gartered."

observes, the play is "much like the Commedy of Errores, or Menechmi in Plautus, but most like and neere to that in Italian called *Inganni*." Manningham might have added Shakespeare's *Two Gentlemen of Verona* as another early instance, since it too employs the device of the heroine Julia disguised in the service of her unresponsive lover Proteus.

The carnival atmosphere is appropriate to the season designated in the play's title: the twelfth night of Christmas, January 6, the Feast of Epiphany. (The prologue to *Gl'Ingannati*, perhaps the Italian play referred to by Manningham, speaks of "La Notte di Beffania," Epiphany night.) Although Epiphany has of course a primary Christian significance as the Feast of the Magi, it was also in Renaissance times the last day of the Christmas revels. Over a twelve-day period, from Christmas until January 6, noble households sponsored numerous performances of plays, masks, banquets, and every kind of festivity. (Leslie Hotson argues, in fact, that *Twelfth Night* was first performed on twelfth night in early 1601, in the presence of Queen Elizabeth.) Students left schools for vacations, celebrating release from study with plays and revels of their own. The stern rigors of a rule-bound society gave way temporarily to playful inversions of authority. The reign of the Boy Bishop and the Feast of Fools, for example, gave choristers and minor church functionaries the cherished opportunity to boss the hierarchy around, mock the liturgy with outrageous lampooning, and generally let off steam. Although such customs occasionally got out of hand, the idea was to channel potentially destructive insubordination into playacting and thereby promote harmony. Behind these Elizabethan midwinter customs lies the Roman Saturnalia, with its pagan spirit of gift-giving, sensual indulgence, and satirical hostility to those who would curb merriment.

Shakespeare's choice of sources for *Twelfth Night* underscores his commitment to mirth. Renaissance literature offered numerous instances of mistaken identity among twins, and of the disguised heroine serving as page to her beloved. Among those in English were the anonymous play *Sir Clyomon and Sir Clamydes* (c. 1570–1583), Sidney's *Arcadia* (1590), and the prose romance *Parismus* by Emanuel Forde (1598), featuring both a shipwreck and two characters with the names of Olivia and Violetta. Of particular significance, but largely for negative reasons, is Barnabe Riche's tale of "Apolonius and Silla" in *Riche his Farewell to Militarie profession*, 1581, based on Belleforest's 1571 French version of Bandello's *Novelle*, 1554. Here we find most of the requisite plot elements: the shipwreck, Silla's disguise as a page in Duke Apolonius' court, her office as ambassador of love from Apolonius to the Lady Julina who thereupon falls in love with Silla, the arrival of Silla's twin brother Silvio and his consequent success in winning Julina's affection. To Riche, however, this tale is merely a long testimonial to the enervating power of infatuation. Silvio gets Julina with child and disappears forthwith, making his belated reappearance almost too late to save the wrongly accused Silla (who is, of course, sexually incapable of fatherhood). Riche's moralizing, in the cautionary vein of Geoffrey Fenton's 1567 translation of Belleforest, puts the blame on the gross and drunken appetite of carnal love. The total mismatching of affection with which the story begins, and the sudden realignments of desire based on mere outward resemblances, are seen as proofs of love's unreasonableness. Shakespeare of course retains and capitalizes on the irrational quality of love, as in *A Midsummer Night's Dream*, but in doing so he minimizes the harm done (Olivia is not made pregnant) and repudiates any negative moral judgments. The added subplot, with its rebuking of Malvolio's censoriousness, may have been conceived as a further answer to Riche, Fenton, and their sober school.

Shakespeare's festive spirit owes much, as Manningham observed, to Plautus and the neoclassical Italian comic writers. At least three Italian comedies called *Gl'Inganni* ("The Frauds") employ the motif of mistaken identity, and one of them, by Curzio Gonzaga, 1592, supplies Viola's assumed name of "Cesare" or Cesario. Another play with the same title appeared in 1562. More useful is *Gl'Ingannati* ("The Deceived"), acted 1531, translated into French in 1543. Besides a plot line generally similar to *Twelfth Night*, and the reference to La Notte di Beffania (Epiphany), this play offers the suggestive name *Malevolti*, evil-faced, and *Fabio* (resembling "Fabian"). It also contains possible hints for Malvolio, Toby, and company, although the plot of the counterfeit letter is original with Shakespeare. Essentially, Shakespeare superimposes his own subplot on an Italianate novelle plot, as he did in *The Taming of the Shrew* and *Much Ado*. And it is in the Malvolio story that Shakespeare most pointedly defends merriment. Feste the professional fool, an original stage type for Shakespeare in *Twelfth Night* and in *As You Like It*, also reinforces the theme of seizing the moment of mirth.

This great lesson, of savoring life's pleasures while one is still young, is something that Duke Orsino and the Countess Olivia have not yet learned when the play commences. Although suited to one another in rank, wealth, and attractiveness, they are unable to overcome their own willful posturing in the elaborate charade of courtship. Like Silvius in *As You Like It*, Orsino is the conventional Petrarchan wooer trapped in the courtly artifice of love's rules. He opens the play on a cloying note of self-pity. He is fascinated with his own degradation as a rejected suitor, and bores his listeners with his changeable moods and fondness for poetical "conceits." He sees himself as a hart pursued by his desires "like fell and cruel hounds," reminding us that enervating lovesickness has in fact robbed him of his manly occupation, hunting. He sends ornately contrived messages to Olivia but has not seen her in so long that his passion has become unreal and fantastical, feeding on itself.

Olivia plays the predictably opposite role of chaste,

denying womanhood. She explains her retirement from the world as mourning for a dead brother, but this brother (whose name we never learn) is another unreal vision. Olivia's practice of mourning, whereby she will "water once a day her chamber round With eye-offending brine" (I,i), is ritually lifeless. As others view the matter, she is senselessly wasting her beauty and affection on the dead. "What a plague means my niece, to take the death of her brother thus?" Sir Toby expostulates (I,iii). Viola, though she too has seemingly lost a brother, is an important foil in this regard, for she continues to hope for her brother's safety, trusts his soul is in heaven if he is dead, and refuses to give up her commitment to life in any case. We suspect that Olivia takes a willful pleasure in self-denial not unlike Orsino's self-congratulatory suffering. She appears to derive satisfaction from the power she holds over Orsino, a power of refusal. And she must know that she looks stunning in black.

Olivia's household reflects in part her mood of self-denial. She keeps Malvolio as steward because he too dresses somberly, insists on quiet as befits a house in mourning, and maintains order. Yet Olivia also retains the fool, Feste, who is Malvolio's opposite in every way. Hard-pressed to defend his mirthful function in a household so given over to melancholy, Feste must find some way of persuading his mistress that her very gravity is itself the essence of folly. This is a paradox, because sobriety and order appeal to the conventional wisdom of the world. Malvolio, sensing that his devotion to propriety is being challenged by the fool's prating, chides Olivia for taking "delight in such a barren rascal" (I,v).

Feste must argue for an inversion of appearance and reality whereby many of the world's ordinary pursuits can be seen to be ridiculous. As he observes, in his habitually elliptical manner of speech, "*cucullus non facit monachum* [the cowl doesn't make the monk]; that's as much to say as I wear not motley in my brain." Feste wins his case by making Olivia laugh at her own illogic in grieving for a brother whose soul she assumes to be in heaven. By extension, Olivia has indeed been a fool for allowing herself to be deprived of happiness in love by her brother's death ("there is no true cuckold but calamity"), and for failing to consider the brevity of youth ("beauty's a flower"). Yet paradoxically only one who professes to be a fool can point this out, enabled by his detachment and innocence to perceive simple but profound truths denied to supposedly rational persons. This vision of the fool as naturally wise, and of society as self-indulgently insane, fascinated Renaissance writers, as in Erasmus' *In Praise of Folly* to Cervantes' *Don Quixote* to Shakespeare's *King Lear*.

Viola, although not dressed in motley, aligns herself with Feste's rejection of self-denial. Refreshingly, even comically, she challenges the staid artifice of Orsino's and Olivia's lives. She is an ocean traveler, like many of Shakespeare's later heroines (Marina in *Pericles*, Perdita in *The Winter's Tale*), arriving on Illyria's shore plucky and determined. On her first embassy to Olivia from Orsino, she exposes with disarming candor the willfully ritualistic quality of Olivia's existence. Viola discards the flowery set speech she had prepared and memorized at Orsino's behest; despite her charmingly conceited assertion that the speech has been "excellently well penned," she senses that its elegant but empty rhetoric is all too familiar to the disdainful Olivia. Instead, Viola departs from her text to urge seizing the moment of happiness. "You do usurp yourself," she lectures Olivia, "for what is yours to bestow is not yours to reserve" (I,v). Beauty is a gift of nature, and failure to use it is a sin against nature. Or, again, "Lady, you are the cruell'st she alive If you will lead these graces [Olivia's beauty] to the grave And leave the world no copy." An essential argument in favor of love, as in Shakespeare's sonnets, is the necessity of marriage and childbearing in order to perpetuate beauty. Needless to say this line is new to Olivia, and sweeps her off her feet. In part she reacts, like Phebe in *As You Like It*, with perversely feminine logic, rejecting a too-willing wooer for one who is hard to get. Yet Olivia is also attracted by a new note of sincerity, prompting her to reenter life and accept maturely both the risks and rewards of romantic involvement. Her longing for "Cesario" is of course sexually misdirected, but the appearance of Viola's identical twin Sebastian soon puts all to rights.

The motifs of Olivia's attraction for another woman (both are really boy actors), and of Orsino's deep fondness for "Cesario" that matures into sexual love, evoke delicately homosexual titillations as in *As You Like It*. Once again, however, we must approach the notion circumspectly, remembering that these elements are also found in Shakespeare's sources and reflect a convention wholly different from a modern psychological analysis of sexual aberration. Like Rosalind, Viola uses her male attire to win Orsino's pure affection, in a friendship devoid of sexual interest since both are seemingly men. Viola as Cesario can teach Orsino about the conventions of love, in relaxed and frank conversations that would not be possible if she were known to be a woman. She teaches him to avoid the beguiling but misleading myths of Petrarchan love, and so prepares him for the realities of marriage. Comparing men and women in love, she confides, "We men may say more, swear more: but indeed Our shows are more than will; for still we prove Much in our vows, but little in our love" (II,iv). Once she and Orsino are friends on a properly spiritual basis, Viola's unmasking can make possible a physical communion as well. The friendship of Sebastian and Antonio, sorely tested by the mix-ups of the mistaken identity plot, presents further insight into the debate of love and friendship.

The below-stairs characters of the subplot, Sir Toby and the rest, share with Feste and Viola a commitment to joy. As Sir Toby proclaims in his first speech, "care's an enemy to life" (I,iii). Even the simpleton

Sir Andrew, although gulled by Sir Toby into spending his money on a hopeless pursuit of Olivia, seems none the worse for his treatment; he loves to drink in Sir Toby's company, and can afford to pay for his entertainment. Sir Toby gives us some of the richly inventive humor of Falstaff, another lovable fat roguish knight. In this subplot, however, the confrontations between merriment and sobriety are more harshly drawn than in the main plot. Whereas the gracious Olivia is won away from her folly, the obdurate Malvolio can only be exposed to ridicule. He is chiefly to blame for the polarization of attitudes, for he insists on rebuking the mirth of others. His name, Mal-Volio, the ill-wisher, implies a self-satisfied determination to impose his rigid moral code on others. As Sir Toby taunts him, "Dost thou think, because thou art virtuous, there shall be no more cakes and ale?" (II,iii). Malvolio's inflexible hostility provokes a desire for comic vengeance. The method is satiric: the clever manipulators, Maria and Toby, invent a scheme to entrap Malvolio in his own self-deceit. The punishment fits the crime, for he has long dreamed of himself as Count Malvolio, rich, powerful, in a position to demolish Toby and the rest. Without Malvolio's infatuated predisposition to believe that Olivia could actually love him and write such a letter as he finds, Maria's scheme would have no hope of success. He tortures the text to make it yield a suitable meaning, much in the style of Puritan theologizing.

Indeed, Malvolio does in some ways resemble a Puritan, as Maria observes (II,iii), even though she qualifies the assertion by saying that he is not a religious fanatic but a "time-pleaser." She directs her observation not at a religious group but at all who would be killjoys; if the Puritans are like that, she intimates, so much the worse for them. This uncustomary lack of charity gives a sharp tone to the vengeance practiced on Malvolio, evoking from Olivia a protestation that "he hath been most notoriously abus'd" (V,i). The belated attempt to make a reconciliation with him seems, however, doomed to failure, in light of his grim resolve to "be reveng'd on the whole pack of you." At the height of his discomfiture he has been tricked into doing the one thing he hates most: smiling affably, and wearing sportive attire. The appearance of merriment is so grossly unsuited to him that he is declared mad and put into safekeeping. The apostle of sobriety in this play thus comes before us as a declared madman, while the fool Feste offers him sage comment in the guise of a priest. Wisdom and folly have changed places. The upside-down character of the play is epitomized in Malvolio's plaintive remark to Feste (no longer posing as the priest): "I am as well in my wits, fool, as thou art" (IV,ii). Malvolio's comeuppance is richly deserved, but the severity of vengeance and countervengeance suggests that the triumph of festival will not last long. This brevity is, of course, inherent in the nature of such holiday release from responsibility. As Feste sings, "What's to come is still unsure. In delay there lies no plenty."

TWELFTH NIGHT; OR, WHAT YOU WILL

[*Dramatis Personae*

ORSINO, Duke of Illyria.
SEBASTIAN, *brother to Viola.*
ANTONIO, *a sea captain, friend to Sebastian.*
A Sea Captain, *friend to Viola.*
VALENTINE, CURIO, } *gentlemen attending on the Duke.*
SIR TOBY BELCH, *uncle to Olivia.*
SIR ANDREW AGUECHEEK.
MALVOLIO, *steward to Olivia.*
FABIAN, FESTE, a Clown, } *servants to Olivia.*

OLIVIA.
VIOLA.
MARIA, *Olivia's woman.*

Lords, Priests, Sailors, Officers, Musicians, *and other* Attendants.

SCENE: *A city in Illyria, and the sea-coast near it.*]

ACT I.

SCENE I. [*The* DUKE'S *palace.*]

Enter ORSINO DUKE of Illyria, CURIO, *and other* Lords [*with* Musicians].

Duke. If music be the food of love, play on;
Give me excess of it, that, surfeiting,
The appetite may sicken, and so die.
That strain again! it had a dying fall:
O, it came o'er my ear like the sweet sound,
That breathes upon a bank of violets,
Stealing and giving odour! Enough; no more:
'Tis not so sweet now as it was before.
O spirit of love! how quick and fresh art thou,
That, notwithstanding thy capacity
Receiveth as the sea, nought enters there,
Of what validity and pitch soe'er,
But falls into abatement and low price,
Even in a minute: so full of shapes is fancy
That it alone is high fantastical.
Cur. Will you go hunt, my lord?
Duke. What, Curio?
Cur. The hart.
Duke. Why, so I do, the noblest that I have:
O, when mine eyes did see Olivia first,
Methought she purg'd the air of pestilence!
That instant was I turn'd into a hart;
And my desires, like fell and cruel hounds,
E'er since pursue me.

Enter VALENTINE.

How now! what news from her?
Val. So please my lord, I might not be admitted;
But from her handmaid do return this answer:
The element itself, till seven years' heat,
Shall not behold her face at ample view;
But, like a cloistress, she will veiled walk
And water once a day her chamber round
With eye-offending brine: all this to season
A brother's dead love, which she would keep fresh
And lasting in her sad remembrance.
Duke. O, she that hath a heart of that fine frame
To pay this debt of love but to a brother,
How will she love, when the rich golden shaft
Hath kill'd the flock of all affections else
That live in her; when liver, brain and heart,
These sovereign thrones, are all supplied, and fill'd
Her sweet perfections with one self king!
Away before me to sweet beds of flow'rs:
Love-thoughts lie rich when canopied with bow'rs.
Exeunt.

SCENE II. [*The sea-coast.*]

Enter VIOLA, *a* Captain, *and* Sailors.

Vio. What country, friends, is this?
Cap. This is Illyria, lady.
Vio. And what should I do in Illyria?
My brother he is in Elysium.
Perchance he is not drown'd: what think you, sailors?
Cap. It is perchance that you yourself were sav'd.
Vio. O my poor brother! and so perchance may he be.
Cap. True, madam: and, to comfort you with chance,
Assure yourself, after our ship did split,
When you and those poor number sav'd with you
Hung on our driving boat, I saw your brother,
Most provident in peril, bind himself,
Courage and hope both teaching him the practice,
To a strong mast that liv'd upon the sea;
Where, like Arion on the dolphin's back,
I saw him hold acquaintance with the waves
So long as I could see.
Vio. For saying so, there 's gold:
Mine own escape unfoldeth to my hope,
Whereto thy speech serves for authority,
The like of him. Know'st thou this country?
Cap. Ay, madam, well; for I was bred and born
Not three hours' travel from this very place.
Vio. Who governs here?
Cap. A noble duke, in nature as in name.
Vio. What is his name?
Cap. Orsino.
Vio. Orsino! I have heard my father name him:
He was a bachelor then.
Cap. And so is now, or was so very late;
For but a month ago I went from hence,
And then 'twas fresh in murmur,—as, you know,
What great ones do the less will prattle of,—
That he did seek the love of fair Olivia.
Vio. What 's she?
Cap. A virtuous maid, the daughter of a count
That died some twelvemonth since, then leaving her
In the protection of his son, her brother,
Who shortly also died: for whose dear love,
They say, she hath abjur'd the sight
And company of men.
Vio. O that I serv'd that lady
And might not be delivered to the world,
Till I had made mine own occasion mellow,
What my estate is!
Cap. That were hard to compass;
Because she will admit no kind of suit,
No, not the duke's.
Vio. There is a fair behaviour in thee, captain;
And though that nature with a beauteous wall
Doth oft close in pollution, yet of thee
I will believe thou hast a mind that suits
With this thy fair and outward character.
I prithee, and I'll pay thee bounteously,
Conceal me what I am, and be my aid
For such disguise as haply shall become
The form of my intent. I'll serve this duke:
Thou shalt present me as an eunuch to him:
It may be worth thy pains; for I can sing
And speak to him in many sorts of music
That will allow me very worth his service.
What else may hap to time I will commit;
Only shape thou thy silence to my wit.
Cap. Be you his eunuch, and your mute I'll be:
When my tongue blabs, then let mine eyes not see.
Vio. I thank thee: lead me on. *Exeunt.*

SCENE III. [OLIVIA'S *house.*]

Enter SIR TOBY [BELCH] *and* MARIA.

Sir To. What a plague means my niece, to take the death of her brother thus? I am sure care 's an enemy to life.

Mar. By my troth, Sir Toby, you must come in earlier o' nights: your cousin, my lady, takes great exceptions to your ill hours.

Sir To. Why, let her except, before excepted.

TITLE. **Twelfth Night,** the feast of the Epiphany, or the visit of the Magi. It occurred on the twelfth night after Christmas. The association of this name with "What You Will" lends some plausibility to the suggestion that the title came from the Prologue to *Gl' Ingannati*, an Italian comedy on a similar theme, which states that the story came from the brains of its authors "just as you draw your lots on Twelfth Night."

ACT I. SCENE I. 1. **food of love.** See *Antony and Cleopatra*, II, v, 1-2. 4. **fall,** cadence. 12. **validity,** value. **pitch,** superiority (literally, the highest point of a falcon's flight). 14. **fancy,** love. 18. **noblest . . . have,** i.e., his noblest part, his heart. 22. **fell,** fierce. 23. **pursue me,** reference to the story in Ovid of Actaeon, who was transformed into a hart and killed by his own hounds. 30. **season,** keep fresh. 35. **golden shaft,** i.e., of Cupid. 37. **liver, brain and heart.** In medieval and Elizabethan psychology these organs were the seats of the passions. 39. **self,** single.

SCENE II. 2. **Illyria,** a country along the eastern shore of the Adriatic. 4. **Elysium,** abode of the blessed dead. 8. **chance,** i.e., what chance may bring about. 11. **driving,** drifting. 14. **liv'd,** kept afloat. 15. **Arion,** a Greek poet who, leaping into the sea to escape murderous sailors, so charmed the dolphins with his lyre that they saved him. This was a favorite subject for pageants and paintings. 19. **unfoldeth . . . hope,** i.e., reinforces my hope for my brother. 21. **like of him,** i.e., he, too, may be saved. 32. **murmur,** gossip. 42. **delivered,** discovered, made known. 43. **mellow,** ready or convenient (to be made known). 47. **behaviour.** The word means "appearance" as well as "behavior." 51. **character,** face or features as indicating moral qualities; see glossary. 55. **form of my intent,** nature of my purpose, with suggestion of outward appearance in *form*. 59. **allow me,** cause me to be acknowledged. 61. **wit,** plan, invention.

SCENE III. 7. **except, before excepted,** legal phrase, *exceptis excipiendis*, "with the exceptions before named." Sir Toby means that enough exceptions to his behavior have already been taken.

Mar. Ay, but you must confine yourself within the modest limits of order.

Sir To. Confine! I'll confine myself no finer than I am: these clothes are good enough to drink in; and so be these boots too: an they be not, let them hang themselves in their own straps.

Mar. That quaffing and drinking will undo you: I heard my lady talk of it yesterday; and of a foolish knight that you brought in one night here to be her wooer.

Sir To. Who, Sir Andrew Aguecheek?

Mar. Ay, he.

Sir To. He 's as tall a man as any 's in Illyria.

Mar. What 's that to the purpose?

Sir To. Why, he has three thousand ducats a year.

Mar. Ay, but he'll have but a year in all these ducats: he 's a very fool and a prodigal.

Sir To. Fie, that you'll say so! he plays o' the viol-de-gamboys, and speaks three or four languages word for word without book, and hath all the good gifts of nature.

Mar. He hath indeed, almost natural: for besides that he 's a fool, he 's a great quarreller; and but that he hath the gift of a coward to allay the gust he hath in quarrelling, 'tis thought among the prudent he would quickly have the gift of a grave.

Sir To. By this hand, they are scoundrels and substractors that say so of him. Who are they?

Mar. They that add, moreover, he 's drunk nightly in your company.

Sir To. With drinking healths to my niece: I'll drink to her as long as there is a passage in my throat and drink in Illyria: he 's a coward and a coystrill that will not drink to my niece till his brains turn o' the toe like a parish-top. What, wench! Castiliano vulgo! for here comes Sir Andrew Agueface.

Enter SIR ANDREW [AGUECHEEK].

Sir And. Sir Toby Belch! how now, Sir Toby Belch!

Sir To. Sweet Sir Andrew!

Sir And. Bless you, fair shrew.

Mar. And you too, sir.

Sir To. Accost, Sir Andrew, accost.

Sir And. What 's that?

Sir To. My niece's chambermaid.

Sir And. Good Mistress Accost, I desire better acquaintance.

Mar. My name is Mary, sir.

Sir And. Good Mistress Mary Accost,—

Sir To. You mistake, knight: 'accost' is front her, board her, woo her, assail her.

Sir And. By my troth, I would not undertake her in this company. Is that the meaning of 'accost'?

Mar. Fare you well, gentlemen.

Sir To. An thou let part so, Sir Andrew, would thou mightst never draw sword again.

Sir And. An you part so, mistress, I would I might never draw sword again. Fair lady, do you think you have fools in hand?

Mar. Sir, I have not you by the hand.

Sir And. Marry, but you shall have; and here 's my hand.

Mar. Now, sir, 'thought is free:' I pray you, bring your hand to the buttery-bar and let it drink.

Sir And. Wherefore, sweet-heart? what 's your metaphor?

Mar. It 's dry, sir.

Sir And. Why, I think so: I am not such an ass but I can keep my hand dry. But what 's your jest?

Mar. A dry jest, sir.

Sir And. Are you full of them?

Mar. Ay, sir, I have them at my fingers' ends: marry, now I let go your hand, I am barren. *Exit Mar.*

Sir To. O knight, thou lackest a cup of canary: when did I see thee so put down?

Sir And. Never in your life, I think; unless you see canary put me down. Methinks sometimes I have no more wit than a Christian or an ordinary man has: but I am a great eater of beef and I believe that does harm to my wit.

Sir To. No question.

Sir And. An I thought that, I 'ld forswear it. I'll ride home to-morrow, Sir Toby.

Sir To. Pourquoi, my dear knight?

Sir And. What is 'pourquoi'? do or not do? I would I had bestowed that time in the tongues that I have in fencing, dancing and bear-baiting: O, had I but followed the arts!

Sir To. Then hadst thou had an excellent head of hair.

Sir And. Why, would that have mended my hair?

Sir To. Past question; for thou seest it will not curl by nature.

Sir And. But it becomes me well enough, does 't not?

Sir To. Excellent; it hangs like flax on a distaff; and I hope to see a housewife take thee between her legs and spin it off.

Sir And. Faith, I'll home to-morrow, Sir Toby: your niece will not be seen; or if she be, it 's four to one she'll none of me: the count himself here hard by woos her.

Sir To. She'll none o' the count: she'll not match above her degree, neither in estate, years, nor wit; I have heard her swear 't. Tut, there 's life in 't, man.

Sir And. I'll stay a month longer. I am a fellow o' the strangest mind i' the world; I delight in masques and revels sometimes altogether.

Sir To. Art thou good at these kickshawses, knight?

Sir And. As any man in Illyria, whatsoever he be, under the degree of my betters; and yet I will not compare with an old man.

Sir To. What is thy excellence in a galliard, knight?

10. **confine myself,** dress myself. 27. **viol-de-gamboys,** bass viol. 28. **without book,** by heart. Sir Andrew's complete ignorance of languages and lack of all accomplishments is one of the sources of Sir Toby's fun at his expense. 30. **natural,** with pun on the sense "born idiot." 33. **allay the gust,** moderate the taste. 37. **substractors,** for "detractors." 43. **coystrill,** horse-groom, base fellow. 45. **parish-top,** a large top provided by the parish to be spun by whipping, apparently for exercise in cold weather. **Castiliano vulgo,** literally, vulgar Spaniard; possibly a slang phrase, or nonsense. 52. **Accost,** make up to. 54. **chambermaid,** lady's maid. 73. **'thought is free,'** reply to *do you think*, above. 74-75. **bring . . . drink,** said to be a proverbial phrase meaning to ask at once for a kiss and a present (Kenrick, quoted by Luce). The buttery-bar was the hatch or half door of the ale-cellar (buttery) where drinks were served. 77. **dry,** i.e., a sign of age and debility. 81. **dry,** dull. 83. **fingers' ends.** Sir Andrew is holding her by the hand. 86. **canary,** sack, a wine from the Canary Islands. 90. **beef,** traditional cause of dull wits. The English were frequently twitted on account of the coarseness and quantity of their food and the dullness of their wit. 95. **Pourquoi,** why. 98. **tongues,** languages and "tongs" (used for curling hair). 99. **arts.** Cf. *nature*, below. 122. **kickshawses,** corruption of the French words *quelque chose;* delicacies, fancy dishes. 126. **old man,** a puzzling reference. Furness suggests that Sir Andrew wishes to express deference to age. 128. **galliard,** lively dance in triple time. 129. **cut a caper.** Sir Andrew uses the phrase in the ordinary sense. Sir

Sir And. Faith, I can cut a caper.

Sir To. And I can cut the mutton to 't.

Sir And. And I think I have the back-trick simply as strong as any man in Illyria.

Sir To. Wherefore are these things hid? wherefore have these gifts a curtain before 'em? are they like to take dust, like Mistress Mall's picture? why dost thou not go to church in a galliard and come home in a coranto? My very walk should be a jig; I would not so much as make water but in a sink-a-pace. What dost thou mean? Is it a world to hide virtues in? I did think, by the excellent constitution of thy leg, it was formed under the star of a galliard.

Sir And. Ay, 'tis strong, and it does indifferent well in a flame-coloured stock. Shall we set about some revels?

Sir To. What shall we do else? were we not born under Taurus?

Sir And. Taurus! That 's sides and heart.

Sir To. No, sir; it is legs and thighs. Let me see thee caper: ha! higher: ha, ha! excellent! *Exeunt.*

SCENE IV. [*The* DUKE'S *palace.*]

Enter VALENTINE, *and* VIOLA *in man's attire.*

Val. If the duke continue these favours towards you, Cesario, you are like to be much advanced: he hath known you but three days, and already you are no stranger.

Vio. You either fear his humour or my negligence, that you call in question the continuance of his love: is he inconstant, sir, in his favours?

Val. No, believe me.

Enter DUKE, CURIO, *and* Attendants.

Vio. I thank you. Here comes the count.
Duke. Who saw Cesario, ho?
Vio. On your attendance, my lord; here.
Duke. Stand you a while aloof. Cesario,
Thou know'st no less but all; I have unclasp'd
To thee the book even of my secret soul:
Therefore, good youth, address thy gait unto her;
Be not denied access, stand at her doors,
And tell them, there thy fixed foot shall grow
Till thou have audience.
Vio. Sure, my noble lord,
If she be so abandon'd to her sorrow
As it is spoke, she never will admit me.
Duke. Be clamorous and leap all civil bounds
Rather than make unprofited return.
Vio. Say I do speak with her, my lord, what then?
Duke. O, then unfold the passion of my love,
Surprise her with discourse of my dear faith:
It shall become thee well to act my woes;
She will attend it better in thy youth
Than in a nuncio's of more grave aspect.
Vio. I think not so, my lord.
Duke. Dear lad, believe it;
For they shall yet belie thy happy years,
That say thou art a man: Diana's lip
Is not more smooth and rubious; thy small pipe
Is as the maiden's organ, shrill and sound,
And all is semblative a woman's part.
I know thy constellation is right apt
For this affair. Some four or five attend him;
All, if you will; for I myself am best
When least in company. Prosper well in this,
And thou shalt live as freely as thy lord,
To call his fortunes thine.
Vio. I'll do my best
To woo your lady: [*Aside*] yet, a barful strife!
Whoe'er I woo, myself would be his wife. *Exeunt.*

SCENE V. [OLIVIA'S *house.*]

Enter MARIA *and* CLOWN.

Mar. Nay, either tell me where thou hast been, or I will not open my lips so wide as a bristle may enter in way of thy excuse: my lady will hang thee for thy absence.

Clo. Let her hang me: he that is well hanged in this world needs to fear no colours.

Mar. Make that good.

Clo. He shall see none to fear.

Mar. A good lenten answer: I can tell thee where that saying was born, of 'I fear no colours.'

Clo. Where, good Mistress Mary?

Mar. In the wars; and that may you be bold to say in your foolery.

Clo. Well, God give them wisdom that have it; and those that are fools, let them use their talents.

Mar. Yet you will be hanged for being so long absent; or to be turned away, is not that as good as a hanging to you?

Clo. Many a good hanging prevents a bad marriage; and, for turning away, let summer bear it out.

Mar. You are resolute, then?

Clo. Not so, neither; but I am resolved on two points.

Mar. That if one break, the other will hold; or, if both break, your gaskins fall.

Clo. Apt, in good faith; very apt. Well, go thy way; if Sir Toby would leave drinking, thou wert as witty a piece of Eve's flesh as any in Illyria.

Mar. Peace, you rogue, no more o' that. Here comes my lady: make your excuse wisely, you were best. [*Exit.*]

Enter Lady OLIVIA *with* MALVOLIO.

Toby makes a pun referring to *caper* sauce. 131. **back-trick,** some figure in the galliard; apparently, dancing backward. 135. **Mistress Mall's picture.** It has been suggested (1) that this refers to Moll Cutpurse or some other notorious female criminal; (2) that it is Maria's picture; (3) that it is a picture of no particular person. 138. **coranto,** lively dance. 140. **sink-a-pace,** French, *cinque-pace*, a dance. 143. **under the star,** i.e., a dancing star. Men's destinies and characters were thought to be influenced by the stars. 145. **flame-coloured,** so Rowe; F: *dam'd colour'd;* Collier: *dun-coloured.* **stock,** stocking. 147, 148. **Taurus,** zodiacal sign. Sir Andrew is mistaken, since Leo governed *sides and hearts* in medical astrology.

SCENE IV. 12. **you,** addressed to the attendants. 15. **address thy gait,** go. 21. **civil bounds,** bounds of civility. 28. **nuncio's,** messenger's. 30. **yet,** i.e., for a long time to come. 32. **rubious,** ruby red. **pipe,** voice. 33. **sound,** clear. 34. **semblative,** resembling, like. 41. **barful,** full of impediments.

SCENE V. *Stage Direction:* **Clown,** the technical word for those who played comic parts in the theatre. *Fool* is more commonly used in the text to denote the jester or domestic fool. 6. **fear no colours,** fear no enemies, with pun on "colors" and "collars" (halters). 9. **lenten,** meager, scanty (like lenten fare). 27. **gaskins,** hose, breeches, held up by laces or *points;* hence Maria's quibble. 29. **Sir Toby.** The Clown hints at a match between Maria and Sir Toby.

Clo. Wit, an 't be thy will, put me into good fooling! Those wits, that think they have thee, do very oft prove fools; and I, that am sure I lack thee, may pass for a wise man: for what says Quinapalus? 'Better a witty fool than a foolish wit.'—God bless thee, lady!

Oli. Take the fool away.

Clo. Do you not hear, fellows? Take away the lady.

Oli. Go to, y' are a dry fool; I'll no more of you: besides, you grow dishonest.

Clo. Two faults, madonna, that drink and good counsel will amend: for give the dry fool drink, then is the fool not dry: bid the dishonest man mend himself; if he mend, he is no longer dishonest; if he cannot let the botcher mend him. Any thing that 's mended is but patched: virtue that transgresses is but patched with sin; and sin that amends is but patched with virtue. If that this simple syllogism will serve, so; if it will not, what remedy? As there is no true cuckold but calamity, so beauty 's a flower. The lady bade take away the fool; therefore, I say again, take her away.

Oli. Sir, I bade them take away you.

Clo. Misprision in the highest degree! Lady, cucullus non facit monachum; that 's as much to say as I wear not motley in my brain. Good madonna, give me leave to prove you a fool.

Oli. Can you do it?

Clo. Dexteriously, good madonna.

Oli. Make your proof.

Clo. I must catechize you for it, madonna: good my mouse of virtue, answer me.

Oli. Well, sir, for want of other idleness, I'll bide your proof.

Clo. Good madonna, why mournest thou?

Oli. Good fool, for my brother's death.

Clo. I think his soul is in hell, madonna.

Oli. I know his soul is in heaven, fool.

Clo. The more fool, madonna, to mourn for your brother's soul being in heaven. Take away the fool, gentlemen.

Oli. What think you of this fool, Malvolio? doth he not mend?

Mal. Yes, and shall do till the pangs of death shake him: infirmity, that decays the wise, doth ever make the better fool.

Clo. God send you, sir, a speedy infirmity, for the better increasing your folly! Sir Toby will be sworn that I am no fox; but he will not pass his word for two pence that you are no fool.

Oli. How say you to that, Malvolio?

Mal. I marvel your ladyship takes delight in such a barren rascal: I saw him put down the other day with an ordinary fool that has no more brain than a stone. Look you now, he 's out of his guard already; unless you laugh and minister occasion to him, he is gagged. I protest, I take these wise men, that crow so at these set kind of fools, no better than the fools' zanies.

Oli. O, you are sick of self-love, Malvolio, and taste with a distempered appetite. To be generous, guiltless and of free disposition, is to take those things for bird-bolts that you deem cannon-bullets: there is no slander in an allowed fool, though he do nothing but rail; nor no railing in a known discreet man, though he do nothing but reprove.

Clo. Now Mercury endue thee with leasing, for thou speakest well of fools!

Enter MARIA.

Mar. Madam, there is at the gate a young gentleman much desires to speak with you.

Oli. From the Count Orsino, is it?

Mar. I know not, madam: 'tis a fair young man, and well attended.

Oli. Who of my people hold him in delay?

Mar. Sir Toby, madam, your kinsman.

Oli. Fetch him off, I pray you; he speaks nothing but madman: fie on him! [*Exit Maria.*] Go you, Malvolio: if it be a suit from the count, I am sick, or not at home; what you will, to dismiss it. *(Exit Malvolio.)* Now you see, sir, how your fooling grows old, and people dislike it.

Clo. Thou hast spoke for us, madonna, as if thy eldest son should be a fool; whose skull Jove cram with brains! for,—here he comes,—one of thy kin has a most weak pia mater.

Enter SIR TOBY.

Oli. By mine honour, half drunk. What is he at the gate, cousin?

Sir To. A gentleman.

Oli. A gentleman! what gentleman?

Sir To. 'Tis a gentleman here—a plague o' these pickle-herring! How now, sot!

Clo. Good Sir Toby.

Oli. Cousin, cousin, how have you come so early by this lethargy?

Sir To. Lechery! I defy lechery. There 's one at the gate.

Oli. Ay, marry, what is he?

Sir To. Let him be the devil, an he will, I care not: give me faith, say I. Well, it 's all one. *Exit.*

Oli. What 's a drunken man like, fool?

Clo. Like a drowned man, a fool and a mad man: one draught above heat makes him a fool; the second mads him; and a third drowns him.

Oli. Go thou and seek the crowner, and let him sit o' my coz; for he 's in the third degree of drink, he 's drowned: go, look after him.

Clo. He is but mad yet, madonna; and the fool shall look to the madman. [*Exit.*]

Enter MALVOLIO.

Mal. Madam, yond young fellow swears he will speak with you. I told him you were sick; he takes on him to understand so much, and therefore comes to

39. **Quinapalus,** apparently an invented authority. 45. **dry,** dull. 46. **dishonest,** unreliable. 52. **botcher,** mender of old clothes and shoes. 56-57. **As . . . flower,** i.e., since Fortune, to which every man is wedded, is notoriously unfaithful, our best course is to seize the moment of youth and beauty before we lose it. 61. **Misprision,** mistake, misunderstanding, with suggestion of the legal use meaning "contempt," the arrest or imprisonment of the wrong person. 62. **cucullus . . . monachum,** the cowl does not make the monk. 63. **motley,** the many-colored garment of jesters. 69. **mouse of virtue,** term of endearment. 70. **idleness,** pastime. 91. **ordinary fool,** probably a fool from the street not regularly attached to a household. 92-93. **out of his guard,** defenseless. 93-94. **minister occasion,** provide opportunity (for his fooling). 96. **zanies,** fools' subordinates or imitators. 100. **bird-bolts,** blunt arrows for shooting small birds. 102. **allowed,** licensed. 105. **Mercury,** god of guile and trickery. **leasing,** lying. 115. **madman,** i.e., the words of madness. 119. **old,** stale. 123. **pia mater,** soft inner lining of the brain. 128. **here.** Sir Toby hiccoughs at this point and tries to conceal his condition. 137. **give me faith,** i.e., to resist the devil. 140. **above heat,** above the point needed to make him normally warm. 142. **crowner,** coroner. 157.

speak with you. I told him you were asleep; he seems to have a foreknowledge of that too, and therefore comes to speak with you. What is to be said to him, lady? he 's fortified against any denial.

Oli. Tell him he shall not speak with me.

Mal. Has been told so; and he says, he'll stand at your door like a sheriff's post, and be the supporter to a bench, but he'll speak with you.

Oli. What kind o' man is he?

Mal. Why, of mankind.

Oli. What manner of man?

Mal. Of very ill manner; he'll speak with you, will you or no.

Oli. Of what personage and years is he?

Mal. Not yet old enough for a man, nor young enough for a boy; as a squash is before 'tis a peascod, or a codling when 'tis almost an apple: 'tis with him in standing water, between boy and man. He is very well-favoured and he speaks very shrewishly; one would think his mother's milk were scarce out of him.

Oli. Let him approach: call in my gentlewoman.

Mal. Gentlewoman, my lady calls. *Exit.*

Enter MARIA.

Oli. Give me my veil: come, throw it o'er my face.
We'll once more hear Orsino's embassy.

Enter VIOLA.

Vio. The honourable lady of the house, which is she?

Oli. Speak to me; I shall answer for her. Your will?

Vio. Most radiant, exquisite and unmatchable beauty,—I pray you, tell me if this be the lady of the house, for I never saw her: I would be loath to cast away my speech, for besides that it is excellently well penned, I have taken great pains to con it. Good beauties, let me sustain no scorn; I am very comptible, even to the least sinister usage.

Oli. Whence came you, sir?

Vio. I can say little more than I have studied, and that question 's out of my part. Good gentle one, give me modest assurance if you be the lady of the house, that I may proceed in my speech.

Oli. Are you a comedian?

Vio. No, my profound heart: and yet, by the very fangs of malice I swear, I am not that I play. Are you the lady of the house?

Oli. If I do not usurp myself, I am.

Vio. Most certain, if you are she, you do usurp yourself; for what is yours to bestow is not yours to reserve. But this is from my commission: I will on with my speech in your praise, and then show you the heart of my message.

Oli. Come to what is important in 't: I forgive you the praise.

Vio. Alas, I took great pains to study it, and 'tis poetical.

Oli. It is the more like to be feigned: I pray you, keep it in. I heard you were saucy at my gates, and allowed your approach rather to wonder at you than to hear you. If you be not mad, be gone; if you have reason, be brief: 'tis not that time of moon with me to make one in so skipping a dialogue.

Mar. Will you hoist sail, sir? here lies your way.

Vio. No, good swabber; I am to hull here a little longer. Some mollification for your giant, sweet lady. Tell me your mind: I am a messenger.

Oli. Sure, you have some hideous matter to deliver, when the courtesy of it is so fearful. Speak your office.

Vio. It alone concerns your ear. I bring no overture of war, no taxation of homage: I hold the olive in my hand; my words are as full of peace as matter.

Oli. Yet you began rudely. What are you? what would you?

Vio. The rudeness that hath appeared in me have I learned from my entertainment. What I am, and what I would, are as secret as maidenhead; to your ears, divinity, to any other's, profanation.

Oli. Give us the place alone; we will hear this divinity. [*Exeunt Maria and Attendants.*]
Now, sir, what is your text?

Vio. Most sweet lady,—

Oli. A comfortable doctrine, and much may be said of it. Where lies your text?

Vio. In Orsino's bosom.

Oli. In his bosom! In what chapter of his bosom?

Vio. To answer by the method, in the first of his heart.

Oli. O, I have read it: it is heresy. Have you no more to say?

Vio. Good madam, let me see your face.

Oli. Have you any commission from your lord to negotiate with my face? You are now out of your text: but we will draw the curtain and show you the picture. Look you, sir, such a one I was this present: is 't not well done? [*Unveiling.*]

Vio. Excellently done, if God did all.

Oli. 'Tis in grain,. sir; 'twill endure wind and weather.

Vio. 'Tis beauty truly blent, whose red and white
Nature's own sweet and cunning hand laid on:
Lady, you are the cruell'st she alive,
If you will lead these graces to the grave
And leave the world no copy.

Oli. O, sir, I will not be so hard-hearted; I will give out divers schedules of my beauty: it shall be inventoried, and every particle and utensil labelled to my will: as, item, two lips, indifferent red; item, two grey eyes, with lids to them; item, one neck, one chin, and so forth. Were you sent hither to praise me?

Vio. I see you what you are, you are too proud;
But, if you were the devil, you are fair.
My lord and master loves you: O, such love
Could be but recompens'd, though you were crown'd
The nonpareil of beauty!

Oli. How does he love me?

Vio. With adorations, fertile tears,

sheriff's post, post before the sheriff's door on which proclamations and notices were fixed. 165-171. **Not yet . . . him.** Nowhere else does Malvolio speak in this vein. 166. **squash,** unripe pea pod. 167. **peascod,** pea pod. **codling,** unripe apple. 170. **shrewishly,** sharply; possibly, like a woman. 181. **Most . . . beauty.** This line is a part of Viola's prepared speech. 186. **con,** learn by heart. 188. **comptible,** susceptible, sensitive. **sinister,** discourteous. 196. **that,** that which. 201. **from,** outside of. 204-205. **forgive you,** excuse you from repeating. 213. **moon,** as affecting lunatics. 214. **skipping,** flighty, frivolous. 217. **swabber,** one who washes the decks; a nautical retort to *hoist sail* (l. 215). 218-219. **Some . . . giant,** pray pacify your giant; alluding ironically to Maria's small size. 222. **courtesy,** ceremonious introduction. 223. **office,** commission. 225. **taxation,** demand for the payment of. 239. **comfortable,** comforting. 244. **method,** i.e., your method, your metaphor. 253. **this present,** just now, presently. Since it was customary to hang curtains in front of pictures, Olivia in unveiling speaks as if she were displaying a picture of herself. 255. **in grain,** fast dyed. 263. **schedules,** inventories. 265. **labelled,** added as a codicil. 274. **fertile,** copious.

With groans that thunder love, with sighs of fire.
Oli. Your lord does know my mind; I cannot love him:
Yet I suppose him virtuous, know him noble,
Of great estate, of fresh and stainless youth;
In voices well divulg'd, free, learn'd and valiant;
And in dimension and the shape of nature
A gracious person: but yet I cannot love him;
He might have took his answer long ago.
Vio. If I did love you in my master's flame,
With such a suff'ring, such a deadly life,
In your denial I would find no sense;
I would not understand it.
Oli. Why, what would you?
Vio. Make me a willow cabin at your gate,
And call upon my soul within the house;
Write loyal cantons of contemned love
And sing them loud even in the dead of night;
Halloo your name to the reverberate hills
And make the babbling gossip of the air
Cry out 'Olivia!' O, you should not rest
Between the elements of air and earth,
But you should pity me!
Oli. You might do much.
What is your parentage?
Vio. Above my fortunes, yet my state is well:
I am a gentleman.
Oli. Get you to your lord;
I cannot love him: let him send no more;
Unless, perchance, you come to me again,
To tell me how he takes it. Fare you well:
I thank you for your pains: spend this for me.
Vio. I am no fee'd post, lady; keep your purse:
My master, not myself, lacks recompense.
Love make his heart of flint that you shall love;
And let your fervour, like my master's, be
Plac'd in contempt! Farewell, fair cruelty. *Exit.*
Oli. 'What is your parentage?'
'Above my fortunes, yet my state is well:
I am a gentleman.' I'll be sworn thou art;
Thy tongue, thy face, thy limbs, actions and spirit,
Do give thee five-fold blazon: not too fast: soft, soft!
Unless the master were the man. How now!
Even so quickly may one catch the plague?
Methinks I feel this youth's perfections
With an invisible and subtle stealth
To creep in at mine eyes. Well, let it be.
What ho, Malvolio!

Enter MALVOLIO.

Mal. Here, madam, at your service.
Oli. Run after that same peevish messenger,
The county's man: he left this ring behind him,
Would I or not: tell him I'll none of it.
Desire him not to flatter with his lord,
Nor hold him up with hopes; I am not for him:
If that the youth will come this way to-morrow,
I'll give him reasons for 't: hie thee, Malvolio.
Mal. Madam, I will. *Exit.*
Oli. I do I know not what, and fear to find
Mine eye too great a flatterer for my mind.
Fate, show thy force: ourselves we do not owe;
What is decreed must be, and be this so. [*Exit.*]

ACT II.

SCENE I. [*The sea-coast.*]

Enter ANTONIO *and* SEBASTIAN.

Ant. Will you stay no longer? nor will you not that I go with you?

Seb. By your patience, no. My stars shine darkly over me: the malignancy of my fate might perhaps distemper yours; therefore I shall crave of you your leave that I may bear my evils alone: it were a bad recompense for your love, to lay any of them on you.

Ant. Let me yet know of you whither you are bound.

Seb. No, sooth, sir: my determinate voyage is mere extravagancy. But I perceive in you so excellent a touch of modesty, that you will not extort from me what I am willing to keep in; therefore it charges me in manners the rather to express myself. You must know of me then, Antonio, my name is Sebastian, which I called Roderigo. My father was that Sebastian of Messaline, whom I know you have heard of. He left behind him myself and a sister, both born in an hour: if the heavens had been pleased, would we had so ended! but you, sir, altered that; for some hour before you took me from the breach of the sea was my sister drowned.

Ant. Alas the day!

Seb. A lady, sir, though it was said she much resembled me, was yet of many accounted beautiful: but, though I could not with such estimable wonder overfar believe that, yet thus far I will boldly publish her; she bore a mind that envy could not but call fair. She is drowned already, sir, with salt water, though I seem to drown her remembrance again with more.

Ant. Pardon me, sir, your bad entertainment.

Seb. O good Antonio, forgive me your trouble.

Ant. If you will not murder me for my love, let me be your servant.

Seb. If you will not undo what you have done, that is, kill him whom you have recovered, desire it not. Fare ye well at once: my bosom is full of kindness, and I am yet so near the manners of my mother, that upon the least occasion more mine eyes will tell tales of me. I am bound to the Count Orsino's court: farewell. *Exit.*

Ant. The gentleness of all the gods go with thee!
I have many enemies in Orsino's court,
Else would I very shortly see thee there.
But, come what may, I do adore thee so,
That danger shall seem sport, and I will go. *Exit.*

---

283. **flame,** passion. 284. **deadly,** death-doomed. 287. **willow cabin,** arbor. Willow is a symbol of unrequited love. 288. **my soul,** i.e., Olivia. 289. **cantons,** songs. **contemned,** rejected. 292. **babbling . . . air,** echo. 303. **fee'd post,** messenger to be tipped. 305. **Love . . . love,** may Love make the heart of the man you love as hard as flint. 310. **thou,** suggestive of tenderness. She has used *your* before (l. 308). 312. **blazon,** heraldic description. 317. **eyes.** Love was thought to enter through the eye.

ACT II. SCENE I. 4. **malignancy,** malevolence (of the stars). 12. **extravagancy,** aimless wandering. 15. **it charges me,** I am bound. 16. **express,** reveal. 19. **Messaline,** possibly, Mytilene or Messina in Sicily. 21. **an,** one. 29. **estimable wonder,** admiring judgment. 34. **entertainment,** reception. 41. **kindness,** tenderness. 42. **manners . . . mother,** womanish qualities.

SCENE II. *Stage Direction: several,* different. 8. **desperate,** without hope. 10. **hardy,** audacious. 13. **She . . . it.** Viola tells a quick and friendly lie to shield Olivia. 21. **lost,** caused her to lose. 29. **pregnant,** quick, resourceful; possibly alluding to Satan. 30. **proper-false,** handsome and deceitful. 31. **set their forms,** stamp their images. 34. **fadge,** turn out. 35. **monster,** i.e., being both man and woman.

SCENE III. 3. **'diluculo surgere'** (*saluberrimum est*), to rise early is most healthful; a sentence from Lilly's *Latin Grammar*. 13. **Th' art**

SCENE II. [*A street.*]

Enter VIOLA *and* MALVOLIO *at several doors.*

Mal. Were not you even now with the Countess Olivia?

Vio. Even now, sir; on a moderate pace I have since arrived but hither.

Mal. She returns this ring to you, sir: you might have saved me my pains, to have taken it away yourself. She adds, moreover, that you should put your lord into a desperate assurance she will none of him: and one thing more, that you be never so hardy to come again in his affairs, unless it be to report your lord's taking of this. Receive it so.

Vio. She took the ring of me: I'll none of it.

Mal. Come, sir, you peevishly threw it to her; and her will is, it should be so returned: if it be worth stooping for, there it lies in your eye; if not, be it his that finds it. *Exit.*

Vio. I left no ring with her: what means this lady?
Fortune forbid my outside have not charm'd her!
She made good view of me; indeed, so much,
That sure methought her eyes had lost her tongue,
For she did speak in starts distractedly.
She loves me, sure; the cunning of her passion
Invites me in this churlish messenger.
None of my lord's ring! why, he sent her none.
I am the man: if it be so, as 'tis,
Poor lady, she were better love a dream.
Disguise, I see, thou art a wickedness,
Wherein the pregnant enemy does much.
How easy is it for the proper-false
In women's waxen hearts to set their forms!
Alas, our frailty is the cause, not we!
For such as we are made of, such we be.
How will this fadge? my master loves her dearly;
And I, poor monster, fond as much on him;
And she, mistaken, seems to dote on me.
What will become of this? As I am man,
My state is desperate for my master's love;
As I am woman,—now alas the day!—
What thriftless sighs shall poor Olivia breathe!
O time! thou must untangle this, not I;
It is too hard a knot for me t' untie! [*Exit.*]

SCENE III. [OLIVIA'S *house.*]

Enter SIR TOBY *and* SIR ANDREW.

Sir To. Approach, Sir Andrew: not to be abed after midnight is to be up betimes; and 'diluculo surgere,' thou know'st,—

Sir And. Nay, by my troth, I know not: but I know, to be up late is to be up late.

Sir To. A false conclusion: I hate it as an unfilled can. To be up after midnight and to go to bed then, is early: so that to go to bed after midnight is to go to bed betimes. Does not our lives consist of the four elements?

Sir And. Faith, so they say; but I think it rather consists of eating and drinking.

Sir To. Th' art a scholar; let us therefore eat and drink. Marian, I say! a stoup of wine!

Enter CLOWN.

Sir And. Here comes the fool, i' faith.

Clo. How now, my hearts! did you never see the picture of 'we three'?

Sir To. Welcome, ass. Now let's have a catch.

Sir And. By my troth, the fool has an excellent breast. I had rather than forty shillings I had such a leg, and so sweet a breath to sing, as the fool has. In sooth, thou wast in very gracious fooling last night, when thou spokest of Pigrogromitus, of the Vapians passing the equinoctial of Queubus: 'twas very good, i' faith. I sent thee sixpence for thy leman: hadst it?

Clo. I did impeticos thy gratillity; for Malvolio's nose is no whipstock: my lady has a white hand, and the Myrmidons are no bottle-ale houses.

Sir And. Excellent! why, this is the best fooling, when all is done. Now, a song.

Sir To. Come on; there is sixpence for you: let's have a song.

Sir And. There's a testril of me too: if one knight give a—

Clo. Would you have a love-song, or a song of good life?

Sir To. A love-song, a love-song.

Sir And. Ay, ay: I care not for good life.

Clo. (Sings)

O mistress mine, where are you roaming?
O, stay and hear; your true love's coming,
That can sing both high and low:
Trip no further, pretty sweeting;
Journeys end in lovers meeting,
Every wise man's son doth know.

Sir And. Excellent good, i' faith.

Sir To. Good, good.

Clo. [*Sings*]

What is love? 'tis not hereafter;
Present mirth hath present laughter;
What's to come is still unsure:
In delay there lies no plenty;
Then come kiss me, sweet and twenty,
Youth's a stuff will not endure.

Sir And. A mellifluous voice, as I am true knight.

Sir To. A contagious breath.

Sir And. Very sweet and contagious, i' faith.

Sir To. To hear by the nose, it is dulcet in contagion. But shall we make the welkin dance indeed? shall we rouse the night-owl in a catch that will draw three souls out of one weaver? shall we do that?

Sir And. An you love me, let's do 't: I am dog at a catch.

Clo. By 'r lady, sir, and some dogs will catch well.

a scholar. Sir Toby is making fun of him. 14. **stoup,** drinking vessel. 17. **picture of 'we three,'** picture of two asses inscribed "we three," the spectator being the third. 18. **catch,** a song so arranged that the second singer takes up the first line just as the first singer is beginning the second line, and so on. 20. **breast,** voice. 21. **leg,** probably, obeisance made by drawing back one leg and bending the other. 24-25. **Pigrogromitus . . . Queubus,** mock erudition. 26. **leman,** sweetheart. 27. **impeticos thy gratillity,** suggests "impetticoat (or pocket up) thy gratuity." 28. **whipstock,** whip handle. 29. **Myrmidons,** followers of Achilles; here, perhaps, taverns of high grade. **bottle-ale,** used contemptuously of taverns because they sold low-class drink. 34. **testril,** a coin worth sixpence. 37. **good life,** respectability. 40. **O mistress mine.** This song is found in several Elizabethan songbooks, but is nevertheless thought by some authorities to be Shakespeare's. 43. **sweeting,** sweet one. 52. **sweet and twenty,** possibly meant originally "twenty times as sweet," *twenty* being used as an intensive; or, kiss me twenty times again. 59. **welkin dance,** drink till the sky seems to turn round (Johnson). 61-62. **draw . . . weaver,** usually explained as a reference to psalm-singing weavers, Protestant refugees from Belgium. There is a reference also to the Renaissance conception of the soul which was held to be threefold, the vegetal, the sensible, and the intellectual soul. 64. **dog at,** clever at.

Sir And. Most certain. Let our catch be, 'Thou knave.'

Clo. 'Hold thy peace, thou knave,' knight? I shall be constrained in 't to call thee knave, knight.

Sir And. 'Tis not the first time I have constrained one to call me knave. Begin, fool: it begins 'Hold thy peace.'

Clo. I shall never begin if I hold my peace.

Sir And. Good, i' faith. Come, begin. *Catch sung.*

Enter MARIA.

Mar. What a caterwauling do you keep here! If my lady have not called up her steward Malvolio and bid him turn you out of doors, never trust me.

Sir To. My lady 's a Cataian, we are politicians, Malvolio 's a Peg-a-Ramsey, and 'Three merry men be we.' Am not I consanguineous? am I not of her blood? Tillyvally. Lady! [*Sings*] 'There dwelt a man in Babylon, lady, lady!'

Clo. Beshrew me, the knight 's in admirable fooling.

Sir And. Ay, he does well enough if he be disposed, and so do I too: he does it with a better grace, but I do it more natural.

Sir To. [*Sings*] 'O, the twelfth day of December,'—

Mar. For the love o' God, peace!

Enter MALVOLIO.

Mal. My masters, are you mad? or what are you? Have you no wit, manners, nor honesty, but to gabble like tinkers at this time of night? Do ye make an alehouse of my lady's house, that ye squeak out your coziers' catches without any mitigation or remorse of voice? Is there no respect of place, persons, nor time in you?

Sir To. We did keep time, sir, in our catches. Sneck up!

Mal. Sir Toby, I must be round with you. My lady bade me tell you, that, though she harbours you as her kinsman, she 's nothing allied to your disorders. If you can separate yourself and your misdemeanours, you are welcome to the house; if not, an it would please you to take leave of her, she is very willing to bid you farewell.

Sir To. [*Sings.*] 'Farewell, dear heart, since I must needs be gone.'

Mar. Nay, good Sir Toby.

Clo. 'His eyes do show his days are almost done.'

Mal. Is 't even so?

Sir To. 'But I will never die.'

Clo. Sir Toby, there you lie.

Mal. This is much credit to you.

Sir To. 'Shall I bid him go?'

Clo. 'What an if you do?'

Sir To. 'Shall I bid him go, and spare not?'

Clo. 'O no, no, no, no, you dare not.'

Sir To. Out o' tune, sir: ye lie. Art any more than a steward? Dost thou think, because thou art virtuous, there shall be no more cakes and ale?

Clo. Yes, by Saint Anne, and ginger shall be hot i' the mouth too.

Sir To. Th' art i' the right. Go, sir, rub your chain with crums. A stoup of wine, Maria!

Mal. Mistress Mary, if you prized my lady's favour at any thing more than contempt, you would not give means for this uncivil rule: she shall know of it, by this hand. *Exit.*

Mar. Go shake your ears.

Sir And. 'Twere as good a deed as to drink when a man 's a-hungry, to challenge him the field, and then to break promise with him and make a fool of him.

Sir To. Do 't, knight: I'll write thee a challenge; or I'll deliver thy indignation to him by word of mouth.

Mar. Sweet Sir Toby, be patient for to-night: since the youth of the count's was to-day with my lady, she is much out of quiet. For Monsieur Malvolio, let me alone with him: if I do not gull him into a nayword, and make him a common recreation, do not think I have wit enough to lie straight in my bed: I know I can do it.

Sir To. Possess us, possess us; tell us something of him.

Mar. Marry, sir, sometimes he is a kind of puritan.

Sir And. O, if I thought that, I 'ld beat him like a dog!

Sir To. What, for being a puritan? thy exquisite reason, dear knight?

Sir And. I have no exquisite reason for 't, but I have reason good enough.

Mar. The devil a puritan that he is, or any thing constantly, but a time-pleaser; an affectioned ass, that cons state without book and utters it by great swarths: the best persuaded of himself, so crammed, as he thinks, with excellencies, that it is his grounds of faith that all that look on him love him; and on that vice in him will my revenge find notable cause to work.

Sir To. What wilt thou do?

Mar. I will drop in his way some obscure epistles of love; wherein, by the colour of his beard, the shape of his leg, the manner of his gait, the expressure of his eye, forehead, and complexion, he shall find himself most feelingly personated. I can write very like my lady your niece: on a forgotten matter we can hardly make distinction of our hands.

Sir To. Excellent! I smell a device.

Sir And. I have 't in my nose too.

Sir To. He shall think, by the letters that thou wilt drop, that they come from my niece, and that she 's in love with him.

Mar. My purpose is, indeed, a horse of that colour.

Sir And. And your horse now would make him an ass.

Mar. Ass, I doubt not.

Sir And. O, 'twill be admirable!

Mar. Sport royal, I warrant you: I know my physic will work with him. I will plant you two, and

80. **Cataian,** explained as Chinese, i.e., from Cathay, suggested by *caterwauling.* **politicians,** schemers, intriguers. 81. **Peg-a-Ramsey,** common name of a tune, evidently of low character. 83. **Tillyvally,** a term of contempt, possibly from a song. 84. **'There . . . lady,'** first line of a ballad having the refrain "Lady, lady." Sir Toby's use of the word, above, suggested the song. 89. **natural,** unconsciously suggesting idiocy. 90-91. **'O . . . December.'** Kittredge suggests that this is the ballad of "Musselburgh Field" in Child's *English and Scottish Popular Ballads,* IV, 507. 97. **coziers',** cobblers'. 98. **mitigation or remorse,** considerate lowering. 101. **Sneck up!** Go hang! 102. **round,** plain. 109-110. **'Farewell . . . gone,'** from the ballad, "Corydon's Farewell to Phyllis." 125. **cakes and ale,** reveling (proverbial). 126. **Saint Anne,** invoked because of her care for material welfare. 128-129. **Go . . . crums,** i.e., scour your steward's chain with crumbs; attend to your own business. 132. **give means,** i.e., by supplying drink. 133. **rule,** conduct. 146. **nayword,** byword. 147. **recreation,** laughingstock. 152. **puritan.** Note that Maria is careful in her distinctions; she raises the prospect of regarding Malvolio as a kind of puritan, but then refuses to regard him simply as a satirical type of the Puritan sect. The extent of the resemblance is left unstated. 160. **time-pleaser,**

let the fool make a third, where he shall find the letter: observe his construction of it. For this night, to bed, and dream on the event. Farewell. *Exit.*

Sir To. Good night, Penthesilea.

Sir And. Before me, she 's a good wench.

Sir To. She 's a beagle, true-bred, and one that adores me: what o' that?

Sir And. I was adored once too.

Sir To. Let 's to bed, knight. Thou hadst need send for more money.

Sir And. If I cannot recover your niece, I am a foul way out.

Sir To. Send for money, knight: if thou hast her not i' the end, call me cut.

Sir And. If I do not, never trust me, take it how you will.

Sir To. Come, come, I'll go burn some sack; 'tis too late to go to bed now: come, knight; come, knight. *Exeunt.*

SCENE IV. [*The* DUKE'S *Palace.*]

Enter DUKE, VIOLA, CURIO, *and others.*

Duke. Give me some music. Now, good morrow, friends.
Now, good Cesario, but that piece of song,
That old and antique song we heard last night:
Methought it did relieve my passion much,
More than light airs and recollected terms
Of these most brisk and giddy-paced times:
Come, but one verse.

Cur. He is not here, so please your lordship, that should sing it.

Duke. Who was it?

Cur. Feste, the jester, my lord; a fool that the lady Olivia's father took much delight in. He is about the house.

Duke. Seek him out, and play the tune the while.
[*Exit Curio.*] *Music plays.*
Come hither, boy: if ever thou shalt love,
In the sweet pangs of it remember me;
For such as I am all true lovers are,
Unstaid and skittish in all motions else,
Save in the constant image of the creature
That is belov'd. How dost thou like this tune?

Vio. It gives a very echo to the seat
Where Love is thron'd.

Duke. Thou dost speak masterly:
My life upon 't, young though thou art, thine eye
Hath stay'd upon some favour that it loves:
Hath it not, boy?

Vio. A little, by your favour.

Duke. What kind of woman is 't?

Vio. Of your complexion.

Duke. She is not worth thee, then. What years, i' faith?

Vio. About your years, my lord.

Duke. Too old, by heaven: let still the woman take
An elder than herself; so wears she to him,
So sways she level in her husband's heart:
For, boy, however we do praise ourselves,
Our fancies are more giddy and unfirm,
More longing, wavering, sooner lost and worn,
Than women's are.

Vio. I think it well, my lord.

Duke. Then let thy love be younger than thyself,
Or thy affection cannot hold the bent;
For women are as roses, whose fair flow'r
Being once display'd, doth fall that very hour.

Vio. And so they are: alas, that they are so;
To die, even when they to perfection grow!

Enter CURIO *and* CLOWN.

Duke. O, fellow, come, the song we had last night.
Mark it, Cesario, it is old and plain;
The spinsters and the knitters in the sun
And the free maids that weave their thread with bones
Do use to chant it: it is silly sooth,
And dallies with the innocence of love,
Like the old age.

Clo. Are you ready, sir?

Duke. Ay; prithee, sing. *Music.*

THE SONG.

[*Clo.*] Come away, come away, death,
And in sad cypress let me be laid;
Fly away, fly away, breath;
I am slain by a fair cruel maid.
My shroud of white, stuck all with yew,
O, prepare it!
My part of death, no one so true
Did share it.

Not a flower, not a flower sweet,
On my black coffin let there be strown;
Not a friend, not a friend greet
My poor corpse, where my bones shall be thrown:
A thousand thousand sighs to save,
Lay me, O, where
Sad true lover never find my grave,
To weep there!

Duke. There 's for thy pains.

Clo. No pains, sir; I take pleasure in singing, sir.

Duke. I'll pay thy pleasure then.

Clo. Truly, sir, and pleasure will be paid, one time or another.

Duke. Give me now leave to leave thee.

Clo. Now, the melancholy god protect thee; and the tailor make thy doublet of changeable taffeta, for thy mind is a very opal. I would have men of such constancy put to sea, that their business might be every

time-server, sycophant. 161. **cons . . . book,** learns the phrases of high society by heart. 162. **best persuaded,** has the best opinion. 171. **expressure,** expression. 173. **personated,** described. 193. **Penthesilea,** queen of the Amazons; another ironical allusion to Maria's stature. 195. **beagle,** small hound; possibly also alluding to Maria's size. 200. **recover,** win. 201. **foul way out,** explained as "out of pocket" and as "off the track." 203. **cut,** a horse with a docked tail.

SCENE IV. 3. **antique,** quaint. 5. **recollected terms,** studied and artificial expressions. 21. **seat,** i.e., the heart. 25. **stay'd . . . favour,** rested upon some face. 30. **still,** always. 31. **wears she,** adapts herself. 32. **sways she level,** keeps steady, constant. 33. **praise,** appraise. 35. **worn,** F: *worne;* Hanmer: *won* (for *wonne*), which is possibly correct. 38. **bent,** degree of tension (as in archery). 45. **spinsters,** spinners. 46. **bones,** bobbins with which bone-lace was made. 47. **silly sooth,** simple truth. 49. **old age,** good old times. 53. **cypress,** interpreted as meaning coffin of cypress wood, or bier strewn with sprigs of cypress. 58-59. **My . . . it,** no one died for love so true to love as I (Luce). 75. **melancholy god,** Saturn, if the Clown has any god in mind. 76. **doublet,** close-fitting body garment with or without sleeves. 77. **taffeta,** silk.

thing and their intent every where; for that 's it that always makes a good voyage of nothing. Farewell. *Exit.*

Duke. Let all the rest give place.
[*Curio and Attendants retire.*]
Once more, Cesario,
Get thee to yond same sovereign cruelty:
Tell her, my love, more noble than the world,
Prizes not quantity of dirty lands;
The parts that fortune hath bestow'd upon her,
Tell her, I hold as giddily as fortune;
But 'tis that miracle and queen of gems
That nature pranks her in attracts my soul.

Vio. But if she cannot love you, sir?

Duke. I cannot be so answer'd.

Vio. Sooth, but you must.
Say that some lady, as perhaps there is,
Hath for your love as great a pang of heart
As you have for Olivia: you cannot love her;
You tell her so; must she not then be answer'd?

Duke. There is no woman's sides
Can bide the beating of so strong a passion
As love doth give my heart; no woman's heart
So big, to hold so much; they lack retention.
Alas, their love may be call'd appetite,
No motion of the liver, but the palate,
That suffer surfeit, cloyment and revolt;
But mine is all as hungry as the sea,
And can digest as much: make no compare
Between that love a woman can bear me
And that I owe Olivia.

Vio. Ay, but I know—

Duke. What dost thou know?

Vio. Too well what love women to men may owe:
In faith, they are as true of heart as we.
My father had a daughter lov'd a man,
As it might be, perhaps, were I a woman,
I should your lordship.

Duke. And what's her history?

Vio. A blank, my lord. She never told her love,
But let concealment, like a worm i' th' bud,
Feed on her damask cheek: she pin'd in thought,
And with a green and yellow melancholy
She sat like Patience on a monument,
Smiling at grief. Was not this love indeed?
We men may say more, swear more: but indeed
Our shows are more than will; for still we prove
Much in our vows, but little in our love.

Duke. But died thy sister of her love, my boy?

Vio. I am all the daughters of my father's house,
And all the brothers too: and yet I know not.
Sir, shall I to this lady?

Duke. Ay, that 's the theme.
To her in haste; give her this jewel; say,
My love can give no place, bide no denay. *Exeunt.*

SCENE V. [OLIVIA's *garden.*]

Enter SIR TOBY, SIR ANDREW, *and* FABIAN.

Sir To. Come thy ways, Signior Fabian.

Fab. Nay, I'll come: if I lose a scruple of this sport, let me be boiled to death with melancholy.

Sir To. Wouldst thou not be glad to have the niggardly rascally sheep-biter come by some notable shame?

Fab. I would exult, man: you know, he brought me out o' favour with my lady about a bear-baiting here.

Sir To. To anger him we'll have the bear again; and we will fool him black and blue: shall we not, Sir Andrew?

Sir And. An we do not, it is pity of our lives.

Enter MARIA.

Sir To. Here comes the little villain. How now, my metal of India!

Mar. Get ye all three into the box-tree: Malvolio 's coming down this walk: he has been yonder i' the sun practising behaviour to his own shadow this half hour: observe him, for the love of mockery; for I know this letter will make a contemplative idiot of him. Close, in the name of jesting! Lie thou there [*throws down a letter*]; for here comes the trout that must be caught with tickling. *Exit.*

Enter MALVOLIO.

Mal. 'Tis but fortune; all is fortune. Maria once told me she did affect me: and I have heard herself come thus near, that, should she fancy, it should be one of my complexion. Besides, she uses me with a more exalted respect than any one else that follows her. What should I think on 't?

Sir To. Here 's an overweening rogue!

Fab. O, peace! Contemplation makes a rare turkey-cock of him: how he jets under his advanced plumes!

Sir And. 'Slight, I could so beat the rogue!

Sir To. Peace, I say.

Mal. To be Count Malvolio!

Sir To. Ah, rogue!

Sir And. Pistol him, pistol him.

Sir To. Peace, peace!

Mal. There is example for 't; the lady of the Strachy married the yeoman of the wardrobe.

Sir And. Fie on him, Jezebel!

Fab. O, peace! now he 's deeply in: look how imagination blows him.

Mal. Having been three months married to her, sitting in my state,—

Sir To. O, for a stone-bow, to hit him in the eye!

Mal. Calling my officers about me, in my branched velvet gown; having come from a daybed, where I have left Olivia sleeping,—

80-81. **for . . . nothing,** possibly ironical, meaning that such changeable enterprise will make a good voyage come to nothing. 86. **parts,** gifts, as wealth or rank. 87. **giddily,** carelessly, indifferently. 89. **pranks,** adorns. 96-106. **There . . . Olivia.** The duke has just said in lines 33-36 that men are more inconstant than women. 99. **retention,** constancy, power of retaining. 101. **liver . . . palate.** The distinction seems to be that real love is a passion of the liver, whereas fancy (light love) is born in the eye and nourished in the palate. 102. **That suffer,** that suffers. *That* is sometimes thought to refer back to *their* (l. 100). **cloyment,** satiety to the point of losing appetite. **revolt,** sickness, revulsion. 113. **blank,** i.e., her history is a blank. 115. **damask,** pink like the damask rose. 116. **green and yellow.** Green denoted hopefulness and yellow jealousy; so that a green and yellow melancholy was a melancholy in which there was jealousy, yet hope. This accords exactly with the state of mind of Viola (Hunter). 127. **denay,** denial.

SCENE V. 3. **boiled to death.** Melancholy being a settled passion, the spirits descended to the intestines, carrying with them their boiling heat. 6. **sheep-biter,** i.e., a sneaky dog. 17. **metal,** gold, probably with pun on "mettle," spirit. 23. **contemplative,** i.e., from contemplating himself. 26. **tickling,** groping gently with the hands—a method of fishing. 28. **she,** i.e., Olivia. 30. **fancy,** fall in love. 36. **jets,** struts. 44. **lady of the Strachy,** apparently a lady who had married below her station; no satisfactory explanation. 46. **Jezebel,** a blunder of Sir Andrew, unless, as has been suggested, we should read *her* for *him* in this line. 48. **blows,** puffs up. 51. **stone-bow,** crossbow that shoots stones. 54. **branched,** adorned with a figured pattern suggesting

Sir To. Fire and brimstone!

Fab. O, peace, peace!

Mal. And then to have the humour of state; and after a demure travel of regard, telling them I know my place as I would they should do theirs, to ask for my kinsman Toby,—

Sir To. Bolts and shackles!

Fab. O peace, peace, peace! now, now.

Mal. Seven of my people, with an obedient start, make out for him: I frown the while; and perchance wind up my watch, or play with my—some rich jewel. Toby approaches; courtesies there to me,—

Sir To. Shall this fellow live?

Fab. Though our silence be drawn from us with cars, yet peace.

Mal. I extend my hand to him thus, quenching my familiar smile with an austere regard of control,—

Sir To. And does not Toby take you a blow o' the lips then?

Mal. Saying, 'Cousin Toby, my fortunes having cast me on your niece give me this prerogative of speech,'—

Sir To. What, what?

Mal. 'You must amend your drunkenness.'

Sir To. Out, scab!

Fab. Nay, patience, or we break the sinews of our plot.

Mal. 'Besides, you waste the treasure of your time with a foolish knight,'—

Sir And. That 's me, I warrant you.

Mal. 'One Sir Andrew,'—

Sir And. I knew 'twas I; for many do call me fool.

Mal. What employment have we here?

[*Taking up the letter.*]

Fab. Now is the woodcock near the gin.

Sir To. O, peace! and the spirit of humours intimate reading aloud to him!

Mal. By my life, this is my lady's hand: these be her very C's, her U's and her T's; and thus makes she her great P's. It is, in contempt of question, her hand.

Sir And. Her C's, her U's and her T's: why that?

Mal. [*Reads*] 'To the unknown beloved, this, and my good wishes:'—her very phrases! By your leave, wax. Soft! and the impressure her Lucrece, with which she uses to seal: 'tis my lady. To whom should this be?

Fab. This wins him, liver and all.

Mal. [*Reads*]

Jove knows I love:
But who?
Lips, do not move;
No man must know.

'No man must know.' What follows? the numbers altered! 'No man must know:' if this should be thee, Malvolio?

Sir To. Marry, hang thee, brock!

Mal. [*Reads*]

I may command where I adore;
But silence, like a Lucrece knife,
With bloodless stroke my heart doth gore:
M, O, A, I, doth sway my life.

Fab. A fustian riddle!

Sir To. Excellent wench, say I.

Mal. 'M, O, A, I, doth sway my life.' Nay, but first, let me see, let me see, let me see.

Fab. What dish o' poison has she dressed him!

Sir To. And with what wing the staniel checks at it!

Mal. 'I may command where I adore.' Why, she may command me: I serve her; she is my lady. Why, this is evident to any formal capacity; there is no obstruction in this: and the end,—what should that alphabetical position portend? If I could make that resemble something in me,—Softly! M, O, A, I,—

Sir To. O, ay, make up that: he is now at a cold scent.

Fab. Sowter will cry upon 't for all this, though it be as rank as a fox.

Mal. M,—Malvolio; M,—why, that begins my name.

Fab. Did not I say he would work it out? the cur is excellent at faults.

Mal. M,—but then there is no consonancy in the sequel; that suffers under probation: A should follow, but O does.

Fab. And O shall end, I hope.

Sir To. Ay, or I'll cudgel him, and make him cry O!

Mal. And then I comes behind.

Fab. Ay, an you had any eye behind you, you might see more detraction at your heels than fortunes before you.

Mal. M, O, A, I; this simulation is not as the former: and yet, to crush this a little, it would bow to me, for every one of these letters are in my name. Soft! here follows prose.

[*Reads*] 'If this fall into thy hand, revolve. In my stars I am above thee; but be not afraid of greatness: some are born great, some achieve greatness and some have greatness thrust upon 'em. Thy Fates open their hands; let thy blood and spirit embrace them; and, to inure thyself to what thou art like to be, cast thy humble slough and appear fresh. Be opposite with a kinsman, surly with servants; let thy tongue tang arguments of state; put thyself into the trick of singularity: she thus advises thee that sighs for thee. Remember who commended thy yellow stockings, and wished to see thee ever cross-gartered: I say, remember. Go to, thou art made, if thou desirest to be so; if not, let me see thee a steward still, the fellow of servants, and not worthy to touch Fortune's fingers. Farewell. She that would alter services with thee,

THE FORTUNATE-UNHAPPY.'

branches. 55. **daybed,** sofa, couch. 58. **humour of state,** imperious manner of authority. 59. **demure . . . regard,** grave survey of the company. 61. **Toby,** i.e., not *Sir* Toby. 66. **wind up my watch,** an impressive act in those days. 71. **cars,** used like "team of horses." 74. **regard of control,** look of authority. 82. **scab,** scurvy fellow. 92. **woodcock,** proverbial for its stupidity. **gin,** snare. 94. **intimate,** suggest. 98. **in contempt of question,** i.e., it is absurd to question it. 103. **By . . . wax,** addressed to the seal on the letter. **impressure,** impression. 104. **Lucrece,** a seal engraved with the picture of Lucrece. 114. **brock,** badger; used contemptuously. 119. **fustian,** bombastic, ridiculously pompous. 123. **dressed,** prepared for. 124. **staniel,** an inferior kind of hawk; F: *stallion,* which may be a dialectal form of the same word. 125. **checks.** A hawk "checked" when it left its quarry and flew at a chance bird. 128. **formal capacity,** normal mind. 134. **cold scent,** cold trail. 135. **Sowter,** cobbler; probably, the name for a hound. 136. **rank as a fox,** i.e., Malvolio is so crude a hunter that he will leave the trail of a hare and follow the rank scent of a fox. 140. **faults,** breaks in the line of scent. 141. **consonancy,** consistency. 142. **probation,** when put to trial. 144. **O,** interpreted as a hempen collar (Johnson), or as a sigh (Steevens), or as an outcry of pain. 151. **simulation,** disguised meaning. 152. **crush,** force. 155. **revolve,** consider. 156. **stars,** fortunes. 159. **blood and spirit,** i.e., as the agents of passion. 161. **slough,** skin of a snake. 162. **opposite,** contradictory. 163. **tang,** sound loud with. 164. **trick of singularity,** eccentricity of manner. 167. **cross-gartered,** wearing garters above and below the knee so as to cross behind it (Onions).

Daylight and champain discovers not more: this is open. I will be proud, I will read politic authors, I will baffle Sir Toby, I will wash off gross acquaintance, I will be point-devise the very man. I do not now fool myself, to let imagination jade me; for every reason excites to this, that my lady loves me. She did commend my yellow stockings of late, she did praise my leg being cross-gartered; and in this she manifests herself to my love, and with a kind of injunction drives me to these habits of her liking. I thank my stars I am happy. I will be strange, stout, in yellow stockings, and cross-gartered, even with the swiftness of putting on. Jove and my stars be praised! Here is yet a postscript. [*Reads*] 'Thou canst not choose but know who I am. If thou entertainest my love, let it appear in thy smiling; thy smiles become thee well; therefore in my presence still smile, dear my sweet, I prithee.'

Jove, I thank thee: I will smile; I will do everything that thou wilt have me. *Exit.*

Fab. I will not give my part of this sport for a pension of thousands to be paid from the Sophy.

Sir To. I could marry this wench for this device.

Sir And. So could I too.

Sir To. And ask no other dowry with her but such another jest.

Enter MARIA.

Sir And. Nor I neither.

Fab. Here comes my noble gull-catcher.

Sir To. Wilt thou set thy foot o' my neck?

Sir And. Or o' mine either?

Sir To. Shall I play my freedom at tray-trip, and become thy bond-slave?

Sir And. I' faith, or I either?

Sir To. Why, thou hast put him in such a dream, that when the image of it leaves him he must run mad.

Mar. Nay, but say true; does it work upon him?

Sir To. Like aqua-vitæ with a midwife.

Mar. If you will then see the fruits of the sport, mark his first approach before my lady: he will come to her in yellow stockings, and 'tis a colour she abhors, and cross-gartered, a fashion she detests; and he will smile upon her, which will now be so unsuitable to her disposition, being addicted to a melancholy as she is, that it cannot but turn him into a notable contempt. If you will see it, follow me.

Sir To. To the gates of Tartar, thou most excellent devil of wit!

Sir And. I'll make one too. *Exeunt.*

ACT III.

SCENE I. [OLIVIA'S *garden*.]

Enter VIOLA, *and* CLOWN [*with a tabor*].

Vio. Save thee, friend, and thy music: dost thou live by thy tabor?

Clo. No, sir, I live by the church.

Vio. Art thou a churchman?

Clo. No such matter, sir: I do live by the church; for I do live at my house, and my house doth stand by the church.

Vio. So thou mayst say, the king lies by a beggar, if a beggar dwell near him; or, the church stands by thy tabor, if thy tabor stand by the church.

Clo. You have said, sir. To see this age! A sentence is but a cheveril glove to a good wit: how quickly the wrong side may be turned outward!

Vio. Nay, that 's certain; they that dally nicely with words may quickly make them wanton.

Clo. I would, therefore, my sister had had no name, sir.

Vio. Why, man?

Clo. Why, sir, her name 's a word; and to dally with that word might make my sister wanton. But indeed words are very rascals since bonds disgraced them.

Vio. Thy reason, man?

Clo. Troth, sir, I can yield you none without words; and words are grown so false, I am loath to prove reason with them.

Vio. I warrant thou art a merry fellow and carest for nothing.

Clo. Not so, sir, I do care for something; but in my conscience, sir, I do not care for you: if that be to care for nothing, sir, I would it would make you invisible.

Vio. Art not thou the Lady Olivia's fool?

Clo. No, indeed, sir; the Lady Olivia has no folly: she will keep no fool, sir, till she be married; and fools are as like husbands as pilchers are to herrings; the husband 's the bigger: I am indeed not her fool, but her corrupter of words.

Vio. I saw thee late at the Count Orsino's.

Clo. Foolery, sir, does walk about the orb like the sun, it shines every where. I would be sorry, sir, but the fool should be as oft with your master as with my mistress: I think I saw your wisdom there.

Vio. Nay, an thou pass upon me, I'll no more with thee. Hold, there 's expenses for thee.

Clo. Now Jove, in his next commodity of hair, send thee a beard!

Vio. By my troth, I'll tell thee, I am almost sick for one; [*Aside*] though I would not have it grow on my chin. Is thy lady within?

Clo. Would not a pair of these have bred, sir?

Vio. Yes, being kept together and put to use.

Clo. I would play Lord Pandarus of Phrygia, sir, to bring a Cressida to this Troilus.

Vio. I understand you, sir; 'tis well begged.

Clo. The matter, I hope, is not great, sir, begging but a beggar: Cressida was a beggar. My lady is within, sir. I will conster to them whence you come; who you are and what you would are out of my welkin, I might say 'element,' but the word is over-worn. *Exit.*

Vio. This fellow is wise enough to play the fool;
And to do that well craves a kind of wit:
He must observe their mood on whom he jests,
The quality of persons, and the time,

174. **champain,** open country. 175. **open,** obvious. 176. **politic,** dealing with state affairs. 177. **point-devise,** extremely precise (in following the letter). 179. **jade,** trick. 185. **stout,** haughty. 198. **Sophy,** Shah of Persia. 208. **tray-trip,** a game with dice, success in which depended on throwing a three. 216. **aqua-vitæ,** distilled liquors.

ACT III. SCENE I. 2. **tabor,** drum used by clowns and jesters. 13. **cheveril,** kidskin. 25. **bonds disgraced them,** i.e., were needed to make them good. 40. **pilchers,** fish resembling herring. 43. **orb,** earth. 44. **but,** but that. 48. **pass upon me,** make jokes at my expense. 50. **commodity,** supply. 55. **pair of these,** two coins like the one he had just received. 58. **Pandarus,** the go-between in the story of Troilus and Cressida; uncle to Cressida. 62. **begging . . . Cressida,** a reference to Henryson's *Testament of Cresseid* in which the heroine becomes a leper and a beggar. The Clown desires another coin to be the mate of the one he has, as Cressida, the beggar, was mate to Troilus. 64. **conster,** construe. 65. **welkin,** sky; here used with play upon *element,* one of whose meanings was "sky." 71. **haggard,** untrained hawk. **check,** forsake quarry for another game. 75. **folly-fall'n,** having fallen into

And, like the haggard, check at every feather
That comes before his eye. This is a practice
As full of labour as a wise man's art:
For folly that he wisely shows is fit;
But wise men, folly-fall'n, quite taint their wit.

Enter Sir Toby *and* [Sir] Andrew.

Sir To. Save you, gentleman.

Vio. And you, sir.

Sir And. Dieu vous garde, monsieur.

Vio. Et vous aussi; votre serviteur.

Sir And. I hope, sir, you are; and I am yours.

Sir To. Will you encounter the house? my niece is desirous you should enter, if your trade be to her.

Vio. I am bound to your niece, sir; I mean, she is the list of my voyage.

Sir To. Taste your legs, sir; put them to motion.

Vio. My legs do better understand me, sir, than I understand what you mean by bidding me taste my legs.

Sir To. I mean, to go, sir, to enter.

Vio. I will answer you with gait and entrance. But we are prevented.

Enter Olivia *and Gentlewoman* [Maria].

Most excellent accomplished lady, the heavens rain odours on you!

Sir And. That youth 's a rare courtier: 'Rain odours;' well.

Vio. My matter hath no voice, lady, but to your own most pregnant and vouchsafed ear.

Sir And. 'Odours,' 'pregnant' and 'vouchsafed;' I'll get 'em all three all ready.

Oli. Let the garden door be shut, and leave me to my hearing. [*Exeunt Sir Toby, Sir Andrew, and Maria.*] Give me your hand, sir.

Vio. My duty, madam, and most humble service.
Oli. What is your name?
Vio. Cesario is your servant's name, fair princess.
Oli. My servant, sir! 'Twas never merry world
Since lowly feigning was call'd compliment:
Y' are servant to the Count Orsino, youth.
Vio. And he is yours, and his must needs be yours:
Your servant's servant is your servant, madam.
Oli. For him, I think not on him: for his thoughts,
Would they were blanks, rather than fill'd with me!
Vio. Madam, I come to whet your gentle thoughts
On his behalf.
Oli. O, by your leave, I pray you,
I bade you never speak again of him:
But, would you undertake another suit,
I had rather hear you to solicit that
Than music from the spheres.
Vio. Dear lady,—
Oli. Give me leave, beseech you. I did send,
After the last enchantment you did here,
A ring in chase of you: so did I abuse
Myself, my servant and, I fear me, you:
Under your hard construction must I sit,
To force that on you, in a shameful cunning,
Which you knew none of yours: what might you think?
Have you not set mine honour at the stake
And baited it with all th' unmuzzled thoughts
That tyrannous heart can think? To one of your receiving
Enough is shown: a cypress, not a bosom,
Hides my heart. So, let me hear you speak.
Vio. I pity you.
Oli. That 's a degree to love.
Vio. No, not a grize; for 'tis a vulgar proof,
That very oft we pity enemies.
Oli. Why, then, methinks 'tis time to smile again.
O world, how apt the poor are to be proud!
If one should be a prey, how much the better
To fall before the lion than the wolf! *Clock strikes.*
The clock upbraids me with the waste of time.
Be not afraid, good youth, I will not have you:
And yet, when wit and youth is come to harvest,
Your wife is like to reap a proper man:
There lies your way, due west.
Vio. Then westward-ho! Grace and good disposition
Attend your ladyship!
You'll nothing, madam, to my lord by me?
Oli. Stay:
I prithee, tell me what thou think'st of me.
Vio. That you do think you are not what you are.
Oli. If I think so, I think the same of you.
Vio. Then think you right: I am not what I am.
Oli. I would you were as I would have you be!
Vio. Would it be better, madam, than I am?
I wish it might, for now I am your fool.
Oli. O, what a deal of scorn looks beautiful
In the contempt and anger of his lip!
A murd'rous guilt shows not itself more soon
Than love that would seem hid: love's night is noon.
Cesario, by the roses of the spring,
By maidhood, honour, truth and every thing,
I love thee so, that, maugre all thy pride,
Nor wit nor reason can my passion hide.
Do not extort thy reasons from this clause,
For that I woo, thou therefore hast no cause;
But rather reason thus with reason fetter,
Love sought is good, but given unsought is better.
Vio. By innocence I swear, and by my youth,
I have one heart, one bosom and one truth,
And that no woman has; nor never none
Shall mistress be of it, save I alone.
And so adieu, good madam: never more
Will I my master's tears to you deplore.
Oli. Yet come again; for thou perhaps mayst move
That heart, which now abhors, to like his love. *Exeunt.*

Scene II. [Olivia's *house.*]

Enter Sir Toby, Sir Andrew, *and* Fabian.

Sir And. No, faith, I'll not stay a jot longer.

folly. **taint their wit,** lose their reputation for wisdom. 78. **Dieu . . . monsieur,** God keep you, sir. 79. **Et . . . serviteur.** And you, too; I am your servant. 82. **encounter,** high-sounding word to express "enter." 86. **list,** destination. 87. **Taste,** try. 110. **lowly feigning,** affected humility. 121. **music from the spheres,** reference to the belief that the heavenly bodies were fixed in hollow concentric spheres which revolved one about the other, producing a harmony too exquisite to be heard by human ears. 126. **hard construction,** harsh interpretation. 127. **To force,** for forcing. 129. **stake.** The figure of speech is from bearbaiting.

131. **receiving,** capacity, intelligence. 132. **cypress,** described as a thin, gauzelike material, mostly black in color. 135. **grize,** step corresponding to *degree* in the preceding line. 146. **westward-ho,** the cry of Thames watermen to attract westward-bound passengers. 151. **That . . . are,** that you think you are in love with a man, and you are mistaken (Luce). 152. **If . . . you.** If I think I lower myself, I think the same of you, i.e., that you are a nobleman in disguise. 156. **now . . . fool.** You are making a fool of me, but implying, also, I am making a fool of you. 163. **maugre,** in spite of.

Sir To. Thy reason, dear venom, give thy reason.

Fab. You must needs yield your reason, Sir Andrew.

Sir And. Marry, I saw your niece do more favours to the count's serving-man than ever she bestowed upon me; I saw 't i' the orchard.

Sir To. Did she see thee the while, old boy? tell me that.

Sir And. As plain as I see you now.

Fab. This was a great argument of love in her toward you.

Sir And. 'Slight, will you make an ass o' me?

Fab. I will prove it legitimate, sir, upon the oaths of judgement and reason.

Sir To. And they have been grand-jurymen since before Noah was a sailor.

Fab. She did show favour to the youth in your sight only to exasperate you, to awake your dormouse valour, to put fire in your heart, and brimstone in your liver. You should then have accosted her; and with some excellent jests, fire-new from the mint, you should have banged the youth into dumbness. This was looked for at your hand, and this was balked: the double gilt of this opportunity you let time wash off, and you are now sailed into the north of my lady's opinion; where you will hang like an icicle on a Dutchman's beard, unless you do redeem it by some laudable attempt either of valour or policy.

Sir And. An 't be any way, it must be with valour; for policy I hate: I had as lief be a Brownist as a politician.

Sir To. Why, then, build me thy fortunes upon the basis of valour. Challenge me the count's youth to fight with him; hurt him in eleven places: my niece shall take note of it; and assure thyself, there is no love-broker in the world can more prevail in man's commendation with woman than report of valour.

Fab. There is no way but this, Sir Andrew.

Sir And. Will either of you bear me a challenge to him?

Sir To. Go, write it in a martial hand; be curst and brief; it is no matter how witty, so it be eloquent and full of invention: taunt him with the license of ink: if thou thou'st him some thrice, it shall not be amiss; and as many lies as will lie in thy sheet of paper, although the sheet were big enough for the bed of Ware in England, set 'em down: go, about it. Let there be gall enough in thy ink, though thou write with a goose-pen, no matter: about it.

Sir And. Where shall I find you?

Sir To. We'll call thee at the cubiculo: go.

Exit Sir Andrew.

Fab. This is a dear manakin to you, Sir Toby.

Sir To. I have been dear to him, lad, some two thousand strong, or so.

Fab. We shall have a rare letter from him: but you'll not deliver 't?

Sir To. Never trust me, then; and by all means stir on the youth to an answer. I think oxen and wainropes cannot hale them together. For Andrew, if he were opened, and you find so much blood in his liver as will clog the foot of a flea, I'll eat the rest of the anatomy.

Fab. And his opposite, the youth, bears in his visage no great presage of cruelty.

Enter MARIA.

Sir To. Look, where the youngest wren of nine comes.

Mar. If you desire the spleen, and will laugh yourselves into stitches, follow me. Yond gull Malvolio is turned heathen, a very renegado; for there is no Christian, that means to be saved by believing rightly, can ever believe such impossible passages of grossness. He 's in yellow stockings.

Sir To. And cross-gartered?

Mar. Most villanously; like a pedant that keeps a school i' the church. I have dogged him, like his murderer. He does obey every point of the letter that I dropped to betray him: he does smile his face into more lines than is in the new map with the augmentation of the Indies: you have not seen such a thing as 'tis. I can hardly forbear hurling things at him. I know my lady will strike him: if she do, he'll smile and take 't for a great favour.

Sir To. Come, bring us, bring us where he is.

Exeunt omnes.

SCENE III. [*A street.*]

Enter SEBASTIAN *and* ANTONIO.

Seb. I would not by my will have troubled you;
But, since you make your pleasure of your pains,
I will no further chide you.

Ant. I could not stay behind you: my desire,
More sharp than filed steel, did spur me forth;
And not all love to see you, though so much
As might have drawn one to a longer voyage,
But jealousy what might befall your travel,
Being skilless in these parts; which to a stranger,
Unguided and unfriended, often prove
Rough and unhospitable: my willing love,
The rather by these arguments of fear,
Set forth in your pursuit.

Seb. My kind Antonio,
I can no other answer make but thanks,
†And thanks; and ever . . . . . . oft good turns
Are shuffled off with such uncurrent pay:
But, were my worth as is my conscience firm,
You should find better dealing. What 's to do?
Shall we go see the reliques of this town?

Ant. To-morrow, sir: best first go see your lodging.

Seb. I am not weary, and 'tis long to night:
I pray you, let us satisfy our eyes
With the memorials and the things of fame
That do renown this city.

Ant. Would you 'ld pardon me;
I do not without danger walk these streets:
Once, in a sea-fight, 'gainst the count his galleys

SCENE II. 8. **orchard,** garden. 14. **'Slight,** oath, by God's light. 21. **dormouse valour.** The dormouse was proverbially sleepy. 27. **double gilt,** twice plated; quibble on "guilt." 28. **north,** i.e., out of the warmth and sunshine of her favor. 31. **valour or policy,** frequently associated as the qualities of a nobleman; *policy* means "discretion." 34. **Brownist,** early name of the Congregationalists, from the name of the founder, Robert Brown (1582). **politician,** intriguer. 39. **love-broker,** one who acts as an agent between lovers. 48. **thou'st.** "Thou" was used only between friends or to inferiors. 51. **bed of Ware,** a famous bedstead capable of holding twelve persons, said to have been at the Stag Inn in Ware, Hertfordshire. 56. **cubiculo,** Italian or Latin for "lodging." 64. **wainropes,** cart ropes. 71. **nine.** Wrens have many young birds all of which are small; presumably the last hatched would be smallest. 75. **renegado,** Spanish, *renegado,* "deserter." 77. **passages of grossness,** grossly foolish tricks. 80. **pedant,** schoolmaster. 85. **new map.** This is regarded as a reference to a map published in the 1599 edition of Hakluyt's *Voyages,* which showed more of the East Indies than had ever been mapped before. The reference is used in dating the play.

I did some service; of such note indeed,
That were I ta'en here it would scarce be answer'd.

Seb. Belike you slew great number of his people.

Ant. Th' offence is not of such a bloody nature;
Albeit the quality of the time and quarrel
Might well have given us bloody argument.
It might have since been answer'd in repaying
What we took from them; which, for traffic's sake,
Most of our city did: only myself stood out;
For which, if I be lapsed in this place,
I shall pay dear.

Seb. Do not then walk too open.

Ant. It doth not fit me. Hold, sir, here 's my purse.
In the south suburbs, at the Elephant,
Is best to lodge: I will bespeak our diet,
Whiles you beguile the time and feed your knowledge
With viewing of the town: there shall you have me.

Seb. Why I your purse?

Ant. Haply your eye shall light upon some toy
You have desire to purchase; and your store,
I think, is not for idle markets, sir.

Seb. I'll be your purse-bearer and leave you
For an hour.

Ant. To th' Elephant.

Seb. I do remember. *Exeunt.*

SCENE IV. [OLIVIA'S *garden.*]

Enter OLIVIA *and* MARIA.

Oli. I have sent after him: he says he'll come;
How shall I feast him? what bestow of him?
For youth is bought more oft than begg'd or borrow'd.
I speak too loud.
Where's Malvolio? he is sad and civil,
And suits well for a servant with my fortunes:
Where is Malvolio?

Mar. He 's coming, madam; but in very strange manner. He is, sure, possessed, madam.

Oli. Why, what 's the matter? does he rave?

Mar. No, madam, he does nothing but smile: your ladyship were best to have some guard about you. if he come; for, sure, the man is tainted in 's wits.

Oli. Go call him hither. [*Exit Maria.*] I am as mad as he,
If sad and merry madness equal be.

Enter [MARIA, *with*] MALVOLIO.

How now, Malvolio!

Mal. Sweet lady, ho, ho.

Oli. Smilest thou?
I sent for thee upon a sad occasion.

Mal. Sad, lady! I could be sad: this does make some obstruction in the blood, this cross-gartering; but what of that? if it please the eye of one, it is with me as the very true sonnet is, 'Please one, and please all.'

Oli. Why, how dost thou, man? what is the matter with thee?

Mal. Not black in my mind, though yellow in my legs. It did come to his hands, and commands shall be executed: I think we do know the sweet Roman hand.

Oli. Wilt thou go to bed, Malvolio?

Mal. To bed! ay, sweet-heart, and I'll come to thee.

Oli. God comfort thee! Why dost thou smile so and kiss thy hand so oft?

Mar. How do you, Malvolio?

Mal. At your request! yes; nightingales answer daws.

Mar. Why appear you with this ridiculous boldness before my lady?

Mal. 'Be not afraid of greatness:' 'twas well writ.

Oli. What meanest thou by that, Malvolio?

Mal. 'Some are born great,'—

Oli. Ha?

Mal. 'Some achieve greatness,'—

Oli. What sayest thou?

Mal. 'And some have greatness thrust upon them.'

Oli. Heaven restore thee!

Mal. 'Remember who commended thy yellow stockings,'—

Oli. Thy yellow stockings!

Mal. 'And wished to see thee cross-gartered.'

Oli. Cross-gartered!

Mal. 'Go to, thou art made, if thou desirest to be so;'—

Oli. Am I made?

Mal. 'If not, let me see thee a servant still.'

Oli. Why, this is very midsummer madness.

Enter Servant.

Ser. Madam, the young gentleman of the Count Orsino's is returned: I could hardly entreat him back: he attends your ladyship's pleasure.

Oli. I'll come to him. [*Exit Servant.*] Good Maria, let this fellow be looked to. Where 's my cousin Toby? Let some of my people have a special care of him: I would not have him miscarry for the half of my dowry. *Exit* [*with Maria*].

Mal. O, ho! do you come near me now? no worse man than Sir Toby to look to me! This concurs directly with the letter: she sends him on purpose, that I may appear stubborn to him; for she incites me to that in the letter. 'Cast thy humble slough,' says she; 'be opposite with a kinsman, surly with servants; let thy tongue tang with arguments of state; put thyself into the trick of singularity;' and consequently sets down the manner how; as, a sad face, a reverend carriage, a slow tongue, in the habit of some sir of note, and so forth. I have limed her; but it is Jove's doing, and Jove make me thankful! And when she went away now, 'Let this fellow be looked to:' fellow! not Malvolio, nor after my degree, but fellow. Why, every thing adheres together, that no dram of a scruple, no scruple of a scruple, no obstacle, no incredulous or unsafe circumstance—What can be said? Nothing that can be can come between me and the full prospect of my hopes. Well, Jove, not I, is the doer of this, and he is to be thanked.

Enter [SIR] TOBY, FABIAN, *and* MARIA.

SCENE III. 6. **not all love,** not altogether love. 8. **jealousy,** anxiety. 9. **skilless,** ignorant, unacquainted with. 15. **And thanks,** etc. This corrupt line is usually made to read, *And thanks and ever thanks. Too oft*, etc. 17. **worth,** wealth. 19. **reliques,** antiquities. 26. **count his,** count's. 32. **argument,** cause. 33. **answer'd,** compensated. 34. **traffic's,** trade's. 36. **lapsed,** caught. 39. **Elephant,** name of an inn. 40. **diet,** dinner, food. 46. **idle markets,** unnecessary purchases.

SCENE IV. 1. **he . . . come,** i.e., suppose he says, etc. 9. **possessed,** i.e., with an evil spirit. 25. **sonnet,** song, ballad. **'Please . . . all,'** the refrain of a ballad. 31. **Roman hand,** fashionable Italian cursive style of handwriting. 38. **nightingales answer daws,** i.e. (to Maria), do you suppose a fine fellow like me would answer a lowly creature like you? 61. **midsummer madness,** a proverbial phrase; the midsummer moon was supposed to cause madness. 69. **miscarry,** come to harm. 71. **come near,** understand. 79. **consequently,** thereafter. 82. **limed,** caught like a bird with birdlime. 86. **fellow.** Malvolio takes the original meaning, companion; Olivia had used it in its degenerated sense. 88. **incredulous,** incredible.

Sir To. Which way is he, in the name of sanctity? If all the devils of hell be drawn in little, and Legion himself possessed him, yet I'll speak to him.

Fab. Here he is, here he is. How is 't with you, sir? how is 't with you, man?

Mal. Go off; I discard you: let me enjoy my private: go off.

Mar. Lo, how hollow the fiend speaks within him! did not I tell you? Sir Toby, my lady prays you to have a care of him.

Mal. Ah, ha! does she so?

Sir To. Go to, go to; peace, peace; we must deal gently with him: let me alone. How do you, Malvolio? how is 't with you? What, man! defy the devil: consider, he 's an enemy to mankind.

Mal. Do you know what you say?

Mar. La you, an you speak ill of the devil, how he takes it at heart! Pray God, he be not bewitched!

Fab. Carry his water to the wise woman.

Mar. Marry, and it shall be done to-morrow morning, if I live. My lady would not lose him for more than I'll say.

Mal. How now, mistress!

Mar. O Lord!

Sir To. Prithee, hold thy peace; this is not the way: do you not see you move him? let me alone with him.

Fab. No way but gentleness; gently, gently: the fiend is rough, and will not be roughly used.

Sir To. Why, how now, my bawcock! how dost thou, chuck?

Mal. Sir!

Sir To. Ay, Biddy, come with me. What, man! 'tis not for gravity to play at cherry-pit with Satan: hang him, foul collier!

Mar. Get him to say his prayers, good Sir Toby, get him to pray.

Mal. My prayers, minx!

Mar. No, I warrant you, he will not hear of godliness.

Mal. Go, hang yourselves all! you are idle shallow things: I am not of your element: you shall know more hereafter. *Exit.*

Sir To. Is 't possible?

Fab. If this were played upon a stage now, I could condemn it as an improbable fiction.

Sir To. His very genius hath taken the infection of the device, man.

Mar. Nay, pursue him now, lest the device take air and taint.

Fab. Why, we shall make him mad indeed.

Mar. The house will be the quieter.

Sir To. Come, we'll have him in a dark room and bound. My niece is already in the belief that he 's mad: we may carry it thus, for our pleasure and his penance, till our very pastime, tired out of breath, prompt us to have mercy on him: at which time we will bring the device to the bar and crown thee for a finder of madmen. But see, but see.

Enter Sir Andrew.

Fab. More matter for a May morning.

Sir And. Here 's the challenge, read it: I warrant there 's vinegar and pepper in 't.

Fab. Is 't so saucy?

Sir And. Ay, is 't, I warrant him: do but read.

Sir To. Give me. [*Reads*] 'Youth, whatsoever thou art, thou art but a scurvy fellow.'

Fab. Good, and valiant.

Sir To. [*Reads*] 'Wonder not, nor admire not in thy mind, why I do call thee so, for I will show thee no reason for 't.'

Fab. A good note; that keeps you from the blow of the law.

Sir To. [*Reads*] 'Thou comest to the lady Olivia, and in my sight she uses thee kindly: but thou liest in thy throat; that is not the matter I challenge thee for.'

Fab. Very brief, and to exceeding good sense—less.

Sir To. [*Reads*] 'I will waylay thee going home; where if it be thy chance to kill me,'—

Fab. Good.

Sir To. [*Reads*] 'Thou killest me like a rogue and a villain.'

Fab. Still you keep o' the windy side of the law: good.

Sir To. [*Reads*] 'Fare thee well; and God have mercy upon one of our souls! He may have mercy upon mine; but my hope is better, and so look to thyself. Thy friend, as thou usest him, and thy sworn enemy,

Andrew Aguecheek.'

If this letter move him not, his legs cannot: I'll give 't him.

Mar. You may have very fit occasion for 't: he is now in some commerce with my lady, and will by and by depart.

Sir To. Go, Sir Andrew; scout me for him at the corner of the orchard like a bum-baily: so soon as ever thou seest him, draw; and, as thou drawest, swear horrible; for it comes to pass oft that a terrible oath, with a swaggering accent sharply twanged off, gives manhood more approbation than ever proof itself would have earned him. Away!

Sir And. Nay, let me alone for swearing. *Exit.*

Sir To. Now will not I deliver his letter: for the behaviour of the young gentleman gives him out to be of good capacity and breeding; his employment between his lord and my niece confirms no less: therefore this letter, being so excellently ignorant, will breed no terror in the youth: he will find it comes from a clodpole. But, sir, I will deliver his challenge by word of mouth; set upon Aguecheek a notable report of valour; and drive the gentleman, as I know his youth will aptly receive it, into a most hideous opinion of his rage, skill, fury and impetuosity. This will so fright them both that they will kill one another by the look, like cockatrices.

Enter Olivia *and* Viola.

Fab. Here he comes with your niece: give them way till he take leave, and presently after him.

Sir To. I will meditate the while upon some horrid message for a challenge.

[*Exeunt Sir Toby, Fabian, and Maria.*]

94-95. **in little,** in miniature. 95. **Legion,** evil spirits mentioned in the Scriptures; Mark 5:9. 100. **private,** privacy. 114. **water,** urine (for medical analysis). 125. **bawcock,** French, *beau-coq,* fine fellow. 126. **chuck,** a form of "chick," term of endearment. 129. **for gravity,** suitable to your dignity. **cherry-pit,** a children's game consisting of throwing cherry stones into a hole. 130. **collier,** Satan. 142. **genius,** soul, spirit. 145. **take air,** become exposed. **taint,** spoil. 154. **bar,** court (in order to be judged). 156. **May,** reference to the many Mayings and holidays in May. 168. **note,** observation, remark. 181. **windy,** to windward; so that the law may get no scent of you. 191. **commerce,** conversation. 194. **bum-baily,** minor sheriff's officer. 199. **approbation,** reputation (for courage). 209. **clodpole,** blockhead. 215. **cockatrices,** basilisks, fabulous serpents reputed to be able to kill by a mere look. 218. **presently,** immediately. 228. **jewel,** used of

Oli. I have said too much unto a heart of stone
And laid mine honour too unchary on 't.
There 's something in me that reproves my fault;
But such a headstrong potent fault it is,
That it but mocks reproof.

Vio. With the same 'haviour that your passion bears
Goes on my master's griefs.

Oli. Here, wear this jewel for me, 'tis my picture;
Refuse it not; it hath no tongue to vex you;
And I beseech you come again to-morrow.
What shall you ask of me that I'll deny,
That honour sav'd may upon asking give?

Vio. Nothing but this; your true love for my master.

Oli. How with mine honour may I give him that
Which I have given to you?

Vio. I will acquit you.

Oli. Well, come again to-morrow: fare thee well:
A fiend like thee might bear my soul to hell. [*Exit.*]

Enter [SIR] TOBY *and* FABIAN.

Sir To. Gentleman, God save thee.

Vio. And you, sir.

Sir To. That defence thou hast, betake thee to 't: of what nature the wrongs are thou hast done him, I know not; but thy intercepter, full of despite, bloody as the hunter, attends thee at the orchard-end: dismount thy tuck, be yare in thy preparation, for thy assailant is quick, skilful and deadly.

Vio. You mistake, sir; I am sure no man hath any quarrel to me: my remembrance is very free and clear from any image of offence done to any man.

Sir To. You'll find it otherwise, I assure you: therefore, if you hold your life at any price, betake you to your guard; for your opposite hath in him what youth, strength, skill and wrath can furnish man withal.

Vio. I pray you, sir, what is he?

Sir To. He is knight, dubbed with unhatched rapier and on carpet consideration; but he is a devil in private brawl: souls and bodies hath he divorced three; and his incensement at this moment is so implacable, that satisfaction can be none but by pangs of death and sepulchre. Hob, nob, is his word; give 't or take 't.

Vio. I will return again into the house and desire some conduct of the lady. I am no fighter. I have heard of some kind of men that put quarrels purposely on others, to taste their valour: belike this is a man of that quirk.

Sir To. Sir, no, his indignation derives itself out of a very competent injury: therefore, get you on and give him his desire. Back you shall not to the house, unless you undertake that with me which with as much safety you might answer him: therefore, on, or strip your sword stark naked; for meddle you must, that 's certain, or forswear to wear iron about you.

Vio. This is as uncivil as strange. I beseech you, do me this courteous office, as to know of the knight what my offence to him is: it is something of my negligence, nothing of my purpose.

Sir To. I will do so. Signior Fabian, stay you by this gentleman till my return. *Exit Toby.*

Vio. Pray you, sir, do you know of this matter?

Fab. I know the knight is incensed against you, even to a mortal arbitrement; but nothing of the circumstance more.

Vio. I beseech you, what manner of man is he?

Fab. Nothing of that wonderful promise, to read him by his form, as you are like to find him in the proof of his valour. He is, indeed, sir, the most skilful, bloody and fatal opposite that you could possibly have found in any part of Illyria. Will you walk towards him? I will make your peace with him if I can.

Vio. I shall be much bound to you for 't: I am one that had rather go with sir priest than sir knight: I care not who knows so much of my mettle. *Exeunt.*

Enter [SIR] TOBY *and* [SIR] ANDREW.

Sir To. Why, man, he 's a very devil; I have not seen such a firago. I had a pass with him, rapier, scabbard and all, and he gives me the stuck in with such a mortal motion, that it is inevitable; and on the answer, he pays you as surely as your feet hit the ground they step on. They say he has been fencer to the Sophy.

Sir And. Pox on 't, I'll not meddle with him.

Sir To. Ay, but he will not now be pacified: Fabian can scarce hold him yonder.

Sir And. Plague on 't, an I thought he had been valiant and so cunning in fence, I 'ld have seen him damned ere I 'ld have challenged him. Let him let the matter slip, and I'll give him my horse, grey Capilet.

Sir To. I'll make the motion: stand here, make a good show on 't: this shall end without the perdition of souls. [*Aside*] Marry, I'll ride your horse as well as I ride you.

Enter FABIAN *and* VIOLA.

[*To Fab.*] I have his horse to take up the quarrel: I have persuaded him the youth 's a devil.

Fab. He is as horribly conceited of him; and pants and looks pale, as if a bear were at his heels.

Sir To. [*To Vio.*] There 's no remedy, sir; he will fight with you for 's oath sake: marry, he hath better bethought him of his quarrel, and he finds that now scarce to be worth talking of: therefore draw, for the supportance of his vow; he protests he will not hurt you.

Vio. [*Aside*] Pray God defend me! A little thing would make me tell them how much I lack of a man.

Fab. Give ground, if you see him furious.

Sir To. Come, Sir Andrew, there 's no remedy; the gentleman will, for his honour's sake, have one bout with you; he cannot by the duello avoid it: but he has promised me, as he is a gentleman and a soldier, he will not hurt you. Come on; to 't.

Sir And. Pray God, he keep his oath!

Vio. I do assure you, 'tis against my will. [*They draw.*]

Enter ANTONIO.

Ant. Put up your sword. If this young gentleman
Have done offence, I take the fault on me:

any piece of jewelry. 235. **acquit you,** release you of your promise. 242. **intercepter,** i.e., he who lies in wait. 243. **despite,** spite, malice. 244-245. **dismount thy tuck,** draw thy sword. 245. **yare,** ready, nimble. 257. **unhatched,** for "unhacked." 258. **carpet consideration,** i.e., he is a carpet knight, not a warrior. A carpet knight was one whose title was obtained only through connections at court. 263. **Hob, nob,** originally, have or have not; here, hit or miss. 265. **conduct,** escort. 268. **quirk,** peculiar humor. 273. **that,** i.e., to give satisfaction. 275. **meddle,** engage in conflict. 286. **mortal arbitrement,** trial to the death. 294. **opposite,** antagonist. 299. **sir,** commonly used as the title of priests as well as knights. 302. **firago,** virago. 304. **stuck in,** stoccado, a thrust in fencing. 315. **Capilet,** from "capel," a nag. 320. **take up,** make up. 322. **is as horribly conceited,** has as horrible a conception. 338. **duello,** duelling code.

If you offend him, I for him defy you.
Sir To. You, sir! why, what are you?
Ant. One, sir, that for his love dares yet do more
Than you have heard him brag to you he will.
Sir To. Nay, if you be an undertaker, I am for you. [*They draw.*]

Enter Officers.

Fab. O good Sir Toby, hold! here come the officers.
Sir To. I'll be with you anon.
Vio. Pray, sir, put your sword up, if you please.
Sir And. Marry, will I, sir; and, for that I promised you, I'll be as good as my word: he will bear you easily and reins well.
First Off. This is the man; do thy office.
Sec. Off. Antonio, I arrest thee at the suit of Count Orsino.
Ant. You do mistake me, sir.
First Off. No, sir, no jot; I know your favour well,
Though now you have no sea-cap on your head.
Take him away: he knows I know him well.
Ant. I must obey. [*To Vio.*] This comes with seeking you:
But there 's no remedy; I shall answer it.
What will you do, now my necessity
Makes me to ask you for my purse? It grieves me
Much more for what I cannot do for you
Than what befalls myself. You stand amaz'd;
But be of comfort.
Sec. Off. Come, sir, away.
Ant. I must entreat of you some of that money.
Vio. What money, sir?
For the fair kindness you have show'd me here,
And, part, being prompted by your present trouble,
Out of my lean and low ability
I'll lend you something: my having is not much;
I'll make division of my present with you:
Hold, there's half my coffer.
Ant. Will you deny me now?
Is 't possible that my deserts to you
Can lack persuasion? Do not tempt my misery,
Lest that it make me so unsound a man
As to upbraid you with those kindnesses
That I have done for you.
Vio. I know of none;
Nor know I you by voice or any feature:
I hate ingratitude more in a man
Than lying, vainness, babbling, drunkenness,
Or any taint of vice whose strong corruption
Inhabits our frail blood
Ant. O heavens themselves!
Sec. Off. Come, sir, I pray you, go.
Ant. Let me speak a little. This youth that you see here
I snatch'd one half out of the jaws of death,
Reliev'd him with such sanctity of love,
And to his image, which methought did promise
Most venerable worth, did I devotion.
First Off. What 's that to us? The time goes by: away!
Ant. But O how vile an idol proves this god!
Thou hast, Sebastian, done good feature shame.
In nature there 's no blemish but the mind;
None can be call'd deform'd but the unkind:
Virtue is beauty, but the beauteous evil
Are empty trunks o'erflourish'd by the devil.
First Off. The man grows mad: away with him! Come, come, sir.
Ant. Lead me on. *Exit* [*with Officers*].
Vio. Methinks his words do from such passion fly,
That he believes himself: so do not I.
Prove true, imagination, O, prove true,
That I, dear brother, be now ta'en for you!
Sir To. Come hither, knight; come hither, Fabian: we'll whisper o'er a couplet or two of most sage saws.
Vio. He nam'd Sebastian: I my brother know
Yet living in my glass; even such and so
In favour was my brother, and he went
Still in this fashion, colour, ornament,
For him I imitate: O, if it prove,
Tempests are kind and salt waves fresh in love. [*Exit.*]
Sir To. A very dishonest paltry boy, and more a coward than a hare: his dishonesty appears in leaving his friend here in necessity and denying him; and for his cowardship, ask Fabian.
Fab. A coward, a most devout coward, religious in it.
Sir And. 'Slid, I'll after him again and beat him.
Sir To. Do; cuff him soundly, but never draw thy sword.
Sir And. An I do not,— [*Exit.*]
Fab. Come, let 's see the event.
Sir To. I dare lay any money 'twill be nothing yet. *Exeunt.*

ACT IV.

SCENE I. [*Before* OLIVIA'S *house.*]

Enter SEBASTIAN *and* CLOWN.

Clo. Will you make me believe that I am not sent for you?
Seb. Go to, go to, thou art a foolish fellow:
Let me be clear of thee.
Clo. Well held out, i' faith! No, I do not know you; nor I am not sent to you by my lady, to bid you come speak with her; nor your name is not Master Cesario; nor this is not my nose neither. Nothing that is so is so.
Seb. I prithee, vent thy folly somewhere else:
Thou know'st not me.
Clo. Vent my folly! he has heard that word of some great man and now applies it to a fool. Vent my folly! I am afraid this great lubber, the world, will prove a cockney. I prithee now, ungird thy strangeness and tell me what I shall vent to my lady: shall I vent to her that thou art coming?
Seb. I prithee, foolish Greek, depart from me:

349. **undertaker,** one who takes upon himself a task or business; here, suggests meddling. 377. **part,** partly. 379. **having,** wealth; see glossary. 380. **present,** present store. 381. **coffer,** purse. 382-383. **deserts . . . persuasion,** claims on you can fail to persuade you to help me. 389. **vainness,** boastfulness. 396. **image,** what he appeared to be. 397. **venerable,** worthy of honor (no reference to age). 400-404. **Thou . . . devil.** It was a widespread belief in the Renaissance that the outward and inward parts of man correspond in quality. 404. **o'erflourish'd,** covered with ornamental carvings. 408. **so do not I,** may mean "I do not believe him" or "I do not believe myself" (in the hope that has arisen in me). 418. **prove,** prove true. 421. **dishonesty,** dishonorable character. 427. **'Slid,** oath, "by God's (eye-) lid."

ACT IV. SCENE I. 15. **cockney,** effeminate or foppish fellow. 19. **Greek,** jester. 24. **fourteen years' purchase,** reference to the valuation

There 's money for thee: if you tarry longer,
I shall give worse payment.

Clo. By my troth, thou hast an open hand. These wise men that give fools money get themselves a good report—after fourteen years' purchase.

Enter [SIR] ANDREW, [SIR] TOBY, *and* FABIAN.

Sir And. Now, sir, have I met you again? there 's for you. [*Strikes Seb.*]

Seb. Why, there 's for thee, and there, and there.
Are all the people mad? [*Strikes Sir And.*]

Sir To. Hold, sir, or I'll throw your dagger o'er the house.

Clo. This will I tell my lady straight: I would not be in some of your coats for two pence. [*Exit.*]

Sir To. Come on, sir; hold.

Sir And. Nay, let him alone: I'll go another way to work with him; I'll have an action of battery against him, if there be any law in Illyria: though I struck him first, yet it 's no matter for that.

Seb. Let go thy hand.

Sir To. Come, sir, I will not let you go. Come, my young soldier, put up your iron: you are well fleshed; come on.

Seb. I will be free from thee. What wouldst thou now?
If thou dar'st tempt me further, draw thy sword.

Sir To. What, what? Nay, then I must have an ounce or two of this malapert blood from you.

Enter OLIVIA.

Oli. Hold, Toby; on thy life I charge thee, hold!

Sir To. Madam!

Oli. Will it be ever thus? Ungracious wretch,
Fit for the mountains and the barbarous caves,
Where manners ne'er were preach'd! out of my sight!
Be not offended, dear Cesario.
Rudesby, be gone!
[*Exeunt Sir Toby, Sir Andrew, and Fabian.*]
I prithee, gentle friend,
Let thy fair wisdom, not thy passion, sway
In this uncivil and unjust extent
Against thy peace. Go with me to my house,
And hear thou there how many fruitless pranks
This ruffian hath botch'd up, that thou thereby
Mayst smile at this: thou shalt not choose but go:
Do not deny. Beshrew his soul for me,
He started one poor heart of mine in thee.

Seb. What relish is in this? how runs the stream?
Or I am mad, or else this is a dream:
Let fancy still my sense in Lethe steep;
If it be thus to dream, still let me sleep!

Oli. Nay, come, I prithee; would thou 'ldst be rul'd by me!

Seb. Madam, I will.

Oli. O, say so, and so be! *Exeunt.*

SCENE II. [OLIVIA'S *house.*]

Enter MARIA *and* CLOWN.

Mar. Nay, I prithee, put on this gown and this beard; make him believe thou art Sir Topas the curate: do it quickly; I'll call Sir Toby the whilst. [*Exit.*]

Clo. Well, I'll put it on, and I will dissemble myself in 't; and I would I were the first that ever dissembled in such a gown. I am not tall enough to become the function well, nor lean enough to be thought a good student; but to be said an honest man and a good housekeeper goes as fairly as to say a careful man and a great scholar. The competitors enter.

Enter [SIR] TOBY [*and* MARIA].

Sir To. Jove bless thee, master Parson.

Clo. Bonos dies, Sir Toby: for, as the old hermit of Prague, that never saw pen and ink, very wittily said to a niece of King Gorboduc, 'That that is is;' so I, being master Parson, am master Parson; for, what is 'that' but 'that,' and 'is' but 'is'?

Sir To. To him, Sir Topas.

Clo. What, ho, I say! peace in this prison!

Sir To. The knave counterfeits well; a good knave.

Mal. (*Within*) Who calls there?

Clo. Sir Topas the curate, who comes to visit Malvolio the lunatic.

Mal. Sir Topas, Sir Topas, good Sir Topas, go to my lady.

Clo. Out, hyperbolical fiend! how vexest thou this man! talkest thou nothing but of ladies?

Sir To. Well said, master Parson.

Mal. Sir Topas, never was man thus wronged: good Sir Topas, do not think I am mad: they have laid me here in hideous darkness.

Clo. Fie, thou dishonest Satan! I call thee by the most modest terms; for I am one of those gentle ones that will use the devil himself with courtesy: sayest thou that house is dark?

Mal. As hell, Sir Topas.

Clo. Why, it hath bay windows transparent as barricadoes, and the clerestories toward the south north are as lustrous as ebony; and yet complainest thou of obstruction?

Mal. I am not mad, Sir Topas: I say to you, this house is dark.

Clo. Madman, thou errest: I say, there is no darkness but ignorance; in which thou art more puzzled than the Egyptians in their fog.

Mal. I say, this house is as dark as ignorance, though ignorance were as dark as hell; and I say, there was never man thus abused. I am no more mad than you are: make the trial of it in any constant question.

Clo. What is the opinion of Pythagoras concerning wild fowl?

Mal. That the soul of our grandam might haply inhabit a bird.

Clo. What thinkest thou of his opinion?

Mal. I think nobly of the soul, and no way approve his opinion.

Clo. Fare thee well. Remain thou still in darkness:

of land at the price of twelve years' rental. The fool adds two years; see *purchase* in glossary. 47. **malapert,** saucy, impudent. 55. **Rudesby,** ruffian. 57. **extent,** attack. 60. **botch'd up,** clumsily contrived. 63. **heart,** with play on "hart." 66. **Lethe,** forgetfulness.

SCENE II. 4. **the whilst,** in the meantime. 5. **dissemble,** disguise. 9. **said,** called. 10. **housekeeper,** good liver, hospitable person. 15. **hermit of Prague,** usually thought to refer to Jerome of Prague, but the allusion is obscure. 16. **niece of King Gorboduc.** Gorboduc was an ancient British king; his niece is apparently an invention of the Clown's. 29. **hyperbolical,** boisterous. 41. **clerestories,** upper walls of a building containing windows by which it is lighted. 48. **Egyptians . . . fog.** See Exodus 10:21, 22. 53. **constant question,** consistent discussion. 54-55. **Pythagoras . . . wild fowl,** an opening for the discussion of transmigration of souls, a doctrine held by Pythagoras.

thou shalt hold the opinion of Pythagoras ere I will allow of thy wits, and fear to kill a woodcock, lest thou dispossess the soul of thy grandam. Fare thee well.

Mal. Sir Topas, Sir Topas!

Sir To. My most exquisite Sir Topas!

Clo. Nay, I am for all waters.

Mar. Thou mightst have done this without thy beard and gown: he sees thee not.

Sir To. To him in thine own voice, and bring me word how thou findest him: I would we were well rid of this knavery. If he may be conveniently delivered, I would he were, for I am now so far in offence with my niece that I cannot pursue with any safety this sport to the upshot. Come by and by to my chamber.
Exit [*with Maria*].

Clo. [*Singing*] 'Hey, Robin, jolly Robin,
Tell me how thy lady does.'

Mal. Fool!

Clo. 'My lady is unkind, perdy.'

Mal. Fool!

Clo. 'Alas, why is she so?'

Mal. Fool, I say!

Clo. 'She loves another'—Who calls, ha?

Mal. Good fool, as ever thou wilt deserve well at my hand, help me to a candle, and pen, ink and paper: as I am a gentleman, I will live to be thankful to thee for 't.

Clo. Master Malvolio?

Mal. Ay, good fool.

Clo. Alas, sir, how fell you besides your five wits?

Mal. Fool, there was never man so notoriously abused: I am as well in my wits, fool, as thou art.

Clo. But as well? then you are mad indeed, if you be no better in your wits than a fool.

Mal. They have here propertied me; keep me in darkness, send ministers to me, asses, and do all they can to face me out of my wits.

Clo. Advise you what you say; the minister is here. —Malvolio, Malvolio, thy wits the heavens restore! endeavour thyself to sleep, and leave thy vain bibble babble.

Mal. Sir Topas!

Clo. Maintain no words with him, good fellow. —Who, I, sir? not I, sir. God be wi' you, good Sir Topas.—Marry, amen.—I will, sir, I will.

Mal. Fool, fool, fool, I say!

Clo. Alas, sir, be patient. What say you, sir? I am shent for speaking to you.

Mal. Good fool, help me to some light and some paper: I tell thee, I am as well in my wits as any man in Illyria.

Clo. Well-a-day that you were, sir!

Mal. By this hand, I am. Good fool, some ink, paper and light; and convey what I will set down to my lady: it shall advantage thee more than ever the bearing of letter did.

Clo. I will help you to 't. But tell me true, are you not mad indeed? or do you but counterfeit?

Mal. Believe me, I am not; I tell thee true.

Clo. Nay, I'll ne'er believe a madman till I see his brains. I will fetch you light and paper and ink.

Mal. Fool, I'll requite it in the highest degree: I prithee, be gone.

Clo. [*Singing*] I am gone, sir,
And anon, sir,
I'll be with you again,
In a trice,
Like to the old Vice,
Your need to sustain;

Who, with dagger of lath,
In his rage and his wrath,
Cries, ah, ha! to the devil:
Like a mad lad,
Pare thy nails, dad;
†Adieu, good man devil. *Exit.*

SCENE III. [OLIVIA's *garden.*]

Enter SEBASTIAN.

Seb. This is the air; that is the glorious sun;
This pearl she gave me, I do feel 't and see 't;
And though 'tis wonder that enwraps me thus,
Yet 'tis not madness. Where 's Antonio, then?
I could not find him at the Elephant:
Yet there he was; and there I found this credit,
That he did range the town to seek me out.
His counsel now might do me golden service;
For though my soul disputes well with my sense,
That this may be some error, but no madness,
Yet doth this accident and flood of fortune
So far exceed all instance, all discourse,
That I am ready to distrust mine eyes
And wrangle with my reason that persuades me
To any other trust but that I am mad
Or else the lady 's mad; yet, if 'twere so,
She could not sway her house, command her followers,
Take and give back affairs and their dispatch
With such a smooth, discreet and stable bearing
As I perceive she does: there 's something in 't.
That is deceiveable. But here the lady comes.

Enter OLIVIA *and* Priest.

Oli. Blame not this haste of mine. If you mean well,
Now go with me and with this holy man
Into the chantry by: there, before him,
And underneath that consecrated roof,
Plight me the full assurance of your faith;
That my most jealous and too doubtful soul
May live at peace. He shall conceal it
Whiles you are willing it shall come to note,
What time we will our celebration keep
According to my birth. What do you say?

64. **woodcock.** The woodcock was a type of stupidity because it was easily caught. 68. **for all waters,** i.e., able to sail in all waters. 73. **knavery,** practical joke. 78-85. **'Hey, Robin . . . another,'** fragments of an old song. 92. **besides,** out of. 92-93. **five wits,** intellectual faculties given as common wit, imagination, fantasy, judgment, and memory. 94-95. **notoriously abused,** shamefully mistreated. 99. **propertied,** explained as "treated me as property and thrown me into the lumber-room"; may mean "have chosen to endow me with madness." 102. **Advise you,** take care. 103. **Malvolio.** The Clown here again impersonates Sir Topas. 112. **shent,** scolded, rebuked. 116. **Well-a-day,** alas, would that. 134. **Vice,** the buffoon of moralities and interludes. 136. **dagger of lath,** symbol of the Vice, who was apparently notorious for using it for paring his nails; cf. *Henry V*, IV, iv, 75-77. 141. **good man,** title for a person of substance but not of gentle birth.

SCENE III. 6. **credit,** belief. 15. **trust,** belief. 17. **sway,** rule. 18. **Take and give back,** undertake and discharge. 21. **deceiveable,** deceptive. 24. **chantry,** chapel privately endowed. 27. **jealous,**

Seb. I'll follow this good man, and go with you;
And, having sworn truth, ever will be true.

Oli. Then lead the way, good father; and heavens so shine,
That they may fairly note this act of mine! *Exeunt.*

ACT V.

SCENE I. [*Before* OLIVIA'S *house.*]

Enter CLOWN *and* FABIAN.

Fab. Now, as thou lovest me, let me see his letter.

Clo. Good Master Fabian, grant me another request.

Fab. Any thing.

Clo. Do not desire to see this letter.

Fab. This is, to give a dog, and in recompense desire my dog again.

Enter DUKE, VIOLA, CURIO, *and* Lords.

Duke. Belong you to the Lady Olivia, friends?

Clo. Ay, sir; we are some of her trappings.

Duke. I know thee well: how dost thou, my good fellow?

Clo. Truly, sir, the better for my foes and the worse for my friends.

Duke. Just the contrary; the better for thy friends.

Clo. No, sir, the worse.

Duke. How can that be?

Clo. Marry, sir, they praise me and make an ass of me; now my foes tell me plainly I am an ass: so that by my foes, sir, I profit in the knowledge of myself, and by my friends I am abused: so that, conclusions to be as kisses, if your four negatives make your two affirmatives, why then, the worse for my friends and the better for my foes.

Duke. Why, this is excellent.

Clo. By my troth, sir, no; though it please you to be one of my friends.

Duke. Thou shalt not be the worse for me: there 's gold.

Clo. But that it would be double-dealing, sir, I would you could make it another.

Duke. O, you give me ill counsel.

Clo. Put your grace in your pocket, sir, for this once, and let your flesh and blood obey it.

Duke. Well, I will be so much a sinner, to be a double-dealer: there 's another.

Clo. Primo, secundo, tertio, is a good play; and the old saying is, the third pays for all: the triplex, sir, is a good tripping measure; or the bells of Saint Bennet, sir, may put you in mind; one, two, three.

Duke. You can fool no more money out of me at this throw: if you will let your lady know I am here to speak with her, and bring her along with you, it may awake my bounty further.

Clo. Marry, sir, lullaby to your bounty till I come again. I go, sir; but I would not have you to think that my desire of having is the sin of covetousness: but, as you say, sir, let your bounty take a nap, I will awake it anon. *Exit.*

Enter ANTONIO *and* Officers.

Vio. Here comes the man, sir, that did rescue me.

Duke. That face of his I do remember well;
Yet, when I saw it last, it was besmear'd
As black as Vulcan in the smoke of war:
A bawbling vessel was he captain of,
For shallow draught and bulk unprizable;
With which such scathful grapple did he make
With the most noble bottom of our fleet,
That very envy and the tongue of loss
Cried fame and honour on him. What 's the matter?

First Off. Orsino, this is that Antonio
That took the Phœnix and her fraught from Candy;
And this is he that did the Tiger board,
When your young nephew Titus lost his leg:
Here in the streets, desperate of shame and state,
In private brabble did we apprehend him.

Vio. He did me kindness, sir, drew on my side;
But in conclusion put strange speech upon me:
I know not what 'twas but distraction.

Duke. Notable pirate! thou salt-water thief!
What foolish boldness brought thee to their mercies,
Whom thou, in terms so bloody and so dear,
Hast made thine enemies?

Ant. Orsino, noble sir,
Be pleas'd that I shake off these names you give me:
Antonio never yet was thief or pirate,
Though I confess, on base and ground enough,
Orsino's enemy. A witchcraft drew me hither:
That most ingrateful boy there by your side,
From the rude sea's enrag'd and foamy mouth
Did I redeem; a wrack past hope he was:
His life I gave him and did thereto add
My love, without retention or restraint,
All his in dedication; for his sake
Did I expose myself, pure for his love,
Into the danger of this adverse town;
Drew to defend him when he was beset:
Where being apprehended, his false cunning,
Not meaning to partake with me in danger,
Taught him to face me out of his acquaintance,
And grew a twenty years removed thing
While one would wink; denied me mine own purse,
Which I had recommended to his use
Not half an hour before.

Viol. How can this be?

Duke. When came he to this town?

Ant. To-day, my lord; and for three months before,
No int'rim, not a minute's vacancy,
Both day and night did we keep company.

Enter OLIVIA *and* Attendants.

Duke. Here comes the countess: now heaven walks on earth.

anxious. 29. **Whiles,** until. **come to note,** become known.

ACT V. SCENE I. 1. **his,** i.e., Malvolio's. 23-24. **conclusions . . . kisses,** i.e., as when a young lady, asked for a kiss, says "no" really meaning "yes," showing that things are the opposite of what they seem. 29. **friends,** probably, flatterers. The duke gives a coin to show that he is sincere. The Clown would ask for two except for seeming to be a *double-dealer*, i.e., insincere in his turn. 35. **grace,** apparently a play on *grace* meaning "favor of God," and the title, "Your *Grace*." 39-40. **Primo, secundo, tertio . . . all,** probably dicing terms. 41. **triplex,** triple time in music. 42. **Saint Bennet,** church of St. Benedict; reference to the sound of the church bell, which may have been embodied in a rhyme. 45. **throw,** i.e., of dice. 48. **lullaby,** suggested by *awake*, above. 57. **bawbling,** insignificant. 58. **unprizable,** of value too slight to be estimated. 59. **scathful,** destructive. 64. **fraught,** cargo. **Candy,** Candia, Crete. 67. **desperate . . . state,** reckless of disgrace and position. 68. **brabble,** brawl. 71. **distraction,** madness. 86. **pure,** entirely. 87. **Into,** unto. **adverse,** hostile. 91. **face . . . acquaintance,** deny he knew me. 94. **recommended,** consigned.

But for thee, fellow; fellow, thy words are madness:
Three months this youth hath tended upon me;
But more of that anon. Take him aside.
Oli. What would my lord, but that he may not have,
Wherein Olivia may seem serviceable?
Cesario, you do not keep promise with me.
Vio. Madam!
Duke. Gracious Olivia,—
Oli. What do you say, Cesario? Good my lord,—
Vio. My lord would speak; my duty hushes me.
Oli. If it be aught to the old tune, my lord,
It is as fat and fulsome to mine ear
As howling after music.
Duke. Still so cruel?
Oli. Still so constant, lord.
Duke. What, to perverseness? you uncivil lady,
To whose ingrate and unauspicious altars
My soul the faithfull'st off'rings have breath'd out
That e'er devotion tender'd! What shall I do?
Oli. Even what it please my lord, that shall become him.
Duke. Why should I not, had I the heart to do it,
Like to th' Egyptian thief at point of death,
Kill what I love?—a savage jealousy
That sometime savours nobly. But hear me this:
Since you to non-regardance cast my faith,
And that I partly know the instrument
That screws me from my true place in your favour,
Live you the marble-breasted tyrant still;
But this your minion, whom I know you love,
And whom, by heaven I swear, I tender dearly,
Him will I tear out of that cruel eye,
Where he sits crowned in his master's spite.
Come, boy, with me; my thoughts are ripe in mischief:
I'll sacrifice the lamb that I do love,
To spite a raven's heart within a dove. [*Going.*]
Vio. And I, most jocund, apt and willingly,
To do you rest, a thousand deaths would die. [*Going.*]
Oli. Where goes Cesario?
Vio. After him I love
More than I love these eyes, more than my life,
More, by all mores, than e'er I shall love wife.
If I do feign, you witnesses above
Punish my life for tainting of my love!
Oli. Ay me, detested! how am I beguil'd!
Vio. Who does beguile you? who does do you wrong?
Oli. Hast thou forgot thyself? is it so long?
Call forth the holy father. [*Exit an Attendant.*]
Duke. [*To Vio.*] Come, away!
Oli. Whither, my lord? Cesario, husband, stay.
Duke. Husband!
Oli. Ay, husband: can he that deny?
Duke. Her husband, sirrah!
Vio. No, my lord, not I.
Oli. Alas, it is the baseness of thy fear
That makes thee strangle thy propriety:
Fear not, Cesario; take thy fortunes up;
Be that thou know'st thou art, and then thou art
As great as that thou fear'st.

Enter Priest.

O, welcome, father!
Father, I charge thee, by thy reverence,
Here to unfold, though lately we intended
To keep in darkness what occasion now
Reveals before 'tis ripe, what thou dost know
Hath newly pass'd between this youth and me.
Priest. A contract of eternal bond of love,
Confirm'd by mutual joinder of your hands,
Attested by the holy close of lips,
Strength'ned by interchangement of your rings;
And all the ceremony of this compact
Seal'd in my function, by my testimony:
Since when, my watch hath told me, toward my grave
I have travell'd but two hours.
Duke. O thou dissembling cub! what wilt thou be
When time hath sow'd a grizzle on thy case?
Or will not else thy craft so quickly grow,
That thine own trip shall be thine overthrow?
Farewell, and take her; but direct thy feet
Where thou and I henceforth may never meet.
Vio. My Lord, I do protest—
Oli. O, do not swear!
Hold little faith, though thou hast too much fear.

Enter SIR ANDREW.

Sir And. For the love of God, a surgeon! Send one presently to Sir Toby.

Oli. What 's the matter?

Sir And. H' as broke my head across and has given Sir Toby a bloody coxcomb too: for the love of God, your help! I had rather than forty pound I were at home.

Oli. Who has done this, Sir Andrew?

Sir And. The count's gentleman, one Cesario: we took him for a coward, but he 's the very devil incardinate.

Duke. My gentleman, Cesario?

Sir And. 'Od's lifelings, here he is! You broke my head for nothing; and that that I did, I was set on to do 't by Sir Toby.

Vio. Why do you speak to me? I never hurt you:
You drew your sword upon me without cause;
But I bespake you fair, and hurt you not.

Sir And. If a bloody coxcomb be a hurt, you have hurt me: I think you set nothing by a bloody coxcomb.

Enter [SIR] TOBY *and* CLOWN.

Here comes Sir Toby halting: you shall hear more: but if he had not been in drink, he would have tickled you othergates than he did.

Duke. How now, gentleman! how is 't with you?

Sir To. That 's all one: has hurt me, and there 's the end on 't. Sot, didst see Dick surgeon, sot?

102. **Three months.** This statement is seemingly inconsistent with the hint found in I, iv, 3; it seems reasonable, however, in this connection. 112. **fat and fulsome,** nauseating. 121. **Egyptian thief,** allusion to the story of Theagenes and Chariclea in the *Ethiopica*, a Greek romance by Heliodorus. The robber chief, Thyamis of Memphis, having captured Chariclea and fallen in love with her, was attacked by a larger band of robbers; threatened with death, he attempted to slay her first. 123. **savours nobly,** is not without nobility. 124. **non-regardance,** neglect. 136. **do you rest,** give you ease. 150. **strangle thy propriety,** disavow thyself. 160. **joinder,** joining. 168. **grizzle,** gray hair. **case,** skin, or possibly, body as containing the soul. 170. **trip,** probably from the trip in wrestling; here, dissembling. 174. **little,** i.e., a little. 179. **coxcomb,** fool's cap with the crest of a cock; here, head. 185. **incardinate,** blunder for "incarnate." 187. **'Od's lifelings,** from the oath "By God's life." 196. **halting,** limping. 198. **othergates,** otherwise. 205. **set,** fixed, closed with drink. 206-207. **passy measures pavin,** so Malone; F reads *panyn*. Explained as connected with Italian, *passo e mezzo* (slow moving) and *pavana* (a

Clo. O, he 's drunk, Sir Toby, an hour agone; his eyes were set at eight i' the morning.

Sir To. Then he 's a rogue, †and a passy measures pavin: I hate a drunken rogue.

Oli. Away with him! Who hath made this havoc with them?

Sir And. I'll help you, Sir Toby, because we'll be dressed together.

Sir To. Will you help? an ass-head and a coxcomb and a knave, a thin-faced knave, a gull!

Oli. Get him to bed, and let his hurt be look'd to.
[*Exeunt Clown, Fabian, Sir Toby, and Sir Andrew.*]

Enter SEBASTIAN.

Seb. I am sorry, madam, I have hurt your kinsman;
But, had it been the brother of my blood,
I must have done no less with wit and safety.
You throw a strange regard upon me, and by that
I do perceive it hath offended you:
Pardon me, sweet one, even for the vows
We made each other but so late ago.

Duke. One face, one voice, one habit, and two persons,
A natural perspective, that is and is not!

Seb. Antonio, O my dear Antonio!
How have the hours rack'd and tortur'd me,
Since I have lost thee!

Ant. Sebastian are you?

Seb. Fear'st thou that, Antonio?

Ant. How have you made division of yourself?
An apple, cleft in two, is not more twin
Than these two creatures. Which is Sebastian?

Oli. Most wonderful!

Seb. Do I stand there? I never had a brother;
Nor can there be that deity in my nature,
Of here and every where. I had a sister,
Whom the blind waves and surges have devour'd.
Of charity, what kin are you to me?
What countryman? what name? what parentage?

Vio. Of Messaline: Sebastian was my father;
Such a Sebastian was my brother too,
So went he suited to his watery tomb:
If spirits can assume both form and suit
You come to fright us.

Seb. A spirit I am indeed;
But am in that dimension grossly clad
Which from the womb I did participate.
Were you a woman, as the rest goes even,
I should my tears let fall upon your cheek,
And say 'Thrice-welcome, drowned Viola!'

Vio. My father had a mole upon his brow.

Seb. And so had mine.

Vio. And died that day when Viola from her birth
Had numb'red thirteen years.

Seb. O, that record is lively in my soul!
He finished indeed his mortal act
That day that made my sister thirteen years.

Vio. If nothing lets to make us happy both
But this my masculine usurp'd attire,
Do not embrace me till each circumstance
Of place, time, fortune, do cohere and jump
That I am Viola: which to confirm,
I'll bring you to a captain in this town,
Where lie my maiden weeds; by whose gentle help
I was preserv'd to serve this noble count.
All the occurrence of my fortune since
Hath been between this lady and this lord.

Seb. [*To Olivia*] So comes it, lady, you have been mistook:
But nature to her bias drew in that.
You would have been contracted to a maid;
Nor are you therein, by my life, deceiv'd,
You are betroth'd both to a maid and man.

Duke. Be not amaz'd; right noble is his blood.
If this be so, as yet the glass seems true,
I shall have share in this most happy wrack.
[*To Viola*] Boy, thou hast said to me a thousand times
Thou never shouldst love woman like to me.

Vio. And all those sayings will I over-swear;
And all those swearings keep as true in soul
As doth that orbed continent the fire
That severs day from night.

Duke. Give me thy hand;
And let me see thee in thy woman's weeds.

Vio. The captain that did bring me first on shore
Hath my maid's garments: he upon some action
Is now in durance, at Malvolio's suit,
A gentleman, and follower of my lady's.

Oli. He shall enlarge him: fetch Malvolio hither:
And yet, alas, now I remember me,
They say, poor gentleman, he 's much distract.

Enter CLOWN *with a letter, and* FABIAN.

A most extracting frenzy of mine own
From my remembrance clearly banish'd his.
How does he, sirrah?

Clo. Truly, madam, he holds Belzebub at the stave's end as well as a man in his case may do: has here writ a letter to you; I should have given 't you to-day morning, but as a madman's epistles are no gospels, so it skills not much when they are delivered.

Oli. Open 't, and read it.

Clo. Look then to be well edified when the fool delivers the madman. [*Reads loudly*] 'By the Lord, madam,'—

Oli. How now! art thou mad?

Clo. No, madam, I do but read madness: an your ladyship will have it as it ought to be, you must allow vox.

Oli. Prithee, read i' thy right wits.

Clo. So I do, madonna; but to read his right wits is to read thus: therefore perpend, my princess, and give ear.

Oli. Read it you, sirrah. [*To Fabian.*]

Fab. (*Reads*) 'By the Lord, madam, you wrong me, and the world shall know it: though you have put me into darkness and given your drunken cousin rule over me, yet have I the benefit of my senses as well as

grave and stately dance). It may thus be connected with Sir Toby's impatience to have his wounds dressed. 218. **with wit and safety,** my wits looking out for my safety. 219. **strange regard,** offended look. 224. **perspective,** any optical device or illusion. 235. **here and every where,** omnipresence. 237. **Of charity,** in kindness. 241. **suited,** dressed. 244. **dimension,** body or bodily shape. **grossly clad,** i.e., in flesh. 245. **participate,** share in common with others. 246. **as . . . even,** since everything else agrees. 253. **record,** recollection. 256. **lets,** hinders. 259. **jump,** coincide, fit exactly; see glossary. 267. **nature . . . that,** nature was true to her bent in that. 272. **glass,** i.e., the *natural perspective* of line 224. 276. **over-swear,** swear again. 278. **orbed continent,** in Ptolemaic astronomy, the sphere of the sun, which divides day from night. 283. **durance,** prison, captivity. 285. **enlarge,** release; see glossary. 288. **extracting,** i.e., that obsessed me and drew me away from all other thoughts. 295. **epistles . . . gospels,** an allusion to readings in the church service. 296. **skills,** matters. 304. **vox,** an appropriately loud voice. 307. **perpend,** consider, attend.

your ladyship. I have your own letter that induced me to the semblance I put on; with the which I doubt not but to do myself much right, or you much shame. Think of me as you please. I leave my duty a little unthought of and speak out of my injury.
THE MADLY-USED MALVOLIO.'

Oli. Did he write this?
Clo. Ay, madam.
Duke. This savours not much of distraction.
Oli. See him deliver'd, Fabian; bring him hither.
[*Exit Fabian.*]
My lord, so please you, these things further thought on,
To think me as well a sister as a wife,
One day shall crown th' alliance on 't, so please you,
Here at my house and at my proper cost.
Duke. Madam, I am most apt t' embrace your offer.
[*To Viola*] Your master quits you; and for your service done him,
So much against the mettle of your sex,
So far beneath your soft and tender breeding,
And since you call'd me master for so long,
Here is my hand: you shall from this time be
Your master's mistress.
Oli. A sister! you are she.

Enter [FABIAN, *with*] MALVOLIO.

Duke. Is this the madman?
Oli. Ay, my lord, this same.
How now, Malvolio!
Mal. Madam, you have done me wrong,
Notorious wrong.
Oli. Have I, Malvolio? no.
Mal. Lady, you have. Pray you, peruse that letter.
You must not now deny it is your hand:
Write from it, if you can, in hand or phrase;
Or say 'tis not your seal, not your invention:
You can say none of this: well, grant it then
And tell me, in the modesty of honour,
Why you have given me such clear lights of favour,
Bade me come smiling and cross-garter'd to you,
To put on yellow stockings and to frown
Upon Sir Toby and the lighter people;
And, acting this in an obedient hope,
Why have you suffer'd me to be imprison'd,
Kept in a dark house, visited by the priest,
And made the most notorious geck and gull
That e'er invention play'd on? tell me why.
Oli. Alas, Malvolio, this is not my writing,
Though, I confess, much like the character:
But out of question 'tis Maria's hand.
And now I do bethink me, it was she
First told me thou wast mad; then cam'st in smiling,
And in such forms which here were presuppos'd
Upon thee in the letter. Prithee, be content:
This practice hath most shrewdly pass'd upon thee;
But when we know the grounds and authors of it,
Thou shalt be both the plaintiff and the judge
Of thine own cause.
Fab. Good madam, hear me speak,
And let no quarrel nor no brawl to come
Taint the condition of this present hour,
Which I have wond'red at. In hope it shall not,
Most freely I confess, myself and Toby
Set this device against Malvolio here,
Upon some stubborn and uncourteous parts
We had conceiv'd against him: Maria writ
The letter at Sir Toby's great importance;
In recompense whereof he hath married her.
How with a sportful malice it was follow'd,
May rather pluck on laughter than revenge;
If that the injuries be justly weigh'd
That have on both sides pass'd.
Oli. Alas, poor fool, how have they baffled thee!

Clo. Why, 'some are born great, some achieve greatness, and some have greatness thrown upon them.' I was one, sir, in this interlude; one Sir Topas, sir; but that 's all one. 'By the Lord, fool, I am not mad.' But do you remember? 'Madam, why laugh you at such a barren rascal? an you smile not, he 's gagged:' and thus the whirligig of time brings in his revenges.

Mal. I'll be reveng'd on the whole pack of you! [*Exit.*]
Oli. He hath been most notoriously abus'd.
Duke. Pursue him, and entreat him to a peace:
He hath not told us of the captain yet:
When that is known and golden time convents,
A solemn combination shall be made
Of our dear souls. Meantime, sweet sister,
We will not part from hence. Cesario, come;
For so you shall be, while you are a man;
But when in other habits you are seen,
Orsino's mistress and his fancy's queen.
Exeunt [*all, except Clown*].

Clo. (*Sings*)
When that I was and a little tiny boy,
With hey, ho, the wind and the rain,
A foolish thing was but a toy,
For the rain it raineth every day.

But when I came to man's estate,
With hey, ho, &c.
'Gainst knaves and thieves men shut their gate,
For the rain, &c.

But when I came, alas! to wive,
With hey, ho, &c.
By swaggering could I never thrive,
For the rain, &c.

But when I came unto my beds,
With hey, ho, &c.
With toss-pots still had drunken heads,
For the rain, &c.

A great while ago the world begun,
With hey, ho, &c.
But that 's all one, our play is done,
And we'll strive to please you every day. [*Exit.*]

324. **these . . . on,** i.e., when they have been considered. 327. **proper,** own. 330. **mettle,** natural disposition. 340. **from it,** differently. 343. **modesty of honour,** sense of propriety belonging to honorable persons. 347. **lighter,** less important. 351. **geck,** dupe. 355. **out of,** beyond. 358. **presuppos'd,** offered beforehand for adoption. 360. **shrewdly,** cruelly. 364. **to come,** i.e., future brawl. 369. **Upon,** on account of. **parts,** qualities. 370. **conceiv'd against,** observed in and charged against. 371. **importance,** importunity. 377. **baffled,** treated ignominiously. 391. **convents,** suits; the word elsewhere means "summons." 412. **toss-pots,** drunkards.

HAMLET, PRINCE OF DENMARK

A recurring motif in *Hamlet* is of a seemingly healthy exterior concealing inward sickness. Mere pretense of virtue, as Hamlet warns his mother, "will but skin and film the ulcerous place, Whiles rank corruption, mining all within, Infects unseen" (III,iv). His mother's shameful deed "takes off the rose From the fair forehead of an innocent love And sets a blister there." Polonius confesses, when he is about to use his daughter as a decoy for Hamlet, that "with devotion's visage And pious action we do sugar o'er The devil himself"; and his observation elicits a more anguished *mea culpa* from Claudius in an aside: "How smart a lash that speech doth give my conscience! The harlot's cheek, beautied with plast'ring art, Is not more ugly to the thing that helps it Than is my deed to my most painted word" (III,i).

This motif of concealed evil and disease continually reminds us that, in both a specific and a broader sense, "Something is rotten in the state of Denmark." The specific source of contamination is a poison: the poison with which Claudius has killed Hamlet Senior, the poison in the players' version of this same murder, and the two poisons (envenomed sword and poisoned drink) with which Claudius and Laertes plot to rid themselves of young Hamlet. More generally, the poison is man's evil nature seeking to destroy his better nature, as in the archetypal murder of Abel by Cain. "O my offence is rank, it smells to heaven," laments Claudius, "It hath the primal curse upon 't, A brother's murther" (III,iii). Hamlet Senior and Claudius typify what is best and worst in man, the sun-god Hyperion compared to a satyr. Claudius is a "serpent" and a "mildew'd ear Blasting his wholesome brother" (III,iv). Too many men, finding this quality in themselves, are perversely drawn in spite of their better qualities to "some vicious mole of nature" in themselves over which they have no control. "Their virtues else—be they as pure as grace, As infinite as man may undergo—Shall in the general censure take corruption From that particular fault." The "dram of evil" pollutes "all the noble substance" (I,iv). Thus poison spreads outward to infect individual men, just as bad men can infect an entire court or nation.

Hamlet, his mind attuned to philosophical matters, is keenly and poetically aware of man's fallen condition. He is, moreover, a shrewd observer of the Danish court, one familiar with its ways and at the same time newly returned from abroad, looking at Denmark with a stranger's eyes. What particularly darkens his view of man, however, is not so much the general condition of mankind as Hamlet's knowledge of a dreadful secret. Even before he learns of his father's murder, Hamlet senses that something is more deeply amiss than his mother's overhasty marriage to her deceased husband's brother. This is serious enough, to be sure, for it violates a widely held taboo (parallel to the marriage of a widower to his deceased wife's sister, long regarded as incestuous by the English), and is thus accurately referred to as "incest" by Hamlet and his father's ghost. The appalling spectacle of Gertrude's "wicked speed, to post With such dexterity to incestuous sheets" overwhelms Hamlet with revulsion at carnal appetite and greatly intensifies the emotional crisis any son goes through when forced to contemplate his father's death and mother's remarriage. Still, the Ghost's revelation is of something far worse, something Hamlet has subconsciously feared and suspected. "O my prophetic soul! My uncle!" Now Hamlet has confirming evidence for his intuition that the world itself is "an unweeded garden That grows to seed; things rank and gross in nature Possess it merely" (I,ii).

Something is indeed rotten in the state of Denmark. The monarch on whom the health and safety of the kingdom should depend is the perpetrator of a lie and an unspeakable crime. Yet few persons know his secret: Hamlet, Horatio only belatedly, Claudius himself, and ourselves as audience. Many ironies and misunderstandings of the play cannot be understood without a proper awareness of this gap between Hamlet's knowledge and most others' ignorance of the murder. For, according to their own lights, Polonius and the rest behave as courtiers normally behave, obeying and flattering a king whom they acknowledge their legitimate ruler. Hamlet, for his part, is so obsessed with the secret murder that he overreacts to those around him, rejecting well-meant overtures of friendship and becoming embittered, callous, brutal, and even violent. His antisocial behavior gives the others good reason to fear him as a menace to the state. Nevertheless, we share with Hamlet a knowledge of the truth, and know that he is right whereas the others are at best unhappily deceived by their own blind complicity in evil.

Rosencrantz and Guildenstern, for instance, are boyhood friends of Hamlet but are now dependent on the favor of King Claudius. Despite their seeming concern for their onetime comrade, and Hamlet's initial pleasure in receiving them, they are faceless courtiers whose very names, like their personalities, are virtually interchangeable. "Thanks, Rosencrantz and gentle Guildenstern," says the king, and "Thanks, Guildenstern and gentle Rosencrantz" echoes the queen (II,ii). They cannot understand why Hamlet increasingly mocks their overtures of friendship, whereas Hamlet cannot stomach their subservience to the king. The secret murder divides Hamlet from them, since only he knows of it. As the confrontation between Hamlet and Claudius grows more deadly, Rosencrantz and Guildenstern, not knowing the true cause, can only interpret Hamlet's behavior as dangerous madness. The wild display he puts on at the players' performance, and the killing of Polonius, are evidence of a treasonous threat to the crown, eliciting from them staunch assertions of the

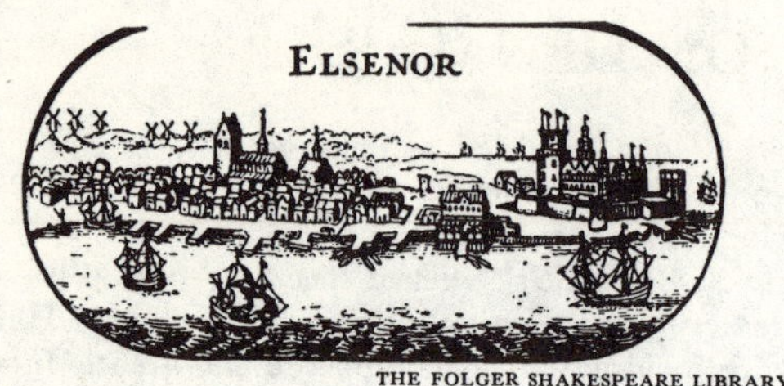

THE FOLGER SHAKESPEARE LIBRARY

Elsinore, the Danish seaport and castle, scene of Hamlet.

divine right of kings. "Most holy and religious fear it is To keep those many many bodies safe That live and feed upon your majesty," professes Guildenstern, and Rosencrantz reiterates the theme: "The cess of majesty Dies not alone; but, like a gulf, doth draw What's near it with it" (III,iii). These sentiments of Elizabethan orthodoxy, which would pass for true current in Shakespeare's history plays, are here undercut by a devastating irony, since they are spoken unwittingly in defense of a murderer. This irony pursues Rosencrantz and Guildenstern to their graves, for they are killed performing what they see as their duty to convey Hamlet safely to England. They are as ignorant of Claudius' secret orders for the murder of Hamlet in England as they are of Claudius' real reason for wishing to be rid of his stepson. That Hamlet should ingeniously remove the secret commission from Rosencrantz and Guildenstern's packet and substitute an order for their execution is ironically fitting, even though they are guiltless of having plotted Hamlet's death. "Why, man, they did make love to this employment," says Hamlet to Horatio. "They are not near my conscience; their defeat Does by their own insinuation grow" (V,ii). In other words, they have condemned themselves by officiously interceding in deadly affairs of which they had no comprehension.

Polonius too must die for meddling. It seems a harsh fate, since he too wishes no physical harm to Hamlet, and is only trying to ingratiate himself with Claudius. Yet Polonius' complicity in jaded court politics is more deep than his fatuous parental sententiousness might lead one to suppose. His famous advice to his son, often quoted out of context as though it were wise counsel, is in fact a worldly gospel of self-interest and concern for appearances. Like his son Laertes he cynically presumes that Hamlet's affection for Ophelia cannot be serious, since princes are not free to marry ladies of the court; accordingly, Polonius obliges his daughter to return the love letters she so cherishes. Polonius' spies are everywhere, seeking to entrap Polonius' own son in fleshly sin or to discover symptoms of Hamlet's presumed lovesickness. Polonius cuts a ridiculous figure as a prattling busybody, but he has actually helped Claudius to the throne and is an essential instrument of royal policy. His ineffectuality and lack of knowledge of the murder do not really lessen the degree of his guilty involvement.

Ophelia is more innocent than her father and brother, and more truly affectionate toward Hamlet. Nevertheless her pitiable story suggests that weak-willed acquiescence becomes poisoned by the evil to which it surrenders. Ophelia is much like Gertrude, who has yielded to Claudius' importunity without ever knowing fully what awful price Claudius has paid for her and for the throne. The resemblance between Ophelia and Gertrude confirms Hamlet's tendency to generalize about feminine weakness—"Frailty, thy name is woman"—and prompts his misogynistic outburst against Ophelia when he realizes she too is spying on him. His rejection of love and friendship (except for Horatio's) seems paranoid in character, and yet is at least partially justified by the fact that so many of the court are in fact conspiring to learn his secret.

It is their oversimplification of his dilemma and their facile analyses that vex Hamlet as much as the meddling. When they presume to diagnose his malady, the courtiers actually reveal more about themselves than about Hamlet. Rosencrantz and Guildenstern think in political terms reflecting their own ambitious natures, and Hamlet takes mordant delight in leading them on. "Sir, I lack advancement," he mockingly answers Rosencrantz' questioning as to the cause of his distemper. Rosencrantz is immediately taken in: "How can that be, when you have the voice of the king himself for your succession in Denmark?" (III,ii). Actually Hamlet does hold a grudge against Claudius for having "Popp'd in between th' election and my hopes" (V,ii), using the Danish custom of "election" by the chief lords of the realm to deprive young Hamlet of the succession that would normally have been his. Nevertheless, it is a gross oversimplification to suppose that political frustration is the key to Hamlet's sorrow. To speculate thus is more presumptuous than to attempt playing the recorder without having studied that musical instrument. "Why, look you now, how unworthy a thing you would make of me!" Hamlet protests to Rosencrantz and Guildenstern. "You would play upon me; you would seem to know my stops; you would pluck out the heart of my mystery" (III,ii). Yet the worst offender in such distortion of complex truth is Polonius, whose diagnosis of lovesickness appears to have been inspired by recollections of Polonius' own far-off youth. ("Truly in my youth I suffered much extremity for love; very near this," II,ii). Polonius' incredibly fatuous complacency in his own powers of analysis—"If circumstances lead me, I will find Where truth is hid, though it were hid indeed Within the centre"—reads like a parody of Hamlet's struggle to discover what is true and what is not.

Thus, although Hamlet may seem to react with excessive bitterness toward those who are set to watch over him, the corruption he decries in Denmark is both real and universal. "The time is out of joint," he laments. "O cursed spite That ever I was born to set it right!" (I,v). How is he to proceed in setting things right? Ever since the nineteenth century it has been fashionable to discover reasons for Hamlet's delaying in revenge. The basic Romantic approach is to find a defect, or tragic flaw, in Hamlet himself. In Coleridge's words, Hamlet suffers from "an overbalance in the contemplative faculty," and is "one who vacillates from sensibility and procrastinates from thought, and loses the power of action in the energy of resolve." More recent psychological interpretations, like that of Freud's disciple, Ernest Jones, are still Romantic in character in that they too seek to explain Hamlet's failure of will. In Jones' interpretation, Hamlet is the victim of an Oedipal trauma; he has longed unconsciously to possess his mother, but cannot bring himself to punish the hated uncle who has supplanted him in his incestuous and forbidden desire. Such interpretations suggest at least that Hamlet continues to serve as a mirror in which analysts who would pluck out the heart of his mystery see an image of themselves—just as Rosencrantz and Guildenstern read politics, and Polonius lovesickness, into Hamlet's distress.

We must ask, however, not only whether the answers to Hamlet's supposed delay are valid but whether the question being asked is itself valid. Is the delay unnecessary or excessive? The question did not even arise until the nineteenth century. Earlier audiences were evidently satisfied that Hamlet must test the Ghost's credibility, since apparitions can tell half-truths to deceive men, and that once Hamlet has confirmed the Ghost's word he proceeds as resolutely as his canny adversary allows. More recent criticism, perhaps reflecting a modern absorption in existentialist philosophy, has proposed that Hamlet's dilemma of action is not a matter of personal failure but of the absurdity of action itself in a corrupt world. Does what Hamlet is asked to do make any sense, given the bestial nature of man and the impossibility of knowing what is right? In part it is a matter of style: Claudius' Denmark is crassly vulgar, and to combat this vulgarity on its own terms seems to require the sort of bad histrionics Hamlet derides in actors who mouth their lines or tear a passion to tatters. Hamlet's dilemma of action can best be studied in the play by comparing him with various characters who are obliged to act in situations similar to his own, and who respond in meaningfully different ways.

Three young men—Hamlet, Laertes, and Fortinbras—are called upon to avenge their fathers' violent deaths. Ophelia too has lost a father by violent means, and her madness and death are another kind of reaction to such a loss. The responses of Laertes and Fortinbras offer implicit object lessons to Hamlet, and in both cases the lesson seems to be the futility of positive and forceful action. Laertes thinks he has received an unambiguous mandate to revenge, since Hamlet has undoubtedly slain Polonius and helped to deprive Ophelia of her sanity. Accordingly Laertes comes back to Denmark in a fury, stirring the rabble to an insurrectionist mood with his demagoguery and spouting Senecan rant about dismissing conscience "to the profoundest pit" in his quest for vengeance (IV,v). When Claudius asks what Laertes would do to Hamlet "To show yourself your father's son in deed More than in words," Laertes fires back: "To cut his throat i' th' church!" (IV,vii). This resolution is wholly understandable. The pity is, however, that Laertes has only superficially identified the murderer in the case. He is too easily deceived by Claudius because he has jumped to easy and fallacious conclusions, and so is doomed to become a pawn in Claudius' sly maneuverings. Too late he sees his error and must die for it, begging and receiving Hamlet's forgiveness. Before we accuse Hamlet of thinking too deliberately before acting, we must consider that Laertes has not thought enough.

Fortinbras of Norway, as his name implies ("strong in arms"), is one who believes in decisive action. At the play's beginning we learn that his father has been slain in battle by old Hamlet, and that Fortinbras has collected an army to win back by force the territory fairly won by the Danes in that encounter. Like Hamlet, young Fortinbras does not succeed his father to the throne, but must now contend with an uncle-king. When this uncle, at Claudius' instigation, forbids Fortinbras to march against the Danes, and rewards him for his restraint with a huge annual income and a commission to fight the Poles instead, Fortinbras cannily embraces the new opportunity. He pockets the money, marches against Poland, and waits for occasion to deliver Denmark as well into his hands. Clearly this is more of a success story than that of Laertes, and Hamlet does after all give his blessing to the "election" of Fortinbras to the Danish throne. Fortinbras is the man of the hour, the representative of a restored political stability. Yet Hamlet's admiration for this man on horseback is qualified by a profound ironic reservation. The spectacle of Fortinbras marching against Poland "to gain a little patch of ground That hath in it no profit but the name" prompts Hamlet to berate himself for inaction, but he cannot ignore the absurdity of the effort. "Two thousand souls and twenty thousand ducats Will not debate the question of this straw." The soldiers will risk their very lives "Even for an egg-shell" (IV,iv). It is only one step from this view of the vanity of ambitious striving to the speculation that great Caesar or Alexander, dead and turned to dust, may one day produce the loam or clay with which to stop the bunghole of a beer barrel. Fortinbras epitomizes the ongoing political order after Hamlet's death, but is that order of any consequence to us after we have experienced with Hamlet the futility of all human endeavor?

To ask such a question is to seek more passive or self-abnegating answers to the riddle of life, and Hamlet is much attuned to such inquiries. Even before he learns of his father's murder he meditates on suicide, wishing "that the Everlasting had not fix'd His canon 'gainst self-slaughter" (I,ii). Once again, as with the alternative of action, other characters serve as foils to Hamlet, revealing both the attractions and perils of withdrawal. Ophelia is destroyed by meekly acquiescing in others' desires. Whether she commits suicide is uncertain, but the very possibility reminds us that Hamlet has considered and reluctantly rejected this despairing path as forbidden by Christian teaching. He has also playacted at the madness to which Ophelia succumbs. Gertrude identifies herself with Ophelia, and like her has surrendered her will to male importunity. We suspect she knows little of the actual murder but dares not think how deeply she may be implicated. Her death may possibly be a suicide also, one of atonement. A more attractive alternative to action for Hamlet is acting, and he is full of advice to the visiting players. Yet playacting is, he recognizes, an escape for him, a way of unpacking his heart with words, of narcissistically verbalizing his situation without doing something to remedy it. Acting and talking remind him too much of Polonius, who was an actor in his youth and who continues to be, like Hamlet, an inveterate punster.

Of the passive responses in the play, the stoicism of Horatio is by far the most attractive to Hamlet. "More an antique Roman than a Dane," Horatio is, as Hamlet praises him, immune to flattering or to opportunities for cheap self-advancement. He is "As one, in suff'ring all, that suffers nothing, A man that fortune's buffets and rewards Hast ta'en with equal thanks" (III,ii). Such a person has a sure defense against the worst that life can offer. Hamlet can trust and love Horatio as he can no one else. Yet even here there are limits, for Horatio's skeptical and Roman philosophy cuts him off from a Christian and metaphysical overview. "There are more things in heaven and earth, Horatio, Than are dreamt of in your philosophy" (I,v). After they have beheld together the skulls of Yorick's graveyard, Horatio cannot share with Hamlet the exulting Christian perception that, although human life is indeed vain, providence will reveal a pattern transcending human sorrow.

Hamlet's path must lie somehow between the rash suddenness of Laertes or the astute *realpolitik* of Fortinbras on the one hand, and the passivity of Ophelia or Gertrude and the stoic resignation of Horatio on the other. Accordingly, he alternates between action and inaction in his attempts to fulfill his mission, finding neither satisfactory. The Ghost has commanded Hamlet to revenge, but has not explained how this is to be done; indeed, Gertrude is to be left passively to heaven and her conscience. If this method will suffice for her (and Christian wisdom taught that such a purgation was as thorough as it was sure), why not for Claudius? If Claudius must be killed, should it be while he is at his sin rather than at his prayers? The play is full of questions, stemming chiefly from the enigmatic commands of the Ghost. "Say, why is this? wherefore? what should we do?" (I,iv). Hamlet is not incapable of action; he shows unusual strength and cunning on the pirate ship, or in his duel with Laertes ("I shall win at the odds"), or especially in his slaying of Polonius. Here is forthright action of the sort Laertes espouses. Yet when the corpse behind his mother's arras turns out to be Polonius rather than Claudius, Hamlet knows he has offended heaven. Even if Polonius deserves what he got, Hamlet has made himself into a cruel "scourge" of providence who must accordingly suffer retribution as well as deal it out. Inconsiderate action has not accomplished what the Ghost commanded.

The Ghost in fact does not appear to speak for providence. His message is of revenge, a pagan concept basic to all primitive societies but at odds with Christian teaching. His wish that Claudius be sent to hell and that Gertrude be more gently treated is not the judgment of an impartial deity but the emotional reaction of a murdered man's restless spirit. This is not to say that Hamlet is being tempted to perform a damnable act, as he fears possible, but that the Ghost's command cannot readily be reconciled with a complex and balanced view of justice. If Hamlet were to spring on Claudius in the fullness of his vice and cut his throat, we would pronounce Hamlet a murderer. What Hamlet learns instead is that he must become the instrument of providence according to *its* plans, not his own. After his return from England, he senses triumphantly that all will be for the best if he allows providence to decide the time and place for his final act. Under these conditions, rash action will be right. "Prais'd be rashness for it, let us know, Our indiscretion sometime serves us well, When our deep plots do pall: and that should teach us There 's a divinity that shapes our ends, Rough-hew them how we will" (V,ii). Passivity too is now a proper course, for Hamlet puts himself wholly at the disposal of providence. What had seemed so impossible when Hamlet tried to formulate his own design now proves elementary once he trusts to heaven's justice. Rashness and passivity are perfectly fused. Hamlet is revenged without having to commit premeditated murder, and is relieved of his painful existence without having to commit suicide.

Providence does indeed accomplish all that Hamlet desires, by a route so circuitous that no man could ever have foreseen or devised it. Polonius' death, as it turns out, was instrumental after all, for it led to Laertes' angry return to Denmark and the challenge to a duel. Every seemingly unrelated event has its place; "There 's a special providence in the fall of a sparrow." Repeatedly the characters stress the role of seeming accident leading to just retribution. Horatio sums up a pattern "Of accidental judgements, casual slaughters . . . And, in this upshot, purposes mistook Fall'n on th' inventors' heads." Laertes confesses himself "a woodcock to mine own springe." As Hamlet had said earlier, of Rosencrantz and Guildenstern, " 'tis the sport to have the enginer Hoist with his own petar" (III,iv). Thus, too, Claudius' poisoned cup, intended for Hamlet, kills the queen for whom Claudius had done such evil.

Divine justice has supplanted all human agencies

of revenge. Yet in its origins *Hamlet* is a revenge story, and these traditions have left some residual savagery in the play. In the *Historia Danica* of Saxo Grammaticus, 1180–1208, and in the rather free translation of Saxo into French by Belleforest, *Histoires Tragiques* (1576), Hamlet is cunning and bloodily resolute throughout. He kills an eavesdropper without a qualm during the interview with his mother, and exchanges letters on his way to England with characteristic shrewdness. Ultimately he returns to Denmark, sets fire to his uncle's hall, slays its courtly inhabitants, and claims his rightful throne from a grateful people. The Ghost, absent in this account, may well have been supplied by Thomas Kyd, author of *The Spanish Tragedy* (c. 1587) and seemingly of a lost *Hamlet* play in existence by 1589. The extant *Spanish Tragedy* bears many resemblances to our *Hamlet*, and suggests what the lost *Hamlet* may well have contained: a sensational murder, a Senecan Ghost demanding revenge, the avenger hampered by court intrigue, his resort to a feigned madness, his difficulty in authenticating the ghostly vision. A German version of *Hamlet*, called *Der bestrafte Brudermord* (1710), based seemingly on the older *Hamlet*, includes such details as the play within the play, the sparing of the king at his prayers in order to damn his soul, Ophelia's madness, the fencing match with poisoned swords and poisoned drink, and the final catastrophe of vengeance and death. Similarly, the early pirated first quarto of *Hamlet* (1603) offers some passages seemingly based on the older play by Kyd.

Although this evidence suggests that Shakespeare received most of his plot material intact, his transformation of that material was nonetheless immeasurable. To be sure, Kyd's *Spanish Tragedy* contains many rhetorical passages on the inadequacy of human justice, but the overall effect is still sensational and the outcome is a triumph for the pagan spirit of revenge. So too in general with the many revenge plays of the 1590's and 1600's which Kyd's dramatic genius had inspired, including Shakespeare's own *Titus Andronicus* (c. 1589–1591). *Hamlet*, written in about 1599–1601 (it is not mentioned by Frances Meres in 1598, and was entered in the Stationers' Register in 1602), is unparalleled in its philosophical richness. Its ending is truly cathartic, for Hamlet dies not as a bloodied avenger but as one who has affirmed the tragic dignity of man. His courage and faith, maintained in the face of great odds, atone for the dismal corruption in which Denmark has festered. His resolutely honest inquiries have taken him beyond the revulsion and doubt that express so eloquently, among other matters, the fearful response of Shakespeare's own generation to a seeming breakdown of established political, theological, and astronomical values. Hamlet finally perceives that "if it be not now, yet it will come," and that "the readiness is all" (V,ii). His discovery in no way denies the tragic circumstance of life, but does provide a philosophic consolation by which man may rise above despair.

HAMLET, PRINCE OF DENMARK

[*Dramatis Personae*

CLAUDIUS, King of Denmark.
HAMLET, *son to the late, and nephew to the present king.*
POLONIUS, *lord chamberlain.*
HORATIO, *friend to Hamlet.*
LAERTES, *son to Polonius.*
VOLTIMAND, CORNELIUS, ROSENCRANTZ, GUILDENSTERN, OSRIC, A Gentleman, — *courtiers.*
A Priest.
MARCELLUS, BERNARDO, — *officers.*
FRANCISCO, *a soldier.*
REYNALDO, *servant to Polonius.*
Players.
Two Clowns, *grave-diggers.*
FORTINBRAS, Prince of Norway.
A Captain.
English Ambassadors.

GERTRUDE, Queen of Denmark, *and mother to Hamlet.*
OPHELIA, *daughter to Polonius.*

Lords, Ladies, Officers, Soldiers, Sailors, Messengers, *and other* Attendants.
Ghost of Hamlet's Father.

SCENE: *Denmark.*]

[ACT I.

SCENE I. *Elsinore. A platform before the castle.*]

Enter BERNARDO *and* FRANCISCO, *two sentinals.*

Ber. Who 's there?
Fran. Nay, answer me: stand, and unfold yourself.
Ber. Long live the king!
Fran. Bernardo?
Ber. He.
Fran. You come most carefully upon your hour.
Ber. 'Tis now struck twelve; get thee to bed, Francisco.
Fran. For this relief much thanks: 'tis bitter cold,
And I am sick at heart.
Ber. Have you had quiet guard?
Fran. Not a mouse stirring.
Ber. Well, good night.
If you do meet Horatio and Marcellus,
The rivals of my watch, bid them make haste.

Enter HORATIO *and* MARCELLUS.

Fran. I think I hear them. Stand, ho! Who is there?
Hor. Friends to this ground.

Mar. And liegemen to the Dane.
Fran. Give you good night.
Mar. O, farewell, honest soldier:
Who hath reliev'd you?
Fran. Bernardo hath my place.
Give you good night. *Exit Fran.*
Mar. Holla! Bernardo!
Ber. Say,
What, is Horatio there?
Hor. A piece of him.
Ber. Welcome, Horatio: welcome, good Marcellus.
Mar. What, has this thing appear'd again to-night?
Ber. I have seen nothing.
Mar. Horatio says 'tis but our fantasy,
And will not let belief take hold of him
Touching this dreaded sight, twice seen of us:
Therefore I have entreated him along
With us to watch the minutes of this night;
That if again this apparition come,
He may approve our eyes and speak to it.
Hor. Tush, tush, 'twill not appear.
Ber. Sit down awhile;
And let us once again assail your ears,
That are so fortified against our story
What we have two nights seen.
Hor. Well, sit we down,
And let us hear Bernardo speak of this.
Ber. Last night of all,
When yond same star that 's westward from the pole
Had made his course t' illume that part of heaven
Where now it burns, Marcellus and myself,
The bell then beating one,—

Enter Ghost.

Mar. Peace, break thee off; look, where it comes again!
Ber. In the same figure, like the king that 's dead.
Mar. Thou art a scholar; speak to it, Horatio.
Ber. Looks 'a not like the king? mark it, Horatio.
Hor. Most like: it harrows me with fear and wonder.
Ber. It would be spoke to.
Mar. Speak to it, Horatio.
Hor. What art thou that usurp'st this time of night,
Together with that fair and warlike form
In which the majesty of buried Denmark
Did sometimes march? by heaven I charge thee, speak!
Mar. It is offended.
Ber. See, it stalks away!
Hor. Stay! speak, speak! I charge thee, speak!
Exit Ghost.
Mar. 'Tis gone, and will not answer.
Ber. How now, Horatio! you tremble and look pale:
Is not this something more than fantasy?
What think you on 't?
Hor. Before my God, I might not this believe
Without the sensible and true avouch
Of mine own eyes.
Mar. Is it not like the king?
Hor. As thou art to thyself:
Such was the very armour he had on
When he the ambitious Norway combated;
So frown'd he once, when, in an angry parle,
He smote the sledded Polacks on the ice.
'Tis strange.
Mar. Thus twice before, and jump at this dead hour,
With martial stalk hath he gone by our watch.
Hor. In what particular thought to work I know not;
But in the gross and scope of my opinion,
This bodes some strange eruption to our state.
Mar. Good now, sit down, and tell me, he that knows,
Why this same strict and most observant watch
So nightly toils the subject of the land,
And why such daily cast of brazen cannon,
And foreign mart for implements of war;
Why such impress of shipwrights, whose sore task
Does not divide the Sunday from the week;
What might be toward, that this sweaty haste
Doth make the night joint-labourer with the day:
Who is 't that can inform me?
Hor. That can I;
At least, the whisper goes so. Our last king,
Whose image even but now appear'd to us,
Was, as you know, by Fortinbras of Norway,
Thereto prick'd on by a most emulate pride,
Dar'd to the combat; in which our valiant Hamlet—
For so this side of our known world esteem'd him—
Did slay this Fortinbras; who, by a seal'd compact,
Well ratified by law and heraldry,
Did forfeit, with his life, all those his lands
Which he stood seiz'd of, to the conqueror:
Against the which, a moiety competent
Was gaged by our king; which had return'd
To the inheritance of Fortinbras,
Had he been vanquisher; as, by the same comart,
And carriage of the article design'd,
His fell to Hamlet. Now, sir, young Fortinbras,
Of unimproved mettle hot and full,
Hath in the skirts of Norway here and there
Shark'd up a list of lawless resolutes,
For food and diet, to some enterprise
That hath a stomach in 't; which is no other—
As it doth well appear unto our state—
But to recover of us, by strong hand
And terms compulsatory, those foresaid lands
So by his father lost: and this, I take it,
Is the main motive of our preparations,
The source of this our watch and the chief head
Of this post-haste and romage in the land.
Ber. I think it be no other but e'en so:

ACT I. SCENE I. *Stage Direction:* **platform,** a level space on the battlements of the royal castle at Elsinore, a Danish seaport; now Helsingör. 2. **me.** This is emphatic, since Francisco is the sentry. 3. **Long live the king,** either a password or greeting; Horatio and Marcellus use a different one in line 15. 13. **rivals,** partners. 16. **Give you,** God give you. 29. **approve,** corroborate. 36. **pole,** polestar. 42. **scholar.** Exorcisms were performed in Latin, which Horatio as an educated man would be able to speak. 44. **harrows,** lacerates the feelings. 45. **It . . . to.** A ghost could not speak until spoken to. 48. **buried Denmark,** the buried King of Denmark. 63. **smote,** defeated. **sledded Polacks,** Polanders using sledges. The Earl of Rochester (1761) explained *sleaded* (Q_1F) or *sledded* (Q_2) as "loaded with lead" and *pollax* ($Q_{1,2}F$) as "pole-ax," the idea being that the elder Hamlet dashed his pole-ax against the ice while engaged in a parley; this is upheld by Schmidt and others. 65. **jump,** exactly. 68. **gross and scope,** general drift. 70. **Good now,** an expression denoting entreaty or expostulation. 72. **toils,** causes or makes to toil. **subject,** people, subjects. 73. **cast,** casting, founding. 74. **mart,** buying and selling, traffic. 75. **impress,** impressment. 83. **prick'd on,** incited. **emulate,** rivaling. 87. **law and heraldry,** heraldic law, governing combat. 89. **seiz'd,** possessed. 90. **moiety competent,** adequate or sufficient portion. 93. **comart,** joint bargain. 94. **carriage,** import, bearing. 96. **unimproved,** not turned to account. **hot and full,** full of fight. 98. **Shark'd up,** got together in haphazard fashion. **resolutes,** desperadoes. 99. **food and diet,** no

Well may it sort that this portentous figure
Comes armed through our watch; so like the king
That was and is the question of these wars.
Hor. A mote it is to trouble the mind's eye.
In the most high and palmy state of Rome,
A little ere the mightiest Julius fell,
The graves stood tenantless and the sheeted dead
Did squeak and gibber in the Roman streets:
†As stars with trains of fire and dews of blood,
Disasters in the sun; and the moist star
Upon whose influence Neptune's empire stands
Was sick almost to doomsday with eclipse:
And even the like precurse of fear'd events,
As harbingers preceding still the fates
And prologue to the omen coming on,
Have heaven and earth together demonstrated
Unto our climatures and countrymen.—

Enter Ghost.

But soft, behold! lo, where it comes again!
I'll cross it, though it blast me. Stay, illusion!
If thou hast any sound, or use of voice,
Speak to me! *It spreads his arms.*
If there be any good thing to be done,
That may to thee do ease and grace to me,
Speak to me!
If thou art privy to thy country's fate,
Which, happily, foreknowing may avoid,
O, speak!
Or if thou hast uphoarded in thy life
Extorted treasure in the womb of earth,
For which, they say, you spirits oft walk in death,
The cock crows.
Speak of it: stay, and speak! Stop it, Marcellus.
Mar. Shall I strike at it with my partisan?
Hor. Do, if it will not stand.
Ber. 'Tis here!
Hor. 'Tis here!
Mar. 'Tis gone! [*Exit Ghost.*]
We do it wrong, being so majestical,
To offer it the show of violence;
For it is, as the air, invulnerable,
And our vain blows malicious mockery.
Ber. It was about to speak, when the cock crew.
Hor. And then it started like a guilty thing
Upon a fearful summons. I have heard,
The cock, that is the trumpet to the morn,
Doth with his lofty and shrill-sounding throat
Awake the god of day; and, at his warning,
Whether in sea or fire, in earth or air,
Th' extravagant and erring spirit hies
To his confine: and of the truth herein
This present object made probation.
Mar. It faded on the crowing of the cock.
Some say that ever 'gainst that season comes
Wherein our Saviour's birth is celebrated,
The bird of dawning singeth all night long:
And then, they say, no spirit dare stir abroad;
The nights are wholesome; then no planets strike,
No fairy takes, nor witch hath power to charm,
So hallow'd and so gracious is that time.
Hor. So have I heard and do in part believe it.
But, look, the morn, in russet mantle clad,
Walks o'er the dew of yon high eastward hill:
Break we our watch up; and by my advice,
Let us impart what we have seen to-night
Unto young Hamlet; for, upon my life,
This spirit, dumb to us, will speak to him.
Do you consent we shall acquaint him with it,
As needful in our loves, fitting our duty?
Mar. Let 's do 't, I pray; and I this morning know
Where we shall find him most conveniently. *Exeunt.*

[SCENE II. *A room of state in the castle.*]

Flourish. Enter CLAUDIUS, KING OF DENMARK, GERTRUDE *the* QUEEN, Councilors, POLONIUS *and his Son* LAERTES, HAMLET, *cum aliis* [*including* VOLTIMAND *and* CORNELIUS].

King. Though yet of Hamlet our dear brother's death
The memory be green, and that it us befitted
To bear our hearts in grief and our whole kingdom
To be contracted in one brow of woe,
Yet so far hath discretion fought with nature
That we with wisest sorrow think on him,
Together with remembrance of ourselves.
Therefore our sometime sister, now our queen,
Th' imperial jointress to this warlike state,
Have we, as 'twere with a defeated joy,—
With an auspicious and a dropping eye,
With mirth in funeral and with dirge in marriage,
In equal scale weighing delight and dole,—
Taken to wife: nor have we herein barr'd
Your better wisdoms, which have freely gone
With this affair along. For all, our thanks.
Now follows, that you know, young Fortinbras,
Holding a weak supposal of our worth,
Or thinking by our late dear brother's death
Our state to be disjoint and out of frame,
Colleagued with this dream of his advantage,
He hath not fail'd to pester us with message,
Importing the surrender of those lands
Lost by his father, with all bands of law,
To our most valiant brother. So much for him.
Now for ourself and for this time of meeting:
Thus much the business is: we have here writ
To Norway, uncle of young Fortinbras,—
Who, impotent and bed-rid, scarcely hears
Of this his nephew's purpose,—to suppress
His further gait herein; in that the levies,
The lists and full proportions, are all made

pay but their keep. 107. **romage,** bustle, commotion. 109. **sort,** suit. 112. **mote,** speck of dust. 113. **palmy state,** triumphant sovereignty. 117. **stars . . . fire,** i.e., comets. 118. **Disasters,** unfavorable aspects. **moist star,** the moon, governing tides. 119. **Neptune's empire,** the sea. 120. **sick . . . doomsday.** See Matthew 24:20; Revelation 6:12. 121. **precurse,** heralding. **fear'd,** Collier: *feard;* Q_2: *feare;* Globe: *fierce,* after Q_4: *fearce.* 127. **cross,** meet, face; thus bringing down the evil influence on the person who crosses it. 129. *Stage Direction:* ***It,*** the Ghost, or perhaps Horatio. 133-139. **If . . . it.** Horatio recites the traditional reasons why ghosts might walk. 140. **partisan,** long-handled spear with a blade having lateral projections. 147. **cock crew.** According to traditional ghost lore, spirits returned to their confines at cockcrow.

154. **extravagant and erring,** wandering. Both words mean the same thing. 155. **confine,** place of confinement. 156. **probation,** proof, trial. 158. **'gainst,** just before. 162. **planets strike.** It was thought that planets were malignant and might strike travelers by night. 164. **gracious,** full of goodness.

SCENE II. *Stage Direction:* ***cum aliis,*** with others. 9. **jointress,** woman possessed of a jointure, or, joint tenancy of an estate. 17. **that,** that which. 18. **weak supposal,** low estimate. 20. **disjoint,** distracted, out of joint. **frame,** order. 21. **Colleagued,** added to. **dream . . . advantage,** visionary hope of success. 23. **Importing,** purporting, pertaining to. 31. **gait,** proceeding.

Out of his subject: and we here dispatch
You, good Cornelius, and you, Voltimand,
For bearers of this greeting to old Norway;
Giving to you no further personal power
To business with the king, more than the scope
Of these delated articles allow.
Farewell, and let your haste commend your duty.
Cor. / *Vol.* In that and all things will we show our duty.
King. We doubt it nothing: heartily farewell.
[*Exeunt Voltimand and Cornelius*.]
And now, Laertes, what 's the news with you?
You told us of some suit; what is 't, Laertes?
You cannot speak of reason to the Dane,
And lose your voice: what wouldst thou beg, Laertes,
That shall not be my offer, not thy asking?
The head is not more native to the heart,
The hand more instrumental to the mouth,
Than is the throne of Denmark to thy father.
What wouldst thou have, Laertes?
Laer. My dread lord,
Your leave and favour to return to France;
From whence though willingly I came to Denmark,
To show my duty in your coronation,
Yet now, I must confess, that duty done,
My thoughts and wishes bend again toward France
And bow them to your gracious leave and pardon.
King. Have you your father's leave? What says Polonius?
Pol. He hath, my lord, wrung from me my slow leave
By laboursome petition, and at last
Upon his will I seal'd my hard consent:
I do beseech you, give him leave to go.
King. Take thy fair hour, Laertes; time be thine,
And thy best graces spend it at thy will!
But now, my cousin Hamlet, and my son,—
Ham. [*Aside*] A little more than kin, and less than kind.
King. How is it that the clouds still hang on you?
Ham. Not so, my lord; I am too much in the sun.
Queen. Good Hamlet, cast thy nighted colour off,
And let thine eye look like a friend on Denmark.
Do not for ever with thy vailed lids
Seek for thy noble father in the dust:
Thou know'st 'tis common; all that lives must die,
Passing through nature to eternity.
Ham. Ay, madam, it is common.
Queen. If it be,
Why seems it so particular with thee?
Ham. Seems, madam! nay, it is; I know not 'seems.'
'Tis not alone my inky cloak, good mother,
Nor customary suits of solemn black,
Nor windy suspiration of forc'd breath,
No, nor the fruitful river in the eye,
Nor the dejected 'haviour of the visage,
Together with all forms, moods, shapes of grief,
That can denote me truly: these indeed seem,
For they are actions that a man might play:
But I have that within which passeth show;
These but the trappings and the suits of woe.
King. 'Tis sweet and commendable in your nature, Hamlet,
To give these mourning duties to your father:
But, you must know, your father lost a father;
That father lost, lost his, and the survivor bound
In filial obligation for some term
To do obsequious sorrow: but to persever
In obstinate condolement is a course
Of impious stubbornness; 'tis unmanly grief;
It shows a will most incorrect to heaven,
A heart unfortified, a mind impatient,
An understanding simple and unschool'd:
For what we know must be and is as common
As any the most vulgar thing to sense,
Why should we in our peevish opposition
Take it to heart? Fie! 'tis a fault to heaven,
A fault against the dead, a fault to nature,
To reason most absurd; whose common theme
Is death of fathers, and who still hath cried,
From the first corse till he that died to-day,
'This must be so.' We pray you, throw to earth
This unprevailing woe, and think of us
As of a father: for let the world take note,
You are the most immediate to our throne;
And with no less nobility of love
Than that which dearest father bears his son,
Do I impart toward you. For your intent
In going back to school in Wittenberg,
It is most retrograde to our desire:
And we beseech you, bend you to remain
Here, in the cheer and comfort of our eye,
Our chiefest courtier, cousin, and our son.
Queen. Let not thy mother lose her prayers, Hamlet:
I pray thee, stay with us; go not to Wittenberg.
Ham. I shall in all my best obey you, madam.
King. Why, 'tis a loving and a fair reply:
Be as ourself in Denmark. Madam, come;
This gentle and unforc'd accord of Hamlet
Sits smiling to my heart: in grace whereof,
No jocund health that Denmark drinks to-day,
But the great cannon to the clouds shall tell,
And the king's rouse the heaven shall bruit again,
Re-speaking earthly thunder. Come away.
Flourish. Exeunt all but Hamlet.
Ham. O, that this too too sullied flesh would melt,
Thaw and resolve itself into a dew!
Or that the Everlasting had not fix'd
His canon 'gainst self-slaughter! O God! God!
How weary, stale, flat and unprofitable,
Seem to me all the uses of this world!
Fie on 't! ah fie! 'tis an unweeded garden,
That grows to seed; things rank and gross in nature
Possess it merely. That it should come to this!
But two months dead: nay, not so much, not two:
So excellent a king; that was, to this,

33. **Out of his subject,** at the expense of Norway's subjects (collectively). 38. **delated,** expressly stated. 44. **the Dane,** Danish king. 45. **lose your voice,** speak in vain. 47. **native,** closely connected, related. 48. **instrumental,** serviceable. 56. **leave and pardon,** permission to depart. 64. **cousin,** any kin not of the immediate family. 65. **A little . . . kind,** my relation to you has become more than kinship warrants; it has also become unnatural. 67. **I am . . . sun.** The senses seem to be: I am too much out of doors, I am too much in the sun of your grace (ironical), I am too much of a son to you. Johnson suggested an allusion to the proverb, "Out of heaven's blessing into the warm sun," i.e., Hamlet is out of house and home in being deprived of the kingship. 74. **Ay . . . common,** it is common, but it hurts nevertheless; possibly a reference to the commonplace quality of the queen's remark. 78. **customary suits,** suits prescribed by custom for mourning. 79. **windy suspiration,** heavy sighing. 92. **obsequious,** dutiful. 93. **condolement,** sorrowing. 95. **incorrect,** untrained, uncorrected. 99. **vulgar thing,** common experience. 107. **unprevailing,** unavailing. 109. **most immediate,** next in succession. 110. **nobility,** high degree. 112. **impart.** The object is apparently *love* (l. 110). 113. **Wittenberg,** famous German university founded in 1502. 114. **retrograde,** contrary. 115. **bend you,** incline

Hyperion to a satyr; so loving to my mother
That he might not beteem the winds of heaven
Visit her face too roughly. Heaven and earth!
Must I remember? why, she would hang on him,
As if increase of appetite had grown
By what it fed on: and yet, within a month—
Let me not think on 't—Frailty, thy name is woman!—
A little month, or ere those shoes were old
With which she followed my poor father's body,
Like Niobe, all tears:—why she, even she—
O God! a beast, that wants discourse of reason,
Would have mourn'd longer—married with my uncle,
My father's brother, but no more like my father
Than I to Hercules: within a month:
Ere yet the salt of most unrighteous tears
Had left the flushing in her galled eyes,
She married. O, most wicked speed, to post
With such dexterity to incestuous sheets!
It is not nor it cannot come to good:
But break, my heart; for I must hold my tongue.

Enter HORATIO, MARCELLUS, *and* BERNARDO.

Hor. Hail to your lordship!
Ham. I am glad to see you well:
Horatio!—or I do forget myself.
Hor. The same, my lord, and your poor servant ever.
Ham. Sir, my good friend; I'll change that name with you:
And what make you from Wittenberg, Horatio?
Marcellus?
Mar. My good lord—
Ham. I am very glad to see you. Good even, sir.
But what, in faith, make you from Wittenberg?
Hor. A truant disposition, good my lord.
Ham. I would not hear your enemy say so,
Nor shall you do my ear that violence,
To make it truster of your own report
Against yourself: I know you are no truant.
But what is your affair in Elsinore?
We'll teach you to drink deep ere you depart.
Hor. My lord, I came to see your father's funeral.
Ham. I prithee, do not mock me, fellow-student;
I think it was to see my mother's wedding.
Hor. Indeed, my lord, it follow'd hard upon.
Ham. Thrift, thrift, Horatio! the funeral bak'd meats
Did coldly furnish forth the marriage tables.
Would I had met my dearest foe in heaven
Or ever I had seen that day, Horatio!
My father!—methinks I see my father.
Hor. Where, my lord?
Ham. In my mind's eye, Horatio.
Hor. I saw him once; 'a was a goodly king.
Ham. 'A was a man, take him for all in all,
I shall not look upon his like again.
Hor. My lord, I think I saw him yesternight.
Ham. Saw? who?
Hor. My lord, the king your father.
Ham. The king my father!
Hor. Season your admiration for a while
With an attent ear, till I may deliver,
Upon the witness of these gentlemen,
This marvel to you.
Ham. For God's love, let me hear.
Hor. Two nights together had these gentlemen,
Marcellus and Bernardo, on their watch,
In the dead waste and middle of the night,
Been thus encount'red. A figure like your father,
Armed at point exactly, cap-a-pe,
Appears before them, and with solemn march
Goes slow and stately by them: thrice he walk'd
By their oppress'd and fear-surprised eyes,
Within his truncheon's length; whilst they, distill'd
Almost to jelly with the act of fear,
Stand dumb and speak not to him. This to me
In dreadful secrecy impart they did;
And I with them the third night kept the watch:
Where, as they had deliver'd, both in time,
Form of the thing, each word made true and good,
The apparition comes: I knew your father;
These hands are not more like.
Ham. But where was this?
Mar. My lord, upon the platform where we watch'd.
Ham. Did you not speak to it?
Hor. My lord, I did;
But answer made it none: yet once methought
It lifted up it head and did address
Itself to motion, like as it would speak;
But even then the morning cock crew loud,
And at the sound it shrunk in haste away,
And vanish'd from our sight.
Ham. 'Tis very strange.
Hor. As I do live, my honour'd lord, 'tis true;
And we did think it writ down in our duty
To let you know of it.
Ham. Indeed, indeed, sirs, but this troubles me.
Hold you the watch to-night?
Mar. } *Ber.* } We do, my lord.
Ham. Arm'd, say you?
Mar. } *Ber.* } Arm'd, my lord.
Ham. From top to toe?
Mar. } *Ber.* } My lord, from head to foot.
Ham. Then saw you not his face?
Hor. O, yes, my lord; he wore his beaver up.
Ham. What, look'd he frowningly?
Hor. A countenance more in sorrow than in anger.
Ham. Pale or red?
Hor. Nay, very pale.
Ham. And fix'd his eyes upon you?
Hor. Most constantly.
Ham. I would I had been there.

yourself; imperative. 127. **rouse,** draft of liquor. **heaven,** so Q_2; F and Globe: *heavens.* **bruit again,** echo. 129. **sullied,** so Furness and Cambridge; Qq: *sallied;* F and Globe: *solid.* 137. **merely,** completely, entirely. 140. **Hyperion,** god of the sun in the older regime of ancient gods. 141. **beteem,** allow. 149. **Niobe,** Tantalus' daughter, who boasted that she had more sons and daughters than Leto; for this Apollo and Artemis slew her children. She was turned into stone by Zeus on Mount Sipylus. 150. **discourse of reason,** process or faculty of reason. 155. **galled,** irritated. 157. **dexterity,** facility. 163. **I'll . . . you,** I'll be your servant, you shall be my friend (Johnson); also explained as "I'll exchange the name of friend with you." 179. **hard,** close. 180. **bak'd meats,** meat pies. 182. **dearest,** direst. The adjective *dear* in Shakespeare has two different origins: O. E. *deore,* "beloved," and O. E. *deor,* "fierce." *Dearest* is the superlative of the second. 187. **'A,** he. 192. **Season your admiration,** restrain your astonishment. 200. **cap-a-pe,** from head to foot. 203. **oppress'd,** distressed. 204. **truncheon,** officer's staff. **distill'd,** softened, weakened. 205. **act,** action. 216. **it,** its. 222. **writ down.** Q_1 has *right done,* regarded as an evidence of stenographic reporting. 230. **beaver,** visor on the helmet.

Hor. It would have much amaz'd you.
Ham. Very like, very like. Stay'd it long?
Hor. While one with moderate haste might tell a hundred.
Mar., *Ber.* Longer, longer.
Hor. Not when I saw 't.
Ham. His beard was grizzled,—no?
Hor. It was, as I have seen it in his life,
A sable silver'd.
Ham. I will watch to-night;
Perchance 'twill walk again.
Hor. I warr'nt it will.
Ham. If it assume my noble father's person,
I'll speak to it, though hell itself should gape
And bid me hold my peace. I pray you all,
If you have hitherto conceal'd this sight,
Let it be tenable in your silence still;
And whatsoever else shall hap to-night,
Give it an understanding, but no tongue:
I will requite your loves. So, fare you well:
Upon the platform, 'twixt eleven and twelve,
I'll visit you.
All. Our duty to your honour.
Ham. Your loves, as mine to you: farewell.
Exeunt [all but Hamlet].
My father's spirit in arms! all is not well;
I doubt some foul play: would the night were come!
Till then sit still, my soul: foul deeds will rise,
Though all the earth o'erwhelm them, to men's eyes.
Exit.

[SCENE III. *A room in Polonius' house.*]

Enter LAERTES *and* OPHELIA, *his Sister.*

Laer. My necessaries are embark'd: farewell:
And, sister, as the winds give benefit
And convoy is assistant, do not sleep,
But let me hear from you.
Oph. Do you doubt that?
Laer. For Hamlet and the trifling of his favour,
Hold it a fashion and a toy in blood,
A violet in the youth of primy nature,
Forward, not permanent, sweet, not lasting,
The perfume and suppliance of a minute;
No more.
Oph. No more but so?
Laer. Think it no more:
For nature, crescent, does not grow alone
In thews and bulk, but, as this temple waxes,
The inward service of the mind and soul
Grows wide withal. Perhaps he loves you now,
And now no soil nor cautel doth besmirch
The virtue of his will: but you must fear,
His greatness weigh'd, his will is not his own;
For he himself is subject to his birth:
He may not, as unvalued persons do,
Carve for himself; for on his choice depends
The safety and health of this whole state;
And therefore must his choice be circumscrib'd
Unto the voice and yielding of that body
Whereof he is the head. Then if he says he loves you,
It fits your wisdom so far to believe it
As he in his particular act and place
May give his saying deed; which is no further
Than the main voice of Denmark goes withal.
Then weigh what loss your honour may sustain,
If with too credent ear you list his songs,
Or lose your heart, or your chaste treasure open
To his unmast'red importunity.
Fear it, Ophelia, fear it, my dear sister,
And keep you in the rear of your affection,
Out of the shot and danger of desire.
The chariest maid is prodigal enough,
If she unmask her beauty to the moon:
Virtue itself 'scapes not calumnious strokes:
The canker galls the infants of the spring,
Too oft before their buttons be disclos'd,
And in the morn and liquid dew of youth
Contagious blastments are most imminent.
Be wary then; best safety lies in fear:
Youth to itself rebels, though none else near.
Oph. I shall the effect of this good lesson keep,
As watchman to my heart. But, good my brother,
Do not, as some ungracious pastors do,
Show me the steep and thorny way to heaven;
Whiles, like a puff'd and reckless libertine,
Himself the primrose path of dalliance treads,
And recks not his own rede.

Enter POLONIUS.

Laer. O, fear me not.
I stay too long: but here my father comes.
A double blessing is a double grace;
Occasion smiles upon a second leave.
Pol. Yet here, Laertes? aboard, aboard, for shame!
The wind sits in the shoulder of your sail,
And you are stay'd for. There; my blessing with thee!
And these few precepts in thy memory
Look thou character. Give thy thoughts no tongue,
Nor any unproportion'd thought his act.
Be thou familiar, but by no means vulgar.
Those friends thou hast, and their adoption tried,
Grapple them to thy soul with hoops of steel;
But do not dull thy palm with entertainment
Of each new-hatch'd, unfledg'd comrade. Beware
Of entrance to a quarrel, but being in,
Bear 't that th' opposed may beware of thee.
Give every man thy ear, but few thy voice;
Take each man's censure, but reserve thy judgement.
Costly thy habit as thy purse can buy,

242. **sable,** black color. 256. **doubt,** fear.

SCENE III. 3. **convoy is assistant,** means of conveyance are available. 6. **fashion,** custom, prevailing usage. **toy in blood,** passing amorous fancy. 7. **primy,** in its prime. 8. **Forward,** precocious. 9. **suppliance of a minute,** diversion to fill up a minute. 10. **so.** Q_2F place a period after this word. The punctuation concerns the extent to which Ophelia is obedient to Laertes' suggestion. 11. **crescent,** growing, waxing. 12. **thews,** bodily strength. **temple,** body. 15. **soil,** blemish. **cautel,** crafty device. 17. **greatness weigh'd,** high position considered. 23. **voice and yielding,** assent, approval. 27. **deed,** effect. 30. **credent,** credulous. 32. **unmast'red,** unrestrained. 36. **chariest,** most scrupulously modest. 39. **The canker . . . spring,** the cankerworm destroys the young plants of spring. 40. **buttons,** buds. **disclos'd,** opened. 41. **liquid dew,** i.e., time when dew is fresh. 42. **blastments,** blights. 47. **ungracious,** graceless. 49. **puff'd,** bloated. 51. **recks,** heeds. **rede,** counsel. 53. **double,** i.e., Laertes has already bade his father good-by. 54. **Occasion,** opportunity. 58. **precepts.** Many parallels have been found to the series of maxims which follows, one of the closest being that in Lyly's *Euphues*. 59. **Look,** so Q_2; Globe, following F: *See*. **character,** inscribe. 60. **unproportion'd,** inordinate. 61. **vulgar,** common. 65. **unfledg'd,** immature. 71. **express'd in fancy,** fantastical in design. 74. **Are . . . that.** Onions defines *chief* as "in chief," "mainly," "principally." *Chief* is usually taken as a substantive meaning "head," "eminence." 77. **husbandry,** thrift. 81. **season,** mature. 94. **put on,** impressed on. 99, 103. **tenders,** offers. 102. **Unsifted,** untried. 106. **tenders,** promises to pay. 107. **sterling,** legal currency.

But not express'd in fancy; rich, not gaudy;
For the apparel oft proclaims the man,
And they in France of the best rank and station
†Are of a most select and generous chief in that.
Neither a borrower nor a lender be;
For loan oft loses both itself and friend,
And borrowing dulleth edge of husbandry.
This above all: to thine own self be true,
And it must follow, as the night the day,
Thou canst not then be false to any man.
Farewell: my blessing season this in thee!

Laer. Most humbly do I take my leave, my lord.

Pol. The time invites you; go; your servants tend.

Laer. Farewell, Ophelia; and remember well
What I have said to you.

Oph. 'Tis in my memory lock'd,
And you yourself shall keep the key of it.

Laer. Farewell. *Exit Laertes.*

Pol. What is 't, Ophelia, he hath said to you?

Oph. So please you, something touching the Lord Hamlet.

Pol. Marry, well bethought:
'Tis told me, he hath very oft of late
Given private time to you; and you yourself
Have of your audience been most free and bounteous:
If it be so, as so 't is put on me,
And that in way of caution, I must tell you,
You do not understand yourself so clearly
As it behoves my daughter and your honour.
What is between you? give me up the truth.

Oph. He hath, my lord, of late made many tenders
Of his affection to me.

Pol. Affection! pooh! you speak like a green girl,
Unsifted in such perilous circumstance.
Do you believe his tenders, as you call them?

Oph. I do not know, my lord, what I should think.

Pol. Marry, I will teach you: think yourself a baby;
That you have ta'en these tenders for true pay,
Which are not sterling. Tender yourself more dearly;
Or—not to crack the wind of the poor phrase,
Running it thus—you'll tender me a fool.

Oph. My lord, he hath importun'd me with love
In honourable fashion.

Pol. Ay, fashion you may call it; go to, go to.

Oph. And hath given countenance to his speech, my lord,
With almost all the holy vows of heaven.

Pol. Ay, springes to catch woodcocks. I do know,
When the blood burns, how prodigal the soul
Lends the tongue vows: these blazes, daughter,
Giving more light than heat, extinct in both,
Even in their promise, as it is a-making,
You must not take for fire. From this time
Be somewhat scanter of your maiden presence;
Set your entreatments at a higher rate
Than a command to parley. For Lord Hamlet,
Believe so much in him, that he is young,
And with a larger tether may he walk
Than may be given you: in few, Ophelia,
Do not believe his vows; for they are brokers,
Not of that dye which their investments show,
But mere implorators of unholy suits,
Breathing like sanctified and pious bawds,
The better to beguile. This is for all:
I would not, in plain terms, from this time forth,
Have you so slander any moment leisure,
As to give words or talk with the Lord Hamlet.
Look to 't, I charge you: come your ways.

Oph. I shall obey, my lord. *Exeunt.*

[SCENE IV. *The platform.*]

Enter HAMLET, HORATIO, *and* MARCELLUS.

Ham. The air bites shrewdly; it is very cold.

Hor. It is a nipping and an eager air.

Ham. What hour now?

Hor. I think it lacks of twelve.

Mar. No, it is struck.

Hor. Indeed? I heard it not: then it draws near the season
Wherein the spirit held his wont to walk.

A flourish of trumpets, and two pieces go off.

What does this mean, my lord?

Ham. The king doth wake to-night and takes his rouse,
Keeps wassail, and the swagg'ring up-spring reels;
And, as he drains his draughts of Rhenish down,
The kettle-drum and trumpet thus bray out
The triumph of his pledge.

Hor. Is it a custom?

Ham. Ay, marry, is 't:
But to my mind, though I am native here
And to the manner born, it is a custom
More honour'd in the breach than the observance.
This heavy-headed revel east and west
Makes us traduc'd and tax'd of other nations:
They clepe us drunkards, and with swinish phrase
Soil our addition; and indeed it takes
From our achievements, though perform'd at height,
The pith and marrow of our attribute.
So, oft it chances in particular men,
That for some vicious mole of nature in them,
As, in their birth—wherein they are not guilty,
Since nature cannot choose his origin—
By the o'ergrowth of some complexion,
Oft breaking down the pales and forts of reason,
Or by some habit that too much o'er-leavens
The form of plausive manners, that these men,
Carrying, I say, the stamp of one defect,
Being nature's livery, or fortune's star,—
Their virtues else—be they as pure as grace,

Tender, hold. 108. **crack the wind,** i.e., run it until it is broken-winded. 109. **tender . . . fool,** show me a fool (for a daughter). 112. **fashion,** mere form, pretense. 113. **countenance,** credit, support. 115. **springes,** snares. **woodcocks,** birds easily caught; type of stupidity. 122. **entreatments,** conversations, interviews. 123. **command to parley,** mere invitation to talk. 124. **so . . . him,** this much concerning him. 126. **in few,** briefly. 127. **brokers,** go-betweens, procurers. 128. **dye,** color or sort. **investments,** clothes. 129. **implorators of,** solicitors of. 130. **Breathing,** speaking. **bawds,** so Theobald. Many editors follow the Q_2 reading, *bonds*, which would mean "agreements." 133. **slander,** bring disgrace or reproach upon.

SCENE IV. 8. **wake,** stay awake, hold revel. **rouse,** carouse, drinking bout. 9. **wassail,** carousal. **up-spring,** last and wildest dance at German merry-makings (Elze). **reels,** reels through. 10. **Rhenish,** Rhine wine. 12. **triumph . . . pledge,** his glorious achievement as a drinker. 15. **to . . . born,** destined by birth to be subject to the custom in question (Onions). 17-38. **This . . . scandal.** The omission of this passage from F may be due to deference to the queen of James I, who was a Danish princess. 19. **clepe,** call. **with swinish phrase,** by calling us swine. 20. **addition,** reputation. 22. **attribute,** reputation. 24. **mole of nature,** natural blemish in one's constitution. 28. **pales,** palings (as of a fortification). 29. **o'er-leavens,** induces a change throughout (as yeast works in bread). 30. **plausive,** pleasing. 32. **nature's livery,** endowment from nature. **fortune's star,** the position in which one is placed by fortune; a reference to astrology. The two phrases are aspects of the same thing.

As infinite as man may undergo—
Shall in the general censure take corruption
From that particular fault: the dram of †eale
Doth all the noble substance †of a doubt
To his own scandal.

Enter Ghost.

Hor. Look, my lord, it comes!

Ham. Angels and ministers of grace defend us!
Be thou a spirit of health or goblin damn'd,
Bring with thee airs from heaven or blasts from hell,
Be thy intents wicked or charitable,
Thou com'st in such a questionable shape
That I will speak to thee: I'll call thee Hamlet,
King, father, royal Dane: O, answer me!
Let me not burst in ignorance; but tell
Why thy canoniz'd bones, hearsed in death,
Have burst their cerements; why the sepulchre,
Wherein we saw thee quietly interr'd,
Hath op'd his ponderous and marble jaws,
To cast thee up again. What may this mean,
That thou, dead corse, again in complete steel
Revisits thus the glimpses of the moon,
Making night hideous; and we fools of nature
So horridly to shake our disposition
With thoughts beyond the reaches of our souls?
Say, why is this? wherefore? what should we do?

[*Ghost*] *beckons* [*Hamlet*].

Hor. It beckons you to go away with it,
As if it some impartment did desire
To you alone.

Mar. Look, with what courteous action
It waves you to a more removed ground:
But do not go with it.

Hor. No, by no means.

Ham. It will not speak; then I will follow it.

Hor. Do not, my lord!

Ham. Why, what should be the fear?
I do not set my life at a pin's fee;
And for my soul, what can it do to that,
Being a thing immortal as itself?
It waves me forth again: I'll follow it.

Hor. What if it tempt you toward the flood, my lord,
Or to the dreadful summit of the cliff
That beetles o'er his base into the sea,
And there assume some other horrible form,
Which might deprive your sovereignty of reason
And draw you into madness? think of it:
The very place puts toys of desperation,
Without more motive, into every brain
That looks so many fathoms to the sea
And hears it roar beneath.

Ham. It waves me still.
Go on; I'll follow thee.

Mar. You shall not go, my lord.

Ham. Hold off your hands!

Hor. Be rul'd; you shall not go.

Ham. My fate cries out,
And makes each petty artere in this body
As hardy as the Nemean lion's nerve.
Still am I call'd. Unhand me, gentlemen.
By heaven, I'll make a ghost of him that lets me!
I say, away! Go on; I'll follow thee.

Exeunt Ghost and Hamlet.

Hor. He waxes desperate with imagination.

Mar. Let 's follow; 'tis not fit thus to obey him.

Hor. Have after. To what issue will this come?

Mar. Something is rotten in the state of Denmark.

Hor. Heaven will direct it.

Mar. Nay, let 's follow him. *Exeunt.*

[SCENE V. *Another part of the platform.*]

Enter GHOST *and* HAMLET.

Ham. Whither wilt thou lead me? speak; I'll go no further.

Ghost. Mark me.

Ham. I will.

Ghost. My hour is almost come,
When I to sulphurous and tormenting flames
Must render up myself.

Ham. Alas, poor ghost!

Ghost. Pity me not, but lend thy serious hearing
To what I shall unfold.

Ham. Speak; I am bound to hear.

Ghost. So art thou to revenge, when thou shalt hear.

Ham. What?

Ghost. I am thy father's spirit,
Doom'd for a certain term to walk the night,
And for the day confin'd to fast in fires,
Till the foul crimes done in my days of nature
Are burnt and purg'd away. But that I am forbid
To tell the secrets of my prison-house,
I could a tale unfold whose lightest word
Would harrow up thy soul, freeze thy young blood,
Make thy two eyes, like stars, start from their spheres,
Thy knotted and combined locks to part
And each particular hair to stand an end,
Like quills upon the fretful porpentine:
But this eternal blazon must not be
To ears of flesh and blood. List, list, O, list!
If thou didst ever thy dear father love—

Ham. O God!

Ghost. Revenge his foul and most unnatural murder.

Ham. Murder!

Ghost. Murder most foul, as in the best it is;
But this most foul, strange and unnatural.

Ham. Haste me to know 't, that I, with wings as swift

36-38. **the dram . . . scandal,** a famous crux; *dram of eale* has had various interpretations, the preferred one being probably, "a dram of evil." The following emendations of *of a doubt* have been offered: (1) *oft adoubt* or *adout* (often erase or "do out"), (2) *antidote* (counteract). Dowden suggests that *scandal* may be a verb to be read with *Doth,* giving the general interpretation, "Out of a mere doubt or suspicion the dram of evil degrades in reputation all the noble substance to its own [substance]." 39. **ministers of grace,** messengers of God. 43. **questionable,** inviting question or conversation. 47. **canoniz'd,** buried according to the canons of the church. **hearsed,** coffined. 48. **cerements,** grave-clothes. 49. **interr'd,** so Qq; F: *enurn'd;* Globe: *inurn'd.* 53. **glimpses of the moon,** the earth by night. 54. **fools of nature,** mere men, limited to natural knowledge. 59. **impartment,** communication. 61. **removed,** remote. 71. **beetles o'er,** overhangs threateningly. 73. **deprive . . . reason,** take away the sovereignty of your reason. It was thought that evil spirits would sometimes assume the form of departed spirits in order to work madness in a human creature. 75. **toys of desperation,** freakish notions of suicide. 82. **artere,** artery. 83. **Nemean lion's.** The Nemean lion was one of the monsters slain by Hercules. **nerve,** sinew, tendon. The point is that the arteries which were carrying the spirits out into the body were functioning and were as stiff and hard as the sinews of the lion. 85. **lets,** hinders. 89. **issue,** outcome. 91. **it,** i.e., the outcome.

SCENE V. 1. **Whither,** Q_2: *Whether;* F and Globe: *Where.* 11. **fast,** probably, do without food. It has been sometimes taken in the sense of doing general penance. 17. **spheres,** orbits. 18. **knotted,** perhaps,

As meditation or the thoughts of love,
May sweep to my revenge.
Ghost. I find thee apt;
And duller shouldst thou be than the fat weed
That roots itself in ease on Lethe wharf,
Wouldst thou not stir in this. Now, Hamlet, hear:
'Tis given out that, sleeping in my orchard,
A serpent stung me; so the whole ear of Denmark
Is by a forged process of my death
Rankly abus'd: but know, thou noble youth,
The serpent that did sting thy father's life
Now wears his crown.
Ham. O my prophetic soul!
My uncle!
Ghost. Ay, that incestuous, that adulterate beast,
With witchcraft of his wit, with traitorous gifts,—
O wicked wit and gifts, that have the power
So to seduce!—won to his shameful lust
The will of my most seeming-virtuous queen:
O Hamlet, what a falling-off was there!
From me, whose love was of that dignity
That it went hand in hand even with the vow
I made to her in marriage, and to decline
Upon a wretch whose natural gifts were poor
To those of mine!
But virtue, as it never will be moved,
Though lewdness court it in a shape of heaven,
So lust, though to a radiant angel link'd,
Will sate itself in a celestial bed,
And prey on garbage.
But, soft! methinks I scent the morning air;
Brief let me be. Sleeping within my orchard,
My custom always of the afternoon,
Upon my secure hour thy uncle stole,
With juice of cursed hebona in a vial,
And in the porches of my ears did pour
The leperous distilment; whose effect
Holds such an enmity with blood of man
That swift as quicksilver it courses through
The natural gates and alleys of the body,
And with a sudden vigour it doth posset
And curd, like eager droppings into milk,
The thin and wholesome blood: so did it mine;
And a most instant tetter bark'd about,
Most lazar-like, with vile and loathsome crust,
All my smooth body.
Thus was I, sleeping, by a brother's hand
Of life, of crown, of queen, at once dispatch'd:
Cut off even in the blossoms of my sin,
Unhous'led, disappointed, unanel'd,
No reck'ning made, but sent to my account
With all my imperfections on my head:
O, horrible! O, horrible! most horrible!
If thou hast nature in thee, bear it not;
Let not the royal bed of Denmark be
A couch for luxury and damned incest.
But, howsomever thou pursues this act,
Taint not thy mind, nor let thy soul contrive
Against thy mother aught: leave her to heaven
And to those thorns that in her bosom lodge,
To prick and sting her. Fare thee well at once!
The glow-worm shows the matin to be near,
And 'gins to pale his uneffectual fire:
Adieu, adieu, adieu! remember me. [*Exit.*]
Ham. O all you host of heaven! O earth! what else?
And shall I couple hell? O, fie! Hold, hold, my heart;
And you, my sinews, grow not instant old,
But bear me stiffly up. Remember thee!
Ay, thou poor ghost, whiles memory holds a seat
In this distracted globe. Remember thee!
Yea, from the table of my memory
I'll wipe away all trivial fond records,
All saws of books, all forms, all pressures past,
That youth and observation copied there;
And thy commandment all alone shall live
Within the book and volume of my brain,
Unmix'd with baser matter: yes, by heaven!
O most pernicious woman!
O villain, villain, smiling, damned villain!
My tables,—meet it is I set it down,
That one may smile, and smile, and be a villain;
At least I am sure it may be so in Denmark: [*Writing.*]
So, uncle, there you are. Now to my word;
It is 'Adieu, adieu! remember me.'
I have sworn 't.

Enter HORATIO *and* MARCELLUS.

Hor. My lord, my lord,—
Mar. Lord Hamlet,—
Hor. Heavens secure him!
Ham. So be it!
Mar. Hillo, ho, ho, my lord!
Ham. Hillo, ho, ho, boy! come, bird, come.
Mar. How is 't, my noble lord?
Hor. What news, my lord?
Ham. O, wonderful!
Hor. Good my lord, tell it.
Ham. No; you will reveal it.
Hor. Not I, my lord, by heaven.
Mar. Nor I, my lord.
Ham. How say you, then; would heart of man once think it?
But you'll be secret?
Hor. } *Mar.* } Ay, by heaven, my lord.
Ham. There 's ne'er a villain dwelling in all Denmark
But he 's an arrant knave.
Hor. There needs no ghost, my lord, come from the grave
To tell us this.
Ham. Why, right; you are in the right;

intricately arranged (Onions). **combined,** tied, bound. 20. **fretful,** so Q_1F; Q_2: *fearefull*, which is defensible. **porpentine,** porcupine. 21. **eternal blazon,** promulgation or proclamation of eternity, revelation of the hereafter. 25. **unnatural,** i.e., pertaining to fratricide. 32. **fat weed.** Many suggestions have been offered as to the particular plant intended, including asphodel; probably, a general figure for plants growing along rotting wharves and piles. 33. **Lethe wharf,** bank of the river of forgetfulness in Hades. 42. **adulterate,** adulterous. 61. **secure,** confident, unsuspicious. 62. **hebona,** generally supposed to mean henbane. Elze conjectured *hemlock;* Nicholson, *ebenus*, meaning "yew." 64. **leperous,** causing leprosy. 68. **posset,** coagulate, curdle. 69. **eager,** sour, acid. 72. **lazar-like,** leperlike. 75. **dispatch'd,** suddenly bereft. 77. **Unhous'led,** without having received the sacrament. **disappointed,** unready, without equipment for the last journey. **unanel'd,** without having received extreme unction. 80. **O . . . horrible.** Many editors give this line to Hamlet; Garrick and Sir Henry Irving spoke it in that part. 83. **luxury,** lechery. 85. **Taint . . . mind,** probably, deprave not thy character, do nothing except in the pursuit of a natural revenge. 89. **matin,** morning. 90. **uneffectual fire,** cold light. 93. **couple,** add. 97. **distracted globe,** confused head. 100. **saws,** wise sayings. **pressures,** impressions stamped. 107. **tables,** probably a small portable writing-tablet carried at the belt. 110. **word,** watchword. 115. **Hillo, ho, ho,** a falconer's call to a hawk in air. 124. **arrant,** thoroughgoing.

And so, without more circumstance at all,
I hold it fit that we shake hands and part:
You, as your business and desire shall point you;
For every man has business and desire,
Such as it is; and for my own poor part,
Look you, I'll go pray.
Hor. These are but wild and whirling words, my lord.
Ham. I am sorry they offend you, heartily;
Yes, 'faith, heartily.
Hor. There 's no offence, my lord.
Ham. Yes, by Saint Patrick, but there is, Horatio,
And much offence too. Touching this vision here,
It is an honest ghost, that let me tell you:
For your desire to know what is between us,
O'ermaster 't as you may. And now, good friends,
As you are friends, scholars and soldiers,
Give me one poor request.
Hor. What is 't, my lord? we will.
Ham. Never make known what you have seen to-night.
Hor. } *Mar.* } My lord, we will not.
Ham. Nay, but swear 't.
Hor. In faith,
My lord, not I.
Mar. Nor I, my lord, in faith.
Ham. Upon my sword.
Mar. We have sworn, my lord, already.
Ham. Indeed, upon my sword, indeed.
Ghost cries under the stage.
Ghost. Swear.
Ham. Ah, ha, boy! say'st thou so? art thou there, truepenny?
Come on—you hear this fellow in the cellarage—
Consent to swear.
Hor. Propose the oath, my lord.
Ham. Never to speak of this that you have seen,
Swear by my sword.
Ghost. [*Beneath*] Swear.
Ham. Hic et ubique? then we'll shift our ground.
Come hither, gentlemen,
And lay your hands again upon my sword:
Swear by my sword,
Never to speak of this that you have heard.
Ghost. [*Beneath*] Swear by his sword.
Ham. Well said, old mole! canst work i' th' earth so fast?
A worthy pioner! Once more remove, good friends.
Hor. O day and night, but this is wondrous strange!
Ham. And therefore as a stranger give it welcome.
There are more things in heaven and earth, Horatio,
Than are dreamt of in your philosophy.
But come;
Here, as before, never, so help you mercy,
How strange or odd soe'er I bear myself,
As I perchance hereafter shall think meet
To put an antic disposition on,
That you, at such times seeing me, never shall,
With arms encumb'red thus, or this head-shake,
Or by pronouncing of some doubtful phrase,
As 'Well, well, we know,' or 'We could, an if we would,'
Or 'If we list to speak,' or 'There be, an if they might,'
Or such ambiguous giving out, to note
That you know aught of me: this not to do,
So grace and mercy at your most need help you,
Swear.
Ghost. [*Beneath*] Swear.
Ham. Rest, rest, perturbed spirit! [*They swear*]. So, gentlemen,
With all my love I do commend me to you:
And what so poor a man as Hamlet is
May do, t' express his love and friending to you,
God willing, shall not lack. Let us go in together;
And still your fingers on your lips, I pray.
The time is out of joint: O cursed spite,
That ever I was born to set it right!
Nay, come, let 's go together. *Exeunt.*

[ACT II.

SCENE I. *A room in Polonius' house.*]

Enter old POLONIUS *with his man* [REYNALDO].

Pol. Give him this money and these notes, Reynaldo.
Rey. I will, my lord.
Pol. You shall do marvellous wisely, good Reynaldo,
Before you visit him, to make inquire
Of his behaviour.
Rey. My lord, I did intend it.
Pol. Marry, well said; very well said. Look you, sir,
Inquire me first what Danskers are in Paris;
And how, and who, what means, and where they keep,
What company, at what expense; and finding
By this encompassment and drift of question
That they do know my son, come you more nearer
Than your particular demands will touch it:
Take you, as 'twere, some distant knowledge of him;
As thus, 'I know his father and his friends,
And in part him:' do you mark this, Reynaldo?
Rey. Ay, very well, my lord.
Pol. 'And in part him; but' you may say 'not well:
But, if 't be he I mean, he 's very wild;
Addicted so and so:' and there put on him
What forgeries you please; marry, none so rank
As may dishonour him; take heed of that;
But, sir, such wanton, wild and usual slips
As are companions noted and most known
To youth and liberty.
Rey. As gaming, my lord.

136. **Saint Patrick.** St. Patrick was keeper of Purgatory and patron saint of all blunders and confusion. 138. **honest,** i.e., a real ghost and not an evil spirit. 147. **sword,** i.e., the hilt in the form of a cross. 150. **truepenny,** good old boy, or the like. 156. **Hic et ubique?** Here and everywhere? 159-160. F and Globe transpose these lines. 161. **by his sword.** F and Globe omit. 163. **pioner,** digger, miner. 172. **antic,** fantastic. 174. **encumb'red,** folded or entwined. 178. **giving out,** profession of knowledge. **to note,** to give a sign. 186. **friending,** friendliness.

ACT II. SCENE I. *Stage Direction:* Q_2 has *Polonius with his man or two;* possible confusion for *Montano*, name of Reynaldo in Q_1. 7. **Danskers.** Danke was a common variant for "Denmark"; hence "Dane." 8. **keep,** dwell. 10. **encompassment,** roundabout talking. **drift,** gradual approach or course. 11-12. **come . . . it,** i.e., you will find out more this way than by asking pointed questions. 13. **Take,** assume, pretend. 19. **put on,** impute to. 20. **forgeries,** invented tales. 22. **wanton,** sportive, unrestrained. 25. **fencing,** indicative of the ill repute of professional fencers and fencing schools in Elizabethan times. 26. **Drabbing,** associating with immoral women. 30. **incontinency,** habitual loose behavior. Malone's interpretation would make this habitual incontinency the *scandal* described; Hudson would read *open to* as *open of*, meaning "open in his practice of." 31. **quaintly,** delicately, ingeniously. 32. **taints of liberty,** blemishes due to freedom. 34. **unreclaimed,** untamed. 35. **general assault,** tendency that assails all

Pol. Ay, or drinking, fencing, swearing, quarrelling,
Drabbing: you may go so far.
Rey. My lord, that would dishonour him.
Pol. 'Faith, no; as you may season it in the charge.
You must not put another scandal on him,
That he is open to incontinency;
That 's not my meaning: but breathe his faults so quaintly
That they may seem the taints of liberty,
The flash and outbreak of a fiery mind,
A savageness in unreclaimed blood,
Of general assault.
Rey. But, my good lord,—
Pol. Wherefore should you do this?
Rey. Ay, my lord,
I would know that.
Pol. Marry, sir, here 's my drift;
And, I believe, it is a fetch of wit:
You laying these slight sullies on my son,
As 'twere a thing a little soil'd i' th' working,
Mark you,
Your party in converse, him you would sound,
Having ever seen in the prenominate crimes
The youth you breathe of guilty, be assur'd
He closes with you in this consequence;
'Good sir,' or so, or 'friend,' or 'gentleman,'
According to the phrase or the addition
Of man and country.
Rey. Very good, my lord.
Pol. And then, sir, does 'a this—'a does—what was I about to say? By the mass, I was about to say something: where did I leave?
Rey. At 'closes in the consequence,' at 'friend or so,' and 'gentleman.'
Pol. At 'closes in the consequence,' ay, marry;
He closes thus: 'I know the gentleman;
I saw him yesterday, or t' other day,
Or then, or then; with such, or such; and, as you say,
There was 'a gaming; there o'ertook in 's rouse;
There falling out at tennis:' or perchance,
'I saw him enter such a house of sale,'
Videlicet, a brothel, or so forth.
See you now;
Your bait of falsehood takes this carp of truth:
And thus do we of wisdom and of reach,
With windlasses and with assays of bias,
By indirections find directions out:
So by my former lecture and advice,
Shall you my son. You have me, have you not?
Rey. My lord, I have.
Pol. God bye ye; fare ye well.
Rey. Good my lord!
Pol. Observe his inclination in yourself.
Rey. I shall, my lord.
Pol. And let him ply his music.
Rey. Well, my lord.
Pol. Farewell! *Exit Reynaldo.*

Enter OPHELIA.

How now, Ophelia! what 's the matter?
Oph. O, my lord, my lord, I have been so affrighted!
Pol. With what, i' th' name of God?
Oph. My lord, as I was sewing in my closet,
Lord Hamlet, with his doublet all unbrac'd;
No hat upon his head; his stockings foul'd,
Ungart'red, and down-gyved to his ankle;
Pale as his shirt; his knees knocking each other;
And with a look so piteous in purport
As if he had been loosed out of hell
To speak of horrors,—he comes before me.
Pol. Mad for thy love?
Oph. My lord, I do not know;
But truly, I do fear it.
Pol. What said he?
Oph. He took me by the wrist and held me hard;
Then goes he to the length of all his arm;
And, with his other hand thus o'er his brow,
He falls to such perusal of my face
As 'a would draw it. Long stay'd he so;
At last, a little shaking of mine arm
And thrice his head thus waving up and down,
He rais'd a sigh so piteous and profound
As it did seem to shatter all his bulk
And end his being: that done, he lets me go:
And, with his head over his shoulder turn'd,
He seem'd to find his way without his eyes;
For out o' doors he went without their helps,
And, to the last, bended their light on me.
Pol. Come, go with me: I will go seek the king.
This is the very ecstasy of love,
Whose violent property fordoes itself
And leads the will to desperate undertakings
As oft as any passion under heaven
That does afflict our natures. I am sorry.
What, have you given him any hard words of late?
Oph. No, my good lord, but, as you did command,
I did repel his letters and denied
His access to me.
Pol. That hath made him mad.
I am sorry that with better heed and judgement
I had not quoted him: I fear'd he did but trifle,
And meant to wrack thee; but, beshrew my jealousy!
By heaven, it is as proper to our age
To cast beyond ourselves in our opinions
As it is common for the younger sort
To lack discretion. Come, go we to the king:
This must be known; which, being kept close, might move
More grief to hide than hate to utter love.
Come. *Exeunt.*

[SCENE II. *A room in the castle.*]

Flourish. Enter KING *and* QUEEN, ROSENCRANTZ, *and* GUILDENSTERN [*with others*].

untrained youth. 38. **fetch of wit,** clever trick. The F reading, *fetch of warrant*, would mean "a warranted device." 43. **ever,** at any time. **prenominate,** before-mentioned. 45. **closes . . . consequence,** agrees with you in this conclusion. 49-51. **And then . . . leave.** Malone's arrangement of Q_2F as prose is probably correct, since Polonius is represented as letting his mind wander in confusion. 58. **o'ertook in 's rouse,** overcome by drink. 61. **Videlicet,** namely. 64. **reach,** capacity, ability. 65. **windlasses,** i.e., circuitous paths. **assays of bias,** attempts that resemble the course of the bowl, which, being weighted on one side, has a curving motion. 66. **indirections,** devious courses. **directions,** straight courses, i.e., the truth. 67. **lecture,** admonition. 69. **bye ye,** be with you. 71. **Observe . . . yourself,** in your own person, not by spies (Johnson), or conform your own conduct to his inclination (Clarendon Press); or test him by studying yourself. 73. **ply his music,** probably to be taken literally. 77. **closet,** private chamber. 78. **doublet,** close-fitting coat. **unbrac'd,** unfastened. 80. **down-gyved,** fallen to the ankles (like gyves or fetters). 95. **bulk,** body. 103. **property,** nature. **fordoes,** destroys. 112. **quoted,** observed. 113. **beshrew my jealousy,** curse my suspicions. 115. **cast beyond,** overshoot, miscalculate. 118-119. **might . . . love,** i.e., I might cause more grief to others by hiding the knowledge of Hamlet's love to Ophelia than hatred to me and mine by telling of it.

King. Welcome, dear Rosencrantz and Guildenstern!
Moreover that we much did long to see you,
The need we have to use you did provoke
Our hasty sending. Something have you heard
Of Hamlet's transformation; so call it,
Sith nor th' exterior nor the inward man
Resembles that it was. What it should be,
More than his father's death, that thus hath put him
So much from th' understanding of himself,
I cannot dream of: I entreat you both,
That, being of so young days brought up with him,
And sith so neighbour'd to his youth and haviour,
That you vouchsafe your rest here in our court
Some little time: so by your companies
To draw him on to pleasures, and to gather,
So much as from occasion you may glean,
Whether aught, to us unknown, afflicts him thus,
That, open'd, lies within our remedy.
Queen. Good gentlemen, he hath much talk'd of you;
And sure I am two men there are not living
To whom he more adheres. If it will please you
To show us so much gentry and good will
As to expend your time with us awhile,
For the supply and profit of our hope,
Your visitation shall receive such thanks
As fits a king's remembrance.
Ros. Both your majesties
Might, by the sovereign power you have of us,
Put your dread pleasures more into command
Than to entreaty.
Guil. But we both obey,
And here give up ourselves, in the full bent
To lay our service freely at your feet,
To be commanded.
King. Thanks, Rosencrantz and gentle Guildenstern.
Queen. Thanks, Guildenstern and gentle Rosencrantz:
And I beseech you instantly to visit
My too much changed son. Go, some of you,
And bring these gentlemen where Hamlet is.
Guil. Heavens make our presence and our practices
Pleasant and helpful to him!
Queen. Ay, amen!
Exeunt Rosencrantz and Guildenstern [*with some Attendants*].

Enter POLONIUS.

Pol. Th' ambassadors from Norway, my good lord,
Are joyfully return'd.
King. Thou still hast been the father of good news.
Pol. Have I, my lord? I assure my good liege,
I hold my duty, as I hold my soul,
Both to my God and to my gracious king:
And I do think, or else this brain of mine
Hunts not the trail of policy so sure
As it hath us'd to do, that I have found
The very cause of Hamlet's lunacy.
King. O, speak of that; that do I long to hear.
Pol. Give first admittance to th' ambassadors;
My news shall be the fruit to that great feast.
King. Thyself do grace to them, and bring them in.
[*Exit Polonius.*]
He tells me, my dear Gertrude, he hath found
The head and source of all your son's distemper.
Queen. I doubt it is no other but the main;
His father's death, and our o'erhasty marriage.
King. Well, we shall sift him.

Enter Ambassadors [VOLTIMAND *and* CORNELIUS, *with* POLONIUS].

Welcome, my good friends!
Say, Voltimand, what from our brother Norway?
Volt. Most fair return of greetings and desires.
Upon our first, he sent out to suppress
His nephew's levies; which to him appear'd
To be a preparation 'gainst the Polack;
But, better look'd into, he truly found
It was against your highness: whereat griev'd,
That so his sickness, age and impotence
Was falsely borne in hand, sends out arrests
On Fortinbras; which he, in brief, obeys;
Receives rebuke from Norway, and in fine
Makes vow before his uncle never more
To give th' assay of arms against your majesty.
Whereon old Norway, overcome with joy,
Gives him three score thousand crowns in annual fee,
And his commission to employ those soldiers,
So levied as before, against the Polack:
With an entreaty, herein further shown, [*Giving a paper.*]
That it might please you to give quiet pass
Through your dominions for this enterprise,
On such regards of safety and allowance
As therein are set down.
King. It likes us well;
And at our more consider'd time we'll read,
Answer, and think upon this business.
Meantime we thank you for your well-took labour:
Go to your rest; at night we'll feast together:
Most welcome home! *Exeunt Ambassadors.*
Pol. This business is well ended.
My liege, and madam, to expostulate
What majesty should be, what duty is,
Why day is day, night night, and time is time,
Were nothing but to waste night, day and time.
Therefore, since brevity is the soul of wit,
And tediousness the limbs and outward flourishes,
I will be brief: your noble son is mad:
Mad call I it; for, to define true madness,
What is 't but to be nothing else but mad?
But let that go.
Queen. More matter, with less art.
Pol. Madam, I swear I use no art at all.
That he is mad, 'tis true: 'tis true 'tis pity;
And pity 'tis 'tis true: a foolish figure;
But farewell it, for I will use no art.
Mad let us grant him, then: and now remains
That we find out the cause of this effect,

SCENE II. 2. **Moreover that,** besides the fact that. 6. **Sith,** since. 11. **of . . . days,** from such early youth. 13. **vouchsafe your rest,** please to stay. 22. **gentry,** courtesy. 24. **supply and profit,** aid and successful outcome. 30. **in . . . bent,** to the utmost degree of our mental capacity. 56. **doubt,** fear. **main,** chief point, principal concern. 67. **borne in hand,** deluded. 69. **in fine,** in the end. 71. **assay,** assault, trial (of arms). 73. **three score,** so Q_2; Globe, following F: *three.* 79. **safety and allowance,** pledges of safety to the country and terms of permission for the troops to pass. 80. **likes,** pleases. 81. **consider'd,** suitable for deliberation. 90. **wit,** sound sense or judgment. 91. **flourishes,** ostentation embellishments. 98. **figure,** figure of speech. 105. **Perpend,** consider. 120. **ill . . . numbers,** unskilled at writing verses. 121. **reckon,** number metrically, scan (Yale). 124. **machine,** bodily frame. 126. **more above,** moreover. 127. **fell out,** occurred. **means,** opportunities (of access). 136. **play'd . . . table-book,** i.e., remained shut up, concealed his information. 137. **given . . . winking,** given my heart a signal to keep silent. 140. **bespeak,** address. 141. **out . . . star,** above thee in position. 146. **repelled,** so Q_2; F and Globe:

Or rather say, the cause of this defect,
For this effect defective comes by cause:
Thus it remains, and the remainder thus.
Perpend.
I have a daughter—have while she is mine—
Who, in her duty and obedience, mark,
Hath given me this: now gather, and surmise. [*Reads*] *the letter*. 'To the celestial and my soul's idol, the most beautified Ophelia,'—
That 's an ill phrase, a vile phrase; 'beautified' is a vile phrase: but you shall hear. Thus: [*Reads.*]
'In her excellent white bosom, these, &c.'
Queen. Came this from Hamlet to her?
Pol. Good madam, stay awhile; I will be faithful. [*Reads.*]
'Doubt thou the stars are fire;
Doubt that the sun doth move;
Doubt truth to be a liar;
But never doubt I love.
'O dear Ophelia, I am ill at these numbers; I have not art to reckon my groans: but that I love thee best, O most best, believe it. Adieu.
'Thine evermore, most dear lady, whilst this machine is to him, HAMLET.'
This, in obedience, hath my daughter shown me,
And more above, hath his solicitings,
As they fell out by time, by means and place,
All given to mine ear.
King. But how hath she
Receiv'd his love?
Pol. What do you think of me?
King. As of a man faithful and honourable.
Pol. I would fain prove so. But what might you think,
When I had seen this hot love on the wing—
As I perceiv'd it, I must tell you that,
Before my daughter told me—what might you,
Or my dear majesty your queen here, think,
If I had play'd the desk or table-book,
Or given my heart a winking, mute and dumb,
Or look'd upon this love with idle sight;
What might you think? No, I went round to work,
And my young mistress thus I did bespeak:
'Lord Hamlet is a prince, out of thy star;
This must not be:' and then I prescripts gave her,
That she should lock herself from his resort,
Admit no messengers, receive no tokens.
Which done, she took the fruits of my advice;
And he, repelled—a short tale to make—
Fell into a sadness, then into a fast,
Thence to a watch, thence into a weakness,
Thence to a lightness, and, by this declension,
Into the madness wherein now he raves,
And all we mourn for.
King. Do you think 'tis this?
Queen. It may be, very like.
Pol. Hath there been such a time—I would fain know that—
That I have positively said ''Tis so,'
When it prov'd otherwise?
King. Not that I know.
Pol. [*Pointing to his head and shoulder*] Take this from this, if this be otherwise:
If circumstances lead me, I will find
Where truth is hid, though it were hid indeed
Within the centre.
King. How may we try it further?
Pol. You know, sometimes he walks four hours together
Here in the lobby.
Queen. So he does indeed.
Pol. At such a time I'll loose my daughter to him:
Be you and I behind an arras then;
Mark the encounter: if he love her not
And be not from his reason fall'n thereon,
Let me be no assistant for a state,
But keep a farm and carters.
King. We will try it.

Enter HAMLET [*reading on a book*].

Queen. But, look, where sadly the poor wretch comes reading.
Pol. Away, I do beseech you both, away:
Exeunt King and Queen [*with Attendants*].
I'll board him presently. O, give me leave.
How does my good Lord Hamlet?

Ham. Well, God-a-mercy.

Pol. Do you know me, my lord?

Ham. Excellent well; you are a fishmonger.

Pol. Not I, my lord.

Ham. Then I would you were so honest a man.

Pol. Honest, my lord!

Ham. Ay, sir; to be honest, as this world goes, is to be one man picked out of ten thousand.

Pol. That 's very true, my lord.

Ham. For if the sun breed maggots in a dead dog, being a good kissing carrion,—Have you a daughter?

Pol. I have, my lord.

Ham. Let her not walk i' the sun: conception is a blessing: but as your daughter may conceive—Friend, look to 't.

Pol. [*Aside*] How say you by that? Still harping on my daughter: yet he knew me not at first; 'a said I was a fishmonger: 'a is far gone, far gone: and truly in my youth I suffered much extremity for love; very near this. I'll speak to him again. What do you read, my lord?

Ham. Words, words, words.

Pol. What is the matter, my lord?

Ham. Between who?

Pol. I mean, the matter that you read, my lord.

Ham. Slanders, sir: for the satirical rogue says here that old men have grey beards, that their faces are wrinkled, their eyes purging thick amber and plum-tree gum and that they have a plentiful lack of wit, together with most weak hams: all which, sir, though I most powerfully and potently believe, yet I hold it not honesty to have it thus set down, for yourself, sir,

repulsed. 148. **watch,** state of sleeplessness. 149. **lightness,** light-headedness. **declension,** decline, deterioration. 152. **like,** so Q_2; Globe, following F: *likely*. 159. **centre,** middle point of the earth. 163. **arras,** hanging, tapestry. 165. **thereon,** on that account. 170. **board,** accost. 174. **fishmonger,** an opprobrious expression meaning "bawd," "procurer." 182. **good kissing carrion,** i.e., a good piece of flesh for kissing (?). Many editors, including Globe, emend to *God kissing carrion,* signifying the sun god shining on a dead body. 185. **i' the sun,** in the sunshine of princely favors (Chambers). **conception,** quibble on "understanding" and "pregnancy." 188. **by,** concerning. 195. **matter,** substance. 196. **Between who.** Hamlet deliberately takes *matter* as meaning "basis of dispute"; modern usage demands *whom* instead of *who*. 200. **purging,** discharging. 205. **honesty,** decency.

should be old as I am, if like a crab you could go backward.

Pol. [*Aside*] Though this be madness, yet there is method in 't.—Will you walk out of the air, my lord?

Ham. Into my grave.

Pol. Indeed, that 's out of the air. [*Aside*] How pregnant sometimes his replies are! a happiness that often madness hits on, which reason and sanity could not so prosperously be delivered of. I will leave him, and suddenly contrive the means of meeting between him and my daughter.—My honourable lord, I will most humbly take my leave of you.

Ham. You cannot, sir, take from me any thing that I will more willingly part withal: except my life, except my life, except my life.

Enter GUILDENSTERN *and* ROSENCRANTZ.

Pol. Fare you well, my lord.

Ham. These tedious old fools!

Pol. You go to seek the Lord Hamlet; there he is.

Ros. [*To Polonius*] God save you, sir! [*Exit Polonius.*]

Guil. My honoured lord!

Ros. My most dear lord!

Ham. My excellent good friends! How dost thou, Guildenstern? Ah, Rosencrantz! Good lads, how do ye both?

Ros. As the indifferent children of the earth.

Guil. Happy, in that we are not over-happy;
On Fortune's cap we are not the very button.

Ham. Nor the soles of her shoe?

Ros. Neither, my lord.

Ham. Then you live about her waist, or in the middle of her favours?

Guil. 'Faith, her privates we.

Ham. In the secret parts of Fortune? O, most true; she is a strumpet. What 's the news?

Ros. None, my lord, but that the world 's grown honest.

Ham. Then is doomsday near: but your news is not true. Let me question more in particular: what have you, my good friends, deserved at the hands of Fortune, that she sends you to prison hither?

Guil. Prison, my lord!

Ham. Denmark 's a prison.

Ros. Then is the world one.

Ham. A goodly one; in which there are many confines, wards and dungeons, Denmark being one o' the worst.

Ros. We think not so, my lord.

Ham. Why, then, 'tis none to you; for there is nothing either good or bad, but thinking makes it so: to me it is a prison.

Ros. Why then, your ambition makes it one; 'tis too narrow for your mind.

Ham. O God, I could be bounded in a nutshell and count myself a king of infinite space, were it not that I have bad dreams.

Guil. Which dreams indeed are ambition, for the very substance of the ambitious is merely the shadow of a dream.

Ham. A dream itself is but a shadow.

Ros. Truly, and I hold ambition of so airy and light a quality that it is but a shadow's shadow.

Ham. Then are our beggars bodies, and our monarchs and outstretched heroes the beggars' shadows. Shall we to the court? for, by my fay, I cannot reason.

Ros. } *Guil.* } We'll wait upon you.

Ham. No such matter: I will not sort you with the rest of my servants, for, to speak to you like an honest man, I am most dreadfully attended. But, in the beaten way of friendship, what make you at Elsinore?

Ros. To visit you, my lord; no other occasion.

Ham. Beggar that I am, I am even poor in thanks; but I thank you: and sure, dear friends, my thanks are too dear a halfpenny. Were you not sent for? Is it your own inclining? Is it a free visitation? Come, come, deal justly with me: come, come; nay, speak.

Guil. What should we say, my lord?

Ham. Why, any thing, but to the purpose. You were sent for; and there is a kind of confession in your looks which your modesties have not craft enough to colour: I know the good king and queen have sent for you.

Ros. To what end, my lord?

Ham. That you must teach me. But let me conjure you, by the rights of our fellowship, by the consonancy of our youth, by the obligation of our ever-preserved love, and by what more dear a better proposer could charge you withal, be even and direct with me, whether you were sent for, or no?

Ros. [*Aside to Guil.*] What say you?

Ham. [*Aside*] Nay, then, I have an eye of you.—If you love me, hold not off.

Guil. My lord, we were sent for.

Ham. I will tell you why; so shall my anticipation prevent your discovery, and your secrecy to the king and queen moult no feather. I have of late—but wherefore I know not—lost all my mirth, forgone all custom of exercises; and indeed it goes so heavily with my disposition that this goodly frame, the earth, seems to me a sterile promontory, this most excellent canopy, the air, look you, this brave o'erhanging firmament, this majestical roof fretted with golden fire, why, it appeareth nothing to me but a foul and pestilent congregation of vapours. What a piece of work is a man! how noble in reason! how infinite in faculties! in form and moving how express and ad-

213. **happiness,** felicity of expression. 214. **prosperously,** successfully. 231. **indifferent,** ordinary. 238. **privates,** i.e., ordinary men (with sexual pun on *private parts*). 252. **confines,** places of confinement. 264. **very . . . ambitious,** that seemingly most substantial thing which the ambitious pursue (Hudson). 272. **fay,** faith. **reason,** argue. 273. **wait upon,** accompany. 274. **sort,** class. 276. **dreadfully attended,** poorly provided with servants. 277. **in the . . . friendship,** as a matter of course among friends. 282. **a,** i.e., at a. 294. **conjure,** adjure, entreat. 295. **consonancy of our youth,** the fact that we are of the same age. 297. **better proposer,** one more skillful in finding proposals. 305. **prevent your discovery,** forestall your disclosure. 313. **fretted,** adorned. 317. **faculties,** capacity. 318. **express,** well-framed (?), exact (?). 319. **apprehension,** understanding. 321. **quintessence,** the fifth essence of ancient philosophy, supposed to be the substance of the heavenly bodies and to be latent in all things. 329. **lenten,** meager.

330. **coted,** overtook and passed beyond. 334. **foil and target,** sword and shield; see *target* in glossary. 336. **humorous man,** actor who takes the part of the humor characters. 338. **tickle o' the sere,** easy on the trigger. 338-340. **the lady . . . for 't,** the lady (fond of talking) shall have opportunity to talk, blank verse or no blank verse. 344. **residence,** remaining in one place. 346. **inhibition,** formal prohibition (from acting plays in the city or, possibly, at court). 347. **innovation,** the new fashion in satirical plays performed by boy actors in the "private" theatres. 352-379. **How . . . load too.** The passage (omitted from Qq) is the famous one dealing with the War of the Theatres (1599-1602), namely, the rivalry between the children's companies and the adult actors. 354. **aery,** nest. 355. **eyases,** young hawks. 355-356. **cry . . . question,** speak in a high key dominating conversation (Clarendon Press); clamor forth the height of controversy (Dowden); probably "excel" (cf. l. 459); perhaps intended to decry leaders of the dramatic

mirable! in action how like an angel! in apprehension how like a god! the beauty of the world! the paragon of animals! And yet, to me, what is this quintessence of dust? man delights not me: no, nor woman neither, though by your smiling you seem to say so.

Ros. My lord, there was no such stuff in my thoughts.

Ham. Why did you laugh then, when I said 'man delights not me'?

Ros. To think, my lord, if you delight not in man, what lenten entertainment the players shall receive from you: we coted them on the way; and hither are they coming, to offer you service.

Ham. He that plays the king shall be welcome; his majesty shall have tribute of me; the adventurous knight shall use his foil and target; the lover shall not sigh gratis; the humorous man shall end his part in peace; the clown shall make those laugh whose lungs are tickle o' the sere; and the lady shall say her mind freely, or the blank verse shall halt for 't. What players are they?

Ros. Even those you were wont to take delight in, the tragedians of the city.

Ham. How chances it they travel? their residence, both in reputation and profit, was better both ways.

Ros. I think their inhibition comes by the means of the late innovation.

Ham. Do they hold the same estimation they did when I was in the city? are they so followed?

Ros. No, indeed, are they not.

Ham. How comes it? do they grow rusty?

Ros. Nay, their endeavour keeps in the wonted pace: but there is, sir, an aery of children, little eyases, that cry out on the top of question, and are most tyrannically clapped for 't: these are now the fashion, and so berattle the common stages—so they call them—that many wearing rapiers are afraid of goose-quills and dare scarce come thither.

Ham. What, are they children? who maintains 'em? how are they escoted? Will they pursue the quality no longer than they can sing? will they not say afterwards, if they should grow themselves to common players—as it is most like, if their means are no better—their writers do them wrong, to make them exclaim against their own succession?

Ros. 'Faith, there has been much to do on both sides; and the nation holds it no sin to tarre them to controversy: there was, for a while, no money bid for argument, unless the poet and the player went to cuffs in the question.

Ham. Is 't possible?

Guil. O, there has been much throwing about of brains.

Ham. Do the boys carry it away?

Ros. Ay, that they do, my lord; Hercules and his load too.

Ham. It is not very strange; for my uncle is king of Denmark, and those that would make mows at him while my father lived, give twenty, forty, fifty, a hundred ducats a-piece for his picture in little. 'Sblood, there is something in this more than natural, if philosophy could find it out.

A flourish [of trumpets within].

Guil. There are the players.

Ham. Gentlemen, you are welcome to Elsinore. Your hands, come then: the appurtenance of welcome is fashion and ceremony: let me comply with you in this garb, lest my extent to the players, which, I tell you, must show fairly outwards, should more appear like entertainment than yours. You are welcome: but my uncle-father and aunt-mother are deceived.

Guil. In what, my dear lord?

Ham. I am but mad north-north-west: when the wind is southerly I know a hawk from a handsaw.

Enter POLONIUS.

Pol. Well be with you, gentlemen!

Ham. Hark you, Guildenstern; and you too: at each ear a hearer: that great baby you see there is not yet out of his swaddling-clouts.

Ros. Happily he is the second time come to them; for they say an old man is twice a child.

Ham. I will prophesy he comes to tell me of the players; mark it.—You say right, sir: o' Monday morning; 'twas then indeed.

Pol. My lord, I have news to tell you.

Ham. My lord, I have news to tell you. When Roscius was an actor in Rome,—

Pol. The actors are come hither, my lord.

Ham. Buz, buz!

Pol. Upon my honour,—

Ham. Then came each actor on his ass,—

Pol. The best actors in the world, either for tragedy, comedy, history, pastoral, pastoral-comical, historical-pastoral, tragical-historical, tragical-comical-historical-pastoral, scene individable, or poem unlimited: Seneca cannot be too heavy, nor Plautus too light. For the law of writ and the liberty, these are the only men.

Ham. O Jephthah, judge of Israel, what a treasure hadst thou!

Pol. What a treasure had he, my lord?

Ham. Why,

'One fair daughter, and no more,
The which he loved passing well.'

Pol. [*Aside*] Still on my daughter.

Ham. Am I not i' the right, old Jephthah?

profession. 356. **tyrannically,** outrageously. 358. **berattle,** berate. **common stages,** public theatres. 359. **many wearing rapiers,** many men of fashion, who were afraid to patronize the common players for fear of being satirized by the poets who wrote for the children. 360. **goose-quills,** i.e., pens of satirists. 362. **escoted,** maintained. 363. **quality,** acting profession. 363-364. **no longer . . . sing,** i.e., until their voices change. 365. **common,** regular, adult. 368. **succession,** future careers. 370. **tarre,** set on (as dogs). 372. **argument,** probably, plot for a play. 373. **went to cuffs,** came to blows. **question,** controversy. 377. **carry it away,** win the day. 378-379. **Hercules . . . load,** regarded as an allusion to the sign of the Globe Theatre, which was Hercules bearing the world on his shoulder. 381. **mows,** grimaces. 382. **ducats,** gold coins worth 9s. 4d. 383. **in little,** in miniature. 390. **comply,** observe the formalities of courtesy. **garb,** manner. 391. **extent,** showing of kindness. 396. **I am . . . north-north-west,** I am only partly mad, i.e., in only one point of the compass. 397. **handsaw.** Hanmer's proposed reading *hernshaw* would mean "heron"; *handsaw* may be an early corruption of *hernshaw*. Another view regards *hawk* as the variant of *hack*, a tool of the pickax type, and *handsaw* as a saw operated by hand. 401. **swaddling-clouts,** cloths in which to wrap a newborn baby. 407. **o' Monday morning,** said to mislead Polonius. 410. **Roscius,** a famous Roman actor. 412. **Buz, buz,** according to Blackstone, an interjection used at Oxford to denote stale news. 418. **scene individable,** a play observing the unity of place. **poem unlimited,** a play disregarding the unities of time and place. 419. **Seneca,** writer of Latin tragedies, model of early Elizabethan writers of tragedy. **Plautus,** writer of Latin comedy. 420. **law . . . liberty,** pieces written according to rules and without rules, i.e., "classical" and "romantic" dramas (Chambers). 422. **Jephthah . . . Israel.** Jephthah had to sacrifice his daughter; see Judges 11.

Pol. If you call me Jephthah, my lord, I have a daughter that I love passing well.

Ham. Nay, that follows not.

Pol. What follows, then, my lord?

Ham. Why,

'As by lot, God wot,'

and then, you know,

'It came to pass, as most like it was,'—

the first row of the pious chanson will show you more; for look, where my abridgement comes.

Enter the Players.

You are welcome, masters; welcome, all. I am glad to see thee well. Welcome, good friends. O, old friend! why, thy face is valanced since I saw thee last: comest thou to beard me in Denmark? What, my young lady and mistress! By 'r lady, your ladyship is nearer to heaven than when I saw you last, by the altitude of a chopine. Pray God, your voice, like a piece of uncurrent gold, be not cracked within the ring. Masters, you are all welcome. We'll e'en to 't like French falconers, fly at any thing we see: we'll have a speech straight: come, give us a taste of your quality; come, a passionate speech.

First Play. What speech, my good lord?

Ham. I heard thee speak me a speech once, but it was never acted; or, if it was, not above once; for the play, I remember, pleased not the million; 'twas caviary to the general: but it was—as I received it, and others, whose judgements in such matters cried in the top of mine—an excellent play, well digested in the scenes, set down with as much modesty as cunning. I remember, one said there were no sallets in the lines to make the matter savoury, nor no matter in the phrase that might indict the author of affectation; but called it an honest method, as wholesome as sweet, and by very much more handsome than fine. One speech in 't I chiefly loved: 'twas Æneas' tale to Dido; and thereabout of it especially, where he speaks of Priam's slaughter: if it live in your memory, begin at this line: let me see, let me see—

'The rugged Pyrrhus, like th' Hyrcanian beast,'—

'tis not so:—it begins with Pyrrhus:—

'The rugged Pyrrhus, he whose sable arms,
Black as his purpose, did the night resemble
When he lay couched in the ominous horse,
Hath now this dread and black complexion
smear'd
With heraldry more dismal; head to foot
Now is he total gules; horridly trick'd
With blood of fathers, mothers, daughters, sons,
Bak'd and impasted with the parching streets,
That lend a tyrannous and a damned light
To their lord's murder: roasted in wrath and fire,
And thus o'er-sized with coagulate gore,
With eyes like carbuncles, the hellish Pyrrhus
Old grandsire Priam seeks.'

So, proceed you.

Pol. 'Fore God, my lord, well spoken, with good accent and good discretion.

First Play. 'Anon he finds him
Striking too short at Greeks; his antique sword,
Rebellious to his arm, lies where it falls,
Repugnant to command: unequal match'd,
Pyrrhus at Priam drives; in rage strikes wide;
But with the whiff and wind of his fell sword
Th' unnerved father falls. Then senseless Ilium,
Seeming to feel this blow, with flaming top
Stoops to his base, and with a hideous crash
Takes prisoner Pyrrhus' ear: for, lo! his sword,
Which was declining on the milky head
Of reverend Priam, seem'd i' th' air to stick:
So, as a painted tyrant, Pyrrhus stood,
And like a neutral to his will and matter,
Did nothing.
But, as we often see, against some storm,
A silence in the heavens, the rack stand still,
The bold winds speechless and the orb below
As hush as death, anon the dreadful thunder
Doth rend the region, so, after Pyrrhus' pause,
Aroused vengeance sets him new a-work;
And never did the Cyclops' hammers fall
On Mars's armour forg'd for proof eterne
With less remorse than Pyrrhus' bleeding sword
Now falls on Priam.
Out, out, thou strumpet, Fortune! All you gods,
In general synod, take away her power;
Break all the spokes and fellies from her wheel,
And bowl the round nave down the hill of heaven,
As low as to the fiends!'

Pol. This is too long.

Ham. It shall to the barber's, with your beard. Prithee, say on: he 's for a jig or a tale of bawdry, or he sleeps: say on: come to Hecuba.

First Play. 'But who, ah woe! had seen the mobled queen—'

Ham. 'The mobled queen?'

Pol. That 's good; 'mobled queen' is good.

First Play. 'Run barefoot up and down, threat'ning
the flames
With bisson rheum; a clout upon that head
Where late the diadem stood, and for a robe,
About her lank and all o'er-teemed loins,
A blanket, in the alarm of fear caught up;
Who this had seen, with tongue in venom steep'd,
'Gainst Fortune's state would treason have
pronounc'd:
But if the gods themselves did see her then
When she saw Pyrrhus make malicious sport
In mincing with his sword her husband's limbs,
The instant burst of clamour that she made,
Unless things mortal move them not at all,

431. **passing,** surpassingly. 437. **like,** probable. 438. **row,** stanza. **chanson,** ballad. 439. **abridgement comes,** opportunity comes for cutting short the conversation. 442. **valanced,** fringed (with a beard). 447. **chopine,** kind of shoe raised by the thickness of the heel; worn in Italy, particularly at Venice. 448. **uncurrent,** not passable as lawful coinage. 449. **cracked within the ring.** In the center of coins were rings enclosing the sovereign's head; if the coin was cracked within this ring, it was unfit for currency. 457. **caviary to the general,** not relished by the multitude. 459. **cried in the top of,** spoke with greater authority than. 461. **cunning,** skill. 462. **sallets,** salads; here, spicy improprieties. 464. **indict,** convict. 466-467. **as wholesome . . . fine.** Its beauty was not that of elaborate ornament, but that of order and proportion (Chambers). 468. **Æneas' tale to Dido.** The lines recited by the player are imitated from Marlowe and Nashe's *Dido Queen of Carthage* (II, i, 214 ff.). They are written in such a way that the conventionality of the play within a play is raised above that of ordinary drama. 472. **Pyrrhus,** a Greek hero in the Trojan War. **Hyrcanian beast,** the tiger; see Virgil, *Aeneid*, IV, 266. 476. **ominous horse,** Trojan horse. 479. **gules,** red; a heraldic term. **trick'd,** spotted, smeared. 481. **impasted,** made into a paste. 484. **o'er-sized,** covered as with size or glue. 493. **Repugnant,** disobedient. 496. **Then senseless Ilium,** insensate Troy. 502. **painted tyrant,** tyrant in a picture. 503. **matter,** task. 505. **against,** before. 506. **rack,** mass of clouds. 509. **region,** sky. 512. **proof eterne,** eternal resistance to assault. 516. **synod,** assembly. 517. **fellies,** pieces of wood forming the rim of a wheel. 518. **nave,** hub. 522. **jig,** comic performance given at the end or in an interval of a play.

Would have made milch the burning eyes
of heaven,
And passion in the gods.'

Pol. Look, whe'r he has not turned his colour and has tears in 's eyes. Prithee, no more.

Ham. 'Tis well; I'll have thee speak out the rest soon. Good my lord, will you see the players well bestowed? Do you hear, let them be well used; for they are the abstract and brief chronicles of the time: after your death you were better have a bad epitaph than their ill report while you live.

Pol. My lord, I will use them according to their desert.

Ham. God's bodykins, man, much better: use every man after his desert, and who shall 'scape whipping? Use them after your own honour and dignity: the less they deserve, the more merit is in your bounty. Take them in.

Pol. Come, sirs.

Ham. Follow him, friends: we'll hear a play to-morrow. [*Aside to First Player.*] Dost thou hear me, old friend; can you play the Murder of Gonzago?

First Play. Ay, my lord.

Ham. We'll ha 't to-morrow night. You could, for a need, study a speech of some dozen or sixteen lines, which I would set down and insert in 't, could you not?

First Play. Ay, my lord.

Ham. Very well. Follow that lord; and look you mock him not.—My good friends, I'll leave you till night: you are welcome to Elsinore.

Exeunt Pol. and Players.

Ros. Good my lord!

Exeunt [*Ros. and Guil*].

Ham. Ay, so, God bye to you.—Now I am alone.
O, what a rogue and peasant slave am I!
Is it not monstrous that this player here,
But in a fiction, in a dream of passion,
Could force his soul so to his own conceit
That from her working all his visage wann'd,
Tears in his eyes, distraction in 's aspect,
A broken voice, and his whole function suiting
With forms to his conceit? and all for nothing!
For Hecuba!
What 's Hecuba to him, or he to Hecuba,
That he should weep for her? What would he do,
Had he the motive and the cue for passion
That I have? He would drown the stage with tears
And cleave the general ear with horrid speech,
Make mad the guilty and appal the free,
Confound the ignorant, and amaze indeed
The very faculties of eyes and ears.
Yet I,
A dull and muddy-mettled rascal, peak,
Like John-a-dreams, unpregnant of my cause,
And can say nothing; no, not for a king,
Upon whose property and most dear life
A damn'd defeat was made. Am I a coward?
Who calls me villain? breaks my pate across?
Plucks off my beard, and blows it in my face?
Tweaks me by the nose? gives me the lie i' th' throat,
As deep as to the lungs? who does me this?
Ha!
'Swounds, I should take it: for it cannot be
But I am pigeon-liver'd and lack gall
To make oppression bitter, or ere this
I should have fatted all the region kites
With this slave's offal: bloody, bawdy villain!
Remorseless, treacherous, lecherous, kindless villain!
O, vengeance!
Why, what an ass am I! This is most brave,
That I, the son of a dear father murder'd,
Prompted to my revenge by heaven and hell,
Must, like a whore, unpack my heart with words,
And fall a-cursing, like a very drab,
A stallion!
Fie upon 't! foh! About, my brains! Hum, I have
heard
That guilty creatures sitting at a play
Have by the very cunning of the scene
Been struck so to the soul that presently
They have proclaim'd their malefactions;
For murder, though it have no tongue, will speak
With most miraculous organ. I'll have these players
Play something like the murder of my father
Before mine uncle: I'll observe his looks;
I'll tent him to the quick: if 'a do blench,
I know my course. The spirit that I have seen
May be the devil: and the devil hath power
T' assume a pleasing shape; yea, and perhaps
Out of my weakness and my melancholy,
As he is very potent with such spirits,
Abuses me to damn me: I'll have grounds
More relative than this: the play 's the thing
Wherein I'll catch the conscience of the king. *Exit.*

[ACT III.

SCENE I. *A room in the castle.*]

Enter KING, QUEEN, POLONIUS, OPHELIA, ROSENCRANTZ, GUILDENSTERN, Lords.

King. And can you, by no drift of conference,
Get from him why he puts on this confusion,
Grating so harshly all his days of quiet
With turbulent and dangerous lunacy?

Ros. He does confess he feels himself distracted;
But from what cause 'a will by no means speak.

Guil. Nor do we find him forward to be sounded,
But, with a crafty madness, keeps aloof,
When we would bring him on to some confession
Of his true state.

Queen. Did he receive you well?

Ros. Most like a gentleman.

523. **bawdry,** indecency. **Hecuba,** wife of Priam, king of Troy. 525. **mobled,** muffled. 529. **bisson rheum,** blinding tears. **clout,** piece of cloth. 531. **o'er-teemed,** worn out with bearing children. 534. **pronounc'd,** proclaimed. 540. **milch,** moist with tears. 542. **turned,** changed. 548. **abstract,** summary account. 554. **bodykins,** diminutive form of the oath, "by God's body." 567. **dozen or sixteen lines.** Critics have amused themselves by trying to locate Hamlet's lines. Lucianus' speech, III, ii, 266, ff., is the best guess. 576. **peasant,** base. 580. **wann'd,** grew pale. 582-583. **his whole . . . conceit,** his whole being responded with forms to suit his thought. 594. **muddy-mettled,** dull-spirited. **peak,** mope, pine. 595. **John-a-dreams,** an expression occurring elsewhere in Elizabethan literature to indicate a dreamer. **unpregnant of,** not quickened by. 597. **property,** proprietorship (of crown and life). 605. **pigeon-liver'd.** The pigeon was supposed to secrete no gall; if Hamlet, so he says, had had gall, he would have felt the bitterness of oppression, and avenged it. 607. **region kites,** kites of the air. 609. **kindless,** unnatural. 615. **drab,** prostitute. 616. **stallion,** prostitute (male or female). Many editors, including Globe, follow F reading of *scullion.* 617. **About,** about it, or turn thou right about. 626. **tent,** probe. **blench,** quail, flinch. 628. **May be the devil.** Hamlet's suspicion is properly grounded in the belief of the time. 631. **spirits,** humors. 633. **relative,** closely related, definite. **this,** i.e., the ghost's story.

ACT III. SCENE I. 1. **drift of conference,** device of conversation; so Q_2; Globe, following F: *circumstance.* 7. **forward,** willing.

Guil. But with much forcing of his disposition.
Ros. Niggard of question; but, of our demands,
Most free in his reply.
Queen. Did you assay him
To any pastime?
Ros. Madam, it so fell out, that certain players
We o'er-raught on the way: of these we told him;
And there did seem in him a kind of joy
To hear of it: they are here about the court,
And, as I think, they have already order
This night to play before him.
Pol. 'Tis most true:
And he beseech'd me to entreat your majesties
To hear and see the matter.
King. With all my heart; and it doth much content me
To hear him so inclin'd.
Good gentlemen, give him a further edge,
And drive his purpose into these delights.
Ros. We shall, my lord.
Exeunt Rosencrantz and Guildenstern.
King. Sweet Gertrude, leave us too;
For we have closely sent for Hamlet hither,
That he, as 'twere by accident, may here
Affront Ophelia:
Her father and myself, lawful espials,
Will so bestow ourselves that, seeing, unseen,
We may of their encounter frankly judge,
And gather by him, as he is behav'd,
If 't be th' affliction of his love or no
That thus he suffers for.
Queen. I shall obey you.
And for your part, Ophelia, I do wish
That your good beauties be the happy cause
Of Hamlet's wildness: so shall I hope your virtues
Will bring him to his wonted way again,
To both your honours.
Oph. Madam, I wish it may. [*Exit Queen.*]
Pol. Ophelia, walk you here. Gracious, so please you,
We will bestow ourselves. [*To Ophelia*] Read on this book;
That show of such an exercise may colour
Your loneliness. We are oft to blame in this,—
'Tis too much prov'd—that with devotion's visage
And pious action we do sugar o'er
The devil himself.
King. [*Aside*] O, 'tis too true!
How smart a lash that speech doth give my conscience!
The harlot's cheek, beautied with plast'ring art,
Is not more ugly to the thing that helps it
Than is my deed to my most painted word:
O heavy burthen!
Pol. I hear him coming: let 's withdraw, my lord.
[*Exeunt King and Polonius.*]

Enter HAMLET.

Ham. To be, or not to be: that is the question:
Whether 'tis nobler in the mind to suffer
The slings and arrows of outrageous fortune,
Or to take arms against a sea of troubles,
And by opposing end them? To die: to sleep;
No more; and by a sleep to say we end
The heart-ache and the thousand natural shocks
That flesh is heir to, 'tis a consummation
Devoutly to be wish'd. To die, to sleep;
To sleep: perchance to dream: ay, there 's the rub;
For in that sleep of death what dreams may come
When we have shuffled off this mortal coil,
Must give us pause: there 's the respect
That makes calamity of so long life;
For who would bear the whips and scorns of time,
Th' oppressor's wrong, the proud man's contumely,
The pangs of despis'd love, the law's delay,
The insolence of office and the spurns
That patient merit of th' unworthy takes,
When he himself might his quietus make
With a bare bodkin? who would fardels bear,
To grunt and sweat under a weary life,
But that the dread of something after death,
The undiscover'd country from whose bourn
No traveller returns, puzzles the will
And makes us rather bear those ills we have
Than fly to others that we know not of?
Thus conscience does make cowards of us all;
And thus the native hue of resolution
Is sicklied o'er with the pale cast of thought,
And enterprises of great pitch and moment
With this regard their currents turn awry,
And lose the name of action.—Soft you now!
The fair Ophelia! Nymph, in thy orisons
Be all my sins rememb'red.
Oph. Good my lord,
How does your honour for this many a day?
Ham. I humbly thank you; well, well, well.
Oph. My lord, I have remembrances of yours,
That I have longed long to re-deliver;
I pray you, now receive them.
Ham. No, not I;
I never gave you aught.
Oph. My honour'd lord, you know right well you did;
And, with them, words of so sweet breath compos'd
As made the things more rich: their perfume lost,
Take these again; for to the noble mind
Rich gifts wax poor when givers prove unkind.
There, my lord.
Ham. Ha, ha! are you honest?
Oph. My lord?
Ham. Are you fair?
Oph. What means your lordship?

12. **forcing of his disposition,** i.e., against his will. 13. **Niggard of question,** sparing of conversation. 14. **assay,** try to win. 17. **o'er-raught,** overtook. 26. **edge,** incitement. 28. **too,** so F; Q_2: *two*. 29. **closely,** secretly. 31. **Affront,** confront. 32. **lawful espials,** legitimate spies. 40. **wildness,** madness. 43. **Gracious,** your grace (addressed to the king). 45. **exercise,** act of devotion. (The book she reads is one of devotion.) **colour,** give a plausible appearance to. 52. **to,** compared to. **thing,** i.e., the cosmetic. 59. **sea.** The mixed metaphor of this speech has often been commented on; Theobald's emendation *siege* has sometimes been spoken on the stage. 67. **shuffled,** sloughed, cast. **coil,** usually means "turmoil"; here, possibly "body" (conceived of as wound about the soul like rope); *clay*, *soil*, *veil*, have been suggested as emendations. 68. **respect,** consideration. 69. **of . . . life,** so long-lived. 70. **time,** the world. 72. **despis'd,** rejected. 73. **office,** office-holders. **spurns,** insults. 75. **quietus,** acquittance; here, death. 76. **bare bodkin,** mere dagger; *bare* is sometimes understood as "unsheathed." **fardels,** burdens. 79. **bourn,** boundary. 83. **conscience,** probably, inhibition by the faculty of reason restraining the will from doing wrong. 84. **native hue,** natural color; metaphor derived from the color of the face. 85. **sicklied o'er,** given a sickly tinge. **cast,** shade of color. 86. **pitch,** height (as of a falcon's flight). **moment,** importance. 87. **regard,** respect, consideration. **currents,** courses. 89. **orisons,** prayers. 103-108. **are you . . . beauty.** *Honest* meaning "truthful" (l. 103) and "chaste" (l. 107), and *fair* meaning "just, honorable" (l. 105) and "beautiful" (l. 107) are not mere quibbles; the speech has the irony of a *double entendre*. 108. **your honesty,** your chastity. **discourse to,** familiar inter-

Ham. That if you be honest and fair, your honesty should admit no discourse to your beauty.

Oph. Could beauty, my lord, have better commerce than with honesty?

Ham. Ay, truly; for the power of beauty will sooner transform honesty from what it is to a bawd than the force of honesty can translate beauty into his likeness: this was sometime a paradox, but now the time gives it proof. I did love you once.

Oph. Indeed, my lord, you made me believe so.

Ham. You should not have believed me; for virtue cannot so inoculate our old stock but we shall relish of it: I loved you not.

Oph. I was the more deceived.

Ham. Get thee to a nunnery: why wouldst thou be a breeder of sinners? I am myself indifferent honest; but yet I could accuse me of such things that it were better my mother had not borne me: I am very proud, revengeful, ambitious, with more offences at my beck than I have thoughts to put them in, imagination to give them shape, or time to act them in. What should such fellows as I do crawling between earth and heaven? We are arrant knaves, all; believe none of us. Go thy ways to a nunnery. Where 's your father?

Oph. At home, my lord.

Ham. Let the doors be shut upon him, that he may play the fool no where but in 's own house. Farewell.

Oph. O, help him, you sweet heavens!

Ham. If thou dost marry, I'll give thee this plague for thy dowry: be thou as chaste as ice, as pure as snow, thou shalt not escape calumny. Get thee to a nunnery, go: farewell. Or, if thou wilt needs marry, marry a fool; for wise men know well enough what monsters you make of them. To a nunnery, go, and quickly too. Farewell.

Oph. O heavenly powers, restore him!

Ham. I have heard of your paintings too, well enough; God hath given you one face, and you make yourselves another: you jig, you amble, and you lisp; you nick-name God's creatures, and make your wantonness your ignorance. Go to, I'll no more on 't; it hath made me mad. I say, we will have no moe marriage: those that are married already, all but one, shall live; the rest shall keep as they are. To a nunnery, go. *Exit.*

Oph. O, what a noble mind is here o'er-thrown!
The courtier's, soldier's, scholar's, eye, tongue, sword;
Th' expectancy and rose of the fair state,
The glass of fashion and the mould of form,
Th' observ'd of all observers, quite, quite down!
And I, of ladies most deject and wretched,
That suck'd the honey of his music vows,
Now see that noble and most sovereign reason,
Like sweet bells jangled, out of time and harsh;
That unmatch'd form and feature of blown youth
Blasted with ecstasy: O, woe is me,
T' have seen what I have seen, see what I see!

Enter KING *and* POLONIUS.

King. Love! his affections do not that way tend;
Nor what he spake, though it lack'd form a little,
Was not like madness. There 's something in his soul,
O'er which his melancholy sits on brood;
And I do doubt the hatch and the disclose
Will be some danger: which for to prevent,
I have in quick determination
Thus set it down: he shall with speed to England,
For the demand of our neglected tribute:
Haply the seas and countries different
With variable objects shall expel
This something-settled matter in his heart,
Whereon his brains still beating puts him thus
From fashion of himself. What think you on 't?

Pol. It shall do well: but yet do I believe
The origin and commencement of his grief
Sprung from neglected love. How now, Ophelia!
You need not tell us what Lord Hamlet said;
We heard it all. My lord, do as you please;
But, if you hold it fit, after the play
Let his queen mother all alone entreat him
To show his grief: let her be round with him;
And I'll be plac'd, so please you, in the ear
Of all their conference. If she find him not,
To England send him, or confine him where
Your wisdom best shall think.

King. It shall be so:
Madness in great ones must not unwatch'd go. *Exeunt.*

[SCENE II. *A hall in the castle.*]

Enter HAMLET *and three of the* Players.

Ham. Speak the speech, I pray you, as I pronounced it to you, trippingly on the tongue: but if you mouth it, as many of your players do, I had as lief the town-crier spoke my lines. Nor do not saw the air too much with your hand, thus, but use all gently; for in the very torrent, tempest, and, as I may say, whirlwind of your passion, you must acquire and beget a temperance that may give it smoothness. O, it offends me to the soul to hear a robustious periwig-pated fellow tear a passion to tatters, to very rags, to split the ears of the groundlings, who for the most part are capable of nothing but inexplicable dumb-shows and noise: I would have such a fellow whipped for o'er-doing Termagant; it out-herods Herod: pray you, avoid it.

First Play. I warrant your honour.

Ham. Be not too tame neither, but let your own discretion be your tutor: suit the action to the word, the word to the action; with this special observance, that you o'er-step not the modesty of nature: for any

course with. 110. **commerce,** intercourse. 115. **the time,** the present age. 119. **inoculate,** graft (metaphorical). 120. **but . . . it,** i.e., that we do not still have about us a taste of the old stock; i.e., retain our sinfulness. 124. **indifferent honest,** moderately virtuous. 128. **beck,** command. 145. **monsters,** an allusion to the horns of a cuckold. 148. **your,** indefinite use. 150. **jig,** move with jerky motion; probably allusion to the *jig*, or song and dance, of the current stage. 152-153. **make . . . ignorance,** i.e., excuse your wantonness on the ground of your ignorance. 156. **one,** i.e., the king. 160. **expectancy and rose,** source of hope. 161. **The glass . . . form,** the mirror of fashion and the pattern of courtly behavior. 162. **observ'd . . . observers,** i.e., the center of attention in the court. 167. **blown,** blooming. 168. **ecstasy,** madness. 174. **doubt,** fear. **disçlose,** disclosure or revelation (by chipping of the shell). 180. **variable,** various. 181. **something-settled,** somewhat settled. 183. **From . . . himself,** out of his natural manner. 191. **round,** blunt.

SCENE II. 4. **your,** indefinite use. 8. **your,** so Q_2; F and Globe omit. 10. **robustious,** violent, boisterous. **periwig-pated,** wearing a wig. 12. **groundlings,** those who stood in the yard of the theatre. 13. **capable of,** susceptible of being influenced by. 14. **inexplicable,** of no significance worth explaining. 16. **Termagant,** a god of the Saracens; a character in the St. Nicholas play, where one of his worshipers, leaving him in charge of goods, returns to find them stolen; whereupon he beats the god (or idol), which howls vociferously. **Herod,** Herod of Jewry; a character in *The Slaughter of the Innocents* and other cycle plays. The part was played with great noise and fury.

thing so overdone is from the purpose of playing, whose end, both at the first and now, was and is, to hold, as 't were, the mirror up to nature; to show virtue her own feature, scorn her own image, and the very age and body of the time his form and pressure. Now this overdone, or come tardy off, though it make the unskilful laugh, cannot but make the judicious grieve; the censure of the which one must in your allowance o'erweigh a whole theatre of others. O, there be players that I have seen play, and heard others praise, and that highly, not to speak it profanely, that, neither having the accent of Christians nor the gait of Christian, pagan, nor man, have so strutted and bellowed that I have thought some of nature's journeymen had made men and not made them well, they imitated humanity so abominably.

First Play. I hope we have reformed that indifferently with us, sir.

Ham. O, reform it altogether. And let those that play your clowns speak no more than is set down for them; for there be of them that will themselves laugh, to set on some quantity of barren spectators to laugh too; though, in the mean time, some necessary question of the play be then to be considered: that 's villanous, and shows a most pitiful ambition in the fool that uses it. Go, make you ready. [*Exeunt Players.*]

Enter POLONIUS, GUILDENSTERN, *and* ROSENCRANTZ.

How now, my lord! will the king hear this piece of work?

Pol. And the queen too, and that presently.

Ham. Bid the players make haste. [*Exit Polonius.*]
Will you two help to hasten them?

Ros.
Guil. } We will, my lord.

Exeunt they two.

Ham. What ho! Horatio!

Enter HORATIO.

Hor. Here, sweet lord, at your service.

Ham. Horatio, thou art e'en as just a man
As e'er my conversation cop'd withal.

Hor. O, my dear lord,—

Ham. Nay, do not think I flatter;
For what advancement may I hope from thee
That no revenue hast but thy good spirits,
To feed and clothe thee? Why should the poor be flatter'd?
No, let the candied tongue lick absurd pomp,
And crook the pregnant hinges of the knee
Where thrift may follow fawning. Dost thou hear?
Since my dear soul was mistress of her choice
And could of men distinguish her election,
S' hath seal'd thee for herself; for thou hast been
As one, in suff'ring all, that suffers nothing,
A man that fortune's buffets and rewards
Hast ta'en with equal thanks: and blest are those
Whose blood and judgement are so well commeddled,
That they are not a pipe for fortune's finger
To sound what stop she please. Give me that man
That is not passion's slave, and I will wear him
In my heart's core, ay, in my heart of heart,
As I do thee.—Something too much of this.—
There is a play to-night before the king;
One scene of it comes near the circumstance
Which I have told thee of my father's death:
I prithee, when thou seest that act afoot,
Even with the very comment of thy soul
Observe my uncle: if his occulted guilt
Do not itself unkennel in one speech,
It is a damned ghost that we have seen,
And my imaginations are as foul
As Vulcan's stithy. Give him heedful note;
For I mine eyes will rivet to his face,
And after we will both our judgements join
In censure of his seeming.

Hor. Well, my lord:
If 'a steal aught the whilst this play is playing,
And 'scape detecting, I will pay the theft.

Enter trumpets and kettledrums, KING, QUEEN, POLONIUS, OPHELIA [, ROSENCRANTZ, GUILDENSTERN, *and others*].

Ham. They are coming to the play; I must be idle:
Get you a place.

King. How fares our cousin Hamlet?

Ham. Excellent, i' faith; of the chameleon's dish: I eat the air, promise-crammed: you cannot feed capons so.

King. I have nothing with this answer, Hamlet; these words are not mine.

Ham. No, nor mine now. [*To Polonius*] My lord, you played once i' the university, you say?

Pol. That did I, my lord; and was accounted a good actor.

Ham. What did you enact?

Pol. I did enact Julius Cæsar: I was killed i' the Capitol; Brutus killed me.

Ham. It was a brute part of him to kill so capital a calf there. Be the players ready?

Ros. Ay, my lord; they stay upon your patience.

Queen. Come hither, my dear Hamlet, sit by me.

Ham. No, good mother, here 's metal more attractive.

Pol. [*To the King*] O, ho! do you mark that?

Ham. Lady, shall I lie in your lap?

[*Lying down at Ophelia's feet.*]

Oph. No, my lord.

Ham. I mean, my head upon your lap?

Oph. Ay, my lord.

Ham. Do you think I meant country matters?

Oph. I think nothing, my lord.

Ham. That 's a fair thought to lie between maids' legs.

Oph. What is, my lord?

27. **pressure,** stamp, impressed character. 28. **come tardy off,** inadequately done. 31. **the censure . . . one,** the judgment of even one of whom. 38. **journeymen,** laborers not yet masters in their trade. 40. **abominably.** Q_2F: *abhominably*, a word thought to be derived from *ab homine*, a circumstance which brings out better the contrast with *humanity*. 41. **indifferently,** fairly, tolerably. 44. **of,** i.e., some among them. 46. **barren,** i.e., of wit. 59. **just,** honest, honorable. 63. **revenue,** accent on second syllable. 66. **pregnant,** pliant. 67. **thrift,** profit. 69-70. Text follows Q_2; Globe, following F, places comma after *distinguish* and reads *Hath*. 74. **commeddled,** so Q_2; Globe, following F: *commingléd*. 76. **stop,** hole in a wind instrument for controlling the sound. 84. **very . . . soul,** inward and sagacious criticism (Dowden). 85. **occulted,** hidden. 87. **damned,** in league with Satan. 89. **stithy,** smithy, place of *stiths* (anvils). 92. **censure . . . seeming,** judgment of his appearance or behavior. 95. **idle,** crazy, or not attending to anything serious. 98. **chameleon's dish.** Chameleons were supposed to feed on air. (Hamlet deliberately misinterprets the King's "fares" as "feeds.") 101. **have . . . with,** make nothing of. 102. **are not mine,**

Ham. Nothing.

Oph. You are merry, my lord.

Ham. Who, I?

Oph. Ay, my lord.

Ham. O God, your only jig-maker. What should a man do but be merry? for, look you, how cheerfully my mother looks, and my father died within's two hours.

Oph. Nay, 'tis twice two months, my lord.

Ham. So long? Nay then, let the devil wear black, for I'll have a suit of sables. O heavens! die two months ago, and not forgotten yet? Then there's hope a great man's memory may outlive his life half a year: but, by 'r lady, 'a must build churches, then; or else shall 'a suffer not thinking on, with the hobby-horse, whose epitaph is 'For, O, for, O, the hobby-horse is forgot.'

The trumpets sound. Dumb show follows.

Enter a King *and a* Queen [*very lovingly*]; *the* Queen *embracing him, and he her.* [*She kneels, and makes show of protestation unto him.*] *He takes her up, and declines his head upon her neck: he lies him down upon a bank of flowers: she, seeing him asleep, leaves him. Anon comes in another man, takes off his crown, kisses it, pours poison in the sleeper's ears, and leaves him. The* Queen *returns; finds the* King *dead, makes passionate action. The* Poisoner, *with some three or four come in again, seem to condole with her. The dead body is carried away. The* Poisoner *wooes the* Queen *with gifts: she seems harsh awhile, but in the end accepts love.* [*Exeunt.*]

Oph. What means this, my lord?

Ham. Marry, this is miching mallecho; it means mischief.

Oph. Belike this show imports the argument of the play.

Enter Prologue.

Ham. We shall know by this fellow: the players cannot keep counsel; they'll tell all.

Oph. Will 'a tell us what this show meant?

Ham. Ay, or any show that you'll show him: be not you ashamed to show, he'll not shame to tell you what it means.

Oph. You are naught, you are naught: I'll mark the play.

Pro. For us, and for our tragedy,
Here stooping to your clemency,
We beg your hearing patiently. [*Exit.*]

Ham. Is this a prologue, or the posy of a ring?

Oph. 'Tis brief, my lord.

Ham. As woman's love.

Enter [*two* Players *as*] King *and* Queen.

P. King. Full thirty times hath Phœbus' cart gone round
Neptune's salt wash and Tellus' orbed ground,
And thirty dozen moons with borrowed sheen
About the world have times twelve thirties been,
Since love our hearts and Hymen did our hands
Unite commutual in most sacred bands.

P. Queen. So many journeys may the sun and moon
Make us again count o'er ere love be done!
But, woe is me, you are so sick of late,
So far from cheer and from your former state,
That I distrust you. Yet, though I distrust,
Discomfort you, my lord, it nothing must:
For women's fear and love holds quantity;
In neither aught, or in extremity.
Now, what my love is, proof hath made you know;
And as my love is siz'd, my fear is so:
Where love is great, the littlest doubts are fear;
Where little fears grow great, great love grows there.

P. King. 'Faith, I must leave thee, love, and shortly too;
My operant powers their functions leave to do:
And thou shalt live in this fair world behind,
Honour'd, belov'd; and haply one as kind
For husband shalt thou—

P. Queen. O, confound the rest!
Such love must needs be treason in my breast:
In second husband let me be accurst!
None wed the second but who kill'd the first.

Ham. [*Aside*] Wormwood, wormwood.

P. Queen. The instances that second marriage move
Are base respects of thrift, but none of love:
A second time I kill my husband dead,
When second husband kisses me in bed.

P. King. I do believe you think what now you speak;
But what we do determine oft we break.
Purpose is but the slave to memory,
Of violent birth, but poor validity:
Which now, like fruit unripe, sticks on the tree;
But fall, unshaken, when they mellow be.
Most necessary 'tis that we forget
To pay ourselves what to ourselves is debt:
What to ourselves in passion we propose,
The passion ending, doth the purpose lose.
The violence of either grief or joy
Their own enactures with themselves destroy:
Where joy most revels, grief doth most lament;
Grief joys, joy grieves, on slender accident.
This world is not for aye, nor 'tis not strange
That even our loves should with our fortunes change;
For 'tis a question left us yet to prove,
Whether love lead fortune, or else fortune love.
The great man down, you mark his favourite flies;
The poor advanc'd makes friends of enemies.
And hitherto doth love on fortune tend;
For who not needs shall never lack a friend,
And who in want a hollow friend doth try,
Directly seasons him his enemy.
But, orderly to end where I begun,
Our wills and fates do so contrary run
That our devices still are overthrown;

do not respond to what I asked. 123. **country,** with a bawdy pun. 132. **your only,** only your. **jig-maker,** composer of jigs (song and dance). 138. **suit of sables,** garments trimmed with the fur of the sable, with a quibble on *sable* meaning "black." 143. **suffer . . . on,** undergo oblivion. 144-145. **'For . . . forgot,'** verse of a song occurring also in *Love's Labour's Lost*, III, i, 30. The hobbyhorse was a character in the Morris Dance. 147. **miching mallecho,** sneaking mischief. 158. **naught,** indecent. 160. **stooping,** bowing. 162. **posy,** motto. 166. **salt wash,** the sea. **Tellus,** goddess of the earth (*orbed ground*).

167. **borrowed,** i.e., reflected. 169. **Hymen,** god of matrimony. 170. **commutual,** mutually. 175. **distrust,** am anxious about. 176. After this line Q_2 has *For women feare too much, euen as they loue.* 177. **hold quantity,** keeps proportion between. 184. **operant,** active. **leave,** cease. 207. **enactures,** fulfillments. 210. **aye,** ever. 218. **who,** whoever. 219. **seasons,** matures, ripens.

Our thoughts are ours, their ends none of our own:
So think thou wilt no second husband wed;
But die thy thoughts when thy first lord is dead.
P. Queen. Nor earth to me give food, nor heaven light!
Sport and repose lock from me day and night!
To desperation turn my trust and hope!
An anchor's cheer in prison be my scope!
Each opposite that blanks the face of joy
Meet what I would have well and it destroy!
Both here and hence pursue me lasting strife,
If, once a widow, ever I be wife!
Ham. If she should break it now!
P. King. 'Tis deeply sworn. Sweet, leave me here awhile;
My spirits grow dull, and fain I would beguile
The tedious day with sleep. [*Sleeps.*]
P. Queen. Sleep rock thy brain;
And never come mischance between us twain! *Exit.*

Ham. Madam, how like you this play?

Queen. The lady doth protest too much, methinks.

Ham. O, but she'll keep her word.

King. Have you heard the argument? Is there no offence in 't?

Ham. No, no, they do but jest, poison in jest; no offence i' the world.

King. What do you call the play?

Ham. The Mouse-trap. Marry, how? Tropically. This play is the image of a murder done in Vienna: Gonzago is the duke's name; his wife, Baptista: you shall see anon; 't is a knavish piece of work: but what o' that? your majesty and we that have free souls, it touches us not: let the galled jade winch, our withers are unwrung.

Enter LUCIANUS.

This is one Lucianus, nephew to the king.

Oph. You are as good as a chorus, my lord.

Ham. I could interpret between you and your love, if I could see the puppets dallying.

Oph. You are keen, my lord, you are keen.

Ham. It would cost you a groaning to take off my edge.

Oph. Still better, and worse.

Ham. So you mistake your husbands. Begin, murderer; pox, leave thy damnable faces, and begin. Come: the croaking raven doth bellow for revenge.

Luc. Thoughts black, hands apt, drugs fit, and time agreeing;
Confederate season, else no creature seeing;
Thou mixture rank, of midnight weeds collected,
With Hecate's ban thrice blasted, thrice infected,
Thy natural magic and dire property,
On wholesome life usurp immediately.
[*Pours the poison into the sleeper's ears.*]

Ham. 'A poisons him i' the garden for his estate. His name 's Gonzago: the story is extant, and written in very choice Italian: you shall see anon how the murderer gets the love of Gonzago's wife.

Oph. The king rises.

Ham. What, frighted with false fire!

Queen. How fares my lord?

Pol. Give o'er the play.

King. Give me some light: away!

Pol. Lights, lights, lights!

Exeunt all but Hamlet and Horatio.

Ham. Why, let the strucken deer go weep,
The hart ungalled play;
For some must watch, while some must sleep:
Thus runs the world away.
Would not this, sir, and a forest of feathers—if the rest of my fortunes turn Turk with me—with two Provincial roses on my razed shoes, get me a fellowship in a cry of players, sir?

Hor. Half a share.

Ham. A whole one, I.
For thou dost know, O Damon dear,
This realm dismantled was
Of Jove himself; and now reigns here
A very, very—pajock.

Hor. You might have rhymed.

Ham. O good Horatio, I'll take the ghost's word for a thousand pound. Didst perceive?

Hor. Very well, my lord.

Ham. Upon the talk of the poisoning?

Hor. I did very well note him.

Ham. Ah, ha! Come, some music! come, the recorders!
For if the king like not the comedy,
Why then, belike, he likes it not, perdy.
Come, some music!

Enter ROSENCRANTZ *and* GUILDENSTERN.

Guil. Good my lord, vouchsafe me a word with you.

Ham. Sir, a whole history.

Guil. The king, sir,—

Ham. Ay, sir, what of him?

Guil. Is in his retirement marvellous distempered.

Ham. With drink, sir?

Guil. No, my lord, rather with choler.

Ham. Your wisdom should show itself more richer to signify this to his doctor; for, for me to put him to his purgation would perhaps plunge him into far more choler.

Guil. Good my lord, put your discourse into some frame and start not so wildly from my affair.

Ham. I am tame, sir: pronounce.

Guil. The queen, your mother, in most great affliction of spirit, hath sent me to you.

Ham. You are welcome.

Guil. Nay, good my lord, this courtesy is not of the right breed. If it shall please you to make me a whole-

223. **ends,** results. 229. **An anchor's,** an anchorite's. **cheer,** fare; sometimes printed as *chair*. 230. **opposite,** adverse thing. **blanks,** causes to *blanch* or grow pale. 248. **Tropically,** figuratively. The Q_1 reading, *trapically*, suggests a pun on *trap* in *Mouse-trap* (l. 247). 249. **Gonzago.** In 1538 Luigi Gonzago murdered the Duke of Urbano by pouring poisoned lotion in his ears. 253. **galled jade,** horse whose hide is rubbed by saddle or harness. **winch,** wince. **withers,** the part between the horse's shoulder blades. **unwrung,** not wrung or twisted. 255. **chorus.** In many Elizabethan plays the action was explained by an actor known as the "chorus"; at a puppet show the actor who explained the action was known as an "interpreter," as indicated by the lines following. 258. **dallying,** with sexual suggestion, continued in *keen* (sexually aroused), *groaning* (i.e., in pregnancy), and *edge* (i.e., sexual desire or impetuosity). 261. **Still . . . worse,** more keen, less decorous (Caldecott). 262. **mistake,** err in taking. 263. **pox,** an imprecation. 267. **Confederate,** conspiring (to assist the murderer). 269. **Hecate,** the goddess of witchcraft. **ban,** curse. 277. **false fire,** fireworks, or a blank discharge. 282-285. **Why . . . away,** probably from an old ballad, with allusion to the popular belief that a wounded deer retires to weep and die. Cf. *As You Like It*, II, i, 66. 286. **this,** i.e., the play. **feathers,** allusion to the plumes which Elizabethan actors were fond of wearing. 287. **turn Turk with,** go back on. 288. **two Provincial roses,** rosettes of ribbon like the roses of Provins near Paris, or else the roses of Provence. **razed,** cut, slashed (by way of ornament). 289. **fellowship . . . players,** partnership in a theatrical company. **cry,** pack (as of hounds). 290. **Half a share,** allusion to the custom in dramatic companies of dividing the ownership into a number of shares among the householders. 292-295. **For . . . very,** probably from an old

some answer, I will do your mother's commandment: if not, your pardon and my return shall be the end of my business.

Ham. Sir, I cannot.

Guil. What, my lord?

Ham. Make you a wholesome answer; my wit 's diseased: but, sir, such answer as I can make, you shall command; or, rather, as you say, my mother: therefore no more, but to the matter: my mother, you say,—

Ros. Then thus she says; your behaviour hath struck her into amazement and admiration.

Ham. O wonderful son, that can so 'stonish a mother! But is there no sequel at the heels of this mother's admiration? Impart.

Ros. She desires to speak with you in her closet, ere you go to bed.

Ham. We shall obey, were she ten times our mother. Have you any further trade with us?

Ros. My lord, you once did love me.

Ham. And do still, by these pickers and stealers.

Ros. Good my lord, what is your cause of distemper? you do, surely, bar the door upon your own liberty, if you deny your griefs to your friend.

Ham. Sir, I lack advancement.

Ros. How can that be, when you have the voice of the king himself for your succession in Denmark?

Ham. Ay, sir, but 'While the grass grows,'—the proverb is something musty.

Enter the Players *with recorders.*

O, the recorders! let me see one. To withdraw with you:—why do you go about to recover the wind of me, as if you would drive me into a toil?

Guil. O, my lord, if my duty be too bold, my love is too unmannerly.

Ham. I do not well understand that. Will you play upon this pipe?

Guil. My lord, I cannot.

Ham. I pray you.

Guil. Believe me, I cannot.

Ham. I do beseech you.

Guil. I know no touch of it, my lord.

Ham. 'Tis as easy as lying: govern these ventages with your fingers and thumb, give it breath with your mouth, and it will discourse most eloquent music. Look you, these are the stops.

Guil. But these cannot I command to any utterance of harmony; I have not the skill.

Ham. Why, look you now, how unworthy a thing you make of me! You would play upon me; you would seem to know my stops; you would pluck out the heart of my mystery; you would sound me from my lowest note to the top of my compass: and there is much music, excellent voice, in this little organ; yet cannot you make it speak. 'Sblood, do you think I am easier to be played on than a pipe? Call me what instrument you will, though you can fret me, you cannot play upon me.

Enter Polonius.

God bless you, sir!

Pol. My lord, the queen would speak with you, and presently.

Ham. Do you see yonder cloud that 's almost in shape of a camel?

Pol. By the mass, and 'tis like a camel, indeed.

Ham. Methinks it is like a weasel.

Pol. It is backed like a weasel.

Ham. Or like a whale?

Pol. Very like a whale.

Ham. Then I will come to my mother by and by. [*Aside*] They fool me to the top of my bent.—I will come by and by.

Pol. I will say so. [*Exit.*]

Ham. By and by is easily said.
Leave me, friends. [*Exeunt all but Hamlet.*]
'Tis now the very witching time of night,
When churchyards yawn and hell itself breathes out
Contagion to this world: now could I drink hot blood,
And do such bitter business as the day
Would quake to look on. Soft! now to my mother.
O heart, lose not thy nature; let not ever
The soul of Nero enter this firm bosom:
Let me be cruel, not unnatural:
I will speak daggers to her, but use none;
My tongue and soul in this be hypocrites;
How in my words somever she be shent,
To give them seals never, my soul, consent! *Exit.*

[SCENE III. *A room in the castle:*]

Enter King, Rosencrantz, *and* Guildenstern.

King. I like him not, nor stands it safe with us
To let his madness range. Therefore prepare you;
I your commission will forthwith dispatch,
And he to England shall along with you:
The terms of our estate may not endure
Hazard so near us as doth hourly grow
Out of his brows.

Guil. We will ourselves provide:
Most holy and religious fear it is
To keep those many many bodies safe
That live and feed upon your majesty.

Ros. The single and peculiar life is bound,
With all the strength and armour of the mind,
To keep itself from noyance; but much more
That spirit upon whose weal depend and rest
The lives of many. The cess of majesty
Dies not alone; but, like a gulf, doth draw
What 's near it with it: it is a massy wheel,

ballad having to do with Damon and Pythias. 293. **dismantled,** stripped, divested. 295. **pajock,** peacock (a bird with a bad reputation). Skeat suggested that the word was *patchock*, diminutive of *patch*, clown. 303. **recorders,** wind instruments of the flute kind. 305. **perdy,** corruption of *par dieu*. 315. **choler,** bilious disorder, with quibble on the sense "anger." 321. **frame,** order. 328. **wholesome,** sensible. 337. **matter,** matter in hand. 349. **pickers and stealers,** hands, so called from the catechism, "to keep my hands from picking and stealing." 356. **voice,** support. 358. **'While . . . grows.'** The rest of the proverb is "the silly horse starves." Hamlet may be destroyed while he is waiting for the succession to the kingdom (Malone). 360. **withdraw,** speak in private. 361. **recover the wind,** get to the windward side. 362. **toil,** snare. 363-364. **if . . . unmannerly,** if I am using an unmannerly boldness, it is my love which occasions it. 373. **ventages,** stops of the recorders. 384. **compass,** range of voice. 385. **organ,** musical instrument, i.e., the pipe. 388. **fret,** quibble on meaning "irritate" and the piece of wood, gut, or metal which regulates the fingering. 401. **top of my bent,** limit of endurance, i.e., extent to which a bow may be bent. 402. **by and by,** immediately. 406. **witching time,** i.e., time when spells are cast. 412. **Nero,** murderer of his mother, Agrippina. 416. **shent,** rebuked. 417. **give them seals,** confirm with deeds.

Scene iii. 3. **dispatch,** prepare. 5. **terms,** condition, circumstances. **estate,** state. 7. **brows,** effronteries. 11. **single and peculiar,** individual and private. 13. **noyance,** harm. 15. **cess,** decease. 16. **gulf,** whirlpool.

Fix'd on the summit of the highest mount,
To whose huge spokes ten thousand lesser things
Are mortis'd and adjoin'd; which, when it falls,
Each small annexment, petty consequence,
Attends the boist'rous ruin. Never alone
Did the king sigh, but with a general groan.

King. Arm you, I pray you, to this speedy voyage;
For we will fetters put about this fear,
Which now goes too free-footed.

Ros. We will haste us.

Exeunt Gentlemen [*Ros. and Guil*].

Enter POLONIUS.

Pol. My lord, he 's going to his mother's closet:
Behind the arras I'll convey myself,
To hear the process; I'll warrant she'll tax him home:
And, as you said, and wisely was it said,
'Tis meet that some more audience than a mother,
Since nature makes them partial, should o'erhear
The speech, of vantage. Fare you well, my liege:
I'll call upon you ere you go to bed,
And tell you what I know.

King. Thanks, dear my lord.

Exit [*Polonius*].

O, my offence is rank, it smells to heaven;
It hath the primal eldest curse upon 't,
A brother's murder. Pray can I not,
Though inclination be as sharp as will:
My stronger guilt defeats my strong intent;
And, like a man to double business bound,
I stand in pause where I shall first begin,
And both neglect. What if this cursed hand
Were thicker than itself with brother's blood,
Is there not rain enough in the sweet heavens
To wash it white as snow? Whereto serves mercy
But to confront the visage of offence?
And what 's in prayer but this two-fold force,
To be forestalled ere we come to fall,
Or pardon'd being down? Then I'll look up;
My fault is past. But, O, what form of prayer
Can serve my turn? 'Forgive me my foul murder'?
That cannot be: since I am still possess'd
Of those effects for which I did the murder,
My crown, mine own ambition and my queen.
May one be pardon'd and retain th' offence?
In the corrupted currents of this world
Offence's gilded hand may shove by justice,
And oft 'tis seen the wicked prize itself
Buys out the law: but 'tis not so above;
There is no shuffling, there the action lies
In his true nature; and we ourselves compell'd,
Even to the teeth and forehead of our faults,
To give in evidence. What then? what rests?
Try what repentance can: what can it not?
Yet what can it when one can not repent?
O wretched state! O bosom black as death!
O limed soul, that, struggling to be free,
Art more engag'd! Help, angels! Make assay!
Bow, stubborn knees; and, heart with strings of steel,
Be soft as sinews of the new-born babe!
All may be well. [*He kneels*.]

Enter HAMLET.

Ham. Now might I do it pat, now he is praying;
And now I'll do 't. And so 'a goes to heaven;
And so am I reveng'd. That would be scann'd:
A villain kills my father; and for that,
I, his sole son, do this same villain send
To heaven.
Why, this is hire and salary, not revenge.
'A took my father grossly, full of bread;
With all his crimes broad blown, as flush as May;
And how his audit stands who knows save heaven?
But in our circumstance and course of thought,
'Tis heavy with him: and am I then reveng'd,
To take him in the purging of his soul,
When he is fit and season'd for his passage?
No!
Up, sword; and know thou a more horrid hent:
When he is drunk asleep, or in his rage,
Or in th' incestuous pleasure of his bed;
At game, a-swearing, or about some act
That has no relish of salvation in 't;
Then trip him, that his heels may kick at heaven,
And that his soul may be as damn'd and black
As hell, whereto it goes. My mother stays:
This physic but prolongs thy sickly days. *Exit*.

King. [*Rising*] My words fly up, my thoughts remain below:
Words without thoughts never to heaven go. *Exit*.

[SCENE IV. *The Queen's closet*.]

Enter [QUEEN] GERTRUDE *and* POLONIUS.

Pol. 'A will come straight. Look you lay home to him:
Tell him his pranks have been too broad to bear with,
And that your grace hath screen'd and stood between
Much heat and him. I'll sconce me even here.
Pray you, be round with him.

Ham. (*Within*) Mother, mother, mother!

Queen. I'll warrant you,
Fear me not: withdraw, I hear him coming.

[*Polonius hides behind the arras*.]

Enter HAMLET.

Ham. Now, mother, what 's the matter?

Queen. Hamlet, thou hast thy father much offended.

Ham. Mother, you have my father much offended.

22. **Attends,** participates in. 24. **Arm,** prepare. 25. **about,** so Q_2; Globe, following F: *upon*. 28. **arras,** screen of tapestry placed around the walls of household apartments. **convey,** implication of secrecy; *convey* was often used to mean "steal." 29. **process,** proceedings. **tax him home,** reprove him severely. 33. **of vantage,** from an advantageous place. 37. **primal eldest curse,** the curse of Cain, the first to kill his brother. 39. **sharp as will,** i.e., his desire is as strong as his determination. 47. **confront,** oppose directly. 49. **forestalled,** prevented. 55. **ambition,** i.e., realization of ambition. 56. **offence,** benefit accruing from offense. 57. **currents,** courses. 58. **gilded hand,** hand offering gold as a bribe. 59. **wicked prize,** prize won by wickedness. 61. **shuffling,** escape by trickery. **lies,** is sustainable. 63. **teeth and forehead,** very face. 64. **rests,** remains. 68. **limed,** caught as with birdlime. 69. **engag'd,** embedded. **assay,** trial. 73. **pat,** opportunely. 75. **would be scann'd,** needs to be looked into. 79. **hire and salary,** so F; Q_2: *base and silly*, which can be defended; Wilson: *bait and salary*. 80. **full of bread,** enjoying his worldly pleasures (see Ezekiel 16:49). 81. **broad blown,** in full bloom. **flush,** lusty. 83. **in . . . course,** as we see it in our mortal situation. 86. **fit . . . passage,** i.e., reconciled to heaven by forgiveness of his sins. 88. **hent,** seizing; or, more probably, occasion of seizure. 89. **drunk asleep,** in a drunken sleep. 96. **physic,** purging (by prayer).

SCENE IV. 1. **lay,** thrust. 2. **broad,** unrestrained. 4. **Much heat,** i.e., the king's anger. **sconce,** hide. 5. **round,** blunt. 9-10. **thy father, my father,** i.e., Claudius, the elder Hamlet. 14. **rood,** cross. 37. **braz'd,** brazened, hardened. 44. **sets a blister,** brands as a harlot.

Queen. Come, come, you answer with an idle tongue.
Ham. Go, go, you question with a wicked tongue.
Queen. Why, how now, Hamlet!
Ham. What 's the matter now?
Queen. Have you forgot me?
Ham. No, by the rood, not so:
You are the queen, your husband's brother's wife;
And—would it were not so!—you are my mother.
Queen. Nay, then, I'll set those to you that can speak.
Ham. Come, come, and sit you down; you shall not budge;
You go not till I set you up a glass
Where you may see the inmost part of you.
Queen. What wilt thou do? thou wilt not murder me?
Help, help, ho!
Pol. [*Behind*] What, ho! help, help, help!
Ham. [*Drawing*] How now! a rat? Dead, for a ducat, dead! [*Makes a pass through the arras.*]
Pol. [*Behind*] O, I am slain! [*Falls and dies.*]
Queen. O me, what hast thou done?
Ham. Nay, I know not:
Is it the king?
Queen. O, what a rash and bloody deed is this!
Ham. A bloody deed! almost as bad, good mother,
As kill a king, and marry with his brother.
Queen. As kill a king!
Ham. Ay, lady, it was my word.
[*Lifts up the arras and discovers Polonius.*]
Thou wretched, rash, intruding fool, farewell!
I took thee for thy better: take thy fortune;
Thou find'st to be too busy is some danger.
Leave wringing of your hands: peace! sit you down,
And let me wring your heart; for so I shall,
If it be made of penetrable stuff,
If damned custom have not braz'd it so
That it be proof and bulwark against sense.
Queen. What have I done, that thou dar'st wag thy tongue
In noise so rude against me?
Ham. Such an act
That blurs the grace and blush of modesty,
Calls virtue hypocrite, takes off the rose
From the fair forehead of an innocent love
And sets a blister there, makes marriage-vows
As false as dicers' oaths: O, such a deed
As from the body of contraction plucks
The very soul, and sweet religion makes
A rhapsody of words: heaven's face does glow
O'er this solidity and compound mass
With heated visage, as against the doom
Is thought-sick at the act.
Queen. Ay me, what act,
That roars so loud, and thunders in the index?
Ham. Look here, upon this picture, and on this.
The counterfeit presentment of two brothers.
See, what a grace was seated on this brow;
Hyperion's curls; the front of Jove himself;
An eye like Mars, to threaten and command;
A station like the herald Mercury
New-lighted on a heaven-kissing hill;
A combination and a form indeed,
Where every god did seem to set his seal,
To give the world assurance of a man:
This was your husband. Look you now, what follows:
Here is your husband; like a mildew'd ear,
Blasting his wholesome brother. Have you eyes?
Could you on this fair mountain leave to feed,
And batten on this moor? Ha! have you eyes?
You cannot call it love; for at your age
The hey-day in the blood is tame, it 's humble,
And waits upon the judgement: and what judgement
Would step from this to this? Sense, sure, you have,
Else could you not have motion; but sure, that sense
Is apoplex'd; for madness would not err,
Nor sense to ecstasy was ne'er so thrall'd
But it reserv'd some quantity of choice,
To serve in such a difference. What devil was 't
That thus hath cozen'd you at hoodman-blind?
Eyes without feeling, feeling without sight,
Ears without hands or eyes, smelling sans all,
Or but a sickly part of one true sense
Could not so mope.
O shame! where is thy blush? Rebellious hell,
If thou canst mutine in a matron's bones,
To flaming youth let virtue be as wax,
And melt in her own fire: proclaim no shame
When the compulsive ardour gives the charge,
Since frost itself as actively doth burn
And reason pandars will.
Queen. O Hamlet, speak no more:
Thou turn'st mine eyes into my very soul;
And there I see such black and grained spots
As will not leave their tinct.
Ham. Nay, but to live
In the rank sweat of an enseamed bed,
Stew'd in corruption, honeying and making love
Over the nasty sty,—
Queen. O, speak to me no more;
These words, like daggers, enter in mine ears;
No more, sweet Hamlet!
Ham. A murderer and a villain;
A slave that is not twentieth part the tithe
Of your precedent lord; a vice of kings;
A cutpurse of the empire and the rule,
That from a shelf the precious diadem stole,
And put it in his pocket!
Queen. No more!

Enter GHOST.

Ham. A king of shreds and patches,—

46. **contraction,** the marriage contract. 47. **religion,** religious vows. 48. **rhapsody,** senseless string. 48-51. **heaven's . . . act,** heaven's face blushes to look down upon this world, compounded of the four elements, with hot face as though the day of doom were near, and thought-sick at the deed (i.e., Gertrude's marriage). 50. **heated,** so Q_2; Globe, following F: *tristful*. **doom,** Last Judgment. 52. **index,** prelude or preface. 54. **counterfeit presentment,** portrayed representation. 56. **Hyperion,** the sun god. **front,** brow. 58. **station,** manner of standing. 62. **assurance,** pledge, guarantee. 64. **mildew'd ear.** See Genesis 41:5-7. 67. **batten,** grow fat. **moor,** barren upland. 69. **hey-day,** state of excitement. 71-72. **Sense . . . motion.** Sense and motion are functions of the middle or sensible soul, the possession of sense being the basis of motion. 73. **apoplex'd,** paralyzed. Mental derangement was thus of three sorts: apoplexy, ecstasy, and diabolic possession. 74. **thrall'd,** enslaved. 75. **quantity of choice,** fragment of the power to choose. 77. **cozen'd,** tricked, cheated. **hoodman-blind,** blindman's buff. 79. **sans,** without. 81. **mope,** be in a depressed, spiritless state, act aimlessly. 83. **mutine,** mutiny, rebel. 86. **gives the charge,** delivers the attack. 88. **reason pandars will.** The normal and proper situation was one in which reason guided the will in the direction of good; here, reason is perverted and leads in the direction of evil. 90. **grained,** dyed in grain. 92. **enseamed,** loaded with grease, greased. 98. **precedent lord,** i.e., the elder Hamlet. **vice of kings,** buffoon of kings; a reference to the Vice, or clown, of the morality plays and interludes. 102. **shreds and patches,** i.e., motley, the traditional costume of the Vice.

Save me, and hover o'er me with your wings,
You heavenly guards! What would your gracious
figure?
Queen. Alas, he 's mad!
Ham. Do you not come your tardy son to chide,
That, laps'd in time and passion, lets go by
Th' important acting of your dread command?
O, say!
Ghost. Do not forget: this visitation
Is but to whet thy almost blunted purpose.
But, look, amazement on thy mother sits:
O, step between her and her fighting soul:
Conceit in weakest bodies strongest works:
Speak to her, Hamlet.
Ham. How is it with you, lady?
Queen. Alas, how is 't with you,
That you do bend your eye on vacancy
And with th' incorporal air do hold discourse?
Forth at your eyes your spirits wildly peep;
And, as the sleeping soldiers in th' alarm,
Your bedded hair, like life in excrements,
Start up, and stand an end. O gentle son,
Upon the heat and flame of thy distemper
Sprinkle cool patience. Whereon do you look?
Ham. On him, on him! Look you, how pale he
glares!
His form and cause conjoin'd, preaching to stones,
Would make them capable.—Do not look upon me;
Lest with this piteous action you convert
My stern effects: then what I have to do
Will want true colour; tears perchance for blood.
Queen. To whom do you speak this?
Ham. Do you see nothing there?
Queen. Nothing at all; yet all that is I see.
Ham. Nor did you nothing hear?
Queen. No, nothing but ourselves.
Ham. Why, look you there! look, how it steals away!
My father, in his habit as he liv'd!
Look, where he goes, even now, out at the portal!
Exit Ghost.
Queen. This is the very coinage of your brain:
This bodiless creation ecstasy
Is very cunning in.
Ham. Ecstasy!
My pulse, as yours, doth temperately keep time,
And makes as healthful music: it is not madness
That I have utt'red: bring me to the test,
And I the matter will re-word, which madness
Would gambol from. Mother, for love of grace,
Lay not that flattering unction to your soul,
That not your trespass, but my madness speaks:
It will but skin and film the ulcerous place,
Whiles rank corruption, mining all within,
Infects unseen. Confess yourself to heaven;
Repent what 's past; avoid what is to come;
And do not spread the compost on the weeds,
To make them ranker. Forgive me this my virtue;
For in the fatness of these pursy times
Virtue itself of vice must pardon beg,
Yea, curb and woo for leave to do him good.
Queen. O Hamlet, thou hast cleft my heart in twain.
Ham. O, throw away the worser part of it,
And live the purer with the other half.
Good night: but go not to my uncle's bed;
Assume a virtue, if you have it not.
That monster, custom, who all sense doth eat,
Of habits devil, is angel yet in this,
That to the use of actions fair and good
He likewise gives a frock or livery,
That aptly is put on. Refrain to-night,
And that shall lend a kind of easiness
To the next abstinence: the next more easy;
For use almost can change the stamp of nature,
†And either . . . the devil, or throw him out
With wondrous potency. Once more, good night:
And when you are desirous to be bless'd,
I'll blessing beg of you. For this same lord,
[*Pointing to Polonius*.]
I do repent: but heaven hath pleas'd it so,
To punish me with this and this with me,
That I must be their scourge and minister.
I will bestow him, and will answer well
The death I gave him. So, again, good night.
I must be cruel, only to be kind:
Thus bad begins and worse remains behind.
One word more, good lady.
Queen. What shall I do?
Ham. Not this, by no means, that I bid you do:
Let the bloat king tempt you again to bed;
Pinch wanton on your cheek; call you his mouse;
And let him, for a pair of reechy kisses,
Or paddling in your neck with his damn'd fingers,
Make you to ravel all this matter out,
That I essentially am not in madness,
But mad in craft. 'Twere good you let him know;
For who, that 's but a queen, fair, sober, wise,
Would from a paddock, from a bat, a gib,
Such dear concernings hide? who would do so?
No, in despite of sense and secrecy,
Unpeg the basket on the house's top,
Let the birds fly, and, like the famous ape,
To try conclusions, in the basket creep,
And break your own neck down.
Queen. Be thou assur'd, if words be made of breath,
And breath of life, I have no life to breathe
What thou hast said to me.
Ham. I must to England; you know that?
Queen. Alack,
I had forgot: 'tis so concluded on.
Ham. There 's letters seal'd: and my two
schoolfellows,
Whom I will trust as I will adders fang'd,

107. **laps'd . . . passion,** having suffered time to slip and passion to cool (Johnson); also explained as "engrossed in casual events and lapsed into mere fruitless passion, so that he no longer entertains a rational purpose." 108. **important,** urgent. 112. **amazement,** frenzy, distraction. 118. **incorporal,** immaterial. 121. **bedded,** laid in smooth layers. **excrements.** The hair was considered an excrement or voided part of the body. 122. **an,** on. 126. **conjoin'd,** united. 128-129. **convert . . . effects,** divert me from my stern duty. For *effects* Singer conjectures *affects* (affections of the mind). 130. **want true colour,** lack good reason so that (with a play on the normal sense of *colour*) I shall shed tears instead of blood. 143. **re-word,** repeat in words. 144. **gambol,** skip away. 145. **unction,** ointment used medicinally or as a rite; suggestion that forgiveness for sin may not be so easily achieved. 148. **mining,** working under the surface. 150. **what is to come,** i.e., the sins of the future. 151. **compost,** manure. 152. **this my virtue,** my virtuous talk in reproving you. 153. **fatness,** grossness. **pursy,** short-winded, corpulent. 155. **curb,** bow, bend the knee. 169. Defective line usually emended by inserting *master* after *either*, following Q_4 and early editors. 171. **be bless'd,** become blessed, i.e., repentant. 182. **bloat,** bloated. 184. **reechy,** dirty, filthy. 187. **essentially,** in my essential nature. 190. **paddock,** toad. **gib,** tomcat. 191. **dear concernings,** important affairs. 194. **the famous ape.** A letter from Sir John Suckling seems to supply other details of the story, otherwise not identified: "It is the story of the jackanapes and the partridges; thou starest after a beauty till it be lost to thee, then let'st out another, and starest after that till it is gone too." 195. **con-**

They bear the mandate; they must sweep my way,
And marshal me to knavery. Let it work;
For 'tis the sport to have the enginer
Hoist with his own petar: and 't shall go hard
But I will delve one yard below their mines,
And blow them at the moon: O, 'tis most sweet,
When in one line two crafts directly meet.
This man shall set me packing:
I'll lug the guts into the neighbour room.
Mother, good night. Indeed this counsellor
Is now most still, most secret and most grave,
Who was in life a foolish prating knave.
Come, sir, to draw toward an end with you.
Good night, mother.

Exeunt [severally; Hamlet dragging in Polonius].

[ACT IV.

SCENE I. *A room in the castle.*]

Enter KING *and* QUEEN, *with* ROSENCRANTZ *and* GUILDENSTERN.

King. There 's matter in these sighs, these profound heaves:
You must translate: 'tis fit we understand them.
Where is your son?

Queen. Bestow this place on us a little while.

[*Exeunt Rosencrantz and Guildenstern.*]

Ah, mine own lord, what have I seen to-night!

King. What, Gertrude? How does Hamlet?

Queen. Mad as the sea and wind, when both contend
Which is the mightier: in his lawless fit,
Behind the arras hearing something stir,
Whips out his rapier, cries, 'A rat, a rat!'
And, in this brainish apprehension, kills
The unseen good old man.

King. O heavy deed!
It had been so with us, had we been there:
His liberty is full of threats to all;
To you yourself, to us, to every one.
Alas, how shall this bloody deed be answer'd?
It will be laid to us, whose providence
Should have kept short, restrain'd and out of haunt,
This mad young man: but so much was our love,
We would not understand what was most fit;
But, like the owner of a foul disease,
To keep it from divulging, let it feed
Even on the pith of life. Where is he gone?

Queen. To draw apart the body he hath kill'd:
O'er whom his very madness, like some ore
Among a mineral of metals base,
Shows itself pure; 'a weeps for what is done.

King. O Gertrude, come away!
The sun no sooner shall the mountains touch,
But we will ship him hence: and this vile deed
We must, with all our majesty and skill,
Both countenance and excuse. Ho, Guildenstern!

Enter ROSENCRANTZ *and* GUILDENSTERN.

Friends both, go join you with some further aid:
Hamlet in madness hath Polonius slain,
And from his mother's closet hath he dragg'd him:
Go seek him out; speak fair, and bring the body
Into the chapel. I pray you, haste in this.

[*Exeunt Rosencrantz and Guildenstern.*]

Come, Gertrude, we'll call up our wisest friends;
And let them know, both what we mean to do,
†And what 's untimely done . . . .
Whose whisper o'er the world's diameter,
As level as the cannon to his blank,
Transports his pois'ned shot, may miss our name,
And hit the woundless air. O, come away!
My soul is full of discord and dismay. *Exeunt.*

[SCENE II. *Another room in the castle.*]

Enter HAMLET.

Ham. Safely stowed.

Ros.
Guil. } (*Within*) Hamlet! Lord Hamlet!

Ham. But soft, what noise? who calls on Hamlet? O, here they come.

Enter ROSENCRANTZ *and* GUILDENSTERN.

Ros. What have you done, my lord, with the dead body?

Ham. Compounded it with dust, whereto 'tis kin.

Ros. Tell us where 'tis, that we may take it thence
And bear it to the chapel.

Ham. Do not believe it.

Ros. Believe what?

Ham. That I can keep your counsel and not mine own. Besides, to be demanded of a sponge! what replication should be made by the son of a king?

Ros. Take you me for a sponge, my lord?

Ham. Ay, sir, that soaks up the king's countenance, his rewards, his authorities. But such officers do the king best service in the end: he keeps them, like an ape an apple, in the corner of his jaw; first mouthed, to be last swallowed: when he needs what you have gleaned, it is but squeezing you, and, sponge, you shall be dry again.

Ros. I understand you not, my lord.

Ham. I am glad of it: a knavish speech sleeps in a foolish ear.

Ros. My lord, you must tell us where the body is, and go with us to the king.

Ham. The body is with the king, but the king is not with the body. The king is a thing—

Guil. A thing, my lord!

clusions, experiments. 204. **sweep my way,** clear my path. 206. **enginer,** constructor of military works, or possibly, artilleryman. 207. **Hoist,** blown up. **petar,** defined as a small engine of war used to blow in a door or make a breach, and as a case filled with explosive materials. 210. **two crafts,** two acts of guile, with quibble on the sense of "two ships." 211. **set me packing,** set me to making schemes, and set me to lugging (him), and, also, send me off in a hurry. 216. **draw,** come, with quibble on literal sense.

ACT IV. SCENE I. 11. **brainish,** headstrong, passionate. **apprehension,** conception, imagination. 17. **providence,** foresight. 18. **short,** i.e., on a short tether. **out of haunt,** secluded. 22. **divulging,** becoming evident. 26. **mineral,** mine. 40. Defective line; Capell and others: *so, haply, slander;* Theobald and others: *for, haply, slander;* other conjectures. 41. **diameter,** extent from side to side. 42. **level,** straight. **blank,** white spot in the center of a target. 44. **woundless,** invulnerable.

SCENE II. 11. **keep your counsel.** Hamlet is aware of their treachery but says nothing about it. 13. **replication,** reply. 17. **authorities,** authoritative backing. 19. **like . . . apple,** so Farmer; F: *like an ape* (Globe); Q_2: *like an apple.* 29-30. **The body . . . body.** There are many interpretations; possibly, "The body lies in death with the king, my father; but my father walks disembodied" (Dowden); or "Claudius has the bodily possession of kingship, but kingliness, or justice of inheritance, is not with him." Yale editor explains, "The King is still alive (i.e., with *his* body), but he is not with the dead body (i.e., Polonius)."

Ham. Of nothing: bring me to him. Hide fox, and all after. *Exeunt.*

[SCENE III. *Another room in the castle.*]

Enter KING, *and two or three.*

King. I have sent to seek him, and to find the body.
How dangerous is it that this man goes loose!
Yet must not we put the strong law on him:
He 's lov'd of the distracted multitude,
Who like not in their judgement, but their eyes;
And where 'tis so, th' offender's scourge is weigh'd,
But never the offence. To bear all smooth and even,
This sudden sending him away must seem
Deliberate pause: diseases desperate grown
By desperate appliance are reliev'd,
Or not at all.

Enter ROSENCRANTZ, [GUILDENSTERN,] *and all the rest.*

How now! what hath befall'n?
Ros. Where the dead body is bestow'd, my lord,
We cannot get from him.
King. But where is he?
Ros. Without, my lord; guarded, to know your pleasure.
King. Bring him before us.
Ros. Ho! bring in the lord.

They enter [*with* HAMLET].

King. Now, Hamlet, where 's Polonius?
Ham. At supper.
King. At supper! where?
Ham. Not where he eats, but where 'a is eaten: a certain convocation of politic worms are e'en at him. Your worm is your only emperor for diet: we fat all creatures else to fat us, and we fat ourselves for maggots: your fat king and your lean beggar is but variable service, two dishes, but to one table: that 's the end.
King. Alas, alas!
Ham. A man may fish with the worm that hath eat of a king, and eat of the fish that hath fed of that worm.
King. What dost thou mean by this?
Ham. Nothing but to show you how a king may go a progress through the guts of a beggar.
King. Where is Polonius?
Ham. In heaven; send thither to see: if your messenger find him not there, seek him i' the other place yourself. But if indeed you find him not within this month, you shall nose him as you go up the stairs into the lobby.
King. Go seek him there, [*To some Attendants.*]
Ham. 'A will stay till you come. [*Exeunt Attendants.*]
King. Hamlet, this deed, for thine especial safety,—
Which we do tender, as we dearly grieve
For that which thou hast done,—must send thee hence
With fiery quickness: therefore prepare thyself;
The bark is ready, and the wind at help,
Th' associates tend, and everything is bent
For England.
Ham. For England!
King. Ay, Hamlet.
Ham. Good.
King. So is it, if thou knew'st our purposes.
Ham. I see a cherub that sees them. But, come; for England! Farewell, dear mother.
King. Thy loving father, Hamlet.
Ham. My mother: father and mother is man and wife; man and wife is one flesh; and so, my mother. Come, for England! *Exit.*
King. Follow him at foot; tempt him with speed aboard;
Delay it not; I'll have him hence to-night:
Away! for every thing is seal'd and done
That else leans on th' affair: pray you, make haste.
[*Exeunt all but the King.*]
And, England, if my love thou hold'st at aught—
As my great power thereof may give thee sense,
Since yet thy cicatrice looks raw and red
After the Danish sword, and thy free awe
Pays homage to us— thou mayst not coldly set
Our sovereign process; which imports at full,
By letters congruing to that effect,
The present death of Hamlet. Do it, England;
For like the hectic in my blood he rages,
And thou must cure me: till I know 'tis done,
Howe'er my haps, my joys were ne'er begun. *Exit.*

[SCENE IV. *A plain in Denmark.*]

Enter FORTINBRAS *with his Army over the stage.*

For. Go, captain, from me greet the Danish king;
Tell him that, by his license, Fortinbras
Craves the conveyance of a promis'd march
Over his kingdom. You know the rendezvous.
If that his majesty would aught with us,
We shall express our duty in his eye;
And let him know so.
Cap. I will do 't, my lord.
For. Go softly on. [*Exeunt all but Captain.*]

Enter HAMLET, ROSENCRANTZ, [GUILDENSTERN,] *&c.*

Ham. Good sir, whose powers are these?
Cap. They are of Norway, sir.
Ham. How purpos'd, sir, I pray you?
Cap. Against some part of Poland.
Ham. Who commands them, sir?
Cap. The nephew to old Norway, Fortinbras.
Ham. Goes it against the main of Poland, sir,
Or for some frontier?
Cap. Truly to speak, and with no addition,
We go to gain a little patch of ground
That hath in it no profit but the name.

32-33. **Hide . . . after,** an old signal cry in the game of hide-and-seek. SCENE III. 4. **distracted,** i.e., without power of forming logical judgments. 6. **scourge,** punishment. **weigh'd,** taken into consideration. 9. **Deliberate pause,** considered action. 21. **convocation . . . worms,** allusion to the Diet of Worms (1521). **politic,** crafty. 25. **variable service,** a variety of dishes. 33. **progress,** royal journey of state. 43. **tender,** regard, hold dear. 50. **cherub.** Cherubim are angels of knowledge (Dowden). 56. **at foot,** close behind, at heel. 62. **cicatrice,** scar. 63. **free awe,** voluntary show of respect. 68. **hectic,** fever. 70. **haps,** fortunes.

SCENE IV. 2. **license,** leave. 3. **conveyance,** escort, convoy. 6. **in his eye,** in his presence. 8. **softly,** slowly. 15. **main,** country itself. 20. **farm it,** take a lease of it. 22. **fee,** fee simple. 26. **debate . . . straw,** settle this trifling matter. 27. **imposthume,** purulent abscess or swelling. 32. **occasions,** incidents, events. **inform against,** generally defined as "show," "betray" (i.e., his tardiness); more probably *inform* means "take shape," as in *Macbeth*, II, i, 48. 34. **market of his time,** the best use he makes of his time, or, that for which he sells his time (Johnson). 39. **fust,** grow moldy. 58. **Excitements of,** incentives to. 61. **trick,** toy, trifle. 62. **plot,** i.e., of ground.

To pay five ducats, five, I would not farm it;
Nor will it yield to Norway or the Pole
A ranker rate, should it be sold in fee.
Ham. Why, then the Polack never will defend it.
Cap. Yes, it is already garrison'd.
Ham. Two thousand souls and twenty thousand ducats
Will not debate the question of this straw:
This is th' imposthume of much wealth and peace,
That inward breaks, and shows no cause without
Why the man dies. I humbly thank you, sir.
Cap. God be wi' you, sir. [*Exit.*]
Ros. Will 't please you go, my lord?
Ham. I'll be with you straight. Go a little before.
[*Exeunt all except Hamlet.*]
How all occasions do inform against me,
And spur my dull revenge! What is a man,
If his chief good and market of his time
Be but to sleep and feed? a beast, no more.
Sure, he that made us with such large discourse,
Looking before and after, gave us not
That capability and god-like reason
To fust in us unus'd. Now, whether it be
Bestial oblivion, or some craven scruple
Of thinking too precisely on th' event,
A thought which, quarter'd, hath but one part wisdom
And ever three parts coward, I do not know
Why yet I live to say 'This thing 's to do;'
Sith I have cause and will and strength and means
To do 't. Examples gross as earth exhort me:
Witness this army of such mass and charge
Led by a delicate and tender prince,
Whose spirit with divine ambition puff'd
Makes mouths at the invisible event,
Exposing what is mortal and unsure
To all that fortune, death and danger dare,
Even for an egg-shell. Rightly to be great
Is not to stir without great argument,
But greatly to find quarrel in a straw
When honour 's at the stake. How stand I then,
That have a father kill'd, a mother stain'd,
Excitements of my reason and my blood,
And let all sleep? while, to my shame, I see
The imminent death of twenty thousand men,
That, for a fantasy and trick of fame,
Go to their graves like beds, fight for a plot
Whereon the numbers cannot try the cause,
Which is not tomb enough and continent
To hide the slain? O, from this time forth,
My thoughts be bloody, or be nothing worth! *Exit.*

[SCENE V. *Elsinore. A room in the castle.*]

Enter HORATIO, [QUEEN] GERTRUDE, *and a* Gentleman.

Queen. I will not speak with her.
Gent. She is importunate, indeed distract:
Her mood will needs be pitied.
Queen. What would she have?
Gent. She speaks much of her father; says she hears
There 's tricks i' th' world; and hems, and beats her heart;
Spurns enviously at straws; speaks things in doubt,
That carry but half sense: her speech is nothing,
Yet the unshaped use of it doth move
The hearers to collection; they yawn at it,
And botch the words up fit to their own thoughts;
Which, as her winks, and nods, and gestures yield them,
Indeed would make one think there might be thought,
Though nothing sure, yet much unhappily.
Hor. 'Twere good she were spoken with: for she may strew
Dangerous conjectures in ill-breeding minds.
Queen. Let her come in. [*Exit Gentleman.*]
[*Aside*] To my sick soul, as sin's true nature is,
Each toy seems prologue to some great amiss:
So full of artless jealousy is guilt,
It spills itself in fearing to be spilt.

Enter OPHELIA [*distracted*].

Oph. Where is the beauteous majesty of Denmark?
Queen. How now, Ophelia!
Oph. (*She sings*) How should I your true love know
From another one?
By his cockle hat and staff,
And his sandal shoon.
Queen. Alas, sweet lady, what imports this song?
Oph. Say you? nay, pray you, mark.
He is dead and gone, lady, (*Song*)
He is dead and gone;
At his head a grass-green turf,
At his heels a stone.
O, ho!
Queen. Nay, but, Ophelia,—
Oph. Pray you, mark
[*Sings*] White his shroud as the mountain snow,—

Enter KING.

Queen. Alas, look here, my lord.
Oph. Larded all with flowers; (*Song*)
Which bewept to the grave did not go
With true-love showers.
King. How do you, pretty lady?
Oph. Well, God 'ild you! They say the owl was a baker's daughter. Lord, we know what we are, but know not what we may be. God be at your table!
King. Conceit upon her father.
Oph. Pray let 's have no words of this; but when they ask you what it means, say you this:
To-morrow is Saint Valentine's day, (*Song*)
All in the morning betime,
And I a maid at your window,
To be your Valentine.
Then up he rose, and donn'd his clothes,

SCENE V. 5. **tricks,** deceptions. **heart,** i.e., breast. 6. **Spurns . . . straws,** kicks spitefully at small objects in her path. 8. **unshaped,** unformed, artless. 9. **collection,** inference, a guess at some sort of meaning. **yawn,** wonder; so Q_2; Globe, following F: *aim*. 10. **botch,** patch. 11. **yield,** deliver, bring forth (her words). 13. **much unhappily,** expressive of much unhappiness. 15. **ill-breeding minds,** minds bent on mischief. 18. **great amiss,** calamity, disaster. 19-20. **So . . . spilt,** guilt is so full of suspicion that it unskillfully betrays itself in fearing to be betrayed (Onions). 25. **cockle hat,** hat with cockleshell stuck in it as a sign that the wearer had been a pilgrim to the shrine of St. James of Compostella. The pilgrim's garb was a conventional disguise for lovers. 26. **shoon,** shoes. 37. **Larded . . . flowers,** so Q_2; Globe, following F: *Larded with sweet flowers*. **Larded,** decorated. 38. **not,** so Q_2F; Globe, following Pope, omits. 41. **God 'ild,** God yield or reward. 42. **owl,** reference to a monkish legend that a baker's daughter was turned into an owl for refusing bread to the Saviour; quoted by Douce. 51. **Valentine.** This song alludes to the belief that the first girl seen by a man on the morning of this day was his valentine or truelove (Halliwell).

And dupp'd the chamber-door;
Let in the maid, that out a maid
Never departed more.

King. Pretty Ophelia!

Oph. Indeed, la, without an oath, I'll make an end on 't:

[*Sings*] By Gis and by Saint Charity,
Alack, and fie for shame!
Young men will do 't, if they come to 't;
By cock, they are to blame.
Quoth she, before you tumbled me,
You promis'd me to wed.
So would I ha' done, by yonder sun,
An thou hadst not come to my bed.

King. How long hath she been thus?

Oph. I hope all will be well. We must be patient: but I cannot choose but weep, to think they would lay him i' the cold ground. My brother shall know of it: and so I thank you for your good counsel. Come, my coach! Good night, ladies; good night, sweet ladies; good night, good night. [*Exit.*]

King. Follow her close; give her good watch, I pray you. [*Exit Horatio.*]
O, this is the poison of deep grief; it springs
All from her father's death. O Gertrude, Gertrude,
When sorrows come, they come not single spies,
But in battalions. First, her father slain:
Next, your son gone; and he most violent author
Of his own just remove: the people muddied,
Thick and unwholesome in their thoughts and whispers,
For good Polonius' death; and we have done but greenly,
In hugger-mugger to inter him: poor Ophelia
Divided from herself and her fair judgement,
Without the which we are pictures, or mere beasts:
Last, and as much containing as all these,
Her brother is in secret come from France;
Feeds on his wonder, keeps himself in clouds,
And wants not buzzers to infect his ear
With pestilent speeches of his father's death;
Wherein necessity, of matter beggar'd,
Will nothing stick our person to arraign
In ear and ear. O my dear Gertrude, this,
Like to a murd'ring-piece, in many places
Gives me superfluous death. *A noise within.*

Queen. Alack, what noise is this?

King. Where are my Switzers? Let them guard the door.

Enter a Messenger.

What is the matter?

Mess. Save yourself, my lord:
The ocean, overpeering of his list,
Eats not the flats with more impiteous haste
Than young Laertes, in a riotous head,
O'erbears your officers. The rabble call him lord;
And, as the world were now but to begin,
Antiquity forgot, custom not known,
The ratifiers and props of every word,
They cry 'Choose we: Laertes shall be king:'
Caps, hands, and tongues, applaud it to the clouds:
'Laertes shall be king, Laertes king!' *A noise within.*

Queen. How cheerfully on the false trail they cry!
O, this is counter, you false Danish dogs!

King. The doors are broke.

Enter LAERTES *with others.*

Laer. Where is this king? Sirs, stand you all without.

Danes. No, let 's come in.

Laer. I pray you, give me leave.

Danes. We will, we will. [*They retire without the door.*]

Laer. I thank you: keep the door. O thou vile king,
Give me my father!

Queen. Calmly, good Laertes.

Laer. That drop of blood that 's calm proclaims me bastard,
Cries cuckold to my father, brands the harlot
Even here, between the chaste unsmirched brow
Of my true mother.

King. What is the cause, Laertes,
That thy rebellion looks so giant-like?
Let him go, Gertrude; do not fear our person:
There 's such divinity doth hedge a king,
That treason can but peep to what it would,
Acts little of his will. Tell me, Laertes,
Why thou art thus incens'd. Let him go, Gertrude.
Speak, man.

Laer. Where is my father?

King. Dead.

Queen. But not by him.

King. Let him demand his fill.

Laer. How came he dead? I'll not be juggled with:
To hell, allegiance! vows, to the blackest devil!
Conscience and grace, to the profoundest pit!
I dare damnation. To this point I stand,
That both the worlds I give to negligence,
Let come what comes; only I'll be reveng'd
Most throughly for my father.

King. Who shall stay you?

Laer. My will, not all the world's:
And for my means, I'll husband them so well,
They shall go far with little.

King. Good Laertes,
If you desire to know the certainty
Of your dear father, is 't writ in your revenge,
That, swoopstake, you will draw both friend and foe,
Winner and loser?

Laer. None but his enemies.

King. Will you know them then?

Laer. To his good friends thus wide I'll ope my arms;
And like the kind life-rend'ring pelican,
Repast them with my blood.

King. Why, now you speak
Like a good child and a true gentleman.
That I am guiltless of your father's death,
And am most sensibly in grief for it,

53. **dupp'd,** opened. 59. **Gis,** Jesus. 62. **cock,** perversion of "God" in oaths. 83. **greenly,** foolishly. 84. **hugger-mugger,** secret haste. 89. **in clouds,** invisible. 90. **buzzers,** gossipers. 92. **of matter beggar'd,** unprovided with facts. 93. **nothing stick,** not hesitate. 94. **In ear and ear,** in everybody's ears. 95. **murd'ring-piece,** small cannon or mortar; suggestion of numerous missiles fired. 97. **Switzers,** Swiss guards, mercenaries. 99. **overpeering,** overflowing. **list,** shore. 105. **word,** promise. 110. **counter,** a hunting term meaning to follow the trail in a direction opposite to that which the game has taken. 124. **peep to,** i.e., look at from afar off. **would,** wishes to do. 134. **give to negligence.** He despises both the here and the hereafter. 137. **My will.** He will not be stopped except by his own will. 142. **swoopstake,** literally, drawing the whole stake at once, i.e., indiscriminately. 146. **pelican,** reference to the belief that the pelican feeds its young with its own blood. 147. **Repast,** feed. 151. **'pear,** so Q_2; Globe, following F: *pierce.* 154. **heat,** probably the heat generated by the passion of grief. 172. **wheel,** spinning wheel as accompaniment to the song (Onions); refrain (Steevens). **false steward.** The story is unknown. 175. **rosemary,**

It shall as level to your judgement 'pear
As day does to your eye.
A noise within: 'Let her come in.'
Laer. How now! what noise is that?

Enter Ophelia.

O heat, dry up my brains! tears seven times salt,
Burn out the sense and virtue of mine eye!
By heaven, thy madness shall be paid with weight,
Till our scale turn the beam. O rose of May!
Dear maid, kind sister, sweet Ophelia!
O heavens! is 't possible, a young maid's wits
Should be as mortal as an old man's life?
Nature is fine in love, and where 'tis fine,
It sends some precious instance of itself
After the thing it loves.
Oph. *(Song)*
They bore him barefac'd on the bier;
Hey non nonny, nonny, hey nonny;
And in his grave rain'd many a tear:—
Fare you well, my dove!
Laer. Hadst thou thy wits, and didst persuade revenge,
It could not move thus.
Oph. [*Sings*] You must sing a-down a-down,
An you call him a-down-a.
O, how the wheel becomes it! It is the false steward, that stole his master's daughter.
Laer. This nothing 's more than matter.
Oph. There 's rosemary, that 's for remembrance; pray you, love, remember: and there is pansies, that 's for thoughts.
Laer. A document in madness, thoughts and remembrance fitted.
Oph. There 's fennel for you, and columbines: there 's rue for you; and here 's some for me: we may call it herb of grace o' Sundays: O, you must wear your rue with a difference. There 's a daisy: I would give you some violets, but they withered all when my father died: they say 'a made a good end,—
[*Sings*] For bonny sweet Robin is all my joy.
Laer. Thought and affliction, passion, hell itself,
She turns to favour and to prettiness.
Oph. And will 'a not come again? *(Song)*
And will 'a not come again?
No, no, he is dead:
Go to thy death-bed:
He never will come again.

His beard was as white as snow,
All flaxen was his poll:
He is gone, he is gone,
And we cast away moan:
God ha' mercy on his soul!
And of all Christian souls, I pray God. God be wi' you.
[*Exit.*]
Laer. Do you see this, O God?
King. Laertes, I must commune with your grief,
Or you deny me right. Go but apart,
Make choice of whom your wisest friends you will,
And they shall hear and judge 'twixt you and me:
If by direct or by collateral hand
They find us touch'd, we will our kingdom give,
Our crown, our life, and all that we call ours,
To you in satisfaction; but if not,
Be you content to lend your patience to us,
And we shall jointly labour with your soul
To give it due content.
Laer. Let this be so;
His means of death, his obscure funeral—
No trophy, sword, nor hatchment o'er his bones,
No noble rite nor formal ostentation—
Cry to be heard, as 'twere from heaven to earth,
That I must call 't in question.
King. So you shall;
And where th' offence is let the great axe fall.
I pray you, go with me. *Exeunt.*

[Scene vi. *Another room in the castle.*]

Enter Horatio *and others.*

Hor. What are they that would speak with me?
Gent. Sea-faring men, sir: they say they have letters for you.
Hor. Let them come in. [*Exit Gent.*]
I do not know from what part of the world
I should be greeted, if not from lord Hamlet.

Enter Sailors.

First Sail. God bless you, sir.
Hor. Let him bless thee too.
First Sail. 'A shall, sir, an 't please him. There 's a letter for you, sir; it comes from the ambassador that was bound for England; if your name be Horatio, as I am let to know it is.
Hor. [*Reads*] 'Horatio, when thou shalt have overlooked this, give these fellows some means to the king: they have letters for him. Ere we were two days old at sea, a pirate of very warlike appointment gave us chase. Finding ourselves too slow of sail, we put on a compelled valour, and in the grapple I boarded them: on the instant they got clear of our ship; so I alone became their prisoner. They have dealt with me like thieves of mercy: but they knew what they did; I am to do a good turn for them. Let the king have the letters I have sent; and repair thou to me with as much speed as thou wouldest fly death. I have words to speak in thine ear will make thee dumb; yet are they much too light for the bore of the matter. These good fellows will bring thee where I am. Rosencrantz and Guildenstern hold their course for England: of them I have much to tell thee. Farewell.
'He that thou knowest thine, Hamlet.'
Come, I will give you way for these your letters;
And do 't the speedier, that you may direct me
To him from whom you brought them. *Exeunt.*

---

used as a symbol of remembrance both at weddings and at funerals. 177. **pansies,** emblems of love and courtship. Cf. French *pensées*. 178. **document,** piece of instruction or lesson. 180. **fennel,** emblem of flattery. **columbines,** emblem of unchastity (?) or ingratitude (?) 181. **rue,** emblem of repentance. It was usually mingled with holy water and then known as *herb of grace*. F and Globe: *herb-grace*. Ophelia is probably playing on the two meanings of *rue*, "repentant" and "even for ruth (pity)"; the former signification is for the queen, the latter for herself. 184. **daisy,** emblem of dissembling, faithlessness. **violets,** emblems of faithfulness. 187. **For . . . joy,** probably a line from a Robin Hood ballad. 188. **Thought,** melancholy thought. 190. **And . . . again.** This song appeared in the songbooks as "The Merry Milkmaids' Dumps." 196. **poll,** head. 198. **cast away,** shipwrecked. 203. **right,** my rights. 206. **collateral,** indirect. 207. **touch'd,** implicated. 214. **hatchment,** tablet displaying the armorial bearings of a deceased person.

Scene vi. 14. **means,** means of access. 21. **thieves of mercy,** merciful thieves. 27. **bore,** caliber, importance.

[SCENE VII. *Another room in the castle.*]

Enter KING *and* LAERTES.

King. Now must your conscience my acquittance seal,
And you must put me in your heart for friend,
Sith you have heard, and with a knowing ear,
That he which hath your noble father slain
Pursued my life.
Laer. It well appears: but tell me
Why you proceeded not against these feats,
So criminal and so capital in nature,
As by your safety, wisdom, all things else,
You mainly were stirr'd up.
King. O, for two special reasons;
Which may to you, perhaps, seem much unsinew'd,
But yet to me th' are strong. The queen his mother
Lives almost by his looks; and for myself—
My virtue or my plague, be it either which—
She 's so conjunctive to my life and soul,
That, as the star moves not but in his sphere,
I could not but by her. The other motive,
Why to a public count I might not go,
Is the great love the general gender bear him;
Who, dipping all his faults in their affection,
Would, like the spring that turneth wood to stone,
Convert his gyves to graces; so that my arrows,
Too slightly timber'd for so loud a wind,
Would have reverted to my bow again,
And not where I had aim'd them.
Laer. And so have I a noble father lost;
A sister driven into desp'rate terms,
Whose worth, if praises may go back again,
Stood challenger on mount of all the age
For her perfections: but my revenge will come.
King. Break not your sleeps for that: you must not think
That we are made of stuff so flat and dull
That we can let our beard be shook with danger
And think it pastime. You shortly shall hear more:
I lov'd your father, and we love ourself;
And that, I hope, will teach you to imagine—

Enter a Messenger *with letters.*

How now! what news?
Mess. Letters, my lord, from Hamlet:
These to your majesty; this to the queen.
King. From Hamlet! who brought them?
Mess. Sailors, my lord, they say; I saw them not:
They were given me by Claudio; he receiv'd them
Of him that brought them.
King. Laertes, you shall hear them.
Leave us. [*Exit Messenger.*]

[*Reads*] 'High and mighty, You shall know I am set naked on your kingdom. To-morrow shall I beg leave to see your kingly eyes: when I shall, first asking your pardon thereunto, recount the occasion of my sudden and more strange return. 'HAMLET.'

What should this mean? Are all the rest come back?
Or is it some abuse, and no such thing?
Laer. Know you the hand?
King. 'Tis Hamlet's character. 'Naked!'
And in a postscript here, he says 'alone.'
Can you devise me?
Laer. I 'm lost in it, my lord. But let him come;
It warms the very sickness in my heart,
That I shall live and tell him to his teeth,
'Thus didst thou.'
King. If it be so, Laertes—
As how should it be so? how otherwise?—
Will you be rul'd by me?
Laer. Ay, my lord;
So you will not o'errule me to a peace.
King. To thine own peace. If he be now return'd,
As checking at his voyage, and that he means
No more to undertake it, I will work him
To an exploit, now ripe in my device,
Under the which he shall not choose but fall:
And for his death no wind of blame shall breathe,
But even his mother shall uncharge the practice
And call it accident.
Laer. My lord, I will be rul'd;
The rather, if you could devise it so
That I might be the organ.
King. It falls right.
You have been talk'd of since your travel much,
And that in Hamlet's hearing, for a quality
Wherein, they say, you shine: your sum of parts
Did not together pluck such envy from him
As did that one, and that, in my regard,
Of the unworthiest siege.
Laer. What part is that, my lord?
King. A very riband in the cap of youth,
Yet needful too; for youth no less becomes
The light and careless livery that it wears
Than settled age his sables and his weeds,
Importing health and graveness. Two months since,
Here was a gentleman of Normandy:—
I have seen myself, and serv'd against, the French,
And they can well on horseback: but this gallant
Had witchcraft in 't; he grew unto his seat;
And to such wondrous doing brought his horse,
As had he been incorps'd and demi-natur'd
With the brave beast: so far he topp'd my thought,
That I, in forgery of shapes and tricks,
Come short of what he did.
Laer. A Norman was 't?
King. A Norman.
Laer. Upon my life, Lamord.
King. The very same.

SCENE VII. 1. **conscience,** knowledge that this is true. 7. **criminal,** so Q_2; Globe, following F: *crimeful.* **capital,** punishable by death. 9. **mainly,** greatly. 10. **unsinew'd,** weak. 14. **conjunctive,** comformable (the next line suggesting planetary conjunction). 15. **sphere,** the hollow sphere in which, according to Ptolemaic astronomy, the planets were supposed to move. 17. **count,** account, reckoning. 18. **general gender,** common people. 20. **spring,** i.e., one heavily charged with lime. 21. **gyves,** fetters; here, faults, or possibly, punishments inflicted (on him). 22. **slightly timber'd,** light. **loud,** strong. For *loud a wind* Jennens would retain the Q_2 reading *loved Arm'd*, explaining, "one so loved and armed with the affections of the people"; for *so loud a wind* Elze suggests *solid arms* to agree with his reading *grieves* (for *gyves*) in line 21. 26. **terms,** state, condition. 27. **go back,** i.e., to Ophelia's former virtues. 28. **on mount,** set up on high (Onions), mounted (on horseback). **of all the age,** qualifies *challenger* and not *mount.* 37. **to the queen.** One hears no more of the letter to the queen. 40. **Claudio.** This character does not appear in the play. 44. **naked,** unprovided (with retinue). 54. **devise,** explain to. 59. **As . . . otherwise?** How can this (Hamlet's return) be true? (yet) how otherwise than true (since we have the evidence of his letter)? Some editors read *How should it not be so*, etc., making the words refer to Laertes' desire to meet with Hamlet. 63. **checking at,** used in falconry of a hawk's leaving the quarry to fly at a chance bird, turn aside. 68. **uncharge the practice,** acquit the stratagem of being a plot. 71. **organ,** agent, instrument. 77. **siege,** rank. 81. **sables,** rich garments. 85. **can well,** are skilled. 88. **incorps'd and demi-natur'd,** of one body and nearly of one nature (like the centaur). 89. **topp'd,** surpassed. 90. **forgery,** invention. 93. **Lamord.** This refers possibly to Pietro Monte,

Laer. I know him well: he is the brooch indeed
And gem of all the nation.
King. He made confession of you,
And gave you such a masterly report
For art and exercise in your defence
And for your rapier most especial,
That he cried out, 'twould be a sight indeed,
If one could match you: the scrimers of their nation,
He swore, had neither motion, guard, nor eye,
If you oppos'd them. Sir, this report of his
Did Hamlet so envenom with his envy
That he could nothing do but wish and beg
Your sudden coming o'er, to play with you.
Now, out of this,—
Laer. What out of this, my lord?
King. Laertes, was your father dear to you?
Or are you like the painting of a sorrow,
A face without a heart?
Laer. Why ask you this?
King. Not that I think you did not love your father;
But that I know love is begun by time;
And that I see, in passages of proof,
Time qualifies the spark and fire of it.
There lives within the very flame of love
A kind of wick or snuff that will abate it;
And nothing is at a like goodness still;
For goodness, growing to a plurisy,
Dies in his own too much: that we would do,
We should do when we would; for this 'would' changes
And hath abatements and delays as many
As there are tongues, are hands, are accidents;
And then this 'should' is like a spendthrift sigh,
That hurts by easing. But, to the quick o' th' ulcer:—
Hamlet comes back: what would you undertake,
To show yourself your father's son in deed
More than in words?
Laer. To cut his throat i' th' church.
King. No place, indeed, should murder sanctuarize;
Revenge should have no bounds. But, good Laertes,
Will you do this, keep close within your chamber.
Hamlet return'd shall know you are come home:
We'll put on those shall praise your excellence
And set a double varnish on the fame
The Frenchman gave you, bring you in fine together
And wager on your heads: he, being remiss,
Most generous and free from all contriving,
Will not peruse the foils; so that, with ease,
Or with a little shuffling, you may choose
A sword unbated, and in a pass of practice
Requite him for your father.
Laer. I will do 't:
And, for that purpose, I'll anoint my sword.
I bought an unction of a mountebank,
So mortal that, but dip a knife in it,
Where it draws blood no cataplasm so rare,
Collected from all simples that have virtue
Under the moon, can save the thing from death
That is but scratch'd withal: I'll touch my point
With this contagion, that, if I gall him slightly,
It may be death.
King. Let 's further think of this;
Weigh what convenience both of time and means
May fit us to our shape: if this should fail,
And that our drift look through our bad performance,
'Twere better not assay'd: therefore this project
Should have a back or second, that might hold,
If this should blast in proof. Soft! let me see:
We'll make a solemn wager on your cunnings:
I ha 't:
When in your motion you are hot and dry—
As make your bouts more violent to that end—
And that he calls for drink, I'll have prepar'd him
A chalice for the nonce, whereon but sipping,
If he by chance escape your venom'd stuck,
Our purpose may hold there. But stay, what noise?

Enter QUEEN.

Queen. One woe doth tread upon another's heel,
So fast they follow: your sister 's drown'd, Laertes.
Laer. Drown'd! O, where?
Queen. There is a willow grows askant the brook,
That shows his hoar leaves in the glassy stream;
There with fantastic garlands did she make
Of crow-flowers, nettles, daisies, and long purples
That liberal shepherds give a grosser name,
But our cold maids do dead men's fingers call them:
There, on the pendent boughs her crownet weeds
Clamb'ring to hang, an envious sliver broke;
When down her weedy trophies and herself
Fell in the weeping brook. Her clothes spread wide;
And, mermaid-like, awhile they bore her up:
Which time she chanted snatches of old lauds;
As one incapable of her own distress,
Or like a creature native and indued
Unto that element: but long it could not be
Till that her garments, heavy with their drink,
Pull'd the poor wretch from her melodious lay
To muddy death.
Laer. Alas then, she is drown'd?
Queen. Drown'd, drown'd.
Laer. Too much of water hast thou, poor Ophelia,
And therefore I forbid my tears: but yet
It is our trick; nature her custom holds,
Let shame say what it will: when these are gone,
The woman will be out. Adieu, my lord:
I have a speech of fire, that fain would blaze,
But that this folly drowns it. *Exit.*
King. Let 's follow, Gertrude:
How much I had to do to calm his rage!

instructor to Louis XII's master of the horse (Hudson). 96. **confession,** grudging admission of superiority. 98. **art and exercise,** skillful exercise. **defence,** science of defense in sword practice. 101. **scrimers,** fencers. 106. **play,** fence. 113. **passages of proof,** proved instances. 118. **plurisy,** excess, plethora. 119. **in his own too much,** of its own excess. 121. **abatements,** diminutions. 122. **accidents,** occurrences, incidents. 123. **spendthrift,** an allusion to the belief that each sigh cost the heart a drop of blood. 124. **quick o' th' ulcer,** heart of the difficulty. 128. **sanctuarize,** protect from punishment; allusion to the right of sanctuary with which certain religious places were invested. 139. **unbated,** not blunted, having no button. **pass of practice,** treacherous thrust. 142. **mountebank,** quack doctor. 144. **cataplasm,** plaster or poultice. 145. **simples,** herbs. 146. **Under the moon,** i.e., when collected by moonlight to add to their medicinal value. 148. **gall,** graze, wound. 151. **shape,** part we propose to act. 152. **drift . . . performance,** intention be disclosed by our bungling. 155. **blast in proof,** burst in the test (like a cannon). 156. **cunnings,** skills. The F reading, *commings*, is explained by Caldecott and Knight as "bouts at fence." 161. **chalice,** cup. 162. **stuck,** thrust (from *stoccado*). 167. **willow,** for its significance of forsaken love. **askant,** aslant. 168. **hoar,** white (i.e., on the underside). 169. **make,** so Q_2; Globe, following F, *come*. 170. **crow-flowers,** buttercups. **long purples,** early purple orchis. 171. **liberal,** probably, free-spoken. 173. **crownet,** coronet; made into a chaplet. 174. **sliver,** branch. 175. **weedy,** i.e., of plants. 178. **lauds,** hymns. 179. **incapable,** lacking capacity to apprehend. 180. **indued,** endowed with qualities fitting her for living in water. 188. **trick,** way. 189-190. **when . . . out,** when my tears are all shed, the woman in me will be satisfied.

Now fear I this will give it start again;
Therefore let 's follow. *Exeunt.*

[ACT V.

SCENE I. *A churchyard.*]

Enter two Clowns [*with spades, &c.*].

First Clo. Is she to be buried in Christian burial when she wilfully seeks her own salvation?

Sec. Clo. I tell thee she is; therefore make her grave straight: the crowner hath sat on her, and finds it Christian burial.

First Clo. How can that be, unless she drowned herself in her own defence?

Sec. Clo. Why, 'tis found so.

First Clo. It must be 'se offendendo;' it cannot be else. For here lies the point: if I drown myself wittingly, it argues an act: and an act hath three branches; it is, to act, to do, and to perform: argal, she drowned herself wittingly.

Sec. Clo. Nay, but hear you, goodman delver,—

First Clo. Give me leave. Here lies the water; good: here stands the man; good: if the man go to this water, and drown himself, it is, will he, nill he, he goes,—mark you that; but if the water come to him and drown him, he drowns not himself: argal, he that is not guilty of his own death shortens not his own life.

Sec. Clo. But is this law?

First Clo. Ay, marry, is 't; crowner's quest law.

Sec. Clo. Will you ha' the truth on 't? If this had not been a gentlewoman, she should have been buried out o' Christian burial.

First Clo. Why, there thou say'st: and the more pity that great folk should have countenance in this world to drown or hang themselves, more than their even Christian. Come, my spade. There is no ancient gentlemen but gardeners, ditchers, and grave-makers: they hold up Adam's profession.

Sec. Clo. Was he a gentleman?

First Clo. 'A was the first that ever bore arms.

Sec. Clo. Why, he had none.

First Clo. What, art a heathen? How dost thou understand the Scripture? The Scripture says 'Adam digged:' could he dig without arms? I'll put another question to thee: if thou answerest me not to the purpose, confess thyself—

Sec. Clo. Go to.

First Clo. What is he that builds stronger than either the mason, the shipwright, or the carpenter?

Sec. Clo. The gallows-maker; for that frame outlives a thousand tenants.

First Clo. I like thy wit well, in good faith: the gallows does well; but how does it well? it does well to those that do ill: now thou dost ill to say the gallows is built stronger than the church: argal, the gallows may do well to thee. To 't again, come.

Sec. Clo. 'Who builds stronger than a mason, a shipwright, or a carpenter?'

First Clo. Ay, tell me that, and unyoke.

Sec. Clo. Marry, now I can tell.

First Clo. To 't.

Sec. Clo. Mass, I cannot tell.

Enter HAMLET *and* HORATIO [*at a distance.*]

First Clo. Cudgel thy brains no more about it, for your dull ass will not mend his pace with beating; and, when you are asked this question next, say 'a grave-maker:' the houses he makes lasts till doomsday. Go, get thee in, and fetch me a stoup of liquor. [*Exit Sec. Clown.*]

Song. [*He digs.*]

In youth, when I did love, did love,
Methought it was very sweet,
To contract—O—the time, for—a—my behove,
O, methought, there—a—was nothing—a—meet.

Ham. Has this fellow no feeling of his business, that 'a sings at grave-making?

Hor. Custom hath made it in him a property of easiness.

Ham. 'Tis e'en so: the hand of little employment hath the daintier sense.

First Clo. *Song.*

But age, with his stealing steps,
Hath claw'd me in his clutch,
And hath shipped me into the land,
As if I had never been such. [*Throws up a skull.*]

Ham. That skull had a tongue in it, and could sing once: how the knave jowls it to the ground, as if 'twere Cain's jaw-bone, that did the first murder! This might be the pate of a politician, which this ass now o'er-reaches; one that would circumvent God, might it not?

Hor. It might, my lord.

Ham. Or of a courtier; which could say 'Good morrow, sweet lord! How dost thou, sweet lord?' This might be my lord such-a-one, that praised my lord such-a-one's horse, when he meant to beg it; might it not?

Hor. Ay, my lord.

Ham. Why, e'en so: and now my Lady Worm's; chapless, and knocked about the mazzard with a sexton's spade: here 's fine revolution, an we had the trick to see 't. Did these bones cost no more the breeding, but to play at loggats with 'em? mine ache to think on 't.

First Clo. *Song.*

A pick-axe, and a spade, a spade,
For and a shrouding sheet:
O, a pit of clay for to be made
For such a guest is meet. [*Throws up another skull.*]

ACT V. SCENE I. *Stage Direction:* **Clowns.** The word *clown* was used to denote peasants as well as humorous characters; here applied to the rustic type of clown. 4. **straight,** straightway, immediately; Johnson interprets "from east to west in a direct line, parallel with the church." **crowner,** coroner. 9. **'se offendendo,'** for *se defendendo,* term used in verdicts of justifiable homicide. 11. **wittingly,** intentionally. 12. **three branches,** parody of legal phraseology. 13. **argal,** corruption of *ergo,* therefore. 15. **delver,** digger. 24. **quest,** inquest. 29. **there thou say'st,** that's right. 31. **countenance,** privilege. 32. **even,** fellow. 35. **hold up,** maintain, continue. 44. **confess thyself,** "and be hanged" completes the proverb. 45. **Go to,** perhaps, "begin," or some other form of concession. 59. **unyoke,** after this great effort you may unharness the team of your wits (Dowden). 62. **Mass,** by the Mass. 68. **in, and,** so Q_2; F: *to Yaughan,* probably a London tavern keeper. **stoup,** two-quart measure. 69. **In . . . love.** This and the two following stanzas, with nonsensical variations, are from a poem attributed to Lord Vaux and printed in *Tottel's Miscellany* (1557). The *O* and *ah* are possibly grunts of the digger or (Clarendon Press) represent drawling notes. 71. **behove,** benefit. 76. **property of easiness,** a peculiarity that now is easy. 81. **into,** so Q_2; Globe, following F: *intil.* 84. **jowls,** dashes. 85. **Cain's jaw-bone,** allusion to the old tradition that Cain slew Abel with the jawbone of an ass. 87. **politician,** schemer, plotter. **o'er-reaches,** quibble on the literal sense and the sense "circumvent"; the F reading, *o'er Offices,* Onions

Ham. There 's another: why may not that be the skull of a lawyer? Where be his quiddities now, his quillities, his cases, his tenures, and his tricks? why does he suffer this mad knave now to knock him about the sconce with a dirty shovel, and will not tell him of his action of battery? Hum! This fellow might be in 's time a great buyer of land, with his statutes, his recognizances, his fines, his double vouchers, his recoveries: is this the fine of his fines, and the recovery of his recoveries, to have his fine pate full of fine dirt? will his vouchers vouch him no more of his purchases, and double ones too, than the length and breadth of a pair of indentures? The very conveyances of his lands will scarcely lie in this box; and must the inheritor himself have no more, ha?

Hor. Not a jot more, my lord.

Ham. Is not parchment made of sheep-skins?

Hor. Ay, my lord, and of calf-skins too.

Ham. They are sheep and calves which seek out assurance in that. I will speak to this fellow. Whose grave 's this, sirrah?

First Clo. Mine, sir.

[*Sings*] O, a pit of clay for to be made
For such a guest is meet.

Ham. I think it be thine, indeed; for thou liest in 't.

First Clo. You lie out on 't, sir, and therefore 't is not yours: for my part, I do not lie in 't, yet it is mine.

Ham. Thou dost lie in 't, to be in 't and say it is thine: 'tis for the dead, not for the quick; therefore thou liest.

First Clo. 'Tis a quick lie, sir; 'twill away again, from me to you.

Ham. What man dost thou dig it for?

First Clo. For no man, sir.

Ham. What woman, then?

First Clo. For none, neither.

Ham. Who is to be buried in 't?

First Clo. One that was a woman, sir; but, rest her soul, she 's dead.

Ham. How absolute the knave is! we must speak by the card, or equivocation will undo us. By the Lord, Horatio, these three years I have taken note of it; the age is grown so picked that the toe of the peasant comes so near the heel of the courtier, he galls his kibe. How long hast thou been a grave-maker?

First Clo. Of all the days i' the year, I came to 't that day that our last king Hamlet overcame Fortinbras.

Ham. How long is that since?

First Clo. Cannot you tell that? every fool can tell that: it was the very day that young Hamlet was born; he that is mad, and sent into England.

Ham. Ay, marry, why was he sent into England?

First Clo. Why, because 'a was mad: 'a shall recover his wits there; or, if 'a do not, 'tis no great matter there.

Ham. Why?

First Clo. 'Twill not be seen in him there; there the men are as mad as he.

Ham. How came he mad?

First Clo. Very strangely, they say.

Ham. How strangely?

First Clo. Faith, e'en with losing his wits.

Ham. Upon what ground?

First Clo. Why, here in Denmark: I have been sexton here, man and boy, thirty years.

Ham. How long will a man lie i' the earth ere he rot?

First Clo. Faith, if 'a be not rotten before 'a die—as we have many pocky corses now-a-days, that will scarce hold the laying in—'a will last you some eight year or nine year: a tanner will last you nine year.

Ham. Why he more than another?

First Clo. Why, sir, his hide is so tanned with his trade, that 'a will keep out water a great while; and your water is a sore decayer of your whoreson dead body. Here 's a skull now hath lain you i' th' earth three and twenty years.

Ham. Whose was it?

First Clo. A whoreson mad fellow's it was: whose do you think it was?

Ham. Nay, I know not.

First Clo. A pestilence on him for a mad rogue! 'a poured a flagon of Rhenish on my head once. This same skull, sir, was Yorick's skull, the king's jester.

Ham. This?

First Clo. E'en that.

Ham. Let me see. [*Takes the skull.*] Alas, poor Yorick! I knew him, Horatio: a fellow of infinite jest, of most excellent fancy: he hath borne me on his back a thousand times; and now, how abhorred in my imagination it is! my gorge rises at it. Here hung those lips that I have kissed I know not how oft. Where be your gibes now? your gambols? your songs? your flashes of merriment, that were wont to set the table on a roar? Not one now, to mock your own grinning? quite chap-fallen? Now get you to my lady's chamber, and tell her, let her paint an inch thick, to this favour she must come; make her laugh at that. Prithee, Horatio, tell me one thing.

Hor. What 's that, my lord?

Ham. Dost thou think Alexander looked o' this fashion i' the earth?

Hor. E'en so.

Ham. And smelt so? pah! [*Puts down the skull.*]

Hor. E'en so, my lord.

Ham. To what base uses we may return, Horatio! Why may not imagination trace the noble dust of Alexander, till 'a find it stopping a bung-hole?

Hor. 'Twere to consider too curiously, to consider so.

Ham. No, faith, not a jot; but to follow him thither with modesty enough, and likelihood to lead it: as thus: Alexander died, Alexander was buried, Alex-

defines as "lords it over by virtue of his office." 97. **chapless,** having no lower jaw. 98. **mazzard,** head. 100. **loggats,** a game in which six sticks are thrown to lie as near as possible to a stake fixed in the ground, or block of wood on a floor. 103. **For and,** and moreover. 107. **quiddities,** subtleties, quibbles. 108. **quillities,** verbal niceties, subtle distinctions. **tenures,** the holding of a piece of property or office or the conditions or period of such holding. 110. **sconce,** head. 114. **statutes, recognizances,** legal terms connected with the transfer of land. 115. **vouchers,** persons called on to warrant a tenant's title. **recoveries,** process for transfer of entailed estate. 116. **fine.** The four uses of this word are as follows: (1) end, (2) legal process, (3) elegant, (4) small. 119. **indentures,** conveyances or contracts. 121. **inheritor,** possessor, owner. 124. **calf-skins,** parchments. 126. **assurance in that,** safety in legal parchments. 148. **absolute,** positive, decided. 149. **by the card,** with precision, i.e., by the mariner's card on which the points of the compass were marked. **equivocation,** ambiguity in the use of terms. 152. **picked,** refined, fastidious. 153. **galls,** chafes. **kibe,** chilblain. 177. **thirty years.** This statement with that in line 160 shows Hamlet's age to be thirty years. 181. **pocky,** rotten, diseased. 189-190. **hath . . . earth,** so Q_2 (*lien*); F (Globe): *this skull has lain in the earth.* 227. **curiously,** minutely.

ander returneth into dust; the dust is earth; of earth we make loam; and why of that loam, whereto he was converted, might they not stop a beer-barrel?

Imperious Cæsar, dead and turn'd to clay,
Might stop a hole to keep the wind away:
O, that that earth, which kept the world in awe,
Should patch a wall t' expel the winter's flaw!
But soft! but soft awhile! here comes the king,

Enter KING, QUEEN, LAERTES, *and the* Corse [*of* OPHELIA, *in procession, with* Priest, Lords, *etc.*].

The queen, the courtiers: who is this they follow?
And with such maimed rites? This doth betoken
The corse they follow did with desp'rate hand
Fordo it own life: 'twas of some estate.
Couch we awhile, and mark. [*Retiring with Horatio.*]

Laer. What ceremony else?

Ham. That is Laertes,
A very noble youth: mark.

Laer. What ceremony else?

First Priest. Her obsequies have been as far enlarg'd
As we have warranty: her death was doubtful;
And, but that great command o'ersways the order,
She should in ground unsanctified have lodg'd
Till the last trumpet; for charitable prayers,
Shards, flints and pebbles should be thrown on her:
Yet here she is allow'd her virgin crants,
Her maiden strewments and the bringing home
Of bell and burial.

Laer. Must there no more be done?

First Priest. No more be done:
We should profane the service of the dead
To sing a requiem and such rest to her
As to peace-parted souls.

Laer. Lay her i' th' earth:
And from her fair and unpolluted flesh
May violets spring! I tell thee, churlish priest,
A minist'ring angel shall my sister be,
When thou liest howling.

Ham. What, the fair Ophelia!

Queen. Sweets to the sweet: farewell! [*Scattering flowers.*]
I hop'd thou shouldst have been my Hamlet's wife;
I thought thy bride-bed to have deck'd, sweet maid,
And not have strew'd thy grave.

Laer. O, treble woe
Fall ten times treble on that cursed head,
Whose wicked deed thy most ingenious sense
Depriv'd thee of! Hold off the earth awhile,
Till I have caught her once more in mine arms:
[*Leaps into the grave.*]
Now pile your dust upon the quick and dead,
Till of this flat a mountain you have made,
T' o'ertop old Pelion, or the skyish head
Of blue Olympus.

Ham. [*Advancing*] What is he whose grief
Bears such an emphasis? whose phrase of sorrow
Conjures the wand'ring stars, and makes them stand
Like wonder-wounded hearers? This is I,
Hamlet the Dane. [*Leaps into the grave.*]

Laer. The devil take thy soul!
[*Grappling with him.*]

Ham. Thou pray'st not well.
I prithee, take thy fingers from my throat;
For, though I am not splenitive and rash,
Yet have I in me something dangerous,
Which let thy wisdom fear: hold off thy hand.

King. Pluck them asunder.

Queen. Hamlet, Hamlet!

All. Gentlemen,—

Hor. Good my lord, be quiet.
[*The Attendants part them, and they come out of the grave.*]

Ham. Why, I will fight with him upon this theme
Until my eyelids will no longer wag.

Queen. O my son, what theme?

Ham. I lov'd Ophelia: forty thousand brothers
Could not, with all their quantity of love,
Make up my sum. What wilt thou do for her?

King. O, he is mad, Laertes.

Queen. For love of God, forbear him.

Ham. 'Swounds, show me what thou 'lt do:
Woo 't weep? woo 't fight? woo 't fast? woo 't tear thyself?
Woo 't drink up eisel? eat a crocodile?
I'll do 't. Dost thou come here to whine?
To outface me with leaping in her grave?
Be buried quick with her, and so will I:
And, if thou prate of mountains, let them throw
Millions of acres on us, till our ground,
Singeing his pate against the burning zone,
Make Ossa like a wart! Nay, an thou 'lt mouth,
I'll rant as well as thou.

Queen. This is mere madness:
And thus awhile the fit will work on him;
Anon, as patient as the female dove,
When that her golden couplets are disclos'd,
His silence will sit drooping.

Ham. Hear you, sir;
What is the reason that you use me thus?
I lov'd you ever: but it is no matter;
Let Hercules himself do what he may,
The cat will mew and dog will have his day.

King. I pray thee, good Horatio, wait upon him.
Exit Hamlet and Horatio.
[*To Laertes*] Strengthen your patience in our last night's speech;
We'll put the matter to the present push.
Good Gertrude, set some watch over your son.
This grave shall have a living monument:

234. **loam,** clay paste for brickmaking. 236. **Imperious,** imperial. 239. **flaw,** gust of wind; see glossary. 244. **Fordo,** destroy. **it,** its. 245. **Couch,** hide, lurk. 249. **enlarg'd,** extended, referring to the fact that suicides are not given full burial rites. 254. **Shards,** broken bits of pottery. 255. **crants,** garlands customarily hung upon the biers of unmarried women. 256. **strewments,** traditional strewing of flowers. 256-257. **bringing . . . burial,** the laying to rest of the body, to the sound of the bell. 261. **peace-parted,** allusion to the text, "Lord, now lettest thou thy servant depart in peace." 265. **howling,** i.e., in hell. 271. **ingenious sense,** mind endowed with finest qualities. 276. **Pelion.** Olympus, Pelion, and Ossa are mountains in the north of Thessaly. 279. **wand'ring stars,** planets. 284. **splenitive,** quick-tempered. 285. **in me something,** so Q_2; F (Globe): *something in me.* 290. **wag,** move (not used ludicrously). 293. **quantity.** Dowden suggests that the word is used in a deprecatory sense (little bits, fragments). 296. **forbear,** leave alone. 297. **'Swounds,** oath, "God's wounds." 298. **Woo 't,** wilt thou. 299. **eisel,** vinegar. Some editors have taken this to be the name of a river, such as the Yssel, the Weissel, and the Nile. 305. **burning zone,** sun's orbit. 310. **golden couplets.** The pigeon lays two eggs; the young when hatched are covered with golden down (Dowden). 317. **in,** by recalling. 318. **present push,** immediate test. 320. **living,** lasting; also refers (for Laertes' benefit) to the plot against Hamlet.

SCENE II. 6. **mutines,** mutineers. **bilboes,** shackles. **Rashly,** goes with line 12. 9. **pall,** fail. 11. **Rough-hew,** shape roughly. Dowden suggests that it may mean "bungle." 13. **sea-gown,** "a sea-gown, or a

An hour of quiet shortly shall we see;
Till then, in patience our proceeding be. *Exeunt.*

[SCENE II. *A hall in the castle.*]

Enter HAMLET *and* HORATIO.

Ham. So much for this, sir: now shall you see the other;
You do remember all the circumstance?
Hor. Remember it, my lord!
Ham. Sir, in my heart there was a kind of fighting,
That would not let me sleep: methought I lay
Worse than the mutines in the bilboes. Rashly,
And prais'd be rashness for it, let us know,
Our indiscretion sometime serves us well,
When our deep plots do pall: and that should learn us
There 's a divinity that shapes our ends,
Rough-hew them how we will,—
Hor. That is most certain.
Ham. Up from my cabin,
My sea-gown scarf'd about me, in the dark
Grop'd I to find out them; had my desire,
Finger'd their packet, and in fine withdrew
To mine own room again; making so bold,
My fears forgetting manners, to unseal
Their grand commission; where I found, Horatio,—
O royal knavery!—an exact command,
Larded with many several sorts of reasons
Importing Denmark's health and England's too,
With, ho! such bugs and goblins in my life,
That, on the supervise, no leisure bated,
No, not to stay the grinding of the axe,
My head should be struck off.
Hor. Is 't possible?
Ham. Here 's the commission: read it at more leisure.
But wilt thou hear me how I did proceed?
Hor. I beseech you.
Ham. Being thus be-netted round with villanies,—
Ere I could make a prologue to my brains,
They had begun the play—I sat me down,
Devis'd a new commission, wrote it fair:
I once did hold it, as our statists do,
A baseness to write fair and labour'd much
How to forget that learning, but, sir, now
It did me yeoman's service: wilt thou know
Th' effect of what I wrote?
Hor. Ay, good my lord.
Ham. An earnest conjuration from the king,
As England was his faithful tributary,
As love between them like the palm might flourish,
As peace should still her wheaten garland wear
And stand a comma 'tween their amities,
And many such-like 'As'es of great charge,
That, on the view and knowing of these contents,
Without debatement further, more or less,
He should the bearers put to sudden death,
Not shriving-time allow'd.
Hor. How was this seal'd?
Ham. Why, even in that was heaven ordinant.
I had my father's signet in my purse,
Which was the model of that Danish seal;
Folded the writ up in the form of th' other,
Subscrib'd it, gave 't th' impression, plac'd it safely,
The changeling never known. Now, the next day
Was our sea-fight; and what to this was sequent
Thou know'st already.
Hor. So Guildenstern and Rosencrantz go to 't.
Ham. Why, man, they did make love to this employment;
They are not near my conscience; their defeat
Does by their own insinuation grow:
'Tis dangerous when the baser nature comes
Between the pass and fell incensed points
Of mighty opposites.
Hor. Why, what a king is this!
Ham. Does it not, think thee, stand me now upon—
He that hath kill'd my king and whor'd my mother,
Popp'd in between th' election and my hopes,
Thrown out his angle for my proper life,
And with such coz'nage—is 't not perfect conscience,
To quit him with this arm? and is 't not to be damn'd,
To let this canker of our nature come
In further evil?
Hor. It must be shortly known to him from England
What is the issue of the business there.
Ham. It will be short: the interim is mine;
And a man's life 's no more than to say 'One.'
But I am very sorry, good Horatio,
That to Laertes I forgot myself;
For, by the image of my cause, I see
The portraiture of his: I'll court his favours:
But, sure, the bravery of his grief did put me
Into a tow'ring passion.
Hor. Peace! who comes here?

Enter a Courtier [OSRIC].

Osr. Your lordship is right welcome back to Denmark.

Ham. I humbly thank you, sir. [To *Hor.*] Dost know this water-fly?

Hor. No, my good lord.

Ham. Thy state is the more gracious; for 'tis a vice to know him. He hath much land, and fertile: let a beast be lord of beasts, and his crib shall stand at the king's mess: 'tis a chough; but, as I say, spacious in the possession of dirt.

Osr. Sweet lord, if your lordship were at leisure, I should impart a thing to you from his majesty.

coarse, high-collered, and short-sleeved gowne, reaching down to the mid-leg, and used most by seamen and saylors" (Cotgrave, quoted by Singer). 15. **Finger'd,** pilfered, filched. **in fine,** finally. 20. **Larded,** enriched. 22. **such . . . life,** such imaginary dangers if I were allowed to live. **bugs,** bugbears. 23. **supervise,** perusal. **leisure bated,** delay allowed. 30-31. **prologue . . . play,** i.e., before I could begin to think, my mind had made its decision. 33. **statists,** statesmen. 34. **fair,** in a clear hand. 36. **yeoman's,** i.e., faithful. 41. **wheaten garland,** symbol of peace. 42. **comma,** smallest break or separation (Gollancz). Here *amity* begins and *amity* ends the period, and *peace* stands between like a dependent clause (Dowden). The comma indicates continuity, link. 43. **'As'es,** the "whereases" of a formal document, with play on the word *ass*. **charge,** import, and burden. 47. **shriving-time,** time for absolution. 48. **ordinant,** directing. 54. **sequent,** subsequent. 59. **insinuation,** interference. 61. **pass,** thrust. **fell incensed,** fiercely angered. 63. **stand,** become incumbent. 65. **election.** The Danish throne was filled by election. 66. **angle,** fishing line. 67. **coz'nage,** trickery. 68. **quit,** repay. 69. **canker,** ulcer, or possibly the worm which destroys buds and leaves. 79. **bravery,** bravado. 84. **water-fly,** vain or busily idle person. 88. **lord of beasts.** Cf. Genesis 1:26, 28. 89. **his crib . . . mess,** he shall eat at the king's table, i.e., be one of the group of persons (usually four) constituting a *mess* at a banquet. 90. **chough,** probably, chattering jackdaw; also explained as *chuff*, provincial boor or churl.

Ham. I will receive it, sir, with all diligence of spirit. Put your bonnet to his right use; 'tis for the head.

Osr. I thank your lordship, it is very hot.

Ham. No, believe me, 'tis very cold; the wind is northerly.

Osr. It is indifferent cold, my lord, indeed.

Ham. But yet methinks it is very sultry and hot for my complexion.

Osr. Exceedingly, my lord; it is very sultry,—as 'twere,—I cannot tell how. But, my lord, his majesty bade me signify to you that 'a has laid a great wager on your head: sir, this is the matter,—

Ham. I beseech you, remember—

[*Hamlet moves him to put on his hat.*]

Osr. Nay, good my lord; for mine ease, in good faith. Sir, here is newly come to court Laertes; believe me, an absolute gentleman, full of most excellent differences, of very soft society and great showing: indeed, to speak feelingly of him, he is the card or calendar of gentry, for you shall find in him the continent of what part a gentleman would see.

Ham. Sir, his definement suffers no perdition in you; though, I know, to divide him inventorially would dozy the arithmetic of memory, †and yet but yaw neither, in respect of his quick sail. But, in the verity of extolment, I take him to be a soul of great article; and his infusion of such dearth and rareness, as, to make true diction of him, his semblable is his mirror; and who else would trace him, his umbrage, nothing more.

Osr. Your lordship speaks most infallibly of him.

Ham. The concernancy, sir? why do we wrap the gentleman in our more rawer breath?

Osr. Sir?

Hor. [*Aside to Ham.*] Is 't not possible to understand in another tongue? You will do 't, sir, really.

Ham. What imports the nomination of this gentleman?

Osr. Of Laertes?

Hor. [*Aside to Ham.*] His purse is empty already; all 's golden words are spent.

Ham. Of him, sir.

Osr. I know you are not ignorant—

Ham. I would you did, sir; yet, in faith, if you did, it would not much approve me. Well, sir?

Osr. You are not ignorant of what excellence Laertes is—

Ham. I dare not confess that, lest I should compare with him in excellence; but, to know a man well, were to know himself.

Osr. I mean, sir, for his weapon; but in the imputation laid on him by them, in his meed he 's unfellowed.

Ham. What 's his weapon?

Osr. Rapier and dagger.

Ham. That 's two of his weapons: but, well.

Osr. The king, sir, hath wagered with him six Barbary horses: against the which he has impawned, as I take it, six French rapiers and poniards, with their assigns, as girdle, hangers, and so: three of the carriages, in faith, are very dear to fancy, very responsive to the hilts, most delicate carriages, and of very liberal conceit.

Ham. What call you the carriages?

Hor. [*Aside to Ham.*] I knew you must be edified by the margent ere you had done.

Osr. The carriages, sir, are the hangers.

Ham. The phrase would be more german to the matter, if we could carry cannon by our sides: I would it might be hangers till then. But, on: six Barbary horses against six French swords, their assigns, and three liberal-conceited carriages; that 's the French bet against the Danish. Why is this 'impawned,' as you call it?

Osr. The king, sir, hath laid, that in a dozen passes between yourself and him, he shall not exceed you three hits: he hath laid on twelve for nine; and it would come to immediate trial, if your lordship would vouchsafe the answer.

Ham. How if I answer 'no'?

Osr. I mean, my lord, the opposition of your person in trial.

Ham. Sir, I will walk here in the hall: if it please his majesty, it is the breathing time of day with me; let the foils be brought, the gentleman willing, and the king hold his purpose, I will win for him an I can; if not, I will gain nothing but my shame and the odd hits.

Osr. Shall I re-deliver you e'en so?

Ham. To this effect, sir; after what flourish your nature will.

Osr. I commend my duty to your lordship.

Ham. Yours, yours. [*Exit Osric.*] He does well to commend it himself; there are no tongues else for 's turn.

Hor. This lapwing runs away with the shell on his head.

Ham. 'A did comply, sir, with his dug, before 'a sucked it. Thus has he—and many more of the same breed that I know the drossy age dotes on—only got the tune of the time and out of an habit of encounter; a kind of yesty collection, which carries them through and through the most †fann'd and winnowed opinions; and do but blow them to their trial, the bubbles are out.

Enter a Lord.

Lord. My lord, his majesty commended him to you by young Osric, who brings back to him, that you attend him in the hall: he sends to know if your pleasure hold to play with Laertes, or that you will take longer time.

Ham. I am constant to my purposes; they follow

100. **indifferent,** somewhat. 108. **remember,** i.e., remember thy courtesy; conventional phrase for "Be covered." 109. **mine ease,** conventional reply declining the invitation of "Remember thy courtesy." 112. **soft,** gentle. 113. **showing,** distinguished appearance. 114. **feelingly,** with just perception. **card,** chart, map. 115. **gentry,** good breeding. 117. **definement,** definition. **perdition,** loss, diminution. 118. **divide him inventorially,** i.e., enumerate his graces. 119. **dozy,** dizzy. 120. **yaw,** to move unsteadily (of a ship). Dowden's note: To enumerate in detail the perfections of Laertes would bewilder the computations of memory, yet for all that—in spite of the calculations—the enumeration would stagger to and fro (and so fall behind) in comparison with Laertes' quick sailing (or, possibly, considering *its* quick sail, which ought to steady the ship). 122. **article,** moment or importance. 123. **infusion,** infused temperament, character imparted by nature. **dearth and rareness,** rarity. 124. **semblable,** true likeness. 125. **trace,** follow. 126. **umbrage,** shadow. 128. **concernancy,** import. 129. **breath,** speech. 131-132. **Is 't . . . tongue?** i.e., can one converse with Osric only in this outlandish jargon? 133. **nomination,** naming. 141. **approve,** commend. 146-147. **but . . . himself,** but to know a man as excellent were to know Laertes. 149. **imputation,** reputation. 150. **meed,** merit. 155-156. **he has impawned,** he has wagered. 158. **hangers,** straps on the sword belt from which the sword hung. 159. **dear to fancy,** fancifully made. **responsive,** probably, well balanced; corresponding closely (Onions). 160. **delicate,** i.e., in workmanship. **liberal conceit,** elaborate design. 163. **margent,** margin of a book, place for explanatory notes. 165. **german,** germain, appropriate.

the king's pleasure: if his fitness speaks, mine is ready; now or whensoever, provided I be so able as now.

Lord. The king and queen and all are coming down.

Ham. In happy time.

Lord. The queen desires you to use some gentle entertainment to Laertes before you fall to play.

Ham. She well instructs me. [*Exit Lord*.]

Hor. You will lose this wager, my lord.

Ham. I do not think so; since he went into France, I have been in continual practice; I shall win at the odds. But thou wouldst not think how ill all 's here about my heart: but it is no matter.

Hor. Nay, good my lord,—

Ham. It is but foolery; but it is such a kind of gain-giving, as would perhaps trouble a woman.

Hor. If your mind dislike any thing, obey it: I will forestal their repair hither, and say you are not fit.

Ham. Not a whit, we defy augury: there 's a special providence in the fall of a sparrow. If it be now, 'tis not to come; if it be not to come, it will be now; if it be not now, yet it will come: the readiness is all: since no man of aught he leaves knows, what is 't to leave betimes? Let be.

A table prepared. [*Enter*] *Trumpets*, *Drums*, *and* Officers *with cushions;* KING, QUEEN, [OSRIC,] *and all the State; foils*, *daggers*, [*and wine borne in;*] *and* LAERTES.

King. Come, Hamlet, come, and take this hand
from me. [*The King puts Laertes' hand into Hamlet's*.]
Ham. Give me your pardon, sir: I have done you
wrong;
But pardon 't, as you are a gentleman.
This presence knows,
And you must needs have heard, how I am punish'd
With a sore distraction. What I have done,
That might your nature, honour and exception
Roughly awake, I here proclaim was madness.
Was 't Hamlet wrong'd Laertes? Never Hamlet:
If Hamlet from himself be ta'en away,
And when he 's not himself does wrong Laertes,
Then Hamlet does it not, Hamlet denies it.
Who does it, then? His madness: if 't be so,
Hamlet is of the faction that is wrong'd;
His madness is poor Hamlet's enemy.
Sir, in this audience,
Let my disclaiming from a purpos'd evil
Free me so far in your most generous thoughts,
That I have shot mine arrow o'er the house,
And hurt my brother.
Laer. I am satisfied in nature,
Whose motive, in this case, should stir me most
To my revenge: but in my terms of honour
I stand aloof; and will no reconcilement,
Till by some elder masters, of known honour,
I have a voice and precedent of peace,
To keep my name ungor'd. But till that time,
I do receive your offer'd love like love,
And will not wrong it.
Ham. I embrace it freely;
And will this brother's wager frankly play.
Give us the foils. Come on.
Laer. Come, one for me.
Ham. I'll be your foil, Laertes: in mine ignorance
Your skill shall, like a star i' th' darkest night,
Stick fiery off indeed.
Laer. You mock me, sir.
Ham. No, by this hand.
King. Give them the foils, young Osric. Cousin
Hamlet,
You know the wager?
Ham. Very well, my lord;
Your grace has laid the odds o' th' weaker side.
King. I do not fear it; I have seen you both:
But since he is better'd, we have therefore odds.
Laer. This is too heavy, let me see another.
Ham. This likes me well. These foils have all a
length? [*They prepare to play*.]
Osr. Ay, my good lord.
King. Set me the stoups of wine upon that table.
If Hamlet give the first or second hit,
Or quit in answer of the third exchange,
Let all the battlements their ordnance fire;
The king shall drink to Hamlet's better breath;
And in the cup an union shall he throw,
Richer than that which four successive kings
In Denmark's crown have worn. Give me the cups;
And let the kettle to the trumpet speak,
The trumpet to the cannoneer without,
The cannons to the heavens, the heavens to earth,
'Now the king drinks to Hamlet.' Come, begin:
Trumpets the while.
And you, the judges, bear a wary eye.
Ham. Come on, sir.
Laer. Come, my lord. [*They play*.]
Ham. One.
Laer. No.
Ham. Judgement.
Osr. A hit, a very palpable hit.
Drum, *trumpets*, *and shot*. *Flourish*. *A piece goes off*.
Laer. Well; again.
King. Stay; give me drink. Hamlet, this pearl is
thine;
Here 's to thy health. Give him the cup.
Ham. I'll play this bout first; set it by awhile.
Come. [*They play*.] Another hit; what say you?
Laer. A touch, a touch, I do confess 't.
King. Our son shall win.
Queen. He 's fat, and scant of breath.
Here, Hamlet, take my napkin, rub thy brows:
The queen carouses to thy fortune, Hamlet.
Ham. Good madam!

181. **breathing time,** exercise period. 193. **lapwing,** peewit; note its wiliness in drawing a visitor away from its nest and its supposed habit of running about when newly hatched with its head in the shell; Ruth Cline suggests allusion to Osric's hat. 195. **did comply . . . dug,** paid compliments to his mother's breast. 197. **drossy,** frivolous. 198. **tune,** temper, mood. 199. **out of an,** so Q_2; F (Globe): *outward*. **habit of encounter,** demeanor of social intercourse. **yesty,** frothy. 201. **fann'd and winnowed,** select and refined. Q_2: *prophane and trennowed*; F: *fond and winnowed* (trivial and sensible; so Globe, following W. J. Craig); text follows Warburton. 202. **blow . . . out,** i.e., put them to the test, and their ignorance is exposed. 214. **In happy time,** a phrase of courtesy. 226. **gain-giving,** misgiving. 233. **all,** all that matters. 239. **presence,** royal assembly. 242. **exception,** disapproval. 255. **brother.** With reference to the F reading, *mother*, Dowden calls attention to Gertrude's request to *use some gentle entertainment* to Laertes. **nature,** i.e., he is personally satisfied, but his honor must be satisfied by the rules of the code of honor. 260. **voice,** authoritative pronouncement. 266. **foil,** quibble on the two senses, "background which sets something off," and "blunted rapier for fencing." 268. **Stick fiery off,** stand out brilliantly. 283. **union,** pearl. 286. **kettle,** kettledrum. 293. **pearl,** i.e., the poison. 297. **confess 't,** Q_2: *confest;* F (Globe): *confess*. 298. **fat,** not physically fit, out of training. Some earlier editors speculated that the term applied to the corpulence of Richard Burbage, who originally played the part, but the allusion now appears unlikely. *Fat* may also suggest "sweaty." 300. **carouses,** drinks a toast.

King. Gertrude, do not drink.
Queen. I will, my lord; I pray you, pardon me. [*Drinks.*]
King. [*Aside*] It is the poison'd cup: it is too late.
Ham. I dare not drink yet, madam; by and by.
Queen. Come, let me wipe thy face.
Laer. My lord, I'll hit him now.
King. I do not think't.
Laer. [*Aside*] And yet 'tis almost 'gainst my conscience.
Ham. Come, for the third, Laertes: you but dally;
I pray you, pass with your best violence;
I am afeard you make a wanton of me.
Laer. Say you so? come on. [*They play.*]
Osr. Nothing, neither way.
Laer. Have at you now!
[*Laertes wounds Hamlet; then, in scuffling, they change rapiers, and Hamlet wounds Laertes.*]
King. Part them; they are incens'd.
Ham. Nay, come, again. [*The Queen falls.*]
Osr. Look to the queen there, ho!
Hor. They bleed on both sides. How is it, my lord?
Osr. How is 't, Laertes?
Laer. Why, as a woodcock to mine own springe, Osric;
I am justly kill'd with mine own treachery.
Ham. How does the queen?
King. She swounds to see them bleed.
Queen. No, no, the drink, the drink,—O my dear Hamlet,—
The drink, the drink! I am poison'd. [*Dies.*]
Ham. O villany! Ho! let the door be lock'd:
Treachery! Seek it out. [*Laertes falls.*]
Laer. It is here, Hamlet: Hamlet, thou art slain;
No med'cine in the world can do thee good;
In thee there is not half an hour of life;
The treacherous instrument is in thy hand,
Unbated and envenom'd: the foul practice
Hath turn'd itself on me; lo, here I lie,
Never to rise again: thy mother 's poison'd:
I can no more: the king, the king 's to blame.
Ham. The point envenom'd too!
Then, venom, to thy work. [*Stabs the King.*]
All. Treason! treason!
King. O, yet defend me, friends; I am but hurt.
Ham. Here, thou incestuous, murd'rous, damned Dane,
Drink off this potion. Is thy union here?
Follow my mother. [*King dies.*]
Laer. He is justly serv'd;
It is a poison temper'd by himself.
Exchange forgiveness with me, noble Hamlet:
Mine and my father's death come not upon thee,
Nor thine on me! [*Dies.*]
Ham. Heaven make thee free of it! I follow thee.
I am dead, Horatio. Wretched queen, adieu!
You that look pale and tremble at this chance,
That are but mutes or audience to this act,
Had I but time—as this fell sergeant, Death,
Is strict in his arrest—O, I could tell you—
But let it be. Horatio, I am dead;
Thou livest; report me and my cause aright
To the unsatisfied.
Hor. Never believe it:
I am more an antique Roman than a Dane:
Here 's yet some liquor left.
Ham. As th' art a man,
Give me the cup: let go; by heaven, I'll ha 't.
O God! Horatio, what a wounded name,
Things standing thus unknown, shall live behind me!
If thou didst ever hold me in thy heart,
Absent thee from felicity awhile,
And in this harsh world draw thy breath in pain,
To tell my story. [*A march afar off.*]
What warlike noise is this?
Osr. Young Fortinbras, with conquest come from Poland,
To the ambassadors of England gives
This warlike volley.
Ham. O, I die, Horatio;
The potent poison quite o'er-crows my spirit:
I cannot live to hear the news from England;
But I do prophesy th' election lights
On Fortinbras: he has my dying voice;
So tell him, with th' occurrents, more and less,
Which have solicited. The rest is silence. [*Dies.*]
Hor. Now cracks a noble heart. Good night, sweet prince;
And flights of angels sing thee to thy rest!
Why does the drum come hither? [*March within.*]

Enter FORTINBRAS, *with the* [English] Ambassadors [*and others*].

Fort. Where is this sight?
Hor. What is it you would see?
If aught of woe or wonder, cease your search.
Fort. This quarry cries on havoc. O proud Death,
What feast is toward in thine eternal cell,
That thou so many princes at a shot
So bloodily hast struck?
First Amb. The sight is dismal;
And our affairs from England come too late:
The ears are senseless that should give us hearing,
To tell him his commandment is fulfill'd,
That Rosencrantz and Guildenstern are dead:
Where should we have our thanks?
Hor. Not from his mouth,
Had it th' ability of life to thank you:
He never gave commandment for their death.
But since, so jump upon this bloody question,
You from the Polack wars, and you from England,
Are here arriv'd, give order that these bodies
High on a stage be placed to the view;
And let me speak to th' yet unknowing world
How these things came about: so shall you hear
Of carnal, bloody, and unnatural acts,
Of accidental judgements, casual slaughters,
Of deaths put on by cunning and forc'd cause,
And, in this upshot, purposes mistook

310. **wanton,** spoiled child. 313. *Stage Direction: **in scuffling, they change rapiers.*** Occurs in F. According to a widespread stage tradition, Hamlet receives a scratch, realizes that Laertes' sword is unbated, and accordingly forces an exchange. 317. **woodcock,** as type of stupidity or as decoy. **springe,** trap, snare. 319. **swounds,** swoons. 328. **Unbated,** not blunted with a button. 339. **temper'd,** mixed. 346. **mutes,** performers in a play who speak no words. 347. **sergeant,** sheriff's officer. Chambers takes the word to mean the officer who enforces a judgment of a tribunal or the commands of a person in authority. 352. **Roman.** It was the Roman custom to follow masters in death (Yale). 355. **God,** so Q_2; F (Globe): *good.* 364. **o'er-crows,** triumphs over. 368. **occurrents,** events, incidents. 369. **solicited,** moved, urged. 375. **quarry,** heap of dead. **cries on havoc,** proclaims a general slaughter. 383. **his mouth,** i.e., the king's. 386. **jump,** precisely. **question,** dispute. 389. **stage,** platform. 400. **of memory,** traditional, remembered. 403. **voice . . . more,** vote will influence still others. 406. **On,** on account of.

Fall'n on th' inventors' heads: all this can I
Truly deliver.
Fort. Let us haste to hear it,
And call the noblest to the audience.
For me, with sorrow I embrace my fortune:
I have some rights of memory in this kingdom,
Which now to claim my vantage doth invite me.
Hor. Of that I shall have also cause to speak,
And from his mouth whose voice will draw on more:
But let this same be presently perform'd,
Even while men's minds are wild; lest more mischance,
On plots and errors, happen.
Fort. Let four captains
Bear Hamlet, like a soldier, to the stage;
For he was likely, had he been put on,
To have prov'd most royal: and, for his passage,
The soldiers' music and the rites of war
Speak loudly for him.
Take up the bodies: such a sight as this
Becomes the field, but here shows much amiss.
Go, bid the soldiers shoot.
Exeunt [marching, bearing off the dead bodies; after which a peal of ordnance is shot off].

or possibly, on top of, in addition to. 409. **royal,** so Q_2; F (Globe): *royally*. **passage,** death. 413. **field,** i.e., of battle.

KING LEAR

In *King Lear*, Shakespeare pushes to its limit the hypothesis of a malign or at least indifferent universe in which man's life is meaningless and brutal. Few plays other than *Hamlet* and *Macbeth* approach *King Lear* in evoking the wretchedness of human existence, and even they cannot match the devastating spectacle of Gloucester blinded or Cordelia dead in Lear's arms. The responses of the chief characters are correspondingly searing. "Is man no more than this?" rages Lear. "Unaccommodated man is no more but such a poor, bare, forked animal as thou art" (III,iv). Life he calls a "great stage of fools," an endless torment: "the first time that we smell the air, We wawl and cry" (IV,vi). Gloucester's despair takes the form of accusing the gods of gleeful malice toward man: "As flies to wanton boys, are we to th' gods, They kill us for their sport" (IV,i). Gloucester's ministering son Edgar can offer him no greater consolation than stoic resolve: "Men must endure Their going hence, even as their coming hither: Ripeness is all" (V,ii). These statements need not be read as choric expressions of "meaning" for the play as a whole, but they do attest to the depth of suffering. In no other Shakespearean play does injustice appear to triumph so ferociously, for so long, and with such impunity. Will the heavens countenance this reign of injustice on earth? Retribution is late in coming and is not certainly the work of the heavens themselves. For, at the last, we must confront the wanton death of the innocent Cordelia, a death no longer willed even by the villain who arranged her execution. "Is this the promis'd end?" asks Kent, stressing the unparalleled horror of the catastrophe.

Throughout its earlier history, in fact, the ancient story of King Lear had always ended happily. In the popular folktale of Cinderella, to which the legend of Lear's daughters bears a significant resemblance, the youngest and virtuous daughter triumphs over her two older wicked sisters and is married to her princely wooer. Geoffrey of Monmouth's *Historia Regum Britanniae* (c. 1136), the earliest known version of the Lear story, records that after Lear is overthrown by his sons-in-law (more than by his daughters), he is restored to his throne by the intervention of the French king and is allowed to enjoy his kingdom and Cordelia's love until his natural death. (Cordelia, as his successor, is later dethroned and murdered by her wicked nephews, but that is another story.) Subsequent Tudor versions of the Lear story with which Shakespeare was familiar—John Higgins' account

COLLECTION OF DR. LOUIS MARDER, UNIVERSITY OF ILLINOIS

In this painting by Fuseli from the Boydell edition of Shakespeare (1803), King Lear fiercely denounces Cordelia while Regan and Goneril watch, thus setting the stage for Lear's eventual tragic end.

in *The First parte of the Mirour for Magistrates* (1574), Holinshed's *Chronicles* (1587), Spenser's *The Faerie Queene*, II,x,27–32, and a play called *The True Chronicle History of King Leir* (by 1594, published 1605)—all retain the happy ending. The tragic pattern may have been suggested instead by Shakespeare's probable source for the Gloucester-Edgar-Edmund plot, Sir Philip Sidney's *Arcadia*, II,10, in which the Paphlagonian king is the victim of filial ingratitude and deceit. Shakespeare's genius linked the two plots, employing in both the themes of exile, cruel persecution, and the barrenness of human existence.

Yet even Shakespeare's great authority was not sufficient to put down the craving for a romantic solution. Nahum Tate's adaptation (1681), which banished the Fool as indecorous for a tragedy and united Edgar and Cordelia in marriage, placing Lear once again on his throne, actually held the English stage for about 150 years. David Garrick restored some of Shakespeare's lines, and Edmund Kean restored the tragic ending, but not until 1838 was Shakespeare's play again performed more or less as he wrote it. Dr. Johnson evidently spoke for most eighteenth-century audiences when he confessed that he could not bring himself to read Shakespeare's text. Cordelia's slaughter violated that age's longing for "poetic justice." Her death implied a wanton universe and so counseled philosophic despair. Today, however, the relentless honesty of Shakespeare's tragic vision, and his refusal to accept easy answers, convince us that Shakespeare was right to defy the conventions of his source. He evidently wrote *King Lear* some time before it was performed at court in December of 1606, probably in 1605 and certainly no earlier than 1603–1604; Edgar's speeches as Tom o' Bedlam contain references to Samuel Harsnett's *Declaration of Egregious Popishe Impostures* which was registered for publication in March of 1603. Thus *King Lear* was probably written between *Othello* (c. 1603–1604) and *Macbeth* (c. 1606–1607), when Shakespeare was at the very height of his tragic power.

It seems a paradox that Shakespeare should have chosen for this supremely mature work a fable derived from folklore and legend, with many of the wondrous and implausible circumstances of popular romance. A prose rendition might almost begin, "Once upon a time there was a king who had three daughters. . . ." In part, Shakespeare's purpose seems to have been to arouse romantic expectations only to crush them by aborting the conventional happy ending, thus setting up a dramatic tension between an idealized world of make-believe and the actual world of disappointed hopes. Just as importantly, however, the folktale element focuses our attention on the archetypal situations with which the story is concerned: rivalry between siblings, fear of parental rejection, and, conversely, parental fear of children's ingratitude. The "unrealistic" contrast between Cordelia and her wicked sisters, or between Edgar and Edmund, is something we accept as a convention of storytelling because it expresses so vividly the psychic truth of rivalry between brothers and sisters. We identify with Cordelia and Edgar as virtuous children whose worth is misunderstood, and who are losing to hated siblings the contest for parental approval. (In folklore the rejecting parent is usually a stepparent, to signify our conviction that he or she is not a true parent at all.) Similarly, we accept as a convention of storytelling the equally "unrealistic" device by which Lear tests the love of his daughters. Here we identify with Lear's universal longing to be loved and appreciated in return for the kindnesses he has performed. This identification is particularly strong for middle-aged readers or viewers of Shakespeare with grown children of their own. Is it too much to ask, after parents have provided for their children and grown old, that those children should express their gratitude and look after the parents?

The difficulty is that the parable of Lear and his children presents two contrasting viewpoints, that of the unappreciated child and that of the unwanted aging parent. Tragic misunderstanding is inevitable and outweighs the question of assessing blame. From Lear's point of view, Cordelia's silence is a truculent scanting of obedience. What he has devised is, after all, only a prearranged formality, with Cordelia to receive the richest third of England. Cannot such a ceremony be answered with the conventional hyperbole of courtly language, to which the king's ear is attuned? Don't parents have a right to be verbally reassured of their children's love? How can children be so laconic about such a precious matter? For her part, however, Cordelia senses that Lear is demanding love as payment for his parental kindliness, *quid pro quo*. True love ought rather to be selfless, as the King of France tells Burgundy: "Love's not love When it is mingled with regards that stand Aloof from th' entire point." Is Cordelia being asked to prefer Lear before her own husband-to-be? Is this the price she must pay for her upbringing? Lear's ego seems fully capable of demanding this self-sacrifice from his daughters, especially his favorite, Cordelia: he has given them his whole kingdom, now let them care for him as befits his royal rank and patriarchal role. The "second childishness" of old age can often bring with it such a self-centered longing to monopolize the lives of one's children, and to be oneself a child again. Besides, as king, Lear has long grown accustomed to flattery and absolute obedience. Goneril and Regan are content to flatter and promise obedience, knowing they will turn him out once he has relinquished his authority. Cordelia, of course, refuses to lie in this fashion, but she also will not yield to Lear's implicit request for her undivided affection. Part of her must be loyal to her own husband and her children, in the natural cycle of the generations. "When I shall wed, That lord whose hand must take my plight shall carry Half my love with him, half my care and duty." Marriage will not prevent her from loving, honoring, and obeying her father as is fit, but will establish a new priority. To

Lear, as to many fathers contemplating a daughter's marriage, this savors of desertion.

Lear is sadly deficient in self-knowledge. As Regan drily observes, "he hath ever but slenderly known himself," and has grown ever more changeable and imperious with age. By dividing his kingdom in three, ostensibly so that "future strife May be prevented now," he instead guarantees a civil war and French invasion. His intention of setting aside his regal authority while still retaining "The name, and all th' additions to a king," betrays an abysmal lack of comprehension of the realities of power. He hearkens to poisoned flattery but interprets well-intended criticism, whether from Cordelia or Kent, as treason. These failures in no sense justify what Lear's ungrateful children do to him; as he later says, just before going mad, "I am a man More sinn'd against than sinning" (III,ii). They are, however, tokens of his worldly insolence from which he must fall. The process is a painful one, but since it brings self-discovery it is not without its compensations. Indeed a central paradox of the play is that by no other way could Lear have learned what human suffering and need are all about.

Lear's Fool is instrumental in elucidating this paradox. The Fool offers Lear advice in palatable form as mere foolery or entertainment, and thus obtains a hearing when Kent and Cordelia have been angrily dismissed. Beneath his seemingly innocent jibes, however, are plain warnings of the looming disaster Lear blindly refuses to acknowledge. The Fool knows, as indeed any fool could tell, that Goneril and Regan are remorseless and unnatural. The real fool, therefore, is Lear himself, for having placed himself in their power. In a metaphor of which the Renaissance was incessantly fond—as in Erasmus' *In Praise of Folly*, Cervantes' *Don Quixote*, and Shakespeare's own earlier *As You Like It* and *Twelfth Night*—folly and wisdom exchange places. By a similar inversion of logic, the Fool offers his coxcomb to Kent for siding with Lear in his exile, "for taking one's part that 's out of favour" (I,iv). Worldly wisdom is to serve those whose fortunes are on the rise, as does the obsequious and servile Oswald. Indeed, the sinister progress of the first half of the play seems to confirm the Fool's contention that kindness and love are a sure way to exile and poverty. "Let go thy hold when a great wheel runs down a hill, lest it break thy neck with following; but the great one that goes upward, let him draw thee after" (II,iv). Yet the Fool resolves to ignore his own cynical advice: "I would have none but knaves follow it, since a fool gives it." Beneath his mocking, the Fool expresses the deeper truth that it is better to be a "fool" and suffer than to win on the world's terms. The greatest fools in the truest sense are those who prosper through cruelty and so become hardened in sin. As the Fool puts it, deriving a seemingly contrary lesson from Lear's rejection of Cordelia: "Why, this fellow has banished two on 's daughters, and did the third a blessing against his will" (I,iv).

These paradoxes find a parallel in Christian teaching, although the play is nominally pagan in setting. (The lack of explicit Christian reference may be in part the result of a recent Parliamentary order banning references to "God" on stage as blasphemous.) Christianity does not hold a monopoly on the idea that one must lose the world to win a better world, but its expressions of that idea were plentifully available to Shakespeare: "Blessed are the meek, for they shall inherit the earth" (the Sermon on the Mount); "Go and sell that thou hast, and give to the poor, and thou shalt have treasure in heaven" (Matthew 19:21); "He hath put down the mighty from their seats, and exalted them of low degree" (Luke 1:52). Cordelia's vision of true love is of this exalted spiritual order. She is, as the King of France extols her, "most rich, being poor; Most choice, forsaken; and most lov'd, despis'd" (I,i). This is the sense in which Lear has bestowed on her an unintended blessing, by exiling her from a worldly prosperity that is inherently pernicious. Now, with poetic fitness, Lear must learn the same lesson himself. He does so, paradoxically, at the very moment he goes mad, parting ways with the conventional truths of the corrupted world. "My wits begin to turn," he says, and then speaks his first kind words to the Fool, who is his companion in the storm. Lear senses companionship with a fellow mortal who is cold and outcast as he is. In his madness he perceives both the worth of this insight and the need for suffering to attain it: "The art of our necessities is strange, That can make vile things precious" (III,ii). Misery teaches Lear things he never could know as king about other "Poor naked wretches" who "bide the pelting of this pitiless storm." How are such poor persons to be fed and clothed? "O, I have ta'en Too little care of this! Take physic, pomp; Expose thyself to feel what wretches feel, That thou mayst shake the superflux to them, And show the heavens more just" (III,iv). This vision of perfect justice is visionary and utopian, utterly mad in fact, but it is also spiritual wisdom dearly bought.

Gloucester learns a similar truth and expresses it in much the same way. Like Lear he had driven into exile a virtuous child and has placed himself in the power of the wicked. Enlightenment comes only through suffering. Just as Lear achieves spiritual wisdom when he goes mad, Gloucester achieves spiritual vision when he is physically blinded. His eyes having been ground out by the heel of Cornwall's boot, Gloucester asks for Edmund only to learn that Edmund has betrayed him for siding with Lear in the approaching civil war. Gloucester's response, however, is not to accuse Edmund of treachery but to beg forgiveness of the wronged Edgar. No longer does Gloucester need eyes to see this truth; "I stumbled when I saw." Although the discovery is shattering, Gloucester perceives, as does Lear, that adversity is a blessing in disguise since prosperity had previously caused him to be so spiritually blind. "Full oft 'tis seen, Our means secure us, and our mere defects

Prove our commodities." And this realization leads him, as it does Lear, to express a longing for utopian social justice in which arrogant men will be humbled and the poor raised up by their redistributed wealth. "Heavens, deal so still! Let the superfluous and lust-dieted man, That slaves your ordinance, that will not see Because he does not feel, feel your pow'r quickly; So distribution should undo excess, And each man have enough" (IV,i).

To say that Lear and Gloucester learn something precious is not, however, to deny that they are also devastated and broken by their savage humiliation. Indeed, Gloucester is driven to a despairing attempt at suicide, and Lear remains obsessed with the rotten stench of his own mortality, "bound Upon a wheel of fire" (IV,vii). Every value, every decency that we like to associate with civilization is grotesquely inverted during the storm scenes. Justice, for example, is portrayed in two sharply contrasting scenes: the mere "form of justice" by which Cornwall condemns Gloucester for treason (III,vii), and the earnestly play-acted trial by which the mad Lear arraigns Goneril and Regan of filial ingratitude (III,vi). The appearance and the reality of justice have exchanged places, as have folly and wisdom or blindness and seeing. The trial of Gloucester is correct in outward show, for Cornwall possesses the legal authority to try his subjects, and at least goes through the motions of interrogating his prisoner. The outcome is, however, cruelly predetermined. In the playacting trial concurrently taking place in a wretched hovel, the outward appearance of justice is pathetically absurd. Here justice on earth is personified by a madman (Lear), Edgar disguised as another madman (Tom o' Bedlam), and a Fool, the latter two addressed by Lear as "Thou robed man of justice" and "thou, his yoke-fellow of equity." They are caught up in a pastime of illusion, using a footstool to represent Lear's ungrateful daughters. Yet true justice is here and not inside the manor house.

Similar contrasts invert the values of loyalty, obedience, and family bonds. Edmund becomes, in the language of the villains, the "loyal" son whose loyalty is demonstrated by turning on his own "traitorous" father. Cornwall becomes a new father to Edmund ("thou shalt find a dearer father in my love"). Conversely, a servant who tries to restrain Cornwall from criminally blinding Gloucester is, in Regan's eyes, monstrously insubordinate. "A peasant stand up thus!"

All these inversions are subsumed in the inversion of the word "natural." Edmund is the "natural" son of Gloucester, meaning literally that he is illegitimate. Figuratively he therefore represents a violation of traditional moral order. In appearance he is smooth and plausible, but in reality he is an archdeceiver like the Vice in the morality play, a superb actor who boasts to the audience in soliloquy of his protean villainy. (See the Introduction to *Othello* for a comparison with Iago.) "Nature" is his goddess, and by this he means something like a naturalistic universe in which the race goes to the swiftest and in which conscience, morality, and religion are empty myths. Whereas Lear invokes Nature as a goddess who will punish ungrateful daughters and defend rejected fathers (I,iv), and whereas Gloucester believes in a cosmic correspondence between eclipses of the moon or sun and mutinous discords among men (I,ii), Edmund scoffs at all such metaphysical speculations. He spurns, in other words, the Boethian conception of a divine harmony uniting the cosmos and man, with man at the Ptolemaic center of the universe. As a rationalist, Edmund echoes Jacobean challenges of the older world order in politics and religion as well as in science. He is a Machiavellian, atheist, Epicurean, everything inimical to traditional Elizabethan order. To him, "natural" means precisely what Lear and Gloucester call "unnatural."

His creed provides the play with its supreme test. Which idea of "natural" is true? Do the heavens exist, and will they let Edmund and his cohorts get away with their evil? The question is frequently asked, but the answers are ambiguous. "If you do love old men," Lear implores the gods, "if your sweet sway Allow obedience, if you yourselves are old, Make it your cause" (II,iv). His exhortations mount into frenzied rant, until finally the heavens do send down a terrible storm—on Lear himself. Witnesses agree that the absence of divine order in the universe would have the gravest consequences. "If that the heavens do not their visible spirits Send quickly down to tame these vile offences," says Albany of Lear's ordeal, "It will come, Humanity must perforce prey on itself, Like monsters of the deep" (IV,ii). And Cornwall's servants have perceived earlier the dire implications of their masters' evil deeds. "I'll never care what wickedness I do, If this man come to good," says one, and his fellow agrees: "If she [Regan] live long, And in the end meet the old course of death, Women will all turn monsters" (III,vii). Yet these servants do in fact obey their own best instincts, turning on Cornwall and ministering to Gloucester despite danger to themselves. Similarly, Albany abandons his mild attempts at conciliation and uses his power for good. The crimes of the villains are punished, and Albany sees divine cause in this. Just as plausibly, however, one can postulate a fundamental decency in humankind that has at last asserted itself, revulsed by what it has seen. In part, too, villainy destroys itself, for Edmund's insatiable ambition extends past Cornwall to the English throne, and Goneril and Regan would willingly kill one another to be Edmund's queen. Whatever force oversees the restoration of at least some semblance of justice cannot prevent the death of Cordelia. Yet her ability to forgive and cherish her father, and Edgar's comparable ministering to Gloucester, give the lie to Edmund's "natural" or amoral view of humanity. Cordelia and Edgar show that, with or without the gods, mankind can atone for its own vicious tendencies by a will to believe in goodness.

KING LEAR

[*Dramatis Personae*

LEAR, King of Britain.
KING OF FRANCE.
DUKE OF BURGUNDY.
DUKE OF CORNWALL.
DUKE OF ALBANY.
EARL OF KENT.
EARL OF GLOUCESTER.
EDGAR, *son to Gloucester.*
EDMUND, *bastard son to Gloucester.*
CURAN, *a courtier.*
Old Man, *tenant to Gloucester.*
Doctor.
Fool.
OSWALD, *steward to Goneril.*
A Captain employed by Edmund.
Gentleman attendant on Cordelia.
A Herald.
Servants to Cornwall.

GONERIL,
REGAN, } *daughters to Lear.*
CORDELIA,

Knights of Lear's train, Captains, Messengers, Soldiers, *and* Attendants.

SCENE: *Britain.*]

ACT I.

SCENE I. [*King Lear's palace.*]

Enter KENT, GLOUCESTER, *and* EDMUND.

Kent. I thought the king had more affected the Duke of Albany than Cornwall.

Glou. It did always seem so to us: but now, in the division of the kingdom, it appears not which of the dukes he values most; for equalities are so weighed, that curiosity in neither can make choice of either's moiety.

Kent. Is not this your son, my lord?

Glou. His breeding, sir, hath been at my charge: I have so often blushed to acknowledge him, that now I am brazed to 't.

Kent. I cannot conceive you.

Glou. Sir, this young fellow's mother could: whereupon she grew round-wombed, and had, indeed, sir, a son for her cradle ere she had a husband for her bed. Do you smell a fault?

Kent. I cannot wish the fault undone, the issue of it being so proper.

Glou. But I have a son, sir, by order of law, some year elder than this, who yet is no dearer in my account: though this knave came something saucily to the world before he was sent for, yet was his mother fair; there was good sport at his making, and the whoreson must be acknowledged. Do you know this noble gentleman, Edmund?

Edm. No, my lord.

Glou. My lord of Kent: remember him hereafter as my honourable friend.

Edm. My services to your lordship.

Kent. I must love you, and sue to know you better.

Edm. Sir, I shall study deserving.

Glou. He hath been out nine years, and away he shall again. The king is coming.

Sennet. Enter KING LEAR, CORNWALL, ALBANY, GONERIL, REGAN, CORDELIA, *and* Attendants.

Lear. Attend the lords of France and Burgundy, Gloucester.

Glou. I shall, my lord. *Exit* [*with Edmund*].

Lear. Meantime we shall express our darker purpose.
Give me the map there. Know that we have divided
In three our kingdom: and 'tis our fast intent
To shake all cares and business from our age;
Conferring them on younger strengths, while we
Unburthen'd crawl toward death. Our son of Cornwall,
And you, our no less loving son of Albany,
We have this hour a constant will to publish
Our daughters' several dowers, that future strife
May be prevented now. The princes, France and Burgundy,
Great rivals in our youngest daughter's love,
Long in our court have made their amorous sojourn,
And here are to be answer'd. Tell me, my daughters,—
Since now we will divest us, both of rule,
Interest of territory, cares of state,—
Which of you shall we say doth love us most?
That we our largest bounty may extend
Where nature doth with merit challenge. Goneril,
Our eldest-born, speak first.

Gon. Sir, I love you more than word can wield the matter;
Dearer than eye-sight, space, and liberty;
Beyond what can be valued, rich or rare;
No less than life, with grace, health, beauty, honour;
As much as child e'er lov'd, or father found;
A love that makes breath poor, and speech unable;
Beyond all manner of so much I love you.

Cor. [*Aside*] What shall Cordelia speak? Love, and be silent.

Lear. Of all these bounds, even from this line to this,
With shadowy forests and with champains rich'd,
With plenteous rivers and wide-skirted meads,
We make thee lady: to thine and Albany's issue
Be this perpetual. What says our second daughter,
Our dearest Regan, wife of Cornwall? Speak.

Reg. Sir, I am made
Of that self mettle as my sister,
And prize me at her worth. In my true heart
I find she names my very deed of love;
Only she comes too short: that I profess
Myself an enemy to all other joys,

ACT I. SCENE I. 5. **equalities,** equivalences (in the lands assigned). 6. **curiosity,** nicety, close scrutiny. 11. **brazed,** hardened. 39. **fast intent,** firm intention. 44. **constant,** fixed. 54. **Where . . . challenge,** where both natural affection and merit claim it as due. 56. **wield the matter,** avail in expressing. 64. **bounds.** The division of Lear's kingdom seems to be a traditional one; it appears also in *1 Henry IV*, III, i, 70 ff. 65. **shadowy,** shady. **champains,** plains. 73. **deed of love,** love in very deed. 74. **that,** in that.

Which the most precious square of sense possesses;
And find I am alone felicitate
In your dear highness' love.
Cor. [*Aside*] Then poor Cordelia!
And yet not so; since, I am sure, my love 's
More ponderous than my tongue.
Lear. To thee and thine hereditary ever
Remain this ample third of our fair kingdom;
No less in space, validity, and pleasure,
Than that conferr'd on Goneril. Now, our joy,
Although our last and least; to whose young love
The vines of France and milk of Burgundy
Strive to be interess'd; what can you say to draw
A third more opulent than your sisters? Speak.
Cor. Nothing, my lord.
Lear. Nothing!
Cor. Nothing.
Lear. Nothing will come of nothing: speak again.
Cor. Unhappy that I am, I cannot heave
My heart into my mouth: I love your majesty
According to my bond; no more nor less.
Lear. How, how, Cordelia! mend your speech a little,
Lest you may mar your fortunes.
Cor. Good my lord,
You have begot me, bred me, lov'd me: I
Return those duties back as are right fit,
Obey you, love you, and most honour you.
Why have my sisters husbands, if they say
They love you all? Haply, when I shall wed,
That lord whose hand must take my plight shall carry
Half my love with him, half my care and duty:
Sure, I shall never marry like my sisters,
To love my father all.
Lear. But goes thy heart with this?
Cor. Ay, my good lord.
Lear. So young, and so untender?
Cor. So young, my lord, and true.
Lear. Let it be so; thy truth, then, be thy dower.
For, by the sacred radiance of the sun,
The mysteries of Hecate, and the night;
By all the operation of the orbs
From whom we do exist, and cease to be;
Here I disclaim all my paternal care,
Propinquity and property of blood,
And as a stranger to my heart and me
Hold thee, from this, for ever. The barbarous Scythian,
Or he that makes his generation messes
To gorge his appetite, shall to my bosom
Be as well neighbour'd, pitied, and reliev'd,
As thou my sometime daughter.
Kent. Good my liege,—
Lear. Peace, Kent!
Come not between the dragon and his wrath.
I lov'd her most, and thought to set my rest
On her kind nursery. Hence, and avoid my sight!
So be my grave my peace, as here I give
Her father's heart from her! Call France; who stirs?
Call Burgundy. Cornwall and Albany,
With my two daughters' dowers digest this third:
Let pride, which she calls plainness, marry her.
I do invest you jointly with my power,
Pre-eminence, and all the large effects
That troop with majesty. Ourself, by monthly course,
With reservation of an hundred knights,
By you to be sustain'd, shall our abode
Make with you by due turns. Only we shall retain
The name, and all th' addition to a king;
The sway, revenue, execution of the rest,
Beloved sons, be yours: which to confirm,
This coronet part between you.
Kent. Royal Lear,
Whom I have ever honour'd as my king,
Lov'd as my father, as my master follow'd,
As my great patron thought on in my prayers,—
Lear. The bow is bent and drawn, make from the shaft.
Kent. Let it fall rather, though the fork invade
The region of my heart: be Kent unmannerly,
When Lear is mad. What wouldst thou do, old man?
Think'st thou that duty shall have dread to speak,
When power to flattery bows? To plainness honour 's bound,
When majesty falls to folly. Reserve thy state,
And, in thy best consideration, check
This hideous rashness: answer my life my judgement,
Thy youngest daughter does not love thee least;
Nor are those empty-hearted whose low sounds
Reverb no hollowness.
Lear. Kent, on thy life, no more.
Kent. My life I never held but as a pawn
To wage against thine enemies; nor fear to lose it,
Thy safety being motive.
Lear. Out of my sight!
Kent. See better, Lear; and let me still remain
The true blank of thine eye.
Lear. Now, by Apollo,—
Kent. Now, by Apollo, king,
Thou swear'st thy gods in vain.
Lear. O, vassal! miscreant!
[*Laying his hand on his sword.*]
Alb., *Corn.* Dear sir, forbear.
Kent. Do;
Kill thy physician, and the fee bestow
Upon thy foul disease. Revoke thy gift;
Or, whilst I can vent clamour from my throat,
I'll tell thee thou dost evil.
Lear. Hear me, recreant!
On thine allegiance, hear me!
That thou hast sought to make us break our vows,
Which we durst never yet, and with strain'd pride
To come betwixt our sentence and our power,
Which nor our nature nor our place can bear,
Our potency made good, take thy reward.
Five days we do allot thee, for provision
To shield thee from disasters of the world;
And on the sixth to turn thy hated back
Upon our kingdom: if, on the tenth day following,

76. **square of sense,** criterion of the senses. 77. **felicitate,** made happy. 83. **validity,** value. 85. **least,** smallest. 86. **vines,** vineyards. **milk,** pastures. 87. **to be interess'd,** to a right in. 95. **bond,** duty, obligation. 102. **Haply,** perhaps. 103. **plight,** pledge. 112. **Hecate,** goddess of witchcraft. 118. **this,** this time forth. **Scythian,** typical of barbarity from the time of Herodotus. 119. **makes . . . messes,** makes meals of his children. 125. **set my rest,** repose myself; a phrase from a game of cards meaning "to stake all." 126. **nursery,** nursing. 127. **So . . . peace, as,** let me rest peacefully in my grave, only as. 133. **effects,** outward shows. 141. **coronet,** i.e., the crown intended for Cordelia. 145. **make from,** get out of the way of. 146. **fall,** strike. **fork,** barbed head of an arrow. 150-151. **To . . . folly.** Allegiance demands frankness when kingship stoops to folly. 151. **Reserve thy state,** retain your royal authority. 153. **answer my life,** let my life answer. 157. **pawn,** stake, wager. 158. **wage,** hazard, wager. 161. **blank,** white center of the target. 162. **by Apollo.** The play of *King*

Thy banish'd trunk be found in our dominions,
The moment is thy death. Away! by Jupiter,
This shall not be revok'd.
Kent. Fare thee well, king: sith thus thou wilt appear,
Freedom lives hence, and banishment is here.
[*To Cordelia*] The gods to their dear shelter take thee, maid,
That justly think'st, and hast most rightly said!
[*To Regan and Goneril*] And your large speeches may your deeds approve,
That good effects may spring from words of love.
Thus Kent, O princes, bids you all adieu;
He'll shape his old course in a country new. *Exit.*

Flourish. Enter GLOUCESTER, *with* FRANCE *and* BURGUNDY; Attendants.

Glou. Here's France and Burgundy, my noble lord.
Lear. My lord of Burgundy,
We first address toward you, who with this king
Hath rivall'd for our daughter: what, in the least,
Will you require in present dower with her,
Or cease your quest of love?
Bur. Most royal majesty,
I crave no more than hath your highness offer'd,
Nor will you tender less.
Lear. Right noble Burgundy,
When she was dear to us, we did hold her so;
But now her price is fall'n. Sir, there she stands:
If aught within that little seeming substance,
Or all of it, with our displeasure piec'd,
And nothing more, may fitly like your grace,
She 's there, and she is yours.
Bur. I know no answer.
Lear. Will you, with those infirmities she owes,
Unfriended, new-adopted to our hate,
Dow'r'd with our curse, and stranger'd with our oath,
Take her, or leave her?
Bur. Pardon me, royal sir;
Election makes not up on such conditions.
Lear. Then leave her, sir; for, by the pow'r that made me,
I tell you all her wealth. [*To France*] For you, great king,
I would not from your love make such a stray,
To match you where I hate; therefore beseech you
T' avert your liking a more worthier way
Than on a wretch whom nature is asham'd
Almost t' acknowledge hers.
France. This is most strange,
That she, whom even but now was your best object,
The argument of your praise, balm of your age,
The best, the dearest, should in this trice of time
Commit a thing so monstrous, to dismantle
So many folds of favour. Sure, her offence
Must be of such unnatural degree,
That monsters it, or your fore-vouch'd affection
Fall'n into taint: which to believe of her,
Must be a faith that reason without miracle
Should never plant in me.
Cor. I yet beseech your majesty,—
If for I want that glib and oily art,
To speak and purpose not; since what I well intend,
I'll do 't before I speak,—that you make known
It is no vicious blot, murder, or foulness,
No unchaste action, or dishonoured step,
That hath depriv'd me of your grace and favour;
But even for want of that for which I am richer,
A still-soliciting eye, and such a tongue
As I am glad I have not, though not to have it
Hath lost me in your liking.
Lear. Better thou
Hadst not been born than not t' have pleas'd me better.
France. Is it but this,—a tardiness in nature
Which often leaves the history unspoke
That it intends to do? My lord of Burgundy,
What say you to the lady? Love 's not love
When it is mingled with regards that stands
Aloof from th' entire point. Will you have her?
She is herself a dowry.
Bur. Royal king,
Give but that portion which yourself propos'd,
And here I take Cordelia by the hand,
Duchess of Burgundy.
Lear. Nothing: I have sworn; I am firm.
Bur. I am sorry, then, you have so lost a father
That you must lose a husband.
Cor. Peace be with Burgundy!
Since that respects of fortune are his love,
I shall not be his wife.
France. Fairest Cordelia, that art most rich, being poor;
Most choice, forsaken; and most lov'd, despis'd!
Thee and thy virtues here I seize upon:
Be it lawful I take up what 's cast away.
Gods, gods! 'tis strange that from their cold'st neglect
My love should kindle to inflam'd respect.
Thy dow'rless daughter, king, thrown to my chance,
Is queen of us, of ours, and our fair France:
Not all the dukes of wat'rish Burgundy
Can buy this unpriz'd precious maid of me.
Bid them farewell, Cordelia, though unkind:
Thou losest here, a better where to find.
Lear. Thou hast her, France: let her be thine; for we
Have no such daughter, nor shall ever see
That face of hers again. Therefore be gone
Without our grace, our love, our benison.
Come, noble Burgundy.
Flourish. Exeunt [*all but France, Goneril, Regan, and Cordelia*].
France. Bid farewell to your sisters.
Cor. The jewels of our father, with wash'd eyes
Cordelia leaves you: I know you what you are;
And like a sister am most loath to call
Your faults as they are nam'd. Love well our father:
To your professed bosoms I commit him:
But yet, alas, stood I within his grace,
I would prefer him to a better place.
So, farewell to you both.

Lear is rather carefully pagan in all its externals. 172. **strain'd,** excessive. 175. **Our potency made good,** our authority being maintained. 180. **trunk,** body. 193. **address,** address ourself. 201. **seeming,** probably, specious, insincere; taken also with *little* to mean "seemingly small." 202. **piec'd,** added. 207. **stranger'd,** estranged. 209. **Election . . . conditions,** no choice is possible under such conditions. 212. **make such a stray,** stray so far. 218. **argument,** theme. 223. **monsters,** makes monstrous. **fore-vouch'd,** hitherto affirmed. 224. **taint,** decay. 234. **still-soliciting,** ever-begging. 242. **regards,** considerations. 261. **wat'rish,** well-watered (with rivers); used contemptuously, water being the symbol of fickleness. 262. **unpriz'd,** not appreciated or priceless. 264. **here . . . where,** used as nouns. 275. **professed,** i.e., full of professions (avowals).

Reg. Prescribe not us our duty.
Gon. Let your study
Be to content your lord, who hath receiv'd you
At fortune's alms. You have obedience scanted,
And well are worth the want that you have wanted.
Cor. Time shall unfold what plighted cunning hides:
Who covers faults, at last shame them derides.
Well may you prosper!
France. Come, my fair Cordelia.
Exeunt France and Cordelia.

Gon. Sister, it is not little I have to say of what most nearly appertains to us both. I think our father will hence to-night.

Reg. That 's most certain, and with you; next month with us.

Gon. You see how full of changes his age is; the observation we have made of it hath not been little: he always loved our sister most; and with what poor judgement he hath now cast her off appears too grossly.

Reg. 'Tis the infirmity of his age: yet he hath ever but slenderly known himself.

Gon. The best and soundest of his time hath been but rash; then must we look from his age to receive not alone the imperfections of long-engraffed condition, but therewithal the unruly waywardness that infirm and choleric years bring with them.

Reg. Such unconstant starts are we like to have from him as this of Kent's banishment.

Gon. There is further compliment of leave-taking between France and him. Pray you, let us hit together: if our father carry authority with such disposition as he bears, this last surrender of his will but offend us.

Reg. We shall further think of it.

Gon. We must do something, and i' the heat. *Exeunt.*

SCENE II. [*The Earl of Gloucester's castle.*]

Enter Bastard [EDMUND, *with a letter*].

Edm. Thou, nature, art my goddess; to thy law
My services are bound. Wherefore should I
Stand in the plague of custom, and permit
The curiosity of nations to deprive me,
For that I am some twelve or fourteen moonshines
Lag of a brother? Why bastard? wherefore base?
When my dimensions are as well compact,
My mind as generous, and my shape as true,
As honest madam's issue? Why brand they us
With base? with baseness? bastardy? base, base?
Who, in the lusty stealth of nature, take
More composition and fierce quality
Than doth, within a dull, stale, tired bed,
Go to th' creating a whole tribe of fops,
Got 'tween asleep and wake? Well, then,
Legitimate Edgar, I must have your land:
Our father's love is to the bastard Edmund
As to th' legitimate: fine word,—legitimate!
Well, my legitimate, if this letter speed,
And my invention thrive, Edmund the base
Shall top th' legitimate. I grow; I prosper:
Now, gods, stand up for bastards!

Enter GLOUCESTER.

Glou. Kent banish'd thus! and France in choler parted!
And the king gone to-night! prescrib'd his pow'r!
Confin'd to exhibition! All this done
Upon the gad! Edmund, how now! what news?
Edm. So please your lordship, none.
[*Putting up the letter.*]
Glou. Why so earnestly seek you to put up that letter?
Edm. I know no news, my lord.
Glou. What paper were you reading?
Edm. Nothing, my lord.

Glou. No? What needed, then, that terrible dispatch of it into your pocket? the quality of nothing hath not such need to hide itself. Let 's see: come, if it be nothing, I shall not need spectacles.

Edm. I beseech you, sir, pardon me: it is a letter from my brother, that I have not all o'er-read; and for so much as I have perused, I find it not fit for your o'er-looking.

Glou. Give me the letter, sir.

Edm. I shall offend, either to detain or give it. The contents, as in part I understand them, are to blame.

Glou. Let 's see, let 's see.

Edm. I hope, for my brother's justification, he wrote this but as an essay or taste of my virtue.

Glou. (*Reads*) 'This policy and reverence of age makes the world bitter to the best of our times; keeps our fortunes from us till our oldness cannot relish them. I begin to find an idle and fond bondage in the oppression of aged tyranny; who sways, not as it hath power, but as it is suffered. Come to me, that of this I may speak more. If our father would sleep till I waked him, you should enjoy half his revenue for ever, and live the beloved of your brother,

EDGAR.'

Hum—conspiracy!—'Sleep till I waked him,—you should enjoy half his revenue,'—My son Edgar! Had he a hand to write this? a heart and brain to breed it in?—When came this to you? who brought it?

Edm. It was not brought me, my lord; there 's the cunning of it; I found it thrown in at the casement of my closet.

Glou. You know the character to be your brother's?

Edm. If the matter were good, my lord, I durst swear it were his; but, in respect of that, I would fain think it were not.

Glou. It is his.

Edm. It is his hand, my lord; but I hope his heart is not in the contents.

281. **At,** i.e., priced at. 282. **well . . . wanted,** well deserve the lack of affection which you yourself have shown; *want* may, however, refer to her dowry. 283. **plighted,** pleated, enfolded. 295. **grossly,** obviously. 298. **time,** lifetime. 301. **long-engraffed condition,** long-implanted habit. 308. **hit,** agree. 310. **offend,** harm, injure. 312. **i' the heat,** i.e., while the iron is hot.

SCENE II. 1. **nature,** i.e., the material world, governed by mechanistic forces rather than by divine hierarchy. 3. **plague,** vexatious injustice. Warburton suggested *plage* meaning "place," "boundary." 4. **curiosity,** nicety, fastidiousness. 5. **moonshines,** months. 6. **Lag of,** later than. 7. **dimensions,** bodily parts or proportions. **compact,** knit together. 8. **generous,** befitting a nobleman. 12. **composition,** completeness. 15. **Got,** begotten. 24. **prescrib'd,** limited. 25. **exhibition,** allowance. 26. **Upon the gad,** suddenly, as if pricked by a gad. 32. **terrible,** terrified. 47. **essay,** assay, trial. 48. **policy and reverence of,** i.e., policy of reverencing; hendiadys, a construction common in *King Lear*. 65. **closet,** private room. 77. **declined,** having become feeble. 82. **detested,** detestable. 89. **where,** whereas.

Glou. Has he never before sounded you in this business?

Edm. Never, my lord: but I have heard him oft maintain it to be fit, that, sons at perfect age, and fathers declined, the father should be as ward to the son, and the son manage his revenue.

Glou. O villain, villain! His very opinion in the letter! Abhorred villain! Unnatural, detested, brutish villain! worse than brutish! Go, sirrah, seek him; I'll apprehend him: abominable villain! Where is he?

Edm. I do not well know, my lord. If it shall please you to suspend your indignation against my brother till you can derive from him better testimony of his intent, you should run a certain course; where, if you violently proceed against him, mistaking his purpose, it would make a great gap in your own honour, and shake in pieces the heart of his obedience. I dare pawn down my life for him, that he hath writ this to feel my affection to your honour, and to no other pretence of danger.

Glou. Think you so?

Edm. If your honour judge it meet, I will place you where you shall hear us confer of this, and by an auricular assurance have your satisfaction; and that without any further delay than this very evening.

Glou. He cannot be such a monster—

Edm. Nor is not, sure.

Glou. To his father, that so tenderly and entirely loves him. Heaven and earth! Edmund, seek him out; wind me into him, I pray you: frame the business after your own wisdom. I would unstate myself, to be in a due resolution.

Edm. I will seek him, sir, presently; convey the business as I shall find means, and acquaint you withal.

Glou. These late eclipses in the sun and moon portend no good to us: though the wisdom of nature can reason it thus and thus, yet nature finds itself scourged by the sequent effects: love cools, friendship falls off, brothers divide: in cities, mutinies; in countries, discord; in palaces, treason; and the bond cracked 'twixt son and father. This villain of mine comes under the prediction; there 's son against father: the king falls from bias of nature; there 's father against child. We have seen the best of our time: machinations, hollowness, treachery, and all ruinous disorders, follow us disquietly to our graves. Find out this villain, Edmund; it shall lose thee nothing; do it carefully. And the noble and true-hearted Kent banished! his offence, honesty! 'Tis strange. *Exit.*

Edm. This is the excellent foppery of the world, that, when we are sick in fortune,—often the surfeits of our own behaviour,—we make guilty of our disasters the sun, the moon, and stars: as if we were villains on necessity; fools by heavenly compulsion; knaves, thieves, and treachers, by spherical predominance; drunkards, liars, and adulterers, by an enforced obedience of planetary influence; and all that we are evil in, by a divine thrusting on: an admirable evasion of whoremaster man, to lay his goatish disposition on the charge of a star! My father compounded with my mother under the Dragon's Tail; and my nativity was under Ursa Major; so that it follows, I am rough and lecherous. Fut, I should have been that I am, had the maidenliest star in the firmament twinkled on my bastardizing. Edgar—

Enter EDGAR.

and pat he comes like the catastrophe of the old comedy: my cue is villanous melancholy, with a sigh like Tom o' Bedlam. O, these eclipses do portend these divisions! fa, sol, la, mi.

Edg. How now, brother Edmund! what serious contemplation are you in?

Edm. I am thinking, brother, of a prediction I read this other day, what should follow these eclipses.

Edg. Do you busy yourself with that?

Edm. I promise you, the effects he writes of succeed unhappily; as of unnaturalness between the child and the parent; death, dearth, dissolutions of ancient amities; divisions in state, menaces and maledictions against king and nobles; needless diffidences, banishment of friends, dissipation of cohorts, nuptial breaches, and I know not what.

Edg. How long have you been a sectary astronomical?

Edm. Come, come; when saw you my father last?

Edg. Why, the night gone by.

Edm. Spake you with him?

Edg. Ay, two hours together.

Edm. Parted you in good terms? Found you no displeasure in him by word nor countenance?

Edg. None at all.

Edm. Bethink yourself wherein you may have offended him: and at my entreaty forbear his presence until some little time hath qualified the heat of his displeasure; which at this instant so rageth in him, that with the mischief of your person it would scarcely allay.

Edg. Some villain hath done me wrong.

Edm. That 's my fear. I pray you, have a continent forbearance till the speed of his rage goes slower; and, as I say, retire with me to my lodging, from whence I will fitly bring you to hear my lord speak: pray ye, go; there 's my key: if you do stir abroad, go armed.

Edg. Armed, brother!

Edm. Brother, I advise you to the best; go armed: I am no honest man if there be any good meaning toward you: I have told you what I have seen and heard; but faintly, nothing like the image and horror of it: pray you, away.

Edg. Shall I hear from you anon?

Edm. I do serve you in this business. *Exit* [*Edgar*].

A credulous father! and a brother noble,
Whose nature is so far from doing harms,

95. **pretence,** intention, purpose. 106. **wind me into him,** insinuate yourself into his confidence; *me* is an ethical dative. 108. **unstate myself,** give up my position and dignity. **due resolution,** actual certainty. 109. **convey,** manage with secrecy. 112-127. **These . . . strange.** The fact that there were eclipses of the sun and moon in the autumn of 1605 has been regarded as an indication of the date of the play; also the references to discord, mutinies, and treason have been thought to refer to the Gunpowder Plot (Nov. 5, 1605). 114. **wisdom of nature,** natural science. 115. **sequent,** consequent, following.

128. **foppery,** foolishness. 131. **disasters,** unfavorable aspects. 134. **treachers,** traitors. **spherical predominance,** ascendancy of planets. Edmund's denial of planetary influence must be set down as a sort of religious infidelity. 145. **catastrophe,** conclusion. 148. **Tom o' Bedlam.** See II, iii, 14, note below. 157. **succeed,** come to pass. 161. **diffidences,** distrust of others. 162. **dissipation of cohorts,** the falling away of supporters. 164. **sectary astronomical,** student of astrology. 175. **qualified,** moderated. 178. **mischief of,** harm to. 179. **allay,** be allayed. 182. **continent,** restraining.

That he suspects none; on whose foolish honesty
My practices ride easy! I see the business.
Let me, if not by birth, have lands by wit:
All with me 's meet that I can fashion fit. *Exit.*

SCENE III. [*The Duke of Albany's palace.*]

Enter GONERIL, *and* [OSWALD, *her*] *steward.*

Gon. Did my father strike my gentleman for chiding of his fool?
Osw. Yes, madam.
Gon. By day and night he wrongs me; every hour
He flashes into one gross crime or other,
That sets us all at odds: I'll not endure it:
His knights grow riotous, and himself upbraids us
On every trifle. When he returns from hunting,
I will not speak with him; say I am sick:
If you come slack of former services,
You shall do well; the fault of it I'll answer.
Osw. He 's coming, madam; I hear him.
[*Horns within.*]
Gon. Put on what weary negligence you please,
You and your fellows; I 'ld have it come to question:
If he distaste it, let him to my sister,
Whose mind and mine, I know, in that are one,
Not to be over-rul'd. Idle old man,
That still would manage those authorities
That he hath given away! Now, by my life,
Old fools are babes again; and must be us'd
With checks as flatteries,—when they are seen abus'd.
Remember what I have said.
Osw. Well, madam.
Gon. And let his knights have colder looks among you;
What grows of it, no matter; advise your fellows so:
I would breed from hence occasions, and I shall
That I may speak: I'll write straight to my sister,
To hold my very course. Prepare for dinner. *Exeunt.*

SCENE IV. [*A hall in the same.*]

Enter KENT [*disguised*].

Kent. If but as well I other accents borrow,
That can my speech defuse, my good intent
May carry through itself to that full issue
For which I raz'd my likeness. Now, banish'd Kent,
If thou canst serve where thou dost stand condemn'd,
So may it come, thy master, whom thou lov'st,
Shall find thee full of labours.

Horns within. Enter LEAR, [Knights,] *and* Attendants.

Lear. Let me not stay a jot for dinner; go get it ready. [*Exit an Attendant.*] How now! what art thou?

Kent. A man, sir.

Lear. What dost thou profess? what wouldst thou with us?

Kent. I do profess to be no less than I seem; to serve him truly that will put me in trust; to love him that is honest; to converse with him that is wise, and says little; to fear judgement; to fight when I cannot choose; and to eat no fish.

Lear. What art thou?

Kent. A very honest-hearted fellow, and as poor as the king.

Lear. If thou be'st as poor for a subject as he 's for a king, thou art poor enough. What wouldst thou?

Kent. Service.

Lear. Who wouldst thou serve?

Kent. You.

Lear. Dost thou know me, fellow?

Kent. No, sir; but you have that in your countenance which I would fain call master.

Lear. What 's that?

Kent. Authority.

Lear. What services canst thou do?

Kent. I can keep honest counsel, ride, run, mar a curious tale in telling it, and deliver a plain message bluntly: that which ordinary men are fit for, I am qualified in; and the best of me is diligence.

Lear. How old art thou?

Kent. Not so young, sir, to love a woman for singing, nor so old to dote on her for any thing: I have years on my back forty eight.

Lear. Follow me; thou shalt serve me: if I like thee no worse after dinner, I will not part from thee yet. Dinner, ho, dinner! Where 's my knave? my fool? Go you, and call my fool hither. [*Exit an Attendant.*]

Enter Steward [OSWALD].

You, you, sirrah, where 's my daughter?

Osw. So please you,— *Exit.*

Lear. What says the fellow there? Call the clotpoll back. [*Exit a Knight.*] Where 's my fool, ho? I think the world 's asleep.

[*Enter* Knight.]

How now! where 's that mongrel?

Knight. He says, my lord, your daughter is not well.

Lear. Why came not the slave back to me when I called him?

Knight. Sir, he answered me in the roundest manner, he would not.

Lear. He would not!

Knight. My lord, I know not what the matter is; but, to my judgement, your highness is not entertained with that ceremonious affection as you were wont; there 's a great abatement of kindness appears as well in the general dependants as in the duke himself also and your daughter.

Lear. Ha! sayest thou so?

Knight. I beseech you, pardon me, my lord, if I be mistaken; for my duty cannot be silent when I think your highness wronged.

Lear. Thou but rememberest me of mine own conception: I have perceived a most faint neglect of late; which I have rather blamed as mine own jealous

SCENE III. 14. **distaste,** dislike. 16. **Idle,** foolish, silly. 20. **With . . . abus'd,** with rebukes instead of flattery, when they (old men) act unselfknowingly (as Lear does). 24-25. **I would . . . speak,** I wish to create incidents from this sort of thing, and thus give me the opportunity to speak to Lear.

SCENE IV. 2. **defuse,** confuse; hence, disguise. 4. **raz'd,** erased. 12. **What . . . profess?** What is thy profession? 16. **judgement,** i.e., God's judgment. 18. **eat no fish.** Warburton's explanation is usually followed: Roman Catholics, who observed the custom of eating fish on Fridays, were thought of as enemies of the government. 51. **clotpoll,** blockhead. 72. **rememberest,** remindest. 74. **faint,** slight, or indifferent, half-hearted. 75. **jealous curiosity,** overscrupulous regard for minutiae. 76. **very pretence,** true intention, purpose. 92. **bandy,** strike a ball to and fro, as in tennis; here figurative, give and take. 95. **foot-ball player.** Football was a rough, dangerous, public sport without organization or officials, and under statutory ban; it was played in the curiosity than as a very pretence and purpose of unkindness: I will look further into 't. But where 's my fool? I have not seen him this two days.

Knight. Since my young lady 's going into France, sir, the fool hath much pined away.

Lear. No more of that; I have noted it well. Go you, and tell my daughter I would speak with her. [*Exit an Attendant*.] Go you, call hither my fool.

[*Exit an Attendant*.]

Enter Steward [Oswald].

O, you sir, you, come you hither, sir: who am I, sir?

Osw. My lady's father.

Lear. 'My lady's father'! my lord's knave: you whoreson dog! you slave! you cur!

Osw. I am none of these, my lord; I beseech your pardon.

Lear. Do you bandy looks with me, you rascal? [*Striking him*.]

Osw. I'll not be strucken, my lord.

Kent. Nor tripped neither, you base foot-ball player. [*Tripping up his heels*.]

Lear. I thank thee, fellow; thou servest me, and I'll love thee.

Kent. Come, sir, arise, away! I'll teach you differences: away, away! If you will measure your lubber's length again, tarry: but away! go to; have you wisdom? so. [*Pushes Oswald out*.]

Lear. Now, my friendly knave, I thank thee: there 's earnest of thy service. [*Giving Kent money*.]

Enter Fool.

Fool. Let me hire him too: here 's my coxcomb. [*Offering Kent his cap*.]

Lear. How now, my pretty knave! how dost thou?

Fool. Sirrah, you were best take my coxcomb.

Kent. Why, fool?

Fool. Why, for taking one's part that 's out of favour: nay, an thou canst not smile as the wind sits, thou 'lt catch cold shortly: there, take my coxcomb: why, this fellow has banished two on 's daughters, and did the third a blessing against his will; if thou follow him, thou must needs wear my coxcomb. How now, nuncle! Would I had two coxcombs and two daughters!

Lear. Why, my boy?

Fool. If I gave them all my living, I 'ld keep my coxcombs myself. There 's mine; beg another of thy daughters.

Lear. Take heed, sirrah; the whip.

Fool. Truth 's a dog must to kennel; he must be whipped out, when Lady the brach may stand by the fire and stink.

Lear. A pestilent gall to me!

Fool. Sirrah, I'll teach thee a speech.

Lear. Do.

Fool. Mark it, nuncle:

Have more than thou showest,
Speak less than thou knowest,
Lend less than thou owest,
Ride more than thou goest,
Learn more than thou trowest,
Set less than thou throwest;
Leave thy drink and thy whore,
And keep in-a-door,
And thou shalt have more
Than two tens to a score.

Kent. This is nothing, fool.

Fool. Then 'tis like the breath of an unfee'd lawyer; you gave me nothing for 't. Can you make no use of nothing, nuncle?

Lear. Why, no, boy; nothing can be made out of nothing.

Fool. [*To Kent*] Prithee, tell him, so much the rent of his land comes to: he will not believe a fool.

Lear. A bitter fool!

Fool. Dost thou know the difference, my boy, between a bitter fool and a sweet one?

Lear. No, lad; teach me.

Fool. That lord that counsell'd thee
To give away thy land,
Come place him here by me,
Do thou for him stand:
The sweet and bitter fool
Will presently appear;
The one in motley here,
The other found out there.

Lear. Dost thou call me fool, boy?

Fool. All thy other titles thou hast given away; that thou wast born with.

Kent. This is not altogether fool, my lord.

Fool. No, faith, lords and great men will not let me; if I had a monopoly out, they would have part on 't: and ladies too, they will not let me have all the fool to myself; they'll be snatching. Give me an egg, nuncle, and I'll give thee two crowns.

Lear. What two crowns shall they be?

Fool. Why, after I have cut the egg i' the middle, and eat up the meat, the two crowns of the egg. When thou clovest thy crown i' the middle, and gavest away both parts, thou borest thine ass on thy back o'er the dirt: thou hadst little wit in thy bald crown, when thou gavest thy golden one away. If I speak like myself in this, let him be whipped that first finds it so.

[*Singing*] Fools had ne'er less grace in a year;
For wise men are grown foppish,
And know not how their wits to wear,
Their manners are so apish.

Lear. When were you wont to be so full of songs, sirrah?

Fool. I have used it, nuncle, e'er since thou madest thy daughters thy mothers: for when thou gavest them the rod, and put'st down thine own breeches,

[*Singing*] Then they for sudden joy did weep,
And I for sorrow sung,
That such a king should play bo-peep,
And go the fools among.

Prithee, nuncle, keep a schoolmaster that can teach thy fool to lie: I would fain learn to lie.

streets by the rowdiest element of the population. 97. **differences,** distinctions in rank. 105. **coxcomb,** fool's cap. 112. **smile . . . sits,** i.e., play along with those in power. 115. **banished,** i.e., alienated. 117. **nuncle,** contraction of "mine uncle," customary address of the licensed fool to his superior. 120. **living,** property. 125. **brach,** a female hound. 131. **showest,** seemest to have. 133. **owest,** ownest. 134. **goest,** i.e., on foot. 136. **Set . . . throwest,** stake less at dice than you have a chance to throw, i.e., don't bet all you can. 138. **in-a-door,** at home. 154. **That lord.** A lord, Skalliger, in the old play of *King Leir* is apparently referred to; no such advice is given to Lear in this play. 160. **motley,** the particolored dress of the fool. 167. **monopoly.** This allusion would be well understood, since the granting of monopolies by King James was a current abuse. **out,** taken out, granted. 179. **like myself,** i.e., like a fool. 181. **grace in a year,** favor at any time. 182. **foppish,** foolish. 191-194. **Then . . . among.** These lines, and probably others below, are no doubt taken from old songs.

Lear. An you lie, sirrah, we'll have you whipped.

Fool. I marvel what kin thou and thy daughters are: they'll have me whipped for speaking true, thou 'lt have me whipped for lying; and sometimes I am whipped for holding my peace. I had rather be any kind o' thing than a fool: and yet I would not be thee, nuncle; thou hast pared thy wit o' both sides, and left nothing i' the middle: here comes one o' the parings.

Enter GONERIL.

Lear. How now, daughter! what makes that frontlet on? Methinks you are too much of late i' the frown.

Fool. Thou wast a pretty fellow when thou hadst no need to care for her frowning; now thou art an O without a figure: I am better than thou art now; I am a fool, thou art nothing. [*To Gon.*] Yes, forsooth, I will hold my tongue; so your face bids me, though you say nothing. Mum, mum,

He that keeps nor crust nor crum,
Weary of all, shall want some.

[*Pointing to Lear*] That 's a sheal'd peascod.

Gon. Not only, sir, this your all-licens'd fool,
But other of your insolent retinue
Do hourly carp and quarrel; breaking forth
In rank and not-to-be-endured riots. Sir,
I had thought, by making this well known unto you,
To have found a safe redress; but now grow fearful,
By what yourself too late have spoke and done,
That you protect this course, and put it on
By your allowance; which if you should, the fault
Would not 'scape censure, nor the redresses sleep,
Which, in the tender of a wholesome weal,
Might in their working do you that offence,
Which else were shame, that then necessity
Will call discreet proceeding.

Fool. For, you know, nuncle,
The hedge-sparrow fed the cuckoo so long,
That it had it head bit off by it young.
So, out went the candle, and we were left darkling.

Lear. Are you our daughter?

Gon. Come, sir,
I would you would make use of your good wisdom,
Whereof I know you are fraught; and put away
These dispositions, which of late transport you
From what you rightly are.

Fool. May not an ass know when the cart draws the horse? Whoop, Jug! I love thee.

Lear. Does any here know me? This is not Lear:
Does Lear walk thus? speak thus? Where are his eyes?
Either his notion weakens, his discernings
Are lethargied—Ha! waking? 'tis not so.
Who is it that can tell me who I am?

Fool. Lear's shadow.

Lear. I would learn that; for, by the marks of sovereignty, knowledge, and reason, I should be false persuaded I had daughters.

Fool. Which they will make an obedient father.

Lear. Your name, fair gentlewoman?

Gon. This admiration, sir, is much o' th' savour
Of other your new pranks. I do beseech you
To understand my purposes aright:
As you are old and reverend, should be wise.
Here do you keep a hundred knights and squires;
Men so disorder'd, so debosh'd and bold,
That this our court, infected with their manners,
Shows like a riotous inn: epicurism and lust
Makes it more like a tavern or a brothel
Than a grac'd palace. The shame itself doth speak
For instant remedy: be then desir'd
By her, that else will take the thing she begs,
A little to disquantity your train;
And the remainders, that shall still depend,
To be such men as may besort your age,
Which know themselves and you.

Lear. Darkness and devils!
Saddle my horses; call my train together.
Degenerate bastard! I'll not trouble thee:
Yet have I left a daughter.

Gon. You strike my people; and your disorder'd rabble
Make servants of their betters.

Enter ALBANY.

Lear. Woe, that too late repents,—[*To Alb.*] O, sir, are you come?
Is it your will? Speak, sir. Prepare my horses.
Ingratitude, thou marble-hearted fiend,
More hideous when thou show'st thee in a child
Than the sea-monster!

Alb. Pray, sir, be patient.

Lear. [*To Gon.*] Detested kite! thou liest:
My train are men of choice and rarest parts,
That all particulars of duty know,
And in the most exact regard support
The worships of their name. O most small fault,
How ugly didst thou in Cordelia show!
Which, like an engine, wrench'd my frame of nature
From the fix'd place; drew from my heart all love,
And added to the gall. O Lear, Lear, Lear!
Beat at this gate, that let thy folly in, [*Striking his head.*]
And thy dear judgement out! Go, go, my people.

Alb. My lord, I am guiltless, as I am ignorant
Of what hath moved you.

Lear. It may be so, my lord.
Hear, nature, hear; dear goddess, hear!
Suspend thy purpose, if thou didst intend
To make this creature fruitful!
Into her womb convey sterility!
Dry up in her the organs of increase;
And from her derogate body never spring
A babe to honour her! If she must teem,
Create her child of spleen; that it may live,
And be a thwart disnatur'd torment to her!
Let it stamp wrinkles in her brow of youth;
With cadent tears fret channels in her cheeks;
Turn all her mother's pains and benefits
To laughter and contempt; that she may feel
How sharper than a serpent's tooth it is

208. **frontlet,** a band worn on the forehead; forehead; here, frowning visage. 212. **O without a figure,** cipher of no value unless joined to a figure. 219. **sheal'd peascod,** shelled pea pod. 221. **other,** others. 227. **put it on,** encourage it. 228. **allowance,** approval. 229. **redresses sleep,** punishment for the riotous conduct of Lear's attendants lie dormant. 230. **tender . . . weal,** preservation of the peace of the state. 232-233. **necessity . . . proceeding,** i.e., everyone will justify the action of chastisement as prudent under the circumstances. 236. **it.** The second and third *it's* are possessives. 237. **darkling,** in the dark. 241. **fraught,** filled. 245. **Whoop, Jug! I love thee,** regarded as a quotation from an old song; used by the Fool to cover up his impertinence. *Jug,* probably, Joan. 248. **notion,** intellectual power. 255. **Which,** whom. 258. **admiration,** wonderment. 263. **debosh'd,** debauched. 265. **epicurism,** luxury. 267. **grac'd,** honorable. 270. **disquantity,** diminish. 271. **depend,** be dependents. 272. **besort,** befit. 283. **sea-monster,** possible allusion to the hippopotamus, reputed in Egyptian mythology to be a monster of ingratitude; the whale has also been suggested. W. J. Craig suggests that no particular monster is

To have a thankless child! Away, away! *Exit.*
Alb. Now, gods that we adore, whereof comes this?
Gon. Never afflict yourself to know more of it;
But let his disposition have that scope
That dotage gives it.

Enter LEAR.

Lear. What, fifty of my followers at a clap!
Within a fortnight!
Alb. What 's the matter, sir?
Lear. I'll tell thee: [*To Gon.*] Life and death! I am asham'd
That thou hast power to shake my manhood thus;
That these hot tears, which break from me perforce,
Should make thee worth them. Blasts and fogs upon thee!
Th' untented woundings of a father's curse
Pierce every sense about thee! Old fond eyes,
Beweep this cause again, I'll pluck ye out,
And cast you, with the waters that you loose,
To temper clay. Yea, is it come to this?
Ha! Let it be so: I have another daughter,
Who, I am sure, is kind and comfortable:
When she shall hear this of thee, with her nails
She'll flay thy wolvish visage. Thou shalt find
That I'll resume the shape which thou dost think
I have cast off for ever: thou shalt, I warrant thee.
Exit [*Lear, with Kent, and Attendants*].
Gon. Do you mark that, my lord?
Alb. I cannot be so partial, Goneril,
To the great love I bear you,—
Gon. Pray you, content. What, Oswald, ho!
[*To the Fool*] You, sir, more knave than fool, after your master.
Fool. Nuncle Lear, nuncle Lear, tarry and take the fool with thee.

A fox, when one has caught her,
And such a daughter,
Should sure to the slaughter,
If my cap would buy a halter:
So the fool follows after. *Exit.*

Gon. This man hath had good counsel:—a hundred knights!
'Tis politic and safe to let him keep
At point a hundred knights: yes, that, on every dream,
Each buzz, each fancy, each complaint, dislike,
He may enguard his dotage with their pow'rs,
And hold our lives in mercy. Oswald, I say!
Alb. Well, you may fear too far.
Gon. Safer than trust too far:
Let me still take away the harms I fear,
Not fear still to be taken: I know his heart.
What he hath utter'd I have writ my sister:
If she sustain him and his hundred knights,
When I have show'd th' unfitness,—

Enter Steward [OSWALD].

How now, Oswald!
What, have you writ that letter to my sister?
Osw. Ay, madam.
Gon. Take you some company, and away to horse:
Inform her full of my particular fear;
And thereto add such reasons of your own
As may compact it more. Get you gone;
And hasten your return. [*Exit Oswald.*] No, no, my lord,
This milky gentleness and course of yours
Though I condemn not, yet, under pardon,
You are much more attask'd for want of wisdom
Than prais'd for harmful mildness.
Alb. How far your eyes may pierce I cannot tell:
Striving to better, oft we mar what 's well.
Gon. Nay, then—
Alb. Well, well; th' event. *Exeunt.*

[SCENE V. *Court before the same.*]

Enter LEAR, KENT, *and* Fool.

Lear. Go you before to Gloucester with these letters. Acquaint my daughter no further with any thing you know than comes from her demand out of the letter. If your diligence be not speedy, I shall be there afore you.

Kent. I will not sleep, my lord, till I have delivered your letter. *Exit.*

Fool. If a man's brains were in 's heels, were 't not in danger of kibes?

Lear. Ay, boy.

Fool. Then, I prithee, be merry; thy wit shall not go slip-shod.

Lear. Ha, ha, ha!

Fool. Shalt see thy other daughter will use thee kindly; for though she 's as like this as a crab 's like an apple, yet I can tell what I can tell.

Lear. What canst tell, boy?

Fool. She will taste as like this as a crab does to a crab. Thou canst tell why one's nose stands i' the middle on 's face?

Lear. No.

Fool. Why, to keep one's eyes of either side 's nose; that what a man cannot smell out, he may spy into.

Lear. I did her wrong—

Fool. Canst tell how an oyster makes his shell?

Lear. No.

Fool. Nor I neither; but I can tell why a snail has a house.

Lear. Why?

Fool. Why, to put 's head in; not to give it away to his daughters, and leave his horns without a case.

Lear. I will forget my nature. So kind a father! Be my horses ready?

Fool. Thy asses are gone about 'em. The reason why the seven stars are no moe than seven is a pretty reason.

Lear. Because they are not eight?

Fool. Yes, indeed: thou wouldst make a good fool.

meant, but that the allusion is to the monsters of classical mythology. 287. **in . . . regard,** with extreme care. 288. **worships,** honors. 290. **engine,** possibly machines for razing houses. 302. **derogate,** debased. 303. **teem,** increase. 305. **thwart,** contrary. **disnatur'd,** without natural affection. 307. **cadent,** falling. 322. **untented,** not cleansed with lint, and therefore liable to fester. 323. **fond,** foolish. 324. **Beweep,** if you weep for. 328. **comfortable,** willing to comfort. 347. **At point,** under arms. 348. **buzz,** idle rumor. 349. **enguard,** surround with a guard. 353. **taken,** overtaken (by the *harms*). 362. **compact,** confirm.

364. **This . . . yours,** the cowardly weakness of your course. 366. **attask'd,** taken to task, blamed. 371. **th' event,** time will show.

SCENE V. 9. **kibes,** chilblains, or ulcerated sores on the heels. 12. **slip-shod,** in slippers. There are no brains, thinks the Fool, in Lear's heels when they are on their way to visit Regan. 15. **kindly,** double sense: according to filial nature and according to her own nature. 16. **a crab 's . . . apple,** seems proverbial for "a crab-apple's an apple." 25. **her.** Lear again thinks of Cordelia. 38. **seven stars,** the Pleiades.

Lear. To take 't again perforce! Monster ingratitude!

Fool. If thou wert my fool, nuncle, I 'ld have thee beaten for being old before thy time.

Lear. How 's that?

Fool. Thou shouldst not have been old till thou hadst been wise.

Lear. O, let me not be mad, not mad, sweet heaven!
Keep me in temper: I would not be mad!

[*Enter*] Gentleman.

How now! are the horses ready?

Gent. Ready, my lord.

Lear. Come, boy.

Fool. She that 's a maid now, and laughs at my departure,
Shall not be a maid long, unless things be cut shorter.

Exeunt.

ACT II.

SCENE I. [*The Earl of Gloucester's castle.*]

Enter Bastard [EDMUND] *and* CURAN, *severally.*

Edm. Save thee, Curan.

Cur. And you, sir. I have been with your father, and given him notice that the Duke of Cornwall and Regan his duchess will be here with him this night.

Edm. How comes that?

Cur. Nay, I know not. You have heard of the news abroad; I mean the whispered ones, for they are yet but ear-kissing arguments?

Edm. Not I: pray you, what are they?

Cur. Have you heard of no likely wars toward, 'twixt the Dukes of Cornwall and Albany?

Edm. Not a word.

Cur. You may do, then, in time. Fare you well, sir.

Exit.

Edm. The duke be here to-night? The better! best!
This weaves itself perforce into my business.
My father hath set guard to take my brother;
And I have one thing, of a queasy question,
Which I must act: briefness and fortune, work!
Brother, a word; descend: brother, I say!

Enter EDGAR.

My father watches: O sir, fly this place;
Intelligence is given where you are hid;
You have now the good advantage of the night:
Have you not spoken 'gainst the Duke of Cornwall?
He 's coming hither; now, i' th' night, i' th' haste,
And Regan with him: have you nothing said
Upon his party 'gainst the Duke of Albany?
Advise yourself.

Edg. I am sure on 't, not a word.

Edm. I hear my father coming: pardon me;
In cunning I must draw my sword upon you:
Draw; seem to defend yourself; now quit you well.
Yield! come before my father!—Light, ho, here!
Fly, brother.—Torches, torches!—So, farewell.

Exit Edgar.

Some blood drawn on me would beget opinion [*Wounds his arm.*]
Of my more fierce endeavour: I have seen drunkards
Do more than this in sport. Father, father!
Stop, stop! No help?

Enter GLOUCESTER, *and* Servants *with torches.*

Glou. Now, Edmund, where 's the villain?

Edm. Here stood he in the dark, his sharp sword out,
Mumbling of wicked charms, conjuring the moon
To stand auspicious mistress,—

Glou. But where is he?

Edm. Look, sir, I bleed.

Glou. Where is the villain, Edmund?

Edm. Fled this way, sir. When by no means he could—

Glou. Pursue him, ho! Go after. [*Exeunt some Servants.*] By no means what?

Edm. Persuade me to the murder of your lordship;
But that I told him, the revenging gods
'Gainst parricides did all the thunder bend;
Spoke, with how manifold and strong a bond
The child was bound to th' father; sir, in fine,
Seeing how loathly opposite I stood
To his unnatural purpose, in fell motion,
With his prepared sword, he charges home
My unprovided body, latch'd mine arm:
But when he saw my best alarum'd spirits,
Bold in the quarrel's right, rous'd to th' encounter,
Or whether gasted by the noise I made,
Full suddenly he fled.

Glou. Let him fly far:
Not in this land shall he remain uncaught;
And found—dispatch. The noble duke my master,
My worthy arch and patron, comes to-night:
By his authority I will proclaim it,
That he which finds him shall deserve our thanks,
Bringing the murderous coward to the stake;
He that conceals him, death.

Edm. When I dissuaded him from his intent,
And found him pight to do it, with curst speech
I threaten'd to discover him: he replied,
'Thou unpossessing bastard! dost thou think,
If I would stand against thee, would the reposal
Of any trust, virtue, or worth in thee
Make thy words faith'd? No: what I should deny,—
As this I would; ay, though thou didst produce
My very character,—I 'ld turn it all
To thy suggestion, plot, and damned practice:
And thou must make a dullard of the world,
If they not thought the profits of my death
Were very pregnant and potential spirits

58. **cut shorter,** a bawdy joke addressed to the audience, implying universal carnality.

ACT II, SCENE I. 1. **Save thee,** i.e., God save thee. 8. **ear-kissing arguments,** lightly whispered topics. 19. **queasy question,** hazardous, or ticklish, nature. 20. **briefness,** promptitude. 28. **Upon his party 'gainst,** i.e., concerning Cornwall's feud with Albany. 29. **Advise yourself,** probably, recollect. 31. **cunning,** pretense. 32. **quit you.** acquit yourself. 35. **beget,** create (for me). 50. **fine,** conclusion, 51. **loathly opposite,** loathingly opposed. 52. **fell motion,** deadly thrust. 54. **latch'd,** wounded. 55. **best alarum'd,** thoroughly aroused to action as by a trumpet. 57. **gasted,** frightened. 60. **dispatch,** I will dispatch him. 61. **arch,** chief. 64. **stake,** an allusion to tying prisoners to a stake, or a figure from bearbaiting. 67. **pight,** determined. **curst,** angry. 69. **unpossessing,** unable to inherit, beggarly. 70. **I would,** I should. **reposal,** placing. 72. **faith'd,** believed. 74. **character,** written testimony. 75. **practice,** plot. 76. **make . . . world,** think the world an idiot. 77. **If . . . thought,** if they had not thought. 78. **pregnant,** teeming (with urgings). **potential spirits,** potent evil spirits. 79. **fast'ned,** confirmed. 80. **got,** begot. 99. **consort,** set, company. 101. **put . . . on,** incited him to. 102. **expense and waste,** squandering. 109. **bewray his practice,** expose Edgar's plot. 114. **in my strength,** by my power and authority. **For,** as for. 121. **threading,** passing

To make thee seek it.'
Glou. O strange and fast'ned villain!
Would he deny his letter, said he? I never got him.
Tucket within.
Hark, the duke's trumpets! I know not why he comes.
All ports I'll bar; the villain shall not 'scape;
The duke must grant me that: besides, his picture
I will send far and near, that all the kingdom
May have due note of him; and of my land,
Loyal and natural boy, I'll work the means
To make thee capable.

Enter CORNWALL, REGAN, *and* Attendants.

Corn. How now, my noble friend! since I came hither,
Which I can call but now, I have heard strange news.
Reg. If it be true, all vengeance comes too short
Which can pursue th' offender. How dost, my lord?
Glou. O, madam, my old heart is crack'd, it's crack'd!
Reg. What, did my father's godson seek your life?
He whom my father nam'd? your Edgar?
Glou. O, lady, lady, shame would have it hid!
Reg. Was he not companion with the riotous knights
That tended upon my father?
Glou. I know not, madam: 'tis too bad, too bad.
Edm. Yes, madam, he was of that consort.
Reg. No marvel, then, though he were ill affected:
'Tis they have put him on the old man's death,
To have th' expense and waste of his revenues.
I have this present evening from my sister
Been well inform'd of them; and with such cautions,
That if they come to sojourn at my house,
I'll not be there.
Corn. Nor I, assure thee, Regan.
Edmund, I hear that you have shown your father
A child-like office.
Edm. It was my duty, sir.
Glou. He did bewray his practice; and receiv'd
This hurt you see, striving to apprehend him.
Corn. Is he pursued?
Glou. Ay, my good lord.
Corn. If he be taken, he shall never more
Be fear'd of doing harm: make your own purpose,
How in my strength you please. For you, Edmund,
Whose virtue and obedience doth this instant
So much commend itself, you shall be ours:
Natures of such deep trust we shall much need;
You we first seize on.
Edm. I shall serve you, sir,
Truly, however else.
Glou. For him I thank your grace.
Corn. You know not why we came to visit you,—
Reg. Thus out of season, threading dark-ey'd night:
Occasions, noble Gloucester, of some prize,
Wherein we must have use of your advice:
Our father he hath writ, so hath our sister,
Of differences, which I least thought it fit
To answer from our home; the several messengers
From hence attend dispatch. Our good old friend,
Lay comforts to your bosom; and bestow
Your needful counsel to our businesses,
Which craves the instant use.
Glou. I serve you, madam:
Your graces are right welcome. *Exeunt. Flourish.*

SCENE II. [*Before Gloucester's castle.*]

Enter KENT *and Steward* [OSWALD], *severally.*

Osw. Good dawning to thee, friend: art of this house?

Kent. Ay.

Osw. Where may we set our horses?

Kent. I' the mire.

Osw. Prithee, if thou lovest me, tell me.

Kent. I love thee not.

Osw. Why, then, I care not for thee.

Kent. If I had thee in Lipsbury pinfold, I would make thee care for me.

Osw. Why dost thou use me thus? I know thee not.

Kent. Fellow, I know thee.

Osw. What dost thou know me for?

Kent. A knave; a rascal; an eater of broken meats; a base, proud, shallow, beggarly, three-suited, hundred-pound, filthy, worsted-stocking knave; a lily-livered, action-taking, whoreson, glass-gazing, superserviceable, finical rogue; one-trunk-inheriting slave; one that wouldst be a bawd, in way of good service, and art nothing but the composition of a knave, beggar, coward, pandar, and the son and heir of a mongrel bitch: one whom I will beat into clamorous whining, if thou deniest the least syllable of thy addition.

Osw. Why, what a monstrous fellow art thou, thus to rail on one that is neither known of thee nor knows thee!

Kent. What a brazen-faced varlet art thou, to deny thou knowest me! Is it two days since I tripped up thy heels, and beat thee before the king? Draw, you rogue: for, though it be night, yet the moon shines; I'll make a sop o' the moonshine of you: draw, you whoreson cullionly barber-monger, draw. [*Drawing his sword.*]

Osw. Away! I have nothing to do with thee.

Kent. Draw, you rascal: you come with letters against the king; and take Vanity the puppet's part against the royalty of her father: draw, you rogue, or I'll so carbonado your shanks: draw, you rascal; come your ways.

Osw. Help, ho! murder! help!

Kent. Strike, you slave; stand, rogue, stand; you neat slave, strike. [*Beating him.*]

Osw. Help, ho! murder! murder!

through (as thread through the eye of a needle). 122. **prize,** price, significance. 125. **which,** the letter. 127. **attend dispatch,** wait to be dispatched.

SCENE II. 9. **Lipsbury pinfold.** This phrase is unexplained. *Pinfold* means "pound for stray animals." Critics have tried to see in it an allusion to the prize ring; Nares supposes the allusion may be to the teeth within the pinfold of the lips. 17. **three-suited,** probable allusion to three suits a year allowed to servants. **hundred-pound,** possible allusion to the minimum property qualification for the status of gentleman; sometimes seen as a reference to James I's wholesale creation of knights. **worsted-stocking,** too poor and menial to wear silk stockings.
18. **action-taking,** settling quarrels by resort to law instead of arms, cowardly. 19. **glass-gazing,** fond of looking in the mirror. **superserviceable,** officious. 20. **finical,** excessively particular, probably, in dress. **one-trunk-inheriting,** possessing effects sufficient for one trunk only. 26. **addition,** title. 35. **sop o' the moonshine,** supposed punning allusion to a dish called "eggs in moonshine." 36. **cullionly barber-monger,** base frequenter of barber shops, fop. 39-40. **Vanity the puppet's part.** Vanity was a character in the morality plays. 41. **carbonado,** cut you crosswise like meat for broiling. 45. **neat,** foppish.

Enter Bastard [EDMUND, *with his rapier drawn*], CORNWALL, REGAN, GLOUCESTER, Servants.

Edm. How now! What 's the matter? Part!
Kent. With you, goodman boy, if you please: come, I'll flesh ye: come on, young master.
Glou. Weapons! arms! What 's the matter here?
Corn. Keep peace, upon your lives;
He dies that strikes again. What is the matter?
Reg. The messengers from our sister and the king.
Corn. What is your difference? speak.
Osw. I am scarce in breath, my lord.
Kent. No marvel, you have so bestirred your valour. You cowardly rascal, nature disclaims in thee: a tailor made thee.
Corn. Thou art a strange fellow: a tailor make a man?
Kent. A tailor, sir: a stone-cutter or a painter could not have made him so ill, though they had been but two years o' the trade.
Corn. Speak yet, how grew your quarrel?
Osw. This ancient ruffian, sir, whose life I have spared at suit of his gray beard,—
Kent. Thou whoreson zed! thou unnecessary letter! My lord, if you will give me leave, I will tread this unbolted villain into mortar, and daub the walls of a jakes with him. Spare my gray beard, you wagtail?
Corn. Peace, sirrah!
You beastly knave, know you no reverence?
Kent. Yes, sir; but anger hath a privilege.
Corn. Why art thou angry?
Kent. That such a slave as this should wear a sword,
Who wears no honesty. Such smiling rogues as these,
Like rats, oft bite the holy cords a-twain
Which are too intrinse t' unloose; smooth every passion
That in the natures of their lords rebel;
Bring oil to fire, snow to their colder moods;
Renege, affirm, and turn their halcyon beaks
With every gale and vary of their masters,
Knowing nought, like dogs, but following.
A plague upon your epileptic visage!
Smile you my speeches, as I were a fool?
Goose, if I had you upon Sarum plain,
I 'ld drive ye cackling home to Camelot.
Corn. What, art thou mad, old fellow?
Glou. How fell you out? say that.
Kent. No contraries hold more antipathy
Than I and such a knave.
Corn. Why dost thou call him knave? What is his fault?
Kent. His countenance likes me not.
Corn. No more, perchance, does mine, nor his, nor hers.
Kent. Sir, 'tis my occupation to be plain:
I have seen better faces in my time
Than stands on any shoulder that I see
Before me at this instant.
Corn. This is some fellow,
Who, having been prais'd for bluntness, doth affect
A saucy roughness, and constrains the garb
Quite from his nature: he cannot flatter, he,
An honest mind and plain, he must speak truth!
An they will take it, so; if not, he 's plain.
These kind of knaves I know, which in this plainness
Harbour more craft and more corrupter ends
Than twenty silly ducking observants
That stretch their duties nicely.
Kent. Sir, in good faith, in sincere verity,
Under th' allowance of your great aspect,
Whose influence, like the wreath of radiant fire
On flick'ring Phœbus' front,—
Corn. What mean'st by this?
Kent. To go out of my dialect, which you discommend so much. I know, sir, I am no flatterer: he that beguiled you in a plain accent was a plain knave; which for my part I will not be, though I should win your displeasure to entreat me to 't.
Corn. What was th' offence you gave him?
Osw. I never gave him any:
It pleas'd the king his master very late
To strike at me, upon his misconstruction;
When he, compact, and flattering his displeasure,
Tripp'd me behind; being down, insulted, rail'd,
And put upon him such a deal of man,
That worthied him, got praises of the king
For him attempting who was self-subdu'd;
And, in the fleshment of this dread exploit,
Drew on me here again.
Kent. None of these rogues and cowards
But Ajax is their fool.
Corn. Fetch forth the stocks!
You stubborn ancient knave, you reverent braggart,
We'll teach you—
Kent. Sir, I am too old to learn:
Call not your stocks for me: I serve the king;
On whose employment I was sent to you:
You shall do small respect, show too bold malice
Against the grace and person of my master,
Stocking his messenger.
Corn. Fetch forth the stocks! As I have life and honour,
There shall he sit till noon.
Reg. Till noon! till night, my lord; and all night too.
Kent. Why, madam, if I were your father's dog,
You should not use me so.
Reg. Sir, being his knave, I will.
Corn. This is a fellow of the self-same colour
Our sister speaks of. Come, bring away the stocks!
Stocks brought out.
Glou. Let me beseech your grace not to do so:
His fault is much, and the good king his master
Will check him for 't: your purpos'd low correction

47. **matter.** Kent takes the secondary meaning, "cause for quarrel." 48. **goodman boy,** contemptuously. 60. **disclaims in,** disowns. 69. **zed,** the letter Z, a Greek character; in the spelling of English words, known but unnecessary, and often not included in dictionaries. 71. **unbolted,** unsifted; hence, coarse. 72. **jakes,** privy. 73. **wagtail,** name of a bird; epithet to denote pertness. 75. **beastly,** in literal sense, beastlike. 80. **holy cords,** natural bonds of affection. 81. **intrinse,** defined as "entangled" and as "very tightly drawn." **smooth,** flatter, humor. 84. **Renege,** deny. **halcyon beaks.** The halcyon or kingfisher, if hung up, would turn his beak against the wind. 85. **vary,** variation. 87. **epileptic,** indication of Oswald's visage, pale with fright and distorted with a grin. 89-90. **Sarum . . . Camelot.** The allusion is to Sarum plain, the Salisbury plain (where large flocks of geese were bred), and to Camelot, the seat of King Arthur and his Round Table, said to have been at Cadbury and at Winchester. 101. **some,** a (sort of). 103-104. **constrains . . . nature,** distorts plainness to the point of caricature. 109. **ducking observants,** bowing, obsequious courtiers. 110. **nicely,** punctiliously. 111. **Sir, in good faith,** etc., Kent assumes the speech of courtly decorum. 124. **misconstruction,** misunderstanding (me). 125. **compact,** joined, united with him. 127. **put . . . man,** acted like such a hero. 128. **worthied,** won reputation. 129. **attempting,** assailing. 130. **fleshment,** excitement resulting from a first success. 132. **Ajax is their fool,** Ajax, traditional braggart, is outdone by them in boasting. 138. **grace . . . master,** who as a messenger Kent represented. 161.

Is such as basest and contemned'st wretches
For pilf'rings and most common trespasses
Are punish'd with: the king must take it ill,
That he, so slightly valued in his messenger,
Should have him thus restrain'd.

Corn. I'll answer that.

Reg. My sister may receive it much more worse,
To have her gentleman abus'd, assaulted,
For following her affairs. Put in his legs.
[*Kent is put in the stocks.*]
Come, my lord, away.
Exit [*with all but Gloucester and Kent*].

Glou. I am sorry for thee, friend; 'tis the duke's pleasure,
Whose disposition, all the world well knows,
Will not be rubb'd nor stopp'd: I'll entreat for thee.

Kent. Pray, do not, sir: I have watch'd and travell'd hard;
Some time I shall sleep out, the rest I'll whistle.
A good man's fortune may grow out at heels:
Give you good morrow!

Glou. The duke 's to blame in this; 'twill be ill taken. *Exit.*

Kent. Good king, that must approve the common saw,
Thou out of heaven's benediction com'st
To the warm sun!
Approach, thou beacon to this under globe,
That by thy comfortable beams I may
Peruse this letter! Nothing almost sees miracles
But misery: I know 'tis from Cordelia,
Who hath most fortunately been inform'd
Of my obscured course; and shall find time
†From this enormous state, seeking to give
Losses their remedies. All weary and o'er-watch'd,
Take vantage, heavy eyes, not to behold
This shameful lodging.
Fortune, good night: smile once more; turn thy wheel! [*Sleeps.*]

[SCENE III. *The same.*]

Enter EDGAR.

Edg. I heard myself proclaim'd;
And by the happy hollow of a tree
Escap'd the hunt. No port is free; no place,
That guard, and most unusual vigilance,
Does not attend my taking. Whiles I may 'scape,
I will preserve myself: and am bethought
To take the basest and most poorest shape
That ever penury, in contempt of man,
Brought near to beast: my face I'll grime with filth;
Blanket my loins; elf all my hairs in knots;
And with presented nakedness out-face
The winds and persecutions of the sky.
The country gives me proof and precedent
Of Bedlam beggars, who, with roaring voices,
Strike in their numb'd and mortified bare arms
Pins, wooden pricks, nails, sprigs of rosemary;
And with this horrible object, from low farms,
Poor pelting villages, sheep-cotes, and mills,
Sometime with lunatic bans, sometime with prayers,
Enforce their charity. Poor Turlygod! poor Tom!
That's something yet: Edgar I nothing am. *Exit.*

[SCENE IV. *The same. Kent still in the stocks.*]

Enter LEAR, Fool, *and* Gentleman.

Lear. 'Tis strange that they should so depart from home,
And not send back my messenger.

Gent. As I learn'd,
The night before there was no purpose in them
Of this remove.

Kent. Hail to thee, noble master!

Lear. Ha!
Mak'st thou this shame thy pastime?

Kent. No, my lord.

Fool. Ha, ha! he wears cruel garters. Horses are tied by the heads, dogs and bears by the neck, monkeys by the loins, and men by the legs: when a man 's over-lusty at legs, then he wears wooden nether-stocks.

Lear. What 's he that hath so much thy place mistook
To set thee here?

Kent. It is both he and she;
Your son and daughter.

Lear. No.

Kent. Yes.

Lear. No, I say.

Kent. I say, yea.

Lear. No, no, they would not.

Kent. Yes, they have.

Lear. By Jupiter, I swear, no.

Kent. By Juno, I swear, ay.

Lear. They durst not do 't;
They could not, would not do 't; 'tis worse than murder,
To do upon respect such violent outrage:
Resolve me, with all modest haste, which way
Thou mightst deserve, or they impose, this usage,
Coming from us.

Kent. My lord, when at their home
I did commend your highness' letters to them,
Ere I was risen from the place that show'd
My duty kneeling, came there a reeking post,
Stew'd in his haste, half breathless, panting forth
From Goneril his mistress salutations;
Deliver'd letters, spite of intermission,
Which presently they read: on whose contents,
They summon'd up their meiny, straight took horse;

rubb'd, hindered, obstructed; term from bowls. 163. **sleep out,** sleep through. 165. **Give you,** i.e., God give you. 167. **approve,** prove true. **saw,** proverb: "To run out of God's blessing into the warm sun," meaning "to go from better to worse." 175-177. **and . . . remedies,** an obscure passage. Daniel's conjecture of *she'll* for *shall* makes a sort of sense. 177. **o'er-watch'd,** exhausted with watching.

SCENE III. The scene is continuous; Kent is still in the stocks. 3. **port,** means of exit. 5. **attend,** watch, wait for. 6. **am bethought,** it has occurred to me. 10. **elf,** tangle into elf-locks. 14. **Bedlam beggars,** called also "Tom o' Bedlams" and "Abraham men"; they were lunatic patients of Bethlehem Hospital turned out to beg for their bread. Dekker in the *Bellman of London,* 1608, gives a description of their characteristics which closely parallels the one in the text. 15. **mortified,** numbed, insensible. 16. **wooden pricks,** skewers. 17. **object,** appearance. **low,** lowly. 18. **pelting,** paltry, petty. 19. **bans,** curses. 20. **Turlygod,** meaning unknown; Warburton proposed *Turlipin,* the name of an order of mad beggars in France. 21. **nothing,** probably, not at all, in no respect.

SCENE IV. 4. **remove,** change of residence (of royalty). 7. **cruel.** Q: *crewell,* a double meaning: (1) "unkind," (2) "crewel," a thin yarn of which garters were made. 11. **nether-stocks,** stockings. 24. **upon respect,** deliberately. 28. **commend,** deliver, commit. 33. **spite of intermission,** in spite of interrupting me. 35. **meiny,** household.

Commanded me to follow, and attend
The leisure of their answer; gave me cold looks:
And meeting here the other messenger,
Whose welcome, I perceiv'd, had poison'd mine,—
Being the very fellow which of late
Display'd so saucily against your highness,—
Having more man than wit about me, drew:
He rais'd the house with loud and coward cries.
Your son and daughter found this trespass worth
The shame which here it suffers.

Fool. Winter 's not gone yet, if the wild-geese fly that way.

Fathers that wear rags
Do make their children blind;
But fathers that bear bags
Shall see their children kind.
Fortune, that arrant whore,
Ne'er turns the key to th' poor.

But, for all this, thou shalt have as many dolours for thy daughters as thou canst tell in a year.

Lear. O, how this mother swells up toward my heart!
Hysterica passio, down, thou climbing sorrow,
Thy element 's below! Where is this daughter?

Kent. With the earl, sir, here within.

Lear. Follow me not;
Stay here. *Exit.*

Gent. Made you no more offence but what you speak of?

Kent. None.
How chance the king comes with so small a number?

Fool. An thou hadst been set i' the stocks for that question, thou'dst well deserved it.

Kent. Why, fool?

Fool. We'll set thee to school to an ant, to teach thee there 's no labouring i' the winter. All that follow their noses are led by their eyes but blind men; and there 's not a nose among twenty but can smell him that 's stinking. Let go thy hold when a great wheel runs down a hill, lest it break thy neck with following; but the great one that goes upward, let him draw thee after. When a wise man gives thee better counsel, give me mine again: I would have none but knaves follow it, since a fool gives it.

That sir which serves and seeks for gain,
And follows but for form,
Will pack when it begins to rain,
And leave thee in the storm.
But I will tarry; the fool will stay,
And let the wise man fly:
The knave turns fool that runs away;
The fool no knave, perdy.

Kent. Where learned you this, fool?

Fool. Not i' th' stocks, fool.

Enter LEAR *and* GLOUCESTER.

Lear. Deny to speak with me? They are sick? they are weary?
They have travell'd all the night? Mere fetches;
The images of revolt and flying off.
Fetch me a better answer.

Glou. My dear lord,
You know the fiery quality of the duke;
How unremoveable and fix'd he is
In his own course.

Lear. Vengeance! plague! death! confusion!
Fiery? what quality? Why, Gloucester, Gloucester,
I 'ld speak with the Duke of Cornwall and his wife.

Glou. Well, my good lord, I have inform'd them so.

Lear. Inform'd them! Dost thou understand me, man?

Glou. Ay, my good lord.

Lear. The king would speak with Cornwall; the dear father
Would with his daughter speak, commands her service:
Are they inform'd of this? My breath and blood!
Fiery? the fiery duke? Tell the hot duke that—
No, but not yet: may be he is not well:
Infirmity doth still neglect all office
Whereto our health is bound; we are not ourselves
When nature, being oppress'd, commands the mind
To suffer with the body: I'll forbear;
And am fallen out with my more headier will,
To take the indispos'd and sickly fit
For the sound man. Death on my state! wherefore
[*Looking on Kent.*]
Should he sit here? This act persuades me
That this remotion of the duke and her
Is practice only. Give me my servant forth.
Go tell the duke and 's wife I 'ld speak with them,
Now, presently: bid them come forth and hear me,
Or at their chamber-door I'll beat the drum
Till it cry sleep to death.

Glou. I would have all well betwixt you. *Exit.*

Lear. O me, my heart, my rising heart! but, down!

Fool. Cry to it, nuncle, as the cockney did to the eels when she put 'em i' the paste alive; she knapped 'em o' the coxcombs with a stick, and cried 'Down, wantons, down!' 'Twas her brother that, in pure kindness to his horse, buttered his hay.

Enter CORNWALL, REGAN, GLOUCESTER, [*and*] Servants.

Lear. Good morrow to you both.

Corn. Hail to your grace!
Kent here set at liberty.

Reg. I am glad to see your highness.

Lear. Regan, I think you are; I know what reason
I have to think so: if thou shouldst not be glad,
I would divorce me from thy mother's tomb,
Sepulchring an adultress. [*To Kent*] O, are you free?
Some other time for that. Beloved Regan,
Thy sister 's naught: O Regan, she hath tied
Sharp-tooth'd unkindness, like a vulture, here:
[*Points to his heart.*]
I can scarce speak to thee; thou 'lt not believe
With how deprav'd a quality—O Regan!

Reg. I pray you, sir, take patience: I have hope

41. **Display'd,** behaved ostentatiously. 42. **drew,** i.e., my sword. 49. **blind,** i.e., indifferent. 50. **bags,** i.e., of gold. 53. **turns the key,** i.e., opens the door. 55. **dolours,** griefs, with pun on "dollars." **tell,** count. 56, 57. **mother, Hysterica passio,** i.e., hysteria, giving the sensation of choking or suffocating. 58. **element's,** proper place is. 64. **chance,** chances it. 69-73. **All . . . stinking,** i.e., one who is out of favor can be easily detected (he smells of misfortune), and so is easily avoided by timeservers. 81. **pack,** take himself off. 90. **fetches,** pretexts, dodges. 91. **flying off,** desertion. 111-112. **am . . . take,** now disapprove of my more impetuous will in taking. 115. **remotion,** removal. 120. **cry sleep to death,** i.e., put an end to sleep. 123. **cockney,** i.e., a Londoner, ignorant of ways of cooking eels. 124. **paste,** pastry pie. 125. **knapped,** rapped. **coxcombs,** heads. 126. **wantons,** playful creatures. 127-128. **'Twas . . . hay.** Another city ignorance; the act is well-intended, but horses do not like greasy hay. 150. **confine,** assigned boundary. 151. **discretion,** discreet person.

You less know how to value her desert
Than she to scant her duty.
Lear. Say, how is that?
Reg. I cannot think my sister in the least
Would fail her obligation: if, sir, perchance
She have restrain'd the riots of your followers,
'Tis on such ground, and to such wholesome end,
As clears her from all blame.
Lear. My curses on her!
Reg. O, sir, you are old;
Nature in you stands on the very verge
Of her confine: you should be rul'd and led
By some discretion, that discerns your state
Better than you yourself. Therefore, I pray you,
That to our sister you do make return;
Say you have wrong'd her, sir.
Lear. Ask her forgiveness?
Do you but mark how this becomes the house:
'Dear daughter, I confess that I am old; [*Kneeling.*]
Age is unnecessary: on my knees I beg
That you'll vouchsafe me raiment, bed, and food.'
Reg. Good sir, no more; these are unsightly tricks:
Return you to my sister.
Lear. [*Rising*] Never, Regan:
She hath abated me of half my train;
Look'd black upon me; struck me with her tongue,
Most serpent-like, upon the very heart:
All the stor'd vengeances of heaven fall
On her ingrateful top! Strike her young bones,
You taking airs, with lameness!
Corn. Fie, sir, fie!
Lear. You nimble lightnings, dart your blinding flames
Into her scornful eyes! Infect her beauty,
You fen-suck'd fogs, drawn by the pow'rful sun,
To fall and blast her pride!
Reg. O the blest gods! so will you wish on me,
When the rash mood is on.
Lear. No, Regan, thou shalt never have my curse:
Thy tender-hefted nature shall not give
Thee o'er to harshness: her eyes are fierce; but thine
Do comfort and not burn. 'Tis not in thee
To grudge my pleasures, to cut off my train,
To bandy hasty words, to scant my sizes,
And in conclusion to oppose the bolt
Against my coming in: thou better know'st
The offices of nature, bond of childhood,
Effects of courtesy, dues of gratitude:
Thy half o' th' kingdom hast thou not forgot,
Wherein I thee endow'd.
Reg. Good sir, to th' purpose.
Lear. Who put my man i' th' stocks? *Tucket within.*
Corn. What trumpet 's that?
Reg. I know 't, my sister's: this approves her letter,
That she would soon be here.

Enter Steward [OSWALD].

Is your lady come?
Lear. This is a slave, whose easy-borrowed pride
Dwells in the fickle grace of her he follows.
Out, varlet, from my sight!
Corn. What means your grace?
Lear. Who stock'd my servant? Regan, I have good hope
Thou didst not know on 't.

Enter GONERIL.

Who comes here? O heavens,
If you do love old men, if your sweet sway
Allow obedience, if you yourselves are old,
Make it your cause; send down, and take my part!
[*To Gon.*] Art not asham'd to look upon this beard?
O Regan, will you take her by the hand?
Gon. Why not by th' hand, sir? How have I offended?
All 's not offence that indiscretion finds
And dotage terms so.
Lear. O sides, you are too tough;
Will you yet hold? How came my man i' th' stocks?
Corn. I set him there, sir: but his own disorders
Deserv'd much less advancement.
Lear. You! did you?
Reg. I pray you, father, being weak, seem so.
If, till the expiration of your month,
You will return and sojourn with my sister,
Dismissing half your train, come then to me:
I am now from home, and out of that provision
Which shall be needful for your entertainment.
Lear. Return to her, and fifty men dismiss'd?
No, rather I abjure all roofs, and choose
To wage against the enmity o' th' air;
To be a comrade with the wolf and owl,—
Necessity's sharp pinch! Return with her?
Why, the hot-blooded France, that dowerless took
Our youngest born, I could as well be brought
To knee his throne, and, squire-like, pension beg
To keep base life afoot. Return with her?
Persuade me rather to be slave and sumpter
To this detested groom. [*Pointing at Oswald.*]
Gon. At your choice, sir.
Lear. I prithee, daughter, do not make me mad:
I will not trouble thee, my child; farewell:
We'll no more meet, no more see one another:
But yet thou art my flesh, my blood, my daughter;
Or rather a disease that 's in my flesh,
Which I must needs call mine: thou art a boil,
A plague-sore, or embossed carbuncle,
In my corrupted blood. But I'll not chide thee;
Let shame come when it will, I do not call it:
I do not bid the thunder-bearer shoot,
Nor tell tales of thee to high-judging Jove:
Mend when thou canst; be better at thy leisure:
I can be patient; I can stay with Regan,
I and my hundred knights.
Reg. Not altogether so:
I look'd not for you yet, nor am provided
For your fit welcome. Give ear, sir, to my sister;
For those that mingle reason with your passion
Must be content to think you old, and so—
But she knows what she does.

155. **how . . . house,** how this would be suitable to our position. 165. **ingrateful top,** ungrateful head. **young bones,** i.e., unborn child. 166. **taking,** infectious. 169. **fen-suck'd.** It was supposed that the sun sucked up poisons from fens or marshes. 174. **tender-hefted,** set in a tender, delicate frame (Wright); gentle. 178. **sizes,** allowances. 186. **approves,** confirms. 188. **easy-borrowed,** put on without justification; hyphen comes from Theobald; perhaps *easy* has an independent meaning, "cool," "impudent." 191. **stock'd,** put into the stocks.

195. **Make . . . cause,** make my cause yours. 200. **sides . . . tough.** This is not figurative but indicates belief in an actual swelling of the heart so that it might break through the sides. 212. **wage,** wage war. 215. **hot-blooded,** passionate, angry. In I, ii, 23, France is said to have "in choler parted," his blood heated by passion. 217. **knee,** fall on my knees before. 219. **sumpter,** pack horse; hence, drudge. 227. **embossed,** swollen, tumid. 230. **thunder-bearer,** Jupiter.

Lear. Is this well spoken?
Reg. I dare avouch it, sir: what, fifty followers?
Is it not well? What should you need of more?
Yea, or so many, sith that both charge and danger
Speak 'gainst so great a number? How, in one house,
Should many people, under two commands,
Hold amity? 'Tis hard; almost impossible.
Gon. Why might not you, my lord, receive attendance
From those that she calls servants or from mine?
Reg. Why not, my lord? If then they chanc'd to slack ye,
We could control them. If you will come to me,—
For now I spy a danger,—I entreat you
To bring but five and twenty: to no more
Will I give place or notice.
Lear. I gave you all—
Reg. And in good time you gave it.
Lear. Made you my guardians, my depositaries;
But kept a reservation to be followed
With such a number. What, must I come to you
With five and twenty, Regan? said you so?
Reg. And speak 't again, my lord; no more with me.
Lear. Those wicked creatures yet do look well-favour'd,
When others are more wicked; not being the worst
Stands in some rank of praise. [*To Gon.*] I'll go with thee:
Thy fifty yet doth double five-and-twenty,
And thou art twice her love.
Gon. Hear me, my lord:
What need you five and twenty, ten, or five,
To follow in a house where twice so many
Have a command to tend you?
Reg. What need one?
Lear. O, reason not the need! Our basest beggars
Are in the poorest thing superfluous:
Allow not nature more than nature needs,
Man's life is cheap as beast's: thou art a lady;
If only to go warm were gorgeous,
Why, nature needs not what thou gorgeous wear'st,
Which scarcely keeps thee warm. But, for true need,—
You heavens, give me that patience, patience I need!
You see me here, you gods, a poor old man,
As full of grief as age; wretched in both!
If it be you that stirs these daughters' hearts
Against their father, fool me not so much
To bear it tamely; touch me with noble anger,
And let not women's weapons, water-drops,
Stain my man's cheeks! No, you unnatural hags,
I will have such revenges on you both,
That all the world shall—I will do such things,—
What they are, yet I know not; but they shall be
The terrors of the earth. You think I'll weep;
No, I'll not weep:
I have full cause of weeping; but this heart
Shall break into a hundred thousand flaws,
Or ere I'll weep. O fool, I shall go mad!
Storm and tempest. Exeunt [Lear, Gloucester, Kent, and Fool].
Corn. Let us withdraw; 'twill be a storm.
Reg. This house is little: the old man and 's people
Cannot be well bestow'd.
Gon. 'Tis his own blame; hath put himself from rest,
And must needs taste his folly.
Reg. For his particular, I'll receive him gladly,
But not one follower.
Gon. So am I purpos'd.
Where is my lord of Gloucester?
Corn. Follow'd the old man forth: he is return'd.

Enter GLOUCESTER.

Glou. The king is in high rage.
Corn. Whither is he going?
Glou. He calls to horse; but will I know not whither.
Corn. 'Tis best to give him way; he leads himself.
Gon. My lord, entreat him by no means to stay.
Glou. Alack, the night comes on, and the high winds
Do sorely ruffle; for many miles about
There 's scarce a bush.
Reg. O, sir, to wilful men,
The injuries that they themselves procure
Must be their schoolmasters. Shut up your doors:
He is attended with a desperate train;
And what they may incense him to, being apt
To have his ear abus'd, wisdom bids fear.
Corn. Shut up your doors, my lord; 'tis a wild night:
My Regan counsels well: come out o' th' storm.
Exeunt.

ACT III.

SCENE I. [*A heath.*]

Storm still. Enter KENT *and a* Gentleman, *severally.*

Kent. Who 's there, besides foul weather?
Gent. One minded like the weather, most unquietly.
Kent. I know you. Where 's the king?
Gent. Contending with the fretful elements;
Bids the wind blow the earth into the sea,
Or swell the curled waters 'bove the main,
That things might change or cease; tears his white hair,
Which the impetuous blasts, with eyeless rage,
Catch in their fury, and make nothing of;
Strives in his little world of man to out-scorn
The to-and-fro-conflicting wind and rain.
This night, wherein the cub-drawn bear would couch,
The lion and the belly-pinched wolf
Keep their fur dry, unbonneted he runs,
And bids what will take all.
Kent. But who is with him?

240. **avouch,** swear by. 242. **sith that,** since. **charge,** expense. 245. **Hold amity,** maintain friendship. 248. **slack,** be careless in their attendance on. 252. **notice,** countenance. 254. **my guardians.** Lear understands his contract to be that the daughters were guardians, or stewardesses, of his realm under him. 261. **Stands . . . praise,** is at least relatively worthy of praise. 265. **follow,** attend on. 266. **tend,** wait on. 267. **reason,** scrutinize. 268. **Are . . . superfluous,** have some wretched possession they can dispense with. 269. **Allow,** if you allow. **needs,** i.e., to survive. 271-273. **If . . . warm,** i.e., if fashions in clothes were determined only by the need for warmth, this natural standard wouldn't justify the rich robes you wear to be gorgeous—which don't serve well for warmth in any case. 278. **fool,** humiliate. 279. **To bear,** as to make me bear. 288. **flaws,** fragments; also, gusts of passion. 292. **bestow'd,** lodged. 293. **blame,** fault. **from rest,** i.e., out of the house; also, lacking peace of mind. 295. **For his particular,** as for him individually. 304. **ruffle,** bluster. 308. **desperate train,** body of desperate followers. 309. **incense him to,** incite him to undertake. 309-310. **being . . . abus'd,** being inclined to hearken to wild counsel.

ACT III. SCENE I. 6. **main,** mainland. 10. **little world of man,** the microcosm; allusion to the theory that man is an epitome of the macrocosm, or universe, and moves in accordance with its laws and influences. 12. **cub-drawn,** famished, with udders sucked dry (and hence

Gent. None but the fool; who labours to out-jest
His heart-struck injuries.
Kent. Sir, I do know you;
And dare, upon the warrant of my note,
Commend a dear thing to you. There is division,
Although as yet the face of it is cover'd
With mutual cunning, 'twixt Albany and Cornwall;
Who have—as who have not, that their great stars
Thron'd and set high?—servants, who seem no less,
Which are to France the spies and speculations
Intelligent of our state; what hath been seen,
Either in snuffs and packings of the dukes,
Or the hard rein which both of them have borne
Against the old kind king; or something deeper,
Whereof perchance these are but furnishings;
But, true it is, from France there comes a power
Into this scattered kingdom; who already,
Wise in our negligence, have secret feet
In some of our best ports, and are at point
To show their open banner. Now to you:
If on my credit you dare build so far
To make your speed to Dover, you shall find
Some that will thank you, making just report
Of how unnatural and bemadding sorrow
The king hath cause to plain.
I am a gentleman of blood and breeding;
And, from some knowledge and assurance, offer
This office to you.
Gent. I will talk further with you.
Kent. No, do not.
For confirmation that I am much more
Than my out-wall, open this purse, and take
What it contains. If you shall see Cordelia,—
As fear not but you shall,—show her this ring;
And she will tell you who that fellow is
That yet you do not know. Fie on this storm!
I will go seek the king.
Gent. Give me your hand: have you no more to say?
Kent. Few words, but, to effect, more than all yet;
That, when we have found the king,—in which your pain
That way, I'll this,—he that first lights on him
Holla the other. *Exeunt* [*severally*].

SCENE II. [*Another part of the heath.*]

Storm still. Enter LEAR *and* Fool.

Lear. Blow, winds, and crack your cheeks! rage! blow!
You cataracts and hurricanoes, spout
Till you have drench'd our steeples, drown'd the cocks!
You sulph'rous and thought-executing fires,
Vaunt-couriers of oak-cleaving thunderbolts,
Singe my white head! And thou, all-shaking thunder,
Strike flat the thick rotundity o' th' world!
Crack nature's moulds, all germens spill at once,
That makes ingrateful man!
Fool. O nuncle, court holy-water in a dry house is better than this rain-water out o' door. Good nuncle, in, ask thy daughters' blessing: here 's a night pities neither wise men nor fools.
Lear. Rumble thy bellyful! Spit, fire! spout, rain!
Nor rain, wind, thunder, fire, are my daughters:
I tax not you, you elements, with unkindness;
I never gave you kingdom, call'd you children,
You owe me no subscription: then let fall
Your horrible pleasure; here I stand, your slave,
A poor, infirm, weak, and despis'd old man:
But yet I call you servile ministers,
That will with two pernicious daughters join
Your high engender'd battles 'gainst a head
So old and white as this. O! O! 'tis foul!
Fool. He that has a house to put 's head in has a good head-piece.
The cod-piece that will house
Before the head has any,
The head and he shall louse;
So beggars marry many.
The man that makes his toe
What he his heart should make
Shall of a corn cry woe,
And turn his sleep to wake.
For there was never yet fair woman but she made mouths in a glass.
Lear. No, I will be the pattern of all patience;
I will say nothing.

Enter KENT.

Kent. Who 's there?
Fool. Marry, here 's grace and a cod-piece; that 's a wise man and a fool.
Kent. Alas, sir, are you here? things that love night
Love not such nights as these; the wrathful skies
Gallow the very wanderers of the dark,
And make them keep their caves: since I was man,
Such sheets of fire, such bursts of horrid thunder,
Such groans of roaring wind and rain, I never
Remember to have heard: man's nature cannot carry
Th' affliction nor the fear.
Lear. Let the great gods,
That keep this dreadful pudder o'er our heads,
Find out their enemies now. Tremble, thou wretch,
That hast within thee undivulged crimes,
Unwhipp'd of justice: hide thee, thou bloody hand;
Thou perjur'd, and thou simular of virtue
That art incestuous: caitiff, to pieces shake,
That under covert and convenient seeming
Hast practis'd on man's life: close pent-up guilts,
Rive your concealing continents, and cry
These dreadful summoners grace. I am a man
More sinn'd against than sinning.
Kent. Alack, bare-headed!

---

ravenous). **couch,** lie close. 18. **upon . . . note,** on the strength of what I know. 19. **Commend,** entrust. 24. **speculations,** scouts, spies. Johnson conjectured *speculators*. 26. **snuffs,** quarrels. **packings,** intrigues. 29. **furnishings,** outward shows. 31. **scattered,** divided. 33. **at point,** ready. 38. **bemadding,** distracting. 39. **plain,** complain of. 45. **out-wall,** exterior. 52. **to effect,** to the purpose. 53-54. **your pain That way,** laborious quest (take you) that way.

SCENE II. 2. **hurricanoes,** waterspouts. 3. **cocks,** weathercocks. 4. **thought-executing,** probably, acting with the quickness of thought. 5. **Vaunt-couriers,** forerunners. 8. **germens,** germs, seeds. **spill,** destroy. 10. **court holy-water,** flattery. 18. **subscription,** allegiance. 23. **high engender'd battles,** battalions levied in the heavens. 27-34. **The cod-piece . . . wake,** a man who cohabits sexually but improvidently can expect penury; and one who elevates what is base above what is noble can expect misery also (as Lear has done with his daughters). **cod-piece,** front part of close-fitting hose worn by men; hence, the sexual member. 44. **Gallow,** frighten, terrify. 50. **pudder,** turmoil. 54. **simular,** pretender. 56. **seeming,** hypocrisy. 58. **Rive,** split. **continents,** covering. 58-59. **cry . . . grace,** pray for mercy at the hands of the officers of divine justice. A *summoner* was the police officer of an ecclesiastical court.

Gracious my lord, hard by here is a hovel;
Some friendship will it lend you 'gainst the tempest:
Repose you there; while I to this hard house—
More harder than the stones whereof 'tis rais'd;
Which even but now, demanding after you,
Denied me to come in—return, and force
Their scanted courtesy.

Lear. My wits begin to turn.
Come on, my boy: how dost, my boy? art cold?
I am cold myself. Where is this straw, my fellow?
The art of our necessities is strange,
That can make vile things precious. Come, your hovel.
Poor fool and knave, I have one part in my heart
That 's sorry yet for thee.

Fool. [*Singing*] He that has and a little tiny wit,—
With hey, ho, the wind and the rain,—
Must make content with his fortunes fit,
Though the rain it raineth every day.

Lear. True, boy. Come, bring us to this hovel. *Exit* [*with Kent*].

Fool. This is a brave night to cool a courtezan.
I'll speak a prophecy ere I go:
When priests are more in word than matter;
When brewers mar their malt with water;
When nobles are their tailors' tutors;
No heretics burn'd, but wenches' suitors;
When every case in law is right;
No squire in debt, nor no poor knight;
When slanders do not live in tongues;
Nor cutpurses come not to throngs;
When usurers tell their gold i' th' field;
And bawds and whores do churches build;
Then shall the realm of Albion
Come to great confusion:
Then comes the time, who lives to see 't,
That going shall be us'd with feet.
This prophecy Merlin shall make; for I live before his time. *Exit.*

SCENE III. [*Gloucester's castle.*]

Enter GLOUCESTER *and* EDMUND.

Glou. Alack, alack, Edmund, I like not this unnatural dealing. When I desired their leave that I might pity him, they took from me the use of mine own house; charged me, on pain of perpetual displeasure, neither to speak of him, entreat for him, or any way sustain him.

Edm. Most savage and unnatural!

Glou. Go to; say you nothing. There is division between the dukes; and a worse matter than that: I have received a letter this night; 'tis dangerous to be spoken; I have locked the letter in my closet: these injuries the king now bears will be revenged home; there is part of a power already footed: we must incline to the king. I will look him, and privily relieve him: go you and maintain talk with the duke, that my charity be not of him perceived: if he ask for me, I am ill, and gone to bed. If I die for it, as no less is threatened me, the king my old master must be relieved. There is strange things toward, Edmund; pray you, be careful. *Exit.*

Edm. This courtesy, forbid thee, shall the duke
Instantly know; and of that letter too:
This seems a fair deserving, and must draw me
That which my father loses; no less than all:
The younger rises when the old doth fall. *Exit.*

SCENE IV. [*The heath. Before a hovel.*]

Enter LEAR, KENT, *and* Fool.

Kent. Here is the place, my lord; good my lord, enter:
The tyranny of the open night 's too rough
For nature to endure. *Storm still.*

Lear. Let me alone.

Kent. Good my lord, enter here.

Lear. Wilt break my heart?

Kent. I had rather break mine own. Good my lord, enter.

Lear. Thou think'st 'tis much that this contentious storm
Invades us to the skin: so 'tis to thee;
But where the greater malady is fix'd,
The lesser is scarce felt. Thou 'ldst shun a bear;
But if thy flight lay toward the roaring sea,
Thou 'ldst meet the bear i' th' mouth. When the mind 's free,
The body 's delicate: the tempest in my mind
Doth from my senses take all feeling else
Save what beats there. Filial ingratitude!
Is it not as this mouth should tear this hand
For lifting food to 't? But I will punish home:
No, I will weep no more. In such a night
To shut me out! Pour on; I will endure.
In such a night as this! O Regan, Goneril!
Your old kind father, whose frank heart gave all,—
O, that way madness lies; let me shun that;
No more of that.

Kent. Good my lord, enter here.

Lear. Prithee, go in thyself; seek thine own ease:
This tempest will not give me leave to ponder
On things would hurt me more. But I'll go in.
[*To the Fool*] In, boy; go first. You houseless poverty,—
Nay, get thee in. I'll pray, and then I'll sleep.
Exit [*Fool into the hovel*].
Poor naked wretches, wheresoe'er you are,
That bide the pelting of this pitiless storm,
How shall your houseless heads and unfed sides,
Your loop'd and window'd raggedness, defend you

---

63. **hard,** cruel. 65. **Which,** i.e., the owners of the house. **demanding,** I inquiring. 80-95. **I'll . . . time.** Omitted in Q and usually regarded as an interpolation in the text of F. Merlin was a magician of King Arthur's court; a prophecy of Merlin, somewhat like these lines, is found in Holinshed and other places. 81. **matter,** i.e., the truth of the Gospel. 89. **tell,** count. **i' th' field,** i.e., openly. 92. **confusion,** i.e., the ironic result of an impossible reform. 94. **going,** i.e., walking (an anticlimax suggesting normality).

SCENE III. 14. **footed,** landed. 15. **look,** look for. 22. **courtesy, forbid thee,** i.e., this kindness to Lear you were forbidden to show. 24. **fair deserving,** meritorious action.

SCENE IV. 8. **greater malady.** There was a familiar belief that one passion might drive out or allay another. 28-36. **Poor naked wretches,** etc. Lear's error has been a violation of that law of nature which is called justice. His sufferings have brought him round to a complete recognition and expression of general distributive justice. 29. **bide,** endure. 31. **loop'd and window'd,** full of openings like windows and loopholes. 33. **Take physic, pomp,** cure yourself, O distempered great man. 35. **superflux,** superfluity, a word suggestive of the ethics of ownership in society. 58. **over four-inched bridges,** i.e., take mad risks. **course,** chase. 59. **five wits,** the five mental faculties: common wit, imagination, fantasy, judgment, memory. 61. **star-blasting,** blighting by influence of the stars. **taking,** pestilence. 65. **pass,** evil plight. 69. **pendulous,** suspended. 77. **pelican,** greedy; a reference

From seasons such as these? O, I have ta'en
Too little care of this! Take physic, pomp;
Expose thyself to feel what wretches feel,
That thou mayst shake the superflux to them,
And show the heavens more just.

Edg. [*Within*] Fathom and half, fathom and half! Poor Tom! *Enter Fool* [*from the hovel*].

Fool. Come not in here, nuncle, here 's a spirit. Help me, help me!

Kent. Give me thy hand. Who 's there?

Fool. A spirit, a spirit: he says his name 's poor Tom.

Kent. What art thou that dost grumble there i' the straw? Come forth.

Enter EDGAR [*disguised as a madman*].

Edg. Away! the foul fiend follows me!
Through the sharp hawthorn blows the cold wind.
Hum! go to thy bed, and warm thee.

Lear. Didst thou give all to thy daughters?
And art thou come to this?

Edg. Who gives any thing to poor Tom? whom the foul fiend hath led through fire and through flame, through ford and whirlpool, o'er bog and quagmire; that hath laid knives under his pillow, and halters in his pew; set ratsbane by his porridge; made him proud of heart, to ride on a bay trotting-horse over four-inched bridges, to course his own shadow for a traitor. Bless thy five wits! Tom 's a-cold,—O, do de, do de, do de. Bless thee from whirlwinds, star-blasting, and taking! Do poor Tom some charity, whom the foul fiend vexes: there could I have him now,—and there,—and there again, and there. *Storm still.*

Lear. What, have his daughters brought him to this pass?
Couldst thou save nothing? Wouldst thou give 'em all?

Fool. Nay, he reserved a blanket, else we had been all shamed.

Lear. Now, all the plagues that in the pendulous air
Hang fated o'er men's faults light on thy daughters!

Kent. He hath no daughters, sir.

Lear. Death, traitor! nothing could have subdu'd nature
To such a lowness but his unkind daughters.
Is it the fashion, that discarded fathers
Should have thus little mercy on their flesh?
Judicious punishment! 'twas this flesh begot
Those pelican daughters.

Edg. Pillicock sat on Pillicock-hill:
Halloo, halloo, loo, loo!

Fool. This cold night will turn us all to fools and madmen.

Edg. Take heed o' the foul fiend: obey thy parents; keep thy word's justice; swear not; commit not with man's sworn spouse; set not thy sweet heart on proud array. Tom 's a-cold.

Lear. What hast thou been?

Edg. A serving-man, proud in heart and mind; that curled my hair; wore gloves in my cap; served the lust of my mistress' heart, and did the act of darkness with her; swore as many oaths as I spake words, and broke them in the sweet face of heaven: one that slept in the contriving of lust, and waked to do it: wine loved I deeply, dice dearly; and in woman out-paramoured the Turk: false of heart, light of ear, bloody of hand; hog in sloth, fox in stealth, wolf in greediness, dog in madness, lion in prey. Let not the creaking of shoes nor the rustling of silks betray thy poor heart to woman: keep thy foot out of brothels, thy hand out of plackets, thy pen from lenders' books, and defy the foul fiend.
Still through the hawthorn blows the cold wind:
Says suum, mun, nonny.
Dolphin my boy, boy, sessa! let him trot by.
Storm still.

Lear. Thou wert better in a grave than to answer with thy uncovered body this extremity of the skies. Is man no more than this? Consider him well. Thou owest the worm no silk, the beast no hide, the sheep no wool, the cat no perfume. Ha! here 's three on 's are sophisticated! Thou art the thing itself: unaccommodated man is no more but such a poor, bare, forked animal as thou art. Off, off, you lendings! come, unbutton here. [*Tearing off his clothes.*]

Fool. Prithee, nuncle, be contented; 'tis a naughty night to swim in. Now a little fire in a wild field were like an old lecher's heart; a small spark, all the rest on 's body cold. Look, here comes a walking fire.

Enter GLOUCESTER, *with a torch.*

Edg. This is the foul Flibbertigibbet: he begins at curfew, and walks till the first cock; he gives the web and the pin, squints the eye, and makes the hare-lip; mildews the white wheat, and hurts the poor creature of earth.
S. Withold footed thrice the 'old;
He met the night-mare, and her nine-fold;
    Bid her alight,
    And her troth plight,
And, aroint thee, witch, aroint thee!

Kent. How fares your grace?

Lear. What 's he?

Kent. Who 's there? What is 't you seek?

Glou. What are you there? Your names?

Edg. Poor Tom; that eats the swimming frog, the toad, the tadpole, the wall-newt and the water; that in the fury of his heart, when the foul fiend rages, eats cow-dung for sallets; swallows the old rat and the ditch-dog; drinks the green mantle of the standing pool; who is whipped from tithing to tithing, and stock-punished, and imprisoned; who hath had three suits to his back, six shirts to his body, horse to ride, and weapon to wear;
But mice and rats, and such small deer,
Have been Tom's food for seven long year.

to the belief that young pelicans fed on the blood of their mother's breasts. 78. **Pillicock,** from an old rhyme (suggested by *pelican*). *Pillicock* seems to have been used to mean "darling." 83. **commit not,** i.e., adultery. 88. **gloves,** as his mistress' favors. 95. **light of ear,** foolishly credulous (Schmidt), frivolous (Onions). 99. **plackets,** slits in skirts. 100. **pen . . . books,** sign a contract for a loan. 103-104. **suum . . . sessa,** imitative of the wind. 104. **Dolphin my boy,** a slang phrase, or bit of song. 110. **cat,** civet cat. 111. **sophisticated,** clad in the trappings of civilized life; Schmidt defines as "adulterated." 112. **unaccommodated man,** man unprovided with clothes and necessaries; also, man without social modification. 120. **Flibbertigibbet,** a fiend whose name Shakespeare borrowed from Harsnet's *Declaration* (1603).

121. **first cock,** midnight. 122. **web and the pin,** cataract of the eye. **squints,** makes to squint or cross. 124. **white wheat,** approaching ripeness. 125. **S. Withold,** understood as a corruption of St. Vitalis, who is said to have been invoked against nightmare. **footed thrice the 'old,** thrice traversed the wold (tract of hilly upland). 126. **nine-fold,** nine familiars; suggestive also certainly of nine foals. 129. **aroint thee,** begone. 135. **wall-newt,** lizard. 136. **water,** i.e., water newt. 137. **sallets,** salads. 139. **mantle,** scum. 140. **tithing to tithing,** i.e., from one ward or parish to another. **stock-punished,** punished by being put into the stocks. 144. **deer,** probably, animals generally.

Beware my follower. Peace, Smulkin; peace, thou fiend!

Glou. What, hath your grace no better company?

Edg. The prince of darkness is a gentleman:
Modo he 's call'd, and Mahu.

Glou. Our flesh and blood, my lord, is grown so vile
That it doth hate what gets it.

Edg. Poor Tom 's a-cold.

Glou. Go in with me: my duty cannot suffer
T' obey in all your daughters' hard commands:
Though their injunction be to bar my doors,
And let this tyrannous night take hold upon you,
Yet have I ventured to come seek you out,
And bring you where both fire and food is ready.

Lear. First let me talk with this philosopher.
What is the cause of thunder?

Kent. Good my lord, take his offer; go into th' house.

Lear. I'll talk a word with this same learned Theban.
What is your study?

Edg. How to prevent the fiend, and to kill vermin.

Lear. Let me ask you one word in private.

Kent. Importune him once more to go, my lord;
His wits begin t' unsettle.

Glou. Canst thou blame him? *Storm still.*
His daughters seek his death; ah, that good Kent!
He said it would be thus, poor banish'd man!
Thou sayest the king grows mad; I'll tell thee, friend,
I am almost mad myself: I had a son,
Now outlaw'd from my blood; he sought my life,
But lately, very late: I lov'd him, friend:
No father his son dearer: truth to tell thee,
The grief hath craz'd my wits. What a night 's this!
I do beseech your grace,—

Lear. O, cry you mercy, sir.
Noble philosopher, your company.

Edg. Tom 's a-cold.

Glou. In, fellow, there, into th' hovel: keep thee warm.

Lear. Come, let 's in all.

Kent. This way, my lord.

Lear. With him;
I will keep still with my philosopher.

Kent. Good my lord, soothe him; let him take the fellow.

Glou. Take him you on.

Kent. Sirrah, come on; go along with us.

Lear. Come, good Athenian.

Glou. No words, no words: hush.

Edg. Child Rowland to the dark tower came,
His word was still,—Fie, foh, and fum,
I smell the blood of a British man. *Exeunt.*

SCENE V. [*Gloucester's castle.*]

Enter CORNWALL *and* EDMUND.

Corn. I will have my revenge ere I depart his house.

Edm. How, my lord, I may be censured, that nature thus gives way to loyalty, something fears me to think of.

Corn. I now perceive, it was not altogether your brother's evil disposition made him seek his death; but a provoking merit, set a-work by a reproveable badness in himself.

Edm. How malicious is my fortune, that I must repent to be just! This is the letter he spoke of, which approves him an intelligent party to the advantages of France. O heavens! that this treason were not, or not I the detector!

Corn. Go with me to the duchess.

Edm. If the matter of this paper be certain, you have mighty business in hand.

Corn. True or false, it hath made thee Earl of Gloucester. Seek out where thy father is, that he may be ready for our apprehension.

Edm. [*Aside*] If I find him comforting the king, it will stuff his suspicion more fully.—I will persevere in my course of loyalty, though the conflict be sore between that and my blood.

Corn. I will lay trust upon thee; and thou shalt find a dearer father in my love. *Exeunt.*

SCENE VI. [*A chamber in a farmhouse adjoining the castle.*]

Enter KENT *and* GLOUCESTER.

Glou. Here is better than the open air; take it thankfully. I will piece out the comfort with what addition I can: I will not be long from you.

Kent. All the power of his wits have given way to his impatience: the gods reward your kindness!
Exit [*Gloucester*].

Enter LEAR, EDGAR, *and* FOOL.

Edg. Frateretto calls me; and tells me Nero is an angler in the lake of darkness. Pray, innocent, and beware the foul fiend.

Fool. Prithee, nuncle, tell me whether a madman be a gentleman or a yeoman?

Lear. A king, a king!

Fool. No, he 's a yeoman that has a gentleman to his son; for he 's a mad yeoman that sees his son a gentleman before him.

Lear. To have a thousand with red burning spits
Come hizzing in upon 'em,—

Edg. The foul fiend bites my back.

Fool. He 's mad that trusts in the tameness of a wolf, a horse's health, a boy's love, or a whore's oath.

Lear. It shall be done; I will arraign them straight.
[*To Edgar*] Come, sit thou here, most learned justice;
[*To the Fool*] Thou, sapient sir, sit here. Now, you she foxes!

Edg. Look, where he stands and glares!
Want'st thou eyes at trial, madam?
Come o'er the bourn, Bessy, to me,—

146. **Smulkin,** another name occurring in Harsnet. 149. **Modo, Mahu,** two superior fiends in Harsnet. 151. **gets,** begets. 162. **learned Theban,** possibly a current phrase to indicate a philosopher. 182. **soothe,** humor, indulge. 187. **Child Rowland,** etc., fragments of the ballad *Child Rowland and Burd Ellen*. The theme of Browning's *Childe Roland to the Dark Tower Came* is derived from these lines.

SCENE V. 8. **provoking merit,** etc., i.e., an evil justice (in Edgar) incited by the badness of Gloucester. 12. **approves him,** proves him to be. **intelligent,** aware (in the legal sense). 25. **blood,** natural feeling.

SCENE VI. 7. **Frateretto,** another of the fiends from Harsnet. 8. **Nero is an angler,** pointed out as an allusion to Rabelais, ii, 30, where Nero is described as a fiddler and Trajan as an angler. 9. **innocent,** simpleton, fool. 17. **hizzing,** hissing. (Lear is contemplating revenge.) 23. **justice,** judge. 25. **he,** perhaps Lear, or one of Edgar's devils. 26. **Want'st . . . trial,** meaning doubtful. Possibly Edgar alludes to the staring fiend. 27. **Come . . . me,** first line of a ballad by William Birche (1558). (The Fool makes a ribald reply; see *hath a leak.*) 32. **Hoppedance.** Harsnet mentions "Hobberdidance." 33. **white,** unsmoked (contrasted with *black devil*). **Croak,** make a rumbling sound in the stomach to denote hunger. 37. **evidence,** witnesses. 39.

Fool. Her boat hath a leak,
And she must not speak
Why she dares not come over to thee.

Edg. The foul fiend haunts poor Tom in the voice of a nightingale. Hoppedance cries in Tom's belly for two white herring. Croak not, black angel; I have no food for thee.

Kent. How do you, sir? Stand you not so amaz'd.
Will you lie down and rest upon the cushions?

Lear. I'll see their trial first. Bring in the evidence.
[*To Edgar*] Thou robed man of justice, take thy place;
[*To the Fool*] And thou, his yoke-fellow of equity,
Bench by his side: [*To Kent*] you are o' th' commission,
Sit you too.

Edg. Let us deal justly.
Sleepest or wakest thou, jolly shepherd?
Thy sheep be in the corn;
And for one blast of thy minikin mouth,
Thy sheep shall take no harm.
Pur! the cat is gray.

Lear. Arraign her first; 'tis Goneril. I here take my oath before this honourable assembly, she kicked the poor king her father.

Fool. Come hither, mistress. Is your name Goneril?

Lear. She cannot deny it.

Fool. Cry you mercy, I took you for a joint-stool.

Lear. And here 's another, whose warp'd looks proclaim
What store her heart is made on. Stop her there!
Arms, arms, sword, fire! Corruption in the place!
False justicer, why hast thou let her 'scape?

Edg. Bless thy five wits!

Kent. O pity! Sir, where is the patience now,
That you so oft have boasted to retain?

Edg. [*Aside*] My tears begin to take his part so much,
They'll mar my counterfeiting.

Lear. The little dogs and all,
Tray, Blanch, and Sweet-heart, see, they bark at me.

Edg. Tom will throw his head at them.
Avaunt, you curs!
Be thy mouth or black or white,
Tooth that poisons if it bite;
Mastiff, greyhound, mongrel grim,
Hound or spaniel, brach or lym,
Or bobtail tike or trundle-tail,
Tom will make him weep and wail:
For, with throwing thus my head,
Dogs leap'd the hatch, and all are fled.
Do de, de, de. Sessa! Come, march to wakes and fairs and market-towns. Poor Tom, thy horn is dry.

Lear. Then let them anatomize Regan; see what breeds about her heart. Is there any cause in nature that makes these hard hearts? [*To Edgar*] You, sir, I entertain for one of my hundred; only I do not like the fashion of your garments: you will say they are Persian; but let them be changed.

Kent. Now, good my lord, lie here and rest awhile.

Lear. Make no noise, make no noise; draw the curtains: so, so. We'll go to supper i' th' morning. So, so, so.

Fool. And I'll go to bed at noon.

Enter GLOUCESTER.

Glou. Come hither, friend: where is the king my master?

Kent. Here, sir; but trouble him not, his wits are gone.

Glou. Good friend, I prithee, take him in thy arms;
I have o'erheard a plot of death upon him:
There is a litter ready; lay him in 't,
And drive toward Dover, friend, where thou shalt meet
Both welcome and protection. Take up thy master:
If thou shouldst dally half an hour, his life,
With thine, and all that offer to defend him,
Stand in assured loss: take up, take up;
And follow me, that will to some provision
Give thee quick conduct.

Kent. Oppressed nature sleeps:
This rest might yet have balm'd thy broken sinews,
Which, if convenience will not allow,
Stand in hard cure. [*To the Fool*] Come, help to bear thy master;
Thou must not stay behind.

Glou. Come, come, away.

Exeunt [*all but Edgar*].

Edg. When we our betters see bearing our woes,
We scarcely think our miseries our foes.
Who alone suffers suffers most i' th' mind,
Leaving free things and happy shows behind:
But then the mind much sufferance doth o'erskip,
When grief hath mates, and bearing fellowship.
How light and portable my pain seems now,
When that which makes me bend makes the king bow,
He childed as I fathered! Tom, away!
Mark the high noises; and thyself bewray,
When false opinion, whose wrong thoughts defile thee,
In thy just proof, repeals and reconciles thee.
What will hap more to-night, safe 'scape the king!
Lurk, lurk. [*Exit*.]

SCENE VII. [*Gloucester's castle*.]

Enter CORNWALL, REGAN, GONERIL, *Bastard* [EDMUND], *and* Servants.

Corn. Post speedily to my lord your husband; show him this letter: the army of France is landed. Seek out the traitor Gloucester. [*Exeunt some of the Servants*.]

Reg. Hang him instantly.

Gon. Pluck out his eyes.

Corn. Leave him to my displeasure. Edmund, keep you our sister company: the revenges we are bound to

yoke-fellow, partner. 40. **Bench,** sit on the judgment seat. **o' th' commission,** a justice of peace. 45. **minikin,** pretty, dainty. 47. **Pur.** Perhaps for the sound of a cat, or the name of a demon, or both. There is a fiend in Harsnet named Purre. 55. **joint-stool,** chair made by a joiner, possibly ornamented. Proverbially this phrase meant "I beg your pardon for failing to notice you." The reference is also presumably to a real stool on stage. 57. **store,** material. 58. **Corruption in the place,** i.e., there is iniquity or bribery in this court. 72. **lym,** lymmer, a species of bloodhound which runs by scent. 73. **tike,** small dog, cur. **trundle-tail,** curly tail. 76. **hatch,** lower half of a divided door. 77. **Sessa,** away! **wakes,** parish feasts. 79. **horn,** horn bottle used by beggars to beg for drinks. 86. **Persian,** rich, gorgeous attire (ironic). 96. **upon,** against. 102. **Stand in assured loss,** will assuredly be lost. 105. **balm'd,** cured, healed. **sinews,** nerves. 106. **convenience,** fortunate circumstance. 107. **Stand . . . cure,** will be hard to cure. 109. **our woes,** woes like ours. 110. **our foes,** i.e., ours alone. 113. **sufferance,** suffering. 114. **bearing,** tribulation. 115. **portable,** endurable. 117. **He . . . fathered,** he has found the same cruelty in his children which I found in my father. 118. **bewray,** betray, reveal. 120. **In . . . proof,** in vindication of your just conduct. **repeals,** recalls, restores.

take upon your traitorous father are not fit for your beholding. Advise the duke, where you are going, to a most festinate preparation: we are bound to the like. Our posts shall be swift and intelligent betwixt us. Farewell, dear sister: farewell, my lord of Gloucester.

Enter Steward [OSWALD].

How now! where 's the king?
Osw. My lord of Gloucester hath convey'd him hence:
Some five or six and thirty of his knights,
Hot questrists after him, met him at gate;
Who, with some other of the lord's dependants,
Are gone with him toward Dover; where they boast
To have well-armed friends.
Corn. Get horses for your mistress.
[*Exit Oswald.*]
Gon. Farewell, sweet lord, and sister.
Corn. Edmund, farewell.
Exit [*Goneril with Edmund*].
Go seek the traitor Gloucester,
Pinion him like a thief, bring him before us.
[*Exeunt other Servants.*]
Though well we may not pass upon his life
Without the form of justice, yet our power
Shall do a court'sy to our wrath, which men
May blame, but not control. Who 's there? the traitor?

Enter GLOUCESTER *and* Servants.

Reg. Ingrateful fox! 'tis he.
Corn. Bind fast his corky arms.
Glou. What means your graces? Good my friends, consider
You are my guests: do me no foul play, friends.
Corn. Bind him, I say. [*Servants bind him.*]
Reg. Hard, hard. O filthy traitor!
Glou. Unmerciful lady as you are, I'm none.
Corn. To this chair bind him. Villain, thou shalt find— [*Regan plucks his beard.*]
Glou. By the kind gods, 'tis most ignobly done
To pluck me by the beard.
Reg. So white, and such a traitor!
Glou. Naughty lady,
These hairs, which thou dost ravish from my chin,
Will quicken, and accuse thee: I am your host:
With robbers' hands my hospitable favours
You should not ruffle thus. What will you do?
Corn. Come, sir, what letters had you late from France?
Reg. Be simple answer'd, for we know the truth.
Corn. And what confederacy have you with the traitors
Late footed in the kingdom?
Reg. To whose hands you have sent the lunatic king:
Speak.
Glou. I have a letter guessingly set down,
Which came from one that 's of a neutral heart,
And not from one oppos'd.
Corn. Cunning.
Reg. And false.
Corn. Where hast thou sent the king?
Glou. To Dover.
Reg. Wherefore to Dover? Wast thou not charg'd at peril—
Corn. Wherefore to Dover? Let him answer that.
Glou. I am tied to th' stake, and I must stand the course.
Reg. Wherefore to Dover?
Glou. Because I would not see thy cruel nails
Pluck out his poor old eyes; nor thy fierce sister
In his anointed flesh stick boarish fangs.
The sea, with such a storm as his bare head
In hell-black night endur'd, would have buoy'd up,
And quench'd the stelled fires:
Yet, poor old heart, he holp the heavens to rain.
If wolves had at thy gate howl'd that stern time,
Thou shouldst have said 'Good porter, turn the key.'
All cruels else subscribe: but I shall see
The winged vengeance overtake such children.
Corn. See 't shalt thou never. Fellows, hold the chair.
Upon these eyes of thine I'll set my foot.
Glou. He that will think to live till he be old,
Give me some help! O cruel! O you gods!
Reg. One side will mock another; th' other too.
Corn. If you see vengeance,—
First Serv. Hold your hand, my lord:
I have serv'd you ever since I was a child;
But better service have I never done you
Than now to bid you hold.
Reg. How now, you dog!
First Serv. If you did wear a beard upon your chin,
I'd shake it on this quarrel. What do you mean?
Corn. My villain! [*They draw and fight.*]
First Serv. Nay, then, come on, and take the chance of anger.
Reg. Give me thy sword. A peasant stand up thus!
[*Takes a sword, and runs at him behind.*] *Kills him.*
First Serv. O, I am slain! My lord, you have one eye left
To see some mischief on him. O! [*Dies.*]
Corn. Lest it see more, prevent it. Out, vile jelly!
Where is thy lustre now?
Glou. All dark and comfortless. Where 's my son Edmund?
Edmund, enkindle all the sparks of nature,
To quit this horrid act.
Reg. Out, treacherous villain!
Thou call'st on him that hates thee: it was he
That made the overture of thy treasons to us;
Who is too good to pity thee.
Glou. O my follies! then Edgar was abus'd.
Kind gods, forgive me that, and prosper him!
Reg. Go thrust him out at gates, and let him smell
His way to Dover. *Exit* [*one*] *with Gloucester.* How is 't, my lord? how look you?

SCENE VII. 9-10. **Advise . . . to,** i.e., advise him to make. 10. **festinate,** hasty. 11. **bound,** ready. 12. **intelligent,** serviceable in bearing intelligence. 13. **my . . . Gloucester,** i.e., Edmund. In line 15 the reference is to Gloucester himself. 17. **questrists,** searchers. 24. **pass upon,** pass sentence upon. 29. **corky,** withered with age. 39. **quicken,** come to life. 40. **hospitable favours.** Gloucester appeals to the sacredness of hospitality; the meaning is "the features of me, your host." 42. **late,** lately. 43. **simple answer'd,** i.e., straightforward in your answers. 45. **footed,** landed. 54. **tied to th' stake,** like a bear to be baited with dogs. 60. **buoy'd,** lifted itself. 61. **stelled,** fixed; sometimes defined as "starry." 63. **stern,** so F; Q: *heard that dearn.* Many editors follow Capell, *howl'd that dearn*, in which *dearn* means "dire," "dreary." 64. **turn the key,** i.e., let them in. 65. **All . . . subscribe,** all other cruel creatures show forgiveness except you. 78. **villain,** servant, bondman. 87. **quit,** requite. 89. **overture,** disclosure. 98. **Untimely,** inopportunely. 101. **old,** customary, natural.

Corn. I have receiv'd a hurt: follow me, lady.
Turn out that eyeless villain; throw this slave
Upon the dunghill. Regan, I bleed apace:
Untimely comes this hurt: give me your arm.
Exeunt [*Cornwall, led by Regan*].

Sec. Serv. I'll never care what wickedness I do,
If this man come to good.
Third Serv. If she live long,
And in the end meet the old course of death,
Women will all turn monsters.
Sec. Serv. Let 's follow the old earl, and get the Bedlam
To lead him where he would: his roguish madness
Allows itself to any thing.
Third Serv. Go thou: I'll fetch some flax and whites of eggs
To apply to his bleeding face. Now, heaven help him!
[*Exeunt severally.*]

ACT IV.

SCENE I. [*The heath.*]

Enter EDGAR.

Edg. Yet better thus, and known to be contemn'd,
Than still contemn'd and flatter'd. To be worst,
The lowest and most dejected thing of fortune,
Stands still in esperance, lives not in fear:
The lamentable change is from the best;
The worst returns to laughter. Welcome, then,
Thou unsubstantial air that I embrace!
The wretch that thou hast blown unto the worst
Owes nothing to thy blasts. But who comes here?

Enter GLOUCESTER, *and an* Old Man.

My father, poorly led? World, world, O world!
But that thy strange mutations make us hate thee,
Life would not yield to age.
Old Man. O, my good lord, I have been your tenant, and your father's tenant, these fourscore years.
Glou. Away, get thee away; good friend, be gone:
Thy comforts can do me no good at all;
Thee they may hurt.
Old Man. You cannot see your way.
Glou. I have no way, and therefore want no eyes;
I stumbled when I saw: full oft 'tis seen,
Our means secure us, and our mere defects
Prove our commodities. O dear son Edgar,
The food of thy abused father's wrath!
Might I but live to see thee in my touch,
I 'ld say I had eyes again!
Old Man. How now! Who 's there?
Edg. [*Aside*] O gods! Who is 't can say 'I am at the worst'?
I am worse than e'er I was.
Old Man. 'Tis poor mad Tom.
Edg. [*Aside*] And worse I may be yet: the worst is not
So long as we can say 'This is the worst.'
Old Man. Fellow, where goest?
Glou. Is it a beggar-man?
Old Man. Madman and beggar too.
Glou. He has some reason, else he could not beg.
I' th' last night's storm I such a fellow saw;
Which made me think a man a worm: my son
Came then into my mind; and yet my mind
Was then scarce friends with him: I have heard more since.
As flies to wanton boys, are we to th' gods,
They kill us for their sport.
Edg. [*Aside*] How should this be?
Bad is the trade that must play fool to sorrow,
Ang'ring itself and others.—Bless thee, master!
Glou. Is that the naked fellow?
Old Man. Ay, my lord.
Glou. Then, prithee, get thee gone: if, for my sake,
Thou wilt o'ertake us, hence a mile or twain,
I' th' way toward Dover, do it for ancient love;
And bring some covering for this naked soul,
Which I'll entreat to lead me.
Old Man. Alack, sir, he is mad.
Glou. 'Tis the times' plague, when madmen lead the blind.
Do as I bid thee, or rather do thy pleasure;
Above the rest, be gone.
Old Man. I'll bring him the best 'parel that I have,
Come on 't what will. *Exit.*
Glou. Sirrah, naked fellow,—
Edg. Poor Tom 's a-cold. [*Aside*] I cannot daub it further.
Glou. Come hither, fellow.
Edg. [*Aside*] And yet I must.—Bless thy sweet eyes, they bleed.
Glou. Know'st thou the way to Dover?
Edg. Both stile and gate, horse-way and foot-path. Poor Tom hath been scared out of his good wits: bless thee, good man's son, from the foul fiend! five fiends have been in poor Tom at once; of lust, as Obidicut; Hobbididance, prince of dumbness; Mahu, of stealing; Modo, of murder; Flibbertigibbet, of mopping and mowing, who since possesses chambermaids and waiting-women. So, bless thee, master!
Glou. Here, take this purse, thou whom the heavens' plagues
Have humbled to all strokes: that I am wretched
Makes thee the happier: heavens, deal so still!
Let the superfluous and lust-dieted man,
That slaves your ordinance, that will not see
Because he does not feel, feel your pow'r quickly;
So distribution should undo excess,
And each man have enough. Dost thou know Dover?
Edg. Ay, master.
Glou. There is a cliff, whose high and bending head
Looks fearfully in the confined deep:
Bring me but to the very brim of it,
And I'll repair the misery thou dost bear
With something rich about me: from that place
I shall no leading need.
Edg. Give me thy arm:

103. **Bedlam,** Bedlamite, lunatic.
ACT IV. SCENE I. 3. **dejected . . . of,** debased or humbled by. 4. **esperance,** hope. 6. **The worst . . . laughter,** i.e., every terrible extreme must turn some day to better fortune. 11. **mutations,** changes, variations. 12. **age,** aging and death. 22. **Our means secure us,** our prosperity makes us overconfident. **mere defects,** sheer afflictions. 23. **commodities,** benefits. 51. **'parel,** apparel. 54. **daub it further,** keep up the disguise. 62-64. **Obidicut . . . Flibbertigibbet,** fiends borrowed, as before, from Harsnet. 65. **mopping and mowing,** making grimaces and mouths. 70. **superfluous,** having a superfluity. **lust-dieted,** probably, feeding luxuriously. 71. **slaves your ordinance,** i.e., makes the laws of heaven his slaves. 73. **distribution,** the principle of distributive justice in ethics.

Poor Tom shall lead thee. *Exeunt.*

SCENE II. [*Before the Duke of Albany's palace.*]

Enter GONERIL [*and*] *Bastard* [EDMUND].

Gon. Welcome, my lord: I marvel our mild husband
Not met us on the way.

[*Enter*] *Steward* [OSWALD].

Now, where 's your master?
Osw. Madam, within; but never man so chang'd.
I told him of the army that was landed;
He smil'd at it: I told him you were coming;
His answer was 'The worse:' of Gloucester's treachery,
And of the loyal service of his son,
When I inform'd him, then he call'd me sot,
And told me I had turn'd the wrong side out:
What most he should dislike seems pleasant to him;
What like, offensive.
Gon. [*To Edm.*] Then shall you go no further.
It is the cowish terror of his spirit,
That dares not undertake: he'll not feel wrongs
Which tie him to an answer. Our wishes on the way
May prove effects. Back, Edmund, to my brother;
Hasten his musters and conduct his pow'rs:
I must change names at home, and give the distaff
Into my husband's hands. This trusty servant
Shall pass between us: ere long you are like to hear,
If you dare venture in your own behalf,
A mistress's command. Wear this; spare speech;
[*Giving a favour.*]
Decline your head: this kiss, if it durst speak,
Would stretch thy spirits up into the air:
Conceive, and fare thee well.
Edm. Yours in the ranks of death. *Exit.*
Gon. My most dear Gloucester!
O, the difference of man and man!
To thee a woman's services are due:
My fool usurps my body.
Osw. Madam, here comes my lord. [*Exit.*]

Enter ALBANY.

Gon. I have been worth the whistle.
Alb. O Goneril!
You are not worth the dust which the rude wind
Blows in your face. I fear your disposition:
That nature, which contemns its origin,
Cannot be bordered certain in itself;
She that herself will sliver and disbranch
From her material sap, perforce must wither
And come to deadly use.
Gon. No more; the text is foolish.
Alb. Wisdom and goodness to the vile seem vile:
Filths savour but themselves. What have you done?
Tigers, not daughters, what have you perform'd?
A father, and a gracious aged man,
Whose reverence even the head-lugg'd bear would lick,
Most barbarous, most degenerate! have you madded.
Could my good brother suffer you to do it?
A man, a prince, by him so benefited!
If that the heavens do not their visible spirits
Send quickly down to tame these vile offences,
It will come,
Humanity must perforce prey on itself,
Like monsters of the deep.
Gon. Milk-liver'd man!
That bear'st a cheek for blows, a head for wrongs:
Who hast not in thy brows an eye discerning
Thine honour from thy suffering; that not know'st
Fools do those villains pity who are punish'd
Ere they have done their mischief. Where 's thy drum?
France spreads his banners in our noiseless land,
With plumed helm thy state begins to threat;
Whilst thou, a moral fool, sits still, and cries
'Alack, why does he so?'
Alb. See thyself, devil!
Proper deformity seems not in the fiend
So horrid as in woman.
Gon. O vain fool!
Alb. Thou changed and self-cover'd thing, for shame,
Be-monster not thy feature. Were 't my fitness
To let these hands obey my blood,
They are apt enough to dislocate and tear
Thy flesh and bones: howe'er thou art a fiend,
A woman's shape doth shield thee.
Gon. Marry, your manhood, mew!

Enter a Messenger.

Alb. What news?
Mess. O, my good lord, the Duke of Cornwall 's dead;
Slain by his servant, going to put out
The other eye of Gloucester.
Alb. Gloucester's eyes!
Mess. A servant that he bred, thrill'd with remorse,
Oppos'd against the act, bending his sword
To his great master; who, thereat enrag'd,
Flew on him, and amongst them fell'd him dead;
But not without that harmful stroke, which since
Hath pluck'd him after.
Alb. This shows you are above,
You justicers, that these our nether crimes
So speedily can venge! But, O poor Gloucester!
Lost he his other eye?
Mess. Both, both, my lord.
This letter, madam, craves a speedy answer;
'Tis from your sister.
Gon. [*Aside*] One way I like this well;
But being widow, and my Gloucester with her,
May all the building in my fancy pluck
Upon my hateful life: another way,

SCENE II. 1. **Welcome.** Goneril, who has just arrived home from Gloucester escorted by Edmund, bids him brief welcome before he must return. **mild,** used ironically. 8. **sot,** fool. 9. **turn'd the wrong side out,** put a wrong interpretation on the matter. 12. **cowish,** cowardly. 13-14. **he'll . . . answer,** i.e., in his cowardice he will ignore injuries he ought to resent. 14. **Our . . . way,** my wishes expressed to you on the way. 15. **prove effects,** come to pass. 17. **change names,** i.e., exchange the roles of master and mistress of the household. **distaff,** spinning staff, symbolizing the wife's role. 24. **Conceive,** understand, take my meaning; with sexual double entendre, continuing from *stretch thy spirits* in the previous line. 29. **whistle.** She alludes to the proverb: "It is a poor dog that is not worth the whistling." 33. **bordered,** kept within bounds. 34. **sliver,** tear off. 35. **material sap,** nourishing substance. 39. **savour but,** care only for. 42. **head-lugg'd,** dragged by the head and infuriated. 43. **madded,** driven mad. 47. **offences,** offenders. 50. **Milk-liver'd,** cowardly. 54. **Fools,** only fools. 55. **thy drum,** i.e., your military preparations. 56. **noiseless,** peaceful, having none of the bustle of war. 58. **moral,** moralizing. 60. **Proper,** i.e., the deformity appropriate to the fiend. 62. **self-cover'd,** having the true self concealed. 63. **Be-monster . . . feature,** do not, being

The news is not so tart.—I'll read, and answer. [*Exit.*]
Alb. Where was his son when they did take his eyes?
Mess. Come with my lady hither.
Alb. He is not here.
Mess. No, my good lord; I met him back again.
Alb. Knows he the wickedness?
Mess. Ay, my good lord; 'twas he inform'd against him;
And quit the house on purpose, that their punishment
Might have the freer course.
Alb. Gloucester, I live
To thank thee for the love thou show'dst the king,
And to revenge thine eyes. Come hither, friend:
Tell me what more thou know'st. *Exeunt.*

SCENE [III. *The French camp near Dover.*]

Enter KENT *and a* Gentleman.

Kent. Why the King of France is so suddenly gone back know you no reason?

Gent. Something he left imperfect in the state, which since his coming forth is thought of; which imports to the kingdom so much fear and danger, that his personal return was most required and necessary.

Kent. Who hath he left behind him general?

Gent. The Marshal of France, Monsieur La Far.

Kent. Did your letters pierce the queen to any demonstration of grief?

Gent. Ay, sir; she took them, read them in my presence;
And now and then an ample tear trill'd down
Her delicate cheek: it seem'd she was a queen
Over her passion; who, most rebel-like,
Sought to be king o'er her.
Kent. O, then it moved her.
Gent. Not to a rage: patience and sorrow strove
Who should express her goodliest. You have seen
Sunshine and rain at once: her smiles and tears
†Were like a better way: those happy smilets,
That play'd on her ripe lip, seem'd not to know
What guests were in her eyes; which parted thence,
As pearls from diamonds dropp'd. In brief,
Sorrow would be a rarity most beloved,
If all could so become it.
Kent. Made she no verbal question?
Gent. 'Faith, once or twice she heav'd the name of 'father'
Pantingly forth, as if it press'd her heart;
Cried 'Sisters! sisters! Shame of ladies! sisters!
Kent! father! sisters! What, i' th' storm? i' th' night?
Let pity not be believ'd!' There she shook
The holy water from her heavenly eyes,
And clamour moisten'd: then away she started
To deal with grief alone.
Kent. It is the stars,
The stars above us, govern our conditions;
Else one self mate and make could not beget
Such different issues. You spoke not with her since?
Gent. No.
Kent. Was this before the king return'd?
Gent. No, since.
Kent. Well, sir, the poor distressed Lear 's i' th' town;
Who sometime, in his better tune, remembers
What we are come about, and by no means
Will yield to see his daughter.
Gent. Why, good sir?
Kent. A sovereign shame so elbows him: his own unkindness,
That stripp'd her from his benediction, turn'd her
To foreign casualties, gave her dear rights
To his dog-hearted daughters, these things sting
His mind so venomously, that burning shame
Detains him from Cordelia.
Gent. Alack, poor gentleman!
Kent. Of Albany's and Cornwall's powers you heard not?
Gent. 'Tis so, they are afoot.
Kent. Well, sir, I'll bring you to our master Lear,
And leave you to attend him: some dear cause
Will in concealment wrap me up awhile;
When I am known aright, you shall not grieve
Lending me this acquaintance. I pray you, go
Along with me. *Exeunt.*

SCENE [IV. *The same. A tent.*]

Enter, with drum and colours, CORDELIA, Doctor, *and* Soldiers.

Cor. Alack, 'tis he: why, he was met even now
As mad as the vex'd sea; singing aloud;
Crown'd with rank fumiter and furrow-weeds,
With har-docks, hemlock, nettles, cuckoo-flow'rs,
Darnel, and all the idle weeds that grow
In our sustaining corn. A century send forth;
Search every acre in the high-grown field,
And bring him to our eye. [*Exit an Officer.*] What can man's wisdom
In the restoring his bereaved sense?
He that helps him take all my outward worth.
Doct. There is means, madam:
Our foster-nurse of nature is repose,
The which he lacks; that to provoke in him,
Are many simples operative, whose power
Will close the eye of anguish.
Cor. All blest secrets,
All you unpublish'd virtues of the earth,
Spring with my tears! be aidant and remediate
In the good man's distress! Seek, seek for him;
Lest his ungovern'd rage dissolve the life
That wants the means to lead it.

Enter Messenger.

Mess. News, madam;

fiend, take on the outward form of a fiend. **my fitness,** suitable for me. 66. **howe'er,** although. 68. **mew,** an exclamation of disgust. 73. **thrill'd,** deeply moved. **remorse,** pity. 74-75. **bending . . . To,** directing his sword against. 88. **tart,** painful. 91. **back,** going back.
SCENE III. 5. **imports,** portends. 14. **trill'd,** trickled. 21. **like a better way,** possibly, better than this. **smilets,** smiles. 22. **ripe,** probably, red (W. J. Craig). 27. **heav'd,** breathed out. 36. **Else . . . make,** otherwise, one couple (husband and wife). 41. **better tune,** saner moments. 44. **elbows,** thrusts away, or possibly, stands at his elbow. 45. **turn'd,** expelled.

SCENE IV. 3. **fumiter,** the weed "earth-smoke." **furrow-weeds,** weeds growing in the furrows of plowed land. 4. **har-docks,** perhaps burdocks, or hoar-docks, white-leaved. **cuckoo-flow'rs,** possibly, cowslips. 5. **Darnel,** a weed of the grass kind. The plants mentioned in this passage are probably selected because of their bitter and poisonous quality. 6. **sustaining,** giving sustenance. **century,** usually interpreted as a troop of 100 men, as in the Roman army; also taken to mean "sentry" or "scout." 8. **wisdom,** science. 9. **bereaved,** snatched away. 14. **simples,** medicinal plants. **operative,** effective. 16. **unpublish'd,** little known. 17. **aidant and remediate,** helpful and remedial.

The British pow'rs are marching hitherward.
Cor. 'Tis known before; our preparation stands
In expectation of them. O dear father,
It is thy business that I go about;
Therefore great France
My mourning and importun'd tears hath pitied.
No blown ambition doth our arms incite,
But love, dear love, and our ag'd father's right:
Soon may I hear and see him! *Exeunt.*

SCENE [V. *Gloucester's castle.*]

Enter REGAN *and Steward* [OSWALD].

Reg. But are my brother's pow'rs set forth?
Osw. Ay, madam.
Reg. Himself in person there?
Osw. Madam, with much ado:
Your sister is the better soldier.
Reg. Lord Edmund spake not with your lord at home?
Osw. No, madam.
Reg. What might import my sister's letter to him?
Osw. I know not, lady.
Reg. 'Faith, he is posted hence on serious matter.
It was great ignorance, Gloucester's eyes being out,
To let him live: where he arrives he moves
All hearts against us: Edmund, I think, is gone,
In pity of his misery, to dispatch
His nighted life; moreover, to descry
The strength o' th' enemy.
Osw. I must needs after him, madam, with my letter.
Reg. Our troops set forth to-morrow: stay with us;
The ways are dangerous.
Osw. I may not, madam:
My lady charg'd my duty in this business.
Reg. Why should she write to Edmund? Might not you
Transport her purposes by word? Belike,
Something—I know not what: I'll love thee much,
Let me unseal the letter.
Osw. Madam, I had rather—
Reg. I know your lady does not love her husband;
I am sure of that: and at her late being here
She gave strange œillades and most speaking looks
To noble Edmund. I know you are of her bosom.
Osw. I, madam?
Reg. I speak in understanding; y' are, I know 't:
Therefore I do advise you, take this note:
My lord is dead; Edmund and I have talk'd;
And more convenient is he for my hand
Than for your lady's: you may gather more.
If you do find him, pray you, give him this;
And when your mistress hears thus much from you,
I pray, desire her call her wisdom to her.
So, fare you well.
If you do chance to hear of that blind traitor,
Preferment falls on him that cuts him off.
Osw. Would I could meet him, madam! I should show
What party I do follow.
Reg. Fare thee well. *Exeunt.*

SCENE [VI. *Fields near Dover.*]

Enter GLOUCESTER, *and* EDGAR [*dressed like a peasant*].

Glou. When shall I come to th' top of that same hill?
Edg. You do climb up it now: look, how we labour.
Glou. Methinks the ground is even.
Edg. Horrible steep.
Hark, do you hear the sea?
Glou. No, truly.
Edg. Why, then, your other senses grow imperfect
By your eyes' anguish.
Glou. So may it be, indeed:
Methinks thy voice is alter'd; and thou speak'st
In better phrase and matter than thou didst.
Edg. Y' are much deceiv'd: in nothing am I chang'd
But in my garments.
Glou. Methinks y' are better spoken.
Edg. Come on, sir; here 's the place: stand still. How fearful
And dizzy 'tis, to cast one's eyes so low!
The crows and choughs that wing the midway air
Show scarce so gross as beetles: half way down
Hangs one that gathers samphire, dreadful trade!
Methinks he seems no bigger than his head:
The fishermen, that walk upon the beach,
Appear like mice; and yond tall anchoring bark,
Diminish'd to her cock; her cock, a buoy
Almost too small for sight: the murmuring surge,
That on th' unnumb'red idle pebbles chafes,
Cannot be heard so high. I'll look no more;
Lest my brain turn, and the deficient sight
Topple down headlong.
Glou. Set me where you stand.
Edg. Give me your hand: you are now within a foot
Of th' extreme verge: for all beneath the moon
Would I not leap upright.
Glou. Let go my hand.
Here, friend, 's another purse; in it a jewel
Well worth a poor man's taking: fairies and gods
Prosper it with thee! Go thou further off;
Bid me farewell, and let me hear thee going.
Edg. Now fare ye well, good sir.
Glou. With all my heart.
Edg. Why I do trifle thus with his despair
Is done to cure it.
Glou. [*Kneeling*] O you mighty gods!
This world I do renounce, and, in your sights,
Shake patiently my great affliction off:
If I could bear it longer, and not fall

26. **importun'd,** importunate. 27. **blown,** puffed up with pride. (Cordelia is at pains to stress that France is invading England not for territorial advantage.)

SCENE V. 6. **import,** to bear as its purport, to express (Onions). 8. **is posted,** has hurried. 9. **ignorance,** error. 18. **charg'd,** ordered strictly. 20. **word,** word of mouth. **Belike,** it may be. 24. **late,** recent. 25. **œillades,** amorous glances. 26. **of her bosom,** in her confidence. 29. **take this note,** take note of this. 30. **have talk'd,** are affianced to one another (W. J. Craig). 32. **gather more,** i.e., infer what I am trying to suggest. 35. **call her wisdom,** recall herself to her senses. 38. **Preferment,** advancement.

SCENE VI. 13. **choughs,** jackdaws. **midway,** halfway down. 14. **gross,** large. 15. **samphire,** an herb called sea-fennel and the herb of St. Pierre, used for pickles. 19. **Diminish'd . . . cock,** reduced to the size of her cock-boat. 21. **unnumb'red,** innumerable. 23-24. **the deficient sight Topple,** my failing sight topple me. 27. **upright,** i.e., up and down, much less forward. 38. **opposeless,** irresistible. 39. **snuff,** useless residue; the metaphor is taken from the smoking wick of a candle. 42. **conceit,** imagination. 47. **pass,** die. 53. **at each,** end to end. 57. **bourn,** limit, boundary. 58. **a-height,** on high.

To quarrel with your great opposeless wills,
My snuff and loathed part of nature should
Burn itself out. If Edgar live, O, bless him!
Now, fellow, fare thee well. [*He falls forward.*]
Edg. Gone, sir: farewell.—
And yet I know not how conceit may rob
The treasury of life, when life itself
Yields to the theft: had he been where he thought,
By this, had thought been past.—Alive or dead?
Ho, you sir! friend! Hear you, sir! speak!—
Thus might he pass indeed: yet he revives.
What are you, sir?
Glou. Away, and let me die.
Edg. Hadst thou been aught but gossamer, feathers, air,
So many fathom down precipitating,
Thou 'dst shiver'd like an egg: but thou dost breathe;
Hast heavy substance; bleed'st not; speak'st; art sound.
Ten masts at each make not the altitude
Which thou hast perpendicularly fell:
Thy life 's a miracle. Speak yet again.
Glou. But have I fall'n, or no?
Edg. From the dread summit of this chalky bourn.
Look up a-height; the shrill-gorg'd lark so far
Cannot be seen or heard: do but look up.
Glou. Alack, I have no eyes.
Is wretchedness depriv'd that benefit,
To end itself by death? 'Twas yet some comfort,
When misery could beguile the tyrant's rage,
And frustrate his proud will.
Edg. Give me your arm:
Up: so. How is 't? Feel you your legs? You stand.
Glou. Too well, too well.
Edg. This is above all strangeness.
Upon the crown o' th' cliff, what thing was that
Which parted from you?
Glou. A poor unfortunate beggar.
Edg. As I stood here below, methought his eyes
Were two full moons; he had a thousand noses,
Horns whelk'd and waved like the enridged sea:
It was some fiend; therefore, thou happy father,
Think that the clearest gods, who make them honours
Of men's impossibilities, have preserved thee.
Glou. I do remember now: henceforth I'll bear
Affliction till it do cry out itself
'Enough, enough,' and die. That thing you speak of,
I took it for a man; often 'twould say
'The fiend, the fiend:' he led me to that place.
Edg. Bear free and patient thoughts. But who comes here?

Enter LEAR [*fantastically dressed with wild flowers*].

The safer sense will ne'er accommodate
His master thus.
Lear. No, they cannot touch me for coining;
I am the king himself.
Edg. O thou side-piercing sight!

Lear. Nature 's above art in that respect. There 's your press-money. That fellow handles his bow like a crow-keeper: draw me a clothier's yard. Look, look, a mouse! Peace, peace; this piece of toasted cheese will do 't. There 's my gauntlet; I'll prove it on a giant. Bring up the brown bills. O, well flown, bird! i' the clout, i' the clout: hewgh! Give the word.

Edg. Sweet marjoram.

Lear. Pass.

Glou. I know that voice.

Lear. Ha! Goneril, with a white beard! They flattered me like a dog; and told me I had white hairs in my beard ere the black ones were there. To say 'ay' and 'no' to every thing that I said!—'Ay' and 'no' too was no good divinity. When the rain came to wet me once, and the wind to make me chatter; when the thunder would not peace at my bidding; there I found 'em, there I smelt 'em out. Go to, they are not men o' their words: they told me I was every thing; 'tis a lie, I am not ague-proof.

Glou. The trick of that voice I do well remember:
Is 't not the king?
Lear. Ay, every inch a king:
When I do stare, see how the subject quakes.
I pardon that man's life. What was thy cause?
Adultery?
Thou shalt not die: die for adultery! No:
The wren goes to 't, and the small gilded fly
Does lecher in my sight.
Let copulation thrive; for Gloucester's bastard son
Was kinder to his father than my daughters
Got 'tween the lawful sheets.
To 't, luxury, pell-mell! for I lack soldiers.
Behold yond simp'ring dame,
Whose face between her forks presages snow;
That minces virtue, and does shake the head
To hear of pleasure's name;
The fitchew, nor the soiled horse, goes to 't
With a more riotous appetite.
Down from the waist they are Centaurs,
Though women all above:
But to the girdle do the gods inherit,
Beneath is all the fiends';
There 's hell, there 's darkness, there is the sulphurous pit,
Burning, scalding, stench, consumption; fie, fie, fie! pah, pah! Give me an ounce of civet, good apothecary, to sweeten my imagination: there 's money for thee.

Glou. O, let me kiss that hand!

Lear. Let me wipe it first; it smells of mortality.

Glou. O ruin'd piece of nature! This great world
Shall so wear out to nought. Dost thou know me?

Lear. I remember thine eyes well enough. Dost thou squiny at me? No, do thy worst, blind Cupid; I'll not love. Read thou this challenge; mark but the penning of it.

Glou. Were all thy letters suns, I could not see one.

shrill-gorg'd, shrill-throated. 63. **beguile,** outwit. 71. **whelk'd,** explained as "twisted"; also as "swollen, as with whelks or knobs." **enridged,** furrowed. 73. **clearest,** most righteous. 74. **men's impossibilities,** things impossible to men. 80. **free,** probably, free from despair. 81. **safer,** saner. **accommodate,** furnish, accoutre. 83. **touch,** arrest, prosecute. **coining,** minting coins (a royal prerogative). 87. **press-money,** bonus given soldiers when they were pressed into service. 89. **clothier's yard,** arrow the length of a cloth yard. 91. **prove it on,** maintain it against. 92. **brown bills,** soldiers carrying pikes, or the pikes themselves. **well flown, bird.** Lear may think he is hawking, or he may be speaking of the flight of an arrow. 93. **clout,** target. **word,** password. 102. **no good divinity,** not good theology, contrary to biblical teaching; see II Cor. 1:18 and James 5:12. 104. **peace,** hold its peace. 108. **trick,** peculiar characteristic. 119. **luxury,** lust. 121. **Whose . . . snow,** whose frosty countenance seems to suggest frigidity between her legs. 122. **minces,** affects. 123. **pleasure's,** i.e., sexual pleasure's. 124. **fitchew,** polecat. **soiled horse,** horse turned out to grass. 126. **Centaurs,** fabulous monsters, half man, half horse. 128. **But,** only. **inherit,** possess. 137. **piece,** masterpiece. 140. **squiny,** squint, look askance.

Edg. [*Aside*] I would not take this from report; it is,
And my heart breaks at it.

Lear. Read.

Glou. What, with the case of eyes?

Lear. O, ho, are you there with me? No eyes in your head, nor no money in your purse? Your eyes are in a heavy case, your purse in a light: yet you see how this world goes.

Glou. I see it feelingly.

Lear. What, art mad? A man may see how this world goes with no eyes. Look with thine ears: see how yond justice rails upon yond simple thief. Hark, in thine ear: change places; and, handy-dandy, which is the justice, which is the thief? Thou hast seen a farmer's dog bark at a beggar?

Glou. Ay, sir.

Lear. And the creature run from the cur? There thou mightst behold the great image of authority: a dog 's obeyed in office.
Thou rascal beadle, hold thy bloody hand!
Why dost thou lash that whore? Strip thy own back;
Thou hotly lusts to use her in that kind
For which thou whipp'st her. The usurer hangs the
cozener.
Through tatter'd clothes small vices do appear;
Robes and furr'd gowns hide all. Plate sin with gold,
And the strong lance of justice hurtless breaks;
Arm it in rags, a pigmy's straw does pierce it.
None does offend, none, I say, none; I'll able 'em:
Take that of me, my friend, who have the power
To seal th' accuser's lips. Get thee glass eyes;
And, like a scurvy politician, seem
To see the things thou dost not. Now, now, now, now:
Pull off my boots: harder, harder: so.

Edg. O, matter and impertinency mix'd!
Reason in madness!

Lear. If thou wilt weep my fortunes, take my eyes.
I know thee well enough; thy name is Gloucester:
Thou must be patient; we came crying hither:
Thou know'st, the first time that we smell the air,
We wawl and cry. I will preach to thee: mark.

Glou. Alack, alack the day!

Lear. When we are born, we cry that we are come
To this great stage of fools: this' a good block;
It were a delicate stratagem, to shoe
A troop of horse with felt: I'll put 't in proof;
And when I have stol'n upon these son-in-laws,
Then, kill, kill, kill, kill, kill, kill!

Enter a Gentleman [*with* Attendants].

Gent. O, here he is: lay hand upon him. Sir,
Your most dear daughter—

Lear. No rescue? What, a prisoner? I am even
The natural fool of fortune. Use me well;
You shall have ransom. Let me have surgeons;
I am cut to th' brains.

Gent. You shall have any thing.

Lear. No seconds? all myself?
Why, this would make a man a man of salt,
To use his eyes for garden water-pots,
Ay, and laying autumn's dust.

Gent. Good sir,—

Lear. I will die bravely, like a smug bridegroom.
What!
I will be jovial: come, come; I am a king;
Masters, know you that.

Gent. You are a royal one, and we obey you.

Lear. Then there 's life in 't. Come, an you get it, you shall get it by running. Sa, sa, sa, sa.

Exit [*running; Attendants follow*].

Gent. A sight most pitiful in the meanest wretch,
Past speaking of in a king! Thou hast one daughter,
Who redeems nature from the general curse
Which twain have brought her to.

Edg. Hail, gentle sir.

Gent. Sir, speed you: what 's your will?

Edg. Do you hear aught, sir, of a battle toward?

Gent. Most sure and vulgar: every one hears that,
Which can distinguish sound.

Edg. But, by your favour,
How near 's the other army?

Gent. Near and on speedy foot; the main descry
Stands on the hourly thought.

Edg. I thank you, sir: that 's all.

Gent. Though that the queen on special cause is
here,
Her army is mov'd on.

Edg. I thank you, sir. *Exit* [*Gent*.].

Glou. You ever-gentle gods, take my breath from
me;
Let not my worser spirit tempt me again
To die before you please!

Edg. Well pray you, father.

Glou. Now, good sir, what are you?

Edg. A most poor man, made tame to fortune's
blows;
Who, by the art of known and feeling sorrows,
Am pregnant to good pity. Give me your hand,
I'll lead you to some biding.

Glou. Hearty thanks:
The bounty and the benison of heaven
To boot, and boot!

Enter Steward [OSWALD].

Osw. A proclaim'd prize! Most
happy!
That eyeless head of thine was first fram'd flesh
To raise my fortunes. Thou old unhappy traitor,
Briefly thyself remember: the sword is out
That must destroy thee.

Glou. Now let thy friendly hand
Put strength enough to 't. [*Edgar interposes*.]

Osw. Wherefore, bold peasant,
Dar'st thou support a publish'd traitor? Hence;
Lest that th' infection of his fortune take
Like hold on thee. Let go his arm.

Edg. Chill not let go, zir, without vurther 'casion.

Osw. Let go, slave, or thou diest!

Edg. Good gentleman, go your gait, and let poor volk pass. An chud ha' bin zwaggered out of my life,

147. **case,** mere sockets. 148. **are . . . me?** Is that your situation? 157. **handy-dandy,** take your choice of hands, as in a well-known child's game. 161-171. **And the . . . pierce it.** Into these ravings should be read the conception of a state resting upon authority solely, and this state fallen into ruin because the holders of this divinely constituted authority are themselves corrupt. 167. **cozener,** cheater. 172. **able,** give warrant to. 175. **politician,** opportunist. 187. **this',** this is. **block,** probably, hat, from the form on which it was molded.

189. **in proof,** to the test. 199. **man of salt,** of salt tears. 212. **speed you,** God speed you. 214. **vulgar,** in everyone's mouth, generally known. 215. **Which,** who. 217-218. **the main . . . thought,** the full view of the main body is expected every hour. 226. **feeling,** heartfelt, deep. 227. **pregnant,** prone. 228. **biding,** abiding place. 230. **To boot, and boot,** i.e., in addition (to my thanks), I wish you the bounty of heaven. 231. **fram'd flesh,** born. 233. **thyself remember,** confess thy sins. 239. **Chill,** I will. Edgar adopts a dialect, apparently of the

'twould not ha' bin zo long as 'tis by a vortnight. Nay, come not near th' old man; keep out, che vor ye, or ise try whether your costard or my ballow be the harder: chill be plain with you.

Osw. Out, dunghill!

Edg. Chill pick your teeth, zir: come; no matter vor your foins. [*They fight, and Edgar knocks him down.*]

Osw. Slave, thou hast slain me: villain, take my purse:
If ever thou wilt thrive, bury my body;
And give the letters which thou find'st about me
To Edmund Earl of Gloucester; seek him out
Upon the English party: O, untimely death! [*Dies.*]

Edg. I know thee well: a serviceable villain;
As duteous to the vices of thy mistress
As badness would desire.

Glou. What, is he dead?

Edg. Sit you down, father; rest you.
Let 's see these pockets: the letters that he speaks of
May be my friends. He 's dead; I am only sorry
He had no other death's-man. Let us see:
Leave, gentle wax; and, manners, blame us not:
To know our enemies' minds, we rip their hearts;
Their papers, is more lawful. (*Reads the letter.*)

'Let our reciprocal vows be remembered. You have many opportunities to cut him off: if your will want not, time and place will be fruitfully offered. There is nothing done, if he return the conqueror: then am I the prisoner, and his bed my gaol; from the loathed warmth whereof deliver me, and supply the place for your labour.

'Your—wife, so I would say—
'Affectionate servant, GONERIL.'

O indistinguish'd space of woman's will!
A plot upon her virtuous husband's life;
And the exchange my brother! Here, in the sands,
Thee I'll rake up, the post unsanctified
Of murderous lechers: and in the mature time
With this ungracious paper strike the sight
Of the death-practis'd duke: for him 'tis well
That of thy death and business I can tell.

Glou. The king is mad: how stiff is my vile sense,
That I stand up, and have ingenious feeling
Of my huge sorrows! Better I were distract:
So should my thoughts be sever'd from my griefs,
And woes by wrong imaginations lose
The knowledge of themselves.

Edg. Give me your hand:
Drum afar off.
Far off, methinks, I hear the beaten drum:
Come, father, I'll bestow you with a friend. *Exeunt.*

SCENE VII. [*A tent in the French camp.*]

Enter CORDELIA, KENT, [DOCTOR,] *and* Gentleman.

Cor. O thou good Kent, how shall I live and work,
To match thy goodness? My life will be too short,
And every measure fail me.

Kent. To be acknowledg'd, madam, is o'er-paid.
All my reports go with the modest truth;
Nor more nor clipp'd, but so.

Cor. Be better suited:
These weeds are memories of those worser hours:
I prithee, put them off.

Kent. Pardon, dear madam;
Yet to be known shortens my made intent:
My boon I make it, that you know me not
Till time and I think meet.

Cor. Then be 't so, my good lord. [*To the Doctor*] How does the king?

Doct. Madam, sleeps still.

Cor. O you kind gods,
Cure this great breach in his abused nature!
Th' untun'd and jarring senses, O, wind up
Of this child-changed father!

Doct. So please your majesty
That we may wake the king: he hath slept long.

Cor. Be govern'd by your knowledge, and proceed
I' th' sway of your own will. Is he array'd?

Enter LEAR *in a chair carried by* Servants.

Gent. Ay, madam; in the heaviness of sleep
We put fresh garments on him.

Doct. Be by, good madam, when we do awake him;
I doubt not of his temperance.

Cor. Very well. [*Music.*]

Doct. Please you, draw near. Louder the music there!

Cor. O my dear father! Restoration hang
Thy medicine on my lips; and let this kiss
Repair those violent harms that my two sisters
Have in thy reverence made!

Kent. Kind and dear princess!

Cor. Had you not been their father, these white flakes
Did challenge pity of them. Was this a face
To be oppos'd against the warring winds?
To stand against the deep dread-bolted thunder?
In the most terrible and nimble stroke
Of quick, cross lightning? to watch—poor perdu!—
With this thin helm? Mine enemy's dog,
Though he had bit me, should have stood that night
Against my fire; and wast thou fain, poor father,
To hovel thee with swine, and rogues forlorn,
In short and musty straw? Alack, alack!
'Tis wonder that thy life and wits at once
Had not concluded all. He wakes; speak to him.

Doct. Madam, do you; 'tis fittest.

Cor. How does my royal lord? How fares your majesty?

Lear. You do me wrong to take me out o' th' grave:
Thou art a soul in bliss; but I am bound
Upon a wheel of fire, that mine own tears
Do scald like molten lead.

Cor. Sir, do you know me?

Lear. You are a spirit, I know: when did you die?

Cor. Still, still, far wide!

Doct. He 's scarce awake: let him alone awhile.

south country. 242. **go your gait,** go your own way. 243. **An chud,** if I could. 246. **che vor ye,** I warn you. 247. **ise,** I shall. **costard,** an apple, slang for "head." **ballow,** cudgel. 249. **dunghill,** person of the lowest extraction. 251. **foins,** thrusts in fencing. 263. **death's-man,** executioner. 264. **Leave,** by your leave. 270. **fruitfully,** amply, fully. 276. **servant,** lover. 278. **indistinguish'd . . . will,** incalculable range of woman's appetite. 281. **rake up,** cover up. 283. **ungracious,** wicked. 284. **death-practis'd,** whose death is plotted. 286. **stiff,** obstinate. **sense,** consciousness. 287. **ingenious,** conscious. 288. **distract,** distracted, crazy.

SCENE VII. 6. **clipp'd,** curtailed. **suited,** dressed. 7. **memories,** remembrances. 9. **made intent,** carefully thought-out purpose. 17. **child-changed,** changed (in mind) by children's cruelty. 24. **temperance,** sanity. 33. **dread-bolted,** furnished with the dreadful thunderstone. 35. **perdu,** soldier placed in a position of peculiar danger. 42. **concluded all,** come to an end all together.

Lear. Where have I been? Where am I? Fair daylight?
I am mightily abus'd. I should e'en die with pity,
To see another thus. I know not what to say.
I will not swear these are my hands: let 's see;
I feel this pin prick. Would I were assur'd
Of my condition!
Cor. O, look upon me, sir,
And hold your hand in benediction o'er me:
You must not kneel.
Lear. Pray, do not mock me:
I am a very foolish fond old man,
Fourscore and upward, not an hour more nor less;
And, to deal plainly,
I fear I am not in my perfect mind.
Methinks I should know you, and know this man;
Yet I am doubtful: for I am mainly ignorant
What place this is; and all the skill I have
Remembers not these garments; nor I know not
Where I did lodge last night. Do not laugh at me;
For, as I am a man, I think this lady
To be my child Cordelia.
Cor. And so I am, I am.
Lear. Be your tears wet? yes, 'faith. I pray, weep not:
If you have poison for me, I will drink it.
I know you do not love me; for your sisters
Have, as I do remember, done me wrong:
You have some cause, they have not.
Cor. No cause, no cause.
Lear. Am I in France?
Kent. In your own kingdom, sir.
Lear. Do not abuse me.
Doct. Be comforted, good madam: the great rage,
You see, is kill'd in him: and yet it is danger
To make him even o'er the time he has lost.
Desire him to go in; trouble him no more
Till further settling.
Cor. Will 't please your highness walk?
Lear. You must bear with me:
Pray you now, forget and forgive: I am old and foolish. *Exeunt* [*all but Kent and Gentleman*].

Gent. Holds it true, sir, that the Duke of Cornwall was so slain?

Kent. Most certain, sir.

Gent. Who is conductor of his people?

Kent. As 'tis said, the bastard son of Gloucester.

Gent. They say Edgar, his banished son, is with the Earl of Kent in Germany.

Kent. Report is changeable. 'Tis time to look about; the powers of the kingdom approach apace.

Gent. The arbitrement is like to be bloody. Fare you well, sir. [*Exit*.]

Kent. My point and period will be throughly wrought,
Or well or ill, as this day's battle 's fought. *Exit*.

ACT V.

SCENE I. [*The British camp, near Dover.*]

Enter, with drum and colours, EDMUND, REGAN, Gentlemen, *and* Soldiers.

Edm. Know of the duke if his last purpose hold,
Or whether since he is advis'd by aught
To change the course: he 's full of alteration
And self-reproving: bring his constant pleasure.
[*To a Gentleman, who goes out.*]
Reg. Our sister's man is certainly miscarried.
Edm. 'Tis to be doubted, madam.
Reg. Now, sweet lord,
You know the goodness I intend upon you:
Tell me—but truly—but then speak the truth,
Do you not love my sister?
Edm. In honour'd love.
Reg. But have you never found my brother's way
To the forfended place?
Edm. That thought abuses you.
Reg. I am doubtful that you have been conjunct
And bosom'd with her, as far as we call hers.
Edm. No, by mine honour, madam.
Reg. I never shall endure her: dear my lord,
Be not familiar with her.
Edm. Fear me not:
She and the duke her husband!

Enter, with drum and colours, ALBANY, GONERIL, [*and*] Soldiers.

Gon. [*Aside*] I had rather lose the battle than that sister
Should loosen him and me.
Alb. Our very loving sister, well be-met.
Sir, this I hear; the king is come to his daughter,
With others whom the rigour of our state
Forc'd to cry out. Where I could not be honest,
I never yet was valiant: for this business,
It touches us, as France invades our land,
Not bolds the king, with others, whom, I fear,
Most just and heavy causes make oppose.
Edm. Sir, you speak nobly.
Reg. Why is this reason'd?
Gon. Combine together 'gainst the enemy;
For these domestic and particular broils
Are not the question here.
Alb. Let 's then determine
With th' ancient of war on our proceeding.
Edm. I shall attend you presently at your tent.
Reg. Sister, you'll go with us?
Gon. No.
Reg. 'Tis most convenient; pray you, go with us.
Gon. [*Aside*] O, ho, I know the riddle.—I will go.

[*As they are going out*,] *enter* EDGAR [*disguised*].

Edg. [*To Albany*] If e'er your grace had speech with man so poor,
Hear me one word.
Alb. I'll overtake you.—Speak.
Exeunt both the armies.
Edg. Before you fight the battle, ope this letter.
If you have victory, let the trumpet sound
For him that brought it: wretched though I seem,

65. **mainly,** perfectly. 77. **abuse,** deceive. 80. **even o'er,** give an account of, go over in his mind. 82. **settling,** composing of his mind. 94. **powers,** armies. 95. **arbitrement,** decision by arms. 98. **period,** end aimed at.

ACT V. SCENE I. 1. **Know,** inquire. 2. **advis'd,** persuaded. 4. **constant pleasure,** settled decision. 5. **miscarried,** lost, perished. 6. **doubted,** feared. 9. **honour'd,** honorable. 11. **forfended,** forbidden. **abuses,** deceives; also, degrades. 12. **doubtful,** fearful. **conjunct,** joined (both sexually and in spirit). 13. **bosom'd with her,** in her confidence; suggesting also her embraces. 23. **honest,** honorable. 26. **Not . . . others,** not because France encourages the king and others. 27. **heavy causes,** weighty reasons. **make oppose,** compel to fight (against us). 28. **reason'd,** argued. 32. **ancient of war,** veteran soldiers. 36. **convenient,** proper, befitting. 44. **avouched,** formally asserted. **miscarry,** perish, come to destruction. 50. **o'erlook,** peruse. 53. **discovery,** reconnoitering. 54. **greet the time,** face the situation.

I can produce a champion that will prove
What is avouched there. If you miscarry,
Your business of the world hath so an end,
And machination ceases. Fortune love you!
Alb. Stay till I have read the letter.
Edg. I was forbid it.
When time shall serve, let but the herald cry,
And I'll appear again.
Alb. Why, fare thee well: I will o'erlook thy paper.
Exit [Edgar].

Enter EDMUND.

Edm. The enemy 's in view; draw up your powers.
Here is the guess of their true strength and forces
By diligent discovery; but your haste
Is now urg'd on you.
Alb. We will greet the time. *Exit.*
Edm. To both these sisters have I sworn my love;
Each jealous of the other, as the stung
Are of the adder. Which of them shall I take?
Both? one? or neither? Neither can be enjoy'd,
If both remain alive: to take the widow
Exasperates, makes mad her sister Goneril;
And hardly shall I carry out my side,
Her husband being alive. Now then we'll use
His countenance for the battle; which being done,
Let her who would be rid of him devise
His speedy taking off. As for the mercy
Which he intends to Lear and to Cordelia,
The battle done, and they within our power,
Shall never see his pardon; for my state
Stands on me to defend, not to debate. *Exit.*

SCENE II. [*A field between the two camps.*]

Alarum within. Enter, with drum and colours, LEAR, CORDELIA, *and* Soldiers, *over the stage; and exeunt.*

Enter EDGAR *and* GLOUCESTER.

Edg. Here, father, take the shadow of this tree
For your good host; pray that the right may thrive:
If ever I return to you again,
I'll bring you comfort.
Glou. Grace go with you, sir!
Exit [Edgar].

Alarum and retreat within. Enter EDGAR.

Edg. Away, old man; give me thy hand; away!
King Lear hath lost, he and his daughter ta'en:
Give me thy hand; come on.
Glou. No further, sir; a man may rot even here.
Edg. What, in ill thoughts again? Men must endure
Their going hence, even as their coming hither:
Ripeness is all: come on.
Glou. And that's true too. *Exeunt.*

SCENE III. [*The British camp near Dover.*]

Enter, in conquest, with drum and colours, EDMUND; LEAR *and* CORDELIA, *as prisoners;* Soldiers, Captain, [&c.].

Edm. Some officers take them away: good guard,
Until their greater pleasures first be known
That are to censure them.
Cor. We are not the first
Who, with best meaning, have incurr'd the worst.
For thee, oppressed king, am I cast down;
Myself could else out-frown false fortune's frown.
Shall we not see these daughters and these sisters?
Lear. No, no, no, no! Come, let 's away to prison:
We two alone will sing like birds i' th' cage:
When thou dost ask me blessing, I'll kneel down,
And ask of thee forgiveness: so we'll live,
And pray, and sing, and tell old tales, and laugh
At gilded butterflies, and hear poor rogues
Talk of court news; and we'll talk with them too,
Who loses and who wins; who 's in, who 's out;
And take upon 's the mystery of things,
As if we were God's spies: and we'll wear out,
In a wall'd prison, packs and sects of great ones,
That ebb and flow by th' moon.
Edm. Take them away.
Lear. Upon such sacrifices, my Cordelia,
The gods themselves throw incense. Have I caught thee?
He that parts us shall bring a brand from heaven,
And fire us hence like foxes. Wipe thine eyes;
The good-years shall devour them, flesh and fell,
Ere they shall make us weep: we'll see 'em starv'd first.
Come. *Exit [with Cordelia, guarded].*
Edm. Come hither, captain; hark.
Take thou this note [*giving a paper*]; go follow them to prison:
One step I have advanc'd thee; if thou dost
As this instructs thee, thou dost make thy way
To noble fortunes: know thou this, that men
Are as the time is: to be tender-minded
Does not become a sword: thy great employment
Will not bear question; either say thou 'lt do 't,
Or thrive by other means.
Capt. I'll do 't, my lord.
Edm. About it; and write happy when th' hast done.
Mark, I say, instantly; and carry it so
As I have set it down.
Capt. I cannot draw a cart, nor eat dried oats;
If it be man's work, I'll do 't. *Exit Captain.*

Flourish. Enter ALBANY, GONERIL, REGAN, [*another* Captain, *and*] Soldiers.

Alb. Sir, you have show'd to-day your valiant strain,
And fortune led you well: you have the captives
Who were the opposites of this day's strife:
I do require them of you, so to use them
As we shall find their merits and our safety
May equally determine.
Edm. Sir, I thought it fit
To send the old and miserable king
To some retention and appointed guard;
Whose age had charms in it, whose title more,
To pluck the common bosom on his side,

56. **jealous,** suspicious. 61. **carry out my side,** fulfill my ambition, and satisfy her. 63. **countenance,** backing. 68-69. **my state . . . debate,** my position depends upon maintenance by force, not on debate.
SCENE II. 11. **Ripeness,** fulfillment of one's allotted years.
SCENE III. 13. **gilded butterflies,** courtiers. 17. **wear out,** outlast. 18-19. **packs . . . moon,** i.e., followers and cliques attached to persons of high station, whose fortunes change erratically and constantly. 23. **fire . . . foxes,** i.e., as foxes are driven out of their holes by fire and smoke; reminiscent of Samson's stratagem, Judges 15:4. 24. **good-years,** apparently a general word for evil; thought sometimes to be the name of a disease. Compare, however, the story of Pharaoh's dream, Genesis 41. **flesh and fell,** flesh and skin. 33. **bear question,** admit of discussion. 35. **write happy,** call yourself happy. 47. **retention,** custody. 49. **common bosom,** the affection of the mob.

And turn our impress'd lances in our eyes
Which do command them. With him I sent the queen;
My reason all the same; and they are ready
To-morrow, or at further space, t' appear
Where you shall hold your session. At this time
We sweat and bleed: the friend hath lost his friend;
And the best quarrels, in the heat, are curs'd
By those that feel their sharpness:
The question of Cordelia and her father
Requires a fitter place.

Alb. Sir, by your patience,
I hold you but a subject of this war,
Not as a brother.

Reg. That 's as we list to grace him.
Methinks our pleasure might have been demanded,
Ere you had spoke so far. He led our powers;
Bore the commission of my place and person;
The which immediacy may well stand up,
And call itself your brother.

Gon. Not so hot:
In his own grace he doth exalt himself,
More than in your addition.

Reg. In my rights,
By me invested, he compeers the best.

Gon. That were the most, if he should husband you.

Reg. Jesters do oft prove prophets.

Gon. Holla, holla!
That eye that told you so look'd but a-squint.

Reg. Lady, I am not well; else I should answer
From a full-flowing stomach. General,
Take thou my soldiers, prisoners, patrimony;
Dispose of them, of me; the walls is thine:
Witness the world, that I create thee here
My lord and master.

Gon. Mean you to enjoy him?

Alb. The let-alone lies not in your good will.

Edm. Nor in thine, lord.

Alb. Half-blooded fellow, yes.

Reg. [*To Edmund*] Let the drum strike, and prove my title thine.

Alb. Stay yet; hear reason. Edmund, I arrest thee
On capital treason; and, in thy attaint,
This gilded serpent [*pointing to Gon.*]. For your claim, fair sister,
I bar it in the interest of my wife;
'Tis she is sub-contracted to this lord,
And I, her husband, contradict your banes.
If you will marry, make your loves to me,
My lady is bespoke.

Gon. An interlude!

Alb. Thou art arm'd, Gloucester: let the trumpet sound:
If none appear to prove upon thy person
Thy heinous, manifest, and many treasons,
There is my pledge [*throwing down a glove*]; I'll make it on thy heart,
Ere I taste bread, thou art in nothing less
Than I have here proclaim'd thee.

Reg. Sick, O, sick!

Gon. [*Aside*] If not, I'll ne'er trust medicine.

Edm. There 's my exchange [*throwing down a glove*]: what in the world he is
That names me traitor, villain-like he lies:
Call by the trumpet: he that dares approach,
On him, on you, who not? I will maintain
My truth and honour firmly.

Alb. A herald, ho!

Edm. A herald, ho, a herald!

Alb. Trust to thy single virtue; for thy soldiers,
All levied in my name, have in my name
Took their discharge.

Reg. My sickness grows upon me.

Alb. She is not well; convey her to my tent.

[*Exit Regan, led.*]

Enter a Herald.

Come hither, herald,—Let the trumpet sound,—
And read out this.

Capt. Sound, trumpet! *A trumpet sounds.*

Her. (*Reads*) 'If any man of quality or degree within the lists of the army will maintain upon Edmund, supposed Earl of Gloucester, that he is a manifold traitor, let him appear by the third sound of the trumpet: he is bold in his defence.'

Edm. Sound! *First trumpet.*

Her. Again! *Second trumpet.*

Her. Again! *Third trumpet.*

Trumpet answers within.

Enter EDGAR, [*at the third sound,*] *armed* [*with a trumpeter before him*].

Alb. Ask him his purposes, why he appears
Upon this call o' th' trumpet.

Her. What are you?
Your name, your quality? and why you answer
This present summons?

Edg. Know, my name is lost;
By treason's tooth bare-gnawn and canker-bit:
Yet am I noble as the adversary
I come to cope.

Alb. Which is that adversary?

Edg. What 's he that speaks for Edmund Earl of Gloucester?

Edm. Himself: what say'st thou to him?

Edg. Draw thy sword,
That, if my speech offend a noble heart,
Thy arm may do thee justice: here is mine.
Behold, it is the privilege of mine honours,
My oath, and my profession: I protest,
Maugre thy strength, place, youth, and eminence,
Despite thy victor sword and fire-new fortune,
Thy valour and thy heart, thou art a traitor;
False to thy gods, thy brother, and thy father;
Conspirant 'gainst this high-illustrious prince;
And, from th' extremest upward of thy head
To the descent and dust below thy foot,
A most toad-spotted traitor. Say thou 'No,'
This sword, this arm, and my best spirits, are bent
To prove upon thy heart, whereto I speak,
Thou liest.

Edm. In wisdom I should ask thy name;

50. **impress'd lances,** weapons of troops impressed into service. 53. **space,** time. 58. **question,** cause. 61. **list,** please. 65. **immediacy,** next in authority, or nearness of his being my agent. 69. **compeers,** is equal with. 72. **That . . . a-squint,** reference to a proverb: Love being jealous makes a good eye look asquint. 74. **full-flowing stomach,** full tide of angry rejoinder. 76. **the walls is thine,** probably a phrase signifying complete surrender; many conjectures. 80. **Half-blooded,** partly of mean blood. 83. **in thy attaint,** i.e., as partner in your treason. 87. **banes,** banns. 89. **interlude,** play, i.e., you are melodramatic. 93. **make,** prove. 96. **medicine,** i.e., poison. 119. **What,**

But, since thy outside looks so fair and warlike,
And that thy tongue some say of breeding breathes,
What safe and nicely I might well delay
By rule of knighthood, I disdain and spurn:
Back do I toss these treasons to thy head;
With the hell-hated lie o'erwhelm thy heart;
Which, for they yet glance by and scarcely bruise,
This sword of mine shall give them instant way,
Where they shall rest for ever. Trumpets, speak!

Alarums. Fight. [*Edmund falls.*]

Alb. Save him, save him!
Gon. This is practice, Gloucester:
By th' law of war thou wast not bound to answer
An unknown opposite; thou art not vanquish'd,
But cozen'd and beguil'd.
Alb. Shut your mouth, dame,
Or with this paper shall I stop it. Hold, sir;
Thou worse than any name, read thine own evil:
No tearing, lady; I perceive you know it.
Gon. Say, if I do, the laws are mine, not thine:
Who can arraign me for 't?
Alb. Most monstrous! oh!
Know'st thou this paper?
Gon. Ask me not what I know. *Exit.*
Alb. Go after her: she 's desperate; govern her.

[*Exit an Officer.*]

Edm. What you have charg'd me with, that have I done;
And more, much more; the time will bring it out:
'Tis past, and so am I. But what art thou
That hast this fortune on me? If thou 'rt noble,
I do forgive thee.
Edg. Let 's exchange charity.
I am no less in blood than thou art, Edmund;
If more, the more th' hast wrong'd me.
My name is Edgar, and thy father's son.
The gods are just, and of our pleasant vices
Make instruments to plague us:
The dark and vicious place where thee he got
Cost him his eyes.
Edm. Th' hast spoken right, 'tis true;
The wheel is come full circle; I am here.
Alb. Methought thy very gait did prophesy
A royal nobleness: I must embrace thee:
Let sorrow split my heart, if ever I
Did hate thee or thy father!
Edg. Worthy prince, I know 't.
Alb. Where have you hid yourself?
How have you known the miseries of your father?
Edg. By nursing them, my lord. List a brief tale;
And when 'tis told, O, that my heart would burst!
The bloody proclamation to escape,
That follow'd me so near,—O, our lives' sweetness!
That we the pain of death would hourly die
Rather than die at once!—taught me to shift
Into a madman's rags; t' assume a semblance
That very dogs disdain'd: and in this habit
Met I my father with his bleeding rings,
Their precious stones new lost; became his guide,
Led him, begg'd for him, sav'd him from despair;
Never,—O fault!—reveal'd myself unto him,
Until some half-hour past, when I was arm'd:
Not sure, though hoping, of this good success,
I ask'd his blessing, and from first to last
Told him our pilgrimage: but his flaw'd heart,
Alack, too weak the conflict to support!
'Twixt two extremes of passion, joy and grief,
Burst smilingly.
Edm. This speech of yours hath mov'd me,
And shall perchance do good: but speak you on;
You look as you had something more to say.
Alb. If there be more, more woeful, hold it in;
For I am almost ready to dissolve,
Hearing of this.
Edg. This would have seem'd a period
To such as love not sorrow; but another,
To amplify too much, would make much more,
And top extremity.
Whilst I was big in clamour came there in a man,
Who, having seen me in my worst estate,
Shunn'd my abhorr'd society; but then, finding
Who 'twas that so endur'd, with his strong arms
He fasten'd on my neck, and bellow'd out
As he 'ld burst heaven; threw him on my father;
Told the most piteous tale of Lear and him
That ever ear receiv'd: which in recounting
His grief grew puissant, and the strings of life
Began to crack: twice then the trumpets sounded,
And there I left him tranc'd.
Alb. But who was this?
Edg. Kent, sir, the banish'd Kent; who in disguise
Follow'd his enemy king, and did him service
Improper for a slave.

Enter a Gentleman [*with a bloody knife*].

Gent. Help, help, O, help!
Edg. What kind of help?
Alb. Speak, man.
Edg. What means this bloody knife?
Gent. 'Tis hot, it smokes;
It came even from the heart of—O, she 's dead!
Alb. Who dead? speak, man.
Gent. Your lady, sir, your lady: and her sister
By her is poisoned; she confesses it.
Edm. I was contracted to them both: all three
Now marry in an instant.
Edg. Here comes Kent.
Alb. Produce the bodies, be they alive or dead:
This judgement of the heavens, that makes us tremble,
Touches us not with pity. [*Exit Gentleman.*]

Enter Kent.

O, is this he?
The time will not allow the compliment
Which very manners urges.
Kent. I am come
To bid my king and master aye good night:
Is he not here?
Alb. Great thing of us forgot!
Speak, Edmund, where 's the king? and where 's Cordelia?

who. 122. **canker-bit,** withered, i.e., bitten by the caterpillar. 131. **Maugre,** in spite of. 132. **fire-new,** freshly gained. 136. **upward,** top. 138. **toad-spotted,** venomous, or having spots of infamy. 141. **wisdom,** prudence; i.e., Edmund might have demanded that his adversary be his equal in rank. 143. **say,** flavor, indication; possibly for "assay," proof.

146. **head,** i.e., to thy teeth. 147. **hell-hated,** hated as hell is hated. 161. **govern,** restrain. 165. **fortune,** victory, success. 170. **pleasant,** pleasurable. 172. **got,** begot. 174. **wheel,** wheel of fortune. 189. **rings,** sockets. 196. **flaw'd,** cracked, damaged by a flaw. 204. **a period,** the limit. 218. **tranc'd,** entranced, senseless.

See'st thou this object, Kent?
Goneril's and Regan's bodies [*are*] *brought out.*
Kent. Alack, why thus?
Edm. Yet Edmund was belov'd:
The one the other poison'd for my sake,
And after slew herself.
Alb. Even so. Cover their faces.
Edm. I pant for life: some good I mean to do,
Despite of mine own nature. Quickly send,
Be brief in it, to th' castle; for my writ
Is on the life of Lear and on Cordelia:
Nay, send in time.
Alb. Run, run, O, run!
Edg. To who, my lord? Who has the office? send
Thy token of reprieve.
Edm. Well thought on: take my sword,
Give it the captain.
Edg. Haste thee, for thy life.
[*Exit Officer*].
Edm. He hath commission from thy wife and me
To hang Cordelia in the prison, and
To lay the blame upon her own despair,
That she fordid herself.
Alb. The gods defend her! Bear him hence awhile.
[*Edmund is borne off.*]

Enter LEAR, *with* CORDELIA *in his arms* [; Gentleman *and others following*].

Lear. Howl, howl, howl, howl! O, you are men of stones:
Had I your tongues and eyes, I 'ld use them so
That heaven's vault should crack. She 's gone for ever!
I know when one is dead, and when one lives;
She 's dead as earth. Lend me a looking-glass;
If that her breath will mist or stain the stone,
Why, then she lives.
Kent. Is this the promis'd end?
Edg. Or image of that horror?
Alb. Fall, and cease!
Lear. This feather stirs; she lives! if it be so,
It is a chance which does redeem all sorrows
That ever I have felt.
Kent. [*Kneeling*] O my good master!
Lear. Prithee, away.
Edg. 'Tis noble Kent, your friend.
Lear. A plague upon you, murderers, traitors all!
I might have sav'd her; now she 's gone for ever!
Cordelia, Cordelia! stay a little. Ha!
What is 't thou say'st? Her voice was ever soft,
Gentle, and low, an excellent thing in woman.
I kill'd the slave that was a-hanging thee.
Capt. 'Tis true, my lords, he did.
Lear. Did I not, fellow?
I have seen the day, with my good biting falchion
I would have made them skip: I am old now,
And these same crosses spoil me. Who are you?
Mine eyes are not o' th' best: I'll tell you straight.
Kent. If Fortune brag of two she lov'd and hated,
One of them we behold.
Lear. This is a dull sight. Are you not Kent?
Kent. The same,
Your servant Kent. Where is your servant Caius?
Lear. He 's a good fellow, I can tell you that;
He'll strike, and quickly too: he 's dead and rotten.
Kent. No, my good lord; I am the very man,—
Lear. I'll see that straight.
Kent. That, from your first of difference and decay,
Have follow'd your sad steps.
Lear. You are welcome hither.
Kent. Nor no man else: all 's cheerless, dark, and deadly.
Your eldest daughters have fordone themselves,
And desperately are dead.
Lear. Ay, so I think.
Alb. He knows not what he says: and vain it is
That we present us to him.
Edg. Very bootless.

Enter a Messenger.

Mess. Edmund is dead, my lord.
Alb. That 's but a trifle here.
You lords and noble friends, know our intent.
What comfort to this great decay may come
Shall be applied: for us, we will resign,
During the life of this old majesty,
To him our absolute power: [*To Edgar and Kent*] you, to your rights;
With boot, and such addition as your honours
Have more than merited. All friends shall taste
The wages of their virtue, and all foes
The cup of their deservings. O, see, see!
Lear. And my poor fool is hang'd! No, no, no life!
Why should a dog, a horse, a rat, have life,
And thou no breath at all? Thou 'lt come no more,
Never, never, never, never, never!
Pray you, undo this button: thank you, sir.
Do you see this? Look on her, look, her lips,
Look there, look there! *He dies.*
Edg. He faints! My lord, my lord!
Kent. Break, heart; I prithee, break!
Edg. Look up, my lord.
Kent. Vex not his ghost: O, let him pass! he hates him
That would upon the rack of this tough world
Stretch him out longer.
Edg. He is gone, indeed.
Kent. The wonder is, he hath endur'd so long:
He but usurp'd his life.
Alb. Bear them from hence. Our present business
Is general woe. [*To Kent and Edgar*] Friends of my soul, you twain
Rule in this realm, and the gor'd state sustain.
Kent. I have a journey, sir, shortly to go;
My master calls me, I must not say no.
Edg. The weight of this sad time we must obey;
Speak what we feel, not what we ought to say.
The oldest hath borne most: we that are young
Shall never see so much, nor live so long.
Exeunt, with a dead march.

249. **office,** commission. 255. **fordid,** destroyed. 262. **mist,** becloud. **stone,** crystal (of which the mirror is made). 263. **end,** Last Judgment. 264. **image,** duplicate. **Fall, and cease.** Let the heavens fall and all things cease. 276. **falchion,** sword; properly, a sword curved at the point with the edge on the convex side. 278. **these . . . spoil me,** all these misfortunes weaken me. 279. **I'll tell you straight,** I'll admit to you; or, I'll recognize you in a moment. 280. **two,** i.e., Lear, and a hypothetical individual whose misfortunes are without parallel. **lov'd and hated,** i.e., first raised and then lowered. 282. **dull sight,** melancholy spectacle; and (Lear's) clouded vision. 283. **Caius,** Kent's disguise name. 287. **see that straight,** attend to that soon; or, comprehend that soon. 288. **first of difference,** beginning of your change for the worst. 292. **desperately,** in despair. 305. **my poor fool,** i.e., Cordelia. It has sometimes been wrongly thought that this refers to the Fool, but *fool*, as here used, is a term of endearment.

THE TEMPEST

In *The Tempest* Shakespeare creates sublimely and perhaps for the last time an idealized world of his imagination, a place of magical rejuvenation like the forests of *A Midsummer Night's Dream* and *As You Like It*. The journey to Shakespeare's island is to a visionary realm existing only in art, where everything is controlled by the artist. Yet the journey is no mere escape from reality, for the island shows men what they ought to be. Even its location juxtaposes the "real" world with an idealized landscape: like Plato's New Atlantis or Thomas More's Utopia, Shakespeare's island is to be found both somewhere and nowhere. On the narrative level it is certainly located in the Mediterranean Sea, since King Alonso and his party are shipwrecked during their return from Africa to Naples, following the marriage of Alonso's daughter to the King of Tunis. Yet there are also insistent overtones of the New World, the Western Hemisphere, where Thomas More had situated his island of Utopia. Ariel fetches dew at Prospero's command from the "Bermoothes," or Bermudas (I,ii). Caliban's name is an anagram of "cannibal," calling to mind those dark and fascinating savages brought back to Jacobean England by adventurers to America. And one inspiration for Shakespeare's story (for which no direct literary source has been found) may well have been various accounts of an actual shipwreck in the Bermudas of the *Sea Venture*, in 1609, carrying supplies and settlers to the new Virginian colonies. Shakespeare certainly borrowed details from Sylvester Jourdain's *A Discovery of the Barmudas, otherwise called the Isle of Divels*, published in 1610, and from William Strachey's *A true Reportory of the Wracke and Redemption . . . from the Ilands of the Bermudas*, which Shakespeare must have seen in manuscript since it is dated 1610 but was not published until after his death. He evidently wrote the play shortly after reading these works, for *The Tempest* was acted at court in 1611. His fascination with the Western Hemisphere gave him not the "actual" location of his story, which remains Mediterranean, but a state of mind associated with newness and hope. Miranda sees on the island a "brave new world" in which mankind appears beauteous; and, although her wonderment must be tempered both by Prospero's melancholy rejoinder ("'Tis new to thee") and by Aldous Huxley's ironic use of her phrase (in his satirical novel called *Brave New World*), the island still endures as a restorative vision. Even though we experience it only fleetingly, as in a dream, this nonexistent realm assumes a permanence which only the artist can create.

Prospero rules as the artist-figure over this imaginary world, conjuring up trials and visions with which to test men's intentions and guide them toward a renewed faith in goodness. To his island come an assortment of men who, because they require different sorts of ordeals, are separated by Prospero and Ariel into three groups: King Alonso and those accompanying him; Alonso's son Ferdinand; and Stephano and Trinculo. Prospero's authority over them, though strong, has certain clearly defined limits. As Duke of Milan he was bookishly inattentive to political matters, and thus was vulnerable to the Machiavellian conniving of his younger brother Antonio. Only in this world apart, the artist's world, do his powers derived from learning find their proper sphere. Because he cannot control the world beyond his isle, he must wait for "strange, bountiful Fortune (Now my dear lady)" to bring his enemies to his shore. Moreover, he eschews the black arts of diabolism. His is a "white" magic, always devoted to good and merciful ends: rescuing Ariel from the spell of the witch Sycorax, curbing the appetite of Caliban, spying on Antonio and Sebastian in the role of Conscience. He believes that Fortune has delivered his enemies into his hands so that he may forgive and restore them, not be revenged. Such a use of power imitates the divine, though Prospero is no god. His chief power, learned from books and exercised through Ariel, is to control the elements so as to create illusion—of separation, of

THE FOLGER SHAKESPEARE LIBRARY

The frontispiece of Nicholas Rowe's 1709 edition of The Tempest *shows Ariel and other spirits churning up the seas in order to force the travelers to land on Prospero's enchanted island.*

death, of the gods' blessing. Yet since he is a man, even this power is an immense burden. Prospero's responsibilities cause him to behave managerially and to be resented by the spirits of the isle. Even Ariel longs to be free, and it is with genuine relief as well as melancholy that Prospero finally lays aside his demanding role as creative moral intelligence.

Alonso and the members of his court party variously illustrate the unregenerate world left behind in Naples and Milan. We first see them on shipboard, panicky and desperate, their titles and their finery mocked by the roaring of the waves. Futile worldly ambition seems destined for a watery grave. Yet death by water in this play is a transfiguration rather than an end, a mystical rebirth as in the regenerative cycle of the seasons from winter to summer. Ariel suggests this in his song about a drowned father: "Those are pearls that were his eyes. Nothing of him that doth fade But doth suffer a sea-change Into something rich and strange" (I,ii). Still, this miracle is not apparent at first to those who are caught in the illusion of death. As in T. S. Eliot's *The Waste Land*, which repeatedly alludes to *The Tempest*, self-blinded men fear an apparent disaster that is ironically the prelude to reawakening.

Prospero creates this illusion of loss to test his enemies and cause them to reveal their true selves. Only Gonzalo, no enemy at all but one who long ago aided Prospero and Miranda when they were banished from Milan, responds affirmatively. He alone notices that his garments and those of his shipwrecked companions have miraculously been left unharmed by the salt water. His ideal commonwealth (II,i), drawn from an essay by Montaigne, naively postulates a natural goodness in man and makes no allowance for the dark propensities of Caliban, but at least Gonzalo's cheerfulness is in refreshing contrast to the jaded sneers of his companions. Sebastian and Antonio react to the magic isle, as to Gonzalo's commonwealth, with cynical rejection of faith in the miraculous. Confident that they are unobserved, they seize the opportunity of Alonso's sleeping to plot a murder and political coup. This attempt is not only despicable but madly ludicrous, for they are all shipwrecked and no longer have any kingdoms over which to quarrel. Even more ironically, however, Sebastian and Antonio are being observed despite their insolent belief in their self-sufficiency. The villains must be taught that an unseen omniscient power does keep track of their misdeeds. They will probably revert to type when returned to their usual habitat, but even they are at last briefly moved to a faith in the unseen (III,iii). Alonso, more worthy than they even though burdened with sin, responds to his situation with guilt and despair, for he assumes that his son Ferdinand's death is the just punishment of the gods for Alonso's part in the earlier overthrow of Prospero. He must be led, by Prospero's curative illusions, through the purgative experience of contrition to the reward he thinks impossible and undeserved: reunion with his lost son.

Alonso is thus, like Posthumus in *Cymbeline* or Leontes in *The Winter's Tale*, a tragicomic figure—sinful, contrite, forgiven. Alonso's son Ferdinand must also undergo ordeals and visions devised by Prospero to test his worth, but much more on the level of romantic comedy. Ferdinand is young, innocent, and hopeful, well-matched to Miranda. Prospero obviously approves from the start of his prospective son-in-law. Yet Prospero invents difficulties, imposing tasks of logbearing (much like those assigned to Caliban) and issuing stern warnings against premarital lust. These illusions of parental opposition conform to the comic mode, in which parents are expected to cross their children in matters of the heart. More seriously, however, Prospero is convinced by long experience that prizes too easily won are too lightly esteemed. Manifold are the temptations urging Ferdinand to surrender to the "natural" rhythms of the isle, and to fulfill his desire like Caliban. Because there are no churches on the island, Prospero must create the illusion of ceremony by his art. The marriage of Ferdinand and Miranda accordingly unites the best of both worlds: the natural innocence of the island, which teaches them to avoid the corruptions of civilization at its worst, and the higher law of nature achieved through moral wisdom at its best. To this marriage, the goddesses Iris, Ceres, and Juno bring promises of bounteous harvest, of "refreshing show'rs," of celestial harmony, and of a springtime brought back to the earth by Proserpina's return from Hades (IV,i). In Ferdinand and Miranda, "nurture" is wedded to "nature." This bond unites spirit and flesh, legitimizing erotic pleasure by subordinating it to a cosmic moral order in the universe.

At the lowest level of this same cosmic and moral framework are Stephano and Trinculo. Their comic scenes juxtapose them with Caliban, for he represents untutored nature whereas they represent the unnatural depths to which men brought up in civilized society can fall. In this they also resemble Sebastian and Antonio, who have learned in supposedly civilized Italy the arts of intrigue and political murder. The antics of Stephano and Trinculo burlesque the conduct of their presumed betters, thereby exposing to ridicule the self-deceptions of ambitious men. The clowns desire to exploit the natural wonders of the isle by taking Caliban back to England or Naples to be shown in carnivals, or by plying him with strong drink and whetting his resentment against authority. These plottings are in vain, however, for like Sebastian and Antonio the clowns are being watched. They teach Caliban to cry out for "freedom," by which they mean license to do as one pleases, but are foiled by Ariel as comic nemesis. Because they are degenerate buffoons, their exposure is appropriately humiliating and satirical, with little attempt at spiritual recovery. They are irredeemable, the dregs of a corrupted civilization.

In contrast with them, Caliban is almost an attractive and sympathetic character. Although he grumbles and curses at his servitude, he is dangerous only when aroused by the clowns and their strong drink. Even his desire to rape Miranda and people the isle with little Calibans is a natural procreative instinct. His sensitivity to natural beauty, as in his descriptions of the "nimble marmoset" or the dreaming music he so often hears (II,ii and III,ii), is entirely appropriate to this child of nature. He is, to be sure, the child of a witch also, and is called many harsh names such as "Abhorred slave" and "a born devil, on whose nature Nurture can never stick." Yet he protests with some justification that the island was his in the first place, and that Prospero and Miranda are the interlopers and exploiters. His very existence calls radically into question the value of Western civilization, which has shown itself capable of limitless depravity. What profit has Caliban derived from learning Prospero's language other than, as he puts it, to "know how to curse"? With instinctive cunning he senses that books are his chief enemy, and plots to destroy them first in his attempt at rebellion. The unspoiled natural world does indeed offer to civilized man a perspective obtainable in no other way. Ultimately, however, Shakespeare's play celebrates man's highest achievement in the union of the island with the civilized world, as in the marriage of Ferdinand and Miranda. Even Caliban is at last reconciled to this solution. Prospero speaks of him as a "thing of darkness I Acknowledge mine," and Caliban vows to "be wise hereafter And seek for grace" (V,i). This synthesis suggests that the natural man within all of us is more contented, better understood, and more truly free when harmonized with reason.

Caliban is a part of humanity, Ariel is not. Ariel can comprehend what compassion and forgiveness would be like, "were I human," and takes part amusedly in Prospero's designs to castigate or reform his fellow man, but Ariel longs to be free in quite another sense from that meant by Caliban. Ariel takes no part in the final integration of human society. This woodland spirit belongs to a magic world of song, music, and illusion which the artist borrows for his use but which exists eternally outside of him. Like the elements of air, earth, fire, and water in which it mysteriously dwells, this force is morally neutral but incredibly vital. From it the artist achieves his powers of imagination, enabling him to bedim the noontide sun or call forth the dead from their graves. These visions are illusory in the profound sense that all life is illusory, an "insubstantial pageant" melted into thin air. Prospero the artist cherishes his own humanity, as a promise of surcease from his labors. Yet the artifact created by the artist endures, existing apart from time and place as does Ariel: "Then to the elements Be free, and fare thou well!" No doubt it is a romantic fiction to associate the dramatist Shakespeare with Prospero's farewell to his art, but it is an almost irresistible idea because we are so moved by the sense of completion and yet humility, the exultation and yet the calm.

THE TEMPEST

Names of the Actors

ALONSO, King of Naples.
SEBASTIAN, *his brother*.
PROSPERO, the right Duke of Milan.
ANTONIO, *his brother, the usurping* Duke of Milan.
FERDINAND, *son to the King of Naples*.
GONZALO, *an honest old Counsellor*.
ADRIAN *and* FRANCISCO, *Lords*.
CALIBAN, *a savage and deformed Slave*.
TRINCULO, *a Jester*.
STEPHANO, *a drunken Butler*.
Master of a Ship.
Boatswain.
Mariners.

MIRANDA, *daughter to Prospero*.

ARIEL, *an airy Spirit*.
IRIS, CERES, JUNO, Nymphs, Reapers, [*presented by*] *Spirits*.

[Other Spirits attending on Prospero.]

THE SCENE: *An uninhabited island.*

ACT I.

SCENE I. [*On a ship at sea:*] *a tempestuous noise of thunder and lightning heard.*

Enter a Ship-Master *and* a Boatswain.

Mast. Boatswain!

Boats. Here, master: what cheer?

Mast. Good, speak to the mariners: fall to 't, yarely, or we run ourselves aground: bestir, bestir. *Exit.*

Enter Mariners.

Boats. Heigh, my hearts! cheerly, cheerly, my hearts! yare, yare! Take in the topsail. Tend to the master's whistle. Blow, till thou burst thy wind, if room enough!

Enter ALONSO, SEBASTIAN, ANTONIO, FERDINAND, GONZALO, *and others.*

Alon. Good boatswain, have care. Where 's the master? Play the men.

Boats. I pray now, keep below.

Ant. Where is the master, bos'n?

Boats. Do you not hear him? You mar our labour: keep your cabins: you do assist the storm.

Gon. Nay, good, be patient.

Boats. When the sea is. Hence! What cares these roarers for the name of king? To cabin: silence! trouble us not.

Gon. Good, yet remember whom thou hast aboard.

Boats. None that I more love than myself. You are a counsellor; if you can command these elements to silence, and work the peace of the present, we will not hand a rope more; use your authority: if you cannot, give thanks you have lived so long, and make yourself ready in your cabin for the mischance of the hour, if it so hap. Cheerly, good hearts! Out of our way, I say. *Exit.*

Gon. I have great comfort from this fellow: methinks he hath no drowning mark upon him; his complexion is perfect gallows. Stand fast, good Fate, to his hanging: make the rope of his destiny our cable, for our own doth little advantage. If he be not born to be hanged, our case is miserable. *Exeunt.*

Enter Boatswain.

Boats. Down with the topmast! yare! lower, lower! Bring her to try with main-course. *(A cry within.)* A plague upon this howling! they are louder than the weather or our office.

Enter SEBASTIAN, ANTONIO, *and* GONZALO.

Yet again! what do you here? Shall we give o'er and drown? Have you a mind to sink?

Seb. A pox o' your throat, you bawling, blasphemous, incharitable dog!

Boats. Work you then.

Ant. Hang, cur! hang, you whoreson, insolent noisemaker! We are less afraid to be drowned than thou art.

Gon. I'll warrant him for drowning; though the ship were no stronger than a nutshell and as leaky as an unstanched wench.

Boats. Lay her a-hold, a-hold! set her two courses off to sea again! lay her off!

Enter Mariners *wet.*

Mariners. All lost! to prayers, to prayers! all lost! [*Exeunt.*]

Boats. What, must our mouths be cold?

Gon. The king and prince at prayers! let 's assist them,
For our case is theirs.

Seb. I 'm out of patience.

Ant. We are merely cheated of our lives by drunkards:
This wide-chapp'd rascal—would thou mightst lie drowning
The washing of ten tides!

Gon. He'll be hang'd yet,
Though every drop of water swear against it
And gape at wid'st to glut him.

A confused noise within: 'Mercy on us!'—
'We split, we split!'—'Farewell my wife and children!'—
'Farewell, brother!'—'We split, we split, we split!'
[*Exit Boats.*]

Ant. Let 's all sink wi' th' king.

Seb. Let 's take leave of him. *Exit* [*with Ant.*]

Gon. Now would I give a thousand furlongs of sea for an acre of barren ground, long heath, brown furze, any thing. The wills above be done! but I would fain die a dry death. *Exit.*

SCENE II. [*The island. Before* PROSPERO'*s cell.*]

Enter PROSPERO *and* MIRANDA.

Mir. If by your art, my dearest father, you have
Put the wild waters in this roar, allay them.
The sky, it seems, would pour down stinking pitch,
But that the sea, mounting to th' welkin's cheek,
Dashes the fire out. O, I have suffered
With those that I saw suffer: a brave vessel,
Who had, no doubt, some noble creature in her,
Dash'd all to pieces. O, the cry did knock
Against my very heart. Poor souls, they perish'd.
Had I been any god of power, I would
Have sunk the sea within the earth or ere
It should the good ship so have swallow'd and
The fraughting souls within her.

Pros. Be collected:
No more amazement: tell your piteous heart
There 's no harm done.

Mir. O, woe the day!

Pros. No harm.
I have done nothing but in care of thee,
Of thee, my dear one, thee, my daughter, who
Art ignorant of what thou art, nought knowing
Of whence I am, nor that I am more better
Than Prospero, master of a full poor cell,
And thy no greater father.

Mir. More to know
Did never meddle with my thoughts.

Pros. 'Tis time
I should inform thee farther. Lend thy hand,
And pluck my magic garment from me. So:
[*Lays down his mantle.*]
Lie there, my art. Wipe thou thine eyes; have comfort.
The direful spectacle of the wrack, which touch'd
The very virtue of compassion in thee,
I have with such provision in mine art
So safely ordered that there is no soul—
No, not so much perdition as an hair
Betid to any creature in the vessel
Which thou heard'st cry, which thou saw'st sink. Sit down;
For thou must now know farther.

Mir. You have often
Begun to tell me what I am, but stopp'd

ACT I. SCENE I. 1. **Boatswain,** under-officer in a ship, having to do with sails and rigging and the supervision of the crew at work. 3. **Good,** probably, good friend. 3-4. **fall . . . yarely,** set to work nimbly. 8. **Tend,** attend. 9. **Blow,** addressed to the wind. **if room enough,** as long as we have sea-room enough. 11. **Play the,** act like. 19. **cares,** described as a singular verb used with a plural subject on account of haste; also as an old northern plural of the verb in *s.* **roarers,** waves or winds, or both; allusion to *roarer* meaning "bully," "blusterer." 24-25. **work . . . present,** calm the storm. 25. **hand,** handle. 32. **complexion . . . gallows,** appearance shows he was born to be hanged. 35. **doth little advantage,** is of little benefit. 38. **Bring . . . course,** heave to and sail her close to the wind by means of the mainsail. 40. **they . . . office,** the passengers make more noise than the winds or than we do at work. 49. **warrant him for drowning,** guarantee that he will never be drowned. 51. **unstanched,** wide open. 52. **a-hold,** close to the wind. 53. **courses,** sails; i.e., they would set her foresail as well as her mainsail. 56. **must . . . cold,** let us heat up our mouths with liquor. 59. **merely,** absolutely, entirely. 60. **wide-chapp'd,** with mouth wide open. 60-61. **lie . . . tides.** Pirates were hanged on the shore and left until three tides had come in. 63. **glut,** swallow. 64. **split,** i.e., on the rocks. 69. **long heath,** defined as "open barren ground"; also as "heather." 70. **furze,** broom, or gorse (a prickly shrub); F: *firrs,* taken to mean "firs" (New Cambridge).

SCENE II. 3. **stinking pitch,** suggestion of heat. 4. **But that,** were it not that. **welkin's cheek,** sky's face. 13. **fraughting,** forming the cargo. 14. **amazement,** consternation. 20. **full,** very, exceedingly.

And left me to a bootless inquisition,
Concluding 'Stay: not yet.'
Pros. The hour 's now come;
The very minute bids thee ope thine ear;
Obey and be attentive. Canst thou remember
A time before we came unto this cell?
I do not think thou canst, for then thou wast not
Out three years old.
Mir. Certainly, sir, I can.
Pros. By what? by any other house or person?
Of any thing the image tell me that
Hath kept with thy remembrance.
Mir. 'Tis far off
And rather like a dream than an assurance
That my remembrance warrants. Had I not
Four or five women once that tended me?
Pros. Thou hadst, and more, Miranda. But how is it
That this lives in thy mind? What seest thou else
In the dark backward and abysm of time?
If thou remembr'st aught ere thou cam'st here,
How thou cam'st here thou mayst.
Mir. But that I do not.
Pros. Twelve year since, Miranda, twelve year since,
Thy father was the Duke of Milan and
A prince of power.
Mir. Sir, are not you my father?
Pros. Thy mother was a piece of virtue, and
She said thou wast my daughter; and thy father
Was Duke of Milan; and thou his only heir
And princess no worse issued.
Mir. O the heavens!
What foul play had we, that we came from thence?
Or blessed was 't we did?
Pros. Both, both, my girl:
By foul play, as thou say'st, were we heav'd thence,
But blessedly holp hither.
Mir. O, my heart bleeds
To think o' th' teen that I have turn'd you to,
Which is from my remembrance! Please you, farther.
Pros. My brother and thy uncle, call'd Antonio—
I pray thee, mark me—that a brother should
Be so perfidious!—he whom next thyself
Of all the world I lov'd and to him put
The manage of my state; as at that time
Through all the signories it was the first
And Prospero the prime duke, being so reputed
In dignity, and for the liberal arts
Without a parallel; those being all my study,
The government I cast upon my brother
And to my state grew stranger, being transported
And rapt in secret studies. Thy false uncle—
Dost thou attend me?
Mir. Sir, most heedfully.
Pros. Being once perfected how to grant suits,
How to deny them, who t' advance and who
To trash for over-topping, new created
The creatures that were mine, I say, or chang'd 'em,
Or else new form'd 'em; having both the key
Of officer and office, set all hearts i' th' state
To what tune pleas'd his ear; that now he was
The ivy which had hid my princely trunk,
And suck'd my verdure out on 't. Thou attend'st not.
Mir. O, good sir, I do.
Pros. I pray thee, mark me.
I, thus neglecting worldly ends, all dedicated
To closeness and the bettering of my mind
With that which, but by being so retir'd,
O'er-priz'd all popular rate, in my false brother
Awak'd an evil nature; and my trust,
Like a good parent, did beget of him
A falsehood in its contrary as great
As my trust was; which had indeed no limit,
A confidence sans bound. He being thus lorded,
Not only with what my revenue yielded,
But what my power might else exact, like one
†Who having into truth, by telling of it,
Made such a sinner of his memory,
To credit his own lie, he did believe
He was indeed the duke; out o' th' substitution,
And executing th' outward face of royalty,
With all prerogative: hence his ambition growing—
Dost thou hear?
Mir. Your tale, sir, would cure deafness.
Pros. To have no screen between this part he play'd
And him he play'd it for, he needs will be
Absolute Milan. Me, poor man, my library
Was dukedom large enough: of temporal royalties
He thinks me now incapable; confederates—
So dry he was for sway—wi' th' King of Naples
To give him annual tribute, do him homage,
Subject his coronet to his crown and bend
The dukedom yet unbow'd—alas, poor Milan!—
To most ignoble stooping.
Mir. O the heavens!
Pros. Mark his condition and th' event; then tell me
If this might be a brother.
Mir. I should sin
To think but nobly of my grandmother:
Good wombs have borne bad sons.
Pros. Now the condition.
This King of Naples, being an enemy
To me inveterate, hearkens my brother's suit;
Which was, that he, in lieu o' th' premises
Of homage and I know not how much tribute,
Should presently extirpate me and mine
Out of the dukedom and confer fair Milan
With all the honours on my brother: whereon,
A treacherous army levied, one midnight
Fated to th' purpose did Antonio open
The gates of Milan, and, i' th' dead of darkness,
The ministers for th' purpose hurried thence

22. **meddle,** mingle. 24. **So,** used with a gesture, meaning "good," "very well." 28. **provision,** foresight. 29. **no soul,** i.e., lost; many emendations. 30. **perdition,** loss. 35. **bootless inquisition,** profitless inquiry. 41. **Out,** fully. 45-46. **assurance . . . warrants,** certainty that my memory guarantees. 56. **piece,** masterpiece. 59. **issued,** born. 64. **teen . . . to,** trouble I've caused you to remember. 65. **from,** i.e., has no place in. 71. **signories,** states of northern Italy. 73. **liberal arts,** allusion to the learned studies of the Middle Ages. 76. **state,** position as ruler. 77. **secret studies,** magic, the occult. 79. **perfected,** grown skillful. 81. **trash,** check a hound by tying a weight to its neck. **over-topping,** running too far ahead of the pack. 83. **key,** tool for tuning stringed instruments, with suggestion of the usual meaning. 90. **closeness,** retirement, seclusion. 91-92. **but . . . rate,** except that it was done in retirement, (would have) surpassed in value all popular estimate. 93. **Awak'd.** *I* in line 89 is the subject. 95. **in its contrary,** of an opposite kind. 97. **lorded,** raised to lordship. 100-102. **Who . . . lie,** a difficult passage; the meaning is: He had lied so long that he believed his own lies. New Cambridge editors read *minted* for *into*, interpreting the passage as a figure from coining of baser metals, so that *telling* means "counting," *substitution* means "the substituting of baser metals for gold," and *executing . . . royalty* means "stamping the coins." 103. **out o',** as a result of. 109. **Absolute Milan,** actual duke of Milan. 110. **royalties,** prerogatives and rights of a sovereign. 111. **confederates,** conspires. 112. **dry,** thirsty. 117. **condition,** pact. **event,** outcome. 123. **in . . . premises,** in return for the stipulations.

Me and thy crying self.
Mir. Alack, for pity!
I, not rememb'ring how I cried out then,
Will cry it o'er again: it is a hint
That wrings mine eyes to 't.
Pros. Hear a little further
And then I'll bring thee to the present business
Which now 's upon 's; without the which this story
Were most impertinent.
Mir. Wherefore did they not
That hour destroy us?
Pros. Well demanded, wench:
My tale provokes that question. Dear, they durst not,
So dear the love my people bore me, nor set
A mark so bloody on the business, but
With colours fairer painted their foul ends.
In few, they hurried us aboard a bark,
Bore us some leagues to sea; where they prepar'd
A rotten carcass of a butt, not rigg'd,
Nor tackle, sail, nor mast; the very rats
Instinctively have quit it: there they hoist us,
To cry to th' sea that roar'd to us, to sigh
To th' winds whose pity, sighing back again,
Did us but loving wrong.
Mir. Alack, what trouble
Was I then to you!
Pros. O, a cherubin
Thou wast that did preserve me. Thou didst smile,
Infused with a fortitude from heaven,
When I have deck'd the sea with drops full salt,
Under my burthen groan'd; which rais'd in me
An undergoing stomach, to bear up
Against what should ensue.
Mir. How came we ashore?
Pros. By Providence divine.
Some food we had and some fresh water that
A noble Neapolitan, Gonzalo,
Out of his charity, who being then appointed
Master of this design, did give us, with
Rich garments, linens, stuffs and necessaries,
Which since have steaded much; so, of his gentleness,
Knowing I lov'd my books, he furnish'd me
From mine own library with volumes that
I prize above my dukedom.
Mir. Would I might
But ever see that man!
Pros. Now I arise: [*Resumes his mantle.*]
Sit still, and hear the last of our sea-sorrow.
Here in this island we arriv'd; and here
Have I, thy schoolmaster, made thee more profit
Than other princesses can that have more time
For vainer hours and tutors not so careful.
Mir. Heavens thank you for 't! And now, I pray you, sir,
For still 'tis beating in my mind, your reason
For raising this sea-storm?
Pros. Know thus far forth.
By accident most strange, bountiful Fortune,
Now my dear lady, hath mine enemies
Brought to this shore; and by my prescience
I find my zenith doth depend upon
A most auspicious star, whose influence
If now I court not but omit, my fortunes
Will ever after droop. Here cease more questions:
Thou art inclin'd to sleep; 'tis a good dulness,
And give it way: I know thou canst not choose.
[*Miranda sleeps.*]
Come away, servant, come. I am ready now.
Approach, my Ariel, come.

Enter ARIEL.

Ari. All hail, great master! grave sir, hail! I come
To answer thy best pleasure; be 't to fly,
To swim, to dive into the fire, to ride
On the curl'd clouds, to thy strong bidding task
Ariel and all his quality.
Pros. Hast thou, spirit,
Perform'd to point the tempest that I bade thee?
Ari. To every article.
I boarded the king's ship; now on the beak,
Now in the waist, the deck, in every cabin,
I flam'd amazement: sometime I 'ld divide,
And burn in many places; on the topmast,
The yards and boresprit, would I flame distinctly,
Then meet and join. Jove's lightnings, the precursors
O' th' dreadful thunder-claps, more momentary
And sight-outrunning were not; the fire and cracks
Of sulphurous roaring the most mighty Neptune
Seem to besiege and make his bold waves tremble,
Yea, his dread trident shake.
Pros. My brave spirit!
Who was so firm, so constant, that this coil
Would not infect his reason?
Ari. Not a soul
But felt a fever of the mad and play'd
Some tricks of desperation. All but mariners
Plung'd in the foaming brine and quit the vessel,
Then all afire with me: the king's son, Ferdinand,
With hair up-staring,—then like reeds, not hair,—
Was the first man that leap'd; cried, 'Hell is empty,
And all the devils are here.'
Pros. Why, that 's my spirit!
But was not this nigh shore?
Ari. Close by, my master.
Pros. But are they, Ariel, safe?
Ari. Not a hair perish'd;
On their sustaining garments not a blemish,
But fresher than before: and, as thou bad'st me,
In troops I have dispers'd them 'bout the isle.
The king's son have I landed by himself;
Whom I left cooling of the air with sighs
In an odd angle of the isle and sitting,
His arms in this sad knot. [*Folds his arms.*]
Pros. Of the king's ship
The mariners say how thou hast dispos'd
And all the rest o' th' fleet.
Ari. Safely in harbour
Is the king's ship; in the deep nook, where once
Thou call'dst me up at midnight to fetch dew
From the still-vex'd Bermoothes, there she 's hid:

134. **hint,** occasion. 138. **impertinent,** irrelevant. 139. **wench,** used as a term of affectionate address. 144. **few,** few words. 146. **butt,** tub; Globe: *boat*. 151. **loving wrong,** figure of speech called oxymoron, in which, to emphasize a contrast, contradictory terms are associated; the *wrong* done by sea and winds was wrought by seeming sympathy. 152. **cherubin,** plural used as singular; applied to an angelic woman. 155. **deck'd,** covered (with salt tears). 156. **which,** i.e., the smile. 157. **undergoing stomach,** courage to undergo. 181. **zenith,** height of fortune; astrological term. 185. **dulness,** drowsiness. 187. **Come away,** come. 192. **task,** make demands upon. 193. **quality,** fellow-spirits. 194. **point,** i.e., to the smallest detail. 196. **beak,** prow. 197. **waist,** midship. **deck,** poopdeck at the stern. 200. **boresprit,** bowsprit. **distinctly,** separately. 202. **momentary,** instantaneous. 209. **fever of the mad,** i.e., such as madmen feel. 213. **up-staring,** standing on end. 218. **sustaining garments,** garments that buoyed them up in the sea. 223. **angle,** corner. 227. **nook,** bay. 228. **fetch**

The mariners all under hatches stow'd;
Who, with a charm join'd to their suff'red labour,
I have left asleep: and for the rest o' th' fleet
Which I dispers'd, they all have met again
And are upon the Mediterranean flote,
Bound sadly home for Naples,
Supposing that they saw the king's ship wrack'd
And his great person perish.
Pros. Ariel, thy charge
Exactly is perform'd: but there 's more work.
What is the time o' th' day?
Ari. Past the mid season.
Pros. At least two glasses. The time 'twixt six and now
Must by us both be spent most preciously.
Ari. Is there more toil? Since thou dost give me pains,
Let me remember thee what thou hast promis'd,
Which is not yet perform'd me.
Pros. How now? moody?
What is 't thou canst demand?
Ari. My liberty.
Pros. Before the time be out? no more!
Ari. I prithee,
Remember I have done thee worthy service;
Told thee no lies, made thee no mistakings, serv'd
Without or grudge or grumblings: thou didst promise
To bate me a full year.
Pros. Dost thou forget
From what a torment I did free thee?
Ari. No.
Pros. Thou dost, and think'st it much to tread the ooze
Of the salt deep,
To run upon the sharp wind of the north,
To do me business in the veins o' th' earth
When it is bak'd with frost.
Ari. I do not, sir.
Pros. Thou liest, malignant thing! Hast thou forgot
The foul witch Sycorax, who with age and envy
Was grown into a hoop? hast thou forgot her?
Ari. No, sir.
Pros. Thou hast. Where was she born? speak; tell me.
Ari. Sir, in Argier.
Pros. O, was she so? I must
Once in a month recount what thou hast been,
Which thou forget'st. This damn'd witch Sycorax,
For mischiefs manifold and sorceries terrible
To enter human hearing, from Argier,
Thou know'st, was banish'd: for one thing she did
They would not take her life. Is not this true?
Ari. Ay, sir.
Pros. This blue-ey'd hag was hither brought with child
And here was left by th' sailors. Thou, my slave,
As thou report'st thyself, wast then her servant;
And, for thou wast a spirit too delicate
To act her earthy and abhorr'd commands,
Refusing her grand hests, she did confine thee,
By help of her more potent ministers
And in her most unmitigable rage,
Into a cloven pine; within which rift
Imprison'd thou didst painfully remain
A dozen years; within which space she died
And left thee there; where thou did'st vent thy groans
As fast as mill-wheels strike. Then was this island—
Save for the son that she did litter here,
A freckled whelp hag-born—not honour'd with
A human shape.
Ari. Yes, Caliban her son.
Pros. Dull thing, I say so; he, that Caliban
Whom now I keep in service. Thou best know'st
What torment I did find thee in; thy groans
Did make wolves howl and penetrate the breasts
Of ever angry bears: it was a torment
To lay upon the damn'd, which Sycorax
Could not again undo: it was mine art,
When I arriv'd and heard thee, that made gape
The pine and let thee out.
Ari. I thank thee, master.
Pros. If thou more murmur'st, I will rend an oak
And peg thee in his knotty entrails till
Thou hast howl'd away twelve winters.
Ari. Pardon, master;
I will be correspondent to command
And do my spiriting gently.
Pros. Do so, and after two days
I will discharge thee.
Ari. That 's my noble master!
What shall I do? say what; what shall I do?
Pros. Go make thyself like a nymph o' th' sea: be subject
To no sight but thine and mine, invisible
To every eyeball else. Go take this shape
And hither come in 't: go, hence with diligence!
Exit [*Ariel*].
Awake, dear heart, awake! thou hast slept well;
Awake!
Mir. The strangeness of your story put
Heaviness in me.
Pros. Shake it off. Come on;
We'll visit Caliban my slave, who never
Yields us kind answer.
Mir. 'Tis a villain, sir,
I do not love to look on.
Pros. But, as 'tis,
We cannot miss him: he does make our fire,
Fetch in our wood and serves in offices
That profit us. What, ho! slave! Caliban!
Thou earth, thou! speak.
Cal. (*Within*) There 's wood enough within.
Pros. Come forth, I say! there 's other business for thee:
Come, thou tortoise! when?

Enter ARIEL *like a water-nymph.*

Fine apparition! My quaint Ariel,

dew, for some incantation. 229. **Bermoothes,** Bermudas; a possible reference to *A Discovery of the Barmudas* (1609), one of the sources of the play. 234. **flote,** sea, or possibly, flotilla, i.e., making for the Mediterranean flotilla (New Cambridge). 240. **glasses,** i.e., hour-glasses. 243. **remember,** remind. 248. **mistakings,** errors. 250. **bate . . . year,** remit me a year of service. Ariel, as a spirit, longs for freedom; as a spirit, he is also incapable of affection or gratitude as entertained by human beings. 261. **Argier,** Algiers. 266. **one thing she did,** allusion not explained; taken by New Cambridge editors as evidence of a cut in the play. Lamb suggested that Shakespeare was thinking of the witch who saved Algiers from Charles v in 1541 by raising a storm that dispersed his fleet. 269. **blue-ey'd,** usually interpreted as referring to dark circles under the eyes. Staunton suggested *blear-eyed*. 274. **hests,** commands. 283. **freckled,** spotted. 297. **correspondent,** responsive, submissive. 311. **miss,** do without.

Hark in thine ear. [*Whispers.*]
Ari. My lord, it shall be done. *Exit.*
Pros. Thou poisonous slave, got by the devil himself
Upon thy wicked dam, come forth!

Enter CALIBAN.

Cal. As wicked dew as e'er my mother brush'd
With raven's feather from unwholesome fen
Drop on you both! a south-west blow on ye
And blister you all o'er!
Pros. For this, be sure, to-night thou shalt have cramps,
Side-stitches that shall pen thy breath up; urchins
Shall, for that vast of night that they may work,
All exercise on thee; thou shalt be pinch'd
As thick as honeycomb, each pinch more stinging
Than bees that made 'em.
Cal. I must eat my dinner.
This island 's mine, by Sycorax my mother,
Which thou tak'st from me. When thou cam'st first,
Thou strok'st me and made much of me, wouldst give me
Water with berries in 't, and teach me how
To name the bigger light, and how the less,
That burn by day and night: and then I lov'd thee
And show'd thee all the qualities o' th' isle,
The fresh springs, brine-pits, barren place and fertile:
Curs'd be I that did so! All the charms
Of Sycorax, toads, beetles, bats, light on you!
For I am all the subjects that you have,
Which first was mine own king: and here you sty me
In this hard rock, whiles you do keep from me
The rest o' th' island.
Pros. Thou most lying slave,
Whom stripes may move, not kindness! I have us'd thee,
Filth as thou art, with humane care, and lodg'd thee
In mine own cell, till thou didst seek to violate
The honour of my child.
Cal. O ho, O ho! would 't had been done!
Thou didst prevent me; I had peopled else
This isle with Calibans.
Mir. Abhorred slave,
Which any print of goodness wilt not take,
Being capable of all ill! I pitied thee,
Took pains to make thee speak, taught thee each hour
One thing or other: when thou didst not, savage,
Know thine own meaning, but wouldst gabble like
A thing most brutish, I endow'd thy purposes
With words that made them known. But thy vile race,
Though thou didst learn, had that in 't which good natures
Could not abide to be with; therefore wast thou
Deservedly confin'd into this rock,
Who hadst deserv'd more than a prison.
Cal. You taught me language; and my profit on 't
Is, I know how to curse. The red plague rid you
For learning me your language!
Pros. Hag-seed, hence!
Fetch us in fuel; and be quick, thou 'rt best,
To answer other business. Shrug'st thou, malice?
If thou neglect'st or dost unwillingly
What I command, I'll rack thee with old cramps,
Fill all thy bones with aches, make thee roar
That beasts shall tremble at thy din.
Cal. No, pray thee.
[*Aside*] I must obey: his art is of such pow'r,
It would control my dam's god, Setebos,
And make a vassal of him.
Pros. So, slave; hence! *Exit Caliban.*

Enter FERDINAND; *and* ARIEL, *invisible, playing and singing.*

ARIEL'S *song.*

Come unto these yellow sands,
And then take hands:
Courtsied when you have and kiss'd
The wild waves whist,
Foot it featly here and there;
And, sweet sprites, the burthen bear.
Burthen (*dispersedly*). Hark, hark!
Bow-wow.
The watch-dogs bark:
Bow-wow.
Ari. Hark, hark! I hear
The strain of strutting chanticleer
Cry, Cock-a-diddle-dow.
Fer. Where should this music be? i' th' air or th' earth?
It sounds no more: and, sure, it waits upon
Some god o' th' island. Sitting on a bank,
Weeping again the king my father's wrack,
This music crept by me upon the waters,
Allaying both their fury and my passion
With its sweet air: thence I have follow'd it,
Or it hath drawn me rather. But 'tis gone.
No, it begins again.

ARIEL'S *song.*

Full fathom five thy father lies;
Of his bones are coral made;
Those are pearls that were his eyes:
Nothing of him that doth fade
But doth suffer a sea-change
Into something rich and strange.
Sea-nymphs hourly ring his knell:
Burthen. Ding-dong.
[*Ari.*] Hark! now I hear them,—Ding-dong, bell.
Fer. The ditty does remember my drown'd father.
This is no mortal business, nor no sound
That the earth owes. I hear it now above me.
Pros. The fringed curtains of thine eye advance
And say what thou seest yond.
Mir. What is 't? a spirit?
Lord, how it looks about! Believe me, sir,
It carries a brave form. But 'tis a spirit.
Pros. No, wench; it eats and sleeps and hath such senses
As we have, such. This gallant which thou seest
Was in the wrack; and, but he 's something stain'd

321. **wicked,** mischievous, harmful. 323. **south-west,** i.e., wind (bringing disease). 326. **urchins,** hedgehogs; here, suggesting goblins. 327. **vast,** long hours. 328. **exercise,** practice, work. 334. **berries.** Strachey's *Reportory*, one of the sources, says that the Bermudas were full of thickets of "goodly Cedar . . . the Berries whereof, our men seething, straining, and letting stand some three or foure daies, made a kind of pleasant drinke." 338. **brine-pits,** salt springs. 342. **sty,** put in sty. 351-362. **Abhorred . . . prison.** Sometimes assigned to Prospero (as in Globe). 357-358. **endow'd . . . known,** enabled you to make known what was going on in your mind. 358. **race,** natural disposition. 364. **red plague,** bubonic plague. **rid,** destroy, with play on *red*. 365. **Hag-seed,** hag's offspring. 369. **old,** plenty of. 370. **aches,** pronounced "aitches." 373. **Setebos,** mentioned in Eden's *History of Travel* (1577) as a deity, or devil, of the Patagonians. 376-378. **Come . . . kiss'd,** three motions before the dance—take hands, curtsy, kiss (New Cambridge). 379. **whist,** silent. 380. **featly,** neatly. 381.

With grief that 's beauty's canker, thou mightst call him
A goodly person: he hath lost his fellows
And strays about to find 'em.
Mir. I might call him
A thing divine, for nothing natural
I ever saw so noble.
Pros. [*Aside*] It goes on, I see,
As my soul prompts it. Spirit, fine spirit! I'll free thee
Within two days for this.
Fer. Most sure, the goddess
On whom these airs attend! Vouchsafe my pray'r
May know if you remain upon this island;
And that you will some good instruction give
How I may bear me here: my prime request,
Which I do last pronounce, is, O you wonder!
If you be maid or no?
Mir. No wonder, sir;
But certainly a maid.
Fer. My language! heavens!
I am the best of them that speak this speech,
Were I but where 'tis spoken.
Pros. How? the best?
What wert thou, if the King of Naples heard thee?
Fer. A single thing, as I am now, that wonders
To hear thee speak of Naples. He does hear me;
And that he does I weep: myself am Naples,
Who with mine eyes, never since at ebb, beheld
The king my father wrack'd.
Mir. Alack, for mercy!
Fer. Yes, faith, and all his lords; the Duke of Milan
And his brave son being twain.
Pros. [*Aside*] The Duke of Milan
And his more braver daughter could control thee,
If now 'twere fit to do 't. At the first sight
They have chang'd eyes. Delicate Ariel,
I'll set thee free for this. [*To Fer.*] A word, good sir;
I fear you have done yourself some wrong: a word.
Mir. Why speaks my father so ungently? This
Is the third man that e'er I saw, the first
That e'er I sigh'd for: pity move my father
To be inclin'd my way!
Fer. O, if a virgin,
And your affection not gone forth, I'll make you
The queen of Naples.
Pros. Soft, sir! one word more.
[*Aside*] They are both in either's pow'rs; but this swift business
I must uneasy make, lest too light winning
Make the prize light. [*To Fer.*] One word more; I charge thee
That thou attend me: thou dost here usurp
The name thou ow'st not; and hast put thyself
Upon this island as a spy, to win it
From me, the lord on 't.
Fer. No, as I am a man.
Mir. There 's nothing ill can dwell in such a temple:
If the ill spirit have so fair a house,
Good things will strive to dwell with 't.
Pros. Follow me.
Speak not you for him; he 's a traitor. [*To Fer.*] Come;
I'll manacle thy neck and feet together:
Sea-water shalt thou drink; thy food shall be
The fresh-brook mussels, wither'd roots and husks
Wherein the acorn cradled. Follow.
Fer. No;
I will resist such entertainment till
Mine enemy has more pow'r.
He draws, and is charmed from moving.
Mir. O dear father,
Make not too rash a trial of him, for
He 's gentle and not fearful.
Pros. What? I say,
My foot my tutor? [*To Fer.*] Put thy sword up, traitor;
Who mak'st a show but dar'st not strike, thy conscience
Is so possess'd with guilt: come, from thy ward,
For I can here disarm thee with this stick
And make thy weapon drop.
Mir. Beseech you, father.
Pros. Hence! hang not on my garments.
Mir. Sir, have pity;
I'll be his surety.
Pros. Silence! one word more
Shall make me chide thee, if not hate thee. What!
An advocate for an impostor! hush!
Thou think'st there is no more such shapes as he,
Having seen but him and Caliban: foolish wench!
To th' most of men this is a Caliban
And they to him are angels.
Mir. My affections
Are then most humble; I have no ambition
To see a goodlier man.
Pros. [*To Fer.*] Come on; obey:
Thy nerves are in their infancy again
And have no vigour in them.
Fer. So they are;
My spirits, as in a dream, are all bound up.
My father's loss, the weakness which I feel,
The wrack of all my friends, nor this man's threats,
To whom I am subdu'd, are but light to me,
Might I but through my prison once a day
Behold this maid: all corners else o' th' earth
Let liberty make use of; space enough
Have I in such a prison.
Pros. [*Aside*] It works. [*To Fer.*] Come on.
Thou hast done well, fine Ariel! [*To Fer.*] Follow me.
[*To Ari.*] Hark what thou else shalt do me.
Mir. Be of comfort;
My father 's of a better nature, sir,
Than he appears by speech: this is unwonted
Which now came from him.
Pros. Thou shalt be as free
As mountain winds: but then exactly do
All points of my command.
Ari. To th' syllable.
Pros. Come, follow. [*To Mir.*] Speak not for him.
Exeunt.

burthen, refrain. 382. **dispersedly,** i.e., from all parts of the stage. 405. **remember,** commemorate. 407. **owes,** owns. 415. **canker,** cankerworm (feeding on buds and leaves). 419. **It goes on,** my charm works. 423. **remain,** dwell. 425. **bear me,** conduct myself. 429. **best,** i.e., in birth. 432. **single,** solitary, with a suggestion of feebleness. 438. **son,** the only reference to a son of Antonio. 439. **control,** confute. 441. **chang'd eyes,** exchanged amorous glances. 443. **done . . . wrong,** are mistaken. 451. **uneasy,** difficult. 451, 452. **light, light,** easy, cheap. 454. **ow'st,** ownest. 465. **entertainment,** treatment. 468. **gentle,** wellborn, high-spirited. **not fearful,** not dangerous (because incapable of treachery). 469. **foot,** subordinate. Miranda (the foot) presumes to instruct Prospero (the head). 471. **ward,** defensive posture (in fencing). 472. **stick,** his wand. 484. **nerves,** sinews. 491-492. **all . . . of,** those who are free may have all the rest of the world.

ACT II.

SCENE I. [*Another part of the island.*]

Enter ALONSO, SEBASTIAN, ANTONIO, GONZALO, ADRIAN, FRANCISCO, *and others.*

Gon. Beseech you, sir, be merry; you have cause,
So have we all, of joy; for our escape
Is much beyond our loss. Our hint of woe
Is common; every day some sailor's wife,
The masters of some merchant and the merchant
Have just our theme of woe; but for the miracle,
I mean our preservation, few in millions
Can speak like us: then wisely, good sir, weigh
Our sorrow with our comfort.

Alon. Prithee, peace.

Seb. [*To Ant.*] He receives comfort like cold porridge.

Ant. [*To Seb.*] The visitor will not give him o'er so.

Seb. Look, he 's winding up the watch of his wit; by and by it will strike.

Gon. Sir,—

Seb. [*To Ant.*] One: tell.

Gon. When every grief is entertain'd that 's offer'd,
Comes to th' entertainer—

Seb. A dollar.

Gon. Dolour comes to him, indeed: you have spoken truer than you purposed.

Seb. You have taken it wiselier than I meant you should.

Gon. Therefore, my lord,—

Ant. Fie, what a spendthrift is he of his tongue!

Alon. I prithee, spare.

Gon. Well, I have done: but yet,—

Seb. He will be talking.

Ant. Which, of he or Adrian, for a good wager, first begins to crow?

Seb. The old cock.

Ant. The cockerel.

Seb. Done. The wager?

Ant. A laughter.

Seb. A match!

Adr. Though this island seem to be desert,—

Seb. Ha, ha, ha! So, you 're paid.

Adr. Uninhabitable and almost inaccessible,—

Seb. Yet,—

Adr. Yet,—

Ant. He could not miss 't.

Adr. It must needs be of subtle, tender and delicate temperance.

Ant. Temperance was a delicate wench.

Seb. Ay, and a subtle; as he most learnedly delivered.

Adr. The air breathes upon us here most sweetly.

Seb. As if it had lungs and rotten ones.

Ant. Or as 'twere perfumed by a fen.

Gon. Here is every thing advantageous to life.

Ant. True; save means to live.

Seb. Of that there 's none, or little.

Gon. How lush and lusty the grass looks! how green!

Ant. The ground indeed is tawny.

Seb. With an eye of green in 't.

Ant. He misses not much.

Seb. No; he doth but mistake the truth totally.

Gon. But the rarity of it is,—which is indeed almost beyond credit,—

Seb. As many vouched rarities are.

Gon. That our garments, being, as they were, drenched in the sea, hold notwithstanding their freshness and glosses, being rather new-dyed than stained with salt water.

Ant. If but one of his pockets could speak, would it not say he lies?

Seb. Ay, or very falsely pocket up his report.

Gon. Methinks our garments are now as fresh as when we put them on first in Afric, at the marriage of the king's fair daughter Claribel to the King of Tunis.

Seb. 'Twas a sweet marriage, and we prosper well in our return.

Adr. Tunis was never graced before with such a paragon to their queen.

Gon. Not since widow Dido's time.

Ant. Widow! a pox o' that! How came that widow in? widow Dido!

Seb. What if he had said 'widower Æneas' too? Good Lord, how you take it!

Adr. 'Widow Dido' said you? you make me study of that: she was of Carthage, not of Tunis.

Gon. This Tunis, sir, was Carthage.

Adr. Carthage?

Gon. I assure you, Carthage.

Seb. His word is more than the miraculous harp; he hath raised the wall and houses too.

Ant. What impossible matter will he make easy next?

Seb. I think he will carry this island home in his pocket and give it his son for an apple.

Ant. And, sowing the kernels of it in the sea, bring forth more islands.

Gon. Ay.

Ant. Why, in good time.

Gon. [*To Alon.*] Sir, we were talking that our garments seem now as fresh as when we were at Tunis at the marriage of your daughter, who is now queen.

Ant. And the rarest that e'er came there.

Seb. Bate, I beseech you, widow Dido.

Ant. O, widow Dido! ay, widow Dido.

Gon. Is not, sir, my doublet as fresh as the first day I wore it? I mean, in a sort.

Ant. That sort was well fished for.

Gon. When I wore it at your daughter's marriage?

Alon. You cram these words into mine ears against
The stomach of my sense. Would I had never
Married my daughter there! for, coming thence,

ACT II. SCENE I. 3. **hint of,** occasion for. 5. **merchant, merchant,** merchant vessel, merchant. 11. **visitor,** one taking nourishment to the sick. 15. **tell,** keep count. 18. **dollar,** widely circulated coin, the German *Thaler* and the Spanish *piece of eight*. 28-29. **Which . . . crow,** which of the two, Gonzalo or Adrian, do you bet will speak (crow) first? 30. **old cock,** i.e., Gonzalo. 33. **laughter,** sitting of eggs. When Adrian (the *cockerel*) begins to speak (l. 35), Sebastian loses the bet and pays with a *laugh* (*Ha, ha, ha!* l. 36) for a *laughter*. 34. **A match,** a bargain; agreed. 40. **He . . . miss 't,** i.e., even if it is uninhabitable and inaccessible, he could not refrain from talking about it. 42. **temperance,** temperature. 43. **Temperance,** a Puritan name for women, thought also to refer to Temperance, a character in Chapman's *May Day* (1611). 54. **tawny,** dull brown. 55. **eye,** tinge. 65. **pockets,** i.e., because they are muddy. 76. **widow Dido,** queen of Carthage deserted by Aeneas, and thus not really a widow. 86. **miraculous harp,** allusion to Amphion's harp with which he raised the walls of Thebes; Gonzalo has exceeded that deed by rebuilding a modern Carthage. 95. **in good time,** vague expression of agreement or approbation. 100. **Bate,** except. 104. **sort,** lucky catch after much angling; probable suggestion of the age of the garment, with a play on *sort* in line 103. 109. **rate,** opinion. 113-122. **Sir . . . land,** Francisco's only speech. 120. **that . . . bow'd,** that hung out over its wave-worn foot. 125.

My son is lost and, in my rate, she too,
Who is so far from Italy remov'd
I ne'er again shall see her. O thou mine heir
Of Naples and of Milan, what strange fish
Hath made his meal on thee?
Fran. Sir, he may live:
I saw him beat the surges under him,
And ride upon their backs; he trod the water,
Whose enmity he flung aside, and breasted
The surge most swoln that met him; his bold head
'Bove the contentious waves he kept, and oar'd
Himself with his good arms in lusty stroke
To th' shore, that o'er his wave-worn basis bow'd,
As stooping to relieve him: I not doubt
He came alive to land.
Alon. No, no, he 's gone.
Seb. Sir, you may thank yourself for this great loss,
That would not bless our Europe with your daughter,
But rather loose her to an African;
Where she at least is banish'd from your eye,
Who hath cause to wet the grief on 't.
Alon. Prithee, peace.
Seb. You were kneel'd to and importun'd otherwise
By all of us, and the fair soul herself
Weigh'd between loathness and obedience, at
Which end o' th' beam should bow. We have lost your son,
I fear, for ever: Milan and Naples have
Moe widows in them of this business' making
Than we bring men to comfort them:
The fault 's your own.
Alon. So is the dear'st o' th' loss.
Gon. My lord Sebastian,
The truth you speak doth lack some gentleness
And time to speak it in: you rub the sore,
When you should bring the plaster.
Seb. Very well.
Ant. And most chirurgeonly.
Gon. It is foul weather in us all, good sir,
When you are cloudy.
Seb. [*To Ant.*] Foul weather?
Ant. [*To Seb.*] Very foul.
Gon. Had I plantation of this isle, my lord,—
Ant. He 'ld sow 't with nettle-seed.
Seb. Or docks, or mallows.
Gon. And were the king on 't, what would I do?
Seb. 'Scape being drunk for want of wine.
Gon. I' th' commonwealth I would by contraries
Execute all things; for no kind of traffic
Would I admit; no name of magistrate;
Letters should not be known; riches, poverty,
And use of service, none; contract, succession,
Bourn, bound of land, tilth, vineyard, none;
No use of metal, corn, or wine, or oil;
No occupation; all men idle, all;
And women too, but innocent and pure;
No sovereignty;—
Seb. Yet he would be king on 't.

Ant. The latter end of his commonwealth forgets the beginning.

Gon. All things in common nature should produce
Without sweat or endeavour: treason, felony,
Sword, pike, knife, gun, or need of any engine,
Would I not have; but nature should bring forth,
Of it own kind, all foison, all abundance,
To feed my innocent people.
Seb. No marrying 'mong his subjects?
Ant. None, man; all idle: whores and knaves.
Gon. I would with such perfection govern, sir,
T' excel the golden age.
Seb. 'Save his majesty!
Ant. Long live Gonzalo!
Gon. And,—do you mark me, sir?

Alon. Prithee, no more: thou dost talk nothing to me.

Gon. I do well believe your highness; and did it to minister occasion to these gentlemen, who are of such sensible and nimble lungs that they always use to laugh at nothing.

Ant. 'Twas you we laughed at.

Gon. Who in this kind of merry fooling am nothing to you: so you may continue and laugh at nothing still.

Ant. What a blow was there given!

Seb. An it had not fallen flat-long.

Gon. You are gentlemen of brave mettle; you would lift the moon out of her sphere, if she would continue in it five weeks without changing.

Enter ARIEL [*invisible*] *playing solemn music.*

Seb. We would so, and then go a bat-fowling.

Ant. Nay, good my lord, be not angry.

Gon. No, I warrant you; I will not adventure my discretion so weakly. Will you laugh me asleep, for I am very heavy?

Ant. Go sleep, and hear us.

[*All sleep except Alon., Seb., and Ant.*]

Alon. What, all so soon asleep! I wish mine eyes
Would, with themselves, shut up my thoughts: I find
They are inclin'd to do so.
Seb. Please you, sir,
Do not omit the heavy offer of it:
It seldom visits sorrow; when it doth,
It is a comforter.
Ant. We two, my lord,
Will guard your person while you take your rest,
And watch your safety.
Alon. Thank you. Wondrous heavy.
[*Alonso sleeps. Exit Ariel.*]
Seb. What a strange drowsiness possesses them!
Ant. It is the quality o' th' climate.
Seb. Why
Doth it not then our eyelids sink? I find not
Myself dispos'd to sleep.

loose, so F; Globe: *lose*. 127. **Who,** which (eye). 129-131. **the fair . . . bow,** Claribel herself was poised uncertain between unwillingness and obedience as to which end of the scale should sink. 140. **chirurgeonly,** like a skilled surgeon. 143. **plantation,** colonization; subsequent play on the literal meaning. 147-156. **I' th' . . . sovereignty.** This passage on man in his primitive state is based on Montaigne, *Essays*, I, xxx, perhaps derived from Florio's translation (1603). 150. **Letters,** learning. 151. **use of service,** custom of employing servants. **succession,** holding of property by right of inheritance. 152. **Bourn,** boundaries. **bound of land,** landmarks. **tilth,** tillage of soil. 161. **engine,** instrument of warfare. 163. **it,** its. **foison,** plenty. 173. **minister occasion,** furnish opportunity. 174. **sensible,** sensitive. 181. **flat-long,** with the flat of the sword. 182. **mettle,** temper, nature. 183. **lift . . . sphere.** As a planet in the old astronomy, the moon had a crystal sphere in which she moved. Gonzalo means that they would lift the moon out of her sphere if she remained steady in it. 185. **bat-fowling,** hunting birds at night with lantern and stick; also, gulling a simpleton. Gonzalo is the simpleton (or fowl), and Sebastian will use the moon as his lantern. 187. **adventure,** risk. 190. **Go . . . us,** let our laughing send you to sleep, or, go to sleep and hear us laugh at you. 194. **omit,** neglect. **heavy,** drowsy.

Ant. Nor I; my spirits are nimble.
They fell together all, as by consent;
They dropp'd, as by a thunder-stroke. What might,
Worthy Sebastian? O, what might?—No more:—
And yet methinks I see it in thy face,
What thou shouldst be: th' occasion speaks thee, and
My strong imagination sees a crown
Dropping upon thy head.
Seb. What, art thou waking?
Ant. Do you not hear me speak?
Seb. I do; and surely
It is a sleepy language and thou speak'st
Out of thy sleep. What is it thou didst say?
This is a strange repose, to be asleep
With eyes wide open; standing, speaking, moving,
And yet so fast asleep.
Ant. Noble Sebastian,
Thou let'st thy fortune sleep—die, rather; wink'st
Whiles thou art waking.
Seb. Thou dost snore distinctly;
There 's meaning in thy snores.
Ant. I am more serious than my custom: you
Must be so too, if heed me; which to do
Trebles thee o'er.
Seb. Well, I am standing water.
Ant. I'll teach you how to flow.
Seb. Do so: to ebb
Hereditary sloth instructs me.
Ant. O,
If you but knew how you the purpose cherish
Whiles thus you mock it! how, in stripping it,
You more invest it! Ebbing men, indeed,
Most often do so near the bottom run
By their own fear or sloth.
Seb. Prithee, say on:
The setting of thine eye and cheek proclaim
A matter from thee, and a birth indeed
Which throes thee much to yield.
Ant. Thus, sir:
Although this lord of weak remembrance, this,
Who shall be of as little memory
When he is earth'd, hath here almost persuaded,—
For he 's a spirit of persuasion, only
Professes to persuade,—the king his son 's alive,
'Tis as impossible that he 's undrown'd
As he that sleeps here swims.
Seb. I have no hope
That he 's undrown'd.
Ant. O, out of that 'no hope'
What great hope have you! no hope that way is
Another way so high a hope that even
Ambition cannot pierce a wink beyond,
But doubt discovery there. Will you grant with me
That Ferdinand is drown'd?
Seb. He 's gone.
Ant. Then, tell me,
Who 's the next heir of Naples?
Seb. Claribel.
Ant. She that is queen of Tunis; she that dwells
Ten leagues beyond man's life; she that from Naples
Can have no note, unless the sun were post—
The man i' th' moon 's too slow—till new-born chins
Be rough and razorable; she that from whom
We all were sea-swallow'd, though some cast again,
And by that destiny to perform an act
Whereof what 's past is prologue, what to come
In yours and my discharge.
Seb. What stuff is this! how say you?
'Tis true, my brother's daughter 's queen of Tunis;
So is she heir of Naples; 'twixt which regions
There is some space.
Ant. A space whose ev'ry cubit
Seems to cry out, 'How shall that Claribel
Measure us back to Naples? Keep in Tunis,
And let Sebastian wake.' Say, this were death
That now hath seiz'd them; why, they were no worse
Than now they are. There be that can rule Naples
As well as he that sleeps; lords that can prate
As amply and unnecessarily
As this Gonzalo; I myself could make
A chough of as deep chat. O, that you bore
The mind that I do! what a sleep were this
For your advancement! Do you understand me?
Seb. Methinks I do.
Ant. And how does your content
Tender your own good fortune?
Seb. I remember
You did supplant your brother Prospero.
Ant. True:
And look how well my garments sit upon me;
Much feater than before: my brother's servants
Were then my fellows; now they are my men.
Seb. But, for your conscience?
Ant. Ay, sir; where lies that? if 'twere a kibe,
'Twould put me to my slipper: but I feel not
This deity in my bosom: twenty consciences,
That stand 'twixt me and Milan, candied be they
And melt ere they molest! Here lies your brother,
No better than the earth he lies upon,
If he were that which now he 's like, that 's dead;
Whom I, with this obedient steel, three inches of it,
Can lay to bed for ever; whiles you, doing thus,
To the perpetual wink for aye might put
This ancient morsel, this Sir Prudence, who
Should not upbraid our course. For all the rest,
They'll take suggestion as a cat laps milk;
They'll tell the clock to any business that
We say befits the hour.
Seb. Thy case, dear friend,
Shall be my precedent; as thou got'st Milan,
I'll come by Naples. Draw thy sword: one stroke
Shall free thee from the tribute which thou payest;
And I the king shall love thee.
Ant. Draw together;
And when I rear my hand, do you the like,
To fall it on Gonzalo. [*They draw.*]
Seb. O, but one word!

203. **consent,** agreement as to a course of action. 207. **speaks,** calls upon, proclaims (thee) king. 216. **wink'st,** shuts the eyes. 217. **distinctly,** with separate and individual sounds. 221. **Trebles thee o'er,** makes thee three times as great. **standing water,** water which neither flows nor ebbs. 224. **purpose,** i.e., of being king. 225. **stripping it,** stripping off all pretense, revealing it. 226. **Ebbing men,** men whose fortunes ebb, leaving them stranded. 229. **setting,** set expression. 230. **matter,** matter of importance. 231. **throes,** pains. 232. **this lord,** Gonzalo. **remembrance,** power of remembering. 234. **earth'd,** buried. 236. **Professes to persuade,** he was a privy councilor. 240. **that way,** i.e., in regard to Ferdinand's being saved. 242-243. **Ambition . . . there,** ambition itself cannot see any further than that hope (of the crown) without doubting the reality of the objects it sees. 247. **Ten . . . life,** it would take more than a lifetime to get there. 248. **note,** intimation. **post,** messenger. 249-250. **till . . . razorable,** till babies born today will be old enough to shave. **from,** on our voyage from. 251. **cast,** were disgorged, with pun on *casting* (of parts for a play). 254. **discharge,** performance, i.e., to get done. 259.

Enter ARIEL [*invisible*], *with music and song.*

Ari. My master through his art foresees the danger
That you, his friend, are in; and sends me forth—
For else his project dies—to keep them living.
Sings in Gonzalo's ear.

While you here do snoring lie,
Open-ey'd conspiracy
His time doth take.
If of life you keep a care,
Shake off slumber, and beware:
Awake, awake!

Ant. Then let us both be sudden.
Gon. [*Wakes*] Now, good angels
Preserve the king. [*The others wake.*]
Alon. Why, how now? ho, awake! Why are you drawn?
Wherefore this ghastly looking?
Gon. What 's the matter?
Seb. Whiles we stood here securing your repose,
Even now, we heard a hollow burst of bellowing
Like bulls, or rather lions: did 't not wake you?
It struck mine ear most terribly.
Alon. I heard nothing.
Ant. O, 'twas a din to fright a monster's ear,
To make an earthquake! sure, it was the roar
Of a whole herd of lions.
Alon. Heard you this, Gonzalo?
Gon. Upon mine honour, sir, I heard a humming,
And that a strange one too, which did awake me:
I shak'd you, sir, and cried: as mine eyes open'd,
I saw their weapons drawn: there was a noise,
That 's verily. 'Tis best we stand upon our guard,
Or that we quit this place: let 's draw our weapons.
Alon. Lead off this ground; and let 's make further search
For my poor son.
Gon. Heavens keep him from these beasts!
For he is, sure, i' th' island.
Alon. Lead away.
Ari. Prospero my lord shall know what I have done:
So, king, go safely on to seek thy son. *Exeunt.*

SCENE II. [*Another part of the island.*]

Enter CALIBAN *with a burden of wood. A noise of thunder heard.*

Cal. All the infections that the sun sucks up
From bogs, fens, flats, on Prosper fall and make him
By inch-meal a disease! His spirits hear me
And yet I needs must curse. But they'll nor pinch,
Fright me with urchin-shows, pitch me i' th' mire,
Nor lead me, like a firebrand, in the dark
Out of my way, unless he bid 'em; but
For every trifle are they set upon me;
Sometime like apes that mow and chatter at me
And after bite me, then like hedgehogs which
Lie tumbling in my barefoot way and mount
Their pricks at my footfall; sometime am I
All wound with adders who with cloven tongues
Do hiss me into madness.

Enter TRINCULO.

Lo, now, lo!
Here comes a spirit of his, and to torment me
For bringing wood in slowly. I'll fall flat;
Perchance he will not mind me. [*Lies down.*]

Trin. Here 's neither bush nor shrub, to bear off any weather at all, and another storm brewing; I hear it sing i' the wind: yond same black cloud, yond huge one, looks like a foul bombard that would shed his liquor. If it should thunder as it did before, I know not where to hide my head: yond same cloud cannot choose but fall by pailfuls. What have we here? a man or a fish? dead or alive? A fish: he smells like a fish; a very ancient and fish-like smell; a kind of not of the newest Poor-John. A strange fish! Were I in England now, as once I was, and had but this fish painted, not a holiday fool there but would give a piece of silver: there would this monster make a man; any strange beast there makes a man: when they will not give a doit to relieve a lame beggar, they will lay out ten to see a dead Indian. Legged like a man! and his fins like arms! Warm o' my troth! I do now let loose my opinion; hold it no longer: this is no fish, but an islander, that hath lately suffered by a thunderbolt. [*Thunder.*] Alas, the storm is come again! my best way is to creep under his gaberdine; there is no other shelter hereabout: misery acquaints a man with strange bed-fellows. I will here shroud till the dregs of the storm be past. [*Creeps under Caliban's garment.*]

Enter STEPHANO, *singing* [, *a bottle in his hand*].

Ste. I shall no more to sea, to sea,
Here shall I die ashore—
This is a very scurvy tune to sing at a man's funeral: well, here 's my comfort. *Drinks.*
[*Sings.*]
The master, the swabber, the boatswain and I,
The gunner and his mate
Lov'd Mall, Meg and Marian and Margery,
But none of us car'd for Kate;
For she had a tongue with a tang,
Would cry to a sailor, Go hang!
She lov'd not the savour of tar nor of pitch,
Yet a tailor might scratch her where'er she did itch:
Then to sea, boys, and let her go hang!

This is a scurvy tune too: but here 's my comfort. *Drinks.*

Cal. Do not torment me: Oh!

Ste. What 's the matter? Have we devils here? Do you put tricks upon 's with savages and men of Ind, ha? I have not 'scaped drowning to be afeard now of your four legs; for it hath been said, As proper a man as ever went on four legs cannot make him give

Measure us, find (her) way. 259-260. **Keep . . . wake,** let her stay in Tunis, and let Sebastian wake (to his good fortune). 265-266. **I . . . chat,** I could teach a jackdaw to talk as wisely. 269. **content,** desire, contentment. 270. **Tender,** provide for; or, regard. 273. **feater,** more becomingly. 276. **kibe,** sore on the heel. 279. **candied,** frozen, congealed. 289. **tell the clock,** answer appropriately. 302. **time,** opportunity. 306. **sudden,** swift in action. 317. **humming,** i.e., Ariel's song.

SCENE II. 3. **inch-meal,** little by little. 9. **mow,** make faces. 19. **bear off,** keep off. 22. **foul bombard,** dirty leathern bottle. 29. **Poor-John,** salted hake, type of poor fare. **fish.** Malone cites a license issued by the Master of the Revels (1632) "to shew a strange fish for half a yeare." 30. **painted,** i.e., on a sign set up outside a booth or tent at a fair. 33. **make a man,** i.e., make his fortune. 35. **doit,** small coin. 40. **gaberdine,** cloak, loose upper garment. 43. **shroud,** take shelter. **dregs,** last remains. 61. **Ind,** India, or, vaguely, the East.

ground; and it shall be said so again while Stephano breathes at' nostrils.

Cal. The spirit torments me; Oh!

Ste. This is some monster of the isle with four legs, who hath got, as I take it, an ague. Where the devil should he learn our language? I will give him some relief, if it be but for that. If I can recover him and keep him tame and get to Naples with him, he 's a present for any emperor that ever trod on neat's-leather.

Cal. Do not torment me, prithee; I'll bring my wood home faster.

Ste. He 's in his fit now and does not talk after the wisest. He shall taste of my bottle: if he have never drunk wine afore, it will go near to remove his fit. If I can recover him and keep him tame, I will not take too much for him; he shall pay for him that hath him, and that soundly.

Cal. Thou dost me yet but little hurt; thou wilt anon, I know it by thy trembling: now Prosper works upon thee.

Ste. Come on your ways; open your mouth; here is that which will give language to you, cat: open your mouth; this will shake your shaking, I can tell you, and that soundly. [*Gives Caliban drink.*] You cannot tell who 's your friend: open your chaps again.

Trin. I should know that voice: it should be—but he is drowned; and these are devils: O defend me!

Ste. Four legs and two voices: a most delicate monster! His forward voice now is to speak well of his friend; his backward voice is to utter foul speeches and to detract. If all the wine in my bottle will recover him, I will help his ague. Come. [*Gives drink.*] Amen! I will pour some in thy other mouth.

Trin. Stephano!

Ste. Doth thy other mouth call me? Mercy, mercy! This is a devil, and no monster: I will leave him; I have no long spoon.

Trin. Stephano! If thou beest Stephano, touch me and speak to me; for I am Trinculo—be not afeard—thy good friend Trinculo.

Ste. If thou beest Trinculo, come forth: I'll pull thee by the lesser legs: if any be Trinculo's legs, these are they. [*Pulls him out.*] Thou art very Trinculo indeed! How camest thou to be the siege of this moon-calf? can he vent Trinculos?

Trin. I took him to be killed with a thunder-stroke. But art thou not drowned, Stephano? I hope now thou art not drowned. Is the storm overblown? I hid me under the dead moon-calf's gaberdine for fear of the storm. And art thou living, Stephano? O Stephano, two Neapolitans 'scaped!

Ste. Prithee, do not turn me about; my stomach is not constant.

Cal. [*Aside*] These be fine things, an if they be not
sprites.
That 's a brave god and bears celestial liquor.
I will kneel to him.

Ste. How didst thou 'scape? How camest thou hither? swear by this bottle how thou camest hither. I escaped upon a butt of sack which the sailors heaved o'erboard—by this bottle, which I made of the bark of a tree with mine own hands since I was cast ashore.

Cal. I'll swear upon that bottle to be thy true subject; for the liquor is not earthly.

Ste. Here; swear then how thou escapedst.

Trin. Swum ashore, man, like a duck: I can swim like a duck, I'll be sworn.

Ste. Here, kiss the book. Though thou canst swim like a duck, thou art made like a goose. [*Gives drink.*]

Trin. O Stephano, hast any more of this?

Ste. The whole butt, man: my cellar is in a rock by the sea-side where my wine is hid. How now, moon-calf! how does thine ague?

Cal. Hast thou not dropp'd from heaven?

Ste. Out o' the moon, I do assure thee: I was the man i' the moon when time was.

Cal. I have seen thee in her and I do adore thee:
My mistress show'd me thee and thy dog and thy
bush.

Ste. Come, swear to that; kiss the book: I will furnish it anon with new contents: swear. [*Gives drink.*]

Trin. By this good light, this is a very shallow monster! I afeard of him! A very weak monster! The man i' the moon! A most poor credulous monster! Well drawn, monster, in good sooth!

Cal. I'll show thee every fertile inch o' th' island;
And I will kiss thy foot: I prithee, be my god.

Trin. By this light, a most perfidious and drunken monster! when 's god 's asleep, he'll rob his bottle.

Cal. I'll kiss thy foot; I'll swear myself thy subject.

Ste. Come on then; down, and swear.

Trin. I shall laugh myself to death at this puppy-headed monster. A most scurvy monster! I could find in my heart to beat him,—

Ste. Come, kiss.

Trin. But that the poor monster 's in drink: an abominable monster!

Cal. I'll show thee the best springs; I'll pluck thee
berries;
I'll fish for thee and get thee wood enough.
A plague upon the tyrant that I serve!
I'll bear him no more sticks, but follow thee,
Thou wondrous man.

Trin. A most ridiculous monster, to make a wonder of a poor drunkard!

Cal. I prithee, let me bring thee where crabs grow;
And I with my long nails will dig thee pig-nuts;
Show thee a jay's nest and instruct thee how
To snare the nimble marmoset; I'll bring thee
To clust'ring filberts and sometimes I'll get thee
Young scamels from the rock. Wilt thou go with me?

Ste. I prithee now, lead the way without any more talking. Trinculo, the king and all our company else being drowned, we will inherit here: here; bear my bottle: fellow Trinculo, we'll fill him by and by again.

Cal. (Sings drunkenly)
Farewell, master; farewell, farewell!

Trin. A howling monster; a drunken monster!

Cal. No more dams I'll make for fish;
Nor fetch in firing

71. **recover,** restore. 73. **neat's-leather,** leather from the skin of an ox or cow. 80. **take too much,** i.e., no sum can be too much. 83. **trembling,** suggestion of demonic possession. 87. **cat . . . mouth,** allusion to the proverb, "Good liquor will make a cat speak." 103. **long spoon,** allusion to the proverb, "He that sups with the devil has need of a long spoon." 111. **siege,** excrement. **moon-calf,** monster, abortion (supposed to be caused by the influence of the moon). 120. **not constant,** unsteady. 126. **butt of sack,** barrel of Canary wine. 134. **kiss the book.** He gives him the bottle instead of the Bible on which to make his oath. 142. **when time was,** once upon a time. 144. **dog . . . bush.** See *A Midsummer Night's Dream,* V, i, 136. 150. **Well drawn.** Caliban takes a good draft of the wine. 171. **crabs,** crab

At requiring;
Nor scrape trenchering, nor wash dish:
'Ban, 'Ban, Cacaliban
Has a new master: get a new man.
Freedom, hey-day! hey-day, freedom! freedom, hey-day, freedom!
Ste. O brave monster! Lead the way. *Exeunt.*

ACT III.

SCENE I. [*Before* PROSPERO'S *cell.*]

Enter FERDINAND, *bearing a log.*

Fer. There be some sports are painful, and their labour
Delight in them sets off: some kinds of baseness
Are nobly undergone and most poor matters
Point to rich ends. This my mean task
Would be as heavy to me as odious, but
The mistress which I serve quickens what 's dead
And makes my labours pleasures: O, she is
Ten times more gentle than her father 's crabbed,
And he 's compos'd of harshness. I must remove
Some thousands of these logs and pile them up,
Upon a sore injunction: my sweet mistress
Weeps when she sees me work, and says, such baseness
Had never like executor. I forget:
But these sweet thoughts do even refresh my labours,
†Most busy lest, when I do it.

Enter MIRANDA; *and* PROSPERO [*at a distance, unseen*].

Mir. Alas, now, pray you,
Work not so hard: I would the lightning had
Burnt up those logs that you are enjoin'd to pile!
Pray, set it down and rest you: when this burns,
'Twill weep for having wearied you. My father
Is hard at study; pray now, rest yourself;
He 's safe for these three hours.
Fer. O most dear mistress,
The sun will set before I shall discharge
What I must strive to do.
Mir. If you'll sit down,
I'll bear your logs the while: pray, give me that;
I'll carry it to the pile.
Fer. No, precious creature;
I had rather crack my sinews, break my back,
Than you should such dishonour undergo,
While I sit lazy by.
Mir. It would become me
As well as it does you: and I should do it
With much more ease; for my good will is to it,
And yours it is against.
Pros. [*Aside*] Poor worm, thou art infected!
This visitation shows it.
Mir. You look wearily.
Fer. No, noble mistress; 'tis fresh morning with me
When you are by at night. I do beseech you—
Chiefly that I might set it in my prayers—
What is your name?
Mir. Miranda.—O my father,
I have broke your hest to say so!
Fer. Admir'd Miranda!
Indeed the top of admiration! worth
What 's dearest to the world! Full many a lady
I have ey'd with best regard and many a time
Th' harmony of their tongues hath into bondage
Brought my too diligent ear: for several virtues
Have I lik'd several women; never any
With so full soul, but some defect in her
Did quarrel with the noblest grace she ow'd
And put it to the foil: but you, O you,
So perfect and so peerless, are created
Of every creature's best!
Mir. I do not know
One of my sex; no woman's face remember,
Save, from my glass, mine own; nor have I seen
More that I may call men than you, good friend,
And my dear father: how features are abroad,
I am skilless of; but, by my modesty,
The jewel in my dower, I would not wish
Any companion in the world but you,
Nor can imagination form a shape,
Besides yourself, to like of. But I prattle
Something too wildly and my father's precepts
I therein do forget.
Fer. I am in my condition
A prince, Miranda; I do think, a king;
I would, not so!—and would no more endure
This wooden slavery than to suffer
The flesh-fly blow my mouth. Hear my soul speak:
The very instant that I saw you, did
My heart fly to your service; there resides,
To make me slave to it; and for your sake
Am I this patient log-man.
Mir. Do you love me?
Fer. O heaven, O earth, bear witness to this sound
And crown what I profess with kind event
If I speak true! if hollowly, invert
What best is boded me to mischief! I
Beyond all limit of what else i' th' world
Do love, prize, honour you.
Mir. I am a fool
To weep at what I am glad of.
Pros. [*Aside*] Fair encounter
Of two most rare affections! Heavens rain grace
On that which breeds between 'em!
Fer. Wherefore weep you?
Mir. At mine unworthiness that dare not offer
What I desire to give, and much less take
What I shall die to want. But this is trifling;
And all the more it seeks to hide itself,
The bigger bulk it shows. Hence, bashful cunning!
And prompt me, plain and holy innocence!
I am your wife, if you will marry me;
If not, I'll die your maid: to be your fellow
You may deny me; but I'll be your servant,
Whether you will or no.
Fer. My mistress, dearest;
And I thus humble ever.
Mir. My husband, then?

apples. 172. **pig-nuts,** earth-chestnuts. 174. **marmoset,** small monkey. 176. **scamels,** not explained. Keightley conjectured *seamels* (sea-gulls); Theobald: *stannels* (kestrels); New Cambridge editors call attention to the fact that "seamews" occurs in Strachey's letter. 179. **inherit,** take possession. 187. **trenchering,** trenchers, wooden plates.
ACT III. SCENE I. 11. **sore,** grievous, severe. 15. **Most . . . lest,** unexplained; Spedding suggests *Most busiest when idlest;* New Cambridge editors suggest *busy-idlest,* employed in trifles. 45. **ow'd,** owned. 46. **put . . . foil,** disgraced it; a wrestling phrase. 53. **skilless,** ignorant. 70. **hollowly,** insincerely, falsely.

Fer. Ay, with a heart as willing
As bondage e'er of freedom: here 's my hand.
Mir. And mine, with my heart in 't: and now
farewell
Till half an hour hence.
Fer. A thousand thousand!
Exeunt [*Fer. and Mir. severally*].
Pros. So glad of this as they I cannot be,
Who are surpris'd withal; but my rejoicing
At nothing can be more. I'll to my book,
For yet ere supper-time must I perform
Much business appertaining. *Exit.*

SCENE II. [*Another part of the island.*]

Enter CALIBAN, STEPHANO, *and* TRINCULO.

Ste. Tell not me; when the butt is out, we will drink water; not a drop before: therefore bear up, and board 'em. Servant-monster, drink to me.

Trin. Servant-monster! the folly of this island! They say there 's but five upon this isle: we are three of them; if th' other two be brained like us, the state totters.

Ste. Drink, servant-monster, when I bid thee: thy eyes are almost set in thy head.

Trin. Where should they be set else? he were a brave monster indeed, if they were set in his tail.

Ste. My man-monster hath drown'd his tongue in sack: for my part, the sea cannot drown me; I swam, ere I could recover the shore, five and thirty leagues off and on. By this light, thou shalt be my lieutenant, monster, or my standard.

Trin. Your lieutenant, if you list; he 's no standard.

Ste. We'll not run, Monsieur Monster.

Trin. Nor go neither; but you'll lie like dogs and yet say nothing neither.

Ste. Moon-calf, speak once in thy life, if thou beest a good moon-calf.

Cal. How does thy honour? Let me lick thy shoe.
I'll not serve him; he is not valiant.

Trin. Thou liest, most ignorant monster: I am in case to justle a constable. Why, thou deboshed fish, thou, was there ever man a coward that hath drunk so much sack as I to-day? Wilt thou tell a monstrous lie, being but half a fish and half a monster?

Cal. Lo, how he mocks me! wilt thou let him, my lord?

Trin. 'Lord' quoth he. That a monster should be such a natural!

Cal. Lo, lo, again! bite him to death, I prithee.

Ste. Trinculo, keep a good tongue in your head: if you prove a mutineer,—the next tree! The poor monster 's my subject and he shall not suffer indignity.

Cal. I thank my noble lord. Wilt thou be pleased to hearken once again to the suit I made to thee?

Ste. Marry, will I: kneel and repeat it; I will stand, and so shall Trinculo.

Enter ARIEL, *invisible.*

Cal. As I told thee before, I am subject to a tyrant, a sorcerer, that by his cunning hath cheated me of the island.

Ari. Thou liest.

Cal. Thou liest, thou jesting monkey, thou: I would my valiant master would destroy thee! I do not lie.

Ste. Trinculo, if you trouble him any more in 's tale, by this hand, I will supplant some of your teeth.

Trin. Why, I said nothing.

Ste. Mum, then, and no more. Proceed.

Cal. I say, by sorcery he got this isle;
From me he got it. If thy greatness will
Revenge it on him,—for I know thou dar'st,
But this thing dare not,—
Ste. That 's most certain.
Cal. Thou shalt be lord of it and I'll serve thee.
Ste. How now shall this be compass'd?
Canst thou bring me to the party?
Cal. Yea, yea, my lord: I'll yield him thee asleep,
Where thou mayst knock a nail into his head.
Ari. Thou liest; thou canst not.
Cal. What a pied ninny 's this! Thou scurvy patch!
I do beseech thy greatness, give him blows
And take his bottle from him: when that 's gone
He shall drink nought but brine; for I'll not show him
Where the quick freshes are.

Ste. Trinculo, run into no further danger: interrupt the monster one word further, and, by this hand, I'll turn my mercy out o' doors and make a stock-fish of thee.

Trin. Why, what did I? I did nothing. I'll go farther off.

Ste. Didst thou not say he lied?

Ari. Thou liest.

Ste. Do I so? take thou that. [*Beats Trin.*] As you like this, give me the lie another time.

Trin. I did not give the lie. Out o' your wits and hearing too? A pox o' your bottle! this can sack and drinking do. A murrain on your monster, and the devil take your fingers!

Cal. Ha, ha, ha!

Ste. Now, forward with your tale. [*To Trin.*] Prithee, stand further off.

Cal. Beat him enough: after a little time
I'll beat him too.
Ste. Stand farther. Come, proceed.
Cal. Why, as I told thee, 'tis a custom with him,
I' th' afternoon to sleep: there thou mayst brain him,
Having first seiz'd his books, or with a log
Batter his skull, or paunch him with a stake,
Or cut his wezand with thy knife. Remember
First to possess his books; for without them
He 's but a sot, as I am, nor hath not
One spirit to command: they all do hate him
As rootedly as I. Burn but his books.
He has brave utensils,—for so he calls them,—
Which, when he has a house, he'll deck withal.
And that most deeply to consider is
The beauty of his daughter; he himself
Calls her a nonpareil: I never saw a woman,
But only Sycorax my dam and she;
But she as far surpasseth Sycorax
As great'st does least.

SCENE II. 3. **bear up,** put the helm up so as to bring the ship into the wind. **board 'em,** climb aboard; both phrases refer to drinking. 10. **thy eyes . . . head,** current description of drunkenness meaning that the eyes are fixed in a stare, or dimmed by drink. 19. **standard,** standard-bearer. 20. **standard,** something that stands up. 29. **case,** condition. 30. **deboshed,** debauched. 37. **natural,** idiot. 71. **pied ninny,** fool in motley. **patch,** common word for *fool.* 75. **quick freshes,** running springs. 79. **stock-fish,** dried cod beaten before boiling. 88. **murrain,** plague. 99. **wezand,** windpipe. 101. **sot,** fool. 108. **nonpareil,** one having no equal. 126. **troll the catch,** sing the

Ste. Is it so brave a lass?
Cal. Ay, lord; she will become thy bed, I warrant.
And bring thee forth brave brood.

Ste. Monster, I will kill this man: his daughter and I will be king and queen,—save our graces!—and Trinculo and thyself shall be viceroys. Dost thou like the plot, Trinculo?

Trin. Excellent.

Ste. Give me thy hand: I am sorry I beat thee; but, while thou livest, keep a good tongue in thy head.

Cal. Within this half hour will he be asleep:
Wilt thou destroy him then?
Ste. Ay, on mine honour.
Ari. This will I tell my master.
Cal. Thou mak'st me merry; I am full of pleasure:
Let us be jocund: will you troll the catch
You taught me but while-ere?

Ste. At thy request, monster, I will do reason, any reason. Come on, Trinculo, let us sing. *Sings.*

Flout 'em and scout 'em
And scout 'em and flout 'em;
Thought is free.

Cal. That 's not the tune.

Ariel plays the tune on a tabor and pipe.

Ste. What is this same?

Trin. This is the tune of our catch, played by the picture of Nobody.

Ste. If thou beest a man, show thyself in thy likeness: if thou beest a devil, take 't as thou list.

Trin. O, forgive me my sins!

Ste. He that dies pays all debts: I defy thee. Mercy upon us!

Cal. Art thou afeard?

Ste. No, monster, not I.

Cal. Be not afeard; the isle is full of noises,
Sounds and sweet airs, that give delight and hurt not.
Sometimes a thousand twangling instruments
Will hum about mine ears, and sometime voices
That, if I then had wak'd after long sleep,
Will make me sleep again: and then, in dreaming,
The clouds methought would open and show riches
Ready to drop upon me, that, when I wak'd,
I cried to dream again.

Ste. This will prove a brave kingdom to me, where I shall have my music for nothing.

Cal. When Prospero is destroyed.

Ste. That shall be by and by: I remember the story.

Trin. The sound is going away; let 's follow it, and after do our work.

Ste. Lead, monster; we'll follow. I would I could see this taborer; he lays it on.

Trin. Wilt come? I'll follow, Stephano. *Exeunt.*

SCENE III. [*Another part of the island.*]

Enter ALONSO, SEBASTIAN, ANTONIO, GONZALO, ADRIAN, FRANCISCO, *&c.*

Gon. By 'r lakin, I can go no further, sir;
My old bones ache: here 's a maze trod indeed
Through forth-rights and meanders! By your patience,
I needs must rest me.
Alon. Old lord, I cannot blame thee,
Who am myself attach'd with weariness,
To th' dulling of my spirits: sit down, and rest.
Even here I will put off my hope and keep it
No longer for my flatterer: he is drown'd
Whom thus we stray to find, and the sea mocks
Our frustrate search on land. Well, let him go.
Ant. [*Aside to Seb.*] I am right glad that he 's so out of hope.
Do not, for one repulse, forego the purpose
That you resolv'd t' effect.
Seb. [*Aside to Ant.*] The next advantage
Will we take throughly.
Ant. [*Aside to Seb.*] Let it be to-night;
For, now they are oppress'd with travel, they
Will not, nor cannot, use such vigilance
As when they are fresh.
Seb. [*Aside to Ant.*] I say, to-night: no more.

Solemn and strange music.

Alon. What harmony is this? My good friends, hark!
Gon. Marvellous sweet music!

[*Enter*] PROSPERO *on the top, invisible. Enter several strange Shapes, bringing in a banquet; they dance about it with gentle actions of salutations; and, inviting the King, &c. to eat, they depart.*

Alon. Give us kind keepers, heavens! What were these?
Seb. A living drollery. Now I will believe
That there are unicorns, that in Arabia
There is one tree, the phœnix' throne, one phœnix
At this hour reigning there.
Ant. I'll believe both;
And what does else want credit, come to me,
And I'll be sworn 'tis true: travellers ne'er did lie,
Though fools at home condemn 'em.
Gon. If in Naples
I should report this now, would they believe me?
If I should say, I saw such islanders—
For, certes, these are people of the island—
Who, though they are of monstrous shape, yet, note,
Their manners are more gentle-kind than of
Our human generation you shall find
Many, nay, almost any.
Pros. [*Aside*] Honest lord,
Thou hast said well; for some of you there present
Are worse than devils.
Alon. I cannot too much muse
Such shapes, such gesture and such sound, expressing,
Although they want the use of tongue, a kind
Of excellent dumb discourse.
Pros. [*Aside*] Praise in departing.
Fran. They vanish'd strangely.
Seb. No matter, since
They have left their viands behind; for we have stomachs.
Will 't please you taste of what is here?
Alon. Not I.
Gon. Faith, sir, you need not fear. When we were boys,
Who would believe that there were mountaineers

round. 127. **while-ere,** a while since. 130. **scout,** deride. New Cambridge editors emend, *cout* (befool). 133. *Stage Direction:* **tabor,** small drum. 136. **picture of Nobody,** a figure with head, arms, and legs, but no trunk, used by John Trundle, bookseller and printer.
SCENE III. 1. **By 'r lakin,** by our Lady. 3. **forth-rights and meanders,** paths straight and crooked. 19. *Stage Direction:* **on the top,** in the gallery above the stage or some higher point. 20. **keepers,** guardian angels. 21. **drollery,** puppet show. 30. **certes,** certainly. 39. **Praise in departing.** Save your praise until the end of the performance.

Dew-lapp'd like bulls, whose throats had hanging at 'em
Wallets of flesh? or that there were such men
Whose heads stood in their breasts? which now we find
Each putter-out of five for one will bring us
Good warrant of.
Alon. I will stand to and feed,
Although my last: no matter, since I feel
The best is past. Brother, my lord the duke,
Stand to and do as we.

Thunder and lightning. Enter Ariel, *like a harpy; claps his wings upon the table; and, with a quaint device, the banquet vanishes.*

Ari. You are three men of sin, whom Destiny,
That hath to instrument this lower world
And what is in 't, the never-surfeited sea
Hath caus'd to belch up you; and on this island
Where man doth not inhabit; you 'mongst men
Being most unfit to live. I have made you mad;
And even with such-like valour men hang and drown
Their proper selves. [*Alon., Seb. &c. draw their swords.*]
You fools! I and my fellows
Are ministers of Fate: the elements,
Of whom your swords are temper'd, may as well
Wound the loud winds, or with bemock'd-at stabs
Kill the still-closing waters, as diminish
One dowle that 's in my plume: my fellow-ministers
Are like invulnerable. If you could hurt,
Your swords are now too massy for your strengths
And will not be uplifted. But remember—
For that 's my business to you—that you three
From Milan did supplant good Prospero;
Expos'd unto the sea, which hath requit it,
Him and his innocent child: for which foul deed
The pow'rs, delaying, not forgetting, have
Incens'd the seas and shores, yea, all the creatures,
Against your peace. Thee of thy son, Alonso,
They have bereft; and do pronounce by me
Ling'ring perdition, worse than any death
Can be at once, shall step by step attend
You and your ways; whose wraths to guard you from—
Which here, in this most desolate isle, else falls
Upon your heads—is nothing but heart's sorrow
And a clear life ensuing.

He vanishes in thunder; then, to soft music, enter the Shapes again, and dance, with mocks and mows, and carrying out the table.

Pros. Bravely the figure of this harpy hast thou
Perform'd, my Ariel; a grace it had, devouring:
Of my instruction hast thou nothing bated
In what thou hadst to say: so, with good life
And observation strange, my meaner ministers
Their several kinds have done. My high charms work
And these mine enemies are all knit up
In their distractions; they now are in my pow'r;
And in these fits I leave them, while I visit
Young Ferdinand, whom they suppose is drown'd,
And his and mine lov'd darling. [*Exit above.*]
Gon. I' th' name of something holy, sir, why stand you
In this strange stare?
Alon. O, it is monstrous, monstrous!
Methought the billows spoke and told me of it;
The winds did sing it to me, and the thunder,
That deep and dreadful organ-pipe, pronounc'd
The name of Prosper: it did bass my trespass.
Therefore my son i' th' ooze is bedded, and
I'll seek him deeper than e'er plummet sounded
And with him there lie mudded. *Exit.*
Seb. But one fiend at a time,
I'll fight their legions o'er.
Ant. I'll be thy second.
Exeunt [*Seb. and Ant.*].
Gon. All three of them are desperate: their great guilt,
Like poison given to work a great time after,
Now 'gins to bite the spirits. I do beseech you
That are of suppler joints, follow them swiftly
And hinder them from what this ecstasy
May now provoke them to.
Adr. Follow, I pray you. *Exeunt omnes.*

ACT IV.

SCENE I. [*Before* Prospero's *cell.*]

Enter Prospero, Ferdinand, *and* Miranda.

Pros. If I have too austerely punish'd you,
Your compensation makes amends, for I
Have given you here a third of mine own life,
Or that for which I live; who once again
I tender to thy hand: all thy vexations
Were but my trials of thy love, and thou
Hast strangely stood the test: here, afore Heaven,
I ratify this my rich gift. O Ferdinand,
Do not smile at me that I boast her off,
For thou shalt find she will outstrip all praise
And make it halt behind her.
Fer. I do believe it
Against an oracle.
Pros. Then, as my gift and thine own acquisition
Worthily purchas'd, take my daughter: but
If thou dost break her virgin-knot before
All sanctimonious ceremonies may
With full and holy rite be minist'red,
No sweet aspersion shall the heavens let fall
To make this contract grow; but barren hate,
Sour-ey'd disdain and discord shall bestrew
The union of your bed with weeds so loathly
That you shall hate it both: therefore take heed,
As Hymen's lamps shall light you.

45. **Dew-lapp'd,** having a dewlap, or fold of skin hanging from the neck, as cattle; often supposed to refer to people afflicted with goiter. 48. **putter-out . . . one,** one who invests money, or gambles on the risks of travel on the condition that, if he returns safely, he is to receive five times the amount deposited; hence, any traveler. 52. *Stage Direction:* ***harpy,*** a fabulous monster with a woman's face and vulture's body supposed to be a minister of divine vengeance. ***quaint device,*** ingenious stage contrivance. 54. **to,** as. 59. **such-like valour,** i.e., the reckless valor derived from madness. 62. **temper'd,** composed. 64. **still-closing,** always closing again when parted. 65. **dowle,** soft, fine feather. **plume,** plumage (?) (Onions). 66. **like,** likewise, similarly. **If,** even if. 71. **requit,** requited, avenged. 82. **clear,** unspotted, innocent. 84. **devouring,** i.e., ravishing (?). 85. **bated,** abated, diminished. 86. **so . . . life,** with faithful reproduction. 87. **observation strange,** rare attention to detail. **meaner,** i.e., subordinate to Ariel. 99. **bass my trespass,** proclaimed my trespass like a bass note in music. 106. **bite the spirits,** i.e., conscience troubles them.

Act iv. scene i. 7. **strangely,** extraordinarily. 12. **Against an oracle,** even if an oracle should declare otherwise. 16. **sanctimonious,** sacred. 18. **aspersion,** dew, shower. 23. **Hymen's.** Hymen was the

Fer. As I hope
For quiet days, fair issue and long life,
With such love as 'tis now, the murkiest den,
The most opportune place, the strong'st suggestion
Our worser genius can, shall never melt
Mine honour into lust, to take away
The edge of that day's celebration
When I shall think, or Phœbus' steeds are founder'd,
Or Night kept chain'd below.
Pros. Fairly spoke.
Sit then and talk with her; she is thine own.
What, Ariel! my industrious servant, Ariel!

Enter ARIEL.

Ari. What would my potent master? here I am.
Pros. Thou and thy meaner fellows your last service
Did worthily perform; and I must use you
In such another trick. Go bring the rabble,
O'er whom I give thee pow'r, here to this place:
Incite them to quick motion; for I must
Bestow upon the eyes of this young couple
Some vanity of mine art: it is my promise,
And they expect it from me.
Ari. Presently?
Pros. Ay, with a twink.
Ari. Before you can say 'come' and 'go,'
And breathe twice and cry 'so, so,'
Each one, tripping on his toe,
Will be here with mop and mow.
Do you love me, master? no?
Pros. Dearly, my delicate Ariel. Do not approach
Till thou dost hear me call.
Ari. Well, I conceive. *Exit.*
Pros. Look thou be true; do not give dalliance
Too much the rein: the strongest oaths are straw
To th' fire i' th' blood: be more abstemious,
Or else, good night your vow!
Fer. I warrant you, sir;
The white cold virgin snow upon my heart
Abates the ardour of my liver.
Pros. Well.
Now come, my Ariel! bring a corollary,
Rather than want a spirit: appear, and pertly!
No tongue! all eyes! be silent. *Soft music.*

Enter IRIS.

Iris. Ceres, most bounteous lady, thy rich leas
Of wheat, rye, barley, vetches, oats and pease;
Thy turfy mountains, where live nibbling sheep,
And flat meads thatch'd with stover, them to keep;
Thy banks with pioned and twilled brims,
Which spongy April at thy hest betrims,
To make cold nymphs chaste crowns; and thy broom-groves,
Whose shadow the dismissed bachelor loves,
Being lass-lorn; thy pole-clipt vineyard;
And thy sea-marge, sterile and rocky-hard,
Where thou thyself dost air;—the queen o' th' sky,
Whose wat'ry arch and messenger am I,
Bids thee leave these, and with her sovereign grace,
Juno descends.
Here on this grass-plot, in this very place,
To come and sport: her peacocks fly amain:
Approach, rich Ceres, her to entertain.

Enter CERES.

Cer. Hail, many-colour'd messenger, that ne'er
Dost disobey the wife of Jupiter;
Who with thy saffron wings upon my flow'rs
Diffusest honey-drops, refreshing show'rs,
And with each end of thy blue bow dost crown
My bosky acres and my unshrubb'd down,
Rich scarf to my proud earth; why hath thy queen
Summon'd me hither, to this short-grass'd green?
Iris. A contract of true love to celebrate;
And some donation freely to estate
On the blest lovers.
Cer. Tell me, heavenly bow,
If Venus or her son, as thou dost know,
Do now attend the queen? Since they did plot
The means that dusky Dis my daughter got,
Her and her blind boy's scandal'd company
I have forsworn.
Iris. Of her society
Be not afraid: I met her deity
Cutting the clouds towards Paphos and her son
Dove-drawn with her. Here thought they to have done
Some wanton charm upon this man and maid,
Whose vows are, that no bed-right shall be paid
Till Hymen's torch be lighted: but in vain;
Mars's hot minion is return'd again;
Her waspish-headed son has broke his arrows,
Swears he will shoot no more but play with sparrows
And be a boy right out.

[JUNO *alights.*]

Cer. Highest queen of state,
Great Juno, comes; I know her by her gait.
Juno. How does my bounteous sister? Go with me
To bless this twain, that they may prosperous be
And honour'd in their issue. *They sing:*

Juno. Honour, riches, marriage-blessing,
Long continuance, and increasing,
Hourly joys be still upon you!
Juno sings her blessings on you.

Cer. Earth's increase, foison plenty,
Barns and garners never empty,
Vines with clust'ring bunches growing,
Plants with goodly burthen bowing;

Spring come to you at the farthest
In the very end of harvest!
Scarcity and want shall shun you;
Ceres' blessing so is on you.

Greek and Roman god of marriage. 27. **genius,** evil genius, or evil attendant spirit. 30. **founder'd,** broken down, made lame. 37. **rabble,** band, i.e., the *meaner fellows* of line 35. 41. **vanity,** illusion. 47. **mop and mow,** gestures and grimaces. 56. **liver,** as the seat of the passions. 57. **corollary,** supernumerary. 58. **pertly,** briskly. 63. **stover,** fodder for cattle. 64. **pioned and twilled,** unexplained; excavated(?) or trenched(?) (Onions), ridged (New Cambridge), grown over with peonies and lilies (Hanmer). 66. **broom-groves,** groves of broom (?). 68. **pole-clipt,** hedged in with poles. 71. **wat'ry arch,** rainbow. 72. *Stage Direction: **Juno descends,*** i.e., starts her descent from the "heavens" above the stage (?). 74. **amain,** with full force or speed. 81. **bosky,** covered with shrubs. **unshrubb'd down,** shrubless upland. 89. **Dis . . . got.** Pluto, god of the infernal regions, carried off Persephone, daughter of Ceres, to be his bride in Hades. 90. **scandal'd,** scandalous. 93. **Paphos,** a town in the island of Cyprus, sacred to Venus. 98. **Mars's . . . minion,** Venus, the beloved of Mars. 99. **waspish-headed,** fiery, hot-headed (?). 110. **foison plenty,** plentiful harvest.

Fer. This is a most majestic vision, and
Harmonious charmingly. May I be bold
To think these spirits?
Pros. Spirits, which by mine art
I have from their confines call'd to enact
My present fancies.
Fer. Let me live here ever;
So rare a wond'red father and a wise
Makes this place Paradise.

Juno and Ceres whisper, and send Iris on employment.

Pros. Sweet, now, silence!
Juno and Ceres whisper seriously;
There 's something else to do: hush, and be mute,
Or else our spell is marr'd.
Iris. You nymphs, call'd Naiads, of the windring brooks,
With your sedg'd crowns and ever-harmless looks,
Leave your crisp channels and on this green land
Answer your summons; Juno does command:
Come, temperate nymphs, and help to celebrate
A contract of true love; be not too late.

Enter certain Nymphs.

You sunburnt sicklemen, of August weary,
Come hither from the furrow and be merry:
Make holiday; your rye-straw hats put on
And these fresh nymphs encounter every one
In country footing.

Enter certain Reapers, properly habited: they join with the Nymphs in a graceful dance; towards the end whereof PROSPERO *starts suddenly, and speaks; after which, to a strange, hollow, and confused noise, they heavily vanish.*

Pros. [*Aside*] I had forgot that foul conspiracy
Of the beast Caliban and his confederates
Against my life: the minute of their plot
Is almost come. [*To the Spirits.*] Well done! avoid; no more!
Fer. This is strange: your father 's in some passion
That works him strongly.
Mir. Never till this day
Saw I him touch'd with anger so distemper'd.
Pros. You do look, my son, in a mov'd sort,
As if you were dismay'd: be cheerful, sir.
Our revels now are ended. These our actors,
As I foretold you, were all spirits and
Are melted into air, into thin air:
And, like the baseless fabric of this vision,
The cloud-capp'd tow'rs, the gorgeous palaces,
The solemn temples, the great globe itself,
Yea, all which it inherit, shall dissolve
And, like this insubstantial pageant faded,
Leave not a rack behind. We are such stuff
As dreams are made on, and our little life
Is rounded with a sleep. Sir, I am vex'd;
Bear with my weakness; my old brain is troubled:
Be not disturb'd with my infirmity:
If you be pleas'd, retire into my cell
And there repose: a turn or two I'll walk,
To still my beating mind.
Fer. Mir. We wish your peace. *Exeunt.*
Pros. Come with a thought. I thank thee, Ariel: come.

Enter ARIEL.

Ari. Thy thoughts I cleave to. What 's thy pleasure?
Pros. Spirit,
We must prepare to meet with Caliban.
Ari. Ay, my commander: when I presented Ceres,
I thought to have told thee of it, but I fear'd
Lest I might anger thee.
Pros. Say again, where didst thou leave these varlets?
Ari. I told you, sir, they were red-hot with drinking;
So full of valour that they smote the air
For breathing in their faces; beat the ground
For kissing of their feet; yet always bending
Towards their project. Then I beat my tabor;
At which, like unback'd colts, they prick'd their ears,
Advanc'd their eyelids, lifted up their noses
As they smelt music: so I charm'd their ears
That calf-like they my lowing follow'd through
Tooth'd briers, sharp furzes, pricking goss and thorns,
Which ent'red their frail shins: at last I left them
I' th' filthy-mantled pool beyond your cell,
There dancing up to th' chins, that the foul lake
O'erstunk their feet.
Pros. This was well done, my bird.
Thy shape invisible retain thou still:
The trumpery in my house, go bring it hither,
For stale to catch these thieves.
Ari. I go, I go. *Exit.*
Pros. A devil, a born devil, on whose nature
Nurture can never stick; on whom my pains,
Humanely taken, all, all lost, quite lost;
And as with age his body uglier grows,
So his mind cankers. I will plague them all,
Even to roaring.

Enter ARIEL, *loaden with glistering apparel, &c.*

Come, hang them on this line.

[PROSPERO *and* ARIEL *remain, invisible.*] *Enter* CALIBAN, STEPHANO, *and* TRINCULO, *all wet.*

Cal. Pray you, tread softly, that the blind mole may not
Hear a foot fall: we now are near his cell.
Ste. Monster, your fairy, which you say is a harmless fairy, has done little better than played the Jack with us.
Trin. Monster, I do smell all horse-piss; at which my nose is in great indignation.
Ste. So is mine. Do you hear, monster? If I should take a displeasure against you, look you,—
Trin. Thou wert but a lost monster.
Cal. Good my lord, give me thy favour still.
Be patient, for the prize I'll bring thee to

123. **wond'red,** wonder-performing. 128. **windring,** wandering (?) or winding (?). 130. **crisp,** curled, rippled. 132. **temperate,** chaste. 138. **country footing,** country dancing. 142. **avoid,** depart, withdraw. 144. **works,** affects. 145. **distemper'd,** vexed. 146. **sort,** state, condition. 154. **it inherit,** occupy it. 156. **rack,** mass of cloud driven before the wind in the upper air (Onions). 164. **with a thought,** on the instant. 167. **presented,** acted the part of, or introduced. 176. **unback'd,** unbroken, unridden. 177. **Advanc'd,** lifted up. 180. **goss,** gorse, a prickly shrub. 182. **filthy-mantled,** covered with a vegetable coating, slimy. 184. **feet,** New Cambridge conjectures: *sweat.* **bird,** used as a term of endearment. 186. **trumpery,** cheap goods, the "glistering apparel" mentioned in the following stage direction. 187. **stale,** decoy. 193. **line,** probably, lime tree. 198. **played the Jack,** done a mean trick. *Jack* has a double meaning, "knave" and "will-o-the-wisp." 206. **hoodwink,** cover up; hawking term. 221. **king Stephano,** allusion to the old ballad beginning, "King Stephen was a worthy peer." 226. **frippery,** place where cast-off clothes are sold. 231. **luggage,** impedimenta, heavy stuff to be carried. 236. **jerkin,** jacket made of leather.

Shall hoodwink this mischance: therefore speak softly.
All 's hush'd as midnight yet.

Trin. Ay, but to lose our bottles in the pool,—

Ste. There is not only disgrace and dishonour in that, monster, but an infinite loss.

Trin. That 's more to me than my wetting: yet this is your harmless fairy, monster.

Ste. I will fetch off my bottle, though I be o'er ears for my labour.

Cal. Prithee, my king, be quiet. See'st thou here,
This is the mouth o' th' cell: no noise, and enter.
Do that good mischief which may make this island
Thine own for ever, and I, thy Caliban,
For aye thy foot-licker.

Ste. Give me thy hand. I do begin to have bloody thoughts.

Trin. O king Stephano! O peer! O worthy Stephano! look what a wardrobe here is for thee!

Cal. Let it alone, thou fool; it is but trash.

Trin. O, ho, monster! we know what belongs to a frippery. O king Stephano!

Ste. Put off that gown, Trinculo; by this hand, I'll have that gown.

Trin. Thy grace shall have it.

Cal. The dropsy drown this fool! what do you mean
To dote thus on such luggage? Let 's alone
And do the murder first: if he awake,
From toe to crown he'll fill our skins with pinches,
Make us strange stuff.

Ste. Be you quiet, monster. Mistress line, is not this my jerkin? [*Takes it down.*] Now is the jerkin under the line: now, jerkin, you are like to lose your hair and prove a bald jerkin.

Trin. Do, do: we steal by line and level, an 't like your grace.

Ste. I thank thee for that jest; here 's a garment for 't: wit shall not go unrewarded while I am king of this country. 'Steal by line and level' is an excellent pass of pate; there 's another garment for 't.

Trin. Monster, come, put some lime upon your fingers, and away with the rest.

Cal. I will have none on 't: we shall lose our time,
And all be turn'd to barnacles, or to apes
With foreheads villanous low.

Ste. Monster, lay to your fingers: help to bear this away where my hogshead of wine is, or I'll turn you out of my kingdom: go to, carry this.

Trin. And this.

Ste. Ay, and this.

A noise of hunters heard. Enter divers Spirits, in shape of dogs and hounds, hunting them about, PROSPERO *and* ARIEL *setting them on.*

Pros. Hey, Mountain, hey!

Ari. Silver! there it goes, Silver!

Pros. Fury, Fury! there, Tyrant, there! hark! hark!

[*Cal., Ste., and Trin. are driven out.*]

Go charge my goblins that they grind their joints
With dry convulsions, shorten up their sinews
With aged cramps, and more pinch-spotted make them
Than pard or cat o' mountain.

Ari. Hark, they roar!

Pros. Let them be hunted soundly. At this hour
Lies at my mercy all mine enemies:
Shortly shall all my labours end, and thou
Shalt have the air at freedom: for a little
Follow, and do me service. *Exeunt.*

ACT V.

SCENE I. [*Before* PROSPERO's *cell.*]

Enter PROSPERO *in his magic robes, and* ARIEL.

Pros. Now does my project gather to a head:
My charms crack not; my spirits obey; and time
Goes upright with his carriage. How 's the day?

Ari. On the sixth hour; at which time, my lord,
You said our work should cease.

Pros. I did say so,
When first I rais'd the tempest. Say, my spirit,
How fares the king and 's followers?

Ari. Confin'd together
In the same fashion as you gave in charge,
Just as you left them; all prisoners, sir,
In the line-grove which weather-fends your cell;
They cannot budge till your release. The king,
His brother and yours, abide all three distracted
And the remainder mourning over them,
Brimful of sorrow and dismay; but chiefly
Him that you term'd, sir, 'The good old lord, Gonzalo;'
His tears runs down his beard, like winter's drops
From eaves of reeds. Your charm so strongly works 'em
That if you now beheld them, your affections
Would become tender.

Pros. Dost thou think so, spirit?

Ari. Mine would, sir, were I human.

Pros. And mine shall.
Hast thou, which art but air, a touch, a feeling
Of their afflictions, and shall not myself,
One of their kind, that relish all as sharply,
Passion as they, be kindlier mov'd than thou art?
Though with their high wrongs I am struck to th' quick,
Yet with my nobler reason 'gainst my fury
Do I take part: the rarer action is
In virtue than in vengeance: they being penitent,
The sole drift of my purpose doth extend
Not a frown further. Go release them, Ariel:
My charms I'll break, their senses I'll restore,
And they shall be themselves.

Ari. I'll fetch them, sir. *Exit.*

Pros. Ye elves of hills, brooks, standing lakes and groves,
And ye that on the sands with printless foot
Do chase the ebbing Neptune and do fly him
When he comes back; you demi-puppets that

237. **under the line,** under the lime tree, with punning allusion, probably, to the equinoctial line. 238. **lose your hair,** a reference to tropical fevers experienced by seamen, causing loss of hair. 239. **by line and level,** i.e., by means of instruments, or, methodically, like dishonest carpenters and masons; with pun on *line*, above. 244. **pass of pate,** sally of wit. 246. **lime,** birdlime. 249. **barnacles,** barnacle geese, formerly supposed to be hatched from seashells attached to trees and to fall thence into the water; possibly, the ordinary meaning is intended. 260. **convulsions,** cramps. 262. **pard,** panther or leopard. **cat o' mountain,** wildcat.

ACT V. SCENE I. 2. **crack not,** are flawless (from alchemy). 3. **carriage,** burden; i.e., Time is unstooped, runs smoothly. **How 's the day?** What time is it? 10. **line-grove,** grove of lime trees. **weather-fends,** protects from the weather. 11. **your release,** you release them. 17. **eaves of reed,** thatch. 23. **all,** quite. 27. **rarer,** nobler. 33-57. **Ye . . . book.** This famous passage is an embellished paraphrase of Golding's translation of Ovid's *Metamorphoses*, vii, 197-219. 36. **demi-puppets,** elves and fairies; literally, puppets of half-size.

By moonshine do the green sour ringlets make,
Whereof the ewe not bites, and you whose pastime
Is to make midnight mushrumps, that rejoice
To hear the solemn curfew; by whose aid,
Weak masters though ye be, I have bedimm'd
The noontide sun, call'd forth the mutinous winds,
And 'twixt the green sea and the azur'd vault
Set roaring war: to the dread rattling thunder
Have I given fire and rifted Jove's stout oak
With his own bolt; the strong-bas'd promontory
Have I made shake and by the spurs pluck'd up
The pine and cedar: graves at my command
Have wak'd their sleepers, op'd, and let 'em forth
By my so potent art. But this rough magic
I here abjure, and, when I have requir'd
Some heavenly music, which even now I do,
To work mine end upon their senses that
This airy charm is for, I'll break my staff,
Bury it certain fathoms in the earth,
And deeper than did ever plummet sound
I'll drown my book. *Solemn music.*

Here enters ARIEL *before: then* ALONSO, *with a frantic gesture, attended by* GONZALO; SEBASTIAN *and* ANTONIO *in like manner, attended by* ADRIAN *and* FRANCISCO: *they all enter the circle which* PROSPERO *had made, and there stand charmed; which* PROSPERO *observing, speaks*:

A solemn air and the best comforter
To an unsettled fancy cure thy brains,
Now useless, boil'd within thy skull! There stand,
For you are spell-stopp'd.
Holy Gonzalo, honourable man,
Mine eyes, ev'n sociable to the show of thine,
Fall fellowly drops. The charm dissolves apace,
And as the morning steals upon the night,
Melting the darkness, so their rising senses
Begin to chase the ignorant fumes that mantle
Their clearer reason. O good Gonzalo,
My true preserver, and a loyal sir
To him thou follow'st! I will pay thy graces
Home both in word and deed. Most cruelly
Didst thou, Alonso, use me and my daughter:
Thy brother was a furtherer in the act.
Thou art pinch'd for 't now, Sebastian. Flesh and blood,
You, brother mine, that entertain'd ambition,
Expell'd remorse and nature; who, with Sebastian,
Whose inward pinches therefore are most strong,
Would here have kill'd your king; I do forgive thee,
Unnatural though thou art. Their understanding
Begins to swell, and the approaching tide
Will shortly fill the reasonable shore
That now lies foul and muddy. Not one of them
That yet looks on me, or would know me: Ariel,
Fetch me the hat and rapier in my cell:
I will discase me, and myself present
As I was sometime Milan: quickly, spirit:
Thou shalt ere long be free. [*Exit Ariel and return immediately.*]

ARIEL *sings and helps to attire him.*

Where the bee sucks, there suck I:
In a cowslip's bell I lie;
There I couch when owls do cry.
On the bat's back I do fly
After summer merrily.
Merrily, merrily shall I live now
Under the blossom that hangs on the bough.

Pros. Why, that 's my dainty Ariel! I shall miss thee;
But yet thou shalt have freedom: so, so, so.
To the king's ship, invisible as thou art:
There shalt thou find the mariners asleep
Under the hatches; the master and the boatswain
Being awake, enforce them to this place,
And presently, I prithee.

Ari. I drink the air before me, and return
Or ere your pulse twice beat. *Exit.*

Gon. All torment, trouble, wonder and amazement
Inhabits here: some heavenly power guide us
Out of this fearful country!

Pros. Behold, sir king,
The wronged Duke of Milan, Prospero:
For more assurance that a living prince
Does now speak to thee, I embrace thy body;
And to thee and thy company I bid
A hearty welcome.

Alon. Whe'r thou be'st he or no,
Or some enchanted trifle to abuse me,
As late I have been, I not know: thy pulse
Beats as of flesh and blood; and, since I saw thee,
Th' affliction of my mind amends, with which,
I fear, a madness held me: this must crave,
An if this be at all, a most strange story.
Thy dukedom I resign and do entreat
Thou pardon me my wrongs. But how should Prospero
Be living and be here?

Pros. First, noble friend,
Let me embrace thine age, whose honour cannot
Be measur'd or confin'd.

Gon. Whether this be
Or be not, I'll not swear.

Pros. You do yet taste
Some subtilties o' th' isle, that will not let you
Believe things certain. Welcome, my friends all!
[*Aside to Seb. and Ant.*] But you, my brace of lords, were I so minded,
I here could pluck his highness' frown upon you
And justify you traitors: at this time
I will tell no tales.

Seb. [*Aside*] The devil speaks in him.

Pros. No.
For you, most wicked sir, whom to call brother
Would even infect my mouth, I do forgive
Thy rankest fault; all of them; and require
My dukedom of thee, which perforce, I know,
Thou must restore.

Alon. If thou be'st Prospero,
Give us particulars of thy preservation;
How thou hast met us here, who three hours since
Were wrack'd upon this shore; where I have lost—
How sharp the point of this remembrance is!—
My dear son Ferdinand.

Pros. I am woe for 't, sir.

Alon. Irreparable is the loss, and Patience

37. **green sour ringlets,** fairy rings, circles of grass produced by fungus within the soil. 44-45. **to . . . fire,** the dread rattling thunderbolt I have discharged. 47. **spurs,** roots. 60. **boil'd,** made hot with humors. 63. **sociable,** sympathetic. **show,** appearance. 67. **ignorant fumes.** The fumes which rose up into the brain to produce sleep brought with them unconsciousness. 85. **discase,** undress. 96. **so, so, so,** that will do very well. 112. **trifle,** trick of magic. 124. **subtilties,** illusions. 128. **justify you,** prove you to be. 139. **woe,** sorry. 145. **late,** i.e., as

Says it is past her cure.
Pros. I rather think
You have not sought her help, of whose soft grace
For the like loss I have her sovereign aid
And rest myself content.
Alon. You the like loss!
Pros. As great to me as late; and, supportable
To make the dear loss, have I means much weaker
Than you may call to comfort you, for I
Have lost my daughter.
Alon. A daughter?
O heavens, that they were living both in Naples,
The king and queen there! that they were, I wish
Myself were mudded in that oozy bed
Where my son lies. When did you lose your daughter?
Pros. In this last tempest. I perceive, these lords
At this encounter do so much admire
That they devour their reason and scarce think
Their eyes do offices of truth, their words
Are natural breath: but, howsoev'r you have
Been justled from your senses, know for certain
That I am Prospero and that very duke
Which was thrust forth of Milan, who most strangely
Upon this shore, where you were wrack'd, was landed,
To be the lord on 't. No more yet of this;
For 'tis a chronicle of day by day,
Not a relation for a breakfast nor
Befitting this first meeting. Welcome, sir;
This cell 's my court: here have I few attendants
And subjects none abroad: pray you, look in.
My dukedom since you have given me again,
I will requite you with as good a thing;
At least bring forth a wonder, to content ye
As much as me my dukedom.

Here PROSPERO *discovers* FERDINAND *and* MIRANDA, *playing at chess.*

Mir. Sweet lord, you play me false.
Fer. No, my dearest love,
I would not for the world.
Mir. Yes, for a score of kingdoms you should wrangle,
And I would call it fair play.
Alon. If this prove
A vision of the Island, one dear son
Shall I twice lose.
Seb. A most high miracle!
Fer. Though the seas threaten, they are merciful;
I have curs'd them without cause. [*Kneels.*]
Alon. Now all the blessings
Of a glad father compass thee about!
Arise, and say how thou cam'st here.
Mir. O, wonder!
How many goodly creatures are there here!
How beauteous mankind is! O brave new world,
That has such people in 't!
Pros. 'Tis new to thee.
Alon. What is this maid with whom thou wast at play?
Your eld'st acquaintance cannot be three hours:
Is she the goddess that hath sever'd us,
And brought us thus together?
Fer. Sir, she is mortal;
But by immortal Providence she 's mine:
I chose her when I could not ask my father
For his advice, nor thought I had one. She
Is daughter to this famous Duke of Milan,
Of whom so often I have heard renown,
But never saw before; of whom I have
Receiv'd a second life; and second father
This lady makes him to me.
Alon. I am hers:
But, O, how oddly will it sound that I
Must ask my child forgiveness!
Pros. There, sir, stop:
Let us not burthen our remembrance with
A heaviness that 's gone.
Gon. I have inly wept
Or should have spoke ere this. Look down, you gods,
And on this couple drop a blessed crown!
For it is you that have chalk'd forth the way
Which brought us hither.
Alon. I say, Amen, Gonzalo!
Gon. Was Milan thrust from Milan, that his issue
Should become kings of Naples? O, rejoice
Beyond a common joy, and set it down
With gold on lasting pillars: In one voyage
Did Claribel her husband find at Tunis
And Ferdinand, her brother, found a wife
Where he himself was lost, Prospero his dukedom
In a poor isle and all of us ourselves
When no man was his own.
Alon. [*To Fer. and Mir.*] Give me your hands:
Let grief and sorrow still embrace his heart
That doth not wish you joy!
Gon. Be it so! Amen!

Enter ARIEL, *with the* Master *and* Boatswain *amazedly following.*

O, look, sir, look, sir! here is more of us:
I prophesied, if a gallows were on land,
This fellow could not drown. Now, blasphemy,
That swear'st grace o'erboard, not an oath on shore?
Hast thou no mouth by land? What is the news?
Boats. The best news is, that we have safely found
Our king and company; the next, our ship—
Which, but three glasses since, we gave out split—
Is tight and yare and bravely rigg'd as when
We first put out to sea.
Ari. [*Aside to Pros.*] Sir, all this service
Have I done since I went.
Pros. [*Aside to Ari.*] My tricksy spirit!
Alon. These are not natural events; they strengthen
From strange to stranger. Say, how came you hither?
Boats. If I did think, sir, I were well awake,
I 'ld strive to tell you. We were dead of sleep,
And—how we know not—all clapp'd under hatches;
Where but even now with strange and several noises
Of roaring, shrieking, howling, jingling chains,
And moe diversity of sounds, all horrible,
We were awak'd; straightway, at liberty;
Where we, in all her trim, freshly beheld
Our royal, good and gallant ship, our master
Cap'ring to eye her: on a trice, so please you,

great to me as it is recent. 155. **devour,** render null, destroy. 171. *Stage Direction: **discovers,*** by opening a curtain rear-stage. 174. **score,** double meaning: game or wager in which the score is reckoned by kingdoms, and also twenty kingdoms. **wrangle,** meaning (1) contend in a game or wager, and (2) argue or contend in words. 186. **eld'st,** earliest. 213. **own,** i.e., master of his senses. 223. **glasses,** hours. 224. **yare,** ready.

Even in a dream, were we divided from them
And were brought moping hither.
Ari. [*Aside to Pros.*] Was 't well done?
Pros. [*Aside to Ari.*] Bravely, my diligence. Thou shalt be free.
Alon. This is as strange a maze as e'er men trod;
And there is in this business more than nature
Was ever conduct of: some oracle
Must rectify our knowledge.
Pros. Sir, my liege,
Do not infest your mind with beating on
The strangeness of this business; at pick'd leisure
Which shall be shortly, single I'll resolve you,
Which to you shall seem probable, of every
These happen'd accidents; till when, be cheerful
And think of each thing well. [*Aside to Ari.*] Come hither, spirit:
Set Caliban and his companions free;
Untie the spell. [*Exit Ariel.*] How fares my gracious sir?
There are yet missing of your company
Some few odd lads that you remember not.

Enter ARIEL, *driving in* CALIBAN, STEPHANO *and* TRINCULO, *in their stolen apparel.*

Ste. Every man shift for all the rest, and let no man take care for himself; for all is but fortune. Coragio, bully-monster, coragio!

Trin. If these be true spies which I wear in my head, here 's a goodly sight.

Cal. O Setebos, these be brave spirits indeed!
How fine my master is! I am afraid
He will chastise me.
Seb. Ha, ha!
What things are these, my lord Antonio?
Will money buy 'em?
Ant. Very like; one of them
Is a plain fish, and, no doubt, marketable.
Pros. Mark but the badges of these men, my lords,
Then say if they be true. This mis-shapen knave,
His mother was a witch, and one so strong
That could control the moon, make flows and ebbs,
And deal in her command without her power.
These three have robb'd me; and this demi-devil—
For he 's a bastard one—had plotted with them
To take my life. Two of these fellows you
Must know and own; this thing of darkness I
Acknowledge mine.
Cal. I shall be pinch'd to death.
Alon. Is not this Stephano, my drunken butler?
Seb. He is drunk now: where had he wine?
Alon. And Trinculo is reeling ripe: where should they
Find this grand liquor that hath gilded 'em?
How cam'st thou in this pickle?

Trin. I have been in such a pickle since I saw you last that, I fear me, will never out of my bones: I shall not fear fly-blowing.

Seb. Why, how now, Stephano!
Ste. O, touch me not; I am not Stephano, but a cramp.
Pros. You 'ld be king o' the isle, sirrah?
Ste. I should have been a sore one then.
Alon. This is a strange thing as e'er I look'd on.
[*Pointing to Caliban.*]
Pros. He is as disproportion'd in his manners
As in his shape. Go, sirrah, to my cell;
Take with you your companions; as you look
To have my pardon, trim it handsomely.
Cal. Ay, that I will; and I'll be wise hereafter
And seek for grace. What a thrice-double ass
Was I, to take this drunkard for a god
And worship this dull fool!
Pros. Go to; away!
Alon. Hence, and bestow your luggage where you found it.
Seb. Or stole it, rather. [*Exeunt Cal., Ste., and Trin.*]
Pros. Sir, I invite your highness and your train
To my poor cell, where you shall take your rest
For this one night; which, part of it, I'll waste
With such discourse as, I not doubt, shall make it
Go quick away; the story of my life
And the particular accidents gone by
Since I came to this isle: and in the morn
I'll bring you to your ship and so to Naples,
Where I have hope to see the nuptial
Of these our dear-belov'd solemnized;
And thence retire me to my Milan, where
Every third thought shall be my grave.
Alon. I long
To hear the story of your life, which must
Take the ear strangely.
Pros. I'll deliver all;
And promise you calm seas, auspicious gales
And sail so expeditious that shall catch
Your royal fleet far off. [*Aside to Ari.*] My Ariel, chick,
That is thy charge: then to the elements
Be free, and fare thou well!—Please you, draw near.
Exeunt omnes.

EPILOGUE.

SPOKEN BY PROSPERO.

Now my charms are all o'erthrown,
And what strength I have 's mine own,
Which is most faint: now, 'tis true,
I must be here confin'd by you,
Or sent to Naples. Let me not,
Since I have my dukedom got
And pardon'd the deceiver, dwell
In this bare island by your spell;
But release me from my bands
With the help of your good hands:
Gentle breath of yours my sails
Must fill, or else my project fails,
Which was to please. Now I want
Spirits to enforce, art to enchant,
And my ending is despair,
Unless I be reliev'd by prayer,
Which pierces so that it assaults
Mercy itself and frees all faults.
As you from crimes would pardon'd be,
Let your indulgence set me free. *Exit.*

244. **conduct,** guide, leader. 246. **infest,** harass, disturb. 247. **pick'd.** chosen. 258. **Coragio,** courage. **bully-monster,** gallant monster. 267. **badges,** emblems of cloth or silver worn on the arms of retainers. Prospero refers here to the stolen clothes as emblems of their villainy. 271. **deal . . . power,** wield the moon's power, either without her authority, or beyond her influence. 280. **gilded,** flushed, made drunk. 284. **fly-blowing,** i.e., rotting after death (since he's pickled). 305. **accidents,** occurrences, events. 313. **Take,** take effect upon. **deliver,** declare, relate.
EPILOGUE. 10. **hands,** applause.

SONNETS

Shakespeare seems to have cared more about his reputation as a lyric poet than as a dramatist. He contributed to the major nondramatic genres of his day: to amatory Ovidian narrative in *Venus and Adonis*, to the "Complaint" in *The Rape of Lucrece*, to philosophical poetry in "The Phoenix and the Turtle." He cooperated in the publication of his first two important poems, dedicating them to the young Earl of Southampton with a plea for sponsorship. To write poetry in this vein was more elegantly fashionable than to write plays, which one did mainly for money.

A poet with ambitions of this sort simply had to write a sonnet sequence. Sonneteering was the rage in the early and mid 1590's. It began in 1591, with the publication of Sir Philip Sidney's *Astrophel and Stella*, and ended almost as suddenly as it began in 1596 or 1597. The sonnet-sequences of this brief period bear the names of most well-known and minor poets of the day: *Amoretti* by Edmund Spenser (1595), *Delia* by Samuel Daniel (1591 and 1592), *Caelica* by Fulke Greville (not published until 1633), *Idea's Mirror* by Michael Drayton (1594), *Diana* by Henry Constable (1592), *Phyllis* by Thomas Lodge (1593), and the more imitative sequences of Barnabe Barnes, Giles Fletcher, William Percy, Bartholomew Griffin, William Smith, and Robert Tofte.

Shakespeare wrote sonnets during this heyday of the genre, for in 1598 Francis Meres praised Shakespeare's "sugred Sonnets among his priuate friends." Even though they were not printed at the time, we know from Meres' remark that they were circulated in manuscript among the cognoscenti and commanded great respect. Shakespeare may actually have preferred to delay publication of his sonnets, not through indifference to their literary worth but through a desire not to seem too professional. The "courtly makers" of the English Renaissance, those gentlemen whose chivalric accomplishments were supposed to include versifying, looked on the writing of poetry as a dilettantish avocation designed to amuse one's peers or court a lady. Publication was not quite genteel, and many such authors affected dismay when their verses were pirated into print. The young wits about London of the 1590's, whether aristocratically born or not, sometimes imitated this fashion. Like that gay blade, young John Donne, they sought the favorable verdict of their fellow-wits at the Inns of Court, and professed not to care about wider recognition. Whether Shakespeare was motivated in this way we do not know, but in any event his much-sought-after sonnet sequence was not published until 1609, long after the vogue had passed. The publisher, Thomas Thorpe, seems not to have obtained Shakespeare's authorization. Two sonnets, numbers 138 and 144, had been pirated ten years earlier by William Jaggard in *The Passionate Pilgrim*, 1599. The sonnets were not reprinted until 1640, either because the sonnet vogue had passed or because Thorpe's edition had been suppressed.

The unexplained circumstances of publication have given rise to a host of vexing and apparently unanswerable questions. Probably no puzzle in all English literature has provoked so much speculation and produced so little agreement. To whom are the sonnets addressed? Do they tell a consistent story that can be unraveled, and if so do they tell us anything about Shakespeare's life? The basic difficulty is that we cannot trust the order in which Thorpe published the sonnets, nor can we assume that Thorpe spoke for Shakespeare when he dedicated the sonnets to "Mr. W. H." As they stand, most of the first 126 sonnets appear to be addressed in warm friendship to a handsome young aristocrat, whereas sonnets 127–152 speak of the poet's dark-haired mistress. Yet the last two sonnets, 153–154, seem unrelated to anything previous, and cast some doubt on the authenticity of the collection. Within each large grouping of the sonnets, moreover, we find manifest inconsistencies: jealousies disappear and suddenly reappear, the poet bewails his absolute rejection by the friend and then speaks a few sonnets later of harmonious affection as though nothing had happened, and so on. Some sonnets are closely linked to their predecessors, some are entirely disconnected. We cannot be sure if the friend of sonnets 1–126 is really one person or several. By the same token, we can only speculate that the unhappy love triangle described in 40–42, in which the friend has usurped the poet's mistress, can be identified with the love triangle of the "Dark Lady" sonnets, 127–152. Most readers sense a narrative continuity of the whole, yet find blocks of sonnets stubbornly out of place. The temptation to rearrange the order has proved irresistible, but no alternative order has ever won acceptance. The consensus is that Thorpe's order is defective and non-Shakespearean, but is the only authoritative order we have.

No less frustrating is Thorpe's dedication "To the onlie begetter of these insuing sonnets, Mr. W. H." Given the late and unauthorized publication, we cannot assume that Thorpe speaks for Shakespeare. Quite possibly he is only thanking the person who obtained the sonnets for him, making publication possible. Mundanely enough, Mr. W. H. could be William Hall, an associate of Thorpe's in the publishing business. Yet Elizabethan usage affords few instances of "begetter" in this sense of "obtainer." Besides, Thorpe does offer to Mr. W. H. "that eternitie promised by our ever-living poet," as though Mr. W. H. were the very subject of those sonnets whom Shakespeare vows to immortalize. At any rate, this interpretation of "begetter" as "inspirer" has prompted many enthusiasts to search for a Mr. W. H. in Shakespeare's life, a nobleman who befriended him. The chief candidates are two. First is the young Earl of Southampton, to whom Shakespeare had dedicated *Venus and Adonis* and *The Rape of Lucrece*. The dedication to the second of these poems bespeaks a real warmth and gratitude that had been lacking in the first. The earl's name, Henry Wriothesley, yields initials that are the reverse of W. H.; or, if this lack of correspondence seems unconvincing, W. H. could stand for Sir William Harvey, third husband of Mary, Lady Southampton, the young earl's mother. Some researchers would have us believe that Shakespeare wrote the sonnets for Lady Southampton, especially those urging a young man (her son) to marry and procreate. This entire case is based, however, on pure speculation, and we have no evidence that Shakespeare had any dealings whatever with Southampton after *The Rape of Lucrece*. The plain ascription "Mr. W. H." seems an oddly uncivil way for Thorpe to have addressed an earl. If meant for Southampton, the sonnets must have been written fairly early in the 1590's, for they give no hint of Southampton's later career: his courtship of Elizabeth Vernon, her pregnancy and their secret marriage in 1598, his later involvement in Essex' Irish campaign and abortive uprising against Queen Elizabeth. Those literary sleuths who stress similarities to the Southampton relationship are too willing to overlook dissimilarities.

The second chief candidate for Mr. W. H. is William Herbert, third Earl of Pembroke, to whom, along with his brother, Shakespeare's colleagues dedicated the First Folio of 1623. In 1595 Pembroke's parents were attempting to arrange his marriage with Lady Elizabeth Carey, granddaughter of the first Lord Hunsdon who was Lord Chamberlain and patron of Shakespeare's company. In 1597 another alliance was attempted with Bridget Vere, granddaughter of Lord Burghley. In both negotiations, young Pembroke objected to the girl in question. This hypothesis requires, however, an uncomfortably late date for the sonnets, and postulates a gap in age between Shakespeare and Pembroke that would have afforded little opportunity for genuine friendship. Pembroke was only fifteen in 1595, Shakespeare thirty-one. Besides, no evidence whatever supports the claim other than historical coincidence. The common initials W. H. can be made to produce other candidates as well, such as the Lincolnshire lawyer named William Hatcliffe proposed (to no one's satisfaction) by Leslie Hotson. Hotson wants to date most of the sonnets before 1589, since Hatcliffe came to London in 1587–1588. When such speculations are constructed on the single enigmatic testimonial of Thomas Thorpe, who may well have had no connection with Shakespeare, we are left with a case that would not be worth describing had it not captured the imagination of so many researchers. The whole effort is a dismal tribute to idolatry, to a fervid but empty religiosity that too often takes the place of a genuine critical interest in Shakespeare as a poet.

Other biographical identifications have been proposed for the various personages in the sonnet sequence, predictably with no better success. The rival poet, with "the proud full sail of his great verse" (86), has been linked to Marlowe (who died in 1593), Chapman, and others. The sequence gives us little to go on, other than that the rival poet possesses a considerable enough talent to intimidate the author of the sonnets and ingratiate himself with the author's aristocratic friend. No biographical circumstances even distantly resembling this rivalry have come to light. Similarly, various candidates have been found for the "Dark Lady." One is Mary Fitton, a lady-in-waiting at court who bore a child by Pembroke in 1601. Again, however, no external evidence links Shakespeare with her, nor is he likely to have carried on an affair with one of such high rank. We are left finally without knowing who any of these people were, or if indeed Shakespeare was attempting to be biographical at all.

The same irresolution afflicts dating of the sonnets. Do they give hints of a personal chronicle extending over some years, following Thorpe's arrangement of the sonnets or some alternative order? Sonnet 104 speaks of three years having elapsed since the poet met his friend. Are there other signposts that relate to contemporary events? A line in Sonnet 107 ("The mortal moon hath her eclipse endur'd") is usually linked to the death of Queen Elizabeth (Cynthia) in 1603, though Leslie Hotson prefers to see in it an allusion to the Spanish Armada, shaped for sea battle in a moonlike crescent when it met defeat in 1588. The newly built pyramids in Sonnet 123 remind Hotson of the obelisks built by Pope Sixtus V in Rome, 1586–1589; other researchers have discovered pyramids erected on London's streets in 1603 to celebrate the coronation of James I. As these illustrations suggest, speculative dating can be used to support a hypothesis of early or late composition. Probably the wary consensus of most scholars is that the sonnets were written over a number of years, a large number certainly before 1598 but some perhaps later and even up to the date of publication in 1609.

However fruitless this quest for nonexistent certainties, it does at least direct us to a meaningful critical question: should we expect sonnets of this "personal" nature to be at least partly autobiographical? Shakespeare's sonnets have struck many readers as cries from the heart, voicing fears of rejection, self-hatred, humiliation, and at other times a serene gratitude for reciprocated affection. This power of expression may, however, be a tribute to Shakespeare's unparalleled dramatic gift rather than evidence of personal involvement. Earlier sonnet sequences, both Elizabethan and pre-Elizabethan, had established a variety of artistic conventions that tended to displace biography. Petrarch's famous *Rime*, though addressed to Laura in two sequences (during her life and after her death), idealized her into the unapproachable lady worshiped by the self-abasing and miserable lover. Petrarch's imitators—Aquilano, Bembo, Ariosto, and Tasso among the Italians, Marot, Du Bellay, Ronsard, and Desportes among the French

THE BRITISH LIBRARY BOARD

Convention required passionate courtly lovers to laud their ladies' charms in sonnets. Shakespeare's sonnets to his Dark Lady, on the other hand, are strikingly unconventional in their self-castigating mood and in their disavowal of the standard compliments (see, for example, Sonnet CXXX).

Plèiade—reworked this configuration in countless minor variations. In England the fashion was taken up by Wyatt, Surrey, Gascoigne, Thomas Watson, and others. Spenser's *Amoretti* and Sidney's *Astrophel and Stella*, though inspired at least in part by real women in the poets' lives, are also deeply concerned with theories of writing poetry. The rejection of stereotyped attitudes and relationships that had come to dominate the typical Petrarchan sonnet sequence is evidence not of biographical literalism in art but of a new insistence on lifelike emotion in art; as Sidney's muse urges him, "look in thy heart and write." Thus, both the Petrarchan and the anti-Petrarchan schools avoid biographical writing for its own sake. This is essentially true of all Elizabethan sonneteering, from Drayton's serious pursuit of Platonic abstraction in his *Idea* to the facile chorusing of lesser sonnet-writers about Diana, Phyllis, Zepheria, or Fidessa.

Moreover, the "story" connecting the individual poems of an Elizabethan sonnet sequence is never very important or consistent, even when we can be sure of the order in which the sonnets were written. Dante had used prose links in his *Vita Nuova* to stress narrative continuity, and so had Petrarch, but this sturdy framework had been abandoned by the late sixteenth century. Rather than telling a cohesive story, the typical Elizabethan sonnet sequence offers a loosely connected series of lyrical meditations, chiefly on love but also on poetic theory, the adversities of fortune, death, or what have you. The narrative events mentioned from time to time are not the substance of the sequence but the mere occasion for meditative reflection. Attitudes need not be consistent throughout, and the characters need not be consistently motivated like *dramatis personae* in a play.

Shakespeare's sonnet sequence retains these conventions of Elizabethan sonneteering and employs many archetypal situations and themes that had been explored by his predecessors and contemporaries. His emphasis on friendship seems new, for no other sequence addressed a majority of its sonnets to a friend rather than to a mistress, but even here the anti-Petrarchan quest for spontaneity and candor is paradoxically in the best Elizabethan tradition of Sidney and Spenser. Besides, the exaltation of friendship over love was itself a widespread neo-Platonic commonplace recently popularized in the writings of John Lyly. Structurally, Shakespeare's sonnet sequence follows the pattern of its contemporaries. Even though we cannot reconstruct a rigorously consistent chronological narrative of the sonnets in their present order, and even though the identity of the person being addressed is sometimes in doubt, we can still discern an overall pattern out of which the poet's emotional crises arise and upon which he constructs his meditative lyrics. We can account for most of the poet's dilemmas by postulating four figures: the poet-speaker himself, his friend, his mistress, and a rival poet. The order of events in this tangled relationship is not what the poet wishes to describe; instead, he touches upon this situation from time to time as he introspectively explores his own reaction to love in all its various aspects.

The poet's relationship to his friend is a vulnerable one. This friend to whom he writes is aristocratic, handsome, younger than he is. The poet is beholden to this friend as a sponsor, and must consider himself as subservient no matter how deep their mutual affection. Even at its happiest, their relationship is hierarchical. The poet abases himself in order to extol his friend's beauty and virtues (52–54, 105–106). He confesses that his love would be idolatry, except that the friend's goodness excels all poetic hyperbole. As the older of the two, the poet sententiously urges his young friend to marry and eternize his beauty through the engendering of children (1–17). Such a course, he argues, is the surest way to conquer devouring Time, the enemy of all earthly beauty and love. Yet elsewhere the poet exalts his own art as the surest defense against Time (55, 60, 63–65, etc.). These conclusions are nominally contradictory, offering procreation in one instance and poetry in another as the best hope for immortality, but thematically the two are obviously interrelated. In even the happiest of the sonnets, such as those giving thanks for "the marriage of true minds" (116, 123), Time is always present with his scythe. If love and celebratory poetry can sometimes triumph over Time, the victory is all the more precious because it is achieved in the face of such terrible odds.

Indeed, love and perfect friendship are a refuge for the poet faced with hostile fortune and an indifferent world. He is too often "in disgrace with Fortune and men's eyes" (29), oppressed by his own failings, saddened by the facile success of opportunists (66–68), ashamed of having sold himself cheap in his own profession (110–111). If biographically interpreted, this could mean that Shakespeare was not happy about his career as actor and playwright, but the motif makes complete sense in the sonnet sequence without resort to biography. The poet is pathetically dependent on his friend. Occasional absences torture him with the physical separation, even though he realizes that pure love of the spirit ought not to be hampered by distance or time (43–51). The absence is especially painful when the poet must confess his own disloyalty (117–118). The chronology of these absences cannot be worked out satisfactorily, but the haunting theme of separation is incessant, overwhelming. By extension it includes the fear of separation through death (71–73, 126). Thus the theme of absence is closely related to the poet's obsession with devouring Time.

All the poet's misfortunes would be bearable if love were constant, but his status of dependency on the aristocratic friend leaves him at the mercy of that friend's changeable mood. The poet must not complain when his well-born friend entertains a rival poet (78–86) or forms other emotional attachments, even with the poet's own mistress (40–42). These disloyalties evoke paranoid outbursts. The poet vacillates between forgiveness and angry recrimination. Sometimes even his forgiveness is a form of self-loathing, in which the poet confesses he would take back the friend on any terms (93–95). At times the poet grovels, conceding that he deserves no better treatment (57–58), but at other times his stored-up resentment bursts forth (93–95). The poet's fears, though presented in no clear chronological order, run the gamut from a fatalistic sense that rejection will come one day (49) to an abject and bitter final farewell (87). Sometimes he is tormented by jealousy (61), sometimes by self-hate (88–89).

The sonnets addressed to the poet's mistress, the "Dark Lady," similarly convey fear, self-abasement, and a panicky awareness of loss of self-control. In rare moments of happiness, the poet praises her dark features as proof of her being a real woman, not a Petrarchan goddess (130). Too often, however, her lack of beauty merely reminds the poet of his irrational enchantment (148–150). She is tyrannous, disdainful, spiteful, disloyal, a "female evil" (144) who has tempted away from the poet his better self, his friend. The poet is obsessed not so much with her perfidy as with his own compulsive self-betrayal; he sees with bitter clarity that he is offending his nobler reason by his attachment to the rebellious flesh. He worships what others abhor, and perjures himself by swearing to what he knows to be false (150–152). His only hope for escape is to punish his flesh and renounce the vanity of all worldly striving (146), but this solution evades him as he plunges helplessly back into the perverse enslavement of a sickened appetite.

This inadequate survey of only some themes of the sequence may suggest the range and yet the interconnectedness of Shakespeare's meditations on love, friendship, and poetry. The overall pattern of a sonnet sequence is visible, even if the exact chronology (never important in the Elizabethan sonnet sequence) cannot be determined. This pattern is equally evident in matters of versification and imagery. The sonnets are written throughout in the "Shakespearean" or English form, *abab cdcd efef gg*. (Number 126, written entirely in couplets, is an exception, perhaps because it was intended as the envoy to the series addressed to the poet's friend.) This familiar sonnet form, introduced by Wyatt and developed by Sidney, differs markedly from the octave-sestet division of the Petrarchan, or Italian, sonnet. The English form of three quatrains and a concluding couplet lends itself to a step-by-step development of idea and image, culminating in an epigrammatic two-line conclusion that may summarize the thought of the preceding twelve lines or give a sententious interpretation of the images developed up to this point. Thus, Sonnet 7 pursues the image of the sun at morning, noon, and evening through three quatrains, one for each phase of the day, and then in the couplet "applies" the image to the friend's unwillingness to beget children. Sonnet 29 moves from resentment of misfortune to a rejoicing in the friend's love, and rhetorically mirrors this sudden elevation of mood in the image of the lark "at break of day arising From sullen earth." Shakespeare's rhetorical and imagistic devices cleverly exploit the sonnet structure he inherited and perfected, and remind us again of the strong element of convention and artifice in these supremely "personal" sonnets. The recurring images—the canker on the rose, the pleading of a case at law, the seasonal rhythms of summer and winter or day and night, the harmonies and dissonances of music—also testify to the artistic unity of the whole and to the artist's extraordinary discipline in evoking a sense of helpless loss of self-control.

SONNETS

TO THE ONLIE BEGETTER OF
THESE INSUING SONNETS
MR. W. H. ALL HAPPINESSE
AND THAT ETERNITIE
PROMISED BY
OUR EVER-LIVING POET
WISHETH
THE WELL-WISHING
ADVENTURER IN
SETTING
FORTH
T. T.

I.

FROM fairest creatures we desire increase,
That thereby beauty's rose might never die,
But as the riper should by time decease,
His tender heir might bear his memory:
But thou, contracted to thine own bright eyes,
Feed'st thy light's flame with self-substantial fuel,
Making a famine where abundance lies,
Thyself thy foe, to thy sweet self too cruel.
Thou that art now the world's fresh ornament
And only herald to the gaudy spring,
Within thine own bud buriest thy content
And, tender churl, mak'st waste in niggarding.
  Pity the world, or else this glutton be,
  To eat the world's due, by the grave and thee.

II.

When forty winters shall besiege thy brow,
And dig deep trenches in thy beauty's field,
Thy youth's proud livery, so gaz'd on now,
Will be a totter'd weed, of small worth held:
Then being ask'd where all thy beauty lies,
Where all the treasure of thy lusty days,
To say, within thine own deep-sunken eyes,
Were an all-eating shame and thriftless praise.
How much more praise deserv'd thy beauty's use,
If thou couldst answer 'This fair child of mine
Shall sum my count and make my old excuse,'
Proving his beauty by succession thine!
  This were to be new made when thou art old,
  And see thy blood warm when thou feel'st it cold.

III.

Look in thy glass, and tell the face thou viewest
Now is the time that face should form another;
Whose fresh repair if now thou not renewest,
Thou dost beguile the world, unbless some mother.
For where is she so fair whose unear'd womb
Disdains the tillage of thy husbandry?
Or who is he so fond will be the tomb
Of his self-love, to stop posterity?
Thou art thy mother's glass, and she in thee
Calls back the lovely April of her prime:
So thou through windows of thine age shalt see
Despite of wrinkles this thy golden time.
  But if thou live, rememb'red not to be,
  Die single, and thine image dies with thee.

IV.

Unthrifty loveliness, why dost thou spend
Upon thyself thy beauty's legacy?
Nature's bequest gives nothing but doth lend,
And being frank she lends to those are free.
Then, beauteous niggard, why dost thou abuse
The bounteous largess given thee to give?
Profitless usurer, why dost thou use
So great a sum of sums, yet canst not live?
For having traffic with thyself alone,
Thou of thyself thy sweet self dost deceive.
Then how, when nature calls thee to be gone,
What acceptable audit canst thou leave?
  Thy unus'd beauty must be tomb'd with thee,
  Which, used, lives th' executor to be.

V.

Those hours, that with gentle work did frame
The lovely gaze where every eye doth dwell,
Will play the tyrants to the very same
And that unfair which fairly doth excel;
For never-resting time leads summer on
To hideous winter and confounds him there;
Sap check'd with frost and lusty leaves quite gone,
Beauty o'ersnow'd and bareness every where:
Then, were not summer's distillation left,
A liquid prisoner pent in walls of glass,
Beauty's effect with beauty were bereft,
Nor it nor no remembrance what it was:
  But flowers distill'd, though they with winter meet,
  Leese but their show; their substance still lives
      sweet.

VI.

Then let not winter's ragged hand deface
In thee thy summer, ere thou be distill'd:
Make sweet some vial; treasure thou some place
With beauty's treasure, ere it be self-kill'd.
That use is not forbidden usury
Which happies those that pay the willing loan;
That 's for thyself to breed another thee,
Or ten times happier, be it ten for one;

Sonnets I-XVII are addressed to a young friend of the poet's. In them the young man is urged to marry so that his beauty may be perpetuated in his children.

I. 5. **contracted,** engaged, espoused; Pooler sees a possible allusion to the fable of Narcissus; cf. *Venus and Adonis*, 161, note. 6. **self-substantial,** fuel of the substance of the flame itself (Dowden). 11. **thy content,** that which is contained in you; potential fatherhood (Pooler). 12. **mak'st . . . niggarding,** squander your substance by being miserly. The *Sonnets* are replete with such instances of oxymoron. 14. **by . . . thee,** by death and by your wilfully remaining childless.

II. 4. **totter'd weed,** worn-out garment. 8. **an all-eating . . . praise.** The phrases may be parallel: the shame of gluttony and the praise of extravagance, since you devour the world's due and are an unthrift of your beauty (Pooler). 9. **deserv'd,** would deserve (subjunctive). **use,** investment. Note with what variety this image of usury recurs in the next few sonnets (IV, 7, 13, 14; VI, 5; IX, 12), accompanied often with subtle word play.

III. 3. **fresh repair,** healthful state. 4. **beguile,** cheat. **unbless,** withhold happiness from. 5. **unear'd,** untilled, uncultivated. 7. **fond,** foolish. **will be,** i.e., that he will be (an ellipsis). 9. **thy mother's glass.** Dowden takes this line (comparing XIII, 14) as an indication that the young man's father was not living—a view in which Tucker Brooke concurs. It has been urged, however, that the lines imply only that the boy resembles his mother more than his father. The same image is used in *The Rape of Lucrece*, 1758-1759 (as Malone noted) to indicate parental resemblance. 13. **remembr'red not to be,** in such a way as not to be remembered. Only for the sake of being forgotten (Beeching). 14. **thine image,** any likeness of you.

Ten times thyself were happier than thou art,
If ten of thine ten times refigur'd thee:
Then what could death do, if thou shouldst depart,
Leaving thee living in posterity?
  Be not self-will'd, for thou art much too fair
  To be death's conquest and make worms thine heir.

VII.

Lo! in the orient when the gracious light
Lifts up his burning head, each under eye
Doth homage to his new-appearing sight,
Serving with looks his sacred majesty;
And having climb'd the steep-up heavenly hill,
Resembling strong youth in his middle age,
Yet mortal looks adore his beauty still,
Attending on his golden pilgrimage;
But when from highmost pitch, with weary car,
Like feeble age, he reeleth from the day,
The eyes, 'fore duteous, now converted are
From his low tract and look another way:
  So thou, thyself out-going in thy noon,
  Unlook'd on diest, unless thou get a son.

VIII.

Music to hear, why hear'st thou music sadly?
Sweets with sweets war not, joy delights in joy.
Why lov'st thou that which thou receiv'st not gladly,
Or else receiv'st with pleasure thine annoy?
If the true concord of well-tuned sounds,
By unions married, do offend thine ear,
They do but sweetly chide thee, who confounds
In singleness the parts that thou shouldst bear.
Mark how one string, sweet husband to another,
Strikes each in each by mutual ordering,
Resembling sire and child and happy mother
Who all in one, one pleasing note do sing:
  Whose speechless song, being many, seeming one,
  Sings this to thee: 'thou single wilt prove none.'

IX.

Is it for fear to wet a widow's eye
That thou consum'st thyself in single life?
Ah! if thou issueless shalt hap to die,
The world will wail thee, like a makeless wife;
The world will be thy widow and still weep
That thou no form of thee hast left behind,
When every private widow well may keep
By children's eyes her husband's shape in mind.
Look what an unthrift in the world doth spend
Shifts but his place, for still the world enjoys it;
But beauty's waste hath in the world an end,
And kept unus'd, the user so destroys it.
  No love toward others in that bosom sits
  That on himself such murd'rous shame commits.

X.

For shame! deny that thou bear'st love to any,
Who for thyself art so unprovident.
Grant, if thou wilt, thou art belov'd of many,
But that thou none lov'st is most evident;
For thou art so possess'd with murd'rous hate
That 'gainst thyself thou stick'st not to conspire,
Seeking that beauteous roof to ruinate
Which to repair should be thy chief desire.
O, change thy thought, that I may change my mind!
Shall hate be fairer lodg'd than gentle love?
Be, as thy presence is, gracious and kind,
Or to thyself at least kind-hearted prove:
  Make thee another self, for love of me,
  That beauty still may live in thine or thee.

XI.

As fast as thou shalt wane, so fast thou grow'st
In one of thine, from that which thou departest;
And that fresh blood which youngly thou bestow'st
Thou mayst call thine when thou from youth
    convertest.
Herein lives wisdom, beauty and increase;
Without this, folly, age and cold decay:
If all were minded so, the times should cease
And threescore year would make the world away.
Let those whom Nature hath not made for store,
Harsh, featureless and rude, barrenly perish:
Look whom she best endow'd she gave the more;
Which bounteous gift thou shouldst in bounty
    cherish:
  She carv'd thee for her seal, and meant thereby
  Thou shouldst print more, not let that copy die.

XII.

When I do count the clock that tells the time,
And see the brave day sunk in hideous night;
When I behold the violet past prime,
And sable curls all silver'd o'er with white;
When lofty trees I see barren of leaves
Which erst from heat did canopy the herd,
And summer's green all girded up in sheaves
Borne on the bier with white and bristly beard,
Then of thy beauty do I question make,
That thou among the wastes of time must go,
Since sweets and beauties do themselves forsake
And die as fast as they see others grow;
  And nothing 'gainst Time's scythe can make
    defence
  Save breed, to brave him when he takes thee hence.

XIII.

O, that you were yourself! but, love, you are
No longer yours than you yourself here live:
Against this coming end you should prepare,
And your sweet semblance to some other give.
So should that beauty which you hold in lease
Find no determination; then you were

IV. 4. **frank,** liberal, bounteous. 8. **live,** quibble on the two meanings, "having a livelihood" and "living in your posterity."

V. 1-3. **Those . . . same,** an application of the Renaissance commonplace of Time as both constructive and destructive; frequent in the *Sonnets*. 2. **gaze,** object of gazes. 4. **unfair,** make unlovely; cf. *unbless*, III, 4. **fairly,** i.e., in beauty. 9. **summer's distillation,** distilled perfume of flowers. 14. **Leese,** lose.

VI. 2. **distill'd,** i.e., dissolved in death, quibbling on the uses in the preceding sonnet. 3. **vial,** i.e., continuing the metaphor of distilling perfume from the preceding sonnet; cf. v, 10, *walls of glass*. **treasure,** enrich. 8. **ten for one,** continues the usury metaphor.

VII. 1. **light,** sun. 2. **under,** earthly.

VIII. 1. **Music to hear,** an absolute construction, a verbal noun introducing the subject of hearing music. **sadly.** Cf. *Measure for Measure*, IV, i, 13-15, note. 8. **In singleness,** i.e., by being unmarried.

IX. 4. **makeless wife,** a widow. 9. **Look what,** whatever.

X. 6. **stick'st,** scruple. 7. **beauteous roof,** i.e., your person. 9. **change . . . mind,** give up your aversion from marriage that I may no longer believe that you hate mankind (Pooler). 11. **presence,** appearance, bearing; a repetition of the idea in the words *fairer lodg'd*.

XI. 1-2. **As . . . departest.** Cf. v, 1-3. 6. **Without this,** the antithesis of *Herein* (l. 5). 9. **for store,** as a source of supply (Pooler).

XII. 6. **erst,** formerly. 11. **sweets . . . forsake,** sweetness and beauty forsake sweet and beautiful things. 14. **Save . . . him,** except children whose youth may set the scythe of Time at defiance.

XIII. 3. **Against,** in anticipation of. 6. **determination,** end.

Yourself again after yourself's decease,
When your sweet issue your sweet form should bear.
Who lets so fair a house fall to decay,
Which husbandry in honour might uphold
Against the stormy gusts of winter's day
And barren rage of death's eternal cold?
  O, none but unthrifts! Dear my love, you know
  You had a father: let your son say so.

XIV.

Not from the stars do I my judgement pluck;
And yet methinks I have astronomy,
But not to tell of good or evil luck,
Of plagues, of dearths, or seasons' quality;
Nor can I fortune to brief minutes tell,
Pointing to each his thunder, rain and wind,
Or say with princes if it shall go well,
By oft predict that I in heaven find:
But from thine eyes my knowledge I derive,
And, constant stars, in them I read such art
As truth and beauty shall together thrive,
If from thyself to store thou wouldst convert;
  Or else of thee this I prognosticate:
  Thy end is truth's and beauty's doom and date.

XV.

When I consider every thing that grows
Holds in perfection but a little moment,
That this huge stage presenteth nought but shows
Whereon the stars in secret influence comment;
When I perceive that men as plants increase,
Cheered and check'd even by the self-same sky,
Vaunt in their youthful sap, at height decrease,
And wear their brave state out of memory;
Then the conceit of this inconstant stay
Sets you most rich in youth before my sight,
Where wasteful Time debateth with Decay,
To change your day of youth to sullied night;
  And all in war with Time for love of you,
  As he takes from you, I engraft you new.

XVI.

But wherefore do not you a mightier way
Make war upon this bloody tyrant, Time?
And fortify yourself in your decay
With means more blessed than my barren rhyme?
Now stand you on the top of happy hours,
And many maiden gardens yet unset
With virtuous wish would bear your living flowers,
Much liker than your painted counterfeit:
So should the lines of life that life repair,
Which this time's pencil, or my pupil pen,
Neither in inward worth nor outward fair,
Can make you live yourself in eyes of men.
  To give away yourself keeps yourself still,
  And you must live, drawn by your own sweet skill.

XVII.

Who will believe my verse in time to come,
If it were fill'd with your most high deserts?
Though yet, heaven knows, it is but as a tomb
Which hides your life and shows not half your parts.
If I could write the beauty of your eyes
And in fresh numbers number all your graces,
The age to come would say 'This poet lies;
Such heavenly touches ne'er touch'd earthly faces.'
So should my papers yellowed with their age
Be scorn'd like old men of less truth than tongue,
And your true rights be term'd a poet's rage
And stretched metre of an antique song:
  But were some child of yours alive that time,
  You should live twice; in it and in my rhyme.

XVIII.

Shall I compare thee to a summer's day?
Thou art more lovely and more temperate:
Rough winds do shake the darling buds of May,
And summer's lease hath all too short a date:
Sometime too hot the eye of heaven shines,
And often is his gold complexion dimm'd;
And every fair from fair sometime declines,
By chance or nature's changing course untrimm'd;
But thy eternal summer shall not fade
Nor lose possession of that fair thou ow'st;
Nor shall Death brag thou wand'rest in his shade,
When in eternal lines to time thou grow'st:
  So long as men can breathe or eyes can see,
  So long lives this and this gives life to thee.

XIX.

Devouring Time, blunt thou the lion's paws,
And make the earth devour her own sweet brood;
Pluck the keen teeth from the fierce tiger's jaws,
And burn the long-liv'd phœnix in her blood;
Make glad and sorry seasons as thou fleets,
And do whate'er thou wilt, swift-footed Time,
To the wide world and all her fading sweets;
But I forbid thee one most heinous crime:
O, carve not with thy hours my love's fair brow,
Nor draw no lines there with thine antique pen;

XIV. 1. **pluck,** derive. 5. **to brief minutes,** i.e., foretell events to the precise minute. 6. **Pointing,** appointing. **his,** its. 8. **oft predict,** frequent predictions. 11-12, 14. **truth . . . convert; Thy end . . . date.** Dowden set off these examples of *such art* with quotation marks, a form which makes the structure more immediately clear. 12. **store,** replenishment. **convert,** turn.

XV. 2. **Holds in perfection,** maintains its prime. 3. **this huge stage.** Pooler notes that the metaphor of the stage and the audience is sustained through the next three lines in *comment* (l. 4) and *Cheered* and *check'd* (l. 6). 9. **inconstant stay,** constant or continual change. 11. **debateth with,** combines in battle with; *with* here implies association, not opposition, as is frequently its meaning in this idiom.

XVI. 6. **unset,** unplanted. 8. **Much liker,** i.e., much more like you. 9. **lines of life,** usually explained as lineage, i.e., children. Dowden sees a play in *lines* on the meanings "lines of a picture or portrait," and "lines of verse"; living poems and pictures are children. 10. **this time's pencil,** a portraiture done in this present age. **pupil,** apprenticed, inexpert. 13. **give away yourself,** i.e., beget children. **keeps,** preserves.

XVII. 11. **rage,** exaggerated inspiration. 12. **stretched metre,** overstrained poetry (Dowden); poetic license (Tucker Brooke).

XVIII. This and the following sonnet develop the theme of the immortalizing power of poetry. 7. **fair from fair,** beautiful thing from beauty. 8. **untrimm'd,** stripped of ornaments. 10. **ow'st,** own. 12. **to . . . grow'st.** To grow to time is to be incorporated or become one with it and so to live while time lasts (Pooler).

XIX. 1. **Devouring Time.** Cf. the apostrophe to Time in *The Rape of Lucrece*, 925 ff. 5. **fleets,** fleetest. 11. **untainted,** a metaphor from tilting; a taint was a hit (Pooler).

Sonnets xx and xxi are in praise of the friend's beauty.

XX. 1. **with . . . painted,** i.e., without cosmetics. 5. **rolling,** i.e., roving. 7. **A man . . . controlling,** one who has a manly appearance, and embodies all handsomeness (?). 11. **defeated,** defrauded. 12. **to my purpose nothing,** out of line with my wishes. 13. **prick'd,** designated (with bawdy suggestion; the "thing" in l. 12 is a phallus).

XXI. 1. **Muse,** poet. 4. **every fair,** every lovely thing. **rehearse,** mention. 5. **Making . . . compare,** joining in proud comparison (Dowden); uniting his *fair* to heaven by extravagant comparisons (Pooler). 8. **rondure,** sphere. 12. **gold candles,** stars. 13. **like . . . well,** like to deal in second-hand ideas (Tucker Brooke); like rumors

Him in thy course untainted do allow
For beauty's pattern to succeeding men.
Yet, do thy worst, old Time: despite thy wrong,
My love shall in my verse ever live young.

XX.

A woman's face with Nature's own hand painted
Hast thou, the master-mistress of my passion;
A woman's gentle heart, but not acquainted
With shifting change, as is false women's fashion;
An eye more bright than theirs, less false in rolling,
Gilding the object whereupon it gazeth;
A man in hue, all hues in his controlling,
Which steals men's eyes and women's souls amazeth.
And for a woman wert thou first created;
Till Nature, as she wrought thee, fell a-doting,
And by addition me of thee defeated,
By adding one thing to my purpose nothing.
But since she prick'd thee out for women's pleasure,
Mine be thy love and thy love's use their treasure.

XXI.

So is it not with me as with that Muse
Stirr'd by a painted beauty to his verse,
Who heaven itself for ornament doth use
And every fair with his fair doth rehearse;
Making a couplement of proud compare,
With sun and moon, with earth and sea's rich gems,
With April's first-born flowers, and all things rare
That heaven's air in this huge rondure hems.
O, let me, true in love, but truly write,
And then believe me, my love is as fair
As any mother's child, though not so bright
As those gold candles fix'd in heaven's air:
Let them say more that like of hearsay well;
I will not praise that purpose not to sell.

XXII.

My glass shall not persuade me I am old,
So long as youth and thou are of one date;
But when in thee time's furrows I behold,
Then look I death my days should expiate.
For all that beauty that doth cover thee
Is but the seemly raiment of my heart,
Which in thy breast doth live, as thine in me:
How can I then be elder than thou art?
O, therefore, love, be of thyself so wary
As I, not for myself, but for thee will;
Bearing thy heart, which I will keep so chary
As tender nurse her babe from faring ill.
Presume not on thy heart when mine is slain;
Thou gav'st me thine, not to give back again.

XXIII.

As an unperfect actor on the stage
Who with his fear is put besides his part,
Or some fierce thing replete with too much rage,
Whose strength's abundance weakens his own heart,
So I, for fear of trust, forget to say
The perfect ceremony of love's rite,
And in mine own love's strength seem to decay,
O'ercharg'd with burden of mine own love's might.
O, let my books be then the eloquence
And dumb presagers of my speaking breast,
Who plead for love and look for recompense
More than that tongue that more hath more express'd.
O, learn to read what silent love hath writ:
To hear with eyes belongs to love's fine wit.

XXIV.

Mine eye hath play'd the painter and hath stell'd
Thy beauty's form in table of my heart;
My body is the frame wherein 'tis held,
And perspective it is best painter's art.
For through the painter must you see his skill,
To find where your true image pictur'd lies;
Which in my bosom's shop is hanging still,
That hath his windows glazed with thine eyes.
Now see what good turns eyes for eyes have done:
Mine eyes have drawn thy shape, and thine for me
Are windows to my breast, where-through the sun
Delights to peep, to gaze therein on thee;
Yet eyes this cunning want to grace their art;
They draw but what they see, know not the heart.

XXV.

Let those who are in favour with their stars
Of public honour and proud titles boast,
Whilst I, whom fortune of such triumph bars,
Unlook'd for joy in that I honour most.
Great princes' favourites their fair leaves spread
But as the marigold at the sun's eye,
And in themselves their pride lies buried,
For at a frown they in their glory die.
The painful warrior famoused for fight,
After a thousand victories once foil'd,
Is from the book of honour razed quite,
And all the rest forgot for which he toil'd:
Then happy I, that love and am beloved
Where I may not remove nor be removed.

rather than facts (Pooler). 14. **that . . . sell.** Pooler sees this line as the converse of Proverbs 20:14: "It is naught, it is naught, saith the buyer." Malone notes parallels in *Love's Labour's Lost*, IV, iii, 240, and in *Troilus and Cressida*, IV, i, 78.

Sonnets XXII-XXV are four separate expressions of the poet's joy in his friend's love, introducing themes later elaborated (Tucker Brooke).

XXII. 4. **look I,** I foresee. **expiate,** end. 13. **Presume not on,** do not expect to receive back (Beeching).

XXIII. 5. **for fear of trust,** doubting of being trusted (Schmidt). Dowden thought the comparison was to the *unperfect actor* who dare not trust himself. He observed that in the first eight lines 5 and 6 refer to 1 and 2, 7 and 8 refer to 3 and 4. 9. **books,** the manuscript books in which he writes his *Sonnets* (Dowden); the *Sonnets* themselves (Massey); the most natural interpretation is that the poet refers to *Venus and Adonis* and *The Rape of Lucrece*, which he describes as *dumb presagers* of the love he cannot directly express, an interpretation which favors the Southampton theory (Tucker Brooke). Those who favor Sewell's emendation *looks* justify it on the ground that *books* are not *dumb presagers;* that the love which expresses itself in love poems is not silent. 10. **presagers,** those which indicate. 12. **More, more, more,** to a greater degree; more ardors of love; more fully.

XXIV. 1. **stell'd,** fixed, installed; or possibly *steel'd*, i.e., engraved; Q: *steeld*. 4. **perspective,** optical device for producing fantastic images (Onions); a painter's highest art is to produce the illusion of distance, one thing seeming to lie behind another. You must look through the painter (my eye or myself) to see your picture, the product of his skill, which lies within him, i.e., in my heart (Dowden); the word *perspective* is used quibblingly. 7. **my bosom's shop.** The imagery is here changed; in 1-4 Shakespeare's eye is the brush, his heart the canvas, his body the frame, of his friend's picture. The second quatrain, 5-8, is connected with the first by the punning explanation of *perspective;* but by a turn of this strange kaleidoscope, the body ceases to be the frame, for part of it, viz., the bosom, has become a shop or studio in which the picture hangs. The windows of this shop are the friend's eyes looking in (Pooler). 13-14. **Yet . . . heart.** Cf. *The Merchant of Venice*, III, ii, 63-69.

XXV. 4. **Unlook'd for,** unexpectedly. 9. **painful,** enduring much. **fight,** Theobald's emendation of Q: *worth*, to rhyme with *quite;* he suggested as an alternative the emendation of *forth* for *quite*.

XXVI.

Lord of my love, to whom in vassalage
Thy merit hath my duty strongly knit,
To thee I send this written embassage,
To witness duty, not to show my wit:
Duty so great, which wit so poor as mine
May make seem bare, in wanting words to show it,
But that I hope some good conceit of thine
In thy soul's thought, all naked, will bestow it;
Till whatsoever star that guides my moving
Points on me graciously with fair aspect
And puts apparel on my tottered loving,
To show me worthy of thy sweet respect:
  Then may I dare to boast how I do love thee;
  Till then not show my head where thou mayst
    prove me.

XXVII.

Weary with toil, I haste me to my bed,
The dear repose for limbs with travel tired;
But then begins a journey in my head,
To work my mind, when body's work's expired:
For then my thoughts, from far where I abide,
Intend a zealous pilgrimage to thee,
And keep my drooping eyelids open wide,
Looking on darkness which the blind do see:
Save that my soul's imaginary sight
Presents thy shadow to my sightless view,
Which, like a jewel hung in ghastly night,
Makes black night beauteous and her old face
  new.
  Lo! thus, by day my limbs, by night my mind,
  For thee and for myself no quiet find.

XXVIII.

How can I then return in happy plight,
That am debarr'd the benefit of rest?
When day's oppression is not eas'd by night,
But day by night, and night by day, oppress'd?
And each, though enemies to either's reign,
Do in consent shake hands to torture me;
The one by toil, the other to complain
How far I toil, still farther off from thee.
I tell the day, to please him thou art bright
And dost him grace when clouds do blot the heaven:
So flatter I the swart-complexion'd night,
When sparkling stars twire not thou gild'st the even.
  But day doth daily draw my sorrows longer
  And night doth nightly make grief's strength seem
    stronger.

XXIX.

When, in disgrace with fortune and men's eyes,
I all alone beweep my outcast state
And trouble deaf heaven with my bootless cries
And look upon myself and curse my fate,
Wishing me like to one more rich in hope,
Featur'd like him, like him with friends possess'd,
Desiring this man's art and that man's scope,
With what I most enjoy contented least;
Yet in these thoughts myself almost despising,
Haply I think on thee, and then my state,
Like to the lark at break of day arising
From sullen earth, sings hymns at heaven's gate;
  For thy sweet love rememb'red such wealth brings
  That then I scorn to change my state with kings.

XXX.

When to the sessions of sweet silent thought
I summon up remembrance of things past,
I sigh the lack of many a thing I sought,
And with old woes new wail my dear time's waste:
Then can I drown an eye, unus'd to flow,
For precious friends hid in death's dateless night,
And weep afresh love's long since cancell'd woe,
And moan th' expense of many a vanish'd sight:
Then can I grieve at grievances foregone,
And heavily from woe to woe tell o'er
The sad account of fore-bemoaned moan,
Which I new pay as if not paid before.
  But if the while I think on thee, dear friend,
  All losses are restor'd and sorrows end.

XXXI.

Thy bosom is endeared with all hearts,
Which I by lacking have supposed dead,
And there reigns love and all love's loving parts,
And all those friends which I thought buried.
How many a holy and obsequious tear
Hath dear religious love stol'n from mine eye
As interest of the dead, which now appear
But things remov'd that hidden in thee lie!
Thou art the grave where buried love doth live,
Hung with the trophies of my lovers gone,
Who all their parts of me to thee did give;

XXVI. This is regarded variously as an "envoy" to the twenty-five preceding sonnets and as a dedication to the next sequence (XXVI-XXXII). Its similarity in tone and phrasing to the dedication of *The Rape of Lucrece* has been frequently noted. 8. **all naked,** modifies *Duty* (l. 5). **bestow,** equip, clothe (Tyler). 9. **moving,** life. 11. **tottered,** tattered. 12. **thy,** so Malone; Q: *their*, regarded generally as a misprint; retained by some editors and explained variously as referring to (1) the stars, (2) thy soul's thought, (3) the sweet respect of the star. 14. **prove,** test.

Beginning with XXVII and continuing through the next five, the poet writes as one on a journey which takes him far from his friend.

XXVII. 6. **Intend,** direct. 11. **ghastly,** fearful. 13-14. **by day . . . find,** by day my limbs find no quiet for myself, i.e., on account of business of my own; by night my mind finds no quiet for thee, i.e., on your account, thinking of you (Dowden); this type of construction is called "chiastic," i.e., interlaced. It is not infrequent in Renaissance poetry.

XXVIII. 1. **plight,** state, condition. 6. **consent,** i.e., mutual agreement. 7. **to complain,** by causing me to complain. 9. **to please him.** There is some argument as to whether this phrase modifies *tell* or *bright;* the absence of any punctuation in Q leaves the line ambiguous. 10. **dost . . . heaven,** i.e., that you shine in place of the sun when the sun is overclouded. 12. **twire,** twinkle, peek. **thou gild'st the even,** you make bright the evening.

XXIX. 6. **Featur'd,** situated (Onions); more likely, formed; i.e., envying their good looks, their beauty of face. **like him, like him,** not a repetition but, as Pooler points out, "like a second man, like a third." 7. **scope,** probably implies both "range of powers" and "opportunity."

XXX. 1-2. **sessions . . . summon.** The metaphor is that of a court of law. Malone cites *Othello*, III, iii, 138-141. Unlike many of the sonnets this one does not sustain the figure. 4. **new wail,** lament anew. **dear time's waste,** i.e., the wasting of precious time, or time's erosion of those things held precious (?). 6. **dateless,** endless. 8. **expense,** that which is spent. 9. **foregone,** past. 10. **tell,** count.

XXXI. 1. **endeared,** enhanced in value, made more precious. You have become dearer to me as representing all I have loved (Pooler). 6. **religious,** i.e., as fulfilling a duty. 7. **As interest of the dead.** The phrase carries out the idea of mourning as a duty owed to the dead. 8. **remov'd,** separated by time or space; i.e., absent. 12. **due of many,** i.e., the duty or obligation to many.

XXXII. 1. **my . . . day,** i.e., the day which will content me well. 5. **bett'ring,** i.e., improvement in the writing of poetry. 7. **Reserve,** preserve. 8. **happier,** more gifted. 11. **dearer birth,** i.e., better poem, better artistic creation. 12. **To . . . equipage.** Sir Sidney Lee points

That due of many now is thine alone:
  Their images I lov'd I view in thee,
  And thou, all they, hast all the all of me.

XXXII.

If thou survive my well-contented day,
When that churl Death my bones with dust shall cover,
And shalt by fortune once more re-survey
These poor rude lines of thy deceased lover,
Compare them with the bett'ring of the time,
And though they be outstripp'd by every pen,
Reserve them for my love, not for their rhyme,
Exceeded by the height of happier men.
O, then vouchsafe me but this loving thought:
'Had my friend's Muse grown with this growing age,
A dearer birth than this his love had brought,
To march in ranks of better equipage:
  But since he died and poets better prove,
  Theirs for their style I'll read, his for his love.'

XXXIII.

Full many a glorious morning have I seen
Flatter the mountain-tops with sovereign eye,
Kissing with golden face the meadows green,
Gilding pale streams with heavenly alchemy;
Anon permit the basest clouds to ride
With ugly rack on his celestial face,
And from the forlorn world his visage hide,
Stealing unseen to west with this disgrace:
Even so my sun one early morn did shine
With all-triumphant splendour on my brow;
But out, alack! he was but one hour mine;
The region cloud hath mask'd him from me now.
  Yet him for this my love no whit disdaineth;
  Suns of the world may stain when heaven's sun
      staineth.

XXXIV.

Why didst thou promise such a beauteous day
And make me travel forth without my cloak,
To let base clouds o'ertake me in my way,
Hiding thy brav'ry in their rotten smoke?
'Tis not enough that through the cloud thou break,
To dry the rain on my storm-beaten face,
For no man well of such a salve can speak
That heals the wound and cures not the disgrace:
Nor can thy shame give physic to my grief;
Though thou repent, yet I have still the loss:
Th' offender's sorrow lends but weak relief
To him that bears the strong offence's cross.
  Ah! but those tears are pearl which thy love sheeds,
  And they are rich and ransom all ill deeds.

XXXV.

No more be griev'd at that which thou hast done:
Roses have thorns, and silver fountains mud;
Clouds and eclipses stain both moon and sun,
And loathsome canker lives in sweetest bud.
All men make faults, and even I in this,
Authorizing thy trespass with compare,
Myself corrupting, salving thy amiss,
Excusing thy sins more than thy sins are;
For to thy sensual fault I bring in sense—
Thy adverse party is thy advocate—
And 'gainst myself a lawful plea commence:
Such civil war is in my love and hate
  That I an accessary needs must be
  To that sweet thief which sourly robs from me.

XXXVI.

Let me confess that we two must be twain,
Although our undivided loves are one:
So shall those blots that do with me remain
Without thy help by me be borne alone.
In our two loves there is but one respect,
Though in our lives a separable spite,
Which though it alter not love's sole effect,
Yet doth it steal sweet hours from love's delight.
I may not evermore acknowledge thee,
Lest my bewailed guilt should do thee shame,
Nor thou with public kindness honour me,
Unless thou take that honour from thy name:
  But do not so; I love thee in such sort
  As, thou being mine, mine is thy good report.

XXXVII.

As a decrepit father takes delight
To see his active child do deeds of youth,
So I, made lame by Fortune's dearest spite,
Take all my comfort of thy worth and truth.
For whether beauty, birth, or wealth, or wit,
Or any of these all, or all, or more,
Entitled in thy parts do crowned sit,
I make my love engrafted to this store:
So then I am not lame, poor, nor despis'd,
Whilst that this shadow doth such substance give

out the frequency of this metaphor in Elizabethan literature. Tyler traced the line to a similar treatment of the figure in Marston's *Pygmalion* (1598); Marston was probably the borrower. **of better equipage,** more finely equipped.

XXXIII. This sonnet begins a new theme. The poet has endured some indignity at the friend's hands and the friend has repented. 2. **Flatter,** explained by *sovereign;* the glance of a king is a compliment to a courtier (Pooler). The *NED* definition, "to encourage with hopeful or pleasing representations," is applicable here. 5. **permit,** to be construed as parallel with *Flatter*. 6. **rack,** mass of cloud driven before the wind in the upper air. 7. **forlorn,** accent on the first syllable. 8. **to west,** westward. 12. **region,** pertaining to the upper air. 14. **stain,** grow dim, be obscured, soiled (Pooler); cf. xxxv, 3.

XXXIV. 4. **brav'ry,** finery, fine clothes. 8. **disgrace,** i.e., the scar, the disfigurement caused by his friend's harsh treatment. Pooler points out that this is the *loss* of line 10. 9. **shame,** repentance for the wrong done. **physic,** remedy. 13. **sheeds,** sheds.

XXXV. 3. **stain.** Cf. xxxiii, 14, note. 4. **canker,** canker worm. 6. **Authorizing,** sanctioning, justifying. **with compare,** by comparison. 7. **salving,** parallel in construction with *Authorizing*, *corrupting*, and *Excusing*. **amiss,** misdeed. 8. **Excusing . . . are,** making the excuse more than proportioned to the offense (Steevens). 9. **sensual,** pertaining to the flesh. **sense,** pertaining to the rational faculty; i.e., I reason away your offenses. 14. **sourly,** cruelly.

XXXVI. Another series on the theme of separation begins here, interrupting the group that dwells on the wrongs suffered by the poet. Here it is the friend who has gone on a journey. 1. **twain,** parted. 3. **those blots,** several possible explanations: not moral turpitude but the professional occupation and lower social standing of the poet (Tyler); perhaps his *disgrace with fortune and men's eyes*, xxix, whatever that may have been (Pooler); may be the darkening of soul expressed in sonnets cxlvii and clii (Tucker Brooke). 5. **respect,** i.e., a mutual regard. 6. **separable spite,** spiteful separation (Schmidt); separating spite (Malone). The latter is warranted by Abbott's observation that adjectives in *-able* are active as well as passive. 7. **sole,** unique. 14. **report,** reputation.

XXXVII. 3. **made lame,** i.e., handicapped in life. For other figurative occurrences of the word in Shakespeare, cf. *As You Like It*, I, iii, 6, and *Coriolanus*, IV, vii, 7. **dearest,** most bitter. 4. **of,** in, from. 5-7. **beauty, birth,** etc. These lines are usually accepted as evidence that the *Sonnets* were addressed to a person of high rank. 7. **Entitled,** ennobled (Malone); as rightful owner by a just title (Pooler). 10. **shadow,** reflection, i.e., in the Platonic sense (Wyndham).

That I in thy abundance am suffic'd
And by a part of all thy glory live.
Look, what is best, that best I wish in thee:
This wish I have; then ten times happy me!

XXXVIII.

How can my Muse want subject to invent,
While thou dost breathe, that pour'st into my verse
Thine own sweet argument, too excellent
For every vulgar paper to rehearse?
O, give thyself the thanks, if aught in me
Worthy perusal stand against thy sight;
For who 's so dumb that cannot write to thee,
When thou thyself dost give invention light?
Be thou the tenth Muse, ten times more in worth
Than those old nine which rhymers invocate;
And he that calls on thee, let him bring forth
Eternal numbers to outlive long date.
If my slight Muse do please these curious days,
The pain be mine, but thine shall be the praise.

XXXIX.

O, how thy worth with manners may I sing,
When thou art all the better part of me?
What can mine own praise to mine own self bring?
And what is 't but mine own when I praise thee?
Even for this let us divided live,
And our dear love lose name of single one,
That by this separation I may give
That due to thee which thou deserv'st alone.
O absence, what a torment wouldst thou prove,
Were it not thy sour leisure gave sweet leave
To entertain the time with thoughts of love,
Which time and thoughts so sweetly doth deceive,
And that thou teachest how to make one twain,
By praising him here who doth hence remain!

XL.

Take all my loves, my love, yea, take them all;
What hast thou then more than thou hadst before?
No love, my love, that thou mayst true love call;
All mine was thine before thou hadst this more.
Then if for my love thou my love receivest,
I cannot blame thee for my love thou usest;
But yet be blam'd, if thou this self deceivest
By wilful taste of what thyself refusest.
I do forgive thy robb'ry, gentle thief,
Although thou steal thee all my poverty;
And yet, love knows, it is a greater grief
To bear love's wrong than hate's known injury.
Lascivious grace, in whom all ill well shows,
Kill me with spites; yet we must not be foes.

XLI.

Those pretty wrongs that liberty commits,
When I am sometime absent from thy heart,
Thy beauty and thy years full well befits,
For still temptation follows where thou art.
Gentle thou art and therefore to be won,
Beauteous thou art, therefore to be assailed;
And when a woman woos, what woman's son
Will sourly leave her till she have prevailed?
Ay me! but yet thou mightst my seat forbear,
And chide thy beauty and thy straying youth,
Who lead thee in their riot even there
Where thou art forc'd to break a twofold truth,
Hers, by thy beauty tempting her to thee,
Thine, by thy beauty being false to me.

XLII.

That thou hast her, it is not all my grief,
And yet it may be said I lov'd her dearly;
That she hath thee, is of my wailing chief,
A loss in love that touches me more nearly.
Loving offenders, thus I will excuse ye:
Thou dost love her, because thou know'st I love her;
And for my sake even so doth she abuse me,
Suff'ring my friend for my sake to approve her.
If I lose thee, my loss is my love's gain,
And losing her, my friend hath found that loss;
Both find each other, and I lose both twain,
And both for my sake lay on me this cross:
But here 's the joy; my friend and I are one;
Sweet flattery! then she loves but me alone.

XLIII.

When most I wink, then do mine eyes best see,
For all the day they view things unrespected;
But when I sleep, in dreams they look on thee,
And darkly bright are bright in dark directed.
Then thou, whose shadow shadows doth make bright,
How would thy shadow's form form happy show
To the clear day with thy much clearer light,
When to unseeing eyes thy shade shines so!
How would, I say, mine eyes be blessed made
By looking on thee in the living day,
When in dead night thy fair imperfect shade
Through heavy sleep on sightless eyes doth stay!

XXXVIII. Sir Sidney Lee points out the frequency in dedicatory lines of the conceit developed in this sonnet; viz., that the patron may claim as his own handiwork the protégé's accomplishment because he inspires it. 1. **want . . . invent,** lack something to write about. 2. **that,** who. 3. **argument,** subject. 4. **vulgar,** common. 12. **numbers,** verses. 13. **curious,** critical.

XXXIX. 1. **with manners,** decently, becomingly. 10. **sour,** bitter, harsh; cf. *sourly*, XXXV, 14.

The three following sonnets revert to the theme of XXXIII-XXXV. Tucker Brooke rearranges the six in a continuous series, placing XXXVI-XXXIX after XLII. The commentators are inclined to interpret XL (considering it with five others—XLI, XLII, CXXXIII, CXXXIV, CLXIV) as biographically significant. Sir Sidney Lee finds here "strands of wholly original sentiment" distinguishing these six from the rest of the *Sonnets*, which for the most part are vigorous and original treatments of stereotyped themes (see his chapter, "The Supposed Story of Intrigue in the Sonnets," *Life*, pp. 151-160).

XL. 5. **my love . . . my love,** love of me . . . her whom I love (Dowden). 6. **for,** because. **thou usest,** you enjoy. 7. **this self,** i.e., this other self of yours, the poet. (Often emended to *thyself*, as in Globe.) 10. **steal thee,** take for your own. **all my poverty,** the poor little that I have (Rolfe). 13. **Lascivious grace,** i.e., you who are gracious even in your lasciviousness.

XLI. Dowden points out that this sonnet develops the idea of line 13 of the preceding one. 1. **pretty,** minor. **liberty,** licentiousness. 2. **absent,** probably to be taken in a literal and local as well as figurative sense (Tucker Brooke). 3. **befits.** The subject is *wrongs* (l. 1); Abbott (333) points out the frequency in Shakespeare of the third person plural in *-s*. 5-6. **Gentle . . . assailed.** The phrasing and the sentiment recall *1 Henry VI*, V, iii, 78-79. 9. **seat,** place. 11. **Who,** which. 12. **twofold truth,** her plighted love and your plighted friendship (Pooler).

XLII. 3. **is . . . chief,** is chief cause of my lamentation. 8. **approve,** try, test. 9. **my love's,** hers whom I love (as in LX, 5, 6). 14. **flattery,** gratifying deception (Onions), as in *Othello*, IV, i, 133.

XLIII. This picks up the theme of XXXVI-XXXIX, i.e., the friend's absence, and continues it through XLVII. 2. **unrespected,** unnoticed. 4. **And . . . directed,** and illumined although closed are clearly directed in the darkness (Dowden); is it possible that the phrase *darkly bright* may mean that the eyes are bright most of all in the dark, because of what they see in dreams? (Alden). 5. **whose . . . bright,** whose image makes darkness bright (Pooler). 6. **thy shadow's form,** probably, the substance of the shadow; i.e., your presence. 8. **unseeing eyes,** i.e.,

All days are nights to see till I see thee,
And nights bright days when dreams do show thee me.

XLIV.

If the dull substance of my flesh were thought,
Injurious distance should not stop my way;
For then despite of space I would be brought,
From limits far remote, where thou dost stay.
No matter then although my foot did stand
Upon the farthest earth remov'd from thee;
For nimble thought can jump both sea and land
As soon as think the place where he would be.
But, ah! thought kills me that I am not thought,
To leap large lengths of miles when thou art gone,
But that so much of earth and water wrought
I must attend time's leisure with my moan,
Receiving nought by elements so slow
But heavy tears, badges of either's woe.

XLV.

The other two, slight air and purging fire,
Are both with thee, wherever I abide;
The first my thought, the other my desire,
These present-absent with swift motion slide.
For when these quicker elements are gone
In tender embassy of love to thee,
My life, being made of four, with two alone
Sinks down to death, oppress'd with melancholy;
Until life's composition be recured
By those swift messengers return'd from thee,
Who even but now come back again, assured
Of thy fair health, recounting it to me:
This told, I joy; but then no longer glad,
I send them back again and straight grow sad.

XLVI.

Mine eye and heart are at a mortal war
How to divide the conquest of thy sight;
Mine eye my heart thy picture's sight would bar,
My heart mine eye the freedom of that right.
My heart doth plead that thou in him dost lie,—
A closet never pierc'd with crystal eyes—
But the defendant doth that plea deny
And says in him thy fair appearance lies.
To 'cide this title is impanneled
A quest of thoughts, all tenants to the heart,
And by their verdict is determined
The clear eye's moiety and the dear heart's part:
As thus; mine eye's due is thy outward part,
And my heart's right thy inward love of heart.

XLVII.

Betwixt mine eye and heart a league is took,
And each doth good turns now unto the other:
When that mine eye is famish'd for a look,
Or heart in love with sighs himself doth smother,
With my love's picture then my eye doth feast
And to the painted banquet bids my heart;
Another time mine eye is my heart's guest
And in his thoughts of love doth share a part:
So, either by thy picture or my love,
Thyself away art present still with me;
For thou not farther than my thoughts canst move,
And I am still with them and they with thee;
Or, if they sleep, thy picture in my sight
Awakes my heart to heart's and eye's delight.

XLVIII.

How careful was I, when I took my way,
Each trifle under truest bars to thrust,
That to my use it might unused stay
From hands of falsehood, in sure wards of trust!
But thou, to whom my jewels trifles are,
Most worthy comfort, now my greatest grief,
Thou, best of dearest and mine only care,
Art left the prey of every vulgar thief.
Thee have I not lock'd up in any chest,
Save where thou art not, though I feel thou art,
Within the gentle closure of my breast,
From whence at pleasure thou mayst come and part;
And even thence thou wilt be stol'n, I fear,
For truth proves thievish for a prize so dear.

XLIX.

Against that time, if ever that time come,
When I shall see thee frown on my defects,
When as thy love hath cast his utmost sum,
Call'd to that audit by advis'd respects;
Against that time when thou shalt strangely pass
And scarcely greet me with that sun, thine eye,
When love, converted from the thing it was,
Shall reasons find of settled gravity,—
Against that time do I ensconce me here
Within the knowledge of mine own desart,
And this my hand against myself uprear,
To guard the lawful reasons on thy part:

closed eyes of the dreamer. 11. **imperfect,** unsubstantial (Tyler); perhaps indistinct as in a dream. 13. **All . . . to see,** all days are gloomy to behold (Steevens).

XLIV. 4. **where,** i.e., to the place where. 6. **farthest earth remov'd,** that part of earth farthest removed. 8. **he,** it. 11. **earth and water,** the baser elements; cf. *Antony and Cleopatra,* V, ii, 292-293; *Henry V,* III, vii, 22-23. 14. **either's,** i.e., because the earth is heavy and the sea is salt and wet, both like tears.

XLV. 1. **other two,** i.e., of the four elements discussed in Sonnet XLIV. 4. **present-absent,** now here and immediately gone (Tucker Brooke). 7. **two alone,** i.e., earth and water. 8. **melancholy,** may have been pronounced *melanch'ly;* so printed by some editors. 9. **recured,** restored. 10. **swift messengers,** i.e., fire and air, thought and desire.

The following two sonnets treat a theme that Lee points out is a favorite one with the Elizabethan sonneteers; i.e., the war between the eye and the heart. Pooler and others think it might be a continuation of XXIV, which develops the conceit of a portrait of the poet's beloved painted on his heart.

XLVI. 2. **thy sight,** the sight of you. 6. **crystal,** i.e., because of their clarity. 9. **'cide,** decide; so Malone and most editors; Q: *side* retained by some who explain "to assign to one side or another." 10. **quest,** inquest, jury. 12. **moiety,** portion.

XLVII. 1. **a league is took,** an agreement is reached. 6. **painted banquet,** i.e., a visual feast, or, a picture of the friend. 8. **his,** its, the heart's.

Sonnets XLVIII-LV form another series on the poet's absence from his friend, occasioned by the poet's having gone on a second journey.

XLVIII. 1. **took my way,** set out on my journey. 2. **truest,** most trusty. 4. **hands of falsehood,** thieves. 5. **to whom,** in comparison to whom. 6. **now . . . grief,** i.e., because of his absence. 12. **part,** depart.

XLIX. 3. **cast . . . sum,** added up the sum total. A metaphor from closing accounts on a dissolution of partnership (Pooler). 4. **advis'd respects,** considerations. 5. **strangely,** as a stranger. 8. **reasons . . . gravity,** find reasons for a dignified reserve (Schmidt); *settled gravity* is taken by many editors to mean "weight"; i.e., find reasons of considerable weight. 10. **desart,** (slight) merit. 11-14. **And . . . cause,** I take your part against myself by admitting that you have a legal right to disown me, since I can show no cause why you should love me (Pooler). 11. **against myself,** i.e., to take an oath, not as if with a weapon.

To leave poor me thou hast the strength of laws,
Since why to love I can allege no cause.

L.

How heavy do I journey on the way,
When what I seek, my weary travel's end,
Doth teach that ease and that repose to say
'Thus far the miles are measur'd from thy friend!'
The beast that bears me, tired with my woe,
Plods dully on, to bear that weight in me,
As if by some instinct the wretch did know
His rider lov'd not speed, being made from thee:
The bloody spur cannot provoke him on
That sometimes anger thrusts into his hide;
Which heavily he answers with a groan,
More sharp to me than spurring to his side;
For that same groan doth put this in my mind;
My grief lies onward and my joy behind.

LI.

Thus can my love excuse the slow offence
Of my dull bearer when from thee I speed:
From where thou art why should I haste me thence?
Till I return, of posting is no need.
O, what excuse will my poor beast then find,
When swift extremity can seem but slow?
Then should I spur, though mounted on the wind;
In winged speed no motion shall I know:
Then can no horse with my desire keep pace;
Therefore desire, of perfect'st love being made,
Shall neigh—no dull flesh—in his fiery race;
But love, for love, thus shall excuse my jade;
Since from thee going he went wilful-slow,
Towards thee I'll run, and give him leave to go.

LII.

So am I as the rich, whose blessed key
Can bring him to his sweet up-locked treasure,
The which he will not ev'ry hour survey,
For blunting the fine point of seldom pleasure.
Therefore are feasts so solemn and so rare,
Since, seldom coming, in the long year set,
Like stones of worth they thinly placed are,
Or captain jewels in the carcanet.
So is the time that keeps you as my chest,
Or as the wardrobe which the robe doth hide,
To make some special instant special blest,
By new unfolding his imprison'd pride.
Blessed are you, whose worthiness gives scope,
Being had, to triumph, being lack'd, to hope.

LIII.

What is your substance, whereof are you made,
That millions of strange shadows on you tend?
Since every one hath, every one, one shade,
And you, but one, can every shadow lend.
Describe Adonis, and the counterfeit
Is poorly imitated after you;
On Helen's cheek all art of beauty set,
And you in Grecian tires are painted new:
Speak of the spring and foison of the year;
The one doth shadow of your beauty show,
The other as your bounty doth appear;
And you in every blessed shape we know.
In all external grace you have some part,
But you like none, none you, for constant heart.

LIV.

O, how much more doth beauty beauteous seem
By that sweet ornament which truth doth give!
The rose looks fair, but fairer we it deem
For that sweet odour which doth in it live.
The canker-blooms have full as deep a dye
As the perfumed tincture of the roses,
Hang on such thorns and play as wantonly
When summer's breath their masked buds discloses:
But, for their virtue only is their show,
They live unwoo'd and unrespected fade,
Die to themselves. Sweet roses do not so;
Of their sweet deaths are sweetest odours made:
And so of you, beauteous and lovely youth,
When that shall vade, by verse distills your truth.

LV.

Not marble, nor the gilded monuments
Of princes, shall outlive this pow'rful rhyme;
But you shall shine more bright in these contents
Than unswept stone besmear'd with sluttish time.
When wasteful war shall statues overturn,
And broils root out the work of masonry,
Nor Mars his sword nor war's quick fire shall burn
The living record of your memory.
'Gainst death and all-oblivious enmity
Shall you pace forth; your praise shall still find room
Even in the eyes of all posterity
That wear this world out to the ending doom.

L. 6. **to bear,** at bearing.

LI. 1. **slow offence,** offense which consists in slowness (Beeching). 4. **posting,** hastening. 6. **swift extremity,** extreme swiftness. 10-11. **desire . . . race,** a recurrence with metaphorical application of the concept developed in XLV. 11. **dull.** Cf. *dully*, l. 6. 12. **jade,** nag. 14. **go,** walk, as contrasted with running.

LII. This sonnet is a complement to XLVIII, where the image is that of a man locking up his treasure. 4. **For blunting,** lest it blunt. 5. **feasts,** i.e., chief festivals of the church year—e.g., Christmas, Easter, Corpus Christi, Michaelmas. 5-8. **so solemn,** etc. Malone cites *1 Henry IV*, I, ii, 229-230; and III, ii, 57-59. 8. **captain,** principal. **carcanet,** necklace of jewels. 11. **special instant,** particular moment. **special blest,** particularly blest. The image has a parallel in *1 Henry IV*, III, ii, 56-57. 12. **his,** its.

LIII. 1. **substance.** Pooler finds a touch of Platonism here in the implication that the substance is divine—the idea of which the shadows are the *idola*, or representation. 2, 3, 4. **shadows, shade,** used quibblingly with the meanings "silhouette" and "picture, reflection, symbol." 2. **tend,** attend, wait upon. 4. **And . . . lend,** i.e., and yet you, being only one person, are endowed with the virtues of numerous types of beauty (*you* is the object of *lend*). 5. **counterfeit,** likeness (of beauty). 8. **tires,** clothes, attire. 9. **foison,** abundance; i.e., autumn.

LIV. 2. **truth,** constancy. 5. **canker-blooms,** dog roses (outwardly attractive, but not as sweetly scented as the damask rose). 8. **discloses,** causes to open. 9. **for,** because; i.e., because their appearance is their only virtue. 10. **unrespected,** unnoticed. 11. **to themselves,** i.e., without profit to others (Pooler). 14. **vade,** perish, depart. **by . . . truth,** i.e., by means of (my) verse, your essence will be distilled and so preserved.

LV. 3. **these contents,** i.e., the contents of my poems written in praise of you. 4. **unswept stone,** parallel with *contents;* i.e., *in* is to be supplied from the preceding line (Pooler). 6. **broils,** battles. 9. **all-oblivious,** causing to be forgotten. 12. **wear . . . out,** i.e., outlast (Pooler). 13. **till . . . arise,** till the decree of the judgment day when you will arise from the dead; cf. Abbott, 284.

LVI. This, like the sonnets immediately preceding, is written in absence (Dowden). Perhaps a plea for the renewal of intimacy (Pooler). 1. **Sweet love.** The address is to the spirit of love. The friend is not directly mentioned in this sonnet (Tucker Brooke). 2. **edge,** keenness. 6. **wink,** shut. 9. **sad int'rim,** i.e., the period of love's abatement or absence. 9-12. **like the ocean,** etc. The image is variously explained. Some editors see a reference to the story of Hero and Leander; others regard *the ocean* figuratively as some kind of barrier which separates lovers (even Death has been suggested); still others take *the ocean* more literally as a separating body of water—a bay or estuary which parts the shore. Alden, although he favors the last interpretation, records a

So, till the judgement that yourself arise,
You live in this, and dwell in lovers' eyes.

LVI.

Sweet love, renew thy force; be it not said
Thy edge should blunter be than appetite,
Which but to-day by feeding is allay'd,
To-morrow sharp'ned in his former might:
So, love, be thou; although to-day thou fill
Thy hungry eyes even till they wink with fullness,
To-morrow see again, and do not kill
The spirit of love with a perpetual dullness.
Let this sad int'rim like the ocean be
Which parts the shore, where two contracted new
Come daily to the banks, that, when they see
Return of love, more blest may be the view;
Else call it winter, which being full of care
Makes summer's welcome thrice more wish'd, more rare.

LVII.

Being your slave, what should I do but tend
Upon the hours and times of your desire?
I have no precious time at all to spend,
Nor services to do, till you require.
Nor dare I chide the world-without-end hour
Whilst I, my sovereign, watch the clock for you,
Nor think the bitterness of absence sour
When you have bid your servant once adieu;
Nor dare I question with my jealous thought
Where you may be, or your affairs suppose,
But, like a sad slave, stay and think of nought
Save, where you are how happy you make those.
So true a fool is love that in your will,
Though you do any thing, he thinks no ill.

LVIII.

That god forbid that made me first your slave,
I should in thought control your times of pleasure,
Or at your hand th' account of hours to crave,
Being your vassal, bound to stay your leisure!
O, let me suffer, being at your beck,
Th' imprison'd absence of your liberty;
And patience, tame to sufferance, bide each check,
Without accusing you of injury.
Be where you list, your charter is so strong
That you yourself may privilege your time
To what you will; to you it doth belong
Yourself to pardon of self-doing crime.
I am to wait, though waiting so be hell;
Not blame your pleasure, be it ill or well.

LIX.

If there be nothing new, but that which is
Hath been before, how are our brains beguil'd,
Which, labouring for invention, bear amiss
The second burthen of a former child!
O, that record could with a backward look,
Even of five hundred courses of the sun,
Show me your image in some antique book,
Since mind at first in character was done!
That I might see what the old world could say
To this composed wonder of your frame;
Whether we are mended, or whe'r better they,
Or whether revolution be the same.
O, sure I am, the wits of former days
To subjects worse have given admiring praise.

LX.

Like as the waves make towards the pebbled shore,
So do our minutes hasten to their end;
Each changing place with that which goes before,
In sequent toil all forwards do contend.
Nativity, once in the main of light,
Crawls to maturity, wherewith being crown'd,
Crooked eclipses 'gainst his glory fight,
And Time that gave doth now his gift confound.
Time doth transfix the flourish set on youth
And delves the parallels in beauty's brow,
Feeds on the rarities of nature's truth,
And nothing stands but for his scythe to mow:
†And yet to times in hope my verse shall stand,
Praising thy worth, despite his cruel hand.

LXI.

Is it thy will thy image should keep open
My heavy eyelids to the weary night?
Dost thou desire my slumbers should be broken,
While shadows like to thee do mock my sight?
Is it thy spirit that thou send'st from thee
So far from home into my deeds to pry,
To find out shames and idle hours in me,
The scope and tenour of thy jealousy?
O, no! thy love, though much, is not so great:
It is my love that keeps mine eye awake;
Mine own true love that doth my rest defeat,

suggestion of A. G. Newcomer, who thought *part* might mean "recede" or "depart from." He paraphrased as follows: Let this sad interim be only like waters that recede from their shore where, viz., by this ocean of love (dropping the image of the ocean at this point), two, *contracted new*, come daily to the banks, so that when they see the tide of love come in again, more blest may be the sight. 10. **contracted new,** lately betrothed.

LVII. 1. **tend,** wait. 5. **world-without-end,** interminable. 7. **think,** i.e., dare to think. 10. **suppose,** make conjectures about. 13. **will.** This word, capitalized in the 1609 quarto, is regarded by some as a pun on Shakespeare's name. Dowden explains as possibly: "Love in your Will (i.e., in me) can think no ill of anything you do," and "love can discover no evil in your will." Sir Sidney Lee thinks the Elizabethan practice of capitalizing nouns too common for this instance to have any significance.

LVIII. 3. **to crave,** parallel with *control* (l. 2); *to* might be omitted or *should* (from l. 2) might be inserted instead, but the omission would create ambiguity, and the insertion would be a tedious repetition (Abbott, 416). 4. **to stay,** to await. 6. **Th' . . . liberty,** i.e., your absence from me, due to your independence of me, makes me as one imprisoned, dependent on (or vassal to) you. 7. **tame to,** subdued by; cf. *King Lear*, IV, vi, 225. **bide each check,** endure each rebuke. 9. **charter,** privilege or right recorded in writing. Pooler notes the loose employment of the word to denote any freedom of action. 10. **privilege,** authorize. 12. **self-doing crime,** crime committed by oneself. 14. **blame,** parallel with *wait* (l. 13).

LIX. Most editors discern a break in the sequence here. 3. **labouring for invention,** striving to give birth to a new creation. 4. **The . . . child,** i.e., a mere repetition of something created before. 5. **record,** memory, especially memory preserved by history (Schmidt); accented on the second syllable. 8. **Since . . . done,** since thought was first expressed in writing. 10. **composed wonder,** wonderful composition (Rolfe). 11. **whe'r,** whether. 12. **revolution,** i.e., of the ages.

LX. 4. **sequent,** one after another. 5. **main,** main body. The entrance of a child into the world at birth is an entrance into the main or ocean of light (Dowden). 6. **Crawls.** Cf. *Hamlet*, III, i, 130; the word denotes the abject condition of mankind (Tyler). 7. **Crooked,** perverse, malignant. 9. **transfix,** destroy. **flourish,** decoration, embellishment; the figure is possibly from penmanship, but the general meaning is older than the scribal flourish. 10. **parallels,** wrinkles. 11. **rarities . . . truth,** rare things created by the fidelity of nature (Alden). 13. **times in hope,** times to come.

LXI. The jealous feeling of LVII reappears (Dowden). 7. **shames and idle hours,** a hendiadys, the meaning being "to see how badly I spend my spare time" (Pooler). 8. **scope . . . jealousy,** aim and purport of your suspicion (Pooler).

To play the watchman ever for thy sake:
  For thee watch I whilst thou dost wake elsewhere,
  From me far off, with others all too near.

LXII.

Sin of self-love possesseth all mine eye
And all my soul and all my every part;
And for this sin there is no remedy,
It is so grounded inward in my heart.
Methinks no face so gracious is as mine,
No shape so true, no truth of such account;
And for myself mine own worth do define,
As I all other in all worths surmount.
But when my glass shows me myself indeed,
Beated and chopp'd with tann'd antiquity,
Mine own self-love quite contrary I read;
Self so self-loving were iniquity.
  'Tis thee, myself, that for myself I praise,
  Painting my age with beauty of thy days.

LXIII.

Against my love shall be, as I am now,
With Time's injurious hand crush'd and o'erworn;
When hours have drain'd his blood and fill'd his brow
With lines and wrinkles; when his youthful morn
Hath travell'd on to Age's steepy night,
And all those beauties whereof now he 's king
Are vanishing or vanish'd out of sight,
Stealing away the treasure of his spring;
For such a time do I now fortify
Against confounding Age's cruel knife,
That he shall never cut from memory
My sweet love's beauty, though my lover's life:
  His beauty shall in these black lines be seen,
  And they shall live, and he in them still green.

LXIV.

When I have seen by Time's fell hand defaced
The rich proud cost of outworn buried age;
When sometime lofty towers I see down-razed
And brass eternal slave to mortal rage;
When I have seen the hungry ocean gain
Advantage on the kingdom of the shore,
And the firm soil win of the wat'ry main,
Increasing store with loss and loss with store;
When I have seen such interchange of state,
Or state itself confounded to decay;
Ruin hath taught me thus to ruminate,
That Time will come and take my lovè away.
  This thought is as a death, which cannot choose
  But weep to have that which it fears to lose.

LXV.

Since brass, nor stone, nor earth, nor boundless sea,
But sad mortality o'er-sways their power,
How with this rage shall beauty hold a plea,
Whose action is no stronger than a flower?
O, how shall summer's honey breath hold out
Against the wrackful siege of batt'ring days,
When rocks impregnable are not so stout,
Nor gates of steel so strong, but Time decays?
O fearful meditation! where, alack,
Shall Time's best jewel from Time's chest lie hid?
Or what strong hand can hold his swift foot back?
Or who his spoil of beauty can forbid?
  O, none, unless this miracle have might,
  That in black ink my love may still shine bright.

LXVI.

Tir'd with all these, for restful death I cry,
As, to behold desert a beggar born,
And needy nothing trimm'd in jollity,
And purest faith unhappily forsworn,
And gilded honour shamefully misplac'd,
And maiden virtue rudely strumpeted,
And right perfection wrongfully disgrac'd,
And strength by limping sway disabled,
And art made tongue-tied by authority,
And folly doctor-like controlling skill,
And simple truth miscall'd simplicity,
And captive good attending captain ill:
  Tir'd with all these, from these would I be gone,
  Save that, to die, I leave my love alone.

LXVII.

Ah! wherefore with infection should he live,
And with his presence grace impiety,
That sin by him advantage should achieve
And lace itself with his society?
Why should false painting imitate his cheek
And steal dead seeing of his living hue?
Why should poor beauty indirectly seek

12. **watchman,** one who stays awake. 13. **watch, wake.** The words were originally identical in meaning; i.e., to be awake.

LXII. 1. **Sin of self-love.** Cf. *All's Well that Ends Well*, I, i, 157. 4. **grounded . . . heart,** fixed or established inwardly. 8. **As,** as if. **other,** a sixteenth-century plural; see Abbott, 12. 9. **indeed,** i.e., as I actually am. 10. **Beated,** battered; Malone conjectured *Bated*, i.e., laid low. **chopp'd,** chapped, roughened. 12. **so self-loving,** i.e., to love oneself as the glass *indeed* shows him. 13. **thee, myself,** i.e., my other self. 14. **days,** i.e., youth.

LXIII. 1. **Against,** i.e., anticipating the time when. 5. **steepy,** having a precipitous declivity (Schmidt); difficult to ascend (Onions); Dowden cites VII, 5, 6, and 9, 10, where the sun, likened to youth, climbs the *steep-up heavenly hill*, and like old age, *reeleth from the day.* 9. **For such a time,** etc., parallel in construction with the phrase (l. 1) *Against my love*, etc. **fortify,** raise works of defense; possibly, fortify myself, gird my strength. 10. **confounding,** destroying.

LXIV. 1. **fell,** cruel. 2. **rich proud,** proud on account of its wealth. 4. **brass . . . rage.** *Mortal* may be contrasted with *eternal* in the sense of destroying as opposed to indestructible (Pooler); brass, i.e., bronze, was the enduring material for sculpture. 5-8. **When . . . store.** Lee points out the similarity of these lines to a passage in Ovid's *Metamorphoses*, XV, 288-290. Shakespeare has used similar imagery in *The Rape of Lucrece*, 944 ff.; *1 Henry IV*, III, i. 108-111; *2 Henry IV*, III, i, 46-52. The notion is expressed also in *Timon of Athens*, the opening dialogue between Poet and Painter. 8. **Increasing . . . store,** i.e., one gaining as the other loses, and losing as the other gains. 9, 10. **state, state,** condition . . . pomp or greatness (Schmidt, Beeching, Tyler); Wyndham glosses both as "condition," the first used particularly, the second in the abstract. 13. **which cannot choose,** modifies *thought.* 14. **to have,** i.e., because it now has.

LXV. 1-2. **Since . . . power,** an elliptical clause: Since there is neither brass, etc., but that sad mortality o'ersways, etc. The ellipsis shows the closeness of the idea to the preceding sonnet. 4. **action,** case (for permanence); legal figure. 10. **Time's chest.** The chest of Time is the repository into which he is poetically supposed to throw those things which he designs to be forgotten (Steevens); cf. *time's wallet*, *Troilus and Cressida*, III, iii, 145-146, wherein he puts *alms for oblivion.* 12. **spoil,** act of spoiling; possibly, spoils, booty.

LXVI. The thoughts of death developed in the preceding series bring the poet to thoughts of his own death and his willingness to part from the world. The theme of the world's infection continues from this sonnet through LXX. 1. **all these.** The antecedent is what follows; many commentators point out the similarity to Hamlet's famous soliloquy, especially *Hamlet*, III, i, 70-75. 2. **As,** for instance. **desert,** i.e., those who have merit, as contrasted with *needy nothing* in the next line. 3. **needy nothing,** moral and mental emptiness (Tucker Brooke). **jollity,** finery. 8. **limping sway,** inept leadership. **disabled,** four syllables. 10. **doctor-like,** like a learned person. 11. **simplicity,** silliness,

Roses of shadow, since his rose is true?
Why should he live, now Nature bankrout is,
Beggar'd of blood to blush through lively veins?
For she hath no exchequer now but his,
And, proud of many, lives upon his gains.
O, him she stores, to show what wealth she had
In days long since, before these last so bad.

LXVIII.

Thus is his cheek the map of days outworn,
When beauty liv'd and died as flowers do now,
Before these bastard signs of fair were born,
Or durst inhabit on a living brow;
Before the golden tresses of the dead,
The right of sepulchres, were shorn away,
To live a second life on second head;
Ere beauty's dead fleece made another gay:
In him those holy antique hours are seen,
Without all ornament, itself and true,
Making no summer of another's green,
Robbing no old to dress his beauty new;
And him as for a map doth Nature store,
To show false Art what beauty was of yore.

LXIX.

Those parts of thee that the world's eye doth view
Want nothing that the thought of hearts can mend;
All tongues, the voice of souls, give thee that due,
Utt'ring bare truth, even so as foes commend.
Thy outward thus with outward praise is crown'd;
But those same tongues that give thee so thine own
In other accents do this praise confound
By seeing farther than the eye hath shown.
They look into the beauty of thy mind,
And that, in guess, they measure by thy deeds;
Then, churls, their thoughts, although their eyes were kind,
To thy fair flower add the rank smell of weeds:
But why thy odour matcheth not thy show,
The soil is this, that thou dost common grow.

LXX.

That thou art blam'd shall not be thy defect,
For slander's mark was ever yet the fair;
The ornament of beauty is suspect,
A crow that flies in heaven's sweetest air.
So thou be good, slander doth but approve
Thy worth the greater, being woo'd of time;
For canker vice the sweetest buds doth love,
And thou present'st a pure unstained prime.
Thou hast pass'd by the ambush of young days,
Either not assail'd or victor being charg'd;
Yet this thy praise cannot be so thy praise,
To tie up envy evermore enlarg'd:
If some suspect of ill mask'd not thy show,
Then thou alone kingdoms of hearts shouldst owe.

LXXI.

No longer mourn for me when I am dead
Than you shall hear the surly sullen bell
Give warning to the world that I am fled
From this vile world, with vilest worms to dwell:
Nay, if you read this line, remember not
The hand that writ it; for I love you so
That I in your sweet thoughts would be forgot
If thinking on me then should make you woe.
O, if, I say, you look upon this verse
When I perhaps compounded am with clay,
Do not so much as my poor name rehearse,
But let your love even with my life decay,
Lest the wise world should look into your moan
And mock you with me after I am gone.

LXXII.

O, lest the world should task you to recite
What merit liv'd in me, that you should love
After my death, dear love, forget me quite,
For you in me can nothing worthy prove;
Unless you would devise some virtuous lie,
To do more for me than mine own desert,
And hang more praise upon deceased I
Than niggard truth would willingly impart:
O, lest your true love may seem false in this,
That you for love speak well of me untrue,
My name be buried where my body is,
And live no more to shame nor me nor you.
For I am sham'd by that which I bring forth,
And so should you, to love things nothing worth.

LXXIII.

That time of year thou mayst in me behold
When yellow leaves, or none, or few, do hang

folly. 12. **attending,** waiting on, subordinated to.

LXVII. 1. **with infection,** i.e., the world's ills enumerated in the preceding sonnet. **he,** i.e., *my love* of LXVI, 14. 4. **lace,** trim with ornament. 6. **dead seeing.** Dowden's gloss, "lifeless appearance," would better define Farmer's emendation, *dead seeming*, a reading adopted by some editors. 7. **poor,** inferior. **indirectly,** imitatively. 8. **Roses of shadow,** i.e., color of roses placed on his cheeks. 9. **bankrout,** bankrupt. 10. **Beggar'd,** modifies *Nature.* **to blush,** which blushes. 11. **exchequer,** i.e., treasury of natural beauty. 13. **stores,** keeps in store.

LXVIII. This sonnet contrasts the real beauty of youth with artificial beauty. The subject of the sonnet is the epitome of natural beauty. 1. **map,** picture, image. 3. **bastard . . . fair,** i.e., cosmetics. 9. **antique hours,** ancient times. 10. **itself.** Malone conjectured *himself*, thinking the antecedent to be *him* (l. 9). Pooler refers the pronoun to *holy antique hours*, singular in idea, since the phrase means "the beauty of the past"; *itself* is equivalent to "unadulterated."

LXIX. 2. **Want . . . mend,** lack nothing which the imagination can and customarily does supply. 3. **voice of souls.** This is a Renaissance commonplace, that the tongue (power of speech) is the voice of the soul. 4. **even . . . commend,** as even ill-disposed persons are forced to admit. 6. **thine own,** i.e., *that due* of line 3. 14. **soil.** Globe, following Malone, has *solve* defined as solution; Q: *solye*; the 1640 Q: soyle; most editors, *soil*, but explain it variously: solution (*NED*); blemish, fault (Verity, citing *Hamlet*, I, iii, 15); ground, i.e., origin, source (Tucker Brooke, who explains it as continuing the figure of the garden). **common,** stale, vulgar.

LXX. 2. **slander's mark,** object of slander. 3. **suspect,** suspicion (as also in l. 13). 5. **So,** provided that. The implied reasoning is: Slandered goodness is more than ordinarily good, for slander is evidence of beauty, and beauty of temptation (Pooler). 6. **woo'd of time,** i.e., by fashion, tempted by the world. 8. **thou . . . prime,** i.e., you have a reputation for an unspotted youth. 12. **enlarg'd,** at liberty. Dowden quotes a letter from J. W. Hales, who saw here a reference to Spenser's *Faerie Queene*, Bk. VI, where Calidore bound the Blatant Beast, now broken loose again and always set free; note also in Bk. II that Occasion is always being set free; so is Maleger. 14. **owe,** own.

LXXI. With this sonnet the theme of death as a release from the world's ills gives place to a more contemplative mood, wherein once more the immortalizing power of poetry is the theme; not its immortalizing of the poet, but of his friend. This theme is continued through LXXIV. 14. **with me,** i.e., as they mock me.

LXXII. 1. **task you to recite,** place upon you the task of reciting. 5. **virtuous lie,** lie about my virtue. 7. **I.** The rhyme is accountable for the pronoun. Abbott (205, 209) remarks the tendency to use *I* for *me* after the sounds *d* and *t*. 10. **untrue,** untruly. 11. **My name be,** let my name be.

Upon those boughs which shake against the cold,
Bare ruin'd choirs, where late the sweet birds sang.
In me thou see'st the twilight of such day
As after sunset fadeth in the west,
Which by and by black night doth take away,
Death's second self, that seals up all in rest.
In me thou see'st the glowing of such fire
That on the ashes of his youth doth lie,
As the death-bed whereon it must expire
Consum'd with that which it was nourish'd by.
This thou perceiv'st, which makes thy love more strong,
To love that well which thou must leave ere long.

LXXIV.

But be contented: when that fell arrest
Without all bail shall carry me away,
My life hath in this line some interest,
Which for memorial still with thee shall stay.
When thou reviewest this, thou dost review
The very part was consecrate to thee:
The earth can have but earth, which is his due;
My spirit is thine, the better part of me:
So then thou hast but lost the dregs of life,
The prey of worms, my body being dead,
The coward conquest of a wretch's knife,
Too base of thee to be remembered.
The worth of that is that which it contains,
And that is this, and this with thee remains.

LXXV.

So are you to my thoughts as food to life,
Or as sweet-season'd showers are to the ground;
And for the peace of you I hold such strife
As 'twixt a miser and his wealth is found;
Now proud as an enjoyer and anon
Doubting the filching age will steal his treasure,
Now counting best to be with you alone,
Then better'd that the world may see my pleasure;
Sometime all full with feasting on your sight
And by and by clean starved for a look;
Possessing or pursuing no delight,
Save what is had or must from you be took.
Thus do I pine and surfeit day by day,
Or gluttoning on all, or all away.

LXXVI.

Why is my verse so barren of new pride,
So far from variation or quick change?
Why with the time do I not glance aside
To new-found methods and to compounds strange?
Why write I still all one, ever the same,
And deep invention in a noted weed,
That every word doth almost tell my name,
Showing their birth and where they did proceed?
O, know, sweet love, I always write of you,
And you and love are still my argument;
So all my best is dressing old words new,
Spending again what is already spent:
For as the sun is daily new and old,
So is my love still telling what is told.

LXXVII.

Thy glass will show thee how thy beauties wear,
Thy dial how thy precious minutes waste;
The vacant leaves thy mind's imprint will bear,
And of this book this learning mayst thou taste.
The wrinkles which thy glass will truly show
Of mouthed graves will give thee memory;
Thou by thy dial's shady stealth mayst know
Time's thievish progress to eternity.
Look, what thy memory can not contain
Commit to these waste blanks, and thou shalt find
Those children nurs'd, deliver'd from thy brain,
To take a new acquaintance of thy mind.
These offices, so oft as thou wilt look,
Shall profit thee and much enrich thy book.

LXXVIII.

So oft have I invok'd thee for my Muse
And found such fair assistance in my verse
As every alien pen hath got my use
And under thee their poesy disperse.
Thine eyes that taught the dumb on high to sing
And heavy ignorance aloft to fly,
Have added feathers to the learned's wing
And given grace a double majesty.
Yet be most proud of that which I compile,
Whose influence is thine and born of thee:
In others' works thou dost but mend the style,
And arts with thy sweet graces graced be;
But thou art all my art and dost advance
As high as learning my rude ignorance.

LXXIX.

Whilst I alone did call upon thy aid,
My verse alone had all thy gentle grace,
But now my gracious numbers are decay'd
And my sick Muse doth give another place.
I grant, sweet love, thy lovely argument
Deserves the travail of a worthier pen,
Yet what of thee thy poet doth invent

LXXIII. 4. **choirs,** that part of cathedrals where the service is said; in apposition with *boughs* (l. 3). This image was probably suggested to Shakespeare by our desolated monasteries. The resemblance between the vaulting of a Gothic aisle and an avenue of trees whose upper branches meet and form an arch overhead is too striking not to be acknowledged. When the roof of the one is shattered, and the boughs of the other leafless, the comparison becomes yet more solemn and picturesque (Steevens). 12. **that,** i.e., the ashes of what was formerly the fuel.

LXXIV. 1. **that fell arrest,** i.e., death; Capell cites *Hamlet*, V, ii, 347-348. 3. **line,** verse. **interest,** legal concern, right, or title. 7. **The . . . earth,** an echo, probably, of the medieval earth-upon-earth rhymes; also of the "earth to earth" phrase in the burial service of the prayer book. 11. **coward . . . knife,** i.e., the conquest that even a poor cowardly wretch like Death can make with his scythe (?). Dowden cites LXIII, 10. The line also suggests some of the pictorial representations of death in the Dance of Death motifs. 12. **of thee,** by thee; modifies *remembered*. 13-14. **The worth . . . remains,** the only worth of my body is the spirit it contains—i.e., this verse, which will remain with you.

LXXV. 2. **sweet-season'd,** (of rain) soft (Onions). 3. **of you,** to be found in you (Dowden). 6. **Doubting,** suspecting, fearing. 8. **better'd,** made happier. 10. **clean,** completely, absolutely. 12. **from you,** modifies both verbs, *had* and *must be took*. 14. **Or . . . or,** either . . . or. **all away,** i.e., all food being taken away.

LXXVI. This sonnet implies on the friend's part a not unnatural restiveness at Shakespeare's plain-spokenness and abstention from the fashionable devices of eulogy (Tucker Brooke). 3. **time,** way of the world, fashion. 4. **compounds,** compound words (Onions); Lee refers the phrase to the extravagances of Shakespeare's contemporaries in inventing new words. 6. **noted weed,** dress by which it is recognizable, well-known garment. 8. **where,** from whence.

LXXVII. Apparently these lines accompanied the gift of a book of blank pages, a memorandum book. 3. **vacant leaves,** blank pages. 4. **learning,** mental profit; what it is is explained in line 9 ff. (Tucker Brooke). 6. **mouthed,** all-devouring (Malone); gaping (Schmidt). 7. **shady stealth,** slow progress of the shadow on the dial (Onions).

LXXVIII. With this sonnet the poet begins his complaint that his friend's patronage is being sought by other poets. The theme continues

He robs thee of and pays it thee again.
He lends thee virtue and he stole that word
From thy behaviour; beauty doth he give
And found it in thy cheek; he can afford
No praise to thee but what in thee doth live.
Then thank him not for that which he doth say,
Since what he owes thee thou thyself dost pay.

LXXX.

O, how I faint when I of you do write,
Knowing a better spirit doth use your name,
And in the praise thereof spends all his might,
To make me tongue-tied, speaking of your fame!
But since your worth, wide as the ocean is,
The humble as the proudest sail doth bear,
My saucy bark inferior far to his
On your broad main doth wilfully appear.
Your shallowest help will hold me up afloat,
Whilst he upon your soundless deep doth ride;
Or, being wrack'd, I am a worthless boat,
He of tall building and of goodly pride:
Then if he thrive and I be cast away,
The worst was this; my love was my decay.

LXXXI.

Or I shall live your epitaph to make,
Or you survive when I in earth am rotten;
From hence your memory death cannot take,
Although in me each part will be forgotten.
Your name from hence immortal life shall have,
Though I, once gone, to all the world must die:
The earth can yield me but a common grave,
When you entombed in men's eyes shall lie.
Your monument shall be my gentle verse,
Which eyes not yet created shall o'er-read,
And tongues to be your being shall rehearse
When all the breathers of this world are dead;
You still shall live—such virtue hath my pen—
Where breath most breathes, even in the mouths of men.

LXXXII.

I grant thou wert not married to my Muse
And therefore mayst without attaint o'erlook
The dedicated words which writers use
Of their fair subject, blessing every book.
Thou art as fair in knowledge as in hue,
Finding thy worth a limit past my praise,
And therefore art enforc'd to seek anew
Some fresher stamp of the time-bettering days.
And do so, love; yet when they have devis'd
What strained touches rhetoric can lend,
Thou truly fair wert truly sympathiz'd
In true plain words by thy true-telling friend;
And their gross painting might be better us'd
Where cheeks need blood; in thee it is abus'd.

LXXXIII.

I never saw that you did painting need
And therefore to your fair no painting set;
I found, or thought I found, you did exceed
The barren tender of a poet's debt;
And therefore have I slept in your report,
That you yourself being extant well might show
How far a modern quill doth come too short,
Speaking of worth, what worth in you doth grow.
This silence for my sin you did impute,
Which shall be most my glory, being dumb;
For I impair not beauty being mute,
When others would give life and bring a tomb.
There lives more life in one of your fair eyes
Than both your poets can in praise devise.

LXXXIV.

Who is it that says most? which can say more
Than this rich praise, that you alone are you?
In whose confine immured is the store
Which should example where your equal grew.
Lean penury within that pen doth dwell
That to his subject lends not some small glory;
But he that writes of you, if he can tell
That you are you, so dignifies his story,
Let him but copy what in you is writ,
Not making worse what nature made so clear,
And such a counterpart shall fame his wit,
Making his style admired every where.
You to your beauteous blessings add a curse,
Being fond on praise, which makes your praises worse.

LXXXV.

My tongue-tied Muse in manners holds her still,
While comments of your praise, richly compil'd,
Reserve their character with golden quill
And precious phrase by all the Muses fil'd.
I think good thoughts whilst other write good words,
And like unlettered clerk still cry 'Amen'
To every hymn that able spirit affords
In polish'd form of well-refined pen.
Hearing you prais'd, I say ''Tis so, 'tis true,'
And to the most of praise add something more;
But that is in my thought, whose love to you,

to the close of LXXXVI. 3. **use,** habit; i.e., of writing in celebration of his friend. 4. **under thee,** with you as their muse. 5. **on high,** loftily, exultingly. 5-6. **Thine . . . fly.** Cf. *my rude ignorance* (l. 14). 7-8. **Have . . . majesty,** a complaint of the rival poet. 9. **compile,** write, compose. 10. **influence,** inspiration; suggestion of astrological meaning. 12. **arts,** literary culture, scholarship. 13. **advance,** lift up.

LXXIX. 3. **numbers,** verse. 5. **thy lovely argument,** the celebration of thy loveliness. 11. **afford,** offer.

LXXX: 2. **a better spirit,** i.e., the rival poet, whom Shakespeare admires. 4. **tongue-tied.** Hearing his friend's virtues praised has stricken the poet with awe. 6. **as,** as well as. 10. **soundless,** unfathomable. 13. **cast away,** shipwrecked. 14. **my love . . . decay,** i.e., because it prompted me to write.

LXXXI. After belittling his own verse, the poet here takes courage and asserts his power. 1. **Or,** either. 4. **in . . . part,** every quality of mine. 5. **Your . . . have.** The theme of the perpetuation of the object's name is common throughout the *Sonnets* and is found in practically all sonnet cycles. 12. **breathers,** living people; cf. *As You Like It*, III, ii, 297.

LXXXII. 2. **attaint,** blame, discredit. 3. **dedicated,** devoted (with a punning reference to dedicatory prefaces addressed to patrons). 8. **time-bettering days.** For this theme of progress in the age see XXXII, 5. 11. **truly sympathiz'd,** faithfully described. 13. **gross painting,** extravagant compliment.

LXXXIII. 1-2. **painting . . . painting,** a continuation of the theme of *gross painting* in the preceding sonnet. 2. **fair,** beauty. 5. **slept in your report,** made no poem about you. 7. **modern,** commonplace. 14. **both your poets,** i.e., Shakespeare and the rival poet.

LXXXIV. 3-4. **In . . . grew,** in whom is contained all the qualities needed to serve as a model for any equal. 5-6. **Lean . . . glory,** i.e., it is a poor book that does not confer some honor on the person to whom it is dedicated. 11. **fame,** endow with fame. 13-14. **You . . . worse.** Probably the intended meaning is that the friend's excellence puts to shame those poets who try to praise him.

LXXXV. 2. **While . . . compil'd,** eulogies composed in fine language. 3. **Reserve their character,** preserve their features. 4. **fil'd,** polished. 11. **But that,** i.e., that which I add.

Though words come hindmost, holds his rank before.
Then others for the breath of words respect,
Me for my dumb thoughts, speaking in effect.

LXXXVI.

Was it the proud full sail of his great verse,
Bound for the prize of all too precious you,
That did my ripe thoughts in my brain inhearse,
Making their tomb the womb wherein they grew?
Was it his spirit, by spirits taught to write
Above a mortal pitch, that struck me dead?
No, neither he, nor his compeers by night
Giving him aid, my verse astonished.
He, nor that affable familiar ghost
Which nightly gulls him with intelligence,
As victors of my silence cannot boast;
I was not sick of any fear from thence:
But when your countenance fill'd up his line,
Then lack'd I matter; that enfeebled mine.

LXXXVII.

Farewell! thou art too dear for my possessing,
And like enough thou know'st thy estimate:
The charter of thy worth gives thee releasing;
My bonds in thee are all determinate.
For how do I hold thee but by thy granting?
And for that riches where is my deserving?
The cause of this fair gift in me is wanting,
And so my patent back again is swerving.
Thyself thou gav'st, thy own worth then not knowing,
Or me, to whom thou gav'st it, else mistaking;
So thy great gift, upon misprision growing,
Comes home again, on better judgement making.
Thus have I had thee, as a dream doth flatter,
In sleep a king, but waking no such matter.

LXXXVIII.

When thou shalt be dispos'd to set me light
And place my merit in the eye of scorn,
Upon thy side against myself I'll fight
And prove thee virtuous, though thou art forsworn.
With mine own weakness being best acquainted,
Upon thy part I can set down a story
Of faults conceal'd, wherein I am attainted,
That thou in losing me shalt win much glory:
And I by this will be a gainer too;
For bending all my loving thoughts on thee,
The injuries that to myself I do,
Doing thee vantage, double-vantage me.
Such is my love, to thee I so belong,
That for thy right myself will bear all wrong.

LXXXIX.

Say that thou didst forsake me for some fault,
And I will comment upon that offence;
Speak of my lameness, and I straight will halt,
Against thy reasons making no defence.
Thou canst not, love, disgrace me half so ill,
To set a form upon desired change,
As I'll myself disgrace: knowing thy will,
I will acquaintance strangle and look strange,
Be absent from thy walks, and in my tongue
Thy sweet beloved name no more shall dwell,
Lest I, too much profane, should do it wrong
And haply of our old acquaintance tell.
For thee against myself I'll vow debate,
For I must ne'er love him whom thou dost hate.

XC.

Then hate me when thou wilt; if ever, now;
Now, while the world is bent my deeds to cross,
Join with the spite of fortune, make me bow,
And do not drop in for an after-loss:
Ah, do not, when my heart hath 'scap'd this sorrow,
Come in the rearward of a conquer'd woe;
Give not a windy night a rainy morrow,
To linger out a purpos'd overthrow.
If thou wilt leave me, do not leave me last,
When other petty griefs have done their spite,
But in the onset come; so shall I taste
At first the very worst of fortune's might,
And other strains of woe, which now seem woe,
Compar'd with loss of thee will not seem so.

XCI.

Some glory in their birth, some in their skill,
Some in their wealth, some in their bodies' force,
Some in their garments, though new-fangled ill,
Some in their hawks and hounds, some in their horse;
And every humour hath his adjunct pleasure,
Wherein it finds a joy above the rest:
But these particulars are not my measure;
All these I better in one general best.
Thy love is better than high birth to me,
Richer than wealth, prouder than garments' cost,
Of more delight than hawks or horses be;
And having thee, of all men's pride I boast:
Wretched in this alone, that thou mayst take
All this away and me most wretched make.

XCII.

But do thy worst to steal thyself away,
For term of life thou art assured mine,
And life no longer than thy love will stay,
For it depends upon that love of thine.
Then need I not to fear the worst of wrongs,
When in the least of them my life hath end.
I see a better state to me belongs
Than that which on thy humour doth depend;
Thou canst not vex me with inconstant mind,
Since that my life on thy revolt doth lie.
O, what a happy title do I find,

14. **speaking in effect,** i.e., which have the quality of speech.

LXXXVI. This sonnet is devoted to generous praise of his rival. 3. **inhearse,** coffin up. 4. **Making . . . grew.** Cf. *Romeo and Juliet*, II, iii, 9-10. 7. **compeers by night,** spirits visiting and aiding the poet in his dreams. (See also the *familiar ghost* in line 9.) 8. **astonished,** struck dumb. 10. **gulls . . . intelligence,** deceives him with rumors or secret information (?). 13. **countenance fill'd up,** approval repaired any defect in; also, beauty served as subject for.

LXXXVII. 4. **determinate,** ended, expired (a legal term). 6. **riches,** wealth; a singular noun. 8. **patent,** charter granting rights of monopoly; hence, privilege. 11. **upon misprision growing,** arising out of error or mistake. 13. **as . . . flatter.** Cf. *Romeo and Juliet*, V, i, 1-5. 14. **no such matter,** nothing of the sort.

LXXXVIII. 1. **set me light,** despise me, make light of me. 6. **Upon thy part,** in support of your opinions.

LXXXIX. 3. **halt,** limp. 6. **To . . . change,** to provide a pretext for (in the interest of justifying) your change of affection. 7. **disgrace,** disfigure. 8. **acquaintance,** familiarity (with the friend). **strangle,** put an end to. 9. **walks,** haunts. 12. **haply,** perchance. 13. **vow debate,** entertain hostility, quarrel.

XC. 2. **cross,** thwart. 4. **do . . . after-loss,** i.e., do not casually add to my sorrow at some future time. 6. **in the rearward of,** at the end of. 8. **purpos'd,** intended. 13. **strains,** kinds.

XCI. 4. **horse,** horses. 5. **his,** its.

XCII. 5-6. **Then . . . end,** i.e., my very least misfortune would be my worst—that is, the loss of your friendship. 10. **Since . . . lie,** since

Happy to have thy love, happy to die!
  But what 's so blessed-fair that fears no blot?
  Thou mayst be false, and yet I know it not.

XCIII.

So shall I live, supposing thou art true,
Like a deceived husband; so love's face
May still seem love to me, though alter'd new;
Thy looks with me, thy heart in other place:
For there can live no hatred in thine eye,
Therefore in that I cannot know thy change.
In many's looks the false heart's history
Is writ in moods and frowns and wrinkles strange,
But heaven in thy creation did decree
That in thy face sweet love should ever dwell;
Whate'er thy thoughts or thy heart's workings be,
Thy looks should nothing thence but sweetness tell.
  How like Eve's apple doth thy beauty grow,
  If thy sweet virtue answer not thy show!

XCIV.

They that have pow'r to hurt and will do none,
That do not do the thing they most do show,
Who, moving others, are themselves as stone,
Unmoved, cold, and to temptation slow,
They rightly do inherit heaven's graces
And husband nature's riches from expense;
They are the lords and owners of their faces,
Others but stewards of their excellence.
The summer's flow'r is to the summer sweet,
Though to itself it only live and die,
But if that flow'r with base infection meet,
The basest weed outbraves his dignity:
  For sweetest things turn sourest by their deeds;
  Lilies that fester smell far worse than weeds.

XCV.

How sweet and lovely dost thou make the shame
Which, like a canker in the fragrant rose,
Doth spot the beauty of thy budding name!
O, in what sweets dost thou thy sins enclose!
That tongue that tells the story of thy days,
Making lascivious comments on thy sport,
Cannot dispraise but in a kind of praise;
Naming thy name blesses an ill report.
O, what a mansion have those vices got
Which for their habitation chose out thee,
Where beauty's veil doth cover every blot,
And all things turn to fair that eyes can see!
  Take heed, dear heart, of this large privilege;
  The hardest knife ill-us'd doth lose his edge.

XCVI.

Some say thy fault is youth, some wantonness;
Some say thy grace is youth and gentle sport;
Both grace and faults are lov'd of more and less;
Thou mak'st faults graces that to thee resort.
As on the finger of a throned queen
The basest jewel will be well esteem'd,
So are those errors that in thee are seen
To truths translated and for true things deem'd.
How many lambs might the stern wolf betray,
If like a lamb he could his looks translate!
How many gazers mightst thou lead away,
If thou wouldst use the strength of all thy state!
  But do not so; I love thee in such sort
  As, thou being mine, mine is thy good report.

XCVII.

How like a winter hath my absence been
From thee, the pleasure of the fleeting year!
What freezings have I felt, what dark days seen!
What old December's bareness every where!
And yet this time remov'd was summer's time,
The teeming autumn, big with rich increase,
Bearing the wanton burthen of the prime,
Like widow'd wombs after their lords' decease:
Yet this abundant issue seem'd to me
But hope of orphans and unfathered fruit;
For summer and his pleasures wait on thee,
And, thou away, the very birds are mute;
  Or, if they sing, 'tis with so dull a cheer
  That leaves look pale, dreading the winter's near.

XCVIII.

From you have I been absent in the spring,
When proud-pied April dress'd in all his trim
Hath put a spirit of youth in every thing,
That heavy Saturn laugh'd and leap'd with him.
Yet nor the lays of birds nor the sweet smell
Of different flowers in odour and in hue
Could make me any summer's story tell,
Or from their proud lap pluck them where they grew;
Nor did I wonder at the lily's white,
Nor praise the deep vermilion in the rose;
They were but sweet, but figures of delight,
Drawn after you, you pattern of all those.
  Yet seem'd it winter still, and, you away,
  As with your shadow I with these did play:

XCIX.

The forward violet thus did I chide:
Sweet thief, whence didst thou steal thy sweet that
    smells,
If not from my love's breath? The purple pride
Which on thy soft cheek for complexion dwells
In my love's veins thou hast too grossly dy'd.
The lily I condemned for thy hand,
And buds of marjoram had stol'n thy hair:
The roses fearfully on thorns did stand,
One blushing shame, another white despair;
A third, nor red nor white, had stol'n of both

if you desert me it will cost me my life.
XCIII. 14. **show,** appearance, looks.
XCIV. 1. **and will do none,** i.e., hurt without intending to do so. 2. **show,** i.e., show themselves capable of; or, seem to do. 6. **expense,** waste, expenditure. 7. **They . . . faces,** they are completely masters of themselves. 12. **his,** its. 14. **Lilies . . . weeds.** This line appears in the anonymous tragedy *Edward III*, usually dated before 1595.
XCV. 2. **canker,** worm that destroys buds and leaves. The figure is frequent in the early works of Shakespeare; cf. XXXV, 4 and LXX, 7. 6. **sport,** amours. 14. **his,** its.
XCVI. 3. **more and less,** great and small. 8. **translated,** transformed. 9. **stern,** cruel. 12. **the strength . . . state,** the full glory of thy eminent position. 13-14. **But . . . report.** Cf. XXXVI, 13-14.

XCVII. A new group of three sonnets begins here. They deal with the theme of absence. 5. **time remov'd,** absence. 7. **prime,** spring.
XCVIII. 4. **That,** so that. 5. **nor the lays,** neither the songs. 7. **any summer's story,** any pleasant story. 11. **but sweet . . . delight,** only sweetness, only delightful forms.
XCIX. This sonnet has fifteen lines, the first being merely introductory. It is devoted to the figure, general among sonneteers, of the flowers stealing their beauty from the beloved. 1. **forward,** early. 6. **for thy hand,** i.e., because it has stolen its whiteness from thy hand. 7. **buds of marjoram.** These are dark purple red, and it may be that the reference is to color, although marjoram is noted for its sweet scent.

And to his robb'ry had annex'd thy breath;
But, for his theft, in pride of all his growth
A vengeful canker eat him up to death.
  More flowers I noted, yet I none could see
  But sweet or colour it had stol'n from thee.

C.

Where art thou, Muse, that thou forget'st so long
To speak of that which gives thee all thy might?
Spend'st thou thy fury on some worthless song,
Dark'ning thy pow'r to lend base subjects light?
Return, forgetful Muse, and straight redeem
In gentle numbers time so idly spent;
Sing to the ear that doth thy lays esteem
And gives thy pen both skill and argument.
Rise, resty Muse, my love's sweet face survey,
If Time have any wrinkle graven there;
If any, be a satire to decay,
And make Time's spoils despised every where.
  Give my love fame faster than Time wastes life;
  So thou prevent'st his scythe and crooked knife.

CI.

O truant Muse, what shall be thy amends
For thy neglect of truth in beauty dy'd?
Both truth and beauty on my love depends;
So dost thou too, and therein dignified.
Make answer, Muse: wilt thou not haply say
'Truth needs no colour, with his colour fix'd;
Beauty no pencil, beauty's truth to lay;
But best is best, if never intermix'd'?
Because he needs no praise, wilt thou be dumb?
Excuse not silence so; for 't lies in thee
To make him much outlive a gilded tomb,
And to be prais'd of ages yet to be.
  Then do thy office, Muse; I teach thee how
  To make him seem long hence as he shows now.

CII.

My love is strength'ned, though more weak in seeming;
I love not less, though less the show appear:
That love is merchandiz'd whose rich esteeming
The owner's tongue doth publish every where.
Our love was new and then but in the spring
When I was wont to greet it with my lays,
As Philomel in summer's front doth sing
And stops her pipe in growth of riper days:
Not that the summer is less pleasant now
Than when her mournful hymns did hush the night,
But that wild music burthens every bough
And sweets grown common lose their dear delight.
  Therefore like her I sometime hold my tongue,
  Because I would not dull you with my song.

CIII.

Alack, what poverty my Muse brings forth,
That having such a scope to show her pride,
The argument all bare is of more worth
Than when it hath my added praise beside!
O, blame me not, if I no more can write!
Look in your glass, and there appears a face
That over-goes my blunt invention quite,
Dulling my lines and doing me disgrace.
Were it not sinful then, striving to mend,
To mar the subject that before was well?
For to no other pass my verses tend
Than of your graces and your gifts to tell;
  And more, much more, than in my verse can sit
  Your own glass shows you when you look in it.

CIV.

To me, fair friend, you never can be old,
For as you were when first your eye I ey'd,
Such seems your beauty still. Three winters cold
Have from the forests shook three summers' pride,
Three beauteous springs to yellow autumn turn'd
In process of the seasons have I seen,
Three April perfumes in three hot Junes burn'd,
Since first I saw you fresh, which yet are green.
Ah! yet doth beauty, like a dial-hand,
Steal from his figure and no pace perceiv'd;
So your sweet hue, which methinks still doth stand,
Hath motion and mine eye may be deceiv'd:
  For fear of which, hear this, thou age unbred;
  Ere you were born was beauty's summer dead.

CV.

Let not my love be call'd idolatry,
Nor my beloved as an idol show,
Since all alike my songs and praises be
To one, of one, still such, and ever so.
Kind is my love to-day, to-morrow kind,
Still constant in a wondrous excellence;
Therefore my verse to constancy confin'd,
One thing expressing, leaves out difference.
'Fair, kind, and true' is all my argument,
'Fair, kind, and true' varying to other words;
And in this change is my invention spent,
Three themes in one, which wondrous scope affords.
  'Fair, kind, and true,' have often liv'd alone,
  Which three till now never kept seat in one.

12. **in pride . . . growth,** in his prime.

C. This sonnet marks another break. The implication is that the poet has been using his pen in unworthy themes—possibly plays. 3. **fury,** poetic inspiration. 6. **numbers,** verse. 8. **argument,** subject. 9. **resty,** inactive, inert. 10. **If,** to see if. 11. **satire,** satirist; rebuke (Alden). 14. **prevent'st,** anticipatest, forestallest.

CI. This sonnet has to do, like LXXXII-LXXXIV, with writing in praise of the friend; the main purpose is to preserve his virtues for the future. 5. **haply,** perhaps. 6. **colour . . . colour,** pretense . . . hue; cf. *1 Henry VI*, II, iv, 34-36. 7. **lay,** lay in, as with a brush.

CII. 3. **merchandiz'd,** degraded by being treated as "a thing of sale." 7. **Philomel,** the nightingale; regarded as feminine. **front,** forehead, beginning. 10. **mournful hymns,** reference to the tragic tale of Philomela.

CIII. 2. **her pride,** power of which she is proud. 3. **argument . . . bare,** subject unadorned. 7. **blunt invention,** unpolished style. 8. **Dulling,** making uninteresting. 11. **pass,** result.

CIV. 4. **pride,** splendor. 9-10. **Ah . . . perceiv'd,** beauty slips away like the shadow of the hand on the dial. 11. **hue,** appearance, complexion. 13. **this,** i.e., the poet's message to posterity.

CV. 4. **still,** always. 8. **difference.** Difference in logic divides genus from species; there has been no division in the completeness of the poet's theme. 11. **this change,** variations on this theme. **spent,** expended. 14. **Which . . . one,** the friend alone possesses all three of the virtues.

CVI. 1. **wasted,** past. 2. **wights,** persons. 5. **blazon,** heraldic metaphor, meaning here "glorification." 7. **antique,** accented on the first syllable. 8. **master,** possess, control. 11. **And, for,** and because. **divining,** guessing. 13. **For,** for even.

CVII. 1-2. **soul . . . world.** "Soul of the world" is a conception in the mystical philosophy of Giordano Bruno. 3. **lease,** term, allotted time. 4. **Suppos'd . . . doom.** The fears supposed his love would have an end. But it is not so (Stopes). 5. **mortal moon,** usually taken as a reference to Queen Elizabeth, ill or deceased. She was known as Diana,

CVI.

When in the chronicle of wasted time
I see descriptions of the fairest wights,
And beauty making beautiful old rhyme
In praise of ladies dead and lovely knights,
Then, in the blazon of sweet beauty's best,
Of hand, of foot, of lip, of eye, of brow,
I see their antique pen would have express'd
Even such a beauty as you master now.
So all their praises are but prophecies
Of this our time, all you prefiguring;
And, for they look'd but with divining eyes,
They had not skill enough your worth to sing:
  For we, which now behold these present days,
  Have eyes to wonder, but lack tongues to praise.

CVII.

Not mine own fears, nor the prophetic soul
Of the wide world dreaming on things to come,
Can yet the lease of my true love control,
Suppos'd as forfeit to a confin'd doom.
The mortal moon hath her eclipse endur'd
And the sad augurs mock their own presage;
Incertainties now crown themselves assur'd
And peace proclaims olives of endless age.
Now with the drops of this most balmy time
My love looks fresh, and Death to me subscribes,
Since, spite of him, I'll live in this poor rhyme,
While he insults o'er dull and speechless tribes:
  And thou in this shalt find thy monument,
  When tyrants' crests and tombs of brass are spent.

CVIII.

What 's in the brain that ink may character
Which hath not figur'd to thee my true spirit?
What 's new to speak, what new to register,
That may express my love or thy dear merit?
Nothing, sweet boy; but yet, like prayers divine,
I must each day say o'er the very same,
Counting no old thing old, thou mine, I thine,
Even as when first I hallowed thy fair name.
So that eternal love in love's fresh case
Weighs not the dust and injury of age,
Nor gives to necessary wrinkles place,
But makes antiquity for aye his page,
  Finding the first conceit of love there bred
  Where time and outward form would show it dead.

CIX.

O, never say that I was false of heart,
Though absence seem'd my flame to qualify.
As easy might I from myself depart
As from my soul, which in thy breast doth lie:
That is my home of love: if I have rang'd,
Like him that travels I return again,
Just to the time, not with the time exchang'd,
So that myself bring water for my stain.
Never believe, though in my nature reign'd
All frailties that besiege all kinds of blood,
That it could so preposterously be stain'd,
To leave for nothing all thy sum of good;
  For nothing this wide universe I call,
  Save thou, my rose; in it thou art my all.

CX.

Alas, 'tis true I have gone here and there
And made myself a motley to the view,
Gor'd mine own thoughts, sold cheap what is most
    dear,
Made old offences of affections new;
Most true it is that I have look'd on truth
Askance and strangely: but, by all above,
These blenches gave my heart another youth,
And worse essays prov'd thee my best of love.
Now all is done, have what shall have no end:
Mine appetite I never more will grind
On newer proof, to try an older friend,
A god in love, to whom I am confin'd.
  Then give me welcome, next my heaven the best,
  Even to thy pure and most most loving breast.

CXI.

O, for my sake do you with Fortune chide,
The guilty goddess of my harmful deeds,
That did not better for my life provide
Than public means which public manners breeds.
Thence comes it that my name receives a brand,
And almost thence my nature is subdu'd
To what it works in, like the dyer's hand:
Pity me then and wish I were renew'd;
Whilst, like a willing patient, I will drink
Potions of eisel 'gainst my strong infection;
No bitterness that I will bitter think,
Nor double penance, to correct correction.
  Pity me then, dear friend, and I assure ye
  Even that your pity is enough to cure me.

CXII.

Your love and pity doth th' impression fill
Which vulgar scandal stamp'd upon my brow;
For what care I who calls me well or ill,

Cynthia, and other epithets of the moon goddess. Hotson explains as a reference to the Armada. 6. **And . . . presage,** and the solemn prophets of disaster are mocked by their own predictions. 7. **Incertainties . . . assur'd,** uncertainties have triumphantly given way to certainties. 8. **endless age,** i.e., without foreseen end. 10. **subscribes,** yields. 12. **insults,** triumphs. 14. **crests,** trophies in a tomb.

CVIII. 1. **character,** write. 2. **figur'd,** revealed. 7. **Counting . . . thine,** a summation of themes of praise—perpetuity and unity. 9. **fresh case,** youthful body. 10. **Weighs not,** is unconcerned about. 12. **page,** servant. 13. **conceit,** conception.

CIX. 2. **qualify,** temper, moderate. 5. **rang'd,** traveled, wandered. 7. **Just,** punctual. **exchang'd,** changed. 8. **So . . . stain,** i.e., so that I myself provide the means of excusing my absence. 12. **To . . . good,** to abandon all thy virtues for a mere nothing.

CX. Sometimes taken as an indictment by Shakespeare of the actor's trade. It means, however, only that he has traveled and made new acquaintances, but has now returned to his only permanent attachment. 2. **motley,** parti-colored dress of the professional fool. 4. **offences,** trespasses. **affections,** passions. 5. **truth,** constancy. 6. **Askance,** sidewise. **strangely,** mistrustfully. 7. **blenches,** swervings. 8. **essays,** experiments (in friendship). 9. **have . . . end,** take what is eternal (my friendship). 10. **grind,** whet. 11. **newer proof,** further experiment. 12. **god in love,** i.e., his friend.

CXI. 1. **chide,** argue. 4. **Than . . . breeds,** i.e., than providing me a means of livelihood which depends on catering to the public (a probable reference to Shakespeare's career as an actor). 5. **receives a brand,** is disgraced (through prejudice against his occupation). 8. **renew'd,** restored to what he was by nature. 10. **eisel,** vinegar, used as an antiseptic against the plague. 12. **Nor . . . correction,** i.e., no bitter cure will seem worse to me than the disease it corrects.

CXII. 1. **impression,** scar. Cf. *brand*, CXI, 5. **fill,** efface.

So you o'er-green my bad, my good allow?
You are my all the world, and I must strive
To know my shames and praises from your tongue;
None else to me, nor I to none alive,
That my steel'd sense or changes right or wrong.
In so profound abysm I throw all care
Of others' voices, that my adder's sense
To critic and to flatterer stopped are.
Mark how with my neglect I do dispense:
You are so strongly in my purpose bred
That all the world besides methinks are dead.

CXIII.

Since I left you, mine eye is in my mind;
And that which governs me to go about
Doth part his function and is partly blind,
Seems seeing, but effectually is out;
For it no form delivers to the heart
Of bird, of flow'r, or shape, which it doth latch:
Of his quick objects hath the mind no part,
Nor his own vision holds what it doth catch;
For if it see the rud'st or gentlest sight,
The most sweet favour or deformed'st creature,
The mountain or the sea, the day or night,
The crow or dove, it shapes them to your feature:
Incapable of more, replete with you,
My most true mind thus mak'th mine eye untrue.

CXIV.

Or whether doth my mind, being crown'd with you,
Drink up the monarch's plague, this flattery?
Or whether shall I say, mine eye saith true,
And that your love taught it this alchemy,
To make of monsters and things indigest
Such cherubins as your sweet self resemble,
Creating every bad a perfect best,
As fast as objects to his beams assemble?
O, 'tis the first; 'tis flatt'ry in my seeing,
And my great mind most kingly drinks it up:
Mine eye well knows what with his gust is 'greeing,
And to his palate doth prepare the cup:
If it be poison'd, 'tis the lesser sin
That mine eye loves it and doth first begin.

CXV.

Those lines that I before have writ do lie,
Even those that said I could not love you dearer:
Yet then my judgement knew no reason why
My most full flame should afterwards burn clearer.
But reckoning time, whose million'd accidents
Creep in 'twixt vows and change decrees of kings,
Tan sacred beauty, blunt the sharp'st intents,
Divert strong minds to th' course of alt'ring things;
Alas, why, fearing of time's tyranny,
Might I not then say 'Now I love you best,'
When I was certain o'er incertainty,
Crowning the present, doubting of the rest?
Love is a babe; then might I not say so,
To give full growth to that which still doth grow.

CXVI.

Let me not to the marriage of true minds
Admit impediments. Love is not love
Which alters when it alteration finds,
Or bends with the remover to remove:
O, no! it is an ever-fixed mark
That looks on tempests and is never shaken;
It is the star to every wand'ring bark,
Whose worth 's unknown, although his height be taken.
Love 's not Time's fool, though rosy lips and cheeks
Within his bending sickle's compass come;
Love alters not with his brief hours and weeks,
But bears it out even to the edge of doom.
If this be error and upon me prov'd,
I never writ, nor no man ever lov'd.

CXVII.

Accuse me thus: that I have scanted all
Wherein I should your great deserts repay,
Forgot upon your dearest love to call,
Whereto all bonds do tie me day by day;
That I have frequent been with unknown minds
And given to time your own dear-purchas'd right;
That I have hoisted sail to all the winds
Which should transport me farthest from your sight.
Book both my wilfulness and errors down
And on just proof surmise accumulate;
Bring me within the level of your frown,
But shoot not at me in your wakened hate;
Since my appeal says I did strive to prove
The constancy and virtue of your love.

CXVIII.

Like as, to make our appetites more keen,
With eager compounds we our palate urge,
As, to prevent our maladies unseen,
We sicken to shun sickness when we purge,
Even so, being full of your ne'er-cloying sweetness,
To bitter sauces did I frame my feeding
And, sick of welfare, found a kind of meetness
To be diseas'd ere that there was true needing.
Thus policy in love, t' anticipate
The ills that were not, grew to faults assured

4. **o'er-green my bad,** cover my evil with green leaves. **allow,** approve. 7-8. **None . . . wrong,** i.e., no one else but you affects my fixed sense of what is right and wrong (?). 8. **steel'd sense,** what is engraven on my sense. 10. **adder's sense.** Adders were supposed to be deaf. 12. **Mark . . . dispense,** i.e., see how I disregard the opinion of others. 13. **You . . . bred,** i.e., you are such a powerful influence over my intentions.

CXIII. 2. **governs,** guides. 3. **part his,** divide its. 4. **effectually,** in reality. 5. **For . . . heart,** I have no knowledge of what passes. 6. **latch,** catch or receive (the sight or sound). 12. **shapes . . . feature,** makes them resemble you.

CXIV. 1, 3. **Or whether,** indicates alternative possibilities. 1. **crown'd with you,** elevated by possession of you. 4. **alchemy,** science of transmuting base metals. 5. **indigest,** chaotic, formless. 6. **cherubins,** another suggestion of the youth and beauty of the friend. 10. **it,** i.e., he accepts the cup of flattery. 11. **what . . . 'greeing,** what suits the eye's taste. Steevens sees in this and the following lines an allusion to tasters for the food of kings.

CXV. 5. **But reckoning time,** merely considering the power of Time as a destroyer. 7. **Tan,** darken, i.e., coarsen. 9. **fearing of,** fearing. 13. **then,** therefore. **so,** i.e., "Now I love you best" (l. 10).

CXVI. 4. **Or . . . remove,** or inclines to inconstancy at the demand of the inconstant. 8. **Whose . . . taken.** The star has an influence over and above the determination of its altitude (for purposes of navigation). 9. **fool,** plaything. 11. **his,** i.e., Time's. 12. **But . . . doom,** endures or holds out to the very day of judgment.

CXVII. 4. **bonds,** a pun on the legal sense of the word. 5. **unknown minds,** persons not worth knowing. 6. **And . . . right,** squandered your rights in me on temporary matters and alliances.

CXVIII. 2. **eager,** pungent, bitter. 3. **prevent,** anticipate. 9-12. **Thus . . . cured,** thus the attempt of love to forestall the evils of satiety had brought in sickness, when in health I had taken medicine for disease. 12. **rank of goodness,** sick with good health.

CXIX. 1. **Siren tears,** deceitful tears of seductive women. 2. **lim-**

And brought to medicine a healthful state
Which, rank of goodness, would by ill be cured:
But thence I learn, and find the lesson true,
Drugs poison him that so fell sick of you.

CXIX.

What potions have I drunk of Siren tears,
Distill'd from limbecks foul as hell within,
Applying fears to hopes and hopes to fears,
Still losing when I saw myself to win!
What wretched errors hath my heart committed,
Whilst it hath thought itself so blessed never!
How have mine eyes out of their spheres been fitted
In the distraction of this madding fever!
O benefit of ill! now I find true
That better is by evil still made better;
And ruin'd love, when it is built anew,
Grows fairer than at first, more strong, far greater.
So I return rebuk'd to my content
And gain by ill thrice more than I have spent.

CXX.

That you were once unkind befriends me now,
And for that sorrow which I then did feel
Needs must I under my transgression bow,
Unless my nerves were brass or hammered steel.
For if you were by my unkindness shaken
As I by yours, y' have pass'd a hell of time,
And I, a tyrant, have no leisure taken
To weigh how once I suffered in your crime.
O, that our night of woe might have rememb'red
My deepest sense, how hard true sorrow hits,
And soon to you, as you to me then, tend'red
The humble salve which wounded bosoms fits!
But that your trespass now becomes a fee;
Mine ransoms yours, and yours must ransom me.

CXXI.

'Tis better to be vile than vile esteemed,
When not to be receives reproach of being,
And the just pleasure lost which is so deemed
Not by our feeling but by others' seeing:
For why should others' false adulterate eyes
Give salutation to my sportive blood?
Or on my frailties why are frailer spies,
Which in their wills count bad what I think good?
No, I am that I am, and they that level
At my abuses reckon up their own:
I may be straight, though they themselves be bevel;
By their rank thoughts my deeds must not be shown;
Unless this general evil they maintain,
All men are bad, and in their badness reign.

CXXII.

Thy gift, thy tables, are within my brain
Full character'd with lasting memory,
Which shall above that idle rank remain
Beyond all date, even to eternity;
Or at the least, so long as brain and heart
Have faculty by nature to subsist;
Till each to raz'd oblivion yield his part
Of thee, thy record never can be miss'd.
That poor retention could not so much hold,
Nor need I tallies thy dear love to score;
Therefore to give them from me was I bold,
To trust those tables that receive thee more:
To keep an adjunct to remember thee
Were to import forgetfulness in me.

CXXIII.

No, Time, thou shalt not boast that I do change:
Thy pyramids built up with newer might
To me are nothing novel, nothing strange;
They are but dressings of a former sight.
Our dates are brief, and therefore we admire
What thou dost foist upon us that is old,
And rather make them born to our desire
Than think that we before have heard them told.
Thy registers and thee I both defy,
Not wond'ring at the present nor the past,
For thy records and what we see doth lie,
Made more or less by thy continual haste.
This I do vow and this shall ever be;
I will be true, despite thy scythe and thee.

CXXIV.

If my dear love were but the child of state,
It might for Fortune's bastard be unfather'd,
As subject to Time's love or to Time's hate,
Weeds among weeds, or flowers with flowers gather'd.
No, it was builded far from accident;
It suffers not in smiling pomp, nor falls
Under the blow of thralled discontent,
Whereto th' inviting time our fashion calls:
It fears not Policy, that heretic,
Which works on leases of short-numb'red hours,
But all alone stands hugely politic,
That it nor grows with heat nor drowns with show'rs.
To this I witness call the fools of time,
Which die for goodness, who have liv'd for crime.

CXXV.

Were 't aught to me I bore the canopy,
With my extern the outward honouring,

becks, vessels used in distillation. 7. **How . . . fitted,** how my eyes have popped out in convulsive fit.

CXX. 4. **nerves,** sinews. 9. **our night of woe,** the dark and woeful time of our estrangement. **rememb'red,** reminded. 11. **soon,** as soon. **tend'red,** offered. 13. **fee,** compensation.

CXXI. 2. **When . . . being,** when not to be vile receives the reproach of vileness. 3-4. **which . . . seeing,** which is measured by the opinions of others, not by our own conscience. 5-6. **For . . . blood,** why should others who are really wicked greet as an equal me, who am only mirthful. 8. **in their wills,** at their pleasure. 9. **that,** what. 11. **bevel,** out of square, crooked. 13. **this general evil,** this general principle of evil.

CXXII. 1. **tables,** writing tablets. 2. **Full . . . memory,** written all over in my lasting memory. 3. **above . . . rank,** i.e., the rank or importance of that memorandum book. 7. **raz'd oblivion,** obliterating forgetfulness. 9. **retention,** i.e., the book, an instrument for retaining memoranda. 10. **tallies,** sticks notched to serve for reckoning. 14. **import,** impute.

CXXIII. 2. **Thy . . . might.** Taken by Hotson to refer to the erection by Pope Sixtus v of four obelisks (known as *pyramids*) in Rome in 1586 and succeeding years; see Introduction. 4. **They . . . sight,** they but repeat all objects in new forms; apparent assertion of the indestructibility of matter. 7-8. **And . . . told,** and rather hold the impression that they are our new structures than remember that we have seen them before.

CXXIV. 1. **child of state,** child of rank or power; possibly circumstance, which is always changing (Lee). 10. **leases . . . hours,** possible allusion to short-term leases granted by heretics to their friends to avoid confiscation of property. 11. **politic,** wise, prudent. 13-14. **To . . . crime,** I call to witness the transitory unworthy loves (sports of time; see CVI), whose death was a virtue since their life was a crime (Dowden).

CXXV. 1. **bore the canopy,** i.e., honor you (or another) as those are honored over whose heads a cloth of state is carried (Pooler). 2. **With . . . honouring,** i.e., to honor the outward by the outward (Alden).

Or laid great bases for eternity,
Which prove more short than waste or ruining?
Have I not seen dwellers on form and favour
Lose all, and more, by paying too much rent,
For compound sweet forgoing simple savour,
Pitiful thrivers, in their gazing spent?
No, let me be obsequious in thy heart,
And take thou my oblation, poor but free,
Which is not mix'd with seconds, knows no art,
But mutual render, only me for thee.
  Hence, thou suborn'd informer! a true soul
  When most impeach'd stands least in thy control.

CXXVI.

O thou, my lovely boy, who in thy power
Dost hold Time's fickle glass, his sickle, hour;
Who hast by waning grown, and therein show'st
Thy lovers withering as thy sweet self grow'st;
If Nature, sovereign mistress over wrack,
As thou goest onwards, still will pluck thee back,
She keeps thee to this purpose, that her skill
May time disgrace and wretched minutes kill.
Yet fear her, O thou minion of her pleasure!
She may detain, but not still keep, her treasure:
Her audit, though delay'd, answer'd must be,
And her quietus is to render thee.

CXXVII.

In the old age black was not counted fair,
Or if it were, it bore not beauty's name;
But now is black beauty's successive heir,
And beauty slander'd with a bastard shame:
For since each hand hath put on nature's power,
Fairing the foul with art's false borrow'd face,
Sweet beauty hath no name, no holy bower,
But is profan'd, if not lives in disgrace.
Therefore my mistress' eyes are raven black,
Her eyes so suited, and they mourners seem
At such who, not born fair, no beauty lack,
Sland'ring creation with a false esteem:
  Yet so they mourn, becoming of their woe,
  That every tongue says beauty should look so.

CXXVIII.

How oft, when thou, my music, music play'st,
Upon that blessed wood whose motion sounds
With thy sweet fingers, when thou gently sway'st
The wiry concord that mine ear confounds,
Do I envy those jacks that nimble leap
To kiss the tender inward of thy hand,
Whilst my poor lips, which should that harvest reap,
At the wood's boldness by thee blushing stand!
To be so tickled, they would change their state
And situation with those dancing chips,
O'er whom thy fingers walk with gentle gait,
Making dead wood more blest than living lips.
  Since saucy jacks so happy are in this,
  Give them thy fingers, me thy lips to kiss.

CXXIX.

Th' expense of spirit in a waste of shame
Is lust in action; and till action, lust
Is perjur'd, murd'rous, bloody, full of blame,
Savage, extreme, rude, cruel, not to trust,
Enjoy'd no sooner but despised straight,
Past reason hunted, and no sooner had
Past reason hated, as a swallowed bait
On purpose laid to make the taker mad;
Mad in pursuit and in possession so;
Had, having, and in quest to have, extreme;
A bliss in proof, and prov'd, a very woe;
Before, a joy propos'd; behind, a dream.
  All this the world well knows; yet none knows well
  To shun the heaven that leads men to this hell.

CXXX.

My mistress' eyes are nothing like the sun;
Coral is far more red than her lips' red;
If snow be white, why then her breasts are dun;
If hairs be wires, black wires grow on her head.
I have seen roses damask'd, red and white,
But no such roses see I in her cheeks;
And in some perfumes is there more delight
Than in the breath that from my mistress reeks.
I love to hear her speak, yet well I know
That music hath a far more pleasing sound;
I grant I never saw a goddess go;
My mistress, when she walks, treads on the ground:
  And yet, by heaven, I think my love as rare
  As any she belied with false compare.

CXXXI.

Thou art as tyrannous, so as thou art,
As those whose beauties proudly make them cruel;
For well thou know'st to my dear doting heart
Thou art the fairest and most precious jewel.
Yet, in good faith, some say that thee behold
Thy face hath not the power to make love groan:
To say they err I dare not be so bold,
Although I swear it to myself alone.
And, to be sure that is not false I swear,
A thousand groans, but thinking on thy face,
One on another's neck, do witness bear
Thy black is fairest in my judgement's place.

3. **Or . . . eternity,** laid foundations for lasting fame. 6. **by paying too much rent,** by overdoing their obligations. 7. **For . . . savour,** foregoing actual love for the sake of obsequious flattery. 8. **spent,** wasted (by merely looking at outward honor). 9. **obsequious,** devoted. 10. **oblation,** offering. 11. **seconds,** inferior parts, as of grain. 12. **mutual render,** fair exchange. 13. **suborn'd informer,** perjured witness. 14. **impeach'd,** charged with treason.

CXXVI. With this sonnet (which is made up of six couplets) the first great cycle, that addressed to the friend, comes to an end. 2. **fickle glass,** ever-changing hourglass. Some editors prefer the reading: *fickle hour*. 3. **by waning grown,** grown more youthful as your age increases. 5. **wrack,** ruin. Nature is mistress of decay because of her power of restoration. 10. **She . . . treasure.** The poet warns his friend that, although nature will keep and restore him for a time, Time will ultimately triumph over him. 11. **audit,** i.e., Nature's account to Time. 12. **quietus,** discharge, quittance.

Here begins a separate series of sonnets, apparently belonging to the same period of time as XXXIII-XLII. They are addressed to, or refer to, a dark woman who passes from loving the poet to loving the friend.

CXXVII. 1. **In . . . fair.** Black was traditionally associated with ugliness; cf. *Love's Labour's Lost*, IV, iii, 247, 261 ff. 3. **successive heir,** lawful successor. 6. **borrow'd face,** i.e., cosmetics. 9. **eyes,** i.e., eyebrows. 10. **so suited,** i.e., similarly black. 11. **At,** for. **no beauty lack,** i.e., nonetheless seem attractive. 12. **Sland'ring . . . esteem,** dishonoring nature by a false reputation for beauty. 13. **becoming of,** gracing.

CXXVIII. 5. **jacks,** upright pieces of wood fixed to the key-lever and fitted with a quill which plucked the strings of the virginal (Onions). 6. **tender inward,** delicate inside.

CXXIX. 1. **expense,** expenditure, waste. 5. **Enjoy'd . . . straight.** Cf. *The Rape of Lucrece*, 211-212, 742. 11. **in proof,** while experienced. **prov'd,** i.e., afterwards.

In nothing art thou black save in thy deeds,
And thence this slander, as I think, proceeds.

CXXXII.

Thine eyes I love, and they, as pitying me,
Knowing thy heart torments me with disdain,
Have put on black and loving mourners be,
Looking with pretty ruth upon my pain.
And truly not the morning sun of heaven
Better becomes the grey cheeks of the east,
Nor that full star that ushers in the even
Doth half that glory to the sober west,
As those two mourning eyes become thy face:
O, let it then as well beseem thy heart
To mourn for me, since mourning doth thee grace,
And suit thy pity like in every part.
Then will I swear beauty herself is black
And all they foul that thy complexion lack.

CXXXIII.

Beshrew that heart that makes my heart to groan
For that deep wound it gives my friend and me!
Is 't not enough to torture me alone,
But slave to slavery my sweet'st friend must be?
Me from myself thy cruel eye hath taken,
And my next self thou harder hast engrossed:
Of him, myself, and thee, I am forsaken;
A torment thrice threefold thus to be crossed.
Prison my heart in thy steel bosom's ward,
But then my friend's heart let my poor heart bail;
Whoe'er keeps me, let my heart be his guard;
Thou canst not then use rigour in my gaol:
And yet thou wilt; for I, being pent in thee,
Perforce am thine, and all that is in me.

CXXXIV.

So, now I have confess'd that he is thine,
And I myself am mortgag'd to thy will,
Myself I'll forfeit, so that other mine
Thou wilt restore, to be my comfort still:
But thou wilt not, nor he will not be free,
For thou art covetous and he is kind;
He learn'd but surety-like to write for me
Under that bond that him as fast doth bind.
The statute of thy beauty thou wilt take,
Thou usurer, that put'st forth all to use,
And sue a friend came debtor for my sake;
So him I lose through my unkind abuse.
Him have I lost; thou hast both him and me:
He pays the whole, and yet am I not free.

CXXXV.

Whoever hath her wish, thou hast thy 'Will,'
And 'Will' to boot, and 'Will' in overplus;
More than enough am I that vex thee still,
To thy sweet will making addition thus.
Wilt thou, whose will is large and spacious,
Not once vouchsafe to hide my will in thine?
Shall will in others seem right gracious,
And in my will no fair acceptance shine?
The sea, all water, yet receives rain still
And in abundance addeth to his store;
So thou, being rich in 'Will,' add to thy 'Will'
One will of mine, to make thy large 'Will' more.
Let no unkind, no fair beseechers kill;
Think all but one, and me in that one 'Will.'

CXXXVI.

If thy soul check thee that I come so near,
Swear to thy blind soul that I was thy 'Will,'
And will, thy soul knows, is admitted there;
Thus far for love my love-suit, sweet, fulfil.
'Will' will fulfil the treasure of thy love,
Ay, fill it full with wills, and my will one.
In things of great receipt with ease we prove
Among a number one is reckon'd none:
Then in the number let me pass untold,
Though in thy stores' account I one must be;
For nothing hold me, so it please thee hold
That nothing me, a something, sweet, to thee:
Make but my name thy love, and love that
still,
And then thou lovest me, for my name is 'Will.'

CXXXVII.

Thou blind fool, Love, what dost thou to mine eyes,
That they behold, and see not what they see?
They know what beauty is, see where it lies,
Yet what the best is take the worst to be.
If eyes corrupt by over-partial looks
Be anchor'd in the bay where all men ride,
Why of eyes' falsehood hast thou forged hooks,
Whereto the judgement of my heart is tied?
Why should my heart think that a several plot
Which my heart knows the wide world's common
place?
Or mine eyes seeing this, say this is not,
To put fair truth upon so foul a face?
In things right true my heart and eyes have err'd,
And to this false plague are they now transferr'd.

CXXXVIII.

When my love swears that she is made of truth
I do believe her, though I know she lies,
That she might think me some untutor'd youth,
Unlearned in the world's false subtleties.
Thus vainly thinking that she thinks me young,
Although she knows my days are past the best,

CXXX. 5. **damask'd,** mingled red and white. 8. **reeks,** issues as smell. 11. **go,** walk. 14. **she,** woman. **compare,** comparison.

CXXXI. 1. **so as thou art,** even as you are (dark, not considered handsome). 11. **One on another's neck,** one after another. 12. **my judgement's place,** my critical opinion.

CXXXII. 4. **ruth,** pity. 12. **suit thy pity like,** clothe your pity in the same way.

CXXXIII. 6. **my next self,** my dearest friend. 8. **crossed,** tried. 9. **steel bosom's ward,** the prison cell of thy hard heart.

CXXXIV. 3. **that other mine,** my other self, my friend. 9. **statute,** security; e.g., of a usurer. 11. **came,** i.e., who became. 12. **unkind abuse,** unnatural ill-usage (of me).

CXXXV. This and the following sonnet ring the changes on the word *will*—desire, temper, passion, and the poet's name; possibly also the friend's name. 13. **Let . . . kill,** a puzzling line, in which *unkind* is usually taken as a noun, i.e., unkind one. Several editors favor Tyler's suggestion, "Let no unkind 'no' your beseechers kill."

CXXXVI. 5. **fulfil,** fill full. 7. **receipt,** capacity. 8. **one is reckon'd none,** variant of the common saying "one is no number." 9. **untold,** uncounted. 13-14. **Make . . . Will,** love only my name (something less than loving myself), and then thou lovest me, for my name is Will, and I myself am all will, that is, all desire (Dowden). The lines may also be taken as a surrender of his mistress to his friend, also named Will.

CXXXVII. A vituperative sonnet, in which the poet blames love for blinding his eyes, so that he has chosen the worst for the best; cf. CXIII. 6. **ride,** with an implication of sexual promiscuity. 9. **several plot,** private field. 10. **common,** open, promiscuous.

CXXXVIII. This sonnet is I in *The Passionate Pilgrim.* 2. **believe her,** i.e., pretend to believe her. 3. **That,** let that.

Simply I credit her false-speaking tongue:
On both sides thus is simple truth suppress'd.
But wherefore says she not she is unjust?
And wherefore say not I that I am old?
O, love's best habit is in seeming trust,
And age in love loves not to have years told:
Therefore I lie with her and she with me,
And in our faults by lies we flattered be.

CXXXIX.

O, call not me to justify the wrong
That thy unkindness lays upon my heart;
Wound me not with thine eye but with thy tongue;
Use power with power and slay me not by art.
Tell me thou lov'st elsewhere, but in my sight,
Dear heart, forbear to glance thine eye aside:
What need'st thou wound with cunning when thy might
Is more than my o'er-press'd defence can bide?
Let me excuse thee: ah! my love well knows
Her pretty looks have been mine enemies,
And therefore from my face she turns my foes,
That they elsewhere might dart their injuries:
Yet do not so; but since I am near slain,
Kill me outright with looks and rid my pain.

CXL.

Be wise as thou art cruel; do not press
My tongue-tied patience with too much disdain;
Lest sorrow lend me words and words express
The manner of my pity-wanting pain.
If I might teach thee wit, better it were,
Though not to love, yet, love, to tell me so;
As testy sick men, when their deaths be near,
No news but health from their physicians know;
For if I should despair, I should grow mad,
And in my madness might speak ill of thee:
Now this ill-wresting world is grown so bad,
Mad slanderers by mad ears believed be.
That I may not be so, nor thou belied,
Bear thine eyes straight, though thy proud heart go wide.

CXLI.

In faith, I do not love thee with mine eyes,
For they in thee a thousand errors note;
But 'tis my heart that loves what they despise,
Who in despite of view is pleas'd to dote;
Nor are mine ears with thy tongue's tune delighted,
Nor tender feeling, to base touches prone,
Nor taste, nor smell, desire to be invited
To any sensual feast with thee alone:
But my five wits nor my five senses can
Dissuade one foolish heart from serving thee,
Who leaves unsway'd the likeness of a man,
Thy proud heart's slave and vassal wretch to be:
Only my plague thus far I count my gain,
That she that makes me sin awards me pain.

CXLII.

Love is my sin and thy dear virtue hate,
Hate of my sin, grounded on sinful loving:
O, but with mine compare thou thine own state,
And thou shalt find it merits not reproving;
Or, if it do, not from those lips of thine,
That have profan'd their scarlet ornaments
And seal'd false bonds of love as oft as mine,
Robb'd others' beds' revenues of their rents.
Be it lawful I love thee, as thou lov'st those
Whom thine eyes woo as mine importune thee:
Root pity in thy heart, that when it grows
Thy pity may deserve to pitied be.
If thou dost seek to have what thou dost hide,
By self-example mayst thou be denied!

CXLIII.

Lo! as a careful housewife runs to catch
One of her feathered creatures broke away,
Sets down her babe and makes all swift dispatch
In pursuit of the thing she would have stay,
Whilst her neglected child holds her in chase,
Cries to catch her whose busy care is bent
To follow that which flies before her face,
Not prizing her poor infant's discontent;
So runn'st thou after that which flies from thee,
Whilst I thy babe chase thee afar behind;
But if thou catch thy hope, turn back to me,
And play the mother's part, kiss me, be kind:
So will I pray that thou mayst have thy 'Will,'
If thou turn back, and my loud crying still.

CXLIV.

Two loves I have of comfort and despair,
Which like two spirits do suggest me still:
The better angel is a man right fair,
The worser spirit a woman colour'd ill.
To win me soon to hell, my female evil
Tempteth my better angel from my side,
And would corrupt my saint to be a devil,
Wooing his purity with her foul pride.
And whether that my angel be turn'd fiend
Suspect I may, yet not directly tell;
But being both from me, both to each friend,
I guess one angel in another's hell:
Yet this shall I ne'er know, but live in doubt,
Till my bad angel fire my good one out.

7. **Simply,** pretending to be foolish. **credit,** believe. 9. **unjust,** unfaithful. 11. **habit,** deportment, with play on the idea of habiliment, that which is put on. 12. **told,** counted. 13. **lie with,** deceive (with sexual pun).

CXXXIX. 3. **Wound . . . tongue.** Cf. *Romeo and Juliet*, II, iv, 14, and *3 Henry VI*, V, vi, 26. 4. **with power,** i.e., directly. **art,** artifice. 11. **foes,** i.e., the "pretty looks" of l. 10.

CXL. 4. **The . . . pain,** the nature of my pain, on which you bestow no pity. 5. **wit,** wisdom, prudence. 6. **to tell me so,** to tell me thou dost love me. 11. **ill-wresting,** misinterpreting. 13-14. **That . . . wide,** that I may not be mad and you may not be exposed, control your eyes, whatever course your heart may take.

CXLI. 6. **base touches,** sensual indulgence. 9. **five wits,** intellectual, the same in number as the five senses—the common sense, imagination, fancy, judgment, and memory. 11. **Who . . . man,** i.e., in my foolish heart, which abandons the government of my personality. 14. **pain,** punishment.

CXLII. 2. **Hate . . . loving,** i.e., hatred of the adulterous character of my love. 6. **profan'd,** desecrated, as a temple. **scarlet ornaments,** lips (here likened to the red wax used to seal documents). 7. **seal'd . . . love,** i.e., with kisses; cf. *The Merchant of Venice*, II, vi, 6. 8. **Robb'd . . . rents,** implication of adultery. 13-14. **If . . . denied,** if thou dost seek to have the pity thou hidst from me, thou mayst by thy own example be denied it.

CXLIII. 4. **pursuit,** accented on first syllable. 13. **will . . . Will,** pun on will, desire, and the Christian name. Whether the *Will* refers to the poet or the rival friend is a matter of doubt.

CXLIV. The second sonnet in *The Passionate Pilgrim*. It depicts the conflict in the poet's mind between his affection for his friend and his mistress. 2. **suggest,** tempt (Malone); prompt (to good or evil). 6. **Tempteth . . . side.** Cf. *Othello*, V, ii, 208. 8. **foul,** wicked. 11. **from me,** away from me. The poet suspects they are together. 12. **I . . . hell,** i.e., I suspect the friend lies in the embraces of the woman (referring to her sexual organs as the gates of hell). 14. **fire**

CXLV.

Those lips that Love's own hand did make
Breath'd forth the sound that said 'I hate'
To me that languish'd for her sake;
But when she saw my woeful state,
Straight in her heart did mercy come,
Chiding that tongue that ever sweet
Was us'd in giving gentle doom,
And taught it thus anew to greet;
'I hate' she alter'd with an end,
That follow'd it as gentle day
Doth follow night, who like a fiend
From heaven to hell is flown away;
'I hate' from hate away she threw,
And sav'd my life, saying 'not you.'

CXLVI.

Poor soul, the centre of my sinful earth,
[Thrall to] these rebel pow'rs that thee array,
Why dost thou pine within and suffer dearth,
Painting thy outward walls so costly gay?
Why so large cost, having so short a lease,
Dost thou upon thy fading mansion spend?
Shall worms, inheritors of this excess,
Eat up thy charge? is this thy body's end?
Then, soul, live thou upon thy servant's loss,
And let that pine to aggravate thy store;
Buy terms divine in selling hours of dross;
Within be fed, without be rich no more:
So shalt thou feed on Death, that feeds on men,
And Death once dead, there 's no more dying then.

CXLVII.

My love is as a fever, longing still
For that which longer nurseth the disease,
Feeding on that which doth preserve the ill,
Th' uncertain sickly appetite to please.
My reason, the physician to my love,
Angry that his prescriptions are not kept,
Hath left me, and I desperate now approve
Desire is death, which physic did except.
Past cure I am, now reason is past care,
And frantic-mad with evermore unrest;
My thoughts and my discourse as madmen's are,
At random from the truth vainly express'd;
For I have sworn thee fair and thought thee bright,
Who art as black as hell, as dark as night.

CXLVIII.

O me, what eyes hath Love put in my head,
Which have no correspondence with true sight!
Or, if they have, where is my judgement fled,
That censures falsely what they see aright?
If that be fair whereon my false eyes dote,
What means the world to say it is not so?
If it be not, then love doth well denote
Love's eye is not so true as all men's 'No.'
How can it? O, how can Love's eye be true,
That is so vex'd with watching and with tears?
No marvel then, though I mistake my view;
The sun itself sees not till heaven clears.
O cunning Love! with tears thou keep'st me blind,
Lest eyes well-seeing thy foul faults should find.

CXLIX.

Canst thou, O cruel! say I love thee not,
When I against myself with thee partake?
Do I not think on thee, when I forgot
Am of myself, all tyrant, for thy sake?
Who hateth thee that I do call my friend?
On whom frown'st thou that I do fawn upon?
Nay, if thou lour'st on me, do I not spend
Revenge upon myself with present moan?
What merit do I in myself respect,
That is so proud thy service to despise,
When all my best doth worship thy defect,
Commanded by the motion of thine eyes?
But, love, hate on, for now I know thy mind;
Those that can see thou lov'st and I am blind.

CL.

O, from what pow'r hast thou this pow'rful might
With insufficiency my heart to sway?
To make me give the lie to my true sight,
And swear that brightness doth not grace the day?
Whence hast thou this becoming of things ill,
That in the very refuse of thy deeds
There is such strength and warrantise of skill
That, in my mind, thy worst all best exceeds?
Who taught thee how to make me love thee more
The more I hear and see just cause of hate?
O, though I love what others do abhor,
With others thou shouldst not abhor my state:
If thy unworthiness rais'd love in me,
More worthy I to be belov'd of thee.

CLI.

Love is too young to know what conscience is;
Yet who knows not conscience is born of love?
Then, gentle cheater, urge not my amiss,
Lest guilty of my faults thy sweet self prove:
For, thou betraying me, I do betray
My nobler part to my gross body's treason;
My soul doth tell my body that he may
Triumph in love; flesh stays no farther reason;

. . . out, drive him out with fire (with suggestion of venereal disease).

CXLV. A sonnet in eight-syllable meter. Critics have regarded it as out of place, or have rejected it. It has been compared to Lyly's "Cupid and my Campaspe played." 6-7. **Chiding . . . doom.** Her tongue was accustomed to dismiss her lover's guilt. 13. **'I . . . threw,'** i.e., she took away the pain and danger by saying, "I do not hate you."

CXLVI. 1. **sinful earth,** the body. 2. **[Thrall to],** anonymous conjecture; Q repeats "My sinfull earth" from l. 1; Globe, *et al.*, leave blank. 8. **thy charge,** that on which thou hast expended so much. 10. **aggravate,** increase. 11. **Buy terms divine,** purchase long periods of divine salvation.

CXLVII. This sonnet is associated in theme with CXLI and CXLIV—his hopeless love for an unworthy mistress. 1. **still,** always. 5. **My . . . love.** Cf. *The Merry Wives of Windsor*, II, i, 5. 7-8. **I . . . except,** I, being in despair, now recognize that desire to be fatal, which took exception to the teaching of physic (Stopes). 9. **cure . . . care,** an adaptation of the proverb, things past cure are past care.

CXLVIII. 4. **censures,** judges. 6. **What . . . so.** The opinion of the world refutes the warped judgment of the poet. 11. **mistake my view,** err in what I see. 13. **O cunning Love,** perhaps refers to the mistress as well as to the god of love.

CXLIX. 2. **partake,** take part (against myself). 3-4. **Do . . . sake,** it is for your sake that I neglect and tyrannize over myself. 7. **lour'st,** frown'st.

CL. 2. **insufficiency,** lack of every virtue and charm. 5. **becoming . . . ill,** ability to render evil things attractive. 7. **warrantise of skill,** warrant or pledge of mental ability. 13. **rais'd,** with bawdy suggestion.

CLI. The vein of the preceding sonnet continues; cf. CXLVI. 1. **Love . . . is,** cf. CXV. 2. **Yet . . . love?** Who knows not that the power of love awakens conscience? 3. **cheater,** rogue; with possible reference to "escheater," a king's officer charged with reversions of land. **amiss,** sin. 6. **My . . . treason.** She was the cause of his betraying his nobler part to the lusts of his body. 8. **stays,** awaits. **reason,** reasoning.

But, rising at thy name, doth point out thee
As his triumphant prize. Proud of this pride,
He is contented thy poor drudge to be,
To stand in thy affairs, fall by thy side.
No want of conscience hold it that I call
Her 'love' for whose dear love I rise and fall.

CLII.

In loving thee thou know'st I am forsworn,
But thou art twice forsworn, to me love swearing,
In act thy bed-vow broke and new faith torn
In vowing new hate after new love bearing.
But why of two oaths' breach do I accuse thee,
When I break twenty? I am perjur'd most;
For all my vows are oaths but to misuse thee
And all my honest faith in thee is lost,
For I have sworn deep oaths of thy deep kindness,
Oaths of thy love, thy truth, thy constancy,
And, to enlighten thee, gave eyes to blindness,
Or made them swear against the thing they see;
For I have sworn thee fair; more perjur'd I,
To swear against the truth so foul a lie!

CLIII.

Cupid laid by his brand, and fell asleep:
A maid of Dian's this advantage found,
And his love-kindling fire did quickly steep
In a cold valley-fountain of that ground;
Which borrow'd from this holy fire of Love
A dateless lively heat, still to endure,
And grew a seething bath, which yet men prove
Against strange maladies a sovereign cure.
But at my mistress' eye Love's brand new-fired,
The boy for trial needs would touch my breast;
I, sick withal, the help of bath desired,
And thither hied, a sad distemper'd guest,
But found no cure: the bath for my help lies
Where Cupid got new fire—my mistress' eyes.

CLIV.

The little Love-god lying once asleep
Laid by his side his heart-inflaming brand,
Whilst many nymphs that vow'd chaste life to keep
Came tripping by; but in her maiden hand
The fairest votary took up that fire
Which many legions of true hearts had warm'd;
And so the general of hot desire
Was sleeping by a virgin hand disarm'd.
This brand she quenched in a cool well by,
Which from Love's fire took heat perpetual,
Growing a bath and healthful remedy
For men diseas'd; but I, my mistress' thrall,
Came there for cure, and this by that I prove,
Love's fire heats water, water cools not love.

9. **rising,** with bawdy suggestion (continued in *point, stand, fall*). 10. **Proud of,** swelling with.

CLII. 9. **kindness,** affection, tenderness. 11. **to enlighten thee,** in order to invest thee with brightness; she was a dark lady.

The following two sonnets have no direct connection with those preceding. They are adaptations of epigrams in the Palatine Anthology, Greek poems of the fifth century (translated into Latin in the sixteenth century). The discovery was made by Hertzbert, *Shakespeare Jahrbuch*, XIII (1878), 158-162. Malone suggested that they were early exercises of the poet.

CLIII. 1. **brand,** firebrand, torch. 2. **Dian,** Diana, goddess of chastity. 6. **dateless,** endless, eternal. 7. **seething bath,** spring of hot medicinal waters. 9. **But . . . new-fired,** love has kindled his torch at my mistress' eyes.

CLIV. 7. **general,** cause and commander, i.e., Cupid. 12. **thrall,** slave, bondman. 13. **this by that,** i.e., *this* is what follows in l. 14, *by that* is by my coming which failed to cure me (Pooler).

SUGGESTIONS FOR READING AND RESEARCH

Abbreviations Used

Shakespeare Newsletter	*ShN*
Shakespeare Quarterly	*SQ*
Shakespeare Studies	*ShakS*
Shakespeare Survey	*ShS*

WORKS OF REFERENCE

Abbott, E. A. *A Shakespearian Grammar*. New edition, London, 1870.

Berman, Ronald. *A Reader's Guide to Shakespeare's Plays*. Rev. ed. Glenview, Ill., 1973.

Bullough, Geoffrey. *Narrative and Dramatic Sources of Shakespeare*. 7 vols. London, 1957—.

Campbell, Oscar James, and Edward G. Quinn, eds. *The Reader's Encyclopedia of Shakespeare*. New York, 1966.

Chambers, E. K. *William Shakespeare: A Study of Facts and Problems*. 2 vols. Oxford, 1930.

Ebisch, Walther, in collaboration with L. L. Schücking. *A Shakespeare Bibliography*. Oxford, 1931. *A Supplement for the Years 1930–1935*. Oxford, 1937.

Greg, W. W. *A Bibliography of the English Printed Drama to the Restoration*. 4 vols. London, 1939–1959.

———, ed. *Shakespeare Quarto Facsimiles*. London, 1939—. (An incomplete set; Greg's work is being supplemented by Charlton Hinman.)

Harbage, Alfred. *Annals of English Drama, 975–1700*. Rev. S. Schoenbaum. Philadelphia, 1964.

Hart, Alfred. *Shakespeare and the Homilies*. Melbourne, 1934.

Hinman, Charlton, ed. *The Norton Facsimile: The First Folio of Shakespeare*. New York, 1968.

Hosley, Richard, ed. *Shakespeare's Holinshed*. New York, 1968.

Joseph, Sister Miriam. *Shakespeare's Use of the Arts of Language*. New York, 1947. Reprinted in part as *Rhetoric in Shakespeare's Time* (1962).

Kökeritz, Helge. *Shakespeare's Names*. New Haven, 1959.

———. *Shakespeare's Pronunciation*. New Haven, 1953.

Long, John. *Shakespeare's Use of Music: Comedies*. Gainesville, Fla., 1955. *Final Comedies*, 1961; *Histories and Tragedies*, 1971.

Muir, Kenneth. *Shakespeare's Sources*. 2 vols. London, 1957.

Muir, Kenneth, and S. Schoenbaum, eds. *A New Companion to Shakespeare Studies*. London and New York, 1971.

Munro, John, ed. *The Shakespeare Allusion Book*. 2 vols. London and New York, 1909; reissued 1932.

Naylor, Edward W. *Shakespeare and Music*. New ed., London, 1931.

Noble, Richmond. *Shakespeare's Biblical Knowledge*. London, 1935.

———. *Shakespeare's Use of Song*. London, 1923.

Onions, C. T. *A Shakespeare Glossary*. 2nd ed. Oxford, 1919.

Partridge, Eric. *Shakespeare's Bawdy*. London, 1947, 1955.

Publications of the Modern Language Association of America (*PMLA*). Annual Bibliography.

Satin, Joseph, ed. *Shakespeare and His Sources*. Boston, 1966.

Schmidt, Alexander. *Shakespeare-Lexicon*. 5th ed. Berlin, 1962.

Seng, Peter J. *The Vocal Songs in the Plays of Shakespeare*. Cambridge, Mass., 1967.

Shakespeare Newsletter.

Shakespeare Quarterly.

Shakespeare Studies.

Shakespeare Survey.

Shakespearean Research Opportunities.

Spevack, Marvin. *The Harvard Concordance to Shakespeare*. Cambridge, Mass., 1973.

Sternfeld, Frederick W. *Music in Shakespearean Tragedy*. London, 1963, 1967.

Studies in Philology. Annual Bibliography.

Thomson, James A. K. *Shakespeare and the Classics*. London, 1952.

LIFE IN SHAKESPEARE'S ENGLAND

Allen, Don Cameron. *The Star-Crossed Renaissance*. Durham, N.C., 1941.

Baker, Herschel. *The Image of Man: A Study of the Idea of Human Dignity in Classical Antiquity, the Middle Ages and the Renaissance*. Cambridge, Mass., 1961. (First published in 1947 as *The Dignity of Man*.)

———. *The Wars of Truth: Studies in the Decay of Christian Humanism in the Earlier Seventeenth Century*. Cambridge, Mass., 1952.

Bindoff, S. T., et al., eds. *Elizabethan Government and*

Society. Essays presented to Sir John Neale. London, 1961.
Brown, Ivor. *Shakespeare in His Time*. Edinburgh, 1960.
Bush, Douglas. *The Renaissance and English Humanism*. Toronto, 1939.
Buxton, John. *Elizabethan Taste*. London, 1963.
Byrne, Muriel St. Clare. *Elizabethan Life in Town and Country*. 8th ed. London, 1970.
Caspari, Fritz. *Humanism and the Social Order in Tudor England*. Chicago, 1954.
Cassirer, Ernst. *The Platonic Renaissance in England*, trans. J. E. Pettegrove. Austin, Texas, 1953.
Chambers, R. W. *Thomas More*. London and New York, 1935.
Clapham, John. *A Concise Economic History of Britain from the Earliest Times to 1750*. Cambridge, Eng., 1949.
Craig, Hardin. *The Enchanted Glass*. New York, 1936.
Einstein, Lewis. *Tudor Ideals*. New York, 1921.
Elton, G. R. *The Tudor Revolution in Government*. Cambridge, Eng., 1959.
Ferguson, Arthur B. *The Articulate Citizen and the English Renaissance*. Durham, N.C., 1965.
Fisher, F. J. "Commercial Trends and Policy in Sixteenth-Century England," *The Economic History Review*, X (1940), 95–117.

Harbage, Alfred. *Shakespeare's Audience*. New York, 1941.

Harrison, G. B. *An Elizabethan Journal*. London, 1928; supplements.
———. *A Jacobean Journal . . . 1603–1606*. London, 1941.
———. *A Second Jacobean Journal . . . 1607 to 1610*. Ann Arbor, Mich., 1958.
Haydn, Hiram. *The Counter-Renaissance*. New York, 1950.
Huizinga, Johan. *The Waning of the Middle Ages*. London, 1924; Baltimore, 1955.
Judges, A. V., ed. *The Elizabethan Underworld*. London and New York, 1930.
Kelso, Ruth. *The Doctrine of the English Gentleman in the Sixteenth Century*. Urbana, Ill., 1929.
Knappen, M. M. *Tudor Puritanism*. Chicago, 1939.
Knights, L. C. *Drama and Society in the Age of Jonson*. London, 1937.
Kocher, Paul. *Science and Religion in Elizabethan England*. San Marino, Calif., 1953.
Lovejoy, A. O. *The Great Chain of Being*. Cambridge, Mass., 1936.
Mattingly, Garrett. *The Armada*. Boston, 1959.
Mazzeo, Joseph A. *Renaissance and Revolution*. New York, 1965.
Neale, John E. *Elizabeth I and Her Parliaments*. 2 vols. London and New York, 1953–1958.
———. *The Elizabethan House of Commons*. London, 1949.
———. *Queen Elizabeth I*. London, 1934; New York, 1957.
Nichols, John, ed. *The Progresses and Public Processions of Queen Elizabeth*. 3 vols. London, 1823.
Nicoll, Allardyce, ed. *Shakespeare in His Own Age*. *ShS 17* (1964).
Ramsey, Peter. *Tudor Economic Problems*. London, 1963.
Read, Conyers. *Lord Burghley and Queen Elizabeth*. New York, 1960.
———. *Mr. Secretary Cecil and Queen Elizabeth*. New York, 1955.
———. *Mr. Secretary Walsingham and the Policy of Queen Elizabeth*. 3 vols. Oxford, 1925.
———. *The Tudors: Personalities and Practical Politics in Sixteenth Century England*. New York, 1936.
Rowse, A. L. *The England of Elizabeth: The Structure of Society*. London, 1951.
Seebohm, Frederic. *The Oxford Reformers*. 3rd ed. London, 1887, 1911.
Spencer, Theodore. *Shakespeare and the Nature of Man*. New York, 1942.
Stone, Lawrence. *The Crisis of the Aristocracy, 1558–1641*. Oxford, 1965.
Stow, John. *Survey of London*, ed. C. L. Kingsford. Oxford, 1971.
Strachey, G. Lytton. *Elizabeth and Essex*. London and New York, 1928.
Tawney, R. H. *Religion and the Rise of Capitalism*. New York, 1926, 1962.
Tayler, Edward W. *Nature and Art in Renaissance Literature*. New York, 1964.
Tillyard, E. M. W. *The Elizabethan World Picture*. London, 1943, 1967.
Wilson, F. P. *Elizabethan and Jacobean*. Oxford, 1945.
Wilson, J. Dover, ed. *Life in Shakespeare's England*. Cambridge, Eng., 1911; 2nd ed., 1926.
Wright, Louis B. *Middle-Class Culture in Elizabethan England*. Chapel Hill, N.C., 1935.
Zeeveld, W. Gordon. *Foundations of Tudor Policy*. Cambridge, Mass., 1948.

LONDON THEATRES AND DRAMATIC COMPANIES

Adams, John Cranford. *The Globe Playhouse*. Rev. ed. New York, 1961.
Adams, Joseph Quincy. *Shakespearean Playhouses*. Boston, 1917, 1960.
Armstrong, William A. *The Elizabethan Private Theatres: Facts and Problems*. London, 1958.
Baldwin, T. W. *The Organization and Personnel of the Shakespearean Company*. Princeton, 1927.
Beckerman, Bernard. *Shakespeare at the Globe, 1599–1609*. New York, 1962, 1967.

Bentley, Gerald Eades. *The Jacobean and Caroline Stage.* 7 vols. Oxford, 1941–1968.

———. "Shakespeare and the Blackfriars Theatre," *ShS 1* (1948), 38–50.

Brown, Ivor. *Shakespeare and the Actors.* London, 1970.

Brown, John Russell. *Shakespeare's Plays in Performance.* London, 1966.

Campbell, Lily B. *Scenes and Machines on the English Stage During the Renaissance.* Cambridge, Eng., 1923.

Chambers, E. K. *The Elizabethan Stage.* 4 vols. Oxford, 1923.

Feuillerat, Albert, ed. *Documents Relating to the Office of the Revels in the Time of Queen Elizabeth.* Louvain, 1908.

Foakes, R. A., and R. T. Rickert, eds. *Henslowe's Diary.* London, 1961.

Gildersleeve, Virginia C. *Government Regulation of the Elizabethan Drama.* New York, 1908.

Greg, W. W., ed. *Dramatic Documents from the Elizabethan Playhouses; Stage Plots; Actors' Parts; Prompt Books.* 2 vols. Oxford, 1931.

———, ed. *Henslowe Papers.* London, 1907.

Harbage, Alfred. *Theatre for Shakespeare.* Toronto, 1955.

Harrison, G. B. *Elizabethan Plays and Players.* London, 1940, 1956.

Hillebrand, H. N. *The Child Actors.* Urbana, Ill., 1926.

Hodges, C. Walter. *The Globe Restored.* London, 1953.

Hosley, Richard. "The Discovery-space in Shakespeare's Globe," *ShS 12* (1959), 35–46.

———. "The Gallery over the Stage in the Public Playhouse of Shakespeare's Time," *SQ*, VIII (1957), 15–31.

———. "A Reconstruction of the Second Blackfriars," *The Elizabethan Theatre*, ed. David Galloway. Toronto, 1969.

———. "Shakespeare's Use of a Gallery over the Stage," *ShS 10* (1957), 77–89.

———. "Was There a Music-room in Shakespeare's Globe?" *ShS 13* (1960), 113–123.

Joseph, Bertram L. *Acting Shakespeare.* London, 1960.

Kernodle, G. R. *From Art to Theatre: Form and Convention in the Renaissance.* Chicago, 1944.

King, T. J. *Shakespearean Staging, 1599–1642.* Cambridge, Mass., 1971.

Lawrence, W. J. *The Elizabethan Playhouse and Other Studies.* Stratford-upon-Avon, 1912, 1913; New York, 1963.

———. *The Physical Conditions of the Elizabethan Public Playhouse.* Cambridge, Mass., 1927.

———. *Pre-Restoration Stage Studies.* Cambridge, Mass., 1927.

Linthicum, Marie C. *Costume in the Drama of Shakespeare and His Contemporaries.* Oxford, 1936.

Murray, John T. *English Dramatic Companies, 1558–1642.* London and Boston, 1910.

Nagler, Alois M. *Shakespeare's Stage*, tr. R. Manheim. New Haven, 1958.

Nungezer, Edwin. *A Dictionary of Actors.* London and New Haven, 1929.

Reynolds, George F. *The Staging of Elizabethan Plays at the Red Bull Theater, 1605–1625.* New York, 1940.

Seltzer, Daniel. "Elizabethan Acting in *Othello*," *SQ*, X (1959), 201–210.

———. "The Staging of the Last Plays," *Later Shakespeare*, ed. John Russell Brown and Bernard Harris, pp. 127–165. Stratford-upon-Avon Studies 8. London, 1966.

Smith, Irwin. *Shakespeare's Blackfriars Playhouse.* New York, 1964.

———. *Shakespeare's Globe Playhouse.* New York, 1956.

Thompson, Elbert N. S. *The Controversy Between the Puritans and the Stage.* New Haven, 1903, 1966.

Thorndike, Ashley H. *Shakespeare's Theatre.* New York, 1916.

Venezky, Alice. *Pageantry on the Shakespearean Stage.* New York, 1951.

Wallace, C. W. *The Children of the Chapel at Blackfriars, 1597–1603.* Lincoln, Neb., 1908.

Wickham, Glynne. *Early English Stages, 1300 to 1660.* London, 1959–1972.

SHAKESPEARE'S TEXTS

Bowers, Fredson. *Bibliography and Textual Criticism.* Oxford, 1964.

———. *On Editing Shakespeare.* Charlottesville, Va., 1966.

———. *On Editing Shakespeare and the Elizabethan Dramatists.* Philadelphia, 1955.

———. *Textual and Literary Criticism.* Cambridge, Eng., 1959.

Chambers, E. K. *William Shakespeare: A Study of Facts and Problems.* 2 vols. Oxford, 1930.

Craig, Hardin. *A New Look at Shakespeare's Quartos.* Stanford, 1961.

Duthie, G. I. *Elizabethan Shorthand and the First Quarto of "King Lear."* Oxford, 1949.

Greg, W. W. *Collected Papers*, ed. J. C. Maxwell. Oxford, 1966.

———. *The Editorial Problem in Shakespeare.* 3rd ed. Oxford, 1954.

———. *Principles of Emendation in Shakespeare.* London, 1928.

———. *The Shakespeare First Folio: Its Bibliographical and Textual History.* Oxford, 1955.

Hart, Alfred. *Stolne and Surreptitious Copies: A Comparative Study of Shakespeare's Bad Quartos.* Melbourne and London, 1942.

Hinman, Charlton. *The Printing and Proof-Reading of*

the First Folio of Shakespeare. 2 vols. Oxford, 1963.
Honigmann, E. A. J. *The Stability of Shakespeare's Text*. London and Lincoln, Neb., 1965.
McKerrow, R. B. *An Introduction to Bibliography for Literary Students*. Oxford, 1927.
———. *Prolegomena for the Oxford Shakespeare*. Oxford, 1939.
Pollard, Alfred W. *Shakespeare Folios and Quartos: A Study in the Bibliography of Shakespeare's Plays, 1594–1685*. London, 1909.
———. *Shakespeare's Fight with the Pirates and the Problems of the Transmission of His Text*. Rev. ed. Cambridge, Eng., 1937.
Pollard, Alfred W., and others. *Shakespeare's Hand in the Play of Sir Thomas More*. Cambridge, Eng., 1923.
Sisson, C. J. *New Readings in Shakespeare*. 2 vols. Cambridge, Eng., 1956.
Walker, Alice. *Textual Problems of the First Folio*. Cambridge, Eng., 1953.
Williams, George W., ed. *The Most Excellent and Lamentable Tragedie of Romeo and Juliet: A Critical Edition*. Durham, N.C., 1964.
Wilson, J. Dover. *The Manuscript of Shakespeare's "Hamlet" and the Problems of Its Transmission*. 2 vols. Cambridge, Eng., 1934.

SHAKESPEARE'S LIFE

Adams, Joseph Quincy. *A Life of William Shakespeare*. Boston, 1923.
Alexander, Peter. *Shakespeare's Life and Art*. New ed. New York, 1961.
Baldwin, T. W. *William Shakspere's Small Latine and Lesse Greeke*. 2 vols. Urbana, Ill., 1944.
Bentley, Gerald Eades. *Shakespeare: A Biographical Handbook*. New Haven, 1961.
Chambers, E. K. *William Shakespeare: A Study of Facts and Problems*. 2 vols. Oxford, 1930.
Chute, Marchette. *Shakespeare of London*. New York, 1949.
Eccles, Mark. *Shakespeare in Warwickshire*. Madison, Wis., 1961.
Fripp, Edgar I. *Shakespeare, Man and Artist*. 2 vols. London, 1938.
Halliday, F. E. *Shakespeare: A Pictorial Biography*. London, 1956, 1964.
Harbage, Alfred. *Conceptions of Shakespeare*. Cambridge, Mass., 1966.
Hotson, Leslie. *I, William Shakespeare, do Appoint Thomas Russell, Esquire*. London and New York, 1937, 1938.
———. *Shakespeare Versus Shallow*. London, 1931.
———. *Shakespeare's Sonnets Dated and Other Essays*. London, 1949.
Lee, Sidney. *A Life of William Shakespeare*. New ed. London, 1925.
Quennell, Peter. *Shakespeare: A Biography*. New York, 1963.
Reese, M. M. *Shakespeare: His World and His Work*. London and New York, 1953.
Rowse, A. L. *William Shakespeare: A Biography*. New York, 1963.
Schoenbaum, S. *Shakespeare's Lives*. Oxford and New York, 1970.
Smart, John S. *Shakespeare: Truth and Tradition*. New ed. Oxford, 1966.
Spencer, Hazelton. *The Art and Life of William Shakespeare*. New York, 1940.
Stopes, C. C. *Shakespeare's Family*. London, 1901.
———. *Shakespeare's Warwickshire Contemporaries*. Stratford-upon-Avon, 1897, 1907.
Wilson, J. Dover. *The Essential Shakespeare*. Cambridge, Eng., 1932.

CRITICAL STUDIES RELATING TO MANY OR ALL OF THE WORKS

Arthos, John. *The Art of Shakespeare*. New York, 1964.
Bethell, S. L. *Shakespeare and the Popular Dramatic Tradition*. London and Durham, N.C., 1944.
Bloom, Allan, with Harry T. Jaffa. *Shakespeare's Politics*. New York, 1964.
Bloom, Edward A., ed. *Shakespeare 1564–1964*. Providence, R.I., 1964.
Bradby, Anne, ed. *Shakespeare Criticism, 1919–35*. London, 1936.
Brown, John Russell. *Shakespeare's Plays in Performance*. London, 1966.
Chambers, E. K. *Shakespeare: A Survey*. London, 1925.
Clemen, Wolfgang. *The Development of Shakespeare's Imagery*. Cambridge, Mass., 1951.
Craig, Hardin. *An Interpretation of Shakespeare*. New York, 1948.
Crane, Milton. *Shakespeare's Prose*. Chicago, 1951.
Cruttwell, Patrick. *The Shakespearean Moment and Its Place in the Poetry of the Seventeenth Century*. London, 1954.
Eagleton, Terence. *Shakespeare and Society*. New York and London, 1967.
Ellis-Fermor, Una. *Shakespeare the Dramatist*. New York, 1961.
Frye, Roland M. *Shakespeare and Christian Doctrine*, Princeton, 1963.
Goddard, Harold C. *The Meaning of Shakespeare*. Chicago, 1951.

Granville-Barker, Harley. *Prefaces to Shakespeare*. 2 vols. Princeton, 1946–1947.

Harbage, Alfred. *As They Liked It*. New York, 1947.

———. *Shakespeare and the Rival Traditions*. New York, 1952.

———. *William Shakespeare: A Reader's Guide*. New York, 1963.

Holland, Norman. *Psychoanalysis and Shakespeare*. New York, 1966.

———. *The Shakespearean Imagination*. New York, 1964.

Jorgensen, Paul A. *Shakespeare's Military World*. Berkeley and Los Angeles, 1956.

Kermode, Frank, ed. *Four Centuries of Shakespearean Criticism*. New York, 1965.

Knight, G. Wilson. *The Shakespearian Tempest*. London, 1932, 1953.

Knights, L. C. *Some Shakespearean Themes*. London, 1959.

Kott, Jan. *Shakespeare Our Contemporary*. New York, 1964.

Mahood, M. M. *Shakespeare's Wordplay*. London, 1957.

Murry, John Middleton. *Shakespeare*. London, 1936.

Odell, George C. D. *Shakespeare from Betterton to Irving*. 2 vols. New York, 1920.

Rabkin, Norman, ed. *Approaches to Shakespeare*. New York, 1964.

———. *Shakespeare and the Common Understanding*. New York, 1967.

Ridler, Anne Bradby, ed. *Shakespeare Criticism, 1935–60*. London, 1963.

Righter, Anne. *Shakespeare and the Idea of the Play*. London, 1962.

Rossiter, A. P. *Angel with Horns*. London, 1961.

Schücking, Levin L. *Character Problems in Shakespeare's Plays*. London, 1922, 1948.

Sewell, Arthur. *Character and Society in Shakespeare*. London, 1951.

Smith, David Nichol, ed. *Shakespeare Criticism: A Selection*. World's Classics, Oxford, 1916.

———, ed. *Shakespeare in the Eighteenth Century*. Oxford, 1928.

Soellner, Rolf. *Shakespeare's Patterns of Self-Knowledge*. Columbus, Ohio, 1972.

Spencer, Theodore. *Shakespeare and the Nature of Man*. New York, 1942.

Spivack, Bernard. *Shakespeare and the Allegory of Evil*. New York, 1958.

Sprague, Arthur Colby. *Shakespeare and the Actors*. Cambridge, Mass., 1944.

———. *Shakespearian Players and Performances*. Cambridge, Mass., 1953.

Spurgeon, Caroline. *Shakespeare's Imagery and What It Tells Us*. Cambridge, Eng., 1935.

Stauffer, Donald. *Shakespeare's World of Images*. New York, 1949.

Stirling, Brents. *The Populace in Shakespeare*. New York, 1949.

Stoll, E. E. *Art and Artifice in Shakespeare*. Cambridge, Eng., 1933, 1962.

———. *Shakespeare Studies*. New York, 1942.

Styan, J. L. *Shakespeare's Stagecraft*. Cambridge, Eng., 1967.

Traversi, Derek. *An Approach to Shakespeare*. 2 vols. Rev. ed. London, 1968.

Trewin, J. C. *Shakespeare on the English Stage, 1900–1964*. London, 1964.

Van Doran, Mark. *Shakespeare*. New York, 1939.

Vickers, Brian. *The Artistry of Shakespeare's Prose*. London, 1968.

Whitaker, Virgil K. *Shakespeare's Use of Learning*. San Marino, Calif., 1953.

THE COMEDIES

Barber, C. L. *Shakespeare's Festive Comedy*. Princeton, 1959.

Barry, Ralph. *Shakespeare's Comedies*. Princeton, 1972.

Brown, John Russell. *Shakespeare and His Comedies*. London, 1957, 1968.

Campbell, Oscar James. *Shakespeare's Satire*. London and New York, 1943, 1963.

Champion, Larry S. *The Evolution of Shakespeare's Comedy*. Cambridge, Mass., 1970.

Charlton, H. B. *Shakespearian Comedy*. London, 1938.

Cody, Richard. *The Landscape of the Mind: Pastoralism and Platonic Theory in Tasso's "Aminta" and Shakespeare's Early Comedies*. Oxford, 1969.

Evans, Bertrand. *Shakespeare's Comedies*. Oxford, 1960.

Frye, Northrop. "The Argument of Comedy," *English Institute Essays 1948*. New York, 1949.

———. "Characterization in Shakespearian Comedy," *SQ*, IV (1953), 271–277.

———. *A Natural Perspective: The Development of Shakespearean Comedy and Romance*. New York, 1965.

Hunter, Robert G. *Shakespeare and the Comedy of Forgiveness*. New York, 1965.

Muir, Kenneth, ed. *Shakespeare: The Comedies*. Englewood Cliffs, N.J., 1965.

Palmer, David, and Malcolm Bradbury, eds. *Shakespearian Comedy*. Stratford-upon-Avon Studies 14. London, 1972.

Palmer, John. *Comic Characters of Shakespeare*. London, 1946.

Parrott, T. M. *Shakespearean Comedy*. New York, 1949.

Pettet, E. C. *Shakespeare and the Romance Tradition*. London, 1949.

Phialas, Peter G. *Shakespeare's Romantic Comedies*. Chapel Hill, N.C., 1966.

Sen Gupta, S. C. *Shakespearian Comedy*. London, 1950.

Stevenson, David L. *The Love-Game Comedy*. New

York, 1946.

Tillyard, E. M. W. *Shakespeare's Early Comedies*. London and New York, 1965.

Traversi, Derek. *Shakespeare: The Early Comedies*. London, 1960.

Wilson, J. Dover. *Shakespeare's Happy Comedies*. London and Evanston, Ill., 1962.

THE HISTORIES

Campbell, Lily B. *Shakespeare's "Histories": Mirrors of Elizabethan Policy*. San Marino, Calif., 1947.

Charlton, H. B. *Shakespeare, Politics and Politicians*. Oxford, 1929.

Craig, Hardin. "Shakespeare and the History Play," *J. Q. Adams Memorial Studies*, ed., J. McManaway et al., pp. 55–64. Washington, D.C., 1948.

Dorius, R. J., ed. *Discussions of Shakespeare's Histories*. Boston, 1964.

Ellis-Fermor, Una. *The Frontiers of Drama*, chap. III. 2nd ed. London, 1964.

Jenkins, Harold. "Shakespeare's History Plays: 1900–1951," *ShS 6* (1953), 1–15.

Kelly, Henry A. *Divine Providence in the England of Shakespeare's Histories*. Cambridge, Mass., 1970.

Knights, L. C. "Shakespeare and Political Wisdom," *Sewanee Review*, LXI (1953), 43–55.

———. "Shakespeare's Politics: With Some Reflections on the Nature of Tradition," *Proceedings of the British Academy*, XLIII (1957), 115–132.

Manheim, Michael. *The Weak King Dilemma in the Shakespearean History Play*. Syracuse, N.Y., 1973.

Ornstein, Robert. *A Kingdom for a Stage*. Cambridge, Mass., 1972.

Palmer, John. *Political Characters of Shakespeare*. London, 1945.

Pierce, Robert B. *Shakespeare's History Plays: The Family and the State*. Columbus, Ohio, 1971.

Prior, Moody. *The Drama of Power*. Evanston, Ill., 1973.

Reese, M. M. *The Cease of Majesty*. London and New York, 1961.

Ribner, Irving. *The English History Play in the Age of Shakespeare*. Rev. ed. London, 1965.

Richmond, H. M. *Shakespeare's Political Plays*. New York, 1967.

Riggs, David. *Shakespeare's Heroical Histories*. Cambridge, Mass., 1971.

Rossiter, A. P. "Ambivalence: The Dialectic of the Histories," *Talking of Shakespeare*, ed. John Garrett. London, 1954.

Sen Gupta, S. C. *Shakespeare's Historical Plays*. London, 1964.

Talbert, Ernest William. *The Problem of Order*. Chapel Hill, N.C., 1962.

Tillyard, E. M. W. *Shakespeare's History Plays*. London, 1944, 1961.

Traversi, Derek. *Shakespeare from Richard II to Henry V*. Palo Alto, 1957.

Waith, Eugene M., ed. *Shakespeare: The Histories*. Englewood Cliffs, N.J., 1965.

Wilson, F. P. "The English History Play," *Shakespearian and Other Studies*. Oxford, 1969.

———. *Marlowe and the Early Shakespeare*. Oxford, 1953.

THE TRAGEDIES

Bradley, A. C. *Shakespearean Tragedy*. London, 1904. (*Hamlet*, *Othello*, *King Lear*, *Macbeth*.)

Brooke, Nicholas. *Shakespeare's Early Tragedies*. London and New York, 1968.

Brower, Reuben. *Hero and Saint: Shakespeare and the Græco-Roman Heroic Tradition*. New York and Oxford, 1971.

Campbell, Lily B. *Shakespeare's Tragic Heroes: Slaves of Passion*. Cambridge, Eng., 1930.

Charlton, H. B. *Shakespearian Tragedy*. Cambridge, Eng., 1948.

Cunningham, J. V. *Woe or Wonder: The Emotional Effect of Shakespearean Tragedy*. Denver, 1951. Reprinted in *Tradition and Poetic Structure*. Denver, 1960.

Farnham, Willard. *Shakespeare's Tragic Frontier*. Berkeley, 1950.

Frye, Northrop. *Fools of Time: Studies in Shakespearean Tragedy*. Toronto, 1967.

Harbage, Alfred, ed. *Shakespeare: The Tragedies*. Englewood Cliffs, N.J., 1964.

Holloway, John. *The Story of the Night: Studies in Shakespeare's Major Tragedies*. London and Lincoln, Neb., 1961.

Knight, G. Wilson. *The Imperial Theme: Further Interpretations of Shakespeare's Tragedies Including the Roman Plays*. London, 1931, 1953.

———. *The Wheel of Fire*. London, 1930, 1965.

Lawlor, John. *The Tragic Sense in Shakespeare*. London, 1960.

Leech, Clifford. *Shakespeare's Tragedies and Other Studies in Seventeenth Century Drama*. London, 1950.

———, ed. *Shakespeare: The Tragedies*. Chicago, 1965.

Mack, Maynard. "The Jacobean Shakespeare: Some Observations on the Construction of the Tragedies," *Jacobean Theatre*, ed. John Russell Brown and Bernard Harris. Stratford-upon-Avon Studies 1. London, 1960.

McElroy, Bernard. *Shakespeare's Mature Tragedies*. Princeton, N.J., 1973.

Nevo, Ruth. *Tragic Form in Shakespeare*. Princeton, 1972.

Proser, Matthew N. *The Heroic Image in Five Shakespearean Tragedies*. Princeton, 1965.

Rosen, William. *Shakespeare and the Craft of Tragedy*. Cambridge, Mass., 1960.

Sisson, C. J. *Shakespeare's Tragic Justice*. Scarborough, Ont., 1961.

Speaight, Robert. *Nature in Shakespearian Tragedy*. London, 1955.

Stirling, Brents. *Unity in Shakespearian Tragedy*. New York, 1956.

Whitaker, Virgil. *The Mirror up to Nature*. San Marino, Calif., 1965.

Wilson, Harold S. *On the Design of Shakespearian Tragedy*. Toronto, 1957.

THE ROMANCES

Bentley, Gerald Eades. "Shakespeare and the Blackfriars Theatre," *ShS 1* (1948), 38–50.

Danby, John F. *Poets on Fortune's Hill*. London, 1952.

Edwards, Philip. "Shakespeare's Romances: 1900–1957," *ShS 11* (1958), 1–18. See also other articles in this issue.

Felperin, Howard. *Shakespearean Romance*. Princeton, 1972.

Foakes, R. A. *Shakespeare: From the Dark Comedies to the Last Plays*. London and Charlottesville, Va., 1971.

Frye, Northrop. *Anatomy of Criticism*. Princeton, 1957.

———. *A Natural Perspective: The Development of Shakespearean Comedy and Romance*. New York, 1965.

Hartwig, Joan. *Shakespeare's Tragicomic Vision*. Baton Rouge, La., 1972.

James, D. G. "The Failure of the Ballad-Makers," *Scepticism and Poetry*. London, 1937.

Kermode, Frank. *William Shakespeare: The Final Plays*. London, 1963.

Knight, G. Wilson. *The Crown of Life*. London, 1947, 1966.

———. *The Shakespearian Tempest*. London, 1932, 1953.

Leavis, F. R. "A Criticism of Shakespeare's Last Plays," *Scrutiny*, X (1942), 339–345; reprinted in *The Common Pursuit*. London, 1952.

Peterson, Douglas. *Time, Tide, and Tempest: A Study of Shakespeare's Romances*. San Marino, Calif., 1973.

Pettet, E. C. *Shakespeare and the Romance Tradition*. London, 1949.

Seltzer, Daniel. "The Staging of the Last Plays," *Later Shakespeare*, ed. John Russell Brown and Bernard Harris, pp. 127–165. Stratford-upon-Avon Studies 8. London, 1966.

Smith, Hallett. *Shakespeare's Romances*. San Marino, Calif., 1972.

Spencer, Theodore. "Appearance and Reality in Shakespeare's Last Plays," *Modern Philology*, XXXIX (1942), 265–274.

Strachey, Lytton. "Shakespeare's Final Period," *Books and Characters*. London, 1922.

Tillyard, E. M. W. *Shakespeare's Last Plays*. London, 1938, 1964.

Traversi, Derek. *Shakespeare: The Last Phase*. New York, 1954.

Wells, Stanley. "Shakespeare and Romance," *Later Shakespeare*, ed. John Russell Brown and Bernard Harris, pp. 49–79. Stratford-upon-Avon Studies 8. London, 1966.

ROMEO AND JULIET

Adams, Barry B. "The Prudence of Prince Escalus," *English Literary History*, XXXV (1968), 32–50.

Bowling, Lawrence E. "The Thematic Framework of *Romeo and Juliet*," *PMLA*, LXIV (1949), 208–220.

Brown, John Russell. "S. Franco Zeffirelli's *Romeo and Juliet*," *ShS 15* (1962), 147–155.

Dickey, Franklin M. *Not Wisely But Too Well*. San Marino, Calif., 1957.

Evans, Bertrand. "The Brevity of Friar Lawrence," *PMLA*, LXV (1950), 841–865.

Granville-Barker, Harley. *Prefaces to Shakespeare*, vol. II. Princeton, 1947.

Hill, R. F. "Shakespeare's Early Tragic Mode," *SQ*, IX (1958), 455–469.

Hosley, Richard. "The Use of the Upper Stage in *Romeo and Juliet*," *SQ*, V (1954), 371–379.

Levin, Harry. "Form and Formality in *Romeo and Juliet*," *SQ*, XI (1960), 1–11.

Mahood, M. M. *Shakespeare's Wordplay*. London, 1957.

McArthur, Herbert. "Romeo's Loquacious Friend," *SQ*, X (1959), 35–44.

Moore, Olin H. *The Legend of Romeo and Juliet*. Columbus, Ohio, 1950.

Nevo, Ruth. "Tragic Form in *Romeo and Juliet*," *Studies in English Literature*, IX (1969), 241–258.

Nosworthy, J. M. "The Two Angry Families of Verona," *SQ*, III (1952), 219–226.

Pettet, E. C. "The Imagery of *Romeo and Juliet*," *English*, VIII (1950), 121–126.

Siegel, Paul N. "Christianity and the Religion of Love in *Romeo and Juliet*," *SQ*, XII (1961), 371–392.

Tanselle, G. Thomas. "Time in *Romeo and Juliet*," *SQ*, XV (1964), 349–361.

Williams, George W., ed. *The Most Excellent and Lamentable Tragedie of Romeo and Juliet*. Durham, N.C., 1964.

A MIDSUMMER NIGHT'S DREAM

Barber, C. L. *Shakespeare's Festive Comedy*. Princeton, 1959.

Bethurum, Dorothy. "Shakespeare's Comment on Mediaeval Romance in *Midsummer-Night's Dream*," *Modern Language Notes*, LX (1945), 85–94.

Bonnard, Georges A. "Shakespeare's Purpose in *Midsummer-Night's Dream*," *Shakespeare Jahrbuch*, XCII (1956), 268–279.

Briggs, Katharine M. *The Anatomy of Puck*. London, 1959.

Dent, R. W. "Imagination in *A Midsummer Night's Dream*," *SQ*, XV (1964), 115–129.

Doran, Madeleine. "Pyramus and Thisbe Once More," *Essays . . . in Honor of Hardin Craig*, ed. Richard Hosley, pp. 149–162. Columbia, Mo., 1962.

Hemingway, Samuel B. "The Relation of *A Midsummer Night's Dream* to *Romeo and Juliet*," *Modern Language Notes*, XXVI (1911), 78–80.

Hunter, G. K. *William Shakespeare: The Late Comedies*. London, 1962.

Kersten, Dorelies. "Shakespeares Puck," *Shakespeare Jahrbuch*, XCVIII (1962), 189–200.

Miller, Donald C. "Titania and the Changeling," *English Studies*, XXII (1940), 66–70.

Muir, Kenneth. "Pyramus and Thisbe: A Study in Shakespeare's Method," *SQ*, V (1954), 141–153.

———. "Shakespeare as Parodist," *Notes and Queries*, CXCIX (1954), 467–468.

Nemerov, Howard. "The Marriage of Theseus and Hippolyta," *Kenyon Review*, XVIII (1956), 633–641.

Olsen, Paul A. "*A Midsummer Night's Dream* and the Meaning of Court Marriage," *English Literary History*, XXIV (1957), 95–119.

Reynolds, Lou Agnes, and Paul Sawyer. "Folk Medicine and the Four Fairies of *A Midsummer-Night's Dream*," *SQ*, X (1959), 513–521.

Schanzer, Ernest. "The Central Theme of *A Midsummer Night's Dream*," *University of Toronto Quarterly*, XX (1951), 233–238.

———. "The Moon and the Fairies in *A Midsummer Night's Dream*," *University of Toronto Quarterly*, XXIV (1955), 234–246.

Siegel, Paul N. "*A Midsummer Night's Dream* and the Wedding Guests," *SQ*, IV (1953), 139–144.

Young, David P. *Something of Great Constancy: The Art of "A Midsummer Night's Dream."* New Haven, 1966.

RICHARD THE SECOND

Altick, Richard D. "Symphonic Imagery in *Richard II*," *PMLA*, LXII (1947), 339–365.

Black, Matthew W. "The Sources of Shakespeare's *Richard II*," *J. Q. Adams Memorial Studies*, ed. J. McManaway et al., pp. 199–216. Washington, D.C., 1948.

Bogard, Travis. "Shakespeare's Second Richard," *PMLA*, LXX (1955), 192–209.

Bonnard, Georges A. "The Actor in *Richard II*," *Shakespeare Jahrbuch*, LXXXVII (1952), 87–101.

Dean, Leonard F. "*Richard II:* The State and the Image of the Theater," *PMLA*, LXVII (1952), 211–218.

Dodson, Sarah. "The Northumberland of Shakespeare and Holinshed," *University of Texas Studies in English*, XIX (1939), 74–85.

Doran, Madeleine. "Imagery in *Richard II* and in *Henry IV*," *Modern Language Review*, XXXVII (1942), 113–122.

Dorius, R. J. "A Little More Than a Little," *SQ*, XI (1960), 13–26.

Elliott, John R., Jr., "History and Tragedy in *Richard II*," *Studies in English Literature*, VIII (1968), 253–271.

Forker, Charles R. "Shakespeare's Chronicle Play as Historical-Pastoral," *ShakS 1* (1965), 85–104.

Kantorowicz, Ernst H. *The King's Two Bodies: A Study in Medieval Political Theology*. Princeton, 1957.

Law, R. A. "Deviations from Holinshed in *Richard II*," *University of Texas Studies in English*, XXIX (1950), 91–101.

———. "Links Between Shakespeare's History Plays," *Studies in Philology*, L (1953), 168–187.

Phialas, Peter G. "The Medieval in *Richard II*," *SQ*, XII (1961), 305–310.

Quinn, Michael. " 'The King Is Not Himself': The Personal Tragedy of *Richard II*," *Studies in Philology*, LVI (1959), 169–186.

Ribner, Irving. "The Political Problem in Shakespeare's Lancastrian Tetralogy," *Studies in Philology*, XLIX (1952), 171–184.

Stirling, Brents. "Bolingbroke's 'Decision,' " *SQ*, II (1951), 27–34.

Swinburne, A. C. *Three Plays of Shakespeare*. New York and London, 1909.

Yeats, W. B. "At Stratford-on-Avon," *Ideas of Good and Evil*, collected in *Essays and Introductions*. New York, 1961.

THE FIRST PART OF KING HENRY THE FOURTH

Barish, Jonas A. "The Turning Away of Prince Hal," *ShakS 1* (1965), 9–17.

Boughner, D. C. "Traditional Elements in Falstaff," *Journal of English and Germanic Philology*, XLIII (1944), 417–428.

———. "Vice, Braggart, and Falstaff," *Anglia*, LXXII (1954), 35–61.

Bradley, A. C. "The Rejection of Falstaff," *Oxford Lectures on Poetry*. London, 1909, 1961.

Bryant, J. A., Jr., "Prince Hal and the Ephesians," *Sewanee Review*, LXVII (1959), 204–219.

Dickinson, Hugh. "The Reformation of Prince Hal," *SQ*, XII (1961), 33–46.

Doran, Madeleine. "Imagery in *Richard II* and in *Henry IV*," *Modern Language Review*, XXXVII (1942), 113–122.

Dorius, R. J., ed. *Twentieth Century Interpretations of "Henry IV Part I."* Englewood Cliffs, N.J., 1970.

Empson, William. "Falstaff and Mr. Dover Wilson," *Kenyon Review*, XV (1953), 213–262.

Fish, Charles. "*Henry IV:* Shakespeare and Holinshed," *Studies in Philology*, LXI (1964), 205–218.

Hunter, G. K. "*Henry IV* and the Elizabethan Two-Part Play," *Review of English Studies*, n. s. V (1954), 236–248.

———. "Shakespeare's Politics and the Rejection of Falstaff," *Critical Quarterly*, I (1959), 229–236.

Jenkins, Harold. *The Structural Problem in Shakespeare's "Henry the Fourth."* London, 1956.

Kernan, Alvin. "The Henriad: Shakespeare's Major History Plays," *Yale Review*, LIX (1969), 3–32.

Kleinstück, Johannes. "The Problem of Order in Shakespeare's Histories," *Neophilologus*, XXXVIII (1954), 268–277.

Knights, L. C. "Notes on Comedy," *Scrutiny*, I (1933), 356–367.

Law, R. A. "Structural Unity in the Two Parts of *Henry the Fourth*," *Studies in Philology*, XXIV (1927), 223–242.

McLuhan, Herbert Marshall. "*Henry IV*, A Mirror of Magistrates," *University of Toronto Quarterly*, XVII (1948), 152–160.

Seng, Peter J. "Songs, Time, and the Rejection of Falstaff," *ShS 15* (1962), 31–40.

Shaaber, M. A. "The Unity of *Henry IV*," *J. Q. Adams Memorial Studies*, ed. J. McManaway et al., pp. 217–228. Washington, D.C., 1948.

Shuchter, J. D. "Prince Hal and Francis: The Imitation of an Action," *ShakS 3* (1967), 129–137.

Spivack, Bernard. "Falstaff and the Psychomachia," *SQ*, VIII (1957), 449–459.

Stewart, J. I. M. "The Birth and Death of Falstaff," *Character and Motive in Shakespeare*. London, 1949.

Stoll, E. E. "Falstaff," *Shakespeare Studies*. New York, 1942.

Tolliver, Harold E. "Falstaff, the Prince, and the History Play," *SQ*, XVI (1965), 63–80.

Williams, Philip. "The Birth and Death of Falstaff Reconsidered," *SQ*, VIII (1957), 359–365.

Wilson, J. Dover. *The Fortunes of Falstaff*. London, 1943.

TWELFTH NIGHT

Barnet, Sylvan. "Charles Lamb and the Tragic Malvolio," *Philological Quarterly*, XXXIII (1954), 178–188.

Downer, Alan S. "Feste's Night," *College English*, XIII (1952), 258–265.

Goldsmith, Robert H. *Wise Fools in Shakespeare*. East Lansing, Mich., 1955.

Hollander, John. "*Twelfth Night* and the Morality of Indulgence," *Sewanee Review*, LXVII (1959), 220–238.

Hotson, Leslie. *The First Night of Twelfth Night*. New York, 1954.

Jenkins, Harold. "Shakespeare's *Twelfth Night*," *Rice Institute Pamphlets*, XLV (1959), iv, 19–42.

King, Walter N., ed. *Twentieth Century Interpretations of "Twelfth Night."* Englewood Cliffs, N.J., 1968.

Knight, G. Wilson. *The Shakespearian Tempest*. London, 1932, 1953.

Leech, Clifford. *"Twelfth Night" and Shakespearian Comedy*. Toronto, 1965.

Lewalski, Barbara K. "Thematic Patterns in *Twelfth Night*," *ShakS 1* (1965), 168–181.

Mueschke, Paul, and Jeannette Fleisher. "Jonsonian Elements in the Comic Underplot of *Twelfth Night*," *PMLA*, XLVIII (1933), 722–740.

Salingar, L. D. "The Design of *Twelfth Night*," *SQ*, IX (1958), 117–139.

Seiden, Melvin. "Malvolio Reconsidered," *University of Kansas City Review*, XXVIII (1961), 105–114.

Summers, Joseph H. "The Masks of *Twelfth Night*," *University of Kansas City Review*, XXII (1955), 25–32. Reprinted in *Shakespeare: Modern Essays in Criticism*, ed. Leonard F. Dean. Rev. ed. London and New York, 1967, 1969.

Tilley, Morris P. "The Organic Unity of *Twelfth Night*," *PMLA*, XXIX (1914), 550–566.

Welsford, Enid. *The Fool*. London, 1935.

Williams, Porter, Jr. "Mistakes in *Twelfth Night* and Their Resolution," *PMLA*, LXXVI (1961), 193–199.

HAMLET

Alexander, Peter. *Hamlet: Father and Son.* New York and London, 1955.

Bevington, David, ed. *Twentieth Century Interpretations of "Hamlet."* Englewood Cliffs, N.J., 1968.

Booth, Stephen. "On the Value of *Hamlet*," *Reinterpretations of Elizabethan Drama*, ed. Norman Rabkin. New York, 1969.

Bowers, Fredson T. *Elizabethan Revenge Tragedy, 1587–1642.* Princeton, 1940.

———. "Hamlet as Minister and Scourge," *PMLA*, LXX (1955), 740–749.

Brown, John Russell, and Bernard Harris, eds. *Hamlet.* Stratford-upon-Avon Studies 5. London, 1963.

Charney, Maurice. *Style in "Hamlet."* Princeton, 1969.

Elliott, G. R. *Scourge and Minister: A Study of "Hamlet" as a Tragedy of Revengefulness and Justice.* Durham, N.C., 1951.

Fergusson, Francis. *The Idea of a Theater.* Princeton, 1949.

Granville-Barker, Harley. *Prefaces to Shakespeare*, vol. I. Princeton, 1946.

Grebanier, Bernard D. *The Heart of Hamlet.* New York, 1949, 1967.

James, D. G. *The Dream of Learning.* Oxford, 1951.

Johnson, S. F. "The Regeneration of Hamlet," *SQ*, III (1952), 187–207.

Jones, Ernest. *Hamlet and Oedipus.* Rev. ed. New York, 1949, 1954.

Joseph, Bertram. *Conscience and the King.* London, 1953.

Kitto, H. D. F. *Form and Meaning in Drama.* London, 1956.

Knights, L. C. *An Approach to Hamlet.* London, 1960.

Levin, Harry. *The Question of Hamlet.* New York and London, 1959.

Lewis, C. S. "Hamlet: The Prince or the Poem?" *Proceedings of the British Academy*, XXVIII (1942), 139–154.

Mack, Maynard. "The World of *Hamlet*," *Yale Review*, XLI (1952), 502–523.

Mack, Maynard, Jr. *Killing the King.* New Haven, 1973.

Madariaga, Salvador de. *On Hamlet.* London, 1948, 1964.

Nicoll, Allardyce, ed. *ShS 9* (1956).

Prosser, Eleanor. *Hamlet and Revenge.* Stanford, 1967, 1971.

Rose, Mark. "*Hamlet* and the Shape of Revenge," *English Literary Renaissance*, I (1971), 132–143.

Tillyard, E. M. W. *Shakespeare's Problem Plays.* Toronto, 1949.

Walker, Roy. *The Time Is out of Joint: A Study of "Hamlet."* London and New York, 1948.

Wilson, J. Dover. *What Happens in "Hamlet."* London and New York, 1935, 1951.

KING LEAR

Barnet, Sylvan. "Some Limitations of a Christian Approach to Shakespeare," *English Literary History*, XXII (1955), 81–92.

Danby, John F. *Shakespeare's Doctrine of Nature: A Study of "King Lear."* London, 1949.

Elton, William R. *King Lear and the Gods.* San Marino, Calif., 1966.

Empson, William. *The Structure of Complex Words.* London, 1951.

Felperin, Howard. *Shakespearean Romance.* Princeton, 1972.

Fraser, Russell A. *Shakespeare's Poetics in Relation to "King Lear."* London, 1962.

Freud, Sigmund. "The Theme of the Three Caskets," *Complete Psychological Works of Sigmund Freud*, XII (1911–1913), pp. 291–301. London, 1958.

Granville-Barker, Harley. *Prefaces to Shakespeare*, vol. I. Princeton, 1946.

Heilman, Robert B. *This Great Stage: Image and Structure in "King Lear."* Baton Rouge, La., 1948.

James, D. G. *The Dream of Learning.* Oxford, 1951.

Jorgensen, Paul A. *Lear's Self-Discovery.* Berkeley and Los Angeles, 1967.

Keast, W. "Imagery and Meaning in the Interpretation of *King Lear*," *Modern Philology*, XLVII (1949), 45–64.

Knights, L. C. *Some Shakespearean Themes.* London, 1959.

Lothian, J. M. *"King Lear": A Tragic Reading of Life.* Toronto, 1949.

Mack, Maynard. *King Lear in Our Time.* Berkeley and Los Angeles, 1965.

MacLean, Norman. "Episode, Scene, Speech, and Word: The Madness of Lear," *Critics and Criticism*, ed. R. S. Crane. Chicago, 1952.

Muir, Kenneth, ed. *King Lear.* The Arden Shakespeare. London and Cambridge, Mass., 1952, 1959.

Nicoll, Allardyce, ed. *Shakespeare Survey 13* (1960).

Rosen, William. *Shakespeare and the Craft of Tragedy.* Cambridge, Mass., 1960.

Rosenberg, Marvin. *The Masks of "King Lear."* Berkeley and Los Angeles, 1972.

Sewall, Richard B. *The Vision of Tragedy.* New Haven, 1959.

Sewell, Arthur. *Character and Society in Shakespeare.* London, 1951.

Stoll, E. E. *Art and Artifice in Shakespeare.* Cambridge, Eng., 1933, 1962.

THE TEMPEST

Allen, Don Cameron. *Image and Meaning*. Baltimore, 1960.

Auden, W. H. "The Sea and the Mirror," *The Collected Poetry*. New York, 1945.

Brockbank, Philip. "*The Tempest:* Conventions of Art and Empire," *Later Shakespeare*, ed. John Russell Brown and Bernard Harris, pp. 183–201. Stratford-upon-Avon Studies 8. London, 1966.

Brower, Reuben. "The Mirror of Analogy," *The Fields of Light*. New York, 1951.

Coleridge, S. T. "Lectures on Shakespeare and Milton: The Ninth Lecture," *Shakespearean Criticism*, 2 vols., ed. T. M. Raysor, II, 121–140. 2nd ed. London, 1960.

Curry, Walter Clyde. *Shakespeare's Philosophical Patterns*. Baton Rouge, La., 1937.

Frye, Northrop, ed. *The Tempest*. Pelican Shakespeare. Baltimore, 1959.

Hoeniger, F. D. "Prospero's Storm and Miracle," *SQ*, VII (1956), 33–38.

James, D. G. *The Dream of Prospero*. Oxford, 1967.

Johnson, W. Stacy. "The Genesis of Ariel," *SQ*, II (1951), 205–210.

Kermode, Frank, ed. *The Tempest*. The Arden Shakespeare. London, 1958.

Knox, Bernard. "*The Tempest* and the Ancient Comic Tradition," *English Stage Comedy*, ed. W. K. Wimsatt. *English Institute Essays 1954*. New York, 1955.

McPeek, James. "The Genesis of Caliban," *Philological Quarterly*, XXV (1946), 378–381.

Palmer, D. J., ed. *Shakespeare, "The Tempest": A Casebook*. London, 1968.

Reed, Robert R., Jr. "The Probable Origin of Ariel," *SQ*, XI (1960), 61–65.

Smith, Hallett, ed. *Twentieth Century Interpretations of "The Tempest."* Englewood Cliffs, N.J., 1969.

Still, Colin. *The Timeless Theme*. London, 1936, 1947. Originally published as *Shakespeare's Mystery Play: A Study of "The Tempest,"* 1921

William, David. "*The Tempest* on the Stage," *Jacobean Theatre*, ed. John Russell Brown and Bernard Harris, pp. 133–157. Stratford-upon-Avon Studies 1. London, 1960.

Wilson, J. Dover. *The Meaning of "The Tempest."* Newcastle, 1936.

Young, David. *The Heart's Forest*. New Haven, 1972

THE SONNETS

Beeching, Henry C. *The Sonnets of Shakespeare*. Boston, 1904.

Booth, Stephen. *An Essay on Shakespeare's Sonnets*. New Haven, 1969.

Bradbrook, Muriel C. *Shakespeare and Elizabethan Poetry*. London, 1951.

Bradley, A. C. *Oxford Lectures on Poetry*. London, 1909, 1961.

Bush, Douglas. *Mythology and the Renaissance Tradition in English Poetry*. Minneapolis and London, 1932; rev. ed., 1963.

Chambers, E. K. *Shakespearean Gleanings*. London, 1944.

Cruttwell, Patrick. *The Shakespearean Moment and Its Place in the Poetry of the Seventeenth Century*. London, 1954.

Herrnstein, Barbara, ed. *Discussions of Shakespeare's Sonnets*. Boston, 1964.

Hubler, Edward. *The Sense of Shakespeare's Sonnets*. Princeton, 1952.

Hubler, Edward, Northrop Frye, Leslie A. Fiedler, Stephen Spender, and R. P. Blackmur. *The Riddle of Shakespeare's Sonnets*. New York, 1962.

Knight, G. Wilson. *The Mutual Flame: On Shakespeare's Sonnets and The Phoenix and the Turtle*. London, 1955.

Krieger, Murray. *A Window to Criticism: Shakespeare's Sonnets and Modern Poetics*. Princeton, 1964.

Landry, Hilton. *Interpretations in Shakespeare's Sonnets*. Berkeley, 1963.

Leishman, J. B. *Themes and Variations in Shakespeare's Sonnets*. London, 1961.

Lever, J. W. *The Elizabethan Love Sonnet*. London, 1956.

Maxwell, J. C., ed. *The Poems*. The New Cambridge Shakespeare. London, 1969.

Nicoll, Allardyce, ed. *ShS 15* (1962).

Rollins, Hyder E. *A New Variorum Edition of Shakespeare: The Sonnets*. Philadelphia, 1944.

CANON, DATES, AND EARLY TEXTS

By "canon" we mean a listing of plays that can be ascribed to Shakespeare on the basis of reliable evidence. Such evidence is either "internal," derived from matters of style or poetics in the plays themselves, or "external," derived from outside the play. The latter includes any reference by Shakespeare's contemporaries to his plays, any allusions in the plays themselves to contemporary events, the entering of Shakespeare's plays for publication in the Stationers' Register (S.R.), actual publication of the plays, and records of early performances. These matters of external evidence are also essential in attempting to date the plays.

The greatest single source of information is the First Folio text of Shakespeare's plays, sponsored by Shakespeare's fellow-actors John Heminges and Henry Condell and published in 1623. It contains all the plays usually included in complete editions of Shakespeare except *Pericles*, and offers strong presumptive evidence of being a complete and accurate compilation of Shakespeare's work by men who knew him and cherished his memory. It provides the only texts we have for the following plays: *The Comedy of Errors*, *The Two Gentlemen of Verona*, *The Taming of the Shrew*, *1 Henry VI*, *King John*, *As You Like It*, *Twelfth Night*, *Julius Caesar*, *All's Well that Ends Well*, *Measure for Measure*, *Timon of Athens*, *Macbeth*, *Antony and Cleopatra*, *Coriolanus*, *Cymbeline*, *The Winter's Tale*, *The Tempest*, and *Henry VIII*. This includes nearly half the known canon of Shakespeare's plays. Our debt to the First Folio is incalculable, and confirms our impression of its reliability.

The information of the First Folio is further confirmed by contemporary references. In 1598, a divine and minor writer of the period named Francis Meres wrote in his *Palladis Tamia:*

> As the soule of *Euphorbus* was thought to liue in *Pythagoras:* so the sweete wittie soule of *Ouid* liues in mellifluous & hony-tongued *Shakespeare*, witnes his *Venus* and *Adonis*, his *Lucrece*, his sugred Sonnets among his priuate friends, &c.
>
> As *Plautus* and *Seneca* are accounted the best for Comedy and Tragedy among the Latines: so *Shakespeare* among the English is the most excellent in both kinds for the stage; for Comedy, witnes his *Gentlemen of Verona*, his *Errors*, his *Loue labors lost*, his *Loue labours wonne*, his *Midsummers night dreame*, & his *Merchant of Venice:* for Tragedy his *Richard the* 2. *Richard* the *3. Henry the* 4. *King Iohn*, *Titus Andronicus* and his *Romeo* and *Iuliet*.

Though this list was meant to offer praise, not to be an exhaustive catalogue, it is remarkably full. If the tantalizing *Loue labours wonne* refers to *The Taming of the Shrew*, Meres' list of comedies is entirely complete down to 1598. Naturally the list does not include the great "festive" comedies, *Much Ado about Nothing*, *As You Like it*, and *Twelfth Night*, since these were written at or slightly later than the time of Meres' comment. Meres correctly names all of Shakespeare's history plays except the *Henry VI* trilogy and of course the later histories *Henry V* (1599) and *Henry VIII* (1613). He names both of Shakespeare's early tragedies not based on English history: *Titus Andronicus* and *Romeo and Juliet*. He tells us about the important nondramatic poems, which did not appear in the First Folio since that volume is devoted exclusively to plays. Not much can be made of the order in which Meres names the plays, however, for we learn from other sources that *Richard III* clearly precedes *Richard II* in date of composition and *King John* precedes the *Henry IV* plays.

Other writers of the 1590's add further confirming evidence. John Weever, in an epigram "*Ad Gulielmum Shakespeare*," published in 1599, refers to "Rose-checkt *Adonis*" and "Faire fire-hot *Venus*," to "Chaste *Lucretia*" and "Prowd lust-stung *Tarquine*," and to "*Romea Richard*, more whose names I know not." Richard Barnfield, in *Poems in Divers Humors*, 1598, praises Shakespeare for "*Venus*" and "*Lucrece*." Both Thomas Nashe and Robert Greene seemingly refer to the *Henry VI* plays, missing from Meres' list. Nashe, in his *Pierce Penilesse* (1592), speculates how it would "have ioyed braue *Talbot* (the terror of the French) to thinke that after he had lyne two hundred yeares in his Tombe, hee should triumphe againe on the Stage." Talbot is the hero of *1 Henry VI*, and we know of no other play on the subject. Greene, in his *Greenes Groats-worth of Wit* (1592), lashes out at an "vpstart Crow, beautified with our feathers, that with his *Tygers hart wrapt in a Players hyde*, supposes he is as well able to bombast out a blanke verse as the best of you: and beeing an absolute *Iohannes fac totum*, is in his owne conceit the onely Shake-scene in a countrey." The line about "Tygers hart" is deliberately misquoted from *3 Henry VI*, I,iv,137. (It is possible that this famous attack on Shakespeare was actually written not by Greene himself but by Henry Chettle, his literary executor.)

Romeo and Juliet (1594–1596)

A corrupt and unregistered quarto of *Romeo and Juliet* appeared in 1597 with the following title:

> AN EXCELLENT conceited Tragedie OF Romeo and Iuliet, As it hath been often (with great applause) plaid publiquely, by the right Honourable the L. of *Hunsdon* his Seruants. LONDON, Printed by Iohn Danter. 1597.

This was a pirated edition issued by an unscrupulous publisher, no doubt to capitalize on the play's great popularity. It seems to have been memorially reconstructed by two or more actors, and possibly thereafter used as a prompt-book. Its appearance seems to have caused the issuance two years later of a clearly authoritative version:

THE MOST EXCELLENT and lamentable Tragedie, of Romeo and *Iuliet. Newly corrected, augmented, and amended:* As it hath bene sundry times publiquely acted, by the right Honourable the Lord Chamberlaine his Seruants. LONDON Printed by Thomas Creede, for Cuthbert Burby, and are to be sold at his shop neare the Exchange. 1599.

This text is some 800 lines longer than the first, and corrects errors in that earlier version. Oddly, however, it seems at times to have been contaminated by the first quarto, as though the manuscript source for the second quarto (probably the author's foul papers) was defective at some point. A passage from I,ii,53 to I,iii,34 was apparently set directly from the first quarto. (On this matter, see George W. Williams' old-spelling edition of the play, Duke U. Press, 1964.) Despite this contamination, however, the second quarto is the authoritative text. It served as the basis for the third quarto (1609) which in turn served as copy for the fourth quarto (1622) and the Folio of 1623. A fifth quarto appeared in 1637.

Francis Meres assigns the play to Shakespeare in 1598. So does John Weever in his *Epigrammes* of 1599. Internal evidence on dating is not reliable. The Nurse observes that " 'Tis since the earthquake now eleven years"; but suitable earthquakes have been discovered in 1580, 1583, 1584, and 1585, giving us a wide choice of dates even if we accept the dubious proposition that the Nurse is speaking accurately. Astronomical reckoning of the position of the moon at the time the play purportedly takes place ("a fortnight and odd days" before Lammastide, August 1) indicates the year 1596; again, however, we have no reason to assume Shakespeare cared about this sort of internal accuracy. More suggestive perhaps is the argument that Danter's unauthorized publication in 1597 was seeking to exploit a popular new play, one the acting company certainly did not yet wish to see published since it was a money-maker. Danter assigns the play to Lord Hunsdon's servants, a name that Shakespeare's company could have used only from July 22, 1596 (when the old Lord Chamberlain, Henry Carey, first Lord Hunsdon, died) to April 17, 1597 (when George Carey, second Lord Hunsdon, was appointed to his father's erstwhile position as Lord Chamberlain). Danter could simply have been using the name of the company at the time he pirated the play, but he may also indicate performance in late 1596. Stylistically, the play is clearly of the "lyric" period of *A Midsummer Night's Dream* and *Richard II*. There are also stylistic affinities to the sonnets and to the narrative poems of 1593–1594. A date between 1594 and 1596 is likely, especially toward the latter end of this period. Whether the play comes before or after *A Midsummer Night's Dream* is, however, a matter of conjecture.

A Midsummer Night's Dream (c. 1594–1595)

A Midsummer Night's Dream was entered on the Stationers' Register by Thomas Fisher on October 8, 1600, and printed by him that same year in quarto:

A Midsommer nights dreame. As it hath beene sundry times pub*lickely acted, by the Right honoura*ble, the Lord Chamberlaine his *seruants. Written by William Shakespeare.* Imprinted at London, for *Thomas Fisher*, and are to be soulde at his shoppe, at the Signe of the White Hart, in *Fleetestreete*. 1600.

This text appears to have been set up from Shakespeare's working manuscript. Its inconsistencies in time scheme and other irregularities may reflect some revision, although the inconsistencies are not noticeable in performance. A second quarto appeared in 1619, though falsely dated 1600; it was a reprint of the first quarto, with some minor corrections and many new errors. A copy of this second quarto, evidently with some added stage directions and other minor changes from a theatrical manuscript in the company's possession, served as the basis for the Folio text of 1623. Essentially, the first quarto remains the authoritative text.

Other than Francis Meres' listing of the play in 1598, external clues as to date are elusive. The description of unruly weather (II,i) has been related to the bad summer of 1594, but complaints about the weather are perennial. On the assumption that the play celebrates some noble wedding of the period, scholars have come up with a number of suitable marriages. Chief are those of Sir Thomas Heneage to Mary, Countess of Southampton, in 1594, of William Stanley, Earl of Derby, to Elizabeth Vere, daughter of the Earl of Oxford, in 1595, and of Thomas, son of Lord Berkeley, to Elizabeth, daughter of Lord Carey, in 1596. The Countess of Southampton was the widowed mother of the young Earl of Southampton, to whom Shakespeare had dedicated his *Venus and Adonis* and *The Rape of Lucrece*. No one has ever convincingly proven, however, that the play was written for any occasion other than commercial public performance. The play makes perfect sense for a general audience, and does not need to depend on references to any private marriage. Shakespeare was, after all, in the business of writing plays for his fellow actors, who earned their livelihood chiefly by public acting before large paying audiences. In any event the search for a court marriage is a circular argument in terms of dating; suitable court marriages can be found for any year of the decade. In the last analysis, the play has to be dated on the basis of its stylistic affinity to plays like *Romeo and Juliet* and *Richard II*, works of the "lyric" midcentury period. The "Pyramus and Thisbe" performance in *A Midsummer Night's Dream* would seem to bear an obvious relation to *Romeo and Juliet*, although no one can say for sure which came first.

Richard the Second (*c. 1595–1596*)

On August 29, 1597, "The Tragedye of Richard the Second" was entered in the Stationers' Register by Andrew Wise, and was published by him later that same year:

THE Tragedie of King Richard the second. *As it hath beene publikely acted by the right Honourable the Lorde Chamberlaine his Seruants.* LONDON Printed by Valentine Simmes for Androw Wise, and are to be sold at his shop in Paules church yard at the signe of the Angel. 1597.

This is a good text, printed evidently from the author's papers or a transcript of them. Wise issued two more quartos of this popular play in 1598, each set from the previous quarto, and then in 1603 transferred his rights in the play to Matthew Law. This publisher issued in 1608 a fourth quarto "With new additions of the Parliament Sceane, and the deposing of King Richard" (according to the title page in some copies). The deposition scene had indeed been omitted from the earlier quartos, probably through censorship. A fifth quarto appeared in 1615, based on the fourth. All the quartos after the first attribute the play to Shakespeare. The added deposition scene in quartos four and five seems to have been memorially reconstructed. The Folio text of 1623 gives a better version of the deposition scene, perhaps because the printers of the Folio had access to the manuscript promptbook for this portion of the text. (Some scholars maintain that the Folio text was derived from an earlier quarto or quartos that had been used as a promptbook.) In any event, most of the Folio was probably set from quarto three, and perhaps from the final two leaves of quarto five, so that the most authoritative text for all but the deposition scene is the first quarto.

Francis Meres mentions the play in 1598. Clearly it had been written and performed prior to the Stationers' Register entry in August of 1597. Its earliest probable date is 1595, since the play is seemingly indebted to Samuel Daniel's poem *The First Fowre Bookes of the Civile Wars* published in that year. Shakespeare follows Daniel, for example, in increasing the queen's age from eleven (according to the chronicles) to maturity, and in other significant details. On December 9, 1595, Sir Edward Hoby invited Sir Robert Cecil to his house in Cannon Row "where as late as it shal please you a gate for your supper shal be open: & K. Richard present him selfe to your vewe." Although it is by no means certain that this passage refers to a private performance of Shakespeare's play, stylistic considerations favor a date around 1595 rather than 1597. If, as some scholars contend, Daniel's *Civile Wars* was written after Shakespeare's play rather than before it, *Richard II* might be as early as 1594.

The First Part of King Henry the Fourth (*c. 1597*)

On February 25, 1598, "The historye of Henry the iiijth with his battaile of Shrewsburye against Henry Hottspurre of the Northe with the conceipted mirthe of Sir John Ffalstoff" was entered in the Stationers' Register by Andrew Wise. Later that year appeared the following quarto:

THE HISTORY OF HENRIE THE FOVRTH; With the battell at Shrewsburie, *betweene the King and Lord* Henry Percy, surnamed Henrie Hotspur of the North. *With the humorous conceits of Sir* Iohn Falstalffe. AT LONDON, Printed by *P. S.* [Peter Short] for *Andrew Wise*, dwelling in Paules Churchyard, at the signe of the Angell. 1598.

Actually this was not the first quarto, for an earlier fragment of eight pages has survived, part of a text that served as copy for the first complete extant quarto. Together these quartos make up an excellent authoritative text, based seemingly on the author's papers. Four more quartos appeared before the Folio of 1623, each based on the previous quarto. The Folio itself was based on the last of these.

The play shows signs of revision in the use of characters' names, most notably that of Falstaff. Plainly the original version of the play called him Sir John Oldcastle, after one of the prince's companions in the anonymous *Famous Victories of Henry the Fifth* (c. 1588). Several lines of verse are one syllable short evidently because "Oldcastle" has been altered to "Falstaff," Falstaff is jokingly referred to as "my old lad of the castle" (*1 Henry IV*, I,ii,47–48), and the speech-prefix "Old." is left standing at I,ii,138 in the quarto of *2 Henry IV*. Moreover, there are several contemporary allusions to a play about a fat knight named Oldcastle. Apparently Henry Brooke, Lord Cobham, a living descendant of the Lollard martyr Oldcastle of Henry v's reign, took umbrage at the profane use Shakespeare had made of this revered name, whereupon Shakespeare's company shifted to another less controversial name from the chronicles, Sir John Fastolfe (called "Falstaff" in the Folio text of Shakespeare's *1 Henry VI* and assigned a cowardly role in the French wars of that play). The revision also changed the names of Oldcastle's cronies from Harvey and Russell to Bardolph and Peto.

Cobham was Lord Chamberlain from July 1596 until his death in March 1597, during which interval Shakespeare's company bore the name of Lord Hunsdon's men. Quite possibly the difficulty over the name Oldcastle erupted during that period, for *1 Henry IV* seems to have been written and performed in late 1596 and early 1597 not long after Shakespeare had finished *Richard II* (c. 1595–1596). *2 Henry IV* must have been written before the end of 1598, so that Shakespeare could then begin *Henry V* in early 1599. Since *2 Henry IV* was originally performed using the names

Oldcastle and Russell, however, we are inclined to date it somewhat earlier, in 1597, before the squabble over the names broke out. Scholars who prefer a date in 1597 for *The Merry Wives* also date *2 Henry IV* early in 1597, since it almost surely introduced Shallow and Pistol before they appeared in *The Merry Wives*. Francis Meres refers in 1598 to "*Henry the* 4" without specifying one or two parts. Publication of *1 Henry IV* in 1598 assured the Elizabethan public that the changes in names to Falstaff, Bardolph, and Peto had taken place; similarly, a revised epilogue to the 1600 quarto of *2 Henry IV* protests that "Oldcastle died a martyr, and this [Falstaff] is not the man," as though by way of apology or disclaimer. A play defending the reputation of the Lollard Oldcastle and attacking Falstaff, called *The History of the Life of Sir John Oldcastle, Lord Cobham, with his Martyrdom*, had been performed by the rival Admiral's men in 1599.

Twelfth Night (*1600–1602*)

Twelfth Night was registered in 1623 and first published in the Folio of that year, in a good text set up from a theatre prompt-book or possibly a transcript of it. The play was first mentioned, however, on Candlemas Day, February 2, 1602, in the following entry from the *Diary* of a Middle Temple law student or barrister named John Manningham:

> At our feast wee had a play called "Twelue Night, or What you Will," much like the Commedy of Errores, or Menechmi in Plautus, but most like and neere to that in Italian called *Inganni*. A good practise in it to make the Steward beleeve his Lady widdowe was in love with him, by counterfeyting a letter as from his Lady in generall termes, telling him what shee liked best in him, and prescribing his gesture in smiling, his apparaile, & c., and then when he came to practise making him beleeue they tooke him to be mad.

This entry was once suspected to be a forgery of John Payne Collier, who published the *Diary* in 1831, but its authenticity is now generally accepted. The date accords with several possible allusions in the play itself. When Fabian jokes about "a pension of thousands to be paid from the Sophy" (II,v,198), he seems to be recalling Sir Anthony Shirley's reception by the Shah of Persia (the Sophy) in 1599–1600. An account of this visit was entered in the S. R. in November of 1601. Viola's description of Feste as "wise enough to play the fool" (III,i,67) may recall a poem beginning "True it is, he plays the fool indeed" published in 1600–1601 by Robert Armin (who played the role of Feste). Maria's comparison of Malvolio's smiling face to "the new map with the augmentation of the Indies" (III,ii,85) refers to new maps of about 1600 in which America (the Indies) was increased in size. Leslie Hotson (*The First Night of Twelfth Night*, 1954) has argued for a first performance at court on Twelfth Night in January of 1601, when Queen Elizabeth entertained Don Virginio Orsino, Duke of Bracciano, but this hypothesis has not gained general acceptance partly because the role of Orsino in the play would scarcely flatter such a noble visitor and partly because there is no proof that any of Shakespeare's plays were originally commissioned for private performance. Nevertheless, a date between 1600 and early 1602 seems most likely. Francis Meres does not mention the play in 1598.

Hamlet (*c. 1599–1601*)

Like everything else about *Hamlet*, the textual problem is complicated. On July 26, 1602, James Roberts entered in the Stationers' Register "A booke called the Revenge of Hamlett Prince Denmarke as yt was latelie Acted by the Lord Chamberleyne his servantes." For some reason, however, Roberts did not print his copy of *Hamlet* until 1604, by which time had appeared the following unauthorized edition:

> THE Tragicall Historie of HAMLET *Prince of Denmarke*. By William Shake-speare. As it hath beene diuerse times acted by his Highnesse seruants in the Cittie of London: as also in the two Vniuersities of Cambridge and Oxford, and else-where. At London printed for N. L. [Nicholas Ling] and Iohn Trundell. 1603.

This edition, the bad quarto of *Hamlet*, seems to have been memorially reconstructed by actors who toured the provinces (note the references to Cambridge, Oxford, etc.), with some recollection of an earlier *Hamlet* play (the *Ur-Hamlet*) written before 1589 and acted during the 1590's.

The authorized quarto of *Hamlet* appeared in 1604. Roberts, the printer, seems to have reached some agreement with Ling, one of the publishers of the bad quarto, for their initials are now paired on the title page:

> *THE* Tragicall Historie of HAMLET, *Prince of Denmarke*. By William Shakespeare. Newly imprinted and enlarged to almost as much againe as it was, according to the true and perfect Coppie. AT LONDON, Printed by I. R. [James Roberts] for N. L. [Nicholas Ling] and are to be sold at his shoppe vnder Saint Dunstons Church in Fleetstreet. 1604.

Some copies of this edition are dated 1605. This text was based seemingly on Shakespeare's own papers, but is marred by printing errors and is at times contaminated by the bad quarto—presumably when the printers found Shakespeare's manuscript unreadable. This quarto served as copy for a third quarto in 1611, Ling having meanwhile transferred his rights in the play to John Smethwick. A fourth quarto, undated but before 1623, was based on the third.

The Folio text of 1623 is derived from a manuscript source independent of that used for the second quarto. The Folio text omits more than two hundred lines found in the quarto, but it also supplies some clearly authentic passages. The consensus today is that the Folio text was set from a prompt-book in use at the time of the Folio printing, or a transcript of it. On the other hand, some textual scholars argue that the Folio text was set from an annotated copy of the second quarto rather than directly from a prompt-book. Since in either case the Folio text evidently contains changes and additions made by actors during years of repeated performance, the text of the Folio is not as close to Shakespeare's own draft as is the second quarto. Nevertheless, the Folio and even the bad quarto supply some authentic readings.

Hamlet must have been produced before the Stationers' Register entry of July 26, 1602. Francis Meres does not mention the play in 1598. Gabriel Harvey attributes the "tragedie of Hamlet, Prince of Denmarke" to Shakespeare in a marginal note in Harvey's copy of Speght's Chaucer; Harvey acquired the book in 1598, but could have written the note any time between then and 1601 or even 1603. More helpful in dating is Hamlet's clear reference to the so-called "War of the Theatres," the rivalry between the adult actors and the boy actors who had newly reopened in 1598–1599 after nearly a decade of inactivity. The Children of the Chapel Royal began acting at Blackfriars in 1598, and provided such keen competition in 1599–1601 that the adult actors were at times forced to tour the provinces (see *Hamlet*, II,ii,343–379). Revenge tragedy was also in fashion during these years: Marston's *Antonio's Revenge*, for example, dates from 1599–1601, and *The Malcontent* is from about the same time or slightly later.

King Lear (*c. 1605*)

On November 26, 1607, Nathaniel Butter and John Busby entered on the Stationers' Register "A booke called. Master William Shakespeare his historye of Kinge Lear, as yt was played before the Kinges maiestie at Whitehall vppon Sainct Stephens night at Christmas Last, by his maiesties servantes playinge vsually at the Globe on the Banksyde." Next year appeared the following quarto:

M. William Shak-speare: *HIS* True Chronicle Historie of the life and death of King LEAR and his three Daughters. *With the vnfortunate life of* Edgar, *sonne* and heire to the Earle of Gloster, and his sullen and assumed humor of TOM of Bedlam: *As it was played before the Kings Maiestie at Whitehall vpon S.* Stephans *night in Christmas Hollidayes.* By his Maiesties seruants playing vsually at the Gloabe on the Bancke-side. LONDON, Printed for *Nathaniel Butter*, and are to be sold at his shop in *Pauls* Church-yard at the signe of the Pide Bull neere St. *Austins* Gate. 1608.

This quarto is often called the "Pied Bull" quarto in reference to its place of sale. Twelve copies exist today, in ten different "states," because proofreading was being carried on while the sheets were being run off in the press; the copies variously combine corrected and uncorrected sheets. A second quarto, printed in 1619 by William Jaggard for Thomas Pavier with the fraudulent date of 1608, was based on a copy of the first quarto combining corrected and uncorrected sheets.

The Folio text of 1623 was also set up from a copy of the first quarto in a state of partial correction. The copy used for this occasion, however, had been carefully emended by reference to some authoritative manuscript, probably a prompt-book of a version of the play cut for performance. Although some 300 lines are deleted, some 100 other lines are added, and in general the Folio text gives evidence of being substantially closer to Shakespeare's original than any of its predecessors. The first quarto itself was not a "bad" quarto in the usual sense, but it does seem to have been based on a careless copy of Shakespeare's draft to which some actors were somehow a party. Whether the actors thus involved were the entire company putting together a text on tour to replace a missing prompt-book, or a single reporter, or the boys who played Goneril and Regan, is a matter of dispute; but in any event this quarto text is not generally as reliable as the Folio text except (obviously) for those 300 or so lines which the Folio omits. The modern tendency is to follow the Folio text except where it is manifestly defective or corrupt.

The Stationers' Register entry for November 26, 1607, describes a performance at court on the previous St. Stephen's night, December 26, 1606. The title page of the first quarto confirms this performance on St. Stephen's night. Such a performance at court was not likely to have been the first, however. Shakespeare's repeated use of Samuel Harsnett's *Declaration of Egregious Popishe Impostures*, registered on March 16, 1603, sets an early limit for composition of the play. Other circumstances point to the existence of the play by May of 1605. In that month, an old play called *The True Chronicle History of King Leir* was entered in the Stationers' Register as a "Tragecall historie," a phrase suggesting the influence of Shakespeare's play since the old *King Leir* does not end tragically. Moreover, the title page of the old *King Leir*, issued in 1605, proclaims the text to be "as it hath bene diuers and sundry times lately acted." In view of the unlikelihood that such an old play (written before 1594) would be revived in 1605, scholars have suggested that the title page was the publisher's way of trying to capitalize on the recent popularity of Shakespeare's play. In this case, the likeliest date for the composition of Shakespeare's *King Lear* would be in the winter of 1604–1605. Shakespeare certainly used the old *King Leir* as a chief source, but he need not have waited for its publication in 1605 if, as seems perfectly plausible, his company owned the prompt-book. On the other hand, Gloucester's mentioning of "These late eclipses in the sun and moon" (I,ii) seems to refer to an eclipse of the moon in September and of the sun in October of 1605, and we are left wondering if Shakespeare was so foresighted as to have anticipated these events.

The Tempest (*c.* 1610–1611)

The Tempest was first printed in the Folio of 1623. It occupies first place in the volume, and is a scrupulously prepared text from a transcript by Ralph Crane of a theatre prompt-book or of Shakespeare's draft after it had been annotated for production. Shakespeare's colleagues may have placed it first in the Folio because they considered it his most recent complete play. The first recorded performance was at court on November 1, 1611: "Hallomas nyght was presented att Whithall before ye kinges Maiestie a play Called the Tempest." The actors were "the Kings players" (*Revels Account*). The play was again presented at court during the winter of 1612–1613, this time "before the Princes Highnes the Lady Elizabeth and the Prince Pallatyne Elector." The festivities for this important betrothal and wedding were sumptuous, and included at least thirteen other plays. Various arguments have been put forward that Shakespeare composed parts of *The Tempest*, especially the masque, for this occasion, but there is absolutely no evidence that the play was singled out for special prominence among the many plays presented, and the masque is integral to the play as it stands. Probably the 1611 production was of a fairly new play. Simon Forman, who saw *Cymbeline* and *The Winter's Tale* in 1611, does not mention *The Tempest*. He died in September of 1611. According to every stylistic test, such as run-on and hypermetric lines, the play is very late. Shakespeare probably knew Sylvester Jourdain's *A Discovery of the Barmudas*, published in 1610, and William Strachey's *A true Reportory of the Wracke and Redemption*, dated July 1610 although not published until 1625.

The Sonnets

On May 20, 1609, "Thomas Thorpe Entred for his copie vnder thandes of master Wilson and master Lownes Warden a Booke called Shakespeares sonnettes." In the same year appeared the following volume:

SHAKE-SPEARES SONNETS. Neuer before Imprinted. AT LONDON By *G. Eld* for *T. T.* and are to be solde by *John Wright*, dwelling at Christ Church gate. 1609.

Some copies of this same edition are marked to be sold by William Aspley rather than John Wright; evidently Thorpe had set up two sellers to distribute the volume. The sonnets were not reprinted until John Benson's rearranged edition of 1640, possibly because the first edition had been suppressed or because sonnets were no longer in vogue. The 1609 edition does not give us a good text; it may rest on an authoritative manuscript, but the edition itself is marred by misprints. Clearly it was not supervised through the press as were *Venus and Adonis* and *The Rape of Lucrece*. All the evidence suggests that it was pirated from a manuscript that had been in private circulation (as we know from Francis Meres' 1598 allusion to Shakespeare's "sugred Sonnets among his priuate friends"). Two sonnets, 138 and 144, had appeared in 1599 in *The Passionate Pilgrim*. On questions of dating and order of the sonnets, see Introduction, pp. 301–305 above.

SOURCES

Romeo and Juliet

Shakespeare's chief source for *Romeo and Juliet* was a long narrative poem by Arthur Brooke called *The Tragicall Historye of Romeus and Juliet, written first in Italian by Bandell, and nowe in Englishe by Ar. Br.* (1562). Other English versions of this popular legend were available to Shakespeare, especially in William Painter's *The Palace of Pleasure* (1566), but Shakespeare shows only a passing indebtedness to it. Brooke mentions having seen (prior to 1562) a play about the two lovers, but such an old play is not likely to have been of much service to Shakespeare. Nor does he appear to have consulted extensively the various continental versions that lay behind Brooke's poem. Still, these versions help explain the genesis of the story.

The use of a sleeping potion to escape an unwelcome marriage goes back at least to the *Ephesiaca* of Xenophon of Ephesus (by the fifth century A.D.). Masuccio of Salerno, in his *Il Novellino* (1476), seems to have been the first to combine this sleeping potion story with an ironic aftermath of misunderstanding and suicide (as found in the Pyramus and Thisbe story of Ovid's *Metamorphoses*). In Masuccio's account, the lovers Mariotto and Giannozza of Siena are secretly married by a friar. When Mariotto kills a prominent citizen of Siena in a quarrel, he is banished to Alexandria. Giannozza, to avoid marriage with a suitor of her father's choosing, takes a sleeping potion given her by the friar, and is buried as though dead. She is thereupon taken from the tomb by the friar and sent on her way to Alexandria. Mariotto, however, having failed to hear from her because the messenger is intercepted by pirates, returns in disguise to her tomb where he is discovered and executed. Giannozza, hearing this sad news, retires to a Sienese convent and dies of a broken heart.

In Luigi da Porto's *Hystoria nouellamente ritrouata di due Nobili Amanti* (published c. 1530), based on Masuccio's account, the scene shifts to Verona. Despite the feuding of their two families, the Montecchi and the Cappelletti, Romeo and Guilietta meet and fall in love at a carnival ball. Romeo at once forgets his unrequited passion for a scornful lady. Friar Lorenzo, an experimenter in magic, secretly marries the lovers. Romeo tries to avoid brawling with the Cappelletti, but when some of his own kinsmen suffer defeat, he kills Theobaldo Cappelletti. After Romeo's departure for Mantua, Guilietta's family arranges a match for her with the Count of Lodrone. Friar Lorenzo gives Guilietta a sleeping potion and sends a letter to Romeo by a fellow friar, but this messenger is unable to find Romeo in Mantua. Romeo, hearing of Guilietta's supposed death from her servant Peter, returns to Verona with a poison he already possesses. Guilietta awakens in time to converse with Romeo before he dies. Then, refusing the friar's advice to retire to a convent, she dies by stopping her own breath. This story provides no equivalents for Mercutio and the Nurse, although a young man named Marcuccio appears briefly at the Cappelletti's ball.

Da Porto's version inspired that of Matteo Bandello in his *Novelle* of 1554. Some details are added: Romeo goes to the ball in a vizard, he has a servant named Pietro, a rope ladder is given to the Nurse enabling Romeo to visit Julietta's chamber before their marriage, Romeo obtains a poison from one Spolentino, etc. The young man at the ball, Marcuccio, is now named Mercutio but is still a minor figure. This Bandello version was translated into French by Pierre Boaistuau in his *Histoires Tragiques* (1559); Boaistuau adds the apothecary (who is racked and hanged for his part in the tragedy), and has Romeo die before Juliet awakens and slays herself with Romeo's dagger.

Despite Arthur Brooke's implication on the title page that his version is based on Bandello, the narrative poem *Romeus and Juliet* is taken from Boaistuau. Brooke's is a severely pious work written in "Poulter's Measure," couplets with alternating lines of six and seven feet. Brooke openly disapproves of the lovers' carnality and haste, although fortunately the story itself remains sympathetic to Romeus and Juliet. Brooke stresses the role of star-crossed fortune and the antithesis of love and hate. He reduces Juliet's age from eighteen (as in Bandello) to sixteen. (Shakespeare further reduced her age to less than fourteen.) Brooke's narrative is generally close to Shakespeare's, though with important exceptions. Shakespeare compresses the time scheme from some nine months to a few days. In Brooke, for example, some two weeks elapse between the masked ball and Romeus' encounter with Juliet in her garden, and about two months elapse between the marriage and Tybalt's death. In Shakespeare, Capulet moves the wedding up from Thursday to Wednesday, thereby complicating the time schedule for the lovers. Shakespeare also unifies his play by such devices as introducing Tybalt and Paris early in the story; in Brooke, Tybalt appears only at the time he is slain, and Juliet's proposed marriage to Count Paris emerges as a threat only after Romeus' banishment. Shakespeare's greatest transformation is of the characters. Brooke's Juliet is scheming. His Mercutio remains a shadowy figure as in Bandello et al. Brooke's Nurse is unattractive, although she does occasionally hint at comic greatness: for example, she garrulously confides to Romeus the details of Juliet's infancy, and then keeps Juliet on tenterhooks while she prates about Romeus' fine qualities (ll. 631–714). Even if Shakespeare's play is incomparably superior to Brooke's drably-versified poem, the indebtedness is extensive.

A Midsummer Night's Dream

No single source has been discovered that unites the various elements we find in *A Midsummer Night's Dream*, but the four main strands of action can be individually discussed in terms of sources. The four strands are: (1) the marriage of Duke Theseus and Queen Hippolyta, (2) the romantic tribulations and triumphs of the four young lovers, (3) the quarrel of King Oberon and Queen Titania, together with the fairies' manipulations of human affairs, and (4) the "rude mechanicals" and their play of "Pyramus and Thisbe."

For his conception of Theseus, Shakespeare went chiefly to Chaucer's *Knight's Tale* and to Thomas North's 1579 translation of The Life of Theseus in Plutarch's *Lives of the Noble Grecians and Romanes*. Chaucer's Theseus is a duke of "wysdom" and "chivalrie," renowned for his conquest of the Amazons and his marriage to Hippolyta. Plutarch provides information concerning Theseus' other conquests (to which Oberon alludes in II,i), including that of Antiopa. Shakespeare could have learned more about Theseus from Chaucer's *The Legend of Good Women* and from Ovid's *Metamorphoses*. He seems to have blended all or some of these impressions together with his own ideal of a noble yet popular Renaissance ruler.

The romantic narrative of the four lovers appears to be original with Shakespeare, although one can find many analogous situations of misunderstanding and rivalry in love. Chaucer's *Knight's Tale* tells of two friends battling over one woman. Shakespeare's own *The Two Gentlemen of Verona* gives us four lovers, properly matched at first until one of the men shifts his attentions to his friend's lady-love; eventually all is righted when the false lover recovers his senses. Parallel situations arise in Sidney's *Arcadia* and in Montemayor's *Diana*, a source for *The Two Gentlemen*. What Shakespeare adds in *A Midsummer* is the intervention of the fairies in human love affairs.

Shakespeare's knowledge of fairy lore must have been extensive, and is hard to trace exactly. Doubtless much of it was from oral traditions. In Chaucer's *Merchant's Tale*, Pluto and Proserpina as king and queen of the fairies intervene in the affairs of old January, his young wife May, and her lover Damyan. Fairies appear on stage in Lyly's *Endymion* (1588), protecting true lovers and tormenting those who are morally tainted. Shakespeare later reflects this tradition in *The Merry Wives of Windsor* (1597–1601). The name Oberon probably comes from the French romance *Huon of Bordeaux* (translated by Lord Berners by about 1540), where Oberon is a dwarfish fairy king from the mysterious East who practices enchantment in a haunted wood. In Spenser's *The Faerie Queene*, Oberon is the Elfin father of Queen Gloriana (II,x,75–76). Greene's *James IV* (c. 1591) also features Oberon as the fairy king, and a lost play called *Huon of Bordeaux* was performed by Sussex' men at about this same time. The name Titania comes from Ovid's *Metamorphoses*, where it is used as a synonym for both the enchantress Circe and the chaste goddess Diana. The name Titania does not appear in Golding's translation, suggesting that Shakespeare found it in the original. Puck or Robin Goodfellow is essentially the product of oral tradition, although Reginald Scot's *The Discoverie of Witchcraft* (1584) discusses Robin in pejorative terms as an incubus or hobgoblin in whom intelligent people no longer believe.

Scot also reports the story of a man who finds an ass' head placed on his shoulders by enchantment. Similar legends of transformation occur in Apuleius' *The Golden Ass* (translated by William Adlington, 1566) and in the well-known story of the ass' ears bestowed by Phoebus on King Midas for his presumption. Perhaps the most suggestive possible source for Shakespeare's clownish actors, however, is Anthony Munday's play *John a Kent and John a Cumber* (c. 1587–1590). In it a group of rude artisans, led by the intrepid Turnop, stage a ludicrous interlude written by their churchwarden in praise of his millhorse. Turnop's prologue is a medley of lofty comparisons. The entertainment is presented before noble spectators, who are graciously amused. *John a Kent* also features a lot of magic trickery, a boy named Shrimp whose role is comparable to that of Puck, and a multiple love plot.

"Pyramus and Thisbe" itself is based on the *Metamorphoses* (IV,67 ff.). Other versions Shakespeare may have known include Chaucer's *The Legend of Good Women*, a poem by William Griffith in 1562, George Pettie's *A Petite Pallace of Pettie His Pleasure* (1576), *A Gorgeous Gallery of Gallant Inventions* (1578), and "A New Sonet of Pyramus and Thisbe" from Clement Robinson's *A Handefull of Pleasant Delites* (1584). Several of these, especially the last three, are bad enough to have given Shakespeare materials to lampoon, though the sweep of his parody goes beyond the particular story of Pyramus and Thisbe. The occasionally stilted phraseology of Golding's translation of *The Metamorphoses* contributed to the fun. According to Kenneth Muir (*Shakespeare's Sources*, 1957), Shakespeare must also have known Thomas Mouffet's *Of the Silkewormes and their Flies* (published 1599, but possibly circulated earlier in manuscript), which contains perhaps the most ridiculous of all versions of the Pyramus and Thisbe story.

Richard the Second

Shakespeare's primary source for *Richard II* was the 1587 edition of Holinshed's *Chronicles* covering the years 1398 to 1400. As in his earlier *Henry VI* plays and *Richard III*, Shakespeare departs from historical accuracy in the interests of artistic design. Queen Isabel's part is almost wholly invented, for historically she was a child of eleven at the time the events in this play occurred. Her "Garden Scene" is a fine piece of invention, bringing together images of order and disorder that are woven into the rest of the play. The Duchess of York's role is entirely original; Holinshed reports the scene in which York's son Aumerle (the Earl of Rutland) rides to the king and begs for mercy while his father simultaneously denounces him as a traitor, but the Duchess is never mentioned. Shakespeare has added the poignant conflict between husband and wife. Northumberland's role as conspirator against Richard and as hatchetman for Bolingbroke is greatly enlarged; for example, Holinshed never names the persons who engage in the original plotting against Richard. Another invention is the meeting between John of Gaunt and the Duchess of Gloucester (I,ii). In fact, most of Gaunt's character and behavior has no basis in Holinshed at all. Shakespeare creates him to fill the role of thoughtfully conservative statesman, agonized by his son's banishment but doggedly obedient to his monarch. Finally, and most importantly, Shakespeare has greatly enlarged the role and the poetic nature of King Richard, especially in the final two acts.

Many of these alterations are Shakespeare's own; others derive from his reading in other sources. Samuel Daniel's *The First Fowre Bookes of the Civile Wars*, 1595, may have had an important influence. Although we cannot discount the possibility that Shakespeare's play may have been written first, the consensus today is that he knew Daniel's poem. It gave him the idea of the queen's maturity and grief (although not the Garden Scene), and the final meeting of king and queen. Daniel's Hotspur is unhistorically a young man, as in II,iii of Shakespeare's play. Like Shakespeare, Daniel sees York as a man of "a mild temperateness." Daniel's Richard and Bolingbroke ride together into London, not separately as in Holinshed. In Daniel's poem, Bolingbroke's indirect manner of insinuating his desire for Richard's death ("And wisht that some would so his life esteeme As rid him of these feares wherein he stood") is verbally close to Shakespeare's depiction of this scene. Richard's final soliloquies in these two works show an unmistakable similarity to one another.

Richard II's reign was an explosively controversial subject in the 1590's, and produced other plays of varying political coloration that Shakespeare must have known. *The Life and Death of Jack Straw* (anonymous, 1590–1593) gives a distortedly friendly portrait of Richard in his handling of the Peasants' Revolt of 1381, with a blatant whitewashing of governmental policy. Contrastingly, the anonymous play *Thomas of Woodstock*, sometimes known as *1 Richard II* (1591–1595), is almost a rallying cry to open rebellion against tyranny. Many verbal echoes link this latter play with Shakespeare's *Richard II*, and, although scholars have difficulty in determining which was written first, the wary consensus is that Shakespeare borrowed from *Woodstock*. Such a hypothesis would explain some of the mysterious references to Woodstock's death in the first act of *Richard II*, since the anonymous play deals with historical events preceding those of Shakespeare's play. Shakespeare's debt to *Jack Straw*, on the other hand, is slight even though he probably knew it. Marlowe's *Edward II* (c. 1592), although dealing with another reign, probably taught Shakespeare much about construction of a play in which a deplorably weak king gains sympathy in his suffering while his successful deposer becomes morally tainted by his act.

Other sources have been proposed, so many in fact that Shakespeare's task of writing the play has been compared to that of a historical researcher. More probably he had read several possible sources at one time or another and assimilated them without any formal program of research. He had certainly read Edward Hall's *Union of the Two Noble Famelies*, a chief source for his earlier history plays, but in *Richard II* he seems to have recalled little more than its overall thematic pattern. Shakespeare must have known the complaints of Mowbray and Richard in *A Myrroure for Magistrates*, but the verbal echoes are slight in this case. The same is essentially true of *The Cronycles of Englande* by John Froissart, translated by Lord Berners (1525), and two French eye-witness accounts available to Shakespeare only in manuscript: the anonymous *Chronicque de la Traïson et Mort de Richart Deux Roy Dengleterre* and Jean Créton's *Histoire du Roy d'Angleterre Richard*. The Froissart *Cronycles* perhaps give some hints for Gaunt's refusal to avenge Gloucester's death, for Richard's insensitivity at Gaunt's death, and for Northumberland's role as conspirator. The *Traïson* is notably sympathetic to Richard in his decline, although Shakespeare might also have found this sympathy in Daniel's *Civile Wars*.

Shakespeare's second tetralogy is considerably less wedded to Tudor orthodoxy than his first, less intent on proving a providential design in England's suffering. The second tetralogy does not lead forward by any direct link to the reign of the Tudors, as the first had done. Henry A. Kelly has recently shown (*Divine Providence in the England of Shakespeare's Histories*, 1970), that Shakespeare does not follow a single "Tudor myth" but allows spokesmen for both pro-Lancastrian and anti-Lancastrian sentiment to repeat arguments found in the various chronicles. This practice is especially evident in *Richard II*, in which some spokesmen eloquently warn of the disasters that will follow Bolingbroke's assumption of the throne, while other spokesmen are sympathetic to Bolingbroke's takeover as a political necessity.

The First Part of King Henry the Fourth

Shakespeare's chief source of information for both *Henry IV* plays was the 1587 edition of Holinshed's *Chronicles*, but Shakespeare also found an important guiding spirit in Samuel Daniel's *The First Fowre Bookes of the Civile Wars* (1595). Following Daniel, Shakespeare readjusts the age of Hotspur (who was historically older than Henry IV) to match that of Prince Hal. Daniel's Hotspur is, like Shakespeare's, dauntless and wrongheaded, a turbulent yet noble spirit. The theme of a Nemesis of rebellion afflicting Henry IV for his usurpation owes much to Daniel's presentation, although the idea of Nemesis is to be found also in Holinshed. Both Daniel and Holinshed err in confusing the Edmund Mortimer whom Glendower captured with his nephew Edmund Mortimer, claimant to the throne; Shakespeare perpetuates this error. Hal's killing of Hotspur is unhistorical, since both Holinshed and Daniel report only that Hal bravely helped rescue his father from attack, and that Hotspur was killed in the melee. Shakespeare invents the scenes in which we see Mortimer as a devoted husband and Hotspur as a fond wit-combatant with his wife Kate; Holinshed merely informs us that these two men were married. Shakespeare greatly expands Glendower's fascination with magic and poetry, changing him from a ruthless barbarian (in Holinshed) into a cranky but charismatic Welshman. Hotspur, despite hints from Daniel, is chiefly Shakespeare's creation.

The most impressive transformations are those of Hal and Falstaff. Shakespeare knew many legends of Hal's wild youth, some of them probably from John Stow's *The Chronicles of England* (1580) and *The Annales of England* (1592), others doubtlessly from oral tradition. Sir Thomas Elyot's *The Governour* (1531) gives an account of Hal's encounter with the Lord Chief Justice that is reproduced almost verbatim by Stow. Most of these stories were also available in Holinshed. Shakespeare's readiest source, however, was a rowdy and chauvinistic play called *The Famous Victories of Henry the Fifth*, registered 1594 but usually ascribed to Richard Tarleton around 1587 or 1588. This play covers all the events of the *Henry IV* plays and *Henry V* in one chaotic sequence. Prince Hal has three companions, Sir John Oldcastle, Tom, and Ned (cf. Ned Poins), in whose company he robs the king's receivers of £1,000, visits the old tavern in East Cheap, sorely grieves his father, and strikes the Lord Chief Justice. A crucial difference is that this Hal is truly unregenerate. He not only robs and wenches, but endorses the idea of plundering the rich and encourages his companions to look forward to unrestricted license when he is king. The blow he delivers the Chief Justice is a blow for freedom. Hal seems actively to desire his father's death. Yet he does reform, and banishes his companions beyond a ten-mile limit with a promise to assist them if they mend their ways. Although this reform is crude and sudden, Hal's reputation for the common touch stands him in good stead when he goes to war against the French. He is followed by a comic crew of London artisans and thieves who prove invincible against the effete enemy.

This play suggests the unsophisticated nature of the legends Shakespeare inherited about Hal's riotous youth, and the extent of the transformation. Most of all, Shakespeare's portrayal of Falstaff is essentially his own. Sir John Oldcastle of the anonymous play is a minor character, not even Hal's closest companion. To an extent, Falstaff owes something to the tradition of the guileful and inventive Vice of the Tudor morality play (especially when Falstaff is called jestingly "that reverend vice, that grey iniquity"), but the morality play influence is general rather than specific. To label Falstaff a "Vice" is to reduce him to comic tempter and villain. Falstaff is partly also an allowed fool, a parasite, and a *miles gloriosus* or braggart soldier, but he transcends all these conventionalized types with his own unique vitality.

The *Henry IV* plays may also reveal some acquaintance with the anonymous play *Thomas of Woodstock* (c. 1591–1595), which Shakespeare may also have used in *Richard II*, and with the complaints of Owen Glendower and Northumberland in *A Myrroure for Magistrates* (1559). In neither case is the debt extensive.

Twelfth Night

John Manningham's description of a performance of *Twelfth Night* on February 2, 1602, at the Middle Temple, compares the play to Plautus' *The Menaechmi* and to an Italian play called *Inganni*. The comment offers a helpful hint on sources. *The Menaechmi* had been the chief source for Shakespeare's earlier *The Comedy of Errors*, and that farce of mistaken identity clearly resembles *Twelfth Night* in the hilarious mixups resulting from the confusion of two look-alike twins. Shakespeare undoubtedly profited from his earlier experimenting with this sort of comedy. *Twelfth Night* had no need to be directly indebted to *The Menaechmi*, however, for Renaissance Italian comedy offered many imitations of Plautus from which Shakespeare could have taken his *Twelfth Night* plot. These include *Gl'Inganni* (1562) by Nicolò Secchi, another *Gl'Inganni* (1592) by Curzio Gonzaga, and most importantly an anonymous *Gl'Ingannati* (published 1537). This last play was translated into French by Charles Estienne as *Les Abusés* (1543), and adapted into Spanish by Lope de Rueda in *Los Engaños* (1567). A Latin version, *Laelia*, based on the French, was performed at Cambridge in the 1590's but never printed. Obviously, *Gl'Ingannati* was widely known, and Manningham was probably referring to it in his diary. To trace Shakespeare's own reading in this matter is difficult, owing to the large number of versions available to him, but we can note the suggestive points of comparison in each.

Both *Inganni* plays feature a brother and a sister mistaken for one another. In the later of these plays (by Gonzaga, 1592), the sister uses the disguise name of "Cesare." In Secchi's *Inganni* (1562), the disguised sister is in love with her master, who is told that a woman the exact age of his supposed page is secretly in love with him. Another play by Secchi, *L'Interesse* (1581), has a comic duel involving the disguised heroine. Of the Italian plays here considered, however, *Gl'Ingannati* (1537) is closest to Shakespeare's play. A short prefatory entertainment included with it in most editions features the name Malevolti. In the play itself, the heroine Lelia disguises herself as a page in the service of Flaminio, whom she secretly loves, and is sent on embassies to Flaminio's disdainful mistress Isabella. This lady falls in love with "Fabio," as Lelia calls herself. Lelia's father Virginio, learning of her disguise and resolving to marry her to old Gherardo (Isabella's father), seeks out Lelia but instead mistakenly arrests her long-lost twin brother, Fabrizio, who has just arrived in Modena. Fabrizio is locked up as a madman in Isabella's room, whereupon Isabella takes the opportunity to betroth herself to the person she mistakes for "Fabio." A recognition scene clears up everything and leads to the marriages of Fabrizio to Isabella and Flaminio to Lelia. This story lacks the subplot of Malvolio, Sir Toby et al. Nor is there a shipwreck.

Bandello based one of the stories in his *Novelle* (1554) on *Gl'Ingannati*, and this prose version was then translated into French by Belleforest in his *Histoires Tragiques* (1579 edition). Shakespeare may well have read both, for he consulted these collections of stories in writing *Much Ado about Nothing*. His most direct source, however, seems to have been the story "Of Apolonius and Silla" in *Riche his Farewell to Militarie profession* (1581), derived from Belleforest. Its heroine, Silla, is washed ashore near Constantinople, where, disguised as "Silvio," she takes service with Duke Apolonius. When she is sent on embassies to the lady Julina, this wealthy widow falls in love with "Silvio." The real Silvio, her twin brother, arrives and is invited by Julina to a dinner rendezvous. The next day he departs on his quest for Silla, leaving Julina pregnant. When Apolonius learns of "Silvio's" apparent success with Julina, he throws the page into prison and angrily charges him with hateful abominations. Julina is understandably distressed to learn that the supposed father of her child is in actuality a woman. Finally all is resolved when Silvio returns to marry Julina. The story has only the merest hint of a Malvolio subplot. Shakespeare has minimized the moral predicaments in his source: Sebastian does not get Olivia with child before their marriage, nor does he desert her. Correspondingly, Viola is not thrown into prison. Shakespeare studiously avoids Riche's stern moralizing about the bestiality of lust. He changes the setting to Illyria, though in fact the flavor is Elizabethan English.

Shakespeare's reading may also have included the anonymous play *Sir Clyomon and Sir Clamydes* (c. 1570–1583), Sidney's *Arcadia* (1590), and Emmanuel Forde's prose romance *Parismus* (1598) in which one "Violetta" borrows the disguise of a page. The Malvolio plot may conceivably have reflected an incident at court in which the Comptroller of the Household, Sir William Knollys, interrupted a noisy party late at night dressed only in his nightshirt and a pair of spectacles, with a copy of Aretine in his hand. A similar confrontation between revelry and sobriety occurred in 1598: Ambrose Willoughby quieted a disturbance after the queen had gone to bed, and was afterwards thanked by her for doing his duty. Such incidents were no doubt common, however, and there is no compelling reason to suppose Shakespeare was sketching from real-life situations.

Hamlet

The ultimate source of the *Hamlet* story is Saxo Grammaticus' *Historia Danica* (1180–1208), the saga of one Amlothi or (as Saxo calls him) Amlethus. The outline of the story is essentially that of Shakespeare's play, even though the emphasis of the Danish saga is overwhelmingly on cunning, brutality, and bloody revenge. Amlethus' father is Horwendil, a governor of Jutland, who bravely kills the King of Norway in single combat and thereby wins the hand in marriage of Gerutha, daughter of the King of Denmark. This good fortune goads the envious Feng into slaying his brother Horwendil and marrying Gerutha, "capping unnatural murder with incest." Though the deed is known to everyone, Feng invents excuses and soon wins the approbation of the fawning courtiers. Young Amlethus vows revenge, but perceiving his uncle's cunning he feigns madness. His mingled words of craft and candor awaken suspicions that he may be playing a game of deception.

Two attempts are made to lure Amlethus into betraying his sanity. The first plan is to tempt him into lechery, on the theory that one who lusts for women cannot be truly insane. Feng causes an attractive woman to be placed in a forest where Amlethus will meet her as though by chance; but Amlethus, secretly warned of the trap by a kindly foster brother, spirits the young lady off to a hideaway where they can make love unobserved by Feng's agents. She confesses the plot to Amlethus. In a second stratagem, a courtier who is reported to be "gifted with more assurance than judgment" hides himself under some straw in the queen's chamber in order to overhear her private conversations with Amlethus. The hero, suspecting just such a trap, feigns madness and begins crowing like a noisy rooster, bouncing up and down on the straw until he finds the eavesdropper. Amlethus stabs the man to death, drags him forth, cuts the body into morsels, boils the morsels, and flings them "through the mouth of an open sewer for the swine to eat." Thereupon he returns to his mother to accuse her of being an infamous harlot. He wins her over to repentant virtue and even cooperation. When Feng, returning from a journey, looks around for his counselor, Amlethus jestingly (but in part truly) suggests that the man went to the sewer and fell in.

Feng now sends Amlethus to the King of Britain, with secret orders for his execution. However, Amlethus finds the letter to the British king in the coffers of the two unnamed retainers accompanying him on the journey, and substitutes a new letter ordering their execution instead. The new letter, purportedly written and signed by Feng, goes on to urge that the King of Britain marry his daughter to a young Dane being sent from the Danish court. By this means Amlethus gains an English wife and rids himself of the escorts. A year later Amlethus returns to Jutland, gets the entire court drunk, flings a tapestry (knitted for him by his mother) over the prostrate courtiers, secures the tapestry with stakes, and then sets fire to the palace. Feng escapes this holocaust, but Amlethus cuts him down with the king's own sword. (Amlethus exchanges swords because his own has been rendered useless by his enemies.) Subsequently, Amlethus convinces the people of the justice of his cause and is chosen King of Jutland. After ruling for several years, he returns to Britain, marries a Scottish queen, fights a battle with his first father-in-law, is betrayed by his second wife, and is finally killed in battle.

In Saxo's account we thus find the prototypes of Hamlet, Claudius, Gertrude, Polonius, Ophelia, Rosencrantz, and Guildenstern. Several episodes are close in narrative detail to Shakespeare's play: the original murder and incestuous marriage, the feigned madness, the woman used as a decoy, the eavesdropping counselor, and especially the trip to England. A translation of Saxo into French by François de Belleforest, in *Histoires Tragiques* (1576 edition), adds a few details such as Gertrude's adultery before the murder, and Hamlet's melancholy. Belleforest's version is longer than Saxo's, with more psychological and moral observation and more dialogue. Shakespeare may have consulted it.

Shakespeare need not have depended extensively on these older versions of his story, however. His main source was almost certainly an old play of *Hamlet*. Much evidence proves the existence of such a play. Henslowe's *Diary* records a performance, not marked as "new," of a *Hamlet* at Newington Butts on June 11, 1594, by "my Lord Admeralle men" or "my Lorde Chamberlen men," probably the latter. Thomas Lodge's *Wits Miserie, and the Worlds Madnesse* (1596) refers to "the Visard of the ghost which cried so miserably at the Theator, like an oister wife, Hamlet, revenge." And Thomas Nashe, in his *Epistle* prefixed to Greene's *Menaphon* (1589), offers the following observation:

> It is a common practise now a dayes amongst a sort of shifting companions, that runne through euery Art and thriue by none, to leaue the trade of *Nouerint*, whereto they were borne, and busie themselues with the endeuours of Art, that could scarcely Latinize their neck verse if they should haue neede; yet English *Seneca* read by Candlelight yeelds many good sentences, as *Blood is a begger*, and so forth; and if you intreate him faire in a frostie morning, hee will affoord you whole *Hamlets*, I should say handfuls of Tragical speeches. But O griefe! *Tempus edax rerum*, whats that will last alwayes? The Sea exhaled by droppes will in continuance bee drie, and *Seneca*, let blood line by line and page by page, at length must needes die to our Stage; which makes his famished followers to imitate the Kidde in Æsop, who, enamoured with the Foxes newfangles, forsooke all hopes of life to leape into a newe occupation; and these men, renouncing all possibilities of credite or estimation, to intermeddle with Italian Translations . . .

Nashe's testimonial describes a *Hamlet* play, written in the Senecan style by some person born to the trade of "Noverint" or scrivener who has turned to hack writing and translation. The description has often been fitted to Thomas Kyd, though this identification is not certain. (Nashe could be punning on Kyd's name when he refers to "the Kidde in Æsop.") Certainly Thomas Kyd's *The Spanish Tragedy* (c. 1587) shows many affinities with Shakespeare's play, and provides many Senecan ingredients missing from Saxo and Belleforest: the ghost, the difficulty in ascertaining whether the ghost's words are believable, the resulting need for delay and a feigning of madness, the moral perplexities afflicting a sensitive man called upon to revenge, the play within the play, the clever reversals and ironically-caused deaths in the catastrophe, the rhetoric of tragical passion. Whether or not Kyd in fact wrote the *Ur-Hamlet*, his extant play enables us to see more clearly what that lost play must have contained. The pirated first quarto of *Hamlet* (1603) also offers a few seemingly authentic details that are not found in the good second quarto but are found in the earlier sources and may have been a part of the *Ur-Hamlet*. For example, after Hamlet has killed Corambis (corresponding to Polonius), the queen vows to assist Hamlet in his strategies against the king; and later, when Hamlet has returned to England, the queen sends him a message by Horatio warning him to be careful.

One last document sheds important light on the *Ur-Hamlet*. A German play, *Der bestrafte Brudermord* (*Fratricide Punished*), from a now-lost manuscript dated 1710, seems to have been based on a text used by English actors traveling in Germany in 1586 and afterwards. Though changed by translation and manuscript transmission, and too entirely different from Shakespeare's play to have been based on it, this German version may well have been based on Shakespeare's source-play. Polonius' name in this text, Corambus, is the same as the Corambis of the bad quarto of 1603.

Der bestrafte Brudermord begins with a prologue in the Senecan manner, followed by the appearance of the ghost to Francisco, Horatio, and sentinels of the watch. Within the palace, meanwhile, the king carouses. Hamlet joins the watch, confiding to Horatio that he is "sick at heart" over his father's death and mother's hasty remarriage. The ghost appears to Hamlet, tells him how the juice of hebona was poured into his ear, and urges revenge. When Hamlet swears Horatio and Francisco to silence, the ghost (now invisible) says several times "We swear," his voice following the men as they move from place to place. Hamlet reveals to Horatio the entire circumstance of the murder. Later, in a formal session of the court, the new king speaks hypocritically of his brother's death and explains the reasons for his marriage to the queen. Hamlet is forbidden to return to Wittenberg, though Corambus' son Leonhardus has already set out for France.

Some time afterward, Corambus reports the news of Hamlet's madness to the king and queen, and presumes on the basis of his own youthful passions to diagnose Hamlet's malady as love-sickness. Concealed, he and the king overhear Hamlet tell Ophelia to "go to a nunnery." When players arrive from Germany, Hamlet instructs them in the natural style of acting, and then requests them to perform a play before the king about the murder of King Pyrrus by his brother. (Death is again inflicted by hebona poured in the ear.) After the king's guilty reaction to the play, Hamlet finds him alone at prayers but postpones the killing lest the king's soul be sent to heaven. Hamlet kills Corambus behind the tapestry in the queen's chamber, and is visited again by the ghost (who says nothing, however). Ophelia, her mind deranged, thinks herself in love with a court butterfly named Phantasmo. (This creature is also involved in a comic action to help the clown Jens with a tax problem.)

The king sends Hamlet to England with two unnamed courtiers who are verbally instructed to kill Hamlet after their arrival. A contrary wind takes them instead to an island near Dover, where Hamlet foils his two enemies by kneeling between them and asking them to shoot him on signal; at the proper moment, he ducks and they shoot one another. He finishes them off with their own swords, and discovers letters on their persons ordering Hamlet's execution by the English king if the original plot should fail. When Hamlet returns to Denmark, the king arranges a duel between him and Corambus' son Leonhardus. If Leonhardus' poisoned dagger misses its mark, a beaker of wine containing finely ground oriental diamond dust is to do the rest. Hamlet is informed of the impending duel by Phantasmo (cf. Osric), whom Hamlet taunts condescendingly and calls "Signora Phantasmo." Shortly before the duel takes place, Ophelia is reported to have thrown herself off a hill to her death. The other deaths occur much as in Shakespeare's play. The dying Hamlet bids that the crown be conveyed to his cousin, Duke Fortempras of Norway, of whom we have not heard earlier.

From the extensive similarities between *Hamlet* and this German play, we can see that Shakespeare inherited his narrative material almost intact, though in a jumble and so pitifully mangled that the modern reader can only laugh at the contrast. No source study in Shakespeare reveals so clearly the extent of Shakespeare's wholesale borrowing of plot, and the incredible transformation he achieved in reordering his materials.

King Lear

The *Lear* story goes back into ancient legend. The motif of two wicked sisters and a virtuous youngest sister reminds us of Cinderella. Lear himself appears to come from Celtic mythology. Geoffrey of Monmouth, a Welshman in close contact with Celtic legend, included a Lear or Leir as one of the pseudohistorical kings in his *Historia Regum Britanniae* (c. 1136). This fanciful mixture of history and legend traces a supposed line of descent from Brut, great-grandson of Aeneas of Troy, through Locrine, Bladud, Leir, Gorboduc, Ferrex and Porrex, Lud, Cymbeline, Bonduca, Vortigern, Arthur, etc., to the historical kings of England. The Tudor monarchs made much of their purported claim to such an ancient dynasty, and in Shakespeare's day this mythology had a quasi-official status demanding a certain reverential suspension of disbelief.

King Leir, according to Geoffrey, is the father of three daughters, Gonorilla, Regan, and Cordeilla, among whom he intends to divide his kingdom. To determine who deserves most, he asks them who loves him most. The two eldest sisters protest undying devotion; but Cordeilla, perceiving how the others flatter and deceive him, renounces hyperbole and promises only to love him as a daughter should love a father. Furious, the king denies Cordeilla her third of the kingdom but permits her to marry Aganippus, King of the Franks, without dowry. Thereafter Leir bestows his two eldest daughters on the Dukes of Albania and Cornubia (Albany and Cornwall), together with half the island during his lifetime and the possession of the remainder after his death. In due course his two sons-in-law rebel against Leir and seize his power. Thereafter Maglaunus, Duke of Albania, agrees to maintain Leir with sixty retainers, but after two years of chafing at this arrangement Gonorilla insists that the number be reduced to thirty. Angrily the king goes to Henvin, Duke of Cornubia, where all goes well for a time; within a year, however, Regan demands that Leir reduce his retinue to five knights. When Gonorilla refuses to take him back with more than one retainer, Leir crosses into France and is generously received by Cordeilla and Aganippus. An invasion restores Leir to his throne. Three years later he and Aganippus die, after which Cordeilla rules successfully for five years until overthrown by the sons of Maglaunus and Henvin. In prison she commits suicide.

This story, as part of England's mythic genealogy, was repeated in various Tudor versions such as *The First parte of the Mirour for Magistrates* (1574), William Warner's *Albions England* (1586), and Holinshed's *Chronicles*. Warner refers to the king's sons-in-law as "the Prince of Albany" and "the Cornish prince"; Holinshed refers to them as "the Duke of Albania" and "the Duke of Cornwall," but reports that it is Cornwall who marries the eldest daughter Gonorilla. *The Mirour* closer to Shakespeare in these details, speaks of "Gonerell" as married to "Albany" and of "Cordila" as married to "the king of Fraunce." Spenser's *The Faerie Queene* (II,x,27–32) reports that "Cordeill" or "Cordelia" ends her life by hanging herself. Other retellings appear in Gerard Legh's *Accidence of Armory* and William Camden's *Remaines.* All of these accounts leave the story virtually unchanged.

Shakespeare's immediate source for *King Lear*, however, was an old play called *The True Chronicle History of King Leir*. It was published in 1605 but plainly is much earlier in style. The Stationers' Register for May 14, 1594, lists "A booke called the Tragecall historie of kinge Leir and his Three Daughters &c.," and a short time earlier Henslowe's *Diary* records the performance of a "Kinge Leare" at the Rose theatre on April 6 and 8, 1594. The actors were the Queen's or Sussex' men, probably the Queen's. The play may have been written as early as 1588. Peele, Greene, Lodge, and Kyd have all been suggested as possible authors. Shakespeare probably knew the play before its publication in 1605.

This play of *Leir* ends happily, with the restoration of Leir to his throne. Essentially the play is a legendary history with a strong element of romance. The two wicked sisters are warned of the king's plans for dividing his kingdom by a sycophantish courtier named Skalliger (cf. Oswald). Cordella receives the ineffectual support of an honest courtier, Perillus (cf. Kent), but is disinherited by her angry father. Trusting herself to God's mercy and setting forth alone to live by her own labor, Cordella is found by the Gallian king and his bluff companion Mumford, who have come to England disguised as palmers to see if the English king's daughters are as beautiful as reported. The king hears Cordella's sad story, falls in love with her at first sight, and woos her (still wearing his disguise) in the name of the Gallian king. When she virtuously suggests the palmer woo for himself, he throws off his disguise and marries her forthwith.

Meanwhile the other sons-in-law, Cornwall and Cambria (i.e., Albany), draw lots for their shares of the kingdom. Leir announces that he will sojourn with Cornwall and Gonorill first. Cornwall treats the king with genuine solicitude, but Gonorill, abetted by Skalliger, tauntingly drives her father away. The king acknowledges to his loyal companion Perillus that he has wronged Cordella. Regan, who rules her mild husband as she pleases, receives the king with seeming tenderness but secretly hires an assassin to end his life. (Gonorill is partner in this plot.) The suborned agent, frightened into remorse by a providentially sent thunderstorm, shows his intended victim the letter ordering the assassination.

The Gallian king and Cordella, who have previously sent ambassadors to Leir urging him to come to France, now decide to journey with Mumford into Britain disguised as countryfolk. Before they can do so, however, Leir and Perillus arrive in France, in mariners' garb, where they encounter Cordella and her party dressed as countryfolk. Cordella recognizes Leir's voice, and father and daughter are tearfully reunited. The Gallian king invades England and restores Leir to his throne.

Shakespeare has changed much in the sheer narrative outline of his source. He discards not only the happy ending but the attempted assassination and the numerous romancelike uses of disguise (although Tom o'Bedlam, in an added plot, repeatedly uses disguise). Shakespeare eliminates the humorous Mumford and replaces Perillus with both Kent and the Fool. He turns Cornwall into a villain and Albany into a belated champion of justice. He creates the storm scene out of a mere suggestion about providential thunder.

Most of all, he adds the parallel plot of Gloucester, Edgar, and Edmund. Here Shakespeare derived some of his material from Sidney's *Arcadia* (1590). In Book II, chapter 10 of this greatest of all Elizabethan prose romances, the two heroes Pyrocles and Musidorus encounter a son leading his blind old father. The old man tells his pitiful tale. He is the deposed King of Paphlagonia, father of a bastard son named Plexirtus who, he now bitterly realizes, turned the king against his true son Leonatus—the very son who is now his guide and guardian. The true son, having managed to escape his father's order of execution, has been forced to live poorly as a soldier, while the bastard son has proceeded to usurp his father's throne. In his wretchedness, the king has been succored by his forgiving true son and has been prevented from casting himself off the top of a hill. At the conclusion of this narrative, the villain Plexirtus arrives and attacks Leonatus; reinforcements arrive on both sides, but eventually Plexirtus is driven off, enabling the king to return to his court and bestow the crown on Leonatus. He thereupon dies, his heart having been stretched beyond the limits of endurance.

Other parts of *The Arcadia* may have given Shakespeare further suggestions. Edmund is decidedly indebted to the Vice of the morality-play tradition. For Tom o' Bedlam's mad language, Shakespeare consulted Samuel Harsnett's *Declaration of Egregious Popishe Impostures*, 1603. (See K. Muir's Arden edition of *King Lear*, pp. 253–256, for an extensive comparison.)

The Tempest

No direct literary source for the whole of *The Tempest* has been found. Shakespeare does seem to have drawn material from various accounts of the shipwreck of the *Sea Venture* in the Bermudas, 1609, although the importance of these materials should not be overstated. Several of the survivors wrote narratives of the shipwreck itself and of their life on the islands for some nine months. Sylvester Jourdain, in *A Discovery of the Barmudas*, published 1610, speaks of miraculous preservation despite the island's reputation for being "a most prodigious and inchanted place." William Strachey's letter, written in July of 1610 and published much later (1625) as *A true Reportory of the Wracke and Redemption . . . from the Ilands of the Bermudas*, describes the panic among the passengers and crew, the much-feared reputation of the island as the habitation of devils and wicked spirits, the actual beauty and fertility of the place with its abundance of wild life (cf. Caliban's descriptions), and the treachery of the Indians they later encounter in Virginia. Shakespeare seems to have read Strachey's letter in manuscript, and may have been acquainted with him. He also kept up with travel accounts of Ralegh and Hariot, and knew various classical evocations of a New World. The name "Setebos" came from Richard Eden's *History of Trauayle* (1577), translated from Peter Martyr's *De Novo Orbe* and from various other travel accounts of the period. All these hints are indeed suggestive, but they are scattered and relate only to the setting and general circumstance of Shakespeare's play.

Shakespeare certainly consulted Montaigne's essay "Of the Caniballes," as translated by John Florio in 1603. Gonzalo's reverie on an ideal commonwealth (II,i) contains many verbal echoes of the essay. Montaigne's point is that supposedly civilized men who condemn as "barbarian" any society not conforming with their own are simply refusing to examine their own shortcomings. A supposedly "primitive" society may well embody perfect religion, justice, and harmony; civilized art can never rival the achievements of nature. The ideal commonwealth has no need of magistrates, riches, poverty, and contracts, all of which breed dissimulation and covetousness. The significance of these ideas for *The Tempest* extends well beyond the particular passage in which they are found. And Caliban himself, whose name is an anagram of "cannibal," illustrates (even though he is not an eater of human flesh) the truth of Montaigne's observation: "I thinke there is more barbarisme in eating men alive, than to feed upon them being dead."

Prospero's famous valedictory speech to "Ye elves of hills, brooks, standing lakes, and groves" (V,i) owes its origin to Medea's similar invocation in Ovid's *Metamorphoses* (Book VII), which Shakespeare knew both in the Latin original and in Golding's translation: "Ye Ayres and windes: ye Elves of Hilles, of B[r]ookes, of Woods alone, Of standing Lakes . . ." Medea also anticipates Shakespeare's Sycorax. Medea thus provides material for the representation of both black and white magic in *The Tempest*, so carefully differentiated by Shakespeare. Ariel is part English fairy, like Puck, and part daemon. The pastoral situation in *The Tempest* is perhaps derived from Spenser's *The Faerie Queene*, Book VI (with its distinctions between savage lust and true courtesy, between nature and art). Italian pastoral drama as practiced by Guarini and (in England) by John Fletcher may also have been an influence. The masque element in *The Tempest*, prominent as in much late Shakespeare, bears the imprint of the courtly masque tradition of Jonson, Beaumont, and Fletcher.

A German play, *Die Schöne Sidea* by Jacob Ayrer, written before 1605, was once thought to have been based on an earlier version of *The Tempest* as performed by English players traveling in Germany. Today the similarities between the two plays are generally attributed to conventions found everywhere in romance.

The Sonnets

See the Introduction, pp. 301–305 above, for a discussion of the sonnet vogue in England of the 1590's, and the previous history of the sonnet in England and on the Continent.

TEXTUAL NOTES

The most usual sort of entry in these notes gives first the *adopted* reading (*in italics*), followed by the rejected reading of the original Folio or quarto text. For instance, the entry "70 *swashing* washing" from I,ii of *Romeo and Juliet* means that the original second quarto reading in line 70, "washing," has been emended to "swashing" in Craig's edition of the Globe text and in this present edition.

These textual notes also list the departures of this present edition from Craig's edition of the Globe text [C]. In nearly all instances, these changes represent a return to the original Folio or quarto reading. For instance, the entry "27 *civil* [Q2] cruel [C]" in I,i of *Romeo and Juliet* means that the Craig-Globe emendation, "cruel," has been rejected in favor of the original reading from the second quarto, "civil." When, on the other hand, the reading adopted by his edition is an emendation not found in the Craig-Globe text, the entry reads typically as follows: "207 *pavin* panyn [F,C]." This entry from V,i of *Twelfth Night* means that the original Folio reading, "panyn," though retained in Craig's edition of the Globe text, has been emended to "pavin" in this present edition.

Each dramatic text in this present edition is based on a single original copy text, and follows that copy text closely except for the actual emendations listed in these notes. For a discussion of the reasons lying behind the choice of copy text in each instance, see *Appendix I*, "Canon, Dates, and Early Texts."

Romeo and Juliet

Copy text: the second quarto of 1599 [Q2]. Q1 = the first quarto of 1597.

Chorus, 8 *Doth* [Q2] do [C]

I,i,1 *on* [Q2] o' [C] 5 *out of* [Q2] out o' the [C] 19 *'Tis true* [Q2] True [C] 27 *civil* [Q2] cruel [C] 28 *I will* [Q2] and [C] 32 *it in* [Q1] it 38 *comes two* [Q1] comes 50 *disgrace* [Q2] a disgrace [C] 61 *But if* [Q2] If [C] 70 *swashing* washing 87 *one* [Q2] a [C] 127 *drave* drive 129 *city's* [Q1] Citie 134 *Which . . . self* [Q2] That most are busied when they're most alone [C] 141 *farthest* [Q2] furthest [C] 153 *his* is 159 *sun* same 183 *create* [Q1] created 185 *well-seeming* [Q1] welseeing 196 *rais'd* [Q1] made 198 *lovers'* [Q1] loving 208 *Bid a* [Q1] A *make* [Q1] makes 217 *unharm'd* [Q1] vncharmd 224 *makes* make

I,ii,14 *The earth* Earth 15 *She is* Shees 29 *fennel* [Q2] female [C] 32 *on* one 47 *One* [Q1] on 77–78 *Rom. Whither . . . house* [Q2] Rom. Whither? Serv. To supper; to our house [C] 88 *loves* [Q2] lovest [C] 94 *fires* fier

I,iii,36 *high lone* hylone [Q2] alone [C] 54 *perilous* perillous [Q2] parlous [C] 66, 67 *honour* [Q1] houre 99 *it fly* [Q1] flie

I,iv,7–8 *Nor . . . entrance* [Q1; not in Q2] 23 *Mer.* Horatio. 31 *quote* cote 39 *done* [Q1] dum 42 *Of this sir* [Q1] Or saue you 45 *like lamps* [Q1] lights lights 47 *five* fine 58 *Over* [Q2] Athwart [C] 61 *Her* [Q2] The [C] *spider* [Q2] spider's [C] 62 *Her* [Q2] The [C] 63 *film* Philome 66 *maid* [Q1] man 72 *O'er* [Q1] On 76 *breaths* [Q1] breath 81 *dreams he* [Q1] he dreams 103 *side* [Q2] face [C] 111 *forfeit* [Q1] fofreit 113 *sail* [Q1] sute

I,v,1 [Q2 has stage direction here: "Enter Romeo"] 9 *loves* [Q2] lovest [C] 19 *walk* [Q2] have [C] 20 *Ah ha* [Q1] Ah 43 *lady's* [Q2] lady is [C] 48 *As* [Q2] Like [C] 68 *'A* [Q2] He [C] 71 *this* [Q2] the [C] 94 *bitt'rest* [Q2] bitter [C] 96 *sin* [Q2] fine [C] 97 *ready* [Q1] did readie 109 *thine* [Q2] yours [C] 134 *there* [Q1] here 144 *this . . . this* tis . . . tis

II, Chorus, 4 *match'd* match

II,i,6 *Nay . . . too* [assigned to Benvolio in Q2] 9 *one* [Q1] on 10 *pronounce* [Q1] prouaunt *dove* [Q1] day 12 *heir* [Q1] her 13 *Abraham* [Q2] Adam [C] *true* [Q2] trim [C] 28 *in* [Q2] and in [C] 38 *et cætera* [Q1] or

II,ii,16 *do* [Q1] to 20 *eyes* [Q1] eye 31 *pacing* [Q1] puffing 41–42 *nor any . . . name* o be some other name / Belonging to a man 44 *name* [Q1] word 45 *were* [Q1] wene 59 *uttering* [Q2] utterance [C] 61 *maid* [Q2] saint [C] 69 *let* [Q2] stop [C] 75 *eyes* [Q2] sight [C] 80 *that* [Q2] who [C] 83 *wash'd* [Q1] washeth 84 *should* [Q2] would [C] 99 *'haviour* [Q1] behauior 101 *more cunning* [Q1] coying 104 *true-love* [Q2] true love's [C] 107 *vow* [Q2] swear [C] 110 *circled* [Q1] circle 153 *suit* strife 163 *than mine* then 164 *"my Romeo"* [Q2] my Romeo's name [C] 168 *dear* Neece *What* [Q2] At what [C] 169 *By* [Q2] At [C] 178 *farther* [Q2] further [C] 179 *That* [Q2] Who [C] *her* his 180 *gyves* giues 181 *silken* [Q2] silk [C] 187 *Sleep . . . breast* [Q1; assigned in Q2 to Juliet] 189–190 *Hence . . . tell* [preceded in Q2 by four lines of the next scene] *father's* [Q1] Friers close

II,iii,2 *Chequ'ring* [Q1] Checking 3 *flecked* [Q1] fleckeld 4 *fiery* [Q1] burning 16 *plants, herbs* [Q2] herbs, plants [C] 22 *sometime* [Q2] sometimes [C] 23 *weak* [Q2] small [C] 40 *with* [Q2] by [C] 66 *that* [Q2] whom [C] 74 *ring yet* [Q1] yet ringing *mine* [Q2] my [C] 85 *chide not; she whom* [Q1] chide me not, her 88 *that* [Q2] and [C]

II,iv,4 *Why* [Q2] Ah [C] 6 *to* [Q2] of [C] 14 *run* [Q2] shot [C] *through* [Q2] thorough [C] 18 *Ben.* [Q1] Ro. 19 *I can tell you* [Q1; not in Q2] *he's* [Q2] he is [C] 23 *he rests . . . rests* [Q2] rests me . . . rest [C] 30 *fantasticoes* [Q1] phantacies 35 *perdona-mi's* pardons mees 65 *Sure wit* [Q2] Well said [C] 67 *solely* [Q2] sole [C] 72 *faint* faints 73 *Swits . . . swits* [Q2] Switch . . . switch [C] 75 *am* [Q2] have [C] 85 *not, then* [Q2] not [C] 108 *A sail, a sail* [assigned in C to Mer.] 109 *Two . . . smock* [assigned in C to Ben.] 121 *for himself* [Q1] himself 152 *Marry, farewell* [Q1; not in Q2] 172, 173 *bid* [Q2] bade [C] 176 *into* [Q1] in 210 *I warrant* Warrant 223 *dog's* dog 232 *Peter . . . go* [Q1; not in Q2] S.D. *Exeunt* Exit

II,v,5 *glide* glides 11 *three* there 15 *And* M. And 26 *I had* [Q1] I 51 *ah* a [Q2] O [C] 53 *jauncing* [Q2] jaunting [C]

II,vi,18 *gossamer* gossamours 19 *idles* ydeles 27 *music's* musicke

III,i,2 *Capulets* Capels 9 *him* [Q2] it [C] 37 S.D. *Tybalt,* Tybalt, Petruchio 38 *come* comes 55 *Or* [Q2] And [C] 63 *love* [Q2] hate [C] 71 *injur'd* iniuried 92 *Forbid this* [Q2] Forbidden [C] 93 S.D. *Tybalt* [*etc.*] Away Tybalt 94 *your houses* houses 115 *this* [Q2] his [C] 118 *cousin* [Q2] kinsman [C] 121 *Mercutio is* [Q2] Mercutio's [C] 127 *Alive* [Q1] He gan 129 *fire-ey'd* [Q1] fier end 171 *agile* [Q1] aged 193 *hate's* [Q1] hearts 197 *I* [Q1] It 200 *he is* [Q2] he's [C] 202 S.D. *Exeunt* Exit

III,ii,9 *By* And by 15 *grown* grow 19 *upon* [Q2] on [C] 21 *he* I 37 *weraday* [Q2] well-a-day [C] 49 *shut* shot 51 *of my* my 56 *swounded* sounded 57 *bankrout* [Q2] bankrupt [C] 60 *one* on 66 *dearest* [Q2] dearloved [C] 72 *Nurse.* [Q1; not in Q2] 73 *Jul.* [Q1] Nur. 74 [Q2 has "Iu." here] 76 *Dove-feather'd* Rauenous douefeatherd 79 *damned* dimme 143 S.D. *Exeunt* Exit

III,iii,15 *Hence* [Q1] Here 39 [Q2 follows with a line: "This may flyes do, when I from this must flie"] 43 [printed in Q2 before l. 40] 52 *Thou* [Q1] Then *a little speak* [Q2] but speak a word [C] 61 *madmen* [Q1] mad man 70 S.D. *Knock* Enter Nurse, and knocke 73 S.D. *Knock* They knocke 75 S.D. *Knock* Slud knock 82 *Where is* [Q1] Where's 92 *Well, death's* [Q1] deaths 94 *not she* [Q2] she not [C] 110 *denote* [Q1] deuote 113 *And* [Q2] Or [C] 117 *that in thy life lives* that in thy life lies [Q2] too that lives in thee [C] 138 *happy* [Q2] happy too [C] 143 *misbehav'd* mishaued 144 *pout'st upon* puts vp 168 *disguis'd* disguise

III,iv,8 *times to* [Q2] time to [C] 11 *she's* [Q2] she is [C] 20 *A . . . a* [Q2] O' . . . o' [C] (also elsewhere) 34 *very very* [Q1] very

III,v,13 *exhales* [Q1] exhale 36 S.D. *Nurse* Madame and Nurse 53 *times* [Q2] time [C] 54 *Jul.* Ro. 55 *so low* [Q2] below [C] 66 *It is* [Q2] is it [C] 83 *pardon him* padon 107 *beseech* [Q2] I beseech [C] 111 *expects* [Q2] expect'st [C] 127 *earth* [Q2] air [C] 132 *counterfeits* [Q2] counterfeit'st [C] 140 *gives* giue 146 *bridegroom* Bride 150 *How . . . how* [Q2] How now, now now [C] 173 *God ye god-den* Godigeden 182 *train'd* [Q1] liand 229 *Else* [Q2] Or else [C]

IV,i,7 *talk'd* [Q1] talke 10 *do* [Q2] doth [C] 45 *cure* [Q1] care 46 *Ah* [Q1] O 72 *slay* [Q1] stay 78 *off* [Q1] of *any* [Q2] yonder [C] 81 *hide* [Q2] shut [C] 83 *chapless* [Q1] chapels 85 *his shroud* his 92 *thy nurse* [Q1] the nurse 94 *distilling* [Q2] distilled [C] 98 *breath* [Q1] breast 100 *paly* many 110 *In* Is [Q2 follows with a line: "Be borne to buriall in thy kindreds graue"] 111 *shalt* shall 116 *waking* walking 126 *Exeunt* Exit

IV,ii,14 *will'd* wield 21 *To* [Q2] And [C] 47 *Exeunt* Exit

IV,iii,40 *this* [Q2] these [C] 49 *wake* walke 58 *Romeo . . . do* [Q1] Romeo, Romeo, Romeo, heeres drinke

IV,iv,12 S.D. *Exeunt* Exit 20 *faith* father

IV,v,15 *weraday* [Q2] well-a-day [C] 41 *long* [Q1] loue 65 *cure* care 81 *In all* [Q1] And in 82 *fond* some 100 *by* [Q1] my 101 [Q2 has stage direction here: "Exit omnes"] S.D. *Enter Peter* Enter Will Kemp 107 *full of woe* full 124 *Pet.* [in Q2, before "I will dry-beat"] 128 *grief* [Q1] griefes 129 *And . . . oppress* [Q1; not in Q2] 135, 139 *Pretty* [Q1] Prates 148 *Exeunt* Exit

V,i,15 *fares my* [Q1] doth my lady 25 *e'en* in [Q2] even [Q1, C] *defy* [Q1] denie 38 *'a* [Q2] he [C] 76 *pay* [Q1] pray 81 *murder* [Q2] murders [C]

V,iii,3 *yew* [Q1] young 21 S.D. *Balthasar* [Q1] Peter 40 *you* [Q1] ye 67 *bid* [Q2] bade [C] 68 *conjurations* [Q1] commiration 71 *Page.* Boy. [Q1; not in Q2] 102 *fair?* faire? I will beleeue 107 *pallet* [Q2] palace [C] 108 [Q2 has four undeleted lines here: "Depart againe, come lye thou in my arme, / Heer's to thy health, where ere thou tumblest in. / O true Appothecarie! / Thy drugs are quicke. Thus with a kisse I die"] 136 *unthrifty* [Q2] unlucky [C] 137 *yew* yong 186 *churchyard* Church-yards 187 *too* too too 189 S.D. *Enter . . . others* Enter Capels 190 *is so shriek'd* is so shrike [Q2] they so shriek [C] 191 *O, the* [Q2] The [C] 194 *our* your 199 *slaughter'd* Slaughter 201 *tombs* [Q2 has a stage direction here: "Enter Capulet and his wife"] 209 *more early* [Q1] now earling 232 *that* thats 258 *awakening* [Q2] awaking [C] 299 *raise* raie 300 *whiles* [Q2] while [C]

A Midsummer Night's Dream

Copy text: the first quarto of 1600 [Q].

I,i,4 *wanes* waues 10 *New-bent* Now bent 19 S.D. *Lysander* Lysander and Helena 24 *stand forth, Demetrius* [printed as a stage direction in Q] 26 *stand forth, Lysander* [printed as a stage direction in Q] 74 *their* there 136 *low* loue 187 *Yours would* Your words 191 *I'ld* ile 216 *sweet* sweld 219 *stranger companies* strange companions

II,i,61 *Fairy* [Q] Fairies [C] 69 *steep* steppe 79 *Ægles* Eagles [Q] Ægle [C] 109 *thin* chinne 158 *the west* west 190 *slay* stay *slayeth* stayeth 201 *not, nor* not, not

II,ii,4 *leathern* lethten 39 *Be* Bet 43 *good* god 47 *is* it

III,i,30 *yourselves* your selfe 57 *Bot.* Cet. 71 *and* or 85 *Odours, odours* Odours, odorous 90 *Puck.* Quin. 200 *you of* you [Q] your [C] 206 *lover's* [Q] love's [C] 206 S.D. *Exeunt* Exit

III,ii,S.D. Q: Enter King of Fairies, and Robin goodfellow 19 *mimic* Minnick 80 *I'so* I 85 *bankrout* [Q] bankrupt [C] *sleep* slippe 213 *like* life 220 *passionate words* words 250 *prayers* praise 260 *off* of 264 *O hated* [Q] hated [C] 299 *gentlemen* gentleman 323 *she's* she is 338 *jowl* [Q] jole [C] 344 S.D. *Exit* Exeunt 426 *shalt* shat 451 *To your* your

IV,i,58 *flouriets'* [Q] flowerets' [C] 76 *o'er* or 85 *five* fine 86 *ho!* howe 121 *Seem'd* Seeme 132 *is my* my 143 *Good* The. Good 176 *saw* see 195 *found* fonnd 203 *let us* lets 212 *to expound* expound 214 *a patched* patcht a

IV,ii,S.D. Q reads: Enter Quince, Flute, Thisby and the

rabble 3 *Star.* Flut. 5 *Flu.* Thys. (and at ll. 9, 13, 19)

V,i,34 *our* Or 122 *his* this 152 S.D. *Exeunt* Exit 157 *Snout* Flute 193 *up in thee* now againe 202 *vile* vilde 208 *mural down* Moon vsed 226 *as* [Q] one [C] 275–276 *And . . . vanished* [so Q; these lines are transposed in C] 279 *gleams* beames 325 *mote* moth 357 *Bot.* Lyon. 378 *lion* Lyons 379 *behowls* beholds 426–427 *And . . . rest* [these lines are transposed in Q]

Richard II

Copy text: the first quarto of 1597 as press-corrected in all four extant copies [Q1]; and, for the deposition scene, IV,i,154–320, the First Folio [F].

I,i,118 *by my* by 163 *Obedience bids* [repeated in error in Q1]

I,ii,42 *alas, may* [F] may 47 *sit* set 58 *it* is 59 *empty* [F] emptines 60 *begun* begone 70 *hear* [F] cheere

I,iii,15 *thee* the 33 *comest* comes 58 *thee* the 84 *innocency* innocence 108 *his God* [F] God 128 *civil* [F] cruell 133 *Draws* Draw 136 *wrathful iron* [F] harsh resounding 172 *then but* but 180 *you owe* y'owe 193 *far* fare 222 *night* nightes 239 *had it* had't 289 *strew'd* strowd

I,iv, S.D. *Bagot* [F] Bushie 20 *our cousin* our Coosens 23 *Bagot here and Green* [Q6; not in Q1] 27 *What* With 52 S.D. *Enter Bushy* Enter Bushie with news 53 *Bushy, what news* [F; not in Q1]

II,i,15 *life's* liues 18 *fond* found 48 *as a* a 102 *incaged* inraged 113 *not* not, not 124 *brother* brothers 151 *bankrout* [Q1] bankrupt [C] (and elsewhere) 156 *kerns* kerne 177 *the* a 209 *seize* cease 252 *hath* [Q1] have [C] 257 *king's* King 277 *Le Port Blanc* le Port Blan [Q1] Port le Blanc [C] 278 *Brittaine* [Q1] Brittany [C] 284 *Quoint* Coines 285 *Brittaine* [Q1] Bretagne [C] 292 *drooping* drowping

II,ii,16 *eye* eyes 25 *more's* more is 31 *though* thought 59 *broken* [Q1] broke [C] 110 *disorderly thrust* [Q1] thrust disorderly [C] 112 *Th'* T [Q1] The [C] 129 *that's* that is 138 *The . . . will* Will the hatefull commons

II,iii,9 *Cotshall* [Q1] Cotswold [C] 30 *Lordship* Lo: 36 *Hereford* Herefords 75 *rase* race [Q1] raze [C] 99 *the lord* lord 151 *never* [Q1] ne'er [C] 164 *Bristow* [Q1] Bristol [C] (and elsewhere)

III,i,25 *Ras'd* Rac't [Q1] Razed [C]

III,ii,29 *heaven yields* heauens yeeld 30 *else, if* else 32 *succour* succors 40 *boldly* bouldy 72 *O'erthrows* Ouerthrowes 134 *this offence* [F] this 170 *through* thorough

III,iii,13 *brief with you* [F] briefe 17 *over* [Q1] o'er [C] 52 *tattered* tottered 91 *yon* [Q1] yond [C] 119 *a prince, is* princesse

III,iv,11 *joy* griefe 26 *pins* pines 27 *They will* [Q1] They'll [C] 29 *yon* yong 55 *seiz'd* ceasde 57 *We at* at 67 *you* [Q1] you then [C] 80 *Cam'st* Canst

IV,i,22 *him* them 43 *Fitzwater* Fitzwaters 54 *As may* As it may 55 *sun to sun* sinne to sinne 76 *my bond* bond 89 *he is* [Q1] he's [C] 109 *thee* the 145 *you* yon 154–320 [This deposition scene is based on the First Folio text; Q1 has only: "Let it be so, and loe on wednesday next, / We solemnly proclaime our Coronation, / Lords be ready all". Unless otherwise indicated all the new readings in lines 154–320 are taken from Q4.] 165 *limbs* knee 183 *and on* on *yours* thine 229 *folly* follyes 237 *upon* vpon me 250 *To undeck* T'vndeck 251 *and* a 255 *Nor* No, nor 267 *bankrout* [Q4] bankrupt [C, F] 270 *torments* [F] torment'st [C] 276 *the* that 285 *Was* Is *that* which 286 *And* That 289 *a* an 296 *manners* manner 333 *and I'll* Ile

V,i,25 *stricken* [F] throwne 32 *thy* the 34 *the* [F] a [C] 37 *sometime* sometimes 41 *thee* the 43 *quite* [F] quit [C] 62 *And he* He

V,ii,2 *off* of 11 *thee* the (also at lines 17 and 94) 52 *Do these . . . hold* [Q1] hold these justs and triumphs [C] 65 *bond* band 116 *And* An

V,iii,36 *I may* May 68 *And* An 75 *voic'd* voice 106 *shall* still 111 *Boling.* yorke 122 *sets* [Q1] set'st [C] 135–136 *With . . . him* I pardon him with al my heart 144 *cousin too* cousin

V,iv, S.D. *Enter* Manet *and* & 6 *wishtly* [Q1] wistly [C]

V,v,20 *through* thorow 25 *seely* [Q1] silly [C] 27 *sit* set 76 *ern'd* [Q1] yearn'd [C] 94 *Spurr'd, gall'd* [Q1] Spur-gall'd [C]

V,vi,12 S.D. *Fitzwater* Fitzwaters 43 *thorough* through

1 Henry IV

Copy text: the first complete quarto of 1598 [Q1]; and, for I,iii,201 through II,ii,118, the fragment of an earlier quarto [Q0].

I,i,4 *stronds* [Q1] strands [C] 62 *a dear* deere 76–77 *In faith, It is* [assigned in Q1 to King]

I,ii,68 *fubbed* fubd [Q1] fobbed [C] 89 *similes* smiles 177 *thou* the 182 *Bardolph, Peto* Haruey, Rossill

I,iii,84 *that* [Q1] the [C] 201 *Hot.* [missing in Q0–Q4] 239 *whipp'd* whipt [Q1] whip [Q0] 267 *Bristow* [Q0] Bristol [C]

II,ii,17 *two and twenty* xxii 21 *Bardolph* Bardol (and thus, or "Bardoll," throughout the play) 38 *mine* [Q1] my [Q0] 46 *Go hang* Hang [Q0, Q1] 89 *ah!* a 118 *fat rogue* [Q0] rogue [Q1]

II,iii,4 *In respect* in the respect 51 *thee* the 72 *a roan* Roane

II,iv,37 *precedent* present 39 *Poins.* Prin. 144 *lives* [Q1] live [C] 172 *All's* All is 192 *Prince.* Gad 193, 195, 199 *Gads.* Ross. 363 *talent* [Q1] talon [C] 374 *Owen* O [Q1, C] 434 *tristful* trustfull 521 *lean* lane 540 *mad* made 572 *Good* God (and at l. 573) 580 S.D. *pockets* pocket 584 *Peto.* [not in Q1] 591 *Prince.* [not in Q1]

III,i,70 *here is* [Q1] here's [C] 100 *cantle* scantle 130 *metre* miter 179 *besides* [Q1] beside [C] 194 *she will* sheele

III,ii,38 *do* [Q1] doth [C] 107 *renowned* renowmed 145 *northern* Northren

III,iii,39 *that's* that 66 *tithe* tight 80 *wives* [Q1] wives, and [C] 101 S.D. *them* him 194 *guests* ghesse 224 *o' clock* of clocke

IV,i,20 *lord* mind 55 *Is* tis 99 *Bated* Baited [Q1,

C] 108 *dropp'd* drop 116 *altar* altars 126 *cannot* can 127 *yet* it
IV,ii,3 *Sutton Co' fil'* Sutton cophill 34 *fac'd* fazd 37 *tattered* tottered 45 *but* not 79 *in* [Q1] on [C] 86 S.D. *Exit* Exeunt
IV,iii,21 *horse* horses 28 *ours* our 82 *country's* Countrey 110 *mine* [Q1] my [C]
IV,iv,18 *o'er-rul'd* ouerrulde
V,i,25 *I do* I 88 *off* of 114 S.D. *Exeunt* Exit 140 *will it* wil
V,ii,3 *undone* vnder one 8 *Supposition* [Q1] Suspicion [C] 10 *ne'er* neuer 25 S.D. *Hotspur* Percy 72 *libertine* libertie
V,iii,1 *the battle* battell 41 *stand'st* stands 52 *get'st* gets
V,iv,34 *so* and 68 *Nor* Now 76 S.D. *who* he 92 *thee* the 163 *ours* our
V,v,29–30 *valours . . . Have* [Q1] valour . . . Hath [C]

Twelfth Night

Copy text: the First Folio [F].
I,ii,15 *Arion* Orion 40 *sight* [F] company [C] 41 *company* [F] sight [C]
I,iii,55 *Sir And.* Ma. 104–105 *curl by* coole my 106 *me* we 145 *flame* dam'd *set* sit 148 *That's* That
I,v,176 S.D. *Viola* Uiolenta 320 *county's* Countes 330 S.D. [F adds "Finis, Actus primus"]

II,ii,21 *That sure* That 32 *our* O 33 *of* if

II,iii,2 *diluculo* Deliculo 9 *lives* [F] life [C] 26 *leman* Lemon 146 *a nayword* an ayword
II,iv,54 *Fly . . . fly* Fye . . . fie 56 *yew* Ew 91 *I* It
II,v,17 *metal* Mettle 124 *staniel* stallion 157 *born* become *achieve* atcheeues 193 *dear* deero 228 [F adds "Finis Actus secundus"]
III,i,9 *king* Kings 39 *pilchers* [F] pilchards [C] 64 *conster* [F] construe [C] 75 *wise men* wisemens 133 *Hides* [F] Hideth [C]
III,ii,9 *thee the* the
III,iv,25 *Oli.* Mal. 78 *tang* langer 190 *You* Yon 197 *oft* [F] off [C] 222 *on 't* [F] out [C] 227 *griefs* [F] grief [C] 270 *competent* computent 305 *hit* hits 399 *vile* vilde 432 S.D. *Exeunt* Exit
IV,ii,7 *in* in in 41 *clerestories* cleere stores [F] clearstores [C] 56 *haply* happily 77 *sport to* sport
IV,iii,35 [F adds "Finis Actus Quartus"]
V,i,117 *have* [F] hath [C] 178 *H' as* [F] He has [C] 207 *pavin* panyn [F, C] 415 *With hey* hey

Hamlet

Copy text: the second quarto of 1604–1605 [Q2]. The First Folio text [F] also represents an independently authoritative text; although seemingly not as close to Shakespeare's own draft as Q2, the Folio text is considerably less marred by typographical errors than is Q2. The adopted readings in these notes are from F unless otherwise indicated; [eds.] means that the adopted reading was first proposed by some editor since the time of F. Some readings are also supplied from the pirated first quarto of 1603 [Q1].

I,i,14 *Who is* [Q2] Who's [F, C] 16 *soldier* [Q1, F] souldiers 17 *hath* [Q2] has [F, C] 43 *'a* [Q2] it [F, C] 44 *harrows* horrowes 45 *Speak to* [Q2] Question [F, C] 63 *Polacks* [eds.] pollax 68 *my* mine 73 *why* [Q1, F] with 87 *heraldry* [Q1, F] heraldy *cast* cost 88 *those* these 91 *return'd* returne 93 *comart* [Q2] covenant [F, C] 94 *design'd* [eds.] desseigne 121 *fear'd* [eds.] feare 138 *you* [Q1, F] your 140 *at it* it 164 *that* [Q2] the [F, C] 175 *conveniently* [Q1, F] conuenient
I,ii,S.D. *Councilors* [eds.] Counsaile: as 21 *this* [Q2] the [F, C] 23 *bands* [Q2] Bonds [F, C] 58 *He hath* [Q1, F] Hath 67 *so* so much *in* [Q2] i' [F, C] 77 *good* coold 82 *shapes* [Q4] chapes 85 *passeth* passes 96 *a* or 129 *sullied* [eds.] sallied [Q2] solid [F] 132 *self* seale 133 *weary* wary 137 *to this* thus 143 *would* [Q1, F] should 149 *even she* [F; not in Q2] 171 *my* [Q2] mine [F, C] 175 *to drink deep* for to drinke 177 *prithee* [Q2] pray thee [F, C] 178 *to see* [Q1, F] to 186 *'a* [Q2] he [F, C; and so throughout the play] 198 *waste* [eds.] wast [Q2, F] vast [C] 213 *watch'd* watch 223 *Indeed, indeed* [Q1, F] Indeede 237 *Very like, very like* [Q1, F] Very like 238 *hundred* hundreth 249 *whatsoever* what someuer 251 *fare* farre 257 *foul* [Q1, F] fonde
I,iii,3 *convoy is* conuay, in 12 *bulk* bulkes 18 *For . . . birth* [F; not in Q2] 21 *safety* [Q2] sanctity [F] sanity [C] 49 *like a* a 63 *to* vnto 65 *comrade* courage 74 *Are* Or 75 *be* boy 76 *loan* loue 77 *dulleth* [Q2] dulls the [F, C] 83 *invites* inuests 105 *I will* [Q2] I'll [F, C] 109 *Running* [eds.] Wrong [Q2] Roaming [F] 115 *springes* springs 123 *parley* parle 125 *tether* tider 129 *implorators* imploratotors 130 *bawds* [eds.] bonds 131 *beguile* beguide
I,iv,2 *is a* is 6 S.D. *go* [eds.] goes 17 *revel* [Q4] reueale 27 *the* [eds.] their 33 *Their* [eds.] His 53 *Revisits* [Q2, F] Revisit'st [C] 82 *artere* [eds.] arture [Q2] artery [C] 86 S.D. *Exeunt* Exit 87 *imagination* imagion
I,v,3 *sulphurous* sulphrus 20 *fretful* [Q1, F] fearefull 42 *wit* [eds.] wits 47 *what a* what 55 *lust* [Q1, F] but 56 *sate* [Q1, F] sort 62 *hebona* [Q2] hebanon [F, C] 68 *posset* possesse 84 *howsomever* [Q2] howsoever [F, C] *pursues* [Q2] pursuest [F, C] 91 *adieu, adieu* [Q2] adieu, Hamlet [F, C] 95 *stiffly* swiftly 96 *whiles* [Q2] while [F, C] 109 *I am* [Q2] I'm [F, C] 113 *Heavens* [Q2] Heaven [F, C] 115 *bird* and 119 *you will* [Q2] you'll [F, C] 122 *my lord* [Q1, F; not in Q2] 126 *in* [Q2] i' [F, C] 131 *my* [Q2] mine [F, C] 132 *Look you, I'll* I will 134 *I am* [Q2] I'm [F, C] 150 *Ah ha* Ha, ha 170 *soe'er* so mere 179 *not to do* doe sweare 181 *Swear* [F; not in Q2]
II,i,S.D. *man* [eds.] man or two 3 *marvellous* [eds.] meruiles 28 *no* [F; not in Q2] 39 *sullies* sallies 40 *i' th'* with 52–53 *at 'friend . . . 'gentleman'* [F; not in Q2] 63 *takes* take 69 *bye ye* [eds.] buy ye [Q2] be wi' you [C] *fare ye* [Q2] fare you [F, C] 105 *passion* passions 112 *quoted* coted 119 *Come* [Q2; not in F, C]
II,ii,20 *are* is 57 *o'erhasty* hastie 90 *since* [F; not in Q2] 97 *he is* hee's 126 *above* about 137 *winking*

working 143 *his* her 148 *watch* wath 149 *to a* to 151 *'tis this* this 153 *I would* [Q2] I'd [F, C] 169 S.D. *Exeunt* [eds.] Exit 182 *good* [Q2, F] god [C] 186 *but* [Q2] but not [F, C] 190 *far gone, far gone* far gone [Q2, C] 206 *should be* shall growe 211 *that's out of* [Q2] that is out o' [F, C] 214 *sanity* sanctity 215–216 *suddenly . . . him and* [F; not in Q2] 216 *honourable* [F; not in Q2] 217 *most humbly* [F; not in Q2] 218 *sir* [F; not in Q2] 219 *more* not more 228 *excellent* extent 230 *ye* you 232 *over* euer 233 *cap* lap 240 *What's the* What 241 *that* [F; not in Q2] 244–277 *Let me . . . attended* [F; not in Q2] 280 *even* euer 284 *Come, come* [Q2] Come [F, C] 286 *Why, any* Any 297 *could* can 314 *appeareth nothing to me but* [Q2] appears no other thing to me than [F, C] 315 *a piece* peece 317 *faculties* [Q2] faculty [F, C] 322 *no, nor* nor *woman* [Q1, F] women 326 *you* ye 333 *of* on 337–338 *the clown . . . sere* [F; not in Q2] 339 *blank* black 352–379 *Ham. How . . . too* [F; not in Q2] 358 *berattle* [eds.] be-ratled [F] 366 *most like* [eds.] like most [F] 380 *my* [Q2] mine [F, C] 381 *mows* [Q1, F] mouths 383 *a* [Q2] an [F, C] 390 *lest my* let me 394 *outwards* [Q2] outward [F, C] 402 *he is* [Q2] he's [F, C] 407 *then* [Q2] so [F, C] 413 *my* [Q2] mine [F, C] 416–417 *tragical-historical . . . -pastoral* [F; not in Q2] 441–442 *O, old friend! why* [Q2] O, my old friend! [F, C] 445 *By'r* by 450 *French falconers* friendly Fankners 453 *good lord* [Q2] lord [F, C] 457 *caviary* [Q2] caviare [C] 465 *affectation* affection 467 *in 't* [Q2] in it [F, C] 468 *tale* talke 469 *where* when 473 *'tis* [Q2] it is [F, C] 478 *heraldry* heraldy 482 *and a* [Q2] and [F, C] 496 *Then senseless Ilium* [F; not in Q2] 503 *And like* Like 517 *fellies* [eds.] follies [Q2] Fallies [F] 521 *to* [Q2, F] be to [C] 524 *ah woe* [Q2] O who [F, C] 527 *'mobled queen' is good* [F; not in Q2; F reads "Inobled"] 529 *bisson* Bison 537 *husband's* [Q1, F] husband 542 *whe'r* [Q2, F] whether [C] 543 *Prithee* [Q2] Pray you [F, C] 555 *shall* [Q2] should [F, C] 566 *for a* for 567 *or* [Q1, F] lines, or 572 *till* tell 580 *his* the 581 *in 's* in his 582 *and* an 585 *Hecuba* [Q1, F] her 587 *the cue* that 607 *have* a 610 *O, vengeance* [F; not in Q] 612 *father* [Q1, Q4; not in Q2, F] 615 *stallion* [Q2] scullion [F, C] 616 *brains! Hum, I* [Q2] brain! I [F, C] 626 *'a do* [Q2] he but [F, C] 628 *the devil* a deale

III,i,1 *And* An 19 *here about* [Q2] about [F, C] 27 *into* [Q2] on to [F, C] 28 *too* two 32 *lawful espials* [F; not in Q2] 33 *Will* Wee'le 46 *loneliness* lowlines 55 *let's* [F; not in Q2] 83 *of us all* [Q1, F; not in Q2] 85 *sicklied* sickled 92 *well, well, well* well 99 *the* these 107 *your honesty* you 122 *to a* a 132 *all* [Q1, F; not in Q2] 142 *go* [Q1, F; not in Q2] 147 *O* [F; not in Q2] 148 *too* [F; not in Q2] 149 *hath* [Q2] has [F, C] 151 *you amble* [Q1, F] & amble *lisp* list *you nick-name* [Q2] and nickname [F, C] 153 *your ignorance* ignorance *Go to, I'll* Ile 155 *moe marriage* [Q2] more marriages [F, C] 160 *Th' expectancy* Th' expectation 164 *music* musickt 165 *that* what 166 *time* [Q2] tune [F, C] 167 *feature* stature 169 [Q2 has "Exit" at the end of this line] 196 *unwatch'd* vnmatcht

III,ii,3 *your* our *lief* [eds.] liue 7 *whirlwind* [Q2] the whirlwind [F, C] 11 *tatters* totters *split* [Q1, F] spleet 22 *overdone* ore-doone 26 *virtue her own* vertue her 29 *it make* it makes 30 *of the* of 34 *praise* praysd 42 *sir* [F; not in Q2] 56 *We will* Ay 85 *my* [Q2] mine [F, C] 94 *detecting* detected 121–122 *Ham. I . . . lord* [F; not in Q2] 135 *within 's* [Q2, F] within these [C] 137 *devil* deule [Q2] Diuel [F] 145 S.D. *sound* [Q4] sounds *comes* [Q2] come [F, C] 147 *is miching* [Q1, F] munching 153 *counsel* [Q1, F; not in Q2] 155 *you'll* [Q1, F] you will 166 *orbed* orb'd the 174 *your* our 176 [Q2 follows here with an extraneous unrhymed line: "For women feare too much, euen as they loue"] 177 *For* And *holds* hold 178 *In* Eyther none, in 179 *love* Lord 191 *Wormwood* That's 200 *like* the 209 *joys* ioy 233 *a* [Q1, F] I be a 238 S.D. *Exit* [Q1, F] Exeunt 250 *o'* [Q1, F] of 252 *winch* [Q2, F] wince [C] 259 *my* mine 262 *mistake* [Q2, F] must take [Q1, C] 263 *pox* [F; not in Q2] 267 *Confederate* [Q1, F] Considerat 269 *infected* [Q1, Q4] inuected 271 *usurp* vsurps 272 *for his* [Q2] for 's [F, C] 273 *written* [Q2] writ [F, C] *very* [Q2; not in F, C] 277 *Ham. What . . . fire* [F; not in Q2] 281 *Pol.* [Q2] All. [F, C] 282 *strucken* [F, Q2] stricken [C] 285 *Thus* [Q2] So [F, C] 287 *with two* with 289 *sir* [F; not in Q2] 315 *rather with* with 317 *his* the 318 *far more* more 321 *start* stare 330 *of my* of 332 *Guil.* Ros. 340 *'stonish* [Q2] astonish [F, C] 349 *And* [Q2] So I [F, C] 373 *thumb* the vmber 384 *the top of* [F; not in Q2] 388 *can fret me* [F] fret me not [Q2] can fret me, yet [Q1, C] 405 *Leave me, friends* [so F; Q2 places before "I will say so" and assigns both to Hamlet] 407 *breaths* breakes 409 *bitter . . . day* busines as the bitter day 414 *daggers* dagger; 416 *somever* [Q2, F] soever [C]

III,iii,6 *near us* [eds.] near's 7 *brows* [Q2] lunacies [F, C] 15 *cess* [Q2] cease [F, C] 17 *it is* or it is 19 *huge* hough 22 *ruin* raine 23 *but with* but 50 *pardon'd* pardon 58 *shove* showe 73 *pat . . . praying* but now a is a praying 79 *Why* [Q2] O [F, C] *hire and salary* base and silly 91 *game, a-swearing* [Q2] gaming, swearing [F, C]

III,iv,4 *sconce* [eds.] silence 5–6 *with him . . . mother* [F; not in Q2] 6 *warrant* wait 20 *inmost* most 23 *help, ho* how 24 *help, help, help* help 30 *it was* [Q2] 'twas [F, C] 37 *braz'd* [F] brasd [Q2] brass'd [C] 48 *does* [Q2] doth [F, C] 49 *O'er* [Q2] Yea [F, C] 52 *That . . . index* [so F; assigned in Q2 to Hamlet] 59 *heaven-kissing* heaue, a kissing 88 *pandars* pardons 89 *mine . . . soul* my very eyes into my soule 90 *grained* greeued 91 *not leave* leaue there 95 *mine* my 97 *tithe* kyth 139 *Ecstasy* [F; not in Q2] 143 *I the* the 158 *live* leaue 159 *my* [Q2] mine [F, C] 165 *Refrain to-night* to refrain night 178 *Thus* This 186 *ravel* rouell 215 *a* a most 217 S.D. *Exeunt* [eds.] Exit

IV,ii,1 S.D. [so F; Q2 reads, "Enter Hamlet, Rosencraus, and others"] 2 *Ros. Guil. . . . Hamlet* [F; not in Q2] 4 S.D. [F; not in Q2] 6 *Compounded* Compound 19 *ape an apple* [eds.] apple [Q2] Ape [F] 32 *Hide . . . after* [F; not in Q2]

IV,iii,16 *Ho! bring in the* [Q2] Ho, Guildenstern! bring in my [F, C] 37 *if indeed* [Q2] indeed, if [F, C] 45 *With fiery quickness* [F; not in Q2] 54 *and so* so 70 *were* will *begun* begin

IV,v,16 *Let . . . in* [assigned in Q2 to Horatio] 33 *O ho!* [Q2; not in F, C] 38 *grave* ground 46 *Pray* [Q2] Pray you [F, C] 57 *la* [F; not in Q2] 65 *So* (He answers) So 70 *would* [Q2] should [F, C] 73 *Good* God 77 *O* and now behold, O 82 *in their* in 89 *his* this 100 *impiteous* [Q2, F] impetuous [C] 96 *Queen. Alack . . . this* [F; not in Q2] 97 *Where* Attend, where *are* is 106 *They* The 137 *world's* [Q2] world [F, C] 141 *father* [Q2] father's death [F, C] 142 *swoopstake* [eds.] soopstake 152 S.D. *Let her come in* [so F; Q2 assigns to Laertes] 157 *Till* Tell 160 *an old* a poore 161–163 *Nature . . . loves* [F; not in Q2] 165 *Hey . . . nonny* [F; not in Q2] 176 *pray you* [Q2] pray [F, C] 182 *O you must* you may 188 *affliction* afflictions 196 *All flaxen* Flaxen 200 *Christian* Christians *I pray God* [F; not in Q2] *you* [Q2] ye [F, C] 201 *you see* you

IV,vi,2 *Sea-faring men* [Q2] Sailors [F, C] 8 *an 't* and 22 *good turn* turn 27 *bore* bord 31 *He* So 32 *will give* [F] will [Q2] will make [C]

IV,vii,6 *proceeded* proceede 8 *safety* safetie, greatnes 11 *th' are* [Q2] they are [F, C] 14 *She's so conjunctive* She is so concliue 20 *Would* Worke 21 *gyves* Giues 22 *loud a wind* loued Arm'd 24 *And* But *had* haue 36 *How . . . Hamlet* [F; not in Q2] 37 *These* [Q2] This [F, C] 46 *your pardon* you pardon 48 *and more strange* [F; not in Q2] 54 *devise* [Q2] advise [F, C] 57 *I shall* I 63 *checking* the King 84 *I have* [Q2] I've [F, C] 89 *my* me 93 *Lamord* [Q2] Lamond [F, C] 106 *you* [Q2] him [F, C] 116 *wick* [eds.] weeke 123 *spendthrift* [eds.] spend thirfts 124 *'o* [eds.] of 126 *your . . . deed* indeede your fathers sonne 135 *on* ore 139 *pass* pace 141 *for that* for 155 *should* did 160 *prepar'd* prefard 163 *But stay, what noise* [Q2] how sweet Queene [F] How now, sweet queen [C] 167 *askant the* [Q2] aslant a [F, C] 168 *hoar* horry 172 *cold* cull-cold 173 *crownet* [Q2] coronet [F, C] 178 *lauds* [Q2] tunes [F, C] 192 *drowns* [Q2] douts [F, C]

V,i,1 *when she* [Q2] that [F, C] 3 *therefore* [Q2] and therefore [F, C] 9 *se offendendo* so offended 13 *and to* to *argal* or all 39–42 *Sec. Clo. Why . . . arms* [F; not in Q2] 49 *frame* [F; not in Q2] 66 *he* [Q2] that he [F, C] *lasts* [Q2, F] last [Q1, C] 68 *stoup* [Q1, F] soope 73 *that* [F; not in Q2] 74 *at* in 85 *'twere* [Q2] it were [F, C] *This* [Q2] It [F, C] 91 *thou, sweet* [Q2] thou, good [F, C] 93 *meant* went 98 *mazzard* massene 100 *'em* them 108 *quillities* [Q2] quillets [F, C] 109 *mad* [Q2] rude [F, C] 114–115 *in this . . . recoveries* [F; not in Q2] 116 *his* [F; not in Q2] 118 *double ones too* doubles 120 *scarcely* [Q2] hardly [F, C] 124 *calf-skins* Calues-skinnes 129 *O* Or 130 *For . . . meet* [F; not in Q2] 132 *'tis* [Q2] it is [F, C] 133 *yet* [Q2] and yet [F, C] 150 *taken* tooke 154 *been a* been 155 *all* [F; not in Q2] 160 *the* that 165 *'tis* [Q2] it's [F, C] 180 *Faith* [Q2] I' faith [F, C] 182 *now-a-days* [F; not in Q2] 199 *Yorick's* sir Yoricks 202 *Let me see* [F; not in Q2] 204 borne bore 230 *as thus* [F; not in Q2] 232 *into* to 239 *winter's* waters 240 *awhile* [Q2] aside [F, C] 252 *have* been 254 *Shards* [F; not in Q2] 270 *treble* double 284 *and rash* rash 286 *wisdom* [Q2] wiseness [F, C] 300 *thou* [F; not in Q2] 308 *thus* this 316 *thee* [Q2] you [F, C] 321 *shortly* thereby 322 *Till* Tell

V,ii,5 *methought* my thought 6 *bilboes* bilbo 8 *sometime* [Q2] sometimes [F, C] 9 *pall* fall *learn* [Q2] teach [F, C] 17 *unseal* vnfold 19 *O* A 27 *me* now 30 *Ere* Or 43 *'As'es* as sir 46 *the* those 51 *in the* [Q2] in [F, C] 52 *Subscrib'd* Subscribe 57 *Ham. Why . . . employment* [F; not in Q2] 63 *think* [Q2] think'st [F, C] 68–80 *To . . . here* [F; not in Q2] 73 *interim is* [eds.] interim's [F] 78 *court* [eds.] count 83 *humbly* humble 95 *Put* [F; not in Q2] 101 *sultry* sully *for* or 104 *But* [F; not in Q2] 109 *mine* my 111 *gentleman* [eds.] gentlemen 114 *feelingly* [Q4] fellingly 119 *dozy* [eds.] dazzie [Q2] dizzy [C] 120 *yaw* [eds.] raw 148 *his* [eds.] this 155 *impawned* [Q2] imponed [F, C] 157 *hangers* hanger 164 *carriages* carriage 166 *cannon* a cannon 167 *might be* be might 170 *'impawned,' as* [eds.] all [Q2] 'imponed,' as [F, C] 172 *laid* layd sir 181 *it is* [Q2] 't is [F, C] 186 *re-deliver you e'en* deliver you 190 *yours. He* [F; not in Q2] 195 *comply* so *sir* [Q2; not in F, C] 199 *yesty* histy 200 *fann'd* [eds.] prophane [Q2] fond [F] *winnowed* trennowed 219 *this wager* [F; not in Q2] 222 *But* [F; not in Q2] 230 *there's a* there is 231 *be now* be 233 *will come* well come 234 *of aught he leaves knows* [Q2] has aught of what he leaves [F, C] 237 *I have* [Q2] I've [F, C] 241 *a sore* [Q2] sore [F, C] 251 *Sir . . . audience* [F; not in Q2] 261 *keep* [F; not in Q2] *till* all 265 *Come on* [F; not in Q2] 272 *has* [Q2] hath [F, C] 274 *better'd* better 283 *union* Vnice ("Onixe" in some copies) 288 *heavens* [eds.] heauen 297 *A touch, a touch* [F; not in Q2] 307 *'t is almost 'gainst* it is almost against 308 *you* you doe 310 *afeard* sure 319 *swounds* [eds.] sounds 324 *Hamlet: Hamlet* Hamlet 326 *hour of* houres 327 *thy* [Q1, F] my 336 *murd'rous* [F; not in Q2] 337 *off* of *thy union* [Q1, F] the Onixe 353 *th' art* [Q2, F] thou'rt [C] 354 *ha 't* [eds.] hate [Q2] have 't [F, C] 356 *live* I leaue 361 *Osr.* [Qq, F provide a stage direction here: "Enter Osrick"] 373 *you* [Q2] ye [F, C] 390 *th' yet* yet 394 *forc'd* for no 403 *on* no 410 *rites* right

King Lear

Copy text: the First Folio [F], except for those 300 or so lines found only in the first quarto of 1608 [Q]. Unless otherwise indicated, readings from Q are from the corrected state of that quarto. A few readings are supplied from the second quarto of 1619 [Q2]. All readings subsequent to F are marked as supplied by "eds."

I,i,5 *equalities* [Q] qualities 19 *sir, by* [F] sir, a son by [Q, C] 22 *to* [F] into [Q, C] 36 *lord* [F] liege [Q, C] 56 *word* [F] words [Q, C] 63 *speak* [F] do [Q, C] 67 *issue* [Q] issues 69 *of* [F] to [Q, C] *Speak* [Q; not in F] 70 *Sir, I* [Q] I 71 *that . . . sister* [F] the self-same metal that my sister is [Q, C] 76 *possesses* [Q] professes 80 *ponderous* [F] richer [Q, C] 85 *our last and* [F] the last, not [Q, C] 95 *no* [F] nor [Q, C] 97 *you* [F] it [Q, C] 106 *To . . . all* [Q; not in F] 107 *my good* [F] good my [Q, C] 112 *mysteries* [eds.] miseries [F] mistresse [Q] 137 *turns* turne *shall* [F] still [Q, C] 148 *wouldst* [F] wilt [Q, C] 151 *falls* [F] stoops [Q, C] *Reserve thy state* [F] Reverse thy doom [Q, C] 155 *sounds* [F] sound [Q, C] 156 *Reverb* [F] Reverbs [Q, C] 157 *as a* [Q] as 158 *thine* [F] thy [Q, C] *nor* [Q] nere 159 *motive* [F] the motive [Q, C] 162 *Lear.* [Q] Kear. *Kent.* [Q] Lent. 165 *Do* [Q; not in F] 166 *the* [Q] thy 167 *gift* [F] doom [Q, C] 171 *That* [F] Since [Q, C] *vows* [F] vow [Q, C] 173 *betwixt* [F] between [Q, C] *sentence* [Q] sentences 177 *disasters* [F] diseases [Q, C] 191 *Glou.* [Q] Cor. 193 *toward* [F] towards [Q, C] 197 *hath* [F] what [Q, C] 209 *on* [Q] in 217 *whom* [F] that [Q, C] *best object* [Q] obiect 219 *The best, the* [F] Most best, most [Q, C] 224 *Fall'n* [Q] Fall 226 *Should* [F] Could [Q, C] 228 *well* [Q] will 235 *As* [Q] That 242 *stands* [Q, F] stand [C] 244 *king* [F] Lear [Q, C] 251 *respects of fortune* [Q] respect and Fortunes 274 *Love* [F] Use [Q, C] 279 *duty* [F] duties [Q, C] 283 *plighted* [F] pleated [Q] plaited [C] 284 *covers* [Q, F] cover [C] *shame them* [Q] with shame 285 s.d. *Exeunt* [eds.] Exit 286 *little* [F] a little [Q, C] 292 *not been* [Q] beene 299 *from . . . receive* [F] to receive from his age [Q, C] 307 *let us* [F] let's [Q, C] *hit* [Q] sit 309 *disposition* [F] dispositions [Q, C] 311 *of it* [F] on 't [Q, C]

I,ii,21 *top* [eds.] to' 24 *prescrib'd* [F] subscribed [Q, C] 59 *waked* [Q] wake 62 *this to you* [Q] you to this 74 *Has* [F] Hath [Q, C] *before* [F] heretofore [Q, C] 78 *declined* [F] declining [Q, C] 89 *should* [F, Q] shall [C] 93 *writ* [F] wrote [Q, C] 94 *other* [F] further [Q, C] 103–105 *Edm. Nor . . . earth* [Q; not in F] 129 *surfeits* [F] surfeit [Q, C] 131 *stars* [F] the stars [Q, C] 132 *on* [F] by [Q, C] 139 *on* [F] to [Q, C] 142 *Fut* [Q; not in F] Tut [C] 144 *Edgar* [Q; not in F] 145 *and pat* [eds.] Pat [F] and out [Q] 154 *with* [F] about [Q, C] 156–167 *as of . . . come* [Q; not in F] 168 *Why, the* [Q] The 172 *nor* [F] or [Q, C] 176 *until* [F] till [Q, C] 187 *go armed* [Q; not in F]

I,iii,14 *distaste* [F] dislike [Q, C] 16–20 *Not . . . abus'd* [Q; not in F] 21 *have said* [F] tell you [Q, C] 24–25 *I . . . speak* [Q; not in F] 26 *very course* [Q] course

I,iv,1 *well* [Q] will 22 *be'st* [F] be [Q, C] *he's* [F] he is [Q, C] 54 *daughter* [Q] Daughters 93 *strucken* [F] struck [Q, C] 110 *Kent. Why, Fool?* [Q] Lear. Why my Boy? 125 *Lady the* [eds.] the Lady 152 *one* [F] fool [Q, C] 154–170 *Fool. That . . . snatching* [Q; not in F] 169 *the fool* [Q] fool [C] 170 *Give . . . nuncle* [Q] Nunckle, giue me an egge 175 *crown* [Q] Crownes 176 *thine* [F] thy [Q, C] 181 *grace* [F] wit [Q, C] 183 *And* [F] They [Q, C] 188 *e'er* [F] ever [Q, C] 189 *mothers* [F] mother [Q, C] 194 *fools* [Q] Foole 209 *Methinks you* [Q] You 236 *it had* [Q] it's had 239 *Come, sir* [Q; not in F] 240 *your* [F] that [Q, C] 242 *which of late transport* [F] that of late transform [Q, C] 246, 247 *Does* [F] Doth [Q, C] 252–256 *Lear. I . . . father* [Q; not in F] 261 *should* [Q, F] you should [C] 266 *Makes* [F] Make [Q, C] 271 *remainders* [F] remainder [Q, C] 273 *Which* [F] That [Q] And [C] 279 *O . . . come* [Q; not in F] 313 *more of it* [F] the cause [Q, C] 325 *loose* [F] lose [C] 326 *Yea . . . this* [Q; not in F] *is it* [eds.] is 't [Q] 327 *Ha! let* [F] Let [C] *I have another* [F] yet have I left a [Q, C] 332 *thou . . . thee* [Q; not in F] 333 *my lord* [Q; not in F] 358 *Ay* [F] Yes [Q, C] 366 *You* [eds.] Your *attask'd* [Q] at task

I,v,s.d. *Kent* Kent, Gentleman 11 *not* [F] ne'er [Q, C] 17 *What canst tell* [F] Why, what canst thou tell, my [Q, C] 32 *put 's* [F] put his [Q, C] 38 *moe* [F] more [Q, C] 51 s.d. ["Gentleman" enters at line 1 in F]

II,i,2 *you* [Q] your 9 *ear-kissing* [F] ear-bussing [Q, C] 48 *the thunder* [F] their thunders [Q, C] 54 *latch'd* [F] lancht [Q] lanced [C] 55 *But* [Q] And 64 *coward* [F, Globe] caitiff [Q, F] 70 *would the reposal* [F, Globe] could the reposure [Q, C] 72 *I should* [Q] should I 73 *ay, though* [Q] though 78 *spirits* [F] spurs [Q, C] 79 *O strange* [F] Strong [Q, C] 80 *said he* [F; not in Q, C] *I never got him* [Q; not in F] 81 *why* [Q] wher 89 *strange news* [Q] strangenesse 92 *it 's* [F] is [Q, C] 97 *tended* [F] tends [Q] tend [C] 102 *expense and waste* [F, Globe] waste and spoil [Q, C] 108 *It was* [F] 'Twas [Q, C] 122 *prize* [F] poise [Q, C] 129 *businesses* [F] business [Q, C]

II,ii,17 *whoreson* [F] knave, a whoreson [Q, C] 25 *clamorous* [Q] clamours 31 *since* [F] ago since [Q, C] 35 *you: draw* [Q] you 48 *Part* [F; not in Q, C] 63 *A* [F] Ay, a [Q, C] 64 *they* [F] he [Q, C] 65 *years o'* [F] hours at [Q, C] 81 *too* [Q] t' 83 *Bring . . . their* [Q] Being . . . the 84 *Renege* [Q] Reuenge 85 *gale* [Q] gall 95 *What is his fault* [F] what's his offence [Q, C] 111 *faith* [F] sooth [Q, C] 113 *flick'ring* [eds.] flicking [F] flikering [C] 125 *compact* [F] conjunct [Q, C] 130 *dread* [Q] dead 133 *reverent* [Q, F] reverend [C] 137 *respect* [Q] respects 148–152 *His . . . with* [Q; not in F] *contemned'st* [eds.] temnest [Q] 152 *king* [Q] King his Master, needs 153 *he* [F] he's [Q, C] 157 *For . . . legs* [Q; not in F] 158 *Come . . . away* [F assigns to Cornwall] 159 *duke's* [Q] Duke

II,iii,10 *hairs* [F] hair [Q, C] 15 *bare arms* [Q] Armes 18 *sheep* [Q] Sheeps 19 *Sometime* [Q] Sometimes

II,iv,2 *messenger* [Q] messengers 9 *man's* [Q] man 19–20 *No, no . . . have* [Q; not in F] 31 *panting* [Q] painting 34 *whose* [Q] those 40 *which* [F] that [Q, C] 64 *the* [Q] the the *number* [F] train [Q, C] 66 *thou'dst* [F] thou hadst [Q, C] 75 *following* [F] following it [Q, C] *upward* [F] up the hill [Q, C] 77 *have* [Q] hause 103 *her* [Q] tends 133 *mother's* [Q] Mother 150 *her* [Q] his 154 *her, sir* [Q] her 170 *blast her pride* [Q] blister 189 *fickle* [Q] sickly 194 *if you* [F] if [Q, C] 197 *will you* [F] wilt thou [Q, C] 227 *or* [F] an [Q, C] 248 *ye* [F] you [Q, C] 270 *life is* [F] life as [Q] life's as [C] 277 *stirs* [Q, F] stir [C] 303 high [F] bleak [Q, C]

III,i,4 *elements* [F] element [Q, C] 7–15 *tears . . . all* [Q; not in F] 20 *is* [F] be [Q, C] 27 *have* [eds.] hath 30–42 *But . . . you* [Q; not in F] 48 *that* [F] your [Q, C]

III,ii,3 *drown'd* [Q] drown 5 *of* [F] to [Q, C] 7 *Strike* [F]

Smite [Q, C] 12 *in* [F] in and [Q, C] 13 *men nor fools* [F] man nor fool [Q, C] 22 *will . . . join* [F] have . . . join'd [Q, C] 50 *pudder* [F] pother [Q, C] 54 *of* [F] man of [Q, C] 57 *Hast* [Q] Ha's 71 *That* [Q] And 78 *True, boy* [F] True, my good boy [Q, C]

III,iii,4 *of* [F] of their [Q, C] 6 *or* [F] nor [Q, C] 8 *There is* [F] There's a [Q, C] 9 *between* [F] betwixt [Q, C] 13 *there is* [F] there's [Q, C] 15 *look* [F] seek [Q, C] 18 *If* [F] Though [Q, C] 20 *is* [F] is some [Q, C] *things* [F] thing [Q, C]

III,iv,10 *thy* [Q] they *roaring* [Q, F] raging [C] 38 S.D. *Enter Fool* [F, at line 36: "Enter Edgar, and Foole"] 47 *blows the cold wind* [Q] blow the windes 48 *bed* [F] cold bed [Q, C] 49 Didst . . . thy [F] Hast thou given all to thy two [Q, C] 53 *ford* [Q] Sword 59 *Bless* [Q] Blisse 65 *What, have* [eds.] Ha's [F] What [Q] 66 *Wouldst . . . 'em* [F] Didst . . . them [Q, C] 83 *word's justice* [F] words justly [Q] word justly [C] 93 *deeply* [Q] deerely 103 *mun* [F] mun, ha, no [C] 104 *boy, boy* [F] boy, my boy [Q, C] *sessa* [eds.] Sesey 105 *Thou* [F] Why, thou [Q, C] *a* [F] thy [Q, C] 120 *foul* [F] foul fiend [Q, C] 121 *till the* [Q] at 141 *stock-punished* [Q] stockt, punish'd *hath had* [Q] hath 150 *my . . . vile* is grown so vile, my lord [Q, C]

III,v,11 *letter* [Q] letter which 26 *dearer* [Q] deere

III,vi,17 *hizzing* [F] hissing [C] 18–59 *Edgar. The . . . 'scape* [Q; not in F] 23 *justice* [Q] justicer [C] 24 *Now* [Q2] No [Q] 27 *bourn* [eds.] broome [Q] 32 *Hoppedance* [Q] Hopdance [C] 36 *cushions* [eds.] cushings [Q] 37 *the* [eds.] their [Q] 49 *she kicked* [Q2] kickt [Q] 53 *joint* [eds.] ioyne [Q] 57 *on* [eds.] an [Q] 72 *lym* [eds.] Hym 73 *tike* [Q] tight *trundle* [Q] Troudle 74 *him* [F] them [Q, C] 76 *leap'd* [F] leap [Q, C] 82 *makes* [Q] make 86 *Persian* [F] Persian attire [Q, C] 91 *So, so, so* [Q; not in F] 98 *toward* [F] towards [Q, C] 104–108 *Oppressed . . . behind* [Q; not in F] 109–122 *Edg. When . . . lurk* [Q; not in F] 119 *thoughts defile* [Q] thought defiles [C]

III,vii,3 *traitor* [F] villain [Q, C] 10 *festinate* [eds.] festiuate 19 *toward* [F] towards [Q, C] 30 *means* [Q, F] mean [C] 43 *answer'd* [F] answerer [Q, C] 46 *you have* [F, Q] have you [C] 53 *answer* [F] first answer [Q, C] 55 *Dover* [F] Dover, sir [Q, C] 65 *subscribe* [F] subscribed [Q, C] 99–107 *Sec. Serv. . . . him* [Q; not in F] *Sec. Serv.* [eds.] Seruant [Q] *Third Serv.* [eds.] 2 Seruant [Q] 105 *roguish* [Q2; not in Q]

IV,i,19 *You* [F] Alack, sir, you [Q, C] 43 *Then . . . gone* [Q] Get thee away 47 *Which* [F] Who [Q, C] 61–67 *five . . . master* [Q; not in F] 63 *Flibbertigibbet* [eds.] Stiberdigebit [Q] 64 *mopping and mowing* [eds.] Mobing, & Mohing [Q] 72 *does* [Q, F] doth [C]

IV,ii,S.D. *Bastard* [Q] Bastard, and Steward 17 *names* [F] arms [Q, F] 31–50 *I fear . . . deep* [Q; not in F] 32 *its* [eds.] ith [Q] it [C] 38, 48 *vile* [eds.] vild [Q] (and elsewhere) 47 *these* [eds.] this [Q] 53–59 *that . . . so* [Q; not in F] 57 *to threat* [eds.] thereat [Q] 58 *Whilst* [Q corrected] Whil's [Q uncorrected] Whiles [C] *sits . . . cries* [Q] sit'st . . . criest [C] 68 *mew* [Q corrected] now [Q uncorrected, C] 75 *thereat enrag'd* [Q] threat-enrag'd 79 *justicers* [Q corrected] Iustices

IV,iii,1–57 [Q; not in F] 2 *no* [Q] the [C] 13 *sir* [eds.] say [Q] 18 *strove* [eds.] streme [Q] 22 *seem'd* [eds.] seeme [Q] 33 *moisten'd* [eds.] moystened her [Q] 36 *mate and make* [Q] mate and mate [C] 57 S.D. *Exeunt* [eds.] Exit [C]

IV,iv,S.D. *Doctor* [Q] Gentlemen 3 *fumiter* [eds.] femiter [Q] Fenitar [F] 4 *har-docks* [F] hor-docks [Q] bur-docks [C] 18 *distress* [Q] desires 26 *importun'd* [F] important [Q, C]

IV,v,21 *Something* [Q] Some things 25 *œillades* [eds.] Eliads 28 *y'are* [F] you are [C] 39 *meet him* [Q] meet

IV,vi,1 *I* [F] we [Q, C] 9, 10 *Y'are* [Q, F] You're [C] 17 *walk* [Q] walk'd 30 *further* [F] farther [Q, C] 32 *ye* [F] you [Q, C] 71 *enridged* [Q] enraged 83 *coining* [Q] crying 98 *white* [Q] the white 129 *there is* [F] there's [Q, C] 133 *to sweeten* [Q] sweeten 143 *thy* [F] the [Q, C] *see one* [Q] see 165 *thy* [F] thine [Q, C] 166 *lusts* [Q, F] lust'st [C] 168 *Through* [Q] Thorough *small* [Q] great 169 *Plate sin* [eds.] Place sinnes 190 *son-in-laws* [Q, F] sons-in-law [C] 201 *Ay . . . dust* [Q; not in F] *Gent. Good sir* [Q2; not in F, Q] 202 *a smug* [F] a [Q, C] 204 *Masters* [F] My masters [Q, C] 206 *Come, an* [F] Nay, and [Q] Nay, if [C] 207 *by* [F] with [Q, C] 209 *one* [Q] a 256 *English* [F] British [Q, C] *death* [eds.] death, death 265 *we* [F] we'ld [Q, C] 278 *indistinguish'd* [Q] undinguish'd [F] undistinguish'd [C]

IV,vii,8 *Pardon* [F] Pardon me [Q, C] 13 *Doct.* [Q] Gent. (and at lines 17, 43, 51, 78) 21 *sleep* [F] his sleep [Q, C] 23 *Doct.* [not in F; Q has "Gent."] 24 *doubt not* [Q] doubt 24–25 *Cor. Very . . . there* [Q; not in F] 31 *Did challenge* [F] Had challenged [Q, C] 32 *warring* [Q] iarring 33–36 *To stand . . . helm* [Q; not in F] 49 *when* [eds.] where 58 *hand* [F] hands [Q, C] 59 *You* [F] No, sir, you [Q, C] 79–80 *and yet . . . lost* [Q; not in F] 85–99 *Gent. Holds . . . fought* [Q; not in F]

V,i,11–13 *Edm. That . . . hers* [Q; not in F] 16 *me not* [Q] not 18–19 *Gon. I . . . me* [Q; not in F] 21 *hear* [Q] heard 23–28 *Where . . . nobly* [Q; not in F] 25 *touches* [Q] toucheth [C] 32 *proceeding* [F] proceedings [Q, C] 33 *Edm. I . . . tent* [Q; not in F] 36 *pray you* [Q] pray 46 *love* [Q] loues

V,ii,8 *further* [F] farther [Q, C]

V,iii,35 *th'* [F] thou [Q, C] 38–39 *Capt. I . . . it* [Q; not in F] 39 *do 't* [Q] do it [C] 40 *show'd* [Q, F] shown [C] 42 *Who* [F] That [Q, C] 43 *I* [F] We [Q, C] 47 *and appointed guard* [Q corrected; not in F] 48 *had* [F] has [Q, C] 54–59 *At . . . place* [Q; not in F] 55 *We* [Q corrected] mee [Q uncorrected] 57 *sharpness* [Q corrected] sharpes [Q uncorrected] 70 *Gon.* [Q] Alb. 76 *is* [F] are [Q, C] 83 *attaint* [Q] arrest 84 *sister* [Q] Sisters 85 *bar* [eds.] bare 87 *banes* [Q, F] bans [C] 91 *person* [F] head [Q, C] 93 *make* [F] prove [Q, C] 97 *he is* [Q] hes 99 *the* [F] thy [Q, C] 102 *Edm. A . . . herald* [Q; not in F] 109 *Capt. Sound, trumpet* [Q; not in F] 115 *Edm. Sound* [Q; not in F] 129 *is the* [Q] is my priuiledge, The 131 *place, youth* [F] youth, place [Q, C] 152 *war* [F] arms [Q, C] 160 *Gon.* [Q] Bast. 168 *th'* [F] thou [Q, C] (also at line 173) 196 *our* [F] my [Q, C] 204–221 *Edg. This . . . slave* [Q; not in F] 213 *him* [eds.] me [Q] 223 *this* [F] that [Q, C] 227 *confesses* [F] hath confess'd [Q, C] 230 *the* [F] their [Q, C] 238 *Goneril's* [eds.] Gonerill [at line 230] 248 *has* [F] hath [Q, C] 251 *Edg.* [F] Alb. [Q, C] 257 *Howl, howl, howl, howl* [Q] Howle, howle, howle *you* [Q] your 277 *them* [Q] him 289 *You are* [eds.] Your are [F] You'r [Q] 294 S.D., 295 *Messenger* [F] Captain [Q, C] 313 *hates him* [Q, F] hates him much [C] 323 *Edg.* [F] Alb. [Q, C]

The Tempest

Copy text: the First Folio [F].

Names of the Actors [printed in F at the end of the play]

I,i,36 S.D. *Exeunt* Exit 59 *chapp'd* chopt

I,ii,26 *wrack* [F] wreck [C] (and elsewhere) 146 *butt* [F] boat [C] 173 *princesses* Princesse 200 *boresprit* [F] bowsprit [C] 201 *lightnings* Lightning 271 *wast* was 282 *she* he 333 *made* [F] madest [C] 346 *humane* [F] human [C] 351 *Mir.* [F] Pro. [C] 358 *vile* vild 375, 396 *Ariel's* Ariel 381 *the burthen bear* beare the burthen

II,i,36 *So, you're paid* [assigned in F to Antonio] 86 *His . . . harp* [assigned in F to Antonio] 168 *'Save* [F] God save [C]

II,ii,187 *trenchering* [F] trencher [C] 190 *hey-day* high-day

III,i,2 *sets* set

III,ii,92 *further* [F] farther [C] 130 *scout* cout

III,iii,2 *ache* akes 18 S.D. *[Enter]* and 29 *islanders* Islands 65 *plume* plumbe 81 *heart's sorrow* hearts-sorrow [F] heart-sorrow [C]

IV,i,3 *third* [F] thrid [C] 9 *off* of 13 *gift* guest 110 *Cer.* [not in F] 163 S.D. *Exeunt* Exit 193 *them on* on them 264 *Lies* [F] Lie [C]

V,i,16 *runs* [F] run [C] 39 *mushrumps* [F] mushrooms [C] 60 *boil'd* boile 72 *Didst* Did 75 *entertain'd* entertaine 76 *who* whom 82 *lies* ly 111 *Whe'r* Where [F] Whether [C] 136 *who* whom 157 *howsoev'r* [F] howsoe'er [C] 199 *remembrance* remembrances 236 *her* our

The Sonnets

Copy text: the quarto of 1609 [Q].

2.4 *totter'd* [Q] tatter'd [C] (also at 26.11) 12.4 *all* or 13.7 *Yourself* You selfe 17.12 *metre* miter 19.5 *fleets* fleet'st 20.7 *hues* Hows 23.14 *with* wit *wit* wiht 25.9 *fight* worth 26.12 *thy* their (also at 27.10, 35.8 [twice], 37.7, 43.11, 45.12, 46.3, 46.8, 46.13, 46.14, 69.5, 70.6, 128.11, 128.14) 28.12 *gild'st the* guil'st th' 28.14 *strength* length 31.8 *thee* there 34.12 *cross* losse 34.13 *sheeds* [Q] sheds [C] 39.12 *doth* dost 40.7 *this self* [Q] thyself [C] 41.8 *she* he 44.13 *nought* naughts 47.11 *not* nor 49.10 *desart* [Q] desert [C] 50.6 *dully* duly 54.14 *vade, by* [Q] fade, my [C] 55.1 *monuments* monument 56.13 *Else* As 59.11 *whe'r* where [Q] whether [C] 65.12 *of* or 67.9 *bankrout* [Q] bankrupt [C] 69.3 *due* end 70.1 *art* are 71.4 *vilest* vildest 76.7 *tell* fel 77.10 *blanks* blacks 90.11 *shall* stall 91.9 *better* bitter 95.12 *turn* turnes 110.13 *best* bes 112.14 *are* y'are 113.6 *latch* lack 113.14 *mak'th mine eye* maketh mine [Q] makes mine eye [C] 126.8 *minutes* mynuit 129.11 *prov'd a* proud and 132.2 *torments* torment 144.6 *side* sight 144.9 *fiend* finde 146.2 *Thrall to* My sinfull earth 147.12 *random* randon 153.14 *eyes* eye

GLOSSARY

Shakespearean Words and Meanings of Frequent Occurrence

A

'A: he (unaccented form).
Abate: lessen, diminish; blunt, reduce; deprive; bar, leave out of account, except; depreciate; humble.
Abuse (N): insult, error, misdeed, offense, crime; imposture, deception; also the modern sense.
Abuse (V): deceive, misapply, put to a bad use; maltreat; frequently the modern sense.
Addition: something added to one's name to denote his rank; mark of distinction; title.
Admiration: wonder; object of wonder.
Admire: wonder at.
Advantage (N): profit, convenience, benefit; opportunity, favorable opportunity; pecuniary profit; often shades toward the modern sense.
Advantage (V): profit, be of benefit to, benefit; augment.
Advice: reflection, consideration, deliberation, consultation.
Affect: aim at, aspire to, incline toward; be fond of, be inclined; love; act upon contagiously (as a disease). (PAST PART.) *Affected:* disposed, inclined, in love, loved.
Affection: passion, love; emotion, feeling, mental tendency, disposition; wish, inclination; affectation.
An: if; but; *an if:* if, though, even if.
Anon: at once, soon; presently, by and by.
Answer: return, requite; atone for; render an account of, account for; obey, agree with; also the modern sense.
Apparent: evident, plain; seeming.
Argument: subject, theme, reason, cause; story; excuse.
As: according as; as far as; namely; as if; in the capacity of; that; so that; that is, that they.
Assay: try, attempt; accost, address; challenge.
Atone: reconcile; set at one.
Attach: arrest, seize.
Awful: commanding reverential fear or respect; profoundly respectful or reverential.

B

Band: bond, fetters, manacle (leash for a dog). *Band* and *bond* are etymologically the same word; *band* was formerly used in both senses.
Basilisk: fabulous reptile said to kill by its look. The basilisk of popular superstition was a creature with legs, wings, a serpentine and winding tail, and a crest or comb somewhat like a cock (Sir Thomas Browne). It was the offspring of a cock's egg hatched under a toad or serpent.
Bate: blunt, abate, reduce; deduct, except.
Battle: army; division of an army.
Beshrew: curse, blame; used as a mild curse, "Bad or ill luck to."
Bias: tendency, bent, inclination, swaying influence; term in bowling applied to the form of the bowl, the oblique line in which it runs, and the kind of impetus given to cause it to run obliquely.
Blood: nature, vigor; supposed source of emotion; passion; spirit, animation; one of the four humours (see *humour*).
Boot (N): advantage, profit; something given in addition to the bargain; booty, plunder.
Boot (V): profit, avail.
Brave (ADJ.): fine, gallant; splendid, finely arrayed, showy; ostentatiously defiant.
Brave (V): challenge, defy; make splendid.
Brook: tolerate, endure.

C

Can: can do; know; be skilled; sometimes used for "did."
Capable: comprehensive; sensible, impressible, susceptible; capable of; gifted, intelligent.
Careful: anxious, full of care; provident; attentive.
Carry: manage, execute; be successful, win; conquer; sustain; endure.
Censure (N): judgment, opinion; critical opinion, unfavorable opinion.
Censure (V): judge, estimate; pass sentence or judgment.
Character (N): writing, printing, record; handwriting; cipher; face, features (bespeaking inward qualities).
Character (V): write, engrave, inscribe.
Check (N): reproof; restraint.
Check (V): reprove, restrain, keep from; control.
Circumstance: condition, state of affairs, particulars; adjunct details; detailed narration, argument, or discourse; formality, ceremony.
Clip: embrace; surround.
Close: secret, private; concealed; uncommunicative; enclosed.
Cog: cheat.
Coil: noise, disturbance, turmoil; fuss, to-do, bustle.
Colour: appearance; pretext, pretense; excuse.
Companion: fellow (used contemptuously).
Complete: accomplished, fully endowed; perfect, perfect in quality; also frequently the modern sense.
Complexion: external appearance; temperament, disposition; the four complexions—sanguine, choleric, phlegmatic, and melancholy—correspond to the four humours (see *humour*); also the modern sense.
Composition: compact, agreement, constitution.
Compound: settle, agree.
Conceit: conception, idea, thought; mental faculty, wit; fancy, imagination; opinion, estimate; device, invention, design.
Condition: temperament, disposition; characteristic, property, quality; social or official position, rank or status; covenant, treaty, contract.
Confound: waste, spend, invalidate, destroy; undo, ruin; mingle indistinguishably, mix, blend.
Confusion: destruction, overthrow, ruin; mental agitation.
Continent: that which contains or encloses; earth, globe; sum, summary.
Contrive: plot; plan; spend or pass (time).
Conversation: conduct, deportment; social intercourse, association.
Converse: hold intercourse; associate with, have to do with.

Cope: encounter, meet; have to do with.
Copy: model, pattern; example; minutes or memoranda.
Cousin: any relative not belonging to one's immediate family.
Cry you mercy: beg your pardon.
Cuckold: husband whose wife is unfaithful.
Curious: careful, fastidious; anxious, concerned; made with care, skillfully, intricately or daintily wrought; particular.
Cursed, curst: shrewish, perverse, spiteful.

D

Dainty: minute; scrupulous, particular; particular about (with *of*); refined, elegant; also the modern sense.
Date: duration, termination, term of existence; limit or end of a term or period, term.
Dear: precious; best; costly; important; affectionate; hearty; grievous, dire; also the modern sense.
Debate: discuss; fight.
Decay (N): downfall, ruin; cause of ruin.
Decay (V): perish, be destroyed; destroy.
Defeat (N): destruction, ruin.
Defeat (V): destroy, disfigure, ruin.
Defy: challenge, challenge to a fight; reject; despise.
Demand (N): inquiry; request.
Demand (V): inquire, question; request.
Deny: refuse (to do something); refuse permission; refuse to accept; refuse admittance; disown.
Depart (N): departure.
Depart (V): part; go away from, leave, quit; take leave (of one another); *depart with, withal:* part with, give up.
Derive: gain, obtain; draw upon, direct (to); descend; pass by descent, be descended or inherited; trace the origin of (refl.).
Difference: diversity of opinion, disagreement, dissension, dispute; characteristic or distinguishing feature; alteration or addition to a coat of arms to distinguish a younger or lateral branch of a family.
Digest: arrange, perfect; assimilate, amalgamate; disperse, dissipate; comprehend, understand; put up with (fig. from the physical sense of digesting food).
Discourse (N): reasoning, reflection; talk, act of conversing, conversation; faculty of conversing; familiar intercourse; relating (as by speech).
Discourse (V): speak, talk, converse; pass (the time) in talk; say, utter, tell, give forth; narrate, relate.
Discover: uncover, expose to view; divulge, reveal, make known; spy out, reconnoiter; betray; distinguish, discern; also the modern sense.
Dispose (N): disposal; temperament, bent of mind, disposition; external manner.
Dispose (V): distribute, manage, make use of; deposit, put or stow away; regulate, order, direct; come to terms. (PAST PART.) *Disposed:* in a good frame of mind; inclined to be merry.
Dispute: discuss, reason; strive against, resist.
Distemper: disturb; disorder, ill humor; illness.
Doit: old Dutch coin, one-half an English farthing.
Doubt (N): suspicion, apprehension; fear, danger, risk; also the modern sense.
Doubt (V): suspect, apprehend; fear; also the modern sense.
Doubtful: inclined to suspect, suspicious, apprehensive; not to be relied on; almost certain.
Duty: reverence, respect, expression of respect; submission to authority, obedience; due.

E

Earnest: money paid as an instalment to secure a bargain; partial payment; often used with quibble in the modern sense.
Ease: comfort, assistance, leisure; idleness, sloth, inactivity; also the modern sense.
Ecstasy: frenzy, madness, state of being beside oneself, excitement, bewilderment; swoon; rapture.
Element: used to refer to the simple substances of which all material bodies were thought to be composed; specifically earth, air, fire, and water, corresponding to the four humors (see *humour*); atmosphere, sky; atmospheric agencies or powers; that one of the four elements which is the natural abode of a creature; hence, natural surroundings, sphere.
Engage: pledge, pawn, mortgage; bind by a promise, swear to; entangle, involve; enlist; embark on an enterprise (refl.).
Engine: mechanical contrivance; artifice, device, plot.
Enlarge: give free scope to; set at liberty, release.
Entertain: keep up, maintain, accept; take into one's service; treat; engage (someone's) attention or thoughts; occupy, while or pass away pleasurably; engage (as an enemy); receive.
Envious: malicious, spiteful, malignant.
Envy: ill-will, malice; hate; also the modern sense.
Even: uniform; direct, straightforward; exact, precise; equable, smooth, comfortable; equal, equally balanced.
Event: outcome; affair, business; also frequently the modern sense.
Exclaim: protest, rail; accuse, blame (with *on*), reproach.
Excursion: stage battle or skirmish (in stage directions).
Excuse: seek to extenuate (a fault); maintain the innocence of; clear oneself, justify or vindicate oneself; decline (refl.).

F

Fact: deed, act; crime.
Faction: party, class, group, set (of persons); party strife, dissension; factious quarrel, intrigue.
Fail: die, die out; err, be at fault; omit, leave undone.
Fair (N): fair thing; one of the fair sex; someone beloved; beauty (the abstract concept).
Fair (ADJ.): just; clear, distinct; beautiful.
Fair (ADV.): fairly (q.v.).
Fairly: beautifully, handsomely; courteously, civilly; properly, honorably, honestly; becomingly, appropriately; favorably, fortunately; softly, gently, kindly.
Fall: let fall, drop; happen, come to pass; befall; shades frequently toward the modern senses.
Falsely: wrongly; treacherously; improperly.
Fame: report; rumor; reputation.
Familiar (N): intimate friend; familiar or attendant spirit, demon associated with and obedient to a person.
Familiar (ADJ.): intimate, friendly; belonging to

household or family, domestic; well-known; habitual, ordinary, trivial; plain, easily understood.

Fancy: fantasticalness; imaginative conception, flight of imagination; amorous inclination or passion, love; liking, taste.

Fantasy: fancy, imagination; caprice, whim.

Favour: countenance, face; complexion; aspect, appearance; leave, permission, pardon; attraction, charm, good will; *in favour*, benevolently.

Fear (N): dread, apprehension; dreadfulness; object of dread or fear.

Fear (V): be apprehensive or concerned about, mistrust, doubt; frighten, make afraid.

Fearful: exciting or inspiring fear, terrible, dreadful; timorous, apprehensive, full of fear.

Feature: shape or form of body, figure; shapeliness, comeliness.

Fellow: companion; partaker, sharer (of); equal, match; customrary form of address to a servant or an inferior (sometimes used contemptuously or condescendingly).

Fine (N): end, conclusion; *in fine:* finally.

Fine (ADJ.): highly accomplished or skillful; exquisitely fashioned, delicate; refined, subtle; frequently the modern sense.

Flaw: fragment; crack, fissure; tempest, squall, gust of wind; outburst of passion.

Flesh: reward a hawk or hound with a piece of flesh of the game killed to excite its eagerness of the chase (Onions); hence to inflame by a foretaste of success; initiate or inure to bloodshed (used for a first time in battle); harden, train.

Flourish: fanfare of trumpets (in stage directions).

Fond: foolish, doting; *fond of:* eager for; also the modern sense.

Fool: term of endearment and pity; frequently the modern sense.

For that, for why: because.

Forfend: forbid, avert.

Free: generous, magnanimous; candid, open; guiltless, innocent.

Front: forehead, face; foremost line of battle; beginning.

Furnish: equip, fit out (furnish forth); endow; dress, decorate, embellish.

G

Gear: apparel, dress; stuff, substance, thing, article; discourse, talk; matter, business, affair.

Get: beget.

Gloss: specious fair appearance; lustrous surface.

Go to: expression of remonstrance, impatience, disapprobation, or derision.

Grace (N): kindness, favor, charm, divine favor; fortune, luck; beneficent virtue; sense of duty or propriety; mercy, pardon; embellish; *do grace:* reflect credit on, do honor to, do a favor for.

Grace (V): gratify, delight; honor, favor.

Groat: coin equal to four pence.

H

Habit: dress, garb, costume; bearing, demeanor, manner; occasionally in the modern sense.

Happily: haply, perchance, perhaps.

Hardly: with difficulty.

Have at: I shall come at (you) (i.e., listen to me), I shall attack (a person or thing); let me at.

Have with: I shall go along with; let me go along with; come along.

Having: possession, property, wealth, estate; endowments, accomplishments.

Head: armed force.

Hind: servant, slave; rustic, boor, clown.

His: its. *His* was historically the possessive form of both the masculine and neuter pronouns. *Its*, although not common in Shakespeare's time, occurs in the plays occasionally.

Holp: helped (archaic past tense).

Home: fully, satisfactorily, thoroughly, plainly, effectually; to the quick.

Honest: holding an honorable position, honorable, respectable; decent, kind, seemly, befitting, proper; chaste; genuine; loosely used as an epithet of approbation.

Humour: mood, temper, cast of mind, temperament, disposition; vagary, fancy, whim; moisture (the literal sense); a physiological, and by transference, a psychological term applied to the four chief fluids of the human body—phlegm, blood, choler, and melancholy (the last also called black choler). A person's disposition and his temporary state of mind were determined according to the relative proportions of these fluids in his body; consequently a person was said to be phlegmatic, sanguine, choleric, or melancholy.

I

Image: likeness; visible form; representation; embodiment, type; mental picture, creation of the imagination.

Influence: supposed flowing from the stars or heavens of an ethereal fluid, acting upon the characters and destinies of men (used metaphorically).

Inform: take shape, give form to, imbue, inspire; instruct, teach; charge (against).

Instance: evidence, proof, sign, confirmation; motive, cause.

Invention: power of mental creation, the creative faculty; work of the imagination, artistic creation, premeditated design; device, plan, scheme.

J

Jar (N): discord in music; quarrel, discord.

Jar (V): be out of tune; be discordant, quarrel.

Jump: agree, tally, coincide, fit exactly; risk, hazard.

K

Keep: continue, carry on; dwell, lodge, guard, defend, care for, employ, be with; restrain, control (refl.); confine in prison.

Kind (N): nature, established order of things; manner, fashion, respect; race, class, kindred, family; *by kind:* naturally.

Kind (ADJ.): natural; favorable; affectionate.

Kindly (ADJ.): natural, appropriate; agreeable; innate; benign.

Kindly (ADV.): naturally; gently, courteously.

L

Large: liberal, bounteous, lavish; free, unrestrained; *at large,* at length, in full; in full detail, as a whole, in general.
Late: lately.
Learn: teach; inform (someone of something); also the modern sense.
Let: hinder.
Level: aim; also shades toward the modern sense.
Liberal: possessed of the characteristics and qualities of gentlemen, genteel, becoming in a gentleman, refined; free in speech; unrestrained by prudence or decorum; licentious.
Lie: be in bed; be still; be confined, be kept in prison; dwell, sojourn, reside, lodge.
Like: please, feel affection; liken, compare.
List (N): strip of cloth, selvedge; limit, boundary; desire.
List (V): choose, desire, please; listen to.
'Long of: owing to, on account of.
Look: power to see; take care, see to it; expect; seek, search for.

M

Make: do; have to do (with); consider; go; be effective, make up, complete; also the modern sense.
Manage: management, conduct, administration; action and paces to which a horse is trained; short gallop at full speed.
Marry: mild interjection equivalent to "Indeed!" Originally an oath by the Virgin Mary.
May: can; also frequently the modern sense to denote probability; *might* has corresponding meanings and uses.
Mean (N): instrument, agency, method (also frequent in the plural); effort; opportunity (for doing something); something interposed or intervening; middle position, medium; tenor or alto parts in singing; money, wealth (usually plural form).
Mean (ADJ.): average, moderate, middle; of low degree, station, or position; undignified, base.
Measure (N): grave or stately dance, graceful motion; tune, melody, musical accompaniment; treatment meted out; moderation, proportion; limit; distance, reach.
Measure (V): judge, estimate; traverse.
Mere: absolute, sheer; pure, unmixed; downright, sincere.
Mew (up): coop up (as used of a hawk), shut up, imprison, confine.
Mind (N): thoughts, judgment, opinion, message; purpose, intention, desire; disposition; also the modern sense of the mental faculty.
Mind (V): remind; perceive, notice, attend; intend.
Minion: saucy woman, hussy; follower; favorite, favored person, darling (often used contemptuously).
Misdoubt (N): suspicion.
Misdoubt (V): mistrust, suspect.
Model: pattern, replica, likeness.
Modern: ordinary, commonplace, everyday.
Modest: moderate, marked by moderation, becoming; characterized by decency and propriety; chaste.
Moe: more.
Moiety: half; share; small part, lesser share; portion, part of.
Mortal: fatal; deadly, of or for death; belonging to mankind; human, pertaining to human affairs.
Motion: power of movement; suggestion, proposal; movement of the soul; impulse, prompting; also the modern sense.
Move: make angry; urge, incite, instigate, arouse, prompt; propose, make a proposal to, apply to, appeal to, suggest; also the modern sense.
Muse: wonder, marvel; grumble, complain.

N

Napkin: handkerchief.
Natural: related by blood; having natural or kindly feeling; also the modern sense.
Naught: useless, worthless; wicked, naughty.
Naughty: wicked; good for nothing, worthless.
Nice: delicate; fastidious, dainty, particular, scrupulous; minute, subtle; shy, coy; reluctant, unwilling; unimportant, insignificant, trivial; accurate, precise; wanton, lascivious.
Nothing: not at all.

O

Of: from, away from; during; on; by; as regards; instead of; *out of,* compelled by; made from.
Offer: make an attack; menace; venture, dare, presume.
Opinion: censure; reputation or credit; favorable estimate of oneself; self-conceit, arrogance; self-confidence; public opinion, reputation; also the modern sense.
Or: before; also used conjunctively where no alternative is implied; *or . . . or:* either . . . or; whether . . . or.
Out (ADV.): without, outside; abroad; fully, quite; at an end, finished; at variance, aligned the wrong way.
Out (INTERJ.): an expression of reproach, impatience, indignation, or anger.
Owe: own; also the modern sense.

P

Pack: load; depart, begone; conspire.
Pageant: show, spectacle, spectacular entertainment; device on a moving carriage.
Pain: punishment, penalty; labor, trouble, effort; also frequently the modern sense.
Painted: specious, unreal, counterfeit.
Parle: parley, conference, talk; bugle call for parley.
Part: depart, part from; divide.
Particular: detail; personal interest or concern; details of a private nature; single person.
Party: faction, side, part, cause; partner, ally.
Pass: pass through, traverse; exceed; surpass; pledge.
Passing (ADJ. and ADV.): surpassing, surpassingly, exceedingly.
Passion (N): powerful or violent feeling, violent sorrow or grief; painful affection or disorder of the body; sorrow; feelings or desires of love; passionate speech or outburst.
Passion (V): sorrow, grieve.

Peevish: silly, senseless, childish; perverse, obstinate, stubborn; sullen.
Perforce: by violence or compulsion; forcibly; necessarily.
Physic: medical faculty; healing art, medical treatment; remedy, medicine, healing property.
Pitch: height; specifically, the height to which a falcon soars before stooping on its prey (often used figuratively).
Policy: conduct of affairs (especially public affairs); prudent management; stratagem, trick; contrivance; craft, cunning.
Port: bearing, demeanor; state, style of living, social station; gate.
Possess: have or give possession or command (of something); inform, acquaint; also the modern sense.
Post (N): courier, messenger; post-horse; haste.
Post (V): convey swiftly; hasten, ignore through haste (with *over* or *off*).
Practice: execution; exercise (especially for instruction); stratagem, intrigue; conspiracy, plot, treachery.
Practise: perform, take part in; use stratagem, craft, or artifice; scheme, plot; play a joke on.
Pregnant: resourceful; disposed, inclined; clear, obvious.
Present (ADJ.): ready, immediate, prompt, instant.
Present (V): represent.
Presently: immediately, at once.
Prevent: forestall, anticipate, foresee; also the modern sense.
Process: drift, tenor, gist; narrative, story; formal command, mandate.
Proof: test, trial, experiment; experience; issue, result; proved or tested strength of armor or arms; also the modern sense.
Proper: (one's or its) own; peculiar, exclusive; excellent; honest, respectable; handsome, elegant, fine, good-looking.
Proportion: symmetry; size; form, carriage, appearance, shape; portion, allotment; rhythm.
Prove: make trial of; put to test; show or find out by experience.
Purchase (N): acquisition; spoil, booty.
Purchase (V): acquire, gain, obtain; strive, exert oneself; redeem, exempt.

Q

Quaint: skilled, clever; pretty, fine, dainty; handsome, elegant; carefully or ingeniously wrought or elaborated.
Quality: that which constitutes (something); essential being; good natural gifts; accomplishment, attainment, property; art, skill; rank, position; profession, occupation, business; party, side; manner, style; cause, occasion.
Quick: living (used substantively to mean "living flesh"); alive; lively, sharp, piercing; hasty, impatient; with child.
Quillets: verbal niceties, subtle distinctions.
Quit: requite, reward; set at liberty; acquit, remit; pay for, clear off.

R

Rack (V): stretch or strain beyond normal extent or capacity to endure; strain oneself; distort.
Rage (N): madness, insanity; vehement pain; angry disposition; violent passion or appetite; poetic enthusiasm; warlike ardor or fury.
Rage (V): behave wantonly or riotously; act with fury or violence; enrage; pursue furiously.
Range: extend or lie in the same plane (with); occupy a position; rove, roam; be inconstant; traverse.
Rank: coarsely luxuriant; puffed up, swollen, fat, abundant; full, copious; rancid; lustful; corrupt, foul.
Rate (N): estimate; value or worth; estimation, consideration; standard, style.
Rate (V): allot; calculate, estimate, compute; reckon, consider; be of equal value (with); chide, scold, berate; drive away by chiding or scolding.
Recreant: traitor, coward, cowardly wretch.
Remorse: pity, compassion; also the modern sense.
Remove: removal, absence; period of absence; change.
Resolve: dissolve, melt, dissipate; answer; free from doubt or uncertainty, convince; inform; decide; also the modern sense.
Respect (N): consideration, reflection, act of seeing, view; attention, notice; decency, modest deportment; also the modern sense.
Respect (V): esteem, value, prize; regard, consider; heed, pay attention to; also the modern sense.
Round: spherical; plain, direct, brusque; fair; honest.
Roundly: plainly, unceremoniously.
Rub: obstacle (a term in the game of bowls); unevenness; inequality.

S

Sack: generic term for Spanish and Canary wines; sweet white wine.
Sad: grave, serious; also the modern sense.
Sadness: seriousness; also the modern sense.
Sans: without (French preposition).
Scope: object, aim, limit; freedom, license; free play.
Seal: bring to completion or conclusion, conclude, confirm, ratify, stamp; also the modern sense.
Sennet: a series of notes sounded on a trumpet to herald the approach or departure of a procession (used in stage directions).
Sense: mental faculty, mind; mental perception, import, rational meaning; physical perception; sensual nature; *common sense:* ordinary or untutored perception, observation or knowledge.
Sensible: capable of physical feeling or perception, sensitive; capable of or exhibiting emotion; rational; capable of being perceived.
Serve: be sufficient; be favorable; succeed; satisfy the need for; serve a turn; answer the purpose.
Several: separate, distinct, different; particular, private; various.
Shadow: shade, shelter; reflection; likeness, image; ghost; representation, picture of the imagination, phantom; also the modern sense.
Shift: change; stratagem, strategy, trick, contrivance, device to serve a purpose; *make shift,* manage.
Shrewd: malicious, mischievous, ill-natured; shrewish; bad, of evil import, grievous; severe.
Sirrah: ordinary or customary form of address to inferiors or servants; disrespectful form of address.
Sith: since.

Smock: woman's undergarment; used typically for "a woman."
Something: somewhat.
Sometime: sometimes, from time to time; once, formerly; at times, at one time.
Speed (N): fortune, success; protecting and assisting power; also the modern sense.
Speed (V): fare (well or ill); succeed; be successful; assist, guard, favor.
Spleen: the seat of emotions and passions; violent passion; fiery temper; malice; anger, rage; impulse, fit of passion; caprice; impetuosity.
Spoil: destruction, ruin; plunder; slaughter, massacre.
Starve: die of cold or hunger; be benumbed with cold; paralyze, disable; allow or cause to die.
State: degree, rank; social position, station; pomp, splendor, outward display, clothes; court, household of a great person; shades into the modern sense.
Stay: wait, wait for; sustain; stand; withhold, withstand; stop.
Stead: assist; be of use to, benefit, help.
Still: always, ever, continuously or continually, constant or constantly; silent, mute; also modern senses.
Stomach: appetite, inclination, disposition; resentment; angry temper, resentful feeling; proud spirit, courage.
Straight: immediately.
Strange: belonging to another country or person, foreign, unfriendly; new, fresh; ignorant; estranged.
Success: issue, outcome (good or bad); sequel, succession, descent (as from father to son).
Suggest: tempt; prompt; seduce.
Suggestion: temptation.

T

Table: memorandum, tablet; surface on which something is written or drawn.
Take: strike; bewitch; charm; infect; destroy; repair to for refuge; modern senses.
Tall: goodly, fine; strong in fight, valiant.
Target: shield.
Tax: censure, blame, accuse.
Tell: count; relate.
Thorough: through.
Throughly: thoroughly.
Toward: in preparation; forthcoming, about to take place.
Toy: trifle, idle fancy; folly.
Train: lure, entice, allure, attract.
Trencher: wooden dish or plate.
Trow: think, suppose, believe; know.

U

Undergo: undertake, perform; modern sense.
Undo: ruin.
Unfold: disclose, tell, make known, reveal; communicate.
Unhappy: evil, mischievous; fatal, ill-fated; miserable.
Unjust: untrue, dishonest; unjustified, groundless; faithless, false.
Unkind: unnatural, cruel, faulty; cf. *kind.*
Use (N): custom, habit; interest paid.
Use (V): make practice of; be accustomed; put out at interest.

V

Vail: lower, let fall.
Vantage: advantage; opportunity; benefit, profit; superiority.
Virtue: general excellence; valor, bravery; merit, goodness, honor; good accomplishment, excellence in culture; power; essence, essential part.

W

Want: lack; be in need of; be without.
Watch: be awake, lie awake, sit up at night, lose sleep; keep from sleep (trans.).
Weed: garment, clothes.
Welkin: sky, heavens.
Wink: close the eyes; close the eyes in sleep; have the eyes closed; seem not to see.
Withal: with; with it, this, or these; together with this; at the same time.
Wot: know.

INDEX

The letter n *following a reference indicates a footnote*

2 3 4 5 6 7 8 9 10–ALP–80 79 78 77 76 75